EUGENE O'NEILL

EUGENE O'NEILL

COMPLETE PLAYS
1920–1931

THE LIBRARY OF AMERICA

Diff'rent © 1921, renewed 1948; *The First Man* © 1922, renewed
1949; *The Hairy Ape* © 1922, 1949; *The Fountain* © 1926, renewed
1954; *Welded* © 1923, renewed 1950; *All God's Chillun Got Wings* ©
1923, renewed 1950; *Desire Under the Elms* © 1924, renewed 1952;
Marco Millions © 1925, renewed 1952; *The Great God Brown* © 1926,
renewed 1954; *Lazarus Laughed* © 1927, renewed 1955; *Strange Interlude* © 1928, renewed 1955; *Dynamo* © 1929, renewed 1957;
Mourning Becomes Electra © 1931, renewed 1958. Published by arrangement with Random House, Inc.

The paper used in this publication meets the
minimum requirements of the American National Standard
for Information Sciences—Permanence of Paper for
Printed Library Materials, ANSI Z39.48—1984.

Distributed to the trade in the United States
and Canada by the Viking Press.

Library of Congress Catalog Card Number: 88-50686
For cataloging information, see end of *Notes* section.
ISBN 0-940450-49-6

First Printing
The Library of America—41

Manufactured in the United States of America

Grateful acknowledgment is made to the National Endowment for the Humanities, the Ford Foundation, and the Andrew W. Mellon Foundation for their generous support of this series.

Contents

DIFF'RENT

A Play in Two Acts

CHARACTERS

CAPTAIN CALEB WILLIAMS

EMMA CROSBY

CAPTAIN JOHN CROSBY, *her father*

MRS. CROSBY, *her mother*

JACK CROSBY, *her brother*

HARRIET WILLIAMS, *Caleb's sister* (*later* MRS. ROGERS)

ALFRED ROGERS

BENNY ROGERS, *their son*

SCENES

ACT I

Parlor of the Crosby home on a side street of a seaport village in New England—mid-afternoon of a day in late spring in the year 1890.

ACT II

The same. Late afternoon of a day in the early spring of the year 1920.

Diff'rent

ACT ONE

SCENE—*Parlor of the Crosby home. The room is small and low-ceilinged. Everything has an aspect of scrupulous neatness. On the left, forward, a stiff plush-covered chair. Farther back, in order, a window looking out on a vegetable garden, a black horsehair sofa, and another window. In the far left corner, an old mahogany chest of drawers. To the right of it, in rear, a window looking out on the front yard. To the right of this window is the front door, reached by a dirt path through the small lawn which separates the house from the street. To the right of door, another window. In the far right corner, a diminutive, old-fashioned piano with a stool in front of it. Near the piano on the right, a door leading to the next room. On this side of the room are also a small bookcase half filled with old volumes, a big open fireplace, and another plush-covered chair. Over the fireplace a mantel with a marble clock and a Rogers group. The walls are papered a brown color. The floor is covered with a dark carpet. In the center of the room there is a clumsy, marble-topped table. On the table, a large china lamp, a bulky Bible with a brass clasp, and several books that look suspiciously like cheap novels. Near the table, three plush-covered chairs, two of which are rockers. Several enlarged photos of strained, stern-looking people in uncomfortable poses are hung on the walls.*

It is mid-afternoon of a fine day in late spring of the year 1890. Bright sunlight streams through the windows on the left. Through the window and the screen door in the rear the fresh green of the lawn and of the elm trees that line the street can be seen. Stiff, white curtains are at all the windows.

As the curtain rises, Emma Crosby and Caleb Williams are discovered. Emma is a slender girl of twenty, rather under the medium height. Her face, in spite of its plain features, gives an impression of prettiness, due to her large, soft blue eyes which have an incongruous quality of absent-minded romantic dreaminess about them. Her mouth and chin are heavy, full of a self-willed stubbornness. Although her body is slight and thin, there is a quick, nervous vitality about all her movements that reveals an underlying constitution of reserve power and health. She has light

3

brown hair, thick and heavy. She is dressed soberly and neatly in her black Sunday best, style of the period.

Caleb Williams is tall and powerfully built, about thirty. Black hair, keen, dark eyes, face rugged and bronzed, mouth obstinate but good-natured. He, also, is got up in black Sunday best and is uncomfortably self-conscious and stiff therein.

They are sitting on the horsehair sofa, side by side. His arm is about her waist. She holds one of his big hands in both of hers, her head leaning back against his shoulder, her eyes half closed in a dreamy contentedness. He stares before him rigidly, his whole attitude wooden and fixed as if he were posing for a photograph; yet his eyes are expressively tender and protecting when he glances down at her diffidently out of the corners without moving his head.

EMMA—(*sighing happily*) Gosh, I wish we could sit this way forever! (*then after a pause, as he makes no comment except a concurring squeeze*) Don't you, Caleb?

CALEB—(*with another squeeze—emphatically*) Hell, yes! I'd like it, Emmer.

EMMA—(*softly*) I do wish you wouldn't swear so awful much, Caleb.

CALEB—S'cuse me, Emmer, it jumped out o' my mouth afore I thought. (*then with a grin*) You'd ought to be used to that part o' men's wickedness—with your Pa and Jack cussin' about the house all the time.

EMMA—(*with a smile*) Oh, I haven't no strict religious notions about it. I'm hardened in sin so far's they're concerned. Goodness me, how would Ma and me ever have lived in the same house with them two if we wasn't used to it? I don't even notice their cussing no more. And I don't mind hearing it from the other men, either. Being sea-faring men, away from their women folks most of the time, I know it just gets to be part of their natures and they ain't responsible. (*decisively*) But you're diff'rent. You just got to be diff'rent from the rest.

CALEB—(*amused by her seriousness*) Diff'rent? Ain't I a sea-farin' man, too?

EMMA—You're diff'rent just the same. That's what made me fall in love with you 'stead of any of them. And you've got to stay diff'rent. Promise me, Caleb, that you'll always stay diff'rent from them—even after we're married years and years.

CALEB—(*embarrassed*) Why—I promise to do my best by you, Emmer. You know that, don't ye? On'y don't git the notion in your head I'm any better'n the rest. They're all good men—most of 'em, anyway. Don't tell me, for instance, you think I'm better'n your Pa or Jack—'cause I ain't. And I don't know as I'd want to be, neither.

EMMA—(*excitedly*) But you got to want to be—when I ask it.

CALEB—(*surprised*) Better'n your Pa?

EMMA—(*struggling to convey her meaning*) Why, Pa's all right. He's a fine man—and Jack's all right, too. I wouldn't hear a bad word about them for anything. And the others are all right in their way, too, I s'pose. Only—don't you see what I mean?—I look on you as diff'rent from all of them. I mean there's things that's all right for them to do that wouldn't be for you—in my mind, anyway.

CALEB—(*puzzled and a bit uneasy*) Sailors ain't plaster saints, Emmer,—not a darn one of 'em ain't!

EMMA—(*hurt and disappointed*) Then you won't promise me to stay diff'rent for my sake?

CALEB—(*with rough tenderness*) Oh, hell, Emmer, I'll do any cussed thing in the world you want me to, and you know it!

EMMA—(*lovingly*) Thank you, Caleb. It means a lot to me—more'n you think. And don't you think I'm diff'rent, too—not just the same as all the other girls hereabouts?

CALEB—'Course you be! Ain't I always said that? You're wo'th the whole pack of 'em put together.

EMMA—Oh, I don't mean I'm any better. I mean I just look at things diff'rent from what they do—getting married, for example, and other things, too. And so I've got it fixed in my head that you and me ought to make a married couple—diff'rent from the rest—not that they ain't all right in their way.

CALEB—(*puzzled—uncertainly*) Waal—it's bound to be from your end of it, you bein' like you are. But I ain't so sure o' mine.

EMMA—Well, I am!

CALEB—(*with a grin*) You got me scared, Emmer. I'm scared you'll want me to live up to one of them high-fangled heroes you been readin' about in them books. (*He indicates the novels on the table.*)

EMMA—No, I don't. I want you to be just like yourself, that's all.

CALEB—That's easy. It ain't hard bein' a plain, ordinary cuss.

EMMA—You are not!

CALEB—(*with a laugh*) Remember, I'm warnin' you, Emmer; and after we're married and you find me out, you can't say I got you under no false pretenses.

EMMA—(*laughing*) I won't. I won't ever need to. (*then after a pause*) Just think, it's only two days more before you and me'll be man and wife.

CALEB—(*squeezing her*) Waal, it's about time, ain't it?—after waitin' three years for me to git enough money saved—and us not seein' hide or hair of each other the last two of 'em. (*with a laugh*) Shows ye what trust I put in you, Emmer, when I kin go off on a two year whalin' vige and leave you all 'lone for all the young fellers in town to make eyes at.

EMMA—But lots and lots of the others does the same thing without thinking nothing about it.

CALEB—(*with a laugh*) Yes, but I'm diff'rent, like you says.

EMMA—(*laughing*) Oh, you're poking fun now.

CALEB—(*with a wink*) And you know as well's me that some o' the others finds out some funny things that's been done when they was away.

EMMA—(*laughing at first*) Yes, but you know I'm diff'rent, too. (*then frowning*) But don't let's talk about that sort o' ructions. I hate to think of such things—even joking. I ain't like that sort.

CALEB—Thunder, I know you ain't, Emmer. I was on'y jokin'.

EMMA—And I never doubted you them two years; and I won't when you sail away again, neither.

CALEB—(*with a twinkle in his eye*) No, even a woman'd find it hard to git jealous of a whale!

EMMA—(*laughing*) I wasn't thinking of whales, silly! But there's plenty of diversion going on in the ports you touched, if you'd a mind for it.

CALEB—Waal, I didn't have no mind for it, that's sartin. My fust vige as skipper, you don't s'pose I had time for no monkey-shinin', do ye? Why, I was that anxious to bring back your Pa's ship with a fine vige that'd make him piles o' money, I didn't even think of nothin' else.

EMMA—'Cepting me, I hope?

CALEB—O' course! What was my big aim in doin' it if it wasn't so's we'd git married when I come to home? And then, s'far as ports go, we didn't tech at one the last year—'ceptin' when that durn tempest blowed us south and we put in at one o' the Islands for water.

EMMA—What island? You never told me nothing about that.

CALEB—(*growing suddenly very embarrassed as if some memory occurred to him*) Ain't nothin' to tell, that's why. Just an island near the Line, that's all. O'ny naked heathen livin' there—brown colored savages that ain't even Christians. (*He gets to his feet abruptly and pulls out his watch.*) Gittin' late, must be. I got to go down to the store and git some things for Harriet afore I forgets 'em.

EMMA—(*rising also and putting her hands on his shoulders*) But you did think of me and miss me all the time you was gone, didn't you?—same as I did you.

CALEB—'Course I did. Every minute.

EMMA—(*nestling closer to him—softly*) I'm glad of that, Caleb. Well, good-by for a little while.

CALEB—I'll step in again for a spell afore supper—that is, if you want me to.

EMMA—Yes, of course I do, Caleb. Good-by. (*She lifts her face to his.*)

CALEB—Good-by, Emmer. (*He kisses her and holds her in his arms for a moment. Jack comes up the walk to the screen door. They do not notice his approach.*)

JACK—(*peering in and seeing them—in a joking bellow*) Belay, there! (*They separate with startled exclamations. Jack comes in grinning. He is a hulking, stocky-built young fellow of 25. His heavy face is sunburned, handsome in a coarse, good-natured animal fashion. His small blue eyes twinkle with the unconsciously malicious humor of the born practical joker. He wears high seaboots turned down from the knee, dirty cotton shirt and pants, and a yellow sou'wester pushed jauntily on the back of his head, revealing his disheveled, curly blond hair. He carries a string of cod heads.)*

JACK—(*laughing at the embarrassed expression on their faces*) Caught ye that time, by gum! Go ahead! Kiss her again, Caleb. Don't mind me.

EMMA—(*with flurried annoyance*) You got a head on you just like one of them cod heads you're carrying—that stupid! I should think you'd be ashamed at your age—shouting to scare folks as if you was a little boy.

JACK—(*putting his arm about her waist*) There, kitty, don't git to spittin'. (*stroking her hair*) Puss, puss, puss! Nice kitty! (*He laughs.*)

EMMA—(*forced to smile—pushing him away*) Get away! You'll never get sense. Land sakes, what a brother to have!

JACK—Oh, I dunno. I ain't so bad, as brothers go—eh, Caleb?

CALEB—(*smiling*) I reckon you'll do, Jack.

JACK—See there! Listen to Caleb. You got to take his word—love, honor, and *obey*, ye know, Emmer.

EMMA—(*laughing*) Leave it to men folks to stick up for each other, right or wrong.

JACK—(*cockily*) Waal, I'm willin' to leave it to the girls, too. Ask any of 'em you knows if I ain't a jim-dandy to have for a brother. (*He winks at Caleb who grins back at him.*)

EMMA—(*with a sniff*) I reckon you don't play much brother with them—the kind you knows. You may fool 'em into believing you're some pumpkins but they'd change their minds if they had to live in the same house with you playing silly jokes all the time.

JACK—(*provokingly*) A good lot on 'em 'd be on'y too damn glad to git me in the same house—if I was fool enough to git married.

EMMA—"Pride goeth before a fall." But shucks, what's the good paying any attention to you. (*She smiles at him affectionately.*)

JACK—(*exaggeratedly*) You see, Caleb? See how she misuses

me—her lovin' brother. Now you know what you'll be up against for the rest o' your natural days.

CALEB—Don't see no way but what I got to bear it, Jack.

EMMA—Caleb needn't fear. He's diff'rent.

JACK—(*with a sudden guffaw*) Oh, hell, yes! I was forgittin'. Caleb's a Sunday go-to-meetin' Saint, ain't he? Yes, he is!

EMMA—(*with real resentment*) He's better'n what you are, if that's what you mean.

JACK—(*with a still louder laugh*) Ho-ho! Caleb's one o' them goody-goody heroes out o' them story books you're always readin', ain't he?

CALEB—(*soberly—a bit disturbed*) I was tellin' Emmer not to take me that high.

JACK—No use, Caleb. She won't hear of it. She's got her head sot t'other way. You'd ought to heard her argyin' when you was gone about what a parson's pet you was. Butter won't melt in your mouth, no siree! Waal, love is blind—and deaf, too, as the feller says—and I can't argy no more 'cause I got to give Ma these heads. (*He goes to the door on right— then glances back at his sister maliciously and says meaningly*) You ought to have a talk with Jim Benson, Emmer. Oughtn't she, Caleb? (*He winks ponderously and goes off laughing uproariously.*)

CALEB—(*his face worried and angry*) Jack's a durn fool at times, Emmer—even if he is your brother. He needs a good lickin'.

EMMA—(*staring at him—uneasily*) What'd he mean about Jim Benson, Caleb?

CALEB—(*frowning*) I don't know—ezactly. Makin' up foolishness for a joke, I reckon.

EMMA—You don't know—*exactly*? Then there is—something?

CALEB—(*quickly*) Not as I know on. On'y Jim Benson's one o' them slick jokers, same's Jack; can't keep their mouths shet or mind their own business.

EMMA—Jim Benson was mate with you this last trip, wasn't he?

CALEB—Yes.

EMMA—Didn't him and you get along?

CALEB—(*a trifle impatiently*) 'Course we did. Jim's all right. We got along fust rate. He just can't keep his tongue from waggin', that's all's the matter with him.

EMMA—(*uneasily*) What's it got to wag about? You ain't done nothing wrong, have you?

CALEB—Wrong? No, nothin' a man'd rightly call wrong.

EMMA—Nothing you'd be shamed to tell me?

CALEB—(*awkwardly*) Why—no, Emmer.

EMMA—(*pleadingly*) You'd swear that, Caleb?

CALEB—(*hesitating for a second—then firmly*) Yes, I'd swear. I'd own up to everything fair and square I'd ever done, if it comes to that p'int. I ain't shamed o' anything I ever done, Emmer. On'y—women folks ain't got to know everything, have they?

EMMA—(*turning away from him—frightenedly*) Oh, Caleb!

CALEB—(*preoccupied with his own thoughts—going to the door in rear*) I'll see you later, Emmer. I got to go up street now more'n ever. I want to give that Jim Benson a talkin' to he won't forgit in a hurry—that is, if he's been tellin' tales. Good-by, Emmer.

EMMA—(*faintly*) Good-by, Caleb. (*He goes out. She sits in one of the rockers by the table, her face greatly troubled, her manner nervous and uneasy. Finally she makes a decision, goes quickly to the door on the right and calls*) Jack! Jack!

JACK—(*from the kitchen*) What you want?

EMMA—Come here a minute, will you?

JACK—Jest a second. (*She comes back by the table, fighting to conceal her agitation. After a moment, Jack comes in from the right. He has evidently been washing up, for his face is red and shiny, his hair wet and slicked in a part. He looks around for Caleb.*) Where's Caleb?

EMMA—He had to go up street. (*then coming to the point abruptly—with feigned indifference*) What's that joke about Jim Benson, Jack? It seemed to get Caleb all riled up.

JACK—(*with a chuckle*) You got to ask Caleb about that, Emmer.

EMMA—I did. He didn't seem to want to own up it was anything.

JACK—(*with a laugh*) 'Course he wouldn't. He don't 'preciate a joke when it's on him.

EMMA—How'd you come to hear of it?

JACK—From Jim. Met him this afternoon and me and him had a long talk. He was tellin' me all 'bout their vige.

EMMA—Then it was on the vige this joke happened?

JACK—Yes. It was when they put in to git water at them South Sea Islands where the tempest blowed 'em.

EMMA—Oh. (*suspiciously*) Caleb didn't seem willing to tell me much about their touching there.

JACK—(*chuckling*) 'Course he didn't. Wasn't I sayin' the joke's on him? (*coming closer to her—in a low, confidential tone, chucklingly*) We'll fix up a joke on Caleb, Emmer, what d'ye say?

EMMA—(*tortured by foreboding—resolved to find out what is back of all this by hook or crook—forcing a smile*) All right, Jack. I'm willing.

JACK—Then I'll tell you what Jim told me. And you put it up to Caleb, see, and pertend you're madder'n hell. (*unable to restrain his mirth*) Ho-ho! It'll git him wild if you do that. On'y I didn't tell ye, mind. You heard it from someone else. I don't want to git Caleb down on me. And you'd hear about it from someone sooner or later 'cause Jim and the rest o' the boys has been tellin' the hull town.

EMMA—(*taken aback—frowning*) So all the town knows about it?

JACK—Yes, and they're all laffin' at Caleb. Oh, it ain't nothin' so out o' the ordinary. Most o' the whalin' men hereabout have run up against it in their time. I've heard Pa and all the others tellin' stories like it out o' their experience. On'y with Caleb it ended up so damn funny! (*He laughs.*) Ho-ho! Jimminy!

EMMA—(*in a strained voice*) Well, ain't you going to tell me?

JACK—I'm comin' to it. Waal, seems like they all went ashore on them islands to git water and the native brown women, all naked a'most, come round to meet 'em same as they always does—wantin' to swap for terbaccer and other tradin' stuff with straw mats and whatever other junk they got. Them brown gals was purty as the devil, Jim says—that is, in their heathen, outlandish way—and the boys got makin' up to 'em; and then, o' course, everything happened like it always does, and even after they'd got all the water they needed aboard, it took 'em a week to round up all hands from where they was foolin' about with them nigger women.

EMMA—(*in anguish*) Yes—but Caleb—he ain't like them others. He's diff'rent.

JACK—(*with a sly wink*) Oho, is he? I'm comin' to Caleb. Waal, seems 's if he kept aboard mindin' his own business and winkin' at what the boys was doin'. And one o' them gals— the purtiest on 'em, Jim says—she kept askin', where's the captain? She wouldn't have nothin' to do with any o' the others. She thought on'y the skipper was good enough for her, I reckon. So one night jest afore they sailed some o' the boys, bein' drunk on native rum they'd stole, planned to put up a joke on Caleb and on that brown gal, too. So they tells her the captain had sent for her and she was to swim right out and git aboard the ship where he was waitin' for her alone. That part of it was true enough 'cause Caleb was alone, all hands havin' deserted, you might say.

EMMA—(*letting an involuntary exclamation escape her*) Oh!

JACK—Waal, that fool brown gal b'lieved 'em and she swum right off, tickled to death. What happened between 'em when she got aboard, nobody knows. Some thinks one thing and some another. And I ain't sayin' nothin' 'bout it—(*with a wink*) but I know damn well what I'd 'a done in Caleb's boots, and I guess he ain't the cussed old woman you makes him out. But that part of it's got nothin' to do with the joke nohow. The joke's this: that brown gal took an awful shine to Caleb and when she saw the ship was gittin' ready to sail she raised ructions, standin' on the beach howlin' and screamin', and beatin' her chest with her fists. And when they ups anchors, she dives in the water and swims out after 'em. There's no wind hardly and she kin swim like a fish and catches up to 'em and tries to climb aboard. At fust, Caleb tries to treat her gentle and argy with her to go back. But she won't listen, she gits wilder and wilder, and finally he gits sick of it and has the boys push her off with oars while he goes and hides in the cabin. Even this don't work. She keeps swimmin' round and yellin' for Caleb. And finally they has to p'int a gun at her and shoot in the water near her afore the crazy cuss gives up and swims back to home, howlin' all the time.

(*with a chuckle*) And Caleb lyin' low in the cabin skeered to move out, and all hands splittin' their sides! Gosh, I wish I'd been there! It must have been funnier'n hell! (*He laughs loudly—then noticing his sister's stony expression, stops abruptly.*) What're you pullin' that long face for, Emmer? (*offendedly*) Hell, you're a nice one to tell a joke to!

EMMA—(*after a pause—forcing the words out slowly*) Caleb's comin' back here, Jack. I want you to see him for me. I want you to tell him—

JACK—Not me! You got to play this joke on him yourself or it won't work.

EMMA—(*tensely*) This ain't a joke, Jack—what I mean. I want you to tell him I've changed my mind and I ain't going to marry him.

JACK—What!

EMMA—I been thinking things over, tell him—and I take back my promise—and he can have back his ring—and I ain't going to marry him.

JACK—(*flabbergasted—peering into her face anxiously*) Say— what the hell—? Are you tryin' to josh me, Emmer? Or are you gone crazy all of a sudden?

EMMA—I ain't joking nor crazy neither. You tell him what I said.

JACK—(*vehemently*) I will like— Say, what's come over you, anyhow?

EMMA—My eyes are opened, that's all, and I ain't going to marry him.

JACK—Is it—'count of that joke about Caleb I was tellin' you?

EMMA—(*her voice trembling*) It's 'count of something I got in my own head. What you told only goes to prove I was wrong about it.

JACK—(*greatly perturbed now*) Say, what's the matter? Can't you take a joke? Are you mad at him 'count o' that brown gal?

EMMA—Yes, I am—and I ain't going to marry him and that's all there is to it.

JACK—(*argumentatively*) Jealous of a brown, heathen woman that ain't no better'n a nigger? God sakes, Emmer, I didn't think you was that big a fool. Why, them kind o'

women ain't women like you. They don't count like folks.
They ain't Christians—nor nothin'!

EMMA—That ain't it. I don't care what they are.

JACK—And it wasn't Caleb anyhow. It was all her fixin'.
And how'd you know he had anything to do with her—like
that? I ain't said he did. Jim couldn't swear he did neither.
And even if he did—what difference does it make? It ain't
rightly none o' your business what he does on a vige. He
didn't ask her to marry him, did he?

EMMA—I don't care. He'd ought to have acted diff'rent.

JACK—Oh golly, there you go agen makin' a durned
creepin'-Jesus out of him! What d'you want to marry, anyhow—a man or a sky-pilot? Caleb's a man, ain't he?—and a
damn good man and as smart a skipper as there be in these
parts! What more d'you want, anyhow?

EMMA—(*violently*) I want you to shet up! You're too dumb
stupid and bad yourself to ever know what I'm thinking.

JACK—(*resentfully*) Go to the devil, then! I'm goin' to tell
Ma and sic her onto you. You'll maybe listen to her and git
some sense. (*He stamps out, right, while he is speaking. Emma
bursts into sobs and throws herself on a chair, covering her face
with her hands. Harriet Williams and Alfred Rogers come up the
path to the door in rear. Peering through the screen and catching
sight of Emma, Harriet calls* Emmer! *Emma leaps to her feet
and dabs at her eyes with a handkerchief in a vain effort to conceal
traces of her tears. Harriet has come in, followed by Rogers. Caleb's
sister is a tall, dark girl of twenty. Her face is plainly homely and
yet attracts the eye by a certain boldly-appealing vitality of self-
confident youth. She wears an apron and has evidently just come
out of the kitchen. Rogers is a husky young fisherman of twenty-
four, washed and slicked up in his ill-fitting best.*)

ROGERS—Hello, Emmer.

EMMA—(*huskily, trying to force a smile*) Hello, Harriet.
Hello, Alfred. Won't you set?

HARRIET—No, I jest run over from the house a second to
see if— Where's Caleb, Emmer?

EMMA—He's gone up street.

HARRIET—And here I be waitin' in the kitchen for him to
bring back the things so's I can start his supper. (*with a laugh*

and a roguish look at Rogers) Dearie me, it ain't no use depending' on a man to remember nothin' when he's in love.

ROGERS—(*putting his arm about her waist and giving her a squeeze—grinning*) How 'bout me? Ain't I in love and ain't I as reliable as an old hoss?

HARRIET—Oh, you! You're the worst of 'em all.

ROGERS—You don't think so. (*He tries to kiss her.*)

HARRIET—Stop it. Ain't you got no manners? What'll Emmer think?

ROGERS—Emmer can't throw stones. Her and Caleb is worser at spoonin' than what we are. (*Harriet breaks away from him laughingly and goes to Emma.*)

HARRIET—(*suddenly noticing the expression of misery on Emma's face—astonished*) Why, Emmer Crosby, what's the matter? You look as if you'd lost your last friend.

EMMA—(*trying to smile*) Nothing. It's nothing.

HARRIET—It is, too! Why, I do believe you've been crying!

EMMA—No, I ain't.

HARRIET—You have, too! (*putting her arms about Emma*) Goodness, what's happened? You and Caleb ain't had a spat, have you, with your weddin' only two days off?

EMMA—(*with quick resentful resolution*) There ain't going to be any wedding.

HARRIET—What!

ROGERS—(*pricking up his ears—inquisitively*) Huh?

EMMA—Not in two days nor no time.

HARRIET—(*dumbfounded*) Why, Emmer Crosby! Whatever's got into you? You and Caleb must have had an awful spat!

ROGERS—(*with a man-of-the-world attitude of cynicism*) Don't take her so dead serious, Harriet. Emmer'll git over it like you all does.

EMMA—(*angrily*) You shet up, Alf Rogers! (*Mrs. Crosby enters bustlingly from the right. She is a large, fat, florid woman of fifty. In spite of her two hundred and more pounds she is surprisingly active, and the passive, lazy expression of her round moon face is belied by her quick, efficient movements. She exudes an atmosphere of motherly good nature. She wears an apron on which*

*she is drying her hands as she enters. Jack follows her into the room.
He has changed to a dark suit, is ready for "up street.")*

MRS. CROSBY—(*smiling at Harriet and Rogers*) Afternoon,
Harriet—and Alf.

HARRIET—Afternoon, Ma.

ROGERS—Afternoon.

JACK—(*grinning*) There she be, Ma. (*points to Emma*)
Don't she look like she'd scratch a feller's eyes out! Phew!
Look at her back curve! Meow? Sptt-sptt! Nice puss! (*He
gives a vivid imitation of a cat fight at this last. Then he and
Rogers roar with laughter and Harriet cannot restrain a giggle
and Mrs. Crosby smiles. Emma stares stonily before her as if she
didn't hear.*)

MRS. CROSBY—(*good-naturedly*) Shet up your foolin',
Jack.

JACK—(*pretending to be hurt*) Nobody in this house kin
take a joke. (*He grins and beckons to Rogers.*) Come along, Alf.
You kin 'preciate a joke. Come on in here till I tell you. (*The
grinning Rogers follows him into the next room where they can be
heard talking and laughing during the following scene.*)

MRS. CROSBY—(*smiling, puts her arms around Emma*)
Waal, Emmer, what's this foolishness Jack's been tellin'
about—

EMMA—(*resentfully*) It ain't foolishness, Ma. I've made up
my mind, I tell you that right here and now.

MRS. CROSBY—(*after a quick glance at her face—soothingly*)
There, there! Let's set down and be comfortable. Me, I don't
relish roostin' on my feet. (*She pushes Emma gently into a
rocker—then points to a chair on the other side of the table.*) Set
down, Harriet.

HARRIET—(*torn between curiosity and a sense of being one too
many*) Maybe I'd best go to home and leave you two alone?

MRS. CROSBY—Shucks! Ain't you like one o' the family—
Caleb's sister and livin' right next door ever since you was
all children playin' together. We ain't got no secrets from
you. Set down. (*Harriet does so with an uncertain glance at
the frozen Emma. Mrs. Crosby has efficiently bustled another
rocker beside her daughter's and sits down with a comfortable
sigh.*) There. (*She reaches over and takes one of her daughter's
hands in hers.*) And now, Emmer, what's all this fuss over? (*as*

Emma makes no reply) Jack says as you've sworn you was breakin' with Caleb. Is that true?

EMMA—Yes.

MRS. CROSBY—Hmm. Caleb don't know this yet, does he?

EMMA—No. I asked Jack to tell him when he comes back.

MRS. CROSBY—Jack says he won't.

EMMA—Then I'll tell him myself. Maybe that's better, anyhow. Caleb'll know what I'm driving at and see my reason— (*bitterly*)—which nobody else seems to.

MRS. CROSBY—Hmm. You ain't tried me yet. (*after a pause*) Jack was a dumb fool to tell you 'bout them goin's-on at them islands they teched. Ain't no good repeatin' sech things.

EMMA—(*surprised*) Did you know about it before Jack—

MRS. CROSBY—Mercy, yes. Your Pa heard it from Jim Benson fust thing they landed here, and Pa told me that night.

EMMA—(*resentfully*) And you never told me!

MRS. CROSBY—Mercy, no. 'Course I didn't. They's trouble enough in the world without makin' more. If you was like most folks I'd told it to you. Me, I thought it was a good joke on Caleb.

EMMA—(*with a shudder*) It ain't a joke to me.

MRS. CROSBY—That's why I kept my mouth shet. I knowed you was touchy and diff'rent from most.

EMMA—(*proudly*) Yes, I am diff'rent—and that's just what I thought Caleb was, too—and he ain't.

HARRIET—(*breaking in excitedly*) Is it that story about Caleb and that heathen brown woman you're talking about? Is that what you're mad at Caleb for, Emmer?

MRS. CROSBY—(*as Emma remains silent*) Yes, Harriet, that's it.

HARRIET—(*astonished*) Why, Emmer Crosby, how can you be so silly? You don't s'pose Caleb took it serious, do you, and him makin' them fire shots round her to scare her back to land and get rid of her? Good gracious! (*a bit resentfully*) I hope you ain't got it in your head my brother Caleb would sink so low as to fall in love serious with one of them critters?

EMMA—(*harshly*) He might just as well.

HARRIET—(*bridling*) How can you say sech a thing! (*sarcastically*) I ain't heard that Caleb offered to marry her, have you? Then you might have some cause— But d'you s'pose he's ever give her another thought? Not Caleb! I know him better'n that. He'd forgot all about the hull thing before they was out o' sight of land, I'll bet, and if them fools hadn't started this story going, he'd never remembered it again.

MRS. CROSBY—(*nodding*) That's jest it. Harriet's right, Emmer.

EMMA—Ma!

MRS. CROSBY—Besides, you don't know they was nothin' wrong happened. Nobody kin swear that for sartin. Ain't that so, Harriet?

HARRIET—(*hesitating—then frankly*) I don't know. Caleb ain't no plaster saint and I reckon he's as likely to sin that way as any other man. He wasn't married then and I s'pose he thought he was free to do as he'd a mind to 'til he was hitched up. Goodness sakes, Emmer, all the men thinks that—and a lot of 'em after they're married, too.

MRS. CROSBY—Harriet's right, Emmer. If you've been wide awake to all that's happened in this town since you was old enough to know, you'd ought to realize what men be.

HARRIET—(*scornfully*) Emma'd ought to have fallen in love with a minister, not a sailor. As for me, I wouldn't give a durn about a man that was too goody-goody to raise Cain once in a while—before he married me, I mean. Why, look at Alf Rogers, Emmer. I'm going to marry him some day, ain't I? But I know right well all the foolin' he's done—and still is doing, I expect. I ain't sayin' I like it but I do like him and I got to take him the way he is, that's all. If you're looking for saints, you got to die first and go to heaven. A girl'd never git married hereabouts if she expected too much.

MRS. CROSBY—Harriet's right, Emmer.

EMMA—(*resentfully*) Maybe she is, Ma, from her side. I ain't claiming she's wrong. Her and me just looks at things diff'rent, that's all. And she can't understand the way I feel about Caleb.

HARRIET—Well, there's one thing certain, Emmer. You won't find a man in a day's walk is any better'n Caleb—or as good.

EMMA—(*wearily*) I know that, Harriet.

HARRIET—Then it's all right. You'll make up with him, and I s'pose I'm a fool to be takin' it so serious. (*as Emma shakes her head*) Oh, yes, you will. You wouldn't want to get him all broke up, would you? (*as Emma keeps silent—irritably*) Story book notions, that's the trouble with you, Emmer. You're gettin' to think you're better'n the rest of us.

EMMA—(*vehemently*) No, I don't! Can't you see—

MRS. CROSBY—Thar, now! Don't you two git to fightin'—to make things worse.

HARRIET—(*repentantly, coming and putting her arms around Emma and kissing her*) I'm sorry, Emmer. You know I wouldn't fall out with you for nothing or nobody, don't you? Only it gits me riled to think of how awful broke up Caleb'd be if— But you'll make it all up with him when he comes, won't you? (*Emma stares stubbornly before her. Before she has a chance to reply a roar of laughter comes from the next room as Jack winds up his tale.*)

ROGERS—(*from the next room*) Gosh, I wished I'd been there! (*He follows Jack into the room. Both are grinning broadly. Rogers says teasingly*) Reckon I'll take to whalin' 'stead o' fishin' after this. You won't mind, Harriet? From what I hears o' them brown women, I'm missin' a hull lot by stayin' to home.

HARRIET—(*in a joking tone—with a meaning glance at Emma*) Go on, then! There's plenty of fish in the sea. Anyhow, I'd never git jealous of your foolin' with one o' them heathen critters. They ain't worth notice from a Christian.

JACK—Oho, ain't they! They're purty as pictures, Benson says. (*with a wink*) And mighty accommodatin' in their ways. (*He and Rogers roar delightedly. Emma shudders with revulsion.*)

MRS. CROSBY—(*aware of her daughter's feeling—smilingly but firmly*) Get out o' this, Jack. You, too, Alf. Go on up street if you want to joke. You're in my way.

JACK—Aw right, Ma. Come on up street, Alf.

HARRIET—Wait. I'll go with you a step. I got to see if Caleb's got back with them supper things. (*They all go to the door in rear. Jack and Rogers pass out, talking and laughing.*)

Harriet turns in the doorway—sympathetically) I'll give Caleb a talking-to before he comes over. Then it'll be easy for you to finish him. Treat him firm but gentle and you'll see he won't never do it again in a hurry. After all, he wasn't married, Emmer—and he's a man—and what can you expect? Good-by. (*She goes.*)

EMMA—(*inaudibly*) Good-by.

MRS. CROSBY—(*after a pause in which she rocks back and forth studying her daughter's face—placidly*) Harriet's right, Emmer. You give him a good talkin'-to and he won't do it again.

EMMA—(*coldly*) I don't care whether he does or not. I ain't going to marry him.

MRS. CROSBY—(*uneasy—persuasively*) Mercy, you can't act like that, Emmer. Here's the weddin' on'y two days off, and everythin' fixed up with the minister, and your Pa and Jack has bought new clothes speshul for it, and I got a new dress—

EMMA—(*turning to her mother—pleadingly*) You wouldn't want me to keep my promise to Caleb if you knew I'd be unhappy, would you, Ma?

MRS. CROSBY—(*hesitatingly*) N-no, Emmer. (*then decisively*) 'Course I wouldn't. It's because I know he'll make you happy. (*as Emma shakes her head*) Pshaw, Emmer, you can't tell me you've got over all likin' for him jest 'count o' this one foolishness o' hisn.

EMMA—I don't love him—what he is now. I loved—what I thought he was.

MRS. CROSBY—(*more and more uneasy*) That's all your queer notions, and I don't know where you gits them from. Caleb ain't changed, neither have you. Why, Emmer, it'd be jest like goin' agen an act of Nature for you not to marry him. Ever since you was children you been livin' side by side, goin' round together, and neither you nor him ever did seem to care for no one else. Shucks, Emmer, you'll git me to lose patience with you if you act that stubborn. You'd ought to remember all he's been to you and forget this one little wrong he's done.

EMMA—I can't, Ma. It makes him another person—not Caleb, but someone just like all the others.

MRS. CROSBY—Waal, is the others so bad? Men is men the world over, I reckon.

EMMA—No, they ain't bad. I ain't saying that. Don't I like 'em all? If it was one of the rest—like Jim Benson or Jack, even—had done this I'd thought it was a joke, too. I ain't strict in judging 'em and you know it. But—can't you see, Ma?—Caleb always seemed diff'rent—and I thought he was.

MRS. CROSBY—(somewhat impatiently) Waal, if he ain't, he's a good man jest the same, as good as any sensible girl'd want to marry.

EMMA—(slowly) I don't want to marry nobody no more. I'll stay single.

MRS. CROSBY—(tauntingly) An old maid! (then resentfully) Emmer, d'you s'pose if I'd had your high-fangled notions o' what men ought to be when I was your age, d'you s'pose you'd ever be settin' there now?

EMMA—(slowly) No. I know from what I can guess from his own stories Pa never was no saint.

MRS. CROSBY—(in a tone of finality as if this settled the matter) There, now! And ain't he been as good a husband to me as ever lived, and a good father to you and Jack? You'll find out Caleb'll turn out the same. You think it over. (She gets up—bustlingly) And now I got to git back in the kitchen.

EMMA—(wringing her hands—desperately) Oh, Ma, why can't you see what I feel? Of course, Pa's good—as good as good can be—

CAPTAIN CROSBY—(from outside the door which he has approached without their noticing him—in a jovial bellow) What's that 'bout Pa bein' good? (He comes in laughing. He is a squat, bow-legged, powerful man, almost as broad as he is long—sixty years old but still in the prime of health and strength, with a great, red, weather-beaten face seamed by sun wrinkles. His sandy hair is thick and disheveled. He is dressed in an old baggy suit much the worse for wear—striped cotton shirt open at the neck. He pats Emma on the back with a playful touch that almost jars her off her feet.) Thunderin' Moses, that's the fust time ever I heerd good o' myself by listenin'! Most times it's: "Crosby? D'you mean that drunken, good-for-nothin', mangy old cuss?" That's what I hears usual. Thank ye, Emmer. (turning to his wife) What ye got to say now, Ma? Here's Emmer tellin'

you the truth after you hair-pullin' me all these years 'cause
you thought it wa'n't. I always told ye I was good, ain't I—
good as hell I be! (*He shakes with laughter and kisses his wife a
resounding smack.*)

Mrs. Crosby—(*teasing lovingly*) Emmer don't know you
like I do.

Crosby—(*turning back to Emma again*) Look-a-here, Emmer, I jest seen Jack. He told me some fool story 'bout you
fallin' out with Caleb. Reckon he was joshin', wa'n't he?

Mrs. Crosby—(*quickly*) Oh, that's all settled, John. Don't
you go stirrin' it up again. (*Emma seems about to speak but stops
helplessly after one glance at her father.*)

Crosby—An' all 'count o' that joke they're tellin' 'bout
him and that brown female critter, Jack says. Hell, Emmer,
you ain't a real Crosby if you takes a joke like that serious.
Thunderin' Moses, what the hell d'you want Caleb to be—a
durned, he-virgin, sky-pilot? Caleb's a man wo'th ten o' most
and, spite o' his bein' on'y a boy yit, he's the smartest skipper
out o' this port and you'd ought to be proud you'd got him.
And as for them islands, all whalin' men knows 'em. I've
teched thar for water more'n once myself, and I know them
brown females like a book. And I tells you, after a year or
more aboard ship, a man'd have to be a goll-durned geldin' if
he don't—

Mrs. Crosby—(*glancing uneasily at Emma*) Ssshh! You
come out in the kitchen with me, Pa, and leave Emmer be.

Crosby—God A'mighty, Ma, I ain't sayin' nothin' agen
Emmer, be I? I knows Emmer ain't that crazy. If she ever got
religion that bad, I'd ship her off as female missionary to the
damned yellow Chinks. (*He laughs.*)

Mrs. Crosby—(*taking his arm*) You come with me. I
want to talk with you 'bout somethin'.

Crosby—(*going*) Aye-aye, skipper! You're boss aboard
here. (*He goes out right with her, laughing. Emma stands for a
while, staring stonily before her. She sighs hopelessly, clasping and
unclasping her hands, looking around the room as if she longed to
escape from it. Finally she sits down helplessly and remains fixed
in a strained attitude, her face betraying the conflict that is tormenting her. Slow steps sound from the path in front of the house.*)

Emma recognizes them and her face freezes into an expression of obstinate intolerance.)

CALEB—(*appears outside the screen door. He looks in, coughs— then asks uncertainly*) It's me, Emmer. Kin I come in?

EMMA—(*coldly*) Yes.

CALEB—(*comes in and walks down beside her chair. His face is set emotionlessly but his eyes cannot conceal a worried bewilderment, a look of uncomprehending hurt. He stands uncomfortably, fumbling with his hat, waiting for her to speak or look up. As she does neither, he finally blurts out*) Kin I set a spell?

EMMA—(*in the same cold tone*) Yes. (*He lowers himself carefully to a wooden posture on the edge of a rocker near hers.*)

CALEB—(*after a pause*) I seen Jim Benson. I give him hell. He won't tell no more tales, I reckon. (*another pause*) I stopped to home on the way back from the store. I seen Harriet. She says Jack'd told you that story they're all tellin' as a joke on me. (*clenching his fists—angrily*) Jack's a durn fool. He needs a good lickin' from someone.

EMMA—(*resentfully*) Don't try to put the blame on Jack. He only told me the truth, didn't he? (*Her voice shows that she hopes against hope for a denial.*)

CALEB—(*after a long pause—regretfully*) Waal, I guess what he told is true enough.

EMMA—(*wounded*) Oh!

CALEB—But that ain't no good reason for tellin' it. Them sort o' things ought to be kept among men. (*after a pause— gropingly*) I didn't want nothin' like that to happen, Emmer. I didn't mean it to. I was thinkin' o' how you might feel— even down there. That's why I stayed aboard all the time when the boys was ashore. I wouldn't have b'lieved it could happen—not to me. (*a pause*) I wish you could see them Islands, Emmer, and be there for a time. Then you might see— It's hard 's hell to explain, and you havin' never seen 'em. Everything is diff'rent down there—the weather—and the trees and water. You git lookin' at it all, and you git to feel diff'rent from what you do to home here. It's purty hereabouts sometimes—like now, in spring—but it's purty there all the time—and down there you notice it and you git feelin'—diff'rent. And them native women—they're diff'-

rent. A man don't think of 'em as women—like you. But they're purty—in their fashion—and at night they sings—and it's all diff'rent like something you'd see in a painted picture. (*a pause*) That night when she swum out and got aboard when I was alone, she caught me by s'prise. I wasn't expectin' nothin' o' that sort. I tried to make her git back to land at fust—but she wouldn't go. She couldn't understand enough English for me to tell her how I felt—and I reckon she wouldn't have seed my p'int anyhow, her bein' a native. (*a pause*) And then I was afeerd she'd catch cold goin' round all naked and wet in the moonlight—though it was warm—and I wanted to wrap a blanket round her. (*He stops as if he had finished.*)

EMMA—(*after a long, tense pause—dully*) Then you own up—there really was something happened?

CALEB—(*after a pause*) I was sorry for it, after. I locked myself in the cabin and left her to sleep out on deck.

EMMA—(*after a pause—fixedly*) I ain't going to marry you, Caleb.

CALEB—Harriet said you'd said that; but I didn't b'lieve you'd let a slip like that make—such a diff'rence.

EMMA—(*with finality*) Then you can believe it now, Caleb.

CALEB—(*after a pause*) You got queer, strict notions, Emmer. A man'll never live up to 'em—with never one slip. But you got to act accordin' to your lights, I expect. It sort o' busts everythin' to bits for me— (*His voice betrays his anguish for a second but he instantly regains his iron control.*) But o' course, if you ain't willin' to take me the way I be, there's nothin' to do. And whatever you think is best, suits me.

EMMA—(*after a pause—gropingly*) I wish I could explain my side of it—so's you'd understand. I ain't got any hard feelings against you, Caleb—not now. It ain't plain jealousy—what I feel. It ain't even that I think you've done nothing terrible wrong. I think I can understand—how it happened—and make allowances. I know that most any man would do the same, and I guess all of 'em I ever met has done it.

CALEB—(*with a glimmer of eager hope*) Then—you'll forgive it, Emmer?

EMMA—Yes, I forgive it. But don't think that my forgiving is going to make any diff'rence—'cause I ain't going to marry you, Caleb. That's final. (*after a pause—intensely*) Oh, I wish I could make you see—my reason. You don't. You never will, I expect. What you done is just what any other man would have done—and being like them is exactly what'll keep you from ever seeing my meaning. (*after a pause—in a last effort to make him understand*) Maybe it's my fault more'n your'n. It's like this, Caleb. Ever since we was little I guess I've always had the idea that you was—diff'rent. And when we growed up and got engaged I thought that more and more. And you was diff'rent, too! And that was why I loved you. And now you've proved you ain't. And so how can I love you any more? I don't, Caleb, and that's all there is to it. You've busted something way down inside me—and I can't love you no more.

CALEB—(*gloomily*) I've warned you often, ain't I, you was settin' me up where I'd no business to be. I'm human like the rest and always was. I ain't diff'rent. (*after a pause—uncertainly*) I reckon there ain't no use sayin' nothin' more. I'll go to home. (*He starts to rise.*)

EMMA—Wait. I don't want you to go out of here with no hard feelings. You 'n' me, Caleb, we've been too close all our lives to ever get to be enemies. I like you, Caleb, same's I always did. I want us to stay friends. I want you to be like one of the family same's you've always been. There's no reason you can't. I don't blame you—as a man—for what I wouldn't hold against any other man. If I find I can't love you—that way—no more or be your wife, it's just that I've decided—things being what they be and me being what I am—I won't marry no man. I'll stay single. (*forcing a smile*) I guess there's worse things than being an old maid.

CALEB—I can't picture you that, Emmer. It's natural in some but it ain't in you. (*then with a renewal of hope*) And o' course I want to stay friends with you, Emmer. There's no hard feelin's on my side. You got a right to your own way—even if— (*hopefully*) And maybe if I show you what I done wasn't natural to me—by never doin' it again—maybe the time'll come when you'll be willin' to forget—

EMMA—(*shaking her head—slowly*) It ain't a question of time, Caleb. It's a question of something being dead. And when a thing's died, time can't make no diff'rence.

CALEB—(*sturdily*) You don't know that for sure, Emmer. You're human, too, and as liable to make mistakes as any other. Maybe you on'y think it's dead, and when I come back from the next vige and you've had two years to think it over, you'll see diff'rent and know I ain't as bad as I seem to ye now.

EMMA—(*helplessly*) But you don't seem bad, Caleb. And two years can't make no change in me—that way.

CALEB—(*feeling himself somehow more and more heartened by hope*) I ain't givin' up hope, Emmer, and you can't make me. Not by a hell of a sight. (*with emphasis*) I ain't never goin' to marry no woman but you, Emmer. You can trust my word for that. And I'll wait for ye to change your mind, I don't give a durn how long it'll take—till I'm sixty years old— thirty years if it's needful! (*He rises to his feet as he is speaking this last.*)

EMMA—(*with a mournful smile*) You might just as well say for life, Caleb. In thirty years we'll both be dead and gone, probably. And I don't want you to think it's needful for you to stay single 'cause I—

CALEB—I ain't goin' to stay single. I'm goin' to wait for you. And some day when you realize men was never cut out for angels you'll—

EMMA—(*helplessly*) Me 'n' you'll never understand each other, Caleb, so long as we live. (*getting up and holding out her hand*) Good-by, Caleb. I'm going up and lie down for a spell.

CALEB—(*made hopeless again by her tone—clasps her hand mechanically—dully*) Good-by, Emmer. (*He goes to the door in the rear, opens it, then hesitates and looks back at her as she goes out the door on the right without turning around. Suddenly he blurts out despairingly*) You'll remember what I told ye 'bout waitin', Emmer? (*She is gone, makes no reply. His face sets in its concealment mask of emotionlessness and he turns slowly and goes out the door as*

The Curtain Falls)

ACT TWO

SCENE—*Thirty years after—the scene is the same but not the
same. The room has a grotesque aspect of old age turned flighty
and masquerading as the most empty-headed youth. There is an
obstreperous newness about everything. Orange curtains are at the
windows. The carpet has given way to a varnished hardwood floor,
its glassy surface set off by three small, garish-colored rugs, placed
with precision in front of the two doors and under the table. The
wall paper is now a cream color sprayed with pink flowers. Sea-
scapes, of the painted-to-order quality, four in number, in gilded
frames, are hung on the walls at mathematically spaced intervals.
The plush-covered chairs are gone, replaced by a set of varnished
oak. The horsehair sofa has been relegated to the attic. A cane-
bottomed affair with fancy cushions serves in its stead. A Victrola
is where the old mahogany chest had been. A brand new piano
shines resplendently in the far right corner by the door, and a
bookcase with glass doors that pull up and slide in flanks the fireplace. This bookcase is full of installment-plan sets of uncut volumes. The table at center is of varnished oak. On it are piles of
fashion magazines and an electric reading lamp. Only the old
Bible, which still preserves its place of honor on the table, and the
marble clock on the mantel, have survived the renovation and serve
to emphasize it all the more by contrast.*

It is late afternoon of a day in the early spring of the year 1920.

*As the curtain rises, Emma and Benny Rogers are discov-
ered. She is seated in a rocker by the table. He is standing by the
Victrola on which a jazz band record is playing. He whistles, goes
through the motions of dancing to the music. He is a young fellow
of twenty-three, a replica of his father in Act One, but coarser,
more hardened and cocksure. He is dressed in the khaki uniform
of a private in the United States Army. The thirty years have
transformed Emma into a withered, scrawny woman. But there is
something revoltingly incongruous about her, a pitiable sham, a
too-apparent effort to cheat the years by appearances. The white
dress she wears is too frilly, too youthful for her; so are the high-
heeled pumps and clocked silk stockings. There is an absurd suggestion of rouge on her tight cheeks and thin lips, of penciled
make-up about her eyes. The black of her hair is brazenly un-
truthful. Above all there is shown in her simpering, self-consciously*

27

*coquettish manner that laughable—and at the same time irritat-
ing and disgusting—mockery of undignified age snatching greedily at the empty simulacra of youth. She resembles some passé stock
actress of fifty made up for a heroine of twenty.*

BENNY—(*as the record stops—switches off the machine*) Oh,
baby! Some jazz, I'll tell the world!

EMMA—(*smiling lovingly at his back*) I'm glad you like it.
It's one of them you picked out on the list.

BENNY—Oh, I'm a swell little picker, aw right. (*turning to
her*) Say, you're a regular feller—gettin' them records for me.

EMMA—(*coquettishly*) Well, if that ain't just like a man!
Who told you I got them just for you?

BENNY—Well, didn't you?

EMMA—No indeedy! I only took your advice on what to
get. I knew you'd know, being growed to a man of the world
now since you was overseas. But I got 'em because I like them
jazz tunes myself. They put life and ginger in an old lady like
me—not like them slow, old-timey tunes.

BENNY—(*bends over chair—kiddingly*) You ain't old. That's
all bunk.

EMMA—(*flattered*) Now, now, Benny!

BENNY—You ain't. You're a regular, up-to-date sport—the
only live one in this dead dump. (*with a grin*) And if you fall
for that jazz stuff, all you got to do now is learn to dance
to it.

EMMA—(*giggling*) I will—if you'll teach me.

BENNY—(*struggling with a guffaw*) Oh, oui! Sure I will!
We'll have a circus, me an' you. Say, you're sure one of the
girls aw right, Aunt Emmer.

EMMA—Oh, you needn't think we're *all* so behind the
times to home here just because you've been to France and
all over.

BENNY—*You* ain't, I'll say, Aunt Emmer.

EMMA—And how often have I got to tell you not to call
me Aunt Emmer?

BENNY—(*with a grin*) Oh, oui! My foot slipped. 'Scuse
me, Emmer.

EMMA—(*delighted by his coarse familiarity*) That's better.
Why, you know well enough I ain't your aunt anyway.

BENNY—I got to get used to the plain Emmer. They taught me to call you "aunt" when I was a kid. (*Emma looks displeased at this remark and Benny hastens to add cajolingly*) And you almost was my aunt-in-law one time from what I've heard. (*winks at her cunningly*)

EMMA—(*flustered*) That was ages ago. (*catching herself quickly*) Not so awful long really, but it's all so dead and gone it seems a long while.

BENNY—(*unthinkingly*) It was before I was born, wasn't it? (*Seeing her expression he hurries on.*) Well, that ain't so darned long. Say, here's something I never could make out— how did you ever come to fall for Uncle Caleb?

EMMA—(*bridling quickly*) I never did. That's all talk, Benny. We was good friends and still are. I was young and foolish and got engaged to him—and then discovered I didn't like him that way. That's all there ever was to it.

BENNY—(*resentfully*) I can't figure how anybody'd ever like him anyway. He's a darn stingy, ugly old cuss, if you want my dope on him. I can't see him at all. I've hated him ever since Pa died and Ma and me had to go live next door with him.

EMMA—You oughtn't to say that. He's kind at bottom, spite of his rough ways, and he's brought you up.

BENNY—(*grumpily*) Dragged me up, you mean. (*with a calculating look at her out of the corners of his eyes*) He's a tight-wad and I hate folks that're tight with their coin. Spend and be a good sport, that's my motto. (*flattering*) He'd ought to be more like you that way, Emmer.

EMMA—(*pleased—condescendingly*) Your Uncle Caleb's an old man, remember. He's sot in his ways and believes in being strict with you—too strict, I've told him.

BENNY—He's got piles of money hoarded in the bank but he's too mean even to retire from whalin' himself—goes right on makin' vige after vige to grab more and never spends a nickel less'n he has to. It was always like pryin' open a safe for me to separate him from a cent. (*with extreme disgust*) Aw, he's a piker. I hate him and I always did!

EMMA—(*looking toward the door apprehensively*) Ssshh!

BENNY—What you scared of? He don't get in from New Bedford till the night train and even if he's got to the house by this he'll be busy as a bird dog for an hour getting himself dolled up to pay you a call.

EMMA—(*perfunctorily*) I hope he's had a good vige and is in good health.

BENNY—(*roughly*) You needn't worry. He's too mean ever to get real sick. Gosh, I wish Pa'd lived—or Uncle Jack. They wasn't like him. I was only a kid when they got drowned, but I remember enough about 'em to know they was good sports. Wasn't they?

EMMA—(*rather primly*) They was too sporty for their own good.

BENNY—Don't you hand me that. That don't sound like you. You're a sport yourself. (*after a pause*) Say, it's nutty when you come to think of it—Uncle Caleb livin' next door all these years and comin' to call all the time when he ain't at sea.

EMMA—What's funny about that? We've always been good friends.

BENNY—(*with a grin*) It's just as if the old guy was still mashin' you. And I'll bet anything he's as stuck on you as he ever was—the old fool!

EMMA—(*with a coquettish titter*) Land sakes, Benny, a body'd think you were actually jealous of your uncle the way you go on.

BENNY—(*with a mocking laugh*) Jealous! Oh, oui! Sure I am! Kin you blame me? (*then seriously, with a calculating look at her*) No, all kiddin' aside, I know he'll run me down first second he sees you. Ma'll tell him all her tales, and he'll be sore at me right off. He's always hated me anyway. He was glad when I enlisted, 'cause that got him rid of me. All he was hopin' was that some German'd get me for keeps. Then when I come back he wouldn't do nothin' for me so I enlisted again.

EMMA—(*chiding—playfully*) Now, Benny! Didn't you tell me you enlisted again 'cause you were sick o' this small place and wanted to be out where there was more fun?

BENNY—Well, o' course it was that, too. But I could have a swell time even in this dump if he'd loosen up and give me some kale. (*again with the calculating look at her*) Why, look here, right now there's a buddy of mine wants me to meet him in Boston and he'll show me a good time, and if I had a hundred dollars—

EMMA—A hundred dollars! That's an awful pile to spend, Benny.

BENNY—(*disgustedly*) Now you're talkin' tight like him.

EMMA—(*hastily*) Oh, no, Benny. You know better'n that. What was you sayin'—if you had a hundred dollars—?

BENNY—That ain't such a much these days with everything gone up so. If I went to Boston I'd have to get dolled up and everything. And this buddy of mine is a sport and a spender. Easy come, easy go is his motto. His folks ain't tight-wads like mine. And I couldn't show myself up as a cheap skate by travelin' 'round with him without a nickel in my jeans and just spongin' on him. (*with the calculating glance to see what effect his words are having—pretending to dismiss the subject*) But what's the good of talkin'? I got a swell chance tellin' that to Uncle Caleb. He'd give me one look and then put a double padlock on his roll. But it ain't fair just the same. Here I'm sweatin' blood in the army after riskin' my life in France and when I get a leave to home, everyone treats me like a wet dog.

EMMA—(*softly*) Do you mean me, too, Benny?

BENNY—No, not you. You're diff'rent from the rest. You're regular—and you ain't any of my real folks, either, and ain't got any reason.

EMMA—(*coquettishly*) Oh, yes, I have a reason. I like you very, very much, Benny—better than anyone in the town—especially since you've been to home these last few times and come to call so often and I feel I've growed to know you. When you first came back from France I never would have recognized you as Harriet's Benny, you was so big and strong and handsome.

BENNY—(*uncomfortably*) Aw, you're kiddin'. But you can tell how good I think you are from me bein' over here so much—so you know I ain't lyin'. (*made more and more uncomfortable by the ardent looks Emma is casting at him*) Well, guess I'll be movin' along.

EMMA—(*pleadingly*) Oh, you mustn't go yet! Just when we're gettin' so friendly!

BENNY—Uncle Caleb'll be over soon and I don't want him

to catch me here—nor nowhere else till he gets calmed down after hearin' Ma's kicks about me. So I guess I better beat it up street.

EMMA—He won't come for a long time yet. I know when to expect him. (*pleading ardently and kittenishly*) Do set down a spell, Benny! Land sakes, I hardly get a sight of you before you want to run away again. I'll begin to think you're only pretending to like me.

BENNY—(*seeing his calculations demand it*) Aw right—jest for a second. (*He looks about him, seeking a neutral subject for conversation.*) Gee, you've had this old place fixed up swell since I was to home last.

EMMA—(*coquettishly*) Guess who I had it all done for, mostly?

BENNY—For yourself, of course.

EMMA—(*shaking her head roguishly*) No, not for me, not for me! Not that I don't like it but I'd never have gone to the trouble and expense for myself. (*with a sigh*) I s'pose poor Ma and Pa turned over in their graves when I ordered it done.

BENNY—(*with a sly grin*) Who d'you have it done for, then?

EMMA—For you! Yes, for you, Benny—so's you'd have a nice, up-to-date place to come to when you was on vacation from the horrid old army.

BENNY—(*embarrassed*) Well, it's great aw right. And it sure looks swell—nothing cheap about it.

EMMA—(*delighted*) As long as you like it, I'm satisfied. (*then suddenly, wagging an admonishing finger at him and hiding beneath a joking manner an undercurrent of uneasiness*) I was forgetting I got a bone to pick with you, young man! I heard them sayin' to the store that you'd been up callin' on that Tilly Small evenin' before last.

BENNY—(*with a lady-killer's carelessness*) Aw, I was passin' by and she called me in, that's all.

EMMA—(*frowning*) They said you had the piano goin' and was singing and no end of high jinks.

BENNY—Aw, these small town boobs think you're raising hell if you're up after eleven.

EMMA—(*excitedly*) I ain't blamin' you. But her—she ought

to have better sense—at her age, too, when she's old enough to be your mother.

BENNY—Aw, say, she ain't half as old— (*catching himself*) Oh, she's an old fool, you're right there, Emmer.

EMMA—(*severely*) And I hope you know the kind of woman she is and has been since she was a girl.

BENNY—(*with a wink*) I wasn't born yesterday. I got her number long ago. I ain't in my cradle, get me! I'm in the army! Oui! (*chuckles*)

EMMA—(*fidgeting nervously*) What'd you—what'd you do when you was there?

BENNY—Why, nothin'. I told her to cut the rough work and behave—and a nice time was had by all. (*He grins provokingly.*)

EMMA—(*springs to her feet nervously*) I don't know what to think—when you act so queer about it.

BENNY—(*carelessly*) Well, don't think nothing wrong— 'cause there wasn't. Bill Tinker was with me and we was both wishin' we had a drink. And Bill says, "Let's go see Tilly Small. She always has some buried and if we hand her a line of talk maybe she'll drag out the old bottle." So we did—and she did. We kidded her for a couple of drinks. (*He snickers.*)

EMMA—(*standing in front of him—fidgeting*) I want you to promise you won't go to see her no more. If you—if you want liquor now and again maybe I—maybe I can fix it so's I can get some to keep here for you.

BENNY—(*eagerly*) Say, that'd be great! Will you? (*She nods. He goes on carelessly.*) And sure I'll promise not to see Tilly no more. Gosh, what do you think I care about her? Or about any dame in this town, for that matter—'ceptin' you. These small town skirts don't hand me nothin'. (*with a grin*) You forgot I was in France—and after the dames over there these birds here look some punk.

EMMA—(*sits down—wetting her lips*) And what—what are those French critters like?

BENNY—(*with a wink*) Oh, boy! They're some pippins! It ain't so much that they're better lookin' as that they've got a way with 'em—lots of ways. (*He laughs with a lascivious smirk.*)

EMMA—(*unconsciously hitches her chair nearer his. The turn the conversation has taken seems to have aroused a hectic, morbid intensity in her. She continually wets her lips and pushes back her hair from her flushed face as if it were stifling her.*) What do you mean, Benny? What kind of ways have they got—them French girls?

BENNY—(*smirking mysteriously*) Oh, ways of dressin' and doin' their hair—and lots of ways.

EMMA—(*eagerly*) Tell me! Tell me all about 'em. You needn't be scared—to talk open with me. I ain't as strict as I seem—about hearin' things. Tell me! I've heard French girls was awful wicked.

BENNY—I don't know about wicked, but they're darned good sports. They'd do anything a guy'd ask 'em. Oui, tooty sweet! (*laughs foolishly*)

EMMA—And what—what'd you ask 'em, for instance?

BENNY—(*with a wink*) Curiosity killed a cat! Ask me no questions and I'll tell you no lies.

EMMA—(*with queer, stupid insistence*) But won't you tell me? Go on!

BENNY—Can't be did, Aunt Emmer, can't be did! (*with a silly laugh*) You're too young. No, all I'll say is, that to the boys who've knocked around over there the girls in town here are just rank amatoors. They don't know how to love and that's a fact. (*He gets to his feet.*) And as for an old bum like Tilly—not me! Well, I guess I'll hike along—

EMMA—(*getting up and putting a hand on his arm—feverishly*) No, don't go. Not yet—not yet. No, don't go.

BENNY—(*stepping away with an expression of repulsion*) Why not? What's the matter with you, Aunt Emmer? You look 's if you was gettin' sick. (*Before she can reply, Harriet's voice is heard calling.*)

HARRIET—Benny! Benny! (*This acts like a pail of cold water on Emma who moves away from Benny quickly.*)

EMMA—That's Harriet. It's your Ma calling, Benny.

BENNY—(*impatiently*) I know. That means Uncle Caleb has come and she's told him her stories and it's up to me to go catch hell. (*stopping Emma as she goes toward the door as if to answer Harriet's hail*) Don't answer, Aunt Emmer. Let her come over here to look. I want to speak to her and find out how I stand before he sees me.

EMMA—(*doubtfully*) I don't know as she'll come. She's been actin' funny to me lately, Harriet has, and she ain't put her foot in my door the last month.

BENNY—(*as his mother's voice is heard much nearer, calling* "Benny!") There! Sure she's comin'.

EMMA—(*flustered*) Land sakes, I can't let her see me this way. I got to run upstairs and tidy myself a little. (*She starts for the door at right.*)

BENNY—(*flatteringly*) Aw, you look swell. Them new duds you got looks great.

EMMA—(*turning in the doorway—coquettishly*) Oh, them French girls ain't the only ones knows how to fix up. (*She flounces out. Benny stands looking after her with a derisive grin of contempt. There is a sharp knock on the door in the rear. Benny goes to open it, his expression turning surly and sullen. Harriet enters. She wears an apron over her old-fashioned black dress with a brooch at the neck. Her hair is gray, her face thin, lined, and careworn, with a fretful, continuously irritated expression. Her shoulders stoop, and her figure is flabby and ugly. She stares at her son with resentful annoyance.*)

HARRIET—Ain't you got sense enough, you big lump, to answer me when I call, and not have me shouting my lungs out?

BENNY—I never heard you callin'.

HARRIET—You're lyin' and you know it. (*then severely*) Your uncle's to home. He's waitin' to talk to you.

BENNY—Let him wait. (*in a snarling tone*) I s'pose you've been givin' him an earful of lies about me?

HARRIET—I told him the truth, if that's what you mean. How you stole the money out of the bureau drawer—

BENNY—(*alarmed but pretending scorn*) Aw, you don't know it was me. You don't know nothin' about it.

HARRIET—(*ignoring this*) And about your disgracin' him and me with your drunken carryin's-on with that harlot, Tilly Small, night after night.

BENNY—Aw, wha'd you know about that?

HARRIET—And last but not least, the sneakin' way you're makin' a silly fool out of poor Emmer Crosby.

BENNY—(*with a grin*) You don't notice her kickin' about it, do you? (*brusquely*) Why don't you mind your own business, Ma?

HARRIET—(*violently*) It's a shame, that's what it is! That I should live to see the day when a son of mine'd descend so low he'd tease an old woman to get money out of her, and her alone in the world. Oh, you're low, you're low all through like your Pa was—and since you been in the army you got bold so you ain't even ashamed of your dirtiness no more!

BENNY—(*in a snarling whisper*) That's right! Blame it all on me. I s'pose she ain't got nothin' to do with it. (*with a wink*) You oughter see her perform sometimes. You'd get wise to something then.

HARRIET—Shut up! You've got the same filthy mind your Pa had. As for Emmer, I don't hold her responsible. She's been gettin' flighty the past two years. She couldn't help it, livin' alone the way she does, shut up in this house all her life. You ought to be 'shamed to take advantage of her condition—but shame ain't in you.

BENNY—Aw, give us a rest!

HARRIET—(*angrily*) Your Uncle Caleb'll give you a rest when he sees you! Him and me's agreed not to give you another single penny if you was to get down on your knees for it. So there! You can git along on your army pay from this out.

BENNY—(*worried by the finality in her tone—placatingly*) Aw, say, Ma, what's eatin' you? What've I done that's so bad? Gosh, you oughta know some of the gang I know in the army. You'd think I was a saint if you did. (*trying a confidential tone*) Honest, Ma, this here thing with Aunt Emmer ain't my fault. How can I help it if she goes bugs in her old age and gets nutty about me? (*with a sly grin—in a whisper*) Gee, Ma, you oughta see her today. She's a scream, honest! She's upstairs now gettin' calmed down. She was gettin' crazy when your callin' stopped her. Wait till she comes down and you git a look! She'll put your eye out—all dolled up like a kid of sixteen and enough paint on her mush for a Buffalo Bill Indian—

HARRIET—(*staring at him with stern condemnation*) You're a worthless loafer, Benny Rogers, same as your Pa was.

BENNY—(*frustrated and furious*) Aw, g'wan with that bunk! (*He turns away from her.*)

HARRIET—And I'm goin' to tell Emma about you and try to put some sense back into her head.

BENNY—Go ahead. You'll get fat runnin' me down to her!

HARRIET—And if my word don't have no influence, I'll tell your Uncle Caleb everything, and get him to talk to her. She'll mind him.

BENNY—(*defiantly*) You just try it, that's all!

HARRIET—I've been scared to do more'n hint about it to him. I'm hopin' any day Emma'll come out of this foolishness, and he'll never know.

BENNY—Aw!

HARRIET—If shame was in you, you'd remember your Uncle Caleb's been in love with Emma all his life and waited for her year after year hopin' in the end she'd change her mind and marry him. And she will, too, I believe, if she comes out of this fit in her sane mind—which she won't if you keep fussin' with her.

BENNY—(*with revengeful triumph*) She'll never marry the old cuss—I'll fix that!

HARRIET—Now you're showin' yourself up for what you are! And I kin see it's come to the p'int where I got to tell your Uncle Caleb everythin' no matter how it breaks him up. I got to do it for Emmer's sake as well as his'n. We got to get her cured of your bad influence once and for all. It's the only hope for the two of 'em.

BENNY—You just try it!

HARRIET—And as for you, you get back to the army where you b'long! And don't never expect another cent from me or Caleb 'cause you won't get it! And don't never come to see us again till you've got rid of the meanness and filth that's the Rogers part of you and found the honesty and decency that's the Williams part—if you got any of me in you at all, which I begin to doubt. (*goes to the door in rear*) And now I'm goin' back to Caleb—and you better not let him find you here when he comes less'n you want a good hidin' for once in your life. (*She goes out.*)

BENNY—(*stammering between fear and rage—shouting after her*) G'wan! Tell him! What the hell do I care? I'll fix him! I'll spill the beans for both of you, if you try to gum me! (*He stands in the middle of the room hesitating whether to run away or stay, concentrating his thoughts on finding some way to make good his bluff. Suddenly his face lights up with a cruel grin and he mutters to himself with savage satisfaction*) By God, that's it! I'll bet I kin work it, too! By God, that'll fix 'em! (*He chuckles and goes quickly to the door on right and calls up to the floor above*) Emmer! Emmer!

EMMA—(*her voice faintly heard answering*) Yes, Benny, I'm coming.

BENNY—(*He calls quickly*) Come down! Come down quick! (*He comes back to the center of the room where he stands waiting, planning his course of action.*)

EMMA—(*appears in the doorway. Her face is profusely powdered—with nervous excitement*) Benny! What's the matter? You sounded so—why where's your Ma?

BENNY—Gone. Gone back to home.

EMMA—(*offendedly*) Without waiting to see me? Why, I only sat down for a minute to give you a chance to talk to her. I was coming right down. Didn't she want to see me? Whatever's got into Harriet lately?

BENNY—She's mad as thunder at you 'cause I come over here so much 'stead of stayin' to home with her.

EMMA—(*pleased*) Oh, is that why? Well, if she ain't peculiar! (*She sits in a rocker by the table.*)

BENNY—(*with a great pretense of grief, taking one of her hands in his*) Say, Emmer—what I called you down for was—I want to say good-by and thank you for all you've done—

EMMA—(*frightenedly*) Good-by? How you say that! What—?

BENNY—Good-by for good this time.

EMMA—For good?

BENNY—Yep. I've got to beat it. I ain't got no home here no more. Ma and Uncle Caleb, they've chucked me out.

EMMA—Good gracious, what're you saying?

BENNY—That's what Ma come over to tell me—that Uncle Caleb'd said I'd never get another cent from him, alive or after he's dead, and she said for me to git back to the army and never to come home again.

EMMA—(*gasping*) She was only joking. She—they couldn't mean it.

BENNY—If you'd heard her you wouldn't think she was joking.

EMMA—(*as he makes a movement as if to go away*) Benny! You can't go! Go, and me never see you again, maybe! You can't! I won't have it!

BENNY—I got to, Emmer. What else is there for me to do when they've throwed me out? I don't give a damn about leaving them—but I hate to leave you and never see you again.

EMMA—(*excitedly—grabbing his arm*) You can't! I won't let you go!

BENNY—I don't want to—but what can I do?

EMMA—You can stay here with me.

BENNY—(*his eyes gleaming with satisfaction*) No, I couldn't. You know this dump of a town. Folks would be sayin' all sorts of bad things in no time. I don't care for myself. They're all down on me anyway because I'm diff'rent from small-town boobs like them and they hate me for it.

EMMA—Yes, you are diff'rent. And I'll show 'em I'm diff'rent, too. You can stay with me—and let 'em gossip all they've a mind to!

BENNY—No, it wouldn't be actin' square with you. I got to go. And I'll try to save up my pay and send you back what I've borrowed now and again.

EMMA—(*more and more wrought up*) I won't hear of no such thing. Oh, I can't understand your Ma and your Uncle Caleb bein' so cruel!

BENNY—Folks have been lyin' to her about me, like I told you, and she's told him. He's only too glad to believe it, too, long as it's bad.

EMMA—I can talk to your Uncle Caleb. He's always minded me more'n her.

BENNY—(*hastily*) Don't do that, for God's sake! You'd only make it worse and get yourself in Dutch with him, too!

EMMA—(*bewilderedly*) But—I—don't see—

BENNY—(*roughly*) Well, he's still stuck on you, ain't he?

EMMA—(*with a flash of coquetry*) Now, Benny!

BENNY—I ain't kiddin'. This is dead serious. He's stuck on you and you know it.

EMMA—(*coyly*) I haven't given him the slightest reason to hope in thirty years.

BENNY—Well, he hopes just the same. Sure he does! Why Ma said when she was here just now she'd bet you and him'd be married some day yet.

EMMA—No such thing! Why, she must be crazy!

BENNY—Oh, she ain't so crazy. Ain't he spent every durn evenin' of the time he's to home between trips over here with you—for the last thirty years?

EMMA—When I broke my engagement I said I wanted to stay friends like we'd been before, and we always have; but every time he'd even hint at bein' engaged again I'd always tell him we was friends only and he'd better leave it be that way. There's never been nothing else between us. (*with a coy smile*) And besides, Benny, you know how little time he's had to home between viges.

BENNY—I kin remember the old cuss marchin' over here every evenin' he was to home since I was a kid.

EMMA—(*with a titter of delight*) D'you know, Benny, I do actually believe you're jealous!

BENNY—(*loudly—to lend conviction*) Sure I'm jealous! But that ain't the point just now. The point is *he's* jealous of me—and you can see what a swell chance you've got of talkin' him over now, can't you! You'd on'y make him madder.

EMMA—(*embarrassedly*) He's getting foolish. What cause has he got—

BENNY—When Ma tells him the lies about us—

EMMA—(*excitedly*) What lies?

BENNY—I ain't goin' to repeat 'em to you but you kin guess, can't you, me being so much over here?

EMMA—(*springing to her feet—shocked but pleased*) Oh!

BENNY—(*turning away from her*) And now I'm going to blow. I'll stay at Bill Grainger's tonight and get the morning train.

EMMA—(*grabbing his arm*) No such thing! You'll stay right here!

BENNY—I can't—Emmer. If you was really my aunt, things'd be diff'rent and I'd tell 'em all to go to hell.

EMMA—(*smiling at him coquettishly*) But I'm glad I ain't your aunt.

BENNY—Well, I mean if you was related to me in some way. (*At some noise he hears from without, he starts frightenedly.*) Gosh, that sounded like our front door slamming. It's him and he's coming over. I got to beat it out the back way. (*He starts for the door on the right.*)

EMMA—(*clinging to him*) Benny! Don't go! You mustn't go!

BENNY—(*inspired by alarm and desire for revenge suddenly blurts out*) Say, let's me 'n' you git married, Emmer—tomorrow, eh? Then I kin stay! That'll stop 'em, damn 'em, and make 'em leave me alone.

EMMA—(*dazed with joy*) Married? You 'n' me? Oh, Benny, I'm too old. (*She hides her head on his shoulder.*)

BENNY—(*hurriedly, with one anxious eye on the door*) No, you ain't! Honest, you ain't! You're the best guy in this town! (*shaking her in his anxiety*) Say yes, Emmer! Say you will—first thing tomorrow.

EMMA—(*choking with emotion*) Yes—I will—if I'm not too old for you.

BENNY—(*jubilantly*) Tell him. Then he'll see where he gets off! Listen! I'm goin' to beat it to the kitchen and wait. You come tell me when he's gone. (*A knock comes at the door. He whispers*) That's him. I'm goin'.

EMMA—(*embracing him fiercely*) Oh, Benny! (*She kisses him on the lips. He ducks away from her and disappears off right. The knock is repeated. Emma dabs tremblingly at her cheeks with a handkerchief. Her face is beaming with happiness and looks indescribably silly. She trips lightly to the door and opens it—forcing a light, careless tone*) Oh, it's you, Caleb. Come right in and set. I was kind of expecting you. Benny—I'd heard you was due to home tonight. (*He comes in and shakes the hand she holds out to him in a limp, vague, absent-minded manner. In appearance, he has changed but little in the thirty years save that his hair is now nearly white and his face more deeply lined and wrinkled. His body is still erect, strong and vigorous. He wears dark clothes, much the same as he was dressed in Act One.*)

CALEB—(*mechanically*) Hello, Emmer. (*Once inside the door, he stands staring about the room, frowning. The garish strangeness of everything evidently repels and puzzles him. His face wears its set expression of an emotionless mask but his eyes cannot*) *conceal an inward struggle, a baffled and painful attempt to comprehend, a wounded look of bewildered hurt.*)

EMMA—(*blithely indifferent to this—pleasantly*) Are you looking at the changes I've made? You ain't seen this room since, have you? Of course not. What am I thinking of? They only got through with the work two weeks ago. Well, what d' you think of it?

CALEB—(*frowning—hesitatingly*) Why—it's—all right, I reckon.

EMMA—It was so gloomy and old-timey before, I just couldn't bear it. Now it's light and airy and young-looking, don't you think? (*with a sigh*) I suppose Pa and Ma turned over in their graves.

CALEB—(*grimly*) I reckon they did, too.

EMMA—Why, you don't mean to tell me you don't like it neither, Caleb? (*then as he doesn't reply, —resentfully*) Well, you always was a sot, old-fashioned critter, Caleb Williams, same as they was. (*She plumps herself into a rocker by the table—then, noticing the lost way in which he is looking about him*) Gracious sakes, why don't you set, Caleb? You give me the fidgets standing that way! You ain't a stranger that's got to be invited, are you? (*Then suddenly realizing the cause of his discomfiture, she smiles pityingly, not without a trace of malice.*) Are you looking for your old chair you used to set in? Is that it? Well, I had it put up in the attic. It didn't fit in with them new things.

CALEB—(*dully*) No, I s'pose it wouldn't.

EMMA—(*indicating a chair next to hers*) Do set down and make yourself to home. (*He does so gingerly. After a pause she asks perfunctorily*) Did you have good luck this voyage?

CALEB—(*again dully*) Oh, purty fair. (*He begins to look at her as if he were seeing her for the first time, noting every detail with a numb, stunned astonishment.*)

EMMA—You're looking as well as ever.

CALEB—(*dully*) Oh, I ain't got nothin' to complain of.

EMMA—You're the same as me, I reckon. (*happily*) Why I seem to get feelin' younger and more chipper every day, I declare I do. (*She becomes uncomfortably aware of his examination—nervously*) Land sakes, what you starin' at so?

CALEB—(*brusquely blurting out his disapproval*) You've changed, Emmer—changed so I wouldn't know you, hardly.

EMMA—(*resentfully*) Well, I hope you think it's for the best.

CALEB—(*evasively*) I ain't enough used to it yet—to tell.

EMMA—(*offended*) I ain't old-timey and old-maidy like I was, I guess that's what you mean. Well, I just got tired of mopin' alone in this house, waiting for death to take me and not enjoyin' anything. I was gettin' old before my time. And all at once, I saw what was happenin' and I made up my mind I was going to get some fun out of what Pa'd left me while I was still in the prime of life, as you might say.

CALEB—(*severely*) Be that paint and powder you got on your face, Emmer?

EMMA—(*embarrassed by this direct question*) Why, yes—I got a little mite—it's awful good for your complexion, they say—and in the cities now all the women wears it.

CALEB—(*sternly*) The kind of women I've seed in cities wearin' it— (*He checks himself and asks abruptly*) Wa'n't your hair turnin' gray last time I was to home?

EMMA—(*flustered*) Yes—yes—so it was—but then it started to come in again black as black all of a sudden.

CALEB—(*glancing at her shoes, stockings, and dress*) You're got up in them things like a young girl goin' to a dance.

EMMA—(*forcing a defiant laugh*) Maybe I will go soon's I learn—and Benny's goin' to teach me.

CALEB—(*keeping his rage in control—heavily*) Benny—

EMMA—(*suddenly bursting into hysterical tears*) And I think it's real mean of you, Caleb—nasty mean to come here on your first night to home—and—make—fun—of—my—clothes—and everything. (*She hides her face in her hands and sobs.*)

CALEB—(*overcome by remorse—forgetting his rage instantly—gets up and pats her on the shoulder—with rough tenderness*) Thar, thar, Emmer! Don't cry, now! I didn' mean nothin'. Don't pay no 'tention to what I said. I'm a durned old fool! What the hell do I know o' women's fixin's anyhow? And I reckon I be old-fashioned and sot in my ideas.

EMMA—(*reassured—pressing one of his hands gratefully*) It hurts—hearing you say—me 'n' you such old friends and—

CALEB—Forgit it, Emmer. I won't say no more about it. (*She dries her eyes and regains her composure. He goes back to his seat, his face greatly softened, looking at her with the blind eyes of love. There is a pause. Finally, he ventures in a gentle tone)* D'you know what time this be, Emmer?

EMMA—(*puzzled*) I don't know exactly, but there's a clock in the next room.

CALEB—(*quickly*) Hell, I don't mean that kind o' time. I mean—it was thirty years ago this spring.

EMMA—(*hastily*) Land sakes, don't let's talk of that. It only gets me thinking how old I am.

CALEB—(*with an affectionate smile*) We both got to realize now and then that we're gettin' old.

EMMA—(*bridling*) That's all right for you to say. You're twelve years older 'n me, don't forget, Caleb.

CALEB—(*smiling*) Waal, even that don't make you out no spring chicken, Emmer.

EMMA—(*stiffly*) A body's as old as they feels—and I feel right young.

CALEB—Waal, so do I as far as health goes. I'm as able and sound as ever. (*after a pause*) But, what I meant was, d'you remember what happened thirty years back?

EMMA—I suppose I do.

CALEB—D'you remember what I said that day?

EMMA—(*primly*) You said a lot that it's better to forget, if you ask me.

CALEB—I don't mean—that part of it. I mean when I was sayin' good-by, I said— (*He gasps—then blurts it out.*) I said I'd wait thirty years—if need be. (*after a pause*) I know you told me time and again not to go back to that. On'y—I was thinkin' all this last vige—that maybe—now when the thirty years are past—I was thinkin' that maybe— (*He looks at her humbly, imploring some encouragement. She stares straight before her, her mouth set thinly. He sighs forlornly and blunders on.*) Thirty years—that's a hell of a long time to wait, Emmer —makin' vige after vige always alone—and feelin' even more alone in between times when I was to home livin' right next door to you and callin' on you every evenin'. (*a pause*) I've made money enough, I know—but what the hell good's that to me—long as you're out of it? (*a pause*) Seems to me, Emmer, thirty o' the best years of a man's life ought to be proof enough to you to make you forget—that one slip o' mine.

EMMA—(*rousing herself—forcing a careless tone*) Land sakes, I forgot all about that long ago. And here you go remindin' me of it!

CALEB—(*doggedly*) You ain't answered what I was drivin' at, Emmer. (*A pause; then, as if suddenly afraid of what her answer will be, he breaks out quickly*) And I don't want you to answer right now, neither. I want you to take time to think it all over.

EMMA—(*feebly evasive*) All right, Caleb, I'll think it over.

CALEB—(*after a pause*) Somehow—seems to me 's if—you might really *need* me now. You never did before.

EMMA—(*suspiciously*) Why should I need you now any more'n any other time?

CALEB—(*embarrassedly*) Oh, I just feel that way.

EMMA—It ain't count o' nothin' Harriet's been tellin' you, is it? (*stiffly*) Her 'n' me ain't such good friends no more, if you must know.

CALEB—(*frowning*) Her 'n' me nearly had a fight right before I came over here. (*Emma starts.*) Harriet lets her tongue run away with her and says dumb fool things she don't really mean. I didn't pay much 'tention to what she was sayin'—but it riled me jest the same. She won't repeat such foolishness after the piece o' my mind I gave her.

EMMA—What did she say?

CALEB—Oh, nothin' worth tellin'. (*a pause*) But neither you nor me ought to get mad at Harriet serious. We'd ought, by all rights, to make allowances for her. You know 's well as me what a hard time she's had. Bein' married to Alf Rogers for five years'd pizin' any woman's life.

EMMA—No, he wasn't much good, there's no denyin'.

CALEB—And now there's Benny drivin' her crazy.

EMMA—(*instantly defensive*) Benny's all right!

CALEB—(*staring at her sharply—after a pause*) No, that's jest it. He ain't all right, Emmer.

EMMA—He is, too! He's as good as gold!

CALEB—(*frowning—with a trace of resentment*) You kin say so, Emmer, but the facts won't bear you out.

EMMA—(*excitedly*) What facts, Caleb Williams? If you mean the nasty lies the folks in this town are mean enough to gossip about him, I don't believe any of 'em. I ain't such a fool.

CALEB—(*bitterly*) Then you've changed, Emmer. You didn't stop about believin' the fool stories they gossiped about me that time.

EMMA—You owned up yourself that was true!

CALEB—And Benny'd own up if he was half the man I was! (*angrily*) But he ain't a man noways. He's a mean skunk from truck to keelson!

EMMA—(*springing to her feet*) Oh!

CALEB—(*vehemently*) I ain't judged him by what folks have told me. But I've watched him grow up from a boy and every time I've come to home I've seed he was gittin' more 'n' more like his Pa—and you know what a low dog Alf Rogers turned out to be, and what a hell he made for Harriet. Waal, I'm sayin' this boy Benny is just Alf all over again—on'y worse!

EMMA—Oh!

CALEB—They ain't no Williams' blood left in Benny. He's a mongrel Rogers! (*trying to calm himself a little and be convincing*) Listen, Emmer. You don't suppose I'd be sayin' it, do you, if it wasn't so? Ain't he Harriet's boy? Ain't I brought him up in my own house since he was knee-high? Don't you know I got some feelin's 'bout it and I wouldn't hold nothing agen him less'n I knowed it was true?

EMMA—(*harshly*) Yes, you would! You're only too anxious to believe all the bad you can about him. You've always hated him, he says—and I can see it's so.

CALEB—(*roughly*) You know damned well it ain't, you mean! Ain't I talked him over with you and asked your advice about him whenever I come to home? Ain't I always aimed to do all I could to help him git on right? You know damned well I never hated him! It's him that's always hated me! (*vengefully*) But I'm beginning to hate him now—and I've good cause for it!

EMMA—(*frightenedly*) What cause?

CALEB—(*ignoring her question*) I seed what he was comin' to years back. Then I thought when the war come, and he was drafted into it, that the army and strict discipline'd maybe make a man o' him. But it ain't! It's made him worse! It's killed whatever mite of decency was left in him. And I reckon now that if you put a coward in one of them there uniforms, he thinks it gives him the privilege to be a bully! Put a sneak in one and it gives him the courage to be a thief! That's why when the war was over Benny enlisted again 'stead o' goin' whalin' with me. He thinks he's found a good shield to cover up his natural-born laziness—and crookedness!

EMMA—(*outraged*) You can talk that way about him that went way over to France to shed his blood for you and me!

CALEB—I don't need no one to do my fightin' for me—against German or devil. And you know durned well he was only in the Quartermaster's Department unloadin' and truckin' groceries, as safe from a gun as you and me be this minute. (*with heavy scorn*) If he shed any blood, he must have got a nose bleed.

EMMA—Oh, you do hate him, I can see it! And you're just as mean as mean, Caleb Williams! All you've said is a wicked lie and you've got no cause—

CALEB—I ain't, eh? I got damned good cause, I tell ye! I ain't minded his meanness to me. I ain't even give as much heed to his meanness to Harriet as I'd ought to have, maybe. But when he starts in his sneakin' thievery with you, Emmer, I put my foot down on him for good and all!

EMMA—What sneakin' thievery with me? How dare you say such things?

CALEB—I got proof it's true. Why, he's even bragged all over town about bein' able to borrow all the money from you he'd a mind to—boastin' of what an old fool he was makin' of you, with you fixin' up your house all new to git him to comin' over.

EMMA—(*scarlet—blazing*) It's a lie! He never said it! You're makin' it all up—'cause you're—'cause you're—

CALEB—'Cause I'm what, Emmer?

EMMA—(*flinging it at him like a savage taunt*) 'Cause you're jealous of him, that's what! Any fool can see that!

CALEB—(*getting to his feet and facing her—slowly*) Jealous? Of Benny? How— I don't see your meanin' rightly.

EMMA—(*with triumphant malice*) Yes, you do! Don't pretend you don't! You're jealous 'cause you know I care a lot about him.

CALEB—(*slowly*) Why would I be jealous 'count o' that? What kind o' man d'you take me for? Don't I know you must care for him when you've been a'most as much a mother to him for years as Harriet was?

EMMA—(*wounded to the quick—furiously*) No such thing! You're a mean liar! I ain't never played a mother to him. He's never looked at me that way—never! And I don't care for him that way at all. Just because I'm a mite older 'n him—can't them things happen just as well as any other— what d'you suppose—can't I care for him same as any woman cares for a man? And I do! I care more'n I ever did for you! And that's why you're lying about him! You're jealous of that!

CALEB—(*staring at her with stunned eyes—in a hoarse whisper*) Emmer! Ye don't know what you're sayin', do ye?

EMMA—I do too!

CALEB—Harriet said you'd been actin' out o' your right senses.

EMMA—Harriet's mad because she knows Benny loves me better 'n her. And he does love me! He don't mind my bein' older. He's said so! And I love him, too!

CALEB—(*stepping back from her in horror*) Emmer!

EMMA—And he's asked me to marry him tomorrow. And I'm going to! Then you can all lie all you've a mind to!

CALEB—You're—going to—marry Benny?

EMMA—First thing tomorrow. And since you've throwed him out of his house in your mad jealousness, I've told him he can stay here with me tonight. And he's going to!

CALEB—(*his fists clenching—tensely*) Where—where is the skunk now?

EMMA—(*hastily*) Oh, he ain't here. He's gone up street.

CALEB—(*starting for the door in rear*) I'm goin' to find the skunk.

EMMA—(*seizing his arms—frightenedly*) What're you going to do?

CALEB—(*between his clenched teeth*) I don't know, Emmer —I don't know— On'y he ain't goin' to marry you, by God!

EMMA—Caleb! (*She tries to throw her arms about him to stop his going. He pushes her firmly but gently aside. She shrieks*) Caleb! (*She flings herself on her knees and wraps her arms around his legs in supplicating terror.*) Caleb! You ain't going to kill him, Caleb? You ain't going to hurt him, be you? Say you ain't! Tell me you won't hurt him! (*as she thinks she sees a relenting softness come into his face as he looks down at her*) Oh, Caleb, you used to say you loved me! Don't hurt him then, Caleb,—for my sake! I love him, Caleb! Don't hurt him— just because you think I'm an old woman ain't no reason— and I won't marry you, Caleb. I won't—not even if you have waited thirty years. I don't love you. I love him! And I'm going to marry him—tomorrow. So you won't hurt him, will you, Caleb—not when I ask you on my knees!

CALEB—(*breaking away from her with a shudder of disgust*) No, I won't touch him. If I was wantin' to git even with ye, I wouldn't dirty my hands on him. I'd let you marry the skunk and set and watch what happened—or else I'd offer him money not to marry ye—more money than the little mite you kin bring him—and let ye see how quick he'd turn his back on ye!

EMMA—(*getting to her feet—frenziedly*) It's a lie! He never would!

CALEB—(*unheeding—with a sudden ominous calm*) But I ain't goin' to do neither. You ain't worth it—and he ain't— and no one ain't, nor nothin'. Folks be all crazy and rotten to the core and I'm done with the whole kit and caboodle of 'em. I kin only see one course out for me and I'm goin' to take it. "A dead whale or a stove boat!" we says in whalin'— and my boat is stove! (*He strides away from her, stops, and turns back—savagely*) Thirty o' the best years of my life flung for a yeller dog like him to feed on. God! You used to say you was diff'rent from the rest o' folks. By God, if you are, it's just you're a mite madder'n they be! By God, that's all! (*He goes, letting the door slam to behind him.*)

EMMA—(*in a pitiful whimper*) Caleb! (*She sinks into a chair by the table sobbing hysterically. Benny sneaks through the door on right, hesitates for a while, afraid that his uncle may be coming back.*)

BENNY—(*finally, in a shrill whisper*) Aunt Emmer!

EMMA—(*raising her face to look at him for a second*) Oh, Benny! (*She falls to weeping again.*)

BENNY—Say, you don't think he's liable to come back, do you?

EMMA—No—he'll—never come back here—no more. (*sobs bitterly*)

BENNY—(*his courage returning, comes forward into the room*) Say, he's way up in the air, ain't he? (*with a grin*) Say, that was some bawlin' out he give you!

EMMA—You—you heard what he said?

BENNY—Sure thing. When you got to shoutin' I sneaked out o' the kitchen into there to hear what was goin' on. (*with a complacent grin*) Say, you certainly stood up for me all right. You're a good old scout at that, d'you know it?

EMMA—(*raising her absurd, besmeared face to his, as if expecting him to kiss her*) Oh, Benny, I'm giving up everything I've held dear all my life for your sake.

BENNY—(*turning away from her with a look of aversion*) Well, what about it? Ain't I worth it? Ain't I worth a million played-out old cranks like him? (*She stares at him bewilderedly. He takes a handful of almonds from his pocket and begins cracking and eating them, throwing the shells on the floor with an impudent carelessness.*) Hope you don't mind my havin' a feed? I found them out in the kitchen and helped myself.

EMMA—(*pitifully*) You're welcome to anything that's here, Benny.

BENNY—(*insolently*) Sure, I know you're a good scout. Don't rub it in. (*after a pause—boastfully*) Where did you get that stuff about askin' him not to hurt me? He'd have a swell chance! There's a lot of hard guys in the army have tried to get funny with me till I put one over on 'em. I'd like to see him start something! I could lick him with my hands handcuffed.

EMMA—(*revolted*) Oh!

BENNY—(*resentfully*) Think I'm bluffin'? I'll show you sometime. (*He swaggers about the room—finally stopping beside her. With a cunning leer*) Say, I been thinkin' it over and I guess I'll call his bluff.

EMMA—(*confusedly*) What—do you mean?

BENNY—I mean what he said just before he beat it—that he could get me not to marry you if he offered me more coin than you got. (*very interestedly*) Say, d'you s'pose the old miser really was serious about that?

EMMA—(*dazedly—as if she could not realize the significance of his words*) I—I—don't know, Benny.

BENNY—(*swaggering about again*) If I was only sure he wasn't stallin'! If I could get the old cuss to shell out that way! (*with a tickled chuckle*) Gosh, that'd be the real stunt aw right, aw right. Oui, oui! Maybe he wasn't kiddin' at that, the old simp! It's worth takin' a stab at, damned if it ain't. I ain't got nothin' to lose.

EMMA—(*frightenedly*) What—what're you talkin' about, Benny?

BENNY—Say, I think I'll go over and talk to Ma after a while. You can go over first to make sure he ain't there. I'll get her to put it up to him straight. If he's willin' to dig in his jeans for some real coin—real dough, this time!—I'll agree to beat it and not spill the beans for him with you. (*threateningly*) And if he's too tight, I'll go right through with what I said I would, if only to spite him! That's me!

EMMA—You mean—if he's willing to bribe you with money, you won't marry me tomorrow?

BENNY—Sure! If he'll put up enough money. I won't stand for no pikin'.

EMMA—(*whimpering*) Oh, Benny, you're only jokin', ain't you? You can't—you can't mean it!

BENNY—(*with careless effrontery*) Why can't I? Sure I mean it!

EMMA—(*hiding her face in her hands—with a tortured moan*) Oh, Benny!

BENNY—(*disgustedly*) Aw, don't go bawlin'! (*after a pause—a bit embarrassedly*) Aw, say, what d'you think, anyway? What're you takin' it so damned serious for—me askin' you to marry me, I mean? I was on'y sort of kiddin' anyway—just so you'd tell him and get his goat right. (*as she looks up at him with agonized despair—with a trace of something like pity showing in his tone*) Say, honest, Aunt Emmer, you didn't believe—you didn't think I was really stuck on you, did you? Ah, say, how could I? Have a heart! Why, you're as old as Ma is, ain't you, Aunt Emmer? (*He adds ruthlessly*) And I'll say you look it, too!

EMMA—(*cowering—as if he had struck her*) Oh! Oh!

BENNY—(*a bit irritated*) What's the use of blubberin', for God's sake? Can't you take it like a sport? Hell, I ain't lookin' to marry no one, if I can help it. What do I want a wife for? There's too many others. (*after a pause—as she still sobs—calculatingly*) Aw, come on, be a sport—and say, listen, if he ain't willin' to come across, I'll marry you all right, honest I will. (*more and more calculatingly*) Sure! If they mean that stuff about kickin' me out of home—sure I'll stay here with you! I'll do anything you want. If you want me to marry you, all you've got to do is say so—anytime! Only not tomorrow, we'd better wait and see—

EMMA—(*hysterically*) Oh, go away! Go away!

BENNY—(*looking down at her disgustedly*) Aw, come up for air, can't you? (*He slaps her on the back.*) Buck up! Be a pal! Tell me what your dope is. This thing's got me so balled up I don't know how I stand. (*with sudden fury*) Damn his hide! I'll bet he'll go and leave all he's got to some lousy orphan asylum now.

EMMA—Oh, go away! Go away!

BENNY—(*viciously*) So you're givin' me the gate, too, eh? I'd like to see you try it! You asked me to stay and I'll stick. It's all your fool fault that's got me in wrong. And now you want to shake me! This is what I get for foolin' around with an old hen like you that oughta been planted in the cemetery long ago! Paintin' your old mush and dressin' like a kid! Christ A'mighty!

EMMA—(*in a cry of despair*) Don't! Stop! Go away.

BENNY—(*suddenly alert—sharply*) Sh! I hear someone coming. (*shaking her*) Stop—now, Emmer! Damn it, you gotta go to the door. Maybe it's him. (*He scurries into the room on right. There is a faint knock at the door. Emma lifts her head. She looks horribly old and worn out. Her face is frozen into an expressionless mask, her eyes are red-rimmed, dull and lifeless. The knock is repeated more sharply. Emma rises like a weary automaton and goes to the door and opens it. Harriet is revealed standing outside.*)

HARRIET—(*making no movement to come in—coldly*) I want to speak to Caleb.

EMMA—(*dully*) He ain't here. He left a while back—said he was goin' up street—I think.

HARRIET—(*worriedly*) Oh, land sakes! (*then hostilely*) Do you know where Benny is?

EMMA—(*dully*) Yes, he's here.

HARRIET—(*contemptuously*) I might have guessed that! (*icily formal*) Would you mind tellin' him I want to see him?

EMMA—(*turns and calls*) Benny! Here's your Ma!

BENNY—(*comes from the next room*) Aw right. (*in a fierce whisper as he passes Emma*) What d'you tell her I was here for, you old fool? (*Emma gives no sign of having heard him but comes back to her chair and sits down. Benny slouches to the door*—*sullenly*) What d'you want, Ma?

HARRIET—(*coldly*) I wanted your Uncle Caleb, not you, but you'll have to do, bein' the only man about.

BENNY—(*suspiciously*) What is it?

HARRIET—(*a bit frightenedly*) I just heard a lot of queer noises down to the barn. Someone's in there, Benny, sure as I'm alive. They're stealin' the chickens, must be.

BENNY—(*carelessly*) It's only the rats.

HARRIET—(*angrily*) Don't play the idiot! This was a big thumpin' noise no rat'd make.

BENNY—What'd any guy go stealin' this early— (*as Harriet turns away angrily*—*placatingly*) Aw right, I'm coming. I'll have a look if that'll satisfy you. Don't go gettin' sore at me again. (*While he is speaking he goes out and disappears after his mother. Emma sits straight and stiff in her chair for a while, staring before her with waxy eyes. Then she gets to her feet and goes from window to window taking down all the curtains with quick mechanical movements. She throws them on a pile in the middle of the floor. She lifts down the framed pictures from the walls and piles them on the curtains. She takes the cushions and throws them on; pushes the rugs to the pile with her feet; sweeps everything off the table onto the floor. She does all this without a trace of change in her expression*—*rapidly, but with no apparent effort. There is the noise of running footsteps from outside and Benny bursts into the room panting for breath. He is terribly excited and badly frightened.*)

BENNY—(*stops short as he sees the pile on the floor*) What the hell—

EMMA—(*dully*) The junk man's coming for them in the morning.

BENNY—(*too excited to be surprised*) To hell with that! Say, listen Aunt Emmer, he's hung himself—Uncle Caleb—in the barn—he's dead!

EMMA—(*slowly letting the words fall—like a beginner on the typewriter touching two new letters*) Caleb—dead!

BENNY—(*voluble now*) Dead as a door nail! Neck's busted. I just cut him down and carried him to home. Say, you've got to come over and help look after Ma. She's goin' bugs. I can't do nothin' with her.

EMMA—(*as before*) Caleb hanged himself—in the barn?

BENNY—Yes—and made a sure job of it. (*with morbid interest in the details*) He got a halter and made a noose of the rope for his neck and climbed up in the loft and hitched the leather end to a beam and then let himself drop. He must have kicked in that quick! (*He snaps his fingers—then urgently*) Say, come on. Come on over 'n' help with Ma, can't you? She's goin' wild. I can't do nothin'!

EMMA—(*vaguely*) I'll be over—in a minute. (*then with a sudden air of having decided something irrevocably*) I got to go down to the barn.

BENNY—Barn? Say, are you crazy? He ain't there now. I told you I carried him home.

EMMA—I mean—my barn. I got to go down—

BENNY—(*exasperated*) Oh hell! You're as bad as Ma! Everyone's lost their heads but me. Well, I got to get someone else, that's all. (*He rushes out rear, slamming the door behind him.*)

EMMA—(*after a tense pause—with a sudden outburst of wild grief*) Caleb! (*then in a strange whisper*) Wait, Caleb, I'm going down to the barn. (*She moves like a sleepwalker toward the door in the rear as*

The Curtain Falls)

THE FIRST MAN

A Play in Four Acts

CHARACTERS

CURTIS JAYSON
MARTHA, *his wife*
JOHN JAYSON, *his father, a banker*
JOHN, JR., *his brother*
RICHARD, *his brother*
ESTHER (MRS. MARK SHEFFIELD), *his sister*
LILY, *his sister*
MRS. DAVIDSON, *his father's aunt*
MARK SHEFFIELD, *a lawyer*
EMILY, *John Jr.'s wife*
EDWARD BIGELOW
A MAID
A TRAINED NURSE

SCENES

ACT I

Living-room in the house of Curtis Jayson, Bridgetown,
Conn.—an afternoon in early Fall.

ACT II

Curtis' study—morning of the following day.

ACT III

The same—three o'clock in the morning of a day in early
spring of the next year.

ACT IV

Same as Act I—three days later.

The First Man

ACT ONE

SCENE—*Living-room of Curtis Jayson's house in Bridgetown, Conn.*

A large, comfortable room. On the left, an armchair, a big open fireplace, a writing desk with chair in far left corner. On this side there is also a door leading into Curtis' study. In the rear, center, a double doorway opening on the hall and the entryway. Bookcases are built into the wall on both sides of this doorway. In the far right corner, a grand piano. Three large windows looking out on the lawn, and another armchair, front, are on this right side of the room. Opposite the fireplace is a couch, facing front. Opposite the windows on the right is a long table with magazines, reading lamp, etc. Four chairs are grouped about the table. The walls and ceiling are in a French gray color. A great rug covers most of the hardwood floor.

It is around four o'clock of a fine afternoon in early fall.

As the curtain rises, Martha, Curtis and Bigelow are discovered. Martha is a healthy, fine-looking woman of thirty-eight. She does not appear this age for her strenuous life in the open has kept her young and fresh. She possesses the frank, clear, direct quality of outdoors, outspoken and generous. Her wavy hair is a dark brown, her eyes blue-gray. Curtis Jayson is a tall, rangy, broad-shouldered man of thirty-seven. While spare his figure has an appearance of rugged health, of great nervous strength held in reserve. His square-jawed, large-featured face retains an eager boyish enthusiasm in spite of its prevailing expression of thoughtful, preoccupied aloofness. His crisp dark hair is graying at the temples. Edward Bigelow is a large, handsome man of thirty-nine. His face shows culture and tolerance, a sense of humor, a lazy unambitious contentment. Curtis is reading an article in some scientific periodical, seated by the table. Martha and Bigelow are sitting nearby, laughing and chatting.

BIGELOW—(*is talking with a comically worried but earnest air*) Do you know, I'm getting so I'm actually afraid to leave them alone with that governess. She's too romantic. I'll wager she's got a whole book full of ghost stories, superstitions, and yellow-journal horrors up her sleeve.

MARTHA—Oh, pooh! Don't go milling around for trouble. When I was a kid I used to get fun out of my horrors.

BIGELOW—But I imagine you were more courageous than most of us.

MARTHA—Why?

BIGELOW—Well, Nevada—the Far West at that time—I should think a child would have grown so accustomed to violent scenes—

MARTHA—(*smiling*) Oh, in the mining camps; but you don't suppose my father lugged me along on his prospecting trips, do you? Why, I never saw any rough scenes until I'd finished with school and went to live with father in Goldfield.

BIGELOW—(*smiling*) And then you met Curt.

MARTHA—Yes—but I didn't mean he was a rough scene. He was very mild even in those days. Do tell me what he was like at Cornell.

BIGELOW—A romanticist—and he still is!

MARTHA—(*pointing at Curtis with gay mischief*) What! That sedate man! Never!

CURTIS—(*looking up and smiling at them both affectionately—lazily*) Don't mind him, Martha. He always was crazy.

BIGELOW—(*to Curt—accusingly*) Why did you elect to take up mining engineering at Cornell instead of a classical degree at the Yale of your fathers and brothers? Because you had been reading Bret Harte in prep. school and mistaken him for a modern realist. You devoted four years to grooming yourself for another outcast of Poker Flat. (*Martha laughs.*)

CURTIS—(*grinning*) It was you who were hypnotized by Harte—so much so that his West of the past is still your blinded New England–movie idea of the West at present. But go on. What next?

BIGELOW—Next? You get a job as engineer in that Goldfield mine—but you are soon disillusioned by a laborious life where six-shooters are as rare as nuggets. You try prospecting. You find nothing but different varieties of pebbles. But it is necessary to your nature to project romance into these stones, so you go in strong for geology. As a geologist, you become a slave to the Romance of the Rocks. It is but a step from that to anthropology—the last romance of all. There you find yourself—because there is no further to go. You win fame as the most proficient of young skull-hunters—and wander over the face of the globe, digging up bones like an old dog.

CURTIS—(*with a laugh*) The man is mad, Martha.

BIGELOW—Mad! What an accusation to come from one who is even now considering setting forth on a five-year excavating contest in search of the remains of our gibbering ancestor, the First Man!

CURTIS—(*with sudden seriousness*) I'm not considering it any longer. I've decided to go.

MARTHA—(*starting—the hurt showing in her voice*) When did you decide?

CURTIS—I only really came to a decision this morning. (*with a seriousness that forces Bigelow's interested attention*) It's a case of got to go. It's a tremendous opportunity that it would be a crime for me to neglect.

BIGELOW—And a big honor, too, isn't it, to be picked as a member of such a large affair?

CURTIS—(*with a smile*) I guess it's just that they want all the men with considerable practical experience they can get. There are bound to be hardships and they know I'm hardened to them. (*turning to his wife with an affectionate smile*) We haven't roughed it in the queer corners for the last ten years without knowing how it's done, have we, Martha?

MARTHA—(*dully*) No, Curt.

CURTIS—(*with an earnest enthusiasm*) And this expedition *is* what you call a large affair, Big. It's the largest thing of its kind ever undertaken. The possibilities, from the standpoint of anthropology, are limitless.

BIGELOW—(*with a grin*) Aha! Now we come to the Missing Link!

CURTIS—(*frowning*) Darn your Barnum and Bailey circus lingo, Big. This isn't a thing to mock at. I should think the origin of man would be something that would appeal even to your hothouse imagination. Modern science believes—knows—that Asia was the first home of the human race. That's where we're going, to the great Central Asian plateau north of the Himalayas.

BIGELOW—(*more soberly*) And there you hope to dig up—our first ancestor?

CURTIS—It's a chance in a million, but I believe we may, myself—at least find authentic traces of him so that we can reconstruct his life and habits. I was up in that country a lot while I was mining advisor to the Chinese government—did some of my own work on the side. The extraordinary results I obtained with the little means at my disposal convinced me of the riches yet to be uncovered. The First Man may be among them.

BIGELOW—(*turning to Martha*) And you were with him on that Asian plateau?

MARTHA—Yes, I've always been with him.

CURTIS—You bet she has. (*He goes over and puts his hand on his wife's shoulder affectionately.*) Martha's more efficient than a whole staff of assistants and secretaries. She knows more about what I'm doing than I do half the time. (*He turns toward his study.*) Well, I guess I'll go in and work some.

MARTHA—(*quietly*) Do you need me now, Curt?

BIGELOW—(*starting up*) Yes, if you two want to work together, why just shoo me—

CURTIS—(*puts both hands on his shoulders and forces him to his seat again*) No. Sit down, Big. I don't need Martha now. (*coming over to her, bends down and kisses her—rather mockingly*) I couldn't deprive Big of an audience for his confessions of a fond parent.

BIGELOW—Aha! Now it's you who are mocking at something you know nothing about. (*An awkward silence follows this remark.*)

CURTIS—(*frowning*) I guess you're forgetting, aren't you, Big? (*He turns and walks into his study, closing the door gently behind him.*)

MARTHA—(*after a pause—sadly*) Poor Curt.

BIGELOW—(*ashamed and confused*) I had forgotten—

MARTHA—The years have made me reconciled. They haven't Curt. (*She sighs—then turns to Bigelow with a forced smile.*) I suppose it's hard for any of you back here to realize that Curt and I ever had any children.

BIGELOW—(*after a pause*) How old were they when—?

MARTHA—Three years and two—both girls. (*She goes on sadly.*) We had a nice little house in Goldfield. (*forcing a smile*) We were very respectable home folks then. The wandering came later, after— It was a Sunday in winter when Curt and I had gone visiting some friends. The nurse girl fell asleep— or something—and the children sneaked out in their underclothes and played in the snow. Pneumonia set in—and a week later they were both dead.

BIGELOW—(*shocked*) Good heavens!

MARTHA—We were real lunatics for a time. And then when we'd calmed down enough to realize—how things stood with us—we swore we'd never have children again— to steal away their memory. It wasn't what you thought— romanticism—that set Curt wandering—and me with him. It was a longing to lose ourselves—to forget. He flung himself with all his power into every new study that interested him. He couldn't keep still, mentally or bodily—and I followed. He needed me—then—so dreadfully!

BIGELOW—And is it that keeps driving him on now?

MARTHA—Oh, no. He's found himself. His work has taken the place of the children.

BIGELOW—And with you, too?

MARTHA—(*with a wan smile*) Well, I've helped—all I could. His work has me in it, I like to think—and I have him.

BIGELOW—(*shaking his head*) I think people are foolish to stand by such an oath as you took—forever. (*with a smile*) Children are a great comfort in one's old age, I've tritely found.

MARTHA—(*smiling*) Old age!

BIGELOW—I'm knocking at the door of fatal forty.

MARTHA—(*with forced gayety*) You're not very tactful, I must say. Don't you know I'm thirty-eight?

BIGELOW—(*gallantly*) A woman is as old as she looks. You're not thirty yet.

MARTHA—(*laughing*) After that nice remark I'll have to forgive you everything, won't I? (*Lily Jayson comes in from the rear. She is a slender, rather pretty girl of twenty-five. The stamp of college student is still very much about her. She rather insists on a superior, intellectual air, is full of nervous, thwarted energy. At the sight of them sitting on the couch together, her eyebrows are raised.*)

LILY—(*coming into the room—breezily*) Hello, Martha. Hello, Big. (*They both get up with answering "Hellos."*) I walked right in regardless. Hope I'm not interrupting.

MARTHA—Not at all.

LILY—(*sitting down by the table as Martha and Bigelow resume their seats on the lounge*) I must say it sounded serious. I heard you tell Big you'd forgive him everything, Martha. (*dryly—with a mocking glance at Bigelow*) You're letting yourself in for a large proposition.

BIGELOW—(*displeased but trying to smile it off*) The past is never past for a dog with a bad name, eh, Lily? (*Lily laughs. Bigelow gets up.*) If you want to reward me for my truthfulness, Mrs. Jayson, help me take the kids for an airing in the car. I know it's an imposition but they've grown to expect you. (*glancing at his watch*) By Jove, I'll have to run along. I'll get them and then pick you up here. Is that all right?

MARTHA—Fine.

BIGELOW—I'll run, then. Good-by, Lily. (*She nods. Bigelow goes out rear.*)

MARTHA—(*cordially*) Come on over here, Lily.

LILY—(*sits on couch with Martha—after a pause—with a smile*) You were forgetting, weren't you?

MARTHA—What?

LILY—That you'd invited all the family over here to tea this afternoon. I'm the advance guard.

MARTHA—(*embarrassed*) So I was! How stupid!

LILY—(*with an inquisitive glance at Martha's face but with studied carelessness*) Do you like Bigelow?

MARTHA—Yes, very much. And Curt thinks the world of him.

LILY—Oh, Curt is the last one to be bothered by anyone's morals. Curt and I are the unconventional ones of the family. The trouble with Bigelow, Martha, is that he was too careless to conceal his sins—and that won't go down in this Philistine small town. You have to hide and be a fellow hypocrite or they revenge themselves on you. Bigelow didn't. He flaunted his love-affairs in everyone's face. I used to admire him for it.

No one exactly blamed him, in their secret hearts. His wife was a terrible, strait-laced creature. No man could have endured her. (*disgustedly*) After her death he suddenly acquired a bad conscience. He'd never noticed the children before. I'll bet he didn't even know their names. And then, presto, he's about in our midst giving an imitation of a wet hen with a brood of ducks. It's a bore, if you ask me.

MARTHA—(*flushing*) I think it's very fine of him.

LILY—(*shaking her head*) His reform is too sudden. He's joined the hypocrites, I think.

MARTHA—I'm sure he's no hypocrite. When you see him with the children—

LILY—Oh, I know he's a good actor. Lots of women have been in love with him. (*then suddenly*) You won't be furious if I'm very, very frank, will you, Martha?

MARTHA—(*surprised*) No, of course not, Lily.

LILY—Well, I'm the bearer of a message from the Jayson family.

MARTHA—(*astonished*) A message? For me?

LILY—Don't think that I have anything to do with it. I'm only a Victor record of their misgivings. Shall I switch it going? Well, then, father thinks, brother John and wife, sister Esther and husband all think that you are unwisely intimate with this same Bigelow.

MARTHA—(*stunned*) I? Unwisely intimate—? (*suddenly laughing with amusement*) Well, you sure are funny people!

LILY—No, we're not funny. We'd be all right if we were. On the contrary, we're very dull and deadly. Bigelow really has a villainous rep. for philandering. But, of course, you didn't know that.

MARTHA—(*beginning to feel resentful—coldly*) No, I didn't and I don't care to know it now.

LILY—(*calmly*) I told them you wouldn't relish their silly advice. (*in a very confidential, friendly tone*) Oh, I hate their narrow small-town ethics as much as you do, Martha. I sympathize with you, indeed I do. But I have to live with them and so, for comfort's sake, I've had to make compromises. And you're going to live in our midst from now on, aren't you? Well then, you'll have to make compromises, too—if you want any peace.

MARTHA—But—compromises about what? (*forcing a laugh*) I refuse to take it seriously. How anyone could think—it's too absurd.

LILY—What set them going was Big's being around such an awful lot the weeks Curt was in New York, just after you'd settled down here. You must acknowledge he was—very much present then, Martha.

MARTHA—But it was on account of his children. They were always with him.

LILY—The town doesn't trust this sudden fond parenthood, Martha. We've known him too long, you see.

MARTHA—But he's Curt's oldest and best friend.

LILY—We've found they always are.

MARTHA—(*springing to her feet—indignantly*) It's a case of evil minds, it seems to me—and it would be extremely insulting if I didn't have a sense of humor. (*resentfully*) You can tell your family, that as far as I'm concerned, the town may—

LILY—Go to the devil. I knew you'd say that. Well, fight the good fight. You have all my best wishes. (*with a sigh*) I wish I had something worth fighting for. Now that I'm through with college, my occupation's gone. All I do is read book after book. The only live people are the ones in books, I find, and the only live life.

MARTHA—(*immediately sympathetic*) You're lonely, that's what, Lily.

LILY—(*dryly*) Don't pity me, Martha—or I'll join the enemy.

MARTHA—I'm not. But I'd like to help you if I could. (*after a pause*) Have you ever thought of marrying?

LILY—(*with a laugh*) Martha! How banal! The men I see are enough to banish that thought if I ever had it.

MARTHA—Marriage isn't only the man. It's children. Wouldn't you like to have children?

LILY—(*turning to her bluntly*) Wouldn't you?

MARTHA—(*confused*) But—Lily—

LILY—Oh, I know it wasn't practicable as long as you elected to wander with Curt—but why not now when you've definitely settled down here? I think that would solve things all round. If you could present Father with a grandson, I'm sure he'd fall on your neck. He feels piqued at the John and Esther families because they've had a run of girls. A male Jayson! Aunt Davidson would weep with joy. (*suddenly*) You're thirty-eight, aren't you, Martha?

MARTHA—Yes.

LILY—Then why don't you—before it's too late? (*Martha, struggling with herself, does not answer. Lily goes on slowly.*) You won't want to tag along with Curt to the ends of the earth forever, will you? (*curiously*) Wasn't that queer life like any other? I mean, didn't it get to pall on you?

MARTHA—(*as if confessing it reluctantly*) Yes—perhaps—in the last two years.

LILY—(*decisively*) It's time for both of you to rest on your laurels. Why can't Curt keep on with what he's doing now— stay home and write his books?

MARTHA—Curt isn't that kind. The actual work—the romance of it—that's his life.

LILY—But if he goes and you have to stay, you'll be lonesome—(*meaningly*) alone.

MARTHA—Horribly. I don't know what I'll do.

LILY—Then why—why? Think, Martha. If Curt knew— that was to happen—he'd want to stay here with you. I'm sure he would.

MARTHA—(*shaking her head sadly*) No. Curt has grown to dislike children. They remind him of—ours that were taken. He adored them so. He's never become reconciled.

LILY—If you confronted Curt with the actual fact, he'd be reconciled soon enough, and happy in the bargain.

MARTHA—(*eagerly*) Do you really think so?

LILY—And you, Martha—I can tell from the way you've talked that you'd like to.

MARTHA—(*excitedly*) Yes, I—I never thought I'd ever want to again. For many years after they died I never once dreamed of it— But lately—the last years—I've felt—and when we came to live here—and I saw all around me— homes—and children, I— (*She hesitates as if ashamed at having confessed so much.*)

LILY—(*putting an arm around her —affectionately*) I know. (*vigorously*) You must, that's all there is to it! If you want my advice, you go right ahead and don't tell Curt until it's a fact he'll have to learn to like, willy-nilly. You'll find, in his inmost heart, he'll be tickled to death.

MARTHA—(*forcing a smile*) Yes, I—I'll confess I thought of that. In spite of my fear, I—I've—I mean—I— (*She flushes in a shamed confusion.*)

LILY—(*looking at her searchingly*) Why, Martha, what— (*then suddenly understanding—with excited pleasure*) Martha! I know! It is so, isn't it? It is!

MARTHA—(*in a whisper*) Yes.

LILY—(*kissing her affectionately*) You dear, you! (*then after a pause*) How long have you known?

MARTHA—For over two months. (*There is a ring from the front door bell in the hall.*)

LILY—(*jumping up*) I'll bet that's we Jaysons now. (*She runs to the door in the rear and looks down the hall to the right.*) Yes, it's Esther and husband and Aunt Davidson. (*She comes back to Martha laughing excitedly. The maid is seen going to the door.*) The first wave of attack, Martha! Be brave! The Young Guard dies but never surrenders!

MARTHA—(*displeased but forcing a smile*) You make me feel terribly ill at ease when you put it that way, Lily. (*She rises now and goes to greet the visitors, who enter. Mrs. Davidson is seventy-five years old—a thin, sinewy old lady, old-fashioned, unbending and rigorous in manner. She is dressed aggressively in the fashion of a bygone age. Esther is a stout, middle-aged woman with the round, unmarked, sentimentally-contented face of one who lives unthinkingly from day to day, sheltered in an assured position in her little world. Mark, her husband, is a lean, tall, stooping man of about forty-five. His long face is alert, shrewd, cautious, full of the superficial craftiness of the lawyer mind. Martha kisses the two women, shakes hands with Mark, uttering the usual meaningless greetings in a forced tone. They reply in much the same spirit. There is the buzz of this empty chatter while Martha gets them seated. Lily stands looking on with a cynical smile of amusement. Mrs. Davidson is in the chair at the end of table, left, Esther sits by Martha on couch, Mark in chair at front of table.*) Will you have tea now or shall we wait for the others?

ESTHER—Let's wait. They ought to be here any moment.

LILY—(*maliciously*) Just think, Martha had forgotten you

were coming. She was going motoring with Bigelow. (*There is a dead silence at this—broken diplomatically by Sheffield.*)

SHEFFIELD—Where is Curt, Martha?

MARTHA—Hard at work in his study. I'm afraid he's there for the day.

SHEFFIELD—(*condescendingly*) Still plugging away at his book, I suppose. Well, I hope it will be a big success.

LILY—(*irritated by his smugness*) As big a success as the brief you're writing to restrain the citizens from preventing the Traction Company robbing them, eh, Mark? (*Before anyone can reply, she turns suddenly on her aunt who is sitting rigidly on her chair, staring before her stonily like some old lady in a daguerreotype—in a loud challenging tone*) You don't mind if I smoke, Aunt? (*She takes a cigarette out of case and lights it.*)

ESTHER—(*smiling*) Lily!

MRS. DAVIDSON—(*fixes Lily with her stare—in a tone of irrevocable decision*) We'll get you married, young lady, and that very soon. What you need to bring you down to earth is a husband and the responsibility of children. (*turning her glance to Martha, a challenge in her question*) Every woman who is able should have children. Don't you believe that, Martha Jayson? (*She accentuates the full name.*)

MARTHA—(*taken aback for a moment but restraining her resentment—gently*) Yes, I do, Mrs. Davidson.

MRS. DAVIDSON—(*seemingly placated by this reply—in a milder tone*) You must call me aunt, my dear. (*meaningly*) All the Jaysons do.

MARTHA—(*simply*) Thank you, Aunt.

LILY—(*as if all of this aroused her irritation—in a nervous fuming*) Why don't the others come, darn 'em? I'm dying for my tea. (*The door from the study is opened and Curt appears. They all greet him.*)

CURTIS—(*absent-mindedly*) Hello, everybody. (*then with a preoccupied air to Martha*) Martha, I don't want to interrupt you—but—

MARTHA—(*getting up briskly*) You want my help?

CURTIS—(*with the same absent-minded air*) Yes—not for long—just a few notes before I forget them. (*He goes back into the study.*)

MARTHA—(*seemingly relieved by this interruption and glad of the chance it gives to show them her importance to Curt*) You'll excuse me for a few moments, all of you, won't you? (*They all nod.*)

MRS. DAVIDSON—(*rather harshly*) Why doesn't Curt hire a secretary? That is no work for his wife.

MARTHA—(*quietly*) A paid secretary could hardly give the sympathy and understanding Curt needs, Mrs. Davidson. (*proudly*) And she would have to study for years, as I have done, in order to take my place. (*to Lily*) If I am not here by the time the others arrive, will you see about the tea, Lily—?

LILY—(*eagerly*) Sure. I love to serve drinks. If I were a man, I'd be a bartender—in Mexico or Canada.

MARTHA—(*going toward the study*) I'll be with you again in a minute, I hope. (*She goes in and shuts the door behind her.*)

ESTHER—(*pettishly*) Even people touched by a smattering of science seem to get rude, don't they?

MRS. DAVIDSON—(*harshly*) I have heard much silly talk of this being an age of free women, and I have always said it was tommyrot. (*pointing to the study*) She is an example. She is more of a slave to Curt's hobbies than any of my generation were to anything but their children. (*still more harshly*) Where are her children?

LILY—They died, Aunt, as children have a bad habit of doing. (*then, meaningly*) However, I wouldn't despair if I were you. (*Mrs. Davidson stares at her fixedly.*)

ESTHER—(*betraying a sudden frightened jealousy*) What do you mean, Lily? What are you so mysterious about? What did she say? What—?

LILY—(*mockingly*) Mark, your frau seems to have me on the stand. Can I refuse to answer? (*There is a ring at the bell. Lily jumps to her feet excitedly.*) Here comes the rest of our Grand Fleet. Now I'll have my tea. (*She darts out to the hallway.*)

ESTHER—(*shaking her head*) Goodness, Lily is trying on the nerves. (*Jayson, his two sons, John and Dick, and John's wife, Emily, enter from hallway in rear. Jayson, the father, is a short, stout bald-headed man of sixty. A typical, small-town, New England best-family banker, reserved in pose, unobtrusively important—a placid exterior hiding querulousness and a fussy temper. John Junior is his father over again in appearance, but pompous, obtrusive, purse-and-family-proud, extremely irritating in his self-complacent air of authority, emptily assertive and loud. He is about forty. Richard, the other brother, is a typical young Casino and country club member, college-bred, good-looking, not unlikable. He has been an officer in the war and has not forgotten it. Emily, John Jr.'s wife, is one of those small, mouse-like women who conceal beneath an outward aspect of gentle, unprotected innocence a very active envy, a silly pride, and a mean malice. The people in the room with the exception of Mrs. Davidson rise to greet them. All exchange familiar, perfunctory greetings. Sheffield relinquishes his seat in front of the table to Jayson, going to the chair, right front, himself. John and Dick take the two chairs to the rear of table. Emily joins Esther on the couch and they whisper together excitedly, Esther doing most of the talking. The men remain in uncomfortable silence for a moment.*)

DICK—(*with gay mockery*) Well, the gang's all here. Looks like the League of Nations. (*then with impatience*) Let's get down to cases, folks. I want to know why I've been summoned here. I'm due for tournament mixed-doubles at the Casino at five. Where's the tea—and has Curt a stick in the cellar to put in it?

LILY—(*appearing in the doorway*) Here's tea—but no stick for you, sot. (*The maid brings in tray with tea things.*)

JOHN—(*heavily*) It seems it would be more to the point to inquire where our hostess—

JAYSON—(*rousing himself again*) Yes. And where is Curt?

LILY—Working at his book. He called Martha to take notes on something.

ESTHER—(*with a trace of resentment*) She left us as if she were glad of the excuse.

LILY—Stuff, Esther! She knows how much Curt depends on her—and we don't.

EMILY—(*in her quiet, lisping voice—with the most innocent air*) Martha seems to be a model wife. (*But there is some quality to the way she says it that makes them all stare at her uneasily.*)

LILY—(*insultingly*) How well you say what you don't mean, Emily! Twinkle, twinkle, little bat! But I'm forgetting to do the honors. Tea, everybody? (*without waiting for any answer*) Tea, everybody! (*The tea is served.*)

JAYSON—(*impatiently*) Stop fooling, Lily. Let's get to our muttons. Did you talk with Martha?

LILY—(*briskly*) I did, sir.

JAYSON—(*in a lowered voice*) What did she say?

LILY—She said you could all go to the devil! (*They all look shocked and insulted. Lily enjoys this, then adds quietly*) Oh, not in those words. Martha is a perfect lady. But she made it plain she will thank you to mind your own business.

ESTHER—(*volubly*) And just imagine, she'd even forgotten she'd asked us here this afternoon and was going motoring with Bigelow.

LILY—With his three children, too, don't forget.

EMILY—(*softly*) They have become such well-behaved and intelligent children, they say. (*Again all the others hesitate, staring at her suspiciously.*)

LILY—(*sharply*) You'd better let Martha train yours for a while, Emily. I'm sure she'd improve their manners—though, of course, she couldn't give them any intelligence.

EMILY—(*with the pathos of outraged innocence*) Oh!

DICK—(*interrupting*) So it's Bigelow you're up in the air about? (*He gives a low whistle—then frowns angrily.*) The deuce you say!

LILY—(*mockingly*) Look at our soldier boy home from the wars getting serious about the family honor! It's too bad this is a rough, untutored country where they don't permit dueling, isn't it, Dick?

DICK—(*his pose crumbling—angrily*) Go to the devil!

SHEFFIELD—(*with a calm, judicious air*) This wrangling is getting us nowhere. You say she was resentful about our well-meant word to the wise?

JAYSON—(*testily*) Surely she must realize that some consideration is due the position she occupies in Bridgetown as Curt's wife.

LILY—Martha is properly unimpressed by big frogs in tiny puddles. And there you are.

MRS. DAVIDSON—(*outraged*) The idea! She takes a lot upon herself—the daughter of a Wild Western coal-miner.

LILY—(*mockingly*) Gold miner, Aunt.

MRS. DAVIDSON—It makes no difference—a common miner!

SHEFFIELD—(*keenly inquisitive*) Just before the others came, Lily, you gave out some hints—very definite hints, I should say—

ESTHER—(*excitedly*) Yes, you did, Lily. What did you mean?

LILY—(*uncertainly*) Perhaps I shouldn't have. It's not my secret. (*enjoying herself immensely now that she holds the spotlight—after a pause, in a stage whisper*) Shall I tell you? Yes, I can't help telling. Well, Martha is going to have a son. (*They are all stunned and flabbergasted and stare at her speechlessly.*)

MRS. DAVIDSON—(*her face lighting up—joyously*) A son! Curt's son!

JAYSON—(*pleased by the idea but bewildered*) A son?

DICK—(*smartly*) Lily's kidding you. How can she know it's a son—unless she's a clairvoyant.

ESTHER—(*with glad relief*) Yes, how stupid!

LILY—I am clairvoyant in this case. Allah is great and it will be a son—if only to make you and Emily burst with envy among your daughters.

ESTHER—Lily!

EMILY—Oh!

JAYSON—(*testily*) Keep still for a moment, Lily, for God's sake. This is no subject to joke about, remember.

LILY—Martha told me. I know that.

JAYSON—And does Curt know this?

LILY—No, not yet. Martha has been afraid to tell him.

JAYSON—Ah, that explains matters. You know I asked Curt some time ago—and he said it was impossible.

EMILY—(*with a lift of her eyebrows*) Impossible? Why, what a funny thing to say.

SHEFFIELD—(*keenly lawyer-like*) And why is Martha afraid to tell him, Lily?

LILY—It's all very simple. When the two died years ago, they said they would never have one again. Martha thinks Curt is still haunted by their memory and is afraid he will resent another as an intruder. I told her that was all foolishness—that a child was the one thing to make Curt settle down for good at home here and write his books.

JAYSON—(*eagerly*) Yes, I believe that myself. (*pleased*) Well, this is fine news.

EMILY—Still it was her duty to tell Curt, don't you think? I don't see how she could be afraid of Curt—for those reasons. (*They all stare at her.*)

ESTHER—(*resentfully*) I don't, either. Why, Curt's the biggest-hearted and kindest—

EMILY—I wonder how long she's known—this?

LILY—(*sharply*) Two months, she said.

EMILY—Two months? (*She lets this sink in.*)

JOHN—(*quickly scenting something—eagerly*) What do you mean, Emily? (*then as if he read her mind*) Two months? But before that—Curt was away in New York almost a month!

LILY—(*turning on Emily fiercely*) So! You got someone to say it for you as you always do, Poison Mind! Oh, I wish the ducking stool had never been abolished!

EMILY—(*growing crimson—falteringly*) I—I didn't mean—

JOHN—(*furiously*) Where the honor of the family is at stake—

LILY—(*fiercely*) Ssshh, you empty barrel! I think I hear— (*The door from the study is opened and Martha comes in in the midst of a heavy silence. All the gentlemen rise stiffly. Martha is made immediately self-conscious and resentful by the feeling that they have been discussing her unfavorably.*)

MARTHA—(*coming forward—with a forced cordiality*) How do you do, everybody? So sorry I wasn't here when you came. I hope Lily made proper excuses for me. (*She goes from one to the other of the four latest comers with* "So glad you came," *etc. They reply formally and perfunctorily. Martha finally finds a seat on the couch between Emily and Esther.*) I hope Lily—but I see you've all had tea.

LILY—(*trying to save the situation—gayly*) Yes. You can trust me as understudy for the part of hostess any time.

MARTHA—(*forcing a smile*) Well, I'm glad to know I wasn't missed.

EMILY—(*sweetly*) We were talking about you—at least, we were listening to Lily talk about you.

MARTHA—(*stiffening defensively*) About me?

EMILY—Yes—about how devoted you were to Curt's work. (*Lily gives her a venomous glance of scorn.*)

MARTHA—(*pleased but inwardly uneasy*) Oh, but you see I

consider it my work, too, I've helped him with it so long now.

JAYSON—(*in a forced tone*) And how is Curt's book coming, Martha?

MARTHA—(*more and more stung by their strained attitudes and inquisitive glances. Coldly and cuttingly*) Finely, thank you. The book will cause quite a stir, I believe. It will make the name of Jayson famous in the big world outside of Bridgetown.

MRS. DAVIDSON—(*indignantly*) The name of Jayson has been—

JAYSON—(*pleadingly*) Aunt Elizabeth!

LILY—Aunt means it's world famous already, Martha. (*pointing to the sullen John*) John was once a substitute on the Yale Freshman soccer team, you know. If it wasn't for his weak shins he would have made the team, fancy!

DICK—(*This tickles his sense of humor and he bursts into laughter.*) Lily wins! (*as his brother glares at him—looking at his watch*) Heavens, I'll have to hustle! (*gets to his feet*) I'm due at the Casino. (*comes and shakes Martha's hand formally*) I'm sorry I can't stay.

MARTHA—So glad you came. Do come in again any time. We keep open house, you know—Western fashion. (*She accentuates this.*)

DICK—(*hurriedly*) Delighted to. (*He starts for the door in rear.*)

LILY—(*as if suddenly making up her mind*) Wait a second! I'm coming with you—

DICK—Sure thing—only hurry, darn you! (*He goes out.*)

LILY—(*stops at the door in rear and catching Martha's eye, looks meaningly at the others*) Phew! I need fresh air! (*She makes an encouraging motion as if pummeling someone to Martha, indicating her assembled family as the victim—then goes out laughing. A motor is heard starting—running off.*)

ESTHER—(*with a huge sigh of relief*) Thank goodness, she's gone. What a vixen! What would you do if you had a sister like that, Martha?

MARTHA—I'd love her—and try to understand her.

SHEFFIELD—(*meaningly*) She's a bad ally to rely on—this side of the fence one day, and that the next.

MARTHA—Is that why you advised her to become a lawyer, Mr. Sheffield?

SHEFFIELD—(*stung, but maintaining an unruffled front*) Now, now, that remark must be catalogued as catty.

MARTHA—(*defiantly*) It seems to be in the Bridgetown atmosphere. I never was—not the least bit—in the open air.

JAYSON—(*conciliatingly*) Oh, Bridgetown isn't so bad, Martha, once you get used to us.

JOHN—It's one of the most prosperous and wealthy towns in the U. S.—and that means in the world, nowadays.

EMILY—(*with her sugary smile*) That isn't what Martha means, you silly. I know what she's thinking about us, and I'm not sure that I don't agree with her—partly. She feels that we're so awfully strict—about certain things. It must be so different in the Far West—I suppose—so much freer.

MARTHA—(*acidly*) Then you believe broadmindedness and clean thinking are a question of locality? I can't agree with you. I know nothing of the present Far West, not having lived there for ten years, but Curt and I have lived in the Far East and I'm sure he'd agree with me in saying that Chinese ancestor worship is far more dignified than ours. After all, you know, theirs is religion, not snobbery. (*There is a loud honking of an auto horn before the house. Martha starts, seems to come to a quick decision, and announces with studied carelessness*) That must be Mr. Bigelow. I suppose Lily told you I had an engagement to go motoring with him. So sorry I must leave. But I'm like Lily. I need fresh air. (*She walks to the study door as she is talking.*) I'll call Curt. (*She raps loudly on the door and calls*) Curt! Come out! It's important. (*She turns and goes to the door, smiling fixedly.*) He'll be out when he's through swearing. (*She goes out, rear.*)

JOHN—(*exploding*) Well, of all the damned cheek!

ESTHER—She shows her breeding, I must say.

EMILY—(*with horror*) Oh, how rude—and insulting.

MRS. DAVIDSON—(*rising rigidly to her feet*) I will never set foot in this house again!

JAYSON—(*jumping up to restrain her—worriedly*) Now, Aunt Elizabeth, do keep your head! We must have no scandal of any sort. Remember there are servants about. Do sit down. (*The old lady refuses in stubborn silence.*)

SHEFFIELD—(*judiciously*) One must make allowances for one in her condition, Aunt.

JAYSON—(*snatching at this*) Exactly. Remember her condition, Aunt (*testily*) and do sit down. (*The old lady plumps herself down again angrily.*)

EMILY—(*in her lisp of hidden meanings*) Yes, the family mustn't forget—her condition. (*The door from the study is opened and Curtis appears. His face shows his annoyance at being interrupted, his eyes are preoccupied. They all turn and greet him embarrassedly. He nods silently and comes slowly down front.*)

CURTIS—(*looking around*) Where's Martha? What's the important thing she called me out for?

ESTHER—(*forcing gayety*) To play host, you big bear, you! Don't you think we came to see you, too? Sit down here and be good. (*He sits on sofa.*)

EMILY—(*softly*) Martha had to leave us to go motoring with Mr. Bigelow.

ESTHER—(*hastily*) And the three children.

CURTIS—(*frowning grumpily*) Hm! Big and his eternal kids. (*He sighs. They exchange meaning glances. Curtis seems to feel ashamed of his grumpiness and tries to fling it off—with a cheerful smile*) But what the deuce! I must be getting selfish to grudge Martha her bit of fresh air. You don't know what it means to outdoor animals like us to be pent up. (*He springs to his feet and paces back and forth nervously.*) We're used to living with the sky for a roof— (*then interestedly*) Did Martha tell you I'd definitely decided to go on the five year Asian expedition?

ESTHER—Curt! You're not!

EMILY—And leave Martha here—all alone—for five years?

JAYSON—Yes, you can't take Martha with you this time, you know.

CURTIS—(*with a laugh*) No? What makes you so sure of that? (*As they look mystified, he continues confidentially*) I'll let you in on the secret—only you must all promise not to breathe a word to Martha—until tomorrow. Tomorrow is her birthday, you know, and this is a surprise I've saved for her. (*They all nod.*) I've been intriguing my damnedest for the past month to get permission for Martha to go with me. It was difficult because women are supposed to be barred. (*happily*) But I've succeeded. The letter came this morning. How tickled to death she'll be when she hears! I know she's given up hope. (*thoughtfully*) I suppose it's that has been making her act so out-of-sorts lately.

JAYSON—(*worriedly*) Hmm! But would you persist in going—alone—if you knew it was impossible for her—?

CURTIS—(*frowning*) I can't imagine it without her. You people can't have any idea what a help—a chum—she's been. You can't believe that a woman could be—so much that—in a life of that kind, how I've grown to depend on her. The thousand details—she attends to them all. She remembers everything. Why, I'd be lost. I wouldn't know how to start. (*with a laugh*) I know this sounds like a confession of weakness but it's true just the same. (*frowning again*) However, naturally my work must always be the first consideration. Yes, absolutely! (*then with glad relief*) But what's the use of rambling on this way? We can both go, thank heaven!

MRS. DAVIDSON—(*sternly*) No. *She* cannot go. And it is *your* duty—

CURTIS—(*interrupting her with a trace of impatience*) Oh, come! That's all nonsense, Aunt. You don't understand the kind of woman Martha is.

MRS. DAVIDSON—(*harshly*) The women I understand prefer rearing their children to selfish gallivanting over the world.

CURTIS—(*impatiently*) But we have no children now, Aunt.

MRS. DAVIDSON—I know that, more's the pity. But later—

CURTIS—(*emphatically*) No, I tell you! It's impossible!

MRS. DAVIDSON—(*grimly*) I have said my last word. Go your own road and work your own ruin.

CURTIS—(*brusquely*) I think I'll change my togs and go for a walk. Excuse me for a second. I'll be right down again. (*He goes out, rear.*)

EMILY—(*with her false air of innocence*) Curt acts so funny, doesn't he? Did you notice how emphatic he was about it's being impossible? And he said Martha seemed to him to be acting queer lately—with him, I suppose he meant.

ESTHER—He certainly appeared put out when he heard she'd gone motoring with Big.

JAYSON—(*moodily*) This dislike of the very mention of children. It isn't like Curt, not a bit.

JOHN—There's something rotten in Denmark somewhere. This family will yet live to regret having accepted a stranger—

SHEFFIELD—(*mollifyingly—with a judicial air*) Come now! This is all only suspicion. There is no evidence; you have no case; and the defendant is innocent until you have proved her guilty, remember. (*getting to his feet*) Well, let's break up. Esther, you and I ought to be getting home. (*They all rise.*)

JAYSON—(*testily*) Well, if I were sure it would all blow over without any open scandal, I'd offer up a prayer of thanks.

(*The Curtain Falls*)

ACT TWO

SCENE—*Curtis Jayson's study.*

On the left, forward, a gun rack in which are displayed several varieties of rifles and shotguns. Farther back, three windows looking out on the garden. In the rear wall, an open fireplace with two leather armchairs in front of it. To right of fireplace, a door leading into the living-room. In the far right corner, another chair. In the right wall, three windows looking out on the lawn and garden. On this side, front, a typewriting table with machine and chair. Opposite the windows on the right, a bulky leather couch, facing front. In front of the windows on the left, a long table with stacks of paper piled here and there on it, reference books, etc. On the left of table, a swivel chair. Gray oak bookcases are built into the cream rough plaster walls which are otherwise almost hidden from view by a collection of all sorts of hunter's trophies, animal heads of all kinds. The floor is covered with animal skins—tiger, polar bear, leopard, lion, etc. Skins are also thrown over the backs of the chairs. The sections of the bookcase not occupied by scientific volumes have been turned into a specimen case for all sorts of zoölogical, geographical, anthropological oddities.

It is mid-morning, sunny and bright, of the following day.

Curtis and Bigelow are discovered. Curtis is half-sitting on the corner of the table, left, smoking a pipe. Bigelow is lying sprawled on the couch. Through the open windows on the right come the shouts of children playing. Martha's voice joins in with theirs.

BIGELOW—Listen to that rumpus, will you! The kids are having the time of their lives. (*He goes to the window and looks out—delightedly*) Your wife is playing hide and seek with them. Come and look.

CURTIS—(*with a trace of annoyance*) Oh, I can see well enough from here.

BIGELOW—(*with a laugh*) She seems to get as much fun out of it as they do. (*as a shriek comes from outside—excitedly*) Ah, Eddy discovered her behind the tree. Isn't he tickled now! (*He turns back from the window and lights a cigarette—enthusiastically*) Jove, what a hand she is with children!

78

CURTIS—(*as if the subject bored him*) Oh, Martha gets along well with anyone.

BIGELOW—(*sits on the couch again—with a sceptical smile*) You think so? With everyone?

CURTIS—(*surprised*) Yes—with everyone we've ever come in contact with—even aboriginal natives.

BIGELOW—With the aboriginal natives of Bridgetown? With the well-known Jayson family, for example?

CURTIS—(*getting to his feet—frowning*) Why, everything's all right between Martha and them, isn't it? What do you mean, Big? I certainly imagined—but I'll confess this damn book has had me so preoccupied—

BIGELOW—Too darn preoccupied, if you'll pardon my saying so. It's not fair to leave her to fight it alone.

CURTIS—(*impatiently*) Fight what? Martha has a sense of humor. I'm sure their petty prejudices merely amuse her.

BIGELOW—(*sententiously*) A mosquito is a ridiculous, amusing creature, seen under a microscope; but when a swarm has been stinging you all night—

CURTIS—(*a broad grin coming over his face*) You speak from experience, eh?

BIGELOW—(*smiling*) You bet I do. Touch me anywhere and you'll find a bite. This, my native town, did me the honor of devoting its entire leisure attention for years to stinging me to death.

CURTIS—Well, if I am to believe one-tenth of the family letters I used to receive on the subject of my old friend, Bigelow, they sure had just cause.

BIGELOW—Oh, I'll play fair. I'll admit they did—then. But it's exasperating to know they never give you credit for changing—I almost said, reforming. One ought to be above the gossip of a town like this—but say what you like, it does get under your skin.

CURTIS—(*with an indulgent smile*) So you'd like to be known as a reformed character, eh?

BIGELOW—(*rather ruefully*) Et tu! Your tone is sceptical. But I swear to you, Curt, I'm an absolutely new man since my wife's death, since I've grown to love the children. Before that I hardly knew them. They were hers, not mine, it seemed. (*his face lighting up*) Now we're the best of pals, and

I've commenced to appreciate life from a different angle. I've found a career at last—the children—the finest career a man could have, I believe.

CURTIS—(*indifferently*) Yes, I suppose so—if you're made that way.

BIGELOW—Meaning you're not?

CURTIS—Not any more. (*frowning*) I tried that once.

BIGELOW—(*after a pause—with a smile*) But we're wandering from the subject of Martha versus the mosquitoes.

CURTIS—(*with a short laugh*) Oh, to the deuce with that! Trust Martha to take care of herself. Besides, I'll have her out of this stagnant hole before so very long—six months, to be exact.

BIGELOW—Where do you think of settling her then?

CURTIS—No settling about it. I'm going to take her with me.

BIGELOW—(*surprised*) On the Asian expedition?

CURTIS—Yes. I haven't told her yet but I'm going to today. It's her birthday—and I've been saving the news to surprise her with.

BIGELOW—Her birthday? I wish the children and I had known—but it's not too late yet.

CURTIS—(*with a grin*) Thirty-nine candles, if you're thinking of baking a cake!

BIGELOW—(*meaningly*) That's not old—but it's not young either, Curt.

CURTIS—(*disgustedly*) You talk like an old woman, Big. What have years to do with it? Martha is young in spirit and always will be. (*There is a knock at the door and Martha's voice calling:* "May I come in, people?") Sure thing! (*Bigelow jumps to open the door and Martha enters. She is flushed, excited, full of the joy of life, panting from her exertions.*)

MARTHA—(*laughing*) I've had to run away and leave them with the governess. They're too active for me. (*She throws herself on the couch.*) Phew! I'm all tired out. I must be getting old.

CURTIS—(*with a grin*) Big was just this minute remarking that, Martha. (*Bigelow looks embarrassed.*)

MARTHA—(*laughing at him*) Well, I declare! Of all the horrid things to hear—

BIGELOW—(*still embarrassed but forcing a joking tone*) He—prevaricates, Mrs. Jayson.

MARTHA—There now, Curt! I'm sure it was you who said it. It sounds just like one of your horrid facts.

BIGELOW—And how can I offer my felicitations now? But I do, despite your husband's calumny. May your shadow never grow less!

MARTHA—Thank you. (*She shakes his proffered hand heartily.*)

BIGELOW—And now I'll collect my flock and go home.

CURTIS—So long, Big. Be sure you don't mislay one of your heirs!

BIGELOW—No fear—but they might mislay me. (*He goes. Curtis sits down on couch. Martha goes to the window right, and looks out—after a pause, waving her hand*)

MARTHA—There they go. What darlings they are! (*Curtis grunts perfunctorily. Martha comes back and sits beside Curtis on the couch—with a sigh*) Whoever did say it was right, Curt. I am getting old.

CURTIS—(*taking one of her hands and patting it*) Nonsense!

MARTHA—(*shaking her head and smiling with a touch of sadness*) No. I feel it.

CURTIS—(*puts his arms around her protectingly*) Nonsense! You're not the sort that ever grows old.

MARTHA—(*nestling up to him*) I'm afraid we're all that sort, dear. Even you. (*She touches the white hair about his temples playfully.*) Circumstantial evidence. I'll have to dye it when you're asleep some time—and then nobody'll know.

CURTIS—(*looking at her*) You haven't any silver threads. (*jokingly*) Am I to suspect—?

MARTHA—No, I don't. Honest, cross my heart, I wouldn't even conceal that from you, if I did. But gray hairs prove nothing. I am actually older than you, don't forget.

CURTIS—One whole year! That's frightful, isn't it?

MARTHA—I'm a woman, remember; so that one means at least six. Ugh! Let's not talk about it. Do you know, it really fills me with a queer panic sometimes?

CURTIS—(*squeezing her*) Silly girl!

MARTHA—(*snuggling close to him*) Will you always love

me—even when I'm old and ugly and feeble and you're still young and strong and handsome?

CURTIS—(*kisses her—tenderly*) Martha! What a foolish question, sweetheart. If we ever have to grow old, we'll do it together just as we've always done everything.

MARTHA—(*with a happy sigh*) That's my dream of happiness, Curt. (*enthusiastically*) Oh, it has been a wonderful, strange life we've lived together, Curt, hasn't it? You're sure you've never regretted, never had the weest doubt that it might have been better with—someone else?

CURTIS—(*kisses her again—tenderly reproachful*) Martha!

MARTHA—And I have helped—really helped you, haven't I?

CURTIS—(*much moved*) You've been the best wife a man could ever wish for, Martha. You've been—you are wonderful. I owe everything to you—your sympathy and encouragement. Don't you know I realize that? (*She kisses him gratefully.*)

MARTHA—(*musing happily*) Yes, it's been a wonderful, glorious life. I'd live it over again if I could, every single second of it—even the terrible suffering—the children.

CURTIS—(*wincing*) Don't. I wouldn't want that over again. (*then changing the subject abruptly*) But why have you been putting all our life into the past tense? It seems to me the most interesting part is still ahead of us.

MARTHA—(*softly*) I mean—together—Curt.

CURTIS—So do I!

MARTHA—But you're going away—and I can't go with you this time.

CURTIS—(*smiling to himself over her head*) Yes, that does complicate matters, doesn't it?

MARTHA—(*hurt—looking up at him*) Curt! How indifferently you say that—as if you didn't care!

CURTIS—(*avoiding her eyes—teasingly*) What do you think you'll do all the time I'm gone?

MARTHA—Oh, I'll be lost—dead— I won't know what to do. I'll die of loneliness—(*yearning creeping into her voice*) unless—

CURTIS—(*inquisitively*) Unless what?

MARTHA—(*burying her face on his shoulders—passionately*) Oh, Curt, I love you so! Swear that you'll always love me no matter what I do—no matter what I ask—

CURTIS—(*vaguely uneasy now, trying to peer into her face*) But, sweetheart—

MARTHA—(*giving way weakly to her feelings for a moment— entreatingly*) Then don't go!

CURTIS—(*astonished*) Why, I've got to go. You know that.

MARTHA—Yes, I suppose you have. (*vigorously, as if flinging off a weakness*) Of course you have!

CURTIS—But, Martha, you said you'd be lonely unless— unless what?

MARTHA—Unless I— (*She hesitates, blushing and confused.*) I mean we—oh, I'm so afraid of what you'll—hold me close, very close to you and I'll whisper it. (*She pulls his head down and whispers in his ear. A look of disappointment and aversion forces itself on his face.*)

CURTIS—(*almost indignantly*) But that's impossible, Martha!

MARTHA—(*pleadingly*) Now don't be angry with me, Curt—not till you've heard everything. (*with a trace of defiance*) It isn't impossible, Curt. It's so! It's happened! I was saving it as a secret—to tell you today—on my birthday.

CURTIS—(*stunned*) You mean it's a fact?

MARTHA—Yes. (*then pitifully*) Oh, Curt, don't look that way! You seem so cold—so far away from me. (*straining her arms about him*) Why don't you hold me close to you? Why don't you say you're glad—for my sake?

CURTIS—(*agitatedly*) But Martha, you don't understand. How can I pretend gladness when— (*vehemently*) Why, it would spoil all our plans!

MARTHA—Plans? *Our* plans? What do you mean?

CURTIS—(*excitedly*) Why, you're going with me, of course! I've obtained official permission. I've been working for it for months. The letter came yesterday morning.

MARTHA—(*stunned*) Permission—to go with you—?

CURTIS—(*excitedly*) Yes. I couldn't conceive going without you. And I knew how you must be wishing—

MARTHA—(*in pain*) Oh!

CURTIS—(*distractedly—jumping to his feet and staring at her bewilderedly*) Martha! You don't mean to tell me you weren't!

MARTHA—(*in a crushed voice*) I was wishing you'd finally decide not to go—

CURTIS—(*betraying exasperation*) But you must realize that's impossible. Martha, are you sure you've clearly understood what I've told you? You can go with me, do you hear? Everything is arranged. And I've had to fight so hard—I was running the risk of losing my own chance by my insistence that I couldn't go without you.

MARTHA—(*weakly and helplessly*) I understand all that, Curt.

CURTIS—(*indignantly*) And yet you hesitate! Why, this is the greatest thing of its kind ever attempted! There are unprecedented possibilities! A whole new world of knowledge may be opened up, the very origin of Man himself! And you will be the only woman—

MARTHA—I realize all that, Curt.

CURTIS—You can't—and hesitate! And then—think, Martha!—it will mean that you and I won't have to be separated. We can go on living the old, free life together.

MARTHA—(*growing calm now*) You are forgetting—what I told you, Curt. You must face the fact. I can't go.

CURTIS—(*overwhelmed by the finality of her tone—after a pause*) How long have you known this?

MARTHA—Two months, about.

CURTIS—But why didn't you tell me before?

MARTHA—I was afraid you wouldn't understand—and you haven't, Curt. But why didn't you tell me before what you were planning?

CURTIS—(*eagerly*) You mean—then you would have been glad to go—before this had happened?

MARTHA—I would have accepted it.

CURTIS—(*despairingly*) Martha, how could you ever have allowed this to happen? Oh, I suppose I'm talking foolishness. It wasn't your seeking, I know.

MARTHA—Yes, it was, Curt.

CURTIS—(*indignantly*) Martha! (*then in a hurt tone*) You have broken the promise we made when they died. We were to keep their memories inviolate. They were to be always—our only children.

MARTHA—(*gently*) They forgive me, Curt. And you'll forgive me, too, when you see him—and love him.

CURTIS—Him?

MARTHA—I know it will be a boy.

CURTIS—(*sinking down on the couch beside her—dully*) Martha! You have blown my world to bits.

MARTHA—(*taking one of his hands in hers—gently*) You must make allowances for me, Curt, and forgive me. I *am* getting old. No, it's the truth. I've reached the turning point. Will you listen to my side of it, Curt, and try to see it—with sympathy—with true understanding—(*with a trace of bitterness*)—forgetting your work for the moment?

CURTIS—(*miserably*) That's unfair, Martha. I think of it as *our* work—and I have always believed you did, too.

MARTHA—(*quickly*) I did, Curt! I do! All in the past is our work. It's my greatest pride to think so. But, Curt, I'll have to confess frankly—during the past two years I've felt myself feeling as if I wasn't complete—with that alone.

CURTIS—Martha! (*bitterly*) And all the time I believed that more and more it was becoming the aim of your life, too.

MARTHA—(*with a sad smile*) I'm glad of that, dear. I tried my best to conceal it from you. It would have been so unfair to let you guess while we were still in harness. But oh, how I kept looking forward to the time when we would come back—and rest—in our own home! You know, you said that was your plan—to stay here and write your books—and I was hoping—

CURTIS—(*with a gesture of aversion*) I loathe this book-writing. It isn't my part, I realize now. But when I made the plans you speak of, how could I know that then?

MARTHA—(*decisively*) You've got to go. I won't try to stop you. I'll help all in my power—as I've always done. Only—I can't go with you any more. And you must help me—to do my work—by understanding it. (*He is silent, frowning, his face agitated, preoccupied. She goes on intensely.*) Oh, Curt, I wish I could tell you what I feel, make you feel with me the longing for a child. If you had just the tiniest bit of feminine in you—! (*forcing a smile*) But you're so utterly masculine, dear! That's what has made me love you, I suppose—so I've no right to complain of it. (*intensely*) I don't. I wouldn't have you changed one bit! I love you! And I love the things you love—your work—because it's a part of you. And that's what I want you to do—to reciprocate—to love the creator in me—to desire that I, too, should complete myself with the thing nearest my heart!

CURTIS—(*intensely preoccupied with his own struggle—vaguely*) But I thought—

MARTHA—I know; but, after all, your work is yours, not mine. I have been only a helper, a good comrade, too, I hope, but—somehow—outside of it all. Do you remember two years ago when we were camped in Yunnan, among the aboriginal tribes? It was one night there when we were lying out in our sleeping-bags up in the mountains along the Tibetan frontier. I couldn't sleep. Suddenly I felt oh, so tired—utterly alone—out of harmony with you—with the earth under me. I became horribly despondent—like an outcast who suddenly realizes the whole world is alien. And all the wandering about the world, and all the romance and excitement I'd enjoyed in it, appeared an aimless, futile business, chasing around in a circle in an effort to avoid touching reality. Forgive me, Curt. I meant myself, not you, of course. Oh, it was horrible, I tell you, to feel that way. I tried to laugh at myself, to fight it off, but it stayed and grew worse. It seemed as if I were the only creature alive—who was not alive. And all at once the picture came of a tribeswoman who stood looking at us in a little mountain village as we rode by. She was nursing her child. Her eyes were so curiously sure of herself. She was horribly ugly, poor woman, and yet—as the picture came back to me—I appeared to myself the ugly one while she was beautiful. And I thought of our children who had died—and such a longing for another child came to me that I began sobbing. You were asleep. You didn't hear. (*She pauses—then proceeds slowly.*) And when we came back here—to have a home at last, I was so happy because I saw my chance of fulfillment—before it was too late. (*in a gentle, pleading voice*) Now can you understand, dear? (*She puts her hand on his arm.*)

CURTIS—(*starting as if awaking from a sleep*) Understand? No, I can't understand, Martha.

MARTHA—(*in a gasp of unbearable hurt*) Curt! I don't believe you heard a word I was saying.

CURTIS—(*bursting forth as if releasing all the pent-up struggle that has been gathering within him*) No, I can't understand. I can't! It seems like treachery to me.

MARTHA—Curt!

CURTIS—I've depended on you. This is the crucial point—the biggest thing of my life—and you desert me!

MARTHA—(*resentment gathering in her eyes*) If you'd listened to me—if you'd even tried to feel—

CURTIS—I feel that you're deliberately ruining my highest hope. How can I go on without you? I've been trying to imagine myself alone. I can't! Even with my work—who can I get to take your place? Oh, Martha, why do you have to bring this new element into our lives at this late day? Haven't we been sufficient, you and I together? Isn't that a more difficult, beautiful happiness to achieve than—children? Everyone has children. Don't I love you as much as any man could love a woman? Isn't that enough for you? Doesn't it mean anything to you that I need you so terribly—for myself, for my work—for everything that is best and worthiest in me? Can you expect me to be glad when you propose to introduce a stranger who will steal away your love, your interest—who will separate us and deprive me of you! No, no, I can't! It's asking the impossible. I'm only human.

MARTHA—If you were human you'd think of my life as well as yours.

CURTIS—I do! It's *our* life I am fighting for, not mine—*our* life that you want to destroy.

MARTHA—Our life seems to mean your life to you, Curt—and only your life. I have devoted fifteen years to that. Now I must fight for my own.

CURTIS—(*aghast*) You talk as if we were enemies, Martha! (*striding forward and seizing her in his arms*) No, you don't mean it! I love you so, Martha! You've made yourself part of my life, my work—I need you so! I can't share you with anyone! I won't! Martha, my own! Say that you won't, dear? (*He kisses her passionately again and again.*)

MARTHA—(*all her love and tenderness aroused by his kisses and passionate sincerity—weakening*) Curt! Curt! (*pitiably*) It

won't separate us, dear. Can't you see he will be a link between us—even when we're away from each other—that he
will bring us together all the closer?

CURTIS—But I can't be away from you!

MARTHA—(*miserably*) Oh, Curt, why won't you look the
fact in the face—and learn to accept it with joy? Why can't
you for my sake? I would do that for you.

CURTIS—(*breaking away from her—passionately*) You will
not do what I have implored you—for me! And I am looking
the fact in the face—the fact that there must be no fact!
(*avoiding her eyes—as if defying his own finer feelings*) There are
doctors who—

MARTHA—(*shrinking back from him*) Curt! You propose
that—to me! (*with overwhelming sorrow*) Oh, Curt! When I
feel him—his life within me—like a budding of my deepest
soul—you say what you have just said! (*grief-stricken*) Oh,
you never, never, never will understand!

CURTIS—(*shamefacedly*) Martha, I— (*distractedly*) I don't
know what I'm saying! This whole situation is so unbearable!
Why does it have to happen now?

MARTHA—(*gently*) It must be now—or not at all—at my
age, dear. (*then after a pause—staring at him frightenedly—
sadly*) You've changed, Curt. I remember it used to be your
happiness to sacrifice yourself for me.

CURTIS—I had no work then—no purpose beyond myself. To sacrifice oneself is easy. But when your only meaning
becomes as a searcher for knowledge—you can't sacrifice
that, Martha. You must sacrifice everything for that or lose all
sincerity.

MARTHA—I wonder where your work leaves off and you
begin. Hasn't your work become you?

CURTIS—Yes and no. (*helplessly*) You can't understand,
Martha! . . .

MARTHA—Nor you.

CURTIS—(*with a trace of bitter irony*) And you and your
work? Aren't they one and the same?

MARTHA—So you think mine is selfish, too? (*after a
pause—sadly*) I can't blame you, Curt. It's all my fault. I've
spoiled you by giving up my life so completely to yours.
You've forgotten I have one. Oh, I don't mean that I was a

martyr. I know that in you alone lay my happiness in those years—after the children died. But we are no longer what we were then. We must, both of us, relearn to love and respect—what we have become.

CURTIS—(*violently*) Nonsense! You talk as if love were an intellectual process— (*taking her into his arms—passionately*) I love you— You are me and I am you! What use is all this vivisecting? (*He kisses her fiercely. They look into each other's eyes for a second—then instinctively fall back from one another.*)

MARTHA—(*in a whisper*) Yes, you love me. But who am I? You don't know.

CURTIS—(*frightfully*) Martha! Stop! This is terrible! (*They continue to be held by each other's fearfully questioning eyes.*)

(*The Curtain Falls*)

ACT THREE

Scene—*Same as Act Two.*

As the curtain rises, Jayson is discovered sitting in an arm-chair by the fireplace, in which a log fire is burning fitfully. He is staring into the flames, a strained, expectant expression on his face. It is about three o'clock in the morning. There is no light but that furnished by the fire which fills the room with shifting shadows. The door in the rear is opened and Richard appears, his face harried by the stress of unusual emotion. Through the open door-way, a low, muffled moan of anguish sounds from the upper part of the house. Jayson and Richard both shudder. The latter closes the door behind him quickly as if anxious to shut out the noise.

Jayson—(*looking up anxiously*) Well?

Richard—(*involuntarily straightening up as if about to sa-lute and report to a superior officer*) No change, sir. (*then, as if remembering himself, comes to the fireplace and slumps down in a chair—agitatedly*) God, Dad, I can't stand her moaning and screaming! It's got my nerves shot to pieces. I thought I was hardened. I've heard them out in No Man's Land—dying by inches—when you couldn't get to them or help—but this is worse—a million times! After all, that was war—and they were men—

Jayson—Martha is having an exceptionally hard ordeal.

Richard—Since three o'clock this morning—yesterday morning, I should say. It's a wonder she isn't dead.

Jayson—(*after a pause*) Where is Curt?

Richard—(*harshly*) Still out in the garden, walking around like a lunatic.

Jayson—Why didn't you make him come in?

Richard—Make him! It's easy to say. He's in a queer state, Dad, I can tell you! There's something torturing him besides her pain—

Jayson—(*after a pause*) Yes, there's a lot in all this we don't know about.

Richard—I suppose the reason he's so down on the family is because we've rather cut her since that tea affair.

90

JAYSON—He shouldn't blame us. She acted abominably and has certainly caused enough talk since then—always about with Bigelow—

RICHARD—(*with a sardonic laugh*) And yet he keeps asking everyone to send for Bigelow—says he wants to talk to him—not us. *We* can't understand! (*He laughs bitterly.*)

JAYSON—I'm afraid Curt knows we understand too much. (*agitatedly*) But why does he want Bigelow, in God's name? In his present state—with the suspicions he must have—there's liable to be a frightful scene.

RICHARD—Don't be afraid of a scene. (*with pitying scorn*) The hell of it is he seems to regard Bigelow as his best friend. Damned if I can make it out.

JAYSON—I gave orders that they were always to tell Curt Bigelow was out of town and couldn't be reached. (*with a sigh*) What a frightful situation for all of us! (*after a pause*) It may sound cruel of me—but—I can't help wishing for all our sakes that this child will never—

RICHARD—Yes, Dad, I know what you're thinking. It would be the best thing for it, too—although I hate myself for saying it. (*There is a pause. Then the door in rear is opened and Lily appears. She is pale and agitated. Leaving the door open behind her she comes forward and flings herself on the lounge.*)

JAYSON—(*anxiously*) Well?

LILY—(*irritably, getting up and switching on the lights*) Isn't everything gloomy enough? (*sits down*) I couldn't bear it upstairs one second longer. Esther and Emily are coming down, too. It's too much for them—and they've had personal experience. (*trying to mask her agitation by a pretense at flippancy*) I hereby become a life-member of the birth-control league. Let's let humanity cease—if God can't manage its continuance any better than that!

RICHARD—(*seriously*) Second the motion.

JAYSON—(*peevishly*) You're young idiots. Keep your blasphemous nonsense to yourself, Lily!

LILY—(*jumping up and stamping her foot—hysterically*) I can't stand it. Take me home, Dick, won't you? We're doing no good waiting here. I'll have a fit—or something—if I stay.

RICHARD—(*glad of the excuse to go himself—briskly*) That's how I feel. I'll drive you home. Come along. (*Esther and Emily enter, followed by John.*)

LILY—(*excitedly*) I'll never marry or have a child! Never, never! I'll go into Mark's office tomorrow and make myself independent of marriage.

ESTHER—Sssh! Lily! Don't you know you're shouting? And what silly talk!

LILY—I'll show you whether it's silly! I'll—

RICHARD—(*impatiently*) Are you coming or not?

LILY—(*quickly*) Yes—wait—here I am. (*She pushes past the others and follows Richard out rear. Esther and Emily sit on couch—John on chair, right rear.*)

ESTHER—(*with a sigh*) I thought I went through something when mine were born—but this is too awful.

EMILY—And, according to John, Curt actually says he hates it! Isn't that terrible? (*after a pause—meaningly*) It's almost as if her suffering was a punishment, don't you think?

ESTHER—If it is, she's being punished enough, Heaven knows. It can't go on this way much longer or something dreadful will happen.

EMILY—Do you think the baby—

ESTHER—I don't know. I shouldn't say it but perhaps it would be better if—

EMILY—That's what I think.

ESTHER—Oh, I wish I didn't have such evil suspicions— but the way Curt goes on—how can you help feeling there's something wrong?

JAYSON—(*suddenly*) How is Curt?

EMILY—John just came in from the garden. (*turning around to where John is dozing in his chair—sharply*) John! Well I never! If he isn't falling asleep! John! (*He jerks up his head and stares at her, blinking stupidly. She continues irritably.*) A nice time to pick out for a nap, I must say.

JOHN—(*surlily*) Don't forget I have to be at the bank in the morning.

JAYSON—(*testily*) I have to be at the bank, too—and you don't notice me sleeping. Tell me about Curt. You just left him, didn't you?

JOHN—(*irritably*) Yes, and I've been walking around that damned garden half the night watching over him. Isn't that enough to wear anyone out? I can feel I've got a terrible cold coming on—

ESTHER—(*impatiently*) For goodness' sake, don't you start to pity yourself!

JOHN—(*indignantly*) I'm not. I think I've showed my willingness to do everything I could. If Curt was only the least bit grateful! He isn't. He hates us all and wishes we were out of his home. I would have left long ago if I didn't want to do my part in saving the family from disgrace.

JAYSON—(*impatiently*) Has he quieted down, that's what I want to know?

JOHN—(*harshly*) Not the least bit. He's out of his head—and I'd be out of mine if a child was being born to my wife that—

JAYSON—(*angrily*) Keep that to yourself! Remember you have no proof. (*morosely*) Think all you want—but don't talk.

EMILY—(*pettishly*) The whole town knows it, anyway; I'm sure they must.

JAYSON—There's only been gossip—no real scandal. Let's do our united best to keep it at that. (*after a pause*) Where's Aunt Elizabeth? We'll have to keep an eye on her, too, or she's quite liable to blurt out the whole business before all comers.

ESTHER—You needn't be afraid. She's forgotten all about the scandalous part. No word of it has come to her out in the country and she hasn't set foot in town since that unfortunate tea, remember. And at present she's so busy wishing the child will be a boy, that she hasn't a thought for another thing. (*The door in the rear is opened and Mark Sheffield enters. He comes up to the fire to warm himself. The others watch him in silence for a moment.*)

JAYSON—(*impatiently*) Well, Mark? Where's Curt?

SHEFFIELD—(*frowning*) Inside. I think he'll be with us in a minute. (*with a scornful smile*) Just now he's phoning to Bigelow. (*The others gasp.*)

JAYSON—(*furiously*) For God's sake, couldn't you stop him?

SHEFFIELD—Not without a scene. Your Aunt persuaded him to come into the house—and he rushed for the phone. I think he guessed we had been lying to him—

JAYSON—(*after a pause*) Then he—Bigelow—will be here soon?

SHEFFIELD—(*dryly*) It depends on his sense of decency. As he seems lacking in that quality, I've no doubt he'll come.

JOHN—(*rising to his feet—pompously*) Then I, for one, will go. Come, Emily. Since Curt seems bound to disgrace everyone concerned, I want it thoroughly understood that we wash our hands of the whole disgraceful affair.

EMILY—(*snappishly*) Go if you want to! I won't! (*then with a sacrificing air*) I think it is our duty to stay.

JAYSON—(*exasperated*) Sit down. Wash your hands indeed! Aren't you as much concerned as any of us?

SHEFFIELD—(*sharply*) Sshh! I think I hear Curt now. (*John sits down abruptly. All stiffen into stony attitudes. The door is opened and Curtis enters. He is incredibly drawn and haggard, a tortured, bewildered expression in his eyes. His hair is dishevelled, his boots caked with mud. He stands at the door staring from one to the other of his family with a wild, contemptuous scorn and mutters*)

CURTIS—Liars! Well, he's coming now. (*then bewilderedly*) Why didn't you want him to come, eh? He's my oldest friend. I've got to talk to someone—and I can't to you. (*wildly*) What do you want here, anyway? Why don't you go? (*A scream of Martha's is heard through the doorway. Curt shudders violently, slams the door to with a crash, putting his shoulders against it as if to bar out the sound inexorably—in anguish*) God, why must she go through such agony? Why? Why? (*He goes to the fireplace as Mark makes way for him, flings himself exhaustedly on a chair, his shoulders bowed, his face hidden in his hands. The others stare at him pityingly. There is a long silence. Then the two women whisper together, get up and tiptoe out of the room, motioning for the others to follow them. John does so. Sheffield starts to go, then notices the preoccupied Jayson who is staring moodily into the fire.*)

SHEFFIELD—Sstt! (*as Jayson looks up—in a whisper*) Let's go out and leave him alone. Perhaps he'll sleep.

JAYSON—(*starting to follow Sheffield, hesitates and puts a hand on his son's shoulder*) Curt. Remember I'm your father. Can't you confide in me? I'll do anything to help.

CURTIS—(*harshly*) No, Dad. Leave me alone.

JAYSON—(*piqued*) As you wish. (*He starts to go.*)

CURTIS—And send Big in to me as soon as he comes.

JAYSON—(*stops, appears about to object—then remarks coldly*) Very well—if you insist. (*He switches off the lights. He hesitates at the door uncertainly, then opens it and goes out. There is a pause. Then Curtis lifts his head and peers about the room. Seeing he is alone he springs to his feet and begins to pace back and forth, his teeth clenched, his features working convulsively. Then, as if attracted by an irresistible impulse, he goes to the closed door and puts his ear to the crack. He evidently hears his wife's moans for he starts away—in agony*)

CURTIS—Oh, Martha, Martha! Martha, darling! (*He flings himself in the chair by the fireplace—hides his face in his hands and sobs bitterly. There is a ring from somewhere in the house. Soon after there is a knock at the door. Curtis doesn't hear at first but when it is repeated he mutters huskily*) Come in. (*Bigelow enters. Curtis looks up at him.*) Close that door, Big, for God's sake!

BIGELOW—(*does so—then taking off his overcoat, hat, and throwing them on the lounge comes quickly over to Curtis*) I got over as soon as I could. (*As he sees Curtis' face he starts and says sympathetically*) By Jove, old man, you look as though you'd been through hell!

CURTIS—(*grimly*) I have. I am.

BIGELOW—(*slapping his back*) Buck up! (*then anxiously*) How's Martha?

CURTIS—She's in hell, too—

BIGELOW—(*attempting consolation*) You're surely not worrying, are you? Martha is so strong and healthy there's no doubt of her pulling through in fine shape.

CURTIS—She should never have attempted this. (*after a pause*) I've a grudge against you, Big. It was you bringing your children over here that first planted this in her mind.

BIGELOW—(*after a pause*) I've guessed you thought that. That's why you haven't noticed me—or them—over here so much lately. I'll confess that I felt you— (*angrily*) And the infernal gossip—I'll admit I thought that you—oh, damn this rotten town, anyway!

CURTIS—(*impatiently*) Oh, for God's sake! (*bitterly*) I didn't want you here to discuss Bridgetown gossip.

BIGELOW—I know, old man, forgive me. (*In spite of the closed door one of Martha's agonized moans is heard. They both shudder.*)

CURTIS—(*in a dead, monotonous tone*) She has been moaning like that hour after hour. I'll have those sounds in my ears until the day I die.

BIGELOW—(*trying to distract him*) Deuce take it, Curt, I never thought you'd turn morbid.

CURTIS—(*darkly*) I've changed, Big—I hardly know myself any more.

BIGELOW—Once you're back on the job again, you'll be all right. You're still determined to go on this expedition, aren't you?

CURTIS—Yes. I was supposed to join them this week in New York but I've arranged to catch up with them in China—as soon as it's possible for us to go.

BIGELOW—Us?

CURTIS—(*angrily aggressive*) Yes, certainly! Why not? Martha ought to be able to travel in a month or so.

BIGELOW—Yes, but—do you think it would be safe to take the child?

CURTIS—(*with a bitter laugh*) Yes—I was forgetting the child, wasn't I? (*viciously*) But perhaps— (*then catching himself with a groan*) Oh, damn all children, Big!

BIGELOW—(*astonished*) Curt!

CURTIS—(*in anguish*) I can't help it—I've fought against it. But it's there—deep down in me—and I can't drive it out. I can't!

BIGELOW—(*bewildered*) What, Curt?

CURTIS—Hatred! Yes, hatred! What's the use of denying it? I must tell someone and you're the only one who might understand. (*with a wild laugh*) For you—hated your wife, didn't you?

BIGELOW—(*stunned*) Good God, you don't mean you hate—Martha?

CURTIS—(*raging*) Hate Martha? How dare you, you fool!

I love Martha—love her with every miserable drop of blood in me—with all my life—all my soul! She is my whole world—everything! Hate Martha! God, man, have you gone crazy to say such a mad thing? (*savagely*) No. I hate it. It!

BIGELOW—(*shocked*) Curt! Don't you know you can't talk like that—now—when—

CURTIS—(*harshly*) It has made us both suffer torments—not only now—every day, every hour, for months and months. Why shouldn't I hate it, eh?

BIGELOW—(*staring at his friend's wild, distorted face with growing horror*) Curt! Can't you realize how horrible—

CURTIS—Yes, it's horrible. I've told myself that a million times. (*with emphasis*) But it's true!

BIGELOW—(*severely*) Shut up! What would Martha feel if she heard you going on this way? Why—it would kill her!

CURTIS—(*with a sobbing groan*) Oh, I know, I know! (*after a pause*) She read it in my eyes. Yes, it's horrible, but when I saw her there suffering so frightfully—I couldn't keep it out of my eyes. I tried to force it back—for her sake—but I couldn't. I was holding her hands and her eyes searched mine with such a longing question in them—and she read only my hatred there, not my love for her. And she screamed and seemed to try to push me away. I wanted to kneel down and pray for forgiveness—to tell her it was only my love for her—that I couldn't help it. And then the doctors told me to leave—and now the door is locked against me— (*He sobs.*)

BIGELOW—(*greatly moved*) This is only your damned imagination. They put you out because you were in their way, that's all. And as for Martha, she was probably suffering so much—

CURTIS—No. She read it in my eyes. I saw that look in hers—of horror—horror of me!

BIGELOW—(*gruffly*) You're raving, damn it!

CURTIS—(*unheeding*) It came home to her then—the undeniable truth. (*with a groan*) Isn't it fiendish that I should be the one to add to her torture—in spite of myself—in spite of all my will to conceal it! She'll never forgive me, never! And how can I forgive myself?

BIGELOW—(*distractedly*) For God's sake, don't think about it! It's ridiculous!

CURTIS—(*growing more calm—in a tone of obsession*) She's guessed it ever since that day when we quarreled—her birthday. Oh, you can have no idea of the misery there has been in our lives since then. You haven't seen or guessed the reason. No one has. It's been—the thought of *it*.

BIGELOW—Curt!

CURTIS—(*unheeding*) For years we two were sufficient, each to each. There was no room for a third. And it was a fine, free life we had made.

BIGELOW—But that life was your life, Curt—

CURTIS—(*vehemently*) No, it was her life, too—her work as well as mine. She had made the life, our life—the work, our work. Had she the right to repudiate what she'd built because she suddenly has a fancy for a home, children, a miserable ease?

BIGELOW—Curt!

CURTIS—Oh, I tried to become reconciled. I tried my damnedest. But I couldn't. I grew to dread the idea of this intruder. She saw this. I denied it—but she knew. There was something in each of us the other grew to hate. And still we loved as never before, perhaps, for we grew to pity each other's helplessness.

BIGELOW—Curt! Are you sure you ought to tell anyone this?

CURTIS—(*waving his remark aside*) One day a thought suddenly struck me—a horrible but fascinating possibility that had never occurred to me before. (*with feverish intensity*) Can you guess what it was?

BIGELOW—No. And I think you've done enough morbid raving, if you ask me.

CURTIS—The thought came to me that if a certain thing happened, Martha could still go with me. And I knew, if it did happen, that she'd want to go, that she'd fling herself into the spirit of our work to forget, that she'd be mine more than ever.

BIGELOW—(*afraid to believe the obvious answer*) Curt!

CURTIS—Yes. My thought was that the child might be born dead.

BIGELOW—(*repelled—sternly*) Damn it, man, do you know what you're saying? (*relentingly*) No, Curt, old boy, do stop talking. If you don't I'll send for a doctor, damned if I won't. That talk belongs in an asylum. God, man, can't you realize this is your child—yours as well as hers?

CURTIS—I've tried. I can't. There is some force in me—

BIGELOW—(*coldly*) Do you realize how contemptible this confession makes you out? (*angrily*) Why, if you had one trace of human kindness in you—one bit of unselfish love for your wife—one particle of pity for her suffering—

CURTIS—(*anguished*) I have—all the love and pity in the world for her! That's why I can't help hating—the cause of her suffering.

BIGELOW—Have you never thought that you might repay Martha for giving up all her life to you by devoting the rest of yours to her?

CURTIS—(*bitterly*) She can be happy without me. She'll have this child—to take my place. (*intensely*) You think I wouldn't give up my work for her? But I would! I'll stay here—do anything she wishes—if only we can make a new beginning again—together—*alone!*

BIGELOW—(*agitated*) Curt, for God's sake, don't return to that! Why, good God, man—even now—don't you realize what may be happening? And you can talk as if you were wishing—

CURTIS—(*fiercely*) I can't help but wish it!

BIGELOW—(*distractedly*) For the love of God, if you have such thoughts, keep them to yourself. (*The door in the rear is opened and Jayson enters, pale and unnerved. A succession of quick, piercing shrieks is heard before he can close the door behind him.*)

CURTIS—(*shuddering*) My God! My God! (*with a fierce cry*) Will—this—never—end!

JAYSON—(*tremblingly*) Sh-h-h, they say this is the crisis. (*puts his arm around Curtis*) Bear up, my boy, it'll soon be over now. (*He sits down in the chair Bigelow has vacated, pointedly ignoring the latter. The door is opened again and Emily, Esther, John and Sheffield file in quickly as if escaping from the cries of the woman upstairs. They are all greatly agitated. Curtis groans, pressing his clenched fists against his ears. The two women sit on the lounge. Mark comes forward and stands by Jayson's chair, John sits by the door as before. Bigelow retreats behind Curtis' chair, aware of their hostility. There is a long pause.*)

ESTHER—(*suddenly*) She's stopped— (*They all listen.*)

JAYSON—(*huskily*) Thank God, it's over at last. (*The door is opened and Mrs. Davidson enters. The old lady is radiant, weeping tears of joy.*)

MRS. DAVIDSON—(*calls out exultantly between sobs*) A son, Curt—a son. (*with rapt fervor—falling on her knees*) Let us all give thanks to God!

CURTIS—(*in a horrible cry of rage and anguish*) No! No! (*They all cry out in fright and amazement:* "Curt!" *The door is opened and the nurse appears.*)

NURSE—(*looking at Curtis—in a low voice*) Mr. Jayson, your wife is asking for you.

BIGELOW—(*promptly slapping Curtis on the back*) There! What did I tell you? Run, you chump!

CURTIS—(*with a gasp of joy*) Martha! (*He rushes out after the nurse.*)

BIGELOW—(*comes forward to get his hat and coat from the sofa—coldly*) Pardon me, please. (*They shrink away from him.*)

EMILY—(*as he goes to the door—cuttingly*) Some people seem to have no sense of decency!

BIGELOW—(*stung, stops at the door and looks from one to the other of them—bitingly*) No, I quite agree with you. (*He goes out, shutting the door. They all gasp angrily.*)

JOHN—Scoundrel!

JAYSON—(*testily—going to Mrs. D., who is still on her knees praying*) Do get up, Aunt Elizabeth! How ridiculous! What a scene if anyone should see you like that. (*He raises her to her feet and leads her to a chair by the fire. She obeys unresistingly, seemingly unaware of what she is doing.*)

ESTHER—(*unable to restrain her jealousy*) So it's a boy.

EMILY—Did you hear Curt—how he yelled out "No"? It's plain as the nose on your face he didn't want—

ESTHER—How awful!

JOHN—Well, can you blame him?

EMILY—And the awful cheek of that Bigelow person— coming here—

ESTHER—They appeared as friendly as ever when we came in.

JOHN—(*scornfully*) Curt is a blind simpleton—and that man is a dyed-in-the-wool scoundrel.

JAYSON—(*frightenedly*) Shhh! Suppose we were overheard!

EMILY—When Curt leaves we can put her in her proper place. I'll soon let her know she hasn't fooled me, for one. (*While she is speaking Mrs. D. has gotten up and is going silently toward the door.*)

JAYSON—(*testily*) Aunt Elizabeth, where are you going?

MRS. D.—(*tenderly*) I must see him again, the dear! (*She goes out.*)

ESTHER—(*devoured by curiosity—hesitatingly*) I think I—come on, Emily. Let's go up and see—

EMILY—Not I! I never want to lay eyes on it.

JOHN—Nor I.

ESTHER—I was only thinking—everyone will think it funny if we don't.

JAYSON—(*hastily*) Yes, yes. We must keep up appearances. (*getting to his feet*) Yes, I think we had better all go up—make some sort of inquiry about Martha, you know. It's expected of us and— (*They are all standing, hesitating, when the door in the rear is opened and the nurse appears, supporting Curtis. The latter is like a corpse. His face is petrified with grief, his body seems limp and half-paralyzed.*)

NURSE—(*her eyes flashing, indignantly*) It's a wonder some of you wouldn't come up—here, help me! Take him, can't you? I've got to run back! (*Jayson and Sheffield spring forward and lead Curtis to a chair by the fire.*)

JAYSON—(*anxiously*) Curt! Curt, my boy! What is it, son?

EMILY—(*catching the nurse as she tries to go*) Nurse! What is the matter?

NURSE—(*slowly*) His wife is dead. (*They are all still, stunned.*) She lived just long enough to recognize him.

EMILY—And—the baby?

NURSE—(*with a professional air*) Oh, it's a fine, healthy baby—eleven pounds—that's what made it so difficult. (*She goes. The others all stand in silence.*)

ESTHER—(*suddenly sinking on the couch and bursting into tears*) Oh, I'm so sorry I said—or thought—anything wrong about her. Forgive me, Martha!

SHEFFIELD—(*honestly moved but unable to resist this opportunity for Latin—solemnly*) De mortuis nil nisi bonum.

JAYSON—(*who has been giving all his attention to his son*) Curt! Curt!

EMILY—Hadn't the doctor better—

JAYSON—Shhh! He begins to recognize me. Curt!

CURTIS—(*looking around him bewilderedly*) Yes. (*Suddenly remembrance comes and a spasm of intolerable pain contracts his features. He presses his hands to the side of his head and groans brokenly*) Martha! (*He appeals wildly to the others.*) Her eyes— she knew me—she smiled—she whispered—forgive me, Curt,—forgive her—when it was I who should have said forgive me—but before I could—she— (*He falters brokenly.*)

EMILY—(*looking from one to the other meaningly as if this justified all their suspicions*) Oh!

CURTIS—(*a sudden triumph in his voice*) But she loved me again—only me—I saw it in her eyes! She had forgotten— *it*. (*raging*) It has murdered her! (*springing to his feet*) I hate it—I will never see it—never—never—I take my oath! (*as his father takes his arm—shaking him off*) Let me go! I am going back to her! (*He strides out of the door in a frenzy of grief and rage. They all stand transfixed, looking at each other bewilderedly.*)

EMILY—(*putting all her venomous gratification into one word*) Well!

(*The Curtain Falls*)

ACT FOUR

SCENE—*Same as Act One. It is afternoon of a fine day three days later. Motors are heard coming up the drive in front of the house. There is the muffled sound of voices. The maid is seen going along the hall to the front door. Then the family enter from the rear. First come Jayson and Esther with Mrs. Davidson—then Lily, Dick and Sheffield—then John and his wife. All are dressed in mourning. The only one who betrays any signs of sincere grief is Mrs. Davidson. The others all have a strained look, irritated, worried, or merely gloomy. They seem to be thinking "The worst is yet to come."*

JAYSON—(*leading Mrs. D., who is weeping softly, to the chair at left of table—fretfully*) Please do sit down, Aunt. (*She does so mechanically.*) And do stop crying. (*He sits down in front of table. Esther goes to couch where she is joined by Emily. Mark goes over and stands in back of them. Dick and John sit at rear of table. Lily comes down front and walks about nervously. She seems in a particularly fretful, upset mood.*)

LILY—(*trying to conceal her feelings under a forced flippancy*) What ridiculous things funerals are, anyway! That stupid minister—whining away through his nose! Why does the Lord show such a partiality for men with adenoids, I wonder!

JAYSON—(*testily*) Sshhh! Have you no respect for anything?

LILY—(*resentfully*) If I had, I'd have lost it when I saw all of you pulling such long faces in the church where you knew you were under observation. Pah! Such hypocrisy! And then, to cap it all, Emily has to force out a few crocodile tears at the grave!

EMILY—(*indignantly*) When I saw Curt—that's why I cried—not for her!

JAYSON—What a scene Curt made! I actually believe he wanted to throw himself into the grave!

DICK—You *believe* he wanted to! Why, it was all Mark and I could do to hold him, wasn't it, Mark? (*Sheffield nods.*)

JAYSON—I never expected he'd turn violent like that. He's seemed calm enough the past three days.

LILY—Calm! Yes, just like a corpse is calm!

JAYSON—(*distractedly*) And now this perfectly mad idea of going away today to join that infernal expedition—leaving that child on our hands—the child he has never even looked at! Why, it's too monstrously flagrant! He's deliberately flaunting this scandal in everyone's face!

JOHN—(*firmly*) He must be brought to time.

SHEFFIELD—Yes, we must talk to him—quite openly, if we're forced to. After all, I guess he realizes the situation more keenly than any of us.

LILY—(*who has wandered to window on right*) You mean you think he believes— Well, I don't. And you had better be careful not to let him guess what you think. (*pointing outside*) There's my proof. There he is walking about with Bigelow. Can you imagine Curt doing that—if he thought for a moment—

DICK—Oh, I guess Curt isn't all fool. He knows that's the very best way to keep people from suspecting.

ESTHER—(*indignantly*) But wouldn't you think that Bigelow person— It's disgusting, his sticking to Curt like this.

SHEFFIELD—Well, for one, I'm becoming quite resigned to Bigelow's presence. In the first place, he seems to be the only one who can bring Curt to reason. Then again, I feel that it is to Bigelow's own interest to convince Curt that he mustn't provoke an open scandal by running away without acknowledging this child.

LILY—(*suddenly bursting forth hysterically*) Oh, I hate you, all of you! I loathe your suspicions—and I loathe myself because I'm beginning to be poisoned by them, too.

EMILY—Really, Lily, at this late hour—after the way Curt has acted—and her last words when she was dying—

LILY—(*distractedly*) I know! Shut up! Haven't you told it a million times already? (*Mrs. Davidson gets up and walks to the door, rear. She has been crying softly during this scene, oblivious to the talk around her.*)

JAYSON—(*testily*) Aunt Elizabeth! Where are you going? (*as she doesn't answer but goes out into the hall*) Esther, go with her and see that she doesn't—

ESTHER—(*gets up with a jealous irritation*) She's only going up to see the baby. She's simply forgotten everything else in the world!

LILY—(*indignantly*) She probably realizes what we are too mean to remember—that the baby, at least, is innocent. Wait, Esther. I'll come with you.

JAYSON—Yes, hurry, she shouldn't be left alone. (*Esther and Lily follow the old lady out, rear.*)

DICK—(*after a pause—impatiently*) Well, what next? I don't see what good we are accomplishing. May I run along? (*He gets up restlessly as he is speaking and goes to the window.*)

JAYSON—(*severely*) You will stay, if you please. There's to be no shirking on anyone's part. It may take all of us to induce Curt—

SHEFFIELD—I wouldn't worry. Bigelow is taking that job off our hands, I imagine.

DICK—(*looking out of the window*) He certainly seems to be doing his damnedest. (*with a sneer*) The stage missed a great actor in him.

JAYSON—(*worriedly*) But, if Bigelow should fail—

SHEFFIELD—Then we'll succeed. (*with a grim smile*) By God, we'll have to.

JAYSON—Curt has already packed his trunks and had them taken down to the station—told me he was leaving on the five o'clock train.

SHEFFIELD—But didn't you hint to him there was now this matter of the child to be considered in making his plans?

JAYSON—(*lamely*) I started to. He simply flared up at me with insane rage.

DICK—(*looking out the window*) Say, I believe they're coming in.

JAYSON—Bigelow?

DICK—Yes, they're both making for the front door.

SHEFFIELD—I suggest we beat a retreat to Curt's study and wait there.

JAYSON—Yes, let's do that—come on, all of you. (*They all retire grumblingly but precipitately to the study, closing the door behind them. The front door is heard opening and a moment later Curtis and Bigelow enter the room. Curtis' face is set in an expression of stony grief. Bigelow is flushed, excited, indignant.*)

BIGELOW—(*as Curtis sinks down on the couch—pleading indignantly*) Curt, damn it, wake up! Are you made of stone? Has everything I've said gone in one ear and out the other? I know it's hell for me to torment you at this particular time but it's your own incredibly unreasonable actions that force me to. I know how terribly you must feel but—damn it, man, postpone this going away! Face this situation like a man! Be reconciled to your child, stay with him at least until you can make suitable arrangements—

CURTIS—(*fixedly*) I will never see it! Never!

BIGELOW—How can you keep repeating that—with Martha hardly cold in her grave! I ask you again, what would she think, how would she feel— If you would only consent to see this baby, I know you'd realize how damnably mad and cruel you are. Won't you—just for a second?

CURTIS—No. (*then raging*) If I saw it I'd be tempted to— (*then brokenly*) No more of that talk, Big. I've heard enough. I've reached the limit.

BIGELOW—(*restraining his anger with difficulty—coldly*) That's your final answer, eh? Well, I'm through. I've done all I could. If you want to play the brute—to forget all that was most dear in the world to Martha—to go your own damn selfish way—well, there's nothing more to be said. (*He takes a step toward the door.*) And I—I want you to understand that all friendship ceases between us from this day. You're not the Curt I thought I knew—and I have nothing but a feeling of repulsion—good-by. (*He starts for the door.*)

CURTIS—(*dully*) Good-by, Big.

BIGELOW—(*stops, his features working with grief, and looks back at his friend—then suddenly goes back to him—penitently*) Curt! Forgive me! I ought to know better. This isn't you. You'll come to yourself when you've had time to think it over. The memory of Martha—she'll tell you what you must do. (*He wrings Curtis' hand.*) Good-by, old scout!

CURTIS—(*dully*) Good-by. (*Bigelow hurries out, rear. Curtis sits in a dumb apathy for a while—then groans heart-brokenly.*) Martha! Martha! (*He springs to his feet distractedly. The door of the study is slowly opened and Sheffield peers out cautiously—then comes into the room, followed by the others. They all take seats as before. Curtis ignores them.*)

SHEFFIELD—(*clearing his throat*) Curt—

CURTIS—(*suddenly*) What time is it, do you know?

SHEFFIELD—(*looking at his watch*) Two minutes to four.

CURTIS—(*impatiently*) Still an hour more of this!

JAYSON—(*clearing his throat*) Curt— (*Before he starts what he intends to say, there is the sound of voices from the hall. Esther and Lily help in Mrs. Davidson to her former chair. The old lady's face is again transformed with joy. Esther joins Emily on the couch. Lily sits in chair—front right. There is a long, uncomfortable pause during which Curtis paces up and down.*)

MRS. DAVIDSON—(*suddenly murmuring aloud to herself— happily*) He's such a dear! I could stay watching him forever.

JAYSON—(*testily*) Sshhh! Aunt! (*then clearing his throat again*) Surely you're not still thinking of going on the five o'clock train, are you, Curt?

CURTIS—Yes.

SHEFFIELD—(*dryly*) Then Mr. Bigelow didn't persuade you—

CURTIS—(*coldly and impatiently*) I'm not to be persuaded by Big or anyone else. And I'll thank you not to talk any more about it. (*They all stiffen resentfully at his tone.*)

JAYSON—(*to Curtis—in a pleading tone*) You mustn't be unreasonable, Curt. After all we are your family—your best friends in the world—and we are only trying to help you—

CURTIS—(*with nervous vehemence*) I don't want your help. You'll help me most by keeping silent.

EMILY—(*with a meaning look at the others—sneeringly*) Yes, no doubt.

ESTHER—Sshhh, Emily!

JAYSON—(*helplessly*) But, you see, Curt—

SHEFFIELD—(*with his best judicial air*) If you'll all allow me to be the spokesman, I think perhaps that I— (*They all nod and signify their acquiescence.*) Well, then, will you listen to me, Curt? (*this last somewhat impatiently as Curtis continues to pace, eyes on the floor*)

CURTIS—(*without looking at him—harshly*) Yes, I'm listening. What else can I do when you've got me cornered? Say what you like and let's get this over.

SHEFFIELD—First of all, Curt, I hope it is needless for me to express how very deeply we all feel for you in your sorrow. But we sincerely trust that you are aware of our heartfelt sympathy. (*They all nod. A bitter, cynical smile comes over Lily's face.*)

ESTHER—(*suddenly breaking down and beginning to weep*) Poor Martha! (*Sheffield glances at his wife, impatient at this interruption. The others also show their irritation.*)

EMILY—(*pettishly*) Esther! For goodness' sake! (*Curtis hesitates, stares at his sister frowningly as if judging her sincerity—then bends down over her and kisses the top of her bowed head impulsively—seems about to break down himself—grits his teeth and forces it back—glances around at the others defiantly and resumes his pacing. Esther dries her eyes.*)

SHEFFIELD—(*clearing his throat*) I may truthfully say we all feel—as Esther does—even if we do not give vent— (*with an air of sincere sympathy*) I know how terrible a day this must be for you, Curt. We all do. And we feel guilty in breaking in upon the sanctity of your sorrow in any way. But, if you will pardon my saying so, your own course of action—the suddenness of your plans—have made it imperative that we come to an understanding about certain things—about one thing in particular, I might say. (*He pauses. Curtis goes on pacing back and forth as if he hadn't heard.*)

JAYSON—(*placatingly*) Yes, it is for the best, Curt.

ESTHER—Yes, Curt dear, you mustn't be unreasonable.

DICK—(*feeling called upon to say something*) Yes, old man, you've got to face things like a regular. Facts are facts. (*This makes everybody uneasy.*)

LILY—(*springing to her feet*) Phew! it's close in here. I'm going out in the garden. You can call me when these— orations—are finished. (*She sweeps out scornfully.*)

JAYSON—(*calling after her imperiously*) Lily! (*But she doesn't answer and he gives it up with a hopeless sigh.*)

CURTIS—(*harshly*) What time is it?

SHEFFIELD—You have plenty of time to listen to what I— I should rather say we—have to ask you, Curt. I promise to be brief. But first let me again impress upon you that I am talking in a spirit of the deepest friendliness and sympathy with you—as a fellow-member of the same family, I may say—and with the highest ideals and the honor of that family always in view. (*Curtis makes no comment. Sheffield unconsciously begins to adopt the alert keenness of the cross-examiner.*)

First, let me ask you, is it your intention to take that five o'clock train today?

CURTIS—(*harshly*) I've told you that.

SHEFFIELD—And then you'll join this expedition to Asia?

CURTIS—You know that.

SHEFFIELD—To be gone five years?

CURTIS—(*shrugging his shoulders*) More or less.

SHEFFIELD—Is it your intention to return here at any time before you leave for Asia?

CURTIS—No!

SHEFFIELD—And your determination on these plans is irrevocable?

CURTIS—Irrevocable! Exactly. Please remember that.

SHEFFIELD—(*sharply*) That being your attitude, I will come bluntly to the core of the whole matter—the child whose coming into the world cost Martha her life.

CURTIS—(*savagely*) Her murderer! (*They all look shocked, suspicious.*)

SHEFFIELD—(*remonstratingly but suspiciously*) You can hardly hold the child responsible for the terrible outcome. Women die every day from the same cause. (*keenly*) Why do you attribute guilt to the child in this case, Curt?

CURTIS—It lives and Martha is gone— But I've said I never wanted it mentioned to me. Will you please remember that?

SHEFFIELD—(*sharply*) Its name is Jayson, Curt—in the eyes of the law. Will *you* please remember that?

CURTIS—(*distractedly*) I don't want to remember anything! (*wildly*) Please, for God's sake, leave me alone!

SHEFFIELD—(*coldly*) I am sorry, Curt, but you can't act as if you were alone in this affair.

CURTIS—Why not? Am I not alone—more alone this minute than any creature on God's earth?

SHEFFIELD—(*soothingly*) In your great grief. Yes, yes, of course. We all appreciate—and we hate to— (*persuasively*) Yes, it would be much wiser to postpone these practical considerations until you are in a calmer mood. And if you will only give us the chance—why not put off this precipitate departure—for a month, say—and in the meantime—

CURTIS—(*harshly*) I am going when I said I was. I must

get away from this horrible hole—as far away as I can. I must get back to my work for only in it will I find Martha again. But you—you can't understand that. What is the good of all this talking which leads nowhere?

SHEFFIELD—(*coldly*) You're mistaken. It leads to this: Do you understand that your running away from this child—on the very day of its mother's funeral!—will have a very queer appearance in the eyes of the world?

EMILY—And what are you going to do with the baby, Curt? Do you think you can run off regardless and leave it here—on our hands?

CURTIS—(*distractedly*) I'll give it this home. And some-one—anyone—Esther, Lily—can appoint a nurse to live here and— (*breaking down*) Oh, don't bother me!

SHEFFIELD—(*sharply*) In the world's eyes, it will appear precious like a desertion on your part.

CURTIS—Oh, arrange it to suit yourselves—anything you wish—

SHEFFIELD—(*quickly*) I'll take you at your word. Then let us arrange it this way. You will remain here a month longer at least—

CURTIS—No!

SHEFFIELD—(*ignoring the interruption*) You can make plans for the child's future in that time, become reconciled to it—

CURTIS—No!

JAYSON—(*pleadingly*) Curt—please—for all our sakes—when the honor of the family is at stake.

DICK—Yes, old man, there's that about it, you know.

CURTIS—No.

EMILY—Oh, he's impossible!

SHEFFIELD—Perhaps Curt misunderstood me. (*meaningly*) Be reconciled to it in the eyes of the public, Curt. That's what I meant. Your own private feelings in the matter—are no one's business but your own, of course.

CURTIS—(*bewilderedly*) But—I don't see— Oh, damn your eyes of the public!

EMILY—(*breaking in*) It's all very well for you to ignore what people in town think—you'll be in China or heaven knows where. The scandal won't touch you—but we've got to live here and have our position to consider.

CURTIS—(*mystified*) Scandal? What scandal? (*then with a harsh laugh*) Oh, you mean the imbecile busy-bodies will call me an unnatural father. Well, let them! I suppose I am. But they don't know—

EMILY—(*spitefully*) Perhaps they know more than you think they do.

CURTIS—(*turning on her—sharply*) Just what do you mean by that, eh?

ESTHER—Emily! Shhh!

JAYSON—(*flurriedly*) Be still, Emily. Let Mark do the talking.

SHEFFIELD—(*interposing placatingly*) What Emily means is simply this, Curt: You haven't even been to look at this child since it has been born—not once, have you?

CURTIS—No, and I never intend—

SHEFFIELD—(*insinuatingly*) And don't you suppose the doctors and nurses—and the servants—have noticed this? It is not the usual procedure, you must acknowledge, and they wouldn't be human if they didn't think your action—or lack of action—peculiar and comment on it outside.

CURTIS—Well, let them! Do you think I care a fiddler's curse how people judge me?

SHEFFIELD—It is hardly a case of their judging—you. (*breaking off as he catches Curtis' tortured eyes fixed on him wildly*) This is a small town, Curt, and you know as well as I do, gossip is not the least of its faults. It doesn't take long for such things to get started. (*persuasively*) Now I ask you, frankly, is it wise to provoke deliberately what may easily be set at rest by a little—I'll be frank—a little pretense on your part?

JAYSON—Yes, my boy. As a Jayson, I know you don't wish—

ESTHER—(*with a sigh*) Yes, you really must think of us, Curt.

CURTIS—(*in an acute state of muddled confusion*) But—I—you—how are you concerned? Pretense? You mean you want me to stay and pretend—in order that you won't be disturbed by any silly tales they tell about me? (*with a wild laugh*) Good God, this is too much! Why does a man have to be maddened by fools at such a time! (*raging*) Leave me alone! You're like a swarm of poisonous flies.

JAYSON—Curt! This is—really—when we've tried to be so considerate—

JOHN—(*bursting with rage*) It's an outrage to allow such insults!

DICK—You're not playing the game, Curt.

EMILY—(*spitefully*) It seems to me it's much more for Martha's sake, we're urging you than for our own. After all, the town can't say anything against us.

CURTIS—(*turning on her*) Martha's sake? (*brokenly*) Martha is gone. Leave her out of this.

SHEFFIELD—(*sharply*) But unfortunately, Curt, others will not leave her out of this. They will pry and pry—you know what they are—and—

EMILY—Curt couldn't act the way he is doing if he ever really cared for her.

CURTIS—You dare to say that! (*then controlling himself a bit—with scathing scorn*) What do you know of love—women like you! You call your little rabbit-hutch emotions love—your bread-and-butter passions—and you have the effrontery to judge—

EMILY—(*shrinking from him frightenedly*) Oh! John!

JOHN—(*getting to his feet*) I protest! I cannot allow even my own brother—

DICK—(*grabbing his arm*) Keep your head, old boy.

SHEFFIELD—(*peremptorily*) You are making a fool of yourself, Curt—and you are damned insulting in the bargain. I think I may say that we've all about reached the end of our patience. What Emily said is for your own best interest, if you had the sense to see it. And I put it to you once and for all: Are you or are you not willing to act like a man of honor to protect your own good name, the family name, the name of this child, and your wife's memory? Let me tell you, your wife's good name is more endangered by your stubbornness than anything else.

CURTIS—(*trembling with rage*) I—I begin to think—you—all of you—are aiming at something against Martha in this. Yes—in back of your words—your actions—I begin to feel— (*raging*) Go away! Get out of this house—all of you! Oh, I know your meanness! I've seen how you've tried to hurt her ever since we came—because you resented in your small minds her evident superiority—

EMILY—(*scornfully*) Superiority, indeed!

CURTIS—Her breadth of mind and greatness of soul that you couldn't understand. I've guessed all this, and if I haven't interfered it's only because I knew she was too far above you to notice your sickening malice—

EMILY—(*furiously*) You're only acting—acting for our benefit because you think we don't—

CURTIS—(*turning on her—with annihilating contempt*) Why, you—you poor little nonentity! (*John struggles to get forward but Dick holds him back.*)

EMILY—(*insane with rage—shrilly*) But we know—and the whole town knows—and you needn't pretend you've been blind. You've given the whole thing away yourself—the silly way you've acted—telling everyone how you hated that baby—letting everyone see—

JAYSON—Emily! (*The others are all frightened, try to interrupt her. Curtis stares at her in a stunned bewilderment.*)

EMILY—(*pouring forth all her venom regardless*) But you might as well leave off your idiotic pretending. It doesn't fool us—or anyone else—your sending for Bigelow that night—your hobnobbing with him ever since—your pretending he's as much your friend as ever. They're all afraid of you—but I'm not! I tell you to your face—it's all acting you're doing—just cheap acting to try and pull the wool over our eyes until you've run away like a coward—and left us to face the disgrace for you with this child on our hands!

ESTHER—(*trying to silence her—excitedly*) Emily! Keep still, for Heaven's sake! (*The others all utter exclamations of caution, with fearful glances at Curtis.*)

EMILY—(*becoming exhausted by her outburst—more faintly*) Well, someone had to show him his place. He thinks he's so superior to us just because—telling us how much better she was than— But I won't stand for that. I've always had a clean name—and always will—and my children, too, thank God! (*She sinks down on the couch exhausted, panting but still glaring defiantly at Curtis.*)

CURTIS—(*an awareness of her meaning gradually forcing*)

itself on his mind) Bigelow! Big? Pretending he's as much my friend— (*with a sudden gasp of sickened understanding*) Oh! (*He sways as if he were about to fall, shrinking away from Emily, all horror.*) Oh, you—you—you—filth!

JOHN—(*his fists clenched, tries to advance on his brother*) How dare you insult my wife! (*He is restrained, held back by his remonstrating father and Dick.*)

MRS. DAVIDSON—(*as if suddenly coming out of a dream— frightenedly*) What is the matter? Why is John mad at Curt?

CURTIS—(*his hands over his eyes, acting like a person stricken with a sudden attack of nausea, weakly*) So—that's—what has been in your minds. Oh, this is bestial—disgusting! And there is nothing to be done. I feel defenseless. One would have to be as low as you are— She would have been defenseless, too. It is better she's dead. (*He stares about him—wildly*) And you think—you all think—

ESTHER—(*pityingly*) Curt, dear, we don't think anything except what you've made us think with your crazy carrying-on.

CURTIS—(*looking from one to the other of them*) Yes—all of you—it's on your faces. (*His eyes fix themselves on his aunt.*) No, you don't—you don't—

MRS. DAVIDSON—I? Don't what, Curtis? My, how sick you look, poor boy!

CURTIS—You don't believe—this child—

MRS. DAVIDSON—(*proudly*) He's the sweetest baby I ever saw!

CURTIS—Ah, I know you— (*looking around at the others with loathing and hatred*) But look at them— (*with a burst of fierce determination*) Wait! I'll give you the only answer— (*He dashes for the door in rear, shakes off his father and Dick, who try to stop him, and then is heard bounding up the stairs in hall. Dick runs after him, Jayson as far as the doorway. Esther gives a stifled scream. There is a tense pause. Then Dick re-appears.*)

DICK—It's all right. I saw him go in.

JAYSON—(*frightenedly*) But—good God—he's liable— why didn't you follow him?

DICK—The doctor and nurse are there. They would have called out, wouldn't they, if—

MRS. DAVIDSON—(*getting angrier and angrier as her puzzlement has grown greater—in a stern tone*) I understand less and less of this. Where has Curtis gone? Why did he act so sick? What is the matter with all of you?

ESTHER—Nothing, Aunt dear, nothing!

MRS. DAVIDSON—No, you'll not hush me up! (*accusingly*) You all look guilty. Have you been saying anything against Curtis' baby? That was what Curtis seemed to think. A fine time you've picked out—with his wife not cold in her grave!

JAYSON—Aunt!

MRS. DAVIDSON—I never liked that woman. I never understood her. But now—now I love her and beg her forgiveness. She died like a true woman in the performance of her duty. She died gloriously—and I will always respect her memory. (*suddenly flying into a passion*) I feel that you are all hostile to her baby—poor, little, defenseless creature! Yes, you'd hate the idea of Curtis' having a son—you and your girls! Well, I'll make you bitterly regret the day you— (*She plumps herself down in her chair again, staring stubbornly and angrily before her.*)

EMILY—(*spitefully*) I fear it will be necessary to tell Aunt—

JAYSON—Sshh! You have made enough trouble with your telling already! (*miserably*) It should never have come to this pass. Curt will never forgive us, never!

ESTHER—(*resentfully to Emily*) See what not holding your tongue has done—and my children will have to suffer for it, too!

SHEFFIELD—(*severely*) If Emily had permitted me to conduct this business uninterruptedly, this would never have occurred.

EMILY—That's right! All pick on me! Cowards! (*She breaks down and sobs.*)

DICK—(*from the doorway. Coming back into the room*) Sstt! Here he comes!

CURTIS—(*reënters. There is a look of strange exultation on his face. He looks from one to the other of them. He stammers*) Well— my answer to you—your rotten world—I kissed him—he's mine! He looked at me—it was as if Martha looked at me— through his eyes.

ESTHER—(*voicing the general relief. Joyfully*) Oh, Curt! You won't go now? You'll stay?

CURTIS—(*staring at her, then from one to another of the rest with a withering scorn*) Ha! Now you think you've conquered, do you? No, I'm not going to stay. Do you think your vile slander could influence me to give up my work? And neither shall you influence the life of my son. I leave him here. I must. But not to your tender mercies. No, no! Thank God, there still remains one Jayson with unmuddled integrity to whom I can appeal. (*He goes to Mrs. Davidson.*) I'll leave him in your care, Aunt—while I'm gone.

MRS. DAVIDSON—(*delighted*) It will be a great happiness. He will be—the one God never granted me. (*her lips trembling*) God has answered my prayer at last.

CURTIS—I thank you, Aunt. (*kisses her reverentially*)

MRS. DAVIDSON—(*pleased but morally bound to grumble at him*) But I cannot approve of your running away like this. It isn't natural. (*then with selfish haste, fearing her words may change his mind and she will lose the baby*) But you always were a queer person—and a man must do faithfully the work ordained for him.

CURTIS—(*gladly*) Yes, I must go! What good would I be for him—or anyone—if I stayed? Thank God, you understand. But I'll come back. (*the light of an ideal beginning to shine in his eyes*) When he's old enough, I'll teach him to know and love a big, free life. Martha used to say that he would take her place in time. Martha shall live again for me in him. And you, Aunt, swear to keep him with you—out there in the country—never to let him know this obscene little world. (*He indicates his relatives.*)

MRS. DAVIDSON—Yes, I promise, Curtis. Let anyone dare—! (*She glares about her. The noise of a motor is heard from the drive. It stops in front of the house.*)

CURTIS—I must go. (*He kisses his aunt.*) Teach him his mother was the most beautiful soul that ever lived. Good-by, Aunt.

MRS. DAVIDSON—Good-by, Curtis! (*Without looking at the others, he starts for the door, rear. They all break out into conscience-stricken protestations.*)

JAYSON—(*miserably*) Curt! You're not leaving us that way?

ESTHER—Curt—you're going—without a word! (*They all say this practically together and crowd toward him. John and Emily remain sullenly apart. Curtis turns to face them.*)

LILY—(*enters from the rear*) You're not going, Curt?

CURTIS—(*turning to her*) Yes. Good-by, Lily. (*He kisses her.*) You loved her, didn't you? You're not like— Take my advice and get away before you become— (*He has been staring into her face. Suddenly he pushes her brusquely away from him—coldly*) But I see in your face it's too late.

LILY—(*miserably*) No Curt—I swear—

CURTIS—(*facing them all defiantly*) Yes, I am going without a word—because I can't find the fitting one. Be thankful I can't. (*He again turns and strides to the door.*)

JAYSON—(*his grief overcoming him*) My boy! We are wrong—we know—but—at least say you forgive us.

CURTIS—(*wavers with his back towards them—then turns and forces the words out*) Ask forgiveness of her. She—yes— she was so fine—I feel she—so you are forgiven. Good-by. (*He goes. The motor is heard driving off. There is a tense pause.*)

LILY—Then he did find out? Oh, a fine mess you've made of everything! But no—I should say "we," shouldn't I? Curt guessed that. Oh, I hate you—and myself! (*She breaks down.*)

(*There is strained pause during which they are all silent, their eyes avoiding each other, fixed in dull, stupid stares. Finally, Dick fidgets uncomfortably, heaves a noisy sigh, and blurts out with an attempt at comforting reassurance*)

DICK—Well, it isn't as bad as it might have been, anyway. He did acknowledge the kid—before witnesses, too.

JAYSON—(*testily*) Keep your remarks to yourself, if you please! (*But most of his family are already beginning to look relieved.*)

(*The Curtain Falls*)

THE HAIRY APE

*A Comedy of Ancient and Modern Life
in Eight Scenes*

CHARACTERS

Robert Smith, "Yank"
Paddy
Long
Mildred Douglas
Her Aunt
Second Engineer
A Guard
A Secretary of an Organization
Stokers, Ladies, Gentlemen, etc.

SCENES

Scene I: The firemen's forecastle of an ocean liner—
an hour after sailing from New York.
Scene II: Section of promenade deck, two days out—
morning.
Scene III: The stokehole. A few minutes later.
Scene IV: Same as Scene I. Half an hour later.
Scene V: Fifth Avenue, New York. Three weeks later.
Scene VI: An island near the city. The next night.
Scene VII: In the city. About a month later.
Scene VIII: In the city. Twilight of the next day.

The Hairy Ape

SCENE ONE

The firemen's forecastle of a transatlantic liner an hour after sailing from New York for the voyage across. Tiers of narrow, steel bunks, three deep, on all sides. An entrance in rear. Benches on the floor before the bunks. The room is crowded with men, shouting, cursing, laughing, singing—a confused, inchoate uproar swelling into a sort of unity, a meaning—the bewildered, furious, baffled defiance of a beast in a cage. Nearly all the men are drunk. Many bottles are passed from hand to hand. All are dressed in dungaree pants, heavy ugly shoes. Some wear singlets, but the majority are stripped to the waist.

The treatment of this scene, or of any other scene in the play, should by no means be naturalistic. The effect sought after is a cramped space in the bowels of a ship, imprisoned by white steel. The lines of bunks, the uprights supporting them, cross each other like the steel framework of a cage. The ceiling crushes down upon the men's heads. They cannot stand upright. This accentuates the natural stooping posture which shoveling coal and the resultant over-development of back and shoulder muscles have given them. The men themselves should resemble those pictures in which the appearance of Neanderthal Man is guessed at. All are hairy-chested, with long arms of tremendous power, and low, receding brows above their small, fierce, resentful eyes. All the civilized white races are represented, but except for the slight differentiation in color of hair, skin, eyes, all these men are alike.

The curtain rises on a tumult of sound. Yank is seated in the foreground. He seems broader, fiercer, more truculent, more powerful, more sure of himself than the rest. They respect his superior strength—the grudging respect of fear. Then, too, he represents to them a self-expression, the very last word in what they are, their most highly developed individual.

VOICES—Gif me trink dere, you!
       'Ave a wet!
       Salute!
       Gesundheit!
       Skoal!

Drunk as a lord, God stiffen you!
Here's how!
Luck!
Pass back that bottle, damn you!
Pourin' it down his neck!
Ho, Froggy! Where the devil have you been?
La Touraine.
I hit him smash in yaw, py Gott!
Jenkins—the First—he's a rotten swine—
And the coppers nabbed him—and I run—
I like peer better. It don't pig head gif you.
A slut, I'm sayin'! She robbed me aslape—
To hell with 'em all!
You're a bloody liar!
Say dot again! (*Commotion. Two men about to
    fight are pulled apart.*)
No scrappin' now!
Tonight—
See who's the best man!
Bloody Dutchman!
Tonight on the for'ard square.
I'll bet on Dutchy.
He packa da wallop, I tella you!
Shut up, Wop!
No fightin', maties. We're all chums, ain't we?
(*A voice starts bawling a song.*)
"Beer, beer, glorious beer!
Fill yourselves right up to here."

YANK—(*for the first time seeming to take notice of the uproar
about him, turns around threateningly—in a tone of contemptuous authority*) Choke off dat noise! Where d'yuh get dat
beer stuff? Beer, hell! Beer's for goils—and Dutchmen. Me
for somep'n wit a kick to it! Gimme a drink, one of youse
guys. (*Several bottles are eagerly offered. He takes a tremendous
gulp at one of them; then, keeping the bottle in his hand, glares
belligerently at the owner, who hastens to acquiesce in this robbery
by saying* All righto, Yank. Keep it and have another. *Yank
contemptuously turns his back on the crowd again. For a second
there is an embarrassed silence. Then—*)

VOICES—We must be passing the Hook.

She's beginning to roll to it.

Six days in hell—and then Southampton.

Py Yesus, I vish somepody take my first vatch for me!

Gittin' seasick, Square-head?

Drink up and forget it!

What's in your bottle?

Gin.

Dot's nigger trink.

Absinthe? It's doped. You'll go off your chump, Froggy!

Cochon!

Whisky, that's the ticket!

Where's Paddy?

Going asleep.

Sing us that whisky song, Paddy.

(*They all turn to an old, wizened Irishman who is dozing, very drunk, on the benches forward. His face is extremely monkey-like with all the sad, patient pathos of that animal in his small eyes.*)

Singa da song, Caruso Pat!

He's gettin' old. The drink is too much for him. He's too drunk.

PADDY—(*blinking about him, starts to his feet resentfully, swaying, holding on to the edge of a bunk*) I'm never too drunk to sing. 'Tis only when I'm dead to the world I'd be wishful to sing at all. (*with a sort of sad contempt*) "Whisky Johnny," ye want? A chanty, ye want? Now that's a queer wish from the ugly like of you, God help you. But no matther. (*He starts to sing in a thin, nasal, doleful tone*)

Oh, whisky is the life of man!

Whisky! O Johnny! (*They all join in on this.*)

Oh, whisky is the life of man!

Whisky for my Johnny! (*again chorus*)

Oh, whisky drove my old man mad!

Whisky! O Johnny!

Oh, whisky drove my old man mad!

Whisky for my Johnny!

YANK—(*again turning around scornfully*) Aw hell! Nix on dat old sailing ship stuff! All dat bull's dead, see? And you're dead, too, yuh damned old Harp, on'y yuh don't know it.

Take it easy, see. Give us a rest. Nix on de loud noise. (*with a cynical grin*) Can't youse see I'm tryin' to t'ink?

ALL—(*repeating the word after him as one with the same cynical amused mockery*) Think! (*The chorused word has a brazen metallic quality as if their throats were phonograph horns. It is followed by a general uproar of hard, barking laughter.*)

VOICES—Don't be cracking your head wit ut, Yank.
        You gat headache, py yingo!
        One thing about it—it rhymes with drink!
        Ha, ha, ha!
        Drink, don't think!
        Drink, don't think!
        Drink, don't think!

(*A whole chorus of voices has taken up this refrain, stamping on the floor, pounding on the benches with fists.*)

YANK—(*taking a gulp from his bottle—good-naturedly*) Aw right. Can de noise. I got yuh de foist time. (*The uproar subsides. A very drunken sentimental tenor begins to sing*)
        "Far away in Canada,
        Far across the sea,
      There's a lass who fondly waits
        Making a home for me—"

YANK—(*fiercely contemptuous*) Shut up, yuh lousy boob! Where d'yuh get dat tripe? Home? Home, hell! I'll make a home for yuh! I'll knock yuh dead. Home! T'hell wit home! Where d'yuh get dat tripe? Dis is home, see? What d'yuh want wit home? (*proudly*) I runned away from mine when I was a kid. On'y too glad to beat it, dat was me. Home was lickings for me, dat's all. But yuh can bet your shoit no one ain't never licked me since! Wanter try it, any of youse? Huh! I guess not. (*in a more placated but still contemptuous tone*) Goils waitin' for yuh, huh? Aw, hell! Dat's all tripe. Dey don't wait for no one. Dey'd double-cross yuh for a nickel. Dey're all tarts, get me? Treat 'em rough, dat's me. To hell wit 'em. Tarts, dat's what, de whole bunch of 'em.

LONG—(*very drunk, jumps on a bench excitedly, gesticulating with a bottle in his hand*) Listen 'ere, Comrades! Yank 'ere is right. 'E says this 'ere stinkin' ship is our 'ome. And 'e says as 'ome is 'ell. And 'e's right! This is 'ell. We lives in 'ell, Comrades—and right enough we'll die in it. (*raging*) And who's ter blame, I arsks yer? We ain't. We wasn't born this rotten way. All men is born free and ekal. That's in the bleedin' Bible, maties. But what d'they care for the Bible—them lazy, bloated swine what travels first cabin? Them's the ones. They dragged us down 'til we're on'y wage slaves in the bowels of a bloody ship, sweatin', burnin' up, eatin' coal dust! Hit's them's ter blame—the damned Capitalist clarss! (*There had been a gradual murmur of contemptuous resentment rising among the men until now he is interrupted by a storm of catcalls, hisses, boos, hard laughter.*)

VOICES—Turn it off!
            Shut up!
            Sit down!
            Closa da face!
            Tamn fool! (*etc.*)

YANK—(*standing up and glaring at Long*) Sit down before I knock yuh down! (*Long makes haste to efface himself. Yank goes on contemptuously.*) De Bible, huh? De Cap'tlist class, huh? Aw nix on dat Salvation Army–Socialist bull. Git a soapbox! Hire a hall! Come and be saved, huh? Jerk us to Jesus, huh? Aw g'wan! I've listened to lots of guys like you, see. Yuh're all wrong. Wanter know what I t'ink? Yuh ain't no good for no one. Yuh're de bunk. Yuh ain't got no noive, get me? Yuh're yellow, dat's what. Yellow, dat's you. Say! What's dem slobs in de foist cabin got to do wit us? We're better men dan dey are, ain't we? Sure! One of us guys could clean up de whole mob wit one mit. Put one of 'em down here for one watch in de stokehole, what'd happen? Dey'd carry him off on a stretcher. Dem boids don't amount to nothin'. Dey're just baggage. Who makes dis old tub run? Ain't it us guys? Well den, we belong, don't we? We belong and dey don't. Dat's all. (*A loud chorus of approval. Yank goes on.*) As for dis bein' hell—aw, nuts! Yuh lost your noive, dat's what. Dis is a man's job, get me? It belongs. It runs dis tub. No stiffs need apply. But yuh're a stiff, see? Yuh're yellow, dat's you.

VOICES—(*with a great hard pride in them*)
            Righto!
            A man's job!
            Talk is cheap, Long.

He never could hold up his end.
Divil take him!
Yank's right. We make it go.
Py Gott, Yank say right ting!
We don't need no one cryin' over us.
Makin' speeches.
Throw him out!
Yellow!
Chuck him overboard!
I'll break his jaw for him!

(*They crowd around Long threateningly.*)

YANK—(*half good-natured again—contemptuously*) Aw, take it easy. Leave him alone. He ain't woith a punch. Drink up. Here's how, whoever owns dis. (*He takes a long swallow from his bottle. All drink with him. In a flash all is hilarious amiability again, back-slapping, loud talk, etc.*)

PADDY—(*who has been sitting in a blinking, melancholy daze—suddenly cries out in a voice full of old sorrow*) We belong to this, you're saying? We make the ship to go, you're saying? Yerra then, that Almighty God have pity on us! (*His voice runs into the wail of a keen, he rocks back and forth on his bench. The men stare at him, startled and impressed in spite of themselves.*) Oh, to be back in the fine days of my youth, ochone! Oh, there was fine beautiful ships them days—clippers wid tall masts touching the sky—fine strong men in them—men that was sons of the sea as if 'twas the mother that bore them. Oh, the clean skins of them, and the clear eyes, the straight backs and full chests of them! Brave men they was, and bold men surely! We'd be sailing out, bound down round the Horn maybe. We'd be making sail in the dawn, with a fair breeze, singing a chanty song wid no care to it. And astern the land would be sinking low and dying out, but we'd give it no heed but a laugh, and never a look behind. For the day that was, was enough, for we was free men—and I'm thinking 'tis only slaves do be giving heed to the day that's gone or the day to come—until they're old like me. (*with a sort of religious exaltation*) Oh, to be scudding south again wid the power of the Trade Wind driving her on steady through the nights and the days! Full sail on her! Nights and days! Nights when the foam of the wake would be flaming wid fire, when the sky'd

be blazing and winking wid stars. Or the full of the moon
maybe. Then you'd see her driving through the gray night,
her sails stretching aloft all silver and white, not a sound on
the deck, the lot of us dreaming dreams, till you'd believe
'twas no real ship at all you was on but a ghost ship like the
Flying Dutchman they say does be roaming the seas forever-
more widout touching a port. And there was the days, too. A
warm sun on the clean decks. Sun warming the blood of you,
and wind over the miles of shiny green ocean like strong
drink to your lungs. Work—aye, hard work—but who'd
mind that at all? Sure, you worked under the sky and 'twas
work wid skill and daring to it. And wid the day done, in the
dog watch, smoking me pipe at ease, the lookout would be
raising land maybe, and we'd see the mountains of South
Americy wid the red fire of the setting sun painting their
white tops and the clouds floating by them! (*His tone of exaltation ceases. He goes on mournfully.*) Yerra, what's the use of
talking? 'Tis a dead man's whisper. (*to Yank resentfully*)
'Twas them days men belonged to ships, not now. 'Twas
them days a ship was part of the sea, and a man was part of
a ship, and the sea joined all together and made it one. (*scornfully*) Is it one wid this you'd be, Yank—black smoke from
the funnels smudging the sea, smudging the decks—the
bloody engines pounding and throbbing and shaking—wid
divil a sight of sun or a breath of clean air—choking our
lungs wid coal dust—breaking our backs and hearts in the
hell of the stokehole—feeding the bloody furnace—feeding
our lives along wid the coal, I'm thinking—caged in by steel
from a sight of the sky like bloody apes in the Zoo! (*with a
harsh laugh*) Ho-ho, divil mend you! Is it to belong to that
you're wishing? Is it a flesh and blood wheel of the engines
you'd be?

YANK—(*who has been listening with a contemptuous sneer,
barks out the answer*) Sure ting! Dat's me. What about it?

PADDY—(*as if to himself—with great sorrow*) Me time is
past due. That a great wave wid sun in the heart of it may
sweep me over the side sometime I'd be dreaming of the days
that's gone!

YANK—Aw, yuh crazy Mick! (*He springs to his feet and
advances on Paddy threateningly—then stops, fighting some*

*queer struggle within himself—lets his hands fall to his sides—
contemptuously*) Aw, take it easy. Yuh're aw right, at dat.
Yuh're bugs, dat's all—nutty as a cuckoo. All dat tripe yuh
been pullin'— Aw, dat's all right. On'y it's dead, get me?
Yuh don't belong no more, see. Yuh don't get de stuff. Yuh're
too old. (*disgustedly*) But aw say, come up for air onct in a
while, can't yuh? See what's happened since yuh croaked. (*He
suddenly bursts forth vehemently, growing more and more excited*) Say! Sure! Sure I meant it! What de hell— Say, lemme
talk! Hey! Hey, you old Harp! Hey, youse guys! Say, listen
to me—wait a moment—I gotter talk, see. I belong and he
don't. He's dead but I'm livin'. Listen to me! Sure I'm part
of de engines! Why de hell not! Dey move, don't dey? Dey're
speed, ain't dey! Dey smash trou, don't dey? Twenty-five
knots a hour! Dat's goin' some! Dat's new stuff! Dat belongs! But him, he's too old. He gets dizzy. Say, listen. All
dat crazy tripe about nights and days; all dat crazy tripe about
stars and moons; all dat crazy tripe about suns and winds,
fresh air and de rest of it— Aw hell, dat's all a dope dream!
Hittin' de pipe of de past, dat's what he's doin'. He's old and
don't belong no more. But me, I'm young! I'm in de pink! I
move wit it! It, get me! I mean de ting dat's de guts of all
dis. It ploughs trou all de tripe he's been sayin'. It blows dat
up! It knocks dat dead! It slams dat offen de face of de oith!
It, get me! De engines and de coal and de smoke and all de
rest of it! He can't breathe and swallow coal dust, but I kin,
see? Dat's fresh air for me! Dat's food for me! I'm new, get
me? Hell in de stokehole? Sure! It takes a man to work in
hell. Hell, sure, dat's my fav'rite climate. I eat it up! I git fat
on it! It's me makes it hot! It's me makes it roar! It's me
makes it move! Sure, on'y for me everyting stops. It all goes
dead, get me? De noise and smoke and all de engines movin'
de woild, dey stop. Dere ain't nothin' no more! Dat's what
I'm sayin'. Everyting else dat makes de woild move, somep'n
makes it move. It can't move witout somep'n else, see? Den
yuh get down to me. I'm at de bottom, get me! Dere ain't
nothin' foither. I'm de end! I'm de start! I start somep'n and
de woild moves! It—dat's me!—de new dat's moiderin' de
old! I'm de ting in coal dat makes it boin; I'm steam and oil
for de engines; I'm de ting in noise dat makes yuh hear it;

I'm smoke and express trains and steamers and factory whistles; I'm de ting in gold dat makes it money! And I'm what makes iron into steel! Steel, dat stands for de whole ting! And I'm steel—steel—steel! I'm de muscles in steel, de punch behind it! (*As he says this he pounds with his fist against the steel bunks. All the men, roused to a pitch of frenzied self-glorification by his speech, do likewise. There is a deafening metallic roar, through which Yank's voice can be heard bellowing*) Slaves, hell! We run de whole woiks. All de rich guys dat tink dey're somep'n, dey ain't nothin'! Dey don't belong. But us guys, we're in de move, we're at de bottom, de whole ting is us! (*Paddy from the start of Yank's speech has been taking one gulp after another from his bottle, at first frightenedly, as if he were afraid to listen, then desperately, as if to drown his senses, but finally has achieved complete indifferent, even amused, drunkenness. Yank sees his lips moving. He quells the uproar with a shout.*) Hey, youse guys, take it easy! Wait a moment! De nutty Harp is sayin' somep'n.

PADDY—(*is heard now—throws his head back with a mocking burst of laughter*) Ho-ho-ho-ho-ho—

YANK—(*drawing back his fist, with a snarl*) Aw! Look out who yuh're givin' the bark!

PADDY—(*begins to sing the "Miller of Dee" with enormous good nature*)

> "I care for nobody, no, not I,
> And nobody cares for me."

YANK—(*good-natured himself in a flash, interrupts Paddy with a slap on the bare back like a report*) Dat's de stuff! Now yuh're gettin' wise to somep'n. Care for nobody, dat's de dope! To hell wit 'em all! And nix on nobody else carin'. I kin care for myself, get me! (*Eight bells sound, muffled, vibrating through the steel walls as if some enormous brazen gong were imbedded in the heart of the ship. All the men jump up mechanically, file through the door silently close upon each other's heels in what is very like a prisoners' lockstep. Yank slaps Paddy on the back.*) Our watch, yuh old Harp! (*mockingly*) Come on down in hell. Eat up de coal dust. Drink in de heat. It's it, see! Act like yuh liked it, yuh better—or croak yuhself.

PADDY—(*with jovial defiance*) To the divil wid it! I'll not report this watch. Let thim log me and be damned. I'm no slave the like of you. I'll be sittin' here at me ease, and drinking, and thinking, and dreaming dreams.

YANK—(*contemptuously*) Tinkin' and dreamin', what'll that get yuh? What's tinkin' got to do wit it? We move, don't we? Speed, ain't it? Fog, dat's all you stand for. But we drive trou dat, don't we? We split dat up and smash trou—twenty-five knots a hour! (*turns his back on Paddy scornfully*) Aw, yuh make me sick! Yuh don't belong! (*He strides out the door in rear. Paddy hums to himself, blinking drowsily.*)

(*Curtain*)

SCENE TWO

Two days out. A section of the promenade deck. Mildred Douglas and her aunt are discovered reclining in deck chairs. The former is a girl of twenty, slender, delicate, with a pale, pretty face marred by a self-conscious expression of disdainful superiority. She looks fretful, nervous and discontented, bored by her own anemia. Her aunt is a pompous and proud—and fat—old lady. She is a type even to the point of a double chin and lorgnettes. She is dressed pretentiously, as if afraid her face alone would never indicate her position in life. Mildred is dressed all in white.

The impression to be conveyed by this scene is one of the beautiful, vivid life of the sea all about—sunshine on the deck in a great flood, the fresh sea wind blowing across it. In the midst of this, these two incongruous, artificial figures, inert and disharmonious, the elder like a gray lump of dough touched up with rouge, the younger looking as if the vitality of her stock had been sapped before she was conceived, so that she is the expression not of its life energy but merely of the artificialities that energy had won for itself in the spending.

MILDRED—(*looking up with affected dreaminess*) How the black smoke swirls back against the sky! Is it not beautiful?

AUNT—(*without looking up*) I dislike smoke of any kind.

MILDRED—My great-grandmother smoked a pipe—a clay pipe.

AUNT—(*ruffling*) Vulgar!

MILDRED—She was too distant a relative to be vulgar. Time mellows pipes.

AUNT—(*pretending boredom but irritated*) Did the sociology you took up at college teach you that—to play the ghoul on every possible occasion, excavating old bones? Why not let your great-grandmother rest in her grave?

MILDRED—(*dreamily*) With her pipe beside her—puffing in Paradise.

AUNT—(*with spite*) Yes, you are a natural born ghoul. You are even getting to look like one, my dear.

MILDRED—(*in a passionless tone*) I detest you, Aunt. (*looking at her critically*) Do you know what you remind me of? Of a cold pork pudding against a background of linoleum tablecloth in the kitchen of a—but the possibilities are wearisome. (*She closes her eyes.*)

AUNT—(*with a bitter laugh*) Merci for your candor. But since I am and must be your chaperon—in appearance, at least—let us patch up some sort of armed truce. For my part you are quite free to indulge any pose of eccentricity that beguiles you—as long as you observe the amenities—

MILDRED—(*drawling*) The inanities?

AUNT—(*going on as if she hadn't heard*) After exhausting the morbid thrills of social service work on New York's East Side—how they must have hated you, by the way, the poor that you made so much poorer in their own eyes!—you are now bent on making your slumming international. Well, I hope Whitechapel will provide the needed nerve tonic. Do not ask me to chaperon you there, however. I told your father I would not. I loathe deformity. We will hire an army of detectives and you may investigate everything—they allow you to see.

MILDRED—(*protesting with a trace of genuine earnestness*) Please do not mock at my attempts to discover how the other half lives. Give me credit for some sort of groping sincerity in that at least. I would like to help them. I would like to be some use in the world. Is it my fault I don't know how? I would like to be sincere, to touch life somewhere. (*with weary bitterness*) But I'm afraid I have neither the vitality nor integrity. All that was burnt out in our stock before I was born. Grandfather's blast furnaces, flaming to the sky, melting steel, making millions—then father keeping those home fires burning, making more millions—and little me at the tail-end of it all. I'm a waste product in the Bessemer process—like the millions. Or rather, I inherit the acquired trait of the by-product, wealth, but none of the energy, none of the strength of the steel that made it. I am sired by gold and damned by it, as they say at the race track—damned in more ways than one. (*She laughs mirthlessly.*)

AUNT—(*unimpressed—superciliously*) You seem to be going in for sincerity today. It isn't becoming to you, really—except as an obvious pose. Be as artificial as you are, I advise. There's a sort of sincerity in that, you know. And, after all, you must confess you like that better.

MILDRED—(*again affected and bored*) Yes, I suppose I do. Pardon me for my outburst. When a leopard complains of its spots, it must sound rather grotesque. (*in a mocking tone*) Purr, little leopard. Purr, scratch, tear, kill, gorge yourself and be happy—only stay in the jungle where your spots are camouflage. In a cage they make you conspicuous.

AUNT—I don't know what you are talking about.

MILDRED—It would be rude to talk about anything to you. Let's just talk. (*She looks at her wrist watch.*) Well, thank goodness, it's about time for them to come for me. That ought to give me a new thrill, Aunt.

AUNT—(*affectedly troubled*) You don't mean to say you're really going? The dirt—the heat must be frightful—

MILDRED—Grandfather started as a puddler. I should have inherited an immunity to heat that would make a salamander shiver. It will be fun to put it to the test.

AUNT—But don't you have to have the captain's—or someone's—permission to visit the stokehole?

MILDRED—(*with a triumphant smile*) I have it—both his and the chief engineer's. Oh, they didn't want to at first, in spite of my social service credentials. They didn't seem a bit anxious that I should investigate how the other half lives and works on a ship. So I had to tell them that my father, the president of Nazareth Steel, chairman of the board of directors of this line, had told me it would be all right.

AUNT—He didn't.

MILDRED—How naïve age makes one! But I said he did,

Aunt. I even said he had given me a letter to them—which I had lost. And they were afraid to take the chance that I might be lying. (*excitedly*) So it's ho! for the stokehole. The second engineer is to escort me. (*looking at her watch again*) It's time. And here he comes, I think. (*The second engineer enters. He is a husky, fine-looking man of thirty-five or so. He stops before the two and tips his cap, visibly embarrassed and ill-at-ease.*)

SECOND ENGINEER—Miss Douglas?

MILDRED—Yes. (*throwing off her rugs and getting to her feet*) Are we all ready to start?

SECOND ENGINEER—In just a second, ma'am. I'm waiting for the Fourth. He's coming along.

MILDRED—(*with a scornful smile*) You don't care to shoulder this responsibility alone, is that it?

SECOND ENGINEER—(*forcing a smile*) Two are better than one. (*disturbed by her eyes, glances out to sea—blurts out*) A fine day we're having.

MILDRED—Is it?

SECOND ENGINEER—A nice warm breeze—

MILDRED—It feels cold to me.

SECOND ENGINEER—But it's hot enough in the sun—

MILDRED—Not hot enough for me. I don't like Nature. I was never athletic.

SECOND ENGINEER—(*forcing a smile*) Well, you'll find it hot enough where you're going.

MILDRED—Do you mean hell?

SECOND ENGINEER—(*flabbergasted, decides to laugh*) Ho-ho! No, I mean the stokehole.

MILDRED—My grandfather was a puddler. He played with boiling steel.

SECOND ENGINEER—(*all at sea—uneasily*) Is that so? Hum, you'll excuse me, ma'am, but are you intending to wear that dress?

MILDRED—Why not?

SECOND ENGINEER—You'll likely rub against oil and dirt. It can't be helped.

MILDRED—It doesn't matter. I have lots of white dresses.

SECOND ENGINEER—I have an old coat you might throw over—

MILDRED—I have fifty dresses like this. I will throw this

one into the sea when I come back. That ought to wash it clean, don't you think?

SECOND ENGINEER—(*doggedly*) There's ladders to climb down that are none too clean—and dark alleyways—

MILDRED—I will wear this very dress and none other.

SECOND ENGINEER—No offense meant. It's none of my business. I was only warning you—

MILDRED—Warning? That sounds thrilling.

SECOND ENGINEER—(*looking down the deck—with a sigh of relief*) There's the Fourth now. He's waiting for us. If you'll come—

MILDRED—Go on. I'll follow you. (*He goes. Mildred turns a mocking smile on her aunt.*) An oaf—but a handsome, virile oaf.

AUNT—(*scornfully*) Poser!

MILDRED—Take care. He said there were dark alleyways—

AUNT—(*in the same tone*) Poser!

MILDRED—(*biting her lips angrily*) You are right. But would that my millions were not so anemically chaste!

AUNT—Yes, for a fresh pose I have no doubt you would drag the name of Douglas in the gutter!

MILDRED—From which it sprang. Good-by, Aunt. Don't pray too hard that I may fall into the fiery furnace.

AUNT—Poser!

MILDRED—(*viciously*) Old hag! (*She slaps her aunt insultingly across the face and walks off, laughing gaily.*)

AUNT—(*screams after her*) I said poser!

(*Curtain*)

SCENE THREE

The stokehole. In the rear, the dimly-outlined bulks of the furnaces and boilers. High overhead one hanging electric bulb sheds just enough light through the murky air laden with coal dust to pile up masses of shadows everywhere. A line of men, stripped to the waist, is before the furnace doors. They bend over, looking neither to right nor left, handling their shovels as if they were part of their bodies, with a strange, awkward, swinging rhythm. They use the shovels to throw open the furnace doors. Then from these fiery round holes in the black a flood of terrific light and heat pours full upon the men who are outlined in silhouette in the crouching, inhuman attitudes of chained gorillas. The men shovel with a rhythmic motion, swinging as on a pivot from the coal which lies in heaps on the floor behind to hurl it into the flaming mouths before them. There is a tumult of noise—the brazen clang of the furnace doors as they are flung open or slammed shut, the grating, teeth-gritting grind of steel against steel, of crunching coal. This clash of sounds stuns one's ears with its rending dissonance. But there is order in it, rhythm, a mechanical regulated recurrence, a tempo. And rising above all, making the air hum with the quiver of liberated energy, the roar of leaping flames in the furnaces, the monotonous throbbing beat of the engines.

As the curtain rises, the furnace doors are shut. The men are taking a breathing spell. One or two are arranging the coal behind them, pulling it into more accessible heaps. The others can be dimly made out leaning on their shovels in relaxed attitudes of exhaustion.

PADDY—(*from somewhere in the line—plaintively*) Yerra, will this divil's own watch nivir end? Me back is broke. I'm destroyed entirely.

YANK—(*from the center of the line—with exuberant scorn*) Aw, yuh make me sick! Lie down and croak, why don't yuh? Always beefin', dat's you! Say, dis is a cinch! Dis was made for me! It's my meat, get me! (*A whistle is blown—a thin, shrill note from somewhere overhead in the darkness. Yank curses without resentment.*) Dere's de damn engineer crackin' de whip. He tinks we're loafin'.

PADDY—(*vindictively*) God stiffen him!

YANK—(*in an exultant tone of command*) Come on, youse guys! Git into de game! She's gittin' hungry! Pile some grub in her. Trow it into her belly! Come on now, all of youse! Open her up! (*At this last all the men, who have followed his movements of getting into position, throw open their furnace doors with a deafening clang. The fiery light floods over their shoulders as they bend round for the coal. Rivulets of sooty sweat have traced*

*maps on their backs. The enlarged muscles form bunches of high
light and shadow.*)

YANK—(*chanting a count as he shovels without seeming effort*)
One—two—tree— (*his voice rising exultantly in the joy of
battle*) Dat's de stuff! Let her have it! All togedder now!
Sling it into her! Let her ride! Shoot de piece now! Call de
toin on her! Drive her into it! Feel her move! Watch her
smoke! Speed, dat's her middle name! Give her coal, youse
guys! Coal, dat's her booze! Drink it up, baby! Let's see yuh
sprint! Dig in and gain a lap! Dere she go-o-es. (*This last in
the chanting formula of the gallery gods at the six-day bike race.
He slams his furnace door shut. The others do likewise with as
much unison as their wearied bodies will permit. The effect is of
one fiery eye after another being blotted out with a series of accompanying bangs.*)

PADDY—(*groaning*) Me back is broke. I'm bate out—
bate— (*There is a pause. Then the inexorable whistle sounds
again from the dim regions above the electric light. There is a
growl of cursing rage from all sides.*)

YANK—(*shaking his fist upward—contemptuously*) Take it
easy dere, you! Who d'yuh tinks runnin' dis game, me or you?
When I git ready, we move. Not before! When I git ready,
get me!

VOICES—(*approvingly*) That's the stuff!
　　　　　　　　　　Yank tal him, py golly!
　　　　　　　　　　Yank ain't affeerd.
　　　　　　　　　　Goot poy, Yank!
　　　　　　　　　　Give him hell!
　　　　　　　　　　Tell 'im 'e's a bloody swine!
　　　　　　　　　　Bloody slave-driver!

YANK—(*contemptuously*) He ain't got no noive. He's yellow, get me? All de engineers is yellow. Dey got streaks a mile
wide. Aw, to hell wit him! Let's move, youse guys. We had a
rest. Come on, she needs it! Give her pep! It ain't for him.
Him and his whistle, dey don't belong. But we belong, see!
We gotter feed de baby! Come on! (*He turns and flings his
furnace door open. They all follow his lead. At this instant the
Second and Fourth Engineers enter from the darkness on
the left with Mildred between them. She starts, turns paler, her
pose is crumbling, she shivers with fright in spite of the blazing*

heat, but forces herself to leave the engineers and take a few steps nearer the men. She is right behind Yank. All this happens quickly while the men have their backs turned.)

YANK—Come on, youse guys! (*He is turning to get coal when the whistle sounds again in a peremptory, irritating note. This drives Yank into a sudden fury. While the other men have turned full around and stopped dumfounded by the spectacle of Mildred standing there in her white dress, Yank does not turn far enough to see her. Besides, his head is thrown back, he blinks upward through the murk trying to find the owner of the whistle, he brandishes his shovel murderously over his head in one hand, pounding on his chest, gorilla-like, with the other, shouting*) Toin off dat whistle! Come down outa dere, yuh yellow, brass-buttoned, Belfast bum, yuh! Come down and I'll knock yer brains out! Yuh lousy, stinkin', yellow mut of a Catholic-moiderin' bastard! Come down and I'll moider yuh! Pullin' dat whistle on me, huh? I'll show yuh! I'll crash yer skull in! I'll drive yer teet' down yer troat! I'll slam yer nose trou de back of yer head! I'll cut yer guts out for a nickel, yuh lousy boob, yuh dirty, crummy, muck-eatin' son of a— (*Suddenly he becomes conscious of all the other men staring at something directly behind his back. He whirls defensively with a snarling, murderous growl, crouching to spring, his lips drawn back over his teeth, his small eyes gleaming ferociously. He sees Mildred, like a white apparition in the full light from the open furnace doors. He glares into her eyes, turned to stone. As for her, during his speech she has listened, paralyzed with horror, terror, her whole personality crushed, beaten in, collapsed, by the terrific impact of this unknown, abysmal brutality, naked and shameless. As she looks at his gorilla face, as his eyes bore into hers, she utters a low, choking cry and shrinks away from him, putting both hands up before her eyes to shut out the sight of his face, to protect her own. This startles Yank to a reaction. His mouth falls open, his eyes grow bewildered.*)

MILDRED—(*about to faint—to the engineers, who now have her one by each arm—whimperingly*) Take me away! Oh, the filthy beast! (*She faints. They carry her quickly back, disappearing in the darkness at the left, rear. An iron door clangs shut. Rage and bewildered fury rush back on Yank. He feels himself insulted in some unknown fashion in the very heart of his pride.*

He roars God damn yuh! *and hurls his shovel after them at the door which has just closed. It hits the steel bulkhead with a clang and falls clattering on the steel floor. From overhead the whistle sounds again in a long, angry, insistent command.*)

(*Curtain*)

SCENE FOUR

The firemen's forecastle. Yank's watch has just come off duty and had dinner. Their faces and bodies shine from a soap and water scrubbing but around their eyes, where a hasty dousing does not touch, the coal dust sticks like black make-up, giving them a queer, sinister expression. Yank has not washed either face or body. He stands out in contrast to them, a blackened, brooding figure. He is seated forward on a bench in the exact attitude of Rodin's "The Thinker." The others, most of them smoking pipes, are staring at Yank half-apprehensively, as if fearing an outburst; half-amusedly, as if they saw a joke somewhere that tickled them.

VOICES—He ain't ate nothin'.

      Py golly, a fallar gat to gat grub in him.

      Divil a lie.

      Yank feeda da fire, no feeda da face.

      Ha-ha.

      He ain't even washed hisself.

      He's forgot.

      Hey, Yank, you forgot to wash.

YANK—(*sullenly*) Forgot nothin'! To hell wit washin'.

VOICES—It'll stick to you.

      It'll get under your skin.

      Give yer the bleedin' itch, that's wot.

      It makes spots on you—like a leopard.

      Like a piebald nigger, you mean.

      Better wash up, Yank.

      You sleep better.

      Wash up, Yank.

      Wash up! Wash up!

YANK—(*resentfully*) Aw say, youse guys. Lemme alone. Can't youse see I'm tryin' to tink?

ALL—(*repeating the word after him as one with cynical mockery*) Think! (*The word has a brazen, metallic quality as if their throats were phonograph horns. It is followed by a chorus of hard, barking laughter.*)

YANK—(*springing to his feet and glaring at them belligerently*) Yes, tink! Tink, dat's what I said! What about it? (*They are silent, puzzled by his sudden resentment at what used to be one of his jokes. Yank sits down again in the same attitude of "The Thinker."*)

VOICES—Leave him alone.
              He's got a grouch on.
              Why wouldn't he?

PADDY—(*with a wink at the others*) Sure I know what's the matther. 'Tis aisy to see. He's fallen in love, I'm telling you.

ALL—(*repeating the word after him as one with cynical mockery*) Love! (*The word has a brazen, metallic quality as if their throats were phonograph horns. It is followed by a chorus of hard, barking laughter.*)

YANK—(*with a contemptuous snort*) Love, hell! Hate, dat's what. I've fallen in hate, get me?

PADDY—(*philosophically*) 'Twould take a wise man to tell one from the other. (*with a bitter, ironical scorn, increasing as he goes on*) But I'm telling you it's love that's in it. Sure what else but love for us poor bastes in the stokehole would be bringing a fine lady, dressed like a white quane, down a mile of ladders and steps to be havin' a look at us? (*A growl of anger goes up from all sides.*)

LONG—(*jumping on a bench—hectically*) Hinsultin' us! Hinsultin' us, the bloody cow! And them bloody engineers! What right 'as they got to be exhibitin' us 's if we was bleedin' monkeys in a menagerie? Did we sign for hinsults to our dignity as 'onest workers? Is that in the ship's articles? You kin bloody well bet it ain't! But I knows why they done it. I arsked a deck steward 'o she was and 'e told me. 'Er old man's a bleedin' millionaire, a bloody Capitalist! 'E's got enuf bloody gold to sink this bleedin' ship! 'E makes arf the bloody steel in the world! 'E owns this bloody boat! And you and me, Comrades, we're 'is slaves! And the skipper and mates and engineers, they're 'is slaves! And she's 'is bloody daughter and we're all 'er slaves, too! And she gives 'er orders as 'ow she wants to see the bloody animals below decks and down they takes 'er! (*There is a roar of rage from all sides.*)

YANK—(*blinking at him bewilderedly*) Say! Wait a moment! Is all dat straight goods?

LONG—Straight as string! The bleedin' steward as waits on 'em, 'e told me about 'er. And what're we goin' ter do, I arsks yer? 'Ave we got ter swaller 'er hinsults like dogs? It ain't in the ship's articles. I tell yer we got a case. We kin go to law—

YANK—(*with abysmal contempt*) Hell! Law!

ALL—(*repeating the word after him as one with cynical mockery*) Law! (*The word has a brazen metallic quality as if their throats were phonograph horns. It is followed by a chorus of hard, barking laughter.*)

LONG—(*feeling the ground slipping from under his feet—desperately*) As voters and citizens we kin force the bloody governments—

YANK—(*with abysmal contempt*) Hell! Governments!

ALL—(*repeating the word after him as one with cynical mockery*) Governments! (*The word has a brazen metallic quality as if their throats were phonograph horns. It is followed by a chorus of hard, barking laughter.*)

LONG—(*hysterically*) We're free and equal in the sight of God—

YANK—(*with abysmal contempt*) Hell! God!

ALL—(*repeating the word after him as one with cynical mockery*) God! (*The word has a brazen metallic quality as if their throats were phonograph horns. It is followed by a chorus of hard, barking laughter.*)

YANK—(*witheringly*) Aw, join de Salvation Army!

ALL—Sit down! Shut up! Damn fool! Sea-lawyer! (*Long slinks back out of sight.*)

PADDY—(*continuing the trend of his thoughts as if he had never been interrupted—bitterly*) And there she was standing behind us, and the Second pointing at us like a man you'd hear in a circus would be saying: In this cage is a queerer kind of baboon than ever you'd find in darkest Africy. We roast them in their own sweat—and be damned if you won't hear some of thim saying they like it! (*He glances scornfully at Yank.*)

YANK—(*with a bewildered uncertain growl*) Aw!

PADDY—And there was Yank roarin' curses and turning round wid his shovel to brain her—and she looked at him, and him at her—

YANK—(*slowly*) She was all white. I tought she was a ghost. Sure.

PADDY—(*with heavy, biting sarcasm*) 'Twas love at first sight, divil a doubt of it! If you'd seen the endearin' look on her pale mug when she shriveled away with her hands over her eyes to shut out the sight of him! Sure, 'twas as if she'd seen a great hairy ape escaped from the Zoo!

YANK—(*stung—with a growl of rage*) Aw!

PADDY—And the loving way Yank heaved his shovel at the skull of her, only she was out the door! (*a grin breaking over his face*) 'Twas touching, I'm telling you! It put the touch of home, swate home in the stokehole. (*There is a roar of laughter from all.*)

YANK—(*glaring at Paddy menacingly*) Aw, choke dat off, see!

PADDY—(*not heeding him—to the others*) And her grabbin' at the Second's arm for protection. (*with a grotesque imitation of a woman's voice*) Kiss me, Engineer dear, for it's dark down here and me old man's in Wall Street making money! Hug me tight, darlin', for I'm afeerd in the dark and me mother's on deck makin' eyes at the skipper! (*another roar of laughter*)

YANK—(*threateningly*) Say! What yuh tryin' to do, kid me, yuh old Harp?

PADDY—Divil a bit! Ain't I wishin' myself you'd brained her?

YANK—(*fiercely*) I'll brain her! I'll brain her yet, wait 'n' see! (*coming over to Paddy—slowly*) Say, is dat what she called me—a hairy ape?

PADDY—She looked it at you if she didn't say the word itself.

YANK—(*grinning horribly*) Hairy ape, huh? Sure! Dat's de way she looked at me, aw right. Hairy ape! So dat's me, huh? (*bursting into rage—as if she were still in front of him*) Yuh skinny tart! Yuh white-faced bum, yuh! I'll show yuh who's a ape! (*turning to the others, bewilderment seizing him again*) Say, youse guys. I was bawlin' him out for pullin' de whistle on us. You heard me. And den I seen youse lookin' at somep'n and I tought he'd sneaked down to come up in back of me, and I hopped round to knock him dead wit de shovel. And dere she was wit de light on her! Christ, yuh coulda pushed me over with a finger! I was scared, get me? Sure! I tought she was a ghost, see? She was all in white like dey wrap around stiffs. You seen her. Kin yuh blame me? She didn't belong, dat's what. And den when I come to and seen it was a real skoit and seen de way she was lookin' at me—like Paddy said—Christ, I was sore, get me? I don't stand for dat stuff from nobody. And I flung de shovel—on'y she'd beat it. (*furiously*) I wished it'd banged her! I wished it'd knocked her block off!

LONG—And be 'anged for murder or 'lectrocuted? She ain't bleedin' well worth it.

YANK—I don't give a damn what! I'd be square wit her, wouldn't I? Tink I wanter let her put somep'n over on me? Tink I'm goin' to let her git away wit dat stuff? Yuh don't know me! No one ain't never put nothin' over on me and got away wit it, see!—not dat kind of stuff—no guy and no skoit neither! I'll fix her! Maybe she'll come down again—

VOICE—No chance, Yank. You scared her out of a year's growth.

YANK—I scared her? Why de hell should I scare her? Who de hell is she? Ain't she de same as me? Hairy ape, huh? (*with his old confident bravado*) I'll show her I'm better'n her, if she on'y knew it. I belong and she don't, see! I move and she's dead! Twenty-five knots a hour, dat's me! Dat carries her but I make dat. She's on'y baggage. Sure! (*again bewilderedly*) But, Christ, she was funny lookin'! Did yuh pipe her hands? White and skinny. Yuh could see de bones through 'em. And her mush, dat was dead white, too. And her eyes, dey was like dey'd seen a ghost. Me, dat was! Sure! Hairy ape! Ghost, huh? Look at dat arm! (*He extends his right arm, swelling out the great muscles.*) I coulda took her wit dat, wit' just my little finger even, and broke her in two. (*again bewilderedly*) Say, who is dat skoit, huh? What is she? What's she come from? Who made her? Who give her de noive to look at me like dat? Dis ting's got my goat right. I don't get her. She's new to me. What does a skoit like her mean, huh? She don't belong, get me! I can't see her. (*with growing anger*) But one ting I'm wise to, aw right, aw right! Youse all kin bet your shoits I'll git even wit her. I'll show her if she tinks she— She grinds de organ and I'm on de string, huh? I'll fix her! Let her come down again and I'll fling her in de furnace! She'll move den! She won't shiver at nothin', den! Speed, dat'll be her! She'll belong den! (*He grins horribly.*)

PADDY—She'll never come. She's had her belly-full, I'm telling you. She'll be in bed now, I'm thinking, wid ten doctors and nurses feedin' her salts to clean the fear out of her.

YANK—(*enraged*) Yuh tink I made her sick, too, do yuh? Just lookin' at me, huh? Hairy ape, huh? (*in a frenzy of rage*) I'll fix her! I'll tell her where to git off! She'll git down on her knees and take it back or I'll bust de face offen her! (*shaking one fist upward and beating on his chest with the other*) I'll find yuh! I'm comin', d'yuh hear? I'll fix yuh, God damn yuh! (*He makes a rush for the door.*)

VOICES—Stop him!
He'll get shot!
He'll murder her!
Trip him up!
Hold him!
He's gone crazy!
Gott, he's strong!
Hold him down!
Look out for a kick!
Pin his arms!

(*They have all piled on him and, after a fierce struggle, by sheer weight of numbers have borne him to the floor just inside the door.*)

PADDY—(*who has remained detached*) Kape him down till he's cooled off. (*scornfully*) Yerra, Yank, you're a great fool. Is it payin' attention at all you are to the like of that skinny sow widout one drop of rale blood in her?

YANK—(*frenziedly, from the bottom of the heap*) She done me doit! She done me doit, didn't she? I'll git square wit her! I'll get her some way! Git offen me, youse guys! Lemme up! I'll show her who's a ape!

(*Curtain*)

Scene Five

Three weeks later. A corner of Fifth Avenue in the Fifties on a fine Sunday morning. A general atmosphere of clean, well-tidied, wide street; a flood of mellow, tempered sunshine; gentle, genteel breezes. In the rear, the show windows of two shops, a jewelry establishment on the corner, a furrier's next to it. Here the adornments of extreme wealth are tantalizingly displayed. The jeweler's window is gaudy with glittering diamonds, emeralds, rubies, pearls, etc., fashioned in ornate tiaras, crowns, necklaces, collars, etc. From each piece hangs an enormous tag from which a dollar sign and numerals in intermittent electric lights wink out the incredible prices. The same in the furrier's. Rich furs of all varieties hang there bathed in a downpour of artificial light. The general effect is of a background of magnificence cheapened and made grotesque by commercialism, a background in tawdry disharmony with the clear light and sunshine on the street itself.

Up the side street Yank and Long come swaggering. Long is dressed in shore clothes, wears a black Windsor tie, cloth cap. Yank is in his dirty dungarees. A fireman's cap with black peak is cocked defiantly on the side of his head. He has not shaved for days and around his fierce, resentful eyes—as around those of Long to a lesser degree—the black smudge of coal dust still sticks like make-up. They hesitate and stand together at the corner, swaggering, looking about them with a forced, defiant contempt.

Long—(*indicating it all with an oratorical gesture*) Well, 'ere we are. Fif' Avenoo. This 'ere's their bleedin' private lane, as yer might say. (*bitterly*) We're trespassers 'ere. Proletarians keep orf the grass!

Yank—(*dully*) I don't see no grass, yuh boob. (*staring at the sidewalk*) Clean, ain't it? Yuh could eat a fried egg offen it. The white wings got some job sweepin' dis up. (*looking up and down the avenue—surlily*) Where's all de white-collar stiffs yuh said was here—and de skoits—*her* kind?

Long—In church, blarst 'em! Arskin' Jesus to give 'em more money.

Yank—Choich, huh? I useter go to choich onct—sure—when I was a kid. Me old man and woman, dey made me. Dey never went demselves, dough. Always got too big a head on Sunday mornin', dat was dem. (*with a grin*) Dey was scrappers for fair, bot' of dem. On Satiday nights when dey bot' got a skinful dey could put up a bout oughter been staged at de Garden. When dey got trou dere wasn't a chair or table wit a leg under it. Or else dey bot' jumped on me for somep'n. Dat was where I loined to take punishment. (*with a grin and a swagger*) I'm a chip offen de old block, get me?

LONG—Did yer old man follow the sea?

YANK—Naw. Worked along shore. I runned away when me old lady croaked wit de tremens. I helped at truckin' and in de market. Den I shipped in de stokehole. Sure. Dat belongs. De rest was nothin'. (*looking around him*) I ain't never seen dis before. De Brooklyn waterfront, dat was where I was dragged up. (*taking a deep breath*) Dis ain't so bad at dat, huh?

LONG—Not bad? Well, we pays for it wiv our bloody sweat, if yer wants to know!

YANK—(*with sudden angry disgust*) Aw, hell! I don't see no one, see—like her. All dis gives me a pain. It don't belong. Say, ain't dere a back room around dis dump? Let's go shoot a ball. All dis is too clean and quiet and dolled-up, get me! It gives me a pain.

LONG—Wait and yer'll bloody well see—

YANK—I don't wait for no one. I keep on de move. Say, what yuh drag me up here for, anyway? Tryin' to kid me, yuh simp, yuh?

LONG—Yer wants to get back at 'er, don't yer? That's what yer been sayin' every bloomin' hour since she hinsulted yer.

YANK—(*vehemently*) Sure ting I do! Didn't I try to get even wit her in Southampton? Didn't I sneak on de dock and wait for her by de gangplank? I was goin' to spit in her pale mug, see! Sure, right in her pop-eyes! Dat woulda made me even, see? But no chanct. Dere was a whole army of plainclothes bulls around. Dey spotted me and gimme de bum's rush. I never seen her. But I'll git square wit her yet, you watch! (*furiously*) De lousy tart! She tinks she kin get away wit moider—but not wit me! I'll fix her! I'll tink of a way!

LONG—(*as disgusted as he dares to be*) Ain't that why I brought yer up 'ere—to show yer? Yer been lookin' at this 'ere 'ole affair wrong. Yer been actin' an' talkin' 's if it was all a bleedin' personal matter between yer and that bloody cow. I wants to convince yer she was on'y a representative of 'er clarss. I wants to awaken yer bloody clarss consciousness. Then yer'll see it's 'er clarss yer've got to fight, not 'er alone. There's a 'ole mob of 'em like 'er, Gawd blind 'em!

YANK—(*spitting on his hands—belligerently*) De more de merrier when I gits started. Bring on de gang!

LONG—Yer'll see 'em in arf a mo', when that church lets out. (*He turns and sees the window display in the two stores for the first time.*) Blimey! Look at that, will yer? (*They both walk back and stand looking in the jeweler's. Long flies into a fury.*) Just look at this 'ere bloomin' mess! Just look at it! Look at the bleedin' prices on 'em—more'n our 'ole bloody stokehole makes in ten voyages sweatin' in 'ell! And they—'er and 'er bloody clarss—buys 'em for toys to dangle on 'em! One of these 'ere would buy scoff for a starvin' family for a year!

YANK—Aw, cut de sob stuff! T' hell wit de starvin' family! Yuh'll be passin' de hat to me next. (*with naïve admiration*) Say, dem tings is pretty, huh? Bet yuh dey'd hock for a piece of change aw right. (*then turning away, bored*) But, aw hell, what good are dey? Let her have 'em. Dey don't belong no more'n she does. (*with a gesture of sweeping the jewelers into oblivion*) All dat don't count, get me?

LONG—(*who has moved to the furrier's—indignantly*) And I s'pose this 'ere don't count neither—skins of poor, 'armless animals slaughtered so as 'er and 'ers can keep their bleedin' noses warm!

YANK—(*who has been staring at something inside—with queer excitement*) Take a slant at dat! Give it de once-over! Monkey fur—two t'ousand bucks! (*bewilderedly*) Is dat straight goods—monkey fur? What de hell—?

LONG—(*bitterly*) It's straight enuf. (*with grim humor*) They wouldn't bloody well pay that for a 'airy ape's skin— no, nor for the 'ole livin' ape with all 'is 'ead, and body, and soul thrown in!

YANK—(*clenching his fists, his face growing pale with rage as if the skin in the window were a personal insult*) Trowin' it up in my face! Christ! I'll fix her!

LONG—(*excitedly*) Church is out. 'Ere they come, the bleedin' swine. (*after a glance at Yank's lowering face—uneasily*) Easy goes, Comrade. Keep yer bloomin' temper. Remember force defeats itself. It ain't our weapon. We must impress our demands through peaceful means—the votes of the on-marching proletarians of the bloody world!

YANK—(*with abysmal contempt*) Votes, hell! Votes is a joke, see. Votes for women! Let dem do it!

LONG—(*still more uneasily*) Calm, now. Treat 'em wiv the proper contempt. Observe the bleedin' parasites but 'old yer 'orses.

YANK—(*angrily*) Git away from me! Yuh're yellow, dat's what. Force, dat's me! De punch, dat's me every time, see! (*The crowd from church enter from the right, sauntering slowly and affectedly, their heads held stiffly up, looking neither to right nor left, talking in toneless, simpering voices. The women are rouged, calcimined, dyed, overdressed to the nth degree. The men are in Prince Alberts, high hats, spats, canes, etc. A procession of gaudy marionettes, yet with something of the relentless horror of Frankensteins in their detached, mechanical unawareness.*)

VOICES—Dear Doctor Caiaphas! He is so sincere!

What was the sermon? I dozed off.

About the radicals, my dear—and the false doctrines that are being preached.

We must organize a hundred per cent American bazaar.

And let everyone contribute one one-hundredth per cent of their income tax.

What an original idea!

We can devote the proceeds to rehabilitating the veil of the temple.

But that has been done so many times.

YANK—(*glaring from one to the other of them—with an insulting snort of scorn*) Huh! Huh! (*Without seeming to see him, they make wide detours to avoid the spot where he stands in the middle of the sidewalk.*)

LONG—(*frightenedly*) Keep yer bloomin' mouth shut, I tells yer.

YANK—(*viciously*) G'wan! Tell it to Sweeney! (*He swaggers away and deliberately lurches into a top-hatted gentleman, then glares at him pugnaciously.*) Say, who d'yuh tink yuh're bumpin'? Tink yuh own de oith?

GENTLEMAN—(*coldly and affectedly*) I beg your pardon. (*He has not looked at Yank and passes on without a glance, leaving him bewildered.*)

LONG—(*rushing up and grabbing Yank's arm*) 'Ere! Come away! This wasn't what I meant. Yer'll 'ave the bloody coppers down on us.

YANK—(*savagely—giving him a push that sends him sprawling*) G'wan!

LONG—(*picks himself up—hysterically*) I'll pop orf then. This ain't what I meant. And whatever 'appens, yer can't blame me. (*He slinks off left.*)

YANK—T' hell wit youse! (*He approaches a lady—with a vicious grin and a smirking wink*) Hello, Kiddo. How's every little ting? Got anyting on for tonight? I know an old boiler down to de docks we kin crawl into. (*The lady stalks by without a look, without a change of pace. Yank turns to others— insultingly*) Holy smokes, what a mug! Go hide yuhself before de horses shy at yuh. Gee, pipe de heine on dat one! Say, youse, yuh look like de stoin of a ferryboat. Paint and powder! All dolled up to kill! Yuh look like stiffs laid out for de boneyard! Aw, g'wan, de lot of youse! Yuh give me de eyeache. Yuh don't belong, get me! Look at me, why don't youse dare? I belong, dat's me! (*pointing to a skyscraper across the street which is in process of construction—with bravado*) See dat building goin' up dere? See de steel work? Steel, dat's me! Youse guys live on it and tink yuh're somep'n. But I'm *in* it, see! I'm de hoistin' engine dat makes it go up! I'm it—de inside and bottom of it! Sure! I'm steel and steam and smoke and de rest of it! It moves—speed—twenty-five stories up— and me at de top and bottom—movin'! Youse simps don't move. Yuh're on'y dolls I winds up to see 'm spin. Yuh're de garbage, get me—de leavins—de ashes we dump over de side! Now, what 'a' yuh gotta say? (*But as they seem neither to see nor hear him, he flies into a fury.*) Bums! Pigs! Tarts! Bitches! (*He turns in a rage on the men, bumping viciously into them but not jarring them the least bit. Rather it is he who recoils after each collision. He keeps growling*) Git off de oith! G'wan, yuh bum! Look where yuh're goin', can't yuh? Git outa here! Fight, why don't yuh? Put up yer mits! Don't be a dog! Fight or I'll knock yuh dead! (*But, without seeming to see him, they all answer with mechanical affected politeness:* I beg your pardon. *Then at a cry from one of the women, they all scurry to the furrier's window.*)

THE WOMAN—(*ecstatically, with a gasp of delight*) Monkey fur! (*The whole crowd of men and women chorus after her in the same tone of affected delight:* Monkey fur!)

YANK—(*with a jerk of his head back on his shoulders, as if he had received a punch full in the face—raging*) I see yuh, all in white! I see yuh, yuh white-faced tart, yuh! Hairy ape, huh? I'll hairy ape yuh! (*He bends down and grips at the street curbing as if to pluck it out and hurl it. Foiled in this, snarling with passion, he leaps to the lamp-post on the corner and tries to pull it up for a club. Just at that moment a bus is heard rumbling up. A fat, high-hatted, spatted gentleman runs out from the side street. He calls out plaintively:* Bus! Bus! Stop there! *and runs full tilt into the bending, straining Yank, who is bowled off his balance.*)

YANK—(*seeing a fight—with a roar of joy as he springs to his feet*) At last! Bus, huh? I'll bust yuh! (*He lets drive a terrific swing, his fist landing full on the fat gentleman's face. But the gentleman stands unmoved as if nothing had happened.*)

GENTLEMAN—I beg your pardon. (*then irritably*) You have made me lose my bus. (*He claps his hands and begins to scream*) Officer! Officer! (*Many police whistles shrill out on the instant and a whole platoon of policemen rush in on Yank from all sides. He tries to fight but is clubbed to the pavement and fallen upon. The crowd at the window have not moved or noticed this disturbance. The clanging gong of the patrol wagon approaches with a clamoring din.*)

(*Curtain*)

SCENE SIX

Night of the following day. A row of cells in the prison on Blackwells Island. The cells extend back diagonally from right front to

*left rear. They do not stop, but disappear in the dark background
as if they ran on, numberless, into infinity. One electric bulb from
the low ceiling of the narrow corridor sheds its light through the
heavy steel bars of the cell at the extreme front and reveals part of
the interior. Yank can be seen within, crouched on the edge of his
cot in the attitude of Rodin's "The Thinker." His face is spotted
with black and blue bruises. A blood-stained bandage is wrapped
around his head.*

YANK—(*suddenly starting as if awakening from a dream,
reaches out and shakes the bars—aloud to himself, wonderingly*)
Steel. Dis is de Zoo, huh? (*A burst of hard, barking laughter
comes from the unseen occupants of the cells, runs back down the
tier, and abruptly ceases.*)

VOICES—(*mockingly*) The Zoo? That's a new name for this
          coop—a damn good name!

          Steel, eh? You said a mouthful. This is the old
          iron house.

          Who is that boob talkin'?

          He's the bloke they brung in out of his head.
          The bulls had beat him up fierce.

YANK—(*dully*) I musta been dreamin'. I tought I was in a
cage at de Zoo—but de apes don't talk, do dey?

VOICES—(*with mocking laughter*) You're in a cage aw right.

          A coop!

          A pen!

          A sty!

          A kennel! (*hard laughter—a pause*)

          Say, guy! Who are you? No, never mind lying.
          What are you?

          Yes, tell us your sad story. What's your game?

          What did they jug yuh for?

YANK—(*dully*) I was a fireman—stokin' on de liners. (*then
with sudden rage, rattling his cell bars*) I'm a hairy ape, get me?
And I'll bust youse all in de jaw if yuh don't lay off kiddin'
me.

VOICES—Huh! You're a hard boiled duck, ain't you!

          When you spit, it bounces! (*laughter*)

          Aw, can it. He's a regular guy. Ain't you?

          What did he say he was—a ape?

YANK—(*defiantly*) Sure ting! Ain't dat what youse all are—apes? (*A silence. Then a furious rattling of bars from down the corridor.*)

A VOICE—(*thick with rage*) I'll show yuh who's a ape, yuh bum!

VOICES—Ssshh! Nix!
             Can de noise!
             Piano!
             You'll have the guard down on us!

YANK—(*scornfully*) De guard? Yuh mean de keeper, don't yuh? (*angry exclamations from all the cells*)

VOICE—(*placatingly*) Aw, don't pay no attention to him. He's off his nut from the beatin'-up he got. Say, you guy! We're waitin' to hear what they landed you for—or ain't yuh tellin'?

YANK—Sure, I'll tell youse. Sure! Why de hell not? On'y—youse won't get me. Nobody gets me but me, see? I started to tell de Judge and all he says was: "Toity days to tink it over." Tink it over! Christ, dat's all I been doin' for weeks! (*after a pause*) I was tryin' to git even wit someone, see?—someone dat done me doit.

VOICES—(*cynically*) De old stuff, I bet. Your goil, huh?
               Give yuh the double-cross, huh?
               That's them every time!
               Did yuh beat up de odder guy?

YANK—(*disgustedly*) Aw, yuh're all wrong! Sure dere was a skoit in it—but not what youse mean, not dat old tripe. Dis was a new kind of skoit. She was dolled up all in white—in de stokehole. I tought she was a ghost. Sure. (*a pause*)

VOICES—(*whispering*) Gee, he's still nutty.
               Let him rave. It's fun listenin'.

YANK—(*unheeding—groping in his thoughts*) Her hands—dey was skinny and white like dey wasn't real but painted on somep'n. Dere was a million miles from me to her—twenty-five knots a hour. She was like some dead ting de cat brung in. Sure, dat's what. She didn't belong. She belonged in de window of a toy store, or on de top of a garbage can, see! Sure! (*He breaks out angrily*) But would yuh believe it, she had de noive to do me doit. She lamped me like she was seein' somep'n broke loose from de menagerie. Christ, yuh'd

oughter seen her eyes! (*He rattles the bars of his cell furiously.*)
But I'll get back at her yet, you watch! And if I can't find her
I'll take it out on de gang she runs wit. I'm wise to where dey
hangs out now. I'll show her who belongs! I'll show her
who's in de move and who ain't. You watch my smoke!

VOICES—(*serious and joking*) Dat's de talkin'!

Take her for all she's got!

What was this dame, anyway? Who was she, eh?

YANK—I dunno. First cabin stiff. Her old man's a millionaire, dey says—name of Douglas.

VOICES—Douglas? That's the president of the Steel Trust,
I bet.

Sure. I seen his mug in de papers.

He's filthy with dough.

VOICE—Hey, feller, take a tip from me. If you want to get
back at that dame, you better join the Wobblies. You'll get
some action then.

YANK—Wobblies? What de hell's dat?

VOICE—Ain't you ever heard of the I. W. W.?

YANK—Naw. What is it?

VOICE—A gang of blokes—a tough gang. I been readin'
about 'em today in the paper. The guard give me the *Sunday Times*. There's a long spiel about 'em. It's from a speech
made in the Senate by a guy named Senator Queen. (*He is
in the cell next to Yank's. There is a rustling of paper.*) Wait'll
I see if I got light enough and I'll read you. Listen. (*He reads*)
"There is a menace existing in this country today which
threatens the vitals of our fair Republic—as foul a menace
against the very life-blood of the American Eagle as was the
foul conspiracy of Cataline against the eagles of ancient
Rome!"

VOICE—(*disgustedly*) Aw, hell! Tell him to salt de tail of
dat eagle!

VOICE—(*reading*) "I refer to that devil's brew of rascals,
jailbirds, murderers and cutthroats who libel all honest working men by calling themselves the Industrial Workers of the
World; but in the light of their nefarious plots, I call them
the Industrious *Wreckers* of the World!"

YANK—(*with vengeful satisfaction*) Wreckers, dat's de right
dope! Dat belongs! Me for dem!

Voice—Ssshh! (*reading*) "This fiendish organization is a foul ulcer on the fair body of our Democracy—"

Voice—Democracy, hell! Give him the boid, fellers—the raspberry! (*They do.*)

Voice—*Ssshh!* (*reading*) "Like Cato I say to this Senate, the I. W. W. must be destroyed! For they represent an ever-present dagger pointed at the heart of the greatest nation the world has ever known, where all men are born free and equal, with equal opportunities to all, where the Founding Fathers have guaranteed to each one happiness, where Truth, Honor, Liberty, Justice, and the Brotherhood of Man are a religion absorbed with one's mother milk, taught at our father's knee, sealed, signed, and stamped upon in the glorious Constitution of these United States!" (*a perfect storm of hisses, catcalls, boos, and hard laughter*)

Voices—(*scornfully*) Hurrah for de Fort' of July!
        Pass de hat!
        Liberty!
        Justice!
        Honor!
        Opportunity!
        Brotherhood!

All—(*with abysmal scorn*) Aw, hell!

Voice—Give that Queen Senator guy the bark! All togedder now—one—two—tree— (*a terrific chorus of barking and yapping*)

Guard—(*from a distance*) Quiet there, youse—or I'll git the hose. (*The noise subsides.*)

Yank—(*with growling rage*) I'd like to catch dat senator guy alone for a second. I'd loin him some trute!

Voice—Ssshh! Here's where he gits down to cases on the Wobblies. (*reads*) "They plot with fire in one hand and dynamite in the other. They stop not before murder to gain their ends, nor at the outraging of defenseless womanhood. They would tear down society, put the lowest scum in the seats of the mighty, turn Almighty God's revealed plan for the world topsy-turvy, and make of our sweet and lovely civilization a shambles, a desolation where man, God's masterpiece, would soon degenerate back to the ape!"

VOICE—(*to Yank*) Hey, you guy. There's your ape stuff again.

YANK—(*with a growl of fury*) I got him. So dey blow up tings, do dey? Dey turn tings round, do dey? Hey, lend me dat paper, will yuh?

VOICE—Sure. Give it to him. On'y keep it to yourself, see. We don't wanter listen to no more of that slop.

VOICE—Here you are. Hide it under your mattress.

YANK—(*reaching out*) Tanks. I can't read much but I kin manage. (*He sits, the paper in the hand at his side, in the attitude of Rodin's "The Thinker." A pause. Several snores from down the corridor. Suddenly Yank jumps to his feet with a furious groan as if some appalling thought had crashed on him—bewilderedly*) Sure—her old man—president of de Steel Trust—makes half de steel in de world—steel—where I tought I belonged—drivin' trou—movin'—in dat—to make *her*—and cage me in for her to spit on! Christ (*He shakes the bars of his cell door till the whole tier trembles. Irritated, protesting exclamations from those awakened or trying to get to sleep.*) He made dis—dis cage! Steel! *It* don't belong, dat's what! Cages, cells, locks, bolts, bars—dat's what it means!—holdin' me down wit him at de top! But I'll drive trou! Fire, dat melts it! I'll be fire—under de heap—fire dat never goes out—hot as hell—breakin' out in de night— (*While he has been saying this last he has shaken his cell door to a clanging accompaniment. As he comes to the "breakin' out" he seizes one bar with both hands and, putting his two feet up against the others so that his position is parallel to the floor like a monkey's, he gives a great wrench backwards. The bar bends like a licorice stick under his tremendous strength. Just at this moment the prison guard rushes in, dragging a hose behind him.*)

GUARD—(*angrily*) I'll loin youse bums to wake me up! (*sees Yank*) Hello, it's you, huh? Got the D. Ts., hey? Well, I'll cure 'em. I'll drown your snakes for yuh! (*noticing the bar*) Hell, look at dat bar bended! On'y a bug is strong enough for dat!

YANK—(*glaring at him*) Or a hairy ape, yuh big yellow bum! Look out! Here I come! (*He grabs another bar.*)

GUARD—(*scared now—yelling off left*) Toin de hose on, Ben!—full pressure! And call de others—and a straitjacket!

(The curtain is falling. As it hides Yank from view, there is a splattering smash as the stream of water hits the steel of Yank's cell.)

(Curtain)

SCENE SEVEN

Nearly a month later. An I. W. W. local near the waterfront, showing the interior of a front room on the ground floor, and the street outside. Moonlight on the narrow street, buildings massed in black shadow. The interior of the room, which is general assembly room, office, and reading room, resembles some dingy settlement boys' club. A desk and high stool are in one corner. A table with papers, stacks of pamphlets, chairs about it, is at center. The whole is decidedly cheap, banal, commonplace and unmysterious as a room could well be. The secretary is perched on the stool making entries in a large ledger. An eye shade casts his face into shadows. Eight or ten men, longshoremen, iron workers, and the like, are grouped about the table. Two are playing checkers. One is writing a letter. Most of them are smoking pipes. A big signboard is on the wall at the rear, "Industrial Workers of the World—Local No. 57."

YANK—*(comes down the street outside. He is dressed as in Scene Five. He moves cautiously, mysteriously. He comes to a point opposite the door; tiptoes softly up to it, listens, is impressed by the silence within, knocks carefully, as if he were guessing at the password to some secret rite. Listens. No answer. Knocks again a bit louder. No answer. Knocks impatiently, much louder.)*

SECRETARY—*(turning around on his stool)* What the hell is that—someone knocking? *(shouts)* Come in, why don't you? *(All the men in the room look up. Yank opens the door slowly, gingerly, as if afraid of an ambush. He looks around for secret doors, mystery, is taken aback by the commonplaceness of the room and the men in it, thinks he may have gotten in the wrong place, then sees the signboard on the wall and is reassured.)*

YANK—*(blurts out)* Hello.

MEN—*(reservedly)* Hello.

YANK—(*more easily*) I tought I'd bumped into de wrong dump.

SECRETARY—(*scrutinizing him carefully*) Maybe you have. Are you a member?

YANK—Naw, not yet. Dat's what I come for—to join.

SECRETARY—That's easy. What's your job—longshore?

YANK—Naw. Fireman—stoker on de liners.

SECRETARY—(*with satisfaction*) Welcome to our city. Glad to know you people are waking up at last. We haven't got many members in your line.

YANK—Naw. Dey're all dead to de woild.

SECRETARY—Well, you can help to wake 'em. What's your name? I'll make out your card.

YANK—(*confused*) Name? Lemme tink.

SECRETARY—(*sharply*) Don't you know your own name?

YANK—Sure; but I been just Yank for so long—Bob, dat's it—Bob Smith.

SECRETARY—(*writing*) Robert Smith. (*fills out the rest of card*) Here you are. Cost you half a dollar.

YANK—Is dat all—four bits? Dat's easy. (*gives the Secretary the money*)

SECRETARY—(*throwing it in drawer*) Thanks. Well, make yourself at home. No introductions needed. There's literature on the table. Take some of those pamphlets with you to distribute aboard ship. They may bring results. Sow the seed, only go about it right. Don't get caught and fired. We got plenty out of work. What we need is men who can hold their jobs—and work for us at the same time.

YANK—Sure. (*But he still stands, embarrassed and uneasy.*)

SECRETARY—(*looking at him—curiously*) What did you knock for? Think we had a coon in uniform to open doors?

YANK—Naw. I tought it was locked—and dat yuh'd wanter give me the once-over trou a peep-hole or somep'n to see if I was right.

SECRETARY—(*alert and suspicious but with an easy laugh*) Think we were running a crap game? That door is never locked. What put that in your nut?

YANK—(*with a knowing grin, convinced that this is all camouflage, a part of the secrecy*) Dis burg is full of bulls, ain't it?

SECRETARY—(*sharply*) What have the cops got to do with us? We're breaking no laws.

YANK—(*with a knowing wink*) Sure. Youse wouldn't for woilds. Sure. I'm wise to dat.

SECRETARY—You seem to be wise to a lot of stuff none of us knows about.

YANK—(*with another wink*) Aw, dat's aw right, see. (*then made a bit resentful by the suspicious glances from all sides*) Aw, can it! Youse needn't put me trou de toid degree. Can't youse see I belong? Sure! I'm reg'lar. I'll stick, get me? I'll shoot de woiks for youse. Dat's why I wanted to join in.

SECRETARY—(*breezily, feeling him out*) That's the right spirit. Only are you sure you understand what you've joined? It's all plain and above board; still, some guys get a wrong slant on us. (*sharply*) What's your notion of the purpose of the I. W. W.?

YANK—Aw, I know all about it.

SECRETARY—(*sarcastically*) Well, give us some of your valuable information.

YANK—(*cunningly*) I know enough not to speak outa my toin. (*then resentfully again*) Aw, say! I'm reg'lar. I'm wise to de game. I know yuh got to watch your step wit a stranger. For all youse know, I might be a plain-clothes dick, or somep'n, dat's what yuh're tinkin', huh? Aw, forget it! I belong, see? Ask any guy down to de docks if I don't.

SECRETARY—Who said you didn't?

YANK—After I'm 'nitiated, I'll show yuh.

SECRETARY—(*astounded*) Initiated? There's no initiation.

YANK—(*disappointed*) Ain't there no password—no grip nor nothin'?

SECRETARY—What'd you think this is—the Elks—or the Black Hand?

YANK—De Elks, hell! De Black Hand, dey're a lot of yellow backstickin' Ginees. Naw. Dis is a man's gang, ain't it?

SECRETARY—You said it! That's why we stand on our two feet in the open. We got no secrets.

YANK—(*surprised but admiringly*) Yuh mean to say yuh always run wide open—like dis?

SECRETARY—Exactly.

YANK—Den yuh sure got your noive wit youse!

SECRETARY—(*sharply*) Just what was it made you want to join us? Come out with that straight.

YANK—Yuh call me? Well, I got noive, too! Here's my hand. Yuh wanter blow tings up, don't yuh? Well, dat's me! I belong!

SECRETARY—(*with pretended carelessness*) You mean change the unequal conditions of society by legitimate direct action —or with dynamite?

YANK—Dynamite! Blow it offen de oith—steel—all de cages—all de factories, steamers, buildings, jails—de Steel Trust and all dat makes it go.

SECRETARY—So—that's your idea, eh? And did you have any special job in that line you wanted to propose to us? (*He makes a sign to the men, who get up cautiously one by one and group behind Yank.*)

YANK—(*boldly*) Sure, I'll come out wit it. I'll show youse I'm one of de gang. Dere's dat millionaire guy, Douglas—

SECRETARY—President of the Steel Trust, you mean? Do you want to assassinate him?

YANK—Naw, dat don't get yuh nothin'. I mean blow up de factory, de woiks, where he makes de steel. Dat's what I'm after—to blow up de steel, knock all de steel in de woild up to de moon. Dat'll fix tings! (*eagerly, with a touch of bravado*) I'll do it by me lonesome! I'll show yuh! Tell me where his woiks is, how to git there, all de dope. Gimme de stuff, de old butter—and watch me do de rest! Watch de smoke and see it move! I don't give a damn if dey nab me—long as it's done! I'll soive life for it—and give 'em de laugh! (*half to himself*) And I'll write her a letter and tell her de hairy ape done it. Dat'll square tings.

SECRETARY—(*stepping away from Yank*) Very interesting. (*He gives a signal. The men, huskies all, throw themselves on Yank and before he knows it they have his legs and arms pinioned. But he is too flabbergasted to make a struggle, anyway. They feel him over for weapons.*)

MAN—No gat, no knife. Shall we give him what's what and put the boots to him?

SECRETARY—No. He isn't worth the trouble we'd get into. He's too stupid. (*He comes closer and laughs mockingly in Yank's face.*) Ho-ho! By God, this is the biggest joke they've

put up on us yet. Hey, you Joke! Who sent you—Burns or
Pinkerton? No, by God, you're such a bonehead I'll bet
you're in the Secret Service! Well, you dirty spy, you rotten
agent provocator, you can go back and tell whatever skunk is
paying you blood-money for betraying your brothers that he's
wasting his coin. You couldn't catch a cold. And tell him that
all he'll ever get on us, or ever has got, is just his own sneaking plots that he's framed up to put us in jail. We are what
our manifesto says we are, neither more nor less—and
we'll give him a copy of that any time he calls. And as for
you— (*He glares scornfully at Yank, who is sunk in an oblivious
stupor.*) Oh, hell, what's the use of talking? You're a brainless
ape.

YANK—(*aroused by the word to fierce but futile struggles*)
What's dat, yuh Sheeny bum, yuh!

SECRETARY—Throw him out, boys. (*In spite of his struggles, this is done with gusto and éclat. Propelled by several parting
kicks, Yank lands sprawling in the middle of the narrow cobbled
street. With a growl he starts to get up and storm the closed door,
but stops bewildered by the confusion in his brain, pathetically
impotent. He sits there, brooding, in as near to the attitude of
Rodin's "Thinker" as he can get in his position.*)

YANK—(*bitterly*) So dem boids don't tink I belong, neider. Aw, to hell wit 'em! Dey're in de wrong pew—de same
old bull—soapboxes and Salvation Army—no guts! Cut out
an hour offen de job a day and make me happy! Gimme a
dollar more a day and make me happy! Tree square a day,
and cauliflowers in de front yard—ekal rights—a woman
and kids—a lousy vote—and I'm all fixed for Jesus, huh?
Aw, hell! What does dat get yuh? Dis ting's in your inside,
but it ain't your belly. Feedin' your face—sinkers and coffee—dat don't touch it. It's way down—at de bottom. Yuh
can't grab it, and yuh can't stop it. It moves, and everything
moves. It stops and de whole woild stops. Dat's me now—I
don't tick, see?—I'm a busted Ingersoll, dat's what. Steel
was me, and I owned de woild. Now I ain't steel, and de
woild owns me. Aw, hell! I can't see—it's all dark, get me?
It's all wrong! (*He turns a bitter mocking face up like an ape
gibbering at the moon.*) Say, youse up dere, Man in de Moon,
yuh look so wise, gimme de answer, huh? Slip me de inside

dope, de information right from de stable—where do I get off at, huh?

A POLICEMAN—(*who has come up the street in time to hear this last—with grim humor*) You'll get off at the station, you boob, if you don't get up out of that and keep movin'.

YANK—(*looking up at him—with a hard, bitter laugh*) Sure! Lock me up! Put me in a cage! Dat's de on'y answer yuh know. G'wan, lock me up!

POLICEMAN—What you been doin'?

YANK—Enuf to gimme life for! I was born, see? Sure, dat's de charge. Write it in de blotter. I was born, get me!

POLICEMAN—(*jocosely*) God pity your old woman! (*then matter-of-fact*) But I've no time for kidding. You're soused. I'd run you in but it's too long a walk to the station. Come on now, get up, or I'll fan your ears with this club. Beat it now! (*He hauls Yank to his feet.*)

YANK—(*in a vague mocking tone*) Say, where do I go from here?

POLICEMAN—(*giving him a push—with a grin, indifferently*) Go to hell.

(*Curtain*)

SCENE EIGHT

Twilight of the next day. The monkey house at the Zoo. One spot of clear gray light falls on the front of one cage so that the interior can be seen. The other cages are vague, shrouded in shadow from which chatterings pitched in a conversational tone can be heard. On the one cage a sign from which the word "gorilla" stands out. The gigantic animal himself is seen squatting on his haunches on a bench in much the same attitude as Rodin's "Thinker." Yank enters from the left. Immediately a chorus of angry chattering and screeching breaks out. The gorilla turns his eyes but makes no sound or move.

YANK—(*with a hard, bitter laugh*) Welcome to your city, huh? Hail, hail, de gang's all here! (*At the sound of his voice the chattering dies away into an attentive silence. Yank walks up* to the gorilla's cage and, leaning over the railing, stares in at its occupant, who stares back at him, silent and motionless. There is a pause of dead stillness. Then Yank begins to talk in a friendly confidential tone, half-mockingly, but with a deep undercurrent of sympathy.) Say, yuh're some hard-lookin' guy, ain't yuh? I seen lots of tough nuts dat de gang called gorillas, but yuh're de foist real one I ever seen. Some chest yuh got, and shoulders, and dem arms and mits! I bet yuh got a punch in eider fist dat'd knock 'em all silly! (This with genuine admiration. The gorilla, as if he understood, stands upright, swelling out his chest and pounding on it with his fist. Yank grins sympathetically.) Sure, I get yuh. Yuh challenge de whole woild, huh? Yuh got what I was sayin' even if yuh muffed de woids. (then bitterness creeping in) And why wouldn't yuh get me? Ain't we both members of de same club—de Hairy Apes? (They stare at each other—a pause—then Yank goes on slowly and bitterly.) So yuh're what she seen when she looked at me, de white-faced tart! I was you to her, get me? On'y outa de cage— broke out—free to moider her, see? Sure! Dat's what she tought. She wasn't wise dat I was in a cage, too—worser'n yours—sure—a damn sight—'cause you got some chanct to bust loose—but me— (He grows confused.) Aw, hell! It's all wrong, ain't it? (a pause) I s'pose yuh wanter know what I'm doin' here, huh? I been warmin' a bench down to de Battery—ever since last night. Sure. I seen de sun come up. Dat was pretty, too—all red and pink and green. I was lookin' at de skyscrapers—steel—and all de ships comin' in, sailin' out, all over de oith—and dey was steel, too. De sun was warm, dey wasn't no clouds, and dere was a breeze blowin'. Sure, it was great stuff. I got it aw right—what Paddy said about dat bein' de right dope—on'y I couldn't get in it, see? I couldn't belong in dat. It was over my head. And I kept tinkin'—and den I beat it up here to see what youse was like. And I waited till dey was all gone to git yuh alone. Say, how d'yuh feel sittin' in dat pen all de time, havin' to stand for 'em comin' and starin' at yuh—de white-faced, skinny tarts and de boobs what marry 'em—makin' fun of yuh, laughin' at yuh, gittin' scared of yuh—damn 'em! (He pounds on the rail with his fist. The gorilla rattles the bars of his cage and snarls. All the other monkeys set up an angry chattering

in the darkness. Yank goes on excitedly.) Sure! Dat's de way it
hits me, too. On'y yuh're lucky, see? Yuh don't belong wit
'em and yuh know it. But me, I belong wit 'em—but I don't,
see? Dey don't belong wit me, dat's what. Get me? Tinkin' is
hard— (*He passes one hand across his forehead with a painful
gesture. The gorilla growls impatiently. Yank goes on gropingly.*)
It's dis way, what I'm drivin' at. Youse can sit and dope
dream in de past, green woods, de jungle and de rest of it.
Den yuh belong and dey don't. Den yuh kin laugh at 'em,
see? Yuh're de champ of de woild. But me—I ain't got no
past to tink in, nor nothin' dat's comin', on'y what's now—
and dat don't belong. Sure, you're de best off! Yuh can't tink,
can yuh? Yuh can't talk neider. But I kin make a bluff at
talkin' and tinkin'—a'most git away wit it—a'most!—and
dat's where de joker comes in. (*He laughs.*) I ain't on oith and
I ain't in heaven, get me? I'm in de middle tryin' to separate
'em, takin' all de woist punches from bot' of 'em. Maybe dat's
what dey call hell, huh? But you, yuh're at de bottom. You
belong! Sure! Yuh're de on'y one in de woild dat does, yuh
lucky stiff! (*The gorilla growls proudly.*) And dat's why dey
gotter put yuh in a cage, see? (*The gorilla roars angrily.*) Sure!
Yuh get me. It beats it when you try to tink it or talk it—it's
way down—deep—behind—you 'n' me we feel it. Sure!
Bot' members of dis club! (*He laughs—then in a savage tone*)
What de hell! T' hell wit it! A little action, dat's our meat!
Dat belongs! Knock 'em down and keep bustin' 'em till dey
croaks yuh wit a gat—wit steel! Sure! Are yuh game? Dey've
looked at youse, ain't dey—in a cage? Wanter git even? Wanter wind up like a sport 'stead of croakin' slow in dere? (*The
gorilla roars an emphatic affirmative. Yank goes on with a sort of
furious exaltation.*) Sure! Yuh're reg'lar! Yuh'll stick to de finish! Me 'n' you, huh?—bot' members of this club! We'll put
up one last star bout dat'll knock 'em offen deir seats! Dey'll
have to make de cages stronger after we're trou! (*The gorilla
is straining at his bars, growling, hopping from one foot to the
other. Yank takes a jimmy from under his coat and forces the lock
on the cage door. He throws this open.*) Pardon from de governor! Step out and shake hands! I'll take yuh for a walk down
Fif' Avenoo. We'll knock 'em offen de oith and croak wit de
band playin'. Come on, Brother. (*The gorilla scrambles gingerly*

out of his cage. Goes to Yank and stands looking at him. Yank keeps his mocking tone—holds out his hand.) Shake—de secret grip of our order. (*Something, the tone of mockery, perhaps, suddenly enrages the animal. With a spring he wraps his huge arms around Yank in a murderous hug. There is a crackling snap of crushed ribs—a gasping cry, still mocking, from Yank.*) Hey, I didn't say kiss me! (*The gorilla lets the crushed body slip to the floor; stands over it uncertainly, considering; then picks it up, throws it in the cage, shuts the door, and shuffles off menacingly into the darkness at left. A great uproar of frightened chattering and whimpering comes from the other cages. Then Yank moves, groaning, opening his eyes, and there is silence. He mutters painfully*) Say—dey oughter match him—wit Zybszko. He got me, aw right. I'm trou. Even him didn't tink I belonged. (*then, with sudden passionate despair*) Christ, where do I get off at? Where do I fit in? (*checking himself as suddenly*) Aw, what de hell! No squawkin', see! No quittin', get me! Croak wit your boots on! (*He grabs hold of the bars of the cage and hauls himself painfully to his feet—looks around him bewilderedly— forces a mocking laugh.*) In de cage, huh? (*in the strident tones of a circus barker*) Ladies and gents, step forward and take a slant at de one and only—(*his voice weakening*)—one and original—Hairy Ape from de wilds of— (*He slips in a heap on the floor and dies. The monkeys set up a chattering, whimpering wail. And, perhaps, the Hairy Ape at last belongs.*)

(*Curtain*)

THE FOUNTAIN

A Play in Eleven Scenes

CHARACTERS

IBNU ASWAD, *a Moorish chieftain*

JUAN PONCE DE LEON

PEDRO, *his servant*

MARIA DE CORDOVA

LUIS DE ALVAREDO

YUSEF, *a Moorish minstrel*

DIEGO MENENDEZ, *a Franciscan*

VICENTE DE CORDOVA, *Maria's husband*

ALONZO DE OVIEDO

MANUEL DE CASTILLO } *nobles*

CRISTOVAL DE MENDOZA

CHRISTOPHER COLUMBUS

A SOLDIER

FRIAR QUESADA, *a Franciscan*

BEATRIZ DE CORDOVA, *daughter of Maria and Vicente*

NANO, *an Indian chief*

A CHIEF OF THE INDIANS IN FLORIDA

A MEDICINE MAN

A FIGURE

A POET OF CATHAY

AN OLD INDIAN WOMAN OF THE BAHAMAS

A DOMINICAN MONK

FATHER SUPERIOR OF THE DOMINICANS IN CUBA

JUAN, *nephew of Juan Ponce de Leon*

Nobles, Monks, Soldiers, Sailors, Captive Indians of Porto Rico, Indians in Florida

Time: Late Fifteenth and early Sixteenth Centuries.

SCENES

The Fountain

SCENE ONE

SCENE—*Courtyard of Ibnu Aswad's palace in Granada.*
The section forms a right triangle, its apex at the rear, right.
In the left, center, a massive porte-cochère opens on the street. On
the right, a door leading into the house itself. In the center of the
courtyard, a large splendid fountain of green marble with human
and animal figures in gilt bronze. The peristyle of the gallery run-
ning around the court is supported by slender columns of polished
marble, partly gilded. The interspaces above the horseshoe arches
springing from the columns are filled with arabesques, texts from
the Koran, red, blue and gold in color. Above are the latticed
windows of the women's apartments. Over the house-top a sky with
stars can be seen. It is early night.

As the curtain rises, the court is empty and there is silence except
for the splash of the fountain. Then a loud, imperious knocking, as
of someone pounding with the hilt of a sword, is heard from the
porte-cochère. Ibnu Aswad enters from the right. He is an el-
derly, noble-looking Moor, the lower part of his face covered by a
long, white beard. His expression is one of great pride borne down
by sorrow and humiliation. He goes out through the porte-cochère,
and returns ushering in Juan Ponce de Leon and his servant,
Pedro. Juan is a tall, handsome Spanish noble of thirty-one,
dressed in full uniform. His countenance is haughty, full of a ro-
mantic adventurousness and courage; yet he gives the impression
of disciplined ability, of a confident self-mastery—a romantic
dreamer governed by the ambitious thinker in him. Pedro is a
dull-looking young fellow.

JUAN—(*as they enter—to Aswad*) Your pardon, Sir Moor.

ASWAD—(*haughtily*) You are quartered here? (*Juan bows*
in affirmation.) Welcome then, since it is the will of Allah that
you should conquer.

JUAN—(*graciously*) I am no conquerer here. I am a
stranger grateful for hospitality.

ASWAD—(*unbending a bit*) You are kind. I have seen you
in action on the field. You are brave. Defeat loses its bitterness
when the foe is noble. (*moodily and bitterly—staring at the*

fountain) The waters of the fountain fall—but ever they rise again, Sir Spaniard. Such is the decree of destiny. (*with fervor*) Blessed be Allah who exalteth and debaseth the kings of the earth, according to his divine will, in whose fulfillment consists eternal justice. (*fiercely and defiantly*) Whosoever the victor, there is no conqueror but Allah!

JUAN—(*stiffening—coldly*) Your fortitude does you honor. (*by way of dismissing the subject—abruptly*) I am expecting friends. Will that disturb your household? If so—

ASWAD—(*coldly*) My house is your house. It is decreed. (*He bows with stately grace and goes out, right.*)

JUAN—(*makes a movement as if to detain him—then shrugs his shoulders*) What can I do for him? (*ironically repeating Ibnu's inflection*) It is decreed by Spain if not by Allah. (*seeing Pedro lolling against the wall, drowsily staring at the fountain—amused*) Lazy lout! Does the fountain cause you, too, to dream? (*in a tone of command*) Bring the wine. They will be here soon.

PEDRO—Yes, sir. (*He goes. Juan paces back and forth, humming to himself. Pedro returns and approaches his master cautiously—in a mysterious whisper*) A lady, sir.

JUAN—(*frowning*) Is she alone? (*Pedro nods, Juan smiles cynically.*) Surely you have mistaken her calling. Tell her I am not here. (*As Pedro turns to go, Maria de Cordova appears in the arch of the porte-cochère. A heavy black veil is thrown over her face.*)

MARIA—(*her voice forced and trembling*) Juan!

JUAN—(*immediately the gallant cavalier, makes a motion for Pedro to leave, and bows low—mockery in his voice*) Beautiful lady, you do me an unmerited honor.

MARIA—(*wearily*) Spare me your mockery, Juan. (*She throws back her veil. She is a striking-looking woman of thirty-eight or forty, but discontent and sorrow have marked her age clearly on her face.*)

JUAN—(*astonished*) Maria! (*then with genuine alarm*) In God's name!

MARIA—(*her voice breaking*) Juan, I had to come.

JUAN—(*sternly*) Your husband is my brother in arms. To-night—here—he is to be among my guests. I feel that every word we speak now degrades me in my honor.

MARIA—(*in a tone of great grief*) You are cruel! I had to speak with you alone. This is my one chance. I leave the Court tomorrow.

JUAN—(*with evident relief*) Ah.

MARIA—(*stares at him with a pitiful appeal. He avoids her eyes.*) Oh, what a fool I am—(*with a half-sob, as if the confession were wrung from her*)—to love you, Juan! (*She makes a movement toward him, but he steps back, aloof and cold.*)

JUAN—(*frowning*) That word—we have never uttered it before. You have always been—my friend. (*after a pause, with deep earnestness*) Why must you ruin our rare friendship for a word that every minstrel mouths? (*then with irritation*) Love, love, love we chatter everlastingly. We pretend love alone is why we live! Bah! Life is nobler than the weak lies of poets— or it's nothing!

MARIA—(*wounded and indignant*) If you had had to fight for love as you have fought for glory!—

JUAN—(*struck by the pain in her tone, kneels and kisses her hand—remorsefully*) Forgive me! I would die rather than bring sorrow to a heart as kind as yours. Keep me forever in that heart, I beg—but as a friend—as it has always been.

MARIA—(*with a gasp of pain*) Ah! (*taking her hand from his—with a deep sigh*) God give you knowledge of the heart!

JUAN—(*rises—plainly endeavoring to change the subject*) You are leaving the Court?

MARIA—The Queen has granted my wish to retire to Cordova. (*passionately*) I'm sick of the Court! I long for simple things! I pray to become worthy again of that pure love of God I knew as a girl. I must seek peace in Him! (*after a pause*) Granada is ours. The Moors are driven from Spain. The wars are over. What will you do now, Juan?

JUAN—Peace means stagnation—a slack ease of cavaliers and songs and faded roses. I must go on.

MARIA—Where will you go?

JUAN—(*smiles half-whimsically at an idea*) Perhaps with the Genoese, Christopher Columbus, when he sails to find the western passage to Cathay.

MARIA—(*disturbed*) But they say he is mad.

JUAN—(*seriously now*) Mad or not, he dreams of glory. I

have heard he plans to conquer for Spain that immense realm of the Great Khan which Marco Polo saw.

MARIA—What! Abandon your career at Court now when your exploits have brought you in such favor? No one would ruin himself so senselessly save in despair! (*jealously*) It must be from love you are fleeing! (*fiercely mocking*) Is a woman avenging women? Tell me her name!

JUAN—(*with a mocking laugh*) Love, love, and always love! Can no other motive exist for you? God pity women!

MARIA—(*after a pause—sadly*) God pity me—because pity is what you offer me. (*as Juan seems about to protest wearily*) Don't deny it, Juan. It sneers at me in your pretended scorn of love— You wish to comfort my humiliation! Am I a fool? Have you not loved others? I could name ten—

JUAN—Maria!

MARIA—Do you imagine I haven't guessed the truth? Those others had youth—while I— And my love seems to you—pitiable!

JUAN—(*kneeling and taking her hand—with passionate earnestness*) No, dear friend, no! I swear to you! (*after a pause*) What you call loves—they were merely moods—dreams of a night or two—lustful adventures—gestures of vanity, perhaps—but I have never loved. Spain is the mistress to whom I give my heart, Spain and my own ambitions, which are Spain's. Now do you understand?

MARIA—(*sadly*) No, Juan. (*He rises.*) I understand that I am growing old—that love has passed for me—and that I suffer in my loneliness. Perhaps if God had granted me a child— But His justice punishes. He has seen my secret sin. I have loved you, Juan, for years. But it was only in the last year when my heart, feeling youth die, grew desperate that I dared let you see. And now, farewell, until God's will be done in death. We must not meet again.

JUAN—(*sternly*) No. (*passionately*) I wish to God you had not told me this!

MARIA—(*gently*) If you are still my friend you will not wish it. It was my final penance—that you should know. And, having told you, I am free, for my heart is dead. There is only my soul left that knows the love of God which blesses and does not torture. Farewell once more, Juan. (*He kneels and kisses her hand. She puts the other on his head as if blessing him.*) You are noble, the soul of courage, a man of men. You will go far, soldier of iron—and dreamer. God pity you if those two selves should ever clash! You shall have all my prayers for your success—but I shall add, Dear Savior, let him know tenderness to recompense him when his hard youth dies! (*She turns quickly and goes out.*)

JUAN—(*looks after her in melancholy thought for a while— then sighs deeply and shrugs his shoulders*) Time tarnishes even the pure, difficult things with common weakness. (*Luis de Alvaredo enters through the porte-cochère. He is a dissipated-looking noble, a few years older than Juan. His face is homely but extremely fetching in its nobility, its expression of mocking fun and raillery. He is dressed carelessly, is slightly drunk.*)

LUIS—(*mockingly*) Lover of glory, beloved of women, hail! (*He comes to the startled Juan as voices are heard from the porte-cochère—in a hurried, cautioning whisper*) The devil, Juan! Have you lost your wits—or has she? I recognized her—and Vicente was only ten paces behind. (*then again mockingly*) Discretion, my stainless knight, discretion!

JUAN—(*sternly*) Stop! You wrong her and me. (*Sounds of a loud, angry dispute are heard from without.*) What is that brawling?

LUIS—My Moor. (*explaining hurriedly to Juan*) A fellow poet—a minstrel of their common folk. We found him running amuck about the streets declaiming to the stars that their king, Abdallah, had sold his soul to hell when he surrendered. (*with admiration*) By God, Juan, how he cursed! Oh, he's a precious songster, and as poet to poet I collared him and dragged him with us. Our friend, Diego, would have cut his throat for the Church's glory had I not interfered.

JUAN—(*smiling*) As madman for madman, eh? But why bring him here to howl?

LUIS—He has a lute. It is my whim he should sing some verses. (*with an amused grin*) The dog speaks only Arabic. If he is wily, he will chant such curses on our heads as will blight that fountain dry—and no one of us but me will understand. (*with great glee*) It will be sport, Juan! (*The clamor from outside grows more violent.*) By God, Diego will murder my minstrel—after all my pains. (*starts to hurry out—stops in the entrance*) Remember, Juan. Vicente may have recognized—the lady.

JUAN—(*nods, frowning*) The devil take all women! (*Luis goes out. Pedro enters, carrying two large baskets full of bottles and sets them down, rear.*) Drink and forget sad nonsense. Bring out cushions. We will sit beside the fountain. (*Pedro goes into the house, right. Luis reënters, holding Yusef by the arm—a wizened old Moor dressed in the clothes of the common people, but wearing the turban signifying that he has made the pilgrimage to Mecca. His deep-set eyes smolder with hatred but physically he is so exhausted as to seem resigned to his fate. They are followed by Diego Menendez, a Franciscan monk, about the same age as Juan and Luis. He has a pale, long face, the thin, cruel mouth, the cold, self-obsessed eyes of the fanatic. Just now he is full of helpless fury and indignation. Accompanying him is Vicente de Cordova, a gray-haired, stern, soldierly noble of forty-five. Following them are the three nobles, Oviedo, Castillo and Mendoza. They are the type of adventurous cavaliers of the day—cruel, courageous to recklessness, practically uneducated—knights of the true Cross, ignorant of and despising every first principle of real Christianity—yet carrying the whole off with a picturesque air.*)

MENENDEZ—(*angrily*) I protest to you, Juan. It is heresy to suffer this dog's presence when we offer thanks to God for victory.

JUAN—(*stares at the Moor interestedly for a moment—then carelessly*) I see no desecration, Diego—if he will sing, not howl. (*turning to Vicente, scrutinizing his face keenly—carelessly*) What do you say, Vicente?

VICENTE—(*gives him a dark look of suspicion—coldly and meaningly*) I say nothing—now.

JUAN—Ah! (*He and Luis exchange a look.*)

OVIEDO—Well, I say let him remain. We may have sport with him.

CASTILLO—(*with a cruel smile*) Perhaps with a sword-point we can persuade him to sing where the townsfolk hid their gold.

MENDOZA—Your words are inspired, Manuel!

LUIS—(*scornfully*) Materialists! You would sack heaven and melt the moon for silver. Juan, where is your wine? (*Pedro appears, bringing cushions and goblets for each. He uncorks the bottles and pours their goblets full. Scorning a goblet Luis snatches a bottle from him and drinks from that.*)

JUAN—(*keeping a wary eye on Vicente*) Let us drink. (*takes a goblet from Pedro*) To our most Gracious Sovereigns and to Spain! (*He drinks.*)

MENENDEZ—And to the Church! (*angrily*) But I will not drink until that infidel is moved apart!

VICENTE—I agree.

JUAN—(*impatiently*) Let the Moor go, Luis—since Diego takes himself so seriously.

VICENTE—(*coldly resentful*) And I? (*Juan is about to reply irritably when Luis breaks in hurriedly.*)

LUIS—Shhh! I'll sing a song for you. (*releasing the Moor and pointing to the rear*) Go, brother bard, and take your ease. (*The Moor goes to the right, rear, and squats down in the shadow by the wall. Luis sings*)

> Love is a flower
> Forever blooming.
> Life is a fountain
> Forever leaping
> Upward to catch the golden sunlight,
> Striving to reach the azure heaven;
> Failing, falling,
> Ever returning
> To kiss the earth that the flower may live.

(*They all applaud as he finishes.*)

JUAN—Charming, Sir Poet—but a lie. (*mockingly*) Love, and love, and always love! The devil seize your flower! Do fountains flow only to nourish flowers that bloom a day and die?

LUIS—Roar, lion! You will not wake my dream that life is love!

JUAN—Listen to him, Diego! We know his only love is his old mother; and yet, to judge from his songs, you would think him a greater philanderer than—than—

VICENTE—(*interrupting sneeringly*) Than you, Don Juan?

JUAN—(*turning on him—coldly*) Gossip gives many a false name—but gossip only deludes old women.

VICENTE—(*growing pale*) Do you intend that insult? (*Their hands go to the hilt of their swords. The three nobles quicken to excited interest. Luis leaps between them.*)

LUIS—For God's sake! Is either of you a Moor? (*raises his bottle*) Let us drink again to Spain!

OVIEDO—And to the next war!

CASTILLO—May it be soon!

MENDOZA—With a world to sack! Sing us a song of that, Luis!

LUIS—I am too thirsty. But come, I was forgetting our infidel. Let me use persuasion— (*He goes back to the Moor, and can be heard talking to him in Arabic.*)

JUAN—We were speaking of wars to come. With whom?

OVIEDO—With anyone!

JUAN—But guess. I think it will be in lands beyond strange seas—Cipango and Cathay—the cities of gold that Marco Polo saw.

OVIEDO—But who will lead us there?

JUAN—Why, Christopher Columbus. (*They all laugh.*)

CASTILLO—That Genoese mongrel!—to lead Spaniards!

MENDOZA—He's mad. He claims the earth is round—like an egg! (*They all laugh.*)

JUAN—(*impressively*) I saw him today. He was riding his flea-bitten mule as if he were a Cæsar in a triumph. His eyes were full of golden cities.

CASTILLO—Bah, Juan, you romance! The man's an idiot!

LUIS—(*coming back*) The more fool you to think so! He will yet find for Spain the Western Passage to the East.

CASTILLO—Or fall off the world's edge! I will wager you would not go with him for all the gold in Indies!

LUIS—You would lose!

JUAN—I'm planning to go. (*All are astonished.*) But not on his first voyage. Before I pledge my sword I must have proof that it can serve Spain's glory. There is no profit in staking life for dreams.

LUIS—There is no profit in anything but that! You're from the East, Moor. Tell us of the Great Khan, of Cipango and Cathay and Cambuluc, of golden roofs and emerald-studded lintels to the doors. Your people must have heard these wonders.

MENDOZA—Yes, let him sing of treasure. (*But the Moor remains silent.*)

LUIS—Wait, I'll talk to him. (*He goes back and speaks to the Moor in Arabic. The latter replies.*)

MENENDEZ—(*furiously*) This is all treasonable. The dog had broken the peace. The punishment is death.

JUAN—(*mockingly*) Let him sing of treasure, Diego. Even the Church loves gold.

LUIS—(*coming back—exultantly*) He consents, Juan—because I am a colleague. He will sing of treasure in the East—a tale told to his father by some wandering poet who came from Cathay with a caravan. (*All except the outraged Diego and the sullen, preoccupied Vicente quicken to interested attention. The Moor strikes a few notes on his lute.*) Hush! (*The Moor begins a crooning chant of verses, accompanying himself on the lute. At first they are all held by its strange rhythm, then they begin to betray impatience.*)

OVIEDO—By God, our wolf turns into a sick shepherd.

LUIS—Hush!

CASTILLO—(*impatiently*) What does he sing?

LUIS—(*enrapt—vaguely*) Hush, hush.

MENENDEZ—(*rising to his feet as the Moor's recitative abruptly ends—harshly*) This is the service in a devil's mass!

LUIS—(*passes his hand across his eyes, then stares into the fountain dreamily*) He sang of treasure—but strange to your longing. There is in some far country of the East—Cathay, Cipango, who knows—a spot that Nature has set apart from men and blessed with peace. It is a sacred grove where all things live in the old harmony they knew before man came. Beauty resides there and is articulate. Each sound is music, and every sight a vision. The trees bear golden fruit. And in the center of the grove, there is a fountain—beautiful beyond human dreams, in whose rainbows all of life is mirrored. In that fountain's waters, young maidens play and sing and tend it everlastingly for very joy in being one with it. This is the Fountain of Youth, he said. The wise men of that far-off land have known it many ages. They make it their last pilgrimage when sick with years and weary of their lives. Here they drink, and the years drop from them like a worn-out robe.

Body and mind know youth again, and these young men, who had been old, leap up and join the handmaids' dance. Then they go back to life, but with hearts purified, and the old discords trouble them no more, but they are holy and the folk revere them. (*with a sigh*) That's his tale, my friends— but he added it is hard to find that fountain. Only to the chosen does it reveal itself.

MENENDEZ—(*furiously*) Idolatry!

OVIEDO—Is this his treasure? By God, he mocks us!

LUIS—Fools! Beauty is lost on you. Your souls clink like coppers. (*Menendez slinks back step by step toward the Moor. Luis grabs a bottle.*) Come, let us drink! We'll all to Cathay with Don Christopher. You can burrow for dung there—but I will search for this fountain.

JUAN—(*drinking—a bit tipsily*) Drink and forget sad nonsense! The devil! His song beguiled me until you tricked it into that old woman's mumble. Youth! Is youth a treasure? Then are we all—except Vicente—priceless rich; and yet, God's blood, one has but to look to see how poor we are!

LUIS—Poor in spirit! I understand you, Juan.

JUAN—Fountain of youth, God help us, with love to boot! I wish he'd sung instead of the armies and power of the Great Khan! (*then half-aside to Luis*) The tale is always told to the wrong person. There was one here not long ago who would have given pearls for drops from that same fountain!

VICENTE—(*who has crept vengefully toward Juan in time to hear these last words—with cold fury*) A moment ago you taunted me with age—and now you dare— (*He slaps Juan across the face. They draw their swords.*)

LUIS—(*trying to intervene*) For God's sake, friends!

OVIEDO—(*with excited interest*) A duel! (*The others echo this. Suddenly there is a harsh shriek from the rear. Menendez appears from the shadow, dagger in hand, a look of fanatical triumph on his face. Forgetting the duel, the others stand appalled.*)

MENENDEZ—(*sheathing the dagger*) I have slain the dog. It was high time.

LUIS—Miserable bigot! (*Raging, he tries to throw himself at the monk, but Juan grasps him and forces him down on a cushion. He breaks down, weeping.*)

MENENDEZ—(*coldly scornful*) What! A soldier of Christ weep for an infidel!

JUAN—(*sternly*) Be still, Diego! (*then frowning—curtly, in a tone of dismissal which silences all protest*) Our reveling is under an ill star. There is blood upon it. Good-night. (*turning to Vicente*) Until tomorrow.

(*Vicente bows and goes, accompanied by Menendez. The young nobles troop out behind, disputing noisily about the coming duel.*)

JUAN—(*comes over and puts his hand on Luis' shoulder—in a mocking, but comforting tone*) Come, Luis. Your brother romancer is dead. Tears will not help him. Perhaps even now he drinks of that Fountain of Youth in Dreamland—if he is not in hell.

LUIS—(*raising his head*) Juan, why do you always sneer at beauty—while your heart calls you liar?

JUAN—(*frowning*) I have Spain in my heart—and my ambition. All else is weakness. (*changing his tone—carelessly*) Well, you were right. Vicente recognized—and so, a duel. I'll prick him in the thigh and send him home to bed. She will nurse and love him then—and hate me for a murderer. Thus, all works out for the best in this fair world! But—a rare thing dies—and I'm sad, Luis. (*shaking himself and taking a goblet of wine*) Come, forget sad nonsense. We will drink to voyaging with Don Christopher—and to the battles before those golden cities of Cathay!

LUIS—(*recovering his spirits—grabbing a bottle*) Lucifer fire your cities! I drink to my fountain!

JUAN—Your health, Sir Lying Poet!

LUIS—And yours, Sir Glory-Glutton! (*They laugh, clink goblet and bottle, and drink as*

The Curtain Falls)

SCENE TWO

SCENE—*About a year later—Columbus's flagship on the last day of his second voyage. The section of the vessel shown reveals the main deck amidships, the mainmast, the mainsail with its Maltese*

Cross, the two higher decks of the poop, the lateen sail on the miz-
zenmast, etc. Wooden stairs on the starboard, near the bulwark,
are the means of getting from one deck to another.

It is the time just preceding the dawn. The ship is sailing stead-
ily on a calm sea. There is a large lantern at center of the main
deck, another low down in the rigging on the port side, another
over the cross which hangs over the stern from the high poop. The
ship is crowded with people. On the main deck are the nobles. They
are dressed in rich uniforms, in armor. Most of them are asleep,
lying sprawled on the deck, wrapped in their cloaks—or huddled
in hunched attitudes, their backs propped against the mast or the
bulwarks. But one small group has apparently been awake all
night. They are sitting cross-legged, throwing dice by the light of
the lantern. The faces of the gamesters are haggard and drawn,
their eyes feverish. Prominent among them are Oviedo, Castillo,
Mendoza and Luis.

On the first deck of the poop, the monks, all Franciscans, are
lying asleep. Here, also, are four of the converted Indians Colum-
bus is bringing back. They are dressed in incongruous costumes,
half savage and half civilized. They are huddled in the right cor-
ner, not asleep, but frozen in a helpless apathy.

On the highest deck Juan is seen standing by the pilot who tends
the helm.

LUIS—(*excitedly*) Double or quits!

OVIEDO—Done. (*They play. Luis loses.*)

LUIS—I am ruined again! (*with a comical groan of despair*)
Fortune is a damned mercenary wench. She scorns the poor.
(*takes up the dice to throw*) Once more!

OVIEDO—(*grumblingly*) No. You owe me more than you
can pay.

LUIS—I will soon be rich as Crœsus. Don Columbus says
we will sight land today—the Indies, Isles of Spice, Cipango,
Cathay, who knows what? I will stake my future wealth
against yours. Come! One more cast for anything you wish.

OVIEDO—(*dryly*) For gold—gold I can see and touch.

LUIS—(*disgustedly*) The devil! I must borrow from Juan
then. (*He gets to his feet.*)

OVIEDO—He will not thank you to wake him on a beggar's errand.

Luis—Do you imagine he sleeps with his Promised Land so near? He is astern on the Admiral's poop keeping a watch of his own—for fear the lookout will miss Cathay!

Castillo—Juan is over-eager. He will make the Genoese jealous.

Mendoza—Has already. It is plain Columbus slights him.

Oviedo—From policy. He knows Juan is in disgrace at Court since the duel. Our admiral trims his sails to the wind.

Castillo—Juan paid dearly for Vicente's wound—a pin-prick that hardly drew blood.

Mendoza—It was the scandal.

Luis—(*indignantly*) All false—the malice of envious tongues! Vicente himself apologized to Juan. As for the lady, when I was home in Cordova I saw her with Vicente. You could not find a more married pair. It was even rumored they were to have a child— (*Juan has come down from the Admiral's poop, passed through the sleeping monks and now appears by the light of the lamp in the rigging at the head of the stairs to the main deck. Luis breaks off suddenly.*) Is that you, Juan? Come, be a brother. This son of luck (*he indicates Oviedo*) has won everything but my skin.

Juan—(*with a laugh*) Then stake the Fountain of Youth which you will find—tomorrow! Sold by the cask it should make you the richest man in Spain. (*The nobles laugh.*)

Luis—(*with real aversion*) What trader's scheming—from you! (*then jokingly*) Take care! When the pox of old age is on you will come begging to me! (*then rattling the dice*) But come, loan me gold for a last cast of revenge. (*then with a sudden idea*) And you throw for me. My star is behind a cloud.

Oviedo—Not fair. Juan always wins.

Juan—(*frowning*) This is no time for gaming.

Luis—(*insistently*) Just once, Juan.

Juan—(*consenting unwillingly*) Only once. The stakes are yours. Let the cast be an augury for me. (*He takes gold from his purse. He and Oviedo play. Oviedo wins and there is a mur-mur of astonishment.*)

Oviedo—(*exultantly*) I win. The first time I have ever beat you, Juan.

Juan—(*getting up*) A poor omen. (*then mockingly*) But

here on the under side of earth these signs must run by opposites.

MENDOZA—(*half frightenedly*) Can we be hanging head down and not know it?

CASTILLO—Bah! The Genoese made his first voyage safely. We cannot fall off, it seems.

OVIEDO—Columbus may be a liar.

MENDOZA—(*savagely*) A low-born braggart! He displayed his origin in the hoggish demands he made on the crown. What could the Sovereigns be thinking of—to make this foreign upstart an Admiral and a Viceroy?

JUAN—(*sternly rebuking*) It is not for us to question. (*He pauses—then adds*) His enterprise has served Spain well. He is our commander. That is enough to know. (*He turns his back on them and walks to the port side where he stands by the rigging looking out to sea. The nobles look after him for a moment in an abashed silence.*)

CASTILLO—(*mockingly*) You are a perfect Christian, Juan— to love your enemy.

OVIEDO—(*yawns*) Put out the lantern. Let us sleep. The dawn will wake us. (*Mendoza puts out the lantern. All except Luis wrap themselves in their robes and lie down on the deck. Luis comes over to Juan.*)

LUIS—(*scornfully*) Look at those clods. They would snore through the Last Judgment. (*then as Juan is silent*) What are you dreaming of—Cathay and glory?

JUAN—No. (*then suddenly*) When I came down I heard Vicente's name—and mention of a child. What were you saying?

LUIS—Gossip of Cordova. My mother told me Maria was having masses said that she might bear an heir—and the rumor was her prayers were answered.

JUAN—(*with deep sincerity*) God grant it. She will be happy then. (*with an ironical laugh*) Did I not tell you that night our duel would reconcile them? (*soberly*) But I pay. Well, what matter the cost if Maria wins happiness?

LUIS—(*reassuringly*) One exploit and the Court will be at your feet again.

JUAN—(*shaking his head*) We will be far from Spain—out of sight and mind. Columbus will be king here, and he and I are by nature antagonistic. (*There is a noise from the higher deck of the poop. A tall figure can be made out coming up on deck there from the companionway. He moves back until the light from the lantern above the cross reveals him. It is Columbus. He is in full uniform but wears no hat on his long, white hair. A commanding figure of noble presence, the face full of the ardent, fixed enthusiasm of the religious devotee.*)

LUIS—(*pulling Juan back into the shadow*) Speak the devil's name! (*They stand, watching and listening, but hidden from the poop.*)

COLUMBUS—(*to the helmsman*) Have you held the course?

HELMSMAN—Southwest by west, sir.

COLUMBUS—(*peering about him*) Will the dawn never come? (*He comes to the edge of the deck and calls down where the monks are—in a low voice*) Father Menendez. Are you awake?

MENENDEZ—(*gets up quickly from among the sleeping monks*) I am here, your Excellency. (*He mounts to the deck above and stands waiting respectfully.*)

COLUMBUS—(*begins in a blunt, perfunctory tone*) Toscanelli's map must be in error. We should have sighted land before. (*A pause. He paces back and forth.*) The sun will soon be up. It leaps from the darkness in these parts. (*a pause, then with evident irritation*) A weary voyage, Father! The spirit of these nobles is perverse. They look on this voyage as an escapade in search of easy riches, not as a crusade for the glory of God.

MENENDEZ—(*curtly*) They are brave. Many of them have proven their ability in war—Juan Ponce de Leon, for one.

COLUMBUS—(*resentfully*) A bravo! A duelist!

LUIS—(*in an indignant whisper*) The devil seize him!

JUAN—(*grimly*) Another aftermath of that cursed duel!

MENENDEZ—(*shortly*) You are unjust, Excellency.

COLUMBUS—Oh, I admit he possesses all the attributes but the one which alone gives them virtue—an humble piety. On this great quest there is no place for egotists who seek only selfish ends. We must all feel ourselves unworthy servants of God's Holy Will. (*then breaking off—abruptly*) But I did not call you to speak of him. (*after a pause—despondently*) My soul is overburdened, Father.

MENENDEZ—(*dryly*) You wish to confess?

COLUMBUS—(*surprised*) Confess? (*then in a loud, ringing*

tone) Yes, to all men! Their mouths are full of lies against me. They say the demands I made for my share of discovery prove my low-minded avarice. Knaves! What can they know of my heart? Is it for myself I desire wealth? No! But as a chosen instrument of God, Who led me to His Indies, I need the power that wealth can give. I need it for God's glory, not my own! (*more and more exaltedly*) I have a dream, Father! Listen! From my earliest youth I have hated the infidel. I fought on the ships of Genoa against their corsairs and as I saw my city's commerce with the East cut off by their ruthlessness, I prayed for one glorious last Crusade that would reclaim the Mediterranean for Christendom and, most fervent prayer of all, regain from profanation the Holy Sepulchre of our Lord Jesus! (*He blesses himself. Menendez also. Then he hurries on exultantly.*) And now an answer is granted! With my share of the wealth from Indies, from Cipango and Cathay, I will fit out an army—the Last Crusade! I have promised it to His Holiness, the Pope—fifty thousand men, four thousand horse, with a like force to follow after five years. I shall reconquer the Blessed Tomb of Christ for the True Faith! And to that sacred end I devote my life and all my wealth and power! (*He stands looking up to heaven with the rapt gaze of a devotee.*)

MENENDEZ—(*dryly*) Such a pious ambition does you honor.

JUAN—(*unable to restrain himself, calls mockingly*) The Crusades are dead—and the wealth of the East is still unwon.

COLUMBUS—(*stung—indignantly*) Who dares—?

JUAN—(*proudly*) A noble of Spain who thinks of her greatness while you dream of Genoa and Rome; a soldier of the present, not the ghost of a Crusader! (*then with exasperated mockery*) God's blood, have all our leaders become half monk? There was a time for that when we fought the Moor, but now a new era of world empire dawns for Spain. By living in the past you will consecrate her future to fanaticism!

COLUMBUS—(*angrily*) Insolent!

JUAN—(*vehemently*) No. I respect you, Columbus—but I have my vision, too. Spain can become the mistress of the world, greater than ancient Rome, if she can find leaders who will weld conquest to her, who will dare to govern with tolerance. (*He laughs a bitter, mocking laugh.*) But what a time to speak! Look at the men of this fleet—now when the East dawns for them! I agree with you, Don Christopher—a weary voyage! Adventurers lusting for loot to be had by a murder or two; nobles of Spain dreaming greedy visions of wealth to be theirs by birthright; monks itching for the rack to torture useful subjects of the Crown into slaves of the Church! And for leader to have you, Don Christopher—you who will pillage to resurrect the Crusades! Looters of the land, one and all! There is not one who will see it as an end to build upon! We will loot and loot and, weakened by looting, be easy prey for stronger looters. God pity this land until all looters perish from the earth! (*While he is speaking it has grown perceptibly lighter.*)

COLUMBUS—(*furiously*) Who are you? Stand forth! You dare not!

JUAN—(*jumps up to the lower level of the poop and advances to the ladder to the Admiral's poop—proudly*) It is I—Juan Ponce de Leon! Why should I not dare? Do you want men under your command—or lackeys?

COLUMBUS—(*striving to control his rage*) Silence! (*A wailing cry of* "Land Ho" *comes from the mainmast head. Immediately the same cry can be heard coming over the water from the other vessels of the fleet. Instantly all is confusion. Everyone jumps to their feet, half awake, peering about bewilderedly. The four Indians sense what has happened and hang over the bulwark, staring over the seas with intense longing. A crowd of half-dressed sailors and rabble pour up from below decks. There is a babble of excited shouts. Columbus looks upward to see where the lookout is pointing, then turns to the horizon off the starboard bow. Juan leaps to the ratlines.*)

THE CROWD—Land! Land! Where? I heard the call. He shouted land! Is it Cathay? Where is he pointing? Look where the Admiral looks. When the sun comes— (*Suddenly the ship is flooded by shafts of golden crimson light. They all cry*) The sun!

JUAN—(*pointing*) There! I see! In a haze of gold and purple—Greater Spain!

ALL—(*crowd to the starboard side and to the front. The Indians are pushed away, jostled, thrown aside contemptuously with imprecations until they are hunched disconsolately in the back-*

ground in dumb terror and bewilderment.) Where? I see!
Where? There! There! Cathay. Cipango. Is it Cathay? Where
are the golden cities? Where are the golden roofs? Is it Cipango? The Indies! The Isles of Spice! Marco Polo's land!
(*They all crowd, pushing and elbowing each other, craning their
necks, the eyes of all, rabble, soldiers, nobles, priests, straining with
the same greedy longing, the lust to loot.*)

JUAN—(*exultantly*) Cathay or Cipango or the Isles of
Spice, what difference? It shall be Greater Spain! (*The crowd
cheers vociferously.*)

COLUMBUS—(*trying to quell the tumult*) Silence, I say!
(*fixing his eyes sternly on Juan with undisguised hostility—rebukingly*) The earth is God's! Give thanks to Him! Kneel, I
command you! Raise the cross! (*The monks raise their cross.
They kneel but the nobles and soldiers hesitate waiting for Juan
as if they saw in him their true commander.*)

JUAN—(*leaps down from the rigging, drawing his sword—
with fierce exultance*) This is a cross too, a soldier's cross—the
cross of Spain! (*He sticks his sword-point into the deck before him.
He kneels before it. All the nobles and soldiers do likewise with a
great flourish of gestures and excited shouts. They are all kneeling
with their quivering cross swords, hilts rising above their heads.*)

COLUMBUS—(*from his knees—looking up to heaven de-
voutly*) Te Deum! (*The monks begin to chant. All join in, their
pent-up excitement giving to the hymn a hectic, nervous quality.
Juan does not sing but stares at the land on the distant horizon.*)

(*The Curtain Falls*)

SCENE THREE

SCENE—*Twenty years or so later—the courtyard of the Governor's palace, Porto Rico. Flowers, shrubs, a coco-palm, orange
and banana trees. A large, handsome fountain closely resembling
that of Scene One, is at center. Two marble benches are at front
and rear of fountain. A narrow paved walk encircles the fountain
basin, with other walks leading from it to the different entrances.
Doors to the interior of the house are at left and right. The main
entrance to the courtyard, opening on the road, is at rear center.*

*It is in the late, languid hours of a torrid afternoon. The court-
yard bakes in the heat, the fountain shimmering in the heat-
waves.*

*Juan is seated on the stone bench in front of the basin. He is
dressed in the full uniform of his authority as Governor. His face
is aged, lined, drawn. His hair and beard are gray. His expression
and attitude are full of great weariness. His eyes stare straight
before him blankly in a disillusioned dream. The lines about his
compressed lips are bitter.*

*Luis enters from the left, rear. He is dressed in the robe of a
Dominican monk. His face shows the years but it has achieved a
calm, peaceful expression as if he were at last in harmony with
himself. He comes down to Juan and puts a hand on his shoulder.*

JUAN—(*starts—then greets his friend with a smile*) Ah, it's
you, reverend Father. (*He accents this last mockingly.*)

LUIS—(*good-naturedly*) Yes, illustrious Governor. (*He sits
beside Juan—with a laugh*) You are like a sulky child, Juan.
Come, is it not time, after five years, you forgave me for
being a Dominican?

JUAN—(*bitterly*) My friend deserting to my enemy!

LUIS—(*protestingly*) Come, come! (*then after a pause, with
a sigh*) You have always had the dream of Cathay. What had
I? What had I done with life?—an aimless, posing rake,
neither poet nor soldier, without place nor peace! I had no
meaning even to myself until God awakened me to His Holy
Will. Now I live in truth. You must renounce in order to
possess.

JUAN—The world would be stale indeed if that were true!
(*after a pause—irritably*) I fight the battles; you monks steal
the spoils! I seek to construct; you bind my hands and
destroy!

LUIS—(*remonstrating*) You speak of Diego and his kind.

JUAN—(*frowning*) Whether you convert by clemency or he
by cruelty, the result is the same. All this baptizing of Indians,
this cramming the cross down their throats has proved a ruin-
ous error. It crushes their spirits and weakens their bodies.
They become burdens for Spain instead of valuable servitors.

LUIS—Your army crushed them first—

JUAN—They had to be conquered, but there I would have

stopped. (*then irritably*) God's blood, here we are arguing about this same issue—for the thousandth time! It is too late. Talk is useless. (*with a weary sigh*) We do what we must—and sand covers our bodies and our deeds. (*with a smile*) And the afternoon is too hot, besides. Tell me some news. Will the fleet from Spain make port today?

Luis—Just now I saw them rounding the point under full sail. They should anchor inside soon. (*They are interrupted by the noise of several people approaching from outside. Oviedo and Friar Quesada, a Franciscan, enter, followed by the Indian chief, Nano, who is guarded by two soldiers with drawn swords. Quesada is a thin young monk with the sallow, gaunt face and burning eyes of a fanatic. Oviedo is aged but gives no evidence of having changed in character. Nano is a tall, powerfully built Indian of fifty or so. Although loaded down with chains, he carries himself erect with an air of aloof, stoical dignity. He wears a headdress of feathers. His face and body are painted, ornaments are about his neck. He is naked except for a breechclout and moccasins.*)

Quesada—(*fiercely and arrogantly*) I demand justice on this dog!

Juan—(*freezing—proudly*) Demand?

Quesada—(*with ill-concealed hatred but awed by Juan's manner*) Pardon my zeal in the service of God, Your Excellency. I ask justice. (*then defiantly*) But it is not the Church's custom to be a suppliant.

Juan—So much the worse— (*sternly*) What is this Indian's crime?

Quesada—His tribe will not pay the tithes—and he himself has dared to refuse baptism!

Juan—(*coldly*) I'll question him. (*then as Quesada hesitates, raging inwardly—sternly*) You may go.

Quesada—(*controlling his rage, bows*) Yes, Your Excellency. (*He goes.*)

Juan—(*to Oviedo with a certain contempt*) You also have a charge against this Indian?

Oviedo—(*angrily*) A plea for justice! These dogs will not pay their taxes. And we who own estates cannot get them to work except by force, which you have arbitrarily curtailed. Then why not punish them by leasing their labor to us until their debt's wiped out? Thus the government will be paid, and we will have workers for our mines and fields.

JUAN—(*disgustedly*) Your brain is not inventive, Oviedo! You are well aware that is the same blunder which failed on Espaniola. It means slavery. It defeats its purpose. The Indians die under the lash—and your labor dies with them. (*contemptuously*) Do you think I am Columbus that you ask this folly of me?

OVIEDO—(*haughtily*) You refuse? (*He goes to the rear where he turns—threateningly*) Take care, Juan! There will come a day of reckoning—when Diego returns from Spain. (*He goes out.*)

JUAN—(*frowning*) Diego? What do you mean?

OVIEDO—(*with a revengeful smile*) Nothing. Adios, Don Juan. (*He goes out.*)

JUAN—(*with a bitter laugh*) There you have it! Bah! What use—? (*He suddenly seems to see Nano for the first time. They stare at each other.*) I was forgetting you. Are you not Nano, chief of the last tribe I conquered? (*as the Indian is silent—imperiously*) Speak!

NANO—The devils were with you. Our villages were burned. Women and children were killed—my wives, my children!

JUAN—(*frowning*) Contrary to my command. But, again, what use? The dead are dead. It is too late. (*after a pause—with a sort of weary self-mockery*) Have you ever heard of Cathay—Cipango? Do you know of vast countries to the west—many peoples—great villages with high walls—much gold?

NANO—I have heard.

JUAN—(*surprised—eagerly*) Ah! Where are they? (*Nano points west.*)

LUIS—(*amusedly*) Where the fountain of youth of my drunken days is located—in dreamland!

JUAN—(*with a certain seriousness*) Do you know, they say there is a similar fountain legend among these tribes. (*then to Nano with a mocking smile*) My friend here is growing impatient waiting for immortality in heaven and would rather gain it here on earth—

LUIS—Juan!

JUAN—So tell him, O Mighty Chief, if there is not over there—a fountain—a spring—in which old men bathe or drink and become young warriors again?

NANO—(*to both their surprise*) The tale is told. Not here. In my home—a land that never ends. Our priests told the tale. I was young then. I was captured in war and brought here. I was adopted. I have never returned.

JUAN—(*lost in thought*) So? Where is this land, your home? (*Nano points as before.*) Where Cathay is? And the fountain— the spring—is there?

NANO—(*after a moment's hesitation*) Yes. My people call it the Spring of Life.

LUIS—(*whimsically*) A pretty title, indeed. (*sceptically*) But none can find it, I suppose?

NANO—Those the Gods love can find it.

JUAN—(*scornfully*) Aha, that old trick of poets—evasion of facts! (*turning to Luis*) Do you remember the Moor that night in Granada? "Only to the chosen." Here is the echo! Bah! What jugglery! (*then thoughtfully*) But it is strange. Where there is so much smoke, there must be a spark of fire. The Moor traced his myth back to the East—Cathay—and now we discover it again—still in Cathay—circling the world— (*then, as if ashamed of himself for taking it so seriously—carelessly*) At all events, it is added evidence that Cathay is near. (*The boom of a cannon comes from the harbor.*)

LUIS—The fleet has anchored. Diego will soon be here. If you can give this Indian into my keeping I will attempt his conversion.

JUAN—(*impatiently*) Until his case is investigated, he must go to prison. You may see him there. (*to Nano, sternly*) If it is proven you have encouraged rebellion against Spain, you will be hung. Against any other charge I will try to save you. (*summoning the soldiers*) Guard. (*They salute and lead Nano out, left. Juan paces up and down in frowning thought.*) Diego! Did you hear Oviedo threaten me with him? What mischief will he bring from Spain this time, I wonder? The cursed spider! His intriguing will destroy all my work here— (*with impotent anger*) And the fight is hopeless. His weapons are whispers. A man of honor stands disarmed. (*intensely*) Would to God this fleet brought me the King's patent to discover new lands! I would sail tomorrow for Cathay—or for the moon!

LUIS—(*firmly*) Fight your battle here! This is your land. You conquered it.

JUAN—Columbus discovered it; and I still feel his influence, like a black fog, stifling me!

LUIS—(*mollifyingly*) He is dead. Forgive. He suffered too much injustice to be just.

JUAN—How can my pride forgive? For years I held his solitary outposts; I suffered wounds and fevers; I fought the Indians for him while he went sailing for the Garden of Eden, the mines of Solomon, his Bible-crazed chimeras! He knew my honor would not permit my conspiring against him as others did. So he ignored my services and deliberately condemned me to obscurity! Never one mention of my name in his reports to Spain! It is only since his downfall— (*breaking off*) But this, too, is an old story. (*then with sudden exasperation*) Why should I not sail to find Cathay? He failed in that—but I would succeed! I am no visionary chasing rainbows. (*desperately*) I tell you I loathe this place! I loathe my petty authority! By God, I could sink all Porto Rico under the sea for one glimpse of Cathay!

LUIS—(*alarmed*) Juan!

JUAN—(*after a pause—ironically*) Well, do not fear that I will leave your precious island. The patent will never come— and if it did, there is a flaw— (*despondently, with a great weariness*) It is too late. Cathay is too far. I am too weary. I have fought small things so long that I am small. My spirit has rusted in chains for twenty years. Now it tends to accept them—to gain peace. (*with passionate yearning*) If I could only feel again my old fire, my energy of heart and mind—! If I could be once more the man who fought before Granada—! But the fire smolders. It merely warms my will to dream of the past. It no longer catches flame in deeds. (*with a desolate smile of self-pity*) I begin to dread—another failure. I am too old to find Cathay.

MENENDEZ—(*appears in rear in time to hear this last. He is dressed in a Bishop's robes. He looks his years, but his expression of rabid fanaticism has changed to one, not less cruel, of the crafty schemer made complacent by a successful career, the oily intriguer of Church politics. He hesitates with a suspicious, inquisitive glance from one to the other—then advances with a forced air of joviality.*) What is this I hear? Too old? Tut-tut! This is heresy, Juan. (*The two turn, startled. Juan stares at him resentfully. Menendez exchanges a cold bow of condescension with Luis, then comes to Juan with outstretched hands, smiling oilily.*) Have you no greeting for me, old friend?

JUAN—(*takes his hands perfunctorily—then sarcastically*) Who would expect you unattended—like any eavesdropping monk?

MENENDEZ—(*unruffled*) My eagerness to see you. I have great news. I often spoke to the King about you. He now holds you in the highest esteem, and as a proof of his favor I bring you— (*then with a sly smile*) But, on second thought, I should not say, I bring you. That is reserved for a worthier hand!

JUAN—(*impatiently*) I dislike mysteries.

MENENDEZ—(*provokingly*) I will give you this hint out of respect for the old age you were lamenting! Prepare to welcome youth—and a prize you have sought for all your life in the Indies—a gift more welcome to you than wine was to Luis before he repented! (*With this parting gibe, he turns away.*) Pardon me if I leave you. I must make preparations— for this event. (*He bows mockingly and goes off right.*)

JUAN—(*angrily*) Schemer! (*He paces up and down.*)

LUIS—(*after pondering a moment—suddenly*) I have it! It must be your patent to explore! He has obtained it from the King—because he wishes to get rid of you here! You stand in his way—your policy of clemency. He wants to be dictator to introduce torture and slavery! Yet he is afraid to fight you openly, so what craftier scheme than to send you away contented, grateful for a gift, bribed without knowing it?

JUAN—(*resentfully*) Then I will fool the fox! There is no compulsion in such a patent. (*then confused*) But—it would be my highest hope come true—too late! Too late! I am too old. (*with an attempt at a railing tone*) God's blood, I need to find Cathay—if your Fountain of Youth is there!

LUIS—I hear a crowd coming. I must go. It adds to their spleen to find us together. (*He presses Juan's hand.*) Whatever comes, be firm, old friend. (*He goes out left. The murmur of*

the crowd increases. Juan sinks on the bench before the fountain,
oblivious to it, lost in gloomy thought. Beatriz de Cordova
appears, attended by her duenna and a crowd of richly dressed
nobles. She is a beautiful young girl of eighteen or so, the personi-
fication of youthful vitality, charm and grace. The nobles point out
Juan to her. She dismisses them, motioning for them to be quiet—
then comes in and approaches Juan, keeping the fountain between
them. She holds a sealed document in her hand. Finally she calls
in a trembling, eager voice)

BEATRIZ—Don Juan! *(Juan whirls on his bench and stares*
through the fountain at her. He utters a stunned exclamation as
if he saw a ghost. His eyes are held fascinated by her beauty. Then
suddenly she laughs—a gay, liquid, clear note—and coming
quickly around confronts him.) It is I, Don Juan.

JUAN—*(stares at her still fascinated—then, reminded, springs*
to his feet and bows low with his old mocking gallantry) Pardon!
I am bewitched! I thought you were the spirit of the fountain. *(then more mockingly)* Beautiful lady, you do me unmerited honor!

BEATRIZ—*(hurt and confused by his tone)* You don't know
me? Why, I'm Beatriz. *(as he bows but shows no recognition)* Has
Bishop Menendez not told you—?

JUAN—*(suspiciously)* Nothing of you, my lady.

BEATRIZ—I am Beatriz de Cordova—

JUAN—*(guessing—amazed, stares at her—a pause, slowly)*
Maria's child!—you!

BEATRIZ—*(letting it all pour forth regardless)* She died a
year ago—and—I am your ward now. It was her last wish.
My father was dead. There was no near relative whom she
would trust. I asked the King to send me here to you. He
bade me wait until the Bishop could escort me. He made me
the bearer of this gift for you—your dearest wish, he said.
(She gives him the document.)

JUAN—*(unrolls it—a pause as he stares at it dully, then bit-*
terly) The patent—to find Cathay!

BEATRIZ—Yes! And you can find it where the others
failed, I know! You were my dear mother's ideal of Spanish
chivalry, of a true knight of the Cross! That was her proph-
ecy, that you would be the first to reach Cathay!

JUAN—She spoke of the man she knew. *(staring at her*

fascinatedly—eagerly) She sends me you—and you are youth!
Is it in mockery?

BEATRIZ—(*suddenly*) Oh, Don Juan, I recall something she
said I must remember when we should meet. "Bring him tenderness," she said. "That will repay the debt I owe him for
saving me for you." She said these words were secrets to tell
you alone. What did she mean, Don Juan?

JUAN—(*deeply moved*) Tenderness? Do you bring me that,
Beatriz? (*then as if recalling himself*) No, do not—for it
means weakness. Bring me the past instead. Give me back—
the man your mother knew.

BEATRIZ—(*who has been scrutinizing him without paying attention to his words*) You are older than I dreamed, Don Juan.

JUAN—(*wounded—with harsh violence*) No tenderness
there! Youth! A cuirass of shining steel! A glittering sword!
Laughter above the battle! (*Then seeing her look of frightened
astonishment at his wild words, he controls himself and adds with
a melancholy bitterness*) It was so long ago, Beatriz—that
night in Granada—a dimly-remembered dream— (*then with
a sudden return of his mockingly gallant manner*) Forgive me. I
have become a savage lost to manners. (*He kneels and kisses
her hand with all his old-time gallantry.*) Welcome, dear ward,
to Porto Rico! (*She looks down at his bowed head, blushing with
pleasure and naïve embarrassment, as*

The Curtain Falls)

SCENE FOUR

SCENE—*Three months later—Menendez' official study in
the palace—a large, high-ceilinged, bare room with a heavy table
at center. The color scheme is dark and gloomy, the atmosphere
that of a rigid, narrow ecclesiasticism. In one corner is an altar
with high candles burning before it. Heavy hangings shut out the
light from the lofty, arched windows. An enormous crucifix hangs
on the wall in rear. The room is like an exaggerated monk's cell,
but it possesses a somber power over the imagination by the force of
its concentration. There is a main entrance at rear, center, and a
smaller side door at left, hidden by curtains.*

It is early evening. Menendez is seated at the table. He is frowningly impatient, listening and waiting for someone. There is the sound of approaching footsteps. Menendez turns eagerly in his chair. Quesada enters through the hangings on the left. His face is ominous and set. He wears a sword and pistols over his robe which is tucked up over high riding boots and spurs. He is covered with dust, and has evidently been riding hard. He bows respectfully to Menendez.

MENENDEZ—I had begun to think you would never come. (*then with anxiety*) What news?

QUESADA—The meeting is being held. They have gathered in the fort outside the town.

MENENDEZ—Good! It is moving according to my plan, then.

QUESADA—They all agree that Don Juan must resign his patent.

MENENDEZ—Unless he sails to find Cathay at once?

QUESADA—Yes. They are all mad for the gold (*with a sneer*) over there, the report of which I have had rumored about, as you directed.

MENENDEZ—Good. Then we shall be rid of Juan and all the discontented spirits on the island at one stroke!

QUESADA—(*excitedly*) But they also demand that first the Indian, Nano, must be burned at the stake. They believe he has bewitched the Governor. They know of Don Juan's secret interviews with him.

MENENDEZ—(*angrily*) Who told them?

QUESADA—(*after a moment's hesitation—defiantly*) I did.

MENENDEZ—(*angrily*) Fool!

QUESADA—(*alarmed—humbly*) But the dog still refuses baptism.

MENENDEZ—(*sternly*) Is this a time to consider one Indian? Idiot! You know as well as I that my intention has been to attack Juan on one issue, and only one—his failure to sail for Cathay now that he has the King's patent. What have all the Nanos, hung or unhung, to do with that?

QUESADA—Much! If Don Juan were not bewitched by Nano's spells, he would have sailed long since.

MENENDEZ—And you told the rabble that? God pardon

you! Was it any part of my orders that you should play upon the mob's lust for blood? I have worked for a peaceable revolt that would awaken Juan to his weakness and shame him into leaving. You have dared to evoke a madness which might easily sweep away all recognized authority. Quick! What was the rabble's mood when you left? (*Quesada avoids his eyes. Menendez pounds the table.*) Answer me!

QUESADA—(*evasively*) They had been drinking—

MENENDEZ—(*furiously, a note of alarm creeping in*) Ah!

QUESADA—(*now thoroughly cowed*) They were clamoring to march on the palace. Don Oviedo was trying to restrain them—

MENENDEZ—(*fiercely—with bitter scorn*) You cursed blunderer! No, I am the dolt for having trusted you!

QUESADA—(*kneeling—cowed*) Forgive me, Your Grace!

MENENDEZ—Your action was treachery to me! And I shall punish you! When this expedition sails for that golden fable, Cathay, you shall go with it. Then blunder all you like! (*He rises and strides to the window at rear.*)

QUESADA—(*humbly*) I humbly accept my penance.

MENENDEZ—(*bitterly*) Behold the first fruits of your excessive piety! (*He points.*) The southern horizon is aflame!

QUESADA—(*rising*) They must have set fire to the Indian villages.

MENENDEZ—Blood and fire! Your merry dance begins well! (*He lets the curtains fall back.*) Only Juan can control them now—if he would only promise them to sail at once—but no, he is too proud. He will fight armed rebellion to the last—and we will all go down in the same ruin!

QUESADA—(*scornfully*) He is not the man he was—since Nano bewitched him.

MENENDEZ—(*disgustedly*) Bah! You fool! (*then intently*) Yet there is truth in what you say. He has grown weak—between Luis' influence and the girl's meddling— (*abruptly*) Come! There is still a chance. Summon Don Juan to me at once! (*this last in a shout of impatience*)

JUAN—(*from outside, rear, mockingly*) There is no need for messengers. (*He enters. In the three months he has aged greatly. His hair and beard have grown perceptibly white. Beneath the bitter, mocking mask there is an expression of deep, hidden conflict and suffering on his face as if he were at war with himself.)*

MENENDEZ—(*startled, afraid of what Juan may have overheard*) You heard—?

JUAN—(*scornfully*) Only what you shouted. Am I a monk to listen at keyholes? (*this with a glance at Quesada*) But I know your intrigues. This meeting of yapping curs—you see, I have heard the rumor—you would have me sail at their bidding, and thus you would be free to rule this island in God's Holy Name! Is it not so?

MENENDEZ—(*controlling his anger*) You have lost your senses. You will not realize that things have reached a crisis! The government has slipped through your fingers while you played at being a loving father—

JUAN—(*stung—fiercely*) It's a lie! (*controlling himself*) I tell you again, Diego, I will sail at my pleasure, not yours.

MENENDEZ—(*persuasively*) You have kept repeating that—and meanwhile your apathy has ruined us. Your soldiers and sailors are in open mutiny. The mob has risen. (*urgently*) Juan, do you want rebellion to overwhelm us? You promised them Cathay—

JUAN—(*proudly*) It was you who promised them in my name, you mean, to make certain you would be rid of me!

MENENDEZ—(*tauntingly—noting Juan's reactions craftily*) I promised because I thought you were still Juan Ponce de Leon. But you are not. You have become merely a slave to a girl's sentimental whims! You are too feeble to govern here and too weak for Cathay. (*Juan's hand goes to his sword. Menendez continues cuttingly.*) Then for the sake of Spain, resign your office and surrender your patent for discovery to someone with the youth and courage to dare!

JUAN—(*infuriated, half drawing his sword*) Take care, Diego! Your cloth cannot condone such insults!

MENENDEZ—(*in a softened, oily tone*) Forgive me, Juan. I insult you for your own sake! Push on to your greatest victory! Do not wait here in a stupor for inglorious defeat!

JUAN—(*shaken*) I shall sail—but first I must know—know for a certainty, beyond all doubt—exactly where— (*He stops abruptly.*)

MENENDEZ—(*inquisitively*) What?

JUAN—(*suspiciously*) Nothing.

QUESADA—(*who has been listening with feverish interest—points to Juan accusingly*) He has gone to Nano every day. Look at his eyes! He is bewitched! (*Juan starts guiltily but tries to ignore him contemptuously.*)

MENENDEZ—Be still, Quesada! (*He looks at Juan.*) These interviews *are* mysterious, Juan.

JUAN—(*quickly—half turning away and averting his eyes—with forced carelessness*) I need accurate information for my voyage that only Nano can give me. That is why I have delayed.

MENENDEZ—(*looking at him sharply*) So? I had thought it might be affection for Beatriz that held you.

JUAN—(*vehemently*) No!

MENENDEZ—(*keenly*) Why are you so vehement? It would be natural enough. You have lived alone. To find a daughter in your declining years—

JUAN—(*pale with rage and agony*) Daughter? How could she look upon me—?

MENENDEZ—(*soothingly but with a taunting intent*) She used to regard you as her hero, her great commander. She must wonder now at this old man's weakness in you.

JUAN—(*frenziedly*) Do you dare taunt me in her name? I *will* sail, I say! I will sail the very first day after I discover— (*then distractedly, shaken*) Enough, Diego! I shall do what I wish and when it pleases me! (*He rushes out rear as if furies were hounding him. Menendez looks after him, a sneering smile of satisfaction gradually coming over his face as if something were proven to him.*)

MENENDEZ—(*half to himself, half to Quesada*) I should have guessed it before. Yet, who would have thought— He is bewitched, certainly.

QUESADA—(*eagerly*) Yes!

MENENDEZ—(*dryly*) But you are blaming the wrong witch. The guilty one is sinless. (*Quesada puzzles over this paradox with open eyes. Menendez ponders for a moment, then he turns to Quesada.*) Bring the Lady Beatriz.

QUESADA—Yes, Your Grace. (*He bows and hurries out, left. Menendez sits thoughtfully, evidently planning out his campaign. A moment later Beatriz enters. She bows respectfully.*)

BEATRIZ—(*reservedly*) You wish to see me, Your Grace?

MENENDEZ—(*nods and motions her to a chair. He scrutinizes her face carefully for a moment, then begins in a playful, ironical tone.*) Beauty did not leave a stone on stone of ancient Troy. Are you another Helen, Beatriz?

BEATRIZ—(*confused*) I—don't understand.

MENENDEZ—(*coldly and brusquely*) Not understand that rebellion is seething in Porto Rico?—a rebellion that will deal destruction to us all!

BEATRIZ—(*bewildered*) Rebellion? (*then spiritedly*) Who would dare rebel against Don Juan?

MENENDEZ—(*belittlingly*) Juan is powerless. His own soldiers have taken the lead against him. He is facing ruin! Do you understand? I wish I had words of fire to brand it on your brain! For I tell you on my conscience, as God's minister, you are the one responsible!

BEATRIZ—(*stunned*) I? I? You are jesting! (*then with haughty resentment*) I harm Don Juan, who is my second father!

MENENDEZ—(*seeming to grow more icy under her anger*) Who has done most in influencing him to softness and lax discipline—

BEATRIZ—(*indignantly*) You mean because I have pitied the suffering of the Indians—?

MENENDEZ—(*dryly*) Let us judge your pity by its results. These heathen no longer fear. They defy our Holy Faith. They sneer at baptism. These Indians shirk their labor. And because Don Juan spends his time with you, he has forgotten not only his duty to govern but his oath to seek Cathay. The soldiers and sailors have waited too long in idleness. Now they revere him no longer as a daring general who will lead them to glory but despise him for a dissembler, delaying because he has lost the courage for action! And so they have conspired. Those are the facts. Will you deny your influence is deep at the root of them? (*Beatriz is too overwhelmed by the ruthlessness of his attack to reply. He pushes his advantage.*) And can you deny that a great change has come over Don Juan since your arrival? You cannot have helped but notice this!

BEATRIZ—He has seemed—to become despondent at times.

MENENDEZ—(*vehemently*) Spiritless! Infirm! His thoughts wander like a senile old man's! I believe his mind is failing him!

BEATRIZ—(*horrified*) No! No!

MENENDEZ—You must face the truth! (*sternly*) When you take a life's ambition from a man like Juan, the man withers away. You have made him forget Cathay. Why? Why have you not urged him to go—for his own sake? When you brought out the patent, you dreamed of him as he dreams of himself—a conqueror and hero!

BEATRIZ—(*hesitatingly*) Father Luis told me we must keep him here—or else his good work would be undone—

MENENDEZ—This uprising will undo it in an hour! (*then soothingly*) Father Luis is a good man—but blind. You are a girl—and inexperienced— Come. (*He pauses, watching her keenly, then takes her hand, and leading her to the window, pulls back the curtain.*) Look!

BEATRIZ—(*with a shudder of horror*) Ah!

MENENDEZ—Now do you believe in the rebellion—in Juan's danger?

BEATRIZ—(*horrified*) Fire!

MENENDEZ—And murder! In the Indian villages. See what your pity for them has done! And it will not stop there. That is only the first spark of revolution. They'll march here! (*impressively*) Beatriz, you can save Don Juan. He loves you— as his daughter. Urge him to sail at once! Rouse the hero in him! Give him back his sanity! He is my old friend. I implore you for his sake, Beatriz!

BEATRIZ—(*bewilderedly*) Yes—yes—but give me time to think—to pray for guidance— (*She kneels before the altar.*)

MENENDEZ—(*impatiently*) There is no time! (*There is a noise of hurrying steps and Oviedo enters. He is booted, spurred, covered with dust, his face betraying anxiety and alarm.*)

OVIEDO—(*without stopping to see who is there, bursts forth*) Diego! I tried to check them, but they have gone mad! They are marching on the town! Juan will be lost!

MENENDEZ—(*to Beatriz who has turned around in terror*) You hear!

OVIEDO—The time has come to abandon that sick fool! We must openly lead this rebellion!

BEATRIZ—(*springs to her feet and faces him—her eyes flashing*) Coward! (*He falls back, his hand on his sword, glaring at her.*)

MENENDEZ—(*urgently*) Go, Beatriz! (*She passes Oviedo with a scathing glance, and goes out rear. Menendez turns to Oviedo with an ironical but worried smile.*)

MENENDEZ—If she will but speak to Juan as she did to you, we may still win, my friend!

(*The Curtain Falls*)

SCENE FIVE

SCENE—*Nano's dungeon—a circular cavern, hollowed out by Nature and cut out by man in the solid rock under the Government house. The enclosed space is narrow but lofty, cylindrical in form. A cut-in flight of steps leads from the floor in rear to a trap-door above. The high wall glistens with moisture. A small bench is at right. A lantern stands on one of the lower steps. In the middle of the floor stands a soldier, thick-set, brutal-looking, his sleeves rolled up over his muscular arms. He is blowing with a bellows on a charcoal brazier, glowing red-hot, in which are thrust several irons. On the wall in the rear, his toes barely touching the floor, Nano hangs with his arms outstretched over his head, the wrists bound by chains to iron sockets in the rock. His head hangs on one side as if he were in a state of semi-consciousness. His body is thin and wasted.*

The trap-door is opened and a circular patch of gray light falls on the stairs. This is obscured as someone descends. It is Juan. He shuts the trap-door behind him and comes down. He stops when he is opposite Nano's head, and, leaning over, stares at the savage's face. The latter opens his eyes. His head stiffens proudly erect on his shoulders. He and Juan stare into each other's eyes. Juan drops his guiltily, turns away and descends to the floor, where the soldier is standing at attention.

JUAN—(*harshly*) Has he spoken?

SOLDIER—Not one word, sir.

JUAN—Then you have not obeyed—

SOLDIER—(*indicates the irons in the fire*) I have tried every trick I know—but he's made of iron.

JUAN—(*looks up at Nano with intense hatred*) Dog! (*Then he turns to the soldier.*) Go and keep guard above.

SOLDIER—Yes, sir. (*He bends down to pick up the brazier.*)

JUAN—(*harshly*) No.

SOLDIER—(*with a glance at him—understandingly*) Yes, sir. (*He goes up the stairs, opens the trap-door and disappears, letting it fall shut behind him. Juan sinks on the stone bench at right and stares up at Nano, who looks back at him with unflinching defiance. A pause.*)

JUAN—(*his eyes now fixed dully on the floor—half-aloud to himself*) Diego did not lie. The storm is gathering. (*with bitter hopelessness*) What matter? I could pray that it might be a deluge annihilating mankind—but for Beatriz. (*He groans, then raises his eyes again to Nano.*) Why do you look at me? I can never read your eyes. They see in another world. What are you? Flesh, but not our flesh. Earth. I come after—or before—but lost, blind in a world where my eyes deflect on surfaces. What values give you your loan of life? Answer! I must know the terms in which to make appeal! (*The savage is silent, motionless. A pause. Then Juan, as if suddenly reminded, jumps to his feet in a frenzy of impatience.*) Answer me, dog! I must find the will to act—or be dishonored!

NANO—(*solemnly—in a faint voice*) The Gods are angry.

JUAN—(*with wild joy*) You speak! At last! Nano, why have you kept dumb while I implored—?

NANO—The Gods have stopped your ears.

JUAN—(*going on obsessed, regardless*) Juan Ponce de Leon—to torture a helpless captive! Why did you bring me to such shame? Why would you not answer my question?

NANO—(*with contempt*) My tongue grew weary. For a moon I answered every day.

JUAN—(*fiercely*) But you lied! Tell me the truth now! Where is the fountain?

NANO—(*indifferently, shutting his eyes*) Only the Gods know.

JUAN—The same lie! You told me at first that men of your former tribe knew! You must know! This is your revenge—for the death of your wives and children! Must I swear to you again they were killed in spite of my strict orders? Come! Forget them! I will give you your choice of all your women on the island—your freedom—I will petition the King to honor you—give you back your lands—anything if you will answer me! (*Nano remains silent. Juan utters a furious cry and, rushing to the brazier, takes a red-hot coal with the tongs and holds it before the Indian's eyes.*) Dog! I will burn that scorn from your eyes! (*The Indian stares at the hot iron immovably. Juan lets it fall to the floor with a desperate groan of misery.*) Pardon! Forgiveness in Christ's name! It is you who torture me! Nano, I burn to hell! I love! (*He suddenly stops, chilled to despair by the implacable isolation in the savage's face. He throws himself down on the bench in an apathy. Finally he slowly draws his sword and speaks in a dead voice.*) Either you speak or you die. I swear it.

NANO—(*with aloof contempt*) What is death?

JUAN—(*dully*) I will die, too. Perhaps in the grave there is oblivion and peace. (*after a pause*) You are a fool, Nano. If you would help me I could make you pilot of the fleet to guide us to your land. The fountain once found, you would be free. No harm should come to your people. Do you never long for your old home?

NANO—(*who has been listening with quickened interest*) Home? To the land of flowers. My home of many warriors. (*after a pause*) You will let me guide the great winged canoes —to my home?

JUAN—(*eagerly*) Yes. (*in great suspense*) Will you help me? Tell me! (*He has sprung to his feet.*)

NANO—Only the Gods— (*He checks himself abruptly.*)

JUAN—(*frenziedly*) Ah! (*He raises his sword as if to run the savage through.*)

NANO—(*looking into Juan's eyes without noticing the threat*) The tongues of the white devils are false. How can I trust your word?

JUAN—I take my sacred oath! (*He raises his hand.*)

NANO—Your God is a God of lies.

JUAN—(*wildly*) By your God then—since mine has forsaken me!

NANO—(*lifts his head and murmurs some supplication, as if*

begging forgiveness—*then looks at Juan with savage triumph*) I will guide you—but remember the way is long!

JUAN—(*triumphantly*) At last! What does it matter how long or difficult! (*raising his arms*) Ah, God's blood, I already feel new life, the will to live! I can conquer now! (*A pounding of a sword-butt on the trap-door. Then it is flung open.*)

SOLDIER—Pardon, Excellency—

BEATRIZ' VOICE—(*calls down*) Don Juan! Don Juan!

JUAN—(*exultantly*) Her voice! A happy omen! (*He hurries up the stairs.*)

NANO—(*again lifting his eyes to heaven*—*with religious fervor*) Great Spirit, forgive my lie. His blood shall atone!

(*The Curtain Falls*)

SCENE SIX

SCENE—*Same as Scene Three*—*Courtyard of the Governor's House*—*a stifling twilight. The sky is darkening with clouds.*

Beatriz' voice—*from the left*—*calls down as at the end of preceding scene.*

BEATRIZ—Don Juan! Don Juan! (*His voice is heard,* "Beatriz." *She enters, pale and agitated, runs to rear and looks for signs of the insurrection*—*then hurries back just in time to meet Juan, who enters, left. He is in a tense state of hectic excitement, his face ghastly pale, his obsessed eyes burning feverishly, his drawn sword still in his hand. She starts back from him, frightened by his appearance.*)

JUAN—(*in a strained, high-pitched tone*) Was it the fountain called—or you, Beatriz? You, for you are the fountain! (*He takes her hand impetuously and kisses it.*)

BEATRIZ—(*flurriedly*) I came to warn you—

JUAN—(*with a sharp glance*) Warn? Then you have seen Diego? Bah! (*He makes a gesture of contempt with his sword as if brushing all revolutions aside.*) When the hour comes, I shall be strong. The will breathes in me again. Forget all else, Beatriz. Give me your thoughts! Have you been happy here with me?

BEATRIZ—(*not knowing what to say or do*) Yes—yes. (*trying to return to her mission*) But—

JUAN—You came as a benediction—that cursed me. (*abruptly*) Have you not noticed how much older I have grown?

BEATRIZ—(*convinced he is out of his head—resolved to humor him—frightened but pityingly*) You can become young again.

JUAN—(*exultantly*) I will! (*then mysteriously*) This is a strange world with many wonders still undiscovered.

BEATRIZ—(*seeing a chance to bring in her point—quickly*) Then discover them. The search will make you young.

JUAN—(*deeply and superstitiously impressed*) From your own lips! It is another blessed augury! (*eagerly*) But pretend I am young. What then?

BEATRIZ—Why then you would be happy.

JUAN—(*intensely*) You promise—? Have you never loved?

BEATRIZ—(*bewildered*) Loved?

JUAN—Since you speak of happiness.

BEATRIZ—I loved my mother—my father—I love you, Don Juan.

JUAN—(*avidly*) Ah, say that again! Those words are blood to my heart!

BEATRIZ—(*earnestly*) I love you as I loved my father—

JUAN—(*brusquely—wounded to the quick*) Has love never stolen into your dreams? You are no nun. Come, tell me the image of the one you dream of as a lover.

BEATRIZ—(*resolved to pass this off jestingly*) It is a great secret. You insist? Well then, it is your double— (*Juan utters a cry of joy, bending toward her. She adds hastily*) You as my mother described you in the wars before Granada.

JUAN—(*bitterly*) When I had youth. But I loved only glory then. Did she not tell you that?

BEATRIZ—Why then—that is why she said, bring him tenderness.

JUAN—(*somberly*) You have fulfilled her wish—or was it her revenge? (*then abruptly*) And what if I should myself become that double?—the knight of Granada with your gift of tenderness—what then?

BEATRIZ—(*frightened by his strangeness*) Ah, now, you are jesting, Don Juan. (*She forces a laugh.*)

JUAN—(*passionately*) No, Beatriz! (*She instinctively shrinks away from him. He calms himself.*) No more now. I fear your laughter. First let the consummation— Then you will not laugh. You— (*trying to read her mystified eyes—miserably uncertain*) What will you do?

BEATRIZ—(*controlling her timidity—softly persuasive*) You are ill, Don Juan. Will you listen to my cure for you?

JUAN—Yes.

BEATRIZ—(*with energy*) Sail and find Cathay!

JUAN—(*with a start, tormentedly*) You, too, condemn me! But I swear to you I have longed to go! I have hated my own cowardice! I have played the traitor to every dream, every great hope— But, Beatriz, when I go, I will leave my life behind with you. So—until I knew—I was afraid of losing what I have— (*then with a quick change to something approaching triumphant decision*) But that is past! My will has risen from the dead. It is decreed by your own lips. I shall sail at once!

BEATRIZ—Oh, I am glad!

JUAN—(*sadly*) Glad I am leaving you?

BEATRIZ—No, I shall be sad and lonely. It is for your own welfare—

JUAN—But promise me one boon—

BEATRIZ—(*eagerly*) Anything!

JUAN—Promise you will not marry until I return—or you hear I am dead?

BEATRIZ—(*confused*) I have never even thought of marrying.

JUAN—(*in deadly earnest in spite of his pitiful pretense at a joking tone*) Until I present my double to you—?

BEATRIZ—(*relieved and laughing easily*) Why, I might change my mind then, Don Juan.

JUAN—Will you seal that pledge with a kiss? (*He forces a smile to conceal his longing.*)

BEATRIZ—(*uncertainly—forcing a laugh*) Yes, Don Juan. (*She lifts her face to him. He starts to kiss her on the lips but something in her face stops him and he ends by kissing her reverentially on the forehead—forcing a smile*)

JUAN—There—upon your forehead—for remembrance. The other—for tenderness—is still a promise of my dream. (*There is a sound of hurrying steps and Juan moves away from Beatriz guiltily. Luis enters from the rear. His face is agitated, full of alarm and anxiety.*)

BEATRIZ—(*greeting him eagerly, glad of the interruption*) Father Luis.

LUIS—Juan! I bring you terrible news. (*He sees Juan's drawn sword.*) Ah, you know! It is time you drew your sword.

JUAN—(*scornfully*) You mean the scum rises? When I tell them the fleet sails tomorrow—

LUIS—Will you give them Nano to burn at the stake? That is their first demand. (*Beatriz gives a horrified cry.*)

JUAN—(*stunned—unbelievingly*) Surrender Nano? No, it is impossible. You have heard rumors—

LUIS—Quesada has roused their cruelty to frenzy. (*He points to where a red glow is mounting up in the sky.*) See! They are burning the Indian quarter. May God have mercy!

JUAN—(*in a rage*) Kill Nano? The curs! I shall order a company of my guard—

LUIS—(*looking at him pityingly*) Your guard is leading the mob! (*reproachfully*) Juan, Juan, why have you lived in a dream! I warned you time after time. If you had been governor in anything but name—

JUAN—(*sinking on the bench—stupidly*) Call the guard. I must order them to disperse.

BEATRIZ—(*pityingly*) His mind is sick—

LUIS—(*rather peremptorily*) Will you leave us, Beatriz?

BEATRIZ—(*obediently*) Yes, Father. (*then excitedly*) I must see Bishop Menendez— (*She hurries out, right.*)

LUIS—(*comes and slaps Juan on the back—sternly*) Juan! Awake, in God's name!

JUAN—(*startled to action, springs to his feet*) I shall protect his life with my own!

LUIS—In order to torture him yourself?

JUAN—(*vehemently but guiltily*) A lie! (*suspicious—resentfully*) Have you seen him? I gave orders—

LUIS—It is weeks since I was permitted to see him; and you have avoided meeting me. Why?

JUAN—(*harshly*) I have no patience with your converting.
I need Nano as he is.

LUIS—Because you prefer his heathen myths—

JUAN—(*controlling an outburst of rage*) Myths? Why myths?
Cathay is there. (*He points.*)

LUIS—I was not speaking of Cathay. You are sailing tomorrow? Does this mean you have finally wrung from this
poor Indian's agonies a faith in magic fountains—?

JUAN—(*losing control of himself—raging*) Fool! You are like
those dullards who, when Columbus said the earth was
round, brayed at him for blaspheming! Listen to me! I do not
believe Nano, I believe in Nature. Nature is part of God. She
can perform miracles. Since this land was discovered have we
not found wonders undreamed of before? The points in
Nano's story hold true to the facts we know. His home is a
beautiful mainland—"A land of flowers," in his own words.
Is not Cathay also known as the "Flowery Land"? There are
great walled cities with roofs of gold inland to the West. Is
not that Marco Polo's land beyond all doubt? And the fountain is in Cathay. All the evidence from around the world
proves that! And I shall find it!

LUIS—(*pityingly*) But this evidence is merely fable, legend,
the dreams of poets!

JUAN—(*furiously*) Have praying and fasting made you an
imbecile? What evidence had Columbus? And you—you believe Christ lived and died. Well, have you talked with men
who saw Him in the manger, or on the cross?

LUIS—Juan, this is blasphemy!

JUAN—(*with bitter despair*) Then let it be! I have prayed to
Him in vain.

LUIS—Juan!

JUAN—(*with all the power of his will in the words*) Let me be
damned forever if Nature will only grant me youth upon this
earth again!

LUIS—(*horrified*) Juan! You defy your God!

JUAN—There is no God but Love—no heaven but youth!

LUIS—(*looks at his tortured face intently—suddenly realizes
—in a tone of great pity*) So that is it—I have been blind. I
thought your love saw in her—a child, a daughter!

JUAN—(*intensely*) A child—yes—for a time—but one

morning standing by the fountain she was a woman. More than a woman! She was the Spirit of Youth, Hope, Ambition, Power to dream and dare! She was all that I had lost. She was Love and the Beauty of Love! So I loved her, loved her with all the intensity of Youth's first love—when youth was dead! Oh, it was monstrous folly, I admit. I called myself a senile fool! I suffered with the damned. I lived in hell without the recompense of being dead! And I loved her more—and more! (*His head sinks down on his hands. A great sob racks his whole body.*)

LUIS—(*overcome by compassion, his voice trembling*) Old friend—God in His Mercy have pity on you! (*He is interrupted by the hurried entrance of Beatriz from the right.*)

BEATRIZ—(*indignantly*) Bishop Menendez says he can do nothing—that you must give Nano up! (*The angry tumult of a mob marching is heard from the distance. Frightenedly*) Listen! Oh, Don Juan, you will save him, will you not?

JUAN—(*starting up—in a voice in which rage and apprehension are blended*) I must! (*He listens to the rising murmur of the mob. As he does so his whole body stiffens into defiant determination. He becomes in an instant the commander again.*) Cowardly rabble! (*He springs to the entrance on the left and shouts to the soldier on guard*) Bring Nano! (*He comes back to where Beatriz and Luis are standing and looks around the courtyard as if measuring his position.*) I shall face them here. Take Beatriz away, Luis.

BEATRIZ—I wish to stay with you!

MENENDEZ—(*enters from the right*) Juan! (*seeing his drawn sword—apprehensively*) What? You will defy them? Then you are lost! Yield to them, I advise you. Give Nano to justice. (*While he is speaking Nano is half carried in by the soldiers. He is limp and exhausted.*)

JUAN—(*with wild scorn*) Ah, High Priest! Deliver him up, eh?

MENENDEZ—Juan! You are impious! (*angrily*) It is sacrilege—to compare this Indian dog—you mock our Blessed Savior! You are cursed—I wash my hands—His will be done! (*He turns and strides back into the house, right.*)

LUIS—(*at a nearer roar from the mob*) Juan! Escape! There is still time—

JUAN—Run from jackals! Is my honor dead?

LUIS—(*as a smashing battering sounds from outside*) They are at the outer gate! Come, Beatriz, in God's name! (*She struggles but he succeeds in getting her as far as the entrance, right. A last crashing smash is heard as the outer gate gives way. A moment later the advance guard of the mob pour in—all of the lower rabble, these. Some wave torches above their heads. All are armed with pikes, knives, and various crude weapons that they have picked up or stolen.*)

JUAN—(*in a roar of command*) Back! (*They hesitate for a moment. Then they see Nano and with yells of fury rush for him around the fountain. Juan springs to meet them. With quick thrusts and cuts of his sword he kills or wounds four of the foremost, who drop to the ground. The rest fall back frightened and awed for the moment. In this lull the remainder of the mob pour in from the rear, crowding and jostling each other. They are a non-descript crowd, ranging from nobles, richly dressed, soldiers, sailors, to the riff-raff of the criminal element in bright-colored rags. There are a number of monks among them, Franciscans who urge them on, a few Dominicans who plead for restraint.*)

THE MOB—Don Juan! It's the Governor—push back there!— To the flames with the Indian dog! Seize him! Stand aside, Don Juan! Heretic! He's bewitched! The dog refused baptism! Torture!

JUAN—(*sternly*) I will kill the man who touches this Indian! (*He walks up and down before them, his sword ready to thrust, looking from eye to eye—scathingly*) Scoundrels! Where is your valor now? Prick up your courage! (*mockingly*) Come! Who wishes to die?

A NOBLE—We demand justice! (*Yells of approval from the crowd. They push in closer. Juan levels his sword at the breast of the nearest who springs back with a frightened cry. The mob sways and surges, close packed and indecisive, cowed by Juan's eyes.*)

QUESADA—(*suddenly pushing his way to the front of the crowd—pointing at Nano, frantically*) Give him up! You are bewitched! (*The mob are again aroused. There are cries of* "To the stake! Torture!" *etc.*)

JUAN—No! (*Yells of rage. The mob surges forward. Juan raises his sword.*) I will kill the first one who— (*They recoil again, all but Quesada. With his free hand Juan sweeps him to*

one side contemptuously—then fiercely threatening the crowd)
Will you rebel against the Governor of your King? Then you
are traitors to Spain! And, by God's blood, I will hang one
of you on every tree! (*The crowd gives way by inches, sullenly,
their yells reduced for the moment to a rebellious muttering:* "The
King will remove you! Hang the Indians! Hang them! Hang
Nano!" *etc.*)

A SOLDIER—We mean no harm to you, Don Juan. Keep
your word to us. Order the fleet to sail. (*a yell of acclamation
from the soldiers and sailors*)

QUESADA—And give over that dog! The Inquisition shall
know you protect infidels!

JUAN—I am Spain's soldier, not the Inquisition's! Soldiers
and sailors! I tell you it is in Spain's service this Indian's life
is spared. The fleet sails tomorrow—and we need Nano to
pilot our voyage! (*A tumult from the bewildered crowd. Shouts
of various nature:* "The fleet sails! Tomorrow! Hurrah! He jokes!
He mocks us! Spare him? No luck with a heathen on board!
What does he mean? Guide us? No! The curse of the Church!"
*But the mob is puzzled, blundering, and Juan continues with a
sort of condescension as if he were speaking to children.*) Silence!
Since you are so stupid, I must explain. This Nano was born
on the mainland—Cathay!—our goal, do you understand?—
and I have put off sailing while I questioned him. We must have
his knowledge. He must be our pilot. (*with a fierce glance at
Nano as if to let his threat strike home*) And if he fails in his
promise to me, I will gladly give him to you for punishment.

QUESADA—(*furiously*) You say this to save him!

JUAN—Soldiers, sailors, I appeal to you! Can this mad
monk lead you to conquest? You must decide between us.
(*The crowd are all turning his way, becoming greedily enthusiastic. Juan sees the psychological moment to play a trump card.*) But
to convince you finally, listen to Nano. Speak, Nano! Tell
them what you told me—of the golden cities. Speak! (*Then
under cover of the crowd's shouts of* "Down with the dog! Torture! Hear! Let him speak! Don Juan says let him!" *etc., he
adds in a fierce whisper to the Indian*) If you wish ever to see
your home again!

NANO—(*mechanically, in a clear monotonous voice, with
expressionless face*) A big land—far mighty cities—gold—

JUAN—You hear? The cities of gold! (*The crowd murmurs excitedly.*)

NANO—There is much gold. The houses have gold on them.

A SOLDIER—Cipango! We'll storm their cities for them!

A SAILOR—Loot, my bullies!

JUAN—Glory and gold for all of you! And now go! (*The crowd are jubilant. Shouts of* "Up anchor! Ahoy Cathay! At last! We sail! Sack! Riches! Gold!" *etc. Juan shouts above the tumult*) Go! Disperse! Tomorrow we sail! (*A voice cries,* "Long live Don Juan!" *The whole mob takes it up. Juan begins to give way under the strain—wearily*) Go. Go.

THE MOB—(*led by a sailor, takes up a sort of chanty song in mighty chorus, dancing wildly, waving their torches, crowding out, rear*)

> The Cities of Gold
> In far Cathay—
> Their great Khan is old,
> And his wealth untold
> In prize for our bold
> Who sail away.
> Aye!
> His gold for our bold who sail away!!

BEATRIZ—(*as the last of the mob disappear—rushing up to Juan with great admiration*) You have saved him! What they have said of you is true indeed—lion by nature as well as name!

JUAN—(*bitterly*) Lion? No! Tricky politician! If I had been the Juan of long ago, I would not have plead or bargained with such curs. I would have— (*He raises his sword threateningly—then lets his arm sink limply. The sword slips from his fingers and falls to the ground.*)

BEATRIZ—(*kneels quickly and presents its hilt to him*) I give you back your sword—to bring good fortune. Now you must find the golden cities!

JUAN—(*taking it—longingly*) I care only for the one, Beatriz—the golden city of Youth, where you are queen. (*She looks into his face smilingly, mystified as—*

The Curtain Falls)

SCENE SEVEN

SCENE—*Four months later—a strip of beach on the Florida coast—a bright, moonlight night. The forest runs diagonally from right, front, to left, rear—a wall of black shadow. The sand gleams a pallid white in the moonlight. The rhythmic ebb and flow of waves is heard—their voice on a windless night of calm.*

As the curtain rises, an Indian is discovered, standing in the moonlight, just out of the shadow of the forest. He is old, but still erect and warrior-like, a chief by his demeanor. His body, naked save for a piece of deerskin at his waist, is elaborately painted, as is his face. A knot of feathers is in his hair. A tomahawk and flint knife are at his waist. He is motionless and silent as a statue, one hand clasping his unslung bow as if it were a staff, but he peers intently at some object in the ocean before him. Finally, he gives an ejaculation of surprise and makes a motion of summons to the forest behind him. The Medicine Man glides out of the darkness to his side. This latter is incredibly old and shrunken, daubed with many insignia in paint, wearing many ornaments of bone and shell. They confer together in low tones with much pantomime. A man is evidently swimming toward them from some strange object out at sea. Other Indians steal from the forest, form a group in the shadow behind the two, point out to sea, gesticulate. At a sharp command from the Chief, they unsling their bows, fit arrows to strings, crouch in an ambush in the shadow. The Chief does likewise and stands waiting, prepared for what may come. Nano walks up the beach from front, left. His naked body glistens with drops of water. He sees the Chief and stops, raising his right hand above his head. The Chief makes a sign. The other Indians dart from their ambush and surround Nano.

CHIEF—Bind him.

NANO—(*calmly*) Is a brother an enemy? (*They all start with surprise at hearing their own language. Nano goes on.*) This is the land of my fathers. I am Nano, a son of Boanu, who was a chief. (*They all stare at him. The Chief makes a sign to the Medicine Man, who comes forward and examines Nano's face intently.*)

MEDICINE MAN—His words are truth. He is Nano—or

an evil spirit in his body. (*He shakes a charm at him.*) Are you from the Land of the Dead?

NANO—I am of the living. They did not chain me. They think I fear the sea. I come to warn you. I swam from the great canoes. They are the warships of the Spaniards.

CHIEF—(*mystified*) What are Spaniards? Their winged canoes are like the boats of Gods.

NANO—These are no Gods. They are men who die from wounds. Their faces are white, but they are evil. They wear shirts that arrows cannot pierce. They have strange sticks that spit fire and kill. Their devils make them strong. But they are not true warriors. They are thieves and rapers of women.

CHIEF—Have they no God?

NANO—(*with scorn*) Their God is a thing of earth! It is this! (*He touches a gold ornament that the Chief wears.*)

MEDICINE MAN—(*mystified*) Gold? Gold is sacred to the Sun. It can be no God itself.

NANO—(*contemptuously*) They see only things, not the spirit behind things. Their hearts are muddy as a pool in which deer have trampled. Listen. Their Medicine Men tell of a God who came to them long ago in the form of a man. He taught them to scorn things. He taught them to look for the spirit behind things. In revenge, they killed him. They tortured him as a sacrifice to their Gold Devil. They crossed two big sticks. They drove little sticks through his hands and feet and pinned him on the others—thus. (*He illustrates. A murmur of horror and indignation goes up among them.*)

MEDICINE MAN—To torture a God! How did they dare?

NANO—Their devils protected them. And now each place they go, they carry that figure of a dying God. They do this to strike fear. They command you to submit when you see how even a God who fought their evil was tortured. (*proudly*) But I would not.

MEDICINE MAN—(*suspiciously*) If you defied them, how are you alive?

NANO—I am craftier than they. They have an old chief who is cursed with madness. Him I told of the Spring of Life. I said I would find it for him.

MEDICINE MAN—Only the Gods can reveal it. Why have you told this lie?

NANO—(*fiercely*) Revenge! I have made a plan. Is there a spring near?

CHIEF—(*mystified*) Yes. In the forest.

NANO—(*with satisfaction*) Good! Listen. This mad chief is the mightiest among them. Without him they would turn cowards. Tomorrow night I will lead him to the spring. You must lie hidden. We will kill him there. Is this clear?

CHIEF—Yes.

NANO—I will swim back now. I escaped to tell you of my plan and warn you. They would lay waste your land as they did mine. They killed my wives and children. They burned. They tortured. They chained warriors neck to neck. They beat them with a whip to dig in the fields like squaws. This old chief led them. My heart is fire. Until he dies, it will know no peace.

CHIEF—I begin to feel your hatred.

NANO—Then remember to hide by the spring.

CHIEF—We will not forget.

NANO—It is well. (*He turns and strides down to the sea. They stand watching him in silence.*)

MEDICINE MAN—(*uneasily, thoughtful*) Only devils could build great canoes that fly with wings. My brothers, they are evil spirits. Nano has made war with them. They have beaten him. Can we trust his plan?

CHIEF—What is your counsel?

MEDICINE MAN—I have heard the voice of the Great Spirit speaking in the night. Let us first try to propitiate their devils.

CHIEF—I do not know how to war with devils. That is your duty. Let us summon the council. (*He makes a sign at which his followers disappear silently into the wood. He and the Medicine Man follow as*—

The Curtain Falls)

SCENE EIGHT

SCENE—*The same. High noon of the following day*—*glaring sunlight on the beach, an atmosphere of oppressive heat and languor. The earth seems dead, preserved in some colorless, molten fluid. The forest is a matted green wall. The sound of the sea has the quality of immense exhaustion.*

On the beach, a sort of makeshift altar is being erected—two round boulders supporting a flat slab of rock. On top of the slab is placed a shallow bowl made of bark. A group of Indians, under the direction of the Medicine Man, are hurriedly putting on the finishing touches to this shrine. They keep casting awed apprehensive glances seaward. The Medicine Man is binding two branches of a tree together in the form of a cross. All the Indians are feathered and painted as for an unusual solemn occasion.

THE INDIANS—(*their eyes on the sea as they work—frightenedly*) The small canoes leave the great winged ones. They are coming! The sun gleams on their shirts that arrows cannot pierce. Their fire-sticks glitter in the sun. Their faces are turned. Their faces are pale! They are watching us!

MEDICINE MAN—(*finishing his work*) Keep your hearts brave! (*giving the cross to two Indians*) Here. This is their totem pole. Stand it there. (*They dig a hole in the sand before the altar and set the cross there; but they make the mistake of setting it head down. The Medicine Man grunts with satisfaction.*) They will think we adore the same devil. They will leave us in peace.

INDIAN—(*his eyes on the sea*) The last canoe has left the great ships. (*He gives a cry of fear echoed by the others.*) Aie! Fire and smoke! (*They cower. The hollow boom of a cannon fired in salute reverberates over the sea. They all shrink with terror, bowing their heads.*)

INDIAN—(*awe-struck*) The Thunder fights with them!

INDIAN—They are white Gods!

MEDICINE MAN—(*frightened himself, but rallying his followers sternly*) You have the hearts of squaws. Quick! Where is the gold? (*An Indian comes to him with an earthenware vessel. He empties it out on the bowl on the top of the altar. It is full of gold nuggets of different sizes. They form a heap glowing in the sun.*)

INDIANS—They come! They come!

MEDICINE MAN—(*sternly*) Pretend to worship their gold

devil but pray to our Great Father, the Sun. He can defeat all devils. Pray to him! (*An Indian starts to beat rhythmically on the small drum. The Medicine Man lifts his shrill voice in the first strains of the chant. Immediately the others all join in as if hypnotized.*) Great Father, Mighty One, Ruler of Earth. Maker of Days. Ripener of the Corn. Creator of Life. Look down upon us out of your Sky-Tent. Let our song rise to you. Let it enter your heart. Mighty One, hear us. Hide not your face in clouds. Bless us at the dawn. And at the day's end. (*They form a circle and dance about the altar, their eyes raised to the sun overhead. Their chant hides the noise of the Spaniards landing. Then the Spaniards appear from the left, front. First comes Juan, his face wild and haggard, his eyes obsessed. He is accompanied by Luis. Following him are a squad of soldiers, guarding Nano, who is in chains. Then come four Franciscan monks, led by Quesada, who wears a sword and pistol over his robe. The others carry crosses. Following them is a group of nobles, richly dressed. Then come ranks of soldiers. They all stare at this Indian ceremony with contemptuous scorn.*)

JUAN—(*irritably*) Make them cease their accursed noise, Luis. Let Nano speak to them.

LUIS—(*advancing toward the Indians—in a loud but friendly voice, raising his right hand*) Peace, brothers. (*The Indians stop, petrified, staring with awe at the white men. The Medicine Man lifts his right hand and advances a step toward Luis. Quesada notices the cross, utters a furious exclamation, strides forward to verify his suspicion. When he sees that it is indeed upside down his face grows livid with fury.*)

QUESADA—The cross head down! The black mass! (*He pulls out his pistol.*) Blaspheming dog! (*He fires. The Medicine Man falls. The other Indians who have shrunk back toward the woods in terror at his first move, now turn tail in panic and flee.*)

LUIS—(*in horror*) Stop, Quesada! (*Quesada pulls up the cross and is setting it back upright when the Medicine Man, by a last dying effort, draws his knife, and writhing to his feet, plunges it into Quesada's back. They both fall together, the Indian dead. Quesada shudders and is still. A yell of rage goes up from the Spaniards. They rush forward toward the woods as if to pursue the Indians but Juan shouts a command.*)

JUAN—Halt! Fools! (*They stop prudently but sullenly. Juan turns to Luis, who is kneeling beside Quesada.*) Is he dead?

LUIS—Yes. (*crossing himself*) May his soul rest in peace. (*All echo this, crossing themselves.*)

JUAN—An eye for an eye, a tooth for a tooth. (*mockingly*) And now it is his eye, his tooth. (*then with a shudder*) Take him away. This is a bloody baptism for Cathay. (*turning to Nano as the soldiers carry the bodies aside*) Is this the land, Nano?

NANO—(*his eyes smoldering with hate*) Yes.

JUAN—You said it was a wonder land—a land of flowers. I see no flowers.

NANO—(*in a sinister tone*) In the forest—flowers grow by a spring—

JUAN—(*harshly—with an apprehensive glance about*) Silence!

A NOBLE—(*from the group that has been stirring impatiently*) Your Excellency. The banners of Castile and Aragon wait on your pleasure.

JUAN—(*making a confused gesture as if wiping cobwebs from his brain*) Yes—yes—I must take possession. Bring the banners. (*He kneels on one knee. They all do likewise.*) In the name of Jesus Christ, Our Lord, and of his most gracious Majesty, the sovereign of Castile and Aragon, I do hereby annex to his dominions this land and all its environs. And I call the land Florida. (*He bends and kisses the sand. The banners are planted in the ground, where they hang motionless from their poles. Juan, having made this effort, seems to fall into a stupor.*)

A NOBLE—(*in a mocking whisper*) A pretty name!

A NOBLE—He has grown imbecile. Will he go spring-hunting here, too? My faith, with all the water he has drunk in the past four months, he must be flooded. (*They all snicker at this.*)

A NOBLE—(*impatiently*) Will he never get off his knees and let us rise?

LUIS—(*sensing what is going on behind their backs—to Juan—who seems to be praying with bowed head—plucking his sleeve*) Juan! Come!

JUAN—(*vaguely*) I was praying—to what God, who knows? (*He rises to his feet weakly. At this, they all rise.*)

A NOBLE—(*pointing excitedly*) Look! In that bowl on the

stones. Is it not gold? (*They all rush forward to the altar. The noble picks up a piece of it—his voice hoarse with greedy triumph*) Gold! (*They all grab at the bowl, upsetting its contents on the sand. They bend down and clutch for it crying*) Gold! This must be a rich land! There must be more! The Golden Cities are near! Cathay at last! (*The soldiers forget discipline, break ranks, form a disorderly, pushing crowd about their leaders. Even the monks edge forward inquisitively.*)

LUIS—(*urgently*) Juan! Look! This is disgraceful!

JUAN—(*coming to himself with a start—in a furious tone of command*) Get back to your ranks! A brave example you set, nobles of Spain! (*His personality is compelling. They all slink to their former order again, muttering rebelliously. Juan seems suddenly seized with a wild exultation.*) Cathay! We have found Cathay! This is the land—the Flowery Land! Our dreams lie hidden here! Sing the Te Deum! Sing! (*There is an oppressive silence for a moment, in which the heat, the sun glaring on the beach, the green of the forest, all nature seems to lay upon these men a mysterious spell, a sudden exhausted recognition of their own defeat. Then the Franciscan monks raise their voices mechanically and spiritlessly in the Te Deum. Other listless voices gradually join theirs as—*

The Curtain Falls)

Scene Nine

SCENE—*About midnight—in the forest. Gigantic tree-trunks, entwined with vines in flower, are in the foreground. Festoons of Spanish moss hang clear to the ground from the branches. Through the network one sees a circular clearing, grass-grown, flooded with moonlight. There is the soft murmur of a spring which bubbles from the ground in the center of this open space. Indians are crouched in ambush among the trees, motionless, their eyes fixed on the clearing.*

The stillness is broken by the whistled call of a bird. The Indians stir alertly. One of them whistles in answer to the call. An Indian creeps swiftly in from the left. The Chief comes from his place of ambush to meet him.

CHIEF—He comes?

INDIAN—He has entered the forest.

CHIEF—I will give Nano the signal when we are ready. Go. Hide. (*The Indian takes a place with the others. The Chief fits an arrow to his bow and crouches in the shadow. There is a pause of silence—then the noise of someone pushing his way through the woods at the rear of the clearing. Nano appears there, followed by Juan.*)

JUAN—Why do you stop?

NANO—This is the place.

JUAN—(*looking around him disappointedly*) This?

NANO—There is the spring.

JUAN—(*stepping forward to look at it—with growing anger*) It looks a common spring like any other. Beware, dog! In these past months you have shown me many springs—

NANO—(*quickly*) The voyage was long. There were many islands. You forced me to lead you to a spring on each. But I told you the Spring of Life was here.

JUAN—I feared your revenge might lie. (*relapsed into a mood of somber preoccupation—bitterly*) I drank of every one. I closed my eyes. I felt the stirring of rebirth. Fool! Always the mirror in the spring showed me the same loathsome blighted face— (*He groans—then with a harsh laugh*) A sacred grove, the legend says! Some of those springs bubbled from sandy water! Beautiful maidens? There were none. At one place I found an old hag filling her bowl, who drank and mumbled at me. (*then in a harsh tone of command*) Nano! I command you to tell me if you have lied. (*distractedly*) I must have certainty, be it of faith or despair!

NANO—This is the spring.

JUAN—(*looking around him*) But where are the trees with golden fruit, the maidens, the fountain—? (*bewildered, staring—grasping at hope*) And yet—this spot has singular beauty. I feel enchantment. But why do I shudder? (*A low whistled signal comes from the Chief hidden on the edge of the clearing. Juan starts.*) Sssh! What was that?

NANO—A bird. (*insistently*) It is a magic spring. Drink!

JUAN—(*bending over the spring*) A mirror of moonlight. The dead eyes of a corpse stare back in mine. (*He kneels by the spring as if fascinated.*) I dare not drink. To whom can I pray? Beatriz! Oh, to hear your voice once more, to see your face! And yet I see you everywhere. Your spirit inspires all things wherever there is beauty. I hear you call in the song of the waves, the wind is your breath, the trees reach out with your arms, the dawn and sunset promise with your lips! You are everywhere and nowhere—part of all life but mine! (*He breaks off, turning distrustful, harried eyes on the impatient Nano—bitterly*) I am a spectacle for laughter, eh? A grotesque old fool!

NANO—(*in a fierce tone of command*) Drink!

JUAN—(*hectically—goading himself to action*) The test. Spirit of Eternal Youth, I pray to you! Beatriz! (*He bends down and drinks. As he does so Nano darts away from him to the woods in front.*)

NANO—(*hurriedly*) Kill when he stands again! (*The Indians can be seen raising their bows, taking aim.*)

JUAN—(*having drunk, remains kneeling by the spring—in a trembling tone of hesitating joy*) New life thrills in me! Is it youth? Do I dream? Then let me never wake till the end of time! (*then harshly*) Coward! How often have you looked death in the face. Are you afraid of life? Open! Open and see! (*He opens his eyes and stares down into the spring. A terrible groan tears from his breast.*) O God! (*His grief is turned immediately into a frenzy of rage.*) Treacherous dog. You betrayed me. (*He leaps to his feet, drawing his sword. There is a twanging of many bows, the whiz of a flight of arrows. Juan falls, clutches at the grass, is still. The Indians pour out into the clearing but keep a cautious distance from Juan.*)

NANO—(*With more courage than they, he bends down over the body.*) He wore no shining shirt. He is dead. (*He does a wild dance of savage triumph beside the body—then stops as suddenly.*) Quick. To their camp. The great Spirit has made them helpless. Be brave and kill! (*He runs swiftly into the woods, followed by the whole band, brandishing their weapons. There is a pause. Then the fierce yells of the savages as they fall upon the sleeping camp, the howls of terror of the Spaniards, the screams of the dying, a few futile musket-shots.*)

(*The Curtain Falls*)

SCENE TEN

SCENE—*The same clearing in the woods some hours later.
There is no intervening fringe of trees in this scene, the open space
is in full view. The Spring is at center. The wall of forest forms a
semicircular background. As the curtain rises, there is a pitch-
blackness and silence except for the murmur of the Spring. Then
the sound of someone struggling to rise from the ground, falling
back again with a groan of pain. Juan's voice comes out of the
darkness.*

JUAN—(*as if he had just regained consciousness—then with a
groan of rage and pain as memory returns*) Fool! Why did I
look? I might have died in my dream. (*a pause—weakly*) Sleep
seems humming in my ears. Or is it—death!—death, the
Merciful One! (*He stirs and his voice suddenly grows strident.*)
No, No! Why have I lived! To die alone like a beast in the
wilderness? (*with a bitter mocking despair*) O Son of God, is
this Thy justice? Does not the Savior of Man know magna-
nimity? True, I prayed for a miracle which was not Thine. Let
me be damned then, but (*passionately*) let me believe in Thy
Kingdom! Show me Thy miracle—a sign—a word—a second's vision of what I am that I should have lived and died!
A test, Lord God of Hosts! (*He laughs with a scornful bravado.*) Nothing! (*But even as he speaks a strange unearthly light
begins to flood down upon a spot on the edge of the clearing on the
right. Startled in spite of himself*) This light—the moon has
waned— (*Beneath the growing light a form takes shape—a tall
woman's figure, like a piece of ancient sculpture, shrouded in long
draperies of a blue that is almost black. The face is a pale mask
with features indistinguishable save for the eyes that stare straight
ahead with a stony penetration that sees through and beyond
things. Her arms are rigid at her sides, the palms of the hands
turned outward. Juan stares at her, defiance striving with his
awe.*) What are you? (*forcing a sneer*) An angel in answer to
my prayer? (*He cannot control a shudder—tries to calm himself.
He stares at the figure—after a pause, boldly*) Or are you
Death? Why then I have often laughed in your eyes! (*tauntingly*) Off with your mask, coward! (*mockingly but uneasy*) Delightful Lady, you are enigmatic. One must embrace you with

bold arms, tear off your masquerade. That was my pastime once—to play at love as gaming. Were I the Juan of long ago—but you see I am old now and wounded. (*He pauses. The figure is frozen. He asks a bit falteringly*) Are you—Death? Then wait— (*in passionate invocation*) O Beatriz! Let me hear your voice again in mercy of farewell! (*As if in answer to this the voice of Beatriz sings from the darkness*)

VOICE—Love is a flower
   Forever blooming
   Life is a fountain
   Forever leaping
   Upward to catch the golden sunlight
   Upward to reach the azure heaven
   Failing, falling,
   Ever returning,
   To kiss the earth that the flower may live.

JUAN— (*raptly*) Youth! (*As the song is sung, the same mystical light floods down slowly about the Spring, which is transformed into a gigantic fountain, whose waters, arched with rainbows, seem to join earth and sky, forming a shimmering veil, which hides the background of forest. Juan and the figure are left at the edge of this, on the outside. The form of Beatriz appears within as if rising from the spring. She dances in ecstasy—the personified spirit of the fountain. Juan cries with a voice trembling with joy*) The Fountain! Let me drink! (*He tries to drag himself to it but cannot—in anguish*) Must I die—? (*making a furious gesture of defiance at the figure and struggling to rise*) No! I defy you! (*Exhausted, he sinks back crying beseechingly*) Beatriz! (*But she seems not to see or hear him. Juan half sobs in despair*) She will not see! She will not hear! Fountain, cruel as the heart of youth, what mercy have you for the old and wounded? (*He sinks down overcome by weakness. Beatriz vanishes from the fountain. In her place appears the form of a Chinese poet. He is a venerable old man with the mild face of a dreamer and scholar. He carries a block and writes upon it with a brush, absorbed in contemplation. Juan looking up and seeing him—startled*) What are you? (*groping at some clue in his memory*) I know—that night in Granada—the Moor's tale— (*excitedly*) Of the poet from the East who told his father the Fountain lie! Are you not that poisoner of life? (*The poet raises his hand as if in summons. The form of the Moorish minstrel of Scene One appears at his side.*) The Moor! (*raging*) Infidel dog! Your lie has cursed me! (*The form of Nano appears at the other side of the Chinese poet. Juan struggles to reach his sword in a fury.*) Murderer! (*Then his eyes are caught by a fourth figure which materializes beside the Moor. It is Luis as he was in Scene One. With a cry of joy*) Luis—old friend— (*Then as Luis seems neither to see nor hear him, he sinks back helplessly.*) No—another mocking phantom! (*He watches the Chinese poet, who seems to be reading what he has written to all of them.*) See! The dead lie to the living. It passes on—from East to West—round the round world—from old worlds to new—cheating the old and wounded—Ha! (*He laughs harshly and wildly. The Chinese poet takes the Indian by one hand, the Moor by the other. These latter stretch out their hands to Luis, who takes them, thus completing the circle. Beatriz' voice can be heard singing*)

VOICE—Life is a field
　　　　Forever growing
　　　　Beauty a fountain
　　　　Forever flowing
　　　　Upward beyond the source of sunshine
　　　　Upward beyond the azure heaven,
　　　　Born of God but
　　　　Ever returning
　　　　To merge with earth that the field may live.

(*As she sings, the four forms disappear as if they were dissolved in the fountain.*)

JUAN—(*lost in the ecstasy of her song*) Sing on, Youth! (*with a start as the song stops—stupidly*) The ghosts are gone. What is the answer to their riddle? I am no poet. I have striven for what the hand can grasp. What is left when Death makes the hand powerless? (*addresses the figure pitifully, trying to mock*) O Mighty Relaxer of hands, have you no vision for the graspers of earth? (*The figure raises a summoning hand. One by one, within the fountain, solemn figures materialize. First the Chinese poet, now robed as a Buddhist priest; then the Moorish minstrel, dressed as a priest of Islam; and then the Medicine Man as he was in Scene Eight, decked out in all the paint and regalia of his office; lastly, Luis, the Dominican monk of the present. Each one carries the symbol of his religion before him. They appear clearly for a moment, then fade from sight, seeming to dissolve in the fountain. Juan has stared at them with straining eyes—in a bewildered voice)* All faiths—they vanish—are one and equal—within— *(awe and reverence creeping into his voice)* What are you, Fountain? That from which all life springs and to which it must return—God! Are all dreams of you but the one dream? *(bowing his head miserably)* I do not know. Come back, Youth. Tell me this secret! *(For a moment the voice of Beatriz is heard from the darkness.)*

Death is a mist
Veiling sunrise.

(Juan seems to fall into a rapt spell. The form of an old Indian woman appears from the left. She falters forward, a wooden bowl under her arm, as if she were going to fill it at the fountain.)

JUAN—*(recognizing her aghast)* Damned hag! I remember you waited beside a spring to mock me! Begone! *(But the old woman stretches out her hands to him with a mysterious beseeching. Juan shudders—then after a struggle with himself, gets to his feet painfully.)* So be it. Sit here by me. I am old, too—and, poor woman, you cannot fill your bowl there. Come. *(He grasps her hands. In a flash her mask of age disappears. She is Beatriz. Juan gazes at her in an ecstasy—faltering, his mind groping)* Beatriz! Age—Youth— They are the same rhythm of eternal life! *(Without his noticing it, Beatriz recedes from him and vanishes in the Fountain. He raises his face to the sky—with halting joy)* Light comes! Light creeps into my soul! *(Then he sees the figure walk slowly from its place and vanish in the Fountain.)* Death is no more! *(The figure materializes again within the Fountain but this time there is no mask, the face is that of Beatriz, her form grown tall, majestic, vibrant with power. Her arms are raised above her head. Her whole body soars upward. A radiant, dancing fire, proceeding from the source of the Fountain, floods over and envelops her until her figure is like the heart of its flame. Juan stares at this vision for a moment, then sinks on his knees—exultantly)* I see! Fountain Everlasting, time without end! Soaring flame of the spirit transfiguring Death! All is within! All things dissolve, flow on eternally! O aspiring fire of life, sweep the dark soul of man! Let us burn in thy unity! (*Beatriz' voice rises triumphantly*)

VOICE—God is a flower
        Forever blooming
        God is a fountain
        Forever flowing.

(*The song ceases. The light fades. There is darkness. Juan's voice is heard sobbing with happiness.*)

JUAN—O God, Fountain of Eternity, Thou art the All in One, the One in All—the Eternal Becoming which is Beauty! (*He falls unconscious. A pause. Then the faint misty light of the dawn floats over the clearing. Juan is seen lying where he had fallen. There is the noise of someone approaching from the woods in the rear, Luis and a brother Dominican enter from the forest.*)

LUIS—(*seeing Juan*) God be praised! (*He rushes forward and kneels by Juan's body. Juan stirs and groans.*) He moves! Juan! It's Luis! Our friends were murdered. A boat from the fleet is waiting—

JUAN—(*in a dreaming ecstasy*) God—Thou art all—

DOMINICAN—He prays.

LUIS—Delirium. Let us carry him. We'll sail for the nearest settlement—

JUAN—(*as they raise him*) Light! I see and know!

LUIS—It is the dawn, Juan.

JUAN—(*exultantly*) The dawn! (*They carry him out as*

The Curtain Falls)

SCENE ELEVEN

SCENE—*Some months later. The courtyard of a Dominican monastery in Cuba. A crude little home-made fountain is in center. This is the only adornment of the quadrangle of bald, sun-baked earth, enclosed on the left and in the rear by a high white wall, on the right by the monastery building itself. The entrance to this is an arched doorway surmounted by a crucifix of carved wood. Two niches on either side of this door shelter primitive wooden figures of the Holy Family and Saint Dominic. In the*

*wall, center, is another arched door with a cross above it. Beyond
the wall nature can be seen and felt—vivid, colorful, burgeoning
with the manifold, compelling life of the tropics. Palm trees lean
over the wall casting their graceful shadows within. Vines in
flower have climbed to the top and are starting to creep down
inside.*

A sunset sky of infinite depth glows with mysterious splendor.

*As the curtain rises, Juan and the Father Superior are dis-
covered. Juan is asleep, reclining on a sort of improvised invalid's
chair, his cloak wrapped around him, facing the fountain. He is
pale and emaciated but his wasted countenance has gained an
entirely new quality, the calm of a deep spiritual serenity. The
Father Superior is a portly monk with a simple round face, gray
hair and beard. His large eyes have the opaque calm of a rumi-
nating cow's. The door in the rear is opened and Luis enters. He
closes the door carefully and tiptoes forward.*

LUIS—(*in a whisper*) He is sleeping?

FATHER SUPERIOR—As you see, Father.

LUIS—(*looking down at Juan*) How calm his face is—as if
he saw a vision of peace.

FATHER SUPERIOR—It is a blessed miracle he has lived so
long.

LUIS—He has been waiting. (*sadly*) And now, I am afraid
his desire is fulfilled—but not as he dreamed. Rather the cup
of gall and wormwood—

FATHER SUPERIOR—(*mystified*) You mean the caravel
brings him bad tidings?

LUIS—Yes; and I must wake him to prepare his mind.

FATHER SUPERIOR—I will leave you with him. It is near
vesper time. (*He turns and goes into the monastery.*)

LUIS—(*touching Juan on the arm—gently*) Juan, awake.
(*Juan opens his eyes.*) The caravel has anchored.

JUAN—From Porto Rico?

LUIS—Yes.

JUAN—(*with an air of certainty—with exultant joy*) Then
Beatriz is here!

LUIS—(*disturbed—evasively*) There has been a frightful insurrection of the Indians. Diego was killed. (*hastily*) But I will
not trouble you with that. (*then slowly*) Beatriz comes to nurse

you—(*with warning emphasis*)—her second father, those were her words.

JUAN—(*smiling*) You need not emphasize. I know her heart. (*then earnestly*) But I must tell her my truth. (*then with a sort of pleading for assurance*) It is for that I have waited, to tell her of the love I bore her—now—as farewell—when she cannot misunderstand. (*proudly*) My love was no common thing. It was the one time Beauty touched my life. I wish to live in her memory as what she was to me. (*sinking back— with a flickering smile, weakly*) Come, old friend, are you grown so ascetic you deny my right to lay this Golden City— the only one I ever conquered—at the feet of Beauty?

LUIS—(*kindly persuasive*) Silence is better, Juan. You should renounce—

JUAN—(*gently*) All is renounced. But do you begrudge a traveler if he begs a flower from this earth, a last token of the world's grace, to lend farewell the solace of regret?

LUIS—(*more and more troubled*) Juan—I—I speak be-cause—you have suffered—and now—I would not have you suffer more, dear friend. (*then blurting out most brusquely*) The caravel brings you a surprise. Your nephew, Juan, has arrived from Spain and comes from Porto Rico to greet you.

JUAN—(*vaguely*) My nephew? (*The sound of voices comes from inside the monastery.*) Beatriz! (*The Father Superior appears in the doorway ushering in Beatriz and Juan's nephew. They are followed by the Duenna and the nephew's servant, who carries his master's cloak and a lute. During the following scene these two remain standing respectfully by the door-way for a time, then go back into the monastery, the servant leaving the cloak and lute on the ground beside the doorway. The Father Superior retires immediately. Luis, after a clasp of Juan's hand, also withdraws, exchanging greetings as he passes the nephew and Beatriz. Beatriz glows with fulfillment, is very apparently deeply in love. The nephew is a slender, graceful young cavalier. He is dressed richly.*)

BEATRIZ—(*halting a moment with a shocked exclamation as she sees Juan's wasted face—then rushing forward and flinging herself on her knees beside his chair. Hastily*) Don Juan! Oh, this is happiness—to find you still—recovered from your wounds! Oh, I'll say prayers of thanksgiving! (*Impulsively she kisses him.*)

JUAN—(*thrilled—choked—unable to say but one word*) Beatriz! Beatriz!

NEPHEW—(*kneels and kisses Juan's hand. Startled, Juan's eyes search his face keenly, apprehensive of what he, too, plainly sees there.*) I greet you, sir. God grant you may soon be strong again.

JUAN—(*weakly*) Soon—I shall be strong—against all wounds. (*after a pause*) And so your name is Juan, too?

NEPHEW—In your honor. Though I can add no honor to it, I hope to bear it worthily.

JUAN—(*hostility creeping into his tone*) You come out here adventuring?

NEPHEW—I come to serve Spain!

JUAN—(*harshly*) A heart as steeled as your sword. Have you that?

BEATRIZ—(*eagerly—somewhat hurt by Juan's reception*) Oh, he is brave! When the mob tried to storm the palace it was Juan who led the defenders.

JUAN—(*more and more agitated—trying to hide his growing resentment under effusive amiability*) Bravely done! But you have doubtless heard great tales of mountains of jewels—Golden Cities of Cathay—you hope to grow rich.

NEPHEW—(*proudly*) I do not care for riches; and as for Golden Cities, I only wish to plant Spain's banner on their citadels!

JUAN—(*inspired by respect in spite of himself*) Brave dreams! Echoes blown down the wind of years.

BEATRIZ—(*looking at the nephew with great pride as Juan searches her face*) He is as you were in my mother's tales. (*She and the nephew are held by each other's eyes.*)

JUAN—(*after a conquering struggle with his bitterness—fatalistically*) So—thus old heart—in silence. (*then rousing himself—intensely*) But with joy! with joy! (*They look at him in puzzled alarm. He smiles gently at Beatriz.*) Then you have found him at last—my double?

BEATRIZ—(*blushing, confusedly*) I—I do not know, Don Juan.

JUAN—Then I know. (*musing a bit sadly*) You have stolen my last gesture. An old man had a tale to tell you—oh, so brave a tale!—but now he sees that if youth cannot, age must keep its secrets! A sad old ghost to haunt your memory, that would be a poor wedding gift. (*They again look from him to each other, mystified and apprehensive. Juan suddenly looks up at them—with a startling directness*) You love each other! (*He hurries on with feverish gayety.*) Forgive—I'm a rough soldier—and there is need for haste. Quick. Do you not ask my blessing?

BEATRIZ—(*falling on her knees beside him—happily*) Oh, yes, good Don Juan! (*The nephew kneels beside her.*)

JUAN—(*He raises his hands over their heads.*) Youth of this earth—love—hail—and farewell! May you be blessed forever! (*He touches their heads with his hands—then sinks back, closing his eyes. They rise and stand looking down at him uncertainly.*)

NEPHEW—(*after a pause—in a whisper*) He wishes to sleep.

BEATRIZ—(*as they walk apart, in a whisper, the tears in her eyes*) Oh, Juan, I'm afraid—and yet—I am not sad.

NEPHEW—(*takes her in his arms passionately*) My life! My soul! (*He kisses her.*)

BEATRIZ—My love!

NEPHEW—Life is beautiful! The earth sings for us! Let us sing, too! (*He strides over to where the lute is and picks it up.*)

BEATRIZ—(*happily*) Yes— (*then reminded*) Ssshh! (*She points at Juan.*)

NEPHEW—(*urgingly*) He is asleep. We can go out beyond the walls. (*He puts his arms around her and leads her out through the door in rear.*)

JUAN—(*opening his eyes and looking after them, a tender smile on his lips*) Yes! Go where Beauty is! Sing! (*From outside the voices of Beatriz and his nephew are heard mingling in their version of the fountain song.*)

> Love is a flower
> Forever blooming
> Beauty a fountain
> Forever flowing
> Upward into the source of sunshine,

Upward into the azure heaven;
One with God but
Ever returning
To kiss the earth that the flower may live.

(*Juan listens in an ecstasy, bows his head, weeps. Then he sinks back with closed eyes exhaustedly. Luis enters from the monastery.*)

LUIS—(*hurries forward in alarm*) Juan! (*He hears the song and is indignant.*) Have they lost all feeling? I will soon stop— (*He starts for the door in rear.*)

JUAN—(*in a ringing voice*) No! I am that song! One must accept, absorb, give back, become oneself a symbol! Juan Ponce de Leon is past! He is resolved into the thousand moods of beauty that make up happiness—color of the sunset, of tomorrow's dawn, breath of the great Trade wind— sunlight on grass, an insect's song, the rustle of leaves, an ant's ambitions. (*in an ecstasy*) Oh, Luis, I begin to know eternal youth! I have found my Fountain! O Fountain of Eternity, take back this drop, my soul! (*He dies. Luis bows his head and weeps.*)

FATHER SUPERIOR—(*enters from the right*) Vespers. (*then in a voice of awe as he stares at Juan*) Is he—dead?

LUIS—(*aroused—exaltedly*) No! He lives in God! Let us pray. (*Luis sinks on his knees beside Juan's body, the Father Superior beside him. He lifts his eyes and clasped hands to heaven and prays fervently. The voices of Beatriz and the nephew in the fountain song seem to rise to an exultant pitch. Then the chant of the monks swells out, deep and vibrant. For a moment the two strains blend into harmony, fill the air in an all-comprehending hymn of the mystery of life as*

The Curtain Falls)

WELDED

A Play in Three Acts

CHARACTERS

MICHAEL CAPE
ELEANOR
JOHN
A WOMAN

SCENES

ACT I
SCENE: Studio apartment.

ACT II
SCENE I: Library.
SCENE II: Bedroom.

ACT III
SCENE: Same as Act I.

Welded

ACT ONE

SCENE—*Studio apartment. In the rear, a balcony with a stairway at center leading down to the studio floor.*

The room is in darkness. Then a circle of light reveals Eleanor lying back on a chaise longue. She is a woman of thirty. Her figure is tall. Her face, with its high, prominent cheek-bones, lacks harmony. It is dominated by passionate, blue-gray eyes, restrained by a high forehead from which the mass of her dark brown hair is combed straight back. The first impression of her whole personality is one of charm, partly innate, partly imposed by years of self-discipline.

She picks up a letter from the table, which she opens and reads, an expression of delight and love coming over her face. She kisses the letter impulsively—then gives a gay laugh at herself. She lets the letter fall on her lap and stares straight before her, lost in a sentimental reverie.

A door underneath the balcony is noiselessly opened and Michael comes in. (A circle of light appears with him, follows him into the room. These two circles of light, like auras of egoism, emphasize and intensify Eleanor and Michael throughout the play. There is no other lighting. The two other people and the rooms are distinguishable only by the light of Eleanor and Michael.)

Michael is thirty-five, tall and dark. His unusual face is a harrowed battlefield of super-sensitiveness, the features at war with one another—the forehead of a thinker, the eyes of a dreamer, the nose and mouth of a sensualist. One feels a powerful imagination tinged with somber sadness—a driving force which can be sympathetic and cruel at the same time. There is something tortured about him—a passionate tension, a self-protecting, arrogant defiance of life and his own weakness, a deep need for love as a faith in which to relax.

He has a suitcase, hat, and overcoat which he sets inside on the floor, glancing toward Eleanor, trying not to make the slightest noise. But she suddenly becomes aware of some presence in the room and turns boldly to face it. She gives an exclamation of delighted astonishment when she sees Michael and jumps up to meet him as he strides toward her.

ELEANOR—Michael!

CAPE—(*with a boyish grin*) You've spoiled it, Nelly; I wanted a kiss to announce me. (*They are in each other's arms. He kisses her tenderly.*)

ELEANOR—(*joyously*) This *is* a surprise!

CAPE—(*straining her in his arms and kissing her passionately*) Own little wife!

ELEANOR—Dearest! (*They look into each other's eyes for a long moment.*)

CAPE—(*tenderly*) Happy?

ELEANOR—Yes, yes! Why do you always ask? You know. (*suddenly pushing him at arms' length—with a happy laugh*) It's positively immoral for an old married couple to act this way. (*She leads him by the hand to the chaise longue.*) And you must explain. You wrote not to expect you till the end of the week. (*She sits down.*) Get a cushion. Sit down here. (*He puts a cushion on the floor beside the chaise longue and sits down.*) Tell me all about it.

CAPE—(*notices the letter lying on the floor*) Were you reading my letter? (*She nods. He gives a happy grin.*) Do you mean to say you still read them over—after five years of me?

ELEANOR—(*with a tender smile*) Oh—sometimes.

CAPE—Sweetheart! (*smiling*) What were you dreaming about when I intruded?

ELEANOR—Never mind. You're enough of an egotist already. (*her hand caressing his face and hair*) I've been feeling so lonely—and it's only been a few weeks, hasn't it? (*She laughs.*) How was everything in the country? (*suddenly kissing him*) Oh, I'm so happy you're back. (*with mock severity*) But ought I? Have you finished the fourth act? You know you promised not to return until you did.

CAPE—This afternoon!

ELEANOR—You're sure you didn't force it—(*with a tender smile at him*)—because you were lonely, too?

CAPE—(*with a sudden change in manner that is almost stern*) No. I wouldn't. I couldn't. You know that.

ELEANOR—(*her face showing a trace of hurt in spite of herself*)

I was only fooling. (*then rousing herself as if conquering a growing depression*) I'm terribly anxious to hear what you've done.

CAPE—(*enthusiastically*) You'll see when I read you— And you're going to be marvelous! It's going to be the finest thing we've ever done!

ELEANOR—I love you for saying "we." But the "we" is you. I only—(*with a smile of ironical self-pity*)—act a part you've created.

CAPE—(*impetuously*) Nonsense! You're an artist. Each performance of yours has taught me something. Why, my women used to be—death masks. But now they're as alive as you are—(*with a sudden grin*)—at least, when you play them.

ELEANOR—(*her eyes shining with excited pleasure*) You don't know how much it means to have you talk like that! Oh, I'm going to work so hard, Michael! (*impetuously*) You've simply got to read me that last act right now!

CAPE—(*jumping to his feet eagerly*) All right. (*He walks toward his bag—then stops when he is half-way and, hesitating, turns slowly and comes back. He bends down and lifts her face to his—with a smile*) No. I won't.

ELEANOR—(*disappointed*) Oh. Why not, dear?

CAPE—Because—

ELEANOR—Plagiarist!

CAPE—Because I've been hoping for this night as our own. Let's forget the actress and playwright. Let's just be— us—lovers.

ELEANOR—(*with a tender smile—musingly*) We *have* remained lovers, haven't we?

CAPE—(*with a grin*) Fights and all?

ELEANOR—(*with a little frown*) We don't fight so much.

CAPE—(*frowning himself*) Too much.

ELEANOR—(*forcing a smile*) Perhaps that's the price.

CAPE—Don't grow fatalistic—just when I was about to propose reform.

ELEANOR—(*smiling—quickly*) Oh, I'll promise to be good—if you will. (*gently reproachful*) Do you think I enjoy fighting with you?

CAPE—(*with sudden passion*) It's wrong, Nelly. It's evil!

ELEANOR—Ssshh! We promised.

CAPE—(*hesitatingly*) We've been taking each other too

much for granted. That may do very well with the common loves of the world—but ours—! (*He suddenly pulls her head down and kisses her impulsively.*) But you understand! Oh, Nelly, I love you with all my soul!

ELEANOR—(*deeply moved*) And I love you, Michael—always and forever! (*They sit close, she staring dreamily before her, he watching her face.*)

CAPE—(*after a pause*) What are you thinking?

ELEANOR—(*with a tender smile*) Of the first time we met—at rehearsal, remember? I was thinking of how mistakenly I'd pictured you before that. (*She pauses—then frowning a little*) I'd heard such a lot of gossip about your love affairs.

CAPE—(*with a wry grin*) You must have been disappointed if you expected Don Juan. (*a pause—then forcing a short laugh*) I also had heard a lot of rumors about your previous— (*He stops abruptly with an expression of extreme bitterness.*)

ELEANOR—(*sharply*) Don't! (*a pause—then she goes on sadly*) It was only our past together I wanted to remember. (*a pause—then with a trace of scornful resentment*) I was forgetting your morbid obsession—

CAPE—(*with gloomy irritation*) Obsession? Why—? (*then determinedly throwing off this mood—reproachfully forcing a joking tone*) We're not "starting something" now, are we—after our promise?

ELEANOR—(*impulsively pressing his hand*) No, no—of course not!

CAPE—(*after a pause—a bit awkwardly*) But you guessed my desire, at that. I wanted to dream with you in our past—to find there—a new faith—

ELEANOR—(*smiling*) Another Grand Ideal for our marriage?

CAPE—(*frowning*) Don't mock.

ELEANOR—(*teasingly*) But you're such a relentless idealist. You needn't frown. That was exactly what drew me to you in those first days. (*earnestly*) I'd lost faith in everything. Your love saved me. Your work saved mine. I owe you myself, Michael! (*She kisses him.*) Do you remember—our first night together?

CAPE—Do you imagine I could've forgotten?

ELEANOR—(*continuing as if she hadn't heard*) The play was such a marvelous success! I knew I had finally won—through your work! I loved myself! I loved you! You came to me—(*more and more intensely*) Oh, it was beautiful madness! I lost myself. I began living in you. I wanted to die and become you!

CAPE—(*passionately*) And I, you!

ELEANOR—(*softly*) And do you remember the dawn creeping in—and how we began to plan our future? (*She exclaims impulsively*) Oh, I'd give anything in the world to live those days over again!

CAPE—Why? Hasn't our marriage kept the spirit of that time—with a growth of something deeper—finer—

ELEANOR—Yes,—but— Oh, you know what I mean! It was revelation then—a miracle out of the sky!

CAPE—(*insistently*) But haven't we realized the ideal of our marriage— (*smiling but with deep earnestness nevertheless*) Not for us the ordinary family rite, you'll remember! We swore to have a true sacrament—or nothing! Our marriage must be a consummation demanding and combining the best in each of us! Hard, difficult, guarded from the commonplace, kept sacred as the outward form of our inner harmony! (*With an awkward sense of having become rhetorical he adds self-mockingly*) We'd tend our flame on an altar, not in a kitchen range! (*He forces a grin —then abruptly changing again, with a sudden fierce pleading*) It has been what we dreamed, hasn't it, Nelly?

ELEANOR—Our ideal was difficult. (*sadly*) Sometimes I think we've demanded too much. Now there's nothing left but that something which can't give itself. And I blame you for this—because I can neither take more nor give more—and you blame me! (*She smiles tenderly.*) And then we fight!

CAPE—Then let's be proud of our fight! It began with the splitting of a cell a hundred million years ago into you and me, leaving an eternal yearning to become one life again.

ELEANOR—At moments—we do.

CAPE—Yes! (*He kisses her—then intensely*) You and I—year after year—together—forms of our bodies merging into one form; rhythm of our lives beating against each other, forming slowly the one rhythm—the life of Us—created by us!—

beyond us, above us! (*with sudden furious anger*) God, what I feel of the truth of this—the beauty!—but how can I express it?

ELEANOR—(*kissing him*) I understand.

CAPE—(*straining her to him with fierce passion*) Oh, My Own, My Own—and I your own—to the end of time!

ELEANOR—I love you!

CAPE—(*with passionate exultance*) Why do you regret our first days? Their fire still burns in us—deeper! Don't you feel that? (*kissing her again and again*) I've become you! You've become me! One heart! One blood! Ours! (*He pulls her to her feet.*) My wife! Come!

ELEANOR—(*almost swooning in his arms*) My lover— yes— My lover—

CAPE—Come! (*With his arms around her he leads her to the stairway. As they get to the foot, there is a noise from the hall. She hears it, starts, seems suddenly brought back to herself. Cape is oblivious and continues up the stairs. She stands swaying, holding on to the banister as if in a daze. At the top, Cape turns in surprise at not finding her, as if he had felt her behind him. He looks down passionately, stretching out his arms, his eyes glowing.*) Come!

ELEANOR—(*weakly*) Ssshh! A moment— Listen!

CAPE—(*bewilderedly*) What? What is it?

ELEANOR—Ssshh— Listen— Someone— (*She speaks in an unnatural, mechanical tone. A knock comes at the door. She gives a sort of gasp of relief.*) There!

CAPE—(*still bewilderedly as if something mysterious were happening that he cannot grasp*) What—what—? (*then as she takes a slow, mechanical step toward the door—with tense pleading*) Nelly! Come here! (*She turns to look at him and is held by his imploring eyes. She sways irresolutely toward him, again reaching to the banister for support. Then a sharper knock comes at the door. It acts like a galvanic shock on her. Her eyes move in that direction, she takes another jerky step. Cape stammers in a fierce whisper*) No! Don't go!

ELEANOR—(*without looking at him—mechanically*) I must.

CAPE—(*frantically*) They'll go away. Nelly, don't! Don't! (*Again she stops irresolutely like a hypnotized person torn by two conflicting suggestions. The knock is repeated, this time with authority, assurance. Her body reacts as if she were throwing off a load.*)

ELEANOR—(*with a return to her natural tone—but hysterically*) Please—don't be silly, Michael. It might be—something important. (*She hurries to the door.*)

CAPE—(*rushing down the stairs—frantically*) No! No! (*He just gets to the bottom as she opens the door. He stands there fixed, disorganized, trembling all over.*)

ELEANOR—(*as she sees who it is—in a relieved tone of surprise*) Why, hello, John. Come in! Here's Michael. Michael, it's John. (*John steps into the room. He is a man of about fifty, tall, loose-limbed, a bit stoop-shouldered, with iron-gray hair, and a gaunt, shrewd face. He is not handsome but his personality compels affection. His eyes are round and childlike. He has no nerves. His voice is low and calming.*)

JOHN—(*shaking Eleanor by the hand*) Hello, Nelly. I was on my way home from the theater and I thought I'd drop in for a second. Hello, Michael. When'd you get in? Glad to see you back. (*He comes to him and shakes his hand which Cape extends jerkily, as if in spite of himself, without a word.*)

ELEANOR—(*after a glance at her husband—in a forced tone*) We're so glad you've come. Sit down.

JOHN—(*He becomes aware of the disharmonious atmosphere his appearance has created.*) I can't stay a second. (*to Cape*) I wanted some news. I thought Nelly'd probably have heard from you. (*He slaps Cape on the back with jovial familiarity.*) Well, how's it coming?

CAPE—(*in a frozen tone*) Oh,—all right—all right.

ELEANOR—(*uneasily*) Won't you have a cigarette, John? (*She takes the box from the table and holds it out to him.*)

JOHN—(*taking one*) Thanks, Nelly. (*He half-sits on the arm of a chair. She holds out a light to him.*) Thanks.

ELEANOR—(*nervously*) Why don't you sit down, Michael? (*He doesn't answer. She goes to him with the cigarettes.*) Don't you want a cigarette? (*Cape stares at her with a hot glance of scorn. She recoils from it, turning quickly away from him, visibly shaken. Without appearing to notice, John scrutinizes their faces keenly, sizing up the situation.*)

JOHN—(*breaking in matter-of-factly*) You look done up, Michael.

CAPE—(*with a guilty start*) I—I'm tired out.

ELEANOR—(*with a forced air*) He's been working too hard. He finished the last act only this afternoon.

JOHN—(*with a grunt of satisfaction*) Glad to hear it. (*abruptly*) When can I see it?

CAPE—In a day or so—I want to go over—

JOHN—All right. (*getting to his feet*) Well, that's that. I'll run along.

ELEANOR—(*almost frightenedly*) Do stay. Why don't you read us the last act now, Michael?

CAPE—(*fiercely*) No! It's rotten! I hate the whole play!

JOHN—(*easily*) Reaction. This play's the finest thing you've done. (*He comes to Cape and slaps him on the back reassuringly.*) And it's the biggest chance the lady here has ever had. It'll be a triumph for you both, wait and see. So cheer up—and get a good night's rest. (*Cape smiles with bitter irony.*) Well, good-night. (*Cape nods without speaking, John goes to the door, Eleanor accompanying him.*) Good night, Nelly. Better start on your part—only don't you overdo it, too. (*He pats her on the back.*) Good-night.

ELEANOR—Good-night. (*She closes the door after him. She remains there for a moment staring at the closed door, afraid to turn and meet Cape's fiercely accusing eyes which she feels fixed upon her. Finally, making an effort of will, she walks back to the table, avoiding his eyes, assuming a careless air.*)

CAPE—(*suddenly explodes in furious protest*) Why did you do that?

ELEANOR—(*with an assumed surprise but with a guilty air, turning over the pages of a magazine*) Do what?

CAPE—(*tensely, clutching her by the arm*) You know what I mean! (*Unconsciously he grips her tighter, almost shaking her.*)

ELEANOR—(*coldly*) You're hurting me. (*A bit shamefacedly, Cape lets go of her arm. She glances quickly at his face, then speaks with a kind of dull remorse.*) I suppose I can guess—my going to the door?

CAPE—He would've gone away— (*with anguish*) Nelly, why did you?

ELEANOR—(*defensively*) Wasn't it important you see John?

CAPE—(*with helpless anger*) Don't evade! (*with deep feeling*) I should think you'd be ashamed.

ELEANOR—(*after a pause—dully*) Perhaps—I am. (*a pause*) I couldn't help myself.

CAPE—(*intensely*) You should've been oblivious to everything! (*miserably*) I—I can't understand!

ELEANOR—That's you, Michael. The other is me—or a part of me—I hardly understand myself.

CAPE—(*sinking down on a chair, his head in his hands*) After all we'd been to each other tonight—! (*with bitter despondency*) Ruined now—gone—a rare moment of beauty! It seems at times as if some jealous demon of the commonplace were mocking us. (*with a violent gesture of loathing*) Oh, how intolerably insulting life can be! (*then brokenly*) Nelly, why, why did you?

ELEANOR—(*dully*) I—I don't know. (*Then after a pause she comes over and puts her hand on his shoulder.*) Don't brood, dear. I'm sorry. I hate myself. (*A pause. She looks down at him, seeming to make up her mind to something—in a forced tone*) But—why is it gone—our beautiful moment? (*She strokes his hair.*) We have the whole night— (*He stares up at her wonderingly. She forces a smile, half turning away.*)

CAPE—(*in wild protest*) Nelly, what are you offering me—a sacrifice? Please!

ELEANOR—(*revolted*) Michael! (*then hysterically*) No, forgive me! I'm the disgusting one! Forgive me! (*She turns away from him and throws herself on a chair, staring straight before her. Their chairs are side by side, each facing front, so near that by a slight movement each could touch the other, but during the following scene they stare straight ahead and remain motionless. They speak, ostensibly to the other, but showing by their tone it is a thinking aloud to oneself, and neither appears to hear what the other has said.*)

CAPE—(*after a long pause*) More and more frequently. There's always some knock at the door, some reminder of the life outside which calls you away from me.

ELEANOR—It's so beautiful—and then—suddenly I'm being crushed. I feel a cruel presence in you paralyzing me, creeping over my body, possessing it so it's no longer my body—then grasping at some last inmost thing which makes me me—my soul—demanding to have that, too! I have to rebel with all my strength—seize any pretext! Just now at the foot of the stairs—the knock on the door was—liberation. (*in anguish*) And yet I love you! It's because I love you! If I'm destroyed, what is left to love you, what is left for you to love?

CAPE—I've grown inward into our life. But you keep trying to escape as if it were a prison. You feel the need of what is outside. I'm not enough for you.

ELEANOR—Why is it I can never know you? I try to know you and I can't. I desire to take all of you into my heart, but there's a great alien force— I hate that unknown power in you which would destroy me. (*pleadingly*) Haven't I a right to myself as you have to yourself?

CAPE—You fight against me as if I were your enemy. Every word or action of mine which affects you, you resent. At every turn you feel your individuality invaded—while at the same time, you're jealous of any separateness in me. You demand more and more while you give less and less. And I have to acquiesce. Have to? Yes, because I can't live without you! You realize that! You take advantage of it while you despise me for my helplessness! (*This seems to goad him to desperation.*) But look out! I still have the strength to—! (*He turns his head and stares at her challengingly.*)

ELEANOR—(*as before*) You insist that I have no life at all outside you. Even my work must exist only as an echo of yours. You hate my need of easy, casual associations. You think that weakness. You hate my friends. You're jealous of everything and everybody. (*resentfully*) I have to fight. You're too severe. Your ideal is too inhuman. Why can't you understand and be generous—be just! (*She turns to meet his eyes, staring back with resentful accusation. They look at each other in this manner for a long moment.*)

CAPE—(*averting his eyes and addressing her directly in a cold, sarcastic tone*) Strange—that John should pop in on us suddenly like that.

ELEANOR—(*resentfully*) I don't see anything strange about it.

CAPE—It's past twelve—

ELEANOR—You're in New York now.

CAPE—(*sharply*) I'm quite aware of that. Nevertheless—

ELEANOR—(*shortly*) He explained. Didn't you hear him?

He wanted news of the play and thought I might have a letter—

CAPE—That's just the point. He had no idea he would find me here.

ELEANOR—(*about to fly at him, checks herself after a pause, coldly*) Why shouldn't he come to see me? He's the oldest friend I've got. He gave me my first chance and he's always helped me since. I owe whatever success I've made to his advice and direction.

CAPE—(*stung—sarcastically*) Oh, undoubtedly!

ELEANOR—I suppose you think I ought to have said it's to you I owe everything?

CAPE—(*dryly*) I'd prefer to say it was to yourself, and no one else. (*after a pause—attempting a casual tone*) Has he been in the habit of calling here while I've been gone? (*hurriedly*) Don't misunderstand me. I'm merely asking a question.

ELEANOR—(*scornfully*) Oh! (*A pause. She bites her lips—then coldly*) Yes, he's been here once before. (*mockingly*) And after the theater, too! Think of that!

CAPE—(*sneeringly*) The same insatiable curiosity about my play?

ELEANOR—(*angrily*) Michael! (*a pause—then scornfully*) Don't tell me you're becoming jealous of John again!

CAPE—(*meaningly*) Again. That's just it.

ELEANOR—(*springing from her chair—excitedly*) This is insufferable! (*then calming herself with an effort—with a forced laugh*) Please don't be so ridiculous, Michael. I'll only lose my temper if you keep on. (*Then suddenly she makes up her mind and comes to him.*) Please stop, dear. We've made up our minds not to quarrel. Let's drop it. (*She pats his head with a friendly smile.*)

CAPE—(*impulsively takes her hand and kisses it*) All right. Forgive me. I'm all unstrung. His breaking in on us like that— (*He relapses into frowning brooding again. She sits down, this time facing him, and looks at him uneasily.*)

ELEANOR—(*after a pause—rather irritably*) It's too absolutely silly, your being jealous of John.

CAPE—I'm not jealous of him. I'm jealous of you—the something in you that repulses our love—the stranger in you.

ELEANOR—(*with a short laugh*) I should think after five years—

CAPE—(*unheeding*) And what makes me hate you at those times is that I know you like to make me jealous, that my suffering pleases you, that it satisfies some craving in you—for revenge!

ELEANOR—(*scornfully*) Can't you realize how absurd you are? (*then with a forced placating laugh*) No, really, Michael, it'd be funny—if it weren't so exasperating.

CAPE—(*after a pause—somberly*) You mentioned our years together as proof. What of the years that preceded?

ELEANOR—(*challengingly*) Well, what of them?

CAPE—By their light, I have plausible grounds for jealousy in John's case. Or don't you acknowledge that?

ELEANOR—I deny it absolutely!

CAPE—Why, you've told me yourself he was in love with you for years, and that he once asked you to marry him!

ELEANOR—Well, did I marry him?

CAPE—But he still loves you.

ELEANOR—Don't be stupid!

CAPE—He does, I tell you!

ELEANOR—If you had any sense you'd know that his love has become purely that of an old friend. And I refuse to give up his friendship for your silly whims.

CAPE—(*after a pause in which they each brood resentfully—sarcastically*) You were a shining exception, it appears. The other women he helped could hardly claim he had remained—merely their friend.

ELEANOR—(*vehemently*) It's a lie! And even if it were true, you'd find it was they who offered themselves!

CAPE—(*significantly*) Ah! (*then after a pause*) Perhaps because they felt it necessary for their careers.

ELEANOR—(*dryly*) Perhaps. (*then after a pause*) But they discovered their mistake, then. John isn't that type.

CAPE—(*suddenly*) Why do you act so jealous—of those others?

ELEANOR—(*flushing angrily*) I don't. It's your imagination.

CAPE—Then why lose your temper?

ELEANOR—Because I resent your superior attitude that

John had to bribe women to love him. Isn't he as worthy of love—as you are?

CAPE—(*sarcastically*) If I am to believe your story, you didn't think so.

ELEANOR—(*irritably*) Then let's stop arguing, for heaven's sake! Why do you always have to rake up the past? For the last year or so you've begun to act more and more as you did when we first lived together—jealous and suspicious of everything and everybody! (*hysterically*) I can't bear it, Michael!

CAPE—(*ironically*) You used to love me for it then.

ELEANOR—(*calming herself*) Well, I can't endure it now. It's too degrading. I have a right to your complete faith. (*reaching over and grasping his hands—earnestly*) You know I have in your heart of hearts. You know that there can never be anyone but you. Forget the past. It wasn't us. For your peace—and mine, Michael!

CAPE—(*moved—pressing her hands*) All right. Let's stop. It's only that I've thought I've felt you drawing away—! Perhaps it's all my supersensitiveness— (*patting her hand and forcing a smile*) Let's talk of something else. (*cheerfully—after a pause*) You can't imagine how wonderful it's been up in the country. There's just enough winter in the air to make one energetic. No summer fools about. Solitude and work. I was happy—that is, as happy as I ever can be without you.

ELEANOR—(*withdrawing her hands from his with a quick movement—sarcastically*) Thanks for that afterthought—but do you expect me to believe it? When you're working I might die and you'd never know it.

CAPE—(*amused but irritated*) There you go! You denounce my jealousy, but it seems to me your brand of it is much more ridiculous.

ELEANOR—(*sharply*) You imagine I'm jealous of your work? You—you flatter yourself!

CAPE—(*stung—bitingly*) It's an unnatural passion certainly—in your case. And an extremely ungrateful passion, I might add!

ELEANOR—(*losing her temper completely*) You mean I ought to be grateful for— I suppose you think that without your work I— (*springing to her feet*) Your egotism is making a

fool of you! You're becoming so exaggeratedly conceited no
one can stand you! Everyone notices it!

CAPE—(*angrily*) You know that's untrue. You only say it
to be mean. As for my work, you've acknowledged a million
times—

ELEANOR—If I have—but please remember there are
other playwrights in the world!

CAPE—(*bitingly*) You were on the stage seven years before
I met you. Your appearance in the work of other playwrights—you must admit you were anything but successful!

ELEANOR—(*with a sneer of rage*) And I suppose you were?

CAPE—Yes! Not in your commercial sense, perhaps, but—

ELEANOR—You're contemptible! You know that's the very
last thing you can say of me. It was exactly because I wasn't
that kind—because I was an artist—that I found it so hard!

CAPE—(*unheeding*) My plays had been written. The one
you played in first was written three years before. The work
was done. That's the proof.

ELEANOR—(*scathingly*) That's absurd! You know very well
if it hadn't been for John, you—

CAPE—(*violently*) Nonsense! There were other managers
who—

ELEANOR—They didn't want your work, you know it!

CAPE—(*enraged*) I see what you're driving at! You'd like
to pretend I was as much dependent on John as you were!
(*trembling all over with the violence of his passion*) I should think
you'd be ashamed to boast so brazenly—to me!—of what he
had done for you!

ELEANOR—Why should I be ashamed of my gratitude?

CAPE—To drag that relationship out of the past and throw
it in my face!

ELEANOR—(*very pale—tensely*) What relationship?

CAPE—(*incoherently, strangled by his passion*) Ask anyone!
(*then suddenly with anguished remorse*) No, no! I don't mean
that! (*torturedly*) Wounds! Wounds! For God's sake!

ELEANOR—(*trembling with rage*) I'll never forget you said
that!

CAPE—(*stung—in a passion again at once*) Because I resent
that man's being here—late at night—when I was away? Oh,
I don't mean I suspect you—now—

ELEANOR—(*viciously*) What noble faith! Maybe you're going to discover I don't deserve it!

CAPE—(*unheeding*) But there was scandal enough about you and him, and if you had any respect for me—

ELEANOR—I've lost it now!

CAPE—You wouldn't deliberately open the way—

ELEANOR—(*tensely*) So you believe—that gutter gossip? You think I—? Then all these years you've really believed—? Oh, you mean hypocrite!

CAPE—(*stung—bitingly*) Don't act moral indignation! What else could I have thought? When we first fell in love, you confessed frankly you had had lovers—not John but others—

ELEANOR—(*brokenly—with mingled grief and rage*) I was an idiot! I should have lied to you! But I thought you'd understand—that I'd been searching for something—that I needed love—something I found in you! I tried to make you see—the truth—that those experiences had only made me appreciate you all the more when I found you! I told you how little these men had meant to me, that in the state of mind I had been in they had no significance either one way or the other, and that such an attitude is possible for a woman without her being low. I thought you understood. But you didn't, you're not big enough for that! (*with a wild ironical laugh*) Now I know why the women in your plays are so wooden! You ought to thank me for breathing life into them!

CAPE—(*furiously*) Good God, how dare you criticize creative work, you actress!

ELEANOR—(*violently*) You deny that I create—? Perhaps if I'd have children and a home, take up knitting—! (*She laughs wildly.*) I'd be safe then, wouldn't I—reliable, guaranteed not to— (*Her face seems suddenly to congeal.*) So you think that I was John's mistress—that I loved him—or do you believe I just sold myself?

CAPE—(*in agony*) No, no! For God's sake, not that! I may have thought you once loved—

ELEANOR—(*frozenly*) Well, it was—that—just that! When he first engaged me—I'd heard the gossip—I thought he expected—and I agreed with myself—it meant nothing to me one way or the other—nothing meant anything then but a chance to do my work—yes, I agreed—but you see he didn't, he didn't agree. He loved me but he saw I didn't love him—that way—and he's a finer man than you think!

CAPE—(*hoarsely*) You're lying! (*bewilderedly*) I can't believe—

ELEANOR—(*fiercely*) Oh yes, you can! You want to! You do! And you're glad! It makes me lower than you thought, but you're glad to know it just the same! You're glad because now you can really believe that—nothing ever happened between us! (*She stares into his eyes and seems to read some confirmation of her statement there, for she cries with triumphant bitterness*) You can't deny it!

CAPE—(*wildly*) No! You devil, you, you read thoughts into my mind!

ELEANOR—(*with wild hysterical scorn*) It's true! How could I ever love you?

CAPE—(*clutching her in his arms fiercely*) You do! (*He kisses her frantically. For a moment she submits, appears even to return his kisses in spite of herself. Cape cries triumphantly*) You do! (*She suddenly pushes him away and glares at him at arms' length. Her features are working convulsively. Her whole tortured face expresses an abysmal self-loathing, a frightful hatred for him.*)

ELEANOR—(*as if to herself—in a strangled voice*) No! You can't crush—me! (*Her face becomes deadly calm. She speaks with intense, cold hatred.*) Don't kiss me. I love him. He was—my lover—here—when you were away!

CAPE—(*stares dumbly into her eyes for a long moment—hoarsely, in agony*) You lie! You only want to torture—

ELEANOR—(*deathly calm*) It's true! (*Cape stares at her another second—then, with a snarl of fury like an animal's he seizes her about the throat with both hands. He chokes her, forcing her down to her knees. She does not struggle but continues to look into his eyes with the same defiant hate. At last he comes to himself with a shudder and steps away from her. She remains where she is, only putting out her hand on the floor to support herself.*)

CAPE—(*in a terrible state, sobbing with rage and anguish*) Gone! All our beauty gone! And you don't love him! You lie! You did this out of hatred for me! You dragged our ideal in the gutter—with delight! (*wildly*) And you pride yourself you've killed it, do you, you actress, you barren soul? (*with savage triumph*) But I tell you only a creator can really destroy! (*with a climax of frenzy*) And I will! I will! I won't give your hatred the satisfaction of seeing our love live on in me— to torture me! I'll drag it lower than you! I'll stamp it into the vilest depths! I'll leave it dead! I'll murder it—and be free! (*Again he threatens her, his hands twitching back toward her neck—then he rushes out of the door as if furies were pursuing him, slamming it shut behind him.*)

ELEANOR—(*with a cry of despair*) Michael! (*She stops as hatred and rage overpower her again—leaps up and runs to the door—opens it and screams after him violently*) Go! Go! I'm glad! I hate you. I'll go, too! I'm free! I'll go— (*She turns and runs up the stairs. She disappears for a moment, then comes back with a hat and coat on and, hurrying down the stairs again, rushes out leaving the door open behind her.*)

(*The Curtain Falls*)

ACT TWO

Scene One

Library. A door is in the rear, toward right. A large couch facing front. On the wall, a framed portrait study of Eleanor.

At first the room is in darkness. As the curtain rises, John can be dimly distinguished sitting, bent over wearily, his shoulders bowed, his long arms resting on his knees, his hands dangling. He sits on the extreme edge in the exact middle of the big couch, and this heightens the sense of loneliness about him.

Suddenly he starts as the sound of a motor comes from the driveway. The car is heard driving up; it stops before the front door; its door is slammed, it drives off; a ringing of the doorbell sounds from somewhere back in the house. John has gotten up, gone toward the door in the rear, exclaiming irritably as the bell continues to ring— All right, damn it! Who the devil—? (*He is heard opening the front door—in blank amazement*) Nelly! (*Then her voice in a strained, hysterical pitch*) John! I— (*The rest is lost incoherently. Then his voice soothingly*) Come in! Come in. (*He follows her into the room. Her face is pale, distraught, desperate. She comes quickly to the couch and flings herself down in one corner. He stands nearby uncertainly, watching her. His face holds a confused mixture of alarm, tenderness, perplexity, passionate hope.*)

JOHN—You're trembling.

ELEANOR—(*with a startled movement*) No—I—I'm— (*A pause. He waits for her to speak, not knowing what to think. She gradually collects herself. Memory crowds back on her and her face twitches with pain which turns to hatred and rage. She becomes conscious of John's eyes, forces this back, her face growing mask-like and determined. She looks up at John and forces the words out slowly.*) John—you said, if ever— You once said I might always come—

JOHN—(*His face lights up for a second with a joy that is incongruously savage—at once controlling this—simply*) Yes, Nelly.

ELEANOR—(*a bit brokenly now*) I hope—you meant that.

JOHN—(*simply*) Yes, I meant it.

ELEANOR—I mean—that you still mean it—?

JOHN—(*forcing an awkward smile*) Then—now—forever

252

after, amen—any old time at all, Nelly. (*then overcome by a rush of bewildered joy—stammering*) Why—you ought to know—!

ELEANOR—(*smiling tensely*) Would I still be welcome if I'd come—to stay?

JOHN—(*his voice quivering*) Nelly! (*He starts toward her, then stops—in a low, uncertain voice*) And Michael?

ELEANOR—(*with an exclamation of pain*) Don't! (*quickly recovering herself—in a cold, hard voice*) That's—dead! (*John lets a held-back breath of suspense escape him. Eleanor stammers a bit hysterically*) Don't talk of him! I've forgotten—as if he'd never lived! Do you still love me? Do you? Then tell me! I must know someone—

JOHN—(*still uncertain, but coming nearer to her—simply*) You knew once. Since then— My God, you've guessed, haven't you?

ELEANOR—I need to hear. You've never spoken—for years—

JOHN—There was—Michael.

ELEANOR—(*wildly, putting her hands up to her ears as if to shut out the name*) Don't! (*then, driven by a desperate determination, forces a twisted smile*) Why do you stand there? Are you afraid? I'm beginning to suspect—perhaps, you've only imagined—

JOHN—Nelly! (*He seizes one of her hands awkwardly and covers it with kisses—confusedly, with deep emotion*) I— You know— You know—

ELEANOR—(*with the same fixed smile*) You must put your arms around me—and kiss me—on the lips—

JOHN—(*takes her in his arms awkwardly and kisses her on the lips—with passionate incoherence*) Nelly! I'd given up hoping— I—I can't believe— (*She submits to his kisses with closed eyes, her face like a mask, her body trembling with revulsion. Suddenly he seems to sense something disharmonious—confusedly*) But you—you don't care for me.

ELEANOR—(*still with closed eyes—dully*) Yes. (*With a spurt of desperate energy she kisses him wildly several times, then sinks back again closing her eyes.*) I'm so tired, John—so tired!

JOHN—(*immediately all concern*) You're trembling all over. I'm an idiot not to have seen— Forgive me. (*He puts his hand on her forehead.*) You're feverish. You'd better go to bed, young lady, right away. Come. (*He raises her to her feet.*)

ELEANOR—(*wearily*) Yes, I'm tired. (*bitterly*) Oh, it's good to be loved by someone who is unselfish and kind—

JOHN—Ssshh! (*forcing a joking tone*) I'm cast for the Doctor now. Doctor's orders: don't talk, don't think, sleep. Come, I'll show you your room.

ELEANOR—(*dully*) Yes. (*As if she were not aware of what she is doing, she allows him to lead her to the door at right, rear. There she suddenly starts as if awakening—frightenedly*) Where are we going?

JOHN—(*with gentle bullying*) You're going upstairs to bed.

ELEANOR—(*with a shudder—incoherently*) No, no! Not now—no—wait—you must wait— (*then calming herself and trying to speak matter-of-factly*) I'd rather stay up and sit with you.

JOHN—(*worriedly, but giving in to her at once*) All right. Whatever suits you. (*They go back. She sits in a chair. He puts a cushion in back of her.*) How's that?

ELEANOR—(*with a wan, grateful smile*) You're so kind, John. You've always been kind. You're so different— (*She checks herself, her face growing hard. John watches her. There is a long pause.*)

JOHN—(*finally—in a gentle tone*) Nelly, don't you think it'd help if you told me—everything that's happened?

ELEANOR—(*with a shudder*) No! It was all horror—and disgust! (*wildly resentful*) Why do you make me remember? I've come to you. Why do you ask for reasons? (*with a harsh laugh*) Are you jealous—of him?

JOHN—(*quietly*) I've always envied Michael.

ELEANOR—If you'd seen him tonight, you wouldn't envy him. He's mean and contemptible! He makes everything as low as he is! He went away threatening, boasting he'd— (*hysterically*) Why do you make me think of him? I want to be yours! (*She throws herself into his arms.*)

JOHN—(*straining her to him—with awkward passion*) Nelly! (*Under his kisses her face again becomes mask-like, her body rigid, her eyes closed. John suddenly grows aware of this. He stares down at her face, his own growing bewildered and afraid. He stammers*) Nelly! What is it?

ELEANOR—(*opening her eyes—in alarm*) What—?

JOHN—(*with a sigh of relief*) You gave me a scare. You were like a corpse.

ELEANOR—(*breaks away from him*) I—I believe I do feel ill. I'll go to bed. (*She moves toward the door.*)

JOHN—(*uneasily—with a forced heartiness*) Now you're talking sense. Come on. (*He leads the way into the hall. She goes as far as the doorway—then stops. A queer struggle is apparent in her face, her whole body, as if she were fighting with all her will to overcome some invisible barrier which bars her way. John is watching her keenly now, a sad foreboding coming into his eyes. He steps past her back into the room, saying kindly but with a faint trace of bitterness*) It's the first door upstairs on your right—if you'd rather go alone. (*He walks still further away, then turns to watch her, his face growing more and more aware and melancholy.*)

ELEANOR—(*vaguely*) No—you don't understand— (*She stands swaying, reaching out her hand to the side of the doorway for support—dully*) The first door to the right—upstairs?

JOHN—Yes.

ELEANOR—(*struggles with herself, confused and impotent, trying to will—finally turns to John like a forlorn child.*) John. Can't you help me?

JOHN—(*gravely*) No—not now when I do understand. You must do it alone.

ELEANOR—(*with a desperate cry*) I can! I'm as strong as he! (*This breaks the spell which has chained her. She grows erect and strong. She walks through the doorway.*)

JOHN—(*with a triumphant exclamation of joy*) Ah! (*He strides toward the doorway—then stops as he notices that she also has stopped at the bottom of the stairs, one foot on the first stair, looking up at the top. Then she wavers and suddenly bolts back into the room, gropingly, her face strained and frightened. John questions her with fierce disappointment.*) What is it? Why did you stop?

ELEANOR—(*forcing a twisted smile—wildly*) You're right. I must be feverish. (*trying to control herself—self-mockingly*) Seeing spooks, that's pretty far gone, isn't it? (*laughing hysterically*) Yes—I swear I saw him—standing at the head of the stairs waiting for me—just as he was standing when you knocked at our door, remember? (*She laughs.*) Really, it was too ridiculous—so plain—

JOHN—Ssshh! (*glancing at her worriedly*) Won't you lie down here? Try and rest.

ELEANOR—(*allowing him to make her comfortable on the couch before the fire*) Yes. (*Her eyes glance up into his bewilderedly.*)

JOHN—(*after a long pause—slowly*) You don't love me, Nelly.

ELEANOR—(*pitifully protesting*) But I do, John! I do! You're kind! You're unselfish and fine!

JOHN—(*with a wry smile*) That isn't me.

ELEANOR—(*desperately defiant, leaps to her feet*) I do! (*She takes his face between her hands and bringing her own close to it stares into his eyes. He looks back into hers. She mutters fiercely between her clenched teeth*) I do! (*For a long moment they remain there, as she brings her face nearer and nearer striving with all her will to kiss him on the lips. Finally, her eyes falter, her body grows limp, she turns away and throws herself on the couch in a fit of abandoned sobbing.*)

JOHN—(*with a sad smile*) You see?

ELEANOR—(*her voice muffled—between sobs*) But I—want to! And I will—I know—some day—I promise!

JOHN—(*forcing a light tone*) Well, I'll be resigned to wait and hope then—and trust in your good intentions. (*after a pause—in a calming, serious tone*) You're calmer now? Tell me what happened between you and Michael.

ELEANOR—No! Please!

JOHN—(*smiling but earnestly*) It'll relieve your mind, Nelly—and besides, how can I help you otherwise?

ELEANOR—(*after a pause—with resigned dullness*) We've quarreled, but never like this before. This was final. (*She shudders—then suddenly bursts out wildly*) Oh, John, for God's sake don't ask me! I want to forget! We tore each other to pieces. I realized I hated him! I couldn't restrain my hate! I had to crush him as he was crushing me! (*after a pause—dully again*) And so that was the end.

JOHN—(*tensely, hoping again now—pleadingly*) You're sure, Nelly?

ELEANOR—(*fiercely*) I hate him!

JOHN—(*after a pause—earnestly*) Then stay here. I think I can help you forget. Never mind what people say. Make this your home—and maybe—in time— (*He forces a smile.*) You see, I'm already starting to nurse along that crumb of hope you gave. (*She is looking down, preoccupied with her own thoughts. He looks at her embarrassedly, then goes on gently, timidly persuasive.*) I don't mind waiting. I'm used to it. And I've been hoping ever since I first met you. (*forcing a half laugh*) I'll admit when you married him the waiting and hoping seemed excess labor. I tried to fire them—thought I had— but when you came tonight—they were right onto the job again! (*He laughs—then catching himself awkwardly*) But hell! I don't want to bother you now. Forget me.

ELEANOR—(*in a bland, absent-minded tone which wounds him*) You're so kind, John. (*Then following her own line of thought, she breaks out savagely*) I told him I'd been your mistress while he was away!

JOHN—(*amazed*) Nelly!

ELEANOR—I had to tell that lie! He was degrading me! I had to revenge myself!

JOHN—But certainly he could never believe—

ELEANOR—(*with fierce triumph*) Oh, I made him believe! (*then dully*) He went away. He said he'd kill our love as I had—worse— (*with a twisted smile*) That's what he's doing now. He's gone to one of those women he lived with before— (*laughing harshly*) No! They wouldn't be vile enough—for his beautiful revenge on me! He has a wonderful imagination. Everyone acknowledges that! (*She laughs with wild bitterness.*) My God, why do I think—? Help me, John! Help me to forget.

JOHN—(*after a pause—with a sad, bitter helplessness*) You mean—help you—to revenge yourself! But don't you realize I can't—you can't—because you still love him!

ELEANOR—(*fiercely*) No! (*after a pause—brokenly*) Don't! I know! (*She sobs heartbrokenly.*)

JOHN—(*after a pause, as her sobbing grows quieter—sadly*) Go home.

ELEANOR—No! (*after a pause, brokenly*) He'll never come back now.

JOHN—(*with a bitter humor*) Oh, yes he will; take my word for it. I know—because I happen to love you, too.

ELEANOR—(*faintly*) And do you—hate me?

JOHN—(*after a pause—with melancholy self-disgust*) No. I'm too soft. (*bitterly*) I ought to hate you! Twice now you've treated my love with the most humiliating contempt— Once when you were willing to endure it as the price of a career— again tonight, when you try to give yourself to me out of hate for him! (*in sudden furious revolt*) Christ! What am I, eh? (*then checking his anger and forcing a wry smile*) I think your treatment has been rather hard to take, Nelly—and even now I'm not cured, at that! (*He laughs harshly and turns away to conceal his real hurt.*)

ELEANOR—(*with a deep grief*) Forgive me.

JOHN—(*as if to himself—reassuringly*) Still—I'd have been the poorest slave. I couldn't have fought you like Michael. Perhaps, deep down, I'm glad— (*then bluntly*) You'd better go home right away.

ELEANOR—(*dully*) Even if he—

JOHN—(*brusquely*) No matter what! Face the truth in yourself. Must you—or mustn't you?

ELEANOR—(*after a moment's defiant struggle with herself— forlornly*) Yes. (*after a pause, with a gesture toward the door and a weary, beaten smile*) Upstairs—if I could have gone—I might have been free. But he's trained me too well in his ideal. (*then shrugging her shoulders, fatalistically*) It's broken me. I'm no longer anything. So what does it matter how weak I am? (*a slight pause*) I begin to know—something. (*with a sudden queer, exultant pride*) My love for him is my own, not his! That he can never possess! It's *my* own. It's *my* life! (*She turns to John determinedly.*) I must go home now.

JOHN—(*wonderingly*) Good. I'll drive you back. (*He starts for the door.*)

ELEANOR—(*suddenly grasping his arm*) Wait. (*affectionately*) I was forgetting you—as usual. What can I do—?

JOHN—(*with a wry smile*) Study your part; help Michael; and we'll all three be enormously successful! (*He laughs mockingly.*)

ELEANOR—(*tenderly*) I'll always believe Fate should have let me love you, instead.

JOHN—(*with the same wry smile*) While I begin to suspect that in a way I'm lucky—to be heartbroken. (*with a laugh*) Curtain! You'll want to go upstairs and powder your nose. There's no angel with a flaming sword there now, is there? (*He points to the doorway.*)

ELEANOR—(*with a tired smile*) No. (*She goes to the doorway. He follows her. They both stop there for a moment instinctively and smile forlornly at each other.*)

JOHN—(*impulsively*) That time you stood here and called to me for help—if I could have given you a push, mental, moral, physical—?

ELEANOR—It wouldn't have helped. The angel was here. (*She touches her breast.*)

JOHN—(*with a sigh*) Thanks. That saves me a life-long regret.

ELEANOR—(*earnestly—gripping his right hand in hers and holding his eyes*) There must be no regrets—between old friends.

JOHN—(*gripping her hand in turn*) No, I promise, Nelly. (*then letting her hand drop and turning away to conceal his emotion—forcing a joking tone*) After all, friendship is sounder, saner—more in the picture for my type, eh?

ELEANOR—(*absent-mindedly again now—vaguely*) I don't know. (*then briskly*) We must hurry. I'll be right down. (*She goes out and up the stairway in the hall.*)

JOHN—(*stares up after her for a second, then smiling grimly*) Well, business of living on as usual. (*He walks out, calling up the stairs*) I'm going to get the car, Nelly.

(*The Curtain Falls*)

SCENE TWO

A bedroom. In the rear, center, a door. A chair to left of door. In the left corner, a washstand. In the left wall, center, a small window with a torn dark shade pulled down. On the right, a bed. Ugly wall paper, dirty, stained, criss-crossed with match-strokes.

When the curtain rises, the room is in darkness except for a faint glow on the window shade from some street lamp. Then the door is opened and a woman's figure is silhouetted against the dim, yellow light of a hall. She turns and speaks to someone who is following her. Her voice is heavy and slow with the strong trace of a foreign intonation, although the words are clearly enough defined. A man's figure appears behind hers. The woman is fairly young. Her face, rouged, powdered, penciled, is broad and stupid. Her small eyes have a glazed look. Yet she is not ugly—rather pretty for her bovine, stolid type—and her figure is still attractive although its movements just now are those of a tired scrubwoman's. She takes off her coat, hangs it on a hook, and removes her hat.

The man is Michael. He is bare-headed, his hair disheveled, his eyes wild, his face has a feverish, mad expression. He stands in the doorway watching each movement of the woman's with an unnatural preoccupied concentration.

WOMAN—(*having removed her hat and put it on the washstand, turns to him impatiently*) Ain't you comin' in? (*He starts and nods stupidly, moving his lips as if answering but not making a sound.*) Come in! Shut the door. (*He does so and locks it mechanically—then looks from her around the room with a frightened, puzzled glance as if he were aware of his surroundings for the first time.*)

WOMAN—(*forcing a trade smile—with an attempt at lightness*) Well, here we are, dearie. (*then with a sigh of physical weariness as she sits on the side of the bed*) Gawd, I'm tired! My feet hurt fierce! I been walkin' miles. I got corns, too. (*She sighs again, this time with a sort of restful content.*) It's good 'n' warm in this dump, I'll hand it that. (*a pause*) I'd gave up hope and was beatin' it home when you come along. (*a pause during which she takes him in calculatingly*) How'd you lose your hat? (*He starts, passes a trembling hand through his hair bewilderedly but does not answer. A pause—then the woman sighs and yawns wearily—bored*) Can't you say nothin'? You was full enough of bull when you met me. Gawd, I thought you'd get us both pinched. You acted like you was crazy. Remember kissing me on the corner with a whole mob pipin' us off?

CAPE—(*with a start—evidently answering some train of*

thought in his mind—with a wild laugh) Remember? (*He sinks on the chair with his head in his hands. There is a pause.*)

WOMAN—(*insinuatingly*) Goin' to stay all night? (*He glances up at her stupidly but doesn't answer. The woman insists dully*) Say, you got ear-muffs on? I ast you, d'you wanta stay all night?

CAPE—(*after a moment's groping, nods emphatically again and again, swallowing hard several times as if he were striving to get control of his voice—finally blurts out in a tone of desperation*) Yes—yes—of course!— Where else would I go?

WOMAN—Home. (*indifferently*) That's where most of 'em goes—afterwards.

CAPE—(*with a sudden burst of wild laughter*) Ha-ha-ha. Home! Is that your private brand of revenge—to go with men with homes? I congratulate you! (*He laughs to himself with bitter irony—then suddenly deadly calm*) Yes, I have a home, come to think of it—from now on Hell is my home! I suspect we're fellow-citizens. (*He laughs.*)

WOMAN—(*superstitiously*) You oughtn't to say them things.

CAPE—(*with dull surprise*) Why?

WOMAN—Somep'n might happen. (*a pause*) Don't you believe in no God?

CAPE—I believe in the devil!

WOMAN—(*frightened*) Say! (*then after a pause, forcing a smile*) I'm wise to what's wrong with you. You been lappin' up some bum hooch.

CAPE—(*jerkily*) No. I'm not drunk. I thought of that— but it's evasion. (*wildly*) And I must be conscious—fully conscious, do you understand? I will this as a symbol of release— of the end of all things! (*He stops, shuddering. She looks at him stolidly. A pause. He presses his hands to his forehead.*) Stop thinking, damn you! (*then after a pause—dully*) How long—? What time is it?

WOMAN—Little after two, I guess.

CAPE—(*amazed*) Only that? (*She nods.*) Only two hours—? (*a pause*) I remember streets—lights—dead faces— Then you—your face alone was alive for me, alive with my deliverance! That was why I kissed you.

WOMAN—(*looking up at him queerly*) Say, you talk nutty. Been dopin' up on coke, I bet you.

CAPE—(*with an abrupt exclamation*) Ha! (*He stares at her with unnatural intensity.*) You seem to take it quite casually that men must be either drunk or doped—otherwise—! Marvelous! You,—you're the last depth— (*with a strange, wild exultance, leaps to his feet*) You're my salvation! You have the power—and the right—to murder love! You can satisfy hate! Will you let me kiss you again? (*He strides over to her.*)

WOMAN—(*in a stupid state of bewilderment, feeling she has been insulted but not exactly knowing by what or how to resent it—angrily, pushing him away*) No! Get away from me! (*then afraid she may lose his trade by this rebuff*) Aw, all right. Sure you can. (*Making a tremendous visible effort he kisses her on the lips, then shrinks back with a shudder and forces a harsh laugh. She stares at him and mutters resentfully*) O'ny don't get so fresh, see? I don't like your line of talk. (*He slumps down on the chair again, sunk in a somber stupor. She watches him. She yawns. Finally she asks insinuatingly*) Ain't you gettin' sleepy?

CAPE—(*starting—with wild scorn*) Do you think I—! (*staring at her*) Oh—I see—you mean, what did I come here for?

WOMAN—(*in same tone*) It's gettin' late.

CAPE—(*dully, with no meaning to his question—like an automaton*) A little after two?

WOMAN—Yes. (*She yawns.*) You better let me go to bed and come yourself.

CAPE—(*again staring at her with strange intensity—suddenly with a queer laugh*) How long have you and I been united in the unholy bonds of—bedlock? (*He chuckles sardonically at his own play on words.*)

WOMAN—(*with a puzzled grin*) Say!

CAPE—Ten thousand years—about—isn't it? Or twenty? Don't you remember?

WOMAN—(*keeping her forced grin*) Tryin' to kid me, ain't you?

CAPE—Don't lie about your age! You were beside the cradle of love, and you'll dance dead drunk on its grave!

WOMAN—I'm only twenty-six, honest.

CAPE—(*with a wild laugh*) A fact! You're right. Thoughts keep alive. Only facts kill—deeds! (*He starts to his feet.*) Then hate will let me alone. Love will be dead. I'll be as ugly as the world. My dreams will be low dreams. I'll "lay me down among the swine." Will you promise me this, you?

WOMAN—(*vaguely offended—impatiently*) Sure, I'll promise anything. (*She gets up to start undressing. She has been pulling the pins out of her hair and, as she rises, it falls over her shoulders in a peroxided flood. She turns to him, smiling with childish pride.*) D'you like my hair, kid? I got a lot of it, ain't I?

CAPE—(*laughing sardonically*) "O love of mine, let down your hair and I will make my shroud of it."

WOMAN—(*coquettishly pleased*) What's that—po'try? (*Then suddenly reminded of something she regards him calculatingly—after a pause, coldly*) Say, you ain't broke, are you? Is that what's troubling you?

CAPE—(*startled—then with bitter mockery*) Ha! I see you're a practical person. (*He takes a bill from his pocket and holds it out to her—contemptuously*) Here!

WOMAN—(*stares from the bill to him, flushing beneath her rouge*) Say! I don't like the way you act. (*proudly*) I don't take nothin' for nothin'—not from you, see!

CAPE—(*surprised and ashamed*) I'll leave it here, then. (*He puts it on top of the washstand and turns to her—embarrassedly*) I didn't mean—to offend you.

WOMAN—(*her face clearing immediately*) Aw, never mind. It's all right.

CAPE—(*staring at her intently—suddenly deeply moved*) Poor woman!

WOMAN—(*stung—excitedly*) Hey, none of that! Nix! Cut it out! I don't stand for that from nobody! (*She sits down on the bed angrily.*)

CAPE—(*with unnatural intensity*) Do you know what you are? You're a symbol. You're all the tortures man inflicts on woman—and you're the revenge of woman! You're love revenging itself upon itself! You're the suicide of love—of my love—of all love since the world began! (*wildly*) Listen to me! Two hours ago— (*Then he beats his head with both clenched hands—distractedly*) Leave me alone! Leave me alone, damn you! (*He flings himself on the chair in a violent outburst of dry sobbing.*)

WOMAN—(*bewilderedly*) Say! Say! (*Then touched, she comes to him and puts her arms around his shoulders, on the verge of tears herself.*) Aw, come on, kid. Quit it. It's all right. Everything's all right, see. (*as his sobbing grows quieter—helpfully*) Say, maybe you ain't ate nothin', huh? Maybe soup'd fix you. S'posin' I go round the corner, huh? Sure, all I got to do is put up my hair—

CAPE—(*controlling hysterical laughter—huskily*) No—thanks. (*Then his bitter memories rush back agonizingly. He stammers wildly*) She confessed! She was proud of her hate! She was proud of my torture. She screamed: "I'll go too." Go where? Did she go? Yes, she must—! Oh, my God! Stop! Stop! (*He springs up, his face distorted, and clutches the woman fiercely in his arms.*) Save me, you! Help me to kill! Help me to gain peace! (*He kisses her again and again frenziedly. She submits stolidly. Finally with a groan he pushes her away, shuddering with loathing, and sinks back on the chair.*) No! I can't—I can't!

WOMAN—(*wiping her lips with the back of her hand—a vague comprehension coming into her face—scornfully*) Huh! I got a hunch now what's eatin' you. (*then with a queer sort of savage triumph*) Well, I'm glad one of youse guys got paid back like you oughter!

CAPE—(*with dull impotent rage*) I can't! I can't. I'm the weaker. Our love must live on in me. There's no death for it. There's no freedom—while I live. (*struck by a sudden thought*) Then, why—? (*a pause*) An end of loathing—no wounds, no memories—sleep!

WOMAN—(*with a shudder*) Say, you're beginning to give me the creeps.

CAPE—(*startled—with a forced laugh*) Am I? (*He shakes his head as if to drive some thought from his mind and forces a trembling, mocking smile.*) That's over. The great temptation, isn't it? I suppose you've known it. But also the great evasion. Too simple for the complicated,—too weak for the strong, too strong for the weak. One must go on, eh?—even wounded, on one's knees—if only out of curiosity to see what will happen—to oneself. (*He laughs harshly and turns with a quick movement toward the door.*) Well, good-by, and forgive me. It isn't you, you know. You're the perfect death—but I'm too strong, or weak—and I can't, you understand—can't! So, good-by. (*He goes to the door.*)

WOMAN—(*frightenedly*) Say! What're you goin' to do?

CAPE—Go on in the dark.

WOMAN—You better beat it home, that's what.

CAPE—(*violently*) No!

WOMAN—(*wearily*) Aw, forget it. She's your wife, ain't she?

CAPE—How do you know? (*He comes back to her, curiously attracted.*)

WOMAN—(*cynically*) Aw, I'm wise. Stick to her, see? You'll get over it. You can get used to anything, take it from me!

CAPE—(*in anguish*) Don't! But it's true—it's the insult we all swallow as the price of life. (*rebelliously*) But I—!

WOMAN—(*with a sort of forlorn chuckle*) Oh, you'll go back aw right! Don't kid yourself. You'll go back no matter what, and you'll loin to like it. Don't I know? You love her, don't you? Well, then! There's no use buckin' that game. Go home. Kiss and make up. Ferget it. It's easy to ferget—when you got to! (*She finishes up with a cynical, weary scorn.*)

CAPE—(*very pale—stammering*) You—you make life despicable.

WOMAN—(*angrily*) Say! (*then with groping, growing resentment*) I don't like your talk! You've pulled a lot of bum cracks about—about—never mind, I got you, anyhow! You ain't got no right— What'd you wanter pick me up for, anyway? Wanter just get me up here to say rotten things? Wanter use me to pay her back? Say! Where do I come in? Guys go with me 'cause they like my looks, see?—what I am, understand?—but you, you don't want nothin'. You ain't drunk, neither! You just don't like me. And you was beatin' it leavin' your money there—without nothin'. I was goin' to let you then. I ain't now. (*She suddenly gives him a furious push which sends him reeling back against the wall.*) G'wan! Take your lousy coin and beat it! I wouldn't take nothin', nor have nothin' to do with you if you was to get down on your knees!

CAPE—(*stares at her—an expression comes as if he were seeing her for the first time—with great pity*) So—it still survives in you. They haven't killed it—that lonely life of one's own which suffers in solitude. (*shame-facedly*) I should have known. Can you forgive me?

WOMAN—(*defensively*) No!

CAPE—Through separate ways love has brought us both to this room. As one lonely human being to another, won't you—?

WOMAN—(*struggling with herself—harshly*) No!

CAPE—(*gently*) Not even if I ask it on my knees? (*He kneels before her, looking up into her face.*)

WOMAN—(*bewildered, with hysterical fierceness*) No! Git up, you—! Don't do that, I tell you! Git up or I'll brain yuh! (*She raises her fist threateningly over his head.*)

CAPE—(*gently*) Not until you—

WOMAN—(*exhaustedly*) Aw right—aw right—I forgive—

CAPE—(*gets up and takes her face between his hands and stares into her eyes—then he kisses her on the forehead.*) Sister.

WOMAN—(*with a half sob*) Nix! Lay off of me, can't you?

CAPE—But I learned that from you.

WOMAN—(*stammering*) What?—loined what? (*She goes away from him and sinks on the bed exhaustedly.*) Say, you better beat it.

CAPE—I'm going. (*He points to the bill on the washstand.*) You need this money. You'll accept it from me now, won't you?

WOMAN—(*dully*) Sure. Leave it there.

CAPE—(*in the same gentle tone*) You'll have to give it to him in the morning?

WOMAN—(*dully*) Sure.

CAPE—All of it?

WOMAN—Sure.

CAPE—Or he'd beat you?

WOMAN—Sure. (*then suddenly grinning*) Maybe he'll beat me up, anyway—just for the fun of it.

CAPE—But you love him, don't you?

WOMAN—Sure. I'm lonesome.

CAPE—Yes. (*after a slight pause*) Why did you smile when you said he'd beat you, anyway?

WOMAN—I was thinkin' of the whole game. It's funny, ain't it?

CAPE—(*slowly*) You mean—life?

WOMAN—Sure. You got to laugh, ain't you? You got to loin to like it!

CAPE—(*This makes an intense impression on him. He nods his head several times.*) Yes! That's it! That's exactly it! That goes deeper than wisdom. To learn to love life—to accept it and be exalted—that's the one faith left to us! (*then with a tremulous smile*) Good-by. I've joined your church. I'm going home.

WOMAN—(*with a grin that is queerly affectionate*) Sure. That's the stuff. Close your eyes and your feet'll take you there.

CAPE—(*impressed again*) Yes! Yes! Of course they would! They've been walking there for thousands of years—blindly. However, now, I'll keep my eyes open—(*he smiles back at her affectionately*)—and learn to like it!

WOMAN—(*grinning*) Sure. Good luck.

CAPE—Good-by. (*He goes out, closing the door after him. She stares at the door listening to his footsteps as they die out down the stairs.*)

WOMAN—(*confusedly*) Say—?

(*The Curtain Falls*)

ACT THREE

SCENE—*Same as Act One.*

Eleanor is standing by the table, leaning her back against it, facing the door, her whole attitude strained, expectant but frightened, tremblingly uncertain whether to run and hide from, or run forward and greet Cape, who is standing in the doorway. For a long, tense moment they remain fixed, staring into each other's eyes with an apprehensive questioning. Then, as if unconsciously, falteringly, with trembling smiles, they come toward each other. Their lips move as if they were trying to speak. When they come close, they instinctively reach out their hands in a strange conflicting gesture of a protective warding off and at the same time a seeking possession. Their hands clasp and they again stop, searching each other's eyes. Finally their lips force out words.

ELEANOR—(*penitently*) Michael!

CAPE—(*humbly*) Nelly! (*They smile with a queer understanding, their arms move about each other, their lips meet. They seem in a forgetful, happy trance at finding each other again. They touch each other testingly as if each cannot believe the other is really there. They act for the moment like two persons of different races, deeply in love but separated by a barrier of language.*)

ELEANOR—(*rambling tenderly*) Michael—I—I was afraid—

CAPE—(*stammeringly*) Nelly—it's no good!—I thought—(*They stare at each other—a pause.*)

ELEANOR—(*beginning to be aware—a bit bewilderedly, breaking away from him with a little shiver—stupidly*) I feel—there's a draught, isn't there?

CAPE—(*becoming aware in his turn—heavily*) I'll shut the door. (*He goes and does so. She walks to her chair and sits down. He comes and sits beside her. They are now side by side as in Act One. A pause. They stare ahead, each frowningly abstracted. Then each, at the same moment, steals a questioning side glance at the other. Their eyes meet, they look away, then back, they stare at each other with a peculiar dull amazement, recognition yet non-recognition. They seem about to speak, then turn away again. Their faces grow sad, their eyes begin to suffer, their bodies become nervous and purposeless. Finally Cape exclaims with a dull resent-*

268

ment directed not at her but at life) What is—it? (*He makes a gesture of repulsing something before him.*)

ELEANOR—(*in his tone*) I don't know.

CAPE—(*harshly*) A moment ago—there— (*He indicates where they had stood in an embrace.*) We knew everything. We understood!

ELEANOR—(*eagerly*) Oh, yes!

CAPE—(*bitterly*) Now—we must begin to think—to continue going on, getting lost—

ELEANOR—(*sadly*) It was happy to forget. Let's not think—yet.

CAPE—(*grimly*) We've begun. (*then with a harsh laugh*) Thinking explains. It eliminates the unexplainable—by which we live.

ELEANOR—(*warningly*) By which we love. Sssh! (*a pause*)

CAPE—(*wonderingly—not looking at her*) You have learned that, too?

ELEANOR—(*with a certain exultance*) Oh, yes, Michael—yes! (*She clasps his hand. A pause. Then she murmurs*) Now—we know peace. (*Their hands drop apart. She sighs.*)

CAPE—(*slowly*) Peace isn't our meaning.

ELEANOR—(*suddenly turns and addresses him directly in a sad, sympathetic tone*) You've something you want to ask me, Michael?

CAPE—(*turns to her with an immediate affirmative on his lips, checks it as he meets her eyes, turns away—a pause—then he turns back humbly*) No.

ELEANOR—(*Her head has been averted since he turned away—without looking at him*) Yes.

CAPE—(*decisively*) No, Nelly. (*She still keeps her head averted. After a pause he asks simply*) Why? Is there something you want to ask me?

ELEANOR—No. (*after a pause—with a trace of bitter humor*) I can't be less magnanimous than you, can I?

CAPE—Then there is something—?

ELEANOR—Haven't you something you want to tell?

CAPE—(*looks at her. Their eyes meet again.*) Yes—the truth—if I can. And you?

ELEANOR—Yes, I wish to tell you the truth. (*They look into each other's eyes. Suddenly she laughs with a sad self-mockery.*)

Well, we've both been noble. I haven't asked you; you haven't asked me; and yet— (*She makes a helpless gesture with her hands. A pause. Then abruptly and mechanically*) I'll begin at the beginning. I left here right after you did.

CAPE—(*with an involuntary start*) Oh! (*He checks himself.*)

ELEANOR—(*her eyes reading his—after a pause—a bit dryly*) You thought I'd stayed here all the time? (*mockingly*) Waiting for you?

CAPE—(*wounded*) Don't! (*after a pause—painfully*) When I found you—perhaps I hoped—

ELEANOR—(*dully*) I had only been back a few minutes. (*after a pause*) Was that why you seemed so happy—there—? (*She points to the spot where they had stood embraced.*)

CAPE—(*indignantly*) No, no! Don't think that! I'm not like that—not any more! (*Without looking at her he reaches out and clasps her hand.*)

ELEANOR—(*looks at him—after a pause, understandingly*) I'm sorry—

CAPE—(*self-defensively*) Of course, I knew you must have gone, you'd have been a fool to stay. (*excitedly*) And it doesn't matter—not a damn! I've gotten beyond that.

ELEANOR—(*misunderstanding—coldly*) I'm glad. (*A pause. She asks coldly*) Shall I begin again?

CAPE—(*struggling with himself—disjointedly*) No—not unless—I don't need— I've changed. That doesn't matter. I— (*with a sudden twisted grin*) I'm learning to like it, you see.

ELEANOR—(*looks at him, strangely impressed—a pause—slowly*) I think I know what you mean. We're both learning.

CAPE—(*wonderingly*) You—? (*She has turned away from him. He turns to stare at her.*)

ELEANOR—(*after a pause, taking up her story matter-of-factly*) I went to John.

CAPE—(*trying with agony to take this stoically—mumbling stupidly*) Yes—of course—I supposed—

ELEANOR—(*in the same mechanical tone*) He drove me back here in his car. He predicted you'd be back any moment, so he went right home again.

CAPE—(*A wild, ironical laugh escapes his control.*) Shrewd—Ha!

ELEANOR—(*after a pause—rebukingly*) John is a good man.

CAPE—(*startled, turns and stares at her averted face—then miserably humble, stammers*) Yes, yes—I know—I acknowledge—good— (*He breaks down, cursing pitiably at himself.*) God damn you!

ELEANOR—Oh!

CAPE—Not you! Me! (*Then he turns to her—with fierce defiance*) I love John!

ELEANOR—(*moved, without looking at him, reaches and clasps his hand*) That—is fine, Michael. (*a pause*)

CAPE—(*begins to frown somberly—lets go of her hand*) It's hard—after what you confessed—

ELEANOR—(*frightenedly*) Ssshh! (*then calmly*) That was a lie. I lied to make you suffer more than you were making me suffer. (*A pause—then she turns to him.*) Can you believe this?

CAPE—(*humbly*) I want to believe—

ELEANOR—(*immediately turning away—significantly*) Oh!

CAPE—(*fiercely as if to himself*) I will believe! But what difference does it make—believing or not believing? I've changed, I tell you! I accept!

ELEANOR—I can't be a lie you live with!

CAPE—(*turning to her resentfully*) Well, then— (*as if she were goading him to something against his will—threateningly*) Shall I tell you what happened to me?

ELEANOR—(*facing him defiantly*) Yes. (*He turns away. Immediately her brave attitude crumbles. She seems about to implore him not to speak.*)

CAPE—(*after a pause—hesitatingly*) You said that years ago you had offered yourself—to him— (*He turns suddenly—hopefully*) Was that a lie, too?

ELEANOR—No.

CAPE—(*turns away with a start of pain*) Ah. (*A pause. Suddenly his face grows convulsed. He turns back to her, overcome by a craving for revenge—viciously*) Then I may as well tell you I— (*He checks himself and turns away.*)

ELEANOR—(*defensively—with feigned indifference*) I don't doubt—you kept your threat.

CAPE—(*glares at her wildly*) Oho, you don't doubt that, do you? You saw I'd changed, eh?

ELEANOR—I saw—something.

CAPE—(*with bitter irony*) God! (*a pause*)

ELEANOR—(*turning on him doggedly as if she were impersonally impelled to make the statement*) I want to tell you that to-night—John and I—nothing you may ever suspect— (*She falters, turns away with a bitter smile.*) I only tell you this for my own satisfaction. I don't expect you to believe it.

CAPE—(*with a wry grin*) No. How could you? (*then turning to her—determinedly—after a pause*) But it doesn't matter.

ELEANOR—I wanted revenge as much as you. I wanted to destroy—and be free of you forever! (*after a pause—simply*) I couldn't.

CAPE—(*turns and stares at her—a pause—then he asks wonderingly, eagerly*) Why couldn't you? Tell me that.

ELEANOR—(*simply*) Something stronger.

CAPE—(*with a passionate triumph*) Love! (*with intense pleading*) Nelly! Will you believe that I, too—? (*He tries to force her eyes to return to his.*)

ELEANOR—(*after a pause—looking before her—sadly*) You should have been generous sooner.

CAPE—It's the truth, Nelly! (*desperately*) I swear to you—!

ELEANOR—(*after a pause—wearily*) We've sworn to so much.

CAPE—Everything is changed, I tell you! Something extraordinary happened to me—a revelation!

ELEANOR—(*with bitter cynicism*) A woman?

CAPE—(*wounded, turns away from her*) Don't. (*then after a pause—with deep feeling*) Yes—she was a woman. And I had thought of her only as revenge—the lowest of the low!

ELEANOR—(*with a shudder*) Ah!

CAPE—Don't judge, Nelly. She was—good!

ELEANOR—Not her! You!

CAPE—(*desperately*) I tell you I—! (*He checks himself helplessly. She gives no sign. Then he asks sadly*) If you can think that, how could you come back?

ELEANOR—(*stammering hysterically*) How? How! (*bursting into tears*) Because I love you!

CAPE—(*starting up from his chair and trying to take her in his arms—exultantly*) Nelly!

ELEANOR—(*pushing him away—violently*) No! I didn't

come back to you! It conquered me, not you! Something in me—mine—not you! (*She stares him in the eyes defiantly, triumphantly.*)

CAPE—(*gently*) It doesn't matter. (*after a pause*) Did I come back to you?

ELEANOR—(*taken aback, turning away*) No, I suppose— (*Cape stares at her uncertainly, then sits down in his chair again.*)

CAPE—(*after a pause, looking before him—assertively, as if taking a pledge*) But I have faith!

ELEANOR—(*wearily*) Now—for a moment.

CAPE—No!

ELEANOR—Yes. We'll believe—and disbelieve. We are— that.

CAPE—(*protesting*) Nelly! (*For a time they both sit staring bleakly before them. Suddenly he turns to her—desperately*) If there's nothing left but—resignation!—what use is there? How can we endure having our dream perish in this?

ELEANOR—Have we any choice?

CAPE—(*intensely—he seems to collect all his forces and turns on her with a fierce challenge*) We can choose—an end!

ELEANOR—(*shudders instinctively as she reads his meaning*) Michael! (*a pause—then looking into his eyes—as a calm counter-challenge*) Yes—if *you* wish.

CAPE—(*with passionate self-scorn*) We! We have become ignoble.

ELEANOR—As *you* wish. (*She again accents the you.*)

CAPE—I?

ELEANOR—I accept. (*a pause—gently*) You must not suffer too much. (*She reaches out her hand and clasps his comfortingly.*) It's I who have changed most, Michael. (*Then she speaks sadly but firmly as if she had come to a decision.*) There's only one way we can give life to each other.

CAPE—(*sharply*) How?

ELEANOR—By releasing each other.

CAPE—(*with a harsh laugh*) Are you forgetting we tried that once tonight?

ELEANOR—With hate. This would be because we loved.

CAPE—(*violently*) Don't be a fool! (*controlling himself— forcing a smile*) Forgive me. (*excitedly*) But, my God, what solution—?

ELEANOR—It will give you peace for your work—freedom—

CAPE—Nonsense!

ELEANOR—I'll still love you. I'll work for you! We'll no longer stand between one another. Then I can really give you my soul—

CAPE—(*controlling himself with difficulty*) You're talking rot!

ELEANOR—(*hurt*) Michael!

CAPE—(*suddenly glaring at her suspiciously*) Why did you come back? Why do you want to go? What are you hiding behind all this?

ELEANOR—(*wounded*) Your faith? You see?

CAPE—(*brokenly*) I—I didn't mean— (*then after a struggle—with desperate bitterness*) Well—I accept! Go—if you want to!

ELEANOR—(*hurt*) Michael! It isn't— (*then determinedly*) But even if you misunderstand, I must be strong for you!

CAPE—(*almost tauntingly*) Then go now—if you're strong enough. (*harshly*) Let me see you act nobility! (*then suddenly remorseful, catching her hand and covering it with kisses*) No! Go now before— Be strong! Be free! I—I can't!

ELEANOR—(*brokenly*) We can try— (*She bends down swiftly and kisses his head, turns away quickly.*) Good-by.

CAPE—(*in a strangled voice*) Good-by. (*He sits in anguish, in a tortured restraint. She grabs her cloak from the chair, goes quickly to the door, puts her hand on the knob—then stops as tense as he. Suddenly he can stand it no longer, he leaps to his feet and jumps toward the door with a pleading cry.*) Nelly! (*He stands fixed as he sees her before the door as if he had expected to find her gone. She does not turn but remains staring at the door in front of her. Finally she raises her hand and knocks on the door softly—then stops to listen.*)

ELEANOR—(*in a queer far-away voice*) No. Never again "come out." (*She opens the door and turns to Cape with a strange smile.*) It opens inward, Michael. (*She closes it again, smiles to herself and walks back to the foot of the stairway. Then she turns to face Cape. She looks full of some happy certitude. She smiles at him and speaks with a tender weariness.*) It must be nearly dawn. I'll say good-night instead of good-by. (*They stare into each other's eyes. It is as if now by a sudden flash from within they recognized themselves, shorn of all the ideas, attitudes, cheating gestures which constitute the vanity of personality. Everything, for this second, becomes simple for them—serenely unquestionable. It becomes impossible that they should ever deny life, through each other, again.*)

ELEANOR—(*with a low tender cry as if she were awakening to maternity*) Michael!

CAPE—(*passionately sure of her now—in a low voice*) Nelly! (*then unable to restrain his triumphant exultance*) You've failed!

ELEANOR—(*smiling dimly at herself*) My acting—didn't convince me.

CAPE—We've failed!

ELEANOR—Are we weak? (*dreamily*) I'm happy.

CAPE—Strong! We can live again! (*exultantly—but as if testing her, warningly*) But we'll hate!

ELEANOR—(*in her same tone*) Yes!

CAPE—And we'll torture and tear, and clutch for each other's souls!—fight—fail and hate again—(*he raises his voice in aggressive triumph*)—but!—fail *with pride*—with joy!

ELEANOR—(*exalted by his exultation rather than by his words*) Yes!

CAPE—*Our* life is to bear together our burden which is our goal—on and up! Above the world, beyond its vision—our meaning!

ELEANOR—(*her eyes fixed on him—dreamily*) Your dream!

CAPE—(*half-sobbing as the intensity of his passion breaks the spell of his exultation*) Oh, Nelly, Nelly, I want to say so much what I feel but I can only stutter like an idiot! (*He has fallen on his knees before her.*)

ELEANOR—(*intensely moved—passionately*) I know! (*She bends over and kisses him.*)

CAPE—(*straining passionately for expression*) Listen! Often I wake up in the night—in a black world, alone in a hundred million years of darkness. I feel like crying out to God for mercy because life lives! Then instinctively I seek you—my hand touches you! You are there—beside me—alive—with you I become a whole, a truth! Life guides me back through the hundred million years to you. It reveals a beginning in unity that I may have faith in the unity of the end! (*He bows his head and kisses her feet ecstatically.*) I love you! Forgive me all I've ever done, all I'll ever do.

ELEANOR—(*brokenly*) No. Forgive me—my child, you! (*She begins to sob softly.*)

CAPE—(*looking at her—gently*) Why do you cry?

ELEANOR—Because I'm happy. (*then with a sudden tearful gayety*) You be happy! You ought to be! Isn't our future as hard as you could wish? Haven't we your old dreams back again?

CAPE—Deeper and more beautiful!

ELEANOR—(*smiling*) Deeper and more beautiful! (*She ascends the stairs slowly.*) Come! (*She reaches the top of the stairway and stands there looking down at him—then stretches out her arms with a passionate, tender gesture.*) Come!

CAPE—(*leaping to his feet—intensely*) My Own!

ELEANOR—(*with deep, passionate tenderness*) My lover!

CAPE—My wife! (*His eyes fixed on her he ascends. As he does so her arms move back until they are stretched out straight to right and left, forming a cross. Cape stops two steps below her—in a low, wondering tone*) Why do you stand like that?

ELEANOR—(*her head thrown back, her eyes shut—slowly, dreamily*) Perhaps I'm praying. I don't know. I love.

CAPE—(*deeply moved*) I love you!

ELEANOR—(*as if from a great distance*) We love! (*He moves close to her and his hands reach out for hers. For a moment as their hands touch they form together one cross. Then their arms go about each other and their lips meet.*)

(*The Curtain Falls*)

ALL GOD'S CHILLUN
GOT WINGS

CHARACTERS

JIM HARRIS
MRS. HARRIS, *his mother*
HATTIE, *his sister*
ELLA DOWNEY
SHORTY
JOE
MICKEY
WHITES AND NEGROES

SCENES

ACT I

SCENE I: A corner in lower New York. Years ago. End of an afternoon in Spring.

SCENE II: The same. Nine years later. End of an evening in Spring.

SCENE III: The same. Five years later. A night in Spring.

SCENE IV: The street before a church in the same ward. A morning some weeks later.

ACT II

SCENE I: A flat in the same ward. A morning two years later.

SCENE II: The same. At twilight some months later.

SCENE III: The same. A night some months later.

All God's Chillun Got Wings

ACT ONE

Scene One

A corner in lower New York, at the edge of a colored district. Three narrow streets converge. A triangular building in the rear, red brick, four-storied, its ground floor a grocery. Four-story tenements stretch away down the skyline of the two streets. The fire escapes are crowded with people. In the street leading left, the faces are all white; in the street leading right, all black. It is hot Spring. On the sidewalk are eight children, four boys and four girls. Two of each sex are white, two black. They are playing marbles. One of the black boys is Jim Harris. The little blonde girl, her complexion rose and white, who sits behind his elbow and holds his marbles is Ella Downey. She is eight. They play the game with concentrated attention for a while. People pass, black and white, the Negroes frankly participants in the spirit of Spring, the whites laughing constrainedly, awkward in natural emotion. Their words are lost. One hears only their laughter. It expresses the difference in race. There are street noises—the clattering roar of the Elevated, the puff of its locomotives, the ruminative lazy sound of a horse-car, the hooves of its team clacking on the cobbles. From the street of the whites a high-pitched, nasal tenor sings the chorus of "Only a Bird in a Gilded Cage." On the street of the blacks a Negro strikes up the chorus of: "I Guess I'll Have to Telegraph My Baby." As this singing ends, there is laughter, distinctive in quality, from both streets. Then silence. The light in the street begins to grow brilliant with the glow of the setting sun. The game of marbles goes on.

White Girl—(*tugging at the elbow of her brother*) Come on, Mickey!

Her Brother—(*roughly*) Aw, gwan, youse!

White Girl—Aw right, den. You kin git a lickin' if you wanter. (*gets up to move off*)

Her Brother—Aw, git off de eart'!

White Girl—De old woman'll be madder'n hell!

279

HER BROTHER—(*worried now*) I'm comin', ain't I? Hold your horses.

BLACK GIRL—(*to a black boy*) Come on, you Joe. We gwine git frailed too, you don't hurry.

JOE—Go long!

MICKEY—Bust up de game, huh? I gotta run! (*jumps to his feet*)

OTHER WHITE BOY—Me, too! (*jumps up*)

OTHER BLACK GIRL—Lawdy, it's late!

JOE—Me for grub!

MICKEY—(*to Jim Harris*) You's de winner, Jim Crow. Yeh gotta play tomorrer.

JIM—(*readily*) Sure t'ing, Mick. Come one, come all! (*He laughs.*)

OTHER WHITE BOY—Me, too! I gotta git back at yuh.

JIM—Aw right, Shorty.

LITTLE GIRLS—Hurry! Come on, come on! (*The six start off together. Then they notice that Jim and Ella are hesitating, standing awkwardly and shyly together. They turn to mock.*)

JOE—Look at dat Jim Crow! Land sakes, he got a gal! (*He laughs. They all laugh.*)

JIM—(*ashamed*) Ne'er mind, you Chocolate!

MICKEY—Look at de two softies, will yeh! Mush! Mush! (*He and the two other boys take this up.*)

LITTLE GIRLS—(*pointing their fingers at Ella*) Shame! Shame! Everybody knows your name! Painty Face! Painty Face!

ELLA—(*hanging her head*) Shut up!

LITTLE WHITE GIRL—He's been carrying her books!

COLORED GIRL—Can't you find nuffin' better'n him, Ella? Look at de big feet he got! (*She laughs. They all laugh. Jim puts one foot on top of the other, looking at Ella.*)

ELLA—Mind yer own business, see! (*She strides toward them angrily. They jump up and dance in an ecstasy, screaming and laughing.*)

ALL—Found yeh out! Found yeh out!

MICKEY—Mush-head! Jim Crow de Sissy! Stuck on Painty Face!

JOE—Will Painty Face let you hold her doll, boy?

SHORTY—Sissy! Softy! (*Ella suddenly begins to cry. At this they all howl.*)

ALL—Cry-baby! Cry-baby! Look at her! Painty Face!

JIM—(*suddenly rushing at them, with clenched fists, furiously*) Shut yo' moufs! I kin lick de hull of you! (*They all run away, laughing, shouting, and jeering, quite triumphant now that they have made him, too, lose his temper. He comes back to Ella, and stands beside her sheepishly, stepping on one foot after the other. Suddenly he blurts out*) Don't bawl no more. I done chased 'em.

ELLA—(*comforted, politely*) T'anks.

JIM—(*swelling out*) It was a cinch. I kin wipe up de street wid any one of dem. (*He stretches out his arms, trying to bulge out his biceps.*) Feel dat muscle!

ELLA—(*does so gingerly—then with admiration*) My!

JIM—(*protectingly*) You mustn't never be scared when I'm hanging round, Painty Face.

ELLA—Don't call me that, Jim—please!

JIM—(*contritely*) I didn't mean nuffin'. I didn't know you'd mind.

ELLA—I do—more'n anything.

JIM—You oughtn't to mind. Dey's jealous, dat's what.

ELLA—Jealous? Of what?

JIM—(*pointing to her face*) Of dat. Red 'n' white. It's purty.

ELLA—I hate it!

JIM—It's purty. Yes, it's—it's purty. It's—outa sight!

ELLA—I hate it. I wish I was black like you.

JIM—(*sort of shrinking*) No you don't. Dey'd call you Crow, den—or Chocolate—or Smoke.

ELLA—I wouldn't mind.

JIM—(*somberly*) Dey'd call you nigger sometimes, too.

ELLA—I wouldn't mind.

JIM—(*humbly*) You wouldn't mind?

ELLA—No, I wouldn't mind. (*an awkward pause*)

JIM—(*suddenly*) You know what, Ella? Since I been tuckin' yo' books to school and back, I been drinkin' lots o' chalk 'n' water tree times a day. Dat Tom, de barber, he tole me dat make me white, if I drink enough. (*pleadingly*) Does I look whiter?

ELLA—(*comfortingly*) Yes—maybe—a little bit—

JIM—(*trying a careless tone*) Reckon dat Tom's a liar, an' de joke's on me! Dat chalk only makes me feel kinder sick inside.

ELLA—(*wonderingly*) Why do you want to be white?

JIM—Because—just because—I lak dat better.

ELLA—I wouldn't. I like black. Let's you and me swap. I'd like to be black. (*clapping her hands*) Gee, that'd be fun, if we only could!

JIM—(*hesitatingly*) Yes—maybe—

ELLA—Then they'd call me Crow, and you'd be Painty Face!

JIM—They wouldn't never dast call you nigger, you bet! I'd kill 'em! (*A long pause. Finally she takes his hand shyly. They both keep looking as far away from each other as possible.*)

ELLA—I like you.

JIM—I like you.

ELLA—Do you want to be my feller?

JIM—Yes.

ELLA—Then I'm your girl.

JIM—Yes. (*then grandly*) You kin bet none o' de gang gwine call you Painty Face from dis out! I lam' 'em good! (*The sun has set. Twilight has fallen on the street. An organ grinder comes up to the corner and plays "Annie Rooney." They stand hand-in-hand and listen. He goes away. It is growing dark.*)

ELLA—(*suddenly*) Golly, it's late! I'll git a lickin'!

JIM—Me, too.

ELLA—I won't mind it much.

JIM—Me nuther.

ELLA—See you going to school tomorrow?

JIM—Sure.

ELLA—I gotta skip now.

JIM—Me, too.

ELLA—I like you, Jim.

JIM—I like you.

ELLA—Don't forget.

JIM—Don't you.

ELLA—Good-by.

JIM—So long. (*They run away from each other—then stop abruptly, and turn as at a signal.*)

ELLA—Don't forget.

JIM—I won't, you bet!

ELLA—Here! (*She kisses her hand at him, then runs off in frantic embarrassment.*)

JIM—(*overcome*) Gee! (*Then he turns and darts away, as*

The Curtain Falls)

SCENE TWO

The same corner. Nine years have passed. It is again late Spring at a time in the evening which immediately follows the hour of Scene One. Nothing has changed much. One street is still all white, the other all black. The fire escapes are laden with drooping human beings. The grocery store is still at the corner. The street noises are now more rhythmically mechanical, electricity having taken the place of horse and steam. People pass, white and black. They laugh as in Scene One. From the street of the whites the high-pitched nasal tenor sings: "Gee, I Wish That I Had a Girl," and the Negro replies with "All I Got Was Sympathy." The singing is followed again by laughter from both streets. Then silence. The dusk grows darker. With a spluttering flare the arc-lamp at the corner is lit and sheds a pale glare over the street. Two young roughs slouch up to the corner, as tough in manner as they can make themselves. One is the Shorty of Scene One; the other the Negro, Joe. They stand loafing. A boy of seventeen or so passes by, escorting a girl of about the same age. Both are dressed in their best, the boy in black with stiff collar, the girl in white.

SHORTY—(*scornfully*) Hully cripes! Pipe who's here. (*to the girl, sneeringly*) Wha's matter, Liz? Don't yer recernize yer old fr'ens?

GIRL—(*frightenedly*) Hello, Shorty.

SHORTY—Why de glad rags? Goin' to graduation? (*He tries to obstruct their way, but, edging away from him, they turn and run.*)

JOE—Har-har! Look at dem scoot, will you! (*Shorty grins with satisfaction.*)

SHORTY—(*looking down other street*) Here comes Mickey.

JOE—He won de semi-final last night easy?

SHORTY—Knocked de bloke out in de thoid.

JOE—Dat boy's suah a-comin'! He'll be de champeen yit.

SHORTY—(*judicially*) Got a good chanct—if he leaves de broads alone. Dat's where he's wide open. (*Mickey comes in from the left. He is dressed loudly, a straw hat with a gaudy band cocked over one cauliflower ear. He has acquired a typical "pug's" face, with the added viciousness of a natural bully. One of his eyes is puffed, almost closed, as a result of his battle the night before. He swaggers up.*)

BOTH—Hello, Mickey.

MICKEY—Hello.

JOE—Hear you knocked him col'.

MICKEY—Sure. I knocked his block off. (*changing the subject*) Say. Seen 'em goin' past to de graduation racket?

SHORTY—(*with a wink*) Why? You int'rested?

JOE—(*chuckling*) Mickey's gwine roun' git a good conduct medal.

MICKEY—Sure. Dey kin pin it on de seat o' me pants. (*They laugh.*) Listen. Seen Ella Downey goin'?

SHORTY—Painty Face? No, she ain't been along.

MICKEY—(*with authority*) Can dat name, see! Want a bunch o' fives in yer kisser? Den nix! She's me goil, understan'?

JOE—(*venturing to joke*) Which one? Yo' number ten?

MICKEY—(*flattered*) Sure. De real K. O. one.

SHORTY—(*pointing right—sneeringly*) Gee! Pipe Jim Crow all dolled up for de racket.

JOE—(*with disgusted resentment*) You mean tell me dat nigger's graduatin'?

SHORTY—Ask him. (*Jim Harris comes in. He is dressed in black, stiff white collar, etc.—a quiet-mannered Negro boy with a queerly-baffled, sensitive face.*)

JIM—(*pleasantly*) Hello, fellows. (*They grunt in reply, looking over him scornfully.*)

JOE—(*staring resentfully*) Is you graduatin' tonight?

JIM—Yes.

JOE—(*spitting disgustedly*) Fo' Gawd's sake! You *is* gittin' high-falutin'!

JIM—(*smiling deprecatingly*) This is my second try. I didn't pass last year.

JOE—What de hell does it git you, huh? Whatever is you gwine do wid it now you gits it? Live lazy on yo' ol' woman?

JIM—(*assertively*) I'm going to study and become a lawyer.

JOE—(*with a snort*) Fo' Chris' sake, nigger!

JIM—(*fiercely*) Don't you call me that—not before them!

JOE—(*pugnaciously*) Does you deny you's a nigger? I shows you—

MICKEY—(*gives them both a push—truculently*) Cut it out, see! I'm runnin' dis corner. (*turning to Jim insultingly*) Say you! Painty Face's gittin' her ticket tonight, ain't she?

JIM—You mean Ella—

MICKEY—Painty Face Downey, dat's who I mean! I don't have to be perlite wit' her. She's me goil!

JIM—(*glumly*) Yes, she's graduating.

SHORTY—(*winks at Mickey*) Smart, huh?

MICKEY—(*winks back—meaningly*) Willin' to loin, take it from me! (*Jim stands tensely as if a struggle were going on in him.*)

JIM—(*finally blurts out*) I want to speak to you, Mickey—alone.

MICKEY—(*surprised—insultingly*) Aw, what de hell—!

JIM—(*excitedly*) It's important, I tell you!

MICKEY—Huh? (*stares at him inquisitively—then motions the others back carelessly and follows Jim down front*)

SHORTY—Some noive!

JOE—(*vengefully*) I gits dat Jim alone, you wait!

MICKEY—Well, spill de big news. I ain't got all night. I got a date.

JIM—With—Ella?

MICKEY—What's dat to you?

JIM—(*the words tumbling out*) What—I wanted to say! I know—I've heard—all the stories—what you've been doing around the ward—with other girls—it's none of my business, with them—but she—Ella—it's different—she's not that kind—

MICKEY—(*insultingly*) Who told yuh so, huh?

JIM—(*draws back his fist threateningly*) Don't you dare—! (*Mickey is so paralyzed by this effrontery that he actually steps back.*)

MICKEY—Say, cut de comedy! (*beginning to feel insulted*)

Listen, you Jim Crow! Ain't you wise I could give yuh one poke dat'd knock yuh into next week?

JIM—I'm only asking you to act square, Mickey.

MICKEY—What's it to yuh? Why, yuh lousy goat, she wouldn't spit on yuh even! She hates de sight of a coon.

JIM—(*in agony*) I—I know—but once she didn't mind—we were kids together—

MICKEY—Aw, ferget dat! Dis is *now*!

JIM—And I'm still her friend always—even if she don't like colored people—

MICKEY—*Coons*, why don't yuh say it right! De trouble wit' you is yuh're gittin' stuck up, dat's what! Stay where yeh belong, see! Yer old man made coin at de truckin' game and yuh're tryin' to buy yerself white—graduatin' and law, for Christ sake! Yuh're gittin' yerself in Dutch wit' everyone in de ward—and it ain't cause yer a coon neider. Don't de gang all train wit' Joe dere and lots of others? But yuh're tryin' to buy white and it won't git yuh no place, see!

JIM—(*trembling*) Some day—I'll show you—

MICKEY—(*turning away*) Aw, gwan!

JIM—D'you think I'd change—be you—your dirty white—!

MICKEY—(*whirling about*) What's dat?

JIM—(*with hysterical vehemence*) You act square with her—or I'll show you up—I'll report you—I'll write to the papers—the sporting writers—I'll let them know how white you are!

MICKEY—(*infuriated*) Yuh damn nigger, I'll bust yer jaw in! (*Assuming his ring pose he weaves toward Jim, his face set in a cruel scowl. Jim waits helplessly but with a certain dignity.*)

SHORTY—Cheese it! A couple bulls! And here's de Downey skoit comin', too.

MICKEY—I'll get yuh de next time! (*Ella Downey enters from the right. She is seventeen, still has the same rose and white complexion, is pretty but with a rather repelling bold air about her.*)

ELLA—(*smiles with pleasure when she sees Mickey*) Hello, Mick. Am I late? Say, I'm so glad you won last night. (*She glances from one to the other as she feels something in the air.*) Hello! What's up?

MICKEY—Dis boob. (*He indicates Jim scornfully.*)

JIM—(*diffidently*) Hello, Ella.

ELLA—(*shortly, turning away*) Hello. (*then to Mickey*) Come on, Mick. Walk down with me. I got to hurry.

JIM—(*blurts out*) Wait—just a second. (*painfully*) Ella, do you hate—colored people?

MICKEY—Aw, shut up!

JIM—Please answer.

ELLA—(*forcing a laugh*) Say! What is this—another exam?

JIM—(*doggedly*) Please answer.

ELLA—(*irritably*) Of course I don't! Haven't I been brought up alongside— Why, some of my oldest—the girls I've been to public school the longest with—

JIM—Do you hate me, Ella?

ELLA—(*confusedly and more irritably*) Say, is he drunk? Why should I? I don't hate anyone.

JIM—Then why haven't you ever hardly spoken to me—for years?

ELLA—(*resentfully*) What would I speak about? You and me've got nothing in common any more.

JIM—(*desperately*) Maybe not any more—but—right on this corner—do you remember once—?

ELLA—I don't remember nothing! (*angrily*) Say! What's got into you to be butting into my business all of a sudden like this? Because you finally managed to graduate, has it gone to your head?

JIM—No, I—only want to help you, Ella.

ELLA—Of all the nerve! You're certainly forgetting your place! Who's asking you for help, I'd like to know? Shut up and stop bothering me!

JIM—(*insistently*) If you ever need a friend—a true friend—

ELLA—I've got lots of friends among my own—kind, I can tell you. (*exasperatedly*) You make me sick! Go to the devil! (*She flounces off. The three men laugh. Mickey follows her. Jim is stricken. He goes and sinks down limply on a box in front of the grocery store.*)

SHORTY—I'm going to shoot a drink. Come on, Joe, and I'll blow yuh.

JOE—(*who has never ceased to follow every move of Jim's with angry, resentful eyes*) Go long. I'se gwine stay here a secon'. I got a lil' argyment. (*He points to Jim.*)

SHORTY—Suit yerself. Do a good job. See yuh later. (*He goes, whistling.*)

JOE—(*stands for a while glaring at Jim, his fierce little eyes peering out of his black face. Then he spits on his hands aggressively and strides up to the oblivious Jim. He stands in front of him, gradually working himself into a fury at the other's seeming indifference to his words.*) Listen to me, nigger: I got a heap to whisper in yo' ear! Who is you, anyhow? Who does you think you is? Don't yo' old man and mine work on de docks togidder befo' yo' old man gits his own truckin' business? Yo' ol' man swallers his nickels, my ol' man buys him beer wid dem and swallers dat—dat's the on'y diff'rence. Don't you 'n' me drag up togidder?

JIM—(*dully*) I'm your friend, Joe.

JOE—No, you isn't! I ain't no fren o' yourn! I don't even know who you is! What's all dis schoolin' you doin'? What's all dis dressin' up and graduatin' an' sayin' you gwine study be a lawyer? What's all dis fakin' an' pretendin' and swellin' out grand an' talkin' soft and perlite? What's all dis denyin' you's a nigger—an' wid de white boys listenin' to you say it! Is you aimin' to buy white wid yo' ol' man's dough like Mickey say? What is you? (*in a rage at the other's silence*) You don't talk? Den I takes it out o' yo' hide! (*He grabs Jim by the throat with one hand and draws the other fist back.*) Tell me befo' I wrecks yo' face in! Is you a nigger or isn't you? (*shaking him*) Is you a nigger, Nigger? Nigger, is you a nigger?

JIM—(*looking into his eyes—quietly*) Yes. I'm a nigger. We're both niggers. (*They look at each other for a moment. Joe's rage vanishes. He slumps onto a box beside Jim's. He offers him a cigarette. Jim takes it. Joe scratches a match and lights both their cigarettes.*)

JOE—(*after a puff, with full satisfaction*) Man, why didn't you 'splain dat in de fust place?

JIM—We're both niggers. (*The same hand-organ man of Scene One comes to the corner. He plays the chorus of "Bonbon Buddie The Chocolate Drop." They both stare straight ahead listening. Then the organ man goes away. A silence. Joe gets to his feet.*)

JOE—I'll go get me a cold beer. (*He starts to move off—then turns.*) Time you was graduatin', ain't it? (*He goes. Jim remains sitting on his box staring straight before him as*

The Curtain Falls)

SCENE THREE

The same corner five years later. Nothing has changed much. It is a night in Spring. The arc-lamp discovers faces with a favorless cruelty. The street noises are the same but more intermittent and dulled with a quality of fatigue. Two people pass, one black and one white. They are tired. They both yawn, but neither laughs. There is no laughter from the two streets. From the street of the whites the tenor, more nasal than ever and a bit drunken, wails in high barber-shop falsetto the last half of the chorus of "When I Lost You." The Negro voice, a bit maudlin in turn, replies with the last half of "Waitin' for the Robert E. Lee." Silence. Shorty enters. He looks tougher than ever, the typical gangster. He stands waiting, singing a bit drunkenly, peering down the street.

SHORTY—(*indignantly*) Yuh bum! Ain't yuh ever comin'? (*He begins to sing*) "And sewed up in her yeller kimona, She had a blue-barreled forty-five gun, For to get her man Who'd done her wrong." (*Then he comments scornfully*) Not her, dough! No gat for her. She ain't got de noive. A little sugar. Dat'll fix her. (*Ella enters. She is dressed poorly, her face is pale and hollow-eyed, her voice cold and tired.*)

SHORTY—Yuh got de message?

ELLA—Here I am.

SHORTY—How yuh been?

ELLA—All right. (*A pause. He looks at her puzzledly.*)

SHORTY—(*a bit embarrassedly*) Well, I s'pose yuh'd like me to give yuh some dope on Mickey, huh?

ELLA—No.

SHORTY—Mean to say yuh don't wanter know where he is or what he's doin'?

ELLA—No.

SHORTY—Since when?

ELLA—A long time.

SHORTY—(*after a pause—with a rat-like viciousness*) Between you'n me, kid, you'll get even soon—you'n all de odder dames he's tossed. I'm on de inside. I've watched him trainin'. His next scrap, watch it! He'll go! It won't be de odder guy. It'll be all youse dames he's kidded—and de ones what's kidded him. Youse'll all be in de odder guy's corner. He won't need no odder seconds. Youse'll trow water on him, and sponge his face, and take de kinks out of his socker—and Mickey'll catch it on de button—and he won't be able to take it no more—'cause all your weight—you and de odders—'ll be behind dat punch. Ha ha! (*He laughs an evil laugh.*) And Mickey'll go—down to his knees first— (*He sinks to his knees in the attitude of a groggy boxer.*)

ELLA—I'd like to see him on his knees!

SHORTY—And den—flat on his pan—dead to de world— de boidies singin' in de trees—ten—out! (*He suits his action to the words, sinking flat on the pavement, then rises and laughs the same evil laugh.*)

ELLA—He's been out—for me—a long time. (*a pause*) Why did you send for me?

SHORTY—He sent me.

ELLA—Why?

SHORTY—To slip you dis wad o' dough. (*He reluctantly takes a roll of bills from his pocket and holds it out to her.*)

ELLA—(*looks at the money indifferently*) What for?

SHORTY—For you.

ELLA—No.

SHORTY—For de kid den.

ELLA—The kid's dead. He took diphtheria.

SHORTY—Hell yuh say! When?

ELLA—A long time.

SHORTY—Why didn't you write Mickey—?

ELLA—Why should I? He'd only be glad.

SHORTY—(*after a pause*) Well—it's better.

ELLA—Yes.

SHORTY—You made up wit yer family?

ELLA—No chance.

SHORTY—Livin' alone?

ELLA—In Brooklyn.

SHORTY—Workin'?

ELLA—In a factory.

SHORTY—You're a sucker. There's lots of softer snaps fer you, kid—

ELLA—I know what you mean. No.

SHORTY—Don't yuh wanter step out no more—have fun—live?

ELLA—I'm through.

SHORTY—(*mockingly*) Jump in de river, huh? T'ink it over, baby. I kin start yuh right in my stable. No one'll bodder yuh den. I got influence.

ELLA—(*without emphasis*) You're a dirty dog. Why doesn't someone kill you?

SHORTY—Is dat so! What're you? They say you been travelin' round with Jim Crow.

ELLA—He's been my only friend.

SHORTY—A nigger!

ELLA—The only white man in the world! Kind and white. You're all black—black to the heart.

SHORTY—Nigger-lover! (*He throws the money in her face. It falls to the street.*) Listen, you! Mickey says he's off of yuh for keeps. Dis is de finish! Dat's what he sent me to tell you. (*glances at her searchingly—a pause*) Yuh won't make no trouble?

ELLA—Why should I? He's free. The kid's dead. I'm free. No hard feelings—only—I'll be there in spirit at his next fight, tell him! I'll take your tip—the other corner—second the punch—nine—ten—out! He's free! That's all. (*She grins horribly at Shorty.*) Go away, Shorty.

SHORTY—(*looking at her and shaking his head—maudlinly*) Groggy! Groggy! We're all groggy! Gluttons for punishment! Me for a drink. So long. (*He goes. A Salvation Army band comes toward the corner. They are playing and singing "Till We Meet at Jesus' Feet." They reach the end as they enter and stop before Ella. The Captain steps forward.*)

CAPTAIN—Sister—

ELLA—(*picks up the money and drops it in his hat—mockingly*) Here. Go save yourself. Leave me alone.

A WOMAN SALVATIONIST—Sister—

ELLA—Never mind that. I'm not in your line—yet. (*as

they hesitate, wonderingly) I want to be alone. (*To the thud of the big drum they march off. Ella sits down on a box, her hands hanging at her sides. Presently Jim Harris comes in. He has grown into a quietly-dressed, studious-looking Negro with an intelligent yet queerly-baffled face.*)

JIM—(*with a joyous but bewildered cry*) Ella! I just saw Shorty—

ELLA—(*smiling at him with frank affection*) He had a message from Mickey.

JIM—(*sadly*) Ah!

ELLA—(*pointing to the box behind her*) Sit down. (*He does so. A pause—then she says indifferently*) It's finished. I'm free, Jim.

JIM—(*wearily*) We're never free—except to do what we have to do.

ELLA—What are you getting gloomy about all of a sudden?

JIM—I've got the report from the school. I've flunked again.

ELLA—Poor Jim.

JIM—Don't pity me. I'd like to kick myself all over the block. Five years—and I'm still plugging away where I ought to have been at the end of two.

ELLA—Why don't you give it up?

JIM—No!

ELLA—After all, what's being a lawyer?

JIM—A lot—to me—what it means. (*intensely*) Why, if I was a Member of the Bar right now, Ella, I believe I'd almost have the courage to—

ELLA—What?

JIM—Nothing. (*after a pause—gropingly*) I can't explain—just—but it hurts like fire. It brands me in my pride. I swear I know more'n any member of my class. I ought to, I study harder. I work like the devil. It's all in my head—all fine and correct to a T. Then when I'm called on—I stand up—all the white faces looking at me—and I can feel their eyes—I hear my own voice sounding funny, trembling—and all of a sudden it's all gone in my head—there's nothing remembered—and I hear myself stuttering—and give up—sit down—They don't laugh, hardly ever. They're kind. They're good people. (*in a frenzy*) They're considerate, damn them! But I feel branded!

ELLA—Poor Jim.

JIM—(*going on painfully*) And it's the same thing in the written exams. For weeks before I study all night. I can't sleep anyway. I learn it all, I see it, I understand it. Then they give me the paper in the exam room. I look it over, I know each answer—perfectly. I take up my pen. On all sides are white men starting to write. They're so sure—even the ones that I know know nothing. But I know it all—but I can't remember any more—it fades—it goes—it's gone. There's a blank in my head—stupidity—I sit like a fool fighting to remember a little bit here, a little bit there—not enough to pass—not enough for anything—when I know it all!

ELLA—(*compassionately*) Jim. It isn't worth it. You don't need to—

JIM—I need it more than anyone ever needed anything. I need it to live.

ELLA—What'll it prove?

JIM—Nothing at all much—but everything to me.

ELLA—You're so much better than they are in every other way.

JIM—(*looking up at her*) Then—you understand?

ELLA—Of course. (*affectionately*) Don't I know how fine you've been to me! You've been the only one in the world who's stood by me—the only understanding person—and all after the rotten way I used to treat you.

JIM—But before that—way back so high—you treated me good. (*He smiles.*)

ELLA—You've been white to me, Jim. (*She takes his hand.*)

JIM—White—to you!

ELLA—Yes.

JIM—All love is white. I've always loved you. (*this with the deepest humility*)

ELLA—Even now—after all that's happened!

JIM—Always.

ELLA—I like you, Jim—better than anyone else in the world.

JIM—That's more than enough, more than I ever hoped

for. (*The organ grinder comes to the corner. He plays the chorus of "Annie Laurie." They sit listening, hand in hand.*) Would you ever want to marry me, Ella?

ELLA—Yes, Jim.

JIM—(*as if this quick consent alarmed him*) No, no, don't answer now. Wait! Turn it over in your mind! Think what it means to you! Consider it—over and over again! I'm in no hurry, Ella. I can wait months—years—

ELLA—I'm alone. I've got to be helped. I've got to help someone—or it's the end—one end or another.

JIM—(*eagerly*) Oh, I'll help—I know I can help—I'll give my life to help you—that's what I've been living for—

ELLA—But can I help you? Can I help you?

JIM—Yes! Yes! We'll go abroad where a man is a man—where it don't make that difference—where people are kind and wise to see the soul under skins. I don't ask you to love me—I don't dare to hope nothing like that! I don't want nothing—only to wait—to know you like me—to be near you—to keep harm away—to make up for the past—to never let you suffer any more—to serve you—to lie at your feet like a dog that loves you—to kneel by your bed like a nurse that watches over you sleeping—to preserve and pro-tect and shield you from evil and sorrow—to give my life and my blood and all the strength that's in me to give you peace and joy—to become your slave!—yes, be your slave—your black slave that adores you as sacred! (*He has sunk to his knees. In a frenzy of self-abnegation, as he says the last words he beats his head on the flagstones.*)

ELLA—(*overcome and alarmed*) Jim! Jim! You're crazy! I want to help you, Jim—I want to help—

(*The Curtain Falls*)

SCENE FOUR

Some weeks or so later. A street in the same ward in front of an old brick church. The church sets back from the sidewalk in a yard enclosed by a rusty iron railing with a gate at center. On each side of this yard are tenements. The buildings have a stern, for-

*bidding look. All the shades on the windows are drawn down, giv-
ing an effect of staring, brutal eyes that pry callously at human
beings without acknowledging them. Even the two tall, narrow
church windows on either side of the arched door are blanked with
dull green shades. It is a bright sunny morning. The district is
unusually still, as if it were waiting, holding its breath.*

*From the street of the blacks to the right a Negro tenor sings in
a voice of shadowy richness—the first stanza with a contented,
childlike melancholy—*

> Sometimes I feel like a mourning dove,
> Sometimes I feel like a mourning dove,
> Sometimes I feel like a mourning dove,
> I feel like a mourning dove.
> Feel like a mourning dove.

The second with a dreamy, boyish exultance—

> Sometimes I feel like an eagle in the air,
> Sometimes I feel like an eagle in the air,
> Sometimes I feel like an eagle in the air,
> I feel like an eagle in the air.
> Feel like an eagle in the air.

The third with a brooding, earthbound sorrow—

> Sometimes I wish that I'd never been born,
> Sometimes I wish that I'd never been born,
> Sometimes I wish that I'd never been born,
> I wish that I'd never been born.
> Wish that I'd never been born.

*As the music dies down there is a pause of waiting stillness. This
is broken by one startling, metallic clang of the church-bell. As if
it were a signal, people—men, women, children—pour from the
two tenements, whites from the tenement to the left, blacks from
the one to the right. They hurry to form into two racial lines on
each side of the gate, rigid and unyielding, staring across at each
other with bitter hostile eyes. The halves of the big church door
swing open and Jim and Ella step out from the darkness within
into the sunlight. The doors slam behind them like wooden lips of
an idol that has spat them out. Jim is dressed in black. Ella in
white, both with extreme plainness. They stand in the sunlight,
shrinking and confused. All the hostile eyes are now concentrated
on them. They become aware of the two lines through which they
must pass; they hesitate and tremble; then stand there staring*

back at the people as fixed and immovable as they are. The organ grinder comes in from the right. He plays the chorus of "Old Black Joe." As he finishes the bell of the church clangs one more single stroke, insistently dismissing.

JIM—(*as if the sound had awakened him from a trance, reaches out and takes her hand*) Come. Time we got to the steamer. Time we sailed away over the sea. Come, Honey! (*She tries to answer but her lips tremble; she cannot take her eyes off the eyes of the people; she is unable to move. He sees this and, keeping the same tone of profound, affectionate kindness, he points upward in the sky, and gradually persuades her eyes to look up.*) Look up, Honey! See the sun! Feel his warm eye lookin' down! Feel how kind he looks! Feel his blessing deep in your heart, your bones! Look up, Honey! (*Her eyes are fixed on the sky now. Her face is calm. She tries to smile bravely back at the sun. Now he pulls her by the hand, urging her gently to walk with him down through the yard and gate, through the lines of people. He is maintaining an attitude to support them through the ordeal only by a terrible effort, which manifests itself in the hysteric quality of ecstasy which breaks into his voice.*) And look at the sky! Ain't it kind and blue! Blue for hope. Don't they say blue's for hope? Hope! That's for us, Honey. All those blessings in the sky! What's it the Bible says? Falls on just and unjust alike? No, that's the sweet rain. Pshaw, what am I saying? All mixed up. There's no unjust about it. We're all the same— equally just—under the sky—under the sun—under God— sailing over the sea—to the other side of the world—the side where Christ was born—the kind side that takes count of the soul—over the sea—the sea's blue, too—. Let's not be late—let's get that steamer! (*They have reached the curb now, passed the lines of people. She is looking up to the sky with an expression of trancelike calm and peace. He is on the verge of collapse, his face twitching, his eyes staring. He calls hoarsely*) Taxi! Where is he? Taxi!

(*The Curtain Falls*)

ACT TWO

SCENE ONE

Two years later. A flat of the better sort in the Negro district near the corner of Act One. This is the parlor. Its furniture is a queer clash. The old pieces are cheaply ornate, naïvely, childishly gaudy—the new pieces give evidence of a taste that is diametrically opposed, severe to the point of somberness. On one wall, in a heavy gold frame, is a colored photograph—the portrait of an elderly Negro with an able, shrewd face but dressed in outlandish lodge regalia, a get-up adorned with medals, sashes, a cocked hat with frills—the whole effect as absurd to contemplate as one of Napoleon's Marshals in full uniform. In the left corner, where a window lights it effectively, is a Negro primitive mask from the Congo—a grotesque face, inspiring obscure, dim connotations in one's mind, but beautifully done, conceived in a true religious spirit. In this room, however, the mask acquires an arbitrary accentuation. It dominates by a diabolical quality that contrast imposes upon it.

There are two windows on the left looking out in the street. In the rear, a door to the hall of the building. In the right, a doorway with red and gold portières leading into the bedroom and the rest of the flat. Everything is cleaned and polished. The dark brown wall paper is new, the brilliantly figured carpet also. There is a round mahogany table at center. In a rocking chair by the table Mrs. Harris is sitting. She is a mild-looking, gray-haired Negress of sixty-five, dressed in an old-fashioned Sunday-best dress. Walking about the room nervously is Hattie, her daughter, Jim's sister, a woman of about thirty with a high-strung, defiant face—an intelligent head showing both power and courage. She is dressed severely, mannishly.

It is a fine morning in Spring. Sunshine comes through the windows at the left.

MRS. HARRIS—Time dey was here, ain't it?

HATTIE—(*impatiently*) Yes.

MRS. H.—(*worriedly*) You ain't gwine ter kick up a fuss, is you—like you done wid Jim befo' de weddin'?

HATTIE—No. What's done is done.

MRS. H.—We mustn't let her see we hold it agin' her—de bad dat happened to her wid dat no-count fighter.

HATTIE—I certainly never give that a thought. It's what she's done to Jim—making him run away and give up his fight—!

MRS. H.—Jim loves her a powerful lot, must be.

HATTIE—(*after a pause—bitterly*) I wonder if she loves Jim!

MRS. H.—She must, too. Yes, she must, too. Don't you forget dat it was hard for her—mighty, mighty hard—harder for de white dan for de black!

HATTIE—(*indignantly*) Why should it be?

MRS. H.—(*shaking her head*) I ain't talkin' of shoulds. It's too late for shoulds. Dey's o'ny one should. (*solemnly*) De white and de black shouldn't mix dat close. Dere's one road where de white goes on alone; dere's anudder road where de black goes on alone—

HATTIE—Yes, if they'd only leave us alone!

MRS. H.—Dey leaves your Pa alone. He comes to de top till he's got his own business, lots o' money in de bank, he owns a building even befo' he die. (*She looks up proudly at the picture. Hattie sighs impatiently—then her mother goes on.*) Dey leaves me alone. I bears four children into dis worl', two dies, two lives, I helps you two grow up fine an' healthy and eddicated wid schoolin' and money fo' yo' comfort—

HATTIE—(*impatiently*) Ma!

MRS. H.—I does de duty God set for me in dis worl'. Dey leaves me alone. (*Hattie goes to the window to hide her exasperation. The mother broods for a minute—then goes on.*) The worl' done change. Dey ain't no satisfaction wid nuffin' no more.

HATTIE—Oh! (*then after a pause*) They'll be here any minute now.

MRS. H.—Why didn't you go meet 'em at de dock like I axed you?

HATTIE—I couldn't. My face and Jim's among those hundreds of white faces— (*with a harsh laugh*) It would give her too much advantage!

MRS. H.—(*impatiently*) Don't talk dat way! What makes you so proud? (*then after a pause—sadly*) Hattie.

HATTIE—(*turning*) Yes, Ma.

MRS. H.—I want to see Jim again—my only boy—but—all de same I'd ruther he stayed away. He say in his letter he's happy, she's happy, dey likes it dere, de folks don't think nuffin' but what's natural at seeing 'em married. Why don't dey stay?

HATTIE—(*vehemently*) No! They were cowards to run away. If they believe in what they've done, then let them face it out, live it out here, be strong enough to conquer all prejudice!

MRS. H.—Strong? Dey ain't many strong. Dey ain't many happy neider. Dey was happy ovah yondah.

HATTIE—We don't deserve happiness till we've fought the fight of our race and won it! (*In the pause that follows there is a ring from back in the flat.*) It's the door bell! You go, Ma. I—I—I'd rather not. (*Her mother looks at her rebukingly and goes out agitatedly through the portières. Hattie waits, nervously walking about, trying to compose herself. There is a long pause. Finally the portières are parted and Jim enters. He looks much older, graver, worried.*)

JIM—Hattie!

HATTIE—Jim! (*They embrace with great affection.*)

JIM—It's great to see you again! You're looking fine.

HATTIE—(*looking at him searchingly*) You look well, too—thinner maybe—and tired. (*then as she sees him frowning*) But where's Ella?

JIM—With Ma. (*apologetically*) She sort of—broke down—when we came in. The trip wore her out.

HATTIE—(*coldly*) I see.

JIM—Oh, it's nothing serious. Nerves. She needs a rest.

HATTIE—Wasn't living in France restful?

JIM—Yes, but—too lonely—especially for her.

HATTIE—(*resentfully*) Why? Didn't the people there want to associate—?

JIM—(*quickly*) Oh, no indeedy, they didn't think anything of that. (*after a pause*) But—she did. For the first year it was all right. Ella liked everything a lot. She went out with French folks and got so she could talk it a little—and I learned it—a little. We were having a right nice time. I never thought then we'd ever want to come back here.

HATTIE—(*frowning*) But—what happened to change you?

JIM—(*after a pause—haltingly*) Well—you see—the first year—she and I were living around—like friends—like a brother and sister—like you and I might.

HATTIE—(*her face becoming more and more drawn and tense*) You mean—then—? (*She shudders—then after a pause*) She loves you, Jim?

JIM—If I didn't know that I'd have to jump in the river.

HATTIE—Are you sure she loves you?

JIM—Isn't that why she's suffering?

HATTIE—(*letting her breath escape through her clenched teeth*) Ah!

JIM—(*suddenly springs up and shouts almost hysterically*) Why d'you ask me all those damn questions? Are you trying to make trouble between us?

HATTIE—(*controlling herself—quietly*) No, Jim.

JIM—(*after a pause—contritely*) I'm sorry, Hattie. I'm kind of on edge today. (*He sinks down on his chair—then goes on as if something forced him to speak.*) After that we got to living housed in. Ella didn't want to see nobody, she said just the two of us was enough. I was happy then—and I really guess she was happy, too—in a way—for a while. (*again a pause*) But she never did get to wanting to go out any place again. She got to saying she felt she'd be sure to run into someone she knew—from over here. So I moved us out to the country where no tourist ever comes—but it didn't make any difference to her. She got to avoiding the French folks the same as if they were Americans and I couldn't get it out of her mind. She lived in the house and got paler and paler, and more and more nervous and scarey, always imagining things—until I got to imagining things, too. I got to feeling blue. Got to sneering at myself that I wasn't any better than a quitter because I sneaked away right after getting married, didn't face nothing, gave up trying to become a Member of the Bar—and I got to suspecting Ella must feel that way about me, too—that I wasn't a *real man*!

HATTIE—(*indignantly*) She couldn't!

JIM—(*with hostility*) You don't need to tell me! All this was only in my own mind. We never quarreled a single bit. We never said a harsh word. We were as close to each other as could be. We were all there was in the world to each other. We were alone together! (*a pause*) Well, one day I got so I couldn't stand it. I could see she couldn't stand it. So I just up and said: Ella, we've got to have a plain talk, look everything straight in the face, hide nothing, come out with the exact truth of the way we feel.

HATTIE—And you decided to come back!

JIM—Yes. We decided the reason we felt sort of ashamed was we'd acted like cowards. We'd run away from the thing— and taken it with us. We decided to come back and face it and live it down in ourselves, and prove to ourselves we were strong in our love—and then, and that way only, by being brave we'd free ourselves, and gain confidence, and be really free inside and able then to go anywhere and live in peace and equality with ourselves and the world without any guilty uncomfortable feeling coming up to rile us. (*He has talked himself now into a state of happy confidence.*)

HATTIE—(*bending over and kissing him*) Good for you! I admire you so much, Jim! I admire both of you! And are you going to begin studying right away and get admitted to the Bar?

JIM—You bet I am!

HATTIE—You must, Jim! Our race needs men like you to come to the front and help— (*As voices are heard approaching she stops, stiffens, and her face grows cold.*)

JIM—(*noticing this—warningly*) Remember Ella's been sick! (*losing control—threateningly*) You be nice to her, you hear! (*Mrs. Harris enters, showing Ella the way. The colored woman is plainly worried and perplexed. Ella is pale, with a strange, haunted expression in her eyes. She runs to Jim as to a refuge, clutching his hands in both of hers, looking from Mrs. Harris to Hattie with a frightened defiance.*)

MRS. H.—Dere he is, child, big's life! She was afraid we'd done kidnapped you away, Jim.

JIM—(*patting her hand*) This place ought to be familiar, Ella. Don't you remember playing here with us sometimes as a kid?

ELLA—(*queerly—with a frown of effort*) I remember playing marbles one night—but that was on the street.

JIM—Don't you remember Hattie?

HATTIE—(*coming forward with a forced smile*) It was a long time ago—but I remember Ella. (*She holds out her hand.*)

ELLA—(*taking it—looking at Hattie with the same queer defiance*) I remember. But you've changed so much.

HATTIE—(*stirred to hostility by Ella's manner—condescendingly*) Yes, I've grown older, naturally. (*then in a tone which, as if in spite of herself, becomes bragging*) I've worked so hard. First I went away to college, you know—then I took up postgraduate study—when suddenly I decided I'd accomplish more good if I gave up learning and took up teaching. (*She suddenly checks herself, ashamed, and stung by Ella's indifference.*) But this sounds like stupid boasting. I don't mean that. I was only explaining—

ELLA—(*indifferently*) I didn't know you'd been to school so long. (*a pause*) Where are you teaching? In a colored school, I suppose. (*There is an indifferent superiority in her words that is maddening to Hattie.*)

HATTIE—(*controlling herself*) Yes. A private school endowed by some wealthy members of our race.

ELLA—(*suddenly—even eagerly*) Then you must have taken lots of examinations and managed to pass them, didn't you?

HATTIE—(*biting her lips*) I always passed with honors!

ELLA—Yes, we both graduated from the same High School, didn't we? That was dead easy for me. Why I hardly even looked at a book. But Jim says it was awfully hard for him. He failed one year, remember? (*She turns and smiles at Jim—a tolerant, superior smile but one full of genuine love. Hattie is outraged, but Jim smiles.*)

JIM—Yes, it was hard for me, Honey.

ELLA—And the law school examinations Jim hardly ever could pass at all. Could you? (*She laughs lovingly.*)

HATTIE—(*harshly*) Yes, he could! He can! He'll pass them now—if you'll give him a chance!

JIM—(*angrily*) Hattie!

MRS. HARRIS—Hold yo' fool tongue!

HATTIE—(*sullenly*) I'm sorry. (*Ella has shrunk back against Jim. She regards Hattie with a sort of wondering hatred. Then she looks away about the room. Suddenly her eyes fasten on the primitive mask and she gives a stifled scream.*)

JIM—What's the matter, Honey?

ELLA—(*pointing*) That! For God's sake, what is it?

HATTIE—(*scornfully*) It's a Congo mask. (*She goes and picks it up.*) I'll take it away if you wish. I thought you'd like it. It was my wedding present to Jim.

ELLA—What is it?

HATTIE—It's a mask which used to be worn in religious ceremonies by my people in Africa. But, aside from that, it's beautifully made, a work of Art by a real artist—as real in his way as your Michael Angelo. (*forces Ella to take it*) Here. Just notice the workmanship.

ELLA—(*defiantly*) I'm not scared of it if you're not. (*looking at it with disgust*) Beautiful? Well, some people certainly have queer notions! It looks ugly to me and stupid—like a kid's game—making faces! (*She slaps it contemptuously.*) Pooh! You needn't look hard at me. I'll give you the laugh. (*She goes to put it back on the stand.*)

JIM—Maybe, if it disturbs you, we better put it in some other room.

ELLA—(*defiantly aggressive*) No. I want it here where I can give it the laugh! (*She sets it there again—then turns suddenly on Hattie with aggressive determination.*) Jim's not going to take any more examinations! I won't let him!

HATTIE—(*bursting forth*) Jim! Do you hear that? There's white justice!—their fear for their superiority!—

ELLA—(*with a terrified pleading*) Make her go away, Jim!

JIM—(*losing control—furiously to his sister*) Either you leave here—or we will!

MRS. H.—(*weeping—throws her arms around Hattie*) Let's go, chile! Let's go!

HATTIE—(*calmly now*) Yes, Ma. All right. (*They go through the portières. As soon as they are gone, Jim suddenly collapses into a chair and hides his head in his hands. Ella stands beside him for a moment. She stares distractedly about her, at the portrait, at the mask, at the furniture, at Jim. She seems fighting to escape from some weight on her mind. She throws this off and, completely her old self for the moment, kneels by Jim and pats his shoulder.*)

ELLA—(*with kindness and love*) Don't, Jim! Don't cry, please! You don't suppose I really meant that about the examinations, do you? Why, of course, I didn't mean a word! I couldn't mean it! I want you to take the examinations! I want you to pass! I want you to be a lawyer! I want you to be the best lawyer in the country! I want you to show 'em—all the dirty sneaking, gossiping liars that talk behind our backs— what a man I married. I want the whole world to know you're the whitest of the white! I want you to climb and climb—and step on 'em, stamp right on their mean faces! I love you, Jim. You know that!

JIM—(*calm again—happily*) I hope so, Honey—and I'll make myself worthy.

HATTIE—(*appears in the doorway—quietly*) We're going now, Jim.

ELLA—No. Don't go.

HATTIE—We were going to, anyway. This is your house— Mother's gift to you, Jim.

JIM—(*astonished*) But I can't accept— Where are you going?

HATTIE—We've got a nice flat in the Bronx—(*with bitter pride*) in the heart of the Black Belt—the Congo—among our own people!

JIM—(*angrily*) You're crazy— I'll see Ma— (*He goes out. Hattie and Ella stare at each other with scorn and hatred for a moment, then Hattie goes. Ella remains kneeling for a moment by the chair, her eyes dazed and strange as she looks about her. Then she gets to her feet and stands before the portrait of Jim's father— with a sneer*)

ELLA—It's his Old Man—all dolled up like a circus horse! Well, they can't help it. It's in the blood, I suppose. They're ignorant, that's all there is to it. (*She moves to the mask—forcing a mocking tone*) Hello, sport! Who d'you think you're scaring? Not me! I'll give you the laugh. He won't pass, you wait and see. Not in a thousand years! (*She goes to the window and looks down at the street and mutters*) All black! Every one of them! (*then with sudden excitement*) No, there's one. Why, it's Shorty! (*She throws the window open and calls*) Shorty! Shorty! Hello, Shorty! (*She leans out and waves—then stops, remains there for a moment looking down, then shrinks back on the floor suddenly as if she wanted to hide—her whole face in an anguish.*) Say! Say! I wonder?— No, he didn't hear you. Yes, he did,

too! He must have! I yelled so loud you could hear me in
Jersey! No, what are you talking about? How would he hear
with all the kids yelling down there? He never heard a word,
I tell you! He did, too! He didn't want to hear you! He didn't
want to let anyone know he knew you! Why don't you acknowledge it? What are you lying about? I'm not! Why
shouldn't he? Where does he come in to—for God's sake,
who is Shorty, anyway? A pimp! Yes, and a dope-peddler,
too! D'you mean to say he'd have the nerve to hear me call
him and then deliberately—? Yes, I mean to say it! I do say
it! And it's true, and you know it, and you might as well be
honest for a change and admit it! He heard you but he didn't
want to hear you! He doesn't want to know you any more.
No, not even him! He's afraid it'd get him in wrong with the
old gang. Why? You know well enough! Because you married
a—a—a—well, I won't say it, but you know without my
mentioning names! (*Ella springs to her feet in horror and shakes
off her obsession with a frantic effort.*) Stop! (*then whimpering
like a frightened child*) Jim! Jim! Jim! Where are you? I want
you, Jim! (*She runs out of the room as*

The Curtain Falls)

Scene Two

*The same. Six months later. It is evening. The walls of the room
appear shrunken in, the ceiling lowered, so that the furniture, the
portrait, the mask look unnaturally large and domineering. Jim is
seated at the table studying, law books piled by his elbows. He is
keeping his attention concentrated only by a driving physical effort
which gives his face the expression of a runner's near the tape. His
forehead shines with perspiration. He mutters one sentence from
Blackstone over and over again, tapping his forehead with his fist
in time to the rhythm he gives the stale words. But, in spite of
himself, his attention wanders, his eyes have an uneasy, hunted
look, he starts at every sound in the house or from the street.
Finally, he remains rigid, Blackstone forgotten, his eyes fixed on
the portières with tense grief. Then he groans, slams the book shut,
goes to the window and throws it open and sinks down beside it,*

his arms on the sill, his head resting wearily on his arms, staring out into the night, the pale glare from the arc-lamp on the corner throwing his face into relief. The portières on the right are parted and Hattie comes in.

HATTIE—(*not seeing him at the table*) Jim! (*discovering him*) Oh, there you are. What're you doing?

JIM—(*turning to her*) Resting. Cooling my head. (*forcing a smile*) These law books certainly are a sweating proposition! (*then, anxiously*) How is she?

HATTIE—She's asleep now. I felt it was safe to leave her for a minute. (*after a pause*) What did the doctor tell you, Jim?

JIM—The same old thing. She must have rest, he says, her mind needs rest— (*bitterly*) But he can't tell me any prescription for that rest—leastways not any that'd work.

HATTIE—(*after a pause*) I think you ought to leave her, Jim—or let her leave you—for a while, anyway.

JIM—(*angrily*) You're like the doctor. Everything's so simple and easy. Do this and that happens. Only it don't. Life isn't simple like that—not in this case, anyway—no, it isn't simple a bit. (*after a pause*) I can't leave her. She can't leave me. And there's a million little reasons combining to make one big reason why we can't. (*a pause*) For her sake—if it'd do her good—I'd go—I'd leave—I'd do anything—because I love her. I'd kill myself even—jump out of this window this second—I've thought it over, too—but that'd only make matters worse for her. I'm all she's got in the world! Yes, that isn't bragging or fooling myself. I know that for a fact! Don't you know that's true? (*There is a pleading for the certainty he claims.*)

HATTIE—Yes, I know she loves you, Jim. I know that now.

JIM—(*simply*) Then we've got to stick together to the end, haven't we, whatever comes—and hope and pray for the best? (*a pause—then hopefully*) I think maybe this is the crisis in her mind. Once she settles this in herself, she's won to the other side. And me—once I become a Member of the Bar— then I win, too! We're both free—by our own fighting down our own weakness! We're both really, truly free! Then we can be happy with ourselves here or anywhere. She'll be proud then! Yes, she's told me again and again, she says she'll be actually proud!

HATTIE—(*turning away to conceal her emotion*) Yes, I'm sure—but you mustn't study too hard, Jim! You mustn't study too awfully hard!

JIM—(*gets up and goes to the table and sits down wearily*) Yes, I know. Oh, I'll pass easily. I haven't got any scarey feeling about that any more. And I'm doing two years' work in one here alone. That's better than schools, eh?

HATTIE—(*doubtfully*) It's wonderful, Jim.

JIM—(*his spirit evaporating*) If I can only hold out! It's hard! I'm worn out. I don't sleep. I get to thinking and thinking. My head aches and burns like fire with thinking. Round and round my thoughts go chasing like crazy chickens hopping and flapping before the wind. It gets me crazy mad— 'cause I can't stop!

HATTIE—(*watching him for a while and seeming to force herself to speak*) The doctor didn't tell you all, Jim.

JIM—(*dully*) What's that?

HATTIE—He told me you're liable to break down too, if you don't take care of yourself.

JIM—(*abjectly weary*) Let 'er come! I don't care what happens to me. Maybe if I get sick she'll get well. There's only so much bad luck allowed to one family, maybe. (*He forces a wan smile.*)

HATTIE—(*hastily*) Don't give in to that idea, for the Lord's sake!

JIM—I'm tired—and blue—that's all.

HATTIE—(*after another long pause*) I've got to tell you something else, Jim.

JIM—(*dully*) What?

HATTIE—The doctor said Ella's liable to be sick like this a very long time.

JIM—He told me that too—that it'd be a long time before she got back her normal strength. Well, I suppose that's got to be expected.

HATTIE—(*slowly*) He didn't mean convalescing—what he told me. (*a long pause*)

JIM—(*evasively*) I'm going to get other doctors in to see Ella—specialists. This one's a damn fool.

HATTIE—Be sensible, Jim. You'll have to face the truth—sooner or later.

JIM—(*irritably*) I know the truth about Ella better'n any doctor.

HATTIE—(*persuasively*) She'd get better so much sooner if you'd send her away to some nice sanitarium—

JIM—No! She'd die of shame there!

HATTIE—At least until after you've taken your examinations—

JIM—To hell with me!

HATTIE—Six months. That wouldn't be long to be parted.

JIM—What are you trying to do—separate us? (*He gets to his feet—furiously*) Go on out! Go on out!

HATTIE—(*calmly*) No, I won't. (*sharply*) There's something that's got to be said to you and I'm the only one with the courage— (*intensely*) Tell me, Jim, have you heard her raving when she's out of her mind?

JIM—(*with a shudder*) No!

HATTIE—You're lying, Jim. You must have—if you don't stop your ears—and the doctor says she may develop a violent mania, dangerous for you—get worse and worse until—Jim, you'll go crazy too—living this way. Today she raved on about "Black! Black!" and cried because she said her skin was turning black—that you had poisoned her—

JIM—(*in anguish*) That's only when she's out of her mind.

HATTIE—And then she suddenly called me a dirty nigger.

JIM—No! She never said that ever! She never would!

HATTIE—She did—and kept on and on! (*a tense pause*) She'll be saying that to you soon.

JIM—(*torturedly*) She don't mean it! She isn't responsible for what she's saying!

HATTIE—I know she isn't—yet she is just the same. It's deep down in her or it wouldn't come out.

JIM—Deep down in her people—not deep in her.

HATTIE—I can't make such distinctions. The race in me, deep in me, can't stand it. I can't play nurse to her any more, Jim,—not even for your sake. I'm afraid—afraid of myself—afraid sometime I'll kill her dead to set you free! (*She loses control and begins to cry.*)

JIM—(*after a long pause—somberly*) Yes, I guess you'd better stay away from here. Good-by.

HATTIE—Who'll you get to nurse her, Jim,—a white woman?

JIM—Ella'd die of shame. No, I'll nurse her myself.

HATTIE—And give up your studies?

JIM—I can do both.

HATTIE—You can't! You'll get sick yourself! Why, you look terrible even as it is—and it's only beginning!

JIM—I can do anything for her! I'm all she's got in the world! I've got to prove I can be all to her! I've got to prove worthy! I've got to prove she can be proud of me! I've got to prove I'm the whitest of the white!

HATTIE—(*stung by this last—with rebellious bitterness*) Is that the ambition she's given you? Oh, you soft, weak-minded fool, you traitor to your race! And the thanks you'll get—to be called a dirty nigger—to hear her cursing you because she can never have a child because it'll be born black—!

JIM—(*in a frenzy*) Stop!

HATTIE—I'll say what must be said even though you kill me, Jim. Send her to an asylum before you both have to be sent to one together.

JIM—(*with a sudden wild laugh*) Do you think you're threatening me with something dreadful now? Why, I'd like that. Sure, I'd like that! Maybe she'd like it better, too. Maybe we'd both find it all simple then—like you think it is now. Yes. (*He laughs again.*)

HATTIE—(*frightenedly*) Jim!

JIM—Together! You can't scare me even with hell fire if you say she and I go together. It's heaven then for me! (*with sudden savagery*) You go out of here! All you've ever been aiming to do is to separate us so we can't be together!

HATTIE—I've done what I did for your own good.

JIM—I have no own good. I only got a good together with her. I'm all she's got in the world! Let her call me nigger! Let her call me the whitest of the white! I'm all she's got in the world, ain't I? She's all I've got! You with your fool talk of the black race and the white race! Where does the human race get a chance to come in? I suppose that's simple for you. You lock it up in asylums and throw away the key! (*with fresh violence*) Go along! There isn't going to be no more people coming in here to separate—excepting the doctor. I'm going to lock the door and it's going to stay locked, you hear? Go along, now!

HATTIE—(*confusedly*) Jim!

JIM—(*pushes her out gently and slams the door after her—vaguely*) Go along! I got to study. I got to nurse Ella, too. Oh, I can do it! I can do anything for her! (*He sits down at the table and, opening the book, begins again to recite the line from Blackstone in a meaningless rhythm, tapping his forehead with his fist. Ella enters noiselessly through the portières. She wears a red dressing-gown over her night-dress but is in her bare feet. She has a carving-knife in her right hand. Her eyes fasten on Jim with a murderous mania. She creeps up behind him. Suddenly he senses something and turns. As he sees her he gives a cry, jumping up and catching her wrist. She stands fixed, her eyes growing bewildered and frightened.*)

JIM—(*aghast*) Ella! For God's sake! Do you want to murder me? (*She does not answer. He shakes her.*)

ELLA—(*whimperingly*) They kept calling me names as I was walking along—I can't tell you what, Jim—and then I grabbed a knife—

JIM—Yes! See! This! (*She looks at it frightenedly.*)

ELLA—Where did I—? I was having a nightmare—Where did they go—I mean, how did I get here? (*with sudden terrified pleading—like a little girl*) Oh, Jim—don't ever leave me alone! I have such terrible dreams, Jim—promise you'll never go away!

JIM—I promise, Honey.

ELLA—(*her manner becoming more and more childishly silly*) I'll be a little girl—and you'll be old Uncle Jim who's been with us for years and years— Will you play that?

JIM—Yes, Honey. Now you better go back to bed.

ELLA—(*like a child*) Yes, Uncle Jim. (*She turns to go. He pretends to be occupied by his book. She looks at him for a second—then suddenly asks in her natural woman's voice*) Are you studying hard, Jim?

JIM—Yes, Honey. Go to bed now. You need to rest, you know.

ELLA—(*stands looking at him, fighting with herself. A star-*

tling transformation comes over her face. It grows mean, vicious, full of jealous hatred. She cannot contain herself but breaks out harshly with a cruel, venomous grin) You dirty nigger!

JIM—(*starting as if he'd been shot*) Ella! For the good Lord's sake!

ELLA—(*coming out of her insane mood for a moment, aware of something terrible, frightened*) Jim! Jim! Why are you looking at me like that?

JIM—What did you say to me just then?

ELLA—(*gropingly*) Why, I—I said—I remember saying, are you studying hard, Jim? Why? You're not mad at that, are you?

JIM—No, Honey. What made you think I was mad? Go to bed now.

ELLA—(*obediently*) Yes, Jim. (*She passes behind the portières. Jim stares before him. Suddenly her head is thrust out at the side of the portières. Her face is again that of a vindictive maniac.*) Nigger! (*The face disappears—she can be heard running away, laughing with cruel satisfaction. Jim bows his head on his outstretched arms but he is too stricken for tears.*)

(*The Curtain Falls*)

SCENE THREE

The same, six months later. The sun has just gone down. The Spring twilight sheds a vague, gray light about the room, picking out the Congo mask on the stand by the window. The walls appear shrunken in still more, the ceiling now seems barely to clear the people's heads, the furniture and the characters appear enormously magnified. Law books are stacked in two great piles on each side of the table. Ella comes in from the right, the carving-knife in her hand. She is pitifully thin, her face is wasted, but her eyes glow with a mad energy, her movements are abrupt and spring-like. She looks stealthily about the room, then advances and stands before the mask, her arms akimbo, her attitude one of crazy mockery, fear and bravado. She is dressed in the red dressing-gown, grown dirty and ragged now, and is in her bare feet.

ELLA—I'll give you the laugh, wait and see! (*then in a confidential tone*) He thought I was asleep! He called, Ella, Ella—but I kept my eyes shut, I pretended to snore. I fooled him good. (*She gives a little hoarse laugh.*) This is the first time he's dared to leave me alone for months and months. I've been wanting to talk to you every day but this is the only chance— (*with sudden violence—flourishing her knife*) What're you grinning about, you dirty nigger, you? How dare you grin at me? I guess you forget what you are! That's always the way. Be kind to you, treat you decent, and in a second you've got a swelled head, you think you're somebody, you're all over the place putting on airs; why, it's got so I can't even walk down the street without seeing niggers, niggers everywhere. Hanging around, grinning, grinning—going to school—pretending they're white—taking examinations— (*She stops, arrested by the word, then suddenly*) That's where he's gone—down to the mail-box—to see if there's a letter from the Board—telling him— But why is he so long? (*She calls pitifully*) Jim! (*then in a terrified whimper*) Maybe he's passed! Maybe he's passed! (*in a frenzy*) No! No! He can't! I'd kill him! I'd kill myself! (*threatening the Congo mask*) It's you who're to blame for this! Yes, you! Oh, I'm on to you! (*then appealingly*) But why d'you want to do this to us? What have I ever done wrong to you? What have you got against me? I married you, didn't I? Why don't you let Jim alone? Why don't you let him be happy as he is—with me? Why don't you let me be happy? He's white, isn't he—the whitest man that ever lived? Where do you come in to interfere? Black! Black! Black as dirt! You've poisoned me! I can't wash myself clean! Oh, I hate you! I hate you! Why don't you let Jim and I be happy? (*She sinks down in his chair, her arms outstretched on the table. The door from the hall is slowly opened and Jim appears. His bloodshot, sleepless eyes stare from deep hollows. His expression is one of crushed numbness. He holds an open letter in his hand.*)

JIM—(*seeing Ella—in an absolutely dead voice*) Honey—I thought you were asleep.

ELLA—(*starts and wheels about in her chair*) What's that? You got—you got a letter—?

JIM—(*turning to close the door after him*) From the Board

of Examiners for admission to the Bar, State of New York—
God's country! (*He finishes up with a chuckle of ironic self-pity
so spent as to be barely audible.*)

ELLA—(*writhing out of her chair like some fierce animal, the
knife held behind her—with fear and hatred*) You didn't—you
didn't—you didn't pass, did you?

JIM—(*looking at her wildly*) Pass? Pass? (*He begins to chuckle
and laugh between sentences and phrases, rich, Negro laughter,
but heart-breaking in its mocking grief.*) Good Lord, child, how
come you can ever imagine such a crazy idea? Pass? Me? Jim
Crow Harris? Nigger Jim Harris—become a full-fledged
Member of the Bar! Why the mere notion of it is enough to
kill you with laughing! It'd be against all natural laws, all
human right and justice. It'd be miraculous, there'd be earth-
quakes and catastrophes, the seven Plagues'd come again and
locusts'd devour all the money in the banks, the second
Flood'd come roaring and Noah'd fall overboard, the sun'd
drop out of the sky like a ripe fig, and the Devil'd perform
miracles, and God'd be tipped head first right out of the Judgment seat! (*He laughs, maudlinly uproarious.*)

ELLA—(*her face beginning to relax, to light up*) Then you—
you didn't pass?

JIM—(*spent—giggling and gasping idiotically*) Well, I
should say not! I should certainly say not!

ELLA—(*With a cry of joy, pushes all the law books crashing to
the floor—then with childish happiness she grabs Jim by both
hands and dances up and down.*) Oh, Jim, I knew it! I knew
you couldn't! Oh, I'm so glad, Jim! I'm so happy! You're still
my old Jim—and I'm so glad! (*He looks at her dazedly, a fierce
rage slowly gathering on his face. She dances away from him. His
eyes follow her. His hands clench. She stands in front of the
mask—triumphantly*) There! What did I tell you? I told you
I'd give you the laugh! (*She begins to laugh with wild unre-
straint, grabs the mask from its place, sets it in the middle of the
table and plunging the knife down through it pins it to the table.*)
There! Who's got the laugh now?

JIM—(*his eyes bulging—hoarsely*) You devil! You white devil
woman! (*in a terrible roar, raising his fists above her head*) You
devil!

ELLA—(*looking up at him with a bewildered cry of terror*)

Jim! (*Her appeal recalls him to himself. He lets his arms slowly drop to his sides, bowing his head. Ella points tremblingly to the mask.*) It's all right, Jim! It's dead. The devil's dead. See! It couldn't live—unless you passed. If you'd passed it would have lived in you. Then I'd have had to kill you, Jim, don't you see?—or it would have killed me. But now I've killed it. (*She pats his hand.*) So you needn't ever be afraid any more, Jim.

JIM—(*dully*) I've got to sit down, Honey. I'm tired. I haven't had much chance for sleep in so long— (*He slumps down in the chair by the table.*)

ELLA—(*sits down on the floor beside him and holds his hand. Her face is gradually regaining an expression that is happy, child-like and pretty.*) I know, Jim! That was my fault. I wouldn't let you sleep. I couldn't let you. I kept thinking if he sleeps good then he'll be sure to study good and then he'll pass— and the devil'll win!

JIM—(*with a groan*) Don't, Honey!

ELLA—(*with a childish grin*) That was why I carried that knife around—(*she frowns—puzzled*)—one reason—to keep you from studying and sleeping by scaring you.

JIM—I wasn't scared of being killed. I was scared of what they'd do to you after.

ELLA—(*after a pause—like a child*) Will God forgive me, Jim?

JIM—Maybe He can forgive what you've done to me; and maybe He can forgive what I've done to you; but I don't see how He's going to forgive—Himself.

ELLA—I prayed and prayed. When you were away taking the examinations and I was alone with the nurse, I closed my eyes and pretended to be asleep but I was praying with all my might: O God, don't let Jim pass!

JIM—(*with a sob*) Don't, Honey, don't! For the good Lord's sake! You're hurting me!

ELLA—(*frightenedly*) How, Jim? Where? (*then after a pause—suddenly*) I'm sick, Jim. I don't think I'll live long.

JIM—(*simply*) Then I won't either. Somewhere yonder maybe—together—our luck'll change. But I wanted—here and now—before you—we—I wanted to prove to you—to myself—to become a full-fledged Member—so you could be proud— (*He stops. Words fail and he is beyond tears.*)

ELLA—(*brightly*) Well, it's all over, Jim. Everything'll be all right now. (*chattering along*) I'll be just your little girl, Jim—and you'll be my little boy—just as we used to be, remember, when we were beaux; and I'll put shoe blacking on my face and pretend I'm black and you can put chalk on your face and pretend you're white just as we used to do—and we can play marbles—only you mustn't all the time be a boy. Sometimes you must be my old kind Uncle Jim who's been with us for years and years. Will you, Jim?

JIM—(*with utter resignation*) Yes, Honey.

ELLA—And you'll never, never, never, never leave me, Jim?

JIM—Never, Honey.

ELLA—'Cause you're all I've got in the world—and I love you, Jim. (*She kisses his hand as a child might, tenderly and gratefully.*)

JIM—(*suddenly throws himself on his knees and raises his shining eyes, his transfigured face*) Forgive me, God—and make me worthy! Now I see Your Light again! Now I hear Your Voice! (*He begins to weep in an ecstasy of religious humility.*) Forgive me, God, for blaspheming You! Let this fire of burning suffering purify me of selfishness and make me worthy of the child You send me for the woman You take away!

ELLA—(*jumping to her feet—excitedly*) Don't cry, Jim! You mustn't cry! I've got only a little time left and I want to play. Don't be old Uncle Jim now. Be my little boy, Jim. Pretend you're Painty Face and I'm Jim Crow. Come and play!

JIM—(*still deeply exalted*) Honey, Honey, I'll play right up to the gates of Heaven with you! (*She tugs at one of his hands, laughingly trying to pull him up from his knees as*

The Curtain Falls)

DESIRE UNDER THE ELMS

A Play in Three Parts

CHARACTERS

EPHRAIM CABOT

SIMEON
PETER
EBEN
} *his sons*

ABBIE PUTNAM

Young Girl, Two Farmers, The Fiddler,
A Sheriff, and other folk from the neighboring farms

The action of the entire play takes place in, and immediately outside of, the Cabot farmhouse in New England, in the year 1850. The south end of the house faces front to a stone wall with a wooden gate at center opening on a country road. The house is in good condition but in need of paint. Its walls are a sickly grayish, the green of the shutters faded. Two enormous elms are on each side of the house. They bend their trailing branches down over the roof. They appear to protect and at the same time subdue. There is a sinister maternity in their aspect, a crushing, jealous absorption. They have developed from their intimate contact with the life of man in the house an appalling humaneness. They brood oppressively over the house. They are like exhausted women resting their sagging breasts and hands and hair on its roof, and when it rains their tears trickle down monotonously and rot on the shingles.

There is a path running from the gate around the right corner of the house to the front door. A narrow porch is on this side. The end wall facing us has two windows in its upper story, two larger ones on the floor below. The two upper are those of the father's bedroom and that of the brothers. On the left, ground floor, is the kitchen—on the right, the parlor, the shades of which are always drawn down.

Desire Under the Elms

PART I

SCENE ONE

Exterior of the Farmhouse. It is sunset of a day at the beginning of summer in the year 1850. There is no wind and everything is still. The sky above the roof is suffused with deep colors, the green of the elms glows, but the house is in shadow, seeming pale and washed out by contrast.

A door opens and Eben Cabot comes to the end of the porch and stands looking down the road to the right. He has a large bell in his hand and this he swings mechanically, awakening a deafening clangor. Then he puts his hands on his hips and stares up at the sky. He sighs with a puzzled awe and blurts out with halting appreciation

EBEN—God! Purty! (*His eyes fall and he stares about him frowningly. He is twenty-five, tall and sinewy. His face is well-formed, good-looking, but its expression is resentful and defensive. His defiant, dark eyes remind one of a wild animal's in captivity. Each day is a cage in which he finds himself trapped but inwardly unsubdued. There is a fierce repressed vitality about him. He has black hair, mustache, a thin curly trace of beard. He is dressed in rough farm clothes. He spits on the ground with intense disgust, turns and goes back into the house. Simeon and Peter come in from their work in the fields. They are tall men, much older than their half-brother [Simeon is thirty-nine and Peter thirty-seven], built on a squarer, simpler model, fleshier in body, more bovine and homelier in face, shrewder and more practical. Their shoulders stoop a bit from years of farm work. They clump heavily along in their clumsy thick-soled boots caked with earth. Their clothes, their faces, hands, bare arms and throats are earth-stained. They smell of earth. They stand together for a moment in front of the house and, as if with the one impulse, stare dumbly up at the sky, leaning on their hoes. Their faces have a compressed, unresigned expression. As they look upward, this softens.*)

SIMEON—(*grudgingly*) Purty.

PETER—Ay-eh.

SIMEON—(*suddenly*) Eighteen years ago.

PETER—What?

SIMEON—Jenn. My woman. She died.

PETER—I'd fergot.

SIMEON—I rec'lect—now an' agin. Makes it lonesome. She'd hair long's a hoss' tail—an' yaller like gold!

PETER—Waal—she's gone. (*this with indifferent finality— then after a pause*) They's gold in the West, Sim.

SIMEON—(*still under the influence of sunset—vaguely*) In the sky?

PETER—Waal—in a manner o' speakin'—thar's the promise. (*growing excited*) Gold in the sky—in the West—Golden Gate—Californi-a!—Goldest West!—fields o' gold!

SIMEON—(*excited in his turn*) Fortunes layin' just atop o' the ground waitin' t' be picked! Solomon's mines, they says! (*For a moment they continue looking up at the sky—then their eyes drop.*)

PETER—(*with sardonic bitterness*) Here—it's stones atop o' the ground—stones atop o' stones—makin' stone walls— year atop o' year—him 'n' yew 'n' me 'n' then Eben—makin' stone walls fur him to fence us in!

SIMEON—We've wuked. Give our strength. Give our years. Plowed 'em under in the ground—(*he stamps rebelliously*) —rottin'—makin' soil for his crops! (*a pause*) Waal—the farm pays good for hereabouts.

PETER—If we plowed in Californi-a, they'd be lumps o' gold in the furrow!

SIMEON—Californi-a's t'other side o' earth, a'most. We got t' calc'late—

PETER—(*after a pause*) 'Twould be hard fur me, too, to give up what we've 'arned here by our sweat. (*A pause. Eben sticks his head out of the dining-room window, listening.*)

SIMEON—Ay-eh. (*a pause*) Mebbe—he'll die soon.

PETER—(*doubtfully*) Mebbe.

SIMEON—Mebbe—fur all we knows—he's dead now.

PETER—Ye'd need proof.

SIMEON—He's been gone two months—with no word.

PETER—Left us in the fields an evenin' like this. Hitched up an' druv off into the West. That's plumb onnateral. He hain't never been off this farm 'ceptin' t' the village in thirty year or more, not since he married Eben's maw. (*A pause. Shrewdly*) I calc'late we might git him declared crazy by the court.

SIMEON—He skinned 'em too slick. He got the best o' all on 'em. They'd never b'lieve him crazy. (*a pause*) We got t' wait—till he's under ground.

EBEN—(*with a sardonic chuckle*) Honor thy father! (*They turn, startled, and stare at him. He grins, then scowls.*) I pray he's died. (*They stare at him. He continues matter-of-factly.*) Supper's ready.

SIMEON AND PETER—(*together*) Ay-eh.

EBEN—(*gazing up at the sky*) Sun's downin' purty.

SIMEON AND PETER—(*pointing*) Ay-eh. They's gold in the West.

EBEN—(*pointing*) Ay-eh. Yonder atop o' the hill pasture, ye mean?

SIMEON AND PETER—(*together*) In Californi-a!

EBEN—Hunh? (*stares at them indifferently for a second, then drawls*) Waal—supper's gittin' cold. (*He turns back into kitchen.*)

SIMEON—(*startled—smacks his lips*) I air hungry!

PETER—(*sniffing*) I smells bacon!

SIMEON—(*with hungry appreciation*) Bacon's good!

PETER—(*in same tone*) Bacon's bacon! (*They turn, shouldering each other, their bodies bumping and rubbing together as they hurry clumsily to their food, like two friendly oxen toward their evening meal. They disappear around the right corner of house and can be heard entering the door.*)

(*The Curtain Falls*)

SCENE TWO

The color fades from the sky. Twilight begins. The interior of the kitchen is now visible. A pine table is at center, a cook-stove in the right rear corner, four rough wooden chairs, a tallow candle on the table. In the middle of the rear wall is fastened a big advertizing poster with a ship in full sail and the word "California" in big letters. Kitchen utensils hang from nails. Everything is neat and in order but the atmosphere is of a men's camp kitchen rather than that of a home.

Places for three are laid. Eben takes boiled potatoes and bacon from the stove and puts them on the table, also a loaf of bread and a crock of water. Simeon and Peter shoulder in, slump down in their chairs without a word. Eben joins them. The three eat in silence for a moment, the two elder as naturally unrestrained as beasts of the field, Eben picking at his food without appetite, glancing at them with a tolerant dislike.

SIMEON—(*suddenly turns to Eben*) Looky here! Ye'd oughtn't t' said that, Eben.

PETER—'Twa'n't righteous.

EBEN—What?

SIMEON—Ye prayed he'd died.

EBEN—Waal—don't yew pray it? (*a pause*)

PETER—He's our Paw.

EBEN—(*violently*) Not mine!

SIMEON—(*dryly*) Ye'd not let no one else say that about yer Maw! Ha! (*He gives one abrupt sardonic guffaw. Peter grins.*)

EBEN—(*very pale*) I meant—I hain't his'n—I hain't like him—he hain't me!

PETER—(*dryly*) Wait till ye've growed his age!

EBEN—(*intensely*) I'm Maw—every drop o' blood! (*A pause. They stare at him with indifferent curiosity.*)

PETER—(*reminiscently*) She was good t' Sim 'n' me. A good Step-maw's scurse.

SIMEON—She was good t' everyone.

EBEN—(*greatly moved, gets to his feet and makes an awkward bow to each of them—stammering*) I be thankful t' ye. I'm her—her heir. (*He sits down in confusion.*)

PETER—(*after a pause—judicially*) She was good even t' him.

EBEN—(*fiercely*) An' fur thanks he killed her!

SIMEON—(*after a pause*) No one never kills nobody. It's allus somethin'. That's the murderer.

EBEN—Didn't he slave Maw t' death?

PETER—He's slaved himself t' death. He's slaved Sim 'n' me 'n' yew t' death—on'y none o' us hain't died—yit.

SIMEON—It's somethin'—drivin' him—t' drive us!

EBEN—(*vengefully*) Waal—I hold him t' jedgment! (*then scornfully*) Somethin'! What's somethin'?

SIMEON—Dunno.

EBEN—(*sardonically*) What's drivin' yew to Californi-a, mebbe? (*They look at him in surprise.*) Oh, I've heerd ye! (*then, after a pause*) But ye'll never go t' the gold fields!

PETER—(*assertively*) Mebbe!

EBEN—Whar'll ye git the money?

PETER—We kin walk. It's an a'mighty ways—Californi-a—but if yew was t' put all the steps we've walked on this farm end t' end we'd be in the moon!

EBEN—The Injuns'll skulp ye on the plains.

SIMEON—(*with grim humor*) We'll mebbe make 'em pay a hair fur a hair!

EBEN—(*decisively*) But t'ain't that. Ye won't never go because ye'll wait here fur yer share o' the farm, thinkin' allus he'll die soon.

SIMEON—(*after a pause*) We've a right.

PETER—Two thirds belongs t' us.

EBEN—(*jumping to his feet*) Ye've no right! She wa'n't yewr Maw! It was her farm! Didn't he steal it from her? She's dead. It's my farm.

SIMEON—(*sardonically*) Tell that t' Paw—when he comes! I'll bet ye a dollar he'll laugh—fur once in his life. Ha! (*He laughs himself in one single mirthless bark.*)

PETER—(*amused in turn, echoes his brother*) Ha!

SIMEON—(*after a pause*) What've ye got held agin us, Eben? Year arter year it's skulked in yer eye—somethin'.

PETER—Ay-eh.

EBEN—Ay-eh. They's somethin'. (*suddenly exploding*) Why didn't ye never stand between him 'n' my Maw when he was slavin' her to her grave—t' pay her back fur the kindness she done t' yew? (*There is a long pause. They stare at him in surprise.*)

SIMEON—Waal—the stock'd got t' be watered.

PETER—'R they was woodin' t' do.

SIMEON—'R plowin'.

PETER—'R hayin'.

SIMEON—'R spreadin' manure.

PETER—'R weedin'.

SIMEON—'R prunin'.

PETER—'R milkin'.

EBEN—(*breaking in harshly*) An' makin' walls—stone atop o' stone—makin' walls till yer heart's a stone ye heft up out o' the way o' growth onto a stone wall t' wall in yer heart!

SIMEON—(*matter-of-factly*) We never had no time t' meddle.

PETER—(*to Eben*) Yew was fifteen afore yer Maw died—an' big fur yer age. Why didn't ye never do nothin'?

EBEN—(*harshly*) They was chores t' do, wa'n't they? (*a pause—then slowly*) It was on'y arter she died I come to think o' it. Me cookin'—doin' her work—that made me know her, suffer her sufferin'—she'd come back t' help—come back t' bile potatoes—come back t' fry bacon—come back t' bake biscuits—come back all cramped up t' shake the fire, an' carry ashes, her eyes weepin' an' bloody with smoke an' cinders same's they used t' be. She still comes back—stands by the stove thar in the evenin'—she can't find it nateral sleepin' an' restin' in peace. She can't git used t' bein' free—even in her grave.

SIMEON—She never complained none.

EBEN—She'd got too tired. She'd got too used t' bein' too tired. That was what he done. (*with vengeful passion*) An' sooner'r later, I'll meddle. I'll say the thin's I didn't say then t' him! I'll yell 'em at the top o' my lungs. I'll see t' it my Maw gits some rest an' sleep in her grave! (*He sits down again, relapsing into a brooding silence. They look at him with a queer indifferent curiosity.*)

PETER—(*after a pause*) Whar in tarnation d'ye s'pose he went, Sim?

SIMEON—Dunno. He druv off in the buggy, all spick an' span, with the mare all breshed an' shiny, druv off clackin' his tongue an' wavin' his whip. I remember it right well. I was finishin' plowin', it was spring an' May an' sunset, an' gold in the West, an' he druv off into it. I yells "Whar ye goin', Paw?" an' he hauls up by the stone wall a jiffy. His old snake's eyes was glitterin' in the sun like he'd been drinkin' a jugful an' he says with a mule's grin: "Don't ye run away till I come back!"

PETER—Wonder if he knowed we was wantin' fur Californi-a?

SIMEON—Mebbe. I didn't say nothin' and he says, lookin' kinder queer an' sick: "I been hearin' the hens cluckin' an' the roosters crowin' all the durn day. I been listenin' t' the cows lowin' an' everythin' else kickin' up till I can't stand it no more. It's spring an' I'm feelin' damned," he says. "Damned like an old bare hickory tree fit on'y fur burnin'," he says. An' then I calc'late I must've looked a mite hopeful, fur he adds real spry and vicious: "But don't git no fool idee I'm dead. I've sworn t' live a hundred an' I'll do it, if on'y t' spite yer sinful greed! An' now I'm ridin' out t' learn God's message t' me in the spring, like the prophets done. An' yew git back t' yer plowin'," he says. An' he druv off singin' a hymn. I thought he was drunk—'r I'd stopped him goin'.

EBEN—(*scornfully*) No, ye wouldn't! Ye're scared o' him. He's stronger—inside—than both o' ye put together!

PETER—(*sardonically*) An' yew—be yew Samson?

EBEN—I'm gittin' stronger. I kin feel it growin' in me— growin' an' growin'—till it'll bust out—! (*He gets up and puts on his coat and a hat. They watch him, gradually breaking into grins. Eben avoids their eyes sheepishly.*) I'm goin' out fur a spell—up the road.

PETER—T' the village?

SIMEON—T' see Minnie?

EBEN—(*defiantly*) Ay-eh!

PETER—(*jeeringly*) The Scarlet Woman!

SIMEON—Lust—that's what's growin' in ye!

EBEN—Waal—she's purty!

PETER—She's been purty fur twenty year!

SIMEON—A new coat o' paint'll make a heifer out of forty.

EBEN—She hain't forty!

PETER—If she hain't, she's teeterin' on the edge.

EBEN—(*desperately*) What d'yew know—

PETER—All they is . . . Sim knew her—an' then me arter—

SIMEON—An' Paw kin tell yew somethin' too! He was fust!

EBEN—D'ye mean t' say he . . . ?

SIMEON—(*with a grin*) Ay-eh! We air his heirs in every-thin'!

EBEN—(*intensely*) That's more to it. That grows on it! It'll

bust soon! (*then violently*) I'll go smash my fist in her face!
(*He pulls open the door in rear violently.*)

SIMEON—(*with a wink at Peter—drawlingly*) Mebbe—but
the night's wa'm—purty—by the time ye git thar mebbe ye'll
kiss her instead!

PETER—Sart'n he will! (*They both roar with coarse laughter.
Eben rushes out and slams the door—then the outside front
door—comes around the corner of the house and stands still by the
gate, staring up at the sky.*)

SIMEON—(*looking after him*) Like his Paw.

PETER—Dead spit an' image!

SIMEON—Dog'll eat dog!

PETER—Ay-eh. (*Pause. With yearning*) Mebbe a year from
now we'll be in Californi-a.

SIMEON—Ay-eh. (*A pause. Both yawn.*) Let's git t' bed.
(*He blows out the candle. They go out door in rear. Eben stretches
his arms up to the sky—rebelliously*)

EBEN—Waal—thar's a star, an' somewhar's they's him,
an' here's me, an' thar's Min up the road—in the same night.
What if I does kiss her? She's like t'night, she's soft 'n' wa'm,
her eyes kin wink like a star, her mouth's wa'm, her arms're
wa'm, she smells like a wa'm plowed field, she's purty . . .
Ay-eh! By God A'mighty she's purty, an' I don't give a damn
how many sins she's sinned afore mine or who she's sinned
'em with, my sin's as purty as any one on 'em! (*He strides off
down the road to the left.*)

SCENE THREE

*It is the pitch darkness just before dawn. Eben comes in from
the left and goes around to the porch, feeling his way, chuckling
bitterly and cursing half-aloud to himself.*

EBEN—The cussed old miser! (*He can be heard going in the
front door. There is a pause as he goes upstairs, then a loud knock
on the bedroom door of the brothers.*) Wake up!

SIMEON—(*startledly*) Who's thar?

EBEN—(*pushing open the door and coming in, a lighted*

candle in his hand. The bedroom of the brothers is revealed. Its ceiling is the sloping roof. They can stand upright only close to the center dividing wall of the upstairs. Simeon and Peter are in a double bed, front. Eben's cot is to the rear. Eben has a mixture of silly grin and vicious scowl on his face.) I be!

PETER—(*angrily*) What in hell's-fire . . . ?

EBEN—I got news fur ye! Ha! (*He gives one abrupt sardonic guffaw.*)

SIMEON—(*angrily*) Couldn't ye hold it 'til we'd got our sleep?

EBEN—It's nigh sunup. (*then explosively*) He's gone an' married agen!

SIMEON AND PETER—(*explosively*) Paw?

EBEN—Got himself hitched to a female 'bout thirty-five—an' purty, they says . . .

SIMEON—(*aghast*) It's a durn lie!

PETER—Who says?

SIMEON—They been stringin' ye!

EBEN—Think I'm a dunce, do ye? The hull village says. The preacher from New Dover, he brung the news—told it t' our preacher—New Dover, that's whar the old loon got himself hitched—that's whar the woman lived—

PETER—(*no longer doubting—stunned*) Waal . . . !

SIMEON—(*the same*) Waal . . . !

EBEN—(*sitting down on a bed—with vicious hatred*) Ain't he a devil out o' hell? It's jest t' spite us—the damned old mule!

PETER—(*after a pause*) Everythin'll go t' her now.

SIMEON—Ay-eh. (*a pause—dully*) Waal—if it's done—

PETER—It's done us. (*pause—then persuasively*) They's gold in the fields o' Californi-a, Sim. No good a-stayin' here now.

SIMEON—Jest what I was a-thinkin'. (*then with decision*) S'well fust's last! Let's light out and git this mornin'.

PETER—Suits me.

EBEN—Ye must like walkin'.

SIMEON—(*sardonically*) If ye'd grow wings on us we'd fly thar!

EBEN—Ye'd like ridin' better—on a boat, wouldn't ye? (*fumbles in his pocket and takes out a crumpled sheet of foolscap*) Waal, if ye sign this ye kin ride on a boat. I've had it writ out an' ready in case ye'd ever go. It says fur three hundred dollars t' each ye agree yewr shares o' the farm is sold t' me. (*They look suspiciously at the paper. A pause.*)

SIMEON—(*wonderingly*) But if he's hitched agen—

PETER—An' whar'd yew git that sum o' money, anyways?

EBEN—(*cunningly*) I know whar it's hid. I been waitin'—Maw told me. She knew whar it lay fur years, but she was waitin' . . . It's her'n—the money he hoarded from her farm an' hid from Maw. It's my money by rights now.

PETER—Whar's it hid?

EBEN—(*cunningly*) Whar yew won't never find it without me. Maw spied on him—'r she'd never knowed. (*A pause. They look at him suspiciously, and he at them.*) Waal, is it fa'r trade?

SIMEON—Dunno.

PETER—Dunno.

SIMEON—(*looking at window*) Sky's grayin'.

PETER—Ye better start the fire, Eben.

SIMEON—An' fix some vittles.

EBEN—Ay-eh. (*then with a forced jocular heartiness*) I'll git ye a good one. If ye're startin' t' hoof it t' Californi-a ye'll need somethin' that'll stick t' yer ribs. (*He turns to the door, adding meaningly*) But ye kin ride on a boat if ye'll swap. (*He stops at the door and pauses. They stare at him.*)

SIMEON—(*suspiciously*) Whar was ye all night?

EBEN—(*defiantly*) Up t' Min's. (*then slowly*) Walkin' thar, fust I felt 's if I'd kiss her; then I got a-thinkin' o' what ye'd said o' him an' her an' I says, I'll bust her nose fur that! Then I got t' the village an' heerd the news an' I got madder'n hell an' run all the way t' Min's not knowin' what I'd do— (*He pauses—then sheepishly but more defiantly*) Waal—when I seen her, I didn't hit her—nor I didn't kiss her nuther—I begun t' beller like a calf an' cuss at the same time, I was so durn mad—an' she got scared—an' I jest grabbed holt an' tuk her! (*proudly*) Yes, siree! I tuk her. She may've been his'n—an' your'n, too—but she's mine now!

SIMEON—(*dryly*) In love, air yew?

EBEN—(*with lofty scorn*) Love! I don't take no stock in sech slop!

PETER—(*winking at Simeon*) Mebbe Eben's aimin' t' marry, too.

SIMEON—Min'd make a true faithful he'pmeet! (*They snicker.*)

EBEN—What do I care fur her—'ceptin' she's round an' wa'm? The p'int is she was his'n—an' now she b'longs t' me! (*He goes to the door—then turns—rebelliously*) An' Min hain't sech a bad un. They's worse'n Min in the world, I'll bet ye! Wait'll we see this cow the Old Man's hitched t'! She'll beat Min, I got a notion! (*He starts to go out.*)

SIMEON—(*suddenly*) Mebbe ye'll try t' make her your'n, too?

PETER—Ha! (*He gives a sardonic laugh of relish at this idea.*)

EBEN—(*spitting with disgust*) Her—here—sleepin' with him—stealin' my Maw's farm! I'd as soon pet a skunk 'r kiss a snake! (*He goes out. The two stare after him suspiciously. A pause. They listen to his steps receding.*)

PETER—He's startin' the fire.

SIMEON—I'd like t' ride t' Californi-a—but—

PETER—Min might o' put some scheme in his head.

SIMEON—Mebbe it's all a lie 'bout Paw marryin'. We'd best wait an' see the bride.

PETER—An' don't sign nothin' till we does!

SIMEON—Nor till we've tested it's good money! (*then with a grin*) But if Paw's hitched we'd be sellin' Eben somethin' we'd never git nohow!

PETER—We'll wait an' see. (*then with sudden vindictive anger*) An' till he comes, let's yew 'n' me not wuk a lick, let Eben tend to thin's if he's a mind t', let's us jest sleep an' eat an' drink likker, an' let the hull damned farm go t' blazes!

SIMEON—(*excitedly*) By God, we've 'arned a rest! We'll play rich fur a change. I hain't a-going to stir outa bed till breakfast's ready.

PETER—An' on the table!

SIMEON—(*after a pause—thoughtfully*) What d'ye calc'late she'll be like—our new Maw? Like Eben thinks?

PETER—More'n' likely.

SIMEON—(*vindictively*) Waal—I hope she's a she-devil that'll make him wish he was dead an' livin' in the pit o' hell fur comfort!

PETER—(*fervently*) Amen!

SIMEON—(*imitating his father's voice*) "I'm ridin' out t' learn God's message t' me in the spring like the prophets done," he says. I'll bet right then an' thar he knew plumb well he was goin' whorin', the stinkin' old hypocrite!

SCENE FOUR

Same as Scene Two—shows the interior of the kitchen with a lighted candle on table. It is gray dawn outside. Simeon and Peter are just finishing their breakfast. Eben sits before his plate of untouched food, brooding frowningly.

PETER—(*glancing at him rather irritably*) Lookin' glum don't help none.

SIMEON—(*sarcastically*) Sorrowin' over his lust o' the flesh!

PETER—(*with a grin*) Was she yer fust?

EBEN—(*angrily*) None o' yer business. (*a pause*) I was thinkin' o' him. I got a notion he's gittin' near—I kin feel him comin' on like yew kin feel malaria chill afore it takes ye.

PETER—It's too early yet.

SIMEON—Dunno. He'd like t' catch us nappin'—jest t' have somethin' t' hoss us 'round over.

PETER—(*mechanically gets to his feet. Simeon does the same.*) Waal—let's git t' wuk. (*They both plod mechanically toward the door before they realize. Then they stop short.*)

SIMEON—(*grinning*) Ye're a cussed fool, Pete—and I be wuss! Let him see we hain't wukin'! We don't give a durn!

PETER—(*as they go back to the table*) Not a damned durn! It'll serve t' show him we're done with him. (*They sit down again. Eben stares from one to the other with surprise.*)

SIMEON—(*grins at him*) We're aimin' t' start bein' lilies o' the field.

PETER—Nary a toil 'r spin 'r lick o' wuk do we put in!

SIMEON—Ye're sole owner—till he comes—that's what ye wanted. Waal, ye got t' be sole hand, too.

PETER—The cows air bellerin'. Ye better hustle at the milkin'.

EBEN—(*with excited joy*) Ye mean ye'll sign the paper?

SIMEON—(*dryly*) Mebbe.

PETER—Mebbe.

SIMEON—We're considerin'. (*peremptorily*) Ye better git t' wuk.

EBEN—(*with queer excitement*) It's Maw's farm agen! It's my farm! Them's my cows! I'll milk my durn fingers off fur cows o' mine! (*He goes out door in rear, they stare after him indifferently.*)

SIMEON—Like his Paw.

PETER—Dead spit 'n' image!

SIMEON—Waal—let dog eat dog! (*Eben comes out of front door and around the corner of the house. The sky is beginning to grow flushed with sunrise. Eben stops by the gate and stares around him with glowing, possessive eyes. He takes in the whole farm with his embracing glance of desire.*)

EBEN—It's purty! It's damned purty! It's mine! (*He suddenly throws his head back boldly and glares with hard, defiant eyes at the sky.*) Mine, d'ye hear? Mine! (*He turns and walks quickly off left, rear, toward the barn. The two brothers light their pipes.*)

SIMEON—(*putting his muddy boots up on the table, tilting back his chair, and puffing defiantly*) Waal—this air solid comfort—fur once.

PETER—Ay-eh. (*He follows suit. A pause. Unconsciously they both sigh.*)

SIMEON—(*suddenly*) He never was much o' a hand at milkin', Eben wa'n't.

PETER—(*with a snort*) His hands air like hoofs! (*a pause*)

SIMEON—Reach down the jug thar! Let's take a swaller. I'm feelin' kind o' low.

PETER—Good idee! (*He does so—gets two glasses—they pour out drinks of whisky.*) Here's t' the gold in Californi-a!

SIMEON—An' luck t' find it! (*They drink—puff resolutely—sigh—take their feet down from the table.*)

PETER—Likker don't 'pear t' sot right.

SIMEON—We hain't used t' it this early. (*A pause. They become very restless.*)

PETER—Gittin' close in this kitchen.

SIMEON—(*with immense relief*) Let's git a breath o' air.

(*They arise briskly and go out rear—appear around house and stop by the gate. They stare up at the sky with a numbed appreciation.*)

PETER—Purty!

SIMEON—Ay-eh. Gold's t' the East now.

PETER—Sun's startin' with us fur the Golden West.

SIMEON—(*staring around the farm, his compressed face tightened, unable to conceal his emotion*) Waal—it's our last mornin'—mebbe.

PETER—(*the same*) Ay-eh.

SIMEON—(*stamps his foot on the earth and addresses it desperately*) Waal—ye've thirty year o' me buried in ye—spread out over ye—blood an' bone an' sweat—rotted away—fertilizin' ye—richin' yer soul—prime manure, by God, that's what I been t' ye!

PETER—Ay-eh! An' me!

SIMEON—An' yew, Peter. (*He sighs—then spits.*) Waal—no use'n cryin' over spilt milk.

PETER—They's gold in the West—an' freedom, mebbe. We been slaves t' stone walls here.

SIMEON—(*defiantly*) We hain't nobody's slaves from this out—nor no thin's slaves nuther. (*a pause—restlessly*) Speakin' o' milk, wonder how Eben's managin'?

PETER—I s'pose he's managin'.

SIMEON—Mebbe we'd ought t' help—this once.

PETER—Mebbe. The cows knows us.

SIMEON—An' likes us. They don't know him much.

PETER—An' the hosses, an' pigs, an' chickens. They don't know him much.

SIMEON—They knows us like brothers—an' likes us! (*proudly*) Hain't we raised 'em t' be fust-rate, number one prize stock?

PETER—We hain't—not no more.

SIMEON—(*dully*) I was fergittin'. (*then resignedly*) Waal, let's go help Eben a spell an' git waked up.

PETER—Suits me. (*They are starting off down left, rear, for the barn when Eben appears from there hurrying toward them, his face excited.*)

EBEN—(*breathlessly*) Waal—har they be! The old mule an' the bride! I seen 'em from the barn down below at the turnin'.

PETER—How could ye tell that far?

EBEN—Hain't I as far-sight as he's near-sight? Don't I know the mare 'n' buggy, an' two people settin' in it? Who else . . . ? An' I tell ye I kin feel 'em a-comin', too! (*He squirms as if he had the itch.*)

PETER—(*beginning to be angry*) Waal—let him do his own unhitchin'!

SIMEON—(*angry in his turn*) Let's hustle in an' git our bundles an' be a-goin' as he's a-comin'. I don't want never t' step inside the door agen arter he's back. (*They both start back around the corner of the house. Eben follows them.*)

EBEN—(*anxiously*) Will ye sign it afore ye go?

PETER—Let's see the color o' the old skinflint's money an' we'll sign. (*They disappear left. The two brothers clump upstairs to get their bundles. Eben appears in the kitchen, runs to window, peers out, comes back and pulls up a strip of flooring in under stove, takes out a canvas bag and puts it on table, then sets the floorboard back in place. The two brothers appear a moment after. They carry old carpet bags.*)

EBEN—(*puts his hand on bag guardingly*) Have ye signed?

SIMEON—(*shows paper in his hand*) Ay-eh. (*greedily*) Be that the money?

EBEN—(*opens bag and pours out pile of twenty-dollar gold pieces*) Twenty-dollar pieces—thirty on 'em. Count 'em. (*Peter does so, arranging them in stacks of five, biting one or two to test them.*)

PETER—Six hundred. (*He puts them in bag and puts it inside his shirt carefully.*)

SIMEON—(*handing paper to Eben*) Har ye be.

EBEN—(*after a glance, folds it carefully and hides it under his shirt—gratefully*) Thank yew.

PETER—Thank yew fur the ride.

SIMEON—We'll send ye a lump o' gold fur Christmas. (*A pause. Eben stares at them and they at him.*)

PETER—(*awkwardly*) Waal—we're a-goin'.

SIMEON—Comin' out t' the yard?

EBEN—No. I'm waitin' in here a spell. (*Another silence. The brothers edge awkwardly to door in rear—then turn and stand.*)

SIMEON—Waal—good-by.

PETER—Good-by.

EBEN—Good-by. (*They go out. He sits down at the table, faces the stove and pulls out the paper. He looks from it to the stove. His face, lighted up by the shaft of sunlight from the window, has an expression of trance. His lips move. The two brothers come out to the gate.*)

PETER—(*looking off toward barn*) Thar he be—unhitchin'.

SIMEON—(*with a chuckle*) I'll bet ye he's riled!

PETER—An' thar she be.

SIMEON—Let's wait 'n' see what our new Maw looks like.

PETER—(*with a grin*) An' give him our partin' cuss!

SIMEON—(*grinning*) I feel like raisin' fun. I feel light in my head an' feet.

PETER—Me, too. I feel like laffin' till I'd split up the middle.

SIMEON—Reckon it's the likker?

PETER—No. My feet feel itchin' t' walk an' walk—an' jump high over thin's—an'. . . .

SIMEON—Dance? (*a pause*)

PETER—(*puzzled*) It's plumb onnateral.

SIMEON—(*a light coming over his face*) I calc'late it's 'cause school's out. It's holiday. Fur once we're free!

PETER—(*dazedly*) Free?

SIMEON—The halter's broke—the harness is busted—the fence bars is down—the stone walls air crumblin' an' tumblin'! We'll be kickin' up an' tearin' away down the road!

PETER—(*drawing a deep breath—oratorically*) Anybody that wants this stinkin' old rock-pile of a farm kin hev it. T'ain't our'n, no sirree!

SIMEON—(*takes the gate off its hinges and puts it under his arm*) We harby 'bolishes shet gates, an' open gates, an' all gates, by thunder!

PETER—We'll take it with us fur luck an' let 'er sail free down some river.

SIMEON—(*as a sound of voices comes from left, rear*) Har they comes! (*The two brothers congeal into two stiff, grim-visaged statues. Ephraim Cabot and Abbie Putnam come in. Cabot is seventy-five, tall and gaunt, with great, wiry, concentrated power, but stoop-shouldered from toil. His face is as hard as if it were hewn out of a boulder, yet there is a weakness in it, a petty pride in its own narrow strength. His eyes are small, close together, and extremely near-sighted, blinking continually in the effort to focus on objects, their stare having a straining, ingrowing quality. He is dressed in his dismal black Sunday suit. Abbie is thirty-five, buxom, full of vitality. Her round face is pretty but marred by its rather gross sensuality. There is strength and obstinacy in her jaw, a hard determination in her eyes, and about her whole personality the same unsettled, untamed, desperate quality which is so apparent in Eben.*)

CABOT—(*as they enter—a queer strangled emotion in his dry cracking voice*) Har we be t' hum, Abbie.

ABBIE—(*with lust for the word*) Hum! (*her eyes gloating on the house without seeming to see the two stiff figures at the gate*) It's purty—purty! I can't b'lieve it's r'ally mine.

CABOT—(*sharply*) Yewr'n? Mine! (*He stares at her penetratingly. She stares back. He adds relentingly*) Our'n—mebbe! It was lonesome too long. I was growin' old in the spring. A hum's got t' hev a woman.

ABBIE—(*her voice taking possession*) A woman's got t' hev a hum!

CABOT—(*nodding uncertainly*) Ay-eh. (*then irritably*) Whar be they? Ain't thar nobody about—'r wukin'—'r nothin'?

ABBIE—(*sees the brothers. She returns their stare of cold appraising contempt with interest—slowly*) Thar's two men loafin' at the gate an' starin' at me like a couple o' strayed hogs.

CABOT—(*straining his eyes*) I kin see 'em—but I can't make out. . . .

SIMEON—It's Simeon.

PETER—It's Peter.

CABOT—(*exploding*) Why hain't ye wukin'?

SIMEON—(*dryly*) We're waitin' t' welcome ye hum—yew an' the bride!

CABOT—(*confusedly*) Huh? Waal—this be yer new Maw, boys. (*She stares at them and they at her.*)

SIMEON—(*turns away and spits contemptuously*) I see her!

PETER—(*spits also*) An' I see her!

ABBIE—(*with the conqueror's conscious superiority*) I'll go in an' look at *my* house. (*She goes slowly around to porch.*)

SIMEON—(*with a snort*) *Her* house!

PETER—(*calls after her*) Ye'll find Eben inside. Ye better not tell him it's *yewr* house.

ABBIE—(*mouthing the name*) Eben. (*then quietly*) I'll tell Eben.

CABOT—(*with a contemptuous sneer*) Ye needn't heed Eben. Eben's a dumb fool—like his Maw—soft an' simple!

SIMEON—(*with his sardonic burst of laughter*) Ha! Eben's a chip o' yew—spit 'n' image—hard 'n' bitter's a hickory tree! Dog'll eat dog. He'll eat ye yet, old man!

CABOT—(*commandingly*) Ye git t' wuk!

SIMEON—(*as Abbie disappears in house—winks at Peter and says tauntingly*) So that thar's our new Maw, be it? Whar in hell did ye dig her up? (*He and Peter laugh.*)

PETER—Ha! Ye'd better turn her in the pen with the other sows. (*They laugh uproariously, slapping their thighs.*)

CABOT—(*so amazed at their effrontery that he stutters in confusion*) Simeon! Peter! What's come over ye? Air ye drunk?

SIMEON—We're free, old man—free o' yew an' the hull damned farm! (*They grow more and more hilarious and excited.*)

PETER—An' we're startin' out fur the gold fields o' Californi-a!

SIMEON—Ye kin take this place an' burn it!

PETER—An' bury it—fur all we cares!

SIMEON—We're free, old man! (*He cuts a caper.*)

PETER—Free! (*He gives a kick in the air.*)

SIMEON—(*in a frenzy*) Whoop.

PETER—Whoop! (*They do an absurd Indian war dance about the old man, who is petrified between rage and the fear that they are insane.*)

SIMEON—We're free as Injuns! Lucky we don't skulp ye!

PETER—An' burn yer barn an' kill the stock!

SIMEON—An' rape yer new woman! Whoop! (*He and Peter stop their dance, holding their sides, rocking with wild laughter.*)

CABOT—(*edging away*) Lust fur gold—fur the sinful, easy gold o' Californi-a! It's made ye mad!

SIMEON—(*tauntingly*) Wouldn't ye like us to send ye back some sinful gold, ye old sinner?

PETER—They's gold besides what's in Californi-a! (*He retreats back beyond the vision of the old man and takes the bag of money and flaunts it in the air above his head, laughing.*)

SIMEON—And sinfuller, too!

PETER—We'll be voyagin' on the sea! Whoop! (*He leaps up and down.*)

SIMEON—Livin' free! Whoop! (*He leaps in turn.*)

CABOT—(*suddenly roaring with rage*) My cuss on ye!

SIMEON—Take our'n in trade fur it! Whoop!

CABOT—I'll hev ye both chained up in the asylum!

PETER—Ye old skinflint! Good-by!

SIMEON—Ye old blood sucker! Good-by!

CABOT—Go afore I . . . !

PETER—Whoop! (*He picks a stone from the road. Simeon does the same.*)

SIMEON—Maw'll be in the parlor.

PETER—Ay-eh! One! Two!

CABOT—(*frightened*) What air ye . . . ?

PETER—Three! (*They both throw, the stones hitting the parlor window with a crash of glass, tearing the shade.*)

SIMEON—Whoop!

PETER—Whoop!

CABOT—(*in a fury now, rushing toward them*) If I kin lay hands on ye—I'll break yer bones fur ye! (*But they beat a capering retreat before him, Simeon with the gate still under his arm. Cabot comes back, panting with impotent rage. Their voices as they go off take up the song of the gold-seekers to the old tune of "Oh, Susannah!"*)

> "I jumped aboard the Liza ship,
> And traveled on the sea,
> And every time I thought of home
> I wished it wasn't me!
> Oh! Californi-a,
> That's the land fur me!
> I'm off to Californi-a!
> With my wash bowl on my knee."

(*In the meantime, the window of the upper bedroom on right is raised and Abbie sticks her head out. She looks down at Cabot—with a sigh of relief*)

ABBIE—Waal—that's the last o' them two, hain't it? (*He doesn't answer. Then in possessive tones*) This here's a nice bedroom, Ephraim. It's a r'al nice bed. Is it my room, Ephraim?

CABOT—(*grimly—without looking up*) Our'n! (*She cannot*

control a grimace of aversion and pulls back her head slowly and shuts the window. A sudden horrible thought seems to enter Cabot's head.) They been up to somethin'! Mebbe—mebbe they've pizened the stock—'r somethin'! (*He almost runs off down toward the barn. A moment later the kitchen door is slowly pushed open and Abbie enters. For a moment she stands looking at Eben. He does not notice her at first. Her eyes take him in penetratingly with a calculating appraisal of his strength as against hers. But under this her desire is dimly awakened by his youth and good looks. Suddenly he becomes conscious of her presence and looks up. Their eyes meet. He leaps to his feet, glowering at her speechlessly.*)

ABBIE—(*in her most seductive tones which she uses all through this scene*) Be you—Eben? I'm Abbie— (*She laughs.*) I mean, I'm yer new Maw.

EBEN—(*viciously*) No, damn ye!

ABBIE—(*as if she hadn't heard—with a queer smile*) Yer Paw's spoke a lot o' yew. . . .

EBEN—Ha!

ABBIE—Ye mustn't mind him. He's an old man. (*A long pause. They stare at each other.*) I don't want t' pretend playin' Maw t' ye, Eben. (*admiringly*) Ye're too big an' too strong fur that. I want t' be frens with ye. Mebbe with me fur a fren ye'd find ye'd like livin' here better. I kin make it easy fur ye with him, mebbe. (*with a scornful sense of power*) I calc'late I kin git him t' do most anythin' fur me.

EBEN—(*with bitter scorn*) Ha! (*They stare again, Eben obscurely moved, physically attracted to her—in forced stilted tones*) Yew kin go t' the devil!

ABBIE—(*calmly*) If cussin' me does ye good, cuss all ye've a mind t'. I'm all prepared t' have ye agin me—at fust. I don't blame ye nuther. I'd feel the same at any stranger comin' t' take my Maw's place. (*He shudders. She is watching him carefully.*) Yew must've cared a lot fur yewr Maw, didn't ye? My Maw died afore I'd growed. I don't remember her none. (*a pause*) But yew won't hate me long, Eben. I'm not the wust in the world—an' yew an' me've got a lot in common. I kin tell that by lookin' at ye. Waal—I've had a hard life, too—oceans o' trouble an' nuthin' but wuk fur reward. I was a orphan early an' had t' wuk fur others in other folks' hums. Then I married an' he turned out a drunken spreer an' so he had to wuk fur others an' me too agen in other folks' hums, an' the baby died, an' my husband got sick an' died too, an' I was glad sayin' now I'm free fur once, on'y I diskivered right away all I was free fur was t' wuk agen in other folks' hums, doin' other folks' wuk till I'd most give up hope o' ever doin' my own wuk in my own hum, an' then your Paw come. . . . (*Cabot appears returning from the barn. He comes to the gate and looks down the road the brothers have gone. A faint strain of their retreating voices is heard:* "Oh, Californi-a! That's the place for me." *He stands glowering, his fist clenched, his face grim with rage.*)

EBEN—(*fighting against his growing attraction and sympathy—harshly*) An' bought yew—like a harlot! (*She is stung and flushes angrily. She has been sincerely moved by the recital of her troubles. He adds furiously*) An' the price he's payin' ye—this farm—was my Maw's, damn ye!—an' mine now!

ABBIE—(*with a cool laugh of confidence*) Yewr'n? We'll see 'bout that! (*then strongly*) Waal—what if I did need a hum? What else'd I marry an old man like him fur?

EBEN—(*maliciously*) I'll tell him ye said that!

ABBIE—(*smiling*) I'll say ye're lyin' a-purpose—an' he'll drive ye off the place!

EBEN—Ye devil!

ABBIE—(*defying him*) This be my farm—this be my hum—this be my kitchen!

EBEN—(*furiously, as if he were going to attack her*) Shut up, damn ye!

ABBIE—(*walks up to him—a queer coarse expression of desire in her face and body—slowly*) An' upstairs—that be my bedroom—an' my bed! (*He stares into her eyes, terribly confused and torn. She adds softly*) I hain't bad nor mean—'ceptin' fur an enemy—but I got t' fight fur what's due me out o' life, if I ever 'spect t' git it. (*then putting her hand on his arm—seductively*) Let's yew 'n' me be frens, Eben.

EBEN—(*stupidly—as if hypnotized*) Ay-eh. (*then furiously flinging off her arm*) No, ye durned old witch! I hate ye! (*He rushes out the door.*)

ABBIE—(*looks after him smiling satisfiedly—then half to*

herself, mouthing the word) Eben's nice. (*She looks at the table, proudly.*) I'll wash up *my* dishes now. (*Eben appears outside, slamming the door behind him. He comes around corner, stops on seeing his father, and stands staring at him with hate.*)

CABOT—(*raising his arms to heaven in the fury he can no longer control*) Lord God o' Hosts, smite the undutiful sons with Thy wust cuss!

EBEN—(*breaking in violently*) Yew 'n' yewr God! Allus cussin' folks—allus naggin' em!

CABOT—(*oblivious to him—summoningly*) God o' the old! God o' the lonesome!

EBEN—(*mockingly*) Naggin' His sheep t' sin! T' hell with yewr God! (*Cabot turns. He and Eben glower at each other.*)

CABOT—(*harshly*) So it's yew. I might've knowed it. (*shaking his finger threateningly at him*) Blasphemin' fool! (*then quickly*) Why hain't ye t' wuk?

EBEN—Why hain't yew? They've went. I can't wuk it all alone.

CABOT—(*contemptuously*) Nor noways! I'm wuth ten o' ye yit, old's I be! Ye'll never be more'n half a man! (*then, matter-of-factly*) Waal—let's git t' the barn. (*They go. A last faint note of the "Californi-a" song is heard from the distance. Abbie is washing her dishes.*)

(*The Curtain Falls*)

PART II

Scene One

The exterior of the farmhouse, as in Part One—a hot Sunday afternoon two months later. Abbie, dressed in her best, is discovered sitting in a rocker at the end of the porch. She rocks listlessly, enervated by the heat, staring in front of her with bored, half-closed eyes.

Eben sticks his head out of his bedroom window. He looks around furtively and tries to see—or hear—if anyone is on the porch, but although he has been careful to make no noise, Abbie has sensed his movement. She stops rocking, her face grows animated and eager, she waits attentively. Eben seems to feel her presence, he scowls back his thoughts of her and spits with exaggerated disdain—then withdraws back into the room. Abbie waits, holding her breath as she listens with passionate eagerness for every sound within the house.

Eben comes out. Their eyes meet. His falter, he is confused, he turns away and slams the door resentfully. At this gesture, Abbie laughs tantalizingly, amused but at the same time piqued and irritated. He scowls, strides off the porch to the path and starts to walk past her to the road with a grand swagger of ignoring her existence. He is dressed in his store suit, spruced up, his face shines from soap and water. Abbie leans forward on her chair, her eyes hard and angry now, and, as he passes her, gives a sneering, taunting chuckle.

EBEN—(*stung—turns on her furiously*) What air yew cacklin' 'bout?

ABBIE—(*triumphant*) Yew!

EBEN—What about me?

ABBIE—Ye look all slicked up like a prize bull.

EBEN—(*with a sneer*) Waal—ye hain't so durned purty yerself, be ye? (*They stare into each other's eyes, his held by hers in spite of himself, hers glowingly possessive. Their physical attraction becomes a palpable force quivering in the hot air.*)

ABBIE—(*softly*) Ye don't mean that, Eben. Ye may think ye mean it, mebbe, but ye don't. Ye can't. It's agin nature, Eben. Ye been fightin' yer nature ever since the day I come—tryin' t' tell yerself I hain't purty t' ye. (*She laughs a low humid laugh without taking her eyes from his. A pause—her body squirms desirously—she murmurs languorously*) Hain't the sun strong an' hot? Ye kin feel it burnin' into the earth—Nature—makin' thin's grow—bigger 'n' bigger—burnin' inside ye—makin' ye want t' grow—into somethin' else—till ye're jined with it—an' it's your'n—but it owns ye, too—an' makes ye grow bigger—like a tree—like them elums— (*She laughs again softly, holding his eyes. He takes a step toward her, compelled against his will.*) Nature'll beat ye, Eben. Ye might's well own up t' it fust 's last.

EBEN—(*trying to break from her spell—confusedly*) If Paw'd hear ye goin' on. . . . (*resentfully*) But ye've made such a damned idjit out o' the old devil. . . ! (*Abbie laughs.*)

ABBIE—Waal—hain't it easier fur yew with him changed softer?

EBEN—(*defiantly*) No. I'm fightin' him—fightin' yew— fightin' fur Maw's rights t' her hum! (*This breaks her spell for him. He glowers at her.*) An' I'm onto ye. Ye hain't foolin' me a mite. Ye're aimin' t' swaller up everythin' an' make it your'n. Waal, you'll find I'm a heap sight bigger hunk nor yew kin chew! (*He turns from her with a sneer.*)

ABBIE—(*trying to regain her ascendancy—seductively*) Eben!

EBEN—Leave me be! (*He starts to walk away.*)

ABBIE—(*more commandingly*) Eben!

EBEN—(*stops—resentfully*) What d'ye want?

ABBIE—(*trying to conceal a growing excitement*) Whar air ye goin'?

EBEN—(*with malicious nonchalance*) Oh—up the road a spell.

ABBIE—T' the village?

EBEN—(*airily*) Mebbe.

ABBIE—(*excitedly*) T' see that Min, I s'pose?

EBEN—Mebbe.

ABBIE—(*weakly*) What d'ye want t' waste time on her fur?

EBEN—(*revenging himself now—grinning at her*) Ye can't beat Nature, didn't ye say? (*He laughs and again starts to walk away.*)

ABBIE—(*bursting out*) An ugly old hake!

EBEN—(*with a tantalizing sneer*) She's purtier'n yew be!

ABBIE—That every wuthless drunk in the country has. . . .

EBEN—(*tauntingly*) Mebbe—but she's better'n yew. She owns up fa'r 'n' squar' t' her doin's.

ABBIE—(*furiously*) Don't ye dare compare. . . .

EBEN—She don't go sneakin' an' stealin'—what's mine.

ABBIE—(*savagely seizing on his weak point*) Your'n? Yew mean—my farm?

EBEN—I mean the farm yew sold yerself fur like any other old whore—my farm!

ABBIE—(*stung—fiercely*) Ye'll never live t' see the day when even a stinkin' weed on it'll belong t' ye! (*then in a scream*) Git out o' my sight! Go on t' yer slut—disgracin' yer Paw 'n' me! I'll git Paw t' horsewhip ye off the place if I want t'! Ye're only livin' here 'cause I tolerate ye! Git along! I hate the sight o' ye! (*She stops, panting and glaring at him.*)

EBEN—(*returning her glance in kind*) An' I hate the sight o' yew! (*He turns and strides off up the road. She follows his retreating figure with concentrated hate. Old Cabot appears coming up from the barn. The hard, grim expression of his face has changed. He seems in some queer way softened, mellowed. His eyes have taken on a strange, incongruous dreamy quality. Yet there is no hint of physical weakness about him—rather he looks more robust and younger. Abbie sees him and turns away quickly with unconcealed aversion. He comes slowly up to her.*)

CABOT—(*mildly*) War yew an' Eben quarrelin' agen?

ABBIE—(*shortly*) No.

CABOT—Ye was talkin' a'mighty loud. (*He sits down on the edge of porch.*)

ABBIE—(*snappishly*) If ye heerd us they hain't no need askin' questions.

CABOT—I didn't hear what ye said.

ABBIE—(*relieved*) Waal—it wa'n't nothin' t' speak on.

CABOT—(*after a pause*) Eben's queer.

ABBIE—(*bitterly*) He's the dead spit 'n' image o' yew!

CABOT—(*queerly interested*) D'ye think so, Abbie? (*after a pause, ruminatingly*) Me 'n' Eben's allus fit 'n' fit. I never could b'ar him noways. He's so thunderin' soft—like his Maw.

ABBIE—(*scornfully*) Ay-eh! 'Bout as soft as yew be!

CABOT—(*as if he hadn't heard*) Mebbe I been too hard on him.

ABBIE—(*jeeringly*) Waal—ye're gittin' soft now—soft as slop! That's what Eben was sayin'.

CABOT—(*his face instantly grim and ominous*) Eben was sayin'? Waal, he'd best not do nothin' t' try me 'r he'll soon diskiver. . . . (*A pause. She keeps her face turned away. His gradually softens. He stares up at the sky.*) Purty, hain't it?

ABBIE—(*crossly*) I don't see nothin' purty.

CABOT—The sky. Feels like a wa'm field up thar.

ABBIE—(*sarcastically*) Air yew aimin' to' buy up over the farm too? (*She snickers contemptuously.*)

CABOT—(*strangely*) I'd like t' own my place up thar. (*a pause*) I'm gittin' old, Abbie. I'm gittin' ripe on the bough. (*A pause. She stares at him mystified. He goes on.*) It's allus lonesome cold in the house—even when it's bilin' hot outside. Hain't yew noticed?

ABBIE—No.

CABOT—It's wa'm down t' the barn—nice smellin' an' warm—with the cows. (*a pause*) Cows is queer.

ABBIE—Like yew?

CABOT—Like Eben. (*a pause*) I'm gittin' t' feel resigned t' Eben—jest as I got t' feel 'bout his Maw. I'm gettin' t' learn to b'ar his softness—jest like her'n. I calc'late I c'd a'most take t' him—if he wa'n't sech a dumb fool! (*a pause*) I s'pose it's old age a-creepin' in my bones.

ABBIE—(*indifferently*) Waal—ye hain't dead yet.

CABOT—(*roused*) No. I hain't, yew bet—not by a hell of a sight—I'm sound 'n' tough as hickory! (*then moodily*) But arter three score and ten the Lord warns ye t' prepare. (*a pause*) That's why Eben's come in my head. Now that his cussed sinful brothers is gone their path t' hell, they's no one left but Eben.

ABBIE—(*resentfully*) They's me, hain't they? (*agitatedly*) What's all this sudden likin' ye've tuk to Eben? Why don't ye say nothin' 'bout me? Hain't I yer lawful wife?

CABOT—(*simply*) Ay-eh. Ye be. (*A pause—he stares at her desirously—his eyes grow avid—then with a sudden movement he seizes her hands and squeezes them, declaiming in a queer camp meeting preacher's tempo*) Yew air my Rose o' Sharon! Behold, yew air fair; yer eyes air doves; yer lips air like scarlet; yer two breasts air like two fawns; yer navel be like a round goblet; yer belly be like a heap o' wheat. . . . (*He covers her hand with kisses. She does not seem to notice. She stares before her with hard angry eyes.*)

ABBIE—(*jerking her hands away—harshly*) So ye're plannin' t' leave the farm t' Eben, air ye?

CABOT—(*dazedly*) Leave. . . ? (*then with resentful obstinacy*) I hain't a-givin' it t' no one!

ABBIE—(*remorselessly*) Ye can't take it with ye.

CABOT—(*thinks a moment—then reluctantly*) No, I calc'late not. (*after a pause—with a strange passion*) But if I could, I would, by the Etarnal! 'R if I could, in my dyin' hour, I'd set it afire an' watch it burn—this house an' every ear o' corn an' every tree down t' the last blade o' hay! I'd sit an' know it was all a-dying with me an' no one else'd ever own what was mine, what I'd made out o' nothin' with my own sweat 'n' blood! (*a pause—then he adds with a queer affection*) 'Ceptin' the cows. Them I'd turn free.

ABBIE—(*harshly*) An' me?

CABOT—(*with a queer smile*) Ye'd be turned free, too.

ABBIE—(*furiously*) So that's the thanks I git fur marryin' ye—t' have ye change kind to Eben who hates ye, an' talk o' turnin' me out in the road.

CABOT—(*hastily*) Abbie! Ye know I wa'n't. . . .

ABBIE—(*vengefully*) Just let me tell ye a thing or two 'bout Eben! Whar's he gone? T' see that harlot, Min! I tried fur t' stop him. Disgracin' yew an' me—on the Sabbath, too!

CABOT—(*rather guiltily*) He's a sinner—nateral-born. It's lust eatin' his heart.

ABBIE—(*enraged beyond endurance—wildly vindictive*) An' his lust fur me! Kin ye find excuses fur that?

CABOT—(*stares at her—after a dead pause*) Lust—fur yew?

ABBIE—(*defiantly*) He was tryin' t' make love t' me—when ye heerd us quarrelin'.

CABOT—(*stares at her—then a terrible expression of rage comes over his face—he springs to his feet shaking all over.*) By the A'mighty God—I'll end him!

ABBIE—(*frightened now for Eben*) No! Don't ye!

CABOT—(*violently*) I'll git the shotgun an' blow his soft brains t' the top o' them elums!

ABBIE—(*throwing her arms around him*) No! Ephraim!

CABOT—(*pushing her away violently*) I will, by God!

ABBIE—(*in a quieting tone*) Listen, Ephraim. 'Twa'n't nothin' bad—on'y a boy's foolin'—'twa'n't meant serious—jest jokin' an' teasin'. . . .

CABOT—Then why did ye say—lust?

ABBIE—It must hev sounded wusser'n I meant. An' I was mad at thinkin'—ye'd leave him the farm.

CABOT—(*quieter but still grim and cruel*) Waal then, I'll horsewhip him off the place if that much'll content ye.

ABBIE—(*reaching out and taking his hand*) No. Don't think o' me! Ye mustn't drive him off. 'Tain't sensible. Who'll ye get to help ye on the farm? They's no one hereabouts.

CABOT—(*considers this—then nodding his appreciation*) Ye got a head on ye. (*then irritably*) Waal, let him stay. (*He sits down on the edge of the porch. She sits beside him. He murmurs contemptuously*) I oughtn't t' git riled so—at that 'ere fool calf. (*a pause*) But har's the p'int. What son o' mine'll keep on here t' the farm—when the Lord does call me? Simeon an' Peter air gone t' hell—an Eben's follerin' 'em.

ABBIE—They's me.

CABOT—Ye're on'y a woman.

ABBIE—I'm yewr wife.

CABOT—That hain't me. A son is me—my blood—mine. Mine ought t' git mine. An' then it's still mine—even though I be six foot under. D'ye see?

ABBIE—(*giving him a look of hatred*) Ay-eh. I see. (*She becomes very thoughtful, her face growing shrewd, her eyes studying Cabot craftily.*)

CABOT—I'm gittin' old—ripe on the bough. (*then with a sudden forced reassurance*) Not but what I hain't a hard nut t' crack even yet—an' fur many a year t' come! By the Etarnal, I kin break most o' the young fellers's backs at any kind o' work any day o' the year!

ABBIE—(*suddenly*) Mebbe the Lord'll give *us* a son.

CABOT—(*turns and stares at her eagerly*) Ye mean—a son—t' me 'n' yew?

ABBIE—(*with a cajoling smile*) Ye're a strong man yet,

hain't ye? 'Tain't noways impossible, be it? We know that. Why d'ye stare so? Hain't ye never thought o' that afore? I been thinkin' o' it all along. Ay-eh—an' I been prayin' it'd happen, too.

CABOT—(*his face growing full of joyous pride and a sort of religious ecstasy*) Ye been prayin', Abbie?—fur a son?—t' us?

ABBIE—Ay-eh. (*with a grim resolution*) I want a son now.

CABOT—(*excitedly clutching both of her hands in his*) It'd be the blessin' o' God, Abbie—the blessin' o' God A'mighty on me—in my old age—in my lonesomeness! They hain't nothin' I wouldn't do fur ye then, Abbie. Ye'd hev on'y t' ask it—anythin' ye'd a mind t'!

ABBIE—(*interrupting*) Would ye will the farm t' me then —t' me an' it?

CABOT—(*vehemently*) I'd do anythin' ye axed, I tell ye! I swar it! May I be everlastin' damned t' hell if I wouldn't! (*He sinks to his knees pulling her down with him. He trembles all over with the fervor of his hopes.*) Pray t' the Lord agen, Abbie. It's the Sabbath! I'll jine ye! Two prayers air better nor one. "An' God hearkened unto Rachel"! An' God hearkened unto Abbie! Pray, Abbie! Pray fur him to hearken! (*He bows his head, mumbling. She pretends to do likewise but gives him a side glance of scorn and triumph.*)

SCENE TWO

About eight in the evening. The interior of the two bedrooms on the top floor is shown. Eben is sitting on the side of his bed in the room on the left. On account of the heat he has taken off everything but his undershirt and pants. His feet are bare. He faces front, brooding moodily, his chin propped on his hands, a desperate expression on his face.

In the other room Cabot and Abbie are sitting side by side on the edge of their bed, an old four-poster with feather mattress. He is in his night shirt, she in her nightdress. He is still in the queer, excited mood into which the notion of a son has thrown him. Both rooms are lighted dimly and flickeringly by tallow candles.

CABOT—The farm needs a son.

ABBIE—I need a son.

CABOT—Ay-eh. Sometimes ye air the farm an' sometimes the farm be yew. That's why I clove t' ye in my lonesomeness. (*A pause. He pounds his knee with his fist.*) Me an' the farm has got t' beget a son!

ABBIE—Ye'd best go t' sleep. Ye're gittin' thin's all mixed.

CABOT—(*with an impatient gesture*) No, I hain't. My mind's clear's a well. Ye don't know me, that's it. (*He stares hopelessly at the floor.*)

ABBIE—(*indifferently*) Mebbe. (*In the next room Eben gets up and paces up and down distractedly. Abbie hears him. Her eyes fasten on the intervening wall with concentrated attention. Eben stops and stares. Their hot glances seem to meet through the wall. Unconsciously he stretches out his arms for her and she half rises. Then aware, he mutters a curse at himself and flings himself face downward on the bed, his clenched fists above his head, his face buried in the pillow. Abbie relaxes with a faint sigh but her eyes remain fixed on the wall; she listens with all her attention for some movement from Eben.*)

CABOT—(*suddenly raises his head and looks at her—scornfully*) Will ye ever know me—'r will any man 'r woman? (*shaking his head*) No. I calc'late 'twa'n't t' be. (*He turns away. Abbie looks at the wall. Then, evidently unable to keep silent about his thoughts, without looking at his wife, he puts out his hand and clutches her knee. She starts violently, looks at him, sees he is not watching her, concentrates again on the wall and pays no attention to what he says.*) Listen, Abbie. When I come here fifty odd year ago—I was jest twenty an' the strongest an' hardest ye ever seen—ten times as strong an' fifty times as hard as Eben. Waal—this place was nothin' but fields o' stones. Folks laughed when I tuk it. They couldn't know what I knowed. When ye kin make corn sprout out o' stones, God's livin' in yew! They wa'n't strong enuf fur that! They reckoned God was easy. They laughed. They don't laugh no more. Some died hereabouts. Some went West an' died. They're all under ground—fur follerin' arter an easy God. God hain't easy. (*He shakes his head slowly.*) An' I growed hard. Folks kept allus sayin' he's a hard man like 'twas sinful t' be hard, so's at last I said back at 'em: Waal then, by thunder, ye'll git me hard

an' see how ye like it! (*then suddenly*) But I give in t' weakness
once. 'Twas arter I'd been here two year. I got weak—de-
spairful—they was so many stones. They was a party leavin',
givin' up, goin' West. I jined 'em. We tracked on 'n' on. We
come t' broad medders, plains, whar the soil was black an'
rich as gold. Nary a stone. Easy. Ye'd on'y to plow an' sow
an' then set an' smoke yer pipe an' watch thin's grow. I could
o' been a rich man—but somethin' in me fit me an' fit me—
the voice o' God sayin': "This hain't wuth nothin' t' Me. Git
ye back t' hum!" I got afeerd o' that voice an' I lit out back
t' hum here, leavin' my claim an' crops t' whoever'd a mind
t' take em. Ay-eh. I actooly give up what was rightful mine!
God's hard, not easy! God's in the stones! Build my church
on a rock—out o' stones an' I'll be in them! That's what He
meant t' Peter! (*He sighs heavily—a pause.*) Stones. I picked
'em up an' piled 'em into walls. Ye kin read the years o' my
life in them walls, every day a hefted stone, climbin' over the
hills up and down, fencin' in the fields that was mine, whar
I'd made thin's grow out o' nothin'—like the will o' God,
like the servant o' His hand. It wa'n't easy. It was hard an'
He made me hard fur it. (*He pauses.*) All the time I kept
gittin' lonesomer. I tuk a wife. She bore Simeon an' Peter.
She was a good woman. She wuked hard. We was married
twenty year. She never knowed me. She helped but she never
knowed what she was helpin'. I was allus lonesome. She died.
After that it wa'n't so lonesome fur a spell. (*a pause*) I lost
count o' the years. I had no time t' fool away countin' 'em.
Sim an' Peter helped. The farm growed. It was all mine!
When I thought o' that I didn't feel lonesome. (*a pause*) But
ye can't hitch yer mind t' one thin' day an' night. I tuk another wife—Eben's Maw. Her folks was contestin' me at law
over my deeds t' the farm—my farm! That's why Eben keeps
a-talkin' his fool talk o' this bein' his Maw's farm. She bore
Eben. She was purty—but soft. She tried t' be hard. She
couldn't. She never knowed me nor nothin'. It was lonesomer
'n hell with her. After a matter o' sixteen odd years, she died.
(*a pause*) I lived with the boys. They hated me 'cause I was
hard. I hated them 'cause they was soft. They coveted the
farm without knowin' what it meant. It made me bitter 'n
wormwood. It aged me—them coveting what I'd made fur

mine. Then this spring the call come—the voice o' God cryin' in my wilderness, in my lonesomeness—t' go out an' seek an' find! (*turning to her with strange passion*) I sought ye an' I found ye! Yew air my Rose o' Sharon! Yer eyes air like. . . . (*She has turned a blank face, resentful eyes to his. He stares at her for a moment—then harshly*) Air ye any the wiser fur all I've told ye?

ABBIE—(*confusedly*) Mebbe.

CABOT—(*pushing her away from him—angrily*) Ye don't know nothin'—nor never will. If ye don't hev a son t' redeem ye. . . ! (*This in a tone of cold threat.*)

ABBIE—(*resentfully*) I prayed, hain't I?

CABOT—(*bitterly*) Pray agen—fur understandin'!

ABBIE—(*a veiled threat in her tone*) Ye'll have a son out o' me, I promise ye.

CABOT—How kin ye promise?

ABBIE—I got second-sight, mebbe. I kin foretell. (*She gives a queer smile.*)

CABOT—I believe ye have. Ye give me the chills sometimes. (*He shivers.*) It's cold in this house. It's oneasy. They's thin's pokin' about in the dark—in the corners. (*He pulls on his trousers, tucking in his night shirt, and pulls on his boots.*)

ABBIE—(*surprised*) Whar air ye goin'?

CABOT—(*queerly*) Down whar it's restful—whar it's warm—down t' the barn. (*bitterly*) I kin talk t' the cows. They know. They know the farm an' me. They'll give me peace. (*He turns to go out the door.*)

ABBIE—(*a bit frightenedly*) Air ye ailin' tonight, Ephraim?

CABOT—Growin'. Growin' ripe on the bough. (*He turns and goes, his boots clumping down the stairs. Eben sits up with a start, listening. Abbie is conscious of his movement and stares at the wall. Cabot comes out of the house around the corner and stands by the gate, blinking at the sky. He stretches up his hands in a tortured gesture.*) God A'mighty, call from the dark! (*He listens as if expecting an answer. Then his arms drop, he shakes his head and plods off toward the barn. Eben and Abbie stare at each other through the wall. Eben sighs heavily and Abbie echoes it. Both become terribly nervous, uneasy. Finally Abbie gets up and listens, her ear to the wall. He acts as if he saw every move she was making, he becomes resolutely still. She seems driven into a decision—goes out the door in rear determinedly. His eyes follow her. Then as the door of his room is opened softly, he turns away, waits in an attitude of strained fixity. Abbie stands for a second staring at him, her eyes burning with desire. Then with a little cry she runs over and throws her arms about his neck, she pulls his head back and covers his mouth with kisses. At first, he submits dumbly; then he puts his arms about her neck and returns her kisses, but finally, suddenly aware of his hatred, he hurls her away from him, springing to his feet. They stand speechless and breathless, panting like two animals.)*

ABBIE—(*at last—painfully*) Ye shouldn't, Eben—ye shouldn't—I'd make ye happy!

EBEN—(*harshly*) I don't want t' be happy—from yew!

ABBIE—(*helplessly*) Ye do, Eben! Ye do! Why d'ye lie?

EBEN—(*viciously*) I don't take t' ye, I tell ye! I hate the sight o' ye!

ABBIE—(*with an uncertain troubled laugh*) Waal, I kissed ye anyways—an' ye kissed back—yer lips was burnin'—ye can't lie 'bout that! (*intensely*) If ye don't care, why did ye kiss me back—why was yer lips burnin'?

EBEN—(*wiping his mouth*) It was like pizen on 'em. (*then tauntingly*) When I kissed ye back, mebbe I thought 'twas someone else.

ABBIE—(*wildly*) Min?

EBEN—Mebbe.

ABBIE—(*torturedly*) Did ye go t' see her? Did ye r'ally go? I thought ye mightn't. Is that why ye throwed me off jest now?

EBEN—(*sneeringly*) What if it be?

ABBIE—(*raging*) Then ye're a dog, Eben Cabot!

EBEN—(*threateningly*) Ye can't talk that way t' me!

ABBIE—(*with a shrill laugh*) Can't I? Did ye think I was in love with ye—a weak thin' like yew! Not much! I on'y wanted ye fur a purpose o' my own—an' I'll hev ye fur it yet 'cause I'm stronger'n yew be!

EBEN—(*resentfully*) I knowed well it was on'y part o' yer plan t' swaller everythin'!

ABBIE—(*tauntingly*) Mebbe!

EBEN—(*furious*) Git out o' my room!

ABBIE—This air my room an' ye're on'y hired help!

EBEN—(*threateningly*) Git out afore I murder ye!

ABBIE—(*quite confident now*) I hain't a mite afeerd. Ye want me, don't ye? Yes, ye do! An' yer Paw's son'll never kill what he wants! Look at yer eyes! They's lust fur me in 'em, burnin' 'em up! Look at yer lips now! They're tremblin' an' longin' t' kiss me, an' yer teeth t' bite! (*He is watching her now with a horrible fascination. She laughs a crazy triumphant laugh.*) I'm a-goin' t' make all o' this hum my hum! They's one room hain't mine yet, but it's a-goin' t' be tonight. I'm a-goin' down now an' light up! (*She makes him a mocking bow.*) Won't ye come courtin' me in the best parlor, Mister Cabot?

EBEN—(*staring at her—horribly confused—dully*) Don't ye dare! It hain't been opened since Maw died an' was laid out thar! Don't ye. . . ! (*But her eyes are fixed on his so burningly that his will seems to wither before hers. He stands swaying toward her helplessly.*)

ABBIE—(*holding his eyes and putting all her will into her words as she backs out the door*) I'll expect ye afore long, Eben.

EBEN—(*stares after her for a while, walking toward the door. A light appears in the parlor window. He murmurs*) In the parlor? (*This seems to arouse connotations for he comes back and puts on his white shirt, collar, half ties the tie mechanically, puts on coat, takes his hat, stands barefooted looking about him in bewilderment, mutters wonderingly*) Maw! Whar air yew? (*then goes slowly toward the door in rear*)

SCENE THREE

A few minutes later. The interior of the parlor is shown. A grim, repressed room like a tomb in which the family has been interred alive. Abbie sits on the edge of the horsehair sofa. She has lighted all the candles and the room is revealed in all its preserved ugliness. A change has come over the woman. She looks awed and frightened now, ready to run away.

The door is opened and Eben appears. His face wears an expression of obsessed confusion. He stands staring at her, his arms hanging disjointedly from his shoulders, his feet bare, his hat in his hand.

ABBIE—(*after a pause—with a nervous, formal politeness*) Won't ye set?

EBEN—(*dully*) Ay-eh. (*Mechanically he places his hat carefully on the floor near the door and sits stiffly beside her on the edge of the sofa. A pause. They both remain rigid, looking straight ahead with eyes full of fear.*)

ABBIE—When I fust come in—in the dark—they seemed somethin' here.

EBEN—(*simply*) Maw.

ABBIE—I kin still feel—somethin'.

EBEN—It's Maw.

ABBIE—At fust I was feered o' it. I wanted t' yell an' run. Now—since yew come—seems like it's growin' soft an' kind t' me. (*addressing the air—queerly*) Thank yew.

EBEN—Maw allus loved me.

ABBIE—Mebbe it knows I love yew, too. Mebbe that makes it kind t' me.

EBEN—(*dully*) I dunno. I should think she'd hate ye.

ABBIE—(*with certainty*) No. I kin feel it don't—not no more.

EBEN—Hate ye fur stealin' her place—here in her hum—settin' in her parlor whar she was laid— (*He suddenly stops, staring stupidly before him.*)

ABBIE—What is it, Eben?

EBEN—(*in a whisper*) Seems like Maw didn't want me t' remind ye.

ABBIE—(*excitedly*) I knowed, Eben! It's kind t' me! It don't b'ar me no grudges fur what I never knowed an' couldn't help!

EBEN—Maw b'ars him a grudge.

ABBIE—Waal, so does all o' us.

EBEN—Ay-eh. (*with passion*) I does, by God!

ABBIE—(*taking one of his hands in hers and patting it*) Thar! Don't git riled thinkin' o' him. Think o' yer Maw who's kind t' us. Tell me about yer Maw, Eben.

EBEN—They hain't nothin' much. She was kind. She was good.

ABBIE—(*putting one arm over his shoulder. He does not seem to notice—passionately*) I'll be kind an' good t' ye!

EBEN—Sometimes she used t' sing fur me.

ABBIE—I'll sing fur ye!

EBEN—This was her hum. This was her farm.

ABBIE—This is my hum! This is my farm!

EBEN—He married her t' steal 'em. She was soft an' easy. He couldn't 'preciate her.

ABBIE—He can't 'preciate me!

EBEN—He murdered her with his hardness.

ABBIE—He's murderin' me!

EBEN—She died. (*a pause*) Sometimes she used to sing fur me. (*He bursts into a fit of sobbing.*)

ABBIE—(*both her arms around him—with wild passion*) I'll sing fur ye! I'll die fur ye! (*In spite of her overwhelming desire for him, there is a sincere maternal love in her manner and voice—a horribly frank mixture of lust and mother love.*) Don't cry, Eben! I'll take yer Maw's place! I'll be everythin' she was t' ye! Let me kiss ye, Eben! (*She pulls his head around. He makes a bewildered pretense of resistance. She is tender.*) Don't be afeered! I'll kiss ye pure, Eben—same 's if I was a Maw t' ye—an' ye kin kiss me back 's if yew was my son— my boy—sayin' good-night t' me! Kiss me, Eben. (*They kiss in restrained fashion. Then suddenly wild passion overcomes her. She kisses him lustfully again and again and he flings his arms about her and returns her kisses. Suddenly, as in the bedroom, he frees himself from her violently and springs to his feet. He is trembling all over, in a strange state of terror. Abbie strains her arms toward him with fierce pleading.*) Don't ye leave me, Eben! Can't ye see it hain't enuf—lovin' ye like a Maw— can't ye see it's got t' be that an' more—much more—a hundred times more—fur me t' be happy—fur yew t' be happy?

EBEN—(*to the presence he feels in the room*) Maw! Maw! What d'ye want? What air ye tellin' me?

ABBIE—She's tellin' ye t' love me. She knows I love ye an' I'll be good t' ye. Can't ye feel it? Don't ye know? She's tellin' ye t' love me, Eben!

EBEN—Ay-eh. I feel—mebbe she—but—I can't figger out —why—when ye've stole her place—here in her hum— in the parlor whar she was—

ABBIE—(*fiercely*) She knows I love ye!

EBEN—(*his face suddenly lighting up with a fierce, trium-*

phant grin) I see it! I sees why. It's her vengeance on him—
so's she kin rest quiet in her grave!

ABBIE—(*wildly*) Vengeance o' God on the hull o' us! What
d'we give a durn? I love ye, Eben! God knows I love ye! (*She
stretches out her arms for him.*)

EBEN—(*throws himself on his knees beside the sofa and grabs
her in his arms—releasing all his pent-up passion*) An' I love
yew, Abbie!—now I kin say it! I been dyin' fur want o' ye—
every hour since ye come! I love ye! (*Their lips meet in a fierce,
bruising kiss.*)

SCENE FOUR

*Exterior of the farmhouse. It is just dawn. The front door at
right is opened and Eben comes out and walks around to the gate.
He is dressed in his working clothes. He seems changed. His face
wears a bold and confident expression, he is grinning to himself
with evident satisfaction. As he gets near the gate, the window of
the parlor is heard opening and the shutters are flung back and
Abbie sticks her head out. Her hair tumbles over her shoulders in
disarray, her face is flushed, she looks at Eben with tender, languorous eyes and calls softly*

ABBIE—Eben. (*as he turns—playfully*) Jest one more kiss
afore ye go. I'm goin' t' miss ye fearful all day.

EBEN—An' me yew, ye kin bet! (*He goes to her. They kiss
several times. He draws away, laughingly*) Thar. That's enuf,
hain't it? Ye won't hev none left fur next time.

ABBIE—I got a million o' 'em left fur yew! (*then a bit anxiously*) D'ye r'ally love me, Eben?

EBEN—(*emphatically*) I like ye better'n any gal I ever
knowed! That's gospel!

ABBIE—Likin' hain't lovin'.

EBEN—Waal then—I love ye. Now air yew satisfied?

ABBIE—Ay-eh, I be. (*She smiles at him adoringly.*)

EBEN—I better git t' the barn. The old critter's liable t'
suspicion an' come sneakin' up.

ABBIE—(*with a confident laugh*) Let him! I kin allus pull

the wool over his eyes. I'm goin' t' leave the shutters open and let in the sun 'n' air. This room's been dead long enuf. Now it's goin' t' be my room!

EBEN—(*frowning*) Ay-eh.

ABBIE—(*hastily*) I meant—our room.

EBEN—Ay-eh.

ABBIE—We made it our'n last night, didn't we? We give it life—our lovin' did. (*a pause*)

EBEN—(*with a strange look*) Maw's gone back t' her grave. She kin sleep now.

ABBIE—May she rest in peace! (*then tenderly rebuking*) Ye oughtn't t' talk o' sad thin's—this mornin'.

EBEN—It jest come up in my mind o' itself.

ABBIE—Don't let it. (*He doesn't answer. She yawns.*) Waal, I'm a-goin' t' steal a wink o' sleep. I'll tell the Old Man I hain't feelin' pert. Let him git his own vittles.

EBEN—I see him comin' from the barn. Ye better look smart an' git upstairs.

ABBIE—Ay-eh. Good-by. Don't ferget me. (*She throws him a kiss. He grins—then squares his shoulders and awaits his father confidently. Cabot walks slowly up from the left, staring up at the sky with a vague face.*)

EBEN—(*jovially*) Mornin', Paw. Star-gazin' in daylight?

CABOT—Purty, hain't it?

EBEN—(*looking around him possessively*) It's a durned purty farm.

CABOT—I mean the sky.

EBEN—(*grinning*) How d'ye know? Them eyes o' your'n can't see that fur. (*This tickles his humor and he slaps his thigh and laughs.*) Ho-ho! That's a good un!

CABOT—(*grimly sarcastic*) Ye're feelin' right chipper, hain't ye? Whar'd ye steal the likker?

EBEN—(*good-naturedly*) 'Tain't likker. Jest life. (*suddenly holding out his hand—soberly*) Yew 'n' me is quits. Let's shake hands.

CABOT—(*suspiciously*) What's come over ye?

EBEN—Then don't. Mebbe it's jest as well. (*a moment's pause*) What's come over me? (*queerly*) Didn't ye feel her passin'—goin' back t' her grave?

CABOT—(*dully*) Who?

EBEN—Maw. She kin rest now an' sleep content. She's quits with ye.

CABOT—(*confusedly*) I rested. I slept good—down with the cows. They know how t' sleep. They're teachin' me.

EBEN—(*suddenly jovial again*) Good fur the cows! Waal—ye better git t' work.

CABOT—(*grimly amused*) Air yew bossin' me, ye calf?

EBEN—(*beginning to laugh*) Ay-eh! I'm bossin' yew. Ha-ha-ha! See how ye like it! Ha-ha-ha! I'm the prize rooster o' this roost. Ha-ha-ha! (*He goes off toward the barn laughing.*)

CABOT—(*looks after him with scornful pity*) Soft-headed. Like his Maw. Dead spit 'n' image. No hope in him! (*He spits with contemptuous disgust.*) A born fool! (*then matter-of-factly*) Waal—I'm gittin' peckish. (*He goes toward door.*)

(*The Curtain Falls*)

PART III

SCENE ONE

A night in late spring the following year. The kitchen and the two bedrooms upstairs are shown. The two bedrooms are dimly lighted by a tallow candle in each. Eben is sitting on the side of the bed in his room, his chin propped on his fists, his face a study of the struggle he is making to understand his conflicting emotions. The noisy laughter and music from below where a kitchen dance is in progress annoy and distract him. He scowls at the floor.

In the next room a cradle stands beside the double bed.

In the kitchen all is festivity. The stove has been taken down to give more room to the dancers. The chairs, with wooden benches added, have been pushed back against the walls. On these are seated, squeezed in tight against one another, farmers and their wives and their young folks of both sexes from the neighboring farms. They are all chattering and laughing loudly. They evidently have some secret joke in common. There is no end of winking, of nudging, of meaning nods of the head toward Cabot who, in a state of extreme hilarious excitement increased by the amount he has drunk, is standing near the rear door where there is a small keg of whisky and serving drinks to all the men. In the left corner, front, dividing the attention with her husband, Abbie is sitting in a rocking chair, a shawl wrapped about her shoulders. She is very pale, her face is thin and drawn, her eyes are fixed anxiously on the open door in rear as if waiting for someone.

The musician is tuning up his fiddle, seated in the far right corner. He is a lanky young fellow with a long, weak face. His pale eyes blink incessantly and he grins about him slyly with a greedy malice.

ABBIE—(*suddenly turning to a young girl on her right*) Whar's Eben?

YOUNG GIRL—(*eying her scornfully*) I dunno, Mrs. Cabot. I hain't seen Eben in ages. (*meaningly*) Seems like he's spent most o' his time t' hum since yew come.

ABBIE—(*vaguely*) I tuk his Maw's place.

YOUNG GIRL—Ay-eh. So I've heerd. (*She turns away to retail this bit of gossip to her mother sitting next to her. Abbie*

358

turns to her left to a big stoutish middle-aged man whose flushed face and starting eyes show the amount of "likker" he has consumed.)

ABBIE—Ye hain't seen Eben, hev ye?

MAN—No, I hain't. (*Then he adds with a wink*) If yew hain't, who would?

ABBIE—He's the best dancer in the county. He'd ought t' come an' dance.

MAN—(*with a wink*) Mebbe he's doin' the dutiful an' walkin' the kid t' sleep. It's a boy, hain't it?

ABBIE—(*nodding vaguely*) Ay-eh—born two weeks back— purty's a picter.

MAN—They all is—t' their Maws. (*then in a whisper, with a nudge and a leer*) Listen, Abbie—if ye ever git tired o' Eben, remember me! Don't fergit now! (*He looks at her uncomprehending face for a second—then grunts disgustedly.*) Waal —guess I'll likker agin. (*He goes over and joins Cabot, who is arguing noisily with an old farmer over cows. They all drink.*)

ABBIE—(*this time appealing to nobody in particular*) Wonder what Eben's a-doin'? (*Her remark is repeated down the line with many a guffaw and titter until it reaches the fiddler. He fastens his blinking eyes on Abbie.*)

FIDDLER—(*raising his voice*) Bet I kin tell ye, Abbie, what Eben's doin'! He's down t' the church offerin' up prayers o' thanksgivin'. (*They all titter expectantly.*)

A MAN—What fur? (*another titter*)

FIDDLER—'Cause unto him a—(*he hesitates just long enough*)—brother is born! (*A roar of laughter. They all look from Abbie to Cabot. She is oblivious, staring at the door. Cabot, although he hasn't heard the words, is irritated by the laughter and steps forward, glaring about him. There is an immediate silence.*)

CABOT—What're ye all bleatin' about—like a flock o' goats? Why don't ye dance, damn ye? I axed ye here t' dance—t' eat, drink an' be merry—an' thar ye set cacklin' like a lot o' wet hens with the pip! Ye've swilled my likker an' guzzled my vittles like hogs, hain't ye? Then dance fur me, can't ye? That's fa'r an' squar', hain't it? (*A grumble of resentment goes around but they are all evidently in too much awe of him to express it openly.*)

FIDDLER—(*slyly*) We're waitin' fur Eben. (*a suppressed laugh*)

CABOT—(*with a fierce exultation*) T' hell with Eben! Eben's done fur now! I got a new son! (*his mood switching with drunken suddenness*) But ye needn't t' laugh at Eben, none o' ye! He's my blood, if he be a dumb fool. He's better nor any o' yew! He kin do a day's work a'most up t' what I kin—an' that'd put any o' yew pore critters t' shame!

FIDDLER—An' he kin do a good night's work, too! (*a roar of laughter*)

CABOT—Laugh, ye damn fools! Ye're right jist the same, Fiddler. He kin work day an' night too, like I kin, if need be!

OLD FARMER—(*from behind the keg where he is weaving drunkenly back and forth—with great simplicity*) They hain't many t' touch ye, Ephraim—a son at seventy-six. That's a hard man fur ye! I be on'y sixty-eight an' I couldn't do it. (*a roar of laughter in which Cabot joins uproariously*)

CABOT—(*slapping him on the back*) I'm sorry fur ye, Hi. I'd never suspicion sech weakness from a boy like yew!

OLD FARMER—An' I never reckoned yew had it in ye nuther, Ephraim. (*There is another laugh.*)

CABOT—(*suddenly grim*) I got a lot in me—a hell of a lot—folks don't know on. (*turning to the fiddler*) Fiddle 'er up, durn ye! Give 'em somethin' t' dance t'! What air ye, an ornament? Hain't this a celebration? Then grease yer elbow an' go it!

FIDDLER—(*seizes a drink which the old farmer holds out to him and downs it*) Here goes! (*He starts to fiddle "Lady of the Lake." Four young fellows and four girls form in two lines and dance a square dance. The fiddler shouts directions for the different movements, keeping his words in the rhythm of the music and interspersing them with jocular personal remarks to the dancers themselves. The people seated along the walls stamp their feet and clap their hands in unison. Cabot is especially active in this respect. Only Abbie remains apathetic, staring at the door as if she were alone in a silent room.*)

FIDDLER—Swing your partner t' the right! That's it, Jim! Give her a b'ar hug! Her Maw hain't lookin'. (*laughter*) Change partners! That suits ye, don't it, Essie, now ye got

Reub afore ye? Look at her redden up, will ye? Waal, life is short an' so's love, as the feller says. (*laughter*)

CABOT—(*excitedly, stamping his foot*) Go it, boys! Go it, gals!

FIDDLER—(*with a wink at the others*) Ye're the spryest seventy-six ever I sees, Ephraim! Now if ye'd on'y good eyesight . . . ! (*Suppressed laughter. He gives Cabot no chance to retort but roars*) Promenade! Ye're walkin' like a bride down the aisle, Sarah! Waal, while they's life they's allus hope, I've heerd tell. Swing your partner to the left! Gosh A'mighty, look at Johnny Cook high-steppin'! They hain't goin' t' be much strength left fur howin' in the corn lot t'morrow. (*laughter*)

CABOT—Go it! Go it! (*Then suddenly, unable to restrain himself any longer, he prances into the midst of the dancers, scattering them, waving his arms about wildly.*) Ye're all hoofs! Git out o' my road! Give me room! I'll show ye dancin'. Ye're all too soft! (*He pushes them roughly away. They crowd back toward the walls, muttering, looking at him resentfully.*)

FIDDLER—(*jeeringly*) Go it, Ephraim! Go it! (*He starts "Pop, Goes the Weasel," increasing the tempo with every verse until at the end he is fiddling crazily as fast as he can go.*)

CABOT—(*starts to dance, which he does very well and with tremendous vigor. Then he begins to improvise, cuts incredibly grotesque capers, leaping up and cracking his heels together, prancing around in a circle with body bent in an Indian war dance, then suddenly straightening up and kicking as high as he can with both legs. He is like a monkey on a string. And all the while he intersperses his antics with shouts and derisive comments.*) Whoop! Here's dancin' fur ye! Whoop! See that! Seventy-six, if I'm a day! Hard as iron yet! Beatin' the young 'uns like I allus done! Look at me! I'd invite ye t' dance on my hundredth birthday on'y ye'll all be dead by then. Ye're a sickly generation! Yer hearts air pink, not red! Yer veins is full o' mud an' water! I be the on'y man in the county! Whoop! See that! I'm a Injun! I've killed Injuns in the West afore ye was born—an' skulped 'em too! They's a arrer wound on my backside I c'd show ye! The hull tribe chased me. I outrun 'em all—with the arrer stuck in me! An' I tuk vengeance on 'em. Ten eyes fur an eye, that was my motter!

Whoop! Look at me! I kin kick the ceilin' off the room! Whoop!

FIDDLER—(*stops playing*—*exhaustedly*) God A'mighty, I got enuf. Ye got the devil's strength in ye.

CABOT—(*delightedly*) Did I beat yew, too? Waal, ye played smart. Hev a swig. (*He pours whisky for himself and fiddler. They drink. The others watch Cabot silently with cold, hostile eyes. There is a dead pause. The fiddler rests. Cabot leans against the keg, panting, glaring around him confusedly. In the room above, Eben gets to his feet and tiptoes out the door in rear, appearing a moment later in the other bedroom. He moves silently, even frightenedly, toward the cradle and stands there looking down at the baby. His face is as vague as his reactions are confused, but there is a trace of tenderness, of interested discovery. At the same moment that he reaches the cradle, Abbie seems to sense something. She gets up weakly and goes to Cabot.*)

ABBIE—I'm goin' up t' the baby.

CABOT—(*with real solicitation*) Air ye able fur the stairs? D'ye want me t' help ye, Abbie?

ABBIE—No. I'm able. I'll be down agen soon.

CABOT—Don't ye git wore out! He needs ye, remember— our son does! (*He grins affectionately, patting her on the back. She shrinks from his touch.*)

ABBIE—(*dully*) Don't—tech me. I'm goin'—up. (*She goes. Cabot looks after her. A whisper goes around the room. Cabot turns. It ceases. He wipes his forehead streaming with sweat. He is breathing pantingly.*)

CABOT—I'm a-goin' out t' git fresh air. I'm feelin' a mite dizzy. Fiddle up thar! Dance, all o' ye! Here's likker fur them as wants it. Enjoy yerselves. I'll be back. (*He goes, closing the door behind him.*)

FIDDLER—(*sarcastically*) Don't hurry none on our account! (*A suppressed laugh. He imitates Abbie.*) Whar's Eben? (*more laughter*)

A WOMAN—(*loudly*) What's happened in this house is plain as the nose on yer face! (*Abbie appears in the doorway upstairs and stands looking in surprise and adoration at Eben who does not see her.*)

A MAN—Ssshh! He's li'ble t' be listenin' at the door. That'd be like him. (*Their voices die to an intensive whispering.*)

Their faces are concentrated on this gossip. A noise as of dead leaves in the wind comes from the room. Cabot has come out from the porch and stands by the gate, leaning on it, staring at the sky blinkingly. Abbie comes across the room silently. Eben does not notice her until quite near.)

EBEN—(*starting*) Abbie!

ABBIE—Ssshh! (*She throws her arms around him. They kiss*—*then bend over the cradle together.*) Ain't he purty?—dead spit 'n' image o' yew!

EBEN—(*pleased*) Air he? I can't tell none.

ABBIE—E-zactly like!

EBEN—(*frowningly*) I don't like this. I don't like lettin' on what's mine's his'n. I been doin' that all my life. I'm gittin' t' the end o' b'arin' it!

ABBIE—(*putting her finger on his lips*) We're doin' the best we kin. We got t' wait. Somethin's bound t' happen. (*She puts her arms around him.*) I got t' go back.

EBEN—I'm goin' out. I can't b'ar it with the fiddle playin' an' the laughin'.

ABBIE—Don't git feelin' low. I love ye, Eben. Kiss me. (*He kisses her. They remain in each other's arms.*)

CABOT—(*at the gate, confusedly*) Even the music can't drive it out—somethin'. Ye kin feel it droppin' off the elums, climbin' up the roof, sneakin' down the chimney, pokin' in the corners! They's no peace in houses, they's no rest livin' with folks. Somethin's always livin' with ye. (*with a deep sigh*) I'll go t' the barn an' rest a spell. (*He goes wearily toward the barn.*)

FIDDLER—(*tuning up*) Let's celebrate the old skunk gittin' fooled! We kin have some fun now he's went. (*He starts to fiddle "Turkey in the Straw." There is real merriment now. The young folks get up to dance.*)

SCENE TWO

A half hour later—Exterior—Eben is standing by the gate looking up at the sky, an expression of dumb pain bewildered by itself on his face. Cabot appears, returning from the barn, walking wearily, his eyes on the ground. He sees Eben and his whole mood immediately changes. He becomes excited, a cruel, triumphant grin comes to his lips, he strides up and slaps Eben on the back. From within comes the whining of the fiddle and the noise of stamping feet and laughing voices.

CABOT—So har ye be!

EBEN—(*startled, stares at him with hatred for a moment— then dully*) Ay-eh.

CABOT—(*surveying him jeeringly*) Why hain't ye been in t' dance? They was all axin' fur ye.

EBEN—Let 'em ax!

CABOT—They's a hull passel o' purty gals.

EBEN—T' hell with 'em!

CABOT—Ye'd ought t' be marryin' one o' 'em soon.

EBEN—I hain't marryin' no one.

CABOT—Ye might 'arn a share o' a farm that way.

EBEN—(*with a sneer*) Like yew did, ye mean? I hain't that kind.

CABOT—(*stung*) Ye lie! 'Twas yer Maw's folks aimed t' steal my farm from me.

EBEN—Other folks don't say so. (*after a pause—defiantly*) An' I got a farm, anyways!

CABOT—(*derisively*) Whar?

EBEN—(*stamps a foot on the ground*) Har!

CABOT—(*throws his head back and laughs coarsely*) Ho-ho! Ye hev, hev ye? Waal, that's a good un!

EBEN—(*controlling himself—grimly*) Ye'll see!

CABOT—(*stares at him suspiciously, trying to make him out— a pause—then with scornful confidence*) Ay-eh. I'll see. So'll ye. It's ye that's blind—blind as a mole underground. (*Eben suddenly laughs, one short sardonic bark: Ha. A pause. Cabot peers at him with renewed suspicion.*) What air ye hawin' 'bout? (*Eben turns away without answering. Cabot grows angry.*) God A'mighty, yew air a dumb dunce! They's nothin' in that thick skull o' your'n but noise—like a empty keg it be! (*Eben doesn't seem to hear. Cabot's rage grows.*) Yewr farm! God A'mighty! If ye wa'n't a born donkey ye'd know ye'll never own stick nor stone on it, specially now arter him bein' born. It's his'n, I tell ye—his'n arter I die—but I'll live a hundred jest t' fool ye all—an' he'll be growed then—yewr age a'most! (*Eben laughs again his sardonic* Ha. *This drives Cabot into a fury.*) Ha? Ye think ye kin git 'round that someways, do ye? Waal, it'll be her'n, too—Abbie's—ye won't git 'round her—she knows yer tricks—she'll be too much fur ye—she wants the farm her'n—she was afeerd o' ye—she told me ye was sneakin' 'round tryin' t' make love t' her t' git her on yer side . . . ye . . . ye mad fool, ye! (*He raises his clenched fists threateningly.*)

EBEN—(*is confronting him, choking with rage*) Ye lie, ye old skunk! Abbie never said no sech thing!

CABOT—(*suddenly triumphant when he sees how shaken Eben is*) She did. An' I says, I'll blow his brains t' the top o' them elums—an' she says no, that hain't sense, who'll ye git t' help ye on the farm in his place—an' then she says yew'n me ought t' have a son—I know we kin, she says—an' I says, if we do, ye kin have anythin' I've got ye've a mind t'. An' she says, I wants Eben cut off so's this farm'll be mine when ye die! (*with terrible gloating*) An' that's what's happened, hain't it? An' the farm's her'n! An' the dust o' the road—that's your'n! Ha! Now who's hawin'?

EBEN—(*has been listening, petrified with grief and rage— suddenly laughs wildly and brokenly*) Ha-ha-ha! So that's her sneakin' game—all along!—like I suspicioned at fust—t' swaller it all—an' me, too. . . ! (*madly*) I'll murder her! (*He springs toward the porch, but Cabot is quicker and gets in between.*)

CABOT—No, ye don't!

EBEN—Git out o' my road! (*He tries to throw Cabot aside. They grapple in what becomes immediately a murderous struggle. The old man's concentrated strength is too much for Eben. Cabot gets one hand on his throat and presses him back across the stone wall. At the same moment, Abbie comes out on the porch. With a stifled cry she runs toward them.*)

ABBIE—Eben! Ephraim! (*She tugs at the hand on Eben's throat.*) Let go, Ephraim! Ye're chokin' him!

CABOT—(*removes his hand and flings Eben sideways full length on the grass, gasping and choking. With a cry, Abbie kneels beside him, trying to take his head on her lap, but he pushes her away. Cabot stands looking down with fierce triumph.*) Ye needn't t've fret, Abbie, I wa'n't aimin' t' kill him. He hain't wuth hangin' fur—not by a hell of a sight! (*more and more trium-phantly*) Seventy-six an' him not thirty yit—an' look whar he be fur thinkin' his Paw was easy! No, by God, I hain't easy! An' him upstairs, I'll raise him t' be like me! (*He turns to leave them.*) I'm goin' in an' dance!—sing an' celebrate! (*He walks to the porch—then turns with a great grin.*) I don't calc'late it's left in him, but if he gits pesky, Abbie, ye jest sing out. I'll come a-runnin' an' by the Etarnal, I'll put him across my knee an' birch him! Ha-ha-ha! (*He goes into the house laughing. A moment later his loud "whoop" is heard.*)

ABBIE—(*tenderly*) Eben. Air ye hurt? (*She tries to kiss him, but he pushes her violently away and struggles to a sitting position.*)

EBEN—(*gaspingly*) T' hell—with ye.

ABBIE—(*not believing her ears*) It's me, Eben—Abbie—don't ye know me?

EBEN—(*glowering at her with hatred*) Ay-eh—I know ye—now! (*He suddenly breaks down, sobbing weakly.*)

ABBIE—(*fearfully*) Eben—what's happened t' ye—why did ye look at me 's if ye hated me?

EBEN—(*violently, between sobs and gasps*) I do hate ye! Ye're a whore—a damn trickin' whore!

ABBIE—(*shrinking back horrified*) Eben! Ye don't know what ye're sayin'!

EBEN—(*scrambling to his feet and following her—accusingly*) Ye're nothin' but a stinkin' passel o' lies! Ye've been lyin' t' me every word ye spoke, day an' night, since we fust—done it. Ye've kept sayin' ye loved me. . . .

ABBIE—(*frantically*) I do love ye! (*She takes his hand, but he flings hers away.*)

EBEN—(*unheeding*) Ye've made a fool o' me—a sick, dumb fool—a-purpose! Ye've been on'y playin' yer sneakin', stealin' game all along—gittin' me t' lie with ye so's ye'd hev a son he'd think was his'n, an' makin' him promise he'd give ye the farm and let me eat dust, if ye did git him a son! (*staring at her with anguished, bewildered eyes*) They must be a devil livin' in ye! T'ain't human t' be as bad as that be!

ABBIE—(*stunned—dully*) He told yew. . . ?

EBEN—Hain't it true? It hain't no good in yew lyin'.

ABBIE—(*pleadingly*) Eben, listen—ye must listen—it was

long ago—afore we done nothin'—yew was scornin' me—
goin' t' see Min—when I was lovin' ye—an' I said it t' him
t' git vengeance on ye!

EBEN—(*unheedingly—with tortured passion*) I wish ye was
dead! I wish I was dead along with ye afore this come! (*ragingly*) But I'll git my vengeance too! I'll pray Maw t' come
back t' help me—t' put her cuss on yew an' him!

ABBIE—(*brokenly*) Don't ye, Eben! Don't ye! (*She throws
herself on her knees before him, weeping.*) I didn't mean t' do
bad t' ye! Fergive me, won't ye?

EBEN—(*not seeming to hear her—fiercely*) I'll git squar'
with the old skunk—an' yew! I'll tell him the truth 'bout
the son he's so proud o'! Then I'll leave ye here t' pizen
each other—with Maw comin' out o' her grave at nights
—an' I'll go t' the gold fields o' Californi-a whar Sim an'
Peter be!

ABBIE—(*terrified*) Ye won't—leave me? Ye can't!

EBEN—(*with fierce determination*) I'm a-goin', I tell ye! I'll
git rich thar an' come back an' fight him fur the farm he
stole—an' I'll kick ye both out in the road—t' beg an' sleep
in the woods—an' yer son along with ye—t' starve an' die!
(*He is hysterical at the end.*)

ABBIE—(*with a shudder—humbly*) He's yewr son, too,
Eben.

EBEN—(*torturedly*) I wish he never was born! I wish he'd
die this minit! I wish I'd never sot eyes on him! It's him—
yew havin' him—a-purpose t' steal—that's changed everythin'!

ABBIE—(*gently*) Did ye believe I loved ye—afore he
come?

EBEN—Ay-eh—like a dumb ox!

ABBIE—An' ye don't believe no more?

EBEN—B'lieve a lyin' thief! Ha!

ABBIE—(*shudders—then humbly*) An' did ye r'ally love me
afore?

EBEN—(*brokenly*) Ay-eh—an' ye was trickin' me!

ABBIE—An' ye don't love me now!

EBEN—(*violently*) I hate ye, I tell ye!

ABBIE—An' ye're truly goin' West—goin' t' leave me—all
account o' him being born?

EBEN—I'm a-goin' in the mornin'—or may God strike me t' hell!

ABBIE—(*after a pause—with a dreadful cold intensity— slowly*) If that's what his comin's done t' me—killin' yewr love—takin' yew away—my on'y joy—the on'y joy I ever knowed—like heaven t' me—purtier'n heaven—then I hate him, too, even if I be his Maw!

EBEN—(*brokenly*) Lies! Ye love him! He'll steal the farm fur ye! (*brokenly*) But t'ain't the farm so much—not no more—it's yew foolin' me—gittin' me t' love ye—lyin' yew loved me—jest t' git a son t' steal!

ABBIE—(*distractedly*) He won't steal! I'd kill him fust! I do love ye! I'll prove t' ye. . . !

EBEN—(*harshly*) T'ain't no use lyin' no more. I'm deaf t' ye! (*He turns away.*) I hain't seein' ye agen. Good-by!

ABBIE—(*pale with anguish*) Hain't ye even goin' t' kiss me—not once—arter all we loved?

EBEN—(*in a hard voice*) I hain't wantin' t' kiss ye never agen! I'm wantin' t' forgit I ever sot eyes on ye!

ABBIE—Eben!—ye mustn't—wait a spell—I want t' tell ye. . .

EBEN—I'm a-goin' in t' git drunk. I'm a-goin' t' dance.

ABBIE—(*clinging to his arm—with passionate earnestness*) If I could make it—'s if he'd never come up between us—if I could prove t' ye I wa'n't schemin' t' steal from ye—so's everythin' could be jest the same with us, lovin' each other jest the same, kissin' an' happy the same's we've been happy afore he come—if I could do it—ye'd love me agen, wouldn't ye? Ye'd kiss me agen? Ye wouldn't never leave me, would ye?

EBEN—(*moved*) I calc'late not. (*then shaking her hand off his arm—with a bitter smile*) But ye hain't God, be ye?

ABBIE—(*exultantly*) Remember ye've promised! (*then with strange intensity*) Mebbe I kin take back one thin' God does!

EBEN—(*peering at her*) Ye're gittin' cracked, hain't ye? (*then going towards door*) I'm a-goin' t' dance.

ABBIE—(*calls after him intensely*) I'll prove t' ye! I'll prove I love ye better'n. . . . (*He goes in the door, not seeming to hear. She remains standing where she is, looking after him—then she finishes desperately*) Better'n everythin' else in the world!

SCENE THREE

Just before dawn in the morning—shows the kitchen and Cabot's bedroom. In the kitchen, by the light of a tallow candle on the table, Eben is sitting, his chin propped on his hands, his drawn face blank and expressionless. His carpetbag is on the floor beside him. In the bedroom, dimly lighted by a small whale-oil lamp, Cabot lies asleep. Abbie is bending over the cradle, listening, her face full of terror yet with an undercurrent of desperate triumph. Suddenly, she breaks down and sobs, appears about to throw herself on her knees beside the cradle; but the old man turns restlessly, groaning in his sleep, and she controls herself, and, shrinking away from the cradle with a gesture of horror, backs swiftly toward the door in rear and goes out. A moment later she comes into the kitchen and, running to Eben, flings her arms about his neck and kisses him wildly. He hardens himself, he remains unmoved and cold, he keeps his eyes straight ahead.

ABBIE—(*hysterically*) I done it, Eben! I told ye I'd do it! I've proved I love ye—better'n everythin'—so's ye can't never doubt me no more!

EBEN—(*dully*) Whatever ye done, it hain't no good now.

ABBIE—(*wildly*) Don't ye say that! Kiss me, Eben, won't ye? I need ye t' kiss me arter what I done! I need ye t' say ye love me!

EBEN—(*kisses her without emotion—dully*) That's fur good-by. I'm a-goin' soon.

ABBIE—No! No! Ye won't go—not now!

EBEN—(*going on with his own thoughts*) I been a-thinkin'—an' I hain't goin' t' tell Paw nothin'. I'll leave Maw t' take vengeance on ye. If I told him, the old skunk'd jest be stinkin' mean enuf to take it out on that baby. (*his voice showing emotion in spite of him*) An' I don't want nothin' bad t' happen t' him. He hain't t' blame fur yew. (*He adds with a certain queer pride*) An' he looks like me! An' by God, he's mine! An' some day I'll be a-comin' back an' . . . !

ABBIE—(*too absorbed in her own thoughts to listen to him—pleadingly*) They's no cause fur ye t' go now—they's no sense—it's all the same's it was—they's nothin' come b'tween us now—arter what I done!

EBEN—(*Something in her voice arouses him. He stares at her a bit frightenedly.*) Ye look mad, Abbie. What did ye do?

ABBIE—I—I killed him, Eben.

EBEN—(*amazed*) Ye killed him?

ABBIE—(*dully*) Ay-eh.

EBEN—(*recovering from his astonishment—savagely*) An' serves him right! But we got t' do somethin' quick t' make it look s'if the old skunk'd killed himself when he was drunk. We kin prove by 'em all how drunk he got.

ABBIE—(*wildly*) No! No! Not him! (*laughing distractedly*) But that's what I ought t' done, hain't it? I oughter killed him instead! Why didn't ye tell me?

EBEN—(*appalled*) Instead? What d'ye mean?

ABBIE—Not him.

EBEN—(*his face grown ghastly*) Not—not that baby!

ABBIE—(*dully*) Ay-eh!

EBEN—(*falls to his knees as if he'd been struck—his voice trembling with horror*) Oh, God A'mighty! A'mighty God! Maw, whar was ye, why didn't ye stop her?

ABBIE—(*simply*) She went back t' her grave that night we fust done it, remember? I hain't felt her about since. (*A pause. Eben hides his head in his hands, trembling all over as if he had the ague. She goes on dully.*) I left the piller over his little face. Then he killed himself. He stopped breathin'. (*She begins to weep softly.*)

EBEN—(*rage beginning to mingle with grief*) He looked like me. He was mine, damn ye!

ABBIE—(*slowly and brokenly*) I didn't want t' do it. I hated myself fur doin' it. I loved him. He was so purty—dead spit 'n' image o' yew. But I loved yew more—an' yew was goin' away—far off whar I'd never see ye agen, never kiss ye, never feel ye pressed agin me agen—an' ye said ye hated me fur havin' him—ye said ye hated him an' wished he was dead—ye said if it hadn't been fur him comin' it'd be the same's afore between us.

EBEN—(*unable to endure this, springs to his feet in a fury, threatening her, his twitching fingers seeming to reach out for her throat*) Ye lie! I never said—I never dreamed ye'd— I'd cut off my head afore I'd hurt his finger!

ABBIE—(*piteously, sinking on her knees*) Eben, don't ye look

at me like that—hatin' me—not after what I done fur ye—
fur us—so's we could be happy agen—

EBEN—(*furiously now*) Shut up, or I'll kill ye! I see yer
game now—the same old sneakin' trick—ye're aimin' t'
blame me fur the murder ye done!

ABBIE—(*moaning—putting her hands over her ears*) Don't
ye, Eben! Don't ye! (*She grasps his legs.*)

EBEN—(*his mood suddenly changing to horror, shrinks away
from her*) Don't ye tech me! Ye're pizen! How could ye—t'
murder a pore little critter— Ye must've swapped yer soul
t' hell! (*suddenly raging*) Ha! I kin see why ye done it! Not
the lies ye jest told—but 'cause ye wanted t' steal agen—steal
the last thin' ye'd left me—my part o' him—no, the hull o'
him—ye saw he looked like me—ye knowed he was all
mine—an' ye couldn't b'ar it—I know ye! Ye killed him fur
bein' mine! (*All this has driven him almost insane. He makes a
rush past her for the door—then turns—shaking both fists at her,
violently*) But I'll take vengeance now! I'll git the Sheriff! I'll
tell him everythin'! Then I'll sing "I'm off to Californi-a!" an'
go—gold—Golden Gate—gold sun—fields o' gold in the
West! (*This last he half shouts, half croons incoherently, suddenly
breaking off passionately.*) I'm a-goin' fur the Sheriff t' come
an' git ye! I want ye tuk away, locked up from me! I can't
stand t' luk at ye! Murderer an' thief 'r not, ye still tempt me!
I'll give ye up t' the Sheriff! (*He turns and runs out, around
the corner of house, panting and sobbing, and breaks into a swerv-
ing sprint down the road.*)

ABBIE—(*struggling to her feet, runs to the door, calling after
him*) I love ye, Eben! I love ye! (*She stops at the door weakly,
swaying, about to fall.*) I don't care what ye do—if ye'll on'y
love me agen! (*She falls limply to the floor in a faint.*)

SCENE FOUR

*About an hour later. Same as Scene Three. Shows the kitchen
and Cabot's bedroom. It is after dawn. The sky is brilliant with
the sunrise. In the kitchen, Abbie sits at the table, her body limp
and exhausted, her head bowed down over her arms, her face*

hidden. Upstairs, Cabot is still asleep but awakens with a start. He looks toward the window and gives a snort of surprise and irritation—throws back the covers and begins hurriedly pulling on his clothes. Without looking behind him, he begins talking to Abbie, whom he supposes beside him.

CABOT—Thunder 'n' lightnin', Abbie! I hain't slept this late in fifty year! Looks 's if the sun was full riz a'most. Must've been the dancin' an' likker. Must be gittin' old. I hope Eben's t' wuk. Ye might've tuk the trouble t' rouse me, Abbie. (*He turns—sees no one there—surprised*) Waal—whar air she? Gittin' vittles, I calc'late. (*He tiptoes to the cradle and peers down—proudly*) Mornin', sonny. Purty's a picter! Sleepin' sound. He don't beller all night like most o' 'em. (*He goes quietly out the door in rear—a few moments later enters kitchen—sees Abbie—with satisfaction*) So thar ye be. Ye got any vittles cooked?

ABBIE—(*without moving*) No.

CABOT—(*coming to her, almost sympathetically*) Ye feelin' sick?

ABBIE—No.

CABOT—(*pats her on shoulder. She shudders.*) Ye'd best lie down a spell. (*half jocularly*) Yer son'll be needin' ye soon. He'd ought t' wake up with a gnashin' appetite, the sound way he's sleepin'.

ABBIE—(*shudders—then in a dead voice*) He hain't never goin' t' wake up.

CABOT—(*jokingly*) Takes after me this mornin'. I hain't slept so late in. . . .

ABBIE—He's dead.

CABOT—(*stares at her—bewilderedly*) What. . . .

ABBIE—I killed him.

CABOT—(*stepping back from her—aghast*) Air ye drunk—'r crazy—'r. . . !

ABBIE—(*suddenly lifts her head and turns on him—wildly*) I killed him, I tell ye! I smothered him. Go up an' see if ye don't b'lieve me! (*Cabot stares at her a second, then bolts out the rear door, can be heard bounding up the stairs, and rushes into the bedroom and over to the cradle. Abbie has sunk back lifelessly into her former position. Cabot puts his hand down on the body in the crib. An expression of fear and horror comes over his face.*)

CABOT—(*shrinking away—tremblingly*) God A'mighty! God A'mighty. (*He stumbles out the door—in a short while returns to the kitchen—comes to Abbie, the stunned expression still on his face—hoarsely*) Why did ye do it? Why? (*As she doesn't answer, he grabs her violently by the shoulder and shakes her.*) I ax ye why ye done it! Ye'd better tell me 'r. . . !

ABBIE—(*gives him a furious push which sends him staggering back and springs to her feet—with wild rage and hatred*) Don't ye dare tech me! What right hev ye t' question me 'bout him? He wa'n't yewr son! Think I'd have a son by yew? I'd die fust! I hate the sight o' ye an' allus did! It's yew I should've murdered, if I'd had good sense! I hate ye! I love Eben. I did from the fust. An' he was Eben's son—mine an' Eben's—not your'n!

CABOT—(*stands looking at her dazedly—a pause—finding his words with an effort—dully*) That was it—what I felt—pokin' 'round the corners—while ye lied—holdin' yerself from me—sayin' ye'd a'ready conceived— (*He lapses into crushed silence—then with a strange emotion*) He's dead, sart'n. I felt his heart. Pore little critter! (*He blinks back one tear, wiping his sleeve across his nose.*)

ABBIE—(*hysterically*) Don't ye! Don't ye! (*She sobs unrestrainedly.*)

CABOT—(*with a concentrated effort that stiffens his body into a rigid line and hardens his face into a stony mask—through his teeth to himself*) I got t' be—like a stone—a rock o' jedgment! (*A pause. He gets complete control over himself—harshly*) If he was Eben's, I be glad he air gone! An' mebbe I suspicioned it all along. I felt they was somethin' onnateral—somewhars—the house got so lonesome—an' cold—drivin' me down t' the barn—t' the beasts o' the field. . . . Ay-eh. I must've suspicioned—somethin'. Ye didn't fool me—not altogether, leastways—I'm too old a bird—growin' ripe on the bough. . . . (*He becomes aware he is wandering, straightens again, looks at Abbie with a cruel grin.*) So ye'd liked t' hev murdered me 'stead o' him, would ye? Waal, I'll live to a hundred! I'll live t' see ye hung! I'll deliver ye up t' the jedgment o' God an' the law! I'll git the Sheriff now. (*starts for the door*)

ABBIE—(*dully*) Ye needn't. Eben's gone fur him.

CABOT—(*amazed*) Eben—gone fur the Sheriff?

ABBIE—Ay-eh.

CABOT—T' inform agen ye?

ABBIE—Ay-eh.

CABOT—(*considers this—a pause—then in a hard voice*) Waal, I'm thankful fur him savin' me the trouble. I'll git t' wuk. (*He goes to the door—then turns—in a voice full of strange emotion*) He'd ought t' been my son, Abbie. Ye'd ought t' loved me. I'm a man. If ye'd loved me, I'd never told no Sheriff on ye no matter what ye did, if they was t' brile me alive!

ABBIE—(*defensively*) They's more to it nor yew know, makes him tell.

CABOT—(*dryly*) Fur yewr sake, I hope they be. (*He goes out—comes around to the gate—stares up at the sky. His control relaxes. For a moment he is old and weary. He murmurs despairingly*) God A'mighty, I be lonesomer'n ever! (*He hears running footsteps from the left, immediately is himself again. Eben runs in, panting exhaustedly, wild-eyed and mad looking. He lurches through the gate. Cabot grabs him by the shoulder. Eben stares at him dumbly.*) Did ye tell the Sheriff?

EBEN—(*nodding stupidly*) Ay-eh.

CABOT—(*gives him a push away that sends him sprawling—laughing with withering contempt*) Good fur ye! A prime chip o' yer Maw ye be! (*He goes toward the barn, laughing harshly. Eben scrambles to his feet. Suddenly Cabot turns—grimly threatening*) Git off this farm when the Sheriff takes her—or, by God, he'll have t' come back an' git me fur murder, too! (*He stalks off. Eben does not appear to have heard him. He runs to the door and comes into the kitchen. Abbie looks up with a cry of anguished joy. Eben stumbles over and throws himself on his knees beside her—sobbing brokenly*)

EBEN—Fergive me!

ABBIE—(*happily*) Eben! (*She kisses him and pulls his head over against her breast.*)

EBEN—I love ye! Fergive me!

ABBIE—(*ecstatically*) I'd fergive ye all the sins in hell fur sayin' that! (*She kisses his head, pressing it to her with a fierce passion of possession.*)

EBEN—(*brokenly*) But I told the Sheriff. He's comin' fur ye!

ABBIE—I kin b'ar what happens t' me—now!

EBEN—I woke him up. I told him. He says, wait till I git dressed. I was waiting. I got to thinkin' o' yew. I got to thinkin' how I'd loved ye. It hurt like somethin' was bustin' in my chest an' head. I got t' cryin'. I knowed sudden I loved ye yet, an' allus would love ye!

ABBIE—(*caressing his hair—tenderly*) My boy, hain't ye?

EBEN—I begun t' run back. I cut across the fields an' through the woods. I thought ye might have time t' run away—with me—an'. . . .

ABBIE—(*shaking her head*) I got t' take my punishment— t' pay fur my sin.

EBEN—Then I want t' share it with ye.

ABBIE—Ye didn't do nothin'.

EBEN—I put it in yer head. I wisht he was dead! I as much as urged ye t' do it!

ABBIE—No. It was me alone!

EBEN—I'm as guilty as yew be! He was the child o' our sin.

ABBIE—(*lifting her head as if defying God*) I don't repent that sin! I hain't askin' God t' fergive that!

EBEN—Nor me—but it led up t' the other—an' the murder ye did, ye did 'count o' me—an' it's my murder, too, I'll tell the Sheriff—an' if ye deny it, I'll say we planned it t'gether—an' they'll all b'lieve me, fur they suspicion every-thin' we've done, an' it'll seem likely an' true to 'em. An' it is true—way down. I did help ye—somehow.

ABBIE—(*laying her head on his—sobbing*) No! I don't want yew t' suffer!

EBEN—I got t' pay fur my part o' the sin! An' I'd suffer wuss leavin' ye, goin' West, thinkin' o' ye day an' night, bein' out when yew was in— (*lowering his voice*) 'R bein' alive when yew was dead. (*a pause*) I want t' share with ye, Abbie— prison 'r death 'r hell 'r anythin'! (*He looks into her eyes and forces a trembling smile.*) If I'm sharin' with ye, I won't feel lonesome, leastways.

ABBIE—(*weakly*) Eben! I won't let ye! I can't let ye!

EBEN—(*kissing her—tenderly*) Ye can't he'p yerself. I got ye beat fur once!

ABBIE—(*forcing a smile—adoringly*) I hain't beat—s'long's I got ye!

EBEN—(*hears the sound of feet outside*) Ssshh! Listen! They've come t' take us!

ABBIE—No, it's him. Don't give him no chance to fight ye, Eben. Don't say nothin'—no matter what he says. An' I won't, neither. (*It is Cabot. He comes up from the barn in a great state of excitement and strides into the house and then into the kitchen. Eben is kneeling beside Abbie, his arm around her, hers around him. They stare straight ahead.*)

CABOT—(*stares at them, his face hard. A long pause—vindictively*) Ye make a slick pair o' murderin' turtle doves! Ye'd ought t' be both hung on the same limb an' left thar t' swing in the breeze an' rot—a warnin' t' old fools like me t' b'ar their lonesomeness alone—an' fur young fools like ye t' hobble their lust. (*A pause. The excitement returns to his face, his eyes snap, he looks a bit crazy.*) I couldn't work today. I couldn't take no interest. T' hell with the farm! I'm leavin' it! I've turned the cows an' other stock loose. I've druv 'em into the woods whar they kin be free! By freein' 'em, I'm freein' myself! I'm quittin' here today! I'll set fire t' house an' barn an' watch 'em burn, an' I'll leave yer Maw t' haunt the ashes, an' I'll will the fields back t' God, so that nothin' human kin never touch 'em! I'll be a-goin' to Californi-a—t' jine Simeon an' Peter—true sons o' mine if they be dumb fools—an' the Cabots'll find Solomon's Mines t'gether! (*He suddenly cuts a mad caper.*) Whoop! What was the song they sung? "Oh, Californi-a! That's the land fur me." (*He sings this—then gets on his knees by the floorboard under which the money was hid.*) An' I'll sail thar on one o' the finest clippers I kin find! I've got the money! Pity ye didn't know whar this was hidden so's ye could steal. . . . (*He has pulled up the board. He stares—feels—stares again. A pause of dead silence. He slowly turns, slumping into a sitting position on the floor, his eyes like those of a dead fish, his face the sickly green of an attack of nausea. He swallows painfully several times—forces a weak smile at last.*) So—ye did steal it!

EBEN—(*emotionlessly*) I swapped it t' Sim an' Peter fur their share o' the farm—t' pay their passage t' Californi-a.

CABOT—(*with one sardonic*) Ha! (*He begins to recover. Gets slowly to his feet—strangely*) I calc'late God give it to 'em—not yew! God's hard, not easy! Mebbe they's easy gold in the West, but it hain't God's gold. It hain't fur me. I kin hear His voice warnin' me agen t' be hard an' stay on my farm. I kin see his hand usin' Eben t' steal t' keep me from weakness. I kin feel I be in the palm o' His hand, His fingers guidin' me. (*A pause—then he mutters sadly*) It's a-goin' t' be lonesomer now than ever it war afore—an' I'm gittin' old, Lord—ripe on the bough. . . . (*then stiffening*) Waal—what d'ye want? God's lonesome, hain't He? God's hard an' lonesome! (*A pause. The sheriff with two men comes up the road from the left. They move cautiously to the door. The sheriff knocks on it with the butt of his pistol.*)

SHERIFF—Open in the name o' the law! (*They start.*)

CABOT—They've come fur ye. (*He goes to the rear door.*) Come in, Jim! (*The three men enter. Cabot meets them in doorway.*) Jest a minit, Jim. I got 'em safe here. (*The sheriff nods. He and his companions remain in the doorway.*)

EBEN—(*suddenly calls*) I lied this mornin', Jim. I helped her do it. Ye kin take me, too.

ABBIE—(*brokenly*) No!

CABOT—Take 'em both. (*He comes forward—stares at Eben with a trace of grudging admiration.*) Purty good—fur yew! Waal, I got t' round up the stock. Good-by.

EBEN—Good-by.

ABBIE—Good-by. (*Cabot turns and strides past the men—comes out and around the corner of the house, his shoulders squared, his face stony, and stalks grimly toward the barn. In the meantime the sheriff and men have come into the room.*)

SHERIFF—(*embarrassedly*) Waal—we'd best start.

ABBIE—Wait. (*turns to Eben*) I love ye, Eben.

EBEN—I love ye, Abbie. (*They kiss. The three men grin and shuffle embarrassedly. Eben takes Abbie's hand. They go out the door in rear, the men following, and come from the house, walking hand in hand to the gate. Eben stops there and points to the sunrise sky.*) Sun's a-rizin'. Purty, hain't it?

ABBIE—Ay-eh. (*They both stand for a moment looking up raptly in attitudes strangely aloof and devout.*)

SHERIFF—(*looking around at the farm enviously—to his companion*) It's a jim-dandy farm, no denyin'. Wished I owned it!

(*The Curtain Falls*)

MARCO MILLIONS

Foreword

This play is an attempt to render poetic justice to one long famous as a traveler, unjustly world-renowned as a liar, but sadly unrecognized by posterity in his true eminence as a man and a citizen—Marco Polo of Venice. The failure to appraise Polo at a fair valuation is his own fault. He dictated the book of his travels but left the traveler out. He was no author. He stuck to a recital of what he considered facts and the world called him a liar for his pains. Even in his native Venice, he was scoffingly nicknamed "the millionaire," or "Marco Millions." They could not take seriously his impressive statistics about the "millions" of this and the "millions" of that in the East. Polo, the man of brass tacks, became celebrated as an extravagant romancer and ever since has traveled down the prejudiced centuries, a prophet without honor, or even notoriety, save in false whiskers. This has moved me to an indignant crusade between the lines of his book, the bars of his prison, in order to whitewash the good soul of that maligned Venetian.

CHARACTERS

CHRISTIANS (*in the order in which they appear*):

A TRAVELER

MARCO POLO

DONATA

NICOLO POLO, *Marco's father*

MAFFEO POLO, *Marco's uncle*

TEDALDO, *Legate of Syria (afterward Pope Gregory X)*

A DOMINICAN MONK

A KNIGHT-CRUSADER

A PAPAL COURIER

PAULO LOREDANO, *Donata's father, a gentleman from Venice*

Ladies and gentlemen of Venice, soldiers, people of Acre,
*   musicians, servants, etc.*

HEATHEN (*in the order in which they appear*):

A MAGIAN TRAVELER

A BUDDHIST TRAVELER

A MAHOMETAN CAPTAIN OF GHAZAN'S ARMY

THE ALI BROTHERS, *Mahometan merchants*

A PROSTITUTE

A DERVISH

TWO BUDDHIST MERCHANTS

TWO TARTAR MERCHANTS

A MONGOL PRIEST

EMISSARY FROM KUBLAI

KUBLAI, THE GREAT KAAN

PRINCESS KUKACHIN, *his granddaughter*

CHU-YIN, *a Cathayan sage*

GENERAL BAYAN

A Messenger from Persia

Ghazan, Khan of Persia

A Buddhist Priest

A Taoist Priest

A Confucian Priest

A Moslem Priest

A Tartar Chronicler

*People of Persia, India, Mongolia, Cathay, courtiers, nobles,
    ladies, wives, warriors of Kublai's court, musicians, dancers,
    Chorus of Mourners.*

SCENES

PROLOGUE: A sacred tree in Persia near the confines of India toward the close of the thirteenth century.

ACT ONE

SCENE I: Exterior of Donata's house, Venice—twenty-three years earlier.

SCENE II: Palace of the Papal Legate of Syria at Acre—six months later.

SCENE III: Persia—four months later.

SCENE IV: India—eight months later.

SCENE V: Mongolia—eleven months later.

SCENE VI: Cathay—The Grand Throne Room in Kublai's palace at Cambaluc—one month later.

ACT TWO

SCENE I: The Little Throne Room in Kublai's summer palace at Xanadu, "the city of Peace," fifteen years later.

SCENE II: The royal wharf at the seaport of Zayton, several weeks later.

SCENE III: Deck of the royal junk of the Princess Kukachin at anchor in the harbor of Hormuz, Persia—two years later.

ACT THREE

SCENE I: The Grand Throne Room in the Imperial Palace at Cambaluc, one year later—and later the Dining Room of the Polo Home in Venice at the same time.

SCENE II: The Grand Throne Room at Cambaluc—one year later.

EPILOGUE: The theatre.

Marco Millions
PROLOGUE

SCENE—*A sacred tree on a vast plain in Persia near the confines of India. Votive offerings, pieces of cloth torn from clothing, bangles, armlets, ornaments, tapers, have been nailed on the trunk or tied to the branches. The heavy limbs spread out to a great distance from the trunk. Beneath them is deep cool shade, contrasting with the blinding glare of the noon sun on the sandy plain in the background. A merchant carrying in each hand a strapped box that resembles a modern sample case, plods wearily to the foot of the tree. He puts the boxes down and takes out a handkerchief to mop his forehead. He is a white Christian, middle-aged, average-looking, with a moustache and beard beginning to show gray. His clothes in the style of the Italian merchant class of the thirteenth century are travel-worn. He sighs, tired and hot.*

CHRISTIAN—Phoo!

(*From the left a Magian, a Persian, dressed in the fashion of a trader, comes in. He carries a small, square bag. He also is hot, weary, and dust-covered. In age and appearance, making allowance for the difference in race, he closely resembles the Christian. He and the latter stare at each other, then bow perfunctorily. The Magian sets down his bag and wipes his brow.*)

CHRISTIAN—(*sympathetically*) Hot as hell!

MAGIAN—(*grimly*) Hotter! (*They both chuckle. A Buddhist, a Kashmiri traveling merchant comes in, puffing and sweating, from the right. He has a pack strapped on his back. He resembles the other two in the essential character of his body and face. He stops on seeing them. After eyeing him for an appraising second, the two bow and the Buddhist comes forward to set his pack beside the bags of the others.*)

BUDDHIST—(*with relief*) Phoo! (*then breaking the ice*) The sun would cook you!

MAGIAN—It is hot certainly.

CHRISTIAN—(*as they all sit down to rest, looks from one to the other—jovially*) Funny! You'd think we three had an appointment here. Your faces look familiar. Haven't I seen you somewheres before?

MAGIAN—In the house of the courtezans at Shiraz. You were drunk.

BUDDHIST—I happened to be there that night, too. You danced and sang lewd songs.

CHRISTIAN—(*a bit embarrassed, but grinning*) Humn—oh, yes—I remember. It was my birthday and I'd taken a drop too much—a very unusual thing for me. (*then abruptly changing the subject*) How are conditions down your way?

BUDDHIST—(*pursing his lips*) Slow. I come from Delhi. There is a new import tax and trade is very unsettled. We make prayer beads.

MAGIAN—(*gloomily*) And I, for my sins, am hawking a novelty, a block-printed book, for an Arab house. It contains one thousand Arabian lies, with one over for good measure, all full of lechery—at least so they instructed me to tell people to get them to buy.

CHRISTIAN—Did your trip take you down around Ispahan way?

MAGIAN—I just came from there. It is a sad city now. All the bazaars have been closed by an imperial edict in mourning for Queen Kukachin.

CHRISTIAN—(*bounding to his feet as if a wasp had stung him*) Is Queen Kukachin dead? (*stunned*) Why, I've got a letter of introduction to her from the head of my firm—Marco Polo of Polo Brothers and Son, Venice. He acted as her official escort, and took her from Cathay to Persia to be married! Why, I was counting on selling her and her husband a whole fleet load of goods!

MAGIAN—(*suddenly, pointing off left*) What makes that cloud of dust? (*They all stare and begin to grow worried.*)

CHRISTIAN—It doesn't look like camels.

BUDDHIST—(*fearfully*) It has a strange look!

CHRISTIAN—It's coming directly this way.

MAGIAN—These plains are haunted by evil spirits.

CHRISTIAN—(*very frightened, but striving to put up a brave front*) I've heard those rumors. And I know for a fact that people are sometimes possessed by devils, but I don't believe—

BUDDHIST—(*suddenly, pointing to the tree*) I am going to offer a prayer for protection to this tree sacred to Buddha.

CHRISTIAN—⎫
MAGIAN—⎭ (*in chorus—irritably*) Sacred to Buddha?

BUDDHIST—Certainly! Do you not know the legend of how the Holy Sakya picked a twig to cleanse his teeth, and then throwing it away, it took root, and sprang up into this mighty tree to testify forever to his miraculous power?

CHRISTIAN—(*resentfully*) You're absolutely all wrong! This tree was the staff of our first father, Adam. It was handed down to Moses who used it to tap water out of stones and finally planted it. The cross our Lord was crucified on was made of this wood. And ever since this tree has been sacred to Him!

MAGIAN—(*cuttingly*) You have both of you been duped by childish lies! This tree is sacred to the founder of the one true religion, Zoroaster, who brought a shoot of the Tree of Life down from Paradise and planted it here!

BUDDHIST—(*scornfully*) You are a pair of superstitious sheep!

CHRISTIAN—You are a couple of idolatrous dogs!

MAGIAN—The two of you are blasphemous hogs! (*They glare at each other insultingly, their hands on their daggers. Suddenly they hear a noise from the left. Their eyes at once are turned in that direction and, forgetting personal animosities, they give a startled exclamation at what they see.*)

BUDDHIST—They are pulling a chariot!

CHRISTIAN—They must be slaves. See how the driver lashes them!

BUDDHIST—But what can that be on the wagon—like a coffin!

CHRISTIAN—It must be treasure!

MAGIAN—No. It is a coffin. (*trembling*) Ssst! I have a foreboding of evil. (*They prostrate themselves, their faces to the ground. A moment later, preceded by shouts, a cracking of whips, and the dull stamping of feet, a double file of thirty men of different ages, stripped to the waist, harnessed to each other waist-to-waist and to the long pole of a two-wheeled wagon, stagger in, straining forward under the lashes of two soldiers who run beside them and the long whips of the Captain and a Corporal who are riding on the wagon, the Captain driving. As they reach the middle of the shade they stop. Lashed on the wagon is a coffin covered with a white pall.*)

CAPTAIN—(*a brutal, determined-looking man of forty, bellows*) Halt! (*The files of bleeding and sweating men collapse in panting, groaning heaps. The soldiers sprawl down beside them. The Captain springs off the wagon.*) Phoo! This shade is grateful. (*He looks at the tree—then in an awed tone*) This must be the Holy Tree which was once the staff of Mahomet and, passing down through generations, was buried in the grave of Abu Abdallah where it struck root and grew by the will of Allah into this tree. (*He makes obeisance and prays to the tree as do the soldiers. He gets up and takes a gulp of water— then, looking around, notices the three merchants—with startled surprise, drawing his sword*) Ho! What are you? Get up! (*They do so frightenedly. He stares at them and laughs coarsely with relief.*) By all the demons, you startled me! But you traders are like fleas, one finds you everywhere! (*then with a scowl*) Three dogs of unbelievers, too! (*sharply*) Give an account of yourselves!

BUDDHIST—I was proceeding westward on a business venture, good sir.

MAGIAN—And I to the northward.

CHRISTIAN—And I to the court of Ghazan Khan to present this letter to Queen Kukachin. But I hear she's dead. (*He hands him the letter but the Captain backs away superstitiously.*)

CAPTAIN—Allah forbid I touch what belongs to a corpse. (*then with forced laughter*) You need not journey farther. She is in there! (*His voice has dropped, he points toward the coffin. The others stare at it, dumbfounded and awed. The Captain goes on dryly.*) You cannot cheat her now, Christian! (*then lowering his voice as if afraid he will be overheard*) And yet, to look at her face you would think her only sleeping.

CHRISTIAN—(*astonished*) What? Can you look at her?

CAPTAIN—Her coffin is glass. Her body was anointed by Egyptians so that she preserves the appearance of life. This was done by command of her grandfather Kublai, the Great Kaan. She is being taken home to Cathay for burial—and under penalty of torture I must transport her over the first stage by dark tonight! (*suddenly lamenting*) But Allah afflicted me! When I reached the last village with my camels foundering,

I found the accursed villagers had driven off their beasts to escape requisition. But the dogs could not balk me. I hitched them to the pole instead. (*He looks at the moaning figures with a cruel appraising eye.*) But will they last till night? Hi, there! Water to revive them! (*The soldiers carry around jugs of water which the panting men reach out for avidly, then sink back. But three of the more elderly men are too spent to move.*)

CHRISTIAN—(*timorously—anxious to change the subject*) Was the Queen very beautiful?

CAPTAIN—(*with bravado*) Would you care to see? You had a letter to her. It can do no harm—and it is a very great wonder!

CHRISTIAN—(*reassuringly, because he is now extremely curious*) Dead Queens in the West usually lie in state.

CAPTAIN—You pull back the cloth then, since that is your custom. (*The Christian goes to the wagon and gingerly pulls back the pall from the head of the coffin—then retreats with an exclamation as Kukachin's face, that of a beautiful Tartar princess of twenty-three, is revealed inside the glass. Her calm expression seems to glow with the intense peace of a life beyond death, the eyes are shut as if she were asleep. The men stare fascinatedly.*)

CHRISTIAN—(*after a pause—crossing himself awedly*) Are you certain she's dead?

CAPTAIN—(*in an awed whisper*) In the palace I commanded the company who guarded her coffin at night. I could not take my eyes from her face. It seemed that any moment she must awake and speak! (*While they have been speaking, unnoticed by them, it has grown dark. An unearthly glow, like a halo, lights up the face of Kukachin. From the branches of the tree comes a sound of sweet sad music as if the leaves were tiny harps strummed by the wind. The face of Kukachin becomes more and more living. Finally her lips part and her eyes open to look up at the tree.*)

CAPTAIN—(*kneeling down to pray*) Allah, be pitiful!

BUDDHIST—Buddha, protect Thy servant!

MAGIAN—Mithra, All-Powerful One!

CHRISTIAN—Jesus, have mercy! (*A voice which is Kukachin's and yet more musical than a human voice, comes from the coffin as her lips are seen to move.*)

KUKACHIN—Say this, I loved and died. Now I am love, and live. And living, have forgotten. And loving, can forgive. (*Here her lips part in a smile of beautiful pity.*) Say this for me in Venice! (*A sound of tender laughter, of an intoxicating, supernatural gaiety, comes from her lips and is taken up in chorus in the branches of the tree as if every harp-leaf were laughing in music with her. The laughter recedes heavenward and dies as the halo of light about her face fades and noonday rushes back in a blaze of baking plain. Everyone is prostrate, the harnessed wretches in the exhausted attitudes of sleep, the others visibly trembling with superstitious horror.*)

CHRISTIAN—(*the first to recover—bewilderedly*) Venice! It must have been a message she wished me to take back to Marco Polo!

CAPTAIN—(*his terror going and rage taking its place, leaps to his feet*) It was the voice of some Christian devil you summoned! It bewitched even me until Allah drove it back to hell! (*He draws his sword.*) Cover her face, accursed sorcerer!

CHRISTIAN—(*pulls the covering over the head of the coffin with indecent haste*) I pledge you my word, good Captain—!

CAPTAIN—(*to his soldiers*) Attention! Kick them up! We must get away from here! (*With blows and kicks the soldiers get their human beasts to their feet. There are groans and curses and cries of pain. But three cannot be roused. The Captain growls savagely at the Christian to keep up his courage.*) Pig of an infidel! (*then glaring at the Buddhist and Magian*) You too! You were in league with him! (*He grips his sword.*)

ALL THREE—(*kneeling—pitiably*) Mercy! Spare us!

A CORPORAL—(*comes up and salutes*) We cannot get three of them up, sir.

CAPTAIN—(*raging*) Lash them!

CORPORAL—They are dead, sir.

CAPTAIN—(*glumly*) Oh. (*Then an idea comes—with cruel satisfaction*) Three, did you say? That is fortunate. Allah has provided! Cut them out and put these in their places! (*At a sign, the soldiers fall upon the three merchants, strip off their upper clothes, untie the dead men, and hitch them in their places. All the time the three set up miserable screams of protest, punctuated by the blows and kicks they receive. The others look on with exhausted indifference.*)

CHRISTIAN—(*making himself heard above the tumult*) My letter! It was to the Queen! When Polo Brothers hear of this outrage they'll get the Kaan to flay you alive!

CAPTAIN—(*taken aback a moment—then craftily*) Show me your letter again!

CHRISTIAN—(*holding it out with frantic eagerness*) Here! Now set me free!

CAPTAIN—(*takes it and calmly tears it up*) I cannot read but I think you are lying. At any rate, now you have no letter! (*The Christian sets up a wailing cry and receives a blow. The Captain and Corporals spring up on the wagon.*) And now forward march! (*With a great cracking of whips and shouts of pain the wagon is pulled swiftly away. On the ground under the sacred tree three bodies lie in crumpled heaps. The same sweet sad music comes from the tree again as if its spirit were playing on the leaves a last lamenting farewell to the dead Princess. It rises softly and as softly dies away until it is nothing but a faint sound of wind rustling the leaves.*)

(*Curtain*)

ACT ONE

SCENE ONE

SCENE—*Twenty-three years earlier. A fresh boy's voice is heard singing a love song in a subdued tone. The light slowly reveals the exterior of Donata's home on a canal, Venice. Marco Polo, a boy of fifteen, youthfully handsome and well made, is standing in a gondola beneath a barred window of the house, a guitar over his shoulder. The song finished, he waits anxiously. A hand is thrust out to him through the bars. He kisses it passionately. It is hurriedly withdrawn. Donata's face appears pressed against the bars. She is a girl of twelve, her face pale and pretty in the moonlight.*

DONATA—(*coyly and tenderly*) You mustn't, Mark.

MARCO—There's no harm in that—just kissing your hand!

DONATA—(*demurely*) It's a sin, I'm sure of it.

MARCO—(*with a quick movement of his own hand, captures hers through the bars*) Then I'll have to steal it, and that's a worse sin. (*He pulls her willing hand down toward his lips.*)

DONATA—You're hurting my fingers.

MARCO—(*boldly now*) Then I know how to cure them. (*He kisses them one by one.*) There!

DONATA—(*tenderly*) You silly boy! Why do you do that?

MARCO—(*very seriously*) You know, Donata.

DONATA—Know what? (*softly*) Go on and tell me, Mark.

MARCO—(*blurts out gruffly*) I love you, that's what! I've loved you ever since I can remember. And you've known it right along, too, so there's no good pretending.

DONATA—(*softly*) I wasn't sure.

MARCO—(*recklessly*) And how about you? Do you love me? You've got to answer me that!

DONATA—You know—without my saying it.

MARCO—Please say it!

DONATA—(*in a whisper*) I love you. There, silly!

MARCO—And you'll promise to marry me when I come back?

DONATA—Yes, but you'll have to ask my parents.

MARCO—(*easily*) Don't worry about them. They'll be

392

glad, and my folks, too. It'll bring the two firms into closer contact.

DONATA—(*practically*) Yes, I think so, too. (*A pause. Songs and music come from near and far-off in the night about them. Marco has gained possession of her two hands now and his face is closer to the bars of her window.*)

MARCO—(*with a sigh*) It's beautiful tonight. I wish I didn't have to go away.

DONATA—I wish, too! Do you really have to?

MARCO—Yes. And I want to, too—all but leaving you. I want to travel and see the world and all the different people, and get to know their habits and needs from first-hand knowledge. You've got to do that if you want to become really big and important. That's what Father says—and Uncle.

DONATA—But won't this trip so very far away be full of danger?

MARCO—(*boastfully*) I can take care of myself. Uncle says taking chances—*necessary* chances, of course—is the best schooling for a real merchant; and Father has a saying that where there's nothing risked, there's nothing gained. And they ought to know, oughtn't they, after spending nine years at the court of the Great Kaan and traveling there and back?

DONATA—Is that where you're going?

MARCO—Yes. He's the richest king in the world and Uncle and Father are personal friends of his. They did a lot of work for him. I'll be on the right side of him from the start, and Father and Uncle both say there's millions to be made in his service if you're not afraid of work and keep awake to opportunity.

DONATA—I'm sure you'll succeed. But I wish you weren't going for so long.

MARCO—I'll miss you as much as you miss me. (*huskily*) I hate to leave you, Donata—but I've got to make my own way—so we can marry—

DONATA—(*hurriedly*) Yes—of course—only come back as soon as you can.

MARCO—But you'll wait, won't you, no matter how long?

DONATA—(*solemnly*) Yes, I swear to, Mark.

MARCO—And I swear by God I'll come back and marry you, and I'll always be true and never forget or do anything—

DONATA—(*startled by a noise from within*) Ssshh! There's someone moving inside. You'll have to go. Here. (*She hands him a locket.*) It's a medallion of me painted by an artist who owed Father for spices and couldn't pay with money. Will you keep looking at this all the time you're away and never forget me?

MARCO—(*kissing it passionately*) Every day!

DONATA—And you'll write me?

MARCO—I promise. Every chance I get.

DONATA—(*hesitatingly*) Will you write me—a poem? I won't care how short it is if it's only a poem.

MARCO—I'll try, Donata. I'll do my best.

DONATA—I'll just love it to death, Mark! (*startledly*) Ssshh! I hear it again. It must be Father. I've got to sneak back.

MARCO—(*desperately*) Won't you kiss me—let me really kiss you—just once—for good-bye?

DONATA—I mustn't.

MARCO—Just once—when I'm going so far away? (*desperately*) I—I—I'll die if you don't!

DONATA—Well—just once. (*The moonlight fades into darkness as their lips meet. Then from the darkness are their voices heard in hushed tones.*) Good-bye, Mark.

MARCO—Good-bye, Donata. (*The sentimental singing voices and guitars are heard from all corners of the night in celebration of love. The sound gradually grows fainter and fainter, receding into the distance, as if Marco were already leaving Venice behind him.*)

(*Darkness*)

SCENE TWO

SCENE—*Six months later. The tolling of a church bell is first heard. Then the interior of the Papal Legate's palace at Acre is revealed—a combination of church and government building.*

The Legate, Tedaldo, a man of sixty with a strong, intelligent face, is seated on a sort of throne placed against the rear wall. On his right, stands a warrior noble, a Knight-Crusader, in full armor, leaning on his sword. On his left, a Dominican monk, his adviser. On the left of the room is an altar with candles burning. On the right, an open portal with a sentry pacing up and down, spear in hand.

The two elder Polos, Nicolo and Maffeo, stand in attitudes of patient servility before the throne. Marco's father, Nicolo, is a small thin middle-aged man, with a dry, shrewd face. Maffeo, Marco's uncle, is around the same age, but he is tall and stout with a round, jovial face and small, cunning eyes. There is a strong general resemblance between both of them and Marco. Marco is sitting on a stool in the foreground, his body all screwed up into an awkward intensity, striving with all his might to compose a poem to Donata, but constantly distracted in spite of himself.

TEDALDO—(*bored but tolerantly*) What can I do except advise you to be patient? I'm sure the Conclave of Cardinals must soon select a Pope.

NICOLO—Two years in session! (*then suddenly—consoled*) Well, it's a new world's record, anyway.

MAFFEO—(*shaking his head*) This uncertainty is bad for trade.

TEDALDO—(*with a bored yawn*) No doubt. (*then rather impatiently*) Then, when your business so evidently calls you to the East, why delay longer? Why not simply explain to the Great Kaan, Kublai, that there was no Pope to whom you could deliver his message?

NICOLO—He mightn't understand. His instructions to us were pretty emphatic.

MAFFEO—To request the Pope to send him a hundred wise men of the West—

TEDALDO—(*dryly*) This Kublai is an optimist!

MAFFEO——to argue with his Buddhists and Taoists and Confucians which religion in the world is best.

MONK—(*outraged*) Impudent ignoramus! Does he imagine the Church would stoop to such bickering?

TEDALDO—(*with a weary smile*) I begin to think Kublai is a humorist, too.

MAFFEO—(*craftily*) It'd pay to convert him. He's the richest king in the world. He rules over millions of subjects, his empire covers millions of square miles of great undeveloped natural resources, his personal wealth in cash and jewels and goods alone easily runs into millions of millions!

MARCO—(*stares at his uncle—then mutters fascinatedly*) Millions! (*then, shaking away this interruption, bends to his writing again*)

TEDALDO—(*wearily*) I am bored with your millions, Messrs. Polo. Even if they are true, it is too much effort to conceive them. (*They bow humbly and retire backward. His eyes following them listlessly Tedaldo sees Marco, who at this moment is scratching himself, twisting and turning his legs and feet, tearing his hair in a perfect frenzy of balked inspiration. Tedaldo smiles and addresses him in an affectionate, humorous tone.*) God's mercy on you, Master Marco! Are you suddenly possessed by a devil—or is it only these infernal Mahometan fleas the Almighty sends us for our sins?

MARCO—(*coming out of his fit—sheepishly*) I'm only writing something.

MAFFEO—Mark is surprisingly quick at figures.

NICOLO—But still heedless. A dreamer! (*to Marco, with a condescending paternal air*) What are you writing, son? (*He and Maffeo draw near Marco.*)

MARCO—(*more confused*) Nothing, sir—just—something. (*He tries to hide it.*)

MAFFEO—Why are you so mysterious? Come, let's see.

MARCO—No—please, Uncle.

MAFFEO—(*With a sudden cunning motion, he snatches it from Marco's hand, glances at it and bursts into laughter.*) Look, Nicolo, look!

MARCO—(*rebelliously*) Give that back!

NICOLO—(*sternly*) Behave yourself, Mark! (*to Maffeo*) What is it?

MAFFEO—See for yourself. (*He hands it to him.*) Did you know you'd hatched a nightingale? (*He laughs coarsely. Nicolo reads, a scornful grin coming to his lips.*)

TEDALDO—Surely it cannot be a song he has written?

NICOLO—(*going to him—laughing*) A rhyme! A love poem, no less!

TEDALDO—(*severely, as he takes the poem*) Do not mock at him! Rather be grateful if a thistle can bring forth figs. (*Marco remains sullenly apart, shamefaced and angry, his fists clenched. Tedaldo reads—frowns—laughs—then smilingly to Nicolo*) Your fear that this is a poem is—humn—exaggerated! (*He reads amusedly as Marco squirms.*)

> "You are lovely as the gold in the sun
>   Your skin is like silver in the moon
>   Your eyes are black pearls I have won.
>   I kiss your ruby lips and you swoon,
>   Smiling your thanks as I promise you
>   A large fortune if you will be true,
>   While I am away earning gold
>   And silver so when we are old
>   I will have a million to my credit
>   And in the meantime can easily afford
>   A big wedding that will do us credit
>   And start having children, bless the Lord!"

(*There is a roar of laughter in which Tedaldo joins. Marco looks about for a hole into which to crawl. Tedaldo addresses him amusedly but with kindness.*) Come, Marco. Here is your poem. Your lady is a bit too mineral, your heaven of love a trifle monetary—but, never mind, you will be happier as a Polo than as a poet. Here. (*He gives it to Marco. The latter fiercely crumples it up and throws it on the floor and stamps on it.*)

NICOLO—(*approvingly*) Sensibly done, my boy.

TEDALDO—(*looking searchingly at Marco's face—gently*) Perhaps I was too critical. Your poem had merits of its own. I am sure it would touch your lady's heart.

MARCO—(*with a great bluster of manliness*) Oh, I don't mind your making fun. I can take a joke. It *was* silly. Poetry's all stupid, anyway. I was only trying it for fun, to see if I could. You won't catch me ever being such a fool again!

MONK—(*as a noise of shouting comes toward them*) Ssstt! What's that? (*The knight hurries to the portal.*)

KNIGHT—Someone is running here, and a crowd behind. I hear them shouting "Pope."

MONK—Then the Conclave has chosen!

POLOS—(*joyfully*) At last! (*The cries of many voices. The sentinel and knight admit the messenger but push back the others.*)

MESSENGER—(*exhausted—falls on his knees before Tedaldo, holding out a sealed paper*) I come from the Conclave. You were chosen. Your Holiness— (*He falls fainting. The crowds cheer and sweep in.*)

TEDALDO—(*rising—pale and trembling*) What does he say?

MONK—(*has picked up the document—joyfully*) See! The official seal! You are the Pope! (*He kneels humbly.*) Your Holiness, let me be the first— (*He kisses Tedaldo's hand. All are kneeling now, their heads bowed. The bells of the churches begin to ring.*)

TEDALDO—(*raising his hands to heaven—dazedly*) Lord, I am not worthy! (*then to those about him—tremblingly*) Leave me. I must pray to God for strength—for guidance!

CROWD—(*in a clamor*) Your blessing! (*Tedaldo, with a simple dignity and power, blesses them. They back out slowly, the monk and knight last. The Polos group together in the foreground, holding a whispered conference. Tedaldo kneels before the altar.*)

MAFFEO—Now that he's the Pope, if we could get an answer from him, we could start right away.

NICOLO—We couldn't hope for better weather.

MAFFEO—He seems to have taken a fancy to Mark. You speak to him, Mark.

MARCO—(*unwillingly*) He's praying.

MAFFEO—He'll have time enough for that, but with us time is money. (*giving the unwilling Marco a push*) This will test your nerve, Mark! Don't shirk!

MARCO—(*gritting his teeth*) All right. I'll show you I'm not scared! (*He advances boldly toward the altar, stands there for a moment awkwardly as Tedaldo remains oblivious—then he falls on his knees—humbly but insistently*) Your Holiness. Forgive me, Your Holiness—

TEDALDO—(*turns to him and springs to his feet—imperiously*) I wish to be alone! (*then as Marco is shrinking back—more kindly*) Well, what is it? I owe you a recompense, perhaps—for an injury.

MARCO—(*stammeringly*) Your Holiness—if you could give

us some answer to deliver to the Great Kaan—we could start now—with such favorable weather—

TEDALDO—(*amused in spite of himself*) On the last day one of your seed will interrupt Gabriel to sell him another trumpet! (*then sardonically to the elder Polos*) I have no hundred wise men—nor one! Tell the Great Kaan he must have been imposed upon by your patriotic lies, or he could never make such a request.

POLOS—(*terrified*) But, Your Holiness, we dare not repeat— He'd have us killed!

TEDALDO—I will send him a monk or two. That is quite sufficient to convert a Tartar barbarian!

MAFFEO—But, Your Holiness, he's not a barbarian! Why, every plate on his table is solid gold!

TEDALDO—(*smiling*) And has he millions of plates, too? (*then with a sudden whimsicality*) But if the monks fail, Master Marco can be my missionary. Let him set an example of virtuous Western manhood amid all the levities of paganism, shun the frailty of poetry, have a million to his credit, as he so beautifully phrased it, and I will wager a million of something or other myself that the Kaan will soon be driven to seek spiritual salvation somewhere! Mark my words, Marco will be worth a million wise men—in the cause of wisdom! (*He laughs gaily, raising his hand over Marco's head.*) Go with my blessing! But what need have you for a blessing? You were born with success in your pocket! (*With a last gesture he turns, going quickly out the door in rear.*)

MAFFEO—(*as he goes—approvingly*) Mark is making a good impression already!

NICOLO—Well, he's got a head on him!

MARCO—(*beginning to swell out a bit matter-of-factly*) Never mind about me. When do we start?

POLOS—(*hurriedly*) At once. Let's go and pack. (*They go out left.*) Come, Mark! Hurry!

MARCO—I'm coming. (*He waits, looks after them, picks up the crumpled poem, starts to hide it in his jacket, stops, mutters with brave self-contempt*) Aw! You damn fool! (*He throws the poem down again, starts to go, hesitates, suddenly turns back, picks it up, crams it into his doublet and runs wildly out the door. The scene fades into darkness. For a time the church bells, which have never ceased ringing, are heard acclaiming the new Pope; but the Polos proceed speedily on their journey and the sound is soon left behind them.*)

(*Darkness*)

SCENE THREE

SCENE—*Light comes, gradually revealing the scene. In the rear is the front of a Mahometan mosque. Before the mosque, is a throne on which sits a Mahometan ruler. On the right, the inevitable warrior—on his left, the inevitable priest—the two defenders of the State. At the ruler's feet his wives crouch like slaves. Everything is jeweled, high-colored, gorgeous in this background. Squatted against the side walls, forming a sort of semi-circle with the throne at center, counting from left to right consecutively, are a mother nursing a baby, two children playing a game, a young girl and a young man in a loving embrace, a middle-aged couple, an aged couple, a coffin. All these Mahometan figures remain motionless. Only their eyes move, staring fixedly but indifferently at the Polos, who are standing at center. Marco is carrying in each hand bags which curiously resemble modern sample cases. He sets these down and gazes around with a bewildered awe.*

NICOLO—(*turning on him—genially*) Well, son, here we are in Islam.

MARCO—(*round-eyed*) A man told me that Noah's Ark is still somewhere around here on top of a mountain. (*eagerly*) And he proved it to me, too. Look! (*He shows them a piece of wood.*) He broke this off of the Ark. See, it's got Noah's initials on it!

MAFFEO—(*grimly*) How much did you pay him for it?

MARCO—Ten soldi in silver.

NICOLO—(*dashing it out of Marco's hand—bitterly*) Muttonhead! Do you suppose Almighty God would allow infidels to cut up Noah's Ark into souvenirs to sell to Christians?

MAFFEO—(*teasingly*) Your son and your money are soon

parted, Brother. (*then placatingly*) But he's only a boy. He'll learn. And before we go farther, Nicolo, we better read him from the notes we made on our last trip all there is to remember about this corner of the world.

NICOLO—(*They take out note-books closely resembling a modern business man's date-book and read*) We're now passing through Kingdoms where they worship Mahomet.

MAFFEO—There's one kingdom called Musul and in it a district of Baku where there's a great fountain of oil. There's a growing demand for it. (*then speaking*) Make a mental note of that.

MARCO—Yes, sir.

NICOLO—Merchants make great profits. The people are simple creatures. It's very cold in winter. The women wear cotton drawers. This they do to look large in the hips, for the men think that a great beauty. (*The two Mahometan merchants enter from the left. Maffeo recognizes them immediately—in a swift aside to his brother*)

MAFFEO—There's those damned Ali brothers. They'll cut under our prices with their cheap junk as usual. (*The Ali brothers have seen the Polos and a whispered aside, evidently of the same nature, passes between them. Then simultaneously the two firms advance to meet each other putting on expressions of the utmost cordiality.*) Well, well. You folks are a welcome sight!

ONE ALI—My dear, dear friends! Praise be to Allah! (*They embrace.*)

MAFFEO—(*with a cunning smirk*) Selling a big bill of goods hereabouts, I'll wager, you old rascals?

THE OLDER ALI—(*airily*) My dear friend, don't speak of business. But you, you are on a venture to the court of the Great Kaan, we hear?

MAFFEO—What lies get around! Nothing in it—absolutely nothing!

NICOLO—For heaven's sake, let's not talk business! Let's have a nice friendly chat. (*The four squat together in a circle.*)

MAFFEO—(*with a wink*) I'll tell you a good one an Armenian doily-dealer told me down in Bagdad. (*They all bend their heads toward him with expectant grins. He looks around— then begins in a cautious lowered tone*) Well, there was an old

Jew named Ikey and he married a young girl named Re-
becca— (*He goes on telling the rest of the story with much exaggerated Jewish pantomime but in a voice too low to be heard. In
the meantime, Marco has slipped off, full of curiosity and wonder,
to look at this strange life. He goes first to the left, stops before the
mother and baby, smiles down at it uncertainly, then bends down
to take hold of its hand.*)

MARCO—Hello! (*then to the mother*) He's fat as butter!
(*Both remain silent and motionless, staring at him from a great
distance with indifferent calm. Marco is rebuffed, grows embarrassed, turns away to the children, who, frozen in the midst of
their game of jackstraws, are looking at him. Marco adopts a lofty
condescending air.*) Humh! Do you still play that game here? I
remember it—when I was a kid. (*They stare silently. He mutters disgustedly*) Thickheads! (*and turns to the lovers who with
their arms about each other, cheek to cheek, stare at him. He looks
at them, fascinated and stirred, and murmurs enviously*) She's
pretty. I suppose they're engaged—like Donata and me. (*He
fumbles and pulls out the locket which is hung around his neck on
a ribbon.*) Donata's prettier. (*Then embarrassedly, he holds it out
for them to see.*) Don't you think she's pretty? She and I are
going to be married some day. (*They do not look except into his
eyes. He turns away, hurt and angry.*) Go to the devil, you
infidels! (*He stuffs the locket back—stops before the throne—tries
to stare insolently at the king but, awed in spite of himself, makes
a grudging bow and passes on, stops before the family group, sneers
and passes on, stops before the old couple and cannot restrain his
curiosity.*) Would you tell me how old you are? (*He passes on,
rebuffed again, stops fascinatedly before the coffin, leans out and
touches it with defiant daring, shudders superstitiously and shrinks
away, going to the merchant group who are roaring with laughter
as Maffeo ends his story.*)

THE OLDER ALI—(*to Nicolo*) Your son?

NICOLO—Yes, and a chip of the old block.

THE OLDER ALI—Will he follow in your footsteps?

NICOLO—(*jocosely*) Yes, and you better look out then!
He's as keen as a hawk already.

THE OLDER ALI—(*with a trace of a biting smile*) He greatly
resembles a youth I saw back on the road buying a piece of
Noah's Ark from a wayside sharper.

MAFFEO—(*hastily coming to the rescue as Nicolo cannot hide his chagrin—boastfully*) It wasn't Mark. Mark would have sold him the lions of St. Mark's for good mousers! (*The prostitute enters from the right. She is painted, half-naked, alluring in a brazen, sensual way. She smiles at Marco enticingly.*)

MARCO—(*with a gasp*) Look! Who's that? (*They all turn, and, recognizing her, laugh with coarse familiarity.*)

MAFFEO—(*jokingly*) So here you are again. You're like a bad coin—always turning up.

PROSTITUTE—(*smiling*) Shut up. You can bet it isn't old fools like you that turn me.

NICOLO—(*with a lecherous grin at her*) No? But it's the old who have the money.

PROSTITUTE—Money isn't everything, not always. Now I wouldn't ask money from him. (*She points to Marco.*)

NICOLO—(*crossly and jealously*) Leave him alone, you filth!

MAFFEO—(*broad-mindedly*) Come, come, Nicolo. Let the boy have his fling.

PROSTITUTE—(*her eyes on Marco*) Hello, Handsome.

MARCO—(*bewilderedly*) You've learned our language?

PROSTITUTE—I sell to all nations.

MARCO—What do you sell?

PROSTITUTE—(*mockingly*) A precious jewel. Myself. (*then desirously*) But for you I'm a gift. (*putting her hands on his shoulders and lifting her lips*) Why don't you kiss me?

MARCO—(*terribly confused—strugglingly*) I—I don't know —I mean, I'm sorry but—you see I promised someone I'd never— (*suddenly freeing himself—frightenedly*) Leave go! I don't want your kisses. (*A roar of coarse taunting laughter from the men. Marco runs away, off Left.*)

NICOLO—(*between his teeth*) What a dolt!

MAFFEO—(*slapping the prostitute on the bare shoulder*) Better luck next time. He'll learn!

PROSTITUTE—(*trying to hide her pique—forcing a cynical smile*) Oh, yes, but I won't be a gift then. I'll make him pay, just to show him! (*She laughs harshly and goes out Left. A pause. All four squat again in silence.*)

THE OLDER ALI—(*suddenly*) Many wonders have come to pass in these regions. They relate that in old times three kings from this country went to worship a Prophet that was born and they carried with them three manner of offerings—Gold and Frankincense and Myrrh—and when they had come to the place where the Child was born, they marveled and knelt before him.

MAFFEO—That's written in the Bible. The child was Jesus Christ, our Lord. (*He blesses himself, Nicolo does likewise.*)

THE OLDER ALI—Your Jesus was a great prophet.

NICOLO—(*defiantly*) He was the Son of God!

BOTH ALIS—(*stubbornly*) There is no God but Allah! (*A strained pause. A dervish of the desert runs in shrieking and begins to whirl. No one is surprised except the two Polos who get up to gape at him with the thrilled appreciation inspired by a freak in a sideshow. Marco comes back and joins them.*)

MAFFEO—(*with appreciation*) If we had him in Venice we could make a mint of money exhibiting him. (*Nicolo nods.*)

MARCO—I'll have to write Donata all about this. (*wonderingly*) Is he crazy?

MAFFEO—(*in a low aside to him*) My boy, all Mahometans are crazy. That's the only charitable way to look at it. (*Suddenly the call to prayer sounds from Muezzins in the minarets of the mosque. The dervish falls on his face. Everyone sinks into the attitude of prayer except the Polos who stand embarrassedly, not knowing what to do.*)

MARCO—Are they praying?

NICOLO—Yes, they call it that. Much good it does them!

MAFFEO—Ssshh! Come! This is a good time to move on again. Marco! Wake up! (*They go quickly out Right, Marco following with the sample cases. The scene fades quickly into darkness as the call of the Muezzins is heard again.*)

(*Darkness*)

SCENE FOUR

SCENE—*The slowly-rising light reveals an Indian snake-charmer squatted on his haunches at center. A snake is starting to*

*crawl from the basket in front of him, swaying its head to the thin,
shrill whine of a gourd. Otherwise, the scene, in the placing of its
people and the characters and types represented, is the exact duplicate of the last except that here the locale is Indian. The background for the ruler's throne is now a Buddhist temple instead of
a mosque. The motionless staring figures are all Indians. Looming
directly above and in back of the ruler's throne is an immense
Buddha. The Polos stand at center as before, Marco still lugging
the sample cases. He is seventeen now. Some of the freshness of
youth has worn off.*

*They stare at the snake-charmer, the two older men cynically.
Marco gasps with enthralled horror.*

MARCO—Look at that deadly snake!

MAFFEO—(*cynically*) He's a fake, like everything else here.
His fangs have been pulled out.

MARCO—(*disillusioned*) Oh! (*He turns away. The snake-
charmer glares at them, stops playing, pushes his snake back into
the box and carries it off, after spitting on the ground at their feet
with angry disgust. Marco sits on one of the cases and glances
about with a forced scorn; looks finally at the Buddha—in a
smart-Aleck tone*) So that is Buddha!

NICOLO—(*begins to read from his note-book*) These people
are idolaters. The climate is so hot if you put an egg in their
rivers it will be boiled.

MAFFEO—(*taking up the reading from his book in the same
tone*) The merchants make great profits. Ginger, pepper, and
indigo. Largest sheep in the world. Diamonds of great size.
The Kings have five hundred wives apiece.

MARCO—(*disgustedly*) It's too darn hot here!

MAFFEO—(*warningly*) Sshhh! Don't let the natives hear
you. Remember any climate is healthy where trade is brisk.

MARCO—(*walks sullenly off to left. At the same moment
two merchants, this time Buddhists, come in. The same interplay
goes on with them as with the Ali brothers in the previous
scene, only this time it is all done in pantomime until the loud
laughter at the end of Maffeo's story. As Maffeo tells the story,
Marco is looking at the people but this time he assumes the
casual, indifferent attitude of the worldly-wise. He makes a silly
gesture to attract the baby's attention, passes by the two children*

with only a contemptuous glance, but stops and stares impudently at the lovers—finally spits with exaggerated scorn.) Where do you think you are—home with the light out? Why don't you charge admission? (*He stalks on—pauses before the middle-aged couple who have a bowl of rice between them—in astonishment as though this evidence of a humanity common with his struck him as strange.*) Real rice! (*He ignores the throne, passes quickly by the old people with a glance of aversion and very obviously averts his head from the coffin. As he returns to the group at center, Maffeo has just finished his story. There is a roar of laughter.*)

MARCO—(*grinning eagerly*) What was it, Uncle?

MAFFEO—(*grinning teasingly*) You're too young.

MARCO—(*boastfully*) Is that so?

NICOLO—(*severely*) Mark! (*The prostitute, the same but now in Indian garb, has entered from Left and comes up behind Marco.*)

PROSTITUTE—A chip of the old block, Nicolo!

NICOLO—(*angrily*) You again!

MARCO—(*pleased to see her—embarrassedly*) Why, hello.

PROSTITUTE—(*cynically*) I knew you'd want to see me. (*She raises her lips.*) Will you kiss me now? (*as he hesitates*) Forget your promise. You know you want to.

MAFFEO—(*grinning*) There's no spirit in the youngsters nowadays. I'll bet he won't.

PROSTITUTE—(*her eyes on Marco's*) How much will you bet?

MAFFEO—Ten— (*Marco suddenly kisses her.*)

PROSTITUTE—(*turning to Maffeo*) I win, Uncle.

MARCO—(*with a grin*) No. I kissed you before he said ten what.

MAFFEO—That's right! Good boy, Mark!

PROSTITUTE—(*turning to Marco—cynically*) You're learning, aren't you? You're becoming shrewd even about kisses. You need only me now to make you into a real man—for ten pieces of gold.

MARCO—(*genuinely overcome by a sudden shame*) No, please.—I—I didn't mean it. It was only in fun.

PROSTITUTE—(*with a sure smile*) Later, then—when we meet again. (*She walks off Left.*)

MARCO—(*looks after her. As she evidently turns to look back at him, he waves his hand and grins—then abashed*) She's pretty. It's too bad she's—what she is.

MAFFEO—Don't waste pity. Her kind are necessary evils. All of us are human. (*a long pause*)

THE OLDER BUDDHIST MERCHANT—(*suddenly*) The Buddha taught that one's loving-kindness should embrace all forms of life, that one's compassion should suffer with the suffering, that one's sympathy should understand all things, and last that one's judgment should regard all persons and things as of equal importance.

NICOLO—(*harshly*) Who was this Buddha?

THE OLDER BUDDHIST MERCHANT—The Incarnation of God.

NICOLO—You mean Jesus?

THE OLDER BUDDHIST MERCHANT—(*unheedingly*) He was immaculately conceived. The Light passed into the womb of Maya, and she bore a son who, when he came to manhood, renounced wife and child, riches and power, and went out as a beggar on the roads to seek the supreme enlightenment which would conquer birth and death; and at last he attained the wisdom where all desire has ended and experienced the heaven of peace, Nirvana. And when he died he became a God again. (*The temple bells begin to ring in chorus. All except the Polos prostrate themselves before the Buddha.*)

MARCO—(*to his uncle—in a whispered chuckle*) Died and became a God? So that's what they believe about that stone statue, is it?

MAFFEO—They're all crazy, like the Mahometans. They're not responsible.

MARCO—(*suddenly*) I saw two of them with a bowl of rice—

MAFFEO—Oh, yes. They eat the same as we do. (*then abruptly*) Come on! This is our chance to make a start. Don't forget our cases, Mark. (*They go out Left followed by Marco with the sample cases. The scene fades into darkness. The clamor of the temple bells slowly dies out in the distance.*)

(*Darkness*)

SCENE FIVE

SCENE—*From the darkness comes the sound of a small Tartar kettledrum, its beats marking the rhythm for a crooning, nasal voice, rising and falling in a wordless chant.*

The darkness gradually lifts. In the rear is a section of the Great Wall of China with an enormous shut gate. It is late afternoon, just before sunset. Immediately before the gate is a rude throne on which sits a Mongol ruler with warrior and sorcerer to right and left of him. At the sides are Mongol circular huts. The motionless figures sit before these. The minstrel, squatting at center, is the only one whose body moves. In the back of the throne and above it is a small idol made of felt and cloth. The clothes of the ruler and his court are of rich silk stuffs, lined with costly furs. The squatting figures of the people are clothed in rough robes.

The Polos stand at center, Marco still lugging the battered sample cases. He is now nearly eighteen, a brash, self-confident young man, assertive and talky. All the Polos are weary and their clothes shabby and travel-worn.

MARCO—(*setting down the bags with a thump and staring about with an appraising contempt*) Welcome to that dear old Motherland, Mongolia!

MAFFEO—(*wearily takes out his guide-book and begins to read in the monotone of a boring formula*) Flocks—goats—horses—cattle. The women do all the buying and selling. Business is all in cattle and crops. In short, the people live like beasts.

NICOLO—(*reading from his book*) They have two Gods—a God of Heaven to whom they pray for health of mind, and a God of Earth who watches over their earthly goods. They pray to him also and do many other stupid things.

MARCO—(*boredly*) Well—let them! (*He walks away and makes the circuit of the figures, but now he hardly glances at them. The two Tartar merchants enter and there is the same pantomime of greeting between them and the Polos as with the Buddhist merchants in the previous scene. Marco joins them. It is apparent the whole company is extremely weary. They yawn and prepare to lie down.*)

MAFFEO—We'll have time to steal a nap before they open the Gate.

MARCO—(*with an assertive importance*) Just a moment! I've got a good one an idol-polisher told me in Tibet. This is the funniest story you ever heard! It seems an Irishman got drunk in Tangut and wandered into a temple where he mistook one of the female statues for a real woman and— (*He goes on, laughing and chuckling to himself, with endless comic pantomime. The two Tartar merchants fall asleep. Nicolo stares at his son bitterly, Maffeo with contemptuous pity. Finally Marco finishes to his own uproarious amusement.*)

NICOLO—(*bitterly*) Dolt!

MAFFEO—(*mockingly—with a yawn*) Youth will have its laugh! (*Marco stops open-mouthed and stares from one to the other.*)

MARCO—(*faintly*) What's the matter?

NICOLO—(*pettishly*) Unless your jokes improve you'll never sell anything.

MAFFEO—I'll have to give Marco some lessons in how to tell a short story. (*warningly*) And until I pronounce you graduated, mum's the word, understand! The people on the other side of that wall may look simple but they're not. (*The prostitute enters dressed now as a Tartar. She comes and puts her hand on Marco's head.*)

PROSTITUTE—What has this bad boy been doing now?

MAFFEO—He's getting too witty! (*He rests his head on his arms and goes to sleep.*)

PROSTITUTE—Shall I expect you again tonight?

MARCO—No. You've got all my money. (*suddenly gets to his feet and faces her—disgustedly*) And I'm through with you, anyway.

PROSTITUTE—(*with a scornful smile*) And I with you—now that you're a man. (*She turns away.*)

MARCO—(*angrily*) Listen here! Give me back what you stole! I know I had it on a ribbon around my neck last night and this morning it was gone. (*threateningly*) Give it to me, you, or I'll make trouble!

PROSTITUTE—(*takes a crumpled paper from her bosom*) Do you mean this?

MARCO—(*tries to snatch it*) No!

PROSTITUTE—(*She unfolds it and reads*)

"I'll have a million to my credit
And in the meantime can easily afford
A big wedding that will do us credit
And start having children, Bless the Lord!"

(*She laughs.*) Are you a poet, too?

MARCO—(*abashed and furious*) I didn't write that.

PROSTITUTE—You're lying. You must have. Why deny it? Don't sell your soul for nothing. That's bad business. (*She laughs, waving the poem in her upraised hand, staring mockingly.*) Going! Going! Gone! (*She lets it fall and grinds it under her feet into the earth—laughing*) Your soul! Dead and buried! You strong man! (*She laughs.*)

MARCO—(*threateningly*) Give me what was wrapped up in that, d'you hear!

PROSTITUTE—(*scornfully—takes the miniature from her bosom*) You mean this? I was bringing it back to you. D'you think I want her ugly face around? Here! (*She throws it at his feet. He leans down and picks it up, polishing it on his sleeve remorsefully. The prostitute, walking away, calls back over her shoulder*) I kissed it so you'd remember my kiss whenever you kiss her! (*She laughs. Marco starts as if to run after her angrily. Suddenly a shout rises from the lips of all the Tartars, the minstrel and his drum become silent, and with one accord they raise their arms and eyes to the sky. Then the minstrel chants*)

MINSTREL—God of the Heaven, be in our souls! (*Then they all prostrate themselves on the ground as he chants*) God of the Earth, be in our bodies! (*The Tartars sit up. The minstrel begins again his drum beat, crooning in a low monotone. The Polos rise and stretch sleepily.*)

MARCO—(*inquisitively*) Two Gods? Are they in one Person like our Holy Trinity?

MAFFEO—(*shocked*) Don't be impious! These are degraded pagans—or crazy, that's a more charitable way to— (*From behind the wall comes the sound of martial Chinese music. The gate opens. The blinding glare of the setting sun floods in from beyond. A file of soldiers, accompanying a richly-dressed court messenger, come through. He walks directly up to the Polos and bows deeply.*)

MESSENGER—The Great Kaan, Lord of the World, sent

me— (*He looks around.*) But where are the hundred wise men of the West?

NICOLO—(*confusedly*) We had two monks to start with— but they left us and went back.

MAFFEO—(*warningly*) Ssst!

MESSENGER—(*indifferently*) You will explain to the Kaan. I was ordered to arrange a welcome for them.

MAFFEO—(*claps him on the back*) Well, here we are—and hungry as hunters! So your welcome will be welcome, Brother. (*The messenger bows, starts back, the Polos following him, Maffeo calling*) Get on the job, Mark! (*They pass through the gate.*)

MARCO—(*wearily picks up the cases—then goading himself on*) Giddap! Cathay or bust! (*He struggles through the gate. For a second he is framed in it, outlined against the brilliant sky, tugging a sample case in each hand. Then the gate shuts, the light fades out. The drum beat and the chanting recede into the distance.*)

(*Darkness*)

SCENE SIX

SCENE—*Music from full Chinese and Tartar bands crashes up to a tremendous blaring crescendo of drums, gongs, and the piercing shrilling of flutes. The light slowly comes to a pitch of blinding brightness. Then, as light and sound attain their highest point, there is a sudden dead silence. The scene is revealed as the Grand Throne Room in the palace of Kublai, the Great Kaan, in the city of Cambaluc, Cathay—an immense octagonal room, the lofty walls adorned in gold and silver. In the far rear wall, within a deep recess like the shrine of an idol, is the throne of the Great Kaan. It rises in three tiers, three steps to a tier. On golden cushions at the top Kublai sits dressed in his heavy gold robes of state. He is a man of sixty but still in the full prime of his powers, his face proud and noble, his expression tinged with an ironic humor and bitterness yet full of a sympathetic humanity. In his person are combined the conquering indomitable force of a descendant of Chinghiz with the humanizing culture of the conquered Chinese who have already begun to absorb their conquerors.*

*On the level of the throne below Kublai are: on his right a
Mongol warrior in full armor with shield and spear, his face grim,
cruel and fierce. On his left Chu-Yin, the Cathayan sage and
adviser to the Kaan, a venerable old man with white hair, dressed
in a simple black robe.*

*On the main floor, grouped close to the throne are: on the right,
the sons of the Kaan. Farther away, the nobles and warriors of all
degrees with their wives behind them. On the left, the wives and
concubines of the Kaan, then the courtiers, officers, poets, scholars,
etc. —all the non-military officials and hangers-on of government,
with their women beside them.*

*Marco stands, a sample case in each hand, bewildered and daz-
zled, gawking about him on every side. His father and uncle, bowing, walk to the foot of the throne and kneel before the Kaan. They
make frantic signals to Marco to do likewise but he is too dazed to
notice. All the people in the room are staring at him. The Kaan
is looking at the two brothers with a stern air. An usher of the
palace comes quietly to Marco and makes violent gestures to him to
kneel down.*

MARCO—(*misunderstanding him—gratefully*) Thank you,
Brother. (*He sits down on one of the sample cases to the gasping
horror of all the Court. The Kaan is still looking frowningly at
the two Polos as he listens to the report of their messenger escort.
He does not notice. An outraged chamberlain rushes over to Marco
and motions him to kneel down.*)

MARCO—(*bewilderedly*) What's the trouble now?

KUBLAI—(*dismissing the messenger, having heard his report—addresses the Polos coldly*) I bid you welcome, Messrs.
Polo. But where are the hundred wise men of the West who
were to dispute with my wise men of the sacred teachings of
Lao-Tseu and Confucius and the Buddha and Christ?

MAFFEO—(*hurriedly*) There was no Pope elected until just
before—

NICOLO—And he had no wise men, anyway. (*The Kaan
now sees Marco and a puzzled expression of interest comes over his
face.*)

KUBLAI—Is he with you?

NICOLO—(*hesitantly*) My son, Marco, your Majesty—still
young and graceless.

KUBLAI—Come here, Marco Polo. (*Marco comes forward, trying feebly to assume a bold, confident air.*)

MAFFEO—(*in a loud, furious aside*) Kneel, you ass! (*Marco flounders to his knees.*)

KUBLAI—(*with a smile*) I bid you welcome, Master Marco.

MARCO—Thank you, sir—I mean, your Lordship—your— (*then suddenly*) Before I forget—the Pope gave me a message for you, sir.

KUBLAI—(*smiling*) Are you his hundred wise men?

MARCO—(*confidently*) Well—almost. He sent me in their place. He said I'd be worth a million wise men to you.

NICOLO—(*hastily*) His Holiness meant that Marco, by leading an upright life—not neglecting the practical side, of course—might set an example that would illustrate, better than wise words, the flesh and blood product of our Christian civilization.

KUBLAI—(*with a quiet smile*) I shall study this apotheosis with unwearied interest, I foresee it.

MARCO—(*suddenly—with a confidential air*) Wasn't that just a joke, your asking for the wise men? His Holiness thought you must have a sense of humor. Or that you must be an optimist.

KUBLAI—(*with a smile of appreciation*) I am afraid your Holy Pope is a most unholy cynic. (*trying to solve a riddle in his own mind—musingly*) Could he believe this youth possesses that thing called soul which the West dreams lives after death—and might reveal it to me? (*suddenly to Marco*) Have you an immortal soul?

MARCO—(*in surprise*) Of course! Any fool knows that.

KUBLAI—(*humbly*) But I am not a fool. Can you prove it to me?

MARCO—Why, if you didn't have a soul, what would happen when you die?

KUBLAI—What, indeed?

MARCO—Why, nothing. You'd be dead—just like an animal.

KUBLAI—Your logic is irrefutable.

MARCO—Well, I'm not an animal, am I? That's certainly plain enough. (*then proudly*) No, sir! I'm a man made by Almighty God in His Own Image for His greater glory!

KUBLAI—(*staring at him for a long moment with appalled appreciation*—*ecstatically*) So you are the Image of God! There is certainly something about you, something complete and unanswerable—but wait—a test! (*He claps his hands, pointing to Marco. Soldiers with drawn swords leap forward and seize him, trussing up his hands behind his back.*)

MAFFEO—(*groveling*) Mercy! He is only a boy!

NICOLO—(*groveling*) Mercy! He is only a fool!

KUBLAI—(*sternly*) Silence! (*to Marco with inhuman calm*) Since you possess eternal life, it can do you no harm to cut off your head. (*He makes a sign to a soldier who flourishes his sword.*)

MARCO—(*trying to conceal his fear under a quavering, joking tone*) I might—catch—cold!

KUBLAI—You jest, but your voice trembles. What! Are you afraid to die, immortal youth? Well, then, if you will confess that your soul is a stupid invention of your fear and that when you die you will be dead as a dead dog is dead—

MARCO—(*with sudden fury*) You're a heathen liar! (*He glares defiantly. His father and uncle moan with horror.*)

KUBLAI—(*laughs and claps his hands. Marco is freed. The Kaan studies his sullen but relieved face with amusement.*) Your pardon, Marco! I suspected a flaw but you are perfect. You cannot imagine your death. You are a born hero. I must keep you near me. You shall tell me about your soul and I will listen as to a hundred wise men from the West! Is it agreed?

MARCO—(*hesitatingly*) I know it's a great honor, sir—but forgetting the soul side of it, I've got to eat.

KUBLAI—(*astonished*) To eat?

MARCO—I mean, I'm ambitious. I've got to succeed, and— (*suddenly blurts out*) What can you pay me?

KUBLAI—Ha! Well, you will find me a practical man, too. I can start you upon any career you wish. What is your choice?

MAFFEO—(*interposing eagerly*) If I might speak to the boy in private a minute—give him my humble advice—he is so young— (*Maffeo and Nicolo hurriedly lead Marco down to the foreground.*) You've made a favorable impression—God knows why—but strike while the iron is hot, you ninny! Ask to be appointed a Second Class government commission-agent.

MARCO—(*offendedly*) No! I'll be first-class or nothing!

MAFFEO—Don't be a fool! A First Class agent is all brass buttons and no opportunities. A Second Class travels around, is allowed his expenses, gets friendly with all the dealers, scares them into letting him in on everything—and gets what's rightfully coming to him! (*then with a crafty look and a nudge in the ribs*) And, being always in the secret, you'll be able to whisper to us in time to take advantage—

MARCO—(*a bit flustered—with bluff assertion*) I don't know. The Kaan's been square with me. After all, honesty's the best policy, isn't it?

MAFFEO—(*looking him over scathingly*) You'd think I was advising you to steal—I, Maffeo Polo, whose conservatism is unquestioned!

MARCO—(*awed*) I didn't mean—

MAFFEO—(*solemnly*) Do you imagine the Kaan is such a Nero as to expect you to live on your salary?

MARCO—(*uncertainly*) No, I suppose not. (*He suddenly looks at Maffeo with a crafty wink.*) When I do give you a tip, what do I get from Polo Brothers?

MAFFEO—(*between appreciation and dismay*) Ha! You learn quickly, don't you? (*then hastily*) Why, we—we've already thought of that—trust us to look after your best interests—and decided to—to make you a junior partner in the firm—eh, Nick?—Polo Brothers and Son—doesn't that sound solid, eh?

MARCO—(*with a sly grin*) It's a great honor—a very great honor. (*then meaningly*) But as neither of you are Neros, naturally you'll also offer me—

MAFFEO—(*grinning in spite of himself*) Hmm! Hmm! You Judas!

MARCO—A fair commission—

NICOLO—(*blustering—but his eyes beaming with paternal pride*) You young scamp!

MAFFEO—(*laughing*) Ha-ha! Good boy, Mark! Polos will be Polos! (*They all embrace laughingly. Kublai, who has been observing them intently, turns to Chu-Yin and they both smile.*)

KUBLAI—Did their Pope mean that a fool is a wiser study

for a ruler of fools than a hundred wise men could be? This Marco touches me, as a child might, but at the same time there is something warped, deformed— Tell me, what shall I do with him?

CHU-YIN—Let him develop according to his own inclination and give him also every opportunity for true growth if he so desires. And let us observe him. At least, if he cannot learn, we shall.

KUBLAI—(*smilingly*) Yes. And be amused. (*He calls commandingly*) Marco Polo! (*Marco turns rather frightenedly and comes to the throne and kneels.*) Have you decided?

MARCO—(*promptly*) I'd like to be appointed a commission-agent of the Second Class.

KUBLAI—(*somewhat taken aback, puzzledly*) You are modest enough!

MARCO—(*manfully*) I want to start at the bottom!

KUBLAI—(*with mocking grandeur*) Arise then, Second Class Marco! You will receive your agent's commission at once. (*then with a twinkle in his eye*) But each time you return from a journey you must relate to me all the observations and comments of your soul on the East. Be warned and never fail me in this!

MARCO—(*confused but cocksuredly*) I won't. I'll take copious notes. (*then meaningly*) And I can memorize any little humorous incidents—

MAFFEO—(*apprehensively*) Blessed Savior! (*He gives a violent fit of coughing.*)

MARCO—(*looks around at him questioningly*) Hum? (*misinterpreting his signal*) And may I announce to your Majesty that a signal honor has just been conferred on me? My father and uncle have taken me into the firm. It will be Polo Brothers and Son from now on, and any way we can serve your Majesty—

KUBLAI—(*a light coming over his face*) Aha! I begin to smell all the rats in Cathay! (*The two elder Polos are bowed to the ground, trembling with apprehension. Kublai laughs quietly.*) Well, I am sure you wish to celebrate this family triumph together, so you may go. And accept my congratulations, Marco!

MARCO—Thank you, your Majesty. You will never regret

it. I will always serve your best interests, so help me God!
(*He goes grandly, preceded hurriedly by the trembling Nicolo and Maffeo. Kublai laughs and turns to Chu-Yin who is smiling.*)

(*Curtain*)

ACT TWO

Scene One

SCENE—*The Little Throne Room in the bamboo summer palace of the Kaan at Xanadu, the City of Peace—smaller, more intimate than the one at Cambaluc, but possessing an atmosphere of aloof dignity and simplicity fitting to the philosopher ruler who retreats here to contemplate in peace the vanity of his authority.*

About fifteen years have elapsed. It is a beautiful sunlit morning in late June. The Kaan reclines comfortably on his cushioned bamboo throne. His face has aged greatly. The expression has grown mask-like, full of philosophic calm. He has the detached air of an idol. Kukachin, a beautiful young girl of twenty, pale and delicate, is sitting at his feet. Her air is grief-stricken. A flute player in the garden is playing a melancholy air. Kukachin recites in a low tone:

KUKACHIN—
My thoughts in this autumn are lonely and sad,
A chill wind from the mountain blows in the garden.
The sky is gray, a snowflake falls, the last chrysanthemum
Withers beside the deserted summer-house.
I walk along the path in which weeds have grown.
My heart is bitter and tears blur my eyes.
I grieve for the days when we lingered together
In this same garden, along these paths between flowers.
In the spring we sang of love and laughed with youth
But now we are parted by many leagues and years,
And I weep that never again shall I see your face.
(*She finishes and relapses into her attitude of broken resignation. The flute player ceases his playing. Kublai looks down at her tenderly.*)
KUBLAI—(*musingly*) Sing while you can. When the voice fails, listen to the song. When the heart fails, be sung asleep. (*chidingly*) That is a sad poem, Little Flower. Are you sad because you must soon become Queen of Persia? But Arghun is a great hero, a Khan of the blood of Chinghiz. You will be blessed with strong sons able to dare the proud destiny of our blood.

KUKACHIN—(*dully*) Your will is my law.

KUBLAI—Not my will. The will of life to continue the strong. (*forcing a consoling tone*) Come, Little Flower. You have been fading here. See how pale you have grown! Your eyes are listless! Your lips droop even in smiling! But life at the Court of Persia is gay. There will be feasts, celebrations, diverting pleasures. You will be their Queen of Beauty.

KUKACHIN—(*with a sigh*) A Queen may be only a woman who is unhappy.

KUBLAI—(*teasingly*) What despair! You talk like the ladies in poems who have lost their lovers! (*Kukachin gives a violent start which he does not notice and a spasm of pain comes over her face.*) But, never mind, Arghun of Persia is a hero no woman could fail to love.

KUKACHIN—(*starting to her feet—desperately*) No! I can bear his children, but you cannot force me to— (*She breaks down, weeping.*)

KUBLAI—(*astonished—gazing at her searchingly*) Have I ever forced you to anything? (*then resuming his tone of tender teasing*) I would say, rather, that ever since you were old enough to talk, the Ruler of Earth, as they innocently call your grandfather, has been little better than your slave.

KUKACHIN—(*taking his hand and kissing it*) Forgive me. (*then smiling at him*) Have I been so bad as that? Has my love for you, who have been both father and mother to me, brought you no happiness?

KUBLAI—(*with deep emotion*) You have been a golden bird singing beside a black river. You took your mother's place in my heart when she died. I was younger then. The river was not so black—the river of man's life so deep and silent— flowing with an insane obsession—whither?—and why? (*then suddenly forcing a smile*) Your poem has made me melancholy. And I am too old, if not too wise, to afford anything but optimism! (*then sadly*) But now you in your turn must leave me, the river seems black indeed! (*then after a pause— tenderly*) If it will make you unhappy, you need not marry Arghun Khan.

KUKACHIN—(*recovering herself—resolutely*) No. Your refusal would insult him. It might mean war. (*resignedly*) And Arghun is as acceptable as any other. Forgive my weakness.

You once told me a Princess must never weep. (*She forces a smile.*) It makes no difference whether I stay or go, except that I shall be homesick for you. (*She kisses his hand again.*)

KUBLAI—(*gratefully*) My little one. (*He strokes her hair. After a pause during which he looks at her thoughtfully—tenderly*) We have never had secrets from each other, you and I. Tell me, can you have fallen in love?

KUKACHIN—(*after a pause—tremblingly*) You must not ask that—if you respect my pride! (*with a pitiful smile*) You see— he does not even know— (*She is blushing and hanging her head with confusion. Chu-Yin enters hurriedly from the right. He is very old but still upright. He is a bit breathless from haste but his face is wreathed in smiles.*)

CHU-YIN—(*making an obeisance*) Your Majesty, do you hear that martial music? His Honor, Marco Polo, Mayor of Yang-Chau, seems about to visit you in state! (*The strains of a distant band can be heard.*)

KUBLAI—(*still looking at Kukachin who has started violently at the mention of Marco's name—worriedly*) Impossible! In love? . . . (*then to Chu-Yin—preoccupiedly*) Eh? Marco? I have given no orders for him to return.

CHU-YIN—(*ironically*) No doubt he comes to refresh your humor with new copious notes on his exploits. Our Marco has made an active mayor. Yang-Chau, according to the petition for mercy you have received from its inhabitants, is the most governed of all your cities. I talked recently with a poet who had fled from there in horror. Yang-Chau used to have a soul, he said. Now it has a brand new Court House. And another, a man of wide culture, told me, our Christian mayor is exterminating our pleasures and our rats as if they were twin breeds of vermin!

KUBLAI—(*irritably*) He is beginning to weary me with his grotesque antics. A jester inspires mirth only so long as his deformity does not revolt one. Marco's spiritual hump begins to disgust me. He has not even a mortal soul, he has only an acquisitive instinct. We have given him every opportunity to learn. He has memorized everything and learned nothing. He has looked at everything and seen nothing. He has lusted for everything and loved nothing. He is only a shrewd and crafty greed. I shall send him home to his native wallow.

CHU-YIN—(*in mock alarm*) What? Must we lose our clown?

KUKACHIN—(*who has been listening with growing indignation*) How dare you call him a clown? Just because he is not a dull philosopher you think—

KUBLAI—(*astounded—admonishingly*) Princess!

KUKACHIN—(*turns to him—on the verge of tears—rebelliously*) Why are you both so unjust? Has he not done well everything he was ever appointed to do? Has he not always succeeded where others failed? Has he not by his will-power and determination risen to the highest rank in your service? (*then her anger dying—more falteringly*) He is strange, perhaps, to people who do not understand him, but that is because he is so different from other men, so much stronger! And he has a soul! I know he has!

KUBLAI—(*whose eyes have been searching her face—aghast*) Kukachin! (*She sees he has guessed her secret and at first she quails and shrinks away, then stiffens regally and returns his gaze unflinchingly. Chu-Yin looks from one to the other comprehendingly. Finally Kublai addresses her sternly.*) So, because I have allowed this fool a jester's latitude, because I permitted him to amuse you when you were a little girl, and since then, on his returns, to speak with you—a Princess!— (*then brusquely*) I shall inform the ambassadors you will be ready to sail for Persia within ten days. You may retire. (*She bows with a proud humility and walks off Left. Kublai sits in a somber study, frowning and biting his lips. The blaring of Marco's band grows steadily nearer.*)

CHU-YIN—(*gently*) Is intolerance wisdom? (*A pause. Then he goes on.*) I have suspected her love for him for a long time.

KUBLAI—Why didn't you warn me?

CHU-YIN—Love is to wisdom what wisdom seems to love—a folly. I reasoned, love comes like the breath of wind on water and is gone leaving calm and reflection. I reasoned, but this is an enchanted moment for her and it will remain a poignant memory to recompense her when she is no longer a girl but merely a Queen. And I reasoned, who knows but some day this Marco may see into her eyes and his soul may be born and that will make a very interesting study—for Kukachin, and her grandfather, the Son of Heaven and Ruler of the World! (*He bows mockingly.*) And for the old fool who is I!

KUBLAI—(*bewilderedly*) I cannot believe it! Why, since she was a little girl, she has only talked to him once or twice every two years or so!

CHU-YIN—That was unwise, for thus he has remained a strange, mysterious dream-knight from the exotic West, an enigma with something about him of a likable boy who brought her home each time a humble, foolish, touching little gift! And also remember that on each occasion he returned in triumph, having accomplished a task—a victor, more or less, acting the hero. (*The band has crashed and dinned its way into the courtyard.*) As now! Listen! (*He goes to the window and looks down—with ironical but intense amusement*) Ah! He wears over his Mayor's uniform, the regalia of Cock of Paradise in his secret fraternal order of the Mystic Knights of Confucius! The band of the Xanadu lodge is with him as well as his own! He is riding on a very fat white horse. He dismounts, aided by the steps of your Imperial Palace! He slaps a policeman on the back and asks his name! He chucks a baby under the chin and asks the mother its name. She lies and says "Marco" although the baby is a girl. He smiles. He is talking loudly so everyone can overhear. He gives the baby one yen to start a savings account and encourage its thrift. The mother looks savagely disappointed. The crowd cheers. He keeps his smile frozen as he notices an artist sketching him. He shakes hands with a one-legged veteran of the Manzi campaign and asks his name. The veteran is touched. Tears come to his eyes. He tells him—but the Polo forgets his name even as he turns to address the crowd. He waves one hand for silence. The band stops. It is the hand on which he wears five large jade rings. The other hand rests upon—and pats—the head of a bronze dragon, our ancient symbol of Yang, the celestial, male principle of the Cosmos. He clears his throat, the crowd stands petrified, he is about to draw a deep breath and open his mouth carefully in position one of the five phonetic exercises— (*Here Chu-Yin chuckles.*) But I am an old man full of malice and venom and it embitters me to see others unreasonably happy so— (*Here just as Marco is heard starting to speak, he throws open the window and calls in a loud, commanding tone*) Messer Polo, His Imperial Majesty commands that you stop talking, dismiss your followers, and repair to his presence at once!

MARCO'S VOICE—(*very faint and crestfallen*) Oh—all right—I'll be right there.

KUBLAI—(*cannot control a laugh in spite of himself—helplessly*) How can one deal seriously with such a child-actor?

CHU-YIN—(*coming back from the window—ironically*) Most women, including Kukachin, love children—and all women must take acting seriously in order to love at all. (*Just as he finishes speaking, Kukachin enters from the left. She is terribly alarmed. She throws herself at Kublai's feet.*)

KUKACHIN—Why did you summon him? I told you he does not know. It is all my fault! Punish me, if you will! But promise me you will not harm him!

KUBLAI—(*looking down at her—sadly*) Is it my custom to take vengeance? (*then as people are heard approaching—quickly*) Compose yourself! Remember again, Princesses may not weep! (*She springs to her feet, turns away for a moment, then turns back, her face rigidly calm and emotionless. Kublai nods with appreciation of her control.*) Good. You will make a Queen. (*She bows and retires backward to the left side of the throne. At the same moment, Nicolo and Maffeo Polo enter ceremoniously from the right. They wear the regalia of officers in the Mystic Knights of Confucius over their rich merchants' robes. [This costume is a queer jumble of stunning effects that recall the parade uniforms of our modern Knights Templar, of Columbus, of Pythias, Mystic Shriners, the Klan, etc.] They are absurdly conscious and proud of this get-up—like two old men in a children's play. Kublai and Chu-Yin regard them with amused astonishment. Even Kukachin cannot restrain a smile. They prostrate themselves at the foot of the throne. Then just at the right moment, preceded by a conscious cough, Marco Polo makes his entrance. Over his gorgeous uniform of Mayor, he wears his childishly fantastic regalia as chief of the Mystic Knights of Confucius. As he steps on, he takes off his gilded, laced hat with its Bird of Paradise plumes and bows with a mechanical dignity on all sides. He has the manner and appearance of a successful movie star at a masquerade ball, disguised so that no one can fail to recognize him. His regular, good-looking, well-groomed face is carefully arranged into the grave responsible expression of a Senator from the South of the United States of America about to propose an amendment to the Constitution restricting the migration of non-Nordic birds into Texas, or prohibiting the practice of the laws of biology within the twelve-mile limit. He moves in stately fashion to the throne and prostrates himself before the Kaan. Kukachin stares at him with boundless admiration, hoping to catch his eye. The Kaan looks from her to him and his face grows stern. Chu-Yin is enjoying himself.*)

KUBLAI—Rise. (*Marco does so. Kublai continues dryly.*) To what do I owe the honor of this unexpected visit?

MARCO—(*hastily, but with full confidence*) Well, I was sending in to your treasury the taxes of Yang-Chau for the fiscal year, and I knew you'd be so astonished at the unprecedented amount I had sweated out of them that you'd want to know how I did it—so here I am. (*An awkward pause. Marco is disconcerted at the Kaan's steady impersonal stare. He glances about—sees the Princess—welcomes this opportunity for diverting attention. Bowing with humble respect*) Pardon me, Princess. I didn't recognize you before, you've gotten so grown up. (*flatteringly*) You look like a Queen.

KUKACHIN—(*falteringly*) I bid you welcome, Your Honor.

KUBLAI—(*as a warning to Kukachin to control her emotion*) The Princess will soon be Queen of Persia.

MARCO—(*flustered and awed, bowing to her again—flatteringly*) Then—Your Majesty—if I may be humbly permitted (*bowing to Kublai*)—to offer my congratulations—and before I settle down to discussing business—if her Highness—Majesty—will accept a small token of my esteem— (*Here he stamps his foot. An African slave, dressed in a pink livery with green hat and shoes and stockings and carrying a golden wicker basket, enters. He kneels, presents the basket to Marco, who lifts the cover and pulls out a small chow puppy with a pink ribbon tied around its neck. He steps forward and offers this to the Princess, with a boyish grin.*) A contribution to your zoo—from your most humble servant!

KUKACHIN—(*taking it—flushing with pleasure*) Oh, what a little darling! (*She cuddles the puppy in her arms.*)

MARCO—(*boastfully*) He's a genuine, pedigreed pup. I procured him at great cost—I mean he's extra well-bred.

KUKACHIN—Oh, thank you so much, Marco Polo! (*stammering*) I mean, Your Honor.

KUBLAI—(*warningly*) His Honor wishes to talk business, Princess.

KUKACHIN—(*controlling herself*) I ask pardon. (*She bows and retires to left, rear, where she stands fondling the puppy and watching Marco.*)

MARCO—(*plunging in confidently on what he thinks is a sure point of attack*) My tax scheme, Your Majesty, that got such wonderful results is simplicity itself. I simply reversed the old system. For one thing I found they had a high tax on excess profits. Imagine a profit being excess! Why, it isn't humanly possible! I repealed it. And I repealed the tax on luxuries. I found out the great majority in Yang-Chau couldn't afford luxuries. The tax wasn't democratic enough to make it pay! I crossed it off and I wrote on the statute books a law that taxes every necessity in life, a law that hits every man's pocket equally, be he beggar or banker! And I got results!

CHU-YIN—(*gravely*) In beggars?

KUBLAI—(*with a chilling air*) I have received a petition from the inhabitants of Yang-Chau enumerating over three thousand cases of your gross abuse of power!

MARCO—(*abashed only for a moment*) Oh, so they've sent that vile slander to you, have they? That's the work of a mere handful of radicals—

KUBLAI—(*dryly*) Five hundred thousand names are signed to it. (*still more dryly*) Half a million citizens accuse you of endeavoring to stamp out their ancient culture!

MARCO—What! Why, I even had a law passed that anyone caught interfering with culture would be subject to a fine! It was Section One of a blanket statute that every citizen must be happy or go to jail. I found it was the unhappy ones who were always making trouble and getting discontented. You see, here's the way I figure it; if a man's good, he's happy—and if he isn't happy, it's a sure sign he's no good to himself or anyone else and he better be put where he can't do harm.

KUBLAI—(*a bit helplessly now*) They complain that you have entirely prohibited all free expression of opinion.

MARCO—(*feelingly*) Well, when they go to the extreme of

circulating such treasonable opinions against me, isn't it time to protect your sovereignty by strong measures? (*Kublai stares at this effrontery with amazement. Marco watches this impression and hurries on with an injured dignity.*) I can't believe, Your Majesty, that this minority of malcontents can have alienated your long-standing high regard for me!

KUBLAI—(*conquered—suddenly overpowered by a great smile*) Not so! You are the marvel of mankind! And I would be lost without you!

MARCO—(*flattered but at the same time nonplussed*) I thank you! (*hesitatingly*) But, to tell the truth, I want to resign, anyhow. I've done all I could. I've appointed five hundred committees to carry on my work and I retire confident that with the system I've instituted everything will go on automatically and brains are no longer needed. (*He adds as a bitter afterthought*) And it's lucky they're not or Yang-Chau would soon be a ruin!

KUBLAI—(*with mock seriousness*) In behalf of the population of Yang-Chau I accept your resignation, with deep regret for the loss of your unique and extraordinary services. (*then suddenly in a strange voice*) Do you still possess your immortal soul, Marco Polo?

MARCO—(*flustered*) Ha-ha! Yes, of course—at least I hope so. But I see the joke. You mean that Yang-Chau used to be a good place to lose one. Well, you wouldn't know the old town now. Sin is practically unseen. (*hurrying on to another subject—boisterously*) But however much I may have accomplished there, it's nothing to the big surprise I've got in reserve for you. May I demonstrate? (*without waiting for permission, takes a piece of printed paper like a dollar bill from his pocket*) What is it? Paper. Correct! What is it worth? Nothing. That's where you're mistaken. It's worth ten yen. No, I'm not a liar! See ten yen written on it, don't you? Well, I'll tell you the secret. This is money, legally valued at ten yen's worth of anything you wish to buy, by order of His Imperial Majesty, the Great Kaan! Do you see my point? Its advantages over gold and silver coin are obvious. It's light, easy to carry,— (*here he gives a prodigious wink*) wears out quickly, can be made at very slight expense and yields enormous profit. Think of getting ten yen for this piece of paper. Yet it can be done.

If you make the people believe it's worth it, it is! After all, when you stop to think, who was it first told them gold was money? I'll bet anything it was some quick-thinker who'd just discovered a gold mine! (*Kublai and Chu-Yin stare at him in petrified incredulity. He mistakes it for admiration and is flattered. Bows and lays his paper money on the Kaan's knee.*) You're stunned, I can see that. It's so simple—and yet, who ever thought of it before me? I was amazed myself. Think it over, Your Majesty, and let the endless possibilities dawn on you! And now I want to show another little aid to government that I thought out. (*He makes a sign to his uncle and father. The former takes a mechanical contrivance out of a box and sets it up on the floor. It is a working model of a clumsy cannon. Nicolo, meanwhile, takes children's blocks out of his box and builds them into a fortress wall. Marco is talking. His manner and voice have become grave and portentous.*) It all came to me, like an inspiration, last Easter Sunday when Father and Uncle and I were holding a little service. Uncle read a prayer which spoke of Our Lord as the Prince of Peace. Somehow, that took hold of me. I thought to myself, well, it's funny, there always have been wars and there always will be, I suppose, because I've never read much in any history about heroes who waged peace. Still, that's wrong. War is a waste of money which eats into the profits of life like thunder! Then why war, I asked myself? But how are you going to end it? Then the flash came! There's only one workable way and that's to conquer everybody else in the world so they'll never dare fight you again! An impossible task, you object? Not any more! This invention you see before you makes conquering easy. Let me demonstrate with these models. On our right, you see the fortress wall of a hostile capital. Under your present system with battering rams, to make an effective breach in this wall would cost you the lives of ten thousand men. Valuing each life conservatively at ten yen, this amounts to one hundred thousand yen! This makes the cost of breaching prohibitive. But all of this waste can be saved. How? Just keep your eyes on your right and permit my exclusive invention to solve this problem. (*He addresses the fortress in a matter-of-fact tone.*) So you won't surrender, eh? (*then in a mock-heroic falsetto, answering himself like a ventriloquist*) We die but we never surrender! (*then matter-of-factly*) Well, Brother, those heroic sentiments do you a lot of credit, but this is war and not a tragedy. You're up against new methods this time, and you better give in and avoid wasteful bloodshed. (*answering himself*) No! Victory or Death! (*then again*) All right, Brother, don't blame me. Fire! (*His uncle fires the gun. There is a bang, and a leaden ball is shot out which knocks a big breach in the wall of blocks. Marco beams. Kukachin gives a scream of fright, then a gasp of delight, and claps her hands. Marco bows to her the more gratefully as Kublai and Chu-Yin are staring at him with a queer appalled wonder that puzzles him although he cannot imagine it is not admiration.*) I see you are stunned again. What made it do that, you're wondering? This! (*He takes a little package out of his pocket and pours some black powder out of it on his palm.*) It's the same powder they've been using here in children's fire works. They've had it under their noses for years without a single soul ever having creative imagination enough to visualize the enormous possibilities. But you can bet I did! It was a lad crying with a finger half blown off where he held a firecracker too long that first opened my eyes. I learned the formula, improved on it, experimented in secret, and here's the gratifying result! (*He takes the cannon ball from his father who has retrieved it.*) You see? Now just picture this little ball magnified into one weighing twenty pounds or so and then you'll really grasp my idea. The destruction of property and loss of life would be tremendous! No one could resist you!

KUBLAI—(*after a pause—musingly*) I am interested in the hero of that city who preferred death to defeat. Did you conquer his immortal soul?

MARCO—(*with frankness*) Well, you can't consider souls when you're dealing with soldiers, can you? (*He takes his model and places it on the Kaan's knee with the paper money.*) When you have time, I wish you'd look this over. In fact—and this is the big idea I've been saving for the last—consider these two inventions of mine in combination. You conquer the world with this—(*he pats the cannon-model*) and you pay for it with this. (*He pats the paper money—rhetorically*) You become the bringer of peace on earth and good-will to men, and it doesn't cost you a yen hardly. Your initial expense—

my price—is as low as I can possibly make it out of my deep affection for your Majesty—only a million yen.

KUBLAI—(*quickly*) In paper?

MARCO—(*with a grin and a wink*) No. I'd prefer gold, if you don't mind. (*Silence. Marco goes on meaningly.*) Of course, I don't want to force them on you. I'm confident there's a ready market for them elsewhere.

KUBLAI—(*grimly smiling*) Oh, I quite realize that in self-protection I've got to buy them—or kill you!

MARCO—(*briskly*) Then it's a bargain? But I've still got one proviso—that you give us permission to go home. (*Kukachin gives a little gasp. Marco goes on feelingly.*) We're homesick, Your Majesty. We've served you faithfully, and frankly now that we've made our fortune we want to go home and enjoy it. There's no place like home, Your Majesty! I'm sure even a King in his palace appreciates that.

KUBLAI—(*with smiling mockery*) But—who can play your part? And your mission—your example? What will your Pope say when you tell him I'm still unconverted?

MARCO—(*confidently*) Oh, you will be—on your death-bed, if not before—a man of your common sense.

KUBLAI—(*ironically*) Courtier! (*then solemnly*) But my last objection is insurmountable. You haven't yet proved you have an immortal soul!

MARCO—It doesn't need proving.

KUBLAI—If you could only bring forward one reliable witness.

MARCO—My Father and Uncle can swear—

KUBLAI—They think it is a family trait. Their evidence is prejudiced.

MARCO—(*worried now—looks at Chu-Yin hopefully*) Mr. Chu-Yin ought to be wise enough to acknowledge—

CHU-YIN—(*smiling*) But I believe that what can be proven cannot be true. (*Marco stands puzzled, irritated, looking stubborn, frightened and foolish. His eyes wander about the room, finally resting appealingly on Kukachin.*)

KUKACHIN—(*suddenly steps forward—flushed but proudly*) I will bear witness he has a soul. (*Kublai looks at her with a sad wonderment, Chu-Yin smilingly, Marco with gratitude, Nicolo and Maffeo exchange a glance of congratulation.*)

KUBLAI—How can you know, Princess?

KUKACHIN—Because I have seen it—once, when he bound up my dog's leg, once when he played with a slave's baby, once when he listened to music over water and I heard him sigh, once when he looked at sunrise, another time at sunset, another at the stars, another at the moon, and each time he said that Nature was wonderful. And all the while, whenever he has been with me I have always felt—something strange and different—and that something must be His Honor's soul, must it not?

KUBLAI—(*with wondering bitterness*) The eye sees only its own sight.

CHU-YIN—But a woman may feel life in the unborn.

KUBLAI—(*mockingly but sadly*) I cannot contest the profound intuitions of virgins and mystics. Go home, Your Honor, Immortal Marco, and live forever! (*with forced gaiety*) And tell your Pope your example has done much to convert me to wisdom—if I could find the true one!

KUKACHIN—(*boldly now*) And may I humbly request, since His Honor, and his father and uncle, are experienced masters of navigation, that they be appointed, for my greater safety, to attend me and command the fleet on my voyage to Persia?

KUBLAI—(*astonished at her boldness—rebukingly*) Princess!

KUKACHIN—(*returning his look—simply*) It is the last favor I shall ever ask. I wish to be converted to wisdom, too—one or another—before I become a name.

KUBLAI—(*bitterly*) I cannot deny your last request, even though you wish your own unhappiness. (*to the Polos*) You will accompany the Princess.

MARCO—(*jubilantly*) I'll be only too glad! (*turning to the Princess*) It'll be a great pleasure! (*then briskly*) And have we your permission to trade in the ports along the way?

KUKACHIN—(*to Marco, embarrassedly*) As you please, Your Honor.

MARCO—(*bowing low*) I'll promise it won't disturb you. It's really a scheme to while away the hours, for I warn you in advance this is liable to be a mighty long trip.

KUKACHIN—(*impulsively*) I do not care how long— (*She stops in confusion.*)

MARCO—Now if I had the kind of ships we build in Venice to work with I could promise you a record passage, but with your tubby junks it's just as well to expect the worst and you'll never be disappointed. (*familiarly*) And the trouble with any ship, for a man of action, is that there's so little you can do. I hate idleness where there's nothing to occupy your mind but thinking. I've been so used to being out, overcoming obstacles, getting things done, creating results where there weren't any before, going after the impossible— well—(*here he gives a little deprecating laugh*) all play and no work makes Jack a dull boy. I'm sure I'd make a pretty dull person to have around if there wasn't plenty to do. You might not believe it, but when I'm idle I actually get gloomy sometimes!

KUKACHIN—(*eagerly*) But we shall have dancers on the ship and actors who will entertain us with plays—

MARCO—(*heartily*) That'll be grand. There's nothing better than to sit down in a good seat at a good play after a good day's work in which you know you've accomplished something, and after you've had a good dinner, and just take it easy and enjoy a good wholesome thrill or a good laugh and get your mind off serious things until it's time to go to bed.

KUKACHIN—(*vaguely*) Yes. (*then eager to have him pleased*) And there will be poets to recite their poems—

MARCO—(*not exactly overjoyed*) That'll be nice. (*then very confidentially—in a humorous whisper*) I'll tell you a good joke on me, Your Highness. I once wrote a poem myself; would you ever believe it to look at me?

KUKACHIN—(*smiling at him as at a boy—teasingly*) No?

MARCO—(*smiling back like a boy*) Yes, I did too, when I was young and foolish. It wasn't bad stuff either, considering I'd had no practice. (*frowning with concentration*) Wait! Let me see if I can remember any—oh, yes— "You are lovely as the gold in the sun." (*He hesitates.*)

KUKACHIN—(*thrilled*) That is beautiful!

MARCO—That's only the first line. (*then jokingly*) You can consider yourself lucky. I don't remember the rest.

KUKACHIN—(*dropping her eyes—softly*) Perhaps on the voyage you may be inspired to write another.

KUBLAI—(*who has been staring at them with weary amazement*) Life is so stupid, it is mysterious!

(*Darkness*)

SCENE TWO

SCENE—*The wharves of the Imperial Fleet at the seaport of Zayton—several weeks later. At the left, stern to, is an enormous junk, the flagship. The wharf extends out, rear, to the right of her. At the right is a warehouse, from a door in which a line of half-naked slaves, their necks, waists, and right ankles linked up by chains, form an endless chain which revolves mechanically, as it were, on sprocket wheels in the interiors of the shed and the junk. As each individual link passes out of the shed it carries a bale on its head, moves with mechanical precision across the wharf, disappears into the junk, and reappears a moment later having dumped its load and moves back into the shed. The whole process is a man-power original of the modern devices with bucket scoops that dredge, load coal, sand, etc. By the side of the shed, a foreman sits with a drum and gong with which he marks a perfect time for the slaves, a four beat rhythm, three beats of the drum, the fourth a bang on the gong as one slave at each end loads and unloads. The effect is like the noise of a machine.*

A bamboo stair leads up to the high poop of the junk from front, left. It is just getting dawn. A forest of masts, spars, sails of woven bamboo laths, shuts out all view of the harbor at the end of the wharf. At the foot of the stairs, Chu-Yin stands like a sentinel. Above on top of the poop, the figures of Kublai and Kukachin are outlined against the lightening sky.

KUBLAI—(*brokenly*) I must go. (*He takes her in his arms.*) We have said all we can say. Little Daughter, all rare things are secrets which cannot be revealed to anyone. That is why life must be so lonely. But I love you more dearly than anything on earth. And I know you love me. So perhaps we do not need to understand. (*rebelliously*) Yet I wish some Power could give me assurance that in granting your desire I am acting for your happiness, and for your eventual deliverance from sorrow to acceptance and peace. (*He notices she is weeping—in self-reproach*) Old fool! I have made you weep again! I am death advising life how to live! Be deaf to me! Strive after what your heart desires! Who can ever know which are the mistakes we make? One should be either sad or joyful. Contentment is a warm sty for the eaters and sleepers! (*impulsively*) Do not weep! Even now I can refuse your hand to Arghun. Let it mean war!

KUKACHIN—(*looking up and controlling herself—with a sad finality*) You do not understand. I wish to take this voyage.

KUBLAI—(*desperately*) But I could keep Polo here. (*with impotent anger*) He shall pray for his soul on his knees before you!

KUKACHIN—(*with calm sadness*) Do I want a slave? (*dreamily*) I desire a captain of my ship on a long voyage in dangerous, enchanted seas.

KUBLAI—(*with a fierce defiance of fate*) I am the Great Kaan! I shall have him killed! (*a pause*)

CHU-YIN—(*from below, recites in a calm, soothing tone*) The noble man ignores self. The wise man ignores action. His truth acts without deeds. His knowledge venerates the unknowable. To him birth is not the beginning nor is death the end. (*Kublai's head bends in submission. Chu-Yin continues tenderly*) I feel there are tears in your eyes. The Great Kaan, Ruler of the World, may not weep.

KUBLAI—(*brokenly*) Ruler? I am my slave! (*then controlling himself—forcing an amused teasing tone*) Marco will soon be here, wearing the self-assurance of an immortal soul and his new admiral's uniform! I must fly in retreat from what I can neither laugh away nor kill. Write when you reach Persia. Tell me—all you can tell—particularly what his immortal soul is like! (*then tenderly*) Farewell, Little Flower! Live. There is no other advice possible from one human being to another.

KUKACHIN—Live—and love!

KUBLAI—(*trying to renew his joking tone*) One's ancestors, particularly one's grandfather. Do not forget me!

KUKACHIN—Never! (*They embrace.*)

KUBLAI—(*chokingly*) Farewell. (*He hurries down the ladder—to Chu-Yin*) You remain—see him—bring me word—

(*He turns his head up to Kukachin.*) For the last time, farewell, Little Flower of my life! May you know happiness! (*He turns quickly and goes.*)

KUKACHIN—Farewell! (*She bows her head on the rail and weeps.*)

CHU-YIN—(*after a pause*) You are tired, Princess. Your eyes are red from weeping and your nose is red. You look old—a little homely, even. The Admiral Polo will not recognize you. (*Kukachin dries her eyes hastily.*)

KUKACHIN—(*half-smiling and half-weeping at his teasing*) I think you are a very horrid old man!

CHU-YIN—A little sleep, Princess, and you will be beautiful. The old dream passes. Sleep and awake in the new. Life is perhaps most wisely regarded as a bad dream between two awakenings, and every day is a life in miniature.

KUKACHIN—(*wearily and drowsily*) Your wisdom makes me sleep. (*Her head sinks back on her arms and she is soon asleep.*)

CHU-YIN—(*after a pause—softly*) Kukachin! (*He sees she is asleep—chuckles.*) I have won a convert. (*then speculatively*) Youth needs so much sleep and old age so little. Is that not a proof that from birth to death one grows steadily closer to complete life? Hum. (*He ponders on this. From the distance comes the sound of Polo's band playing the same martial air as in the previous scene. Chu-Yin starts—then smiles. The music quickly grows louder. The Princess awakes with a start.*)

KUKACHIN—(*startledly*) Chu-Yin! Is that the Admiral coming?

CHU-YIN—(*dryly*) I suspect so. It is like him not to neglect a person in the city when saying good-bye.

KUKACHIN—(*flurriedly*) I must go to my cabin for a moment. (*She hurries back.*)

CHU-YIN—(*listens with a pleased, ironical smile as the band gets rapidly nearer. Finally it seems to turn a corner nearby, and a moment later, to a deafening clangor, Marco enters, dressed in a gorgeous Admiral's uniform. Two paces behind, side by side, walk Maffeo and Nicolo, dressed only a trifle less gorgeously as Commodores. Behind them comes the band. Marco halts as he sees Chu-Yin, salutes condescendingly, and signals the band to be silent. Chu-Yin bows gravely and remarks as if answering an argument in his own mind*) Still, even though they cannot be house-broken, I prefer monkeys because they are so much less noisy.

MARCO—(*with a condescending grin*) What's that—more philosophy? (*clapping him on the back*) Well, I like your determination. (*He wipes his brow with a handkerchief.*) Phew! I'll certainly be glad to get back home where I can hear some music that I can keep step to. My feet just won't give in to your tunes. (*with a grin*) And look at the Old Man and Uncle. They're knock-kneed for life. (*confidentially*) Still, I thought the band was a good idea—to sort of cheer up the Princess, and let people know she's leaving at the same time. (*as people begin to come in and stare at the poop of the ship*) See the crowd gather? I got them out of bed, too!

CHU-YIN—(*ironically*) You also woke up the Princess. You sail at sunrise?

MARCO—(*briskly—taking operations in hand*) Thank you for reminding me. I've got to hurry. (*to his father and uncle*) You two better get aboard your ships and be ready to cast off when I signal. (*They go off. He suddenly bawls to someone in the ship*) Much more cargo to load?

A VOICE—Less than a hundred bales, sir.

MARCO—Good. Call all hands on deck and stand by to put sail on her.

A VOICE—Aye-aye, sir.

MARCO—And look lively, damn your lazy souls! (*to Chu-Yin—complacently*) You've got to impose rigid discipline on shipboard.

CHU-YIN—(*inquisitively*) I suppose you feel your heavy responsibility as escort to the future Queen of Persia?

MARCO—(*soberly*) Yes, I do. I'll confess I do. If she were a million yen's worth of silk or spices, I wouldn't worry an instant, but a Queen, that's a different matter. However, when you give my last word to His Majesty, you can tell him that I've always done my duty by him and I won't fail him this time. As long as I've a breath in me, I'll take care of her!

CHU-YIN—(*with genuine appreciation*) That is bravely spoken.

MARCO—I don't know anything about brave speaking. I'm by nature a silent man, and I let my actions do the talking.

But, as I've proved to you people in Cathay time and again, when I say I'll do a thing, I do it!

CHU-YIN—(*suddenly with a sly smile to himself*) I was forgetting. His Majesty gave me some secret last instructions for you. You are, at some time every day of the voyage, to look carefully and deeply into the Princess's eyes and note what you see there.

MARCO—What for? (*then brightly*) Oh, he's afraid she'll get fever in the tropics. Well, you tell him I'll see to it she keeps in good condition. I'll do what's right by her without considering fear or favor. (*then practically*) Then, of course, if her husband thinks at the end of the voyage that my work deserves a bonus—why, that's up to him. (*inquisitively*) She's never seen him, has she?

CHU-YIN—No.

MARCO—(*with an air of an independent thinker*) Well, I believe in love matches myself, even for Kings and Queens. (*with a grin*) Come to think of it, I'll be getting married to Donata myself when I get home.

CHU-YIN—Donata?

MARCO—(*proudly*) The best little girl in the world! She's there waiting for me.

CHU-YIN—You have heard from her?

MARCO—I don't need to hear. I can trust her. And I've been true to her, too. I haven't ever thought of loving anyone else. Of course, I don't mean I've been any he-virgin. I've played with concubines at odd moments when my mind needed relaxation—but that's only human nature. (*his eyes glistening reminiscently*) Some of them were beauties, too! (*with a sigh*) Well, I've had my fun and I suppose it's about time I settled down.

CHU-YIN—Poor Princess!

MARCO—What's that? Oh, I see, yes, I sympathize with her, too—going into a harem. If there's one thing more than another that proves you in the East aren't responsible, it's that harem notion. (*with a grin*) Now in the West we've learned by experience that one at a time is trouble enough.

CHU-YIN—(*dryly*) Be sure and converse on love and marriage often with the Princess. I am certain you will cure her.

MARCO—(*mystified*) Cure her?

CHU-YIN—Cure her mind of any unreasonable imaginings.

MARCO—(*easily*) Oh, I'll guarantee she'll be contented, if that's what you mean. (*The human chain in back finishes its labors and disappears into the shed. The crowd of people has been steadily augmented by new arrivals, until a small multitude is gathered standing in silence staring up at the poop. Marco says with satisfaction*) Well, cargo's all aboard, before schedule, too. We killed six slaves but, by God, we did it! And look at the crowd we've drawn, thanks to my band!

CHU-YIN—(*disgustedly*) They would have come without noise. They love their Princess.

MARCO—(*cynically*) Maybe, but they love their sleep, too. I know 'em! (*A cry of adoration goes up from the crowd. With one movement they prostrate themselves as the Princess comes from the cabin dressed in a robe of silver and stands at the rail looking down.*)

THE CROWD—(*in a long, ululating whisper*) Farewell—farewell—farewell—farewell!

KUKACHIN—(*silences them with a motion of her hand*)
I shall know the long sorrow of an exile
As I sail over the green water and the blue water
Alone under a strange sky amid alien flowers and faces.
My eyes shall be ever red with weeping, my heart bleeding,
While I long for the land of my birth and my childhood
Remembering with love the love of my people.
(*A sound of low weeping comes from the crowd.*) Farewell!

THE CROWD—Farewell—farewell—farewell—farewell!

MARCO—(*feeling foolish because he is moved*) Damn it! Reciting always makes me want to cry about something. Poetry acts worse on me than wine that way. (*He calls up—very respectfully*) Princess! We'll be sailing at once. Would you mind retiring to your cabin? I'm afraid you're going to catch cold standing bareheaded in the night air.

KUKACHIN—(*tremulously—grateful for his solicitude*) I am in your charge, Admiral. I am grateful that you should think of my health, and I obey. (*She turns and goes back into her cabin. The crowd silently filters away, leaving only the band.*)

MARCO—(*proudly and fussily*) You can't have women around when you're trying to get something done. I can see where I'll have to be telling her what to do every second. Well, I hope she'll take it in good part and not forget I'm acting in her husband's interests, not my own. (*very confidentially*) You know, apart from her being a Princess, I've always respected her a lot. She's not haughty and she's—well, human, that's what I mean. I'd do anything I could for her, Princess or not! Yes, sir!

CHU-YIN—(*wonderingly*) There may be hope—after all.

MARCO—What's that?

CHU-YIN—Nothing. Enigma!

MARCO—There's always hope! Don't be a damned pessimist! (*clapping him on the back*) Enigma, eh? Well, if that isn't like a philosopher—to start in on riddles just at the last moment! (*He ascends half-way up the ladder to the poop, then turns back to Chu-Yin with a chuckle.*) Take a fool's advice and don't think so much or you'll get old before your time! (*more oratorically*) If you look before you leap, you'll decide to sit down. Keep on going ahead and you can't help being right! You're bound to get somewhere! (*He suddenly breaks into a grin again.*) There! Don't ever say I never gave you good advice! (*He springs swiftly to the top deck and bellows*) Cast off there amidships! Where the hell are you—asleep? Set that foresail! Hop, you kidney-footed gang of thumb-fingered infidels! (*He turns with a sudden fierceness on the band who are standing stolidly, awaiting orders.*) Hey you! Didn't I tell you to strike up when I set foot on the deck? What do you think I paid you in advance for—to wave me good-bye? (*The band plunges madly into it. A frenzied cataract of sound results. Chu-Yin covers his ears and moves away, shaking his head, as Marco leans over the rail and bawls after him*) And tell the Kaan—anything he wants—write me—just Venice—they all know me there—and if they don't, by God, they're going to!

(*Darkness*)

SCENE THREE

SCENE—*Poop deck of the royal junk of the Princess Kukachin at anchor in the harbor of Hormuz, Persia—a moonlight night some two years later. On a silver throne at center Kukachin is sitting dressed in a gorgeous golden robe of ceremony. Her beauty has grown more intense, her face has undergone a change, it is the face of a woman who has known real sorrow and suffering. In the shadow of the highest deck in rear her women-in-waiting are in a group, sitting on cushions. On the highest deck in rear sailors lower and furl the sail of the mizzenmast, every movement being carried out in unison with a machine-like rhythm. The bulwarks of the junk are battered and splintered, the sail is frayed and full of jagged holes and patches. In the foreground (the port side of deck) the two elder Polos are squatting. Each has a bag of money before him from which they are carefully counting gold coins and packing stacks of these into a chest that stands between them.*

MARCO—(*His voice, hoarse and domineering, comes from the left just before the curtain rises.*) Let go that anchor! (*A meek "Aye-aye, sir," is heard replying and then a great splash and a long rattling of chains. The curtain then rises discovering the scene as above. Marco's voice is again heard.*) Lower that mizzensail! Look lively now!

BOATSWAIN—(*with the sailors*) Aye-aye, sir! (*They lower the sail, and begin to tie it up trimly.*)

MAFFEO—(*looking up and straightening his cramped back—with a relieved sigh*) Here's Persia! I'll be glad to get on dry land again. Two years on this foreign tub are too much.

NICOLO—(*with a grunt, intent on the money*) Keep counting if you want to finish before we go ashore. It's nine hundred thousand now in our money, isn't it?

MAFFEO—(*nods—counting again*) This lot will bring it to a million. (*He begins stacking and packing again.*)

BOATSWAIN—(*chanting as his men work*)
        Great were the waves
        Volcanoes of foam
        Ridge after ridge
        To the rim of the world!
        Great were the waves!

CHORUS OF
SAILORS— Great were the waves!

BOATSWAIN—Fierce were the winds!
    Demons screamed!
    Their claws rended
    Sails into rags,
    Fierce were the winds!
CHORUS—   Fierce were the winds!
BOATSWAIN—Fire was the sun!
    Boiled the blood black,
    Our veins hummed
    Like bronze kettles.
    Fire was the sun!
CHORUS—   Fire was the sun!
BOATSWAIN—Long was the voyage!
    Life drifted becalmed,
    A dead whale awash
    In the toil of tides.
    Long was the voyage!
CHORUS—   Long was the voyage!
BOATSWAIN—Many have died!
    Sleep in green water.
    Wan faces at home
    Pray to the sea.
    Many have died!
CHORUS—   Many have died!
KUKACHIN—(*chants the last line after them—sadly*)
    Many have died!
(*After a brooding pause she rises and chants in a low voice*)
    If I were asleep in green water,
    No pang could be added to my
      sorrow,
    Old grief would be forgotten,
    I would know peace
SAILORS—   There is peace deep in the sea
    But the surface is sorrow.
WOMEN—   Kukachin will be a Queen!
    A Queen may not sorrow
    Save for her King!
KUKACHIN—When love is not loved it loves death.
    When I sank drowning, I loved
      Death.

When the pirate's knife gleamed, I
    loved Death.
When fever burned me I loved
    Death.
But the man I love saved me.

SAILORS— Death lives in a silent sea,
Gray and cold under cold gray
    sky,
Where there is neither sun nor
    wind
Nor joy nor sorrow!

WOMEN— Kukachin will be a wife.
A wife must not sorrow
Save for her man.

KUKACHIN— A hero is merciful to women.
Why could not this man see or
    feel or know?
Then he would have let me die.

SAILORS— There are harbors at every
    voyage-end
Where we rest from the sorrows
    of the sea.

WOMEN— Kukachin will be a mother
A mother may not sorrow
Save for her son.

(*Kukachin bows her head in resignation. A pause of silence.*)

(*Marco Polo enters briskly from below on the left. He is dressed in full uniform, looking spick and span and self-conscious. His face wears an expression of humorous scorn. He bows ceremoniously to the Princess, his attitude a queer mixture of familiarity and an uncertain awe.*)

MARCO—Your Highness—(*then ingratiatingly*)—or I suppose I'd better say Majesty now that we've reached Persia—I've got queer news for you. A boat just came from the shore with an official notification that your intended husband, Arghun Khan, is dead and I'm to hand you over to his son, Ghazan, to marry. (*He hands her a sealed paper.*) See!

KUKACHIN—(*letting the paper slip from her hand without a glance—dully*) What does it matter?

MARCO—(*admiringly—as he picks it up*) I must say you

take it coolly. Of course, come to think of it, never having seen either, one's as good as another. (*He winds up philosophically*) And you'll be Queen just the same, that's the main thing.

KUKACHIN—(*with bitter irony*) So you think that is happiness? (*Then as Marco stares at her uncertainly, she turns away and looks out over the sea with a sigh—after a pause*) There, where I see the lights, is that Hormuz?

MARCO—Yes. And I was forgetting, the messenger said Ghazan Khan would come to take you ashore tonight.

KUKACHIN—(*with sudden fear*) So soon? Tonight? (*then rebelliously*) Is the granddaughter of the Great Kublai no better than a slave? I will not go until it pleases me!

MARCO—Good for you! That's the spirit! (*then alarmed at his own temerity—hastily*) But don't be rash! The Khan probably meant whenever you were willing. And don't mind what I just said.

KUKACHIN—(*looks at him with a sudden dawning of hope—gently*) Why should you be afraid of what you said?

MARCO—(*offended*) I'm not afraid of anything—when it comes to the point!

KUKACHIN—What point?

MARCO—(*nonplussed*) Why—well—when I feel someone's trying to steal what's rightfully mine, for instance.

KUKACHIN—And now—here—you do not feel that?

MARCO—(*with a forced laugh, thinking she is joking*) Ha! Well— (*uncertainly*) That is—I don't catch your meaning— (*then changing the subject abruptly*) But here's something I want to ask you. Your grandfather entrusted you to my care. He relied on me to prove equal to the task of bringing you safe and sound to your husband. Now I want to ask you frankly if you yourself won't be the first to acknowledge that in spite of typhoons, shipwrecks, pirates and every other known form of bad luck, I've brought you through in good shape?

KUKACHIN—(*with an irony almost hysterical*) More than anyone in the world, I can appreciate your devotion to duty! You have been a prodigy of heroic accomplishment! In the typhoon when a wave swept me from the deck, was it not you who swam to me as I was drowning?

MARCO—(*modestly*) It was easy. Venetians make the best swimmers in the world.

KUKACHIN—(*even more ironically*) When the pirates attacked us, was it not your brave sword that warded off their curved knives from my breast and struck them dead at my feet?

MARCO—I was out of practice, too. I used to be one of the crack swordsmen of Venice—and they're the world's foremost, as everyone knows.

KUKACHIN—(*with a sudden change—softly*) And when the frightful fever wasted me, was it not you who tended me night and day, watching by my bedside like a gentle nurse, even brewing yourself the medicines that brought me back to life?

MARCO—(*with sentimental solemnity*) My mother's recipes. Simple home remedies—from the best friend I ever had!

KUKACHIN—(*a trifle wildly*) Oh, yes, you have been a model guardian, Admiral Polo!

MARCO—(*quickly*) Thank you, Princess. If I have satisfied you—then if I might ask you a favor, that you put in writing all you've just said in your first letter to the Great Kaan, and also tell your husband?

KUKACHIN—(*suddenly wildly bitter*) I will assuredly! I will tell them both of your heroic cruelty in saving me from death! (*intensely*) Why could you not let me die?

MARCO—(*confusedly*) You're joking. You certainly didn't want to die, did you?

KUKACHIN—(*slowly and intensely*) Yes!

MARCO—(*puzzled and severe*) Hum! You shouldn't talk that way.

KUKACHIN—(*longingly*) I would be asleep in green water!

MARCO—(*worriedly, suddenly reaches out and takes her hand*) Here now, young lady! Don't start getting morbid!

KUKACHIN—(*with a thrill of love*) Marco!

MARCO—I believe you're feverish. Let me feel your pulse!

KUKACHIN—(*violently*) No! (*She draws her hand from his as if she had been stung.*)

MARCO—(*worriedly*) Please don't be unreasonable. There'd be the devil to pay if you should suffer a relapse of that fever after I sweated blood to pull you through once already! Do you feel hot?

KUKACHIN—(*wildly*) No! Yes! On fire!

MARCO—Are your feet cold?

KUKACHIN—No! Yes! I don't know! (*Gravely Marco kneels, removes a slipper, and feels the sole of her foot—then pats her foot playfully.*)

MARCO—No. They're all right. (*He gets up—professionally*) Any cramps?

KUKACHIN—You fool! No! Yes! My heart feels as if it were bursting!

MARCO—It burns?

KUKACHIN—Like a red ember flaring up for the last time before it chills into gray ash forever!

MARCO—Then something must have disagreed with you. Will you let me see your tongue?

KUKACHIN—(*in a queer hysterical state where she delights in self-humiliation*) Yes! Yes! Anything! I am a Princess of the Imperial blood of Chinghiz and you are a dog! Anything! (*She sticks out her tongue, the tears streaming down her face as he looks at it.*)

MARCO—(*shakes his head*) No sign of biliousness. There's nothing seriously wrong. If you would only try to sleep a while—

KUKACHIN—O Celestial God of the Heavens! What have I done that Thou shouldst torture me? (*then wildly to Marco*) I wished to sleep in the depths of the sea. Why did you awaken me?

MARCO—(*worried again*) Perhaps it's brain fever. Does your head ache?

KUKACHIN—No! Does your immortal soul?

MARCO—Don't blaspheme! You're talking as if you were delirious! (*then pleadingly*) For Heaven's sake, try and be calm, Princess! What if your husband, Ghazan Khan, should find you in such a state?

KUKACHIN—(*calming herself with difficulty—after a pause, bitterly*) I suppose you are relieved to get me here alive and deliver me—like a cow!

MARCO—(*injuredly*) I've only carried out your own grandfather's orders!

KUKACHIN—(*forcing a smile*) Won't you miss being my guardian? (*striving pitifully to arouse his jealousy*) When you think of Ghazan protecting me and nursing me when I am sick—and—and loving me? Yes! I will compel him to love me, even though I never love him! He shall look into my eyes and see that I am a woman and beautiful!

MARCO—That's a husband's privilege.

KUKACHIN—Or a man's—a man who has a soul! (*mockingly but intensely*) And that reminds me, Admiral Polo! You are taking advantage of this being the last day to shirk your duty!

MARCO—Shirk! No one can ever say—!

KUKACHIN—It was my grandfather's special command, given to you by Chu-Yin, you told me, that every day you should look into my eyes.

MARCO—(*resignedly*) Well, it isn't too late yet, is it? (*He moves toward her with a sigh of half-impatience with her whims.*)

KUKACHIN—Wait. This is the one part of your duty in which I shall have to report you incompetent.

MARCO—(*hurt*) I've done my best. I never could discover anything out of the way.

KUKACHIN—There must be something he wished you to find. I myself feel there is something, something I cannot understand, something you must interpret for me! And remember this is your last chance! There is nothing in life I would not give—nothing I would not do—even now it is not too late! See my eyes as those of a woman and not a Princess! Look deeply! I will die if you do not see what is there! (*She finishes hysterically and beseechingly.*)

MARCO—(*worried—soothingly*) There! There! Certainly, Princess! Of course, I'll look. And will you promise me that afterwards you'll lie down?

KUKACHIN—Look! See! (*She throws her head back, her arms outstretched. He bends over and looks into her eyes. She raises her hands slowly above his head as if she were going to pull it down to hers. Her lips part, her whole being strains out to him. He looks for a moment critically, then he grows tense, his face moves hypnotically toward hers, their lips seem about to meet in a kiss. She murmurs*) Marco!

MARCO—(*his voice thrilling for this second with oblivious passion*) Kukachin!

MAFFEO—(*suddenly slapping a stack of coins into the chest with a resounding clank*) One million!

MARCO—(*with a start, comes to himself and backs away from the Princess in terror*) What, Uncle? Did you call?

MAFFEO—One million in God's money! (*He and Nicolo lock and fasten the box jubilantly.*)

KUKACHIN—(*in despair*) Marco!

MARCO—(*flusteredly*) Yes, Princess. I saw something queer! It made me feel feverish too! (*recovering a bit—with a sickly smile*) Oh, there's trouble there, all right! You must be delirious! I advise you to go to sleep.

KUKACHIN—(*with wild despair pulls out a small dagger from the bosom of her dress*) I obey! I shall sleep forever! (*But Marco, the man of action, springs forward and wresting the dagger from her hand, flings it over the side. She confronts him defiantly, her eyes wild with grief and rage. He stares at her, dumbfounded and bewildered.*)

MARCO—(*bewilderedly*) I never believed people—sane people—ever seriously tried—

KUKACHIN—(*intensely*) I implored an ox to see my soul! I no longer can endure the shame of living!

MARCO—(*sheepishly*) You mean it was a terrible insult when I called you—by your name?

KUKACHIN—(*bursting into hysterical laughter*) Yes! How dared you!

MARCO—(*hastily*) I ask pardon, Princess! Please forgive me! My only excuse is, I forgot myself. I guess I'll have to stop overworking or I'll suffer a nervous breakdown. I felt like one of those figures in a puppet show with someone jerking the wires. It wasn't me, you understand. My lips spoke without me saying a word. And here's the funniest part of it all, and what'll explain matters in full, if you can believe it. It wasn't you I was seeing and talking to, not a Princess at all, you'd changed into someone else, someone I've got a good right to—just a girl—

KUKACHIN—(*again clutching at hope*) A girl—a woman— you saw in me?

MARCO—(*enthusiastically, groping in his shirt front*) Yes.

Here she is! (*He jerks the locket out of an under pocket and presents it to her proudly.*) The future Mrs. Marco Polo! (*The Princess takes it mechanically and stares at it in a stupor as Marco rambles on.*)

MARCO—You may believe it or not but like a flash she was standing there in your place and I was talking to her, not you at all!

KUKACHIN—(*dully*) But it was my name you spoke.

MARCO—(*confused*) I meant to say Donata. That's her name. We're going to be married as soon as I get home. (*then as she stares at the miniature—proudly*) Pretty, isn't she?

KUKACHIN—(*dully*) She may have married another.

MARCO—(*confidently*) No. Her family needs an alliance with our house.

KUKACHIN—She may have had lovers.

MARCO—(*simply*) Oh, no. She's not that kind.

KUKACHIN—(*staring at the picture*) She will be middle-aged—fat—and stupid!

MARCO—(*with a grin*) Well, I don't mind a wife being a bit plump—and who wants a great thinker around the house? Sound common sense and a home where everything runs smooth, that's what I'm after.

KUKACHIN—(*looks from him to the miniature*) There is no soul even in your love, which is no better than a mating of swine! And I—! (*A spasm of pain covers her face—then with hatred and disdain*) Pig of a Christian! Will you return to this sow and boast that a Princess and a Queen—? (*with rage*) Shall I ask as my first wedding present from Ghazan Khan that he have you flayed and thrown into the street to be devoured by dogs?

MAFFEO AND NICOLO—(*who have pricked up their ears at this last, rush to the Princess, dragging their box between them and prostrate themselves at her feet*) Mercy! Mercy! (*She seems not to hear or to see them but stares ahead stonily. Marco beckons Maffeo to one side.*)

MARCO—(*in a whisper*) Don't be afraid. She doesn't mean a word of it. She's hysterical. Listen, I just noticed the royal barge coming. I'll go and meet the Khan. You keep her from doing anything rash until he gets here.

MAFFEO—Yes. (*He goes back and crouches again before the Princess, keeping a wary eye on her, but she seems turned to stone. Marco comes down and goes off Left. There is the blare of a trumpet, the reflections of lanterns and torches, the sound of running about on deck and Marco's voice giving commands. The women come out to attend the Princess. She remains rigid, giving no sign.*)

WOMEN—(*in chorus*)
> The lover comes,
> Who becomes a husband,
> Who becomes a son,
> Who becomes a father—
> In this contemplation lives the woman.

KUKACHIN—(*her face now a fatalistic mask of acceptance*)
> I am not.
> Life is.
> A cloud hides the sun.
> A life is lived.
> The sun shines again.
> Nothing has changed.
> Centuries wither into tired dust.
> A new dew freshens the grass.
> Somewhere this dream is being dreamed.

(*From the left Marco comes escorting Ghazan Khan, attended by a train of nobles and slaves with lights. He can be heard saying:* "She is a little feverish—the excitement—" *All are magnificently dressed, glittering with jewels. Ghazan is a young man, not handsome but noble and manly looking. He comes forward and bows low before her, his attendants likewise. Then he looks into her face and stands fascinated by her beauty. She looks back at him with a calm indifference.*)

GHAZAN—(*after a pause—his voice thrilling with admiration*) If it were possible for a son who loved a noble father to rejoice at that father's death, then I should be that guilty son! (*as she makes no reply*) You have heard? Arghun Khan is dead. You must bear the humiliation of accepting his son for husband, a crow to replace an eagle! Forgive me. But with your eyes to watch I may become at least a shadow of his greatness.

KUKACHIN—(*calmly*) What am I? I shall obey the eternal will which governs your destiny and mine.

GHAZAN—(*impetuously*) You are more beautiful than I had dared to dream! It shall not be I who rules, but you! I shall be your slave! Persia shall be your conquest and everywhere where songs are sung they shall be in praise of your beauty! You shall be Queen of Love—!

KUKACHIN—(*sharply with pain*) No! (*She drops the locket on the floor and grinds it into pieces under her foot.*)

MARCO—(*excitedly*) Princess! Look out! You're stepping on— (*She kicks it away from her. Marco stoops on his knees and begins picking up the wreckage in his handkerchief.*)

KUKACHIN—(*turns to Ghazan and points to Marco*) My first request of you, my Lord, is that you reward this Christian who has brought me here in safety. I ask, as a fitting tribute to his character, that you give an immense feast in his honor. Let there be food in tremendous amounts! He is an exquisite judge of quantity. Let him be urged to eat and drink until he can hold no more, until he becomes his own ideal figure, an idol of stuffed self-satisfaction! Will you do this? (*She is a trifle hectic now and her manner has grown wilder.*)

GHAZAN—Your wish is my will!

KUKACHIN—(*pointing to a magnificent lion in diamonds on his breast*) What is that wonderful glittering beast?

GHAZAN—It is the emblem of the Order of the Lion which only great heroes and kings of men may wear.

KUKACHIN—(*gives a laugh of wild irony*) Great heroes— kings of men? (*then eagerly*) Will you give it to me? I implore you! (*Ghazan, fascinated, yet with a wondering glance, unpins it and hands it to her without a word. She prods Marco, who is still collecting the pieces of the locket, with her foot.*) Arise! Let me give you the noble Order of the Lion! (*She pins the blazing diamond figure on the breast of the stunned Marco, laughing with bitter mockery.*) How well it is set off on the bosom of a sheep! (*She laughs more wildly.*) Kneel again! Bring me a chest of gold! (*Ghazan makes a sign. Two slaves bring a chest of gold coins to her. She takes handfuls and throws them over the kneeling forms of the Polos, laughing.*) Here! Guzzle! Grunt! Wallow for our amusement! (*The two elder are surreptitiously snatching at the coins but Marco jumps to his feet, his face flushing.*)

MARCO—(*in a hurt tone*) I don't see why you're trying to insult me—just at the last moment. What have I done? (*then suddenly forcing a smile*) But I realize you're not yourself.

GHAZAN—(*sensing something*) Has this man offended you? Shall he be killed?

KUKACHIN—(*wearily*) No. He has amused me. Let him be fed. Stuff him with food and gold and send him home. And you, My Lord, may I ask that this first night I be allowed to remain on board alone with my women? I am weary!

GHAZAN—Again your wish is my will, even though I will not live until I see you again!

KUKACHIN—(*exhaustedly*) I am humbly grateful. Good night, My Lord. (*She bows. Ghazan and the Court bow before her. They retire toward the left, Marco talking earnestly to the oblivious Ghazan whose eyes are riveted on the Princess, who has turned away from them. The two elder Polos, carrying their chest, their pockets stuffed, trudge along last.*)

MARCO—The close confinement of a long voyage. I think probably her spleen is out of order. (*They are gone from sight. Kukachin's shoulders quiver as, her head bowed in her hands, she sobs quietly. The ship can be heard making off.*)

WOMEN—Weep, Princess of the Wounded Heart,
       Weeping heals the wounds of sorrow
       Till only the scars remain
       And the heart forgets.

KUKACHIN—(*suddenly runs up to the upper deck and stands outlined against the sky, her arms outstretched—in a voice which is a final, complete renunciation, calls*) Farewell, Marco Polo!

MARCO—(*His voice comes from over the water, cheery and relieved.*) Good-bye, Your Majesty—and all best wishes for long life and happiness! (*The Princess sinks to her knees, her face hidden in her arms on the bulwark.*)

(*Curtain*)

ACT THREE

Scene One

Scene—*One year later.*

The Grand Throne Room in the Imperial palace at Cambaluc. Kublai squats on his throne, aged and sad, listening with an impassive face to General Bayan who, dressed in the full military uniform and armor of the Commander-in-Chief is explaining earnestly with several maps in his hand. On Kublai's left stands Chu-Yin, who is reading. Behind Bayan are grouped at attention all the generals of his army with a multitude of young staff officers, all gorgeously uniformed and armored. From the room on the right, the ballroom, a sound of dance music and laughter comes through the closed doors.

BAYAN—(*impressively—pointing to the map*) Here, Your Majesty, is the line of the river Danube which marks the Western boundary of your Empire. Beyond it, lies the West. Our spies report their many petty states are always quarreling. So great is their envy of each other that we could crush each singly and the rest would rejoice. We can mobilize one million horsemen on the Danube within a month. (*proudly*) We would ride their armies down into the sea! Your Empire would extend from ocean to ocean!

KUBLAI—(*wearily*) It is much too large already. Why do you want to conquer the West? It must be a pitiful land, poor in spirit and material wealth. We have everything to lose by contact with its greedy hypocrisy. The conqueror acquires first of all the vices of the conquered. Let the West devour itself.

BAYAN—(*helplessly*) But—everywhere in the East there is peace!

KUBLAI—(*with hopeless irony*) Ah! And you are becoming restless?

BAYAN—(*proudly*) I am a Mongol—a man of action!

KUBLAI—(*looking at him with musing irony*) Hum! You have already conquered the West, I think.

BAYAN—(*puzzled*) What, Your Majesty? (*then persuasively*) The West may not be strong but it is crafty. Remember how that Christian, Polo, invented the engine to batter down walls? It would be better to wipe out their cunning now before they make too many engines to weaken the power of men. (*then with a sudden inspiration*) And it would be a righteous war! We would tear down their Christian Idols and set up the image of the Buddha!

KUBLAI—Buddha, the Prince of Peace?

BAYAN—(*bowing his head as do all his retinue*) The Gentle One, The Good, The Kind, The Pitiful, The Merciful, The Wise, The Eternal Contemplative One!

KUBLAI—In His Name?

BAYAN—(*fiercely*) Death to those who deny Him!

ALL—(*with a great fierce shout and a clanking of swords*) Death!

KUBLAI—(*looks up at the ceiling quizzically*) A thunderbolt? (*waits*) No? Then there is no God! (*then to Bayan with a cynical bitter smile*) August Commander, if you must have war, let it be one without fine phrases—a practical war of few words, as that Polo you admire would say. Leave the West alone. Our interests do not conflict—yet. But there is a group of islands whose silk industry is beginning to threaten the supremacy of our own. Lead your gallant million there—and see to it your war leaves me in peace!

BAYAN—I hear and I obey! (*He turns to his staff exultantly.*) His Majesty has declared war!

ALL—(*with a fierce cheer*) Down with the West!

BAYAN—(*hastily*) No. Not yet. Down with Japan! (*They cheer with equal enthusiasm—then he harangues them with the air of a patriotic exhorter.*) His Majesty's benevolence and patience have been exhausted by the continued outrages against our silk nationals perpetrated by unscrupulous Japanese trade-pirates who, in spite of his protests, are breeding and maintaining silkworms for purposes of aggression! We fight in the cause of moral justice, that our silk-makers may preserve their share of the eternal sunlight! (*a long cheer*)

KUBLAI—(*smiling—distractedly*) War without rhetoric, please! Polo has infected you with cant! The West already invades us! Throw open the doors! Music! (*The doors are thrown open. The dance music sounds loudly.*) Go in and dance, everyone! You, too, General! I revoke my declaration of war—

unless you learn to dance and be silent! (*They all go into the ballroom, Bayan stalking majestically with an injured mien.*) But dancing makes me remember Kukachin whose little dancing feet—! Shut the doors! Music brings back her voice singing! (*turning to Chu-Yin—harshly*) Wisdom! No, do not read! What good are wise writings to fight stupidity? One must have stupid writings that men can understand. In order to live even wisdom must be stupid!

A CHAMBERLAIN—(*enters hurriedly and prostrates himself*) A courier from Persia!

KUBLAI—(*excitedly*) From Kukachin! Bring him here! (*The chamberlain dashes to the door and a moment later the courier enters, travel-stained and weary. He sinks into a heap before the throne. Kublai shouts at him impatiently.*)

KUBLAI—Have you a letter?

COURIER—(*with a great effort holds out a letter*) Here! (*He collapses. Chu-Yin hands the letter up to Kublai who takes it eagerly from him. He begins to read at once. The chamberlain comes back with a cup of wine. The courier is revived and gets to his knees, waiting humbly.*)

CHU-YIN—(*goes back to Kublai who has finished reading the short note and is staring somberly before him*) And did the Little Flower save his Immortal Soul? (*Kublai does not look at him but mutely hands him the letter. Chu-Yin becomes grave. He reads aloud*) "Arghun had died. I am the wife of his son, Ghazan. It does not matter. He is kind but I miss my home and you. I doubt if I shall be blessed with a son. I do not care. I have lost my love of life. My heart beats more and more wearily. Death woos me. You must not grieve. You wish me to be happy, do you not? And my body may resist Death for a long time yet. Too long. My soul he has already possessed. I wish to commend the unremitting attention to his duty of Admiral Polo. He saved my life three times at the risk of his own. He delivered me to Ghazan. Send him another million. You were right about his soul. What I had mistaken for one I discovered to be a fat woman with a patient virtue. By the time you receive this they will be married in Venice. I do not blame him. But I cannot forgive myself—nor forget—nor believe again in any beauty in the world. I love you the best in life. And tell Chu-Yin I love him too."

(*He lets the letter in his hand drop to his side, his eyes filling, his voice grown husky. Kublai stares bleakly ahead of him.*)

KUBLAI—(*at last rouses himself—harshly to the courier*) Did the Queen give you this in person?

COURIER—Yes, Your Majesty—with a generous gift.

KUBLAI—I can be generous too. Did she appear—ill?

COURIER—Yes. I could scarcely hear her voice.

KUBLAI—You brought no other word?

COURIER—Not from the Queen. I came privately from her. But Admiral Polo suspected my departure and gave me a verbal message which he caused me to memorize.

KUBLAI—(*harshly—his eyes beginning to gleam with anger*) Ha! Go on! Repeat!

COURIER—(*stopping for a moment to freshen his memory*) He said, tell the Great Kaan that "in spite of perils too numerous to relate, I have delivered my charge safely to Ghazan Khan. In general, she gave but little trouble on the voyage, for although flighty in temper and of a passionate disposition, she never refused to heed my advice for her welfare and as I informed His Majesty, King Ghazan, the responsibilities of marriage and the duties of motherhood will sober her spirit and she will settle down as a sensible wife should. This much I further add, that in humble obedience to your final instructions given me by Mr. Chu-Yin, I looked daily into her eyes."

KUBLAI—(*bewilderedly to Chu-Yin*) What? Did you—?

CHU-YIN—(*miserably*) Forgive an old fool! I meant it partly in jest as a last chance—to cure her—or to awaken him.

COURIER—(*continuing*) "But I have never noted any unnatural change in them except toward the termination of our trip, particularly on the last day, when I noticed a rather strained expression but this I took to be fever due to her Highness's spleen being sluggish after the long confinement on shipboard."

KUBLAI—(*choking with wrath*) O God of the Somber Heavens!

COURIER—And he gave me no money for delivering the message but he promised that you would reward me nobly.

KUBLAI—(*with wild laughter*) Ha-ha-ha! Stop! Do you dare to madden me? (*then suddenly raging*) Out of my sight, dog, before I have you impaled! (*The terror-stricken courier scrambles out like a flash. Kublai stands up with flashing eyes—revengefully*) I have reconsidered! I shall conquer the West! I shall lead my armies in person! I shall not leave one temple standing nor one Christian alive who is not enslaved! Their cities shall vanish in flame, their fields shall be wasted! Famine shall finish what I leave undone! And of the city of Venice not one vestige shall remain! And of the body of Marco Polo there shall not be a fragment of bone nor an atom of flesh which will not have shrieked through ten days' torture before it died!

CHU-YIN—Master! (*He throws himself on his face at Kublai's feet.*) Do not torture yourself! Is this Wisdom? Is this the peace of the soul?

KUBLAI—(*distractedly*) To revenge oneself—that brings a kind of peace!

CHU-YIN—To revenge equally the wrong of an equal perhaps, but this—? Can you confess yourself weaker than his stupidity?

KUBLAI—He has murdered her!

CHU-YIN—She does not accuse him. What would be her wish?

KUBLAI—(*his anger passing—wearily and bitterly, after a pause*) Rise, my old friend, it is I who should be at your feet, not you at mine! (*He sinks dejectedly on his throne again. After a pause, sadly*) She will die. Why is this? What purpose can it serve? My hideous suspicion is that God is only an infinite, insane energy which creates and destroys without other purpose than to pass eternity in avoiding thought. Then the stupid man becomes the Perfect Incarnation of Omnipotence and the Polos are the true children of God! (*He laughs bitterly.*) Ha! How long before we shall be permitted to die, my friend? I begin to resent life as the insult of an ignoble inferior with whom it is a degradation to fight! (*broodingly—after a pause*) I have had a foreboding she would die. Lately, to while away time, I experimented with the crystal. I do not believe the magic nonsense about it but I do consider that, given a focus, the will can perhaps overcome the limits of the senses. Whatever the explanation be, I looked into the crystal and willed to see Kukachin in Persia and she appeared, sitting alone in a garden, beautiful and sad, apart from life, wait-ing— (*brokenly*) My eyes filled with tears. I cried out to her— and she was gone! (*then suddenly—to the chamberlain*) Bring me the crystal! (*to Chu-Yin as the chamberlain goes*) Marco, the true ruler of the world, will have come to Venice by this time. My loathing grows so intense I feel he must jump into the crystal at my bidding. And—in the cause of wisdom, say—we must see what he is doing now. (*The chamberlain returns with the crystal. Kublai takes it eagerly from his hand and stares fixedly into it.*)

CHU-YIN—(*protestingly*) Why do you wish to hurt your-self further?

KUBLAI—(*staring fixedly*) I shall observe dispassionately. It is a test of myself I want to make as a penalty for my weak-ness a moment ago. (*He sees something.*) Ah—it begins. (*A pause. The light grows dimmer and dimmer on the stage proper as it begins to come up on the extreme foreground.*) I see—a city whose streets are canals—it is evening—a house. I begin to see through the walls— Ah! (*The lights come up again on the back stage as the forestage is fully revealed. The Kaan on his throne and Chu-Yin are seen dimly, behind and above, like beings on another plane. At the center of the forestage is a great banquet table garishly set with an ornate gold service. A tall majordomo in a gorgeous uniform enters and stands at attention as the procession begins. First come the guests, male and female, a crowd of good substantial bourgeois, who stare about with awe and envy and are greatly impressed by the gold plate.*)

A MAN—They've laid out a pile of money here!

A WOMAN—Is that gold service really gold?

ANOTHER—Absolutely. I can tell without biting it.

A MAN—They must have cash, whoever they are.

A WOMAN—Do you think they're really the Polos?

ANOTHER—They looked like greasy Tartars to me.

ANOTHER—That was their queer clothes.

A MAN—And remember they've been gone twenty-odd years.

ANOTHER—In spite of that, I thought I could recognize Maffeo.

A WOMAN—Will Donata know Marco, I wonder?

A MAN—What's more to her point, will he recognize her?

A Woman—Imagine her waiting all this time!

Another—How romantic! He must be terribly rich—if it's really him.

A Man—We'll soon know. That's why we were invited.

A Woman—Ssshh! Here comes Donata now. How old she's getting to look!

Another—And how fat in the hips!

A Man—(*jokingly*) That's the way I like 'em, and perhaps Marco— (*Donata enters on the arm of her father, a crafty, wizened old man. She has grown into a stout middle-age but her face is unlined and still pretty in a bovine, good-natured way. All bow and they return this salutation.*)

All—Congratulations, Donata! (*She blushes and turns aside in an incongruous girlish confusion.*)

Father—(*proud but pretending querulousness*) Don't tease her now! The girl's nervous enough already. And it may not be Marco after all but only a joke someone's put up on us.

A Woman—No one could be so cruel!

All—(*suddenly with a great gasp*) Oh, listen! (*An orchestra vigorously begins a flowery, sentimental Italian tune. This grows into quite a blare as the musicians enter from the right, six in number, in brilliant uniforms.*) Oh, look! (*The musicians form a line, three on each side by the stairs on right.*) Oh, see! (*A procession of servants begins to file one by one through the ranks of musicians, each carrying on his head or upraised hand an enormous platter on which are whole pigs, fowl of all varieties, roasts, vegetables, salads, fruits, nuts, dozens of bottles of wine. The servants arrange these on the table, in symmetrical groups, with the trained eye for display of window-dressers, until the table, with the bright light flooding down on it, closely resembles the front of a pretentious delicatessen store. Meanwhile*) See! What a turkey! Such a goose! The fattest pig I ever saw! What ducks! What vegetables! Look at the wine! A feast for the Gods! And all those servants! An army! And the orchestra! What expense! Lavish! They must be worth millions! (*The three Polos make their grand entrance from the stairs on right, walking with bursting self-importance between the files of musicians who now blare out a triumphant march. The two elder precede Marco. All three are dressed in long robes of embroidered crimson satin reaching almost to the ground. The guests give a new united gasp of aston-*

ishment.) Is it they? Is that old Nicolo? That's Maffeo's nose! No! It isn't them at all! Well, if it's a joke, I don't see the point. But such robes! Such hand embroidery! Such material! They must be worth millions!

DONATA—(*falteringly*) Is that him, father? I can't tell. (*She calls faintly*) Marco! (*But he pretends not to hear. He gives a sign at which the three take off their robes and hand them to the servants. They have even more gorgeous blue ones underneath. Marco addresses the servants in a false voice.*)

MARCO—My good men, you may sell these rich robes and divide the proceeds among yourselves! And here is a little something extra. (*He tosses a handful of gold to the servants and another to the musicians. A mad scramble results. The guests gasp. They seem inclined to join in the scramble.*)

GUESTS—How generous! What prodigality! What indifference to money! They throw it away like dirt. They must be worth millions!

MARCO—(*in the same false voice*) Our guests look thirsty. Pass around the wine. (*The servants do so. The guests gaze, smell, taste.*)

ALL—What a vintage! What flavor! What bouquet! How aged! It must have cost twenty lire a bottle! (*At another signal the three Polos take off their blue robes.*)

MARCO—(*regally*) Give those to the musicians! (*They are revealed now in their old dirty, loose Tartar traveling dress and look quite shabby. The guests gape uncertainly. Then Marco declares grandly*) You look astonished, good people, but this is a moral lesson to teach you not to put too much faith in appearances, for behold! (*He slits up the wide sleeves of his own robe, as do his father and uncle, and now the three, standing beside a big empty space which has been purposely left at the very center of the table at the front, lower their opened sleeves, and, as the musicians, obeying this signal, start up a great blare, let pour from them a perfect stream of precious stones which forms a glittering multicolored heap. This is the final blow. The guests stare popeyed, open-mouthed, speechless for a second. Then their pent-up admiration breaks forth.*)

ALL—Extraordinary! Jewels! Gems! Rubies! Emeralds! Diamonds! Pearls! A king's ransom! Millions!

MARCO—(*suddenly with his hail-fellow-well-met joviality*)

Well, folks, are you all tongue-tied? Isn't one of you going to say welcome home? And Miss Donata, don't I get a kiss? I'm still a bachelor! (*Immediately with mad shouts of* "Bravo!" "Welcome home!" "Hurrah for the Polos!" *etc., etc., the guests bear down on them in a flood. There is a confused whirl of embraces, kisses, back-slaps, handshakes and loud greetings of all sorts. Marco manages to get separated and pulls Donata down front to the foreground.*)

DONATA—(*half swooning*) Marco!

MARCO—(*moved*) My old girl! (*They kiss, then he pushes her away.*) Here! Let me get a good look at you! Why, you're still as pretty as a picture and you don't look a day older!

DONATA—(*exaltedly*) My beloved prince!

MARCO—(*jokingly*) No, if I was a prince I'd never have remained single all these years in the East! I'm a hero, that's what! And all the twenty-odd years I kept thinking of you, and I was always intending to write— (*He pulls the pieces of the miniature wrapped in the handkerchief out of his pocket.*) Here's proof for you! Look at yourself! You're a bit smashed but that was done in a hand-to-hand fight with pirates. Now don't I deserve another kiss?

DONATA—(*giving it*) My hero! (*then jealously*) But I know all the heathen women must have fallen in love with you.

MARCO—Oh, maybe one or two or so—but I didn't have time to waste on females. I kept my nose to the grindstone every minute. (*proudly*) And I got results. I don't mind telling you, Donata, I'm worth over two millions! How's that for keeping my promise? Worth while your waiting, eh? (*He slaps her on the back.*)

DONATA—Yes, my wonder boy! (*then worriedly*) You said there were one or two women? But you were true in spite of them, weren't you?

MARCO—I tell you I wouldn't have married the prettiest girl in Cathay! (*this with emphasis—then abruptly*) But never mind any other girl. (*He chucks her under the chin.*) What I want to know is when this girl is going to marry me?

DONATA—(*softly*) Any time! (*They hug. The guests group about them kittenishly, pointing and murmuring,* "What a romance! What a romance!")

DONATA'S FATHER—(*seizing the opportunity*) Friends, I

take this opportunity to publicly announce the betrothal of my daughter, Donata, to Marco Polo of this City! (*another wild round of congratulations, kisses, etc.*)

MARCO—(*his voice sounding above the hubbub*) Let's eat, friends! (*They swirl to their places behind the long table. When they stand their faces can be seen above the piles of food but when they sit they are out of sight.*) No ceremony among friends. Just pick your chair. All ready? Let's sit down then! (*With one motion they disappear.*)

VOICE OF DONATA'S FATHER—But, first, before we regale ourselves with your cheer, won't you address a few words to your old friends and neighbors who have gathered here on this happy occasion? (*Applause. Marco is heard expostulating but finally he gives in.*)

MARCO—All right, if you'll promise to go ahead and eat and not wait for me. (*His head appears, his expression full of importance. Servants flit about noisily. He coughs and begins with dramatic feeling*) My friend and neighbors of old, your generous and wholehearted welcome touches me profoundly. I would I had the gift of oratory to thank you fittingly, but I am a simple man, an ordinary man, I might almost say,— a man of affairs used to dealing in the hard facts of life, a silent man given to deeds not words— (*Here he falters fittingly.*) And so now—forgive my emotion—words fail me— (*Here he clears his throat with an important cough and bursts forth into a memorized speech in the grand Chamber of Commerce style.*) But I'll be glad to let you have a few instructive facts about the silk industry as we observed it in the Far East, laying especial emphasis upon the keystone of the whole silk business—I refer to the breeding of worms! (*A few hungry guests start to eat. Knives and forks and spoons rattle against plates. Soup is heard. Marco strikes a good listening attitude so he will be sure not to miss a word his voice utters and warms to his work.*) Now, to begin with, there are millions upon millions of capital invested in this industry, millions of contented slaves labor unremittingly millions of hours per annum to obtain the best results in the weaving and dyeing of the finished product, but I don't hesitate to state that all this activity is relatively unimportant beside the astounding fact that in the production of the raw material there are constantly employed millions upon millions upon millions of millions of worms!

ONE VOICE—(*rather muffled by roast pig*) Hear! (*But the rest are all absorbed in eating and a perfect clamor of knives and forks resounds. Marco begins again but this time the clamor is too great, his words are lost, only the one he lays such emphasis upon can be distinguished.*)

MARCO—Millions! . . . millions! . . . millions! . . . millions!

KUBLAI—(*who from the height of his golden throne, crystal in hand, has watched all this with fascinated disgust while Chu-Yin has sat down to read again, now turns away with a shudder of loathing—and, in spite of himself, a shadow of a smile—and lets the crystal fall from his hand and shatter into bits with a loud report. Instantly there is darkness and from high up in the darkness Kublai's voice speaking with a pitying scorn.*) The Word became their flesh, they say. Now all is flesh! And can their flesh become the Word again?

(*Darkness*)

SCENE TWO

SCENE—*Grand Throne Room in the Imperial Palace at Cambaluc, about two years later. The walls tower majestically in shadow, their elaborate detail blurred into a background of half-darkness.*

Kublai sits at the top of his throne, cross-legged in the posture of an idol, motionless, wrapped in contemplation. He wears a simple white robe without adornment of any sort. A brilliant light floods down upon him in one concentrated ray. His eyes are fixed on a catafalque, draped in heavy white silk, which stands in the center of the room, emphasized by another downpouring shaft of light.

Chu-Yin stands on the level below, on Kublai's left. On the main floor are the nobles and people of the court, grouped as in Act One, Scene Six.

There is a long pause clamorous with the pealing of the thousands of bells in the city, big and little, near and far. Every figure

*in the room is as motionless as the Kaan himself. Their eyes are
kept on him with the ardent humility and respect of worship. Behind their impassive faces, one senses a tense expectancy of some
sign from the throne. At last, Kublai makes a slight but imperious
motion of command with his right hand. Immediately the women
all turn with arms outstretched toward the catafalque. Their voices
rise together in a long, rhythmic wail of mourning; their arms
with one motion move slowly up; their voices attain a prolonged
note of unbearable poignancy; their heads are thrown back, their
arms appeal to Heaven in one agonized gesture of despair. Here
the Kaan makes the same barely perceptible sign of command
again. The voices are instantly silenced. With one motion, the
women throw themselves prostrate on the floor. The bells, except for
one slow deep-toned one in the palace itself, are almost instantly
hushed. At the same instant, from outside, at first faint, but growing momentarily in volume, comes the sound of funeral music. A
moment later the funeral procession enters. The men sink to the
cross-legged position of prayer, their heads bowed.*

*First come the musicians, nine in number, men in robes of
bright red. They are followed by the chorus of nine singers, five
men and four women, all of them aged, with bent bodies, their
thin, cracked voices accompanying the music in queer, breaking
waves of lamentation. These are masked, the men with a male
mask of grief, the women with a female. All are dressed in deep
black with white edging to their robes. After them comes a troupe
of young girls and boys, dressed in white with black edging, moving
slowly backward in a gliding, interweaving dance pattern. Their
faces are not masked but are fixed in a disciplined, traditional
expression of bewildered, uncomprehending grief that is like a
mask. They carry silver censers which they swing in unison toward
the corpse of the Princess Kukachin, carried on a bier directly behind them on the shoulders of eight princes of the blood in black
armor.*

*Accompanying the bier, one at each corner, are four priests—
the foremost two, a Confucian and a Taoist, the latter two, a
Buddhist and a Moslem. Each walks with bent head reading aloud
to himself from his Holy Book.*

*The princes lift the bier of Kukachin to the top of the catafalque.
Her body is wrapped in a winding sheet of deep blue, a jeweled
golden head-dress is on her black hair, her face is white and clear*

as a statue's. The young boys and girls place their smoking censers about the catafalque, the incense ascending in clouds about the Princess as if it were bearing her soul with it. The music and the singing cease as the dancers, singers, and musicians form on each side, and to the rear, of the catafalque and sink into attitudes of prayer.

Kublai speaks to the priests in a voice of command in which is weariness and disbelief.

KUBLAI—Peace! She does not need your prayers. She was a prayer! (*With one motion they shut their books, raise their heads and stare before them in silence. Kublai continues—sadly*) Can words recall life to her beauty? (*to the priest of Tao*) Priest of Tao, will you conquer death by your mystic Way?

PRIEST OF TAO—(*bowing his head in submission—fatalistically*) Which is the greater evil, to possess or to be without? Death is.

CHORUS—(*in an echo of vast sadness*) Death is.

KUBLAI—(*to the Confucian*) Follower of Confucius, the Wise, have you this wisdom?

PRIEST OF CONFUCIUS—(*slowly*) Before we know life, how can we know death? (*then as the Taoist, submissively*) Death is.

CHORUS—(*as before*) Death is.

KUBLAI—(*to the Buddhist priest*) Worshiper of Buddha, can your self-overcoming overcome that greatest overcomer of self?

BUDDHIST PRIEST—This is a thing which no god can bring about: that what is subject to death should not die. (*then as the others, submissively*) Death is.

CHORUS—(*as before*) Death is.

KUBLAI—(*wearily*) And your answer, priest of Islam?

PRIEST OF ISLAM—It is the will of Allah! (*submissively*) Death is.

CHORUS—Death is. Death is. Death is. (*Their voices die away.*)

KUBLAI—(*after a pause*) What is death? (*A long pause. His eyes rest in loving contemplation on the body of Kukachin. Finally he speaks tenderly to her with a sad smile.*) Girl whom we call dead, whose beauty is even in death more living than we, smile with infinite silence upon our speech, smile with infinite forbearance upon our wisdom, smile with infinite remoteness upon our sorrow, smile as a star smiles! (*His voice appears about to break. A muffled sound of sobbing comes from the prostrate women. Kublai regains control over his weakness and rises to his feet—with angry self-contempt*) No more! That is for poets! (*with overstressed arrogance—assertively*) I am the Great Kaan! (*Everyone in the room rises with one motion of assertion.*)

CHORUS—(*accompanied by a clangor of brass from the musicians—recite with discordant vigor*)

> Greatest of the Great!
> Son of Heaven!
> Lord of Earth!
> Sovereign of the World!
> Ruler over Life and Death!

KUBLAI—(*silences them by an imperious gesture—and now even the great palace bell is stilled—half-mockingly but assertively*) The Son of Heaven? Then I should know a prayer. Sovereign of the World? Then I command the World to pray! (*With one motion all sink to the position of prayer.*) In silence! Prayer is beyond words! Contemplate the eternal life of Life! Pray thus! (*He himself sinks to the position of prayer—a pause—then slowly*) In silence—for one concentrated moment—be proud of life! Know in your heart that the living of life can be noble! Know that the dying of death can be noble! Be exalted by life! Be inspired by death! Be humbly proud! Be proudly grateful! Be immortal because life is immortal. Contain the harmony of womb and grave within you! Possess life as a lover—then sleep requited in the arms of death! If you awake, love again! If you sleep on, rest in peace! Who knows which? What does it matter? It is nobler not to know! (*A pause of silence. He rises to his feet. With one motion all do likewise. Kublai sits back on his cushions again, withdrawing into contemplation. The Mongol chronicler comes forward to fulfill his function of chanting the official lament for the dead. He declaims in a high wailing voice accompanied by the musicians and by the chorus who sway rhythmically and hum a rising and falling mourning accompaniment.*)

CHRONICLER—We lament the shortness of life. Life at its longest is brief enough.

Too brief for the wisdom of joy, too long for the knowledge of sorrow.

Sorrow becomes despair when death comes to the young, untimely.

Oh, that her beauty could live again, that her youth could be born anew.

Our Princess was young as Spring, she was beautiful as a bird or flower.

Cruel when Spring is smitten by Winter, when birds are struck dead in full song, when the budding blossom is blighted!

Alas that our Princess is dead, she was the song of songs, the perfume of perfumes, the perfect one!

Our sobs stifle us, our tears wet the ground, our lamentations sadden the wind from the West.

(*bows submissively—speaks*)

Yet we must bow humbly before the Omnipotent.

CHORUS—We must be humble.

CHRONICLER—Against Death all Gods are powerless.

CHORUS—All Gods are powerless. (*Their voices die into silence.*)

KUBLAI—(*after a pause—wearily*) Leave her in peace. Go. (*The Court leaves silently at his command in a formal, expressionless order. The four priests go first, beginning to pray silently again. They are followed by the nobles and officials with their women coming after. Finally the young boys and girls take up their censers and dance their pattern out backward, preceded by the musicians. Only the chorus remain, grouped in a semi-circle behind the catafalque, motionless, and Chu-Yin who stays at the left hand of Kublai. The music fades away. Kublai takes his eyes from the dead girl with a sigh of bitter irony.*)

KUBLAI—Oh, Chu-Yin, my Wise Friend, was the prayer I taught them wisdom?

CHU-YIN—It was the wisdom of pride. It was thy wisdom.

CHORUS—(*echoing sadly*) Thy wisdom.

KUBLAI—Was it not truth?

CHU-YIN—It was the truth of power. It was thy truth.

CHORUS—(*as before*) Thy truth.

KUBLAI—My pride, my power? My wisdom, my truth? For me there remains only—her truth! (*then after staring at*

Kukachin for a second, bitterly) Her truth! She died for love of a fool!

CHU-YIN—No. She loved love. She died for beauty.

KUBLAI—Your words are hollow echoes of the brain. Do not wound me with wisdom. Speak to my heart! (*sadly—his eyes again on Kukachin*) Her little feet danced away the stamp of armies. Her smile made me forget the servile grin on the face of the World. In her eyes' mirror I watched myself live protected from life by her affection—a simple old man dying contentedly a little, day after pleasant day.

CHU-YIN—(*bowing—compassionately*) Then weep, old man. Be humble and weep for your child. The old should cherish sorrow. (*He bows again and goes out silently.*)

KUBLAI—(*after a pause, gets up and descending from his throne, slowly approaches the catafalque, speaking to the dead girl softly as he does so—with a trembling smile*) I think you are hiding your eyes, Kukachin. You are a little girl again. You are playing hide and seek. You are pretending. Did we not once play such games together, you and I? You have made your face still, you have made your face cold, you have set your lips in a smile so remote—you are pretending even that you are dead! (*He is very near her now. His voice breaks—more and more intensely*) Let us stop playing! It is late. It is time you were asleep. Open your eyes and laugh! Laugh now that the game is over. Take the blindfold from my dim eyes. Whisper your secret in my ear. I—I am dead and you are living! Weep for me, Kukachin! Weep for the dead! (*He stretches his arms out to her beseechingly—pauses, standing beside the body, staring down at her; then, after a moment, he passes his hand over her face—tremblingly—with a beautiful tenderness of grief*) So, little Kukachin—so, Little Flower—you have come back— they could not keep you—you were too homesick—you wanted to return—to gladden my last days— (*He no longer tries to control his grief. He sobs like a simple old man, bending and kissing his granddaughter on the forehead—with heart-breaking playfulness*) I bid you welcome home, Little Flower! I bid you welcome home! (*He weeps, his tears falling on her calm white face.*)

(*Curtain*)

EPILOGUE

*The play is over. The lights come up brilliantly in the theatre.
In an aisle seat in the first row a man rises, conceals a yawn in
his palm, stretches his legs as if they had become cramped by too
long an evening, takes his hat from under the seat and starts to
go out slowly with the others in the audience. But although there
is nothing out of the ordinary in his actions, his appearance excites
general comment and surprise for he is dressed as a Venetian merchant of the later Thirteenth Century. In fact, it is none other
than Marco Polo himself, looking a bit sleepy, a trifle puzzled, and
not a little irritated as his thoughts, in spite of himself, cling for a
passing moment to the play just ended. He appears quite unaware
of being unusual and walks in the crowd without self-consciousness,
very much as one of them. Arrived in the lobby his face begins to
clear of all disturbing memories of what had happened on the
stage. The noise, the lights of the streets, recall him at once to
himself. Impatiently he waits for his car, casting a glance here and
there at faces in the groups around him, his eyes impersonally spec-
ulative, his bearing stolid with the dignity of one who is sure of his
place in the world. His car, a luxurious limousine, draws up at
the curb. He gets in briskly, the door is slammed, the car edges
away into the traffic and Marco Polo, with a satisfied sigh at the
sheer comfort of it all, resumes his life.*

THE END

THE GREAT GOD BROWN

CHARACTERS

WILLIAM A. BROWN

HIS FATHER, *a contractor*

HIS MOTHER

DION ANTHONY

HIS FATHER, *a builder*

HIS MOTHER

MARGARET

HER THREE SONS

CYBEL

TWO DRAFTSMEN

CLIENT

THREE COMMITTEEMEN

POLICE CAPTAIN

SCENES

The Great God Brown
PROLOGUE

SCENE—*A cross section of the pier of the Casino. In the rear, built out beyond the edge, is a rectangular space with benches on the three sides. A rail encloses the entire wharf at the back.*

It is a moonlight night in mid-June. From the Casino comes the sound of the school quartet rendering "Sweet Adeline" with many ultra-sentimental barber-shop quavers. There is a faint echo of the ensuing hand-clapping—then nothing but the lapping of ripples against the piles and their swishing on the beach—then footsteps on the boards and Billy Brown walks along from right with his mother and father. The mother is a dumpy woman of forty-five, overdressed in black lace and spangles. The father is fifty or more, the type of bustling, genial, successful, provincial business man, stout and hearty in his evening dress.

Billy Brown is a handsome, tall and athletic boy of nearly eighteen. He is blond and blue-eyed, with a likeable smile and a frank good-humored face, its expression already indicating a disciplined restraint. His manner has the easy self-assurance of a normal intelligence. He is in evening dress.

They walk arm in arm, the mother between.

MOTHER—(*always addressing the father*) This Commencement dance is badly managed. Such singing! Such poor voices! Why doesn't Billy sing?

BILLY—(*to her*) Mine is a regular fog horn! (*He laughs.*)

MOTHER—(*to the air*) I had a pretty voice, when I was a girl. (*then, to the father, caustically*) Did you see young Anthony strutting around the ballroom in dirty flannel pants?

FATHER—He's just showing off.

MOTHER—Such impudence! He's as ignorant as his father.

FATHER—The old man's all right. My only kick against him is he's been too damned conservative to let me branch out.

MOTHER—(*bitterly*) He has kept you down to his level—out of pure jealousy.

FATHER—But he took me into partnership, don't forget—

473

MOTHER—(*sharply*) Because you were the brains! Because he was afraid of losing you! (*a pause*)

BILLY—(*admiringly*) Dion came in his old clothes on a bet with me. He's a real sport. He wouldn't have been afraid to appear in his pajamas! (*He grins with appreciation.*)

MOTHER—Isn't the moonlight clear! (*She goes and sits on the center bench. Billy stands at the left corner, forward, his hand on the rail, like a prisoner at the bar, facing the judge. His father stands in front of the bench on right. The mother announces, with finality*) After he's through college, Billy must study for a profession of some sort, I'm determined on that! (*She turns to her husband, defiantly, as if expecting opposition.*)

FATHER—(*eagerly and placatingly*) Just what I've been thinking, my dear. Architecture! How's that? Billy a first-rate, number-one architect! That's my proposition! What I've always wished I could have been myself! Only I never had the opportunity. But Billy—we'll make him a partner in the firm after. Anthony, Brown *and Son*, *architects* and builders—instead of *contractors* and builders!

MOTHER—(*yearning for the realization of a dream*) And we won't lay sidewalks—or dig sewers—ever again?

FATHER—(*a bit ruffled*) I and Anthony can build anything your pet can draw—even if it's a church! (*then, selling his idea*) It's a great chance for him! He'll design—expand us—make the firm famous.

MOTHER—(*to the air—musingly*) When you proposed, I thought your future promised success—my future— (*with a sigh*) —Well, I suppose we've been comfortable. Now, it's his future. How would Billy like to be an architect? (*She does not look at him.*)

BILLY—(*to her*) All right, Mother. (*then sheepishly*) I guess I've never bothered much about what I'd like to do after college—but architecture sounds all right to me, I guess.

MOTHER—(*to the air—proudly*) Billy used to draw houses when he was little.

FATHER—(*jubilantly*) Billy's got the stuff in him to win, if he'll only work hard enough.

BILLY—(*dutifully*) I'll work hard, Dad.

MOTHER—Billy can do anything!

BILLY—(*embarrassed*) I'll try, Mother. (*There is a pause.*)

MOTHER—(*with a sudden shiver*) The nights are so much colder than they used to be! Think of it, I once went moonlight bathing in June when I was a girl—but the moonlight was so warm and beautiful in those days, do you remember, Father?

FATHER—(*puts his arm around her affectionately*) You bet I do, Mother. (*He kisses her. The orchestra at the Casino strikes up a waltz.*) There's the music. Let's go back and watch the young folks dance. (*They start off, leaving Billy standing there.*)

MOTHER—(*suddenly calls back over her shoulder*) I want to watch Billy dance.

BILLY—(*dutifully*) Yes, Mother! (*He follows them. For a moment the faint sound of the music and the lapping of waves is heard. Then footsteps again and the three Anthonys come in. First come the father and mother, who are not masked. The father is a tall lean man of fifty-five or sixty with a grim, defensive face, obstinate to the point of stupid weakness. The mother is a thin frail faded woman, her manner perpetually nervous and distraught, but with a sweet and gentle face that had once been beautiful. The father wears an ill-fitting black suit, like a mourner. The mother wears a cheap, plain, black dress. Following them, as if he were a stranger, walking alone, is their son, Dion. He is about the same height as young Brown but lean and wiry, without repose, continually in restless nervous movement. His face is masked. The mask is a fixed forcing of his own face—dark, spiritual, poetic, passionately supersensitive, helplessly unprotected in its childlike, religious faith in life—into the expression of a mocking, reckless, defiant, gayly scoffing and sensual young Pan. He is dressed in a gray flannel shirt, open at the neck, sneakers over bare feet, and soiled white flannel trousers. The father strides to the center bench and sits down. The mother, who has been holding to his arm, lets go and stands by the bench at the right. They both stare at Dion, who, with a studied carelessness, takes his place at the rail, where young Brown had stood. They watch him, with queer, puzzled eyes.*)

MOTHER—(*suddenly—pleading*) You simply must send him to college!

FATHER—I won't. I don't believe in it. Colleges turn out lazy loafers to sponge on their poor old fathers! Let him slave like I had to! That'll teach him the value of a dollar! College'll only make him a bigger fool than he is already! I never got above grammar school but I've made money and established a sound business. Let him make a man out of himself like I made of myself!

DION—(*mockingly—to the air*) This Mr. Anthony is my father, but he only imagines he is God the Father. (*They both stare at him.*)

FATHER—(*with angry bewilderment*) What—what—what's that?

MOTHER—(*gently remonstrating to her son*) Dion, dear! (*then to her husband—tauntingly*) Brown takes all the credit! He tells everyone the success is all due to his energy—that you're only an old stick-in-the-mud!

FATHER—(*stung, harshly*) The damn fool! He knows better'n anyone if I hadn't held him down to common sense, with his crazy wild-cat notions, he'd have had us ruined long ago!

MOTHER—He's sending Billy to college—Mrs. Brown, just told me—going to have him study architecture afterwards, too, so's he can help expand your firm!

FATHER—(*angrily*) What's that? (*suddenly turns on Dion furiously*) Then you can make up your mind to go, too! And you'll learn to be a better architect than Brown's boy or I'll turn you out in the gutter without a penny! You hear?

DION—(*mockingly—to the air*) It's difficult to choose— but architecture sounds less laborious.

MOTHER—(*fondly*) You ought to make a wonderful architect, Dion. You've always painted pictures so well—

DION—(*with a start—resentfully*) Why must she lie? Is it my fault? She knows I only try to paint. (*passionately*) But I will, some day! (*then quickly, mocking again*) On to college! Well, it won't be home, anyway, will it? (*He laughs queerly and approaches them. His father gets up defensively. Dion bows to him.*) I thank Mr. Anthony for this splendid opportunity to create myself—(*he kisses his mother, who bows with a strange humility as if she were a servant being saluted by the young master—then adds lightly*)—in my mother's image, so she may feel her life comfortably concluded. (*He sits in his father's place at center and his mask stares with a frozen mockery before him. They stand on each side, looking dumbly at him.*)

MOTHER—(*at last, with a shiver*) It's cold. June didn't use to be cold. I remember the June when I was carrying you, Dion—three months before you were born. (*She stares up at the sky.*) The moonlight was warm, then. I could feel the night wrapped around me like a gray velvet gown lined with warm sky and trimmed with silver leaves!

FATHER—(*gruffly—but with a certain awe*) My mother used to believe the full of the moon was the time to sow. She was terrible old-fashioned. (*with a grunt*) I can feel it's bringing on my rheumatism. Let's go back indoors.

DION—(*with intense bitterness*) Hide! Be ashamed! (*They both start and stare at him.*)

FATHER—(*with bitter hopelessness. To his wife—indicating their son*) Who is he? You bore him!

MOTHER—(*proudly*) He's my boy! He's Dion!

DION—(*bitterly resentful*) What else, indeed! The identical son! (*then mockingly*) Are Mr. Anthony and his wife going in to dance? The nights grow cold! The days are dimmer than they used to be! Let's play hide-and-seek! Seek the monkey in the moon! (*He suddenly cuts a grotesque caper, like a harlequin and darts off, laughing with forced abandon. They stare after him—then slowly follow. Again there is silence except for the sound of the lapping waves. Then Margaret comes in, followed by the humbly worshiping Billy Brown. She is almost seventeen, pretty and vivacious, blonde, with big romantic eyes, her figure lithe and strong, her facial expression intelligent but youthfully dreamy, especially now in the moonlight. She is in a simple white dress. On her entrance, her face is masked with an exact, almost transparent reproduction of her own features, but giving her the abstract quality of a Girl instead of the individual, Margaret.*)

MARGARET—(*looking upward at the moon and singing in low tone as they enter*) "Ah, moon of my delight that knowest no wane!"

BILLY—(*eagerly*) I've got that record—John McCormack. It's a peach! Sing some more. (*She looks upward in silence. He keeps standing respectfully in back of her, glancing embarrassedly toward her averted face. He tries to make conversation.*) I think the *Rubáiyát*'s great stuff, don't you? I never could memorize poetry worth a darn. Dion can recite lots of Shelley's poems by heart.

MARGARET—(*slowly takes off her mask—to the moon*) Dion! (*a pause*)

BILLY—(*fidgeting*) Margaret!

MARGARET—(*to the moon*) Dion is so wonderful!

BILLY—(*blunderingly*) I asked you to come out here because I wanted to tell you something.

MARGARET—(*to the moon*) Why did Dion look at me like that? It made me feel so crazy!

BILLY—I wanted to ask you something, too.

MARGARET—That one time he kissed me—I can't forget it! He was only joking—but I felt—and he saw and just laughed!

BILLY—Because that's the uncertain part. My end of it is a sure thing, and has been for a long time, and I guess everybody in town knows it—they're always kidding me—so it's a cinch you must know—how I feel about you.

MARGARET—Dion's so different from all the others. He can paint beautifully and write poetry and he plays and sings and dances so marvelously. But he's sad and shy, too, just like a baby sometimes, and he understands what I'm really like inside—and—and I'd love to run my fingers through his hair—and I love him! Yes, I love him! (*She stretches out her arms to the moon.*) Oh, Dion, I love you!

BILLY—I love you, Margaret.

MARGARET—I wonder if Dion— I saw him looking at me again tonight— Oh, I wonder. . . . !

BILLY—(*takes her hand and blurts out*) Can't you love me? Won't you marry me—after college—

MARGARET—Where is Dion now, I wonder?

BILLY—(*shaking her hand in an agony of uncertainty*) Margaret! Please answer me!

MARGARET—(*her dream broken, puts on her mask and turns to him—matter-of-factly*) It's getting chilly. Let's go back and dance, Billy.

BILLY—(*desperately*) I love you! (*He tries clumsily to kiss her.*)

MARGARET—(*with an amused laugh*) Like a brother! You can kiss me if you like. (*She kisses him.*) A big-brother kiss. It doesn't count. (*He steps back crushed, with head bowed. She turns away and takes off her mask—to the moon*) I wish Dion would kiss me again!

BILLY—(*painfully*) I'm a poor boob. I ought to know better. I'll bet I know. You're in love with Dion. I've seen you look at him. Isn't that it?

MARGARET—Dion! I love the sound of it!

BILLY—(*huskily*) Well—he's always been my best friend—I'm glad it's him—and I guess I know how to lose—(*he takes her hand and shakes it*)—so here's wishing you all the success and happiness in the world, Margaret—and remember I'll always be your best friend! (*He gives her hand a final shake—swallows hard—then manfully*) Let's go back in!

MARGARET—(*to the moon—faintly annoyed*) What is Billy Brown doing here? I'll go down to the end of the dock and wait. Dion is the moon and I'm the sea. I want to feel the moon kissing the sea. I want Dion to leave the sky to me. I want the tides of my blood to leave my heart and follow him! (*She whispers like a little girl*) Dion! Margaret! Peggy! Peggy is Dion's girl—Peggy is Dion's little girl— (*She sings laughingly, elfishly*) Dion is my Daddy-O! (*She is walking toward the end of the dock, off left.*)

BILLY—(*who has turned away*) I'm going. I'll tell Dion you're here.

MARGARET—(*more and more strongly and assertively, until at the end she is a wife and a mother*) And I'll be Mrs. Dion—Dion's wife—and he'll be my Dion—my own Dion—my little boy—my baby! The moon is drowned in the tides of my heart, and peace sinks deep through the sea! (*She disappears off left, her upturned unmasked face like that of a rapturous visionary. There is silence again, in which the dance music is heard. Then this stops and Dion comes in. He walks quickly to the bench at center and throws himself on it, hiding his masked face in his hands. After a moment, he lifts his head, peers about, listens huntedly, then slowly takes off his mask. His real face is revealed in the bright moonlight, shrinking, shy and gentle, full of a deep sadness.*)

DION—(*with a suffering bewilderment*) Why am I afraid to dance, I who love music and rhythm and grace and song and laughter? Why am I afraid to live, I who love life and the beauty of flesh and the living colors of earth and sky and sea? Why am I afraid of love, I who love love? Why am I afraid, I who am not afraid? Why must I pretend to scorn in order to pity? Why must I hide myself in self-contempt in order to understand? Why must I be so ashamed of my strength, so proud of my weakness? Why must I live in a cage like a criminal, defying and hating, I who love peace and friendship? (*clasping his hands above in supplication*) Why was I born without a skin, O God, that I must wear armor in order to touch or to be touched? (*A second's pause of waiting silence—then he suddenly claps his mask over his face again, with a gesture of despair and his voice becomes bitter and sardonic.*) Or rather, Old Graybeard, why the devil was I ever born at all? (*Steps are heard from the right. Dion stiffens and his mask stares straight ahead. Billy comes in from the right. He is shuffling along disconsolately. When he sees Dion, he stops abruptly and glowers resentfully—but at once the "good loser" in him conquers this.*)

BILLY—(*embarrassedly*) Hello, Dion. I've been looking all over for you. (*He sits down on the bench at right, forcing a joking tone*) What are you sitting here for, you nut—trying to get more moonstruck? (*a pause—awkwardly*) I just left Margaret—

DION—(*gives a start—immediately defensively mocking*) Bless you, my children!

BILLY—(*gruffly and slangily*) I'm out of it—she gave me the gate. You're the original white-haired boy. Go on in and win! We've been chums ever since we were kids, haven't we?—and—I'm glad it's you, Dion. (*This huskily—he fumbles for Dion's hand and gives it a shake.*)

DION—(*letting his hand fall back—bitterly*) Chums? Oh no, Billy Brown would despise me!

BILLY—She's waiting for you now, down at the end of the dock.

DION—For me? Which? Who? Oh no, girls only allow themselves to look at what is seen!

BILLY—She's in love with you.

DION—(*moved—a pause—stammers*) Miracle? I'm afraid! (*He chants flippantly*) I love, thou lovest, he loves, she loves! She loves, she loves—what?

BILLY—And I know damn well, underneath your nuttiness, you're gone on her.

DION—(*moved*) Underneath? I love love! I'd love to be loved! But I'm afraid! (*then aggressively*) *Was* afraid! Not now!

Now I can make love—to anyone! Yes, I love Peggy! Why not? Who is she? Who am I? We love, you love, they love, one loves! No one loves! All the world loves a lover, God loves us all and we love Him! Love is a word—a shameless ragged ghost of a word—begging at all doors for life at any price!

BILLY—(*always as if he hadn't listened to what the other said*) Say, let's you and me room together at college—

DION—Billy wants to remain by her side!

BILLY—It's a bet, then! (*forcing a grin*) You can tell her I'll see that you behave! (*turns away*) So long. Remember she's waiting. (*He goes.*)

DION—(*dazedly, to himself*) Waiting—waiting for me! (*He slowly removes his mask. His face is torn and transfigured by joy. He stares at the sky raptly.*) O God in the moon, did you hear? She loves me! I am not afraid! I am strong! I can love! She protects me! Her arms are softly around me! She is warmly around me! She is my skin! She is my armor! Now I am born—I—the I!—one and indivisible—I who love Margaret! (*He glances at his mask triumphantly—in tones of deliverance*) You are outgrown! I am beyond you! (*He stretches out his arms to the sky.*) O God, now I believe! (*From the end of the wharf, her voice is heard.*)

MARGARET—Dion!

DION—(*raptly*) Margaret!

MARGARET—(*nearer*) Dion!

DION—Margaret!

MARGARET—Dion! (*She comes running in, her mask in her hands. He springs toward her with outstretched arms but she shrinks away with a frightened shriek and hastily puts on her mask. Dion starts back. She speaks coldly and angrily.*) Who are you? Why are you calling me? I don't know you!

DION—(*heart-brokenly*) I love you!

MARGARET—(*freezingly*) Is this a joke—or are you drunk?

DION—(*with a final pleading whisper*) Margaret! (*But she only glares at him contemptuously. Then with a sudden gesture he claps his mask on and laughs wildly and bitterly.*) Ha-ha-ha! That's one on you, Peg!

MARGARET—(*with delight, pulling off her mask*) Dion! How did you ever— Why, I never knew you!

DION—(*puts his arm around her boldly*) How? It's the moon—the crazy moon—the monkey in the moon—playing jokes on us! (*He kisses her with his masked face with a romantic actor's passion again and again.*) You love me! You know you do! Say it! Tell me! I want to hear! I want to feel! I want to know! I want to want! To want you as you want me!

MARGARET—(*in ecstasy*) Oh, Dion, I do! I do love you!

DION—(*with ironic mastery—rhetorically*) And I love you! Oh, madly! Oh, forever and ever, amen! You are my evening star and all my Pleiades! Your eyes are blue pools in which gold dreams glide, your body is a young white birch leaning backward beneath the lips of spring. So! (*He has bent her back, his arms supporting her, his face above hers.*) So! (*He kisses her.*)

MARGARET—(*with overpowering passionate languor*) Oh, Dion! Dion! I love you!

DION—(*with more and more mastery in his tone*) I love, you love, we love! Come! Rest! Relax! Let go your clutch on the world! Dim and dimmer! Fading out in the past behind! Gone! Death! Now! Be born! Awake! Live! Dissolve into dew—into silence—into night—into earth—into space— into peace—into meaning—into joy—into God—into the Great God Pan! (*While he has been speaking, the moon has passed gradually behind a black cloud, its light fading out. There is a moment of intense blackness and silence. Then the light gradually comes on again. Dion's voice, at first in a whisper, then increasing in volume with the light, is heard.*) Wake up! Time to get up! Time to exist! Time for school! Time to learn! Learn to pretend! Cover your nakedness! Learn to lie! Learn to keep step! Join the procession! Great Pan is dead! Be ashamed!

MARGARET—(*with a sob*) Oh, Dion, I am ashamed!

DION—(*mockingly*) Sssshh! Watch the monkey in the moon! See him dance! His tail is a piece of string that was left when he broke loose from Jehovah and ran away to join Charley Darwin's circus!

MARGARET—I know you must hate me now! (*She throws her arms around him and hides her head on his shoulder.*)

DION—(*deeply moved*) Don't cry! Don't—! (*He suddenly tears off his mask—in a passionate agony*) Hate you? I love you with all my soul! Love me! Why can't you love me, Margaret?

(*He tries to kiss her but she jumps to her feet with a frightened cry holding up her mask before her face protectingly.*)

MARGARET—Don't! Please! I don't know you! You frighten me!

DION—(*puts on his mask again—quietly and bitterly*) All's well. I'll never let you see again. (*He puts his arm around her—gently mocking*) By proxy, I love you. There! Don't cry! Don't be afraid! Dion Anthony will marry you some day. (*He kisses her.*) "I take this woman—" (*tenderly joking*) Hello, woman! Do you feel older by æons? Mrs. Dion Anthony, shall we go in and may I have the next dance?

MARGARET—(*tenderly*) You crazy child! (*then, laughing with joy*) Mrs. Dion Anthony! It sounds wonderful, doesn't it? (*They go out as

The Curtain Falls)

ACT ONE

SCENE ONE

SCENE—*Seven years later.*

The sitting room of Mrs. Dion Anthony's half of a two-family house in the homes section of the town—one of those one-design districts that daze the eye with multiplied ugliness. The four pieces of furniture shown are in keeping—an armchair at left, a table with a chair in back of it at center, a sofa at right. The same court-room effect of the arrangement of benches in Act One is held to here. The background is a backdrop on which the rear wall is painted with the intolerable lifeless realistic detail of the stereotyped paintings which usually adorn the sitting rooms of such houses. It is late afternoon of a gray day in winter.

Dion is sitting behind the table, staring before him. The mask hangs on his breast below his neck, giving the effect of two faces. His real face has aged greatly, grown more strained and tortured, but at the same time, in some queer way, more selfless and ascetic, more fixed in its resolute withdrawal from life. The mask, too, has changed. It is older, more defiant and mocking, its sneer more forced and bitter, its Pan quality becoming Mephistophelean. It has already begun to show the ravages of dissipation.

DION—(*suddenly reaches out and takes up a copy of the New Testament which is on the table and, putting a finger in at random, opens and reads aloud the text at which it points*) "Come unto me all ye who are heavy laden and I will give you rest." (*He stares before him in a sort of trance, his face lighted up from within but painfully confused—in an uncertain whisper*) I will come—but where are you, Savior? (*The noise of the outer door shutting is heard. Dion starts and claps the mocking mask on his face again. He tosses the Testament aside contemptuously.*) Blah! Fixation on old Mama Christianity! You infant blubbering in the dark, you! (*He laughs, with a bitter self-contempt. Footsteps approach. He picks up a newspaper and hides behind it hurriedly. Margaret enters. She is dressed in stylish, expensive clothes and a fur coat, which look as if they had been remodeled and seen service. She has grown mature and maternal, in spite of her youth. Her pretty face is still fresh and healthy but there is the beginning*

484

of a permanently worried, apprehensive expression about the nose and mouth—an uncomprehending hurt in her eyes. Dion pretends to be engrossed in his paper. She bends down and kisses him.)

MARGARET—(*with a forced gayety*) Good morning—at four in the afternoon! You were snoring when I left!

DION—(*puts his arms around her with a negligent, accustomed gesture—mockingly*) The Ideal Husband!

MARGARET—(*already preoccupied with another thought—comes and sits in chair on left*) I was afraid the children would disturb you, so I took them over to Mrs. Young's to play. (*A pause. He picks up the paper again. She asks anxiously*) I suppose they'll be all right over there, don't you? (*He doesn't answer. She is more hurt than offended.*) I wish you'd try to take more interest in the children, Dion.

DION—(*mockingly*) Become a father—before breakfast? I'm in too delicate a condition. (*She turns away, hurt. Penitently he pats her hand—vaguely*) All right. I'll try.

MARGARET—(*squeezing his hand—with possessive tenderness*) Play with them. You're a bigger kid than they are—underneath.

DION—(*self-mockingly—flipping the Bible*) Underneath— I'm becoming downright infantile! "Suffer these little ones!"

MARGARET—(*keeping to her certainty*) You're my oldest.

DION—(*with mocking appreciation*) She puts the Kingdom of Heaven in its place!

MARGARET—(*withdrawing her hand*) I was serious.

DION—So was I—about something or other. (*He laughs.*) This domestic diplomacy! We communicate in code—when neither has the other's key!

MARGARET—(*frowns confusedly—then forcing a playful tone*) I want to have a serious talk with you, young man! In spite of your promises, you've kept up the hard drinking and gambling you started the last year abroad.

DION—From the time I realized it wasn't in me to be an artist—except in living—and not even in that! (*He laughs bitterly.*)

MARGARET—(*with conviction*) But you *can* paint, Dion— beautifully!

DION—(*with deep pain*) No! (*He suddenly takes her hand and kisses it gratefully.*) I love Margaret! Her blindness surpasseth all understanding! (*then bitterly*)—or is it pity?

MARGARET—We've only got about one hundred dollars left in the bank.

DION—(*with dazed surprise*) What! Is all the money from the sale of the house gone?

MARGARET—(*wearily*) Every day or so you've been cashing checks. You've been drinking—you haven't counted—

DION—(*irritably*) I know! (*a pause—soberly*) No more estate to fall back on, eh? Well, for five years it kept us living abroad in peace. It bought us a little happiness—of a kind—didn't it?—living and loving and having children—(*a slight pause—bitterly*)—thinking one was creating before one discovered one couldn't!

MARGARET—(*this time with forced conviction*) But you *can* paint—beautifully!

DION—(*angrily*) Shut up! (*a pause—then jeeringly*) So my wife thinks it behooves me to settle down and support my family in the meager style to which they'll have to become accustomed?

MARGARET—(*shamefacedly*) I didn't say—still—something's got to be done.

DION—(*harshly*) Will Mrs. Anthony helpfully suggest what?

MARGARET—I met Billy Brown on the street. He said you'd have made a good architect, if you'd stuck to it.

DION—Flatterer! Instead of leaving college when my Old Man died? Instead of marrying Peggy and going abroad and being happy?

MARGARET—(*as if she hadn't heard*) He spoke of how well you used to draw.

DION—Billy was in love with Margaret at one time.

MARGARET—He wanted to know why you've never been in to see him.

DION—He's bound heaven-bent for success. It's the will of Mammon! Anthony and Brown, contractors and builders —death subtracts Anthony and I sell out—Billy graduates— Brown and Son, architects and builders—old man Brown perishes of paternal pride—and now we have William

A. Brown, architect! Why his career itself already has an architectural design! One of God's mud pies!

MARGARET—He particularly told me to ask you to drop in.

DION—(*springs to his feet—assertively*) No! Pride! I have been alive!

MARGARET—Why don't you have a talk with him?

DION—Pride in my failure!

MARGARET—You were always such close friends.

DION—(*more and more desperately*) The pride which came after man's fall—by which he laughs as a creator at his self-defeats!

MARGARET—Not for my sake—but for your own—and, above all, for the children's!

DION—(*with terrible despair*) Pride! Pride without which the Gods are worms!

MARGARET—(*after a pause, meekly and humbly*) You don't want to? It would hurt you? All right, dear. Never mind. We'll manage somehow—you mustn't worry—you must start your beautiful painting again—and I can get that position in the library—it would be such fun for me working there! . . . (*She reaches out and takes his hand—tenderly*) I love you, dear. I understand.

DION—(*slumps down into his chair, crushed, his face averted from hers, as hers is from him, although their hands are still clasped—in a trembling, expiring voice*) Pride is dying! (*As if he were suffocating, he pulls the mask from his resigned, pale, suffering face. He prays like a Saint in the desert, exorcizing a demon.*) Pride is dead! Blessed are the meek! Blessed are the poor in spirit!

MARGARET—(*without looking at him—in a comforting, motherly tone*) My poor boy!

DION—(*resentfully—clapping on his mask again and springing to his feet—derisively*) Blessed are the meek for they shall inherit graves! Blessed are the poor in spirit for they are blind! (*then with tortured bitterness*) All right! Then I ask my wife to go and ask Billy Brown—that's more deadly than if I went myself! (*with wild mockery*) Ask him if he can't find an opening for a talented young man who is only honest when he isn't sober—implore him, beg him in the name of old

love, old friendship—to be a generous hero and save the
woman and her children! (*He laughs with a sort of diabolical,
ironical glee now, and starts to go out.*)

MARGARET—(*meekly*) Are you going up street, Dion?

DION—Yes.

MARGARET—Will you stop at the butchers' and have them
send two pounds of pork chops?

DION—Yes.

MARGARET—And stop at Mrs. Young's and ask the children to hurry right home?

DION—Yes.

MARGARET—Will you be back for dinner, Dion?

DION—No. (*He goes, the outer door slams. Margaret sighs
with a tired incomprehension and goes to the window and stares
out.*)

MARGARET—(*worriedly*) I hope they'll watch out, crossing
the street.

(Curtain)

SCENE TWO

SCENE—*Billy Brown's Office, at five in the afternoon. At
center, a fine mahogany desk with a swivel chair in back of it. To
the left of desk, an office armchair. To the right of desk, an office
lounge. The background is a backdrop of an office wall, treated
similarly to that of Scene One in its over-meticulous representation
of detail.*

*Billy Brown is seated at the desk looking over a blue print by
the light of a desk lamp. He has grown into a fine-looking, well-
dressed, capable, college-bred American business man, boyish still
and with the same engaging personality.*

The telephone rings.

BROWN—(*answering it*) Yes? Who? (*this in surprise—then
with eager pleasure*) Let her come right in. (*He gets up and goes
to the door, expectant and curious. Margaret enters. Her face is
concealed behind the mask of the pretty young matron, still hardly
a woman, who cultivates a naïvely innocent and bravely hopeful*

attitude toward things and acknowledges no wound to the world. She is dressed as in Scene One but with an added touch of effective primping here and there.)

MARGARET—(*very gayly*) Hello, Billy Brown!

BROWN—(*awkward in her presence, shakes her hand*) Come in. Sit down. This is a pleasant surprise, Margaret. (*She sits down on the lounge. He sits in his chair behind the desk, as before.*)

MARGARET—(*looking around*) What lovely offices! My, but Billy Brown is getting grand!

BROWN—(*pleased*) I've just moved in. The old place was too stuffy.

MARGARET—It looks so prosperous—but then, Billy is doing so wonderfully well, everyone says.

BROWN—(*modestly*) Well, to be frank, it's been mostly luck. Things have come my way without my doing much about it. (*then, with an abashed pride*) Still—I have done a little something myself. (*He picks the plan from the desk.*) See this? It's my design for the new Municipal Building. It's just been accepted—provisionally—by the Committee.

MARGARET—(*taking it—vaguely*) Oh? (*She looks at it abstractedly. There is a pause. Suddenly*) You mentioned the other day how well Dion used to draw—

BROWN—(*a bit stiffly*) Yes, he certainly did. (*He takes the drawing from her and at once becomes interested and squints at it frowningly.*) Did you notice that anything seemed lacking in this?

MARGARET—(*indifferently*) Not at all.

BROWN—(*with a cheerful grin*) The Committee want it made a little more American. It's too much of a conventional Greco-Roman tomb, they say. (*laughs*) They want an original touch of modern novelty stuck in to liven it up and make it look different from other town halls. (*putting the drawing back on his desk*) And I've been figuring out how to give it to them but my mind doesn't seem to run that way. Have you any suggestion?

MARGARET—(*as if she hadn't heard*) Dion certainly draws well, Billy Brown was saying?

BROWN—(*trying not to show his annoyance*) Why, yes—he did—and still can, I expect. (*A pause. He masters what he feels to be an unworthy pique and turns to her generously.*) Dion would have made a cracking good architect.

MARGARET—(*proudly*) I know. He could be anything he wanted to.

BROWN—(*a pause*—*embarrassedly*) Is he working at anything these days?

MARGARET—(*defensively*) Oh, yes! He's painting wonderfully! But he's just like a child, he's so impractical. He doesn't try to have an exhibition anywhere, or anything.

BROWN—(*surprised*) The one time I ran into him, I thought he told me he'd destroyed all his pictures—that he'd gotten sick of painting and completely given it up.

MARGARET—(*quickly*) He always tells people that. He doesn't want anyone even to look at his things, imagine! He keeps saying they're rotten—when they're really too beautiful! He's too modest for his own good, don't you think? But it is true he hasn't done so much lately since we've been back. You see the children take up such a lot of his time. He just worships them! I'm afraid he's becoming a hopeless family man, just the opposite of what anyone would expect who knew him in the old days.

BROWN—(*painfully embarrassed by her loyalty and his knowledge of the facts*) Yes, I know. (*He coughs self-consciously.*)

MARGARET—(*aroused by something in his manner*) But I suppose the gossips are telling the same silly stories about him they always did. (*She forces a laugh.*) Poor Dion! Give a dog a bad name! (*Her voice breaks a little in spite of herself.*)

BROWN—(*hastily*) I haven't heard any stories—(*he stops uncertainly, then decides to plunge in*)—except about money matters.

MARGARET—(*forcing a laugh*) Oh, perhaps they're true enough. Dion is such a generous fool with his money, like all artists.

BROWN—(*with a certain doggedness*) There's a rumor that you've applied for a position at the Library.

MARGARET—(*forcing a gay tone*) Yes, indeed! Won't it be fun! Maybe it'll improve my mind! And one of us has got to be practical, so why not me? (*She forces a gay, girlish laugh.*)

BROWN—(*impulsively reaches out and takes her hand*—*awkwardly*) Listen, Margaret. Let's be perfectly frank, will you?

I'm such an old friend, and I want like the deuce to. . . . You know darn well I'd do anything in the world to help you—or Dion.

MARGARET—(*withdrawing her hand, coldly*) I'm afraid I— don't understand, Billy Brown.

BROWN—(*acutely embarrassed*) Well, I—I just meant—you know, if you needed— (*A pause. He looks questioningly at her averted face—then ventures on another tack, matter-of-factly.*) I've got a proposition to make to Dion—if I could ever get hold of him. It's this way: business has been piling up on me—a run of luck—but I'm short-handed. I need a crack chief draftsman darn badly—or I'm liable to lose out. Do you think Dion would consider it—as a temporary stop-gap— until he felt in the painting mood again?

MARGARET—(*striving to conceal her eagerness and relief— judicially*) Yes—I really do. He's such a good sport and Billy and he were such pals once. I know he'd be only too tickled to help him out.

BROWN—(*diffidently*) I thought he might be sensitive about working for—I mean, with me—when, if he hadn't sold out to Dad he'd be my partner now—(*earnestly*)—and, by jingo, I wish he was! (*then, abruptly*) Let's try to nail him down right away, Margaret. Is he home now? (*He reaches for the phone.*)

MARGARET—(*hurriedly*) No, he—he went out for a long walk.

BROWN—Perhaps I can locate him later around town somewhere.

MARGARET—(*with a note of pleading*) Please don't trouble. It isn't necessary. I'm sure when I talk to him—he's coming home to dinner— (*getting up*) Then it's all settled, isn't it? Dion will be so glad to be able to help an old friend—he's so terribly loyal, and he's always liked Billy Brown so much! (*holding out her hand*) I really must go now!

BROWN—(*shakes her hand*) Good-by, Margaret. I hope you'll be dropping in on us a lot when Dion gets here.

MARGARET—Yes. (*She goes.*)

BROWN—(*sits at his desk again, looking ahead in a not un-satisfying melancholy reverie. He mutters admiringly but pity-ingly*) Poor Margaret! She's a game sport, but it's pretty damn tough on her! (*indignantly*) By God, I'm going to give Dion a good talking-to one of these days!

(*Curtain*)

SCENE THREE

SCENE—*Cybel's parlor. An automatic, nickel-in-the-slot player-piano is at center, rear. On its right is a dirty gilt second-hand sofa. At the left is a bald-spotted crimson plush chair. The backdrop for the rear wall is cheap wall-paper of a dull yellow-brown, resembling a blurred impression of a fallow field in early spring. There is a cheap alarm clock on top of the piano. Beside it her mask is lying.*

Dion is sprawled on his back, fast asleep on the sofa. His mask has fallen down on his chest. His pale face is singularly pure, spiritual and sad.

The player-piano is groggily banging out a sentimental medley of "Mother—Mammy" tunes.

Cybel is seated on the stool in front of the piano. She is a strong, calm, sensual, blonde girl of twenty or so, her complexion fresh and healthy, her figure full-breasted and wide-hipped, her movements slow and solidly languorous like an animal's, her large eyes dreamy with the reflected stirring of profound instincts. She chews gum like a sacred cow forgetting time with an eternal end. Her eyes are fixed, incuriously, on Dion's pale face.

CYBEL—(*as the tune runs out, glances at the clock, which indicates midnight, then goes slowly over to Dion and puts her hand gently on his forehead*) Wake up!

DION—(*stirs, sighs and murmurs dreamily*) "And He laid his hands on them and healed them." (*Then with a start he opens his eyes and, half sitting up, stares at her bewilderedly.*) What—where—who are you? (*He reaches for his mask and claps it on defensively.*)

CYBEL—(*placidly*) Only another female. You was camping on my steps, sound asleep. I didn't want to run any risk getting into more trouble with the cops pinching you there and blaming me, so I took you in to sleep it off.

DION—(*mockingly*) Blessed are the pitiful, Sister! I'm broke—but you will be rewarded in Heaven!

CYBEL—(*calmly*) I wasn't wasting my pity. Why should I? You were happy, weren't you?

DION—(*approvingly*) Excellent! You're not a moralist, I see.

CYBEL—(*going on*) And you look like a good boy, too— when you're asleep. Say, you better beat it home to bed or you'll be locked out.

DION—(*mockingly*) Now you're becoming maternal, Miss Earth. Is that the only answer—to pin my soul into every vacant diaper? (*She stares down at his mask, her face growing hard. He laughs.*) But please don't stop stroking my aching brow. Your hand is a cool mud poultice on the sting of thought!

CYBEL—(*calmly*) Stop acting. I hate ham fats. (*She looks at him as if waiting for him to remove his mask—then turns her back indifferently and goes to the piano.*) Well, if you simply got to be a regular devil like all the other visiting sports, I s'pose I got to play with you. (*She takes her mask and puts it on— then turns. The mask is the rouged and eye-blackened countenance of the hardened prostitute. In a coarse, harsh voice*) Kindly state your dishonorable intentions, if any! I can't sit up all night keeping company! Let's have some music! (*She puts a plug in the machine. The same sentimental medley begins to play. The two masks stare at each other. She laughs.*) Shoot! I'm all set! It's your play, Kid Lucifer!

DION—(*slowly removes his mask. She stops the music with a jerk. His face is gentle and sad—humbly*) I'm sorry. It has always been such agony for me to be touched!

CYBEL—(*taking off her mask—sympathetically as she comes back and sits down on her stool*) Poor kid! I've never had one, but I can guess. They hug and kiss you and take you on their laps and pinch you and want to see you getting dressed and undressed—as if they owned you— I bet you I'd never let them treat one of mine that way!

DION—(*turning to her*) You're lost in blind alleys, too. (*suddenly holding out his hand to her*) But you're strong. Let's be friends.

CYBEL—(*with a strange sternness, searches his face*) And never nothing more?

DION—(*with a strange smile*) Let's say, never anything less! (*She takes his hand. There is a ring at the outside door bell. They stare at each other. There is another ring.*)

CYBEL—(*puts on her mask, Dion does likewise. Mockingly*) When you got to love to live it's hard to love living. I better join the A. F. of L. and soap-box for the eight-hour night! Got a nickel, baby? Play a tune. (*She goes out. Dion puts a nickel in. The same sentimental tune starts. Cybel returns, followed by Billy Brown. His face is rigidly composed, but his superior disgust for Dion can be seen. Dion jerks off the music and he and Billy look at each other for a moment, Cybel watching them both—then, bored, she yawns.*) He's hunting for you. Put out the lights when you go. I'm going to sleep. (*She starts to go— then, as if reminded of something—to Dion*) Life's all right, if you let it alone. (*then mechanically flashing a trade smile at Billy*) Now you know the way, Handsome, call again! (*She goes.*)

BROWN—(*after an awkward pause*) Hello, Dion! I've been looking all over town for you. This place was the very last chance. . . . (*another pause—embarrassedly*) Let's take a walk.

DION—(*mockingly*) I've given up exercise. They claim it lengthens your life.

BROWN—(*persuasively*) Come on, Dion, be a good fellow. You're certainly not staying here—

DION—Billy would like to think me taken in *flagrante delicto*, eh?

BROWN—Don't be a damn fool! Listen to me! I've been looking you up for purely selfish reasons. I need your help.

DION—(*astonished*) What?

BROWN—I've a proposition to make that I hope you'll consider favorably out of old friendship. To be frank, Dion, I need you to lend me a hand down at the office.

DION—(*with a harsh laugh*) So it's the job, is it? Then my poor wife did a-begging go!

BROWN—(*repelled—sharply*) On the contrary, I had to beg her to beg you to take it! (*more angrily*) Look here, Dion! I won't listen to you talk that way about Margaret! And you wouldn't if you weren't drunk! (*suddenly shaking him*) What in hell has come over you, anyway! You didn't use to be like this! What the devil are you going to do with yourself—sink into the gutter and drag Margaret with you? If you'd heard her defend you, lie about you, tell me how hard you were working, what beautiful things you were painting, how you stayed at home and idolized the children!—when everyone knows you've been out every night sousing and gambling away the last of your estate. . . . (*He stops, ashamed, controlling himself.*)

DION—(*wearily*) She was lying about her husband, not me, you fool! But it's no use explaining. (*then, in a sudden, excitable passion*) What do you want? I agree to anything— except the humiliation of yelling secrets at the deaf!

BROWN—(*trying a bullying tone—roughly*) Bunk! Don't try to crawl out! There's no excuse and you know it. (*then as Dion doesn't reply—penitently*) But I know I shouldn't talk this way, old man! It's only because we're such old pals—and I hate to see you wasting yourself—you who had more brains than any of us! But, damn it, I suppose you're too much of a rotten cynic to believe I mean what I've just said!

DION—(*touched*) I know Billy was always Dion Anthony's friend.

BROWN—You're damn right I am—and I'd have proved it long ago if you'd only given me half a chance! After all, I couldn't keep chasing after you and be snubbed every time. A man has some pride!

DION—(*bitterly mocking*) Dead wrong! Never more! None whatever! It's unmoral! Blessed are the poor in spirit, Brother! When shall I report?

BROWN—(*eagerly*) Then you'll take the—you'll help me?

DION—(*wearily bitter*) I'll take the job. One must do something to pass away the time, while one is waiting—for one's next incarnation.

BROWN—(*jokingly*) I'd say it was a bit early to be worrying about that. (*trying to get Dion started*) Come along, now. It's pretty late.

DION—(*shakes his hand off his shoulder and walks away from him—after a pause*) Is my father's chair still there?

BROWN—(*turns away—embarrassed*) I—I don't really remember, Dion—I'll look it up.

DION—(*taking off his mask—slowly*) I'd like to sit where he spun what I have spent. What aliens we were to each other!

When he lay dead, his face looked so familiar that I wondered where I had met that man before. Only at the second of my conception. After that, we grew hostile with concealed shame. And my mother? I remember a sweet, strange girl, with affectionate, bewildered eyes as if God had locked her in a dark closet without any explanation. I was the sole doll our ogre, her husband, allowed her and she played mother and child with me for many years in that house until at last through two tears I watched her die with the shy pride of one who has lengthened her dress and put up her hair. And I felt like a forsaken toy and cried to be buried with her, because her hands alone had caressed without clawing. She lived long and aged greatly in the two days before they closed her coffin. The last time I looked, her purity had forgotten me, she was stainless and imperishable, and I knew my sobs were ugly and meaningless to her virginity; so I shrank away, back into life, with naked nerves jumping like fleas, and in due course of nature another girl called me her boy in the moon and married me and became three mothers in one person, while I got paint on my paws in an endeavor to see God! (*He laughs wildly—claps on his mask.*) But that Ancient Humorist had given me weak eyes, so now I'll have to foreswear my quest for Him and go in for the Omnipresent Successful Serious One, the Great God Mr. Brown, instead! (*He makes him a sweeping, mocking bow.*)

BROWN—(*repelled but cajolingly*) Shut up, you nut! You're still drunk. Come on! Let's start! (*He grabs Dion by the arm and switches off the light.*)

DION—(*from the darkness—mockingly*) I am thy shorn, bald, nude sheep! Lead on, Almighty Brown, thou Kindly Light!

(*Curtain*)

ACT TWO

Scene One

SCENE—*Cybel's parlor—about sunset in spring seven years later. The arrangement of furniture is the same but the chair and sofa are new, bright-colored, costly pieces. The old automatic piano at center looks exactly the same. The cheap alarm clock is still on top of it. On either side of the clock, the masks of Dion and Cybel are lying. The background backdrop is brilliant, stunning wallpaper, on which crimson and purple flowers and fruits tumble over one another in a riotously profane lack of any apparent design.*

Dion sits in the chair on left, Cybel on the sofa. A card-table is between them. Both are playing solitaire. Dion is now prematurely gray. His face is that of an ascetic, a martyr, furrowed by pain and self-torture, yet lighted from within by a spiritual calm and human kindliness.

Cybel has grown stouter and more voluptuous, but her face is still unmarked and fresh, her calm more profound. She is like an unmoved idol of Mother Earth.

The piano is whining out its same old sentimental medley. They play their cards intently and contentedly. The music stops.

CYBEL—(*musingly*) I love those rotten old sob tunes. They make me wise to people. That's what's inside them—what makes them love and murder their neighbor—crying jags set to music!

DION—(*compassionately*) Every song is a hymn. They keep trying to find the Word in the Beginning.

CYBEL—They try to know too much. It makes them weak. I never puzzled them with myself. I gave them a Tart. They understood her and knew their parts and acted naturally. And on both sides we were able to keep our real virtue, if you get me. (*She plays her last card—indifferently*) I've made it again.

DION—(*smiling*) Your luck is uncanny. It never comes out for me.

CYBEL—You keep getting closer, but it knows you still

want to win—a little bit—and it's wise all I care about is playing. (*She lays out another game.*) Speaking of my canned music, our Mr. Brown hates that old box. (*At the mention of Brown, Dion trembles as if suddenly possessed, has a terrible struggle with himself, then while she continues to speak, gets up like an automaton and puts on his mask. The mask is now terribly ravaged. All of its Pan quality has changed into a diabolical Mephistophelean cruelty and irony.*) He doesn't mind the music inside. That gets him somehow. But he thinks the case looks shabby and he wants it junked. But I told him that just because he's been keeping me so long, he needn't start bossing like a husband or I'll— (*She looks up and sees the masked Dion standing by the piano—calmly*) Hello! Getting jealous again?

DION—(*jeeringly*) Are you falling in love with your keeper, old Sacred Cow?

CYBEL—(*without taking offense*) Cut it! You've been asking me that for years. Be yourself! He's healthy and handsome— but he's too guilty. What makes you pretend you think love is so important, anyway? It's just one of a lot of things you do to keep life living.

DION—(*in same tone*) Then you've lied when you've said you loved me, have you, Old Filth?

CYBEL—(*affectionately*) You'll never grow up! We've been friends, haven't we, for seven years? I've never let myself want you nor you me. Yes, I love you. It takes all kinds of love to make a world! Ours is the living cream, I say, living rich and high! (*A pause. Coaxingly*) Stop hiding. I know you.

DION—(*taking off his mask, wearily comes and sits down at her feet and lays his head in her lap—with a grateful smile*) You're strong. You always give. You've given my weakness strength to live.

CYBEL—(*tenderly, stroking his hair maternally*) You're not weak. You were born with ghosts in your eyes and you were brave enough to go looking into your own dark—and you got afraid. (*after a pause*) I don't blame your being jealous of Mr. Brown sometimes. I'm jealous of your wife, even though I know you do love her.

DION—(*slowly*) I love Margaret. I don't know who my wife is.

CYBEL—(*after a pause—with a queer broken laugh*) Oh, God, sometimes the truth hits me such a sock between the eyes I can see the stars!—and then I'm so damn sorry for the lot of you, every damn mother's son-of-a-gun of you, that I'd like to run out naked into the street and love the whole mob to death like I was bringing you all a new brand of dope that'd make you forget everything that ever was for good! (*then, with a twisted smile*) But they wouldn't see me, any more than they see each other. And they keep right on moving along and dying without my help anyway.

DION—(*sadly*) You've given me strength to die.

CYBEL—You may be important but your life's not. There's millions of it born every second. Life can cost too much even for a sucker to afford it—like everything else. And it's not sacred—only the you inside is. The rest is earth.

DION—(*gets to his knees and with clasped hands looks up raptly and prays with an ascetic fervor*) "Into thy hands, O Lord," . . . (*then suddenly, with a look of horror*) Nothing! To feel one's life blown out like the flame of a cheap match . . . ! (*He claps on his mask and laughs harshly.*) To fall asleep and know you'll never, never be called to get on the job of existence again! "Swift be thine approaching flight! Come soon—soon!" (*He quotes this last with a mocking longing.*)

CYBEL—(*pats his head maternally*) There, don't be scared. It's born in the blood. When the time comes, you'll find it's easy.

DION—(*jumps to his feet and walks about excitedly*) It won't be long. My wife dragged in a doctor the day before yesterday. He says my heart is gone—booze— He warned me, never another drop or— (*mockingly*) What say? Shall we have a drink?

CYBEL—(*like an idol*) Suit yourself. It's in the pantry. (*then, as he hesitates*) What set you off on this bat? You were raving on about some cathedral plans. . . .

DION—(*wildly mocking*) They've been accepted—Mr. Brown's designs! My designs really! You don't need to be told that. He hands me one mathematically correct barn after another and I doctor them up with cute allurements so that fools will desire to buy, sell, breed, sleep, love, hate, curse and pray in them! I do this with devilish cleverness to their entire delight! Once I dreamed of painting wind on the sea and the skimming flight of cloud shadows over the tops of trees! Now . . . (*He laughs.*) But pride is a sin—even in a memory of the long deceased! Blessed are the poor in spirit! (*He subsides weakly on his chair, his hand pressed to his heart.*)

CYBEL—(*like an idol*) Go home and sleep. Your wife'll be worried.

DION—She knows—but she'll never admit to herself that her husband ever entered your door. (*mocking*) Aren't women loyal—to their vanity and their other things!

CYBEL—Brown is coming soon, don't forget.

DION—He knows too and can't admit. Perhaps he needs me here—unknown. What first aroused his passion to possess you exclusively, do you think? Because he knew you loved me and he felt himself cheated. He wanted what he thought was my love of the flesh! He feels I have no right to love. He'd like to steal it as he steals my ideas—complacently—righteously. Oh, the good Brown!

CYBEL—But you like him, too! You're brothers, I guess, somehow. Well, remember he's paying, he'll pay—in some way or other.

DION—(*raises his head as if starting to remove the mask*) I know. Poor Billy! God forgive me the evil I've done him!

CYBEL—(*reaches out and takes his hand*) Poor boy!

DION—(*presses her convulsively—then with forced harshness*) Well, homeward Christian Soldier! I'm off! By-bye, Mother Earth! (*He starts to go off right. She seems about to let him go.*)

CYBEL—(*suddenly starts and calls with deep grief*) Dion! (*He looks at her. A pause. He comes slowly back. She speaks strangely in a deep, far-off voice—and yet like a mother talking to her little son.*) You mustn't forget to kiss me before you go, Dion. (*She removes his mask.*) Haven't I told you to take off your mask in the house? Look at me, Dion. I've—just—seen—something. I'm afraid you're going away a long, long ways. I'm afraid I won't see you again for a long, long time. So it's good-by, dear. (*She kisses him gently. He begins to sob. She hands him back his mask.*) Here you are. Don't get hurt. Remember, it's all a game, and after you're asleep I'll tuck you in.

DION—(*in a choking, heart-broken cry*) Mother! (*Then he claps on his mask with a terrible effort of will—mockingly*) Go to the devil, you sentimental old pig! See you tomorrow! (*He goes, whistling, slamming the door.*)

CYBEL—(*like an idol again*) What's the good of bearing children? What's the use of giving birth to death? (*She sighs wearily, turns, puts a plug in the piano, which starts up its old sentimental tune. At the same moment Brown enters quietly from the left. He is the ideal of the still youthful, good-looking, well-groomed, successful provincial American of forty. Just now, he is plainly perturbed. He is not able to see either Cybel's face or her mask.*)

BROWN—Cybel! (*She starts, jams off the music and reaches for her mask but has no time to put it on.*) Wasn't that Dion I just saw going out—after all your promises never to see him! (*She turns like an idol, holding the mask behind her. He stares, bewildered—stammers*) I—I beg your pardon—I thought—

CYBEL—(*in her strange voice*) Cybel's gone out to dig in the earth and pray.

BROWN—(*with more assurance*) But—aren't those her clothes?

CYBEL—Cybel doesn't want people to see me naked. I'm her sister. Dion came to see me.

BROWN—(*relieved*) So that's what he's up to, is it? (*then with a pitying sigh*) Poor Margaret! (*then with playful reproof*) You really shouldn't encourage him. He's married and got three big sons.

CYBEL—And you haven't.

BROWN—(*stung*) No, I'm not married.

CYBEL—He and I were friends.

BROWN—(*with a playful wink*) Yes, I can imagine how the platonic must appeal to Dion's pure, innocent type! It's no good your kidding me about Dion. We've been friends since we were kids. I know him in and out. I've always stood up for him whatever he's done—so you can be perfectly frank. I only spoke as I did on account of Margaret—his wife—it's pretty tough on her.

CYBEL—You love his wife.

BROWN—(*scandalized*) What? What are you talking about? (*then uncertainly*) Don't be a fool! (*a pause—then as if impelled by an intense curiosity*) So Dion is your lover, eh? That's very interesting. (*He pulls his chair closer to hers.*) Sit down.

Let's talk. (*She continues to stand, the mask held behind her.*)
Tell me—I've always been curious—what is it that makes
Dion so attractive to women—especially certain types of
women, if you'll pardon me? He always has been and yet I
never could see exactly what they saw in him. Is it his looks—
or because he's such a violent sensualist—or because he poses
as artistic and temperamental—or because he's so wild—or
just what is it?

CYBEL—He's alive!

BROWN—(*suddenly takes one of her hands and kisses it—
insinuatingly*) Well, don't you think I'm alive, too? (*eagerly*)
Listen. Would you consider giving up Dion—and letting me
take care of you under a similar arrangement to the one I've
made with Cybel? I like you, you can see that. I won't bother
you much—I'm much too busy—you can do what you
like—lead your own life—except for seeing him. (*He stops. A
pause. She stares ahead unmoved as if she hadn't heard. He
pleads*) Well—what do you say? Please do!

CYBEL—(*her voice very weary*) Cybel said to tell you she'd
be back next week, Mr. Brown.

BROWN—(*with queer agony*) You mean you won't? Don't
be so cruel! I love you! (*She walks away. He clutches at her,
pleadingly*) At least—I'll give you anything you ask!—please
promise me you won't see Dion Anthony again!

CYBEL—(*with deep grief*) He will never see me again, I
promise you. Good-by!

BROWN—(*jubilantly, kissing her hand—politely*) Thank
you! Thank you! I'm exceedingly grateful. (*tactfully*) I won't
disturb you any further. Please forgive my intrusion, and remember me to Cybel when you write. (*He bows, turns, and
goes off left.*)

(*Curtain*)

SCENE TWO

SCENE—*The drafting room in Brown's office. Dion's drafting
table with a high stool in front is at center. Another stool is to the
left of it. At the right is a bench. It is in the evening of the same*

day. The black wall drop has windows painted on it with a dim, street-lighted view of black houses across the way.

Dion is sitting on the stool in back of the table, reading aloud from the "Imitation of Christ" by Thomas à Kempis to his mask, which is on the table before him. His own face is gentler, more spiritual, more saintlike and ascetic than ever before.

DION—(*like a priest, offering up prayers for the dying*) "Quickly must thou be gone from hence, see then how matters stand with thee. Ah, fool—learn now to die to the world that thou mayst begin to live with Christ! Do now, beloved, do now all thou canst because thou knowst not when thou shalt die; nor dost thou know what shall befall thee after death. Keep thyself as a pilgrim, and a stranger upon earth, to whom the affairs of this world do not—belong! Keep thy heart free and raised upwards to God because thou hast not here a lasting abode. 'Because at what hour you know not the Son of Man will come!' " Amen. (*He raises his hand over the mask as if he were blessing it, closes the book and puts it back in his packet. He raises the mask in his hands and stares at it with a pitying tenderness.*) Peace, poor tortured one, brave pitiful pride of man, the hour of our deliverance comes. Tomorrow we may be with Him in Paradise! (*He kisses it on the lips and sets it down again. There is the noise of footsteps climbing the stairs in the hallway. He grabs up the mask in a sudden panic and, as a knock comes on the door, he claps it on and calls mockingly*) Come in, Mrs. Anthony, come in! (*Margaret enters. In one hand behind her, hidden from him, is the mask of the brave face she puts on before the world to hide her suffering and disillusionment, and which she has just taken off. Her own face is still sweet and pretty but lined, drawn and careworn for its years, sad, resigned, but a bit querulous.*)

MARGARET—(*wearily reproving*) Thank goodness I've found you! Why haven't you been home the last two days? It's bad enough your drinking again without your staying away and worrying us to death!

DION—(*bitterly*) My ears knew her footsteps. One gets to recognize everything—and to see nothing!

MARGARET—I finally sent the boys out looking for you

and came myself. (*with tired solicitude*) I suppose you haven't eaten a thing, as usual. Won't you come home and let me fry you a chop?

DION—(*wonderingly*) Can Margaret still love Dion Anthony? Is it possible she does?

MARGARET—(*forcing a tired smile*) I suppose so, Dion. I certainly oughtn't to, had I?

DION—(*in same tone*) And I love Margaret! What haunted, haunting ghosts we are! We dimly remember so much it will take us so many million years to forget! (*He comes forward, putting one arm around her bowed shoulders, and they kiss.*)

MARGARET—(*patting his hand affectionately*) No, you certainly don't deserve it. When I stop to think of all you've made me go through in the years since we settled down here. . . ! I really don't believe I could ever have stood it if it weren't for the boys! (*forcing a smile*) But perhaps I would, I've always been such a big fool about you.

DION—(*a bit mockingly*) The boys! Three strong sons! Margaret can afford to be magnanimous!

MARGARET—If they didn't find you, they were coming to meet me here.

DION—(*with sudden wildness—torturedly, sinking on his knees beside her*) Margaret! Margaret! I'm lonely! I'm frightened! I'm going away! I've got to say good-by!

MARGARET—(*patting his hair*) Poor boy! Poor Dion! Come home and sleep.

DION—(*springs up frantically*) No! I'm a man! I'm a lonely man! I can't go back! I have conceived myself! (*then with desperate mockery*) Look at me, Mrs. Anthony! It's the last chance! Tomorrow I'll have moved on to the next hell! Behold your man—the sniveling, cringing, life-denying Christian slave you have so nobly ignored in the father of your sons! Look! (*He tears the mask from his face, which is radiant with a great pure love for her and a great sympathy and tenderness.*) O woman—my love—that I have sinned against in my sick pride and cruelty—forgive my sins—forgive my solitude—forgive my sickness—forgive me! (*He kneels and kisses the hem of her dress.*)

MARGARET—(*who has been staring at him with terror,*

raising her mask to ward off his face) Dion! Don't! I can't bear it! You're like a ghost! You're dead! Oh, my God! Help! Help! (*She falls back fainting on the bench. He looks at her— then takes her hand which holds her mask and looks at that face— gently*) And now I am permitted to understand and love you, too! (*He kisses the mask first—then kisses her face, murmuring*) And you, sweetheart! Blessed, thrice blessed are the meek! (*There is a sound of heavy, hurrying footsteps on the stairs. He puts on his mask in haste. The three sons rush into the room. The eldest is about fourteen, the two others thirteen and twelve. They look healthy, normal likeable boys, with much the same quality as Billy Brown's in Act One, Scene One. They stop short and stiffen all in a row, staring from the woman on the bench to their father, accusingly.*)

ELDEST—We heard someone yell. It sounded like Mother.

DION—(*defensively*) No. It was this lady—my wife.

ELDEST—But hasn't Mother come yet?

DION—(*going to Margaret*) Yes. Your Mother is here. (*He stands between them and puts her mask over Margaret's face—then steps back.*) She has fainted. You'd better bring her to.

BOYS—Mother! (*They run to her side, kneel and rub her wrists. The eldest smooths back her hair.*)

DION—(*watching them*) At least I am leaving her well provided for. (*He addresses them directly.*) Tell your mother she'll get word from Mr. Brown's house. I must pay him a farewell call. I am going. Good-by. (*They stop, staring at him fixedly, with eyes a mixture of bewilderment, distrust and hurt.*)

ELDEST—(*awkwardly and shamefacedly*) Honest, I think you ought to have . . .

SECOND—Yes, honest you ought . . .

YOUNGEST—Yes, honest . . .

DION—(*in a friendly tone*) I know. But I couldn't. That's for you who can. You must inherit the earth for her. Don't forget now, boys. Good-by.

BOYS—(*in the same awkward, self-conscious tone, one after another*) Good-by—good-by—good-by. (*Dion goes.*)

(*Curtain*)

SCENE THREE

SCENE—*The library of William Brown's home—night of the same day. A backdrop of carefully painted, prosperous, bourgeois culture, bookcases filled with sets, etc. The heavy table at center is expensive. The leather armchair at left of it and the couch at right are opulently comfortable. The reading lamp on the table is the only light.*

Brown sits in the chair at left reading an architectural periodical. His expression is composed and gravely receptive. In outline, his face suggests a Roman consul on an old coin. There is an incongruous distinction about it, the quality of unquestioning faith in the finality of its achievement.

There is a sudden loud thumping on the front door and the ringing of the bell. Brown frowns and listens as a servant answers. Dion's voice can be heard, raised mockingly.

DION—Tell him it's the devil come to conclude a bargain.

BROWN—(*suppressing annoyance, calls out with forced good nature*) Come on in, Dion. (*Dion enters. He is in a wild state. His clothes are disheveled, his masked face has a terrible deathlike intensity, its mocking irony becomes so cruelly malignant as to give him the appearance of a real demon, tortured into torturing others.*) Sit down.

DION—(*stands and sings*) William Brown's soul lies moldering in the crib but his body goes marching on!

BROWN—(*maintaining the same indulgent, big-brotherly tone, which he tries to hold throughout the scene*) Not so loud, for Pete's sake! I don't mind—but I've got neighbors.

DION—Hate them! Fear thy neighbor as thyself! That's the leaden rule for the safe and sane. (*then advancing to the table with a sort of deadly calm*) Listen! One day when I was four years old, a boy sneaked up behind when I was drawing a picture in the sand he couldn't draw and hit me on the head with a stick and kicked out my picture and laughed when I cried. It wasn't what he'd done that made me cry, but him! I had loved and trusted him and suddenly the good God was disproved in his person and the evil and injustice of Man was born! Everyone called me cry-baby, so I became silent for life and designed a mask of the Bad Boy Pan in which to live and rebel against that other boy's God and protect myself from His cruelty. And that other boy, secretly he felt ashamed but he couldn't acknowledge it; so from that day he instinctively developed into the good boy, the good friend, the good man, William Brown!

BROWN—(*shamefacedly*) I remember now. It was a dirty trick. (*then with a trace of resentment*) Sit down. You know where the booze is. Have a drink, if you like. But I guess you've had enough already.

DION—(*looks at him fixedly for a moment—then strangely*) Thanks be to Brown for reminding me. I must drink. (*He goes and gets a bottle of whisky and a glass.*)

BROWN—(*with a good-humored shrug*) All right. It's your funeral.

DION—(*returning and pouring out a big drink in the tumbler*) And William Brown's! When I die, he goes to hell! Sköal! (*He drinks and stares malevolently. In spite of himself, Brown is uneasy. A pause.*)

BROWN—(*with forced casualness*) You've been on this toot for a week now.

DION—(*tauntingly*) I've been celebrating the acceptance of *my* design for the cathedral.

BROWN—(*humorously*) You certainly helped me a lot on it.

DION—(*with a harsh laugh*) O perfect Brown! Never mind! I'll make him look in my mirror yet—and drown in it! (*He pours out another big drink.*)

BROWN—(*rather tauntingly*) Go easy. I don't want your corpse on my hands.

DION—But I do. (*He drinks.*) Brown will still need me— to reassure him he's alive! I've loved, lusted, won and lost, sang and wept! I've been life's lover! I've fulfilled her will and if she's through with me now it's only because I was too weak to dominate her in turn. It isn't enough to be her creature, you've got to create her or she requests you to destroy yourself.

BROWN—(*good-naturedly*) Nonsense. Go home and get some sleep.

DION—(*as if he hadn't heard—bitingly*) But to be neither creature nor creator! To exist only in her indifference! To be unloved by life! (*Brown stirs uneasily.*) To be merely a success-

ful freak, the result of some snide neutralizing of life forces—
a spineless cactus—a wild boar of the mountains altered into
a packer's hog eating to become food—a Don Juan inspired
to romance by a monkey's glands—and to have Life not even
think you funny enough to see!

BROWN—(*stung—angrily*) Bosh!

DION—Consider Mr. Brown. His parents bore him on
earth as if they were thereby entering him in a baby parade
with prizes for the fattest—and he's still being wheeled along
in the procession, too fat now to learn to walk, let alone to
dance or run, and he'll never live until his liberated dust
quickens into earth!

BROWN—(*gruffly*) Rave on! (*then with forced good-nature*)
Well, Dion, at any rate, I'm satisfied.

DION—(*quickly and malevolently*) No! Brown isn't satisfied! He's piled on layers of protective fat, but vaguely, deeply
he feels at his heart the gnawing of a doubt! And I'm interested in that germ which wriggles like a question mark of
insecurity in his blood, because it's part of the creative life
Brown's stolen from me!

BROWN—(*forcing a sour grin*) Steal germs? I thought you
caught them.

DION—(*as if he hadn't heard*) It's mine—and I'm interested in seeing it thrive and breed and become multitudes and
eat until Brown is consumed!

BROWN—(*cannot restrain a shudder*) Sometimes when
you're drunk, you're positively evil, do you know it?

DION—(*somberly*) When Pan was forbidden the light and
warmth of the sun he grew sensitive and self-conscious and
proud and revengeful—and became Prince of Darkness.

BROWN—(*jocularly*) You don't fit the rôle of Pan, Dion. It
sounds to me like Bacchus, alias the Demon Rum, doing the
talking. (*Dion recovers from his spasm with a start and stares at
Brown with terrible hatred. There is a pause. In spite of himself,
Brown squirms and adopts a placating tone.*) Go home. Be a
good scout. It's all well enough celebrating our design being
accepted but—

DION—(*in a steely voice*) I've been the brains! I've been the
design! I've designed even his success—drunk and laughing
at him—laughing at his career! Not proud! Sick! Sick of

myself and him! Designing and getting drunk! Saving my woman and children! (*He laughs.*) Ha! And this cathedral is my masterpiece! It will make Brown the most eminent architect in this state of God's Country. I put a lot into it—what was left of my life! It's one vivid blasphemy from sidewalk to the tips of its spires!—but so concealed that the fools will never know. They'll kneel and worship the ironic Silenus who tells them the best good is never to be born! (*He laughs triumphantly.*) Well, blasphemy is faith, isn't it? In self-preservation the devil must believe! But Mr. Brown, the Great Brown, has no faith! He couldn't design a cathedral without it looking like the First Supernatural Bank! He only believes in the immortality of the moral belly! (*He laughs wildly—then sinks down in his chair, gasping, his hands pressed to his heart. Then suddenly becomes deadly calm and pronounces like a cruel malignant condemnation*) From now on, Brown will never design anything. He will devote his life to renovating the house of my Cybel into a home for my Margaret!

BROWN—(*springing to his feet, his face convulsed with strange agony*) I've stood enough! How dare you. . . !

DION—(*his voice like a probe*) Why has no woman ever loved him? Why has he always been the Big Brother, the Friend? Isn't their trust—a contempt?

BROWN—You lie!

DION—Why has he never been able to love—since my Margaret? Why has he never married? Why has he tried to steal Cybel, as he once tried to steal Margaret? Isn't it out of revenge—and envy?

BROWN—(*violently*) Rot! I wanted Cybel, and I bought her!

DION—Brown bought her for me! She has loved me more than he will ever know!

BROWN—You lie! (*then furiously*) I'll throw her back on the street!

DION—To me! To her fellow creature! Why hasn't Brown had children—he who loves children—he who loves *my* children—he who envies me *my* children?

BROWN—(*brokenly*) I'm not ashamed to envy you them!

DION—They like Brown, too—as a friend—as an equal—as Margaret has always liked him—

BROWN—(*brokenly*) And as I've liked her!

DION—How many million times Brown has thought how much better for her it would have been if she'd chosen him instead!

BROWN—(*torturedly*) You lie! (*then with sudden frenzied defiance*) All right! If you force me to say it, I do love Margaret! I always have loved her and you've always known I did!

DION—(*with a terrible composure*) No! That is merely the appearance, not the truth! Brown loves me! He loves me because I have always possessed the power he needed for love, because I am love!

BROWN—(*frenziedly*) You drunken bum! (*He leaps on Dion and grabs him by the throat.*)

DION—(*triumphantly, staring into his eyes*) Ah! Now he looks into the mirror! Now he sees his face! (*Brown lets go of him and staggers back to his chair, pale and trembling.*)

BROWN—(*humbly*) Stop, for God's sake! You're mad!

DION—(*sinking in his chair, more and more weakly*) I'm done. My heart, not Brown— (*mockingly*) My last will and testament! I leave Dion Anthony to William Brown—for him to love and obey—for him to become me—then my Margaret will love me—my children will love me—Mr. and Mrs. Brown and sons, happily ever after! (*staggering to his full height and looking upward defiantly*) Nothing more—but Man's last gesture—by which he conquers—to laugh! Ha— (*He begins, stops as if paralyzed, and drops on his knees by Brown's chair, his mask falling off, his Christian Martyr's face at the point of death.*) Forgive me, Billy. Bury me, hide me, forget me for your own happiness! May Margaret love you! May you design the Temple of Man's Soul! Blessed are the meek and the poor in spirit! (*He kisses Brown's feet—then more and more weakly and childishly*) What was the prayer, Billy? I'm getting so sleepy. . . .

BROWN—(*in a trancelike tone*) "Our Father who art in Heaven."

DION—(*drowsily*) "Our Father." . . . (*He dies. A pause. Brown remains in a stupor for a moment—then stirs himself, puts his hand on Dion's breast.*)

BROWN—(*dully*) He's dead—at last. (*He says this mechanically but the last two words awaken him—wonderingly*) At last?

(*then with triumph*) At last! (*He stares at Dion's real face contemptuously.*) So that's the poor weakling you really were! No wonder you hid! And I've always been afraid of you—yes, I'll confess it now, in awe of you! Paugh! (*He picks up the mask from the floor.*) No, not of you! Of this! Say what you like, it's strong if it is bad! And this is what Margaret loved, not you! Not you! This man!—this man who willed himself to me! (*Struck by an idea, he jumps to his feet.*) By God! (*He slowly starts to put the mask on. A knocking comes on the street door. He starts guiltily, laying the mask on the table. Then he picks it up again quickly, takes the dead body and carries it off left. He reappears immediately and goes to the front door as the knocking recommences—gruffly*) Hello! Who's there?

MARGARET—It's Margaret, Billy. I'm looking for Dion.

BROWN—(*uncertainly*) Oh—all right— (*unfastening door*) Come in. Hello, Margaret. Hello, Boys! He's here. He's asleep. I—I was just dozing off too. (*Margaret enters. She is wearing her mask. The three sons are with her.*)

MARGARET—(*seeing the bottle, forcing a laugh*) Has he been celebrating?

BROWN—(*with strange glibness now*) No. I was. He wasn't. He said he'd sworn off tonight—forever—for your sake—and the kids!

MARGARET—(*with amazed joy*) Dion said that? (*then hastily defensive*) But of course he never does drink much. Where is he?

BROWN—Upstairs. I'll wake him. He felt bad. He took off his clothes to take a bath before he lay down. You just wait here. (*She sits in the chair where Dion had sat and stares straight before her. The sons group around her, as if for a family photo. Brown hurries out left.*)

MARGARET—It's late to keep you boys up. Aren't you sleepy?

BOYS—No, Mother.

MARGARET—(*proudly*) I'm glad to have three such strong boys to protect me.

ELDEST—(*boastingly*) We'd kill anyone that touched you, wouldn't we?

NEXT—You bet! We'd make him wish he hadn't!

YOUNGEST—You bet!

MARGARET—You're Mother's brave boys! (*She laughs fondly—then curiously*) Do you like Mr. Brown?

ELDEST—Sure thing! He's a regular fellow.

NEXT—He's all right!

YOUNGEST—Sure thing!

MARGARET—(*half to herself*) Your father claims he steals his ideas.

ELDEST—(*with a sheepish grin*) I'll bet father said that when he was—just talking.

NEXT—Mr. Brown doesn't have to steal, does he?

YOUNGEST—I should say not! He's awful rich.

MARGARET—Do you love your father?

ELDEST—(*scuffling—embarrassed*) Why—of course—

NEXT—(*ditto*) Sure thing!

YOUNGEST—Sure I do.

MARGARET—(*with a sigh*) I think you'd better start on before—right now—before your father comes— He'll be very sick and nervous and he'll want to be quiet. So run along!

BOYS—All right. (*They file out and close the front door as Brown, dressed in Dion's clothes and wearing his mask, appears at left.*)

MARGARET—(*taking off her mask, gladly*) Dion! (*She stares wonderingly at him and he at her; goes to him and puts an arm around him.*) Poor dear, do you feel sick? (*He nods.*) But you look—(*squeezing his arms*)—why, you actually feel stronger and better already! Is it true what Billy told me—about your swearing off forever? (*He nods. She exclaims intensely*) Oh, if you'll only—and get well—we can still be so happy! Give Mother a kiss. (*They kiss. A shudder passes through both of them. She breaks away laughing with aroused desire.*) Why, Dion? Aren't you ashamed? You haven't kissed me like that in ages!

BROWN—(*his voice imitating Dion's and muffled by the mask*) I've wanted to, Margaret!

MARGARET—(*gayly and coquettishly now*) Were you afraid I'd spurn you? Why, Dion, something has happened. It's like a miracle! Even your voice is changed! It actually sounds younger, do you know it? (*then, solicitously*) But you must be worn out. Let's go home. (*With an impulsive movement she flings her arms wide open, throwing her mask away from her as if suddenly no longer needing it.*) Oh, I'm beginning to feel so happy, Dion—so happy!

BROWN—(*stifledly*) Let's go home. (*She puts her arm around him. They walk to the door.*)

(*Curtain*)

ACT THREE
Scene One

SCENE—*The drafting room and private office of Brown are both shown. The former is at left, the latter at right of a dividing wall at center. The arrangement of furniture in each room is the same as in previous scenes. It is ten in the morning of a day about a month later. The backdrop for both rooms is of plain wall with a few tacked-up designs and blue prints painted on it.*

Two draftsmen, a middle-aged and a young man, both stoop-shouldered, are sitting on stools behind what was formerly Dion's table. They are tracing plans. They talk as they work.

OLDER DRAFTSMAN—W. B. is late again.

YOUNGER DRAFTSMAN—Wonder what's got into him the last month? (*A pause. They work silently.*)

OLDER DRAFTSMAN—Yes, ever since he fired Dion. . . .

YOUNGER DRAFTSMAN—Funny his firing him all of a sudden like that. (*A pause. They work.*)

OLDER DRAFTSMAN—I haven't seen Dion around town since then. Have you?

YOUNGER DRAFTSMAN—No, not since Brown told us he'd canned him. I suppose he's off drowning his sorrow!

OLDER DRAFTSMAN—I heard someone had seen him at home and he was sober and looking fine. (*A pause. They work.*)

YOUNGER DRAFTSMAN—What got into Brown? They say he fired all his old servants that same day and only uses his house to sleep in.

OLDER DRAFTSMAN—(*with a sneer*) Artistic temperament, maybe—the real name of which is swelled head! (*There is a noise of footsteps from the hall. Warningly*) Ssstt! (*They bend over their table. Margaret enters. She does not need to wear a mask now. Her face has regained the self-confident spirit of its youth, her eyes shine with happiness.*)

MARGARET—(*heartily*) Good morning! What a lovely day!

BOTH—(*perfunctorily*) Good morning, Mrs. Anthony.

MARGARET—(*looking around*) You've been changing around in here, haven't you? Where is Dion? (*They stare at her*.) I forgot to tell him something important this morning and our phone's out of order. So if you'll tell him I'm here— (*They don't move. A pause. Margaret says stiffly*) Oh, I realize Mr. Brown has given strict orders Dion is not to be disturbed, but surely. . . . (*sharply*) Where is my husband, please?

OLDER DRAFTSMAN—We don't know.

MARGARET—You don't know?

YOUNGER DRAFTSMAN—We haven't seen him.

MARGARET—Why, he left home at eight-thirty!

OLDER DRAFTSMAN—To come here?

YOUNGER DRAFTSMAN—This morning?

MARGARET—(*provoked*) Why, of course, to come here— as he does every day! (*They stare at her. A pause.*)

OLDER DRAFTSMAN—(*evasively*) We haven't seen him.

MARGARET—(*with asperity*) Where is Mr. Brown?

YOUNGER DRAFTSMAN—(*at a noise of footsteps from the hall—sulkily*) Coming now. (*Brown enters. He is now wearing a mask which is an exact likeness of his face as it was in the last scene—the self-assured success. When he sees Margaret, he starts back apprehensively.*)

BROWN—(*immediately controlling himself—breezily*) Hello, Margaret! This is a pleasant surprise! (*He holds out his hand.*)

MARGARET—(*hardly taking it—reservedly*) Good morning.

BROWN—(*turning quickly to the draftsmen*) I hope you explained to Mrs. Anthony how busy Dion . . .

MARGARET—(*interrupting him—stiffly*) I certainly can't understand—

BROWN—(*hastily*) I'll explain. Come in here and be comfortable. (*He throws open the door and ushers her into his private office.*)

OLDER DRAFTSMAN—Dion must be putting over some bluff on her.

YOUNGER DRAFTSMAN—Pretending he's still here—and Brown's helping him. . . .

OLDER DRAFTSMAN—But why should Brown, after he . . . ?

YOUNGER DRAFTSMAN—Well, I suppose— Search me. (*They work.*)

BROWN—Have a chair, Margaret. (*She sits on the chair stiffly. He sits behind the desk.*)

MARGARET—(*coldly*) I'd like some explanation. . . .

BROWN—(*coaxingly*) Now, don't get angry, Margaret! Dion is hard at work on his design for the new State Capitol, and I don't want him disturbed, not even by you! So be a good sport! It's for his own good, remember! I asked him to explain to you.

MARGARET—(*relenting*) He told me you'd agreed to ask me and the boys not to come here—but then, we hardly ever did.

BROWN—But you might! (*then with confidential friendliness*) This is for his sake, Margaret. I know Dion. He's got to be able to work without distractions. He's not the ordinary man, you appreciate that. And this design means his whole future! He's to get full credit for it, and as soon as it's accepted, I take him into partnership. It's all agreed. And after that I'm going to take a long vacation—go to Europe for a couple of years—and leave everything here in Dion's hands! Hasn't he told you all this?

MARGARET—(*jubilant now*) Yes—but I could hardly believe . . . (*proudly*) I'm sure he can do it. He's been like a new man lately, so full of ambition and energy! It's made me so happy! (*She stops in confusion.*)

BROWN—(*deeply moved, takes her hand impulsively*) And it has made me happy, too!

MARGARET—(*confused—with an amused laugh*) Why, Billy Brown! For a moment, I thought it was Dion, your voice sounded so much . . . !

BROWN—(*with sudden desperation*) Margaret, I've got to tell you! I can't go on like this any longer! I've got to confess. . . ! There's something. . . !

MARGARET—(*alarmed*) Not—not about Dion?

BROWN—(*harshly*) To hell with Dion! To hell with Billy Brown! (*He tears off his mask and reveals a suffering face that is ravaged and haggard, his own face tortured and distorted by the demon of Dion's mask.*) Think of me! I love you, Margaret! Leave him! I've always loved you! Come away with me! I'll sell out here! We'll go abroad and be happy!

MARGARET—(*amazed*) Billy Brown, do you realize what

you're saying? (*with a shudder*) Are you crazy? Your face—is terrible. You're sick! Shall I phone for a doctor?

BROWN—(*turning away slowly and putting on his mask—dully*) No. I've been on the verge—of a breakdown—for some time. I get spells. . . . I'm better now. (*He turns back to her.*) Forgive me! Forget what I said! But, for all our sakes, don't come here again.

MARGARET—(*coldly*) After this—I assure you. . . ! (*then looking at him with pained incredulity*) Why, Billy—I simply won't believe—after all these years. . . !

BROWN—It will never happen again. Good-by.

MARGARET—Good-by. (*then, wishing to leave on a pleasant change of subject—forcing a smile*) Don't work Dion to death! He's never home for dinner any more. (*She goes out past the draftsmen and off right, rear. Brown sits down at his desk, taking off the mask again. He stares at it with bitter, cynical amusement.*)

BROWN—You're dead, William Brown, dead beyond hope of resurrection! It's the Dion you buried in your garden who killed you, not you him! It's Margaret's husband who . . . (*He laughs harshly.*) Paradise by proxy! Love by mistaken identity! God! (*This is almost a prayer—then fiercely defiant*) But it *is* paradise! I *do* love! (*As he is speaking, a well-dressed, important, stout man enters the drafting room. He is carrying a rolled-up plan in his hand. He nods condescendingly and goes directly to Brown's door, on which he raps sharply, and, without waiting for an answer, turns the knob. Brown has just time to turn his head and get his mask on.*)

MAN—(*briskly*) Ah, good morning! I came right in. Hope I didn't disturb . . . ?

BROWN—(*the successful architect now—urbanely*) Not at all, sir. How are you? (*They shake hands.*) Sit down. Have a cigar. And now what can I do for you this morning?

MAN—(*unrolling his plan*) It's your plan. My wife and I have been going over it again. We like it—and we don't—and when a man plans to lay out half a million, why he wants everything exactly right, eh? (*Brown nods.*) It's too cold, too spare, too like a tomb, if you'll pardon me, for a liveable home. Can't you liven it up, put in some decorations, make it fancier and warmer—you know what I mean. (*looks at him a bit doubtfully*) People tell me you had an assistant, Anthony, who was a real shark on these details but that you've fired him—

BROWN—(*suavely*) Gossip! He's still with me but, for reasons of his own, doesn't wish it known. Yes, I trained him and he's very ingenious. I'll turn this right over to him and instruct him to carry out your wishes. . . .

(*Curtain*)

SCENE TWO

SCENE—*The same as Act Two, Scene Three—the library of Brown's home about eight the same night. He can be heard feeling his way in through the dark. He switches on the reading lamp on the table. Directly under it on a sort of stand is the mask of Dion, its empty eyes staring front.*

Brown takes off his own mask and lays it on the table before Dion's. He flings himself down in the chair and stares without moving into the eyes of Dion's mask. Finally, he begins to talk to it in a bitter, mocking tone.

BROWN—Listen! Today was a narrow escape—for us! We can't avoid discovery much longer. We must get our plot to working! We've already made William Brown's will, leaving you his money and business. We must hustle off to Europe now—and murder him there! (*a bit tauntingly*) Then you— the I in you—*I* will live with Margaret happily ever after. (*more tauntingly*) She will have children by me! (*He seems to hear some mocking denial from the mask. He bends toward it.*) What? (*then with a sneer*) Anyway, that doesn't matter! Your children already love me more than they ever loved you! And Margaret loves me more! You think you've won, do you— that I've got to vanish into you in order to live? Not yet, my friend! Never! Wait! Gradually Margaret will love what is beneath—me! Little by little I'll teach her to know me, and then finally I'll reveal myself to her, and confess that I stole your place out of love for her, and she'll understand and forgive and love me! And you'll be forgotten! Ha! (*Again he*

bends down to the mask as if listening—torturedly) What's that?
She'll never believe? She'll never see? She'll never understand?
You lie, devil! (*He reaches out his hands as if to take the mask by
the throat, then shrinks back with a shudder of hopeless despair.*)
God have mercy! Let me believe! Blessed are the merciful!
Let me obtain mercy! (*He waits, his face upturned—pleadingly*)
Not yet? (*despairingly*) Never? (*A pause. Then, in a sudden
panic of dread, he reaches out for the mask of Dion like a dope
fiend after a drug. As soon as he holds it, he seems to gain strength
and is able to force a sad laugh.*) Now I am drinking your
strength, Dion—strength to love in this world and die and
sleep and become fertile earth, as you are becoming now in
my garden—your weakness the strength of my flowers, your
failure as an artist painting their petals with life! (*then, with
bravado*) Come with me while Margaret's bridegroom dresses
in your clothes, Mr. Anthony! I need the devil when I'm in
the dark! (*He goes off left, but can be heard talking.*) Your
clothes begin to fit me better than my own! Hurry, Brother!
It's time we were home. Our wife is waiting! (*He reappears,
having changed his coat and trousers.*) Come with me and tell
her again I love her! Come and hear her tell me how she loves
you! (*He suddenly cannot help kissing the mask.*) I love you because she loves you! My kisses on your lips are for her! (*He
puts the mask over his face and stands for a moment, seeming to
grow tall and proud—then with a laugh of bold self-assurance*)
Out by the back way! I mustn't forget I'm a desperate criminal, pursued by God, and by myself! (*He goes out right, laughing with amused satisfaction.*)

(*Curtain*)

Scene Three

SCENE—*Is the same as Scene One of Act One—the sitting-
room of Margaret's home. It is about half an hour after the last
scene. Margaret sits on the sofa, waiting with the anxious, impatient expectancy of one deeply in love. She is dressed with a careful, subtle extra touch to attract the eye. She looks young and
happy. She is trying to read a book. The front door is heard*

opening and closing. She leaps up and runs back to throw her arms around Brown as he enters from right, rear. She kisses him passionately.

MARGARET—(*as he recoils with a sort of guilt—laughingly*) Why, you hateful old thing, you! I really believe you were trying to avoid kissing me! Well, just for that, I'll never . . .

BROWN—(*with fierce, defiant passion, kisses her again and again*) Margaret!

MARGARET—Call me Peggy again. You used to when you really loved me. (*softly*) Remember the school commencement dance—you and I on the dock in the moonlight?

BROWN—(*with pain*) No. (*He takes his arms from around her.*)

MARGARET—(*still holding him—with a laugh*) Well, I like that! You old bear, you! Why not?

BROWN—(*sadly*) It was so long ago.

MARGARET—(*a bit melancholy*) You mean you don't want to be reminded that we're getting old?

BROWN—Yes. (*He kisses her gently.*) I'm tired. Let's sit down. (*They sit on the sofa, his arm about her, her head on his shoulder.*)

MARGARET—(*with a happy sigh*) I don't mind remembering—now I'm happy. It's only when I'm unhappy that it hurts—and I've been so happy lately, dear—and so grateful to you! (*He stirs uneasily. She goes on joyfully.*) Everything's changed! I'd gotten pretty resigned to—and sad and hopeless, too—and then all at once you turn right around and everything is the same as when we were first married—much better even, for I was never sure of you then. You were always so strange and aloof and alone, it seemed I was never really touching you. But now I feel you've become quite human—like me—and I'm so happy, dear! (*She kisses him.*)

BROWN—(*his voice trembling*) Then I have made you happy—happier than ever before—no matter what happens? (*She nods.*) Then—that justifies everything! (*He forces a laugh.*)

MARGARET—Of course it does! I've always known that. But you—you wouldn't be—or you couldn't be—and I could never help you—and all the time I knew you were so lonely! I could always hear you calling to me that you were lost, but I couldn't find the path to you because I was lost, too! That's an awful way for a wife to feel! (*She laughs—joyfully*) But now you're here! You're mine! You're my long-lost lover, and my husband, and my big boy, too!

BROWN—(*with a trace of jealousy*) Where are your other big boys tonight?

MARGARET—Out to a dance. They've all acquired girls, I'll have you know.

BROWN—(*mockingly*) Aren't you jealous?

MARGARET—(*gayly*) Of course! Terribly! But I'm diplomatic. I don't let them see. (*changing the subject*) Believe me, they've noticed the change in you! The eldest was saying to me to-day: "It's great not to have Father so nervous, any more. Why, he's a regular sport when he gets started!" And the other two said very solemnly: "You bet!" (*She laughs.*)

BROWN—(*brokenly*) I—I'm glad.

MARGARET—Dion! You're crying!

BROWN—(*stung by the name, gets up—harshly*) Nonsense! Did you ever know Dion to cry about anyone?

MARGARET—(*sadly*) You couldn't—then. You were too lonely. You had no one to cry to.

BROWN—(*goes and takes a rolled-up plan from the table drawer—dully*) I've got to do some work.

MARGARET—(*disappointedly*) What, has that old Billy Brown got you to work at home again, too?

BROWN—(*ironically*) It's for Dion's good, you know—and yours.

MARGARET—(*making the best of it—cheerfully*) All right. I won't be selfish. It really makes me proud to have you so ambitious. Let me help. (*She brings his drawing-board, which he puts on the table and pins his plan upon. She sits on sofa and picks up her book.*)

BROWN—(*carefully casual*) I hear you were in to see me today?

MARGARET—Yes, and Billy wouldn't hear of it! I was quite furious until he convinced me it was all for the best. When is he going to take you into partnership?

BROWN—Very soon now.

MARGARET—And will he really give you full charge when he goes abroad?

BROWN—Yes.

MARGARET—(*practically*) I'd pin him down if I could. Promises are all right, but—(*she hesitates*) I don't trust him.

BROWN—(*with a start, sharply*) What makes you say that?

MARGARET—Oh, something that happened today.

BROWN—What?

Margaret—I don't mean I blame him, but—to be frank, I think the Great God Brown, as you call him, is getting a bit queer and it's time he took a vacation. Don't you?

BROWN—(*his voice a bit excited—but guardedly*) But why? What did he do?

MARGARET—(*hesitatingly*) Well—it's really too silly—he suddenly got awfully strange. His face scared me. It was like a corpse. Then he raved on some nonsense about he'd always loved me. He went on like a perfect fool! (*She looks at Brown, who is staring at her. She becomes uneasy.*) Maybe I shouldn't tell you this. He simply wasn't responsible. Then he came to himself and was all right and begged my pardon and seemed dreadfully sorry, and I felt sorry for him. (*then with a shudder*) But honestly, Dion, it was just too disgusting for words to hear him! (*with kind, devastating contempt*) Poor Billy!

BROWN—(*with a show of tortured derision*) Poor Billy! Poor Billy the Goat! (*with mocking frenzy*) I'll kill him for you! I'll serve you his heart for breakfast!

MARGARET—(*jumping up—frightenedly*) Dion!

BROWN—(*waving his pencil knife with grotesque flourishes*) I tell you I'll murder this God-damned disgusting Great God Brown who stands like a fatted calf in the way of our health and wealth and happiness!

MARGARET—(*bewilderedly, not knowing how much is pretending, puts an arm about him*) Don't, dear! You're being horrid and strange again. It makes me afraid you haven't really changed, after all.

BROWN—(*unheeding*) And then my wife can be happy! Ha! (*He laughs. She begins to cry. He controls himself—pats her head—gently*) All right, dear. Mr. Brown is now safely in hell. Forget him!

MARGARET—(*stops crying—but still worriedly*) I should never have told you—but I never imagined you'd take it seriously. I've never thought of Billy Brown except as a friend, and lately not even that! He's just a stupid old fool!

BROWN—Ha-ha! Didn't I say he was in hell? They're torturing him! (*then controlling himself again—exhaustedly*) Please leave me alone now. I've got to work.

MARGARET—All right, dear. I'll go into the next room and anything you want, just call. (*She pats his face—cajolingly*) Is it all forgotten?

BROWN—Will you be happy?

MARGARET—Yes.

BROWN—Then it's dead, I promise! (*She kisses him and goes out. He stares ahead, then shakes off his thoughts and concentrates on his work—mockingly*) Our beautiful new Capitol calls you, Mr. Dion! To work! We'll adroitly hide old Silenus on the cupola! Let him dance over their law-making with his eternal leer! (*He bends over his work.*)

(*Curtain*)

ACT FOUR

Scene One

SCENE—*Same as Scene One of Act Three—the drafting room and Brown's office. It is dusk of a day about a month later.*

The two draftsmen are bent over their table, working.

Brown, at his desk, is working feverishly over a plan. He is wearing the mask of Dion. The mask of William Brown rests on the desk beside him. As he works, he chuckles with malicious glee—finally flings down his pencil with a flourish.

BROWN—Done! In the name of the Almighty Brown, amen, amen! Here's a wondrous fair capitol! The design would do just as well for a Home for Criminal Imbeciles! Yet to them, such is my art, it will appear to possess a pure common-sense, a fat-bellied finality, as dignified as the suspenders of an assemblyman! Only to me will that pompous façade reveal itself as the wearily ironic grin of Pan as, his ears drowsy with the crumbling hum of past and future civilizations, he half-listens to the laws passed by his fleas to enslave him! Ha-ha-ha! (*He leaps grotesquely from behind his desk and cuts a few goatish capers, laughing with lustful merriment.*) Long live Chief of Police Brown! District Attorney Brown! Alderman Brown! Assemblyman Brown! Mayor Brown! Congressman Brown! Governor Brown! Senator Brown! President Brown! (*He chants*) Oh, how many persons in one God make up the good God Brown? Hahahaha! (*The two draftsmen in the next room have stopped work and are listening.*)

YOUNGER DRAFTSMAN—Drunk as a fool!

OLDER DRAFTSMAN—At least Dion used to have the decency to stay away from the office—

YOUNGER DRAFTSMAN—Funny how it's got hold of Brown so quick!

OLDER DRAFTSMAN—He was probably hitting it up on the Q.T. all the time.

BROWN—(*has come back to his desk, laughing to himself and out of breath*) Time to become respectable again! (*He takes off the Dion mask and reaches out for the William Brown one—then stops, with a hand on each, staring down on the plan with fascinated loathing. His real face is now sick, ghastly, tortured, hollow-cheeked and feverish-eyed.*) Ugly! Hideous! Despicable! Why must the demon in me pander to cheapness—then punish me with self-loathing and life-hatred? Why am I not strong enough to perish—or blind enough to be content? (*to heaven, bitterly but pleadingly*) Give me the strength to destroy this!—and myself!—and him!—and I will believe in Thee! (*While he has been speaking there has been a noise from the stairs. The two draftsmen have bent over their work. Margaret enters, closing the door behind her. At this sound, Brown starts. He immediately senses who it is—with alarm*) Margaret! (*He grabs up both masks and goes into room off right.*)

MARGARET—(*She looks healthy and happy, but her face wears a worried, solicitous expression—pleasantly to the staring draftsmen*) Good morning. Oh, you needn't look worried, it's Mr. Brown I want to see, not my husband.

YOUNGER D.—(*hesitatingly*) He's locked himself in—but maybe if you'll knock—

MARGARET—(*knocks—somewhat embarrassedly*) Mr. Brown! (*Brown enters his office, wearing the William Brown mask. He comes quickly to the other door and unlocks it.*)

BROWN—(*with a hectic cordiality*) Come on, Margaret! Enter! This is delightful! Sit down! What can I do for you?

MARGARET—(*taken aback—a bit stiffly*) Nothing much.

BROWN—Something about Dion, of course. Well, your darling pet is all right—never better!

MARGARET—(*coldly*) That's a matter of opinion. I think you're working him to death.

BROWN—Oh, no, not him. It's Brown who is to die. We've agreed on that.

MARGARET—(*giving him a queer look*) I'm serious.

BROWN—So am I. Deadly serious! Hahaha!

MARGARET—(*checking her indignation*) That's what I came to see you about. Really, Dion has acted so hectic and on edge lately I'm sure he's on the verge of a breakdown.

BROWN—Well, it certainly isn't drink. He hasn't had a drop. He doesn't need it! Haha! And I haven't either, although the gossips are beginning to say I'm soused all the time! It's because I've started to laugh! Hahaha! They can't believe in joy in this town except by the bottle! What funny little people! Hahaha! When you're the Great God Brown, eh, Margaret? Hahaha!

MARGARET—(*getting up—uneasily*) I'm afraid I—

BROWN—Don't be afraid, my dear! I won't make love to you again! Honor bright! I'm too near the grave for such folly! But it must have been funny for you when you came here the last time—watching a disgusting old fool like me, eh?—too funny for words! Hahaha! (*Then with a sudden movement he flourishes the design before her.*) Look! We've finished it! Dion has finished it! His fame is made!

MARGARET—(*tartly*) Really, Billy, I believe you are drunk!

BROWN—Nobody kisses me—so you can all believe the worst! Hahaha!

MARGARET—(*chillingly*) Then if Dion is through, why can't I see him?

BROWN—(*crazily*) See Dion? See Dion? Well, why not? It's an age of miracles. The streets are full of Lazaruses. Pray! I mean—wait a moment, if you please.

(*Brown disappears into the room off right. A moment later he reappears in the mask of Dion. He holds out his arms and Margaret rushes into them. They kiss passionately. Finally he sits with her on the lounge.*)

MARGARET—So you've finished it!

BROWN—Yes. The Committee is coming to see it soon. I've made all the changes they'll like, the fools!

MARGARET—(*lovingly*) And can we go on that second honeymoon, right away now?

BROWN—In a week or so, I hope—as soon as I've gotten Brown off to Europe.

MARGARET—Tell me—isn't he drinking hard?

BROWN—(*laughing as Brown did*) Haha! Soused to the ears all the time! Soused on life! He can't stand it! It's burning his insides out!

MARGARET—(*alarmed*) Dear! I'm worried about you. You sound as crazy as he did—when you laugh! You must rest!

BROWN—(*controlling himself*) I'll rest in peace—when he's gone!

MARGARET—(*with a queer look*) Why Dion, that isn't your suit. It's just like—

BROWN—It's his! We're getting to be like twins. I'm inheriting his clothes already! (*then calming himself as he sees how frightened she is*) Don't be worried, dear. I'm just a trifle elated, now the job's done. I guess I'm a bit soused on life, too! (*The Committee, three important-looking, average personages, come into the drafting room.*)

MARGARET—(*forcing a smile*) Well, don't let it burn *your* insides out!

BROWN—No danger! Mine were tempered in hell! Hahaha!

MARGARET—(*kissing him, coaxingly*) Come home, dear—please!

OLDER DRAFTSMAN—(*knocks on the door*) The Committee is here, Mr. Brown.

BROWN—(*hurriedly to Margaret*) You receive them. Hand them the design. I'll get Brown. (*He raises his voice.*) Come right in, gentlemen. (*He goes off right, as the Committee enter the office. When they see Margaret, they stop in surprise.*)

MARGARET—(*embarrassedly*) Good afternoon. Mr. Brown will be right with you. (*They bow. Margaret holds out the design to them.*) This is my husband's design. He finished it today.

COMMITTEE—Ah! (*They crowd around to look at it—with enthusiasm*) Perfect! Splendid! Couldn't be better! Exactly what we suggested!

MARGARET—(*joyfully*) Then you accept it? Mr. Anthony will be so pleased!

MEMBER—Mr. Anthony?

ANOTHER—Is he working here again?

THIRD—Did I understand you to say this was your husband's design?

MARGARET—(*excitedly*) Yes! Entirely his! He's worked like a dog— (*appalled*) You don't mean to say—Mr. Brown never told you? (*They shake their heads in solemn surprise.*) Oh, the contemptible cad! I hate him!

BROWN—(*appearing at right—mockingly*) Hate me, Margaret? Hate Brown? How superfluous! (*oratorically*) Gentlemen, I have been keeping a secret from you in order that you might be the more impressed when I revealed it. That design is entirely the inspiration of Mr. Dion Anthony's genius. I had nothing to do with it.

MARGARET—(*contritely*) Oh, Billy! I'm sorry! Forgive me!

BROWN—(*ignoring her, takes the plan from the Committee and begins unpinning it from the board—mockingly*) I can see by your faces you have approved this. You are delighted, aren't you? And why not, my dear sirs? Look at it, and look at you! Hahaha! It'll immortalize you, my good men! You'll be as death-defying a joke as any in Joe Miller! (*then with a sudden complete change of tone—angrily*) You damn fools! Can't you see this is an insult—a terrible, blasphemous insult!—that this embittered failure Anthony is hurling in the teeth of our success—an insult to you, to me, to you, Margaret—and to Almighty God! (*in a frenzy of fury*) And if you are weak and cowardly enough to stand for it, I'm not! (*He tears the plan into four pieces. The Committee stands aghast. Margaret runs forward.*)

MARGARET—(*in a scream*) You coward! Dion! Dion! (*She picks up the plan and hugs it to her bosom.*)

BROWN—(*with a sudden goatish caper*) I'll tell him you're here. (*He disappears, but reappears almost immediately in the mask of Dion. He is imposing a terrible discipline on himself to avoid dancing and laughing. He speaks suavely.*) Everything is all right—all for the best—you mustn't get excited! A little paste, Margaret! A little paste, gentlemen! And all will be well! Life is imperfect, Brothers! Men have their faults, Sister! But with a few drops of glue much may be done! A little dab of pasty resignation here and there—and even broken hearts may be repaired to do yeoman service! (*He has edged toward the door. They are all staring at him with petrified bewilderment. He puts his finger to his lips.*) Ssssh! This is Daddy's bedtime secret for today: Man is born broken. He lives by mending. The grace of God is glue! (*With a quick prancing movement, he has opened the door, gone through, and closed it after him silently, shaking with suppressed laughter. He springs lightly to the side of the petrified draftsmen—in a whisper*) They will find him in the little room. Mr. William Brown is dead! (*With light leaps he vanishes, his head thrown back, shaking with silent laughter. The sound of his feet leaping down the stairs, five at a time, can be heard. Then a pause of silence. The people in the two rooms stare. The younger draftsman is the first to recover.*)

YOUNGER DRAFTSMAN—(*rushing into the next room, shouts in terrified tones*) Mr. Brown is dead!

COMMITTEE—He murdered him! (*They all run into the little room off right. Margaret remains, stunned with horror. They return in a moment, carrying the mask of William Brown, two on each side, as if they were carrying a body by the legs and shoulders. They solemnly lay him down on the couch and stand looking down at him.*)

FIRST COMMITTEEMAN—(*with a frightened awe*) I can't believe he's gone.

SECOND COMMITTEEMAN—(*in same tone*) I can almost hear him talking. (*As if impelled, he clears his throat and addresses the mask importantly.*) Mr. Brown— (*then stops short*)

THIRD COMMITTEEMAN—(*shrinking back*) No. Dead, all right! (*then suddenly, hysterically angry and terrified*) We must take steps at once to run Anthony to earth!

MARGARET—(*with a heart-broken cry*) Dion's innocent!

YOUNGER DRAFTSMAN—I'll phone for the police, sir! (*He rushes to the phone.*)

(*Curtain*)

SCENE TWO

SCENE—*The same as Scene Two of Act Three—the library of William Brown's home. The mask of Dion stands on the table beneath the light, facing front.*

On his knees beside the table, facing front, stripped naked except for a white cloth around his loins, is Brown. The clothes he has torn off in his agony are scattered on the floor. His eyes, his arms, his whole body strain upward, his muscles writhe with his lips as they pray silently in their agonized supplication. Finally a voice seems torn out of him.

BROWN—Mercy, Compassionate Savior of Man! Out of my depths I cry to you! Mercy on thy poor clod, thy clot of unhallowed earth, thy clay, the Great God Brown! Mercy, Savior! (*He seems to wait for an answer—then leaping to his feet he puts out one hand to touch the mask like a frightened child reaching out for its nurse's hand—then with immediate mocking despair*) Bah! I am sorry, little children, but your kingdom is empty. God has become disgusted and moved away to some far ecstatic star where life is a dancing flame! We must die without him. (*then—addressing the mask—harshly*) Together, my friend! You, too! Let Margaret suffer! Let the whole world suffer as I am suffering! (*There is a sound of a door being pushed violently open, padding feet in slippers, and Cybel, wearing her mask, runs into the room. She stops short on seeing Brown and the mask, and stares from one to the other for a second in confusion. She is dressed in a black kimono robe and wears slippers over her bare feet. Her yellow hair hangs down in a great mane over her shoulders. She has grown stouter, has more of the deep objective calm of an idol.*)

BROWN—(*staring at her—fascinated—with great peace as if her presence comforted him*) Cybel! I was coming to you! How did you know?

CYBEL—(*takes off her mask and looks from Brown to the Dion mask, now with a great understanding*) So that's why you never came to me again! You are Dion Brown!

BROWN—(*bitterly*) I am the remains of William Brown! (*He points to the mask of Dion.*) I am his murderer and his murdered!

CYBEL—(*with a laugh of exasperated pity*) Oh, why can't you ever learn to leave yourselves alone and leave me alone!

BROWN—(*boyishly and naïvely*) I am Billy.

CYBEL—(*immediately, with a motherly solicitude*) Then run, Billy, run! They are hunting for someone! They came to my place, hunting for a murderer, Dion! They must find a victim! They've got to quiet their fears, to cast out their devils, or they'll never sleep soundly again! They've got to absolve themselves by finding a guilty one! They've got to kill someone now, to live! You're naked! You must be Satan! Run, Billy, run! They'll come here! I ran here to warn—someone! So run away if you want to live!

BROWN—(*like a sulky child*) I'm too tired. I don't want to.

CYBEL—(*with motherly calm*) All right, you needn't, Billy. Don't sulk. (*as a noise comes from outside*) Anyway, it's too late. I hear them in the garden now.

BROWN—(*listening, puts out his hand and takes the mask of Dion—as he gains strength, mockingly*) Thanks for this one last favor, Dion! Listen! Your avengers! Standing on your grave in the garden! Hahaha! (*He puts on the mask and springs to the left and makes a gesture as if flinging French windows open. Gayly mocking*) Welcome, dumb worshippers! I am your great God Brown! I have been advised to run from you but it is my almighty whim to dance into escape over your prostrate souls! (*Shouts from the garden and a volley of shots. Brown staggers back and falls on the floor by the couch, mortally wounded.*)

CYBEL—(*runs to his side, lifts him on to the couch and takes off the mask of Dion*) You can't take this to bed with you. You've got to go to sleep alone. (*She places the mask of Dion back on its stand under the light and puts on her own, just as, after a banging of doors, crashing of glass, trampling of feet, a squad of police with drawn revolvers, led by a grizzly, brutal-faced captain, run into the room. They are followed by Margaret, still distractedly clutching the pieces of the plan to her breast.*)

CAPTAIN—(*pointing to the mask of Dion—triumphantly*) Got him! He's dead!

MARGARET—(*throws herself on her knees, takes the mask and kisses it—heart-brokenly*) Dion! Dion! (*Her face hidden in her arms, the mask in her hands above her bowed head, she remains, sobbing with deep, silent grief.*)

CAPTAIN—(*noticing Cybel and Brown—startled*) Hey! Look at this! What're you doin' here? Who's he?

CYBEL—You ought to know. You croaked him!

CAPTAIN—(*with a defensive snarl—hastily*) It was Anthony! I saw his mug! This feller's an accomplice, I bet yuh! Serves him right! Who is he? Friend o' yours! Crook! What's his name? Tell me or I'll fix yuh!

CYBEL—Billy.

CAPTAIN—Billy what?

CYBEL—I don't know. He's dying. (*then suddenly*) Leave me alone with him and maybe I'll get him to squeal it.

CAPTAIN—Yuh better! I got to have a clean report. I'll give yuh a couple o' minutes. (*He motions to the policemen, who follow him off left. Cybel takes off her mask and sits down by Brown's head. He makes an effort to raise himself toward her and she helps him, throwing her kimono over his bare body, drawing his head on to her shoulder.*)

BROWN—(*snuggling against her—gratefully*) The earth is warm.

CYBEL—(*soothingly, looking before her like an idol*) Ssshh! Go to sleep, Billy.

BROWN—Yes, Mother. (*then explainingly*) It was dark and I couldn't see where I was going and they all picked on me.

CYBEL—I know. You're tired.

BROWN—And when I wake up . . . ?

CYBEL—The sun will be rising again.

BROWN—To judge the living and the dead! (*frightenedly*) I don't want justice. I want love.

CYBEL—There is only love.

BROWN—Thank you, Mother. (*then feebly*) I'm getting sleepy. What's the prayer you taught me— Our Father—?

CYBEL—(*with calm exultance*) Our Father Who Art!

BROWN—(*taking her tone—exultantly*) Who art! Who art! (*suddenly—with ecstasy*) I know! I have found Him! I hear Him speak! "Blessed are they that weep, for they shall laugh!" Only he that has wept can laugh! The laughter of Heaven sows earth with a rain of tears, and out of Earth's transfigured birth-pain the laughter of Man returns to bless and play again in innumerable dancing gales of flame upon the knees of God! (*He dies.*)

CYBEL—(*gets up and fixes his body on the couch. She bends down and kisses him gently—she straightens up and looks into space—with a profound pain*) Always spring comes again bearing life! Always again! Always, always forever again!— Spring again!—life again!—summer and fall and death and peace again!—(*with agonized sorrow*)—but always, always, love and conception and birth and pain again—spring bearing the intolerable chalice of life again!—(*then with agonized exultance*)—bearing the glorious, blazing crown of life again! (*She stands like an idol of Earth, her eyes staring out over the world.*)

MARGARET—(*lifting her head adoringly to the mask—triumphant tenderness mingled with her grief*) My lover! My husband! My boy! (*She kisses the mask.*) Good-by. Thank you for happiness! And you're not dead, sweetheart! You can never die till my heart dies! You will live forever! You will sleep under my heart! I will feel you stirring in your sleep, forever under my heart! (*She kisses the mask again. There is a pause.*)

CAPTAIN—(*comes just into sight at left and speaks front without looking at them—gruffly*) Well, what's his name?

CYBEL—Man!

CAPTAIN—(*taking a grimy notebook and an inch-long pencil from his pocket*) How d'yuh spell it?

(*Curtain*)

EPILOGUE

SCENE—*Four years later.*

The same spot on the same dock as in Prologue on another moonlight night in June. The sound of the waves and of distant dance music.

Margaret and her three sons appear from the right. The eldest is now eighteen. All are dressed in the height of correct Prep-school elegance. They are all tall, athletic, strong and handsome-looking. They loom up around the slight figure of their mother like protecting giants, giving her a strange aspect of lonely, detached, small femininity. She wears her mask of the proud, indulgent Mother. She has grown appreciably older. Her hair is now a beautiful gray. There is about her manner and voice the sad but contented feeling of one who knows her life-purpose well accomplished but is at the same time a bit empty and comfortless with the finality of it. She is wrapped in a gray cloak.

ELDEST—Doesn't Bee look beautiful tonight, Mother?

NEXT—Don't you think Mabel's the best dancer in there, Mother?

YOUNGEST—Aw, Alice has them both beat, hasn't she, Mother?

MARGARET—(*with a sad little laugh*) Each of you is right. (*then, with strange finality*) Good-by, boys.

BOYS—(*surprised*) Good-by.

MARGARET—It was here on a night just like this your father first—proposed to me. Did you ever know that?

BOYS—(*embarrassedly*) No.

MARGARET—(*yearningly*) But the nights now are so much colder than they used to be. Think of it, I went in moonlight-bathing in June when I was a girl. It was so warm and beautiful in those days. I remember the Junes when I was carrying you boys— (*A pause. They fidget uneasily. She asks pleadingly*) Promise me faithfully never to forget your father!

BOYS—(*uncomfortably*) Yes, Mother.

MARGARET—(*forcing a joking tone*) But you mustn't waste June on an old woman like me! Go in and dance. (*as they hesitate dutifully*) Go on. I really want to be alone—with my Junes.

BOYS—(*unable to conceal their eagerness*) Yes, Mother. (*They go away.*)

MARGARET—(*slowly removes her mask, laying it on the bench, and stares up at the moon with a wistful, resigned sweetness*) So long ago! And yet I'm still the same Margaret. It's only our lives that grow old. We *are* where centuries only count as seconds and after a thousand lives our eyes begin to open— (*she looks around her with a rapt smile*)—and the moon rests in the sea! I want to feel the moon at peace in the sea! I want Dion to leave the sky for me! I want him to sleep in the tides of my heart! (*She slowly takes from under her cloak, from her bosom, as if from her heart, the mask of Dion as it was at the last and holds it before her face.*) My lover! My husband! My boy! You can never die till my heart dies! You will live forever! You are sleeping under my heart! I feel you stirring in your sleep, forever under my heart. (*She kisses him on the lips with a timeless kiss.*)

(*Curtain*)

LAZARUS LAUGHED

A Play for an Imaginative Theatre

CHARACTERS

Lazarus of Bethany
His Father
His Mother
Martha ⎫
Mary ⎭ *his sisters*
Miriam, *his wife*
Seven Guests, *neighbors of Lazarus*
Chorus of Old Men
An Orthodox Priest
Chorus of Lazarus' Followers
A Centurion
Gaius Caligula
Crassus, *a Roman General*
Chorus of Greeks
Seven Citizens of Athens
Chorus of Roman Senators
Seven Senators
Chorus of Legionaries
Flavius, *a centurion*
Marcellus, *a patrician*
Chorus of the Guard
Tiberius Cæsar
Pompeia
Chorus of Youths and Girls
Chorus of the Roman Populace
Crowds

SCENES

Lazarus Laughed

ACT ONE

SCENE ONE

SCENE—*Exterior and interior of Lazarus' home at Bethany. The main room at the front end of the house is shown—a long, low-ceilinged, sparely furnished chamber, with white walls gray in the fading daylight that enters from three small windows at the left. To the left of center several long tables placed lengthwise to the width of the room, around which many chairs for guests have been placed. In the rear wall, right, a door leading into the rest of the house. On the left, a doorway opening on a road where a crowd of men has gathered. On the right, another doorway leading to the yard where there is a crowd of women.*

Inside the house, on the men's side, seven male Guests are grouped by the door, watching Lazarus with frightened awe, talking hesitantly in low whispers. The Chorus of Old Men, seven in number, is drawn up in a crescent, in the far corner, right, facing Lazarus.

(All of these people are masked in accordance with the following scheme: There are seven periods of life shown: Boyhood [or Girlhood], Youth, Young Manhood [or Womanhood], Manhood [or Womanhood], Middle Age, Maturity and Old Age; and each of these periods is represented by seven different masks of general types of character as follows: The Simple, Ignorant; the Happy, Eager; the Self-Tortured, Introspective; the Proud, Self-Reliant; the Servile, Hypocritical; the Revengeful, Cruel; the Sorrowful, Resigned. Thus in each crowd [this includes among the men the Seven Guests who are composed of one male of each period-type as period one—type one, period two—type two, and so on up to period seven—type seven] there are forty-nine different combinations of period and type. Each type has a distinct predominant color for its costumes which varies in kind according to its period. The masks of the Chorus of Old Men are double the size of the others. They are all seven in the Sorrowful, Resigned type of Old Age.)

On a raised platform at the middle of the one table placed lengthwise at center sits Lazarus, his head haloed and his body illumined by a soft radiance as of tiny phosphorescent flames.

Lazarus, freed now from the fear of death, wears no mask.

In appearance Lazarus is tall and powerful, about fifty years of age, with a mass of gray-black hair and a heavy beard. His face recalls that of a statue of a divinity of Ancient Greece in its general structure and particularly in its quality of detached serenity. It is dark-complected, ruddy and brown, the color of rich earth upturned by the plow, calm but furrowed deep with the marks of former suffering endured with a grim fortitude that had never softened into resignation. His forehead is broad and noble, his eyes black and deep-set. Just now he is staring straight before him as if his vision were still fixed beyond life.

Kneeling beside him with bowed heads are his wife, Miriam, his sisters, Martha and Mary, and his Father and Mother.

Miriam is a slender, delicate woman of thirty-five, dressed in deep black, who holds one of his hands in both of hers, and keeps her lips pressed to it. The upper part of her face is covered by a mask which conceals her forehead, eyes and nose, but leaves her mouth revealed. The mask is the pure pallor of marble, the expression that of a statue of Woman, of her eternal acceptance of the compulsion of motherhood, the inevitable cycle of love into pain into joy and new love into separation and pain again and the loneliness of age. The eyes of the mask are almost closed. Their gaze turns within, oblivious to the life outside, as they dream down on the child forever in memory at her breast. The mouth of Miriam is sensitive and sad, tender with an eager, understanding smile of self-forgetful love, the lips still fresh and young. Her skin, in contrast to the mask, is sunburned and earth-colored like that of Lazarus. Martha, Mary and the two parents all wear full masks which broadly reproduce their own characters. Martha is a buxom middle-aged housewife, plain and pleasant. Mary is young and pretty, nervous and high-strung. The Father is a small, thin, feeble old man of over eighty, meek and pious. The Mother is tall and stout, over sixty-five, a gentle, simple woman.

All the masks of these Jews of the first two scenes of the play are pronouncedly Semitic.

A background of twilight sky. A dissolving touch of sunset still lingers on the horizon.

It is some time after the miracle and Jesus has gone away.

CHORUS OF OLD MEN—(*in a quavering rising and falling chant—their arms outstretched toward Lazarus*)
Jesus wept!
Behold how he loved him!
He that liveth,
He that believeth,
Shall never die!
CROWD—(*on either side of house, echo the chant*)
He that believeth
Shall never die!
Lazarus, come forth!
FIRST GUEST—(*a Simple Boy—in a frightened whisper after a pause of dead silence*) That strange light seems to come from within him! (*with awe*) Think of it! For four days he lay in the tomb! (*turns away with a shudder*)
SECOND GUEST—(*a Happy Youth—with reassuring conviction*) It is a holy light. It came from Jesus.
FIFTH GUEST—(*an Envious, Middle-Aged Man*) Maybe if the truth were known, our friend there never really died at all!
FOURTH GUEST—(*a Defiant Man, indignantly*) Do you doubt the miracle? I tell you I was here in this house when Lazarus died!
SEVENTH GUEST—(*an Aged, Sorrowful Man*) And I used to visit him every day. He knew himself his hour was near.
FOURTH GUEST—He wished for death! He said to me one day: "I have known my fill of life and the sorrow of living. Soon I shall know peace." And he smiled. It was the first time I had seen him smile in years.
THIRD GUEST—(*a Self-Tortured Man—gloomily*) Yes, of late years his life had been one long misfortune. One after another his children died—
SIXTH GUEST—(*a Mature Man with a cruel face—with a harsh laugh*) They were all girls. Lazarus had no luck.
SEVENTH GUEST—The last was a boy, the one that died at birth. You are forgetting him.
THIRD GUEST—Lazarus could never forget. Not only did his son die but Miriam could never bear him more children.
FIFTH GUEST—(*practically*) But he could not blame bad luck for everything. Take the loss of his father's wealth since

he took over the management. That was his own doing. He was a bad farmer, a poor breeder of sheep, and a bargainer so easy to cheat it hurt one's conscience to trade with him!

SIXTH GUEST—(*with a sneer—maliciously*) You should know best about that! (*a suppressed laugh from those around him*)

FIRST GUEST—(*who has been gazing at Lazarus—softly*) Ssssh! Look at his face! (*They all stare. A pause.*)

SECOND GUEST—(*with wondering awe*) Do you remember him, neighbors, before he died? He used to be pale even when he worked in the fields. Now he seems as brown as one who has labored in the earth all day in a vineyard beneath the hot sun! (*a pause*)

FOURTH GUEST—The whole look of his face has changed. He is like a stranger from a far land. There is no longer any sorrow in his eyes. They must have forgotten sorrow in the grave.

FIFTH GUEST—(*grumblingly*) I thought we were invited here to eat—and all we do is stand and gape at him!

FOURTH GUEST—(*sternly*) Be silent! We are waiting for him to speak.

THIRD GUEST—(*impressively*) He did speak once. And he laughed!

ALL THE GUESTS—(*amazed and incredulous*) Laughed?

THIRD GUEST—(*importantly*) Laughed! I heard him! It was a moment after the miracle—

MIRIAM—(*her voice, rich with sorrow, exultant now*) Jesus cried, "Lazarus, come forth!" (*She kisses his hand. He makes a slight movement, a stirring in his vision. The Guests stare. A frightened pause.*)

FIFTH GUEST—(*nudging the Second—uneasily*) Go on with your story!

THIRD GUEST—Just as he appeared in the opening of the tomb, wrapped in his shroud—

SECOND GUEST—(*excitedly—interrupting*) My heart stopped! I fell on my face! And all the women screamed! (*sceptically*) You must have sharp ears to have heard him laugh in that uproar!

THIRD GUEST—I helped to pry away the stone so I was right beside him. I found myself kneeling, but between my fingers I watched Jesus and Lazarus. Jesus looked into his face for what seemed a long time and suddenly Lazarus said "Yes" as if he were answering a question in Jesus' eyes.

ALL THE GUESTS—(*mystified*) Yes? What could he mean by yes?

THIRD GUEST—Then Jesus smiled sadly but with tenderness, as one who from a distance of years of sorrow remembers happiness. And then Lazarus knelt and kissed Jesus' feet and both of them smiled and Jesus blessed him and called him "My Brother" and went away; and Lazarus, looking after Him, began to laugh softly like a man in love with God! Such a laugh I never heard! It made my ears drunk! It was like wine! And though I was half-dead with fright I found myself laughing, too!

MIRIAM—(*with a beseeching summons*) Lazarus, come forth!

CHORUS—(*chanting*) Lazarus! Come forth!

CROWD—(*on either side of the house—echoing the chant*) Come forth! Come forth!

LAZARUS—(*suddenly in a deep voice—with a wonderful exultant acceptance in it*) Yes! (*The Guests in the room, the Crowds outside all cry out in fear and joy and fall on their knees.*)

CHORUS—(*chanting exultantly*)
    The stone is taken away!
    The spirit is loosed!
    The soul let go!

LAZARUS—(*rising and looking around him at everyone and everything—with an all-embracing love—gently*) Yes! (*His family and the Guests in the room now throng about Lazarus to embrace him. The Crowds of men and women on each side push into the room to stare at him. He is in the arms of his Mother and Miriam while his Sisters and Father kiss and press his hands. The five are half hysterical with relief and joy, sobbing and laughing.*)

FATHER—My son is reborn to me!

CHORUS—Hosannah!

ALL—(*with a great shout*) Hosannah!

FATHER—Let us rejoice! Eat and drink! Draw up your chairs, friends! Music! Bring wine! (*Music begins in the room off right, rear—a festive dance tune. The company sit down in their places, the Father and Mother at Lazarus' right and left, Miriam next to the Mother, Martha and Mary beside the Father. But Lazarus remains standing. And the Chorus of Old Men remain in their formation at the rear. Wine is poured and all raise their goblets toward Lazarus—then suddenly they stop, the music dies out, and an awed and frightened stillness prevails, for Lazarus is a strange, majestic figure whose understanding smile seems terrible and enigmatic to them.)*

FATHER—(*pathetically uneasy*) You frighten us, my son. You are strange—standing there— (*In the midst of a silence more awkward than before he rises to his feet, goblet in hand—forcing his voice, falteringly*) A toast, neighbors!

CHORUS—(*in a forced echo*) A toast!

ALL—(*echoing them*) A toast!

FATHER—To my son, Lazarus, whom a blessed miracle has brought back from death!

LAZARUS—(*suddenly laughing softly out of his vision, as if to himself, and speaking with a strange unearthly calm in a voice that is like a loving whisper of hope and confidence*) No! There is no death! (*A moment's pause. The people remain with goblets uplifted, staring at him. Then all repeat after him questioningly and frightenedly*)

ALL—There—is—no—death?

SIXTH GUEST—(*suddenly blurts out the question which is in the minds of all*) What did you find beyond there, Lazarus? (*a pause of silence*)

LAZARUS—(*smiles gently and speaks as if to a group of inquisitive children*) O Curious Greedy Ones, is not one world in which you know not how to live enough for you?

SIXTH GUEST—(*emboldened*) Why did you say yes, Lazarus?

FOURTH GUEST—Why did you laugh?

ALL THE GUESTS—(*with insistent curiosity but in low awed tones*) What is beyond there, Lazarus?

CHORUS—(*in a low murmur*) What is beyond there? What is beyond?

CROWD—(*carrying the question falteringly back into silence*) What is beyond?

LAZARUS—(*suddenly again—now in a voice of loving exaltation*) There is only life! I heard the heart of Jesus laughing in my heart; "There is Eternal Life in No," it said, "and there is the same Eternal Life in Yes! Death is the fear between!" And my heart reborn to love of life cried "Yes!" and I laughed in the laughter of God! (*He begins to laugh, softly at first—a laugh so full of a complete acceptance of life, a profound assertion of joy in living, so devoid of all self-consciousness or fear, that it is like a great bird song triumphant in depths of sky, proud and powerful, infectious with love, casting on the listener an enthralling spell. The Crowd in the room are caught by it. Glancing sideways at one another, smiling foolishly and self-consciously, at first they hesitate, plainly holding themselves in for fear of what the next one will think.*)

CHORUS—(*in a chanting murmur*)
Lazarus laughs!
Our hearts grow happy!
Laughter like music!
The wind laughs!
The sea laughs!
Spring laughs from the earth!
Summer laughs in the air!
Lazarus laughs!

LAZARUS—(*on a final note of compelling exultation*) Laugh! Laugh with me! Death is dead! Fear is no more! There is only life! There is only laughter!

CHORUS—(*chanting exultingly now*)
Laugh! Laugh!
Laugh with Lazarus!
Fear is no more!
There is no death!

(*They laugh in a rhythmic cadence dominated by the laughter of Lazarus.*)

CROWD—(*who, gradually, joining in by groups or one by one—including Lazarus' family with the exception of Miriam, who does not laugh but watches and listens to his laughter with a tender smile of being happy in his happiness—have now all begun to laugh in rhythm with the Chorus—in a great, full-throated pæan as the laughter of Lazarus rises higher and higher*)
Laugh! Laugh!
Fear is no more!
There is no death!

CHORUS—
    Laugh! Laugh!
    There is only life!
    There is only laughter!
    Fear is no more!
    Death is dead!
CROWD—(*in a rhythmic echo*)
    Laugh! Laugh!
    Death is dead!
    There is only laughter!

(*The room rocks, the air outside throbs with the rhythmic beat of their liberated laughter—still a bit uncertain of its freedom, harsh, discordant, frenzied, desperate and drunken, but dominated and inspired by the high, free, aspiring, exulting laughter of Lazarus.*)

(*Curtain*)

SCENE TWO

SCENE—*Some months later. Exterior of Lazarus' home in Bethany, now known as the House of Laughter. It is a clear bright night, the sky sparkling with stars. At the extreme front is a road. Between this and the house is a small raised terrace. The house is low, of one story only, its walls white. Four windows are visible with a closed door in the middle of the wall. Steps lead up to this door, and to the left of door a flight of stairs goes up to the balustraded roof. The windows shine brilliantly with the flickering light of many candles which gives them a throbbing star-like effect. From within comes the sound of flutes and dance music. The dancers can be seen whirling swiftly by the windows. There is continually an overtone of singing laughter emphasizing the pulsing rhythm of the dance.*

On the road in the foreground, at left and right, two separate groups of Jews are gathered. They are not divided according to sex as in the previous scene. Each is composed about equally of men and women, forty-nine in each, masked and costumed as before. It is religious belief that now divides them. The adherents of Jesus, the Nazarenes, among whom may be noted Martha and Mary, are on the left; the Orthodox, among whom are Lazarus' Father and Mother and a Priest, are at right. Between the two hostile groups is the same Chorus of Old Men, in a formation like a spearhead, whose point is placed at the foot of the steps leading to the terrace. All these people are staring fascinatedly at the house, listening entranced, their feet moving, their bodies swaying to the music's beat, stiffly, constrainedly, compelled against their wills. Then the music suddenly stops and the chant of youthful voices is heard:

FOLLOWERS OF LAZARUS—(*from within the house*)
  Laugh! Laugh!
  There is only life!
  There is only laughter!

CHORUS OF OLD MEN—(*as if they were subjects moved by hypnotic suggestion—miserably and discordantly*)
  Ha-ha-ha-ha!
  There is only laughter!
  Ha-ha—

CROWD—(*in the same manner*) Ha-ha—

MARY—Ha— (*then frantically—half-weeping with indignant rage—to the Nazarenes*) Stop! Oh, how can we laugh! We are betraying Jesus! My brother Lazarus has become a devil!

THE ORTHODOX PRIEST—(*His mask is that of a religious fanatic. He is sixty or so.*) Ha—ha— (*tearing his beard and stamping with rage*) Stop it, you fools! It is a foul sin in the sight of Jehovah! Why do you come here every night to listen and watch their abominations? The Lord God will punish you!

MARY—(*echoing him—to her people*) Jesus will never forgive you!

THE PRIEST—(*angrily*) Jesus? (*He turns to look at the Nazarenes disdainfully and spits on the ground insultingly. The members of the two groups begin to glare at each other. The Chorus falls back, three on each side, leaving one neutral figure before the steps. The Priest goes on tauntingly.*) Did you hear her, friends? These renegade Nazarenes will soon deny they are Jews at all! They will begin to worship in filthy idolatry the sun and stars and man's body—as Lazarus in there, (*points to the house*) the disciple of their Jesus, has so well set them the example! (*This is followed by an outburst of insulting shouts of accusation and denial from both sides.*)

A NAZARENE—(*the Fourth Guest of Scene One*) You lie! Lazarus is no disciple! He is a traitor to Jesus! We scorn him!

PRIEST—(*sneeringly*) But your pretended Messiah did not scorn him. According to your stupid lies, he raised him from the dead! And answer me, has your Jesus ever denied Lazarus, or denounced his laughter? No! No doubt he is laughing, too, at all you credulous fools—for if Lazarus is not his disciple, in the matter of the false miracle he was his accomplice! (*This provokes a furious protest from the Nazarenes and insulting hoots and jeers from the Orthodox, penetrated by a piercing scream from Lazarus' Mother, who, crushed in the crowd, sinks fainting to the ground. The Father bends over her. The group of the Orthodox falls back from them. With frightened cries Martha and Mary run from the group of Nazarenes and kneel beside her.*)

FATHER—(*pitifully*) Rachel! Darling! Speak to me!

MARTHA—(*practically*) She has only fainted.

MARY—She is opening her eyes! Mother, dear!

MOTHER—(*weakly*) Did I fall? (*recognizing Martha and Mary*) Martha—and Mary—my dear ones! (*They embrace her, weeping.*) I have not kissed you since you left home to follow that Jesus— Oh, if we were only at home again—and if, also, my poor boy, Lazarus— (*She sobs.*)

FATHER—(*gruffly*) You must not speak of him!

MARTHA—Do not worry your head about Lazarus. He is not worth it!

MARY—(*with surprising vindictiveness*) He is accursed! He has betrayed our Lord!

PRIEST—(*to those around him—mockingly*) Do you hear? They already call the Nazarene "Lord!" A Lord who is in the common prison at Jerusalem, I heard today! A fine Lord whom our High Priests have had arrested like a thief!

MARY—(*with fanatic fervor*) He is a king! Whenever He chooses He will gather a great army and He will seize His kingdom and all who deny Him shall be crucified!

PRIEST—(*tauntingly*) Now their jail-bird is a king, no less!

Soon they will make him a god, as the Romans do their Cæsars!

MARY—(*her eyes flashing*) He is the Messiah!

PRIEST—(*furiously*) The Messiah! May Jehovah smite you in your lies! Step back among your kind! You defile us! (*As she stands defiantly he appeals to the Father.*) Have you no authority? She called him the Messiah—that common beggar, that tramp! Curse her!

FATHER—(*confused, pitifully harried, collecting his forces*) Wait! Go back, Mary! You chose to follow that impostor—

MARY—(*defiantly*) The Messiah!

MARTHA—(*trying to calm her*) Ssssh! Remember he is our father!

MARY—(*fanatically*) I deny him! I deny all who deny Jesus!

MOTHER—(*tearfully*) And me, darling?

MARY—You must come to us, Mother! You must believe in Jesus and leave all to follow Him!

FATHER—(*enraged*) So! You want to steal your mother away, to leave me lonely in my old age! You are an unnatural daughter! I disown you! Go, before I curse—

MOTHER—(*beseechingly*) Father!

MARTHA—(*pulling Mary away*) Mary! Jesus teaches to be kind.

MARY—(*hysterically*) He teaches to give up all and follow Him! I want to give Him everything! I want my father to curse me!

FATHER—(*frenziedly*) Then I do curse you! No—not you—but the devil in you! And the devil in Martha! And the great mocking devil that dwells in Lazarus and laughs from his mouth! I curse these devils and that Prince of Devils, that false prophet, Jesus! It is he who has brought division to my home and many homes that were happy before. I curse him! I curse the day he called my good son, Lazarus, from the grave to walk again with a devil inside him! It was not my son who came back but a devil! My son is dead! And you, my daughters, are dead! I am the father only of devils! (*His voice has risen to a wailing lament.*) My children are dead!

LAZARUS—(*His voice rings from within the house in exultant denial.*) Death is dead! There is only laughter! (*He laughs.*)

(*The voices of all his Followers echo his laughter. They pour in
a laughing rout from the doorway onto the terrace. At the same
moment the Chorus of Followers appears on the roof and forms
along the balustrade, facing front.*

(*These Followers of Lazarus, forty-nine in number, composed
about equally of both sexes, wear a mask that, while recognizably
Jewish, is a Lazarus mask, resembling him in its expression of fearless faith in life, the mouth shaped by laughter. The Chorus of
Followers, seven in number, all men, have identical masks of double size, as before. The Period of all these masks is anywhere between Youth and Manhood* [*or Womanhood*].

(*The music continues to come from within. Laughing, the Followers dance to it in weaving patterns on the terrace. They are
dressed in bright-colored diaphanous robes. Their chorused laughter, now high and clear, now dying to a humming murmur,
stresses the rhythmic flow of the dance.*)

CHORUS OF FOLLOWERS—
    Laugh! Laugh!
    There is no death!
    There is only laughter!
FOLLOWERS—
    There is only laughter!
    Death is dead!
    Laugh! Laugh!
CROWD—(*The two groups of Nazarenes and Orthodox, on the
appearance of the Followers, immediately forget their differences
and form into one mob, led by their Chorus of Old Men, whose
jeering howls they echo as one voice.*) Yaah! Yaah! Yaah! (*But they
cannot keep it up. The music and laughter rise above their hooting. They fall into silence. Then they again begin to feel impelled
by the rhythm and laughter, their feet move, their bodies sway.
Their lips quiver, their mouths open as if to laugh. Their Chorus
of Old Men are the first to be affected. It is as if this reaction were
transmitted through the Chorus to the Crowd.*)

PRIEST—(*his mouth twitching—fighting against the compulsion in him—stammers*) Brothers—listen—we must unite—
in one cause—to—stamp out—this abomination! (*It is as if
he can no longer control his speech. He presses his hand over his
mouth convulsively.*)

AN AGED ORTHODOX JEW—(*the Seventh Guest of Scene*

One—starts to harangue the crowd. He fights the spell but cannot control his jerking body nor his ghastly, spasmodic laughter.) Neighbors! Our young people are corrupted! They are leaving our farms—to dance and sing! To laugh! Ha—! Laugh at everything! Ha-ha—! (*He struggles desperately to control himself.*)

CHORUS OF OLD MEN—(*a barking laugh forced from them*) Ha-ha—!

CROWD—(*echoing this*) Ha-ha—!

THE AGED JEW—They have no respect for life! When I said in kindness, "You must go back to work," they laughed at me! Ha—! "We desire joy. We go to Lazarus," they said—and left my fields! I begged them to stay—with tears in my eyes! I even offered them more money! They laughed! "What is money? Can the heart eat gold?" They laughed at money! Ha-ha—! (*He chokes with exasperated rage.*)

CHORUS OF OLD MEN—(*echoing him*) Ha-ha—!

CROWD—(*echoing the Chorus*) Ha-ha—!

AGED JEW—(*shaking his fist at Lazarus' Followers*) That loafer taught them that! They come to him and work for nothing! For nothing! And they are glad, these undutiful ones! While they sow, they dance! They sing to the earth when they are plowing! They tend his flocks and laugh toward the sun! Ha-ha-ha—! (*He struggles again.*)

CHORUS OF OLD MEN—(*as before*) Ha-ha-ha—

CROWD—(*as before*) Ha-ha-ha—

AGED JEW—How can we compete with labor for laughter! We will have no harvest. There will be no food! Our children will starve! Our race will perish! And he will laugh! Ha-ha-ha-ha! (*He howls with furious, uncontained laughter.*)

CHORUS OF OLD MEN—(*echoing his tone*)
　　Our children will starve!
　　Our race will perish!
　　Lazarus laughs!
　　Ha-ha-ha-ha! Ha-ha-ha-ha!

CROWD—(*as before*) Ha-ha-ha-ha! Ha-ha-ha-ha! (*Their former distinctions of Nazarenes and Orthodox are now entirely forgotten. The members of Lazarus' family are grouped in the center as if nothing had ever happened to separate them. The Chorus of Old Men is again joined in its spearhead formation*

*at the stairs. Apparent first in this Chorus, a queer excite-
ment begins to pervade this mob. They begin to weave in and out,
clasping each other's hands now and then, moving mechanically in
jerky steps to the music in a grotesque sort of marionettes' country
dance. At first this is slow but it momentarily becomes more hectic
and peculiar. They raise clenched fists or hands distended into
threatening talons. Their voices sound thick and harsh and ani-
mal-like with anger as they mutter and growl, each one aloud to
himself or herself.)*

CHORUS OF OLD MEN—(*threateningly, gradually rising to
hatred*)

> Hear them laugh!
> See them dance!
> Shameless! Wanton!
> Dirty! Evil!
> Infamous! Bestial!
> Madness! Blood!
> Adultery! Murder!
> We burn!
> We kill!
> We crucify!
> Death! Death!
> Beware, Lazarus!

(*this last in a wild frenzy*)

CROWD—(*frenziedly*)

> Beware, Lazarus!
> We burn! We kill!
> We crucify!
> Death! Death!

(*They crowd toward the gateway, their arms stretched out as if
demanding Lazarus for a sacrificial victim. Meanwhile they
never cease to hop up and down, to mill around, to twist their
bodies toward and away from each other in bestial parody of the
dance of the Followers.*

(*The tall figure of Lazarus, dressed in a white robe, suddenly
appears on the roof of the house. He stands at the balustrade in
the middle of the Chorus. Beside him, a little behind, Miriam
appears dressed in black, her face upturned, her lips praying. She
appears to have grown older, to be forty now. Lazarus' body is softly
illumined by its inner light. The change in him is marked. He*

*seems ten years younger, at the prime of forty. His body has become
less angular and stiff. His movements are graceful and pliant. The
change is even more noticeable in his face, which has filled out,
become purer in outline, more distinctly Grecian. His complexion
is the red-brown of rich earth, the gray in his black, curly beard
has almost disappeared.*

(*He makes a sign and the music ceases. His Followers remain
fixed in their dancing attitudes like figures in a frieze. Each member of the mob remains frozen in a distorted posture. He stares
down at the mob pityingly, his face calm.*)

LAZARUS—(*speaks amid a profound silence. His voice releases
his own dancers and the mob from their fixed attitudes. The music
begins to play again within the house, very soft and barely audible,
swelling up and down like the sound of an organ from a distant
church.*) You laugh, but your laughter is guilty! It laughs a
hyena laughter, spotted, howling its hungry fear of life! That
day I returned did I not tell you your fear was no more, that
there is no death? You believed then—for a moment! You
laughed—discordantly, hoarsely, but with a groping toward
joy. What! Have you so soon forgotten, that now your laughter curses life again as of old? (*He pauses—then sadly*) That is
your tragedy! You forget! You forget the God in you! You
wish to forget! Remembrance would imply the high duty
to live as a son of God—generously!—with love!—with
pride!—with laughter! This is too glorious a victory for you,
too terrible a loneliness! Easier to forget, to become only a
man, the son of a woman, to hide from life against her breast,
to whimper your fear to her resigned heart and be comforted by her resignation! To live by denying life! (*then ex-
hortingly*) Why are your eyes always either fixed on the
ground in weariness of thought, or watching one another
with suspicion? Throw your gaze upward! To Eternal Life!
To the fearless and deathless! The everlasting! To the stars!
(*He stretches out his arms to the sky—then suddenly points.*)
See! A new star has appeared! It is the one that shone over
Bethlehem! (*His voice becomes a little bitter and mocking.*) The
Master of Peace and Love has departed this earth. Let all
stars be for you henceforth symbols of Saviors—Sons of
God who appeared on worlds like ours to tell the saving
truth to ears like yours, inexorably deaf! (*then exaltedly*) But

the greatness of Saviors is that they may not save! The greatness of Man is that no god can save him—until he becomes
a god! (*He stares up at the stars, rapt in contemplation, oblivious to all around him now.*

(*Rapidly approaching from the left a man's voice jarring in
high-pitched cruel laughter is heard. They all listen, huddled together like sheep.*)

MESSENGER—(*The Third Guest of Scene One rushes in
breathlessly, shouting*) The Nazarene has been crucified!

PRIEST—(*with fierce triumph*) Jehovah is avenged! Hosannah!

ORTHODOX—Hosannah! The false prophet is dead! The
pretended Messiah is dead! (*They jump and dance, embracing
one another. The Nazarenes stand paralyzed and stunned. The
two groups mechanically separate to right and left again, the
Chorus of Old Men dividing itself as before.*)

MARY—(*in a frenzy of grief*) Do not believe him! Jesus
could not die! (*But at this moment a Nazarene youth, exhausted
by grief and tears, staggers in from the left.*)

MESSENGER—(*Second Guest of Scene One*) Jesus is dead!
Our Lord is murdered! (*He sinks on his knees sobbing. All the
Nazarenes do likewise, wailing, rending their garments, tearing
their hair, some even beating their heads on the ground in the
agony of their despair.*)

MARY—(*insane with rage now*) They have murdered Him!
(*to her Followers—savagely*) An eye for an eye! Avenge the
Master! (*Their frenzy of grief turned into rage, the Nazarenes
leap to their feet threateningly. Concealed swords and knives are
brought out by both sides.*)

MIRIAM—(*leaning over the balustrade—in a voice of entreaty*) Mary! Brothers! (*But none heed her or seem to see her.
Lazarus and his Followers remain oblivious to men, arms up-
stretched toward the stars, their heads thrown back.*)

MARY—(*wildly*) Vengeance! Death to His murderers!

PRIEST—(*fiercely to his Followers*) Death to the Nazarenes!
(*With cries of rage the two groups rush on one another. There is
a confused tumult of yells, groans, curses, the shrieks of women,
the sounds of blows as they meet in a pushing, whirling, struggling mass in which individual figures are indistinguishable.
Knives and swords flash above the heads of the mass, hands in*

every tense attitude of striking, clutching, tearing are seen upraised. As the fight is at its height a Roman Centurion and a squad of eight Soldiers come tramping up at the double-quick. They all are masked. These Roman masks now and henceforth in the play are carried out according to the same formula of Seven Periods, Seven Types, as those of the Jews seen previously, except that the basis of each face is Roman—heavy, domineering, self-complacent, the face of a confident dominant race. The Centurion differs from his soldiers only in being more individualized. He is middle-aged, his soldiers belong to the Period of Manhood. All are of the Simple, Ignorant Type.)

CENTURION—(*shouts commandingly*) Disperse! (*But no one hears him—with angry disgust to his Soldiers*) Charge! Cut them down! (*The Soldiers form a wedge and charge with a shout. They soon find it necessary to use their swords, and strike down everyone in their way.*)

MIRIAM—Mercy, Romans! (*As they pay no attention to her, in desperation she embraces Lazarus beseechingly, forcing his attention back to earth.*) Lazarus! Mercy!

LAZARUS—(*looks down upon the struggling mass and cries in a ringing voice*) Hold! (*Each person stands transfixed, frozen in the last movement, even the Roman Soldiers and the Centurion himself. Ten dead and mortally wounded lie on the ground, trampled by the feet of friend and foe alike. Lazarus looks at the Crowd. To each he seems to look at him or her alone. His eyes are accusing and stern. As one head, the heads of all are averted. Even the Centurion stares at the ground humbly, in spite of himself. Finally Lazarus speaks in a voice of infinite disdain.*) Sometimes it is hard to laugh—even *at* men! (*He turns his eyes from them, staring straight before him. This seems to release them from their fixed positions. The Nazarenes and the Orthodox separate and slink guiltily apart. The Chorus of Old Men forms again, the apex at the center of the steps as before. A low wail of lamentation arises from them. The two crowds of Nazarenes and Orthodox echo this.*)

CHORUS OF OLD MEN—(*in a wailing chant*)
Woe unto Israel!
Woe unto thee, Jerusalem!
O divided house,
Thou shalt crumble to dust,

And swine shall root
Where thy Temple stood!
Woe unto us!

CROWD—(*in a great echoing cry*) Woe unto us!

CENTURION—(*gruffly to hide his embarrassment at being awed by Lazarus*) Here, you! Drag your carcasses away! (*From each side men and women come forward to identify and mourn their dead. The wail of lamentation rises and falls. The Centurion looks up at Lazarus—harshly*) You, there! Are you he whom they call the Laugher?

LAZARUS—(*without looking at him—his voice seeming to come from some dream within him*) I am Lazarus.

CENTURION—Who was brought back from death by enchantment?

LAZARUS—(*looking down at him now—with a smile, simply*) No. There is no death!

CHORUS OF FOLLOWERS—(*chanting joyously*) There is no death!

FOLLOWERS—(*echoing*) There is no death!

AN ORTHODOX MAN—(*bending beside the body of Lazarus' Father*) Here is your father, Lazarus. He is dead.

AN ORTHODOX WOMAN—This is your mother, Lazarus. She is dead.

A NAZARENE—Here is your sister, Martha, Lazarus. She is dead.

A NAZARENE WOMAN—And this is Mary, Lazarus. She is dead.

MIRIAM—(*suddenly—with deep grief*) And Jesus who was the Son of Man, who loved you and gave you life again has died, Lazarus—has died!

LAZARUS—(*in a great triumphant voice*) Yes! Yes!! Yes!!! Men die! Even a Son of Man must die to show men that Man may live! But there is no death!

CENTURION—(*at first in a tone of great awe—to his Soldiers*) Is he a god? (*then gruffly, ashamed of his question*) Come down, Jew! I have orders to bring you to Rome to Cæsar!

LAZARUS—(*as if he were answering not the Centurion but the command of his fate from the sky*) Yes! (*He walks down the narrow stairs and, Miriam following him, comes down the path to the road. He goes and kneels for a moment each beside the bodies of his Father, Mother, and Sisters and kisses each in turn on the forehead. For a moment the struggle with his grief can be seen in his face. Then he looks up to the stars and, as if answering a question, again says simply and acceptingly)* Yes! *(then exultantly)* Yes!! *(And begins to laugh from the depths of his exalted spirit. The laughter of his Chorus and then of his Followers echoes his. The music and dancing begin again.*

(The Centurion grins sheepishly. The Soldiers chuckle. The Centurion laughs awkwardly. The Soldiers laugh. The music from the house and the laughter of the Followers grow louder. The infection spreads to the Chorus of Old Men whose swaying grief falls into the rhythm of the laughter and music as does that of the mourners.)

LAZARUS' FOLLOWERS—*(led by their Chorus)* Laugh! Laugh!

CHORUS OF OLD MEN—*(torn by the conflict—torturedly)*
Ha-ha-ha—
Woe to us, woe!

CROWD—*(beside the bodies)*
Woe to us, woe!
Ha-ha—!

CENTURION—*(laughingly)* You are brave, you Laugher! Remember Tiberius never laughs! And boast not to Cæsar there is no death, or he will invent a new one for you!

LAZARUS—*(with a smile)* But all death is men's invention! So laugh! *(He laughs and the Centurion and Soldiers laugh with him, half dancing clumsily now to the beat of the music.)*

CHORUS OF LAZARUS' FOLLOWERS—
Laugh! Laugh!
Fear is no more!
There is no death!
There is only life!
There is only laughter!

FOLLOWERS—*(dancing)*
Laugh! Laugh!
Fear is no more!
Death is dead!

CHORUS OF OLD MEN—*(forgetting their grief—their eyes on Lazarus now, their arms outstretched to him as are those of the crowd grouped around the bodies but forgetting them)*

    Death is no more!
    Death is dead!
    Laugh!
CROWD—
    Laugh! Laugh!
    Death is no more!

CENTURION—(*laughing, to his laughing Soldiers*) Forward! (*They tramp, dancing, off. Lazarus and Miriam start to follow.*)

MIRIAM—(*suddenly pointing to his Followers who are dancing and laughing obliviously—pityingly*) But your faithful ones who love you, Lazarus?

LAZARUS—(*simply, with a trace of a sad sternness*) This is their test. Their love must remember—or it must forget. Come! (*With a last gesture back like a blessing on all he is leaving, he goes. The laughter of the Soldiers recedes. That of the Chorus of Old Men and of the Crowd falters and breaks into lamenting grief again, guilt-stricken because of its laughter.*)

CHORUS OF OLD MEN—
    Laugh! Laugh!
    Death is dead!
    Laugh!—But woe!
    There lie our dead!
    Oh shame and guilt!
    We forget our dead!

CROWD—(*with fierce remorseful grief*)
    Woe to us, woe!
    There lie our dead!

CHORUS OF LAZARUS' FOLLOWERS—(*their voices and the music growing more and more hesitating and faint*)
    Laugh! Laugh!
    There is only life!
    There is only—
    Laugh—
(*Their dance is faltering and slow now.*)
    Fear is no—
    Death is—
    Laugh—
(*The music and dancing and voices cease. The lights in the windows, which have been growing dim, go out. There is a second*

of complete, death-like silence. The mourning folk in the fore-
ground are frozen figures of grief. Then a sudden swelling chorus
of forlorn bewilderment, a cry of lost children comes from the
Chorus of Followers and the Followers themselves. They huddle into
groups on the roof and on the terrace. They stretch their arms out
in every direction supplicatingly.)

CHORUS OF FOLLOWERS—
  Oh, Lazarus, laugh!
  Do not forsake us!
  We forget!
  Where is thy love fled?
  Give back thy laughter,
  Thy fearless laughter!
  We forget!
FOLLOWERS—
  Give back thy laughter!
  We forget!
CHORUS OF FOLLOWERS—(*with dull, resigned terror now*)
  Death slinks out
  Of his grave in the heart!
  Ghosts of fear
  Creep back in the brain!
  We remember fear!
  We remember death!
FOLLOWERS—
  Death in the heart!
  Fear in the brain!
  We remember fear!
  We remember death!
CHORUS OF FOLLOWERS—(*wailing hopelessly now*)
  Forgotten is laughter!
  We remember
  Only death!
  Fear is God!
  Forgotten is laughter!
  Life is death!
FOLLOWERS—
  Forgotten is laughter!
  Life is death!

ALL—(*the Chorus of Old Men and the Crowd joining in*)
 Life is a fearing,
 A long dying,
 From birth to death!
 God is a slayer!
 Life is death!

(Curtain)

ACT TWO

SCENE ONE

SCENE—*Some months later. A square in Athens about ten o'clock at night. In the rear, pure and beautiful in the light of a full moon, is the façade of a temple. An excited crowd of Greeks of both sexes is gathered in the square as if for some public festival. They are masked according to the scheme of Seven Periods in Seven Types of Character for each sex. Here, of course, the foundation of the mask is the Grecian type of face.*

On the left, the Chorus of Greeks is grouped, seven in number, facing front, in the spearhead formation. As before the Chorus wears masks double the life size of the Crowd masks. They are all of the Proud Self-Reliant type, in the period of Young Manhood.

These seven are clad in goat skins, their tanned bodies and masks daubed and stained with wine lees, in imitation of the old followers of Dionysus. Rumor has led them to hope and believe that Lazarus may be the reincarnation of this deity.

The people in the crowd are holding themselves in restraint with difficulty, they stir and push about restlessly with an eager curiosity and impatience. All eyes are fixed off left.

A buzz of voices hums in the air.

Acting as police, a number of Roman legionaries (masked like the soldiers of Scene Two) armed with staves, keep back the crowd from the line of the street that runs from left to right, front. They resent this duty, which has already kept them there a long time, and are surly and quick-tempered with the Greeks.

At front, pacing impatiently up and down, is a young Roman noble of twenty-one, clad richly, wearing beautifully wrought armor and helmet. This is Gaius, the heir of Tiberius Cæsar, nicknamed Caligula by the soldiers in whose encampments he was born and where he spent his childhood. His body is bony and angular, almost malformed, with wide, powerful shoulders and long arms and hands, and short, skinny, hairy legs like an ape's. He wears a half-mask of crimson, dark with a purplish tinge, that covers the upper part of his face to below the nose. This mask accentuates his bulging, prematurely wrinkled forehead, his hollow temples and his bulbous, sensual nose. His large troubled eyes, of a glazed greenish-

blue, glare out with a shifty feverish suspicion at everyone. Below his mask his own skin is of an anemic transparent pallor. Above it, his hair is the curly blond hair of a child of six or seven. His mouth also is childish, the red lips soft and feminine in outline. Their expression is spoiled, petulant and self-obsessed, weak but domineering. In combination with the rest of the face there is an appalling morbid significance to his mouth. One feels that its boyish cruelty, encouraged as a manly attribute in the coarse brutality of camps, has long ago become naïvely insensitive to any human suffering but its own.

Walking with Caligula is Cneius Crassus, a Roman general — a squat, muscular man of sixty, his mask that of a heavy battered face full of coarse humor.

CHORUS OF GREEKS—(intoning solemnly)
  Soon the God comes!
  Redeemer and Savior!
  Dionysus, Son of Man and a God!
GREEK CROWD—(echoing)
  Soon the God comes
  Redeemer and Savior!
  Dionysus!
FIRST GREEK—They say an unearthly flame burns in this Lazarus!

SECOND GREEK—The sacred fire! He must be the Fireborn, the son of Zeus!

THIRD GREEK—Many who have seen him swear he is Dionysus, rearisen from Hades!

FOURTH GREEK—(importantly) I saw Lazarus at Antioch where the galley on which they were taking him to Rome had been thrice blown back by a storm. Fear of this warning omen is why they now march with him by land.

FIRST GREEK—Does he truly resemble a god?

FOURTH GREEK—(impressively) One look in his eyes while his laughter sings in your ears and you forget sorrow! You dance! You laugh! It is as if a heavy weight you had been carrying all your life without knowing it suddenly were lifted. You are like a cloud, you can fly, your mind reels with laughter, you are drunk with joy! (solemnly) Take my word for it, he is indeed a god. Everywhere the people have acclaimed him. He heals the sick, he raises the dead, by laughter.

SEVENTH GREEK—But I have heard that when he has gone people cannot remember his laughter, that the dead are dead again and the sick die, and the sad grow more sorrowful.

FIFTH GREEK—Well, we shall soon see with our own eyes. But why should the God return in the body of a Jew?

SIXTH GREEK—What better disguise if he wishes to remain unknown? The fools of Romans will never suspect him!

THIRD GREEK—(*laughing*) Never! They are beginning to claim he is a Roman!

FIFTH GREEK—So much the better! He will be in their confidence!

FOURTH GREEK—He will lead us against Rome! He will laugh our tyrants into the sea! Ha! (*He turns toward the Romans and laughs sneeringly. This is taken up by the Crowd— unpleasant, resentful laughter. They push forward aggressively and almost sweep the Soldiers from their feet.*)

CRASSUS—(*angrily*) Drive them back!

CALIGULA—(*suddenly with a distorted warped smile*) Order them to use their swords, Cneius. Let the scum look at their dead and learn respect for us!

SOLDIERS—(*shoving and whacking*) Back! Step back! Back there! (*The Crowd push back to their former line. There are muttered curses, groans, protests, which subside into the former hum of expectancy.*)

CALIGULA—(*with the same smile*) The sword, my old hyena! Corpses are so educational!

CRASSUS—(*surlily*) I would like to, I promise you! When I see how they hate us—!

CALIGULA—(*carelessly*) Let them hate—so long as they fear us! We must keep death dangling (*he makes the gesture of doing so*) before their eyes! (*He gives a soft, cruel laugh.*) Will you not sacrifice in my honor? What are a few Greeks? (*queerly*) I like to watch men die.

CRASSUS—I dare not, Caligula. Cæsar has forbidden bloodshed.

CALIGULA—Tiberius is a miser. He wants to hoard all of death for his own pleasure! (*He laughs again.*)

CRASSUS—(*with rough familiarity*) I wager no one will make that complaint against you when you are Cæsar! (*He chuckles.*)

CALIGULA—(*with the sudden grandiose posturing of a bad actor unintentionally burlesquing grandeur*) When I, Gaius Caligula, am Cæsar, I— (*then superstitiously looking up at the sky with cringing foreboding*) But it brings bad luck to anticipate fate. (*He takes off his helmet and spits in it—then with a grim smile*) The heirs of a Cæsar take sick so mysteriously! Even with you who used to ride me on your knee, I do not eat nor drink until you have tasted first.

CRASSUS—(*nodding approvingly*) You are sensible. I suppose I, too, have my price—if they were only clever enough to discover it! (*He laughs hoarsely.*)

CALIGULA—(*steps back from him with an uneasy shudder*) You are honest, at least—too honest, Cneius! (*grimly*) If my father Germanicus had had you for his counselor, he might have escaped their poison. (*then gloomily*) I must fear everyone. The world is my enemy.

CRASSUS—Kill it then! (*He laughs again.*)

CHORUS—(*stretching out their arms in the direction from which Lazarus is expected—supplicatingly*)

> Son of the Lightning!
> Deadly thy vengeance!
> Swift thy deliverance!
> Beholding thy Mother,
> Greece, our Mother,
> Her beauty in bondage,
> Her pride in chains!
> Hasten, Redeemer!

CROWD—(*as before—echoing the chant*)

> Hasten, Redeemer!
> Son of the Lightning!
> Deadly thy vengeance!
> Swift thy deliverance!

CALIGULA—(*disdainfully*) What clods! Mob is the same everywhere, eager to worship any new charlatan! They have already convinced themselves this Lazarus is a reincarnation of Dionysus! A Jew become a god! By the breasts of Venus that *is* a miracle! (*He laughs.*)

CRASSUS—(*seriously*) But he must be expert in magic. He was buried four days and came out unharmed. Maybe he is not a Jew. Some say his father was really a legionary of our garrison in Judea. And he teaches people to laugh at death. That smacks of Roman blood!

CALIGULA—(*ironically*) Better still! He tells them there is no death at all! Hence the multitude of fools who have acclaimed him everywhere since he left his own country—and why Tiberius has begun to fear his influence.

CRASSUS—(*sententiously*) Whom Cæsar fears—disappears!

CALIGULA—Yes, the dupes who follow Lazarus will be killed. But Tiberius believes this Lazarus may know a cure for death or for renewing youth, and the old lecher hopes he can worm the secret out of him—before he kills him. (*He laughs ironically, then disgustedly*) That is why I must escort this Jew to Rome—as a special honor! (*with fierce, haughty resentment*) I, the heir of Cæsar! (*savagely*) Oh, if I were Cæsar—!

CRASSUS—(*with a coarse, meaning smirk*) Patience. Tiberius is old.

CALIGULA—(*suddenly becoming terribly uneasy at some thought*) Cneius! What if this Lazarus has really discovered a cure for old age and should reveal it to Tiberius! (*His lips tremble, his eyes are terrified, he shrinks against Crassus for protection—with boyish pleading*) Oh, Cneius, what could I do then?

CRASSUS—(*matter-of-factly*) Kill him before Cæsar can talk to him.

CALIGULA—(*almost in tears*) But if he knows a charm against death how could he be slain, old fool?

CRASSUS—(*gruffly*) Bah! (*then with grim humor*) Death in bed I suspect, but when men are killed I know they stay dead! (*disgustedly*) A moment ago you were laughing at him! (*scornfully*) Do you fear him now?

CALIGULA—(*rather shamefacedly pulls himself together—then broodingly*) I fear everyone who lives. Even you. As you advised me. (*He turns away.*)

CRASSUS—(*contemptuously*) Well, maybe he can teach you to laugh at fear. You would welcome him then, eh, cry baby?

CALIGULA—(*with sudden passionate intensity but only half aloud as if to himself*) I would love him, Cneius! As a father!

As a god! (*He stands staring before him strangely. There is a new stir from the Crowd who again push forward.*)

CRASSUS—(*pointing off right*) Look! I see a great crowd! Your Lazarus must be coming at last!

CHORUS—(*chanting in a deep, rhythmic monotone like the rising and falling cadences of waves on a beach*)

> He comes, the Redeemer and Savior!
> Laughing along the mountains!
> To give back our lost laughter
> To raise from the dead our freedom
> To free us from Rome!

CROWD—(*echoing this chant*)

> Fire-born! Redeemer! Savior!
> Raise from the dead our freedom!
> Give back our lost laughter!
> Free us from Rome!

(*They have been pushing forward, more and more fiercely and defiantly. The Roman Soldiers in spite of their efforts are pushed backward step by step.*)

SOLDIERS—(*angrily*) Back! Back! (*The Soldiers work with a will, dealing out blows with their staves at everyone in reach. But now these blows seem only to infuriate the Crowd which steadily pushes them back into the street. At the same time the distant sound of exultant music, singing and laughter becomes steadily louder. Both Soldiers and Crowd are inspired to battle by these strains without their knowing it. Caligula is listening spell-bound, his mouth open, his body swaying and twitching. Even Crassus stares off at the oncomers, forgetful of the growing plight of his Soldiers.*)

CROWD—(*led by their Chorus—angrily*)

> Cowards! Pigs!
> Strike! Hit!
> Stones! Knives!
> Stab! Kill!
> Death to the Romans!
> Death!

A SOLDIER—(*alarmed, calls to Crassus*) General! Let us use our swords!

SOLDIERS—(*enraged—eagerly*) Yes! Swords!

CROWD—Death!

CRASSUS—(*turning—uneasy but afraid to give any drastic order*) Bah! Staves are enough. Crack their skulls!

CROWD—(*led by the Chorus—defiantly*)

Death to Crassus!

Drunkard! Coward!

Death to him!

(*They continue to push forward, hooting and jeering.*)

CRASSUS—(*exploding for a second*) By the gods—! (*to the Soldiers*) Draw your swords! (*The troops do so eagerly. The Crowd sag back momentarily with exclamations of fear.*)

CALIGULA—(*listening as in a trance to the music and what is going on behind him—in a queer whisper*) Kill, Cneius! Let me dance! Let me sing! (*The music and crashing of cymbals and the ferment of passions around him cause him to lose all control over himself. He gives a crazy leap in the air and begins to dance grotesquely and chant in a thick voice.*) He is coming! Death, the Deliverer! Kill, soldiers! I command you! I, Caligula! I will be Cæsar! Death!

CROWD—(*led by the Chorus—savage now*)

Beast! Cur!

Death to Caligula!

(*They crowd forward.*)

CALIGULA—(*drawing his sword and flourishing it drunkenly—his eyes glazed*) Death!

CRASSUS—(*drawing his own sword in a frenzy*) Strike! Death! (*His Soldiers raise their swords. The Crowd have raised whatever weapons they have found—knives, clubs, daggers, stones, bare fists.*)

CHORUS—(*chanting fiercely*) Death!

ALL—(*Romans and Greeks alike as one great voice*) Death! (*The chorused word beats down all sound into a stricken silence. The wild joyous music ceases. The Romans and Greeks seem to lean back from one another and collect strength to leap forward. At this moment the voice of Lazarus comes ringing through the air like a command from the sky.*)

LAZARUS—There is no death! (*The Soldiers and Greeks remain frozen in their attitudes of murderous hate. Following his words the laughter of Lazarus is heard, exultant and gaily mocking, filling them with the sheepish shame of children caught in mischief. Their hands hang, their arms sink to their sides. The music starts once more with a triumphant clash of cymbals, Laza-rus' laughter is echoed from the throats of the multitude of his Followers who now come dancing into the square, preceded by a band of masked musicians and by their Chorus.*

(This Chorus wears, in double size, the laughing mask of Laz-arus' Followers in the same Period and Type as in the preceding scene, except that here the mask of each member of the Chorus has a different racial basis—Egyptian, Syrian, Cappadocian, Lydian, Phrygian, Cilician, Parthian. The Followers are costumed and masked as in the preceding scene, seven Types in seven Periods, except that, as in the Chorus, racially there are many nations represented. All have wreaths of ivy in their hair and flowers in their hands which they scatter about. They whirl in between the Soldiers and Crowd, forcing them back from each other, teasing them, sifting into the Crowd, their Chorus in a half circle, con-fronting the Chorus of Greeks.)

CHORUS OF FOLLOWERS—
    Laugh! Laugh!
    There is no death!
    There is only life!
    There is only laughter!
FOLLOWERS—(*echoing*)
    Laugh! Laugh!
    There is no death!

(Caligula and Crassus are swept to one side, left. Then the cries and laughter of all become mingled into one exclamation.)

ALL—Lazarus! Lazarus! (*The squad of Roman Soldiers led by the Centurion, who had taken Lazarus prisoner, march in with dancers' steps, like a proud guard of honor now, laughing, pulling a chariot in which Lazarus stands dressed in a tunic of white and gold, his bronzed face and limbs radiant in the halo of his own glowing light.*

(Lazarus now looks less than thirty-five. His countenance now might well be that of the positive masculine Dionysus, closest to the soil of the Grecian Gods, a Son of Man, born of a mortal. Not the coarse, drunken Dionysus, nor the effeminate God, but Dionysus in his middle period, more comprehensive in his symbolism, the soul of the recurring seasons, of living and dying as processes in eternal growth, of the wine of life stirring forever in the sap and blood and loam of things. Miriam is beside him, dressed in black, smiling the

*same sad tender smile, holding Lazarus' arm as if for protection
and in protection. She appears older, a woman over forty-five.*)

CHORUS OF GREEKS—(*rushing to Lazarus' car*)

Hail, Dionysus!

Iacchus!

Lazarus!

Hail!

(*They surround him, throw over his shoulders and head the finely
dressed hide of a bull with great gilded horns, force into his right
hand the mystic rod of Dionysus with a pine cone on top, then
prostrate themselves.*)

Hail, Savior!

Redeemer!

Conqueror of Death!

ALL—(*in a repeated chorus which finally includes even the
Roman Soldiers, raising their arms to him*)

Hail, Lazarus!

Redeemer!

Hail!

(*They are silent. Lazarus looks at them, seeming to see each and
all at the same time, and his laughter, as if in answer to their
greetings, is heard rising from his lips like a song.*)

CRASSUS—(*awed*) Look! He is more than man!

CALIGULA—(*trembling, in a queer agitation*) I dare not look!

CRASSUS—Do you hear his laughter?

CALIGULA—(*chokingly—puts his hands over his ears*) I will
not hear!

CRASSUS—But you must welcome him in Cæsar's name!

CALIGULA—(*his teeth chattering*) I must kill him!

LAZARUS—(*looking directly at him—gaily mocking*) Death is
dead, Caligula! (*He begins to laugh again softly.*)

CALIGULA—(*with an hysterical cry of defiant terror*) You lie!
(*Sword in hand he whirls to confront Lazarus, but at the first
sight of his face he stops in his tracks, trembling, held fascinated by
Lazarus' eyes, mumbling with a last pitiful remainder of defiance*)
But—you lie—whatever you are! I say there *must* be death!
(*The sword has fallen to his side. He stares open-mouthed at
Lazarus. There is something of a shy, wondering child about his
attitude now. Lazarus looks at him, laughing with gentle
understanding. Caligula suddenly drops his sword and covering*

his face with his hands weeps like a boy who has been hurt.) You have murdered my only friend, Lazarus! Death would have been my slave when I am Cæsar. He would have been my jester and made me laugh at fear! (*He weeps bitterly.*)

LAZARUS—(*gaily*) Be your own jester instead, O Caligula! Laugh at yourself, O Cæsar-to-be! (*He laughs. The Crowd now all join in with him.*

(*Caligula suddenly uncovers his face, grins his warped grin, gives a harsh cackle which cracks through the other laughter with a splitting discord, cuts a hopping caper like some grotesque cripple which takes him to the side of Lazarus' chariot where he squats on his hams and, stretching out his hand, fingers Lazarus' robe inquisitively and stares up into his face in the attitude of a chained monkey.*)

CALIGULA—(*with a childish, mischievous curiosity*) Then if there is no death, O Teacher, tell me why I love to kill?

LAZARUS—Because you fear to die! (*then gaily mocking*) But what do you matter, O Deathly-Important One? Put yourself that question—as a jester! (*exultantly*) Are you a speck of dust danced in the wind? Then laugh, dancing! Laugh yes to your insignificance! Thereby will be born your new greatness! As Man, Petty Tyrant of Earth, you are a bubble pricked by death into a void and a mocking silence! But as dust, you are eternal change, and everlasting growth, and a high note of laughter soaring through chaos from the deep heart of God! Be proud, O Dust! Then you may love the stars as equals! (*then mockingly again*) And then perhaps you may be brave enough to love even your fellow men without fear of their vengeance!

CALIGULA—(*dully*) I cannot understand. I hate men. I am afraid of their poison and their swords and the cringing envy in their eyes that only yields to fear!

LAZARUS—(*gaily mocking*) Tragic is the plight of the tragedian whose only audience is himself! Life is for each man a solitary cell whose walls are mirrors. Terrified is Caligula by the faces he makes! But I tell you to laugh in the mirror, that seeing your life gay, you may begin to live as a guest, and not as a condemned one! (*raising his hands for silence—with a playful smile*) Listen! In the dark peace of the grave the man called Lazarus rested. He was still weak, as one who recovers from a long illness—for, living, he had believed his life a sad one! (*He laughs softly, and softly they all echo his laughter.*) He lay dreaming to the croon of silence, feeling as the flow of blood in his own veins the past reënter the heart of God to be renewed by faith into the future. He thought: "Men call this death"—for he had been dead only a little while and he still remembered. Then, of a sudden, a strange gay laughter trembled from his heart as though his life, so long repressed in him by fear, had found at last its voice and a song for singing. "Men call this death," it sang. "Men call life death and fear it. They hide from it in horror. Their lives are spent in hiding. Their fear becomes their living. They worship life as death!"

CHORUS OF FOLLOWERS—(*in a chanting echo*)
Men call life death and fear it.
They hide from it in horror.
Their lives are spent in hiding.
Their fear becomes their living.
They worship life as death!

LAZARUS—And here the song of Lazarus' life grew pitiful. "Men must learn to live," it mourned. "Before their fear invented death they knew, but now they have forgotten. They must be taught to laugh again!" And Lazarus answered "Yes!" (*He now addresses the Crowd—especially Caligula, directly, laughingly.*) Thus sang his life to Lazarus while he lay dead! Man must learn to live by laughter! (*He laughs.*)

CHORUS OF FOLLOWERS—
Laugh! Laugh!
There is only life!
There is only laughter!
Fear is no more!
Death is dead!

CHORUS OF GREEKS—
Laugh! Laugh!
Hail, Dionysus!
Fear is no more!
Thou hast conquered death!

ALL—(*laughing—in a great laughing chorus*)
Laugh! Laugh!
Fear is no more!
Death is dead!

LAZARUS—(*as to a crowd of children—laughingly*) Out with you! Out into the woods! Upon the hills! Cities are prisons wherein man locks himself from life. Out with you under the sky! Are the stars too pure for your sick passions? Is the warm earth smelling of night too desirous of love for your pale introspective lusts? Out! Let laughter be your new clean lust and sanity! So far man has only learned to snicker meanly at his neighbor! Let a laughing away of self be your new right to live forever! Cry in your pride, "I am Laughter, which is Life, which is the Child of God!" (*He laughs and again his voice leads and dominates the rhythmic chorus of theirs. The music and dancing begin again.*)

THE TWO CHORUSES—(*chanting in unison*)
> Laugh! Laugh!
> There is only God!
> We are His Laughter!

ALL—(*echoing*)
> There is only God!
> We are His Laughter!
> Laugh! Laugh!

(*They take hold of his chariot traces, and as he had come, in the midst of a happy multitude, now augmented by all the Greeks, and the Roman Soldiers who had awaited him, dancing, playing, singing, laughing, he is escorted off. The noise of their passing recedes. Caligula and Crassus are left in the empty square, the former squatting on his hams, monkey-wise, and brooding somberly.*)

CRASSUS—(*is swaying and staggering, like a man in a drunken stupor, in a bewildered, stubborn struggle to control himself. He stammers after the Soldiers*) Ha-ha-ha— Halt! Halt, I say! No use—they are gone—mutiny— Halt! (*He continues to stumble toward left.*) Ha-ha— Stop it, curse you! Am I laughing? Where am I going? After Lazarus? Thirty years of discipline and I— Halt, traitor! Remember Cæsar! Remember Rome! Halt, traitor! (*He faints with the violence of his struggle and falls in a limp heap.*)

CALIGULA—(*startled by his fall, terrified, hops to his feet and snatches up his sword defensively, glancing over his shoulder and whirling around as if he expected someone to stab him in the back. Then, forcing a twisted grin of self-contempt—harshly*) Coward!

What do I fear—if there is no death? (*As if he had to cut something, he snatches up a handful of flowers—desperately*) You must laugh, Caligula! (*He starts to lop off the flowers from their stems with a savage intentness.*) Laugh! Laugh! Laugh! (*Finally, impatiently, he cuts off all the remaining with one stroke.*) Laugh! (*He grinds the petals under his feet and breaks out into a terrible hysterical giggle.*) Ha-ha—

(*Curtain*)

Scene Two

SCENE—*A midnight, months later. Immediately inside the walls of Rome. In the foreground is the portico of a temple between whose massive columns one looks across a street on a lower level to the high wall of Rome at the extreme rear. In the center of the wall is a great metal gate. The night is thick and oppressive. In the sky overhead lightning flashes and thunder rumbles and crashes but there is no rain.*

Within the portico on rows of chairs placed on a series of wide steps which are on each side, members of the Senate are seated in their white robes. High hanging lamps cast a wan light over their faces. They are all masked in the Roman mask, refined in them by nobility of blood but at the same time with strength degenerated, corrupted by tyranny and debauchery to an exhausted cynicism. The three periods of Middle Age, Maturity and Old Age are represented in the types of the Self-Tortured, Introspective; Proud, Self-Reliant; the Servile, Hypocritical, the Cruel, Revengeful; and the Resigned, Sorrowful. The Senators are divided into two groups on each side, thirty in each. Seated in the middle of the lower of the three high broad stairs that lead to the level from which the columns rise is the Chorus of Senators, seven in number, facing front, in double-sized masks of the Servile, Hypocritical type of Old Age.

Lazarus, in his robe of white and gold, the aura of light surrounding his body seeming to glow more brightly than ever, stands in the rear at the edge of the portico, center, gazing upward into the pall of sky beyond the wall. His figure appears in its immobility to be the statue of the god of the temple. Near him, but to the rear and to the left of him, facing right, Miriam is kneeling in her black robes, swaying backward and forward, praying silently with moving lips like a nun who asks mercy for the sins of the world. She has grown much older, her hair is gray, her shoulders are bowed.

On the other side, placed similarly in relation to Lazarus and facing Miriam, Caligula is squatting on his hams on a sort of throne-chair of ivory and gold. He is dressed with foppish richness in extreme bright colors, a victory wreath around his head. He stares blinkingly and inquisitively at Lazarus, then at Miriam. He is half-drunk. A large figured goblet of gold is in his hand. A slave with an amphora of wine crouches on the steps by his chair. The slave wears a black negroid mask.

At the opening of the scene there is heard the steady tramp of departing troops, whose masks, helmets and armored shoulders can be seen as they pass through the street before Lazarus to the gate beyond. Finally with a metallic clash the gate is shut behind them and there is a heavy and oppressive silence in which only the murmured prayers of Miriam are heard.

CHORUS OF THE SENATE—(*intones wearily, as if under a boring compulsion*)

> The Roman Senate
> Is the Roman Senate
> The Mighty Voice
> Of the Roman People
> As long as Rome is Rome.

CALIGULA—(*as if he hadn't heard—sings hoarsely an old camp song of the Punic Wars, pounding with his goblet*)

> A bold legionary am I!
> March, oh march on!
> A Roman eagle was my daddy,
> My mother was a drunken drabby
> Oh, march on to the wars!

> Since lived that lady Leda
> March, oh march on!
> Women have loved high-fliers
> And we are eagles of Rome!
> Oh march on to the wars!

Comrades, march to the wars!
There's pretty girls in Carthage
And wine to swill in Carthage,
So we must capture Carthage
And fight for Mother Rome!

(*Holds out his goblet to be refilled. There is silence again. He stares at Lazarus with a somber intentness. He says thickly*) The legions have gone, Lazarus. (*Lazarus gives no evidence of having heard him. Caligula gulps at his wine. The Senators begin to talk to each other in low voices.*)

FIRST SENATOR—How does that Jew make that light come from him, I wonder? It is a well-contrived bit of magic.

SECOND SENATOR—What are we waiting for? A messenger came to me with Cæsar's command that the Senate meet here at midnight.

THIRD SENATOR—(*bored*) Some new whim of Tiberius, naturally—(*with a meaning titter*)—or rather I should say, unnaturally!

FOURTH SENATOR—Perhaps Cæsar has decided to abolish our august body by a massacre in mass!

THIRD SENATOR—(*yawning*) There was a feast at Cinna's last night that lasted until this evening. I could welcome my own murder as an excuse for sleeping!

FIFTH SENATOR—(*pompously*) Tiberius would not dare harm the Senate. He may mistreat individual Senators, but the Roman Senate is the Roman Senate!

CHORUS OF THE SENATE—(*as before—wearily as if under a boring compulsion—intones*)
While Rome is Rome
The Senate is the Senate
The Mighty Voice of the Roman People.

FIRST SENATOR—(*with the ghost of a laugh—wearily*) The Senate is an empty name—a pack of degenerate cowards with no trace of their ancient nobility or courage remaining—that and no more!

THIRD SENATOR—(*flippantly*) You are too severe with yourself, Lucius! (*a titter of laughter*)

FIRST SENATOR—(*wearily*) A degenerate coward. I am, I confess it. So are you too, Sulpicius—a hundred fold!—

whether you admit it or not. (*Sulpicius laughs weakly without taking offense.*)

SIXTH SENATOR—(*after a pause—sighing*) In truth, the Senate is not what it used to be. I can remember—

FIRST SENATOR—Let us forget, if we can! (*then impatiently*) What are we doing here?

SECOND SENATOR—I imagine it has something to do with the followers of this Lazarus encamped outside the wall. Probably the legions are to butcher them in their sleep.

SEVENTH SENATOR—And what part do we play—official witnesses? But how can we witness at night and through a wall? (*with bored resignation*) Ah well, the moods of Tiberius are strange, to say the least. But Cæsar is Cæsar.

CHORUS—(*again with bored weariness as before*)
> Hail!
> Cæsar is Cæsar
> The August One
> Prince of the Senate
> Tribune over Tribunes
> Consul of Consuls
> Supreme Pontiff
> Emperor of Rome
> God among Gods
> Hail!

FIRST SENATOR—(*after a pause of silence—dryly*) Cæsar is a beast—and a madman!

FIFTH SENATOR—(*pompously*) Respect, sir! More respect for Cæsar!

THIRD SENATOR—(*mockingly*) Or caution, Lucius. One of us might repeat your opinion to him.

FIRST SENATOR—You would if it would pay you. But all my money is squandered. My death is worthless to Tiberius. He would not reward you. Moreover, you would not be revenged on me, for I long for death.

THIRD SENATOR—(*dryly*) Your stomach must be out of order.

FIRST SENATOR—The times are out of order. But let us change the subject. Is it true Tiberius has fled to Capri?

FOURTH SENATOR—Yes. He was terrified by the multitude

of laughing idiots who appeared today with that charlatan. (*He points to Lazarus.*)

SECOND SENATOR—There are thousands of them outside the wall. Cæsar refused to let them enter the city. The story is, this Lazarus was dead four days and then restored himself to life by magic.

FIRST SENATOR—I have a mind to question him. (*calls as to a slave*) You, there! Jew, turn round! In the name of the Senate! (*Lazarus seems not to hear him. Lucius remarks with a weary smile*) So much for our authority!

SIXTH SENATOR—(*with injured dignity*) What insolence! (*in a rage*) Ho, barbarian cur, turn round! The Senate commands you! (*Lazarus does not seem to hear, but Caligula turns on them fiercely.*)

CALIGULA—Silence! Leave him alone! (*with insulting scorn*) I, Caligula, command *you*! (*The Senators seem to shrink back from him in fear, all but Lucius, who answers with a mocking servility.*)

FIRST SENATOR—At least, grant us the boon to see this corpse's face, O Gracious Gaius!

CALIGULA—(*fixing his cruel, burning eyes on him—softly*) I heard you wish for death, Lucius. When I am Cæsar you shall scream and pray for it!

FIRST SENATOR—(*dryly and haughtily*) You were bred in camp, Gaius. You should have learned more courage there along with your coarseness. But accept my gratitude for your warning. I shall take care to die before you become Cæsar— and life becomes too idiotic!

CALIGULA—(*his grin becoming ferocious with cruelty*) No. You are too weak to kill yourself. Look at me, Lucius! I am imagining what I shall have done to you! (*The Senators are now trembling. Even Lucius cannot repress a shudder of horror at the face glaring at him. Suddenly Caligula throws the cup from him and springs to his feet.*) What good is wine if it cannot kill thought? Lazarus! It is time. I must give the signal! The legions are waiting. It is Cæsar's command that they spare none of your followers. (*He has walked toward Lazarus.*)

MIRIAM—(*stretches out her hands to Caligula imploringly*) Mercy! Spare them who are so full of life and joy!

CALIGULA—(*harshly*) For their joy I will revenge myself upon them! Mercy? If there is no death, then death is a mercy! Ask that man! (*He points accusingly to Lazarus.*) And why should you plead for them, Jewess? There are few Jews among them. They are mostly those whom your people call idolaters and would gladly see murdered.

MIRIAM—(*with deep grief*) I am a mother of dead children. I plead for the mothers of those about to die.

CALIGULA—(*contemptuously*) Pah! (*He turns from her and puts his hand on Lazarus' shoulder.*) Lazarus! Do you hear? I must signal to the legions!

LAZARUS—(*turns. He has grown more youthful. He seems no more than thirty. His face is exalted and calm and beautiful. His eyes shine with an unearthly glory. The Senators lean forward in their seats, fascinated by his face. A low murmur of admiration comes from them. Lazarus speaks commandingly.*) Wait! I will awaken my beloved ones that their passing may be a symbol to the world that there is no death! (*He turns, throwing back his head and stretching up his arms, and begins to laugh low and tenderly, like caressing music at first but gradually gaining in volume, becoming more and more intense and insistent, finally ending up on a triumphant, blood-stirring call to that ultimate attainment in which all prepossession with self is lost in an ecstatic affirmation of Life. The voices of his Followers from beyond the wall, at first one by one, then several at a time, then multitudes, join in his laughter. Even the Senators are drawn into it. Now every one of these is standing up, stretching out his arms toward Lazarus, laughing harshly and discordantly and awkwardly in his attempt to laugh. Terrific flashes of lightning and crashes of thunder seem a responsive accompaniment from the heavens to this laughter of thousands which throbs in beating waves of sound in the air. Mingled with the laughing from beyond the wall comes the sound of singing and the music of flutes and cymbals. Miriam has crawled on her knees to the edge of the portico where her black figure of grief is outlined below and to the left of Lazarus, her arms raised outward like the arms of a cross.*)

FOLLOWERS OF LAZARUS—(*in a great chanting singing chorus*)

Laugh! Laugh!
There is only God!

Life is His Laughter!
We are His Laughter!
Fear is no more!
Death is dead!

CHORUS OF SENATORS—(*taking it up in a tone between chanting and their old solemn intoning*)
Laugh! Laugh!
Fear is no more!
Death is dead!

ALL—(*the multitude beyond the wall, all the Senators, every-one except the never-laughing Miriam and Caligula and the Men of the Legions*)
Laugh! Laugh!
Death is dead!

CALIGULA—(*in a queer state of mingled exaltation and fear—hopping restlessly about from foot to foot—shouting*) The signal! Shall I give the signal to kill, Lazarus?

MEN OF THE LEGIONS—(*following a brazen trumpet call, are suddenly heard from beyond the wall beginning to laugh their hoarse, bass laughter, a deeper note than all the others*) Laugh! Laugh!

CALIGULA—(*listening—with dismay*) I hear the legions, Lazarus! They are laughing with them! (*He cries with a strange pitifulness and beseeching*) You are playing me false, Lazarus! You are trying to evade death! You are trying to spare your people! You are small and weak like other men when the test comes! You give way to pity! Your great laughter becomes pitiful! (*working himself into a rage*) You are a traitor, Lazarus! You betray Cæsar! Have you forgotten I will be Cæsar? You betray me, Lazarus! (*He rushes to the edge and, making a megaphone of his hands, bellows*) You on the wall! Sentry! It is I, Caligula! Kill! (*The brazen trumpets of the Legions sound from beyond the wall. He springs near Lazarus again, in a fiendish ecstasy, dancing a hopping grotesque sword dance behind him, chanting as he does so*) Kill! Kill laughter! Kill those who deny Cæsar! I will be Cæsar! Kill those who deny Death! I will be Death! My face will be bright with blood! My laughing face, Lazarus! Laughing because men fear me! My face of victorious Fear! Look at me! I am laughing, Lazarus! *My* laughter! Laughter of Gods and Cæsars! Ha-ha-ha-ha! (*He laughs, his laughter fanatically cruel and savage, forced from his lips with a desperate, destroying abandon. For a moment, above all the chorus of other sounds, his voice fights to overcome that of Lazarus, whose laughter seems now to have attained the most exultant heights of spiritual affirmation. Then Caligula's breaks into a cry of fear and a sob, and, casting his sword aside, he hides his face in his hands and cries beseechingly)* Forgive me! I love you, Lazarus! Forgive me! *(At this second the blaring trumpets of the Legions are heard approaching and their great bass chorus of marching tramping laughter.)*

MEN OF THE LEGIONS—*(chanting)*

Laugh! Laugh! Laugh!

Fear, no more!

Death, no more!

Death is dead!

(There is now no sound of the singing or the laughter or music of Lazarus' Followers. Miriam rocks to and fro and raises a low wail of lamentation. The Senators cheer and shout as at a triumph.)

CHORUS OF SENATORS—*(saluting Lazarus)*

Hail, Victor!

Hail, Divine One!

Thou hast slain fear!

Thou hast slain death!

Hail! Triumph!

SENATORS—

Hail! Hail!

Slayer of Fear!

Slayer of Death!

(The gate in the wall is clanged open. The returning Legions burst through and gather in a dense mob in the street below Lazarus, who looks down upon them, silent but smiling gently now. They stare at him with admiration. Only a sea of their masks can be seen, their eyes shining exultantly. Crassus, their general, ascends the steps until he stands a little below Lazarus. Their Chorus of Legionaries in double-sized masks climb to the step below Crassus, forming behind him. They are in the Period of Manhood, of the Simple, Ignorant Type. No weapons can be seen—only their masks and helmets and armor gleaming in the lightning flashes and in the flickering light of torches. Their laughter seems to shake the walls and make the pillars of the temple dance.)

CHORUS OF THE LEGIONS—
  Fear, no more!
  Death, no more!
  Death is dead!
LEGIONARIES—(*echoing*)
  Laugh! Laugh! Laugh!
  Death is dead!
CRASSUS—(*raising his hand*) Silence! (*They obey. He turns to Lazarus and bows his head, falling on one knee, raising his right arm.*) Hail!
  LEGIONARIES—(*as one man—raising their arms*) Hail!
  CALIGULA—(*suddenly pushes forward impudently and strikes a grandiose attitude*) I am here, my brave ones! (*There is a roar of mocking laughter from the Legionaries.*)
  CRASSUS—(*not unkindly*) Not you, Little Killer! We hail the Great Laugher!
  CALIGULA—(*harshly*) Have you killed all his followers?
  CRASSUS—No. They died. They did not wait for our attack. They charged upon us, laughing! They tore our swords away from us, laughing, and we laughed with them! They stabbed themselves, dancing as though it were a festival! They died, laughing, in one another's arms! We laughed, too, with joy because it seemed it was not they who died but death itself they killed! (*He stops uncertainly, bowing to Lazarus, awkwardly*) I do not understand this. I am a soldier. But there is a god in it somewhere! For I know they were drunk, and so were we, with a happiness no mortal ever felt on earth before! And death was dead! (*In a sudden outburst as if he were drunk with excitement, he takes off his helmet and waves it.*) Hail, Deliverer! Death is dead! We left our swords with them! What virtue in killing when there is no death? Your foe laughs. The joke is on you. What a fool's game, eh? One can only laugh! Now we want peace to laugh in—to laugh at war! Let Cæsars fight—that is all they are good for—and not much good for that!
  CALIGULA—(*frenziedly*) Silence, impious traitor!
  CRASSUS—(*smiling drunkenly*) Shut up, yourself, camp-brat! Though you were Cæsar this minute I would laugh at you! Your death is dead! We will make Lazarus Cæsar! What say you? (*He appeals to the Soldiers.*)

CALIGULA—No!

CHORUS OF THE LEGIONS—(*with laughing intoxication*) Hail, Lazarus Cæsar! Hail!

LEGIONARIES—Lazarus Cæsar, hail!

CRASSUS—(*appealing to Senate*) And you, Senators!

CHORUS OF SENATORS—(*with the same joyous intoxication as the Soldiers*) Hail, Lazarus Cæsar! Hail!

SENATORS—Lazarus Cæsar, hail!

CALIGULA—(*piteously*) No, Lazarus! Say no for my sake!

LAZARUS—(*with gay mockery*) What is—Cæsar? (*He begins to laugh with mockery. All except Caligula and Miriam join in this laughter.*)

CRASSUS—Ha-ha! What is Cæsar? You are right! You deserve better from us. A god? How is that? We will build you a temple, Lazarus, and make you a god!

LAZARUS—(*laughingly*) When men make gods, there is no God! (*He laughs. They all laugh.*)

CRASSUS—(*with puzzled good-nature*) I do not understand. But there is a god in it somewhere—a god of peace—a god of happiness! Perhaps you are already he, eh? Are you? Well, never mind now, remember our offer. Give us your answer tomorrow. Good night to you!

LAZARUS—(*As the Soldiers start to march away behind Crassus, and the Senators turn to retire, he stops them all for a moment with a gesture—with a deep earnestness*) Wait! When you awake tomorrow, try to remember! Remember that death is dead! Remember to laugh!

ALL—(*as if taking an oath with one voice*) We will remember, Lazarus!

CRASSUS—(*making a sign to the regimental musicians jovially*) And we will laugh! Play there! (*The bands crash out. The Legions tramp away.*)

CHORUS OF THE LEGIONS—(*chanting to the music*)
Laugh! Laugh! Laugh!
Cæsar, no more!
War, no more!
Wounds, no more!
Death is dead!
Dead! Dead! Dead!

LEGIONARIES—
  Laugh! Laugh! Laugh!
  Death is dead!
  Dead! Dead! Dead!
CHORUS OF SENATORS—(*following them*)
  Cæsar, no more!
  Fear, no more!
  Death, no more!
  Laugh! Laugh! Laugh!
SENATE—(*elated, excited as a crowd of schoolboys going on a vacation. Marching after them.*)
  Laugh! Laugh! Laugh!
  Death is dead!
(*Lazarus, Miriam and Caligula remain.*)
LAZARUS—(*with a great yearning*) If men would remember! If they could! (*He stares after them compassionately.*)
CALIGULA—(*crouching beside Lazarus. Plucks at his robe humbly.*) You will not laugh at Cæsar, Lazarus, will you—when I am Cæsar? You will not laugh at gods when they make me a god? (*Lazarus does not answer. Caligula forces a cruel vindictive smile.*) I swear you shall not laugh at death when I am Death! Ha-ha— (*He starts to laugh harshly—then suddenly, terrified, slinks away and sidles off at right.*)
MIRIAM—(*from where she kneels bowed with grief—brokenly*) Those who have just died were like your children, Lazarus. They believed in you and loved you.
LAZARUS—And I loved them!
MIRIAM—Then how could you laugh when they were dying?
LAZARUS—(*exultingly*) Did they not laugh? That was their victory and glory! (*with more and more of a passionate, proud exultation*) Eye to eye with the Fear of Death, did they not laugh with scorn? "Death to old Death," they laughed! "Once as squirming specks we crept from the tides of the sea. Now we return to the sea! Once as quivering flecks of rhythm we beat down from the sun. Now we reënter the sun! Cast aside is our pitiable pretense, our immortal egohood, the holy lantern behind which cringed our Fear of the Dark! Flung off is that impudent insult to life's nobility which gibbers: 'I, this Jew, this Roman, this noble or this slave, must survive in my

pettiness forever!' Away with such cowardice of spirit! We will to die! We will to change! Laughing we lived with our gift, now with laughter give we back that gift to become again the Essence of the Giver! Dying we laugh with the Infinite. We are the Giver and the Gift! Laughing, we will our own annihilation! Laughing, we give our lives for Life's sake!" (*He laughs up to heaven ecstatically.*) This must Man will as his end and his new beginning! He must conceive and desire his own passing as a mood of eternal laughter and cry with pride, "Take back, O God, and accept in turn a gift from me, my grateful blessing for Your gift—and see, O God, now I am laughing with You! I am Your laughter—and You are mine!" (*He laughs again, his laughter dying lingeringly and tenderly on his lips like a strain of music receding into the silence over still waters.*)

MIRIAM—(*with a sigh—meekly*) I cannot understand, Lazarus. (*sadly*) They were like your children—and they have died. Must you not mourn for them?

LAZARUS—(*gently*) Mourn? When they laughed?

MIRIAM—(*sadly*) They are gone from us. And their mothers weep.

LAZARUS—(*puts his arm around her and raises her to her feet—tenderly*) But God, their Father, laughs! (*He kisses her on the forehead.*)

(*Curtain*)

ACT THREE

Scene One

SCENE—*Some days later—exterior of Tiberius' villa-palace at Capri. It is about two in the morning of a clear black night. In the rear, the walls of the villa, which is built entirely of marble on the brow of a cliff, loom up with a startling clarity against the sky. The rear foreground is a marble terrace at the middle of which is a triumphal arch. On each side, leading up to it, are massive marble columns standing like the mummies of legionaries at attention. In the exact centre of the arch itself a cross is set up on which a full grown male lion has been crucified. A lamp reflecting downward has been fixed at the top of the cross to light up an inscription placed over the lion's head. Below the steps to the terrace, in a line facing front, on each side of the cross, is the Chorus of the Guard in their double masks and gorgeous uniforms and armor. Their masks are the same as the Legionary Chorus of the previous scene.*

The windows of the palace glow crimson-purple with the reflection of many shaded lamps. The sound of music in a strained theme of that joyless abandon which is vice is heard above a confused drunken clamor of voices, punctuated by the high, staccato laughter of women and youths. A squad of the Guard in the same uniforms as the Chorus, masked as all the Roman Soldiers previously, enter from the left, front, climbing up from the beach below. They are commanded by a Centurion, Flavius. His mask is that of a typical young patrician officer. They are followed by Lazarus and Miriam. Caligula walks behind, his drawn sword in his hand. He is in a state of queer conflicting emotion, seeming to be filled with a nervous dread and terror of everything about him, while at the same time perversely excited and elated by his own morbid tension. Lazarus, looking no more than twenty-five, haloed in his own mystic light, walks in a deep, detached serenity.

Miriam, in black, her hair almost white now, her figure bowed and feeble, seems more than ever a figure of a sad, resigned mother of the dead. The Soldiers form in line with the columns.

FLAVIUS—(*saluting Caligula—with an awed glance at*

Lazarus) I will announce your coming—(*as if in spite of him-self he bows awkwardly to Lazarus*)—and that of this man. Cæsar was not expecting you so soon, I think.

CALIGULA—(*forcing a light tone*) Lazarus laughed and the galley slaves forgot their fetters and made their oars fly as if they were bound for the Blessed Isles of Liberty! (*then with an ironic smile*) But you need not tell Tiberius that, good Flavius. Say it was due to my extreme zeal.

FLAVIUS—(*smiles with respectful understanding. Caligula nods in dismissal. Flavius turns to go—apologetically*) You may have to wait. I dare not speak before he questions me. (*Flavius salutes and hastens to the villa, walking under an arm of the cross unconcernedly without an upward glance. As they follow him with their eyes Caligula and Miriam see the lion for the first time. He steps back with a startled exclamation. She gives a cry of horror and covers her eyes with her hands to shut out the sight.*)

LAZARUS—(*immediately puts his arms around her protect-ingly*) What is it, Beloved? (*She hides her face on his breast, pointing toward the lion with a trembling hand.*)

CALIGULA—(*pointing—curiously now, but with entire cal-lousness*) This lion they have crucified. Are you frightened, Jewess? (*with a cruel laugh*) My grandfather frequently plants whole orchards of such trees, but usually they bear human fruit!

MIRIAM—(*with a shudder*) Monster!

CALIGULA—(*with genuine surprise—turning to her*) Who? Why? (*He approaches the cross and stares at it moodily.*) But why did he have it placed here where he knew you must pass? Tiberius does not go to such pains to frighten women. (*His eyes fasten on the inscription above the lion's head.*) Aha! I see! (*He reads*) "From the East, land of false gods and supersti-tion, this lion was brought to Rome to amuse Cæsar." (*A silence. Caligula shrugs his shoulders, turning away—lightly*) A lesson for you, Lazarus. An example for other lions—not to roar—or laugh—at Cæsar! (*He gives a harsh laugh.*) Tiberius must be terribly afraid of you. (*then somberly*) You should never have come here. I would have advised you not to—but what are you to me? My duty, if I wish to become Cæsar, is to Cæsar. Besides, you are no fool. Evidently you must desire your own death. Last night *you* might have been Cæsar. The legions were yours.

LAZARUS—(*smiling without bitterness—with a sad comprehension*) But this morning the legions had forgotten. They only remembered—to go out and pick up their swords! They also pillaged the bodies a little, as their right, believing now that they had slain them! (*this last a bit bitterly*)

CALIGULA—(*tauntingly*) The legions did slay them! It was only by some magician's trick you made them think your followers killed themselves.

LAZARUS—(*not answering him—ironically to himself*) It is too soon. Men still need their swords to slash at ghosts in the dark. Men, those haunted heroes! (*He laughs softly.*)

CALIGULA—(*irritably*) What are you laughing at?

LAZARUS—At Lazarus when I find him feeling wronged because men are men! (*He laughs again, softly and musically.*)

CALIGULA—(*again taunting brutally*) You may be in his place soon! (*He points to the lion.*) Will you laugh then? (*Miriam gives a cry of terror.*)

LAZARUS—(*calmly*) Yes. (*then humbly, bowing his head*) I will laugh with the pride of a beggar set upon the throne of Man!

CALIGULA—(*sneeringly*) You boast. (*then as Lazarus does not answer, touching the lion with intentional provoking brutality*) This one from Africa seems almost gone. They do not last as long as men.

LAZARUS—(*walks up the steps to the cross and, stretching to his full height, gently pushes the lion's hair out of its eyes—tenderly*) Poor brother! Cæsar avenges himself on you because of me. Forgive me your suffering!

CALIGULA—(*with a start backward—with frightened awe*) Gods! He licks your hand! I could swear he smiles—with his last breath! (*then with relief*) Now he is dead!

LAZARUS—(*gently*) There is no death.

CALIGULA—(*pointing to the lion*) What is that then?

LAZARUS—Your fear of life.

CALIGULA—(*impatiently*) Bah! (*then somberly*) A little fear is useful even for lions—or teachers of laughter if they wish to laugh long! (*then with a sudden exasperation*) Escape now, you fool, while there is still time!

LAZARUS—(*laughing softly*) Escape—what?

CALIGULA—(*in a frenzy*) You know, you ass, you lunatic! Escape death! Death! Death! (*to Miriam*) You, woman! Talk to him! Do you want him nailed up like that?

MIRIAM—(*with a pitiful cry*) Lazarus! Come! Caligula will help us!

CALIGULA—(*harshly*) You presume, Jewess! I have no wish to die! (*then with his wry smile*) But I will turn my back—and shut my eyes— (*He walks away to left.*)

MIRIAM—(*beseechingly*) Lazarus! I could not bear that aching hunger of my empty heart if you should die again!

LAZARUS—(*coming to her—tenderly*) I will not leave you! Believe in me! (*He kisses her forehead tenderly.*)

MIRIAM—(*after a pause—slowly and lamentingly*) I wish we were home, Lazarus. This Roman world is full of evil. These skies threaten. These hearts are heavy with hatred. There is a taint of blood in the air that poisons the breath of the sea. These columns and arches and thick walls seem waiting to fall, to crush these rotten men and then to crumble over the bones that raised them until both are dust. It is a world deadly to your joy, Lazarus. Its pleasure is a gorging of dirt, its fulfilled desire a snoring in a sty in the mud among swine. Its will is so sick that it must kill in order to be aware of life at all. I wish we were home, Lazarus. I begin to feel horror gnawing at my breast. I begin to know the torture of the fear of death, Lazarus—not of my death but of yours—not of the passing of your man's body but of the going away from me of your laughter which is to me as my son, my little boy!

LAZARUS—(*soothing her*) Be comforted, Beloved. Your fear shall never be!

MIRIAM—On the hills near Bethany you might pray at noon and laugh your boy's laughter in the sun and there would be echoing laughter from the sky and up from the grass and distantly from the shining sea. We would adopt children whose parents the Romans had butchered, and their laughter would be around me in my home where I cooked and weaved and sang. And in the dawn at your going out, and in the evening on your return, I would hear in the hushed air the bleating of sheep and the tinkling of many little bells and your voice. And my heart would know peace.

LAZARUS—(*tenderly*) Only a little longer! There is God's laughter on the hills of space, and the happiness of children, and the soft healing of innumerable dawns and evenings, and the blessing of peace!

CALIGULA—(*looks around at Lazarus impatiently. Then he makes a beckoning gesture to Miriam.*) Ssstt! (*Wonderingly she leaves Lazarus' side and follows him. Lazarus remains, his eyes fixed on the cross, directly in front of it. Caligula speaks gruffly to Miriam with a sneer.*) Jewess, your Lazarus is mad, I begin to think. (*then confusedly but helplessly inquisitive and confiding— bursting out*) What is it troubles me about him? What makes me dream of him? Why should I—love him, Jewess? Tell me! You love him, too. I do not understand this. Why, wherever he goes, is there joy? You heard even the galley slaves laugh and clank time with their chains! (*then with exasperation*) And yet why can I not laugh, Jewess?

MIRIAM—(*in a tone of hushed grief*) I may not laugh either. My heart remains a little dead with Lazarus in Bethany. The miracle could not revive all his old husband's life in my wife's heart.

CALIGULA—(*disgustedly*) What answer is that to me? (*then brusquely*) But I called you to put you on your guard. (*He points.*) There is death in there—Tiberius' death, a kind from which no miracles can recall one! (*He smiles his twisted smile.*) Since Lazarus will not help himself, you must protect him. I will not, for once in there I am (*mockingly*) the heir of Cæsar, and you are scum whom I will kill at his order as I would two beetles! So keep watch! Taste first of what he eats—even were I the one to give it to him!

LAZARUS—(*suddenly laughs softly*) Why do you delight in believing evil of yourself, Caligula?

CALIGULA—(*flying into a queer rage*) You lie! I am what I am! (*with grandiose pride*) What could you know of a Cæsar?

LAZARUS—(*still laughing with an affectionate understanding*) What—I know! (*As he finishes speaking all the sound of music and voices from the house ceases abruptly and there is a heavy silence.*)

MIRIAM—(*shaking her head and turning away sadly*) That is too far, Lazarus. Let us go home.

CALIGULA—(*harshly*) Sst! Do you hear? Flavius has told

CÆSAR. (*grimly forcing a harsh snicker*) Now we will soon know— (*There is the sudden blaring of a trumpet from within the palace. A wide door is flung open and a stream of reddish light comes out against which the black figures of several men are outlined. The door is shut again quickly. Several slaves bearing lamps on poles escort the patrician, Marcellus, forward to the arch. He passes under the crucified lion without a glance—then stands, cool and disdainful, to look about him. He is a man of about thirty-five, wearing the type mask of a Roman patrician to which are added the dissipated courtier's characteristics of one who leans to evil more through weakness than any instinctive urge. He is dressed richly. His smile is hypocritical and his eyes are hard and cold but when they come to rest on Lazarus he gives a start of genuine astonishment.*)

CALIGULA—(*who has moved to Lazarus' side defensively— in a quick whisper*) Beware of this man, Lazarus! (*then advancing—with a condescending hauteur*) Greeting, Marcellus!

MARCELLUS—(*in an ingratiating tone*) Greeting, Gaius. I have a message from Cæsar for the man called Lazarus.

LAZARUS—(*calmly*) I am Lazarus.

MARCELLUS—(*makes a deep bow—flatteringly*) I had surmised it, sir. Although I cannot pretend to virtue in myself at least I may claim the merit of recognizing it in others. (*He advances toward Lazarus, smiling, with one hand kept hidden beneath his cloak.*)

CALIGULA—(*stepping between them—sharply*) What is your message?

MARCELLUS—(*surprised—placatingly*) I am sorry, Gaius, but it was Cæsar's command I speak to Lazarus alone.

CALIGULA—(*fiercely*) And then, Marcellus? (*Marcellus shrugs his shoulders and smiles deprecatingly.*)

LAZARUS—(*with a compelling dignity*) Let him speak. (*inclining his head to Marcellus—strangely*) Over here where it is dark you will not be seen—nor see yourself. (*He walks to the darkness at right.*)

CALIGULA—(*turning his back on them, with angry boyish resentfulness that is close to tears*) Idiot! Go and die, then!

MIRIAM—(*with a terrified cry*) Lazarus! (*She starts to go to him.*)

LAZARUS—(*motioning her to remain where she is—gently*)

Believe, Beloved! (*He turns his back on them all and stands waiting.*)

MARCELLUS—(*stares at Lazarus—then over his shoulder at Caligula—uncertainly*) What does he mean, Gaius? (*Then suddenly putting on a brave front, he strides up behind Lazarus.*) Cæsar wished me to bid you welcome, to tell you how much regard he has for you, but he desired me to ask whether you propose to laugh here—in Cæsar's palace? He has heard that you laugh at death—that you have caused others to laugh— even his legionaries. (*A pause, Marcellus remains behind Lazarus' back, the latter standing like a victim.*) Briefly, Cæsar requires your pledge that you will not laugh. Will you give it? (*He frees his dagger from under his robe. A pause. Arrogantly*) I am waiting! Answer when Cæsar commands! (*then angrily, baffled*) I will give you while I count three—or take your silence as a refusal! One! Two! Three! (*He raises his hand to stab Lazarus in the back. Miriam stifles a scream. At the same instant, Lazarus begins to laugh, softly and affectionately. Marcellus stops, frozen in mid-action, the dagger upraised. Caligula has whirled around and stands staring, a smile gradually coming to his face. Lazarus turns, his laughter grown a trifle louder, and faces Marcellus. The latter steps back from him, staring open-mouthed, fascinated. His arm sinks to his side. The dagger falls from his fingers. He smiles back at Lazarus—the curious, sheepish, bashful smile of one who has fallen in love and been discovered.*)

LAZARUS—(*going to him, puts both hands on his shoulders and looks in his eyes, laughing affectionately—then quizzically*) Here is another one who believes in death! But soon you will laugh with life! I see it in your eyes. Farewell, Marcellus! (*He turns away from him and walks, laughing, toward the arch in rear. With bowed head the black-robed figure of Miriam follows him. Marcellus hides his face in his hands, half-sobbing, and half-laughing hysterically. Lazarus pauses before the cross for a moment—raises his hand as if blessing the dead lion, then passes below it, moving slowly on toward the palace in the rear. His laughter rises with more and more summoning power. The files of the Guard, as he passes them, two by two join in his laughter, saluting him as if in spite of themselves.*)

CALIGULA—(*sidling up to Marcellus, cruel and mocking*) Are

you weeping, Marcellus? Laugh at that blundering fool, yourself! What will Cæsar say? Will he laugh when he has your
body broken one bone at a time with hammers? Why did you
not kill? For shame! A patrician exposed to laughter by a Jew!
Poor craven! Why could you not strike? There *must* be death!
Coward! Why did you not stab? (*then in a queer awed whisper*)
I know! Was it not because of a sudden you loved him and
could not?

MARCELLUS—(*suddenly—eagerly*) Yes! That was it! I loved
him!

CALIGULA—(*craftily and cruelly*) You were about to murder him!

MARCELLUS—(*tortured with remorse*) No! No! How could
I? What infamy! (*cries tearfully*) Forgive me, Lazarus!

CALIGULA—(*with vindictive insistence*) Judge yourself! (*He
takes up the dagger.*) Here is your dagger! Avenge him on
yourself!

MARCELLUS—(*trying to laugh*) Ha-ha— Yes! (*He stabs
himself and falls. Suddenly his laughter is released.*) I laugh! You
are a fool, Caligula! There is no death! (*He dies, laughing up
at the sky.*)

CALIGULA—(*kicks his body with savage cruelty*) You lie! (*then
suddenly kneels and bends over it imploringly*) Tell me you lie,
Marcellus! Do me that mercy!—and when I am Cæsar, I—
(*He begins to weep like a frightened boy, his head in his hands.
Meanwhile Lazarus has arrived with Miriam at the steps before
the door of the palace. As he starts to ascend these, the crimson-
purple lights of the many windows of the palace go out one by one
as if fleeing in terror from the laughter which now beats at the
walls.*)

CHORUS OF THE GUARD—

   Fear, no more!
   Death, no more!
   Laugh! Laugh! Laugh!
   Death is dead!

ALL THE GUARDS—(*now all in a great chorus, raising their
spears aloft and saluting Lazarus as if they were his own triumphal body guard*)

   Laugh! Laugh! Laugh!
   Death is dead!

(*Lazarus has ascended the steps. He walks into the black archway of the darkened palace, his figure radiant and unearthly in his own light. Miriam follows him. They disappear in the darkness. There is a pause of dead silence.*)

CALIGULA—(*raises his head uneasily, looks back toward the palace, jumps to his feet in a panic of terror, and runs toward the palace door, calling*) Lazarus! Wait! I will defend you! There is death inside there—death! Beware, Lazarus!

CHORUS OF THE GUARD—(*as the laughter of Lazarus is heard again from the dark palace*)
     Laugh! Laugh! Laugh!
     Death is dead!

ALL THE GUARDS—
     Dead! Dead! Dead!
     Death is dead!

(*Curtain*)

SCENE TWO

SCENE—*The banquet hall in the palace of Tiberius—an immense high-ceilinged room. In the rear, center, is a great arched doorway. Smaller arches in the middle of the side walls lead into other rooms. Long couches are placed along the walls at right and left, and along the rear wall on either side of the arch. Before these couches, a series of narrow tables is set. In the center of the room on a high dais is the ivory and gold chair of Cæsar, a table in front of it, couches for him to recline on at either side. On this table, and on all the tables for his guests, gold lamps with shades of crimson-purple are placed.*

Reclining on the couches on the right are young women and girls, on the left, youths of an equal number.

(*The masks are based on the Roman masks of the periods of Boyhood [or Girlhood], Youth, and Young Manhood [or Womanhood] and there are seven individuals of each period and sex in each of the three types of the Introspective, Self-Tortured; the Servile, Hypocritical; and the Cruel, Revengeful—a crowd of forty-two in all. There is a distinctive character to the masks of each sex, the stamp of an effeminate corruption on all the male, while the female have a bold, masculine expression. The male masks are a blotched heliotrope in shade. These youths wear female wigs of curled wire like frizzed hair of a yellow gold. They are dressed in women's robes of pale heliotrope, they wear anklets and bracelets and necklaces. The women are dressed as males in crimson or deep purple. They also wear wire wigs but of straight hair cut in short boyish mode, dyed either deep purple or crimson. Those with crimson hair are dressed in purple, and vice versa. The female voices are harsh, strident, mannish—those of the youths affected, lisping, effeminate. The whole effect of these two groups is of sex corrupted and warped, of invented lusts and artificial vices.*

(The Chorus in this scene and the next is composed of three males and four females—the males in the period of Youth, one in each of the types represented, and three of the females in similar type-period masks. The fourth female is masked in the period of Womanhood in the Proud, Self-Reliant type. They sit, facing front in their double-sized masks, on the side steps of the dais, four on right, three on left.)

Pompeia, a Roman noblewoman, the favorite mistress of Cæsar, sits at front, right.

She wears a half-mask on the upper part of her face, olive-colored with the red of blood smoldering through, with great, dark, cruel eyes—a dissipated mask of intense evil beauty, of lust and perverted passion. Beneath the mask, her own complexion is pale, her gentle, girlish mouth is set in an expression of agonized self-loathing and weariness of spirit. Her body is strong and beautiful. Her wig and dress are purple.

Tiberius Cæsar stands on the dais, dressed in deep purple, fringed and ornamented with crimson and gold. An old man of seventy-six, tall, broad and corpulent but of great muscular strength still despite his age, his shiny white cranium rises like a polished shell above his half-masked face. This mask is a pallid purple blotched with darker color, as if the imperial blood in his veins had been sickened by age and debauchery. The eyes are protuberant, leering, cynical slits, the long nose, once finely modeled, now gross and thickened, the forehead lowering and grim. Beneath the mask, his own mouth looks as incongruous as Caligula's. The lips are thin and stern and self-contained—the lips of an able soldier-statesman of rigid probity. His chin is forceful and severe. The complexion of his own skin is that of a healthy old campaigner.

As the curtain rises, slaves are hurriedly putting out the many lamps. From outside, the laughter of Lazarus rises on the deep ground swell of the Guard's laughter. The walls and massive columns seem to reverberate with the sound. In the banquet room all are listening fascinatedly. Every reaction, from the extreme of panic fear or hypnotized ecstasy to a feigned cynical amusement or a pretended supercilious indifference, is represented in their frozen attitudes. Tiberius stands, shrinking back, staring at the doorway in the rear with superstitious dread. A squad of the Guard surround the dais, commanded by Flavius.

TIBERIUS—(*in a strained voice shaken by apprehension and awe*) Marcellus! Strike him down! Stab him!

SOLDIERS OF THE GUARD—(*from without*)

Laugh! Laugh! Laugh!

Death is dead!

TIBERIUS—(*as he suddenly sees the shining figure of Lazarus appear at the end of the dark hall beyond the archway*) Gods! Flavius, look! (*He points with a shaking finger. Flavius has leaped up to his side.*)

FLAVIUS—(*not without dread himself*) That is the man, Cæsar.

TIBERIUS—Man? Say a dæmon! (*to the slaves who are turning out the few remaining lamps*) Quick! Darkness! (*He puts out the lamp on his table himself. Then as nothing is seen but the light from the approaching Lazarus*) Flavius! Stand here in my place! It will think you are Cæsar! (*He clumps heavily down the steps of the dais.*) Guards! Here! Cover me with your shields! (*He goes to the extreme right corner, front, and crouches there. His Guards follow him. They hold their shields so that they form a wall around him and half over him. Then Caligula's voice is heard screaming above the chorus of laughter as he enters the hall behind Lazarus.*)

CALIGULA—Beware of death! I will defend you, Lazarus! (*He is seen to rush past Lazarus, flourishing his sword and comes running into the room, shouting*) Cæsar! Dare not to murder Lazarus! (*He leaps to the dais and up its steps in a frenzy.*) Dare not, I say! (*He stabs Flavius with a savage cry*) Ah! (*Then, as the body of Flavius falls heavily and rolls down the steps at right, he begins to laugh, at first a clear laughter of selfless joy, sounding*

startlingly incongruous from him.) I have saved you, Lazarus—
at the risk of my own life—and now, hear me, I can laugh!
(*Lazarus appears in the archway, Miriam behind him. He stops
laughing and immediately there is silence, except for Caligula.
Lazarus casts a luminous glow over the whole room in which
the masked faces appear distorted and livid. Caligula stands
with upraised sword by the chair of Cæsar. Suddenly his laughter
cracks, changes, becomes full of his old fear and bloodlust.*)

CALIGULA—Ha-ha-ha! See, Lazarus! (*He points to the body
of Flavius with his sword.*) Welcome in the name of Cæsar, now
Cæsar is slain and I am Cæsar! (*He assumes the absurd grandiose posture of his imperial posing. No one looks at him or hears
him. Their eyes are on Lazarus as he moves directly to where Tiberius crouches behind the shields of the Guards. Miriam follows
him. Caligula turns and stares toward him, and then down at
the body of Flavius and back, in a petrified, bewildered stupor.
Lazarus steps up beside Tiberius. The Guards make way for him
fearfully.*)

TIBERIUS—(*feeling his nearness—straightening himself with
a certain dignity*) Strike! I have been a soldier. Thou canst not
make me fear death, Dæmon! (*He draws his toga over his face.*)

LAZARUS—(*smiling gently*) Then fear not fear, Tiberius!
(*He reaches out and pulls back the toga from his face. Tiberius
looks into his eyes, at first shrinkingly, then with growing reassurance, his own masked face clearly revealed now in the light from
Lazarus.*)

TIBERIUS—(*at first falteringly*) So—thou art not evil?
Thou art not come to contrive my murder? (*As Lazarus smilingly shakes his head, Tiberius frowns.*) Then why dost thou
laugh against Cæsar? (*then bitterly—with a twisted attempt at
a smile*) Yet I like thy laughter. It is young. Once I laughed
somewhat like that—so I pardon thee. I will even laugh at
thee in return. Ha-ha! (*His laughter is cold, cruel and merciless
as the grin of a skeleton.*)

CALIGULA—(*who has been staring in a bewildered stupor from
Tiberius, whom he thought he had killed, to the body of Flavius—quaking with terror now as if this laugh was meant for
him, drops to his knees, his sword clattering down the steps to the
floor*) Mercy, Tiberius! I implore you forgive your Caligula!

TIBERIUS—(*not understanding. Fixing his eyes on Caligula with a malevolent irony.*) Come down from my throne, Caligula. (*Caligula slinks down warily.*) You are too impatient. But I must pardon you, too—for where could I find another heir so perfect for serving my spite upon mankind? (*He has walked toward the throne while he is speaking, Caligula backing away from him. Lazarus remains where he is, Miriam beside and to the rear of him. Tiberius, his eyes fixed on Caligula, stumbles against the body of Flavius. He gives a startled gasp and shrinks back, calling*) Lights! A light here! (*A crowd of masked slaves obey his orders. One runs to him with a lantern. He looks down at Flavius' corpse—half to himself*) I did wisely to stand him in my place. (*to Caligula—with sinister emphasis*) Too impatient, my loving grandchild! Take care lest I become impatient also—with your impatience! (*Caligula shudders and backs away to the extreme left corner, front, where he crouches on his haunches as inconspicuously as possible. Tiberius suddenly whirls around as if he felt a dagger at his back.*)

TIBERIUS—Where—? (*seeing Lazarus where he had been—with relief—staring at his face now that the room is flooded with the purplish-crimson glow from all the lamps*) Ah, you are there. More lights! Darkness leads men into error. My heir mistakes a man for Cæsar and Cæsar, it appears, has mistaken a man for a dæmon! (*scrutinizing him—with sinister finality*) I can deal with men. I know them well. Too well! (*He laughs grimly.*) Therefore I hate them. (*He mounts the steps of the dais and sits on the couch at left of table—staring at Lazarus, wonderingly*) But you seem—something other than man! That light! (*Then he forces a harsh laugh.*) A trick! I had forgotten you are a magician. (*arrogantly*) Stand there, Jew. I would question you about your magic. (*Smilingly Lazarus ascends to where Tiberius points at the top of the dais. Miriam remains standing at the foot. Tiberius stares for a while with somber intensity at Lazarus.*) They say you died and have returned from death?

LAZARUS—(*smiling—as if he were correcting a child*) There is no death, Cæsar.

TIBERIUS—(*with a sneer of scepticism but with an underlying eagerness*) I have heard you teach that folly. (*then threateningly*) You shall be given full opportunity to prove it! (*a pause—then in a low voice, bending down toward Lazarus*) Do you foretell the future? (*trembling but with a pretense of carelessness*) Must I die soon?

LAZARUS—(*simply*) Yes, Cæsar.

TIBERIUS—(*jumping up with a shuddering start*) Soon? Soon? (*then his fear turning to rage*) What do you say? Vile Jew, do you dare threaten me with death! (*Lazarus, looking into his eyes, begins to laugh softly. Tiberius sinks back on his couch, fighting to control himself—confusedly*) Laugh not, I ask you. I am old. It is not seemly. (*Lazarus ceases his low laughter. A pause. Tiberius broods—then suddenly*) And you were really dead? (*He shudders.*) Come nearer. I need to watch your face. I have learned to read the lies in faces. A Cæsar gets much practice—from childhood on—too much! (*with awe*) Your eyes are dark with death. While I watch them, answer me, what cured thee of death?

LAZARUS—(*gently*) There is only life, Cæsar. (*then gaily mocking but compellingly*) And laughter! Look! Look well into my eyes, old Reader of Lies, and see if you can find aught in them that is not life—and laughter! (*He laughs softly. A ripple of soft laughter from the motionless figures about the room echoes his. Tiberius stares into his eyes. In the silence that ensues Pompeia gets up and walks over to the dais. She stops to stare for a moment with cruel contempt at Miriam, then stands and looks up at Lazarus, trying in vain to attract his or Cæsar's attention. Failing in this, she passes over and sits beside Caligula, whose attention is concentrated on Lazarus.*)

POMPEIA—I admire your strange magician, Caligula.

CALIGULA—(*without looking at her*) He is no magician. He is something like a god.

POMPEIA—(*longingly*) His laughter is like a god's. He is strong. I love him.

CALIGULA—(*turning to her—coarsely*) Do not waste your lust. He is faithful to his wife, I warn you.

POMPEIA—(*She points to Miriam.*) Not that ugly slave?

CALIGULA—Yes. And yet, on our journey, whole herds of women—and many as beautiful as you, Pompeia—threw themselves on him and begged for his love.

POMPEIA—(*her voice hardening*) And he?

CALIGULA—He laughed—and passed on. (*She starts. Caligula goes on wonderingly.*) But they seemed as happy as if his laughter had possessed them! You are a woman. Tell me, how could that be?

POMPEIA—(*her voice cruel*) He shall not laugh at me!

CALIGULA—(*tauntingly*) I will bet a string of pearls against your body for a night that he does.

POMPEIA—(*defiantly*) Done! (*Then she laughs—a low, cruel laugh—staring at Miriam*) So he loves that woman?

CALIGULA—(*curiously*) What are you planning?

POMPEIA—I shall offer her the fruit Cæsar preserves for those he fears.

CALIGULA—(*with a careless shrug*) You will not win his love by killing her.

POMPEIA—I no longer want his love. I want to see him suffer, to hear his laughter choke in his throat with pain! (*She speaks with more and more voluptuous satisfaction.*) Then I shall laugh! (*She laughs softly and steps forward.*)

CALIGULA—(*concernedly*) Stop. I am his protector. (*then suddenly*) But what is the Jewess to me? (*with more and more of a spirit of perverse cruelty*) Do it, Pompeia! His laughter is too cruel to us! We must save death from him!

POMPEIA—(*walks to the dais which she ascends slowly until she stands by Cæsar's couch behind him, confronting Lazarus. But the two men remain unmindful of her presence. Tiberius continues to stare into Lazarus' eyes. His whole body is now relaxed, at rest, a dreamy smile softens his thin, compressed mouth. Pompeia leans over and takes a peach from the bowl of fruit on Cæsar's table and, taking Tiberius' hand in her other, she kisses it and calls insistently*) Cæsar. It is I, Pompeia. (*Lazarus does not look at her. She stares at him defiantly. Tiberius blinks his eyes in a daze.*)

TIBERIUS—(*dreamily*) Yes! A cloud came from a depth of sky—around me, softly, warmly, and the cloud dissolved into the sky, and the sky into peace! (*suddenly springing to his feet and staring about him in a confused rage—clutching Pompeia by the shoulder and forcing her to her knees*) What are you doing here?

POMPEIA—Forgive your loving slave! I grew afraid this

magician had put you under a spell. (*She stares at Lazarus, her words challenging him.*)

TIBERIUS—(*confusedly, sinking back on his couch and releasing her*) A spell? Could it be he laid a dream of death upon me, leading me to death? (*He trembles timorously—appealing to Lazarus*) Whatever magic thou didst to me, Dæmon, I beseech thee undo it!

LAZARUS—(*smiling*) Do you fear peace?

POMPEIA—(*harshly and insolently*) Mock not at Cæsar, dog! (*Lazarus continues to smile. His eyes remain on Cæsar. He seems absolutely unaware of Pompeia. This enrages her the more against him. She speaks tauntingly to Tiberius.*) Surely, Cæsar, this magician must have powerful charms since he dares to mock Tiberius to his face!

TIBERIUS—(*stung*) Be still! (*then in a low tone to her*) Do you not know this Lazarus died and then by his magic rose from his tomb.

POMPEIA—(*scornfully*) To believe that, I must have seen it, Cæsar!

TIBERIUS—(*impatiently*) Do you think I would believe without good evidence? I have had them take the statements of many witnesses. The miracle was done in conjunction with another Jew acting as this man's tool. This other Jew, the report states, could not possibly have possessed any magic power Himself, for Pilate crucified Him a short time after and He died in pain and weakness within a few hours. But this Lazarus laughs at death!

LAZARUS—(*looks up, smiling with ironical bitterness*) Couldst Thou but hear, Jesus! And men shall keep on in panic nailing Man's soul to the cross of their fear until in the end they do it to avenge Thee, for Thine Honor and Glory! (*He sighs sadly—then after a struggle overcoming himself—with exultance*) Yes! (*His eyes fall again to Tiberius and he smiles.*) Yes! Yes to the stupid as to the wise! To what is understood and to what cannot be understood! Known and unknown! Over and over! Forever and ever! Yes! (*He laughs softly to himself.*)

TIBERIUS—(*with superstitious dread*) What dost thou mean, Dæmon?

POMPEIA—(*with indignant scorn*) Let him prove there is no

death, Cæsar! (*She appeals to the company who straighten up on their couches with interest.*)

CHORUS—(*chant demandingly*)

Let him prove there is no death!

We are bored!

CROWD—(*echoing*)

Prove there is no death!

We are bored, Cæsar!

TIBERIUS—(*waits to see what Lazarus will say—then as he says nothing, plucking up his courage—his cruelty aroused*) Do you hear, Lazarus?

POMPEIA—Make him perform his miracle again!

CHORUS—(*as before*)

Let him perform a miracle!

We are bored, Cæsar!

CROWD—(*They now stand up and coming from behind their tables, move forward toward the dais.*)

A miracle!

We are bored!

POMPEIA—Let him raise someone from the dead!

CHORUS—(*chanting with a pettish insistence*)

Raise the dead!

We are bored!

CROWD—(*echoing—grouping in a big semicircle as of spectators in a theatre, around and to the sides of the dais, one sex on each side. Caligula moves in from the left in front of them. They form in three ranks, the first squatting on their hams like savages [as Caligula does], the second rank crouching over them, the third leaning over the second, all with a hectic, morbid interest.*)

We are bored!

Raise the dead!

POMPEIA—(*with a cruel smile*) I have thought of a special test for him, Cæsar. (*She whispers in Cæsar's ear and points to Miriam and the fruit in her hand.*) And he must laugh!

TIBERIUS—(*with a harsh, cruel chuckle*) Yes, I shall command him to laugh! (*then disgustedly*) But she is sad and old. I will be only doing him a favor.

CALIGULA—(*rocking back and forth on his haunches—looking at Lazarus with taunting cruelty*) No, Cæsar! I know he loves her!

LAZARUS—Yes! (*He steps down from the dais to Miriam's side and taking her head in both his hands, he kisses her on the lips.*)

TIBERIUS—(*with a malignant grin*) Give her the fruit!

POMPEIA—(*advances and offers the peach to Miriam—with a hard, cruel little laugh*) Cæsar invites you to eat!

MIRIAM—(*to Lazarus—requesting meekly but longingly*) May I accept, Lazarus? Is it time at last? My love has followed you over long roads among strangers and each league we came from home my heart has grown older. Now it is too old for you, a heart too weary for your loving laughter. Ever your laughter has grown younger, Lazarus! Upward it springs like a lark from a field, and sings! Once I knew your laughter was my child, my son of Lazarus; but then it grew younger and I felt at last it had returned to my womb—and ever younger and younger—until, tonight, when I spoke to you of home, I felt new birth-pains as your laughter, grown too young for me, flew back to the unborn—a birth so like a death! (*She sobs and wipes her eyes with her sleeve—then humbly, reaching out for the fruit*) May I accept it, Lazarus? You should have newborn laughing hearts to love you. My old one labors with memories and its blood is sluggish with the past. Your home on the hills of space is too far away. My heart longs for the warmth of close walls of earth baked in the sun. Our home in Bethany, Lazarus, where you and my children lived and died. Our tomb near our home, Lazarus, in which you and my children wait for me. Is it time at last?

LAZARUS—(*deeply moved*) Poor lonely heart! It has been crueler for you than I remembered. Go in peace—to peace! (*His voice trembles in spite of himself.*) I shall be lonely, dear one. (*with a note of pleading*) You have never laughed with my laughter. Will you call back— Yes!—when you know—to tell me you understand and laugh with me at last?

MIRIAM—(*not answering him, to Pompeia, taking the peach and making a humble courtesy before her*) I thank you, pretty lady. (*She raises the peach toward her mouth. Involuntarily one of Lazarus' hands half-reaches out as if to stop her.*)

POMPEIA—(*with savage triumph, pointing*) See! He would stop her! He is afraid of death!

CHORUS—(*pointing—jeeringly*) He is afraid of death! Ha-ha-ha-ha!

CROWD—(*jeeringly*) Ha-ha-ha-ha!

MIRIAM—(*bites into the peach and, chewing, begins, as if immediately affected, to talk like a garrulous old woman, her words coming quicker and quicker as her voice becomes fainter and fainter*) Say what you like, it is much better I should go home first, Lazarus. We have been away so long, there will be so much to attend to about the house. And all the children will be waiting. You would be as helpless as a child, Lazarus. Between you and the children, things would soon be in a fine state! (*more and more confused*) No, no! You cannot help me, dearest one. You are only in my way. No, I will make the fire. When you laid it the last time, we all had to run for our lives, choking, the smoke poured from the windows, the neighbors thought the house was burning! (*She laughs—a queer, vague little inward laugh.*) You are so impractical. The neighbors all get the best of you. Money slips through your fingers. If it was not for me— (*She sighs—then brightly and lovingly*) But, dearest husband, why do you take it so to heart? Why do you feel guilty because you are not like other men? That is why I love you so much. Is it a sin to be born a dreamer? But God, He must be a dreamer, too, or how would we be on earth? Do not keep saying to yourself so bitterly, you are a failure in life! Do not sit brooding on the hilltop in the evening like a black figure of Job against the sky! (*her voice trembling*) Even if God has taken our little ones—yes, in spite of sorrow— have you not a good home I make for you, and a wife who loves you? (*She forces a chuckle.*) Be grateful, then—for me! Smile, my sad one! Laugh a little once in a while! Come home, bringing me laughter of the wind from the hills! (*swaying, looking at the peach in her hand*) What a mellow, sweet fruit! Did you bring it home for me? (*She falls back into his arms. Gently he lets her body sink until it rests against the steps of the dais. Tiberius rises from his couch to bend over with cruel gloating. Pompeia steps nearer to Lazarus, staring at him mockingly. Caligula hops to her side, looking from Lazarus to Miriam. The half-circle of masked figures moves closer, straining forward and downward as if to overwhelm the two figures at the foot of the dais with their concentrated death wish.*)

TIBERIUS—(*thickly*) She is dead, and I do not hear you laugh!

LAZARUS—(*bending down—supplicatingly*) Miriam! Call back to me! Laugh! (*He pauses. A second of dead silence. Then, with a sound that is very like a sob, he kisses her on the lips.*) I am lonely!

POMPEIA—(*with savage malice—jeeringly*) See! He weeps, Cæsar! (*She bursts into strident laughter.*) Ha-ha-ha-ha!

CHORUS—(*echoing her laughter*)
 Ha-ha-ha-ha!
 There is fear!
 There is death!

CROWD—
 There is death!
 Ha-ha-ha-ha!

CALIGULA—(*in a frenzy of despairing rage, hopping up and down*) Liar! Charlatan! Weakling! How you have cheated Caligula! (*He suddenly slaps Lazarus viciously across the face.*) There is death! Laugh, if you dare!

TIBERIUS—(*standing—in a sinister cold rage, the crueler because his dream of a cure for death is baffled, yet feeling his power as Cæsar triumphant nevertheless*) And I thought you might be a dæmon. I thought you might have a magic cure— (*with revengeful fury*) But death is, and death is mine! I shall make you pray for death! And I shall make Death laugh at you! Ha-ha-ha-ha! (*in a frenzy as Lazarus neither makes a sound nor looks up*) Laugh, Lazarus! Laugh at yourself! Laugh with me! (*then to his Soldiers*) Scourge him! Make him laugh!

CALIGULA—(*running to Soldiers—fiercely*) Give me a scourge!

POMPEIA—(*running to the Soldiers—hysterically*) Ha-ha-ha-ha! Let me beat him, Cæsar! (*They group behind him. The rods and scourges are uplifted over his back to strike, when in the dead expectant silence, Miriam's body is seen to rise in a writhing tortured last effort.*)

MIRIAM—(*in a voice of unearthly sweetness*) Yes! There is only life! Lazarus, be not lonely! (*She laughs and sinks back and is still.*

(*A shuddering murmur of superstitious fear comes from them as they shrink back swiftly from Lazarus, remaining huddled one against the other. Pompeia runs to the feet of Tiberius and crouches down on the steps below him, as if for protection, her terrified eyes on Miriam. Caligula runs to her and crouches beside and beneath her.)*

LAZARUS—*(kisses Miriam again and raises his head. His face is radiant with new faith and joy. He smiles with happiness and speaks to himself with a mocking affection as if to an amusing child.)* That much remained hidden in me of the sad old Lazarus who died of self-pity—his loneliness! Lonely no more! Man's loneliness is but his fear of life! Lonely no more! Millions of laughing stars there are around me! And laughing dust, born once of woman on this earth, now freed to dance! New stars are born of dust eternally! The old, grown mellow with God, burst into flaming seed! The fields of infinite space are sown—and grass for sheep springs up on the hills of earth! But there is no death, nor fear, nor loneliness! There is only God's Eternal Laughter! His Laughter flows into the lonely heart! *(He begins to laugh, his laughter clear and ringing—the laughter of a conqueror arrogant with happiness and the pride of a new triumph. He bends and picks up the body of Miriam in his arms and, his head thrown back, laughing, he ascends the dais and places her on the table as on a bier. He touches one hand on her breast, as if he were taking an oath to life on her heart, looks upward and laughs, his voice ringing more and more with a terrible unbearable power and beauty that beats those in the room into an abject submissive panic.*

(Tiberius grovels half under the table, his hands covering his ears, his face on the floor; he is laughing with the agony and terror of death. Pompeia lies face down on the first step and beats it with her fists; she is laughing with horror and self-loathing. Caligula, his hands clutching his head, pounds it against the edge of the steps; he is laughing with grief and remorse. The rest, soldiers, slaves and the prostitutes of both sexes, writhe and twist distractedly, seeking to hide their heads against each other, beating each other and the floor with clenched hands. An agonized moan of supplicating laughter comes from them all.)

ALL—

Ha-ha-ha-ha! Ha-ha-ha-ha!

Let us die, Lazarus!

Mercy, Laughing One!
Mercy of death!
Ha-ha-ha-ha! Ha-ha-ha-ha!
(*But the laughter of Lazarus is as remote now as the laughter of a god.*)

(*Curtain*)

ACT FOUR

Scene One

SCENE—*The same as previous Scene—the same night a short while later. All the lamps are out except the one on the table on the dais which, placed beside the head of Miriam, shines down upon the white mask of her face. In the half-darkness, the walls are lost in shadow, the room seems immense, the dais nearer.*

Lazarus sits on the couch at the right on the dais. His face is strong and proud although his eyes are fixed down on the face of Miriam. He seems more youthful still now, like a young son who keeps watch by the body of his mother, but at the same time retaining the aloof serenity of the statue of a god. His face expresses sorrow and a happiness that transcends sorrow.

On the other side of the table, at the end of the couch, Tiberius sits facing front, his elbows on his knees, his large hands with bloated veins hanging loosely. He keeps his gaze averted from the corpse. He talks to Lazarus half over his shoulder.

On the top step, Pompeia sits, facing right, her hands clasped about one knee, the other leg stretched down to the lower step. Her head is thrown back and she is gazing up into Lazarus' face.

On the step below her, Caligula squats on his haunches, his arms on his knees, his fists pressed to his temples. He is staring straight before him.

Only these four people are in the room now.

TIBERIUS—(*gloomily*) Was she dead, Dæmon, and was it thy power that recalled life to her body for that moment? Or was she still living and her words only the last desire of her love to comfort you, Lazarus? (*Lazarus does not reply.*) If thou dost not tell me, I must always doubt thee, Dæmon.

POMPEIA—(*with a sigh of bewildered happiness, turns to Caligula*) I am glad he laughed, Caligula! Did I say I loved him before? Then it was only my body that wanted a slave. Now it is my heart that desires a master! Now I know love for the first time in my life!

CALIGULA—(*bitterly*) Fool! What does he care for love? (*somberly*) He loves everyone—but no one—not even me! (*He broods frowningly.*)

POMPEIA—(*following her own thoughts*) And now that hag is dead he will need a woman, young and beautiful, to protect and comfort him, to make him a home and bear his children! (*She dreams, her eyes again fixed on Lazarus—then suddenly turning to Caligula*) I am glad I lost our bet. But you must accept some other payment. Now I know love, I may not give myself to any man save him!

CALIGULA—I do not want you! What are you but another animal! Faugh! (*with a grimace of disgust*) Pleasure is dirty and joyless! Or we who seek it are, which comes to the same thing. (*then grimly*) But our bet can rest. This is not the end. There may still be a chance for you to laugh at him!

POMPEIA—No! Now I could not! I should weep for his defeat!

TIBERIUS—(*gloomily arguing, half to himself*) His laughter triumphed over me, but he has not brought her back to life. I think he knows no cure for another's death, as I had hoped. And I must always doubt that it was not some trick— (*harshly*) until I have tested him with his own life! He cannot cheat me then! (*a pause—arguing to himself*) But he was dead—that much has been proved—and before he died he was old and sad. What did he find beyond there? (*suddenly— turning to Lazarus now*) What did you find beyond death, Lazarus?

LAZARUS—(*exaltedly*) Life! God's Eternal Laughter!

TIBERIUS—(*shaking his head*) I want hope—for me, Tiberius Cæsar.

LAZARUS—What is—you? But there is hope for Man! Love is Man's hope—love for his life on earth, a noble love above suspicion and distrust! Hitherto Man has always suspected his life, and in revenge and self-torture his love has been faithless! He has even betrayed Eternity, his mother, with his slave he calls Immortal Soul! (*He laughs softly, gaily, mockingly—then to Tiberius directly*) Hope for you, Tiberius Cæsar? Then dare to love Eternity without your fear desiring to possess her! Be brave enough to be possessed!

TIBERIUS—(*strangely*) My mother was the wife of Cæsar. (*then dully*) I do not understand.

LAZARUS—Men are too cowardly to understand! And so the worms of their little fears eat them and grow fat and terrible and become their jealous gods they must appease with lies!

TIBERIUS—(*wearily*) Your words are meaningless, Lazarus. You are a fool. All laughter is malice, all gods are dead, and life is a sickness.

LAZARUS—(*laughs pityingly*) So say the race of men, whose lives are long dyings! They evade their fear of death by becoming so sick of life that by the time death comes they are too lifeless to fear it! Their disease triumphs over death—a noble victory called resignation! "We are sick," they say, "therefore there is no God in us, therefore there is no God!" Oh, if men would but interpret that first cry of man fresh from the womb as the laughter of one who even then says to his heart, "It is my pride as God to become Man. Then let it be my pride as Man to recreate the God in me!" (*He laughs softly but with exultant pride.*)

POMPEIA—(*laughing with him—proudly*) He will create a god in me! I shall be proud!

CALIGULA—(*pounding his temples with his fists—tortured*) I am Caligula. I was born in a camp among soldiers. My father was Germanicus, a hero, as all men know. But I do not understand this—and though I burst with pride, I cannot laugh with joy!

TIBERIUS—(*gloomily*) Obscurities! I have found nothing in life that merits pride. I am not proud of being Cæsar—and what is a god but a Cæsar over Cæsars? If fools kneel and worship me because they fear me, should I be proud? But Cæsar is a fact, and Tiberius, a man, is one, and I cling to these certainties—and I do not wish to die! If I were sure of eternal sleep beyond there, deep rest and forgetfulness of all I have ever seen or heard or hated or loved on earth, I would gladly die! But surely, Lazarus, nothing is sure—peace the least sure of all—and I fear there is no rest beyond there, that one remembers there as here and cannot sleep, that the mind goes on eternally the same—a long insomnia of memories and regrets and the ghosts of dreams one has poisoned to death passing with white bodies spotted by the leprous fingers of one's lusts. (*bitterly*) I fear the long nights now in which I lie awake and listen to Death dancing round me in the darkness, prancing to the drum beat of my heart! (*He shudders.*) And I am afraid, Lazarus—afraid that there is no sleep beyond there, either!

LAZARUS—There is peace! (*His words are like a benediction he pronounces upon them. Soothed in a mysterious, childlike way, they repeat the word after him, wonderingly.*)

POMPEIA—Peace?

CALIGULA—Peace?

TIBERIUS—Peace? (*For a long moment there is complete silence. Then Tiberius sighs heavily, shaking his head.*) Peace! Another word blurred into a senseless sigh by men's longing! A bubble of froth blown from the lips of the dying toward the stars! No! (*He grins bitterly—then looks at Lazarus— somberly contemptuous and threatening*) You are pleased to act the mysterious, Jew, but I shall solve you! (*then with a lawyer-like incisiveness*) There is one certainty about you and I must know the cause—for there must be a cause and a rational explanation! You were fifty when you died—

LAZARUS—(*smiling mockingly*) Yes. When I died.

TIBERIUS—(*unheeding*) And now your appearance is of one younger by a score. Not alone your appearance! You *are* young. I see the fact, the effect. And I demand an explanation of the cause without mystic nonsense or evasion. (*threateningly*) And I warn you to answer directly in plain words— and not to laugh, you understand!—not to dare!—or I shall lose patience with you and— (*with a grim smile*) I can be terrible! (*Lazarus smiles gently at him. He turns away with confused annoyance, then back to Lazarus, resuming his lawyer-like manner.*) What was it restored your youth? How did you contrive that your body reversed the natural process and grows younger? Is it a charm by which you invoke a super-natural force? Or is it a powder you dissolve in wine? Or a liquid? Or an unguent you rub into the skin to revitalize the old bones and tissues? Or—what is it, Lazarus?

LAZARUS—(*gently*) I know that age and time are but timidities of thought.

TIBERIUS—(*broodingly—as if he had not heard—persuasively*) Perhaps you ask yourself, what would Tiberius do with youth? Then, because you must have heard rumors of my de-pravity, you will conclude the old lecher desires youth for his lusts! (*He laughs harshly.*) Ha! Why, do not my faithful

subjects draw pictures of an old buck goat upon the walls and
write above them, Cæsar? And they are just. In self-contempt
of Man I have made this man, myself, the most swinish and
contemptible of men! Yes! In all this empire there is no man
so base a hog as I! (*He grins bitterly and ironically.*) My claim
to this excellence, at least, is not contested! Everyone admits
therein Tiberius is by right their Cæsar! (*He laughs bitterly.*)
Ha! So who would believe Tiberius if he said, I want youth
again because I loathe lust and long for purity!

LAZARUS—(*gently*) I believe you, Cæsar.

TIBERIUS—(*stares at him—deeply moved*) You—believe—?
(*then gruffly*) You lie! You are not mad—and only a madman
would believe another man! (*then confidingly, leaning over toward Lazarus*) I know it is folly to speak—but—one gets old,
one becomes talkative, one wishes to confess, to say the thing
one has always kept hidden, to reveal one's unique truth—
and there is so little time left—and one is alone! Therefore
the old—like children—talk to themselves, for they have
reached that hopeless wisdom of experience which knows that
though one were to cry it in the streets to multitudes, or
whisper it in the kiss to one's beloved, the only ears that can
ever hear one's secret are one's own! (*He laughs bitterly.*) And
so I talk aloud, Lazarus! I talk to my loneliness!

LAZARUS—(*simply*) I hear, Tiberius.

TIBERIUS—(*again moved and confused—forcing a mocking
smile*) Liar! Eavesdropper! You merely—listen! (*Then he turns
away.*) My mother, Livia, that strong woman, giving birth to
me, desired not a child, but a Cæsar—just as, married to Augustus, she loved him not but loved herself as Cæsar's wife.
She made me feel, in the proud questioning of her scornful
eyes, that to win her mother love I must become Cæsar. She
poisoned Prince Marcellus and young Gaius and Lucius that
the way might be clear for me. I used to see their blood dance
in red specks before my eyes when I looked at the sky.
Now—(*he brushes his hand before his eyes*) it is all a red blot! I
cannot distinguish. There have been too many. My mother—
her blood is in that blot, for I revenged myself on her. I did
not kill her, it is true, but I deprived her of her power and
she died, as I knew she must, that powerful woman who bore
me as a weapon! The murder was subtle and cruel—how

cruel only that passionate, deep-breasted woman unslaked by eighty years of devoured desires could know! Too cruel! I did not go to her funeral. I was afraid her closed eyes might open and look at me! (*then with almost a cry*) I want youth, Lazarus, that I may play again about her feet with the love I felt for her before I learned to read her eyes! (*He half sobs, bowing his head. A pause.*)

CALIGULA—(*nudging Pompeia—with a crafty whisper*) Do you hear? The old lecher talks to himself. He is becoming senile. He will soon die. And I shall be Cæsar. Then I shall laugh!

POMPEIA—(*staring up at Lazarus' face, hearing only Caligula's words without their meaning*) No. My Lazarus does not laugh now. See. His mouth is silent—and a little sad, I think.

LAZARUS—(*gently and comfortingly*) I hear, Tiberius.

TIBERIUS—(*harshly*) I hated that woman, my mother, and I still hate her! Have you ever loved, Lazarus? (*then with a glance at Miriam's body and a shuddering away from it— vaguely*) I was forgetting her. I killed your love, too, did I not? Well, I must! I envy those who are loved. Where I can, I kill love—for retribution's sake—but much of it escapes me. (*then harshly again*) I loved Agrippina. We were married. A son was born to us. We were happy. Then that proud woman, my mother, saw my happiness. Was she jealous of my love? Or did she know no happy man would wish to be Cæsar? Well, she condemned my happiness to death. She whispered to Augustus and he ordered me to divorce Agrippina. I should have opened her veins and mine, and died with her. But my mother stayed by me, Agrippina was kept away, my mother spoke to me and spoke to me and even wept, that tall woman, strong as a great man, and I consented that my love be murdered. Then my mother married me to a whore. Why? The whore was Cæsar's daughter, true—but I feel that was not all of it, that my mother wished to keep me tortured that I might love her alone and long to be Cæsar! (*He laughs harshly.*) Ha! In brief, I married the whore, she tortured me, my mother's scheming prospered—that subtle and crafty woman!—and many years passed in being here and there, in doing this and that, in growing full of hate and revengeful ambition to be Cæsar. At last, Augustus died. I was Cæsar. Then I killed that whore, my wife, and I starved my mother's strength to death until she died, and I began to take pleasure in vengeance upon men, and pleasure in taking vengeance on myself. (*He grins horribly.*) It is all very simple, as you see! (*He suddenly starts to his feet—with harsh arrogance and pride, threateningly*) Enough! Why do I tell you these old tales? Must I explain to you why I want youth? It is my whim! I am Cæsar! And now I must lie down and try to sleep! And it is my command that you reveal the secret of your youth to me when I awake, or else—(*with malignant cruelty*) I will have to revenge the death of a hope on you—and a hope at my age demands a terrible expiation on its slayer! (*He walks down and starts to go off, right—then turns and addresses Lazarus with grim irony.*) Good night to you, Lazarus. And remember there shall be death while I am Cæsar! (*He turns to go.*)

LAZARUS—(*smiling affectionately at him, shakes his head*) Cæsar must believe in death. But does the husband of Agrippina?

TIBERIUS—(*stops short and stares at Lazarus, confused and stuttering*) What—what—do you mean, Lazarus?

LAZARUS—I have heard your loneliness.

TIBERIUS—(*cruelly and grimly again*) So much the more reason why my pride should kill you! Remember that! (*He turns and strides off into the darkness at right.*)

CALIGULA—(*peers after him until sure he is gone—then gets up and begins a grotesque, hopping dance, singing a verse of the legionary's song*)

A bold legionary am I
March, oh march on!
A Roman eagle was my daddy
My mother was a drunken drabby
Oh march on to the wars!

(*He laughs gratingly, posturing and gesticulating up at Lazarus.*) Ha-ha-ha! He is gone! I can breathe! His breath in the same air suffocates me! The gods grant mine do the same for him! But he is failing! He talks to himself like a man in second childhood. His words are a thick babble I could not hear. They well from his lips like clots of blood from a reopened wound. I kept listening to the beating of his heart. It sounded slow, slower than when I last heard it. Did you detect that, Lazarus? Once or twice I thought it faltered— (*He draws in his breath with an avid gasp—then laughs gratingly*) Ha-ha-ha—(*grandiloquently*) Tiberius, the old buck goat, will soon be gone, my friends, and in his place you will be blessed with the beautiful young god, Caligula! Hail to Caligula! Hail! Ha-ha-ha— (*His laughter suddenly breaks off into a whimper and he stands staring around him in a panic of fear that he has been overheard. He slinks noiselessly up the steps of the dais and squats coweringly at Lazarus' feet, blinking up at his face in monkey-wise, clutching Lazarus' hand in both of his. His teeth can be heard chattering together in nervous fear.*

(*Pompeia, whose gaze has remained fixed on Lazarus' throughout, has gradually moved closer to him until she, too, is at his feet, half-kneeling beneath the table on which Miriam lies, side by side with Caligula but as oblivious of him as he is of her.*

(*Having grown calmer now, Caligula speaks again—mournful and bewildered*)

CALIGULA—Why should I love you, Lazarus? Your laughter taunts me! It insults Cæsar! It denies Rome! But I will warn you again. Escape! Tonight Tiberius' mood is to play sentimental, but tomorrow he will jeer while hyenas gnaw at your skull and lick your brain. And then—there is pain, Lazarus! There is pain!

POMPEIA—(*pressing her hand to her own heart—with a shudder*) Yes, there is pain!

LAZARUS—(*smiling down on them—gently*) If you can answer Yes to pain, there is no pain!

POMPEIA—(*passionately*) Yes! Yes! I love Lazarus!

CALIGULA—(*with a bitter grin*) Do not take pain away from us! It is our one truth. Without pain there is nothing— a nothingness in which even your laughter, Lazarus, is swallowed at one gulp like a whining gnat by the cretin's silence of immensity! Ha-ha! No, we must keep pain! Especially Cæsar must! Pain must twinkle with a mad mirth in a Cæsar's eyes—men's pain—or they would become dissatisfied and disrespectful! Ha-ha! (*He stops his grating laughter abruptly and continues mournfully*) I am sick, Lazarus, sick of cruelty and lust and human flesh and all the imbecilities of pleasure—

the unclean antics of half-witted children! (*with a mounting agony of longing*) I would be clean! If I could only laugh your laughter, Lazarus! That would purify my heart. For I could wish to love all men, as you love them—as I love you! If only I did not fear them and despise them! If I could only believe—believe in them—in life—in myself!—believe that one man or woman in the world knew and loved the real Caligula—then I might have faith in Caligula myself—then I might laugh your laughter!

LAZARUS—(*suddenly, in a quiet but compelling voice*) I, who know you, love you, Caligula. (*gently patting his head*) I love Caligula.

CALIGULA—(*staring up at him in pathetic confusion*) You? You? You, Lazarus? (*He begins to tremble all over as if in a seizure—chokingly*) Beware! It is not good—not just—to make fun of me—to laugh at my misery—saying you love— (*In a frenzy, he jumps to his feet threatening Lazarus.*) Are you trying to fool me, hypocrite? Do you think I have become so abject that you dare—? Because I love you, do you presume—? Do you think I am your slave, dog of a Jew, that you can—insult—to my face—the heir of Cæsar— (*He stutters and stammers with rage, hopping up and down grotesquely, shaking his fist at Lazarus, who smiles at him affectionately as at a child in a tantrum.*)

LAZARUS—(*catching his eyes and holding them with his glance—calmly*) Believe, Caligula!

CALIGULA—(*again overcome—stuttering with strange terror*) Believe? But I cannot! I must not! You cannot know me, if— You are a holy man! You are a god in a mortal body—you can laugh with joy to be alive—while I— Oh, no, you cannot love me! There is nothing in me at bottom but a despising and an evil eye! You cannot! You are only being kind! (*hysterically*) I do not want your kindness! I hate your pity! I am too proud! I am too strong! (*He collapses weepingly, kneeling and clutching Lazarus' hand in both of his.*)

LAZARUS—(*smiling*) You are so proud of being evil! What if there is no evil? What if there are only health and sickness? Believe in the healthy god called Man in you! Laugh at Caligula, the funny clown who beats the backside of his shadow with a bladder and thinks thereby he is Evil, the Enemy of

God! (*He suddenly lifts the face of Caligula and stares into his eyes.*) Believe! What if you are a man and men are despicable? Men are also unimportant! Men pass! Like rain into the sea! The sea remains! Man remains! Man slowly arises from the past of the race of men that was his tomb of death! For Man death is not! Man, Son of God's Laughter, *is*! (*He begins to laugh triumphantly, staring deep into Caligula's eyes.*) *Is*, Caligula! Believe in the laughing god within you!

CALIGULA—(*bursting suddenly into choking, joyful laughter —like a visionary*) I believe! I believe there is love even for Caligula! I can laugh—now—Lazarus! Free laughter! Clean! No sickness! No lust for death! My corpse no longer rots in my heart! The tomb is full of sunlight! I am alive! I who love Man, I who can love and laugh! Listen, Lazarus! I dream! When I am Cæsar, I will devote my power to your truth. I will decree that there must be kindness and love! I will make the Empire one great Blessed Isle! Rome shall know happiness, it shall believe in life, it shall learn to laugh your laughter, Lazarus, or I— (*He raises his hand in an imperial autocratic gesture.*)

LAZARUS—(*gaily mocking*) Or you will cut off its head?

CALIGULA—(*fiercely*) Yes! I will—! (*Then meeting Lazarus' eyes, he beats his head with his fists crazily.*) Forgive me! I forget! I forget!

LAZARUS—Go out under the sky! Let your heart climb on laughter to a star! Then make it look down at earth, and watch Caligula commanding Life under pain of death to do his will! (*He laughs.*)

CALIGULA—(*laughing*) I will! I do! I laugh at him! Caligula is a trained ape, a humped cripple! Now I take him out under the sky, where I can watch his monkey tricks, where there is space for laughter and where this new joy, your love of me, may dance! (*Laughing clearly and exultantly, he runs out through the arched doorway at rear.*)

LAZARUS—(*stops laughing—shaking his head, almost sadly*) They forget! It is too soon for laughter! (*then grinning at himself*) What, Lazarus? Are you, too, thinking in terms of time, old fool so soon to reënter infinity? (*He laughs with joyous self-mockery.*)

POMPEIA—(*who has crept to his feet, kisses his hand passion-ately*) I love you, Lazarus!

LAZARUS—(*stops laughing, and looks down at her gently*) And I love you, woman.

POMPEIA—(*with a gasp of delight*) You? (*She stares up into his eyes doubtingly, raising her face toward his.*) Then—put your arms around me. (*He does so, smiling gently.*) And hold me to you. (*He presses her closer to him.*) And kiss me. (*He kisses her on the forehead.*) No, on the lips! (*He kisses her. She flings her arms about his neck passionately and kisses him again and again—then slowly draws away—remains looking into his eyes a long time, shrinking back from him with bewildered pain which speedily turns to rage and revengeful hatred.*) No! No! It is *my* love, not Love! I want you to know *my* love, to give me back love—for me—only for me—Pompeia—my body, my heart—me, a woman—not Woman, women! Do I love Man, men? I hate men! I love you, Lazarus—a man—a lover—a father to children! I want love—as you loved that woman there (*she points to Miriam*) that I poisoned for love of you! But did you love her—or just Woman, wife and mother of men? (*She stares—then as if reading admission in his eyes, she springs to her feet.*) Liar! Cheat! Hypocrite! Thief! (*Half hys-terical with rage, pain and grief, she bends over Miriam and smooths the hair back from her forehead.*) Poor wife! Poor woman! How he must have tortured you! Now I remember the pity in your eyes when you looked at me! Oh, how his soothing gray words must have pecked at the wound in your heart like doves with bloody beaks! (*then with sudden harsh-ness*) But perhaps you were too dull to understand, too poor and tired and ugly and old to care, too slavish—! Pah! (*She turns away with contempt and faces Lazarus with revengeful hatred.*) Did you think I would take her place—become your slave, wait upon you, give you love and passion and beauty in exchange for phrases about man and gods—you who are neither a man nor a god but a dead thing without desire! You dared to hope I would give my body, my love, to you! (*She spits in his face and laughs harshly.*) You insolent fool! I shall punish you! You shall be tortured as you have tortured! (*She laughs wildly—then steps down from the dais and goes off right, crying distractedly*) Cæsar! This man has made you a fool before all the world! Torture him, Cæsar! Now! Let the people witness! Send heralds to wake them! Torture him, Cæsar, the man who laughs at you! Ha-ha-ha-ha! (*Her laughter is caught up by all the girls and youths of the palace, who, as she disappears, led by their Chorus, pour in from each side of the room and dance forward to group themselves around the dais as in the previous scene, staring at Lazarus, laughing cruelly, falsely, stridently.*)

CHORUS—(*tauntingly*)
    Ha-ha-ha-ha!
    Laugh now, Lazarus!
    Let us see you laugh!
    Ha-ha-ha-ha!
CROWD—(*echoing*)
    Ha-ha-ha-ha!
    Ha-ha-ha-ha!

LAZARUS—(*moves, and immediately there is silence. He bends down and kisses Miriam and picks her up in his arms. Talking down to her face—with a tender smile*) Farewell! You are home! And now I will take your body home to earth! Space is too far away, you said! Home in the earth! There will be so much for you to do there! Home! Earth! (*his voice trembling a bit*) Farewell, body of Miriam. My grief is a lonely cry wailing in the home in my heart that you have left forever! (*then exultantly*) But what am I? Now your love has become Eternal Love! Now, since your life passed, I feel Eternal Life made nobler by your selflessness! Love has grown purer! The laughter of God is more profoundly tender! (*He looks up in an ecstasy and descends the dais, carrying her.*) Yes, that is it! That is it, my Miriam! (*Laughing softly and tenderly, he walks around the dais and carries the body out through the doorway in rear.*

(*The Chorus and youths and girls make way for him in awed silence—then scurry around to right and left, forming an aisle through which he passes—then after he has gone out through the arch, they close into a semicircular group again, staring after him, and a whisper of strange, bewildered, tender laughter comes from them.*)

CHORUS—(*in this whisper*)

That is it!
Love is pure!
Laughter is tender!
Laugh!
CROWD—(*echoing*) Laugh! Laugh!

(*Curtain*)

SCENE TWO

SCENE—*The arena of an amphitheatre. It is just before dawn of the same night. Cæsar's throne is on the left at the extreme front, facing right, turned a little toward front. It is lighted by four immense lamps. In front of the throne is a marble railing that tops the wall that encloses the arena. In the rear the towering pile of the circular amphitheatre is faintly outlined in deeper black against the dark sky.*

Tiberius sits on the throne, his eyes fixed on the middle of the arena off right, where, bound to a high stake after he had been tortured, Lazarus is now being burnt alive over a huge pile of faggots. The crackling of the flames is heard. Their billowing rise and fall is reflected on the masked faces of the multitude who sit on the banked tiers of marble behind and to the rear of the throne, with their Chorus, seven men masked in Middle Age in the Ser-vile, Hypocritical type, grouped on each side of the throne of Cæsar on a lower tier.

Half-kneeling before Tiberius, her chin resting on her hands on top of the marble rail, Pompeia also stares at Lazarus.

Before the curtain, the crackle of the flames and an uproar of human voices from the multitude, jeering, hooting, laughing at Lazarus in cruel mockery of his laughter. This sound has risen to its greatest volume as the curtain rises.

CHORUS—(*chanting mockingly*)
Ha-ha-ha-ha!
Burn and laugh!
Laugh now, Lazarus!
Ha-ha-ha-ha!
CROWD—(*chanting with revengeful mockery*) Ha-ha-ha-ha!

TIBERIUS—Who laughs now, Lazarus—thou or Cæsar? Ha-ha—! (*with awe*) His flesh melts in the fire but his eyes shine with peace!

POMPEIA—How he looks at me! (*averting her eyes with a shudder*) Command them to put out his eyes, Cæsar!

TIBERIUS—(*harshly*) No. I want to read his eyes when they see death! (*then averting his face—guiltily*) He is looking at me, not you. I should not have listened to your cries for his death.

POMPEIA—(*turning to him again with a shudder of agony—beseechingly*) Have them put out his eyes, Cæsar! They call to me!

TIBERIUS—(*as if not hearing her—to himself*) Why do I feel remorse? His laughter dies and is forgotten, and the hope it raised dies— (*with sudden excitement*) And yet—he must know something—and if he would—even now he could tell— (*Suddenly rising to his feet he calls imploringly*) Lazarus!

CHORUS—(*chanting in a great imploring chorus now*) Lazarus!

CROWD—(*echoing*) Lazarus!

SOLDIER'S VOICE—(*calling from off beside the stake*) You had us gag him, Cæsar, so he might not laugh. Shall we cut away the gag?

POMPEIA—(*in terror*) No, Cæsar! He will laugh! And I will go to him! (*desperately*) He will laugh at you, Cæsar—and the mob will laugh with him!

TIBERIUS—(*struggles with himself—then calls*) Lazarus! If you hear let your eyes answer, and I will grant the mercy of death to end your agony! Is there hope of love somewhere for men on earth?

CHORUS—(*intoning as before*)
   Is there hope of love
   For us on earth?

CROWD—
   Hope of love
   For us on earth!

SOLDIER'S VOICE—His eyes laugh, Cæsar!

TIBERIUS—(*in a strange frenzy now*) Hear me, thou Dæmon of Laughter! Hear and answer, I beseech thee, who alone hath known joy! (*more and more wildly*) How must we live? Wherein lies happiness?

CHORUS—Wherein lies happiness?

CROWD—Wherein, happiness?

TIBERIUS—Why are we born? To what end must we die?

CHORUS—Why are we born to die?

CROWD—Why are we born?

SOLDIER'S VOICE—His eyes laugh, Cæsar! He is dying! He would speak!

CHORUS AND CROWD—(*in one great cry*) Cæsar! Let Lazarus speak!

POMPEIA—(*terrified*) No, Cæsar! He will laugh—and you will die—and I will go to him!

TIBERIUS—(*torn—arguing with his fear*) But—he may know some hope— (*then making his decision, with grim fatalism*) Hope—or nothing! (*calls to the Soldiers*) Let him speak!

CHORUS AND CROWD—(*cheering*) Hail, Cæsar!

LAZARUS—(*His voice comes, recognizably the voice of Lazarus, yet with a strange, fresh, clear quality of boyhood, gaily mocking with life.*) Hail, Cæsar!

CROWD—(*frantic with hope*) Hail, Lazarus!

TIBERIUS—Pull away the fire from him! I see death in his eyes! (*The flaming reflections in the banked, masked faces dance madly as the Soldiers rake back the fire from the stake. With a forced, taunting mockery*) What do you say now, Lazarus? You are dying!

CHORUS AND CROWD—(*taking his tone—mockingly*) You are dying, Lazarus!

LAZARUS—(*his voice a triumphant assertion of the victory of life over pain and death*) Yes!

TIBERIUS—(*triumphant yet disappointed—with scorn and rage*) Ha! You admit it, do you, coward! Craven! Knave! Duper of fools! Clown! Liar! Die! I laugh at you! Ha-ha-ha-ha— (*His voice breaks chokingly.*)

CROWD—(*led by their Chorus—in the same frenzy of disappointment, with all sorts of grotesque and obscene gestures and noises, thumbing their fingers to their noses, wagging them at their ears, sticking out their tongues, slapping their behinds, barking, crowing like roosters, howling, and hooting in every conceiv-*

able manner) Yah! Yah! Yellow Gut! Bungkisser! Muckheel! Scumwiper! Liar! Pig! Jackal! Die! We laugh at you! Ha-ha-ha— (*Their voices, too, break.*)

POMPEIA—(*rising to her feet like one in a trance, staring toward Lazarus*) They are tormenting him. I hear him crying to me! (*She moves to the top of the steps leading to the arena.*)

LAZARUS—(*his voice thrilling with exultance*) O men, fear not life! You die—but there is no death for Man! (*He begins to laugh, and at the sound of his laughter, a great spell of silence settles upon all his hearers—then as his laughter rises, they begin to laugh with him.*)

POMPEIA—(*descending the steps like a sleep-walker*) I hear his laughter calling. I must go to him.

TIBERIUS—(*as if he realized something was happening that was against his will—trying feebly to be imperial*) I command you not to laugh! Cæsar commands— (*calling feebly to the Soldiers*) Put back—the gag! Stop his laughter! (*The laughter of Lazarus gaily and lovingly mocks back at him.*)

SOLDIER'S VOICE—(*his voice gently remonstrating*) We may not, Cæsar. We love his laughter! (*They laugh with him.*)

CHORUS AND CROWD—(*in a soft, dreamy murmur*)
    We love his laughter!
    We laugh!

TIBERIUS—(*dreamily*) Then—pile the fire back around him. High and higher! Let him blaze to the stars! I laugh with him!

SOLDIER'S VOICE—(*gently and gravely*) That is just, Cæsar. We love men flaming toward the stars! We laugh with him!

CHORUS AND CROWD—(*as the flames, piled back and fed anew by the Soldiers, flare upward and are reflected on their masks in dancing waves of light*)
    We love men flaming toward the stars!
    We laugh!

POMPEIA—(*in the arena*) The fire calls me. My burning heart calls for the fire! (*She laughs softly and passes swiftly across the arena toward Lazarus.*)

TIBERIUS—(*in a sort of childish complaint*) You must pardon me, Lazarus. This is my Cæsar's duty—to kill you! You have no right to laugh—before all these people—at Cæsar.

It is not kind. (*He sobs snuffingly—then begins to laugh at himself.*

(*Suddenly the flames waver, die down, then shoot up again and Pompeia's laughter is heard for a moment, rising clear and passionately with that of Lazarus, then dying quickly out.*)

SOLDIER'S VOICE—A woman has thrown herself in the flames, Cæsar! She laughs with Lazarus!

TIBERIUS—(*in a sudden panicky flurry—feverishly*) Quick, Lazarus! You will soon be silent! Speak!—in the name of man's solitude—his agony of farewell—what is beyond there, Lazarus? (*His voice has risen to a passionate entreaty.*)

CHORUS—(*in a great pleading echo*) What is beyond there, Lazarus?

CROWD—What is beyond?

LAZARUS—(*his voice speaking lovingly, with a surpassing clearness and exaltation*) Life! Eternity! Stars and dust! God's Eternal Laughter! (*His laughter bursts forth now in its highest pitch of ecstatic summons to the feast and sacrifice of Life, the Eternal.*

(*The Crowds laugh with him in a frenzied rhythmic chorus. Led by the Chorus, they pour down from the banked walls of the amphitheatre and dance in the flaring reflection of the flames strange wild measures of liberated joy. Tiberius stands on the raised dais laughing great shouts of clear, fearless laughter.*)

CHORUS—(*chanting as they dance*)
Laugh! Laugh!
We are stars!
We are dust!
We are gods!
We are laughter!

CROWD—
We are dust!
We are gods!
Laugh! Laugh!

CALIGULA—(*enters from behind Tiberius. His aspect is wild, his hair disheveled, his clothes torn, he is panting as if exhausted by running. He stares toward the flames stupidly—then screams despairingly above the chant*) Lazarus! I come to save you! Do you still live, Lazarus?

TIBERIUS—(*has been speaking. His words are now heard as*

the tumult momentarily dies down.) I have lived long enough!
I will die with Lazarus! I no longer fear death! I laugh! I
laugh at Cæsar! I advise you, my brothers, fear not Cæsars!
Seek Man in the brotherhood of the dust! Cæsar is your fear
of Man! I counsel you, laugh away your Cæsars!

CALIGULA—(*with resentful jealousy and rage—in a voice
rising to a scream*) What do I hear, Lazarus? You laugh with
your murderer? You give him your laughter? You have forgotten me—my love—you make him love you—you make
him laugh at Cæsars—at me! (*suddenly springs on Tiberius in
a fury and grabbing him by the throat chokes him, forcing him
back on the throne—screaming*) Die, traitor! Die! (*Tiberius'
body relaxes in his hands, dead, and slips from the chair. Caligula
rushes madly down the stairs into the midst of the oblivious, laughing, dancing crowd, screaming*) You have betrayed me, dog of
a Jew! You have betrayed Cæsar! (*beginning to be caught by the
contagion of the laughter*) Ha-ah— No! I will not laugh! I will
kill you! Give me a spear! (*He snatches a spear from a soldier
and fights his way drunkenly toward the flames, like a man half
overcome by a poisonous gas, shouting, half-laughing in spite of
himself, half-weeping with rage.*) Ha-ha— The gods be with
Cæsar Caligula! O Immortal Gods, give thy brother strength!
You shall die, Lazarus—die— Ha-ah—! (*He disappears toward the flames, his spear held ready to stab.*)

CHORUS AND CROWD—(*who have been entirely oblivious of
him—chanting*)
Laugh! Laugh!
We are gods!
We are dust!

LAZARUS—(*At his first word there is a profound silence in
which each dancer remains frozen in the last movement.*) Hail,
Caligula Cæsar! Men forget! (*He laughs with gay mockery as at
a child.*)

CHORUS AND CROWD—(*starting to laugh*) Laugh! Laugh!
(*Then there is a fierce cry of rage from Caligula and Lazarus'
laughter ceases, and with it the laughter of the Crowd turns to a
wail of fear and lamentation.*)

CALIGULA—(*dashes back among them waving his bloody spear
and rushing up to the throne stands on it and strikes a grandiose
pose*) I have killed God! I am Death! Death is Cæsar!

CHORUS AND CROWD—(*turning and scurrying away—huddled in fleeing groups, crouching close to the ground like a multitude of terrified rats, their voices squeaky now with fright*) Hail, Cæsar! Hail to Death! (*They are gone.*)

CALIGULA—(*keeping his absurd majestic pose, turns and addresses with rhetorical intoning, and flowing gestures, the body of Lazarus, high upon its stake, the flames below it now flickering fitfully*) Hail, Caligula! Hero of heroes, conqueror of the Dæmon, Lazarus, who taught the treason that fear and death were dead! But I am Lord of Fear! I am Cæsar of Death! And you, Lazarus, are carrion! (*then in a more conversational tone, putting aside his grandiose airs, confidentially*) I had to kill you, Lazarus! Surely your good sense tells you— You heard what the old fool, Tiberius, told the mob. A moment more and there would have been a revolution—no more Cæsars—and my dream—! (*He stops—bewilderedly*) My dream? Did I kill laughter? I had just learned to laugh—with love! (*more confusedly*) I must be a little mad, Lazarus. It was one terror too many, to have been laughing your laughter in the night, to have been dreaming great yearning dreams of all the good my love might do for men when I was Cæsar—and then, to hear the old howling of mob lust, and to run here—and there a high white flame amidst the fire—you, Lazarus!—dying! —laughing with him—Tiberius—betraying me—who loved you, Lazarus! Yes, I became mad! I am mad! And I can laugh my own mad laughter, Lazarus—my own! Ha-ha-ha-ha! (*He laughs with a wild triumphant madness and again rhetorically, with sweeping gestures and ferocious capers*) And all of men are vile and mad, and I shall be their madmen's Cæsar! (*He turns as if addressing an amphitheatre full of his subjects.*) O my good people, my faithful scum, my brother swine, Lazarus is dead and we have murdered great laughter, and it befits our madness to have done so, and it is befitting above all to have Caligula for Cæsar! (*then savagely*) Kneel down! Abase yourselves! I am your Cæsar and your God! Hail! (*He stands saluting himself with a crazy intensity that is not without grandeur. A pause. Suddenly the silence seems to crush down upon him; he is aware that he is alone in the vast arena; he whirls about, looking around him as if he felt an assassin at his back; he lunges with his spear at imaginary foes, jumping, dodging from side to side, yelping*) Ho, there! Help! Help! Your Cæsar calls you! Help, my people! To the rescue! (*suddenly throwing his spear away and sinking on his knees, his face toward Lazarus, supplicatingly*) Lazarus! Forgive me! Help me! Fear kills me! Save me from death! (*He is groveling in a paroxysm of terror, grinding his face in his fists as if to hide it.*)

LAZARUS—(*His voice is heard in a gentle, expiring sigh of compassion, followed by a faint dying note of laughter that rises and is lost in the sky like the flight of his soul back into the womb of Infinity.*) Fear not, Caligula! There is no death!

CALIGULA—(*lifts his head at the first sound and rises with the laughter to his feet, until, as it is finally lost, he is on tip-toes, his arms straining upward to the sky, a tender, childish laughter of love on his lips*) I laugh, Lazarus! I laugh with you! (*then grief-stricken*) Lazarus! (*He hides his face in his hands, weeping.*) No more! (*then beats his head with his fists*) I will remember! I will! (*then suddenly, with a return to grotesqueness—harshly*) All the same, I killed him and I proved there is death! (*immediately overcome by remorse, groveling and beating himself*) Fool! Madman! Forgive me, Lazarus! Men forget!

(*Curtain*)

STRANGE INTERLUDE

CHARACTERS

Charles Marsden

Professor Henry Leeds

Nina Leeds, *his daughter*

Edmund Darrell

Sam Evans

Mrs. Amos Evans, *Sam's mother*

Gordon Evans

Madeline Arnold

SCENES

First Part

ACT ONE

Library, the Leeds' home in a small university town of
New England—an afternoon in late summer.

ACT TWO

The same. Fall of the following year. Night.

ACT THREE

Dining room of the Evans' homestead in northern New
York state—late spring of the next year. Morning.

ACT FOUR

The same as Acts One and Two. Fall of the same year.
Evening.

ACT FIVE

Sitting room of small house Evans has rented in a seashore
suburb near New York. The following April. Morning.

Second Part

ACT SIX

The same. A little over a year later. Evening.

ACT SEVEN

Sitting room of the Evans' apartment on Park Avenue.
Nearly eleven years later. Early afternoon.

ACT EIGHT

Section of afterdeck of the Evans' cruiser anchored near the
finish line at Poughkeepsie. Ten years later. Afternoon.

ACT NINE

A terrace on the Evans' estate on Long Island. Several
months later. Late afternoon.

Strange Interlude

FIRST PART

ACT ONE

SCENE—*The library of Professor Leeds' home in a small university town in New England. This room is at the front part of his house with windows opening on the strip of lawn between the house and the quiet residential street. It is a small room with a low ceiling. The furniture has been selected with a love for old New England pieces. The walls are lined almost to the ceiling with glassed-in bookshelves. These are packed with books, principally editions, many of them old and rare, of the ancient classics in the original Greek and Latin, of the later classics in French and German and Italian, of all the English authors who wrote while s was still like an f and a few since then, the most modern probably being Thackeray. The atmosphere of the room is that of a cosy, cultured retreat, sedulously built as a sanctuary where, secure with the culture of the past at his back, a fugitive from reality can view the present safely from a distance, as a superior with condescending disdain, pity, and even amusement.*

There is a fair-sized table, a heavy armchair, a rocker, and an old bench made comfortable with cushions. The table, with the Professor's armchair at its left, is arranged toward the left of the room, the rocker is at center, the bench at right.

There is one entrance, a door in the right wall, rear.

It is late afternoon of a day in August. Sunshine, cooled and dimmed in the shade of trees, fills the room with a soothing light.

The sound of a maid's voice—a middle-aged woman—explaining familiarly but respectfully from the right, and Marsden enters. He is a tall thin man of thirty-five, meticulously well-dressed in tweeds of distinctly English tailoring, his appearance that of an Anglicized New England gentleman. His face is too long for its width, his nose is high and narrow, his forehead broad, his mild blue eyes those of a dreamy self-analyst, his thin lips ironical and a bit sad. There is an indefinable feminine quality about him, but it is nothing apparent in either appearance or act. His manner is cool and poised. He speaks with a careful ease as one who listens to his own conversation. He has long fragile hands, and the stoop to his shoulders of a man weak muscularly, who has never

633

liked athletics and has always been regarded as of delicate consti-tution. The main point about his personality is a quiet charm, a quality of appealing, inquisitive friendliness, always willing to lis-ten, eager to sympathize, to like and to be liked.

MARSDEN—(*standing just inside the door, his tall, stooped fig-ure leaning back against the books—nodding back at the maid and smiling kindly*) I'll wait in here, Mary. (*His eyes follow her for a second, then return to gaze around the room slowly with an appreciative relish for the familiar significance of the books. He smiles affectionately and his amused voice recites the words with a rhetorical resonance.*) Sanctum Sanctorum! (*His voice takes on a monotonous musing quality, his eyes stare idly at his drifting thoughts.*)

How perfectly the Professor's unique haven! . . .
(*He smiles.*)

Primly classical . . . when New Englander meets Greek! . . .
(*looking at the books now*)

He hasn't added one book in years . . . how old was I when I first came here? . . . six . . . with my father . . . father . . . how dim his face has grown! . . . he wanted to speak to me just before he died . . . the hospital . . . smell of iodoform in the cool halls . . . hot summer . . . I bent down . . . his voice had withdrawn so far away . . . I couldn't understand him . . . what son can ever understand? . . . always too near, too soon, too distant or too late! . . .
(*His face has become sad with a memory of the bewildered suffer-ing of the adolescent boy he had been at the time of his father's death. Then he shakes his head, flinging off his thoughts, and makes himself walk about the room.*)

What memories on such a smiling afternoon! . . . this pleasant old town after three months . . . I won't go to Europe again . . . couldn't write a line there . . . how answer the fierce question of all those dead and maimed? . . . too big a job for me! . . .
(*He sighs—then self-mockingly*)

But back here . . . it is the interlude that gently ques-tions . . . in this town dozing . . . decorous bodies

moving with circumspection through the afternoons
. . . their habits affectionately chronicled . . . an excuse for weaving amusing words . . . my novels . . .
not of cosmic importance, hardly . . .

(*then self-reassuringly*)

but there is a public to cherish them, evidently . . .
and I can write! . . . more than one can say of these
modern sex-yahoos! . . . I must start work tomorrow
. . . I'd like to use the Professor in a novel sometime
. . . and his wife . . . seems impossible she's been
dead six years . . . so aggressively his wife! . . . poor
Professor! now it's Nina who bosses him . . . but
that's different . . . she has bossed me, too, ever since
she was a baby . . . she's a woman now . . . known
love and death . . . Gordon brought down in flames
. . . two days before the armistice . . . what fiendish
irony! . . . his wonderful athlete's body . . . her lover
. . . charred bones in a cage of twisted steel . . . no
wonder she broke down . . . Mother said she's become quite queer lately . . . Mother seemed jealous of
my concern . . . why have I never fallen in love with
Nina? . . . could I? . . . that way . . . used to dance
her on my knee . . . sit her on my lap . . . even now
she'd never think anything about it . . . but sometimes the scent of her hair and skin . . . like a dreamy
drug . . . dreamy! . . . there's the rub! . . . all
dreams with me! . . . my sex life among the phan-
toms! . . .

(*He grins torturedly.*)

Why? . . . oh, this digging in gets nowhere . . . to
the devil with sex! . . . our impotent pose of today to
beat the loud drum on fornication! . . . boasters . . .
eunuchs parading with the phallus! . . . giving themselves away . . . whom do they fool? . . . not even
themselves! . . .

(*his face suddenly full of an intense pain and disgust*)

Ugh! . . . always that memory! . . . why can't I ever
forget? . . . as sickeningly clear as if it were yesterday
. . . prep school . . . Easter vacation . . . Fatty
Boggs and Jack Frazer . . . that house of cheap vice

. . . one dollar! . . . why did I go? . . . Jack, the
dead game sport . . . how I admired him! . . . afraid
of his taunts . . . he pointed to the Italian girl . . .
"Take her!" . . . daring me . . . I went . . . miserably frightened . . . what a pig she was! . . . pretty
vicious face under caked powder and rouge . . . surly
and contemptuous . . . lumpy body . . . short legs
and thick ankles . . . slums of Naples . . . "What you
gawkin' about? Git a move on, kid" . . . kid! . . . I
was only a kid! . . . sixteen . . . test of manhood . . .
ashamed to face Jack again unless . . . fool! . . . I
might have lied to him! . . . but I honestly thought
that wench would feel humiliated if I . . . oh, stupid
kid! . . . back at the hotel I waited till they were
asleep . . . then sobbed . . . thinking of Mother . . .
feeling I had defiled her . . . and myself . . . forever! . . .

(*mocking bitterly*)

"Nothing half so sweet in life as love's young dream,"
what? . . .

(*He gets to his feet impatiently.*)

Why does my mind always have to dwell on that? . . .
too silly . . . no importance really . . . an incident
such as any boy of my age . . .

(*He hears someone coming quickly from the right and turns expectantly. Professor Leeds enters, a pleased relieved expression
fighting the flurried worry on his face. He is a small, slender man
of fifty-five, his hair gray, the top of his head bald. His face, pre-
possessing in spite of its too-small, over-refined features, is that of a
retiring, studious nature. He has intelligent eyes and a smile that
can be ironical. Temperamentally timid, his defense is an assump-
tion of his complacent, superior manner of the classroom toward
the world at large. This defense is strengthened by a natural tendency toward a prim provincialism where practical present-day
considerations are concerned (though he is most liberal — even radical — in his tolerant understanding of the manners and morals of
Greece and Imperial Rome!). This classroom poise of his, however,
he cannot quite carry off outside the classroom. There is an un-
convincing quality about it that leaves his larger audience — and
particularly the Professor himself — subtly embarrassed. As*

Marsden is one of his old students, whom, in addition, he has known from childhood, he is perfectly at ease with him.)

MARSDEN—(*holding out his hand—with unmistakable liking*) Here I am again, Professor!

PROFESSOR LEEDS—(*shaking his hand and patting him on the back—with genuine affection*) So glad to see you, Charlie! A surprise, too! We didn't expect you back so soon! (*He sits in his chair on the left of the table while Marsden sits in the rocker. Looking away from Marsden a moment, his face now full of selfish relief as he thinks*)

> Fortunate, his coming back . . . always calming influence on Nina . . .

MARSDEN—And I never dreamed of returning so soon. But Europe, Professor, is the big casualty they were afraid to set down on the list.

PROFESSOR LEEDS—(*his face clouding*) Yes, I suppose you found everything completely changed since before the war. (*He thinks resentfully*)

> The war . . . Gordon! . . .

MARSDEN—Europe has "gone west"—(*he smiles whimsically*) to America, let's hope! (*then frowningly*) I couldn't stand it. There were millions sitting up with the corpse already, who had a family right to be there— (*then matter-of-factly*) I was wasting my time, too. I couldn't write a line. (*then gaily*) But where's Nina? I must see Nina!

PROFESSOR LEEDS—She'll be right in. She said she wanted to finish thinking something out— You'll find Nina changed, Charlie, greatly changed! (*He sighs—thinking with a trace of guilty alarm*)

> The first thing she said at breakfast . . . "I dreamed of Gordon" . . . as if she wanted to taunt me! . . . how absurd! . . . her eyes positively glared! . . .

(*suddenly blurting out resentfully*) She dreams about Gordon.

MARSDEN—(*looking at him with amused surprise*) Well, I'd hardly call that a change, would you?

PROFESSOR LEEDS—(*thinking, oblivious to this remark*)

> But I must constantly bear in mind that she's not herself . . . that she's a sick girl . . .

MARSDEN—(*thinking*)

> The morning news of Gordon's death came . . . her

face like gray putty . . . beauty gone . . . no face
can afford intense grief . . . it's only later when sorrow . . .

(*with concern*) Just what do you mean by changed, Professor?
Before I left she seemed to be coming out of that horrible
numbed calm.

PROFESSOR LEEDS—(*slowly and carefully*) Yes, she has
played a lot of golf and tennis this summer, motored around
with her friends, and even danced a good deal. And she eats
with a ravenous appetite. (*thinking frightenedly*)

>Breakfast . . . "dreamed of Gordon" . . . what a look
>of hate for me in her eyes! . . .

MARSDEN—But that sounds splendid! When I left she
wouldn't see anyone or go anywhere. (*thinking pityingly*)

>Wandering from room to room . . . her thin body and
>pale lost face . . . gutted, love-abandoned eyes! . . .

PROFESSOR LEEDS—Well, now she's gone to the opposite
extreme! Sees everyone—bores, fools—as if she'd lost all dis-
crimination or wish to discriminate. And she talks intermi-
nably, Charlie—intentional nonsense, one would say! Refuses to be serious! Jeers at everything!

MARSDEN—(*consolingly*) Oh, that's all undoubtedly part of
the effort she's making to forget.

PROFESSOR LEEDS—(*absent-mindedly*) Yes. (*arguing with
himself*)

>Shall I tell him? . . . no . . . it might sound silly . . .
>but it's terrible to be so alone in this . . . if Nina's
>mother had lived . . . my wife . . . dead! . . . and for
>a time I actually felt released! . . . wife! . . . helpmeet!
>. . . now I need help! . . . no use! . . . she's gone! . . .

MARSDEN—(*watching him—thinking with a condescending
affection*)

>Good little man . . . he looks worried . . . always
>fussing about something . . . he must get on Nina's
>nerves. . . .

(*reassuringly*) No girl could forget Gordon in a hurry, especially after the shock of his tragic death.

PROFESSOR LEEDS—(*irritably*) I realize that. (*thinking resentfully*)

>Gordon . . . always Gordon with everyone! . . .

MARSDEN—By the way, I located the spot near Sedan where Gordon's machine fell. Nina asked me to, you know.

PROFESSOR LEEDS—(*irritated*—*expostulatingly*) For heaven's sake, don't remind her! Give her a chance to forget if you want to see her well again. After all, Charlie, life must be lived and Nina can't live with a corpse forever! (*trying to control his irritation and talk in an objective tone*) You see, I'm trying to see things through clearly and unsentimentally. If you'll remember, I was as broken up as anyone over Gordon's death. I'd become so reconciled to Nina's love for him—although, as you know, I was opposed at first, and for fair reasons, I think, for the boy, for all his good looks and prowess in sport and his courses, really came of common people and had no money of his own except as he made a career for himself.

MARSDEN—(*a trifle defensively*) I'm sure he would have had a brilliant career.

PROFESSOR LEEDS—(*impatiently*) No doubt. Although you must acknowledge, Charlie, that college heroes rarely shine brilliantly in after life. Unfortunately, the tendency to spoil them in the university is a poor training—

MARSDEN—But Gordon was absolutely unspoiled, I should say.

PROFESSOR LEEDS—(*heatedly*) Don't misunderstand me, Charlie! I'd be the first to acknowledge— (*a bit pathetically*) It isn't Gordon, Charlie. It's his memory, his ghost, you might call it, haunting Nina, whose influence I have come to dread because of the terrible change in her attitude toward me. (*His face twitches as if he were on the verge of tears*—*he thinks desperately*)

> I've got to tell him . . . he will see that I acted for the best . . . that I was justified. . . .

(*He hesitates*—*then blurts out*) It may sound incredible, but Nina has begun to act as if she hated me!

MARSDEN—(*startled*) Oh, come now!

PROFESSOR LEEDS—(*insistently*) Absolutely! I haven't wanted to admit it. I've refused to believe it, until it's become too appallingly obvious in her whole attitude toward me! (*His voice trembles.*)

MARSDEN—(*moved*—*expostulating*) Oh, now you're becoming morbid! Why, Nina has always idolized you! What possible reason—?

PROFESSOR LEEDS—(*quickly*) I can answer that, I think. She has a reason. But why she should blame me when she must know I acted for the best— You probably don't know, but just before he sailed for the front Gordon wanted their marriage to take place, and Nina consented. In fact, from the insinuations she lets drop now, she must have been most eager, but at the time— However, I felt it was ill-advised and I took Gordon aside and pointed out to him that such a precipitate marriage would be unfair to Nina, and scarcely honorable on his part.

MARSDEN—(*staring at him wonderingly*) You said that to Gordon? (*thinking cynically*)

> A shrewd move! . . . Gordon's proud spot, fairness and honor! . . . but was it honorable of you? . . .

PROFESSOR LEEDS—(*with a touch of asperity*) Yes, I said it, and I gave him my reason. There *was* the possibility he might be killed, in the flying service rather more than a possibility, which needless to say, I did not point out, but which Gordon undoubtedly realized, poor boy! If he were killed, he would be leaving Nina a widow, perhaps with a baby, with no resources, since he was penniless, except what pension she might get from the government; and all this while she was still at an age when a girl, especially one of Nina's charm and beauty, should have all of life before her. Decidedly, I told him, in justice to Nina, they must wait until he had come back and begun to establish his position in the world. That was the square thing. And Gordon was quick to agree with me!

MARSDEN—(*thinking*)

> The square thing! . . . but we must all be crooks where happiness is concerned! . . . steal or starve! . . .

(*then rather ironically*) And so Gordon told Nina he'd suddenly realized it wouldn't be fair to her. But I gather he didn't tell her it was your scruple originally?

PROFESSOR LEEDS—No, I asked him to keep what I said strictly confidential.

MARSDEN—(*thinking ironically*)

Trusted to his honor again! . . . old fox! . . . poor Gordon! . . .

But Nina suspects now that you—?

PROFESSOR LEEDS—(*startled*) Yes. That's exactly it. She knows in some queer way. And she acts toward me exactly as if she thought I had deliberately destroyed her happiness, that I had hoped for Gordon's death and been secretly overjoyed when the news came! (*His voice is shaking with emotion.*) And there you have it, Charlie—the whole absurd mess! (*thinking with a strident accusation*)

And it's true, you contemptible . . . !

(*then miserably defending himself*)

No! . . . I acted unselfishly . . . for her sake! . . .

MARSDEN—(*wonderingly*) You don't mean to tell me she has accused you of all this?

PROFESSOR LEEDS—Oh, no, Charlie! Only by hints—looks—innuendos. She knows she has no real grounds, but in the present state of her mind the real and the unreal become confused—

MARSDEN—(*thinking cynically*)

As always in all minds . . . or how could men live? . . .

(*soothingly*) That's just what you ought to bear in your mind—the state of hers—and not get so worked up over what I should say is a combination of imagination on both your parts. (*He gets to his feet as he hears voices from the right.*) Buck up! This must be Nina coming. (*The Professor gets to his feet, hastily composing his features into his bland, cultured expression.*)

MARSDEN—(*thinking self-mockingly but a bit worried about himself*)

My heart pounding! . . . seeing Nina again! . . . how sentimental . . . how she'd laugh if she knew! . . . and quite rightly . . . absurd for me to react as if I loved . . . that way . . . her dear old Charlie . . . ha! . . .

(*He smiles with bitter self-mockery.*)

PROFESSOR LEEDS—(*thinking worriedly*)

I hope she won't make a scene . . . she's seemed on

the verge all day . . . thank God, Charlie's like one of the family . . . but what a life for me! . . . with the opening of the new term only a few weeks off! . . . I can't do it . . . I'll have to call in a nerve specialist . . . but the last one did her no good . . . his outrageous fee . . . he can take it to court . . . I absolutely refuse . . . but if he should bring suit? . . . what a scandal . . . no, I'll have to pay . . . somehow . . . borrow . . . he has me in a corner, the robber! . . .

NINA—(*enters and stands just inside the doorway looking directly at her father with defiant eyes, her face set in an expression of stubborn resolve. She is twenty, tall with broad square shoulders, slim strong hips and long beautifully developed legs—a fine athletic girl of the swimmer, tennis player, golfer type. Her strawblond hair, framing her sunburned face, is bobbed. Her face is striking, handsome rather than pretty, the bone structure prominent, the forehead high, the lips of her rather large mouth clearly modelled above the firm jaw. Her eyes are beautiful and bewildering, extraordinarily large and a deep greenish blue. Since Gordon's death they have a quality of continually shuddering before some terrible enigma, of being wounded to their depths and made defiant and resentful by their pain. Her whole manner, the charged atmosphere she gives off, is totally at variance with her healthy outdoor physique. It is strained, nerve-racked, hectic, a terrible tension of will alone maintaining self-possession. She is dressed in smart sport clothes. Too preoccupied with her resolve to remember or see Marsden, she speaks directly to her father in a voice tensely cold and calm.*) I have made up my mind, Father.

PROFESSOR LEEDS—(*thinking distractedly*)

What does she mean? . . . oh, God help me! . . .
(*flustered—hastily*) Don't you see Charlie, Nina?

MARSDEN—(*troubled—thinking*)

She has changed . . . what has happened? . . .
(*He comes forward toward her—a bit embarrassed but affectionately using his pet name for her.*) Hello, Nina Cara Nina! Are you trying to cut me dead, young lady?

NINA—(*turning her eyes to Marsden, holding out her hand for him to shake, in her cool, preoccupied voice*) Hello, Charlie. (*Her eyes immediately return to her father.*) Listen, Father!

MARSDEN—(*standing near her, concealing his chagrin*)
> That hurts! . . . I mean nothing! . . . but she's a sick
> girl . . . I must make allowance . . .

PROFESSOR LEEDS—(*thinking distractedly*)
> That look in her eyes! . . . hate! . . .

(*with a silly giggle*) Really, Nina, you're absolutely rude! What
has Charlie done?

NINA—(*in her cool tone*) Why, nothing. Nothing at all.
(*She goes to him with a detached, friendly manner.*) Did I seem
rude, Charlie? I didn't mean to be. (*She kisses him with a cool,
friendly smile.*) Welcome home. (*thinking wearily*)
> What has Charlie done? . . . nothing . . . and never
> will . . . Charlie sits beside the fierce river, immacu-
> lately timid, cool and clothed, watching the burning,
> frozen naked swimmers drown at last. . . .

MARSDEN—(*thinking torturedly*)
> Cold lips . . . the kiss of contempt! . . . for dear old
> Charlie! . . .

(*forcing a good-natured laugh*) Rude? Not a bit! (*banteringly*)
As I've often reminded you, what can I expect when the first
word you ever spoke in this world was an insult to me.
"Dog" you said, looking right at me—at the age of one! (*He
laughs. The Professor laughs nervously. Nina smiles perfunctorily.*)

NINA—(*thinking wearily*)
> The fathers laugh at little daughter Nina . . . I must
> get away! . . . nice Charlie doggy . . . faithful
> . . . fetch and carry . . . bark softly in books at the
> deep night. . . .

PROFESSOR LEEDS—(*thinking*)
> What is she thinking? . . . I can't stand living like
> this! . . .

(*giggle gone to a twitching grin*) You are a cool one, Nina!
You'd think you'd just seen Charlie yesterday!

NINA—(*slowly—coolly and reflectively*) Well, the war is over.
Coming back safe from Europe isn't such an unusual feat
now, is it?

MARSDEN—(*thinking bitterly*)
> A taunt . . . I didn't fight . . . physically unfit . . .
> not like Gordon . . . Gordon in flames . . . how she
> must resent my living! . . . thinking of me, scribbling

in press bureau . . . louder and louder lies . . .
drown the guns and the screams . . . deafen the world
with lies . . . hired choir of liars! . . .

(*forcing a joking tone*) Little you know the deadly risks I ran,
Nina! If you'd eaten some of the food they gave me on my
renovated transport, you'd shower me with congratulations!
(*The Professor forces a snicker.*)

NINA—(*coolly*) Well, you're here, and that's that. (*then
suddenly expanding in a sweet, genuinely affectionate smile*) And
I *am* glad, Charlie, always glad you're here! You know that.

MARSDEN—(*delighted and embarrassed*) I hope so, Nina!

NINA—(*turning on her father—determinedly*) I must finish
what I started to say, Father. I've thought it all out and decided that I simply must get away from here at once—or go
crazy! And I'm going on the nine-forty tonight. (*She turns to
Marsden with a quick smile.*) You'll have to help me pack,
Charlie! (*thinking with weary relief*)

> Now that's said . . . I'm going . . . never come back
> . . . oh, how I loathe this room! . . .

MARSDEN—(*thinking with alarm*)

> What's this? . . . going? . . . going to whom? . . .

PROFESSOR LEEDS—(*thinking—terrified*)

> Going? . . . never come back to me? . . . no! . . .

(*desperately putting on his prim severe manner toward an un-
ruly pupil*) This is rather a sudden decision, isn't it? You
haven't mentioned before that you were considering—in fact,
you've led me to believe that you were quite contented
here—that is, of course I mean for the time being, and I
really think—

MARSDEN—(*looking at Nina—thinking with alarm*)

> Going away to whom? . . .

(*then watching the Professor with a pitying shudder*)

> He's on the wrong tack with his professor's manner
> . . . her eyes seeing cruelly through him . . . with
> what terrible recognition! . . . God, never bless me
> with children! . . .

NINA—(*thinking with weary scorn*)

> The Professor of Dead Languages is talking again . . .
> a dead man lectures on the past of living . . . since I
> was born I have been in his class, loving-attentive,

pupil-daughter Nina . . . my ears numb with spiritless
messages from the dead . . . dead words droning on
. . . listening because he is my cultured father . . . a
little more inclined to deafness than the rest (let me be
just) because he is my father . . . father? . . . what is
father? . . .

PROFESSOR LEEDS—(*thinking—terrified*)

I must talk her out of it! . . . find the right words!
. . . oh, I know she won't hear me! . . . oh, wife,
why did you die, you would have talked to her, she
would have listened to you! . . .

(*continuing in his professor's superior manner*) —and I really
think, in justice to yourself above all, you ought to consider
this step with great care before you definitely commit yourself. First and foremost, there is your health to be taken into
consideration. You've been very ill, Nina, how perilously so
perhaps you're not completely aware, but I assure you, and
Charlie can corroborate my statement, that six months ago
the doctors thought it might be years before—and yet, by
staying home and resting and finding healthy outdoor recre-
ation among your old friends, and keeping your mind occupied with the routine of managing the household—(*he forces
a prim playful smile*) and managing me, I might add!—you
have wonderfully improved and I think it most ill-advised
in the hottest part of August, while you're really still a con-
valescent—

NINA—(*thinking*)

Talking! . . . his voice like a fatiguing dying tune
droned on a beggar's organ . . . his words arising
from the tomb of a soul in puffs of ashes . . .

(*torturedly*)

Ashes! . . . oh, Gordon, my dear one! . . . oh, lips
on my lips, oh, strong arms around me, oh, spirit so
brave and generous and gay! . . . ashes dissolving into
mud! . . . mud and ashes! . . . that's all! . . . gone!
. . . gone forever from me! . . .

PROFESSOR LEEDS—(*thinking angrily*)

Her eyes . . . I know that look . . . tender, loving
. . . not for me . . . damn Gordon! . . . I'm glad
he's dead! . . .

(*a touch of asperity in his voice*) And at a couple of hours' notice to leave everything in the air, as it were— (*then judicially*) No, Nina, frankly, I can't see it. You know I'd gladly consent to anything in the world to benefit you, but—surely, you can't have reflected!

NINA—(*thinking torturedly*)

> Gordon darling, I must go away where I can think of you in silence! . . .

(*She turns on her father, her voice trembling with the effort to keep it in control—icily*) It's no use talking, Father. I *have* reflected and I am going!

PROFESSOR LEEDS—(*with asperity*) But I tell you it's quite impossible! I don't like to bring up the money consideration but I couldn't possibly afford— And how will you support yourself, if I may ask? Two years in the University, I am sorry to say, won't be much use to you when applying for a job. And even if you had completely recovered from your nervous breakdown, which it's obvious to anyone you haven't, then I most decidedly think you should finish out your science course and take your degree before you attempt— (*thinking desperately*)

> No use! . . . she doesn't hear . . . thinking of Gordon . . . she'll defy me . . .

NINA—(*thinking desperately*)

> I must keep calm . . . I mustn't let go or I'll tell him everything . . . and I mustn't tell him . . . he's my father . . .

(*with the same cold calculating finality*) I've already had six months' training for a nurse. I will finish my training. There's a doctor I know at a sanitarium for crippled soldiers—a friend of Gordon's. I wrote to him and he answered that he'll gladly arrange it.

PROFESSOR LEEDS—(*thinking furiously*)

> Gordon's friend . . . Gordon again! . . .

(*severely*) You seriously mean to tell me you, in your condition, want to nurse in a soldiers' hospital! Absurd!

MARSDEN—(*thinking with indignant revulsion*)

> Quite right, Professor! . . . her beauty . . . all those men . . . in their beds . . . it's too revolting! . . .

(*with a persuasive quizzing tone*) Yes, I must say I can't see you as a peace-time Florence Nightingale, Nina!

NINA—(*coolly, struggling to keep control, ignoring these remarks*) So you see, Father, I've thought of everything and there's not the slightest reason to worry about me. And I've been teaching Mary how to take care of you. So you won't need me at all. You can go along as if nothing had happened—and really, nothing will have happened that hasn't already happened.

PROFESSOR LEEDS—Why, even the manner in which you address me—the tone you take—proves conclusively that you're not yourself!

NINA—(*her voice becoming a bit uncanny, her thoughts breaking through*) No, I'm not myself yet. That's just it. Not all myself. But I've been becoming myself. And I must finish!

PROFESSOR LEEDS—(*with angry significance—to Marsden*) You hear her, Charlie? She's a sick girl!

NINA—(*slowly and strangely*) I'm not sick. I'm too well. But they are sick and I must give my health to help them to live on, and to live on myself. (*with a sudden intensity in her tone*) I must pay for my cowardly treachery to Gordon! You should understand this, Father, you who— (*She swallows hard, catching her breath. Thinking desperately*)

> I'm beginning to tell him! . . . I mustn't! . . . he's my father! . . .

PROFESSOR LEEDS—(*in a panic of guilty fear, but defiantly*) What do you mean? I am afraid you're not responsible for what you're saying.

NINA—(*again with the strange intensity*) I must pay! It's my plain duty! Gordon is dead! What use is my life to me or anyone? But I must make it of use—by giving it! (*fiercely*) I must learn to give myself, do you hear—give and give until I can make that gift of myself for a man's happiness without scruple, without fear, without joy except in his joy! When I've accomplished this I'll have found myself, I'll know how to start in living my own life again! (*appealing to them with a desperate impatience*) Don't you see? In the name of the commonest decency and honor, I owe it to Gordon!

PROFESSOR LEEDS—(*sharply*) No, I can't see—nor anyone else! (*thinking savagely*)

> I hope Gordon is in hell! . . .

MARSDEN—(*thinking*)

> Give herself? . . . can she mean her body? . . . beautiful body . . . to cripples? . . . for Gordon's sake? . . . damn Gordon! . . .

(*coldly*) What do you mean, you owe it to Gordon, Nina?

PROFESSOR LEEDS—(*bitterly*) Yes, how ridiculous! It seems to me when you gave him your love, he got more than he could ever have hoped—

NINA—(*with fierce self-contempt*) I gave him? What did I give him? It's what I didn't give! That last night before he sailed—in his arms until my body ached—kisses until my lips were numb—knowing all that night—something in me knowing he would die, that he would never kiss me again—knowing this so surely yet with my cowardly brain lying, no, he'll come back and marry you, you'll be happy ever after and feel his children at your breasts looking up with eyes so much like his, possessing eyes so happy in possessing you! (*then violently*) But Gordon never possessed me! I'm still Gordon's silly virgin! And Gordon is muddy ashes! And I've lost my happiness forever! All that last night I knew he wanted me. I knew it was only the honorable code-bound Gordon, who kept commanding from his brain, no, you mustn't, you must respect her, you must wait till you have a marriage license! (*She gives a mocking laugh.*)

PROFESSOR LEEDS—(*shocked*) Nina! This is really going too far!

MARSDEN—(*repelled—with a superior sneer*) Oh, come now, Nina! You've been reading books. Those don't sound like your thoughts.

NINA—(*without looking at him, her eyes on her father's—intensely*) Gordon wanted me! I wanted Gordon! I should have made him take me! I knew he would die and I would have no children, that there would be no big Gordon or little Gordon left to me, that happiness was calling me, never to call again if I refused! And yet I did refuse! I didn't make him take me! I lost him forever! And now I am lonely and not pregnant with anything at all, but—but loathing! (*She hurls this last at her father—fiercely*) Why did I refuse? What was that cowardly something in me that cried, no, you mustn't, what would your father say?

PROFESSOR LEEDS—(*thinking—furiously*)

> What an animal! . . . and my daughter! . . . she
> doesn't get it from me! . . . was her mother like
> that? . . .

(*distractedly*) Nina! I really can't listen!

NINA—(*savagely*) And that's exactly what my father did
say! Wait, he told Gordon! Wait for Nina till the war's over,
and you've got a good job and can afford a marriage license!

PROFESSOR LEEDS—(*crumbling pitifully*) Nina! I—!

MARSDEN—(*flurriedly—going to him*) Don't take her seriously, Professor! (*thinking with nervous repulsion*)

> Nina has changed . . . all flesh now . . . lust . . .
> who would dream she was so sensual? . . . I wish
> I were out of this! . . . I wish I hadn't come here to-
> day! . . .

NINA—(*coldly and deliberately*) Don't lie any more, Father!
Today I've made up my mind to face things. I know now why
Gordon suddenly dropped all idea of marriage before he left,
how unfair to me he suddenly decided it would be! Unfair to
me! Oh, that's humorous! To think I might have had happiness, Gordon, and now Gordon's child— (*then directly accusing him*) You told him it'd be unfair, you put him on his
honor, didn't you?

PROFESSOR LEEDS—(*collecting himself—woodenly*) Yes. I
did it for your sake, Nina.

NINA—(*in the same voice as before*) It's too late for lies!

PROFESSOR LEEDS—(*woodenly*) Let us say then that I *persuaded* myself it was for your sake. That may be true. You are
young. You think one can live with truth. Very well. It is also
true I was jealous of Gordon. I was alone and I wanted to
keep your love. I hated him as one hates a thief one may not
accuse nor punish. I did my best to prevent your marriage. I
was glad when he died. There. Is that what you wish me to
say?

NINA—Yes. Now I begin to forget I've hated you. You
were braver than I, at least.

PROFESSOR LEEDS—I wanted to live comforted by your
love until the end. In short, I am a man who happens to be
your father. (*He hides his face in his hands and weeps softly.*)
Forgive that man!

MARSDEN—(*thinking timidly*)

> In short, forgive us our possessing as we forgive those who possessed before us . . . Mother must be wondering what keeps me so long . . . it's time for tea . . . I must go home . . .

NINA—(*sadly*) Oh, I forgive you. But do you understand now that I must somehow find a way to give myself to Gordon still, that I must pay my debt and learn to forgive myself?

PROFESSOR LEEDS—Yes.

NINA—Mary will look after you.

PROFESSOR LEEDS—Mary will do very well, I'm sure.

MARSDEN—(*thinking*)

> Nina has changed . . . this is no place for me . . . Mother is waiting tea. . . .

(*then venturing on an uncertain tone of pleasantry*) Quite so, you two. But isn't this all nonsense? Nina will be back with us in a month, Professor, what with the depressing heat and humidity, and the more depressing halt and the lame!

PROFESSOR LEEDS—(*sharply*) She must stay away until she gets well. This time I do speak for her sake.

NINA—I'll take the nine-forty. (*turning to Marsden— with a sudden girlishness*) Come on upstairs, Charlie, and help me pack! (*She grabs him by the hand and starts to pull him away.*)

MARSDEN—(*shrugging his shoulders—confusedly*) Well—I don't understand this!

NINA—(*with a strange smile*) But some day I'll read it all in one of your books, Charlie, and it'll be so simple and easy to understand that I won't be able to recognize it, Charlie, let alone understand it! (*She laughs teasingly.*) Dear old Charlie!

MARSDEN—(*thinking in agony*)

> God damn in hell . . . dear old Charlie! . . .

(*then with a genial grin*) I'll have to propose, Nina, if you continue to be my severest critic! I'm a stickler for these little literary conventions, you know!

NINA—All right. Propose while we pack. (*She leads him off, right.*)

PROFESSOR LEEDS—(*blows his nose, wipes his eyes, sighs, clears his throat, squares his shoulders, pulls his coat down in front,*

*sets his tie straight, and starts to take a brisk turn about the room.
His face is washed blandly clean of all emotion.*)

Three weeks now . . . new term . . . I will have to
be looking over my notes. . . .

(*He looks out of window, front.*)

Grass parched in the middle . . . Tom forgotten the
sprinkler . . . careless . . . ah, there goes Mr. Davis
of the bank . . . bank . . . my salary will go farther
now . . . books I really need . . . all bosh two can
live as cheaply as one . . . there are worse things than
being a trained nurse . . . good background of discipline . . . she needs it . . . she may meet rich fellow
there . . . mature . . . only students here for her . . .
and their fathers never approve if they have anything. . . .

(*He sits down with a forced sigh of peace.*)

I am glad we had it out . . . his ghost will be gone
now . . . no more Gordon, Gordon, Gordon, love
and praise and tears, all for Gordon! . . . Mary will
do very well by me . . . I will have more leisure and
peace of mind . . . and Nina will come back home
. . . when she is well again . . . the old Nina! . . .
my little Nina! . . . she knows and she forgave me
. . . she said so . . . said! . . . but could she really?
. . . don't you imagine? . . . deep in her heart? . . .
she still must hate? . . . oh, God! . . . I feel cold!
. . . alone! . . . this home is abandoned! . . . the
house is empty and full of death! . . . there is a pain
about my heart! . . .

(*He calls hoarsely, getting to his feet*) Nina!

NINA'S VOICE—(*Her voice, fresh and girlish, calls from upstairs*) Yes, Father. Do you want me?

PROFESSOR LEEDS—(*struggling with himself—goes to door
and calls with affectionate blandness*) No. Never mind. Just
wanted to remind you to call for a taxi in good time.

NINA'S VOICE—I won't forget.

PROFESSOR LEEDS—(*looks at his watch*)

Five-thirty just . . . nine-forty, the train . . . then
. . . Nina no more! . . . four hours more . . . she'll
be packing . . . then good-bye . . . a kiss . . .

nothing more ever to say to each other . . . and I'll die in here some day . . . alone . . . gasp, cry out for help . . . the president will speak at the funeral . . . Nina will be here again . . . Nina in black . . . too late! . . .

(He calls hoarsely) Nina! *(There is no answer.)*

In other room . . . doesn't hear . . . just as well . . . *(He turns to the bookcase and pulls out the first volume his hands come on and opens it at random and begins to read aloud sonorously like a child whistling to keep up his courage in the dark.)*

"Stetit unus in arcem
Erectus capitis victorque ad sidera mittit
Sidereos oculos propiusque adspectat Olympum
Inquiritque Iovem;" . . .

(Curtain)

ACT TWO

SCENE—*The same as Scene One, Professor Leeds' study. It is about nine o'clock of a night in early fall, over a year later. The appearance of the room is unchanged except that all the shades, of the color of pale flesh, are drawn down, giving the windows a suggestion of lifeless closed eyes and making the room seem more withdrawn from life than before. The reading lamp on the table is lit. Everything on the table, papers, pencils, pens, etc., is arranged in meticulous order.*

Marsden is seated on the chair at center. He is dressed carefully in an English made suit of blue serge so dark as to seem black, and which, combined with the gloomy brooding expression of his face, strongly suggests one in mourning. His tall, thin body sags wearily in the chair, his head is sunk forward, the chin almost touching his chest, his eyes stare sadly at nothing.

MARSDEN—(*his thoughts at ebb, without emphasis, sluggish and melancholy*)

> Prophetic Professor! . . . I remember he once said . . . shortly after Nina went away . . . "some day, in here, . . . you'll find me" . . . did he foresee? . . . no . . . everything in life is so contemptuously accidental! . . . God's sneer at our self-importance! . . .

(*smiling grimly*)

> Poor Professor! he was horribly lonely . . . tried to hide it . . . always telling you how beneficial the training at the hospital would be for her . . . poor old chap! . . .

(*His voice grows husky and uncertain—he controls it—straightens himself*)

> What time is it? . . .

(*He takes out his watch mechanically and looks at it.*)

> Ten after nine. . . . Nina ought to be here. . . .

(*then with sudden bitterness*)

> Will she feel any real grief over his death, I wonder? . . . I doubt it! . . . but why am I so resentful? . . . the two times I've visited the hospital she's been pleasant enough . . . pleasantly evasive! . . . perhaps she thought her father had sent me to spy on her . . .

poor Professor! . . . at least she answered his letters
. . . he used to show them to me . . . pathetically
overjoyed . . . newsy, loveless scripts, telling nothing
whatever about herself . . . well, she won't have to
compose them any more . . . she never answered
mine . . . she might at least have acknowledged
them. . . . Mother thinks she's behaved quite in-
excusably . . .

(*then jealously*)

I suppose every single damned inmate has fallen in
love with her! . . . her eyes seemed cynical . . . sick
with men . . . as though I'd looked into the eyes of a
prostitute . . . not that I ever have . . . except that
once . . . the dollar house . . . hers were like patent
leather buttons in a saucer of blue milk! . . .

(*getting up with a movement of impatience*)

The devil! . . . what beastly incidents our memories
insist on cherishing! . . . the ugly and disgusting . . .
the beautiful things we have to keep diaries to remember! . . .

(*He smiles with a wry amusement for a second—then bitterly*)

That last night Nina was here . . . she talked so brazenly about giving herself . . . I wish I knew the truth
of what she's been doing in that house full of men
. . . particularly that self-important young ass of a
doctor! . . . Gordon's friend! . . .

(*He frowns at himself, determinedly puts an end to his train of
thought and comes and sits down again in the chair—in sneering,
conversational tones as if he were this time actually addressing another person*)

Really, it's hardly a decent time, is it, for that kind of
speculation . . . with her father lying dead upstairs? . . .

(*A silence as if he had respectably squelched himself—then he pulls
out his watch mechanically and stares at it. As he does so a noise
of a car is heard approaching, stopping at the curb beyond the
garden. He jumps to his feet and starts to go to door—then hesitates confusedly.*)

No, let Mary go . . . I wouldn't know what to do
. . . take her in my arms? . . . kiss her? . . . right
now? . . . or wait until she? . . .

(*A bell rings insistently from the back of the house. From the front voices are heard, first Nina's, then a man's. Marsden starts, his face suddenly angry and dejected.*)

>Someone with her! . . . a man! . . . I thought she'd be alone! . . .

(*Mary is heard shuffling to the front door which is opened. Immediately, as Mary sees Nina, she breaks down and there is the sound of her uncontrolled sobbing and choking, incoherent words drowning out Nina's voice, soothing her.*)

NINA—(*As Mary's grief subsides a trifle, her voice is heard, flat and toneless.*) Isn't Mr. Marsden here, Mary? (*She calls*) Charlie!

MARSDEN—(*confused—huskily*) In here—I'm in the study, Nina. (*He moves uncertainly toward the door.*)

NINA—(*comes in and stands just inside the doorway. She is dressed in a nurse's uniform with cap, a raglan coat over it. She appears older than in the previous scene, her face is pale and much thinner, her cheek bones stand out, her mouth is taut in hard lines of a cynical scorn. Her eyes try to armor her wounded spirit with a defensive stare of disillusionment. Her training has also tended to coarsen her fiber a trifle, to make her insensitive to suffering, to give her the nurse's professionally callous attitude. In her fight to regain control of her nerves she has over-striven after the cool and efficient poise, but she is really in a more highly strung, disorganized state than ever, although she is now more capable of suppressing and concealing it. She remains strikingly handsome and her physical appeal is enhanced by her pallor and the mysterious suggestion about her of hidden experience. She stares at Marsden blankly and speaks in queer flat tones.*) Hello, Charlie. He's dead, Mary says.

MARSDEN—(*nodding his head several times—stupidly*) Yes.

NINA—(*in same tones*) It's too bad. I brought Doctor Darrell. I thought there might be a chance. (*She pauses and looks about the room—thinking confusedly*)

>His books . . . his chair . . . he always sat there . . . there's his table . . . little Nina was never allowed to touch anything . . . she used to sit on his lap . . . cuddle against him . . . dreaming into the dark beyond the windows . . . warm in his arms before the fireplace . . . dreams like sparks soaring up to die in

the cold dark . . . warm in his love, safe-drifting into sleep . . . "Daddy's girl, aren't you?" . . .

(*She looks around and then up and down.*)

His home . . . my home . . . he was my father . . . he's dead . . .

(*She shakes her head.*)

Yes, I hear you, little Nina, but I don't understand one word of it. . . .

(*She smiles with a cynical self-contempt.*)

I'm sorry, Father! . . . you see you've been dead for me a long time . . . when Gordon died, all men died . . . what did you feel for me then? . . . nothing . . . and now I feel nothing . . . it's too bad . . .

MARSDEN—(*thinking woundedly*)

I hoped she would throw herself in my arms . . . weeping . . . hide her face on my shoulder . . . "Oh, Charlie, you're all I've got left in the world . . ."

(*then angrily*)

Why did she have to bring that Darrell with her?

NINA—(*flatly*) When I said good-bye that night I had a premonition I'd never see him again.

MARSDEN—(*glad of this opening for moral indignation*) You've never tried to see him, Nina! (*then overcome by disgust with himself—contritely*) Forgive me! It was rotten of me to say that!

NINA—(*shaking her head—flatly*) I didn't want him to see what he would have thought was me. (*ironically*) That's the other side of it you couldn't dissect into words from here, Charlie! (*then suddenly asking a necessary question in her nurse's cool, efficient tones*) Is he upstairs? (*Marsden nods stupidly.*) I'll take Ned up. I might as well. (*She turns and walks out briskly.*)

MARSDEN—(*staring after her—dully*)

That isn't Nina. . . .

(*indignantly*)

They've killed her soul down there! . . .

(*Tears come to his eyes suddenly and he pulls out his handkerchief and wipes them, muttering huskily*)

Poor old Professor! . . .

(*then suddenly jeering at himself*)

For God's sake, stop acting! . . . it isn't the Professor! . . . dear old Charlie is crying because she didn't weep on his shoulder . . . as he had hoped! . . .

(*He laughs harshly—then suddenly sees a man outside the doorway and stares—then calls sharply*) Who's that?

EVANS—(*his voice embarrassed and hesitating comes from the hall*) It's all right. (*He appears in the doorway, grinning bashfully.*) It's me—I, I mean—Miss Leeds told me to come in here. (*He stretches out his hand awkwardly.*) Guess you don't remember me, Mr. Marsden. Miss Leeds introduced us one day at the hospital. You were leaving just as I came in. Evans is my name.

MARSDEN—(*who has been regarding him with waning resentment, forces a cordial smile and shakes hands*) Oh, yes. At first I couldn't place you.

EVANS—(*awkwardly*) I sort of feel I'm butting in.

MARSDEN—(*beginning to be taken by his likable boyish quality*) Not at all. Sit down. (*He sits in the rocker at center as Evans goes to the bench at right. Evans sits uncomfortably hunched forward, twiddling his hat in his hands. He is above the medium height, very blond, with guileless, diffident blue eyes, his figure inclined to immature lumbering outlines. His face is fresh and red-cheeked, handsome in a boyish fashion. His manner is bashful with women or older men, coltishly playful with his friends. There is a lack of self-confidence, a lost and strayed appealing air about him, yet with a hint of some unawakened obstinate force beneath his apparent weakness. Although he is twenty-five and has been out of college three years, he still wears the latest in collegiate clothes and as he looks younger than he is, he is always mistaken for an undergraduate and likes to be. It keeps him placed in life for himself.*)

MARSDEN—(*studying him keenly—amused*)

This is certainly no giant intellect . . . overgrown boy . . . likable quality though . . .

EVANS—(*uneasy under Marsden's eyes*)

Giving me the once-over . . . seems like good egg . . . Nina says he is . . . suppose I ought to say something about his books, but I can't even remember a title of one . . .

(*He suddenly blurts out*) You've known Nina—Miss Leeds—
ever since she was a kid, haven't you?

MARSDEN—(*a bit shortly*) Yes. How long have you known
her?

EVANS—Well—really only since she's been at the hospital,
although I met her once years ago at a Prom with Gordon
Shaw.

MARSDEN—(*indifferently*) Oh, you knew Gordon?

EVANS—(*proudly*) Sure thing! I was in his class! (*with admiration amounting to hero-worship*) He sure was a wonder,
wasn't he?

MARSDEN—(*cynically*)

> Gordon über alles and forever! . . . I begin to appre-
> ciate the Professor's viewpoint . . .

(*casually*) A fine boy! Did you know him well?

EVANS—No. The crowd he went with were mostly fellows
who were good at sports—and I always was a dud. (*forcing
a smile*) I was always one of the first to get bounced off the
squad in any sport. (*then with a flash of humble pride*) But I
never quit trying, anyway!

MARSDEN—(*consolingly*) Well, the sport hero usually
doesn't star after college.

EVANS—Gordon did! (*eagerly—with intense admiration*) In
the war! He was an ace! And he always fought just as cleanly
as he'd played football! Even the Huns respected him!

MARSDEN—(*thinking cynically*)

> This Gordon worshipper must be the apple of Nina's
> eye! . . .

(*casually*) Were you in the army?

EVANS—(*shamefacedly*) Yes—infantry—but I never got to
the front—never saw anything exciting. (*thinking glumly*)

> Won't tell him I tried for flying service . . . wanted to
> get in Gordon's outfit . . . couldn't make the physical
> exam. . . . never made anything I wanted . . . sup-
> pose I'll lose out with Nina, too . . .

(*then rallying himself*)

> Hey, you! . . . what's the matter with you? . . .
> don't quit! . . .

MARSDEN—(*who has been staring at him inquisitively*) How
did you happen to come out here tonight?

EVANS—I was calling on Nina when your wire came. Ned thought I better come along, too—might be of some use.

MARSDEN—(*frowning*) You mean Doctor Darrell? (*Evans nods.*) Is he a close friend of yours?

EVANS—(*hesitatingly*) Well, sort of. Roomed in the same dorm with me at college. He was a senior when I was a freshman. Used to help me along in lots of ways. Took pity on me, I was so green. Then about a year ago when I went to the hospital to visit a fellow who'd been in my outfit I ran into him again. (*then with a grin*) But I wouldn't say Ned was close to anyone. He's a dyed-in-the-wool doc. He's only close to whatever's the matter with you! (*He chuckles—then hastily*) But don't get me wrong about him. He's the best egg ever! You know him, don't you?

MARSDEN—(*stiffly*) Barely. Nina introduced us once. (*thinking bitterly*)

> He's upstairs alone with her . . . I hoped it would be I who . . .

EVANS—

> Don't want him to get the wrong idea of Ned . . . Ned's my best friend . . . doing all he can to help me with Nina . . . he thinks she'll marry me in the end . . . God, if she only would! . . . I wouldn't expect her to love me at first . . . be happy only to take care of her . . . cook her breakfast . . . bring it up to her in bed . . . tuck the pillows behind her . . . comb her hair for her . . . I'd be happy just to kiss her hair! . . .

MARSDEN—(*agitated—thinking suspiciously*)

> What are Darrell's relations with Nina? . . . close to what's the matter with her? . . . damned thoughts! . . . why should I care? . . . I'll ask this Evans . . . pump him while I have a chance . . .

(*with forced indifference*) Is your friend, the Doctor, "close" to Miss Leeds? She's had quite a lot the matter with her since her breakdown, if that's what interests him! (*He smiles casually.*)

EVANS—(*gives a start, awakening from his dream*) Oh—er—yes. He's always trying to bully her into taking better care of herself, but she only laughs at him. (*soberly*) It'd be much better if she'd take his advice.

MARSDEN—(*suspiciously*) No doubt.

EVANS—(*pronounces with boyish solemnity*) She isn't herself, Mr. Marsden. And I think nursing all those poor guys keeps the war before her when she ought to forget it. She ought to give up nursing and be nursed for a change, that's my idea.

MARSDEN—(*struck by this—eagerly*) Exactly my opinion. (*thinking*)

> If she'd settle down here . . . I could come over every day . . . I'd nurse her . . . Mother home . . . Nina here . . . how I could work then! . . .

EVANS—(*thinking*)

> He certainly seems all for me . . . so far! . . .

(*then in a sudden flurry*)

> Shall I tell him? . . . he'll be like her guardian now . . . I've got to know how he stands . . .

(*He starts with a solemn earnestness.*) Mr. Marsden, I—there's something I ought to tell you, I think. You see, Nina's talked a lot about you. I know how much she thinks of you. And now her old man— (*He hesitates in confusion.*) I mean, her father's dead—

MARSDEN—(*in a sort of panic—thinking*)

> What's this? . . . proposal? . . . in form? . . . for her hand? . . . to me? . . . Father Charlie now, eh? . . . ha! . . . God, what a fool! . . . does he imagine she'd ever love him? . . . but she might . . . not bad looking . . . likable, innocent . . . something to mother . . .

EVANS—(*blundering on regardless now*) I know it's hardly the proper time—

MARSDEN—(*interrupting—dryly*) Perhaps I can anticipate. You want to tell me you're in love with Nina?

EVANS—Yes, sir, and I've asked her to marry me.

MARSDEN—What did she say?

EVANS—(*sheepishly*) Nothing. She just smiled.

MARSDEN—(*with relief*) Ah. (*then harshly*) Well, what could you expect? Surely you must know she still loves Gordon?

EVANS—(*manfully*) Sure I know it—and I admire her for it! Most girls forget too easily. She ought to love Gordon for a long time yet. And I know I'm an awful wash-out compared to him—but I love her as much as he did, or anyone could!

And I'll work my way up for her—I know I can!—so I can give her everything she wants. And I wouldn't ask for anything in return except the right to take care of her. (*blurts out confusedly*) I never think of her—that way—she's too beautiful and wonderful—not that I don't hope she'd come to love me in time—

MARSDEN—(*sharply*) And just what do you expect me to do about all this?

EVANS—(*taken aback*) Why—er—nothing, sir. I just thought you ought to know. (*Sheepishly he glances up at ceiling, then down at floor, twiddling his hat.*)

MARSDEN—(*thinking—at first with a grudging appreciation and envy*)

He thinks he means that . . . pure love! . . . it's easy to talk . . . he doesn't know life . . . but he might be good for Nina . . . if she were married to this simpleton would she be faithful? . . . and then I? . . . what a vile thought! . . . I don't mean that! . . .

(*then forcing a kindly tone*) You see, there's really nothing I can do about it. (*with a smile*) If Nina will, she will—and if she won't, she won't. But I can wish you good luck.

EVANS—(*immediately all boyish gratitude*) Thanks! That's darn fine of you, Mr. Marsden!

MARSDEN—But I think we'd better let the subject drop, don't you? We're forgetting that her father—

EVANS—(*guiltily embarrassed*) Yes—sure—I'm a damn fool! Excuse me! (*There is the noise of steps from the hall and Doctor Edmund Darrell enters. He is twenty-seven, short, dark, wiry, his movements rapid and sure, his manner cool and observant, his dark eyes analytical. His head is handsome and intelligent. There is a quality about him, provoking and disturbing to women, of intense passion which he has rigidly trained himself to control and set free only for the objective satisfaction of studying his own and their reactions; and so he has come to consider himself as immune to love through his scientific understanding of its real sexual nature. He sees Evans and Marsden, nods at Marsden silently, who returns it coldly, goes to the table and taking a prescription pad from his pocket, hastily scratches on it.*)

MARSDEN—(*thinking sneeringly*)

Amusing, these young doctors! . . . perspire with the

effort to appear cool! . . . writing a prescription . . .
cough medicine for the corpse, perhaps! . . . good-
looking? . . . more or less . . . attractive to women,
I dare say. . . .

DARRELL—(*tears it off—hands it to Evans*) Here, Sam. Run
along up the street and get this filled.

EVANS—(*with relief*) Sure. Glad of the chance for a walk.
(*He goes out, rear.*)

DARRELL—(*turning to Marsden*) It's for Nina. She's got to
get some sleep tonight. (*He sits down abruptly in the chair at
center. Marsden unconsciously takes the Professor's place behind the
table. The two men stare at each other for a moment, Darrell with
a frank probing, examining look that ruffles Marsden and makes
him all the more resentful toward him.*)

This Marsden doesn't like me . . . that's evident . . .
but he interests me . . . read his books . . . wanted
to know his bearing on Nina's case . . . his novels just
well-written surface . . . no depth, no digging underneath . . . why? . . . has the talent but doesn't dare
. . . afraid he'll meet himself somewhere . . . one of
those poor devils who spend their lives trying not to
discover which sex they belong to! . . .

MARSDEN—

Giving me the fishy, diagnosing eye they practice at
medical school . . . like freshmen from Ioway culti-
vating broad A's at Harvard! . . . what is his spe-
cialty? . . . neurologist, I think . . . I hope not
psychoanalyst . . . a lot to account for, Herr Freud!
. . . punishment to fit his crimes, be forced to listen
eternally during breakfast while innumerable plain
ones tell him dreams about snakes . . . pah, what an
easy cure-all! . . . sex the philosopher's stone . . .
"O Oedipus, O my king! The world is adopting
you!" . . .

DARRELL—

Must pitch into him about Nina . . . have to have his
help . . . damn little time to convince him . . . he's
the kind you have to explode a bomb under to get
them to move . . . but not too big a bomb . . . they
blow to pieces easily . . .

(*brusquely*) Nina's gone to pot again! Not that her father's death is a shock in the usual sense of grief. I wish to God it were! No, it's a shock because it's finally convinced her she can't feel anything any more. That's what she's doing upstairs now—trying to goad herself into feeling something!

MARSDEN—(*resentfully*) I think you're mistaken. She loved her father—

DARRELL—(*shortly and dryly*) We can't waste time being sentimental, Marsden! She'll be down any minute, and I've got a lot to talk over with you. (*as Marsden seems again about to protest*) Nina has a real affection for you and I imagine you have for her. Then you'll want as much as I do to get her straightened out. She's a corking girl. She ought to have every chance for a happy life. (*then sharply driving his words in*) But the way she's conditioned now, there's no chance. She's piled on too many destructive experiences. A few more and she'll dive for the gutter just to get the security that comes from knowing she's touched bottom and there's no farther to go!

MARSDEN—(*revolted and angry, half-springs to his feet*) Look here, Darrell, I'll be damned if I'll listen to such a ridiculous statement!

DARRELL—(*curtly—with authority*) How do you know it's ridiculous? What do you know of Nina since she left home? But she hadn't been nursing with us three days before I saw she really ought to be a patient; and ever since then I've studied her case. So I think it's up to you to listen.

MARSDEN—(*freezingly*) I'm listening. (*with apprehensive terror*)

> Gutter . . . has she . . . I wish he wouldn't tell me! . . .

DARRELL—(*thinking*)

> How much need I tell him? . . . can't tell him the raw truth about her promiscuity . . . he isn't built to face reality . . . no writer is outside of his books . . . have to tone it down for him . . . but not too much! . . .

Nina has been giving way more and more to a morbid longing for martyrdom. The reason for it is obvious. Gordon went away without—well, let's say marrying her. The war killed him. She was left suspended. Then she began to blame

herself and to want to sacrifice herself and at the same time
give happiness to various fellow war-victims by pretending to
love them. It's a pretty idea but it hasn't worked out. Nina's
a bad actress. She hasn't convinced the men of her love—or
herself of her good intentions. And each experience of this
kind has only left her more a prey to a guilty conscience than
before and more determined to punish herself!

MARSDEN—(*thinking*)

> What does he mean? . . . how far did she? . . . how
> many? . . .

(*coldly and sneeringly*) May I ask on what specific actions of
hers this theory of yours is based?

DARRELL—(*coldly in turn*) On her evident craving to make
an exhibition of kissing, necking, petting—whatever you call
it—spooning in general—with any patient in the institution
who got a case on her! (*ironically—thinking*)

> Spooning! . . . rather a mild word for her affairs . . .
> but strong enough for this ladylike soul. . . .

MARSDEN—(*bitterly*)

> He's lying! . . . what's he trying to hide? . . . was he
> one of them? . . . her lover? . . . I must get her away
> from him . . . get her to marry Evans! . . .

(*with authority*) Then she mustn't go back to your hospital,
that's certain!

DARRELL—(*quickly*) You're quite right. And that brings
me to what I want you to urge her to do.

MARSDEN—(*thinking suspiciously*)

> He doesn't want her back . . . I must have been
> wrong . . . but there might be many reasons why he'd
> wish to get rid of her . . .

(*coldly*) I think you exaggerate my influence.

DARRELL—(*eagerly*) Not a bit. You're the last link con-
necting her with the girl she used to be before Gordon's
death. You're closely associated in her mind with that period
of happy security, of health and peace of mind. I know that
from the way she talks about you. You're the only person she
still respects—and really loves. (*as Marsden starts guiltily and
glances at him in confusion—with a laugh*) Oh, you needn't
look frightened. I mean the sort of love she'd feel for an
uncle.

MARSDEN—(*thinking in agony*)

> Frightened? . . . was I? . . . only person she loves
> . . . and then he said "love she'd feel for an uncle"
> . . . Uncle Charlie now! . . . God damn him! . . .

DARRELL—(*eyeing him*)

> Looks damnably upset . . . wants to evade all respon-
> sibility for her, I suppose . . . he's that kind . . . all
> the better! . . . he'll be only too anxious to get her
> safely married. . . .

(*bluntly*) And that's why I've done all this talking. You've got
to help snap her out of this.

MARSDEN—(*bitterly*) And how, if I may ask?

DARRELL—There's only one way I can see. Get her to
marry Sam Evans.

MARSDEN—(*astonished*) Evans? (*He makes a silly gesture toward the door—thinking confusedly*)

> Wrong again . . . why does he want her married to
> . . . it's some trick. . . .

DARRELL—Yes, Evans. He's in love with her. And it's one
of those unselfish loves you read about. And she is fond of
him. In a maternal way, of course—but that's just what she
needs now, someone she cares about to mother and boss and
keep her occupied. And still more important, this would give
her a chance to have children. She's got to find normal outlets
for her craving for sacrifice. She needs normal love objects for
the emotional life Gordon's death blocked up in her. Now
marrying Sam ought to do the trick. Ought to. Naturally, no
one can say for certain. But I think his unselfish love, combined with her real liking for him, will gradually give her back
a sense of security and a feeling of being worth something to
life again, and once she's got that, she'll be saved! (*He has
spoken with persuasive feeling. He asks anxiously*) Doesn't that
seem good sense to you?

MARSDEN—(*suspicious—dryly non-committal*) I'm sorry but
I'm in no position to say. I don't know anything about Evans,
for one thing.

DARRELL—(*emphatically*) Well, I do. He's a fine healthy
boy, clean and unspoiled. You can take my word for that.
And I'm convinced he's got the right stuff in him to succeed,
once he grows up and buckles down to work. He's only a big

kid now, but all he needs is a little self-confidence and a sense of responsibility. He's holding down a fair job, too, considering he's just started in the advertising game—enough to keep them living. (*with a slight smile*) I'm prescribing for Sam, too, when I boost this wedding.

MARSDEN—(*his snobbery coming out*) Do you know his family—what sort of people?—

DARRELL—(*bitingly*) I'm not acquainted with their social qualifications, if that's what you mean! They're upstate country folks—fruit growers and farmers, well off, I believe. Simple, healthy people, I'm sure of that although I've never met them.

MARSDEN—(*a bit shamefacedly—changing the subject hastily*) Have you suggested this match to Nina?

DARRELL—Yes, a good many times lately in a half-joking way. If I were serious she wouldn't listen, she'd say I was prescribing. But I think what I've said has planted it in her mind as a possibility.

MARSDEN—(*thinking suspiciously*)

> Is this Doctor her lover? . . . trying to pull the wool over my eyes? . . . use me to arrange a convenient triangle for him? . . .

(*harshly—but trying to force a joking tone*) Do you know what I'm inclined to suspect, Doctor? That you may be in love with Nina yourself!

DARRELL—(*astonished*) The deuce you do! What in the devil makes you think that? Not that any man mightn't fall in love with Nina. Most of them do. But I didn't happen to. And what's more I never could. In my mind she always belongs to Gordon. It's probably a reflection of her own silly fixed idea about him. (*suddenly, dryly and harshly*) And I couldn't share a woman—even with a ghost! (*thinking cynically*)

> Not to mention the living who have had her! . . . Sam doesn't know about them . . . and I'll bet he couldn't believe it of her even if she confessed! . . .

MARSDEN—(*thinking baffledly*)

> Wrong again! . . . he isn't lying . . . but I feel he's hiding something . . . why does he speak so resentfully of Gordon's memory? . . . why do I sympathize? . . .

(*in a strange mocking ironic tone*) I can quite appreciate your feeling about Gordon. I wouldn't care to share with a ghost-lover myself. That species of dead is so invulnerably alive! Even a doctor couldn't kill one, eh? (*He forces a laugh—then in a friendly confidential tone*) Gordon is too egregious for a ghost. That was the way Nina's father felt about him, too. (*suddenly reminded of the dead man—in penitently sad tones*). You didn't know her father, did you? A charming old fellow!

DARRELL—(*hearing a noise from the hall—warningly*) Sstt! (*Nina enters slowly. She looks from one to the other with a queer, quick, inquisitive stare, but her face is a pale expressionless mask drained of all emotional response to human contacts. It is as if her eyes were acting on their own account as restless, prying, recording instruments. The two men have risen and stare at her anxiously. Darrell moves back and to one side until he is standing in relatively the same place as Marsden had occupied in the previous scene while Marsden is in her father's place and she stops where she had been. There is a pause. Then just as each of the men is about to speak, she answers as if they had asked a question.*)

NINA—(*in a queer flat voice*) Yes, he's dead—my father—whose passion created me—who began me—he is ended. There is only his end living—his death. It lives now to draw nearer me, to draw me nearer, to become my end! (*then with a strange twisted smile*) How we poor monkeys hide from ourselves behind the sounds called words!

MARSDEN—(*thinking frightenedly*)
            How terrible she is! . . . who is she? . . . not my
        Nina! . . .
(*as if to reassure himself—timidly*) Nina! (*Darrell makes an impatient gesture for him to let her go on. What she is saying interests him and he feels talking it out will do her good. She looks at Marsden for a moment startledly as if she couldn't recognize him.*)

NINA—What? (*then placing him—with real affection that is like a galling goad to him*) Dear old Charlie!

MARSDEN—
            Dear damned Charlie! . . . She loves to torture! . . .
(*then forcing a smile—soothingly*) Yes, Nina Cara Nina! Right here!

NINA—(*forcing a smile*) You look frightened, Charlie. Do

I seem queer? It's because I've suddenly seen the lies in the sounds called words. You know—grief, sorrow, love, father —those sounds our lips make and our hands write. You ought to know what I mean. You work with them. Have you written another novel lately? But, stop to think, you're just the one who couldn't know what I mean. With you the lies have become the only truthful things. And I suppose that's the logical conclusion to the whole evasive mess, isn't it? Do you understand me, Charlie? Say lie— (*She says it, drawing it out.*) L-i-i-e! Now say life. L-i-i-f-e! You see! Life is just a long drawn out lie with a sniffling sigh at the end! (*She laughs.*)

MARSDEN—(*in strange agony*)

> She's hard! . . . like a whore! . . . tearing your heart with dirty finger nails! . . . my Nina! . . . cruel bitch! . . . some day I won't bear it! . . . I'll scream out the truth about every woman! . . . no kinder at heart than dollar tarts! . . .

(*then in a passion of remorse*)

> Forgive me, Mother! . . . I didn't mean all! . . .

DARRELL—(*a bit worried himself now—persuasively*) Why not sit down, Nina, and let us two gentlemen sit down?

NINA—(*smiling at him swiftly and mechanically*) Oh, all right, Ned. (*She sits at center. He comes and sits on the bench. Marsden sits by the table. She continues sarcastically.*) Are you prescribing for me again, Ned? This is my pet doctor, Charlie. He couldn't be happy in heaven unless God called him in because He'd caught something! Did you ever know a young scientist, Charlie? He believes if you pick a lie to pieces, the pieces are the truth! I like him because he's so inhuman. But once he kissed me—in a moment of carnal weakness! I was as startled as if a mummy had done it! And then he looked so disgusted with himself! I had to laugh! (*She smiles at him with a pitying scorn.*)

DARRELL—(*good-naturedly smiling*) That's right! Rub it in! (*ruffled but amused in spite of it*)

> I'd forgotten about that kiss . . . I was sore at myself afterwards . . . she was so damned indifferent! . . .

NINA—(*wanderingly*) Do you know what I was doing up-stairs? I was trying to pray. I tried hard to pray to the modern science God. I thought of a million light years to a spiral nebula—one other universe among innumerable others. But how could that God care about our trifling misery of death-born-of-birth? I couldn't believe in Him, and I wouldn't if I could! I'd rather imitate His indifference and prove I had that one trait at least in common!

MARSDEN—(*worriedly*) Nina, why don't you lie down?

NINA—(*jeeringly*) Oh, let me talk, Charlie! They're only words, remember! So many many words have jammed up into thoughts in my poor head! You'd better let them over-flow or they'll burst the dam! I wanted to believe in any God at any price—a heap of stones, a mud image, a drawing on a wall, a bird, a fish, a snake, a baboon—or even a good man preaching the simple platitudes of truth, those Gospel words we love the sound of but whose meaning we pass on to spooks to live by!

MARSDEN—(*again—half-rising—frightenedly*) Nina! You ought to stop talking. You'll work yourself into— (*He glances angrily at Darrell as if demanding that, as a doctor, he do some-thing.*)

NINA—(*with bitter hopelessness*) Oh, all right!

DARRELL—(*answering his look—thinking*)

> You poor fool! . . . it'll do her good to talk this out of her system . . . and then it'll be up to you to bring her around to Sam . . .

(*starts toward the door*) Think I'll go out and stretch my legs.

MARSDEN—(*thinking—in a panic*)

> I don't want to be alone with her! . . . I don't know her! . . . I'm afraid! . . .

(*protestingly*) Well—but—hold on—I'm sure Nina would rather—

NINA—(*dully*) Let him go. I've said everything I can ever say—to him. I want to talk to you, Charlie. (*Darrell goes out noiselessly with a meaning look at Marsden—a pause.*)

MARSDEN—(*thinking tremblingly*)

> Here . . . now . . . what I hoped . . . she and I alone . . . she will cry . . . I will comfort her . . . why am I so afraid? . . . whom do I fear? . . . is it she? . . . or I? . . .

NINA—(*suddenly, with pity yet with scorn*) Why have you

always been so timid, Charlie? Why are you always afraid? What are you afraid of?

MARSDEN—(*thinking in a panic*)

She sneaked into my soul to spy! . . .

(*then boldly*)

Well then, a little truth for once in a way! . . .

(*timidly*) I'm afraid of—of life, Nina.

NINA—(*nodding slowly*) I know. (*after a pause—queerly*) The mistake began when God was created in a male image. Of course, women would see Him that way, but men should have been gentlemen enough, remembering their mothers, to make God a woman! But the God of Gods—the Boss—has always been a man. That makes life so perverted, and death so unnatural. We should have imagined life as created in the birth-pain of God the Mother. Then we would understand why we, Her children, have inherited pain, for we would know that our life's rhythm beats from Her great heart, torn with the agony of love and birth. And we would feel that death meant reunion with Her, a passing back into Her substance, blood of Her blood again, peace of Her peace! (*Marsden has been listening to her fascinatedly. She gives a strange little laugh.*) Now wouldn't that be more logical and satisfying than having God a male whose chest thunders with egotism and is too hard for tired heads and thoroughly comfortless? Wouldn't it, Charlie?

MARSDEN—(*with a strange passionate eagerness*) Yes! It would, indeed! It would, Nina!

NINA—(*suddenly jumping to her feet and going to him—with a horrible moaning desolation*) Oh, God, Charlie, I want to believe in something! I want to believe so I can feel! I want to feel that he is dead—my father! And I can't feel anything, Charlie! I can't feel anything at all! (*She throws herself on her knees beside him and hides her face in her hands on his knees and begins to sob—stifled torn sounds.*)

MARSDEN—(*bends down, pats her head with trembling hands, soothes her with uncertain trembling words*) There— there—don't—Nina, please—don't cry—you'll make yourself sick—come now—get up—do! (*His hands grasping her arms he half raises her to her feet, but, her face still hidden in her hands, sobbing, she slips on to his lap like a little girl and hides*) *her face on his shoulder. His expression becomes transported with a great happiness. In an ecstatic whisper)*

As I dreamed . . . with a deeper sweetness! . . .

(He kisses her hair with a great reverence.)

There . . . this is all my desire . . . I am this kind of lover . . . this is my love . . . she is my girl . . . not woman . . . my little girl . . . and I am brave because of her little girl's pure love . . . and I am proud . . . no more afraid . . . no more ashamed of being pure! . . .

(He kisses her hair again tenderly and smiles at himself. Then soothingly with a teasing incongruous gaiety) This will never do, Nina Cara Nina—never, never do, you know—I can't permit it!

NINA—*(in a muffled voice, her sobbing beginning to ebb away into sighs—in a young girl's voice)* Oh, Charlie, you're so kind and comforting! I've wanted you so!

MARSDEN—*(immediately disturbed)*

Wanted? . . . wanted? . . . not that kind of wanted . . . can she mean? . . .

(questioning hesitatingly) You've wanted me, Nina?

NINA—Yes,—awfully! I've been so homesick. I've wanted to run home and 'fess up, tell how bad I've been, and be punished! Oh, I've got to be punished, Charlie, out of mercy for me, so I can forgive myself! And now Father dead, there's only you. You will, won't you—or tell me how to punish myself? You've simply got to, if you love me!

MARSDEN—*(thinking intensely)*

If I love her! . . . oh, I do love her! . . .

(eagerly) Anything you wish, Nina—anything!

NINA—*(with a comforted smile, closing her eyes and cuddling up against him)* I knew you would. Dear old Charlie! *(as he gives a wincing start)* What is it? *(She looks up into his face.)*

MARSDEN—*(forcing a smile—ironically)* Twinge—rheumatics—getting old, Nina. *(thinking with wild agony)*

Dear old Charlie! . . . descended again into hell! . . .

(then in a flat voice) What do you want to be punished for, Nina?

NINA—*(in a strange, far-away tone, looking up not at him but at the ceiling)* For playing the silly slut, Charlie. For giving my cool clean body to men with hot hands and greedy eyes which they called love! Ugh! (*A shiver runs over her body.*)

MARSDEN—(*thinking with sudden agony*)

   Then she did! . . . the little filth! . . .

(*in his flat voice*) You mean you— (*then pleadingly*) But not— Darrell?

NINA—(*with simple surprise*) Ned? No, how could I? The war hadn't maimed him. There would have been no point in that. But I did with others—oh, four or five or six or seven men, Charlie. I forget—and it doesn't matter. They were all the same. Count them all as one, and that one a ghost of nothing. That is, to me. They were important to themselves, if I remember rightly. But I forget.

MARSDEN—(*thinking in agony*)

   But why? . . . the dirty little trollop! . . . why? . . .

(*in his flat voice*) Why did you do this, Nina?

NINA—(*with a sad little laugh*) God knows, Charlie! Perhaps I knew at the time but I've forgotten. It's all mixed up. There was a desire to be kind. But it's horribly hard to give anything, and frightful to receive! And to give love—oneself—not in this world! And men are difficult to please, Charlie. I seemed to feel Gordon standing against a wall with eyes bandaged and these men were a firing squad whose eyes were also bandaged—and only I could see! No, I was the blindest! I would not see! I knew it was a stupid, morbid business, that I was more maimed than they were, really, that the war had blown my heart and insides out! And I knew too that I was torturing these tortured men, morbidly super-sensitive already, that they loathed the cruel mockery of my gift! Yet I kept on, from one to one, like a stupid, driven animal until one night not long ago I had a dream of Gordon diving down out of the sky in flames and he looked at me with such sad burning eyes, and all my poor maimed men, too, seemed staring out of his eyes with a burning pain, and I woke up crying, my own eyes burning. Then I saw what a fool I'd been—a guilty fool! So be kind and punish me!

MARSDEN—(*thinking with bitter confusion*)

   I wish she hadn't told me this . . . it has upset me terribly! . . . I positively must run home at once . . . Mother is waiting up . . . oh, how I'd love to hate

this little whore! . . . then I could punish! . . . I wish her father were alive . . . "now he's dead there's only you," she said . . . "I've wanted you," . . .
(with intense bitterness)
Dear old Father Charlie now! . . . ha! . . . that's how she wants me! . . .
(then suddenly in a matter-of-fact tone that is mockingly like her father's) Then, under the circumstances, having weighed the pros and cons, so to speak, I should say that decidedly the most desirable course—

NINA—*(drowsily—her eyes shut)* You sound so like Father, Charlie.

MARSDEN—*(in the tone like her father's)* —is for you to marry that young Evans. He is a splendid chap, clean and boyish, with real stuff in him, too, to make a career for himself if he finds a helpmeet who will inspire him to his best efforts and bring his latent ability to the surface.

NINA—*(drowsily)* Sam is a nice boy. Yes, it would be a career for me to bring a career to his surface. I would be busy—surface life—no more depths, please God! But I don't love him, Father.

MARSDEN—*(blandly—in the tone like her father's)* But you like him, Nina. And he loves you devotedly. And it's time you were having children—and when children come, love comes, you know.

NINA—*(drowsily)* I want children. I must become a mother so I can give myself. I am sick of sickness.

MARSDEN—*(briskly)* Then it's all settled?

NINA—*(drowsily)* Yes. *(very sleepily)* Thank you, Father. You've been so kind. You've let me off too easily. I don't feel as if you'd punished me hardly at all. But I'll never, never do it again, I promise—never, never!— *(She falls asleep and gives a soft little snore.)*

MARSDEN—*(still in her father's tones—very paternally—looking down)* She's had a hard day of it, poor child! I'll carry her up to her room. *(He rises to his feet with Nina sleeping peacefully in his arms. At this moment Sam Evans enters from the right with the package of medicine in his hand.)*

EVANS—*(grinning respectfully)* Here's the— *(as he sees Nina)* Oh! *(then excitedly)* Did she faint?

MARSDEN—(*smiling kindly at Evans*—*still in her father's tones*) Sssh! She's asleep. She cried and then she fell asleep—like a little girl. (*then benignantly*) But first we spoke a word about you, Evans, and I'm sure you have every reason to hope.

EVANS—(*overcome, his eyes on his shuffling feet and twiddling cap*) Thanks— I—I really don't know how to thank—

MARSDEN—(*going to door*—*in his own voice now*) I've got to go home. My mother is waiting up for me. I'll just carry Nina upstairs and put her on her bed and throw something over her.

EVANS—Can't I help you, Mr. Marsden?

MARSDEN—(*dully*) No. I cannot help myself. (*As Evans looks puzzled and startled he adds with an ironical, self-mocking geniality*) You'd better call me just Charlie after this. (*He smiles bitterly to himself as he goes out.*)

EVANS—(*looks after him for a moment*—*then cannot restrain a joyful, coltish caper*—*gleefully*) Good egg! Good old Charlie! (*As if he had heard or guessed, Marsden's bitter laugh comes back from the end of the hallway.*)

(*Curtain*)

ACT THREE

SCENE—*Seven months or so later—the dining room of the Evans' homestead in northern New York state—about nine o'clock in the morning of a day in late spring of the following year.*

The room is one of those big, misproportioned dining rooms that are found in the large, jigsaw country houses scattered around the country as a result of the rural taste for grandeur in the eighties. There is a cumbersome hanging lamp suspended from chains over the exact center of the ugly table with its set of straight-backed chairs set back at spaced intervals against the walls. The wall paper, a repulsive brown, is stained at the ceiling line with damp blotches of mildew, and here and there has started to peel back where the strips join. The floor is carpeted in a smeary brown with a dark red design blurred into it. In the left wall is one window with starched white curtains looking out on a covered side porch, so that no sunlight ever gets to this room and the light from the window, although it is a beautiful warm day in the flower garden beyond the porch, is cheerless and sickly. There is a door in the rear, to left of center, that leads to a hall opening on the same porch. To the right of door a heavy sideboard, a part of the set, displaying some "company" china and glassware. In the right wall, a door leading to the kitchen.

Nina is seated at the foot of the table, her back to the window, writing a letter. Her whole personality seems changed, her face has a contented expression, there is an inner calm about her. And her personal appearance has changed in kind, her face and figure have filled out, she is prettier in a conventional way and less striking and unusual; nothing remains of the strange fascination of her face except her unchangeably mysterious eyes.

NINA—(*reading what she has just written over to herself*)

It's a queer house, Ned. There is something wrong with its psyche, I'm sure. Therefore you'd simply adore it. It's a hideous old place, a faded gingerbread with orange fixin's and numerous lightning rods. Around it are acres and acres of apple trees in full bloom, all white and pinkish and beautiful, like brides just tripping out of church with the bridegroom, Spring, by the arm.

Which reminds me, Ned, that it's over six months since Sam and I were married and we haven't seen hide nor hair of you since the ceremony. Do you think that is any nice way to act? You might at least drop me a line. But I'm only joking. I know how busy you must be now that you've got the chance you've always wanted to do research work. Did you get our joint letter of congratulation written after we read of your appointment?

But to get back to this house. I feel it has lost its soul and grown resigned to doing without it. It isn't haunted by anything at all—and ghosts of some sort are the only normal life a house has—like our minds, you know. So although last evening when we got here at first I said "obviously haunted" to myself, now that I've spent one night in it I know that whatever spooks there may once have been have packed up their manifestations a long time ago and drifted away over the grass, wisps of mist between the apple trees, without one backward glance of regret or recollection. It's incredible to think Sam was born and spent his childhood here. I'm glad he doesn't show it! We slept last night in the room he was born in. Or rather he slept, I couldn't. I lay awake and found it difficult to breathe, as if all the life in the air had long since been exhausted in keeping the dying living a little longer. It was hard to believe anyone had ever been born alive there. I know you're saying crossly "She's still morbid" but I'm not. I've never been more normal. I feel contented and placid.

(*looking up from the letter, thinking embarrassedly*)

Should I have told him? . . . no . . . my own secret . . . tell no one . . . not even Sam . . . why haven't I told Sam? . . . it'd do him so much good . . . he'd feel so proud of himself, poor dear . . . no . . . I want to keep it just my baby . . . only mine . . . as long as I can . . . and it will be time enough to let Ned know when I go to New York . . . he can suggest a good obstetrician . . . how delighted he'll be when he hears! . . . he always said it would be the best thing for me . . . well, I do feel happy when I think . . . and I love Sam now . . . in a way . . . it will be his baby too . . .

(*then with a happy sigh, turns back to letter*)

But speaking of Sam's birth, you really must meet his mother sometime. It's amazing how little she is like him, a strange woman from the bit I saw of her last night. She has been writing Sam regularly once a week ever since she's known we were married, the most urgent invitations to visit her. They were really more like commands, or prayers. I suspect she is terribly lonely all by herself in this big house. Sam's feeling toward her puzzles me. I don't believe he ever mentioned her until her letters began coming or that he'd ever have come to see the poor woman if I hadn't insisted. His attitude rather shocked me. It was just as though he'd forgotten he had a mother. And yet as soon as he saw her he was sweet enough. She seemed dreadfully upset to see Charlie with us, until we'd explained it was thanks to his kindness and in his car we were taking this deferred honeymoon. Charlie's like a fussy old woman about his car, he's afraid to let Sam or me drive it—

MARSDEN—(*enters from the rear. He is spruce, dressed immaculately, his face a bit tired and resigned, but smiling kindly. He has a letter in his hand.*) Good morning. (*She gives a start and instinctively covers the letter with her hand.*)

NINA—Good morning. (*thinking amusedly*)

If he knew what I'd just written . . . poor old Charlie! . . .

(*then indicating the letter he carries*) I see you're an early correspondent, too.

MARSDEN—(*with sudden jealous suspicion*)

Why did she cover it up like that? . . . whom is she writing to? . . .

(*coming toward her*) Just a line to Mother to let her know we've not all been murdered by rum-bandits. You know how she worries.

NINA—(*thinking with a trace of pitying contempt*)

Apron strings . . . still his devotion to her is touching

> . . . I hope if mine is a boy he will love me as much
> . . . oh, I hope it is a boy . . . healthy and strong
> and beautiful . . . like Gordon! . . .

(*then suddenly sensing Marsden's curiosity—perfunctorily*) I'm
writing to Ned Darrell. I've owed him one for ages. (*She folds
it up and puts it aside.*)

MARSDEN—(*thinking glumly*)

> I thought she'd forgotten him . . . still I suppose it's
> just friendly . . . and it's none of my business now
> she's married. . . .

(*perfunctorily*) How did you sleep?

NINA—Not a wink. I had the strangest feeling.

MARSDEN—Sleeping in a strange bed, I suppose. (*jokingly*) Did you see any ghosts?

NINA—(*with a sad smile*) No, I got the feeling the ghosts
had all deserted the house and left it without a soul—as the
dead so often leave the living—(*she forces a little laugh*) if you
get what I mean.

MARSDEN—(*thinking worriedly*)

> Slipping back into that morbid tone . . . first time in
> a long while . . .

(*teasingly*) Hello! Do I hear graveyards yawning from their
sleep—and yet I observe it's a gorgeous morning without,
the flowers are flowering, the trees are treeing with one another, and you, if I mistake not, are on your honeymoon!

NINA—(*immediately gaily mocking*) Oh, very well, old
thing! "God's in his heaven, all's right with the world!" And
Pippa's cured of the pip! (*She dances up to him.*)

MARSDEN—(*gallantly*) Pippa is certainly a pippin this
morning!

NINA—(*kisses him quickly*) You deserve one for that! All I
meant was that ghosts remind me of men's smart crack about
women, you can't live with them and can't live without them.
(*stands still and looks at him teasingly*) But there you stand
proving me a liar by every breath you draw! You're ghostless
and womanless—and as sleek and satisfied as a pet seal! (*She
sticks out her tongue at him and makes a face of superior scorn.*)
Bah! That for you, 'Fraid-cat Charlie, you slacker bachelor!
(*She runs to the kitchen door.*) I'm going to bum some more
coffee! How about you?

MARSDEN—(*with a forced smile*) No, thank you. (*She disappears into the kitchen. Thinking with bitter pain*)

Ghostless! . . . if she only knew . . . that joking tone hides her real contempt! . . .

(*self-mockingly*)

"But when the girls began to play 'Fraid-cat Charlie ran away!"

(*then rallying himself*)

Bosh! . . . I haven't had such thoughts . . . not since their marriage . . . happy in her happiness . . . but is she happy? . . . in the first few months she was obviously playing a part . . . kissed him too much . . . as if she'd determined to make herself a loving wife . . . and then all of a sudden she became contented . . . her face filled out . . . her eyes lazily examined peace . . . pregnant . . . yes, she must be . . . I hope so. . . . why? . . . for her sake . . . my own, too . . . when she has a child I know I can entirely accept . . . forget I have lost her . . . lost her? . . . silly ass! . . . how can you lose what you never possessed? . . . except in dreams! . . .

(*shaking his head exasperatedly*)

Round and round . . . thoughts . . . damn pests! . . . mosquitoes of the soul . . . whine, sting, suck one's blood . . . why did I invite Nina and Sam on this tour . . . it's a business trip with me, really . . . I need a new setting for my next novel . . . "Mr. Marsden departs a bit from his familiar field" . . . well, there they were stuck in the Professor's house . . . couldn't afford a vacation . . . never had a honeymoon . . . I've pretended to be done up every night so they could . . . I've gone to bed right after dinner so they could be alone and . . . I wonder if she can really like him . . . that way? . . .

(*The sound of Evans' voice and his mother's is heard from the garden. Marsden goes over and carefully peers out.*)

Sam with his mother . . . peculiar woman . . . strong . . . good character for a novel . . . no, she's too somber . . . her eyes are the saddest . . . and, at the same time, the grimmest . . . they're coming in . . .

I'll drive around the country a bit . . . give them a chance for a family conference . . . discuss Nina's pregnancy, I suppose . . . does Sam know? . . . he gives no indication . . . why do wives hide it from their husbands? . . . ancient shame . . . guilty of continuing life, of bringing fresh pain into the world . . .

(*He goes out, rear. The outside door in the hall is heard being opened and Evans and his mother evidently meet Marsden as he is about to go out. Their voices, his voice explaining, are heard, then the outer door being opened and shut again as Marsden departs. A moment later Evans and his mother enter the dining room. Sam looks timorously happy, as if he could not quite believe in his good fortune and had constantly to reassure himself about it, yet he is riding the crest of the wave, he radiates love and devotion and boyish adoration. He is a charming-looking fresh boy now. He wears a sweater and linen knickers, collegiate to the last degree. His mother is a tiny woman with a frail figure, her head and face, framed in iron-gray hair, seeming much too large for her body, so that at first glance she gives one the impression of a wonderfully made, lifelike doll. She is only about forty-five but she looks at least sixty. Her face with its delicate features must have once been of a romantic, tender, clinging-vine beauty, but what has happened to her has compressed its defenseless curves into planes, its mouth into the thin line around a locked door, its gentle chin has been forced out aggressively by a long reliance on clenched teeth. She is very pale. Her big dark eyes are grim with the prisoner-pain of a walled-in soul. Yet a sweet loving-kindness, the ghost of an old faith and trust in life's goodness, hovers girlishly, fleetingly, about the corners of her mouth and softens into deep sorrow the shadowy grimness of her eyes. Her voice jumps startlingly in tone from a caressing gentleness to a blunted flat assertiveness, as if what she said then was merely a voice on its own without human emotion to inspire it.*)

EVANS—(*as they come in—rattling on in the cocksure boastful way of a boy showing off his prowess before his mother, confident of thrilled adulation*) In a few years you won't have to worry one way or another about the darned old apple crop. I'll be able to take care of you then. Wait and see! Of course, I'm not making so much now. I couldn't expect to. I've only just started. But I'm making good, all right, all right—since I got married—and it's only a question of time when— Why, to show you, Cole—he's the manager and the best egg ever— called me into his office and told me he'd had his eye on me, that my stuff was exactly what they wanted, and he thought I had the makings of a real find. (*proudly*) How's that? That's certainly fair enough, isn't it?

MRS. EVANS—(*vaguely—she has evidently not heard much of what he said*) That's fine, Sammy. (*thinking apprehensively*)

> I do hope I'm wrong! . . . but that old shiver of dread took me the minute she stepped in the door! . . . I don't think she's told Sammy but I got to make sure. . . .

EVANS—(*seeing her preoccupation now—deeply hurt—testily*) I'll bet you didn't hear a word I said! Are you still worrying about how the darn old apples are going to turn out?

MRS. EVANS—(*with a guilty start—protestingly*) Yes, I did hear you, Sammy—every word! That's just what I was thinking about—how proud I am you're doing so wonderful well!

EVANS—(*mollified but still grumbling*) You'd never guess it from the gloomy way you looked! (*but encouraged to go on*) And Cole asked me if I was married—seemed to take a real personal interest—said he was glad to hear it because marriage was what put the right kind of ambition into a fellow— unselfish ambition—working for his wife and not just himself— (*then embarrassedly*) He even asked me if we were expecting an addition to the family.

MRS. EVANS—(*seeing this is her chance—quickly—forcing a smile*) I've been meaning to ask you that myself, Sammy. (*blurts out apprehensively*) She—Nina—she isn't going to have a baby, is she?

EVANS—(*with an indefinable guilty air—as if he were reluctant to admit it*) I—why—you mean, is she now? I don't think so, Mother. (*He strolls over to the window whistling with an exaggeratedly casual air, and looks out.*)

MRS. EVANS—(*thinking with grim relief*)

> He don't know . . . there's that much to be thankful for, anyway. . . .

EVANS—(*thinking with intense longing*)

> If that'd only happen! . . . soon! . . . Nina's begun to love me . . . a little . . . I've felt it the last two

months . . . God, it's made me happy! . . . before
that she didn't . . . only liked me . . . that was all
I asked . . . never dared hope she'd come to love
me . . . even a little . . . so soon . . . sometimes I
feel it's too good to be true . . . don't deserve it . . .
and now . . . if that'd happen . . . then I'd feel sure
. . . it'd be there . . . half Nina, half me . . . living
proof! . . .

(*then an apprehensive note creeping in*)

And I know she wants a baby so much . . . one
reason why she married me . . . and I know she's
felt right along that then she'd love me . . . really love
me . . .

(*gloomily*)

I wonder why . . . ought to have happened before
this . . . hope it's nothing wrong . . . with me! . . .
(*He starts, flinging off this thought—then suddenly clutching at
a straw, turns hopefully to his mother.*) Why did you ask me
that, Mother? D'you think—?

MRS. EVANS—(*hastily*) No, indeed! I don't think she is! I
wouldn't say so at all!

EVANS—(*dejectedly*) Oh—I thought perhaps— (*then
changing the subject*) I suppose I ought to go up and say hello
to Aunt Bessie.

MRS. EVANS—(*her face becoming defensive—in blunted
tones, a trifle pleadingly*) I wouldn't, Sammy. She hasn't seen
you since you were eight. She wouldn't know you. And
you're on your honeymoon, and old age is always sad to
young folks. Be happy while you can! (*then pushing him toward door*) Look here! You catch that friend, he's just getting
his car out. You drive to town with him, give me a chance to
get to know my daughter-in-law, and call her to account for
how she's taking care of you! (*She laughs forcedly.*)

EVANS—(*bursting out passionately*) Better than I deserve!
She's an angel, Mother! I know you'll love her!

MRS. EVANS—(*gently*) I do already, Sammy! She's so
pretty and sweet!

EVANS—(*kisses her—joyously*) I'll tell her that. I'm going
out this way and kiss her good-bye. (*He runs out through the
kitchen door.*)

MRS. EVANS—(*looking after him—passionately*)
   He loves her! . . . he's happy! . . . that's all that
   counts! . . . being happy! . . .
(*thinking apprehensively*)
   If only she isn't going to have a baby . . . if only she
   doesn't care so much about having one . . . I got to
   have it out with her . . . got to! . . . no other way
   . . . in mercy . . . in justice . . . this has got to end
   with my boy . . . and he's got to live happy! . . .
(*At the sound of steps from the kitchen she straightens up in her
chair stiffly.*)
  NINA—(*comes in from the kitchen, a cup of coffee in her hand,
smiling happily*) Good morning—(*she hesitates—then shyly*)
Mother. (*She comes over and kisses her—slips down and sits on
the floor beside her.*)
  MRS. EVANS—(*flusteredly—hurriedly*) Good morning! It's
a real fine day, isn't it? I ought to have been here and got
your breakfast, but I was out gallivanting round the place
with Sammy. I hope you found everything you wanted.
  NINA—Indeed I did! And I ate so much I'm ashamed of
myself! (*She nods at the cup of coffee and laughs.*) See. I'm still
at it.
  MRS. EVANS—Good for you!
  NINA—I ought to apologize for coming down so late. Sam
should have called me. But I wasn't able to get to sleep until
after daylight somehow.
  MRS. EVANS—(*strangely*) You couldn't sleep? Why? Did
you feel anything funny—about this house?
  NINA—(*struck by her tone—looks up*) No. Why? (*thinking*)
   How her face changes! . . . what sad eyes! . . .
  MRS. EVANS—(*thinking in an agony of apprehension*)
   Got to start in to tell her . . . got to . . .
  NINA—(*apprehensive herself now*)
   That sick dead feeling . . . when something is going
   to happen . . . I felt it before I got the cable about
   Gordon . . .
(*then taking a sip of coffee, and trying to be pleasantly casual*)
Sam said you wanted to talk to me.
  MRS. EVANS—(*dully*) Yes. You love my boy, don't
you?

NINA—(*startled—forcing a smile, quickly*) Why, of course! (*reassuring herself*)

> No, it isn't a lie . . . I do love him . . . the father of my baby . . .

MRS. EVANS—(*blurts out*) Are you going to have a baby, Nina?

NINA—(*She presses Mrs. Evans' hand—simply*) Yes, Mother.

MRS. EVANS—(*in her blunt flat tones—with a mechanical rapidity to her words*) Don't you think it's too soon? Don't you think you better wait until Sammy's making more money? Don't you think it'll be a drag on him and you? Why don't you just go on being happy together, just you two?

NINA—(*thinking frightenedly*)

> What is behind what she's saying? . . . that feeling of death again! . . .

(*moving away from her—repulsed*) No, I don't think any of those things, Mrs. Evans. I want a baby—beyond everything! We both do!

MRS. EVANS—(*hopelessly*) I know. (*then grimly*) But you can't! You've got to make up your mind you can't! (*thinking fiercely—even with satisfaction*)

> Tell her! . . . make her suffer what I was made to suffer! . . . I've been too lonely! . . .

NINA—(*thinking with terrified foreboding*)

> I knew it! . . . Out of a blue sky . . . black! . . .

(*springing to her feet—bewilderedly*) What do you mean? How can you say a thing like that?

MRS. EVANS—(*reaching out her hand tenderly, trying to touch Nina*) It's because I want Sammy—and you, too, child—to be happy. (*then as Nina shrinks away from her hand—in her blunted tones*) You just can't.

NINA—(*defiantly*) But I can! I have already! I mean—I am, didn't you understand me?

MRS. EVANS—(*gently*) I know it's hard. (*then inexorably*) But you can't go on!

NINA—(*violently*) I don't believe you know what you're saying! It's too terrible for you—Sam's own mother—how would you have felt if someone—when you were going to have Sam—came to you and said—?

MRS. EVANS—(*thinking fiercely*)

Now's my chance! . . .

(*tonelessly*) They did say it! Sam's own father did—my husband! And I said it to myself! And I did all I could, all my husband could think of, so's I wouldn't—but we didn't know enough. And right to the time the pains come on, I prayed Sammy'd be born dead, and Sammy's father prayed, but Sammy was born healthy and smiling, and we just had to love him, and live in fear. He doubled the torment of fear we lived in. And that's what you'd be in for. And Sammy, he'd go the way his father went. And your baby, you'd be bringing it into torment. (*a bit violently*) I tell you it'd be a crime—a crime worse than murder! (*then recovering—commiseratingly*) So you just can't, Nina!

NINA—(*who has been listening distractedly—thinking*)
> Don't listen to her! . . . feeling of death! . . . what is
> it? . . . she's trying to kill my baby! . . . oh, I hate
> her! . . .

(*hysterically resentful*) What do you mean? Why don't you speak plainly? (*violently*) I think you're horrible! Praying your baby would be born dead! That's a lie! You couldn't!

MRS. EVANS—(*thinking*)
> I know what she's doing now . . . just what I did
> . . . trying not to believe . . .

(*fiercely*)
> But I'll make her! . . . she's got to suffer, too! . . . I
> been too lonely! . . . she's got to share and help me
> save my Sammy! . . .

(*with an even more blunted flat relentless tonelessness*) I thought I was plain, but I'll be plainer. Only remember it's a family secret, and now you're one of the family. It's the curse on the Evanses. My husband's mother—she was an only child— died in an asylum and her father before her. I know that for a fact. And my husband's sister, Sammy's aunt, she's out of her mind. She lives on the top floor of this house, hasn't been out of her room in years, I've taken care of her. She just sits, doesn't say a word, but she's happy, she laughs to herself a lot, she hasn't a care in the world. But I remember when she was all right, she was always unhappy, she never got married, most people around here were afraid of the Evanses in spite of their being rich for hereabouts. They knew about the craziness going back, I guess, for heaven knows how long. I didn't know about the Evanses until after I'd married my husband. He came to the town I lived in, no one there knew about the Evanses. He didn't tell me until after we were married. He asked me to forgive him, he said he loved me so much he'd have gone mad without me, said I was his only hope of salvation. So I forgave him. I loved him an awful lot. I said to myself, I'll be his salvation—and maybe I could have been if we hadn't had Sammy born. My husband kept real well up to then. We'd swore we'd never have children, we never forgot to be careful for two whole years. Then one night we'd both gone to a dance, we'd both had a little punch to drink, just enough—to forget—driving home in the moonlight—that moonlight!—such little things at the back of big things!

NINA—(*in a dull moan*) I don't believe you! I won't believe you!

MRS. EVANS—(*drones on*) My husband, Sammy's father, in spite of all he and I fought against it, he finally gave in to it when Sammy was only eight, he couldn't keep up any more living in fear for Sammy, thinking any minute the curse might get him, every time he was sick, or had a headache, or bumped his head, or started crying, or had a nightmare and screamed, or said something queer like children do naturally. (*a bit stridently*) Living like that with that fear is awful torment! I know that! I went through it by his side! It nearly drove me crazy, too—but I didn't have it in my blood! And that's why I'm telling you! You got to see you can't, Nina!

NINA—(*suddenly breaking out—frenziedly*) I don't believe you! I don't believe Sam would ever have married me if he knew—

MRS. EVANS—(*sharply*) Who said Sammy knew? He don't know a single thing about it! That's been the work of my life, keeping him from knowing. When his father gave up and went off into it I sent Sammy right off to boarding school. I told him his father was sick, and a little while after I sent word his father was dead, and from then on until his father did really die during Sammy's second year to college, I kept him away at school in winter and camp in summers and I went to see him, I never let him come home. (*with a sigh*) It was hard, giving up Sammy, knowing I was making him forget he had a mother. I was glad taking care of them two kept me so busy I didn't get much chance to think then. But here's what I've come to think since, Nina: I'm certain sure my husband might have kept his mind with the help of my love if I hadn't had Sammy. And if I'd never had Sammy I'd never have loved Sammy—or missed him, would I?—and I'd have kept my husband.

NINA—(*not heeding this last—with wild mockery*) And I thought Sam was so normal—so healthy and sane—not like me! I thought he'd give me such healthy, happy children and I'd forget myself in them and learn to love him!

MRS. EVANS—(*horrified, jumping to her feet*) Learn to? You told me you did love Sammy!

NINA—No! Maybe I almost have—lately—but only when I thought of his baby! Now I hate him! (*She begins to weep hysterically. Mrs. Evans goes to her and puts her arms around her. Nina sobs out*) Don't touch me! I hate you, too! Why didn't you tell him he must never marry!

MRS. EVANS—What reason could I give, without telling him everything? And I never heard about you till after you were married. Then I wanted to write to you but I was scared he might read it. And I couldn't leave her upstairs to come away to see you. I kept writing Sammy to bring you here right off, although having him come frightened me to death for fear he might get to suspect something. You got to get him right away from here, Nina! I just kept hoping you wouldn't want children right away—young folks don't nowadays—until I'd seen you and told you everything. And I thought you'd love him like I did his father, and be satisfied with him alone.

NINA—(*lifting her head—wildly*) No! I don't! I won't! I'll leave him!

MRS. EVANS—(*shaking her, fiercely*) You can't! He'd go crazy sure then! You'd be a devil! Don't you see how he loves you?

NINA—(*breaking away from her—harshly*) Well, I don't love him! I only married him because he needed me—and I needed children! And now you tell me I've got to kill my—oh, yes, I see I've got to, you needn't argue any more! I love it too much to make it run that chance! And I hate it too, now, because it's sick, it's not my baby, it's his! (*with terrible ironic bitterness*) And still you can dare to tell me I can't even leave Sam!

MRS. EVANS—(*very sadly and bitterly*) You just said you married him because he needed you. Don't he need you now—more'n ever? But I can't tell you not to leave him, not if you don't love him. But you oughtn't to have married him when you didn't love him. And it'll be your fault, what'll happen.

NINA—(*torturedly*) What will happen?—what do you mean?—Sam will be all right—just as he was before—and it's not my fault anyway!—it's not my fault! (*then thinking conscience-strickenly*)

> Poor Sam . . . she's right . . . it's not his fault . . . it's mine . . . I wanted to use him to save myself . . . I acted the coward again . . . as I did with Gordon. . .

MRS. EVANS—(*grimly*) You know what'll happen to him if you leave him—after all I've told you! (*then breaking into intense pleading*) Oh, I'd get down on my knees to you, don't make my boy run that risk! You got to give one Evans, the last one, a chance to live in this world! And you'll learn to love him, if you give up enough for him! (*then with a grim smile*) Why, I even love that idiot upstairs, I've taken care of her so many years, lived her life for her with my life, you might say. You give your life to Sammy, then you'll love him same as you love yourself. You'll have to! That's sure as death! (*She laughs a queer gentle laugh full of amused bitterness.*)

NINA—(*with a sort of dull stupid wonderment*) And you've found peace?—

MRS. EVANS—(*sardonically*) There's peace in the green fields of Eden, they say! You got to die to find out! (*then proudly*) But I can say I feel proud of having lived fair to them that gave me love and trusted in me!

NINA—(*struck—confusedly*) Yes—that's true, isn't it? (*thinking strangely*)

> Lived fair . . . pride . . . trust . . . play the game! . . . who is speaking to me . . . Gordon! . . . oh, Gordon, do you mean I must give Sam the life I didn't

give you? . . . Sam loved you too . . . he said, if we
have a boy, we'll call him Gordon in Gordon's honor
. . . Gordon's honor! . . . what must I do now in
your honor, Gordon? . . . yes! . . . I know! . . .
(*speaking mechanically in a dull voice*) All right, Mother. I'll
stay with Sam. There's nothing else I can do, is there, when
it isn't his fault, poor boy! (*then suddenly snapping and bursting out in a despairing cry*) But I'll be so lonely! I'll have lost
my baby! (*She sinks down on her knees at Mrs. Evans' feet —
piteously*) Oh, Mother, how can I keep on living?

MRS. EVANS—(*thinking miserably*)

> Now she knows my suffering . . . now I got to help
> her . . . she's got a right to have a baby . . . another
> baby . . . sometime . . . somehow . . . she's giving
> her life to save my Sammy . . . I got to save her! . . .

(*stammeringly*) Maybe, Nina—

NINA—(*dully and resentfully again now*) And how about
Sam? You want him to be happy, don't you? It's just as important for him as it is for me that I should have a baby! If
you know anything at all about him, you ought to see that!

MRS. EVANS—(*sadly*) I know that. I see that in him, Nina.
(*gropingly*) There must be a way—somehow. I remember
when I was carrying Sam, sometimes I'd forget I was a wife,
I'd only remember the child in me. And then I used to wish
I'd gone out deliberate in our first year, without my husband
knowing, and picked a man, a healthy male to breed by,
same's we do with stock, to give the man I loved a healthy
child. And if I didn't love that other man nor him me where
would be the harm? Then God would whisper: "It'd be a sin,
adultery, the worst sin!" But after He'd gone I'd argue back
again to myself, then we'd have a healthy child, I needn't be
afraid! And maybe my husband would feel without ever
knowing how he felt it, that I wasn't afraid and that child
wasn't cursed and so he needn't fear and I could save him.
(*then scornfully*) But I was too afraid of God then to have ever
done it! (*then very simply*) He loved children so, my poor husband did, and the way they took to him, you never saw anything like it, he was a natural born father. And Sammy's the
same.

NINA—(*as from a distance—strangely*) Yes, Sammy's the

same. But I'm not the same as you. (*defiantly*) I don't believe
in God the Father!

MRS. EVANS—(*strangely*) Then it'd be easy for you. (*with
a grim smile*) And I don't believe in Him, neither, not any
more. I used to be a great one for worrying about what's
God and what's devil, but I got richly over it living here with
poor folks that was being punished for no sins of their own,
and me being punished with them for no sin but loving
much. (*with decision*) Being happy, that's the nearest we can
ever come to knowing what's good! Being happy, that's
good! The rest is just talk! (*She pauses—then with a strange
austere sternness*) I love my boy, Sammy. I could see how
much he wants you to have a baby. Sammy's got to feel sure
you love him—to be happy. Whatever you can do to make
him happy is good—is good, Nina! I don't care what! You've
got to have a healthy baby—sometime—so's you can both
be happy! It's your rightful duty!

NINA—(*confusedly—in a half-whisper*) Yes, Mother. (*thinking longingly*)

> I want to be happy! . . . it's my right . . . and my
> duty! . . .

(*then suddenly in guilty agony*)

> Oh, my baby . . . my poor baby . . . I'm forgetting
> you . . . desiring another after you are dead! . . .
> I feel you beating against my heart for mercy . . .
> oh! . . .

(*She weeps with bitter anguish.*)

MRS. EVANS—(*gently and with deep sympathy*) I know what
you're suffering. And I wouldn't say what I just said now only
I know us two mustn't see each other ever again. You and
Sammy have got to forget me. (*as Nina makes a motion of
protest—grimly and inexorably*) Oh, yes, you will—easy. People forget everything. They got to, poor people! And I'm saying what I said about a healthy baby so's you will remember
it when you need to, after you've forgotten—this one.

NINA—(*sobbing pitifully*) Don't! Please, Mother!

MRS. EVANS—(*with sudden tenderness—gathering Nina up
in her arms, brokenly*) You poor child! You're like the daughter
of my sorrow! You're closer to me now than ever Sammy

could be! I want you to be happy! (*She begins to sob, too, kissing Nina's bowed head.*)

(*Curtain*)

ACT FOUR

SCENE—*An evening early in the following winter about seven months later. The Professor's study again. The books in the cases have never been touched, their austere array shows no gaps, but the glass separating them from the world is gray with dust, giving them a blurred ghostly quality. The table, although it is the same, is no longer the Professor's table, just as the other furniture in the room, by its disarrangement, betrays that the Professor's well-ordered mind no longer trims it to his personality. The table has become neurotic. Volumes of the Encyclopedia Britannica mixed up with popular treatises on Mind Training for Success, etc., looking startlingly modern and disturbing against the background of classics in the original, are slapped helter-skelter on top of each other on it. The titles of these books face in all directions, no one volume is placed with any relation to the one beneath it—the effect is that they have no connected meaning. The rest of the table is littered with an ink bottle, pens, pencils, erasers, a box of typewriting paper, and a typewriter at the center before the chair, which is pushed back, setting the rug askew. On the floor beside the table are an overflowing wastepaper basket, a few sheets of paper and the rubber cover for the typewriter like a collapsed tent. The rocking chair is no longer at center but has been pulled nearer the table, directly faces it with its back to the bench. This bench in turn has been drawn much closer, but is now placed more to the rear and half-faces front, its back squarely to the door in the corner.*

Evans is seated in the Professor's old chair. He has evidently been typing, or is about to type, for a sheet of paper can be seen in the machine. He smokes a pipe, which he is always relighting whether it needs it or not, and which he bites and shifts about and pulls in and out and puffs at nervously. His expression is dispirited, his eyes shift about, his shoulders are collapsed submissively. He seems much thinner, his face drawn and sallow. The collegiate clothes are no longer natty, they need pressing and look too big for him.

EVANS—*(turns to his typewriter and pounds out a few words with a sort of aimless desperation—then tears the sheet out of the machine with an exclamation of disgust, crumples it up and*

692

throws it violently on the floor, pushing his chair back and jump-
ing to his feet) Hell! (*He begins pacing up and down the room,*
puffing at his pipe, thinking tormentedly)

> No use . . . can't think of a darn thing . . . well, who
> could dope out a novel ad on another powdered milk,
> anyway? . . . all the stuff been used already . . .
> Tartars conquering on dried mare's milk . . . Metch-
> nikoff, eminent scientist . . . been done to death . . .
> but simply got to work out something or . . . Cole
> said, what's been the matter with you lately? . . . you
> started off so well . . . I thought you were a real find,
> but your work's fallen off to nothing . . .

(*He sits down on the edge of the bench nearby, his shoulders
hunched—despondently*)

> Couldn't deny it . . . been going stale ever since we
> came back from that trip home . . . no ideas . . . I'll
> get fired . . . sterile . . .

(*with a guilty terror*)

> in more ways than one, I guess! . . .

(*He springs to his feet as if this idea were a pin stuck in him—
lighting his already lighted pipe, walks up and down again, forcing his thoughts into other channels.*)

> Bet the old man turns over in his grave at my writing
> ads in his study . . . maybe that's why I can't . . .
> bum influence . . . try tomorrow in my bedroom
> . . . sleeping alone . . . since Nina got sick . . .
> some woman's sickness . . . wouldn't tell me . . . too
> modest . . . still, there are some things a husband has
> a right to know . . . especially when we haven't . . .
> in five months . . . doctor told her she mustn't, she
> said . . . what doctor? . . . she's never said . . . what
> the hell's the matter with you, do you think Nina's
> lying? . . . no . . . but . . .

(*desperately*)

> If I was only sure it was because she's really sick . . .
> not just sick of me! . . .

(*He sinks down in the rocking chair despondently.*)

> Certainly been a big change in her . . . since that visit
> home . . . what happened between Mother and her?
> . . . she says nothing . . . they seemed to like each

other . . . both of them cried when we left . . . still, Nina insisted on going that same day and Mother seemed anxious to get rid of us . . . can't make it out . . . next few weeks Nina couldn't be loving enough . . . I never was so happy . . . then she crashed . . . strain of waiting and hoping she'd get pregnant . . . and nothing happening . . . that's what did it . . . my fault! . . . how d'you know? . . . you can't tell that! . . .

(*He jumps to his feet again—walks up and down again distractedly.*)

God, if we'd only have a kid! . . . then I'd show them all what I could do! . . . Cole always used to say I had the stuff, and Ned certainly thought so. . . .

(*with sudden relieved excitement*)

By gosh, I was forgetting! . . . Ned's coming out tonight . . . forgot to tell Nina . . . mustn't let her get wise I got him to come to look her over . . . she'd hate me for swallowing my pride after he's never been to see us . . . but I had to . . . this has got my goat . . . I've got to know what's wrong . . . and Ned's the only one I can trust . . .

(*He flings himself on chair in front of desk and, picking up a fresh sheet of paper, jams it into the machine.*)

Gosh, I ought to try and get a new start on this before it's time . . .

(*He types a sentence or two, a strained frown of concentration on his face. Nina comes silently through the door and stands just inside it looking at him. She has grown thin again, her face is pale and drawn, her movements are those of extreme nervous tension.*)

NINA—(*before she can stifle her immediate reaction of contempt and dislike*)

How weak he is! . . . he'll never do anything . . . never give me my desire . . . if he'd only fall in love with someone else . . . go away . . . not be here in my father's room . . . I even have to give him a home . . . if he'd disappear . . . leave me free . . . if he'd die . . .

(*checking herself—remorsefully*)

I must stop such thoughts . . . I don't mean it . . . poor Sam! . . . trying so hard . . . loving me so much . . . I give so little in return . . . he feels I'm always watching him with scorn . . . I can't tell him it's with pity . . . how can I help watching him? . . . help worrying over his worry because of what it might lead to . . . after what his mother . . . how horrible life is! . . . he's worried now . . . he doesn't sleep . . . I hear him tossing about . . . I must sleep with him again soon . . . he's only home two nights a week . . . it isn't fair of me . . . I must try . . . I must! . . . he suspects my revulsion . . . it's hurting him . . . oh, poor dead baby I dared not bear, how I might have loved your father for your sake! . . .

EVANS—(*suddenly feeling her presence, jerks himself to his feet—with a diffident guilty air which is noticeable about him now whenever he is in her presence*) Hello, dear. I thought you were lying down. (*guiltily*) Did the noise of my typing bother you? I'm terribly sorry!

NINA—(*irritated in spite of herself*)

Why is he always cringing? . . .

(*She comes forward to the chair at center and sits down—forcing a smile*) But there's nothing to be terribly sorry about! (*As he stands awkward and confused, like a schoolboy who has been called on to recite and cannot and is being "bawled out" before the class, she forces a playful tone.*) Goodness, Sam, how tragic you can get about nothing at all!

EVANS—(*still forced to justify himself—contritely*) I know it isn't pleasant for you having me drag my work out here, trying to pound out rotten ads. (*with a short laugh*) Trying to is right! (*blurts out*) I wouldn't do it except that Cole gave me a warning to buck up—or get out.

NINA—(*stares at him, more annoyed, her eyes hardening, thinking*)

Yes! . . . he'll always be losing one job, getting another, starting with a burst of confidence each time, then . . .

(*cutting him with a careless sneering tone*) Well, it isn't a job to worry much about losing, is it?

EVANS—(*wincing pitiably*) No, not much money. But I

used to think there was a fine chance to rise there—but of course that's my fault, I haven't made good—(*he finishes miserably*) somehow.

NINA—(*her antagonism giving way to remorseful pity*) What makes me so cruel? . . . he's so defenseless . . . his mother's baby . . . poor sick baby! . . . poor Sam! . . .

(*She jumps to her feet and goes over to him.*)

EVANS—(*as she comes—with a defensive, boastful bravery*) Oh, I can get another job just as good, all right—maybe a lot better.

NINA—(*reassuringly*) Certainly, you can! And I'm sure you're not going to lose this one. You're always anticipating trouble. (*She kisses him and sits on the arm of his chair, putting an arm around his neck and pulling his head on to her breast.*) And it isn't your fault, you big goose, you! It's mine. I know how hard it makes everything for you, being tied to a wife who's too sick to be a wife. You ought to have married a big strapping, motherly—

EVANS—(*in the seventh heaven now—passionately*) Bunk! All the other women in the world aren't worth your little finger! It's you who ought to have married someone worth while, not a poor fish like me! But no one could love you more than I do, no matter what he was!

NINA—(*presses his head on her breast, avoiding his eyes, kisses him on the forehead*) And I love you, Sam. (*staring out over his head—with loving pity, thinking*) I almost do . . . poor unfortunate boy! . . . at these moments . . . as his mother loves him . . . but that isn't enough for him . . . I can hear his mother saying, "Sammy's got to feel sure you love him . . . to be happy." . . . I must try to make him feel sure . . .

(*speaking gently*) I want you to be happy, Sam.

EVANS—(*his face transformed with happiness*) I am—a hundred times more than I deserve!

NINA—(*presses his head down on her breast so he cannot see her eyes—gently*) Ssshh. (*thinking sadly*) I promised her . . . but I couldn't see how hard it would be to let him love me . . . after his baby . . .

was gone . . . it was hard even to keep on living . . .
after that operation . . . Gordon's spirit followed me
from room to room . . . poor reproachful ghost! . . .

(*with bitter mockery*)

Oh, Gordon, I'm afraid this is a deeper point of honor
than any that was ever shot down in flames! . . . what
would your honor say now? . . . "Stick to him! . . .
play the game!" . . . oh, yes, I know . . . I'm sticking
. . . but he isn't happy . . . I'm trying to play the game
. . . then why do I keep myself from him? . . .
but I was really sick . . . for a time after . . . since
then, I couldn't . . . but . . . oh, I'll try . . . I'll try
soon . . .

(*tenderly—but having to force herself to say it*) Doesn't my boy
want to sleep with me again—sometime soon?

EVANS—(*passionately—hardly able to believe his ears*) Oh,
it'd be wonderful, Nina! But are you sure you really want me
to—that you'll feel well enough?

NINA—(*repeats his words as if she were memorizing a lesson*)
Yes, I want you to. Yes, I'll feel well enough. (*He seizes her
hand and kisses it in a passionately grateful silence. She thinks
with resigned finality*)

There, Sammy's mother and Gordon . . . I'll play the
game . . . it will make him happy for a while . . . as
he was in those weeks after we'd left his mother . . .
when I gave myself with a mad pleasure in torturing
myself for his pleasure! . . .

(*then with weary hopelessness*)

He'll be happy until he begins to feel guilty again because I'm not pregnant . . .

(*with a grim bitter smile*)

Poor Sam, if he only knew the precautions . . . as if I
wouldn't die rather than take the slightest chance of
that happening! . . . ever again . . . what a tragic
joke it was on both of us! . . . I wanted my baby so!
. . . oh, God! . . . his mother said . . . "You've got
to have a healthy baby . . . sometime . . . it's your
rightful duty" . . . that seemed right then . . . but
now . . . it seems cowardly . . . to betray poor Sam
. . . and vile to give myself . . . without love or de-

sire . . . and yet I've given myself to men before without a thought, just to give them a moment's happiness
. . . can't I do that again? . . . when it's a case of
Sam's happiness? . . . and my own? . . .

(*She gets up from beside him with a hunted movement.*) It must
be half past eight. Charlie's coming to bring his suggestions
on my outline for Gordon's biography.

EVANS—(*his bliss shattered—dejectedly*)
Always happens . . . just as we get close . . . something comes between . . .

(*then confusedly*) Say, I forgot to tell you Ned's coming out
tonight.

NINA—(*astonished*) Ned Darrell?

EVANS—Sure. I happened to run into him the other day
and invited him and he said Saturday evening. He couldn't
tell what train. Said never mind meeting him.

NINA—(*excitedly*) Why didn't you tell me before, you big
booby! (*She kisses him.*) There, don't mind. But it's just like
you. Now someone'll have to go down to the store. And I'll
have to get the spare room ready. (*She hurries to the doorway.
He follows her.*)

EVANS—I'll help you.

NINA—You'll do nothing of the kind! You'll stay right
downstairs and bring them in here and cover up my absence.
Thank heavens, Charlie won't stay long if Ned is here. (*The
doorbell rings—excitedly*) There's one of them now. I'll run
upstairs. Come up and tell me if it's Ned—and get rid of
Charlie. (*She kisses him playfully and hurries out.*)

EVANS—(*looking after her—thinks*)
She seems better tonight . . . happier . . . she seems
to love me . . . if she'll only get all well again, then
everything will . . .

(*The bell rings again.*)
I must give Ned a good chance to talk to her . . .

(*He goes out to the outer door—returns a moment later with
Marsden. The latter's manner is preoccupied and nervous. His face
has an expression of anxiety which he tries to conceal. He seems a
prey to some inner fear he is trying to hide even from himself and
is resolutely warding off from his consciousness. His tall, thin body
stoops as if a part of its sustaining will had been removed.*)

EVANS—(*with a rather forced welcoming note*) Come on in, Charlie. Nina's upstairs lying down.

MARSDEN—(*with marked relief*) Then by all means don't disturb her. I just dropped in to bring back her outline with the suggestions I've made. (*He has taken some papers out of his pocket and hands them to Evans.*) I couldn't have stayed but a minute in any event. Mother is a bit under the weather these days.

EVANS—(*perfunctorily*) Too bad. (*thinking vindictively*)

> Serve her right, the old scandal-monger, after the way she's gossiped about Nina! . . .

MARSDEN—(*with assumed carelessness*) Just a little indigestion. Nothing serious but it annoys her terribly. (*thinking frightenedly*)

> That dull pain she complains of . . . I don't like it . . . and she won't see anyone but old Doctor Tibbetts . . . she's sixty-eight . . . I can't help fearing . . . no! . . .

EVANS—(*bored—vaguely*) Well, I suppose you've got to be careful of every little thing when you get to her age.

MARSDEN—(*positively bristling*) Her age? Mother isn't so old!

EVANS—(*surprised*) Over sixty-five, isn't she?

MARSDEN—(*indignantly*) You're quite out there! She's still under sixty-five—and in health and spirits she isn't more than fifty! Everyone remarks that! (*annoyed at himself*)

> Why did I lie to him about her age? . . . I must be on edge . . . Mother is rather difficult to live with these days, getting me worried to death, when it's probably nothing . . .

EVANS—(*annoyed in his turn—thinking*)

> Why all the fuss? . . . as if I gave a damn if the old girl was a million! . . .

(*indicating the papers*) I'll give these to Nina first thing in the morning.

MARSDEN—(*mechanically*) Righto. Thank you. (*He starts to go toward door—then turns—fussily*) But you'd better take a look while I'm here and see if it's clear. I've written on the margins. See if there's anything you can't make out. (*Evans nods helplessly and begins reading the sheets, going back beneath the lamp.*)

MARSDEN—(*looking around him with squeamish disapproval*)
What a mess they've made of this study . . . poor
Professor! . . . dead and forgotten . . . and his tomb
desecrated . . . does Sam write his ads here of a week-
end now? . . . the last touch! . . . and Nina labors
with love at Gordon's biography . . . whom the Professor hated! . . . "life is so full of a number of
things!" . . . why does everyone in the world think
they can write? . . . but I've only myself to blame
. . . why in the devil did I ever suggest it to her? . . .
because I hoped my helping her while Sam was in the
city would bring us alone together? . . . but I made
the suggestion before she had that abortion performed! . . . how do you know she did? . . . because
I know! . . . there are psychic affinities . . . her body
confessed . . . and since then, I've felt an aversion
. . . as if she were a criminal . . . she is! . . . how
could she? . . . why? . . . I thought she wanted a
child . . . but evidently I don't know her . . . I suppose, afraid it would spoil her figure . . . her flesh
. . . her power to enslave men's senses . . . mine . . .
and I had hoped . . . looked forward to her becoming
a mother . . . for my peace of mind. . . .
(*catching himself—violently*)
Shut up! . . . what a base creature I'm becoming!
. . . to have such thoughts when Mother is sick and I
ought to be thinking only of her! . . . and it's none
of my damn business, anyway! . . .
(*glaring at Evans resentfully as if he were to blame*)
Look at him! . . . he'll never suspect anything!
. . . what a simple-simon! . . . he adored Gordon
as a newsboy does a champion pugilist! . . . and
Nina writes of Gordon as if he had been a demi-god!
. . . when actually he came from the commonest
people! . . .
(*He suddenly speaks to Evans with a really savage satisfaction.*)
Did I tell you I once looked up Gordon's family in Beach-
ampton? A truly deplorable lot! When I remembered Gordon
and looked at his father I had either to suspect a lover in the
wood pile or to believe in an Immaculate Conception . . .

that is, until I saw his mother! Then a stork became the only conceivable explanation!

EVANS—(*who has only half-heard and hasn't understood, says vaguely*) I never saw his folks. (*indicating the papers*) I can make this all out all right.

MARSDEN—(*sarcastically*) I'm glad it's understandable!

EVANS—(*blunderingly*) I'll give it to Nina—and I hope your mother is feeling better tomorrow.

MARSDEN—(*piqued*) Oh, I'm going. Why didn't you tell me if I was interrupting—your writing!

EVANS—(*immediately guilty*) Oh, come on, Charlie, don't get peevish, you know I didn't mean— (*The bell rings. Evans stammers in confusion, trying at a nonchalant air*) Hello! That must be Ned. You remember Darrell. He's coming out for a little visit. Excuse me. (*He blunders out of the door.*)

MARSDEN—(*looking after him with anger mixed with alarmed suspicion and surprise*)

> Darrell? . . . what's he doing here? . . . have they been meeting? . . . perhaps he was the one who performed the . . . no, his idea was she ought to have a child . . . but if she came and begged him? . . . but why should Nina beg not to have a baby? . . .

(*distractedly*)

> Oh, I don't know! . . . it's all a sordid mess! . . . I ought to be going home! . . . I don't want to see Darrell! . . .

(*He starts for the door—then struck by a sudden thought, stops.*)

> Wait . . . I could ask him about Mother . . . yes . . . good idea . . .

(*He comes back to the middle of the room, front, and is standing there when Darrell enters, followed by Evans. Darrell has not changed in appearance except that his expression is graver and more thoughtful. His manner is more convincingly authoritative, more mature. He takes in Marsden from head to foot with one comprehensive glance.*)

EVANS—(*awkwardly*) Ned, you remember Charlie Marsden?

MARSDEN—(*holding out his hand, urbanely polite*) How are you, Doctor?

DARRELL—(*shaking his hand—briefly*) Hello.

EVANS—I'll go up and tell Nina you're here, Ned. (*He goes, casting a resentful glance at Marsden.*)

MARSDEN—(*awkwardly, as Darrell sits down in the chair at center, goes over and stands by the table*) I was on the point of leaving when you rang. Then I decided to stop and renew our acquaintance. (*He stoops and picks up one sheet of paper, and puts it back carefully on the table.*)

DARRELL—(*watching him—thinking*)

> Neat . . . suspiciously neat . . . he's an old maid who seduces himself in his novels . . . so I suspect . . . I'd like a chance to study him more closely. . . .

MARSDEN—(*thinking resentfully*)

> What a boor! . . . he might say something! . . .

(*forcing a smile*) And I wanted to ask a favor of you, a word of advice as to the best specialist, the very best, it would be possible to consult—

DARRELL—(*sharply*) On what?

MARSDEN—(*almost naïvely*) My mother has a pain in her stomach.

DARRELL—(*amused—dryly*) Possibly she eats too much.

MARSDEN—(*as he bends and carefully picks another sheet from the floor to place it as carefully on the table*) She doesn't eat enough to keep a canary alive. It's a dull, constant pain, she says. She's terribly worried. She's terrified by the idea of cancer. But, of course, that's perfect rot, she's never been sick a day in her life and—

DARRELL—(*sharply*) She's showing more intelligence about her pain than you are.

MARSDEN—(*bending down for another sheet, his voice trembling with terror*) I don't understand—quite. Do you mean to say you think—?

DARRELL—(*brutally*) It's possible. (*He has pulled out his pen and a card and is writing. Thinking grimly*)

> Explode a bomb under him, as I did once before . . . only way to get him started doing anything. . . .

MARSDEN—(*angrily*) But—that's nonsense!

DARRELL—(*with satisfaction—unruffledly*) People who are afraid to face unpleasant possibilities until it's too late commit more murders and suicides than— (*holds out card*) Doctor Schultz is your man. Take her to see him—tomorrow!

MARSDEN—(*bursting out in anger and misery*) Damn it, you're condemning her without—! (*He breaks down chokingly.*) You've no damn right!— (*He bends down, trembling all over, to pick up another piece of paper.*)

DARRELL—(*genuinely astonished and contrite*)

> And I thought he was so ingrown he didn't care a damn about anyone! . . . his mother . . . now I begin to see him . . .

(*He jumps from his chair and going to Marsden puts a hand on his shoulder—kindly*) I beg your pardon, Marsden. I only wanted to drive it in that all delay is dangerous. Your mother's pain may be due to any number of harmless causes, but you owe it to her to make sure. Here. (*He hands out the card.*)

MARSDEN—(*straightens up and takes it, his eyes grateful now—humbly*) Thank you. I'll take her to see him tomorrow. (*Evans comes in.*)

EVANS—(*to Marsden, blunderingly*) Say, Charlie, I don't want to hurry you but Nina wants some things at the store before it closes, and if you'd give me a lift—

MARSDEN—(*dully*) Of course. Come along. (*He shakes hands with Darrell.*) Good night, Doctor—and thank you.

DARRELL—Good night. (*Marsden goes, followed by Evans.*)

EVANS—(*turns in the doorway and says meaningly*) Nina'll be right down. For Pete's sake, have a good heart-to-heart talk with her, Ned!

DARRELL—(*frowning—impatiently*) Oh—all right! Run along. (*Evans goes. Darrell remains standing near the table looking after them, thinking about Marsden.*)

> Queer fellow, Marsden . . . mother's boy still . . . if she dies what will he do? . . .

(*then dismissing Marsden with a shrug of his shoulders*)

> Oh, well, he can always escape life in a new book. . . .

(*He moves around the table examining its disorder critically, then sits down in armchair—amused*)

> Evidences of authorship . . . Sam's ads? . . . isn't making good, he said . . . was I wrong in thinking he had stuff in him? . . . hope not . . . always liked Sam, don't know why exactly . . . said Nina'd gotten

into a bad state again . . . what's happened to their marriage? . . . I felt a bit sorry for myself at their wedding . . . not that I'd ever fallen . . . but I did envy him in a way . . . she always had strong physical attraction for me . . . that time I kissed her . . . one reason I've steered clear since . . . take no chances on emotional didos . . . need all my mind on my work . . . got rid of even that slight suspicion . . . I'd forgotten all about her . . . she's a strange girl . . . interesting case . . . I should have kept in touch on that account . . . hope she'll tell me about herself . . . can't understand her not having child . . . it's so obviously the sensible thing . . .

(*cynically*)

Probably why . . . to expect common sense of people proves you're lacking in it yourself! . . .

NINA—(*enters silently. She has fixed herself up, put on her best dress, arranged her hair, rouged, etc.—but it is principally her mood that has changed her, making her appear a younger, prettier person for the moment. Darrell immediately senses her presence, and, looking up, gets to his feet with a smile of affectionate admiration. She comes quickly over to him saying with frank pleasure*) Hello, Ned. I'm certainly glad to see you again—after all these years!

DARRELL—(*as they shake hands—smiling*) Not as long as all that, is it? (*thinking admiringly*)

Wonderful-looking as ever . . . Sam is a lucky devil! . . .

NINA—(*thinking*)

Strong hands like Gordon's . . . take hold of you . . . not like Sam's . . . yielding fingers that let you fall back into yourself . . .

(*teasingly*) I ought to cut you dead after the shameful way you've ignored us!

DARRELL—(*a bit embarrassedly*) I've really meant to write. (*his eyes examining her keenly*)

Been through a lot since I saw her . . . face shows it . . . nervous tension pronounced . . . hiding behind her smile . . .

NINA—(*uneasy under his glance*)

I hate that professional look in his eyes . . . watching symptoms . . . without seeing me . . .

(*with resentful mockery*) Well, what do you suspect is wrong with the patient now, Doctor? (*She laughs nervously.*) Sit down, Ned. I suppose you can't help your diagnosing stare. (*She turns from him and sits down in the rocker at center.*)

DARRELL—(*quickly averting his eyes—sits down—jokingly*) Same old unjust accusation! You were always reading diagnosis into me, when what I was really thinking was what fine eyes you had, or what a becoming gown, or—

NINA—(*smiling*) Or what a becoming alibi you could cook up! Oh, I know you! (*With a sudden change of mood she laughs gaily and naturally.*) But you're forgiven—that is, if you can explain why you've never been to see us.

DARRELL—Honestly, Nina, I've been so rushed with work I haven't had a chance to go anywhere.

NINA—Or an inclination!

DARRELL—(*smiling*) Well—maybe.

NINA—Do you like the Institute so much? (*He nods gravely.*) Is it the big opportunity you wanted?

DARRELL—(*simply*) I think it is.

NINA—(*with a smile*) Well, you're the taking kind for whom opportunities are made!

DARRELL—(*smiling*) I hope so.

NINA—(*sighing*) I wish that could be said of more of us— (*then quickly*)—meaning myself.

DARRELL—(*thinking with a certain satisfaction*)

> Meaning Sam . . . that doesn't look hopeful for future wedded bliss! . . .

(*teasingly*) But I heard you were "taking an opportunity" to go in for literature—collaborating with Marsden.

NINA—No, Charlie is only going to advise. He'd never deign to appear as co-author. And besides, he never appreciated the real Gordon. No one did except me.

DARRELL—(*thinking caustically*)

> Gordon myth strong as ever . . . root of her trouble still . . .

(*keenly inquisitive*) Sam certainly appreciated him, didn't he?

NINA—(*not remembering to hide her contempt*) Sam? Why, he's the exact opposite in every way!

DARRELL—(*caustically thinking*)

>   These heroes die hard . . . but perhaps she can write
>   him out of her system. . . .

(*persuasively*) Well, you're going ahead with the biography,
aren't you? I think you ought to.

NINA—(*dryly*) For my soul, Doctor? (*listlessly*) I suppose I
will. I don't know. I haven't much time. The duties of a wife—
(*teasingly*) By the way, if it isn't too rude to inquire, aren't
you getting yourself engaged to some fair lady or other?

DARRELL—(*smiling—but emphatically*) Not on your life!
Not until after I'm thirty-five, at least!

NINA—(*sarcastically*) Then you don't believe in taking your
own medicine? Why, Doctor! Think of how much good it
would do you!—(*excitedly with a hectic sarcasm*)—if you had
a nice girl to love—or was it learn to love?—and take care
of—whose character you could shape and whose life you
could guide and make what you pleased, in whose unselfish
devotion you could find peace! (*more and more bitterly sarcastic*) And you ought to have a baby, Doctor! You will never
know what life is, you'll never be really happy until you've
had a baby, Doctor—a fine, healthy baby! (*She laughs a bitter,
sneering laugh.*)

DARRELL—(*after a quick, keen glance, thinking*)

>   Good! . . . she's going to tell . . .

(*meekly*) I recognize my arguments. Was I really wrong on
every point, Nina?

NINA—(*harshly*) On every single point, Doctor!

DARRELL—(*glancing at her keenly*) But how? You haven't
given the baby end of it a chance yet, have you?

NINA—(*bitterly*) Oh, haven't I? (*then bursts out with intense
bitterness*) I'll have you know I'm not destined to bear babies,
Doctor!

DARRELL—(*startledly*)

>   What's that? . . . why not? . . .

(*again with a certain satisfaction*)

>   Can she mean Sam? . . . that he . . .

(*soothingly—but plainly disturbed*) Why don't you begin at the
beginning and tell me all about it? I feel responsible.

NINA—(*fiercely*) You are! (*then wearily*) And you're not.
No one is. You didn't know. No one could know.

DARRELL—(*in same tone*) Know what? (*thinking with the same eagerness to believe something he hopes*)

> She must mean no one could know that Sam wasn't . . . but I might have guessed it . . . from his general weakness . . . poor unlucky devil . . .

(*then as she remains silent—urgingly*) Tell me. I want to help you, Nina.

NINA—(*touched*) It's too late, Ned. (*then suddenly*) I've just thought—Sam said he happened to run into you. That isn't so, is it? He went to see you and told you how worried he was about me and asked you out to see me, didn't he? (*as Darrell nods*) Oh, I don't mind! It's even rather touching. (*then mockingly*) Well, since you're out here professionally, and my husband wants me to consult you, I might as well give you the whole case history! (*wearily*) I warn you it isn't pretty, Doctor! But then life doesn't seem to be pretty, does it? And, after all, you aided and abetted God the Father in making this mess. I hope it'll teach you not to be so cocksure in future. (*more and more bitterly*) I must say you proceeded very unscientifically, Doctor! (*then suddenly starts her story in a dull monotonous tone recalling that of Evans' mother in the previous Act*) When we went to visit Sam's mother I'd known for two months that I was going to have a baby.

DARRELL—(*startled—unable to hide a trace of disappointment*) Oh, then you actually were? (*thinking disappointedly and ashamed of himself for being disappointed*)

> All wrong, what I thought . . . she was going to . . . then why didn't she? . . .

NINA—(*with a strange happy intensity*) Oh, Ned, I loved it more than I've ever loved anything in my life—even Gordon! I loved it so it seemed at times that Gordon must be its real father, that Gordon must have come to me in a dream while I was lying asleep beside Sam! And I was happy! I almost loved Sam then! I felt he was a good husband!

DARRELL—(*instantly repelled—thinking with scornful jealousy*)

> Ha! . . . the hero again! . . . comes to her bed! . . . puts horns on poor Sam! . . . becomes the father of his child! . . . I'll be damned if hers isn't the most idiotic obsession I ever . . .

NINA—(*her voice suddenly becoming flat and lifeless*) And then Sam's mother told me I couldn't have my baby. You see, Doctor, Sam's great-grandfather was insane, and Sam's grandmother died in an asylum, and Sam's father had lost his mind for years before he died, and an aunt who is still alive is crazy. So of course I had to agree it would be wrong—and I had an operation.

DARRELL—(*who has listened with amazed horror—profoundly shocked and stunned*) Good God! Are you crazy, Nina? I simply can't believe! It would be too hellish! Poor Sam, of all people! (*bewilderedly*) Nina! Are you absolutely sure?

NINA—(*immediately defensive and mocking*) Absolutely, Doctor! Why? Do you think it's I who am crazy? Sam looks so healthy and sane, doesn't he? He fooled you completely, didn't he? You thought he'd be an ideal husband for me! And poor Sam's fooling himself too because he doesn't know anything about all this—so you can't blame him, Doctor!

DARRELL—(*thinking in a real panic of horror—and a flood of protective affection for her*)

> God, this is too awful! . . . on top of all the rest! . . . how did she ever stand it! . . . she'll lose her mind too! . . . and it's my fault! . . .

(*getting up, comes to her and puts his hands on her shoulders, standing behind her—tenderly*) Nina! I'm so damn sorry! There's only one possible thing to do now. You'll have to make Sam give you a divorce.

NINA—(*bitterly*) Yes? Then what do you suppose would be his finish? No, I've enough guilt in my memory now, thank you! I've got to stick to Sam! (*then with a strange monotonous insistence*) I've promised Sam's mother I'd make him happy! He's unhappy now because he thinks he isn't able to give me a child. And I'm unhappy because I've lost my child. So I must have another baby—somehow—don't you think, Doctor?—to make us both happy? (*She looks up at him pleadingly. For a moment they stare into each other's eyes—then both turn away in guilty confusion.*)

DARRELL—(*bewilderedly thinking*)

> That look in her eyes . . . what does she want me to think? . . . why does she talk so much about being

happy? . . . am I happy? . . . I don't know . . . what
is happiness? . . .

(*confusedly*) Nina, I don't know what to think.

NINA—(*thinking strangely*)

That look in his eyes . . . what did he mean? . . .

(*with the same monotonous insistence*) You must know what to
think. I can't think it out myself any more. I need your advice—your *scientific* advice this time, if you please, Doctor.
I've thought and thought about it. I've told myself it's what
I ought to do. Sam's own mother urged me to do it. It's
sensible and kind and just and good. I've told myself this a
thousand times and yet I can't quite convince something in
me that's afraid of something. I need the courage of someone
who can stand outside and reason it out as if Sam and I were
no more than guinea pigs. You've got to help me, Doctor!
You've got to show me what's the sane—the truly sane, you
understand!—thing I must do for Sam's sake, and my own.

DARRELL—(*thinking confusedly*)

What do I have to do? . . . this was all my fault . . .
I owe her something in return . . . I owe Sam something . . . I owe them happiness! . . .

(*irritably*)

Damn it, there's a humming in my ears! . . . I've
caught some fever . . . I swore to live coolly . . . let
me see. . . .

(*in a cold, emotionless professional voice, his face like a mask of a
doctor*) A doctor must be in full possession of the facts, if he
is to advise. What is it precisely that Sam's wife has thought
so much of doing?

NINA—(*in the same insistent tone*) Of picking out a healthy
male about whom she cared nothing and having a child by
him that Sam would believe was his child, whose life would
give him confidence in his own living, who would be for him
a living proof that his wife loved him. (*confusedly, strangely
and purposefully*)

This doctor is healthy. . . .

DARRELL—(*in his ultra-professional manner—like an automaton of a doctor*) I see. But this needs a lot of thinking over.
It isn't easy to prescribe— (*thinking*)

I have a friend who has a wife . . . I was envious at

his wedding . . . but what has that to do with it? . . .
damn it, my mind won't work! . . . it keeps running
away to her . . . it wants to mate with her mind . . .
in the interest of Science? . . . what damned rot I'm
thinking! . . .

NINA—(*thinking as before*)

This doctor is nothing to me but a healthy male . . .
when he was Ned he once kissed me . . . but I cared
nothing about him . . . so that's all right, isn't it,
Sam's Mother?

DARRELL—(*thinking*)

Let me see. . . . I am in the laboratory and they are
guinea pigs . . . in fact, in the interest of science, I
can be for the purpose of this experiment, a healthy
guinea pig myself and still remain an observer . . . I
observe my pulse is high, for example, and that's obviously because I am stricken with a recurrence of an
old desire . . . desire is a natural male reaction to the
beauty of the female . . . her husband is my friend.
. . . I have always tried to help him . . .

(*coldly*) I've been considering what Sam's wife told me and
her reasoning is quite sound. The child can't be her husband's.

NINA—Then you agree with Sam's mother? She said:
"Being happy is the nearest we can ever come to knowing
what good is!"

DARRELL—I agree with her decidedly. Sam's wife should
find a healthy father for Sam's child at once. It is her sane
duty to her husband. (*worriedly thinking*)

Have I ever been happy? . . . I have studied to cure
the body's unhappiness . . . I have watched happy
smiles form on the lips of the dying . . . I have experienced pleasure with a number of women I desired
but never loved . . . I have known a bit of honor and
a trifle of self-satisfaction . . . this talk of happiness
seems to me extraneous . . .

NINA—(*beginning to adopt a timid, diffident, guilty tone*)
This will have to be hidden from Sam so he can never know!
Oh, Doctor, Sam's wife is afraid!

DARRELL—(*sharply professional*) Nonsense! This is no time

for timidity! Happiness hates the timid! So does Science! Certainly Sam's wife must conceal her action! To let Sam know would be insanely cruel of her—and stupid, for then no one could be the happier for her act! (*anxiously thinking*)

> Am I right to advise this? . . . yes, it is clearly the rational thing to do . . . but this advice betrays my friend! . . . no, it saves him! . . . it saves his wife . . . and if a third party should know a little happiness . . . is he any poorer, am I any the less his friend because I saved him? . . . no, my duty to him is plain . . . and my duty as an experimental searcher after truth . . . to observe these three guinea pigs, of which I am one . . .

NINA—(*thinking determinedly*)

> I must have my baby! . . .

(*timidly—gets from her chair and half-turns toward him—pleadingly*) You must give his wife courage, Doctor. You must free her from her feeling of guilt.

DARRELL—There can only be guilt when one deliberately neglects one's manifest duty to life. Anything else is rot! This woman's duty is to save her husband and herself by begetting a healthy child! (*thinking guiltily and instinctively moving away from her*)

> I am healthy . . . but he is my friend . . . there is such a thing as honor! . . .

NINA—(*determinedly*)

> I must take my happiness! . . .

(*frightenedly—comes after him*) But she is ashamed. It's adultery. It's wrong.

DARRELL—(*moving away again—with a cold sneering laugh of impatience*) Wrong! Would she rather see her husband wind up in an asylum? Would she rather face the prospect of going to pot mentally, morally, physically herself through year after year of devilling herself and him? Really, Madame, if you can't throw overboard all such irrelevant moral ideas, I'll have to give up this case here and now! (*thinking frightenedly*)

> Who is talking? . . . is he suggesting me? . . . but you know very well I can't be the one, Doctor! . . . why not, you're healthy and it's a friendly act for all concerned . . .

NINA—(*thinking determinedly*)

   I must have my baby! . . .

(*Going further toward him—she can now touch him with her hand.*) Please, Doctor, you must give her strength to do this right thing that seems to her so right and then so wrong! (*She puts out her hand and takes one of his.*)

DARRELL—(*thinking frightenedly*)

   Whose hand is this? . . . it burns me . . . I kissed her once . . . her lips were cold . . . now they would burn with happiness for me! . . .

NINA—(*taking his other hand and slowly pulling him around to face her, although he does not look at her—pleadingly*) Now she feels your strength. It gives her the courage to ask you, Doctor, to suggest the father. She has changed, Doctor, since she became Sam's wife. She can't bear the thought now of giving herself to any man she could neither desire nor respect. So each time her thoughts come to the man she must select they are afraid to go on! She needs your courage to choose!

DARRELL—(*as if listening to himself*)

   Sam is my friend . . . well, and isn't she your friend? . . . her two hands are so warm! . . . I must not even hint at my desire! . . .

(*judicially calm*) Well, the man must be someone who is not unattractive to her physically, of course.

NINA—Ned always attracted her.

DARRELL—(*thinking frightenedly*)

   What's that she said? . . . Ned? . . . attracts? . . .

(*in same tone*) And the man should have a mind that can truly understand—a scientific mind superior to the moral scruples that cause so much human blundering and unhappiness.

NINA—She always thought Ned had a superior mind.

DARRELL—(*thinking frightenedly*)

   Did she say Ned? . . . she thinks Ned . . . ?

(*in same tone*) The man should like and admire her, he should be her good friend and want to help her, but he should not love her—although he might, without harm to anyone, desire her.

NINA—Ned does not love her—but he used to like her and, I think, desire her. Does he now, Doctor?

DARRELL—(*thinking*)

Does he? . . . who is he? . . . he is Ned! . . . Ned is
I! . . . I desire her! . . . I desire happiness! . . .
(*tremblingly now—gently*) But, Madame, I must confess the
Ned you are speaking of is I, and I am Ned.

NINA—(*gently*) And I am Nina, who wants her baby.
(*Then she reaches out and turns his head until his face faces hers
but he keeps his eyes down—she bends her head meekly and submissively—softly*) I should be so grateful, Ned. (*He starts, looks
up at her wildly, makes a motion as though to take her in his
arms, then remains fixed for a moment in that attitude, staring
at her bowed head as she repeats submissively*) I should be so
humbly grateful.

DARRELL—(*suddenly falling on his knees and taking her
hand in both of his and kissing it humbly—with a sob*) Yes—yes,
Nina—yes—for your happiness—in that spirit! (*thinking—
fiercely triumphant*)

I shall be happy for a while! . . .

NINA—(*raising her head—thinking—proudly triumphant*)
I shall be happy! . . . I shall make my husband
happy! . . .

(*Curtain*)

ACT FIVE

SCENE—*The sitting room of a small house Evans has rented in a seashore suburb near New York. It is a bright morning in the following April.*

The room is a typical sitting room of the quantity-production bungalow type. Windows on the left look out on a broad porch. A double doorway in rear leads into the hall. A door on right, to the dining room. Nina has tried to take the curse of offensive, banal newness off the room with some of her own things from her old home but the attempt has been half-hearted in the face of such overpowering commonness, and the result is a room as disorganized in character as was the Professor's study in the last Act.

The arrangement of the furniture follows the same pattern as in preceding scenes. There is a Morris chair and a round golden oak table at left of center, an upholstered chair, covered with bright chintz at center, a sofa covered with the same chintz at right.

Nina is sitting in the chair at center. She has been trying to read a book but has let this drop listlessly on her lap. A great change is noticeable in her face and bearing. She is again the pregnant woman of Act Three but this time there is a triumphant strength about her expression, a ruthless self-confidence in her eyes. She has grown stouter, her face has filled out. One gets no impression of neurotic strain from her now, she seems nerveless and deeply calm.

NINA—(*as if listening for something within her—joyfully*)
>   There! . . . that can't be my imagination . . . I felt it
>   plainly . . . life . . . my baby . . . my only baby . . .
>   the other never really lived . . . this is the child of my
>   love! . . . I love Ned! . . . I've loved him ever since
>   that first afternoon . . . when I went to him . . . so
>   scientifically! . . .

(*She laughs at herself.*)

>   Oh, what a goose I was! . . . then love came to me
>   . . . in his arms . . . happiness! . . . I hid it from
>   him . . . I saw he was frightened . . . his own joy
>   frightened him . . . I could feel him fighting with
>   himself . . . during all those afternoons . . . our
>   wonderful afternoons of happiness! . . . and I said

714

nothing . . . I made myself be calculating . . . so when he finally said . . . dreadfully disturbed . . . "Look here, Nina, we've done all that is necessary, playing with fire is dangerous" . . . I said, "You're quite right, Ned, of all things I don't want to fall in love with you!" . . .

(*She laughs.*)

He didn't like that! . . . he looked angry . . . and afraid . . . then for weeks he never even phoned . . . I waited . . . it was prudent to wait . . . but every day I grew more terrified . . . then just as my will was breaking, his broke . . . he suddenly appeared again . . . but I held him to his aloof doctor's pose and sent him away, proud of his will power . . . and sick of himself with desire for me! . . . every week since then he's been coming out here . . . as my doctor . . . we've talked about our child wisely, dispassionately . . . as if it were Sam's child . . . we've never given in to our desire . . . and I've watched love grow in him until I'm sure . . .

(*with sudden alarm*)

But am I? . . . he's never once mentioned love . . . perhaps I've been a fool to play the part I've played . . . it may have turned him against me . . .

(*suddenly with calm confidence*)

No . . . he does . . . I feel it . . . it's only when I start thinking, I begin to doubt . . .

(*She settles back and stares dreamily before her—a pause.*)

There . . . again . . . his child! . . . my child moving in my life . . . my life moving in my child . . . the world is whole and perfect . . . all things are each other's . . . life is . . . and the is is beyond reason . . . questions die in the silence of this peace . . . I am living a dream within the great dream of the tide . . . breathing in the tide I dream and breathe back my dream into the tide . . . suspended in the movement of the tide, I feel life move in me, suspended in me . . . no whys matter . . . there is no why . . . I am a mother . . . God is a Mother . . .

(*She sighs happily, closing her eyes. A pause.*)

EVANS——(*enters from the hallway in rear. He is dressed carefully but his clothes are old ones—shabby collegiate gentility—and he has forgotten to shave. His eyes look pitiably harried, his manner has become a distressingly obvious attempt to cover up a chronic state of nervous panic and guilty conscience. He stops inside the doorway and looks at her with a pitiable furtiveness, arguing with himself, trying to get up his courage.*)

Tell her! . . . go on! . . . you made up your mind to, didn't you? . . . don't quit now! . . . tell her you've decided . . . for her sake . . . to face the truth . . . that she can't love you . . . she's tried . . . she's acted like a good sport . . . but she's beginning to hate you . . . and you can't blame her . . . she wanted children . . . and you haven't been able . . .

(*protesting feebly*)

But I don't know for certain . . . that that's my fault . . .

(*then bitterly*)

Aw, don't kid yourself, if she'd married someone else . . . if Gordon had lived and married her . . . I'll bet in the first month she'd . . . you'd better resign from the whole game . . . with a gun! . . .

(*He swallows hard as if he were choking back a sob—then savagely*)

Stop whining! . . . go on and wake her up! . . . say you're willing to give her a divorce so she can marry some real guy who can give her what she ought to have! . . .

(*then with sudden terror*)

And if she says yes? . . . I couldn't bear it! . . . I'd die without her! . . .

(*then with a somber alien forcefulness*)

All right . . . good riddance! . . . I'd have the guts to bump off then, all right! . . . that'd set her free . . . come on now! . . . ask her! . . .

(*But his voice begins to tremble uncertainly again as he calls*) Nina.

NINA——(*opens her eyes and gazes calmly, indifferently at him*) Yes?

EVANS——(*immediately terrified and beaten—thinking*)

I can't! . . . the way she looks at me! . . . she'd say
yes! . . .

(*stammering*) I hate to wake you up but—it's about time for
Ned to come, isn't it?

NINA—(*calmly*) I wasn't asleep. (*thinking as if she found it
hard to concentrate on him, to realize his existence*)

> This man is my husband . . . it's hard to remember
> that . . . people will say he's the father of my
> child. . . .

(*with revulsion*)

> That's shameful! . . . and yet that's exactly what I
> wanted! . . . wanted! . . . not now! . . . now I love
> Ned! . . . I won't lose him! . . . Sam must give me a
> divorce . . . I've sacrificed enough of my life . . .
> what has he given me? . . . not even a home . . . I
> had to sell my father's home to get money so we could
> move near his job . . . and then he lost his job! . . .
> now he's depending on Ned to help him get another!
> . . . my love! . . . how shameless! . . .

(*then contritely*)

> Oh, I'm unjust . . . poor Sam doesn't know about
> Ned . . . and it was I who wanted to sell the place
> . . . I was lonely there . . . I wanted to be near
> Ned. . . .

EVANS—(*thinking in agony*)

> What's she thinking? . . . probably lucky for me I
> don't know! . . .

(*forcing a brisk air as he turns away from her*) I hope Ned
brings that letter he promised me to the manager of the
Globe company. I'm keen to get on the job again.

NINA—(*with scornful pity*) Oh, I guess Ned will bring the
letter. I asked him not to forget.

EVANS—I hope they'll have an opening right off. We can
use the money. (*hanging his head*) I feel rotten, living on you
when you've got so little.

NINA—(*indifferently but with authority, like a governess to a
small boy*) Now, now!

EVANS—(*relieved*) Well, it's true. (*then coming to her—
humbly ingratiating*) You've felt a lot better lately, haven't
you, Nina?

NINA—(*with a start—sharply*) Why?

EVANS—You look ever so much better. You're getting fat. (*He forces a grin.*)

NINA—(*curtly*) Don't be absurd, please! As a matter of fact, I don't feel a bit better.

EVANS—(*thinking despondently*)

> Lately, she jumps on me every chance she gets . . . as if everything I did disgusted her! . . .

(*He strays over to the window and looks out listlessly.*) I thought we'd get some word from Charlie this morning saying if he was coming down or not. But I suppose he's still too broken up over his mother's death to write.

NINA—(*indifferently*) He'll probably come without bothering to write. (*vaguely—wonderingly*)

> Charlie . . . dear old Charlie . . . I've forgotten him, too. . . .

EVANS—I think that's Ned's car now. Yes. It's stopping. I'll go out and meet him. (*He starts for the door in rear.*)

NINA—(*sharply, before she can restrain the impulse*) Don't be such a fool!

EVANS—(*stops—stammers confusedly*) What—what's the matter?

NINA—(*controlling herself—but irritably*) Don't mind me. I'm nervous. (*thinking guiltily*)

> One minute I feel ashamed of him for making such a fool of himself over my lover . . . the next minute something hateful urges me to drive him into doing it! . . .

(*The maid has answered the ring and opened the outer door. Ned Darrell comes in from the rear. His face looks older. There is an expression of defensive bitterness and self-resentment about his mouth and eyes. This vanishes into one of desire and joy as he sees Nina. He starts toward her impulsively. "Nina!" then stops short as he sees Evans*)

NINA—(*forgetting Evans, gets to her feet as if to receive Darrell in her arms—with love*) Ned!

EVANS—(*affectionately and gratefully*) Hello, Ned! (*He holds out his hand which Darrell takes mechanically.*)

DARRELL—(*trying to overcome his guilty embarrassment*) Hello, Sam. Didn't see you. (*hurriedly reaching in his coat pocket*) Before I forget, here's that letter. I had a talk over the phone with Appleby yesterday. He's pretty sure there's an opening—(*with a condescension he can't help*)—but you'll have to get your nose on the grindstone to make good with him.

EVANS—(*flushing guiltily—forcing a confident tone*) You bet I will! (*then gratefully and humbly*) Gosh, Ned, I can't tell you how grateful I am!

DARRELL—(*brusquely, to hide his embarrassment*) Oh, shut up! I'm only too glad.

NINA—(*watching Evans with a contempt that is almost gloating—in a tone of curt dismissal*) You'd better go and shave, hadn't you, if you're going to town?

EVANS—(*guiltily, passing his hand over his face—forcing a brisk, purposeful air*) Yes, of course. I forgot I hadn't. Excuse me, will you? (*This to Darrell. Evans hurries out, rear.*)

DARRELL—(*as soon as he is out of earshot—turning on Nina accusingly*) How can you treat him that way? It makes me feel—like a swine!

NINA—(*flushing guiltily—protestingly*) What way? (*then inconsequentially*) He's always forgetting to shave lately.

DARRELL—You know what I mean, Nina! (*turns away from her—thinking bitterly*)

>What a rotten liar I've become! . . . and he trusts me absolutely! . . .

NINA—(*thinking frightenedly*)

>Why doesn't he take me in his arms? . . . oh, I feel he doesn't love me now! . . . he's so bitter! . . .

(*trying to be matter-of-fact*) I'm sorry, Ned. I don't mean to be cross but Sam does get on my nerves.

DARRELL—(*thinking bitterly*)

>Sometimes I almost hate her! . . . if it wasn't for her I'd have kept my peace of mind . . . no good for anything lately, damn it! . . . but it's idiotic to feel guilty . . . if Sam only didn't trust me! . . .

(*then impatiently*)

>Bosh! . . . sentimental nonsense! . . . end justifies means! . . . this will have a good end for Sam, I swear to that! . . . why doesn't she tell him she's pregnant? . . . what's she waiting for? . . .

NINA—(*thinking passionately, looking at him*)

> Oh, my lover, why don't you kiss me? . . .

(*imploringly*) Ned! Don't be cross with me, please!

DARRELL—(*fighting to control himself—coldly*) I'm not cross, Nina. Only you must admit these triangular scenes are, to say the least, humiliating. (*resentfully*) I won't come out here again!

NINA—(*with a cry of pain*) Ned!

DARRELL—(*thinking exultingly at first*)

> She loves me! . . . she's forgotten Gordon! . . . I'm happy! . . . do I love her? . . . no! . . . I won't! . . . I can't! . . . think what it would mean to Sam! . . . to my career! . . . be objective about it! . . . you guinea pig! . . . I'm her doctor . . . and Sam's . . . I prescribed child for them . . . that's all there is to it! . . .

NINA—(*torn between hope and fear*)

> What is he thinking? . . . he's fighting his love . . . oh, my lover! . . .

(*again with longing*) Ned!

DARRELL—(*putting on his best professional air, going to her*) How do you feel today? You look as if you might have a little fever. (*He takes her hand as if to feel her pulse. Her hand closes over his. She looks up into his face. He keeps his turned away.*)

NINA—(*straining up toward him—with intense longing—thinking*)

> I love you! . . . take me! . . . what do I care for anything in the world but you! . . . let Sam die! . . .

DARRELL—(*fighting himself—thinking*)

> Christ! . . . touch of her skin! . . . her nakedness! . . . those afternoons in her arms! happiness! . . . what do I care for anything else? . . . to hell with Sam! . . .

NINA—(*breaking out passionately*) Ned! I love you! I can't hide it any more! I won't! I love you, Ned!

DARRELL—(*suddenly taking her in his arms and kissing her frantically*) Nina! Beautiful!

NINA—(*triumphantly—between kisses*) You love me, don't you? Say you do, Ned!

DARRELL—(*passionately*) Yes! Yes!

NINA—(*with a cry of triumph*) Thank God! At last you've
told me! You've confessed it to yourself! Oh, Ned, you've
made me so happy! (*There is a ring from the front door bell.
Darrell hears it. It acts like an electric shock on him. He tears
himself away from her. Instinctively she gets up too and moves to
the lounge at right.*)

DARRELL—(*stupidly*) Someone—at the door. (*He sinks
down in the chair by the table at left. Thinking torturedly*)

    I said I loved her! . . . she won! . . . she used my
    desire! . . . but I don't love her! . . . I won't! . . .
    she can't own my life! . . .

(*violently—almost shouts at her*) I don't, Nina! I tell you I
don't!

NINA—(*The maid has just gone to the front door.*) Sshh!
(*then in a triumphant whisper*) You do, Ned! You do!

DARRELL—(*with dogged stupidity*) I don't! (*The front door
has been opened. Marsden appears in the rear, walks slowly and
woodenly like a man in a trance into the room. He is dressed
immaculately in deep mourning. His face is pale, drawn, haggard
with loneliness and grief. His eyes have a dazed look as if he were
still too stunned to comprehend clearly what has happened to him.
He does not seem conscious of Darrell's presence at first. His shoulders are bowed, his whole figure droops.*)

NINA—(*thinking—in a strange superstitious panic*)

    Black . . . in the midst of happiness . . . black comes
    . . . again . . . death . . . my father . . . comes be-
    tween me and happiness! . . .

(*then recovering herself, scornfully*)

    You silly coward! . . . it's only Charlie! . . .

(*then with furious resentment*)

    The old fool! . . . what does he mean coming in on
    us without warning? . . .

MARSDEN—(*forcing a pitiful smile to his lips*) Hello, Nina.
I know it's an imposition—but—I've been in such a terrible
state since Mother— (*He falters, his face becomes distorted into
an ugly mask of grief, his eyes water.*)

NINA—(*immediately sympathetic, gets up and goes to him impulsively*) There's no question of imposition, Charlie. We were
expecting you. (*She has come to him and put her arms around
him. He gives way and sobs, his head against her shoulder.*)

MARSDEN—(*brokenly*) You don't know, Nina—how terrible—it's terrible!—

NINA—(*leading him to the chair at center, soothingly*) I know, Charlie. (*thinking with helpless annoyance*)

> Oh, dear, what can I say? . . . his mother hated me . . . I'm not glad she's dead . . . but neither am I sorry . . .

(*with a trace of contempt*)

> Poor Charlie . . . he was so tied to her apron strings . . .

(*then kindly but condescendingly, comforting him*) Poor old Charlie!

MARSDEN—(*The words and the tone shock his pride to life. He raises his head and half-pushes her away—resentfully, thinking*)

> Poor old Charlie! . . . damn it, what am I to her? . . . her old dog who's lost his mother? . . . Mother hated her . . . no, poor dear Mother was so sweet, she never hated anyone . . . she simply disapproved . . .

(*coldly*) I'm all right, Nina. Quite all right now, thank you. I apologize for making a scene.

DARRELL—(*has gotten up from his chair—with relief—thinking*)

> Thank God for Marsden . . . I feel sane again . . .

(*He comes to Marsden—cordially*) How are you, Marsden? (*then offering conventional consolation, pats Marsden's shoulder*) I'm sorry, Marsden.

MARSDEN—(*startled, looks up at him in amazement*) Darrell! (*then with instant hostility*) There's nothing to be sorry about that I can discover! (*Then as they both look at him in surprise he realizes what he has said—stammeringly*) I mean—sorry—is hardly the right word—hardly—is it?

NINA—(*worriedly*) Sit down, Charlie. You look so tired. (*He slumps down in the chair at center mechanically. Nina and Darrell return to their chairs. Nina looks across him at Darrell—triumphantly—thinking*)

> You do love me, Ned! . . .

DARRELL—(*thinking—answering her look—defiantly*)

> I don't love you! . . .

MARSDEN—(*stares intensely before him. Thinking suspiciously—morbidly agitated*)

> Darrell! . . . and Nina! . . . there's something in this room! . . . something disgusting! . . . like a brutal, hairy hand, raw and red, at my throat! . . . stench of human life! . . . heavy and rank! . . . outside it's April . . . green buds on the slim trees . . . the sadness of spring . . . my loss at peace in Nature . . . her sorrow of birth consoling my sorrow of death . . . something human and unnatural in this room! . . . love and hate and passion and possession! . . . cruelly indifferent to my loss! . . . mocking my loneliness! . . . no longer any love for me in any room! . . . lust in this room! . . . lust with a loathsome jeer taunting my sensitive timidities! . . . my purity! . . . purity? . . . ha! yes, if you say prurient purity! . . . lust ogling me for a dollar with oily shoe button Italian eyes! . . .

(*in terror*)

> What thoughts! . . . what a low scoundrel you are! . . . and your mother dead only two weeks! . . . I hate Nina! . . . that Darrell in this room! . . . I feel their desires! . . . where is Sam? . . . I'll tell him! . . . no, he wouldn't believe . . . he's such a trusting fool . . . I must punish her some other way . . .

(*remorsefully*)

> What? . . . punish Nina? . . . my little Nina? . . . why, I want her to be happy! . . . even with Darrell? . . . it's all so confused! . . . I must stop thinking! . . . I must talk! . . . forget! . . . say something! . . . forget everything! . . .

(*He suddenly bursts into a flood of garrulity.*) Mother asked for you, Nina—three days before the end. She said, "Where is Nina Leeds now, Charlie? When is she going to marry Gordon Shaw?" Her mind was wandering, poor woman! You remember how fond she always was of Gordon. She used to love to watch the football games when he was playing. He was so handsome and graceful, she always thought. She always loved a strong, healthy body. She took such strict care of her own, she walked miles every day, she loved bathing and boating in the summer even after she was sixty, she was never sick a day in her life until— (*He turns on Darrell— coldly*) You were right, Doctor Darrell. It was cancer. (*then angrily*) But the doctor you sent me to, and the others he called in could do nothing for her—absolutely nothing! I might just as well have imported some witch doctors from the Solomon Islands! They at least would have diverted her in her last hours with their singing and dancing, but your specialists were a total loss! (*suddenly with an insulting, ugly sneer, raising his voice*) I think you doctors are a pack of God-damned ignorant liars and hypocrites!

NINA—(*sharply*) Charlie!

MARSDEN—(*coming to himself—with a groan—shame-facedly*) Don't mind me. I'm not myself, Nina. I've been through hell! (*He seems about to sob—then abruptly springs to his feet, wildly*) It's this room! I can't stand this room! There's something repulsive about it!

NINA—(*soothingly*) I know it's ugly, Charlie. I haven't had a chance to fix it up yet. We've been too broke.

MARSDEN—(*confusedly*) Oh, it's all right. I'm ugly, too! Where's Sam?

NINA—(*eagerly*) Right upstairs. Go on up. He'll be delighted to see you.

MARSDEN—(*vaguely*) Very well. (*He goes to the door, then stops mournfully.*) But from what I saw on that visit to his home, he doesn't love his mother much. I don't think he'll understand, Nina. He never writes to her, does he?

NINA—(*uneasily*) No—I don't know.

MARSDEN—She seemed lonely. He'll be sorry for it some day after she— (*He gulps.*) Well— (*He goes.*)

NINA—(*in a sudden panic—thinking*)

Sam's mother! . . . "Make my boy, Sammy, happy!" . . . I promised . . . oh, why did Charlie have to remember her? . . .

(*then resolutely*)

I can't remember her now! . . . I won't! . . . I've got to be happy! . . .

DARRELL—(*uneasily trying to force a casual conversation*) Poor Marsden is completely knocked off balance, isn't he? (*a pause*) My mother died when I was away at school. I hadn't seen her in some time, so her death was never very real to me; but in Marsden's case—

NINA—(*with a possessive smile of tolerance*) Never mind Charlie, Ned. What do I care about Charlie? I love you! And you love me!

DARRELL—(*apprehensively, forcing a tone of annoyed rebuke*) But I don't! And you don't! You're simply letting your romantic imagination run away with you—(*showing his jealous resentment in spite of himself*)—as you did once before with Gordon Shaw!

NINA—(*thinking*)

> He is jealous of Gordon! . . . how wonderful that is! . . .

(*with provoking calm*) I loved Gordon.

DARRELL—(*irritably ignoring this as if he didn't want to hear it*) Romantic imagination! It has ruined more lives than all the diseases! Other diseases, I should say! It's a form of insanity! (*He gets up forcefully and begins to pace about the room. Thinking uneasily*)

> Mustn't look at her . . . find an excuse and get away . . . and this time never come back! . . .

(*avoiding looking at her, trying to argue reasonably—coldly*) You're acting foolishly, Nina—and very unfairly. The agreement we made has no more to do with love than a contract for building a house. In fact, you know we agreed it was essential that love mustn't enter into it. And it hasn't in spite of what you say. (*A pause. He walks about. She watches him. Thinking*)

> She's got to come back to earth! . . . I've got to break with her! . . . bad enough now! . . . but to go on with it! . . . what a mess it'd make of all our lives! . . .

NINA—(*thinking tenderly*)

> Let his pride put all the blame on me! . . . I'll accept it gladly! . . .

DARRELL—(*irritably*) Of course, I realize I've been to blame, too. I haven't been able to be as impersonal as I thought I could be. The trouble is there's been a dangerous physical attraction. Since I first met you, I've always desired you physically. I admit that now.

NINA—(*smiling tenderly—thinking*)

Oh, he admits that, does he? . . . poor darling! . . . (*enticingly*) And you still do desire me, don't you, Ned?

DARRELL—(*keeping his back turned to her—roughly*) No! That part of it is finished! (*Nina laughs softly, possessively. He whirls around to face her—angrily*) Look here! You're going to have the child you wanted, aren't you?

NINA—(*implacably*) My child wants its father!

DARRELL—(*coming a little toward her—desperately*) But you're crazy! You're forgetting Sam! It may be stupid but I've got a guilty conscience! I'm beginning to think we've wronged the very one we were trying to help!

NINA—You were trying to help me, too, Ned!

DARRELL—(*stammering*) Well—all right—let's say that part of it was all right then. But it's got to stop! It can't go on!

NINA—(*implacably*) Only your love can make me happy now! Sam must give me a divorce so I can marry you.

DARRELL—(*thinking suspiciously*)

Look out! . . . there it is! . . . marry! . . . own me! . . . ruin my career! . . .

(*scornfully*) Marry? Do you think I'm a fool? Get that out of your head quick! I wouldn't marry anyone—no matter what! (*as she continues to look at him with unmoved determination— pleadingly*) Be sensible, for God's sake! We're absolutely un-suited to each other! I don't admire your character! I don't respect you! I know too much about your past! (*then indignantly*) And how about Sam? Divorce him? Have you forgotten all his mother told you? Do you mean to say you'd deliberately—? And you expect me to—? What do you think I am?

NINA—(*inflexibly*) You're my lover! Nothing else matters. Yes, I remember what Sam's mother said. She said, "being happy is the nearest we can come to knowing what good is." And I'm going to be happy! I've lost everything in life so far because I didn't have the courage to take it—and I've hurt everyone around me. There's no use trying to think of others. One human being can't think of another. It's impossible. (*gently and caressingly*) But this time I'm going to think of my own happiness—and that means you—and our child!

That's quite enough for one human being to think of, dear, isn't it? (*She reaches out and takes his hand. A pause. With her other hand she gently pulls him around until he is forced to look into her eyes.*)

DARRELL—(*thinking fascinatedly*)

    I see my happiness in her eyes . . . the touch of her soft skin! . . . those afternoons! . . . God, I was happy! . . .

(*in a strange dazed voice—as if it were forced out of him by an impulse stronger than his will*) Yes, Nina.

NINA—(*in a determined voice*) I've given Sam enough of my life! And it hasn't made him happy, not the least bit! So what's the good? And how can we really know that his thinking our child was his would do him any good? We can't! It's all guesswork. The only thing sure is that we love each other.

DARRELL—(*dazedly*) Yes. (*A noise from the hall and Evans comes in from the rear. He sees their two hands together but mistakes their meaning.*)

EVANS—(*genially—with a forced self-confident air*) Well, Doc, how's the patient? I think she's much better, don't you—although she won't admit it.

DARRELL—(*at the first sound of Evans' voice, pulls his hand from Nina's as if it were a hot coal—avoiding Evans' eyes, moving away from her jerkily and self-consciously*) Yes. Much better.

EVANS—Good! (*He pats Nina on the back. She shrinks away. His confidence vanishes in a flash. Thinking miserably*)

    Why does she shrink away . . . if I even touch her? . . .

NINA—(*matter-of-factly*) I must see how lunch is coming on. You'll stay, of course, Ned?

DARRELL—(*struggling—shakenly*) No, I think I'd better— (*thinking desperately*)

    Got to go! . . . can't go! . . . got to go! . . .

EVANS—Oh, come on, old man!

NINA—(*thinking*)

    He must stay . . . and after lunch we'll tell Sam. . . . (*with certainty*) He'll stay. (*meaningly*) And we want to have a long talk with you after lunch, Sam—don't we, Ned? (*Darrell does not answer. She goes out, right.*)

EVANS—(*vaguely making talk*) I got Charlie to lie down.

He's all in, poor guy. (*then trying to face Darrell who keeps looking away from him*) What did Nina mean, you want a long talk with me? Or is it a secret, Ned?

DARRELL—(*controlling an impulse toward hysterical laughter*) A secret? Yes, you bet it's a secret! (*He flings himself in the chair at left, keeping his face averted. His thoughts bitter and desperate like a cornered fugitive's*)

This is horrible! . . . Sam thinks I'm finest fellow in world . . . and I do this to him! . . . as if he hadn't enough! . . . born under a curse! . . . I finish him! . . . a doctor! . . . God damn it! . . . I can see his end! . . . never forgive myself! . . . never forget! . . . break me! . . . ruin my career! . . .

(*more desperately*)

Got to stop this! . . . while there's time! . . . she said . . . after lunch, talk . . . she meant, tell him . . . that means kill him . . . then she'll marry me! . . .

(*beginning to be angry*)

By God, I won't! . . . she'll find out! . . . smiling! . . . got me where she wants me! . . . then be as cruel to me as she is to him! . . . love me? . . . liar! . . . still loves Gordon! . . . her body is a trap! . . . I'm caught in it! . . . she touches my hand, her eyes get in mine, I lose my will! . . .

(*furiously*)

By God, she can't make a fool of me that way! . . . I'll go away some place! . . . go to Europe! . . . study! . . . forget her in work! . . . keep hidden until boat sails so she can't reach me! . . .

(*He is in a state of strange elation by this time.*)

Go now! . . . no! . . . got to spike her guns with Sam! . . . by God, I see! . . . tell him about baby! . . . that'll stop her! . . . when she knows I've told him that, she'll see it's hopeless! . . . she'll stick to him! . . . poor Nina! . . . I'm sorry! . . . she does love me! . . . hell! . . . she'll forget! . . . she'll have her child! . . . she'll be happy! . . . and Sam'll be happy! . . .

(*He suddenly turns to Evans who has been staring at him, puzzledly—in a whisper*) Look here, Sam. I can't stay to lunch. I haven't time, I've got a million things to do. I'm sailing for Europe in a few days.

EVANS—(*surprised*) You're sailing?

DARRELL—(*very hurriedly*) Yes—going to study over there for a year or so. I haven't told anyone. I came out today to say good-bye. You won't be able to reach me again. I'll be out of town visiting. (*then elatedly*) And now for your secret! It ought to make you very happy, Sam. I know how much you've wished for it, so I'm going to tell you although Nina'll be furious with me. She was saving it to surprise you with at her own proper time—(*still more elatedly*)—but I'm selfish enough to want to see you happy before I go!

EVANS—(*not daring to believe what he hopes—stammering*) What—what is it, Ned?

DARRELL—(*clapping him on the back—with strange joviality*) You're going to be a father, old scout, that's the secret! (*Then as Evans just stares at him dumbly in a blissful satisfaction, he rattles on.*) And now I've got to run. See you again in a year or so. I've said good-bye to Nina. Good-bye, Sam. (*He takes his hand and clasps it.*) Good luck! Buckle down to work now! You've got the stuff in you! When I get back I'll expect to hear you're on the highroad to success! And tell Nina I'll expect to find you both happy in your child—both of you, tell her!—happy in your child! Tell her that, Sam! (*He turns and goes to the door. Thinking as he goes*)

That does it! . . . honorably! . . . I'm free! . . .

(*He goes out—then out the front door—a moment later his motor is heard starting—dies away.*)

EVANS—(*stares after him dumbly in the same state of happy stupefaction—mumbles*) Thank you—Ned. (*thinking disjointedly*)

Why did I doubt myself? . . . now she loves me . . . she's loved me right along . . . I've been a fool . . .

(*He suddenly falls on his knees.*)

Oh, God, I thank you!

(*Nina comes in from the kitchen. She stops in amazement when she sees him on his knees. He jumps to his feet and takes her in his arms with confident happiness and kisses her.*) Oh, Nina, I love you so! And now I know you love me! I'll never be afraid of anything again!

NINA—(*bewildered and terror-stricken, trying feebly to push him away*—*thinking*)

> Has he . . . has he gone crazy? . . .

(*weakly*) Sam! What's come over you, Sam?

EVANS—(*tenderly*) Ned told me—the secret—and I'm so happy, dear! (*He kisses her again.*)

NINA—(*stammering*) Ned told you—what?

EVANS—(*tenderly*) That we're going to have a child, dear. You mustn't be sore at him. Why did you want to keep it a secret from me? Didn't you know how happy it would make me, Nina?

NINA—He told you we—we—you, the father—? (*then suddenly breaking from him*—*wildly*) Ned! Where is Ned?

EVANS—He left a moment ago.

NINA—(*stupidly*) Left? Call him back. Lunch is ready.

EVANS—He's gone. He couldn't stay. He's got so much to do getting ready to sail.

NINA—Sail?

EVANS—Didn't he tell you he was sailing for Europe? He's going over for a year or so to study.

NINA—A year or so! (*wildly*) I've got to call him up! No, I'll go in and see him right now! (*She takes a wavering step toward the door. Thinking in anguish*)

> Go! . . . go to him! . . . find him! . . . my lover! . . .

EVANS—He won't be there, I'm afraid. He said we couldn't reach him, that he'd be visiting friends out of town until he sailed. (*solicitously*) Why, do you have to see him about something important, Nina? Perhaps I could locate—

NINA—(*stammering and swaying*) No. (*She stifles an hysterical laugh.*) No, nothing—nothing important—nothing is important—ha—! (*She stifles another laugh*—*then on the verge of fainting, weakly*) Sam! Help me—

EVANS—(*rushes to her, supports her to sofa at right*) Poor darling! Lie down and rest. (*She remains in a sitting position, staring blankly before her. He chafes her wrists.*) Poor darling! (*thinking jubilantly*)

> Her condition . . . this weakness comes from her condition! . . .

NINA—(*thinking in anguish*)

> Ned doesn't love me! . . . he's gone! . . . gone for-

ever! . . . like Gordon! . . . no, not like Gordon!
. . . like a sneak, a coward! . . . a liar! . . . oh, I hate
him! . . . O Mother God, please let me hate him!
. . . he must have been planning this! . . . he must
have known it today when he said he loved me! . . .
(*thinking frenziedly*)
I won't bear it! . . . he thinks he has palmed me off
on Sam forever! . . . and his child! . . . he can't! . . .
I'll tell Sam he was lying! . . . I'll make Sam hate him!
. . . I'll make Sam kill him! . . . I'll promise to love
Sam if he kills him! . . .
(*suddenly turns to Evans—savagely*) He lied to you!
EVANS—(*letting her wrists drop—appalled—stammers*) You
mean—Ned lied about—?
NINA—(*in same tone*) Ned lied to you!
EVANS—(*stammers*) You're not—going to have a child—
NINA—(*savagely*) Oh, yes! Oh, yes, I am! Nothing can
keep me from that! But you're—you're—I mean, you . . .
(*thinking in anguish*)
I can't say that to him! . . . I can't tell him without
Ned to help me! . . . I can't! . . . look at his face!
. . . oh, poor Sammy! . . . poor little boy! . . . poor
little boy! . . .
(*She takes his head and presses it to her breast and begins to weep.
Weeping*) I mean, you weren't to know about it, Sammy.
EVANS—(*immediately on the crest again—tenderly*) Why?
Don't you want me to be happy, Nina?
NINA—Yes—yes, I do, Sammy. (*thinking strangely*)
Little boy! . . . little boy! . . . one gives birth to
little boys! . . . one doesn't drive them mad and kill
them! . . .
EVANS—(*thinking*)
She's never called me Sammy before . . . someone
used to . . . oh, yes, Mother. . . .
(*tenderly and boyishly*) And I'm going to make you happy from
now on, Nina. I tell you, the moment Ned told me, something happened to me! I can't explain it, but—I'll make good
now, Nina! I know I've said that before but I was only boasting. I was only trying to make myself think so. But now I say
it knowing I can do it! (*softly*) It's because we're going to

have a child, Nina. I knew that you'd never come to really love me without that. That's what I was down on my knees for when you came in. I was thanking God—for our baby!

NINA—(*tremblingly*) Sammy! Poor boy!

EVANS—Ned said when he came back he'd expect to find us both happy—in our baby. He said to tell you that. You will be happy now, won't you, Nina?

NINA—(*brokenly and exhaustedly*) I'll try to make you happy, Sammy. (*He kisses her, then hides his head on her breast. She stares out over his head. She seems to grow older. Thinking as if she were repeating the words of some inner voice of life*)

>Not Ned's child! . . . not Sam's child! . . . mine!
>. . . there! . . . again! . . . I feel my child live . . .
>moving in my life . . . my life moving in my child
>. . . breathing in the tide I dream and breathe my
>dream back into the tide . . . God is a Mother. . . .

(*then with sudden anguish*)

>Oh, afternoons . . . dear wonderful afternoons of love
>with you, my lover . . . you are lost . . . gone from
>me forever! . . .

(*Curtain*)

SECOND PART

ACT SIX

SCENE—*The same—an evening a little over a year later. The room has undergone a significant change. There is a comfortable, homey atmosphere as though now it definitely belonged to the type of person it was built for. It has a proud air of modest prosperity.*

It is soon after dinner—about eight o'clock. Evans is sitting by the table at left, glancing through a newspaper at headlines and reading an article here and there. Nina is in the chair at center, knitting a tiny sweater. Marsden is sitting on the sofa at right, holding a book which he pretends to be looking through, but glancing wonderingly at Evans and Nina.

There is a startling change in Evans. He is stouter, the haggard look of worry and self-conscious inferiority has gone from his face, it is full and healthy and satisfied. There is also, what is more remarkable, a decided look of solidity about him, of a determination moving toward ends it is confident it can achieve. He has matured, found his place in the world.

The change in Nina is also perceptible. She looks noticeably older, the traces of former suffering are marked on her face, but there is also an expression of present contentment and calm.

Marsden has aged greatly. His hair is gray, his expression one of a deep grief that is dying out into a resignation resentful of itself. He is dressed immaculately in dark tweed.

NINA—(*thinking*)

> I wonder if there's a draft in the baby's room? . . .
> maybe I'd better close the window? . . . oh, I guess
> it's all right . . . he needs lots of fresh air . . . little
> Gordon . . . he does remind me of Gordon . . .
> something in his eyes . . . my romantic imagination?
> . . . Ned said that . . . why hasn't Ned ever written?
> . . . it's better he hasn't . . . how he made me suffer!
> . . . but I forgive him . . . he gave me my baby . . .
> the baby certainly doesn't look like him . . . everyone
> says he looks like Sam . . . how absurd! . . . but Sam

makes a wonderful father . . . he's become a new man in the past year . . . and I've helped him . . . he asks me about everything . . . I have a genuine respect for him now . . . I can give myself without repulsion . . . I am making him happy . . . I've written his mother I'm making him happy . . . I was proud to be able to write her that . . . how queerly things work out! . . . all for the best . . . and I don't feel wicked . . . I feel good . . .

(*She smiles strangely.*)

MARSDEN—(*thinking*)

What a change! . . . the last time I was here the air was poisoned . . . Darrell . . . I was sure he was her lover . . . but I was in a morbid state . . . why did Darrell run away? . . . Nina could have got Sam to divorce her if she really loved Darrell . . . then it's evident she couldn't have loved him . . . and she was going to have Sam's baby . . . Darrell's love must have seemed like treachery . . . so she sent him away . . . that must be it . . .

(*with satisfaction*)

Yes, I've got it straight now. . . .

(*with contemptuous pity*)

Poor Darrell . . . I have no use for him but I did pity him when I ran across him in Munich . . . he was going the pace . . . looked desperate . . .

(*then gloomily*)

My running away was about as successful as his . . . as if one could leave one's memory behind! . . . I couldn't forget Mother . . . she haunted me through every city of Europe . . .

(*then irritatedly*)

I must get back to work! . . . not a line written in over a year! . . . my public will be forgetting me! . . . a plot came to me yesterday . . . my mind is coming around again . . . I am beginning to forget, thank God! . . .

(*then remorsefully*)

No, I don't want to forget you, Mother! . . . but let me remember . . . without pain! . . .

EVANS—(*turning over a page of his paper*) There's going to be the biggest boom before long this country has ever known, or I miss my guess, Nina.

NINA—(*with great seriousness*) Do you think so, Sammy?

EVANS—(*decidedly*) I'm dead sure of it.

NINA—(*with a maternal pride and amusement*)

  Dear Sam . . . I can't quite believe in this self-confident business man yet . . . but I have to admit he's proved it . . . he asked for more money and they gave it without question . . . they're anxious to keep him . . . they ought to be . . . how he's slaved! . . . for me and my baby! . . .

EVANS—(*has been looking at Marsden surreptitiously over his paper*)

  Charlie's mother must have hoarded up a half million . . . he'll let it rot in government bonds . . . wonder what he'd say if I proposed that he back me? . . . he's always taken a friendly interest . . . well, it's worth a bet, anyway . . . he'd be an easy partner to handle . . .

MARSDEN—(*staring at Evans wonderingly*)

  What a changed Sam! . . . I preferred him the old way . . . futile but he had a sensitive quality . . . now he's brash . . . a little success . . . oh, he'll succeed all right . . . his kind are inheriting the earth . . . hogging it, cramming it down their tasteless gullets! . . . and he's happy! . . . actually happy! . . . he has Nina . . . a beautiful baby . . . a comfortable home . . . no sorrow, no tragic memories . . . and I have nothing! . . . but utter loneliness! . . .

(*with grieving self-pity*)

  If only Mother had lived! . . . how horribly I miss her! . . . my lonely home . . . who will keep house for me now? . . . it has got to be done sympathetically or I won't be able to work . . . I must write to Jane . . . she'll probably be only too glad . . .

(*turning to Nina*) I think I'll write to my sister in California and ask her to come on and live with me. She's alone now that her youngest daughter is married, and she has very little money. And my hands are tied as far as sharing the estate with her is concerned. According to Mother's will, I'm cut off too if I give her a penny. Mother never got over her bitter feeling about Jane's marriage. In a way, she was right. Jane's husband wasn't much—no family or position or ability—and I doubt if she was ever happy with him. (*sarcastically*) It was one of those love matches!

NINA—(*smiling—teasingly*) There's no danger of your ever making a love match, is there, Charlie?

MARSDEN—(*wincing—thinking*)

> She can't believe any woman could possibly love me! . . .

(*caustically*) I trust I'll never make that kind of a fool of myself, Nina!

NINA—(*teasingly*) Pooh! Aren't you the superior bachelor! I don't see anything to be so proud of! You're simply shirking, Charlie!

MARSDEN—(*wincing but forcing a teasing air*) You were my only true love, Nina. I made a vow of perpetual bachelorhood when you threw me over in Sam's favor!

EVANS—(*has listened to this last—jokingly*) Hello! What's this? I never knew you were my hated rival, Charlie!

MARSDEN—(*dryly*) Oh—didn't you really? (*But Evans has turned back to his paper. Thinking savagely*)

> That fool, too! . . . he jokes about it! . . . as if I were the last one in the world he could imagine . . .

NINA—(*teasingly*) Well, if I'm responsible, Charlie, I feel I ought to do something about it. I'll pick out a wife for you— guaranteed to suit! She must be at least ten years older than you, large and matronly and placid, and a wonderful cook and housekeeper—

MARSDEN—(*sharply*) Don't be stupid! (*thinking angrily*)

> She picks someone beyond the age! . . . she never imagines sex could enter into it! . . .

NINA—(*placatingly—seeing he is really angry*) Why, I was only picking out a type I thought would be good for you, Charlie—and for your work.

MARSDEN—(*sneeringly—with a meaning emphasis*) You didn't mention chaste. I couldn't respect a woman who hadn't respected herself!

NINA—(*thinking—stung*)

>He's thinking of those men in the hospital . . . what a fool I was ever to tell him! . . .

(*cuttingly*) Oh, so you think you deserve an innocent virgin!

MARSDEN—(*coldly—controlling his anger*) Let's drop me, if you please. (*with a look at her that is challenging and malicious*) Did I tell you I ran into Doctor Darrell in Munich?

NINA—(*startled—thinking frightenedly and confusedly*)

>Ned! . . . he saw Ned! . . . why hasn't he told me before? . . . why did he look at me like that? . . . does he suspect? . . .

(*trying to be calm but stammering*) You saw—Ned?

MARSDEN—(*with savage satisfaction*)

>That struck home! . . . look at her! . . . guilty! . . . then I was right that day! . . .

(*casually*) Yes, I chanced to run into him.

NINA—(*more calmly now*) Why on earth didn't you tell us before, Charlie?

MARSDEN—(*coolly*) Why? Is it such important news? You knew he was there, didn't you? I supposed he'd written you.

EVANS—(*looking up from his paper—affectionately*) How was the old scout?

MARSDEN—(*maliciously*) He seemed in fine feather—said he was having a gay time. When I saw him he was with a startling looking female—quite beautiful, if you like that type. I gathered they were living together.

NINA—(*cannot restrain herself—breaks out*) I don't believe it! (*then immediately controlling herself and forcing a laugh*) I mean, Ned was always so serious-minded it's hard to imagine him messed up in that sort of thing. (*thinking in a queer state of jealous confusion*)

>Hard to imagine! . . . my lover! . . . oh, pain again! . . . why? . . . I don't love him now . . . be careful! . . . Charlie's staring at me. . . .

MARSDEN—(*thinking—jealously*)

>Then she did love him! . . . does she still? . . .

(*hopefully*)

>Or is it only pique? . . . no woman likes to lose a man even when she no longer loves him. . . .

(*with malicious insistence*) Why is that hard to imagine, Nina?

Darrell never struck me as a Galahad. After all, why shouldn't
he have a mistress? (*meaningly*) He has no tie over here to
remain faithful to, has he?

NINA—(*struggling with herself—thinking pitiably*)

> He's right . . . why shouldn't Ned? . . . is that why
> he's never written? . . .

(*airily*) I don't know what ties he has or hasn't got. It's nothing to me if he has fifty mistresses. I suppose he's no better
than the rest of you.

EVANS—(*looking over at her—tenderly reproachful*) That
isn't fair, Nina. (*thinking proudly*)

> I'm proud of that . . . never anyone before her . . .

NINA—(*looking at him—with real gratitude*) I didn't mean
you, dear. (*thinking—proudly*)

> Thank God for Sammy! . . . I know he's mine . . .
> no jealousy . . . no fear . . . no pain . . . I've found
> peace . . .

(*then distractedly*)

> Oh, Ned, why haven't you written? . . . stop it! . . .
> what a fool I am! . . . Ned's dead for me! . . . oh, I
> hate Charlie! . . . why did he tell me? . . .

MARSDEN—(*looking at Evans—contemptuously thinking*)

> What a poor simpleton Sam is! . . . boasting of his
> virtue! . . . as if women loved you for that! . . . they
> despise it! . . . I don't want Nina to think I've had no
> experiences with women. . . .

(*mockingly*) So then it's Sam who is the Galahad, eh? Really,
Nina, you should have him put in the Museum among the
prehistoric mammals!

EVANS—(*pleased—comes back kiddingly*) Well, I never had
your chances, Charlie! I couldn't run over to Europe and get
away with murder the way you have!

MARSDEN—(*foolishly pleased—admitting while denying*)
Oh, I wasn't quite as bad as all that, Sam! (*scornfully ashamed
of himself—thinking*)

> Poor sick ass that I am! . . . I want them to think I've
> been a Don Juan! . . . how pitiful and disgusting!
> . . . I wouldn't have a mistress if I could! . . . if I
> could? . . . of course I could! . . . I've simply never
> cared to degrade myself! . . .

NINA—(*thinking—tormentedly*)

> The thought of that woman! . . . Ned forgetting our
> afternoons in nights with her! . . . stop these
> thoughts! . . . I won't give in to them! . . . why did
> Charlie want to hurt me? . . . is he jealous of Ned?
> . . . Charlie has always loved me in some queer way
> of his own . . . how ridiculous! . . . look at him!
> . . . he's so proud of being thought a Don Juan! . . .
> I'm sure he never even dared to kiss a woman except
> his mother! . . .

(*mockingly*) Do tell us about all your various mistresses in foreign parts, Charlie!

MARSDEN—(*in confusion now*) I—I really don't remember,
Nina!

NINA—Why, you're the most heartless person I've ever
heard of, Charlie! Not remember even one! And I suppose
there are little Marsdens—and you've forgotten all about
them too! (*She laughs maliciously—Evans laughs with her.*)

MARSDEN—(*still more confused—with a silly idiotic smirk*) I
can't say about that, Nina. It's a wise father who knows his
own child, you know!

NINA—(*frightenedly—thinking*)

> What does he mean? . . . does he suspect about the
> baby too? . . . I must be terribly careful of Char-
> lie! . . .

EVANS—(*looking up from his paper again*) Did Ned say anything about coming back?

NINA—(*thinking—longingly*)

> Come back? . . . oh, Ned, how I wish! . . .

MARSDEN—(*looking at her—meaningly*) No, he didn't say.
I gathered he was staying over indefinitely.

EVANS—I'd sure like to see him again.

NINA—(*thinking*)

> He has forgotten me . . . if he did come, he'd proba-
> bly avoid me. . . .

MARSDEN—He spoke of you. He asked if I'd heard
whether Nina had had her baby yet or not. I told him I
hadn't.

EVANS—(*heartily*) Too bad you didn't know. You could
have told him what a world-beater we've got! Eh, Nina?

NINA—(*mechanically*) Yes. (*joyfully—thinking*)

> Ned asked about my baby! . . . then he hadn't for-
> gotten! . . . if he came back he'd come to see his
> baby! . . .

EVANS—(*solicitously*) Isn't it time to nurse him again?

NINA—(*starts to her feet automatically*) Yes, I'm going now.
(*She glances at Marsden, thinking calculatingly*)

> I must win Charlie over again . . . I don't feel safe . . .

(*She stops by his chair and takes his hand and looks into his eyes
gently and reproachfully.*)

MARSDEN—(*thinking shamefacedly*)

> Why have I been trying to hurt her? . . . my Nina!
> . . . I am nearer to her than anyone! . . . I'd give my
> life to make her happy! . . .

NINA—(*triumphantly*)

> How his hand trembles! . . . what a fool to be afraid
> of Charlie! . . . I can always twist him round my
> finger! . . .

(*She runs her hand through his hair, and speaks as though she
were hiding a hurt reproach beneath a joking tone.*) I shouldn't
like you any more, do you know it, after you've practically
admitted you've philandered all over Europe! And I thought
you were absolutely true to me, Charlie!

MARSDEN—(*so pleased he can hardly believe his ears*)

> Then she did believe me! . . . she's actually hurt! . . .
> but I can't let her think . . .

(*with passionate earnestness, clasping her hand in both of his, looking into her eyes*) No, Nina! I swear to you!

NINA—(*thinking—cruelly*)

> Pah! . . . how limp his hands are! . . . his eyes are so
> shrinking! . . . is it possible he loves me? . . . like
> that? . . . what a sickening idea! . . . it seems inces-
> tuous somehow! . . . no, it's too absurd! . . .

(*smiling, gently releases her hand*) All right. I forgive you,
Charlie. (*then matter-of-factly*) Excuse me, please, while I go
up and feed my infant, or we're due to hear some lusty howling in a moment. (*She turns away, then impulsively turns back
and kisses Marsden with real affection.*) You're an old dear, do
you know it, Charlie? I don't know what I'd do without you!
(*thinking*)

It's true, too! . . . he's my only dependable friend
. . . I must never lose him . . . never let him suspect
about little Gordon . . .

(*She turns to go.*)

EVANS—(*jumping up, throwing his paper aside*) Wait a second. I'll come with you. I want to say good night to him.
(*He comes, puts his arm about her waist, kisses her and they go
out together.*)

MARSDEN—(*thinking excitedly*)

I almost confessed I loved her! . . . a queer expression
came over her face . . . what was it? . . . was it satisfaction? . . . she didn't mind? . . . was it pleasure?
. . . then I can hope? . . .

(*then miserably*)

Hope for what? . . . what do I want? . . . If Nina
were free, what would I do? . . . would I do anything? . . . would I wish to? . . . what would I offer
her? . . . money? . . . she could get that from others
. . . myself? . . .

(*bitterly*)

What a prize! . . . my ugly body . . . there's nothing
in me to attract her . . . my fame? . . . God, what a
shoddy, pitiful! . . . but I might have done something
big . . . I might still . . . if I had the courage to write
the truth . . . but I was born afraid . . . afraid of
myself . . . I've given my talent to making fools feel
pleased with themselves in order that they'd feel
pleased with me . . . and like me . . . I'm neither
hated nor loved . . . I'm liked . . . women like me
. . . Nina likes me! . . .

(*resentfully*)

She can't help letting the truth escape her! . . .
"You're an old dear, do you know it, Charlie?" Oh,
yes, I know it . . . too damned well! . . . dear old
Charlie! . . .

(*in anguish*)

Dear old Rover, nice old doggie, we've had him for
years, he's so affectionate and faithful but he's growing
old, he's getting cross, we'll have to get rid of him
soon! . . .

(*in a strange rage, threateningly*)
> But you won't get rid of me so easily, Nina! . . .

(*then confusedly and shamefacedly*)
> Good God, what's the matter with me! . . . since
> Mother's death I've become a regular idiot! . . .

EVANS—(*comes back from the right, a beaming look of proud
parenthood on his face*) He was sleeping so soundly an earth-
quake wouldn't have made him peep! (*He goes back to his
chair—earnestly*) He sure is healthy and husky, Charlie. That
tickles me more than anything else. I'm going to start in
training him as soon as he's old enough—so he'll be a crack
athlete when he goes to college—what I wanted to be and
couldn't. I want him to justify the name of Gordon and be a
bigger star than Gordon ever was, if that's possible.

MARSDEN—(*with a sort of pity—thinking*)
> His is an adolescent mind . . . he'll never grow up
> . . . well, in this adolescent country, what greater
> blessing could he wish for? . . .

(*forcing a smile*) How about training his mind?

EVANS—(*confidently*) Oh, that'll take care of itself. Gordon
was always near the top in his studies, wasn't he? And with
Nina for a mother, his namesake ought to inherit a full set of
brains.

MARSDEN—(*amused*) You're the only genuinely modest
person I know, Sam.

EVANS—(*embarrassed*) Oh—me—I'm the boob of the
family. (*then hastily*) Except when it comes to business. I'll
make the money. (*confidently*) And you can bet your sweet life
I will make it!

MARSDEN—I'm quite sure of that.

EVANS—(*very seriously—in a confidential tone*) I couldn't
have said that two years ago—and believed it. I've changed
a hell of a lot! Since the baby was born, I've felt as if I had
a shot of dynamite in each arm. They can't pile on the work
fast enough. (*He grins—then seriously*) It was about time I
got hold of myself. I wasn't much for Nina to feel proud
about having around the house in those days. Now—well—
at least I've improved. I'm not afraid of my own shadow any
more.

MARSDEN—(*thinking strangely*)

Not to be afraid of one's shadow! . . . that must be the highest happiness of heaven! . . .

(*flatteringly*) Yes, you've done wonders in the past year.

EVANS—Oh, I haven't even started yet. Wait till I get my chance! (*glances at Marsden sharply, makes up his mind and leans forward toward him confidentially*) And I see my real chance, Charlie—lying right ahead, waiting for me to grab it—an agency that's been allowed to run down and go to seed. Within a year or so they'll be willing to sell out cheap. One of their people who's become a good pal of mine told me that in confidence, put it up to me. He'd take it on himself but he's sick of the game. But I'm not! I love it! It's great sport! (*then putting the brake on this exuberance—matter-of-factly*) But I'll need a hundred thousand—and where will I get it? (*looking at Marsden keenly but putting on a joking tone*) Any suggestion you can make, Charlie, will be gratefully received.

MARSDEN—(*thinking suspiciously*)

> Does he actually imagine I . . . ? and a hundred thousand, no less! . . . over one-fifth of my entire . . . by Jove, I'll have to throw cold water on that fancy! . . .

(*shortly*) No, Sam, I can't think of anyone. Sorry.

EVANS—(*without losing any confidence—with a grin*)

> Check! . . . That's that! . . . Charlie's out . . . till the next time! . . . but I'll keep after him! . . .

(*contemplating himself with pride*)

> Gee, I have changed all right! I can remember when a refusal like that would have ruined my confidence for six months!

(*heartily*) Nothing to be sorry about, old man. I only mentioned it on the off chance you might know of someone. (*trying a bold closing stroke—jokingly*) Why don't you be my partner, Charlie? Never mind the hundred thousand. We'll get that elsewhere. I'll bet you might have darn fine original ideas to contribute. (*thinking—satisfied*)

> There! . . . That'll keep my proposition pinned up in his mind! . . .

(*then jumping to his feet—briskly*) What do you say to a little stroll down to the shore and back? Come on—do you good.

(*taking his arm and hustling him genially toward the door*) What
you need is exercise. You're soft as putty. Why don't you take
up golf?

MARSDEN—(*with sudden resistance pulls away—determinedly*) No, I won't go, Sam. I want to think out a new plot.

EVANS—Oh, all right! If it's a case of work, go to it! See
you later. (*He goes out. A moment later the front door is heard
closing.*)

MARSDEN—(*looks after him with a mixture of annoyance and
scornful amusement*)

> What a fount of meaningless energy he's tapped!
> . . . always on the go . . . typical terrible child of
> the age . . . universal slogan, keep moving . . .
> moving where? . . . never mind that . . . don't
> think of ends . . . the means are the end . . . keep
> moving! . . .

(*He laughs scornfully and sits down in Evans' chair, picking up
the paper and glancing at it sneeringly*)

> It's in every headline of this daily newer testament
> . . . going . . . going . . . never mind the gone . . .
> we won't live to see it . . . and we'll be so rich, we
> can buy off the deluge anyway! . . . even our new
> God has His price! . . . must have! . . . aren't we
> made in His image? . . . or vice-versa? . . .

(*He laughs again, letting the paper drop disdainfully—then
bitterly*)

> But why am I so superior? . . . where am I going?
> . . . to the same nowhere! . . . worse! . . . I'm not
> even going! . . . I'm there! . . .

(*He laughs with bitter self-pity—then begins to think with
amused curiosity*)

> Become Sam's partner? . . . there's a grotesque no-
> tion! . . . it might revive my sense of humor about
> myself, at least . . . I'm the logical one to help him
> . . . I helped him to Nina . . . logical partner . . .
> partner in Nina? . . . what inane thoughts! . . .

(*with a sigh*)

> No use trying to think out that plot tonight . . . I'll
> try to read. . . .

(*He sees the book he has been reading on the couch and gets up to get it. There is a ring from the front door. Marsden turns toward it uncertainly. A pause. Then Nina's voice calls down the stairs*)

NINA—The maid's out. Will you go to the door, Charlie?

MARSDEN—Surely. (*He goes out and opens the front door. A pause. Then he can be heard saying resentfully*) Hello, Darrell. (*And someone answering* "Hello, Marsden" *and coming in and the door closing.*)

NINA—(*from upstairs, her voice strange and excited*) Who is it, Charlie?

DARRELL—(*comes into view in the hall, opposite the doorway, at the foot of the stairs—his voice trembling a little with suppressed emotion*) It's I, Nina—Ned Darrell.

NINA—(*with a glad cry*) Ned! (*then in a voice which shows she is trying to control herself, and is frightened now*) I—make yourself at home. I'll be down—in a minute or two. (*Darrell remains standing looking up the stairs in a sort of joyous stupor. Marsden stares at him.*)

MARSDEN—(*sharply*) Come on in and sit down. (*Darrell starts, comes into the room, plainly getting a grip on himself. Marsden follows him, glaring at his back with enmity and suspicion. Darrell moves as far away from him as possible, sitting down on the sofa at right. Marsden takes Evans' chair by the table. Darrell is pale, thin, nervous, unhealthy looking. There are lines of desperation in his face, puffy shadows of dissipation and sleeplessness under his restless, harried eyes. He is dressed carelessly, almost shabbily. His eyes wander about the room, greedily taking it in.*)

DARRELL—(*thinking disjointedly*)

> Here again! . . . dreamed of this house . . . from here, ran away . . . I've come back . . . my turn to be happy! . . .

MARSDEN—(*watching him—savagely*)

> Now I know! . . . absolutely! . . . his face! . . . her voice! . . . they did love each other! . . . they do now! . . .

(*sharply*) When did you get back from Europe?

DARRELL—(*curtly*) This morning on the Olympic. (*thinking—cautiously*)

> Look out for this fellow . . . always had it in for me

. . . like a woman . . . smells out love . . . he suspected before . . .

(*then boldly*)

Well, who gives a damn now? . . . all got to come
out! . . . Nina wanted to tell Sam . . . now I'll tell
him myself! . . .

MARSDEN—(*righteously indignant*)

What has brought him back? . . . what a devilish,
cowardly trick to play on poor unsuspecting Sam! . . .

(*revengefully*)

But I'm not unsuspecting! . . . I'm not their
fool! . . .

(*coldly*) What brought you back so soon? When I saw you in
Munich you weren't intending—

DARRELL—(*shortly*) My father died three weeks ago. I've
had to come back about his estate. (*thinking*)

Lie . . . Father's death just gave me an excuse to myself . . . wouldn't have come back for that . . . came
back because I love her! . . . damn his questions! . . .
I want to think . . . before I see her . . . sound of
her voice . . . seemed to burn inside my head . . .
God, I'm licked! . . . no use fighting it . . . I've done
my damnedest . . . work . . . booze . . . other
women . . . no use . . . I love her! . . . always! . . .
to hell with pride! . . .

MARSDEN—(*thinking*)

He has two brothers . . . they'll probably all share
equally . . . his father noted Philadelphia surgeon
. . . rich, I've heard . . .

(*with a bitter grin*)

Wait till Sam hears that! . . . he'll ask Darrell to back
him . . . and Darrell will jump at it . . . chance to
avert suspicion . . . conscience money, too! . . . it's
my duty to protect Sam . . .

(*as he hears Nina coming down the stairs*)

I must watch them . . . it's my duty to protect Nina
from herself . . . Sam is a simpleton . . . I'm all she
has . . .

DARRELL—(*hearing her coming—in a panic—thinking*)

Coming! . . . in a second I'll see her! . . .

(*terrified*)

> Does she still love me? . . . she may have forgotten . . . no, it's my child . . . she can never forget that! . . .

(*Nina comes in from the rear. She has put on a fresh dress, her hair is arranged, her face newly rouged and powdered, she looks extremely pretty and this is heightened by the feverish state of mind she is in—a mixture of love, of triumphant egotism in knowing her lover has come back to her, and of fear and uncertainty in feeling her new peace, her certainties, her contented absorption in her child failing her. She hesitates just inside the door, staring into Darrell's eyes, thinking a fierce question.*)

NINA—

> Does he still love me? . . .

(*then triumphantly as she reads him*)

> Yes! . . . he does! . . . he does! . . .

DARRELL—(*who has jumped to his feet—with a cry of longing*) Nina! (*thinking with alarm now*)

> She's changed! . . . changed! . . . can't tell if she loves! . . .

(*He has started to go to her. Now he hesitates. His voice taking on a pleading uncertain quality*) Nina!

NINA—(*thinking triumphantly—with a certain cruelty*)

> He loves me! . . . he's mine . . . now more than ever! . . . he'll never dare leave me again! . . .

(*Certain of herself now, she comes to him and speaks with confident pleasure.*) Hello, Ned! This is a wonderful surprise! How are you? (*She takes his hand.*)

DARRELL—(*taken aback—confusedly*) Oh—all right, Nina. (*thinking in a panic*)

> That tone! . . . as if she didn't care! . . . can't believe that! . . . she's playing a game to fool Marsden! . . .

MARSDEN—(*who is watching them keenly—thinking*)

> She loves his love for her . . . she's cruelly confident . . . much as I hate this man I can't help feeling sorry . . . I know her cruelty . . . it's time I took a hand in this . . . what a plot for a novel! . . .

(*almost mockingly*) Darrell's father died, Nina. He had to come home to see about the estate.

DARRELL—(*with a glare at Marsden—protestingly*) I was

coming home anyway. I only intended to stay a year, and it's over that since— (*intensely*) I was coming back anyway, Nina!

NINA—(*thinking with triumphant happiness*)

> You dear, you! . . . as if I didn't know that! . . . oh, how I'd love to take you in my arms! . . .

(*happily*) I'm awfully glad you've come, Ned. We've missed you terribly.

DARRELL—(*thinking—more and more at sea*)

> She looks glad . . . but she's changed . . . I don't understand her . . . "we've missed" . . . that means Sam . . . what does that mean? . . .

(*intensely, pressing her hand*) And I've missed you—terribly!

MARSDEN—(*sardonically*) Yes, indeed, Darrell, I can vouch for their missing you—Sam in particular. He was asking about you only a short while ago—how things were going with you when I saw you in Munich. (*maliciously*) By the way, who was the lady you were with that day? She was certainly startling looking.

NINA—(*thinking—triumphantly mocking*)

> A miss, Charlie! . . . he loves me! . . . what do I care about that woman? . . .

(*gaily*) Yes, who was the mysterious beauty, Ned? Do tell us! (*She moves away from him and sits down at center. Darrell remains standing.*)

DARRELL—(*glaring at Marsden, sullenly*) Oh, I don't remember— (*thinking apprehensively with a bitter resentment*)

> She doesn't give a damn! . . . if she loved me she'd be jealous! . . . but she doesn't give a damn! . . .

(*He blurts out resentfully at Nina*) Well, she was my mistress—for a time—I was lonely. (*then with sudden anger turning on Marsden*) But what's all this to you, Marsden?

MARSDEN—(*coolly*) Absolutely nothing. Pardon me. It was a tactless question. (*then with continued open malice*) But I was starting to say how Sam had missed you, Darrell. It's really remarkable. One doesn't encounter such friendship often in these slack days. Why, he'd trust you with anything!

NINA—(*wincing—thinking*)

> That hurts . . . hurts Ned . . . Charlie is being cruel! . . .

DARRELL—(*wincing—in a forced tone*) And I'd trust Sam with anything.

MARSDEN—Of course. He is a person one can trust. They are rare. You're going to be amazed at the change in Sam, Darrell. Isn't he, Nina? He's a new man. I never saw such energy. If ever a man was bound for success Sam is. In fact, I'm so confident he is that as soon as he thinks the time is ripe to start his own firm I'm going to furnish the capital and become his silent partner.

DARRELL—(*puzzled and irritated—thinking confusedly*)

> What's he driving at? . . . why doesn't he get the hell out and leave us alone? . . . but I'm glad Sam is on his feet . . . makes it easier to tell him the truth. . . .

NINA—(*thinking—worriedly*)

> What's Charlie talking about? . . . it's time I talked to Ned . . . Oh, Ned, I do love you! . . . you can be my lover! . . . we won't hurt Sam! . . . he'll never know! . . .

MARSDEN—Yes, ever since the baby was born Sam's been another man—in fact, ever since he knew there was going to be a baby, isn't it, Nina?

NINA—(*agreeing as if she had only half-heard him*) Yes. (*thinking*)

> Ned's baby! . . . I must talk to him about our baby. . . .

MARSDEN—Sam is the proudest parent I've ever seen!

NINA—(*as before*) Yes, Sam makes a wonderful father, Ned. (*thinking*)

> Ned doesn't care for children . . . I know what you're hoping, Ned . . . but if you think I'm going to take Sam's baby from him, you're mistaken! . . . or if you think I'll run away with you and leave my baby . . .

MARSDEN—(*with the same strange driving insistence*) If anything happened to that child I actually believe Sam would lose his reason! Don't you think so, Nina?

NINA—(*with emphasis*) I know I'd lose mine! Little Gordon has become my whole life.

DARRELL—(*thinking—with a sad bitter irony*)

> Sam . . . wonderful father . . . lose his reason . . . little Gordon! . . . Nina called my son after Gordon!

. . . romantic imagination! . . . Gordon is still her lover! . . . Gordon, Sam and Nina! . . . and my son! . . . closed corporation! . . . I'm forced out! . . .

(*then rebelling furiously*)

No! . . . not yet, by God! . . . I'll smash it up! . . . I'll tell Sam the truth no matter what! . . .

NINA—(*thinking with a strange calculation*)

I couldn't find a better husband than Sam . . . and I couldn't find a better lover than Ned . . . I need them both to be happy . . .

MARSDEN—(*with sudden despairing suspicion*)

Good God . . . after all, is it Sam's child? . . . mightn't it be Darrell's! . . . why have I never thought of that? . . . No! . . . Nina couldn't be so vile! . . . to go on living with Sam, pretending . . . and, after all, why should she, you fool? . . . there's no sense! . . . she could have gone off with Darrell, couldn't she? . . . Sam would have given her a divorce . . . there was no possible reason for her staying with Sam, when she loved Darrell, unless exactly because this was Sam's baby . . . for its sake . . .

(*hectically relieved*)

Of course! . . . of course! . . . that's all right! . . . I love that poor baby now! . . . I'll fight for its sake against these two! . . .

(*smilingly gets to his feet—thinking*)

I can leave them alone now . . . for they won't be alone, thanks to me! . . . I leave Sam and his baby in this room with them . . . and their honor . . .

(*suddenly raging*)

Their honor! . . . what an obscene joke! . . . the honor of a harlot and a pimp! . . . I hate them! . . . if only God would strike them dead! . . . now! . . . and I could see them die! . . . I would praise His justice! . . . His kindness and mercy to me! . . .

NINA—(*thinking—with horrified confusion*)

Why doesn't Charlie go? . . . What is he thinking? . . . I suddenly feel afraid of him! . . .

(*She gets to her feet with a confused pleading cry.*) Charlie!

MARSDEN—(*immediately urbane and smiling*) It's all right. I'm going out to find Sam. When he knows you're here he'll come on the run, Darrell. (*He goes to the door. They watch him suspiciously.*) And you two probably have a lot to talk over. (*He chuckles pleasantly and goes into the hall—mockingly warning*) We'll be back before long. (*The front door is heard slamming. Nina and Darrell turn and look at each other guiltily and frightenedly. Then he comes to her and takes both of her hands uncertainly.*)

DARRELL—(*stammeringly*) Nina—I—I've come back to you—do you—do you still care—Nina?

NINA—(*giving way to his love passionately, as if to drown her fears*) I love you, Ned!

DARRELL—(*kisses her awkwardly—stammering*) I—I didn't know—you seemed so cold—damn Marsden—he suspects, doesn't he?—but it makes no difference now, does it? (*then in a flood of words*) Oh, it's been hell, Nina! I couldn't forget you! Other women—they only made me love you more! I hated them and loved you even at the moment when—that's honest! It was always you in my arms—as you used to be— those afternoons—God, how I've thought of them—lying awake—recalling every word you said, each movement, each expression on your face, smelling your hair, feeling your soft body— (*suddenly taking her in his arms and kissing her again and again—passionately*) Nina! I love you so!

NINA—And I've longed for you so much! Do you think I've forgotten those afternoons? (*then in anguish*) Oh, Ned, why did you run away? I can never forgive that! I can never trust you again!

DARRELL—(*violently*) I was a fool! I thought of Sam! And that wasn't all! Oh, I wasn't all noble, I'll confess! I thought of myself and my career! Damn my career! A lot of good that did it! I didn't study! I didn't live! I longed for you—and suffered! I paid in full, believe me, Nina! But I know better now! I've come back! The time for lying is past! You've got to come away with me! (*He kisses her.*)

NINA—(*letting herself go, kissing him passionately*) Yes! My lover! (*then suddenly resisting and pushing him away*) No! You're forgetting Sam—and Sam's baby!

DARRELL—(*staring at her wildly*) Sam's baby? Are you joking? Ours, you mean! We'll take him with us, of course!

NINA—(*sadly*) And Sam?

DARRELL—Damn Sam! He's got to give you a divorce! Let him be generous for a change!

NINA—(*sadly but determinedly*) He would be. You must be just to Sam. He'd give his life for my happiness. And this would mean his life. Could we be happy then? You know we couldn't! And I've changed, Ned. You've got to realize that. I'm not your old mad Nina. I still love you. I will always love you. But now I love my baby too. His happiness comes first with me!

DARRELL—But—he's mine, too!

NINA—No! You gave him to Sam to save Sam!

DARRELL—To hell with Sam! It was to make you happy!

NINA—So I could make Sam happy! That was in it too! I was sincere in that, Ned! If I hadn't been, I could never have gone to you that first day—or if I had, I'd never have forgiven myself. But as it is I don't feel guilty or wicked. I have made Sam happy! And I'm proud! I love Sam's happiness! I love the devoted husband and father in him! And I feel it's his baby—that we've made it his baby!

DARRELL—(*distractedly*) Nina! For God's sake! You haven't come to love Sam, have you? Then—I'll go—I'll go away again—I'll never come back—I tried not to this time—but I had to, Nina!

NINA—(*taking him in her arms—with sudden alarm*) No, don't go away, Ned—ever again. I don't love Sam! I love you!

DARRELL—(*miserably*) But I don't understand! Sam gets everything—and I have nothing!

NINA—You have my love! (*with a strange, self-assured smile at him*) It seems to me you're complaining unreasonably!

DARRELL—You mean—I can be—your lover again?

NINA—(*simply, even matter-of-factly*) Isn't that the nearest we can come to making everyone happy? That's all that counts.

DARRELL—(*with a harsh laugh*) And is that what you call playing fair to Sam?

NINA—(*simply*) Sam will never know. The happiness I
have given him has made him too sure of himself ever to
suspect me now. And as long as we can love each other without danger to him, I feel he owes that to us for all we've done
for him. (*with finality*) That's the only possible solution, Ned,
for all our sakes, now you've come back to me.

DARRELL—(*repulsed*) Nina! How can you be so inhuman
and calculating!

NINA—(*stung—mockingly*) It was you who taught me the
scientific approach, Doctor!

DARRELL—(*shrinking back from her—threateningly*) Then
I'll leave again! I'll go back to Europe! I won't endure—!
(*then in a queer, futile rage*) You think I'll stay—to be your
lover—watching Sam with my wife and my child—you think
that's what I came back to you for? You can go to hell,
Nina!

NINA—(*calmly—sure of him*) But what else can I do, Ned?
(*then warningly*) I hear them coming, dear. It's Sam, you
know.

DARRELL—(*in a frenzy*) What else can you do? Liar! But I
can do something else! I can smash your calculating game for
you! I can tell Sam—and I will—right now—by God, I will!

NINA—(*quietly*) No. You won't, Ned. You can't do that to
Sam.

DARRELL—(*savagely*) Like hell I can't! (*The front door is
opened. Evans' voice is immediately heard, even before he bounds
into the room. He rushes up to Ned hilariously, shakes his hand
and pounds his back, oblivious to Darrell's wild expression.*)

EVANS—You old son of a gun! Why didn't you let a guy
know you were coming? We'd have met you at the dock, and
brought the baby. Let me have a look at you! You look thinner. We'll fatten you up, won't we, Nina? Let us do the prescribing this time! Why didn't you let us know where you
were, you old bum? We wanted to write you about the baby.
And I wanted to boast about how I was getting on! You're
the only person in the world—except Nina and Charlie—I
would boast about that to.

NINA—(*affectionately*) Mercy, Sam, give Ned a chance to
get a word in! (*looking at Ned pityingly but challengingly*) He
wants to tell you something, Sam.

DARRELL—(*crushed—stammers*) No—I mean, yes—I want to tell you how damn glad I am . . . (*He turns away, his face is screwed up in his effort to hold back his tears. Thinking miserably*)

> I can't tell him! . . . God damn him, I can't! . . .

NINA—(*with a strange triumphant calm*)

> There! . . . that's settled for all time! . . . poor Ned! . . . how crushed he looks! . . . I mustn't let Sam look at him! . . .

(*She steps between them protectingly.*) Where's Charlie, Sam?

MARSDEN—(*appearing from the hall*) Here, Nina. Always here! (*He comes to her, smiling with assurance.*)

NINA—(*suddenly with a strange unnatural elation—looking from one to the other with triumphant possession*) Yes, you're here, Charlie—always! And you, Sam—and Ned! (*with a strange gaiety*) Sit down, all of you! Make yourselves at home! You are my three men! This is your home with me! (*then in a strange half-whisper*) Ssshh! I thought I heard the baby. You must all sit down and be very quiet. You must not wake our baby. (*Mechanically the three sit down, careful to make no noise—Evans in his old place by the table, Marsden at center, Darrell on the sofa at right. They sit staring before them in silence. Nina remains standing, dominating them, a little behind and to the left of Marsden.*)

DARRELL—(*thinking abjectly*)

> I couldn't! . . . there are things one may not do and live with oneself afterwards . . . there are things one may not say . . . memory is too full of echoes! . . . there are secrets one must not reveal . . . memory is lined with mirrors! . . . he was too happy! . . . to kill happiness is a worse murder than taking life! . . . I gave him that happiness! . . . Sam deserves my happiness! . . . God bless you, Sam! . . .

(*then in a strange objective tone—thinking*)

> My experiment with the guinea pigs has been a success . . . the ailing ones, Sam, and the female, Nina, have been restored to health and normal function . . . only the other male, Ned, seems to have suffered deterioration. . . .

(*then bitterly humble*)

> Nothing left but to accept her terms . . . I love her
> . . . I can help to make her happy . . . half a loaf is
> better . . . to a starving man. . . .

(*glancing over at Evans—bitterly gloating*)

> And your child is mine! . . . your wife is mine! . . .
> your happiness is mine! . . . may you enjoy my hap-
> piness, her husband! . . .

EVANS—(*looking at Darrell affectionately*)

> Sure good to see Ned again . . . a real friend if there
> ever was one . . . looks blue about something . . .
> oh, that's right, Charlie said his old man had kicked in
> . . . his old man was rich . . . that's an idea . . . I'll
> bet he'd put up that capital . . .

(*then ashamed of himself*)

> Aw hell, what's the matter with me? . . . he's no
> sooner here than I start . . . he's done enough . . .
> forget it! . . . now anyway . . . he looks pretty dissi-
> pated . . . too many women . . . ought to get mar-
> ried and settle down . . . tell him that if I didn't think
> he'd laugh at me giving him advice . . . but he'll soon
> realize I'm not the old Sam he knew . . . I suppose
> Nina's been boasting about that already . . . she's
> proud . . . she's helped me . . . she's a wonderful
> wife and mother . . .

(*looking up at her—solicitously*)

> She acted a bit nervous just now . . . queer . . . like
> she used to . . . haven't noticed her that way in a long
> time . . . suppose it's the excitement of Ned turning
> up . . . mustn't let her get over-excited . . . bad for
> the baby's milk. . . .

MARSDEN—(*glancing furtively over his shoulder at Nina—
broodingly thinking*)

> She's the old queer Nina now . . . the Nina I could
> never fathom . . . her three men! . . . and we are!
> . . . I? . . . yes, more deeply than either of the others
> since I serve for nothing . . . a queer kind of love,
> maybe . . . I am not ordinary! . . . our child . . .
> what could she mean by that? . . . child of us three?
> . . . on the surface, that's insane . . . but I felt when

she said it there was something in it . . . she has
strange devious intuitions that tap the hidden currents
of life . . . dark intermingling currents that become
the one stream of desire . . . I feel, with regard to
Nina, my life queerly identified with Sam's and Darrell's . . . her child is the child of our three loves for
her . . . I would like to believe that . . . I would like
to be her husband in a sense . . . and the father of a
child, after my fashion . . . I could forgive her everything . . . permit everything . . .

(*determinedly*)

And I do forgive! . . . and I will not meddle hereafter
more than is necessary to guard her happiness, and
Sam's and our baby's . . . as for Darrell, I am no
longer jealous of him . . . she is only using his love
for her own happiness . . . he can never take her away
from me! . . .

NINA—(*more and more strangely triumphant*)

My three men! . . . I feel their desires converge in
me! . . . to form one complete beautiful male desire
which I absorb . . . and am whole . . . they dissolve
in me, their life is my life . . . I am pregnant with
the three! . . . husband! . . . lover! . . . father! . . .
and the fourth man! . . . little man! . . . little
Gordon! . . . he is mine too! . . . that makes it
perfect! . . .

(*with an extravagant suppressed exultance*)

Why, I should be the proudest woman on earth! . . .
I should be the happiest woman in the world! . . .

(*then suppressing an outbreak of hysterical triumphant laughter
only by a tremendous effort*)

Ha-ha . . . only I better knock wood . . .

(*She raps with both knuckles in a fierce tattoo on the table.*)

before God the Father hears my happiness! . . .

EVANS—(*as the three turn to her—anxiously*) Nina? What's
the matter?

NINA—(*controlling herself with a great effort comes to him—
forcing a smile—puts her arms around him affectionately*) Nothing, dear. Nerves, that's all. I've gotten over-tired, I guess.

EVANS—(*bullying her—with loving authority*) Then you go right to bed, young lady! We'll excuse you.

NINA—(*quietly and calmly now*) All right, dear. I guess I do need to rest. (*She kisses him as she might kiss a big brother she loved—affectionately*) Good night, you bossy old thing, you!

EVANS—(*with deep tenderness*) Good night, darling.

NINA—(*She goes and kisses Charlie dutifully on the cheek as she might her father—affectionately*) Good night, Charlie.

MARSDEN—(*with a touch of her father's manner*) That's a good girl! Good night, dear.

NINA—(*She goes and kisses Darrell lovingly on the lips as she would kiss her lover.*) Good night, Ned.

DARRELL—(*looks at her with grateful humility*) Thank you. Good night. (*She turns and walks quietly out of the room. The eyes of the three men follow her.*)

(*Curtain*)

ACT SEVEN

SCENE—*Nearly eleven years later. The sitting room of the Evans' apartment on Park Avenue, New York City—a room that is a tribute to Nina's good taste. It is a large, sunny room, the furniture expensive but extremely simple. The arrangement of the furniture shown is as in previous scenes except there are more pieces. Two chairs are by the table at left. There is a smaller table at center, and a chaise longue. A large, magnificently comfortable sofa is at right.*

It is about one in the afternoon of a day in early fall. Nina and Darrell and their son, Gordon, are in the room. Nina is reclining on the chaise longue watching Gordon who is sitting on the floor near her, turning over the pages of a book. Darrell is sitting by the table at left, watching Nina.

Nina is thirty-five, in the full bloom of her womanhood. She is slimmer than in the previous scene. Her skin still retains a trace of summer tan and she appears in the pink of physical condition. But as in the first act of the play, there is beneath this a sense of great mental strain. One notices the many lines in her face at second glance. Her eyes are tragically sad in repose and her expression is set and masklike.

Gordon is eleven—a fine boy with, even at this age, the figure of an athlete. He looks older than he is. There is a grave expression to his face. His eyes are full of a quick-tempered sensitiveness. He does not noticeably resemble his mother. He looks nothing at all like his father. He seems to have sprung from a line distinct from any of the people we have seen.

Darrell has aged greatly. His hair is streaked with gray. He has grown stout. His face is a bit jowly and puffy under the eyes. The features have become blurred. He has the look of a man with no definite aim or ambition to which he can relate his living. His eyes are embittered and they hide his inner self-resentment behind a pose of cynical indifference.

GORDON—(*thinking as he plays—resentfully*)

> I wish Darrell'd get out of here! . . . why couldn't Mother let me run my own birthday? . . . I'd never had him here, you bet! . . . what's he always hanging 'round for? . . . why don't he go off on one of his old

trips again . . . last time he was gone more'n a year
. . . I was hoping he'd died! . . . what makes Mother
like him so much? . . . she makes me sick! . . . I'd
think she'd get sick of the old fool and tell him to get
out and never come back! . . . I'd kick him out if I
was big enough! . . . it's good for him he didn't
bring me any birthday present or I'd smash it first
chance I got! . . .

NINA—(*watching him—brooding with loving tenderness—
sadly*)

No longer my baby . . . my little man . . . eleven
. . . I can't believe it . . . I'm thirty-five . . .
five years more . . . at forty a woman has finished
living . . . life passes by her . . . she rots away in
peace! . . .

(*intensely*)

I want to rot away in peace! . . . I'm sick of the fight
for happiness! . . .

(*smiling with a wry amusement at herself*)

What ungrateful thoughts on my son's birthday! . . .
my love for him has been happiness . . . how handsome he is! . . . not at all like Ned . . . when I was
carrying him I was fighting to forget Ned . . . hoping
he might be like Gordon . . . and he is . . . poor
Ned, I've made him suffer a great deal . . . !

(*She looks over at Darrell—self-mockingly*)

My lover! . . . so very rarely now, those interludes of
passion . . . what has bound us together all these
years? . . . love? . . . if he could only have been contented with what I was able to give him! . . . but he
has always wanted more . . . yet never had the courage to insist on all or nothing . . . proud without
being proud enough! . . . he has shared me for his
comfort's sake with a little gratitude and a big bitterness . . . and sharing me has corrupted him! . . .

(*then bitterly*)

No, I can't blame myself! . . . no woman can make a
man happy who has no purpose in life! . . . why did
he give up his career? . . . because I had made him
weak? . . .

(*with resentful scorn*)

> No, it was I who shamed him into taking up biology and starting the station at Antigua . . . if I hadn't he'd simply have hung around me year after year, doing nothing . . .

(*irritatedly*)

> Why does he stay so long? . . . over six months . . . I can't stand having him around me that long any more! . . . why doesn't he go back to the West Indies? . . . I always get a terrible feeling after he's been back a while that he's waiting for Sam to die! . . . or go insane! . . .

DARRELL—(*thinking—with an apathetic bitterness*)

> What is she thinking? . . . we sit together in silence, thinking . . . thoughts that never know the other's thoughts . . . our love has become the intimate thinking together of thoughts that are strangers . . . our love! . . . well, whatever it is that has bound us together, it's strong! . . . I've broken with her, run away, tried to forget her . . . running away to come back each time more abject! . . . or, if she saw there was some chance I might break loose, she'd find some way to call me back . . . and I'd forget my longing for freedom, I'd come wagging my tail . . . no, guinea pigs have no tails . . . I hope my experiment has proved something! . . . Sam . . . happy and wealthy . . . and healthy! . . . I used to hope he'd break down . . . I'd watch him and read symptoms of insanity into every move he made . . . despicable? . . . certainly, but love makes one either noble or despicable! . . . he only grew healthier . . . now I've given up watching him . . . almost entirely . . . now I watch him grow fat and I laugh! . . . the huge joke has dawned on me! . . . Sam is the only normal one! . . . we lunatics! . . . Nina and I! . . . have made a sane life for him out of our madness! . . .

(*watching Nina—sadly*)

> Always thinking of her son . . . well, I gave him to her . . . Gordon . . . I hate that name . . . why do I continue hanging around here? . . . each time after

a few months my love changes to bitterness . . . I
blame Nina for the mess I've made of life . . .

NINA—(*suddenly turning on him*) When are you going
back to the West Indies, Ned?

DARRELL—(*determinedly*) Soon!

GORDON—(*stops playing to listen—thinking*)
Gosh, I'm glad! . . . How soon, I wonder? . . .

NINA—(*with a trace of a sneer*) I don't see how you can
afford to leave your work for such long periods. Don't you
grow rusty?

DARRELL—(*looking at her meaningly*) My life work is to
rust—nicely and unobtrusively! (*He smiles mockingly.*)

NINA—(*sadly—thinking*)
To rot away in peace . . . that's all he wants now, too!
. . . and this is what love has done to us! . . .

DARRELL—(*bitterly*) My work was finished twelve years
ago. As I believe you know, I ended it with an experiment
which resulted so successfully that any further meddling with
human lives would have been superfluous!

NINA—(*pityingly*) Ned!

DARRELL—(*indifferent and cynical*) But you meant my
present dabbling about. You know better than to call that
work. It's merely my hobby. Our backing Sam has made
Marsden and me so wealthy that we're forced to take up hobbies. Marsden goes in for his old one of dashing off genteel
novels, while I play at biology. Sam argued that golf would
be healthier and less nonsensical for me, but you insisted on
biology. And give it its due, it has kept me out in the open
air and been conducive to travelling and broadening my
mind! (*then forcing a smile*) But I'm exaggerating. I really am
interested, or I'd never keep financing the Station. And when
I'm down there I do work hard, helping Preston. He's doing
remarkable work already, and he's still in his twenties. He'll
be a big man—(*his bitterness cropping up again*) at least if he
takes my advice and never carries his experiments as far as
human lives!

NINA—(*in a low voice*) How can you be so bitter, Ned—
on Gordon's birthday?

DARRELL—(*thinking cynically*)
She expects me to love the child she deliberately took

from me and gave to another man! . . . no, thank
you, Nina! . . . I've been hurt enough! . . . I'll not
leave myself open there! . . .

(*regarding his son bitterly*) Every day he gets more like Sam,
doesn't he?

GORDON—(*thinking*)

He's talking about me . . . he better look out! . . .

NINA—(*resentfully*) I don't think Gordon resembles Sam at
all. He reminds me a great deal of his namesake.

DARRELL—(*touched on a sore spot—with a nasty laugh—
cuttingly*) Gordon Shaw? Not the slightest bit in the world!
And you ought to thank God he doesn't! It's the last thing
I'd want wished on a boy of mine—to be like that rah-rah
hero!

GORDON—(*thinking contemptuously*)

Boy of his! . . . He hasn't got a boy! . . .

NINA—(*amused and pleased by his jealousy*)

Poor Ned! . . . isn't he silly? . . . at his age, after all
we've been through, to still feel jealous . . .

DARRELL—I'd much rather have him (*pointing to Gordon*) grow up to be an exact duplicate of the esteemed
Samuel!

GORDON—(*thinking resentfully*)

He's always making fun of my father! . . . he better
look out! . . .

DARRELL—(*more and more mockingly*) And what could be
fairer? The good Samuel is an A one success. He has a charming wife and a darling boy, and a Park Avenue apartment and
a membership in an expensive golf club. And, above all, he
rests so complacently on the proud assurance that he is self-
made!

NINA—(*sharply*) Ned! You ought to be ashamed! You
know how grateful Sam has always been to you!

DARRELL—(*bitingly*) Would he be grateful if he knew how
much I'd really done for him?

NINA—(*sternly*) Ned!

GORDON—(*suddenly jumps up and confronts Darrell, his fists
clenched, trembling with rage, stammers*) You—shut up—making fun of my father!

NINA—(*in dismay*) Gordon!

DARRELL—(*mockingly*) My dear boy, I wouldn't make fun of your father for the world!

GORDON—(*baffledly—his lips trembling*) You—you did, too! (*then intensely*) I hate you!

NINA—(*shocked and indignant*) Gordon! How dare you talk like that to your Uncle Ned!

GORDON—(*rebelliously*) He's not my uncle! He's not my anything!

NINA—Not another word or you'll be punished, whether it's your birthday or not! If you can't behave better than that, I'll have to phone to all your friends they mustn't come here this afternoon, that you've been so bad you can't have a party! (*thinking remorsefully*)

> Is this my fault? . . . I've done my best to get him to love Ned! . . . but it only makes him worse! . . . it makes him turn against me! . . . turn from me to Sam! . . .

GORDON—(*sullenly*) I don't care! I'll tell Dad!

NINA—(*peremptorily*) Leave the room! And don't come near me again, do you hear, until you've apologized to Uncle Ned! (*thinking angrily*)

> Dad! . . . It's always Dad with him now! . . .

DARRELL—(*boredly*) Oh, never mind, Nina!

GORDON—(*going out—mutters*) I won't 'pologize—never! (*thinking vindictively*)

> I hate her too when she sides with him! . . . I don't care if she is my mother! . . . she has no right! . . .

(*He goes out, rear.*)

DARRELL—(*irritably*) What if he does hate me? I don't blame him! He suspects what I know—that I've acted like a coward and a weakling toward him! I should have claimed him no matter what happened to other people! Whose fault is it if he hates me, and I dislike him because he loves another father? Ours! You gave him to Sam and I consented! All right! Then don't blame him for acting like Sam's son!

NINA—But he shouldn't say he hates you. (*thinking bitterly*)

> Sam's! . . . he's becoming all Sam's! . . . I'm getting to mean nothing! . . .

DARRELL—(*sardonically*) Perhaps he realizes subconsciously that I am his father, his rival in your love; but I'm not his father ostensibly, there are no taboos, so he can come right out and hate me to his heart's content! (*bitterly*) If he realized how little you love me any more, he wouldn't bother!

NINA—(*exasperatedly*) Oh, Ned, do shut up! I can't stand hearing those same old reproaches I've heard a thousand times before! I can't bear to hear myself making the same old bitter counter-accusations. And then there'll be the same old terrible scene of hate and you'll run away—it used to be to drink and women, now it's to the Station. Or I'll send you away, and then after a time I'll call you back, because I'll have gotten so lonely again living this lonely lie of my life, with no one to speak to except Sam's business friends and their deadly wives. (*She laughs helplessly.*) Or else you'll get lonely in your lie a little before I do and come back again of your own desire! And then we'll kiss and cry and love each other again!

DARRELL—(*with an ironical grimace*) Or I might cheat myself into believing I'd fallen in love with some nice girl and get myself engaged to be married again as I did once before! And then you'd be jealous again and have to find some way of getting me to break it off!

NINA—(*forlornly amused*) Yes—I suppose the thought of a wife taking you away from me would be too much—again! (*then helplessly*) Oh, Ned, when are we ever going to learn something about each other? We act like such brainless fools—with our love. It's always so wonderful when you first come back, but you always stay too long—or I always keep you too long! You never leave before we've come to the ugly bitter stage when we blame each other! (*then suddenly forlornly tender*) Is it possible you can still love me, Ned?

DARRELL—(*mournfully smiling*) I must, or I'd never act this fool way, would I?

NINA—(*smiling back*) And I must love you. (*then seriously*) After all, I can never forget that Gordon is the child of your love, Ned.

DARRELL—(*sadly*) You'd better forget that, for his sake and your own. Children have sure intuitions. He feels cheated of your love—by me. So he's concentrating his affections on Sam whose love he knows is secure, and withdrawing from you.

NINA—(*frightened—angrily*) Don't be stupid, Ned! That isn't so at all! I hate you when you talk that way!

DARRELL—(*cynically*) Hate me, exactly. As he does! That's what I'm advising you to do if you want to keep his love! (*He smiles grimly.*)

NINA—(*sharply*) If Gordon doesn't love you it's because you've never made the slightest attempt to be lovable to him! There's no earthly reason why he should like you, when you come right down to it, Ned! Take today, for instance. It's his birthday but you'd forgotten, or didn't care! You never even brought him a present.

DARRELL—(*with bitter sadness*) I did bring him a present. It's out in the hall. I bought him a costly delicate one so he could get full satisfaction and yet not strain himself when he smashed it, as he's smashed every present of mine in the past! And I left it out in the hall, to be given to him after I've gone because, after all, he is my son and I'd prefer he didn't smash it before my eyes! (*trying to mock his own emotion back—with savage bitterness*) I'm selfish, you see! I don't want my son to be too happy at my expense, even on his birthday!

NINA—(*tormented by love and pity and remorse*) Ned! For God's sake! How can you torture us like that! Oh, it's too dreadful—what I have done to you! Forgive me, Ned!

DARRELL—(*his expression changing to one of pity for her— goes to her and puts his hand on her head—tenderly*) I'm sorry. (*with remorseful tenderness*) Dreadful, what you've done, Nina? Why, you've given me the only happiness I've ever known! And no matter what I may say or do in bitterness, I'm proud—and grateful, Nina!

NINA—(*looks up at him with deep tenderness and admiration*) Dearest, it's wonderful of you to say that! (*She gets up and puts her hands on his shoulders and looks into his eyes—tenderly in a sort of pleading*) Can't we be brave enough—for you to go away—now, on this note—sure of our love—with no ugly bitterness for once?

DARRELL—(*joyfully*) Yes! I'll go—this minute if you wish!

NINA—(*playfully*) Oh, you needn't go this minute! Wait and say good-bye to Sam. He'd be terribly hurt if you didn't. (*then seriously*) And will you promise to stay away two

years—even if I call you back before then—and work this
time, really work?

DARRELL—I'll try, Nina!

NINA—And then—surely come back to me!

DARRELL—(*smiling*) Surely—again!

NINA—Then good-bye, dear! (*She kisses him.*)

DARRELL—Again! (*He smiles and she smiles and they kiss
again. Gordon appears in the doorway at rear and stands for a
moment in a passion of jealousy and rage and grief, watching
them.*)

GORDON—(*thinking with a strange tortured shame*)

    I mustn't see her! . . . pretend I didn't see her! . . .
    mustn't never let her know I saw her! . . .

(*He vanishes as silently as he had come.*)

NINA—(*suddenly moving away from Darrell, looking around
her uneasily*) Ned, did you see—? I had the queerest feeling
just then that someone—

GORDON—(*His voice sounds from the hall with a strained
casualness.*) Mother! Uncle Charlie's downstairs. Shall he
come right up?

NINA—(*startled, her own voice straining to be casual*) Yes,
dear—of course! (*then worriedly*) His voice sounded funny.
Did it to you? Do you suppose he—?

DARRELL—(*with a wry smile*) It's possible. To be on the
safe side, you'd better tell him you kissed me good-bye to get
rid of me! (*then angrily*) So Marsden's here again! The
damned old woman! I simply can't go him any more, Nina!
Why Gordon should take such a fancy to that old sissy is
beyond me!

NINA—(*suddenly struck—thinking*)

    Why, he's jealous of Gordon liking Charlie! . . .
(*immediately all affectionate pity*)

    Then he must love Gordon a little! . . .
(*letting her pity escape her*) Poor Ned! (*She makes a movement
toward him.*)

DARRELL—(*startled and afraid she may have guessed something he doesn't acknowledge to himself*) What? Why do you say
that? (*then rudely defensive*) Don't be silly! (*resentfully*) You
know well enough what I've always held against him! I
wanted to put up all the money to back Sam when he started.

I wanted to do it for Sam's sake—but especially for my child's sake. Why did Marsden absolutely insist on Sam letting him in equally? It isn't that I begrudge him the money he's made, but I know there was something queer in his mind and that he did it intentionally to spite me! (*From the hallway comes the sound of Marsden's voice and Gordon's greeting him vociferously as he lets him into the apartment. As Darrell listens his expression becomes furious again. He bursts out angrily*) You're letting that old ass spoil Gordon, you fool, you! (*Marsden comes in from the rear, smiling, immaculately dressed as usual. He looks hardly any older except that his hair is grayer and his tall figure more stooped. His expression and the general atmosphere he gives out are more nearly like those of Act One. If not happy, he is at least living in comparative peace with himself and his environment.*)

MARSDEN—(*comes straight to Nina*) Hello, Nina Cara Nina! Congratulations on your son's birthday! (*He kisses her.*) He's grown so much bigger and stronger in the two months since I've seen him. (*He turns and shakes hands with Darrell coldly—with a trace of a patronizing air*) Hello, Darrell. Last time I was here you were leaving for the West Indies in a week but I see you're still around.

DARRELL—(*furious—with a mocking air*) And here you are around again yourself! You're looking comfortable these days, Marsden. I hope your sister is well. It must be a great comfort, having her to take your mother's place! (*then with a harsh laugh*) Yes, we're two bad pennies, eh, Marsden?—counterfeits—fakes—Sam's silent partners!

NINA—(*thinking irritably*)
> Ned's getting hateful again! . . . Poor Charlie! . . . I won't have him insulted! . . . he's become such a comfort . . . he understands so much . . . without my having to tell him . . .

(*looking rebukingly at Darrell*) Ned is sailing this week, Charlie.

MARSDEN—(*thinking triumphantly*)
> He's trying to insult me . . . I know all he means . . . but what do I care what he says . . . she's sending him away! . . . intentionally before me! . . . it means he's finished! . . .

DARRELL—(*thinking resentfully*)

> Is she trying to humiliate me before him? . . . I'll
> teach her! . . .

(*then struggling with himself—remorsefully*)

> No . . . not this time . . . I promised . . . no quarrel
> . . . remember . . .

(*acquiescing—with a pleasant nod to Marsden*) Yes, I'm going
this week and I expect to be gone at least two years this
time—two years of hard work.

MARSDEN—(*thinking with scornful pity*)

> His work! . . . what a pretense! . . . a scientific dilet-
> tante! . . . could anything be more pitiable? . . .
> poor chap! . . .

(*perfunctorily*) Biology must be an interesting study. I wish I
knew more about it.

DARRELL—(*stung yet amused by the other's tone—ironically*)
Yes, so do I wish you did, Marsden! Then you might write
more about life and less about dear old ladies and devilish
bachelors! Why don't you write a novel about life sometime,
Marsden? (*He turns his back on Marsden with a glance of repulsion and walks to the window and stares out.*)

MARSDEN—(*confusedly*) Yes—decidedly—but hardly in
my line— (*thinking in anguish—picking up a magazine and
turning over the pages aimlessly*)

> That . . . is . . . true! . . . he's full of poison! . . .
> I've never married the word to life! . . . I've been a
> timid bachelor of Arts, not an artist! . . . my poor
> pleasant books! . . . all is well! . . . is this well, the
> three of us? . . . Darrell has become less and less her
> lover . . . Nina has turned more and more to me . . .
> we have built up a secret life of subtle sympathies and
> confidences . . . she has known I have understood
> about her mere physical passion for Darrell . . . what
> woman could be expected to love Sam passionately?
> . . . some day she'll confide all about Darrell to me
> . . . now that he's finished . . . she knows that I love
> her without my telling . . . she even knows the sort
> of love it is. . . .

(*passionately—thinking*)

> My love is finer than any she has known! . . . I do

not lust for her! . . . I would be content if our marriage should be purely the placing of our ashes in the
same tomb . . . our urns side by side and touching
one another . . . could the others say as much, could
they love so deeply? . . .

(*then suddenly miserably self-contemptuous*)

What! . . . platonic heroics at my age! . . . do I believe a word of that? . . . look at her beautiful eyes!
. . . wouldn't I give anything in life to see them desire
me? . . . and the intimacy I'm boasting about, what
more does it mean than that I've been playing the dear
old Charlie of her girlhood again? . . .

(*thinking in anguish*)

Damned coward and weakling! . . .

NINA—(*looking at him—pityingly—thinking*)

What does he always want of me? . . . me? . . . I am
the only one who senses his deep hurt . . . I feel how
life has wounded him . . . is that partly my fault, too?
. . . I have wounded everyone . . . poor Charlie,
what can I do for you? . . . if giving myself to you
would bring you a moment's happiness, could I? . . .
the idea used to be revolting . . . now, nothing about
love seems important enough to be revolting . . .
poor Charlie, he only thinks he ought to desire me!
. . . dear Charlie, what a perfect lover he would make
for one's old age! . . . what a perfect lover when one
was past passion! . . .

(*then with sudden scornful revulsion*)

These men make me sick! . . . I hate all three of them!
. . . they disgust me! . . . the wife and mistress in me
has been killed by them! . . . thank God, I am only a
mother now! . . . Gordon is my little man, my only
man! . . .

(*suddenly*) I've got a job for you, Charlie—make the salad
dressing for lunch. You know, the one I'm so crazy about.

MARSDEN—(*springs to his feet*) Righto! (*He puts his arm
about her waist and they go out together laughingly, without a
glance at Darrell.*)

DARRELL—(*thinking dully*)

I mustn't stay to lunch . . . ghost at my son's feast!

> . . . I better go now . . . why wait for Sam? . . . what is there to say to him I can say? . . . and there's nothing about him I want to see . . . he's as healthy as a pig . . . and as sane . . . I was afraid once his mother had lied to Nina . . . I went upstate and investigated . . . true, every word of it . . . his great-grandfather, his grandmother, his father, were all insane . . .

(*moving uneasily*)

> Stop it! . . . time to go when those thoughts come . . . sail on Saturday . . . not come here again . . . Nina will soon be fighting Sam for my son's love! . . . I'm better out of that! . . . O Christ, what a mess it all is! . . .

GORDON—(*appears in the doorway in rear. He carries a small, expensive yacht's model of a sloop with the sails set. He is in a terrific state of conflicting emotions, on the verge of tears yet stubbornly determined.*)

> I got to do it! . . . Gosh, it's awful . . . this boat is so pretty . . . why did it have to come from him? . . . I can get Dad to buy me another boat . . . but now I love this one . . . but he kissed Mother . . . she kissed him . . .

(*He walks up defiantly and confronts Darrell who turns to him in surprise.*) Hey—Darrell—did you—? (*He stops chokingly.*)

DARRELL—(*immediately realizing what is coming—thinking with somber anguish*)

> So this has to happen! . . . what I dreaded! . . . my fate is merciless, it seems! . . .

(*with strained kindliness*) Did what?

GORDON—(*growing hard—stammers angrily*) I found this—out in the hall. It can't be from anybody else. Is this—your present?

DARRELL—(*hard and defiant himself*) Yes.

GORDON—(*in a rage—tremblingly*) Then—here's what—I think of you! (*Beginning to cry, he breaks off the mast, bowsprit, breaks the mast in two, tears the rigging off and throws the dismantled hull at Darrell's feet.*) There! You can keep it!

DARRELL—(*his anger overcoming him for an instant*) You—you mean little devil, you! You don't get that from me— (*He has taken a threatening step forward. Gordon stands white-faced, defying him. Darrell pulls himself up short—then in a trembling voice of deeply wounded affection*) You shouldn't have done that, son. What difference do I make? It was never my boat. But it was your boat. You should consider the boat, not me. Don't you like boats for themselves? It was a beautiful little boat, I thought. That's why I—

GORDON—(*sobbing miserably*) It was awful pretty! I didn't want to do it! (*He kneels down and gathers up the boat into his arms again.*) Honest I didn't. I love boats! But I hate you! (*this last with passionate intensity*)

DARRELL—(*dryly*) So I've observed. (*thinking with angry anguish*)

He hurts, damn him! . . .

GORDON—No, you don't know! More'n ever now! More'n ever! (*the secret escaping him*) I saw you kissing Mother! I saw Mother, too!

DARRELL—(*startled, but immediately forcing a smile*) But I was saying good-bye. We're old friends. You know that.

GORDON—You can't fool me! This was different! (*explosively*) It would serve you good and right—and Mother, too—if I was to tell Dad on you!

DARRELL—Why, I'm Sam's oldest friend. Don't make a little fool of yourself!

GORDON—You are not his friend. You've always been hanging around cheating him—hanging around Mother!

DARRELL—Keep still! What do you mean cheating him?

GORDON—I don't know. But I know you aren't his friend. And sometime I'm going to tell him I saw you—

DARRELL—(*with great seriousness now—deeply moved*) Listen! There are things a man of honor doesn't tell anyone—not even his mother or father. You want to be a man of honor, don't you? (*intensely*) There are things we don't tell, you and I! (*He has put his hand around Gordon's shoulder impulsively.*)

This is my son! . . . I love him! . . .

GORDON—(*thinking—terribly torn*)

Why do I like him now? . . . I like him awful! . . . (*crying*) We?—who d'you mean?—I've got honor!—more'n you!—you don't have to tell me!—I wasn't going to tell Dad anyway, honest I wasn't! We?—what d'you mean, we?—I'm not like you! I don't want to be ever like you! (*There is the sound of a door being flung open and shut and Evans' hearty voice.*)

EVANS—(*from the entrance hall*) Hello, everybody!

DARRELL—(*slapping Gordon on the back*) Buck up, son! Here he is! Hide that boat or he'll ask questions. (*Gordon runs and hides the boat under the sofa. When Evans enters, Gordon is entirely composed and runs to him joyfully. Evans has grown stouter, his face is heavy now, he has grown executive and used to command, he automatically takes charge wherever he is. He does not look his age except that his hair has grown scanty and there is a perceptible bald spot on top. He is expensively tailored.*)

EVANS—(*hugging Gordon to him—lovingly*) How's the old son? How's the birthday coming along?

GORDON—Fine, Dad!

EVANS—Hello, Ned! Isn't this kid of mine a whopper for his age, though!

DARRELL—(*smiling strainedly*) Yes. (*writhing—thinking*)
> It hurts now! . . . to see my son his son! . . . I've had enough! . . . get out! . . . any excuse! . . . I can phone afterwards! . . . I'll yell out the whole business if I stay! . . .

I was just going, Sam. I've got to step around and see a fellow who lives near—biologist. (*He has gone to the door.*)

EVANS—(*disappointedly*) Then you won't be here for lunch?

DARRELL—(*thinking*)
> I'll yell the truth into your ears if I stay a second longer . . . you damned lunatic! . . .

Can't stay. Sorry. This is important. I'm sailing in a few days—lots to do—see you later, Sam. So long—Gordon.

GORDON—(*as he goes out with awkward haste*) Good-bye—Uncle Ned. (*thinking confusedly*)
> Why did I call him that when I said I never would? . . . I know . . . must be because he said he's sailing and I'm glad . . .

EVANS—So long, Ned. (*thinking—good-naturedly superior*)
> Ned and his biology! . . . He takes his hobby pretty seriously! . . .

(with satisfaction)

> Well, he can afford to have hobbies now! . . . his investment with me has made him a pile. . . .

Where's Mother, son?

GORDON—Out in the kitchen with Uncle Charlie. *(thinking)*

> I hope he never comes back! . . . why did I like him then? . . . it was only for a second . . . I didn't really . . . I never could! . . . why does he always call me Gordon as if he hated to? . . .

EVANS—*(sitting down at left)* I hope lunch is ready soon. I'm hungry as the devil, aren't you?

GORDON—*(absent-mindedly)* Yes, Dad.

EVANS—Come over here and tell me about your birthday. *(Gordon comes over. Evans pulls him up on his lap.)* How'd you like your presents? What'd you get from Uncle Ned?

GORDON—*(evasively)* They were all dandy. *(suddenly)* Why was I named Gordon?

EVANS—Oh, you know all about that—all about Gordon Shaw. I've told you time and again.

GORDON—You told me once he was Mother's beau—when she was a girl.

EVANS—*(teasingly)* What do you know about beaus? You're growing up!

GORDON—Did Mother love him a lot?

EVANS—*(embarrassedly)* I guess so.

GORDON—*(thinking keenly)*

> That's why Darrell hates me being called Gordon . . . he knows Mother loved Gordon better'n she does him . . . now I know how to get back at him . . . I'll be just like Gordon was and Mother'll love me better'n him! . . .

And then that Gordon was killed, wasn't he? Am I anything like him?

EVANS—I hope you are. If when you go to college you can play football or row like Gordon did, I'll—I'll give you anything you ask for! I mean that!

GORDON—*(dreamily)* Tell me about him again, will you, Dad—about the time he was stroking the crew and the fellow who was Number Seven began to crack, and he couldn't see him but he felt him cracking somehow, and he began talking back to him all the time and sort of gave him his strength so that when the race was over and they'd won Gordon fainted and the other fellow didn't.

EVANS—(*with a fond laugh*) Why, you know it all by heart! What's the use of my telling you?

NINA—(*comes in from the rear while they are talking. She comes forward slowly. Thinking resentfully*)

Does he love Sam more than he does me? . . . oh, no, he can't! . . . but he trusts him more! . . . he confides in him more! . . .

GORDON—Did you ever used to fight fellows, Dad?

EVANS—(*embarrassedly*) Oh, a little—when I had to.

GORDON—Could you lick Darrell?

NINA—(*thinking frightenedly*)

Why does he ask that? . . .

EVANS—(*surprised*) Your Uncle Ned? What for? We've always been friends.

GORDON—I mean, if you weren't friends, could you?

EVANS—(*boastfully*) Oh, yes, I guess so. Ned was never as strong as I was.

NINA—(*thinking contemptuously*)

Ned is weak. . . .

(*then apprehensively*)

But you're getting too strong, Sam. . . .

GORDON—But Gordon could have licked you, couldn't he?

EVANS—You bet he could!

GORDON—(*thinking*)

She must have loved Gordon better'n Dad even! . . .

NINA—(*She comes forward to the chair at center, forcing a smile.*) What's all this talk about fighting? That's not nice. For heaven's sake, Sam, don't encourage him—

EVANS—(*grinning*) Never mind the women, Gordon. You've got to know how to fight to get on in this world.

NINA—(*thinking pityingly*)

You poor booby! . . . how brave you are now! . . . (*softly*) Perhaps you're right, dear. (*looking around*) Has Ned gone?

GORDON—(*defiantly*) Yes—and he's not coming back—and he's sailing soon!

NINA—(*with a shudder*)

    Why does he challenge me that way? . . . and cling to
    Sam? . . . he must have seen Ned and me . . . he
    doesn't offer to come to my lap . . . he used to . . .
    Ned was right . . . I've got to lie to him . . . get him
    back . . . here . . . on my lap! . . .

(*with a sneer—to Evans*) I'm glad Ned's gone. I was afraid he
was going to be on our hands all day.

GORDON—(*eagerly, half-getting down from his father's lap*)
You're glad—? (*then cautiously thinking*)

    She's cheating . . . I saw her kiss him. . . .

NINA—Ned's getting to be an awful bore. He's so weak.
He can't get started on anything unless he's pushed.

GORDON—(*moving a little nearer—searching her face—
thinking*)

    She doesn't seem to like him so much . . . but I saw
    her kiss him! . . .

EVANS—(*surprised*) Oh, come now, Nina, aren't you being
a little hard on Ned? It's true he's sort of lost his grip in a
way but he's our best friend.

GORDON—(*moving away from his father again—resentfully—thinking*)

    What's Dad standing up for him to her for? . . .

NINA—(*thinking triumphantly*)

    That's right, Sam . . . just what I wanted you to
    say! . . .

(*boredly*) Oh, I know he is but he gets on my nerves hanging
around all the time. Without being too rude, I urged him to
get back to his work, and made him promise me he wouldn't
return for two years. Finally he promised—and then he became silly and sentimental and asked me to kiss him good-
bye for good luck! So I kissed him to get rid of him! The
silly fool!

GORDON—(*thinking—overjoyed*)

    Then! . . . that's why! . . . that's why! . . . and he'll
    be gone two years! . . . oh, I'm so glad! . . .

(*He goes to her and looks up into her face with shining eyes.*)
Mother!

NINA—Dear! (*She takes him up on her lap and hugs him in
her arms.*)

GORDON—(*kisses her*) There! (*triumphantly thinking*)

> That makes up for his kiss! . . . That takes it off her
> mouth. . . .

EVANS—(*grinning*) Ned must be falling for you—in his
old age! (*then sentimentally*) Poor guy! He's never married,
that's the trouble. He's lonely. I know how he feels. A fellow
needs a little feminine encouragement to help him keep his
head up.

NINA—(*snuggling Gordon's head against hers—laughing
teasingly*) I think your hard-headed Dad is getting mushy and
silly! What do you think, Gordon?

GORDON—(*laughing with her*) Yes, he's mushy, Mother!
He's silly! (*He kisses her and whispers*) I'm going to be like
Gordon Shaw, Mother! (*She hugs him fiercely to her, trium-
phantly happy.*)

EVANS—(*grinning*) You two are getting too hard-boiled
for me. (*He laughs. They all laugh happily together.*)

NINA—(*suddenly overcome by a wave of conscience-stricken remorse and pity*)

> Oh, I am hard on Ned! . . . poor dear generous Ned!
> . . . you told me to lie to your son against you . . .
> for my sake . . . I'm not worthy of your love! . . .
> I'm low and selfish! . . . but I do love you! . . . this
> is the son of our love in my arms! . . . oh, Mother
> God, grant my prayer that some day we may tell our
> son the truth and he may love his father! . . .

GORDON—(*sensing her thoughts, sits up in her lap and stares
into her face, while she guiltily avoids his eyes—in fear and resentment. Thinking*)

> She's thinking about that Darrell now! . . . I know!
> . . . she likes him too! . . . she can't fool me! . . . I
> saw her kissing! . . . she didn't think he was a silly
> fool then! . . . she was lying to Dad and me! . . .

(*He pushes off her lap and backs away from her.*)

NINA—(*thinking frightenedly*)

> He read my thoughts! . . . I mustn't even think of
> Ned when he's around! . . . poor Ned! . . . no, don't
> think of him! . . .

(*leaning forward toward Gordon with her arms stretched out entreatingly but adopting a playful tone*) Why, Gordon, what's

come over you? You jumped off my lap as though you'd sat on a tack! (*She forces a laugh.*)

GORDON—(*his eyes on the floor—evasively*) I'm hungry. I want to see if lunch is nearly ready. (*He turns abruptly and runs out.*)

EVANS—(*in a tone of superior manly understanding, kindly but laying down the law to womanly weakness*) He's sick of being babied, Nina. You forget he's getting to be a big boy. And we want him to grow up a real he-man and not an old lady like Charlie. (*sagaciously*) That's what's made Charlie like he is, I'll bet. His mother never stopped babying him.

NINA—(*submissively—but with a look of bitter scorn at him*) Perhaps you're right, Sam.

EVANS—(*confidently*) I know I am!

NINA—(*thinking with a look of intense hatred*)

 Oh, Mother God, grant that I may some day tell this fool the truth! . . .

(*Curtain*)

ACT EIGHT

SCENE—*Late afternoon in late June, ten years later—the afterdeck of the Evans' motor cruiser anchored in the lane of yachts near the finish line at Poughkeepsie. The bow and amidship of the cruiser are off right, pointed upstream. The portside rail is in the rear, the curve of the stern at left, the rear of the cabin with broad windows and a door is at right. Two wicker chairs are at left and a chaise longue at right. A wicker table with another chair is at center. The afterdeck is in cool shade, contrasted with the soft golden haze of late afternoon sunlight that glows on the river.*

Nina is sitting by the table at center, Darrell in the chair farthest left, Marsden in the chaise longue at right. Evans is leaning over the rail directly back of Nina, looking up the river through a pair of binoculars. Madeline Arnold is standing by his side.

Nina's hair has turned completely white. She is desperately trying to conceal the obvious inroads of time by an over-emphasis on make-up that defeats its end by drawing attention to what it would conceal. Her face is thin, her cheeks taut, her mouth drawn with forced smiling. There is little left of her face's charm except her eyes which now seem larger and more deeply mysterious than ever. But she has kept her beautiful figure. It has the tragic effect of making her face seem older and more worn-out by contrast. Her general manner recalls instantly the Nina of Act Four, neurotic, passionately embittered and torn. She is dressed in a white yachting costume.

Darrell seems to have "thrown back" to the young doctor we had seen at the house of Nina's father in Act Two. He has again the air of the cool, detached scientist regarding himself and the people around him as interesting phenomena. In appearance, he is once more sharply defined, his face and body have grown lean and well-conditioned, the puffiness and jowls of the previous Act are gone. His skin is tanned almost black by his years in the tropics. His thick hair is iron-gray. He wears flannel pants, a blue coat, white buckskin shoes. He looks his fifty-one years, perhaps, but not a day more. Marsden has aged greatly. The stoop of his tall figure is accentuated, his hair has grown whitish. He is an older image of the Marsden of Act Five, who was so prostrated by his mother's death. Now it is his sister's death two months before that has plunged him into despair. His present grief, however, is more resigned to its fate than the old. He is dressed immaculately in black, as in Act Five.

Evans is simply Evans, his type logically developed by ten years of continued success and accumulating wealth, jovial and simple and good-natured as ever, but increasingly stubborn and self-opinionated. He has grown very stout. His jowly broad face has a heavy, flushed, apoplectic look. His head has grown quite bald on top. He is wearing a yachting cap, blue yachting coat, white flannel pants, buckskin shoes.

Madeline Arnold is a pretty girl of nineteen, with dark hair and eyes. Her skin is deeply tanned, her figure tall and athletic, reminding one of Nina's when we first saw her. Her personality is direct and frank. She gives the impression of a person who always knows exactly what she is after and generally gets it, but is also generous and a good loser, a good sport who is popular with her own sex as well as sought after by men. She is dressed in a bright-colored sport costume.

EVANS—(*nervous and excited—on pins and needles—lowering his binoculars impatiently*) Can't see anything up there! There's a damned haze on the river! (*handing the binoculars to Madeline*) Here, Madeline. You've got young eyes.

MADELINE—(*eagerly*) Thank you. (*She looks up the river through the glasses.*)

NINA—(*thinking—bitterly*)

> Young eyes! . . . they look into Gordon's eyes! . . . he sees love in her young eyes! . . . mine are old now! . . .

EVANS—(*pulling out his watch*) Soon be time for the start. (*comes forward—exasperatedly*) Of course, the damned radio has to pick out this time to go dead! Brand new one I had installed especially for this race, too! Just my luck! (*coming to Nina and putting his hand on her shoulder*) Gosh, I'll bet Gordon's some keyed-up right at this moment, Nina!

MADELINE—(*without lowering the glasses*) Poor kid! I'll bet he is!

NINA—(*thinking with intense bitterness*)

> That tone in her voice! . . . her love already possesses him! . . . my son! . . .

(*vindictively*)

But she won't! . . . as long as I live! . . .

(*flatly*) Yes, he must be nervous.

EVANS—(*taking his hand away, sharply*) I didn't mean nervous. He doesn't know what it is to have nerves. Nothing's ever got him rattled yet. (*this last with a resentful look down at her as he moves back to the rail*)

MADELINE—(*with the calm confidence of one who knows*) Yes, you can bank on Gordon never losing his nerve.

NINA—(*coldly*) I'm quite aware my son isn't a weakling—(*meaningly, with a glance at Madeline*) even though he does do weak things sometimes.

MADELINE—(*without lowering the glasses from her eyes—thinking good-naturedly*)

Ouch! . . . that was meant for me! . . .

(*then hurt*)

Why does she dislike me so? . . . I've done my best, for Gordon's sake, to be nice to her. . . .

EVANS—(*looking back at Nina resentfully—thinking*)

Another nasty crack at Madeline! . . . Nina's certainly become the prize bum sport! . . . I thought once her change of life was over she'd be ashamed of her crazy jealousy . . . instead of that it's got worse . . . but I'm not going to let her come between Gordon and Madeline . . . he loves her and she loves him . . . and her folks have got money and position, too . . . and I like her a lot . . . and, by God, I'm going to see to it their marriage goes through on schedule, no matter how much Nina kicks up! . . .

DARRELL—(*keenly observant—thinking*)

Nina hates this young lady . . . of course! . . . Gordon's girl . . . she'll smash their engagement if she can . . . as she did mine once . . . once! . . . thank God my slavery is over! . . . how did she know I was back in town? . . . I wasn't going to see her again . . . but her invitation was so imploring . . . my duty to Gordon, she wrote . . . what duty? . . . pretty late in the day! . . . that's better left dead, too! . . .

EVANS—(*looking at his watch again*) They ought to be lined

up at the start any minute now. (*pounding his fist on the rail — letting his pent-up feelings explode*) Come on, Gordon!

NINA—(*startled—with nervous irritation*) Sam! I told you I have a splitting headache! (*thinking intensely*)

> You vulgar boor! . . . Gordon's engagement to her is all your fault! . . .

EVANS—(*resentfully*) I'm sorry. Why don't you take some aspirin? (*thinking irritably*)

> Nina in the dumps! . . . Charlie in mourning! . . . what a pair of killjoys! . . . I wanted to bring Gordon and his friends on board to celebrate . . . no chance! . . . have to take Madeline . . . stage a party in New York . . . leave this outfit flat . . . Nina'll be sore as the devil but she'll have to like it . . .

DARRELL—(*examining Nina critically—thinking*)

> She's gotten into a fine neurotic state . . . reminds me of when I first knew her . . .

(*then exultantly*)

> Thank God, I can watch her objectively again . . . these last three years away have finally done it . . . complete cure! . . .

(*then remorsefully*)

> Poor Nina! . . . we're all deserting her . . .

(*then glancing at Marsden—with a trace of a sneer*)

> Even Marsden seems to have left her for the dead! . . .

MARSDEN—(*vaguely irritated—thinking*)

> What am I doing here? . . . what do I care about this stupid race? . . . why did I let Nina bully me into coming? . . . I ought to be alone . . . with my memories of dear Jane . . . it will be two months ago Saturday she died . . .

(*His lips tremble, tears come to his eyes.*)

MADELINE—(*with an impatient sigh, lowering the glasses*) It's no use, Mr. Evans, I can't see a thing.

EVANS—(*with angry disgust*) If only that damned radio was working!

NINA—(*exasperatedly*) For heaven's sake, stop swearing so much!

EVANS—(*hurt—indignantly*) What about it if I am excited? Seems to me you could show a little more interest without it hurting you, when it's Gordon's last race, his last appearance on a varsity! (*He turns away from her.*)

MADELINE—(*thinking*)

> He's right . . . she's acting rotten . . . if I were Gordon's mother, I certainly wouldn't . . .

EVANS—(*turning back to Nina—resentfully*) You used to cheer loud enough for Gordon Shaw! And our Gordon's got him beat a mile, as an oarsman, at least! (*turning to Darrell*) And that isn't father stuff either, Ned! All the experts say so!

DARRELL—(*cynically*) Oh, come on, Sam! Surely no one could ever touch Shaw in anything! (*He glances at Nina with a sneer. Immediately angry at himself*)

> What an idiot! . . . that popped out of me! . . . old habit! . . . I haven't loved her in years! . . .

NINA—(*thinking indifferently*)

> Ned still feels jealous . . . that no longer pleases me . . . I don't feel anything . . . except that I must get him to help me. . . .

(*She turns to Darrell bitterly.*) Sam said "our" Gordon. He means his. Gordon's become so like Sam, Ned, you won't recognize him!

MADELINE—(*thinking indignantly*)

> She's crazy! . . . he's nothing like his father! . . . he's so strong and handsome! . . .

EVANS—(*good-naturedly, with a trace of pride*) You flatter me, Nina. I wish I thought that. But he isn't a bit like me, luckily for him. He's a dead ringer for Gordon Shaw at his best.

MADELINE—(*thinking*)

> Shaw . . . I've seen his picture in the gym . . . my Gordon is better looking . . . he once told me Shaw was an old beau of his mother's . . . they say she was beautiful once . . .

NINA—(*shaking her head—scornfully*) Don't be modest, Sam. Gordon *is* you. He may be a fine athlete like Gordon Shaw, because you've held that out to him as your ideal, but there the resemblance ceases. He isn't really like him at all, not the slightest bit!

EVANS—(*restraining his anger with difficulty—thinking*)

>I'm getting sick of this! . . . she's carrying her jealous grouch too far! . . .

(*suddenly exploding, pounds his fist on the rail*) Damn it, Nina, if you had any feeling you couldn't—right at the moment when he's probably getting into the shell— (*He stops, trying to control himself, panting, his face red.*)

NINA—(*staring at him with repulsion—with cool disdain*) I didn't say anything so dire, did I—merely that Gordon resembles you in character. (*with malice*) Don't get so excited. It's bad for your high blood pressure. Ask Ned if it isn't. (*intensely—thinking*)

>If he'd only die! . . .

(*thinking—immediately*)

>Oh, I don't mean that . . . I mustn't . . .

DARRELL—(*thinking keenly*)

>There's a death wish . . . things have gone pretty far . . . Sam does look as if he might have a bad pressure . . . what hope that would have given me at one time! . . . no more, thank God! . . .

(*in a joking tone*) Oh, I guess Sam's all right, Nina.

EVANS—(*gruffly*) I never felt better. (*He jerks out his watch again.*) Time for the start. Come on in the cabin, Ned, and shoot a drink. We'll see if McCabe's getting the damned radio fixed. (*Passing by Marsden he claps him on the shoulder exasperatedly.*) Come on, Charlie! Snap out of it!

MARSDEN—(*startled out of his trance—bewilderedly*) Eh?—what is it?—are they coming?

EVANS—(*recovering his good nature—with a grin, taking his arm*) You're coming to shoot a drink. You need about ten, I think, to get you in the right spirit to see the finish! (*to Darrell who has gotten up but is still standing by his chair*) Come on, Ned.

NINA—(*quickly*) No, leave Ned with me. I want to talk to him. Take Madeline—and Charlie.

MARSDEN—(*looking at her appealingly*) But I'm perfectly contented sitting— (*then after a look in her eyes—thinking*)

>She wants to be alone with Darrell . . . all right . . . doesn't matter now . . . their love is dead . . . but there's still some secret between them she's never told

me . . . never mind . . . she'll tell me sometime . . .
I'm all she will have left . . . soon. . . .
(*then stricken with guilt*)

Poor dear Jane! . . . how can I think of anyone but
you! . . . God, I'm contemptible! . . . I'll get drunk
with that fool! . . . that's all I'm good for! . . .

MADELINE—(*thinking resentfully*)

She takes a fine do-this-little-girl tone toward me!
. . . I'll give in to her now . . . but once I'm married! . . .

EVANS—Come on then, Madeline. We'll give you a small
one. (*impatiently*) Charlie! Head up!

MARSDEN—(*with hectic joviality*) I hope it's strong poison!

EVANS—(*laughing*) That's the spirit! We'll make a sport
out of you yet!

MADELINE—(*laughing, goes and takes Marsden's arm*) I'll
see you get home safe, Mr. Marsden! (*They go into the cabin,
Evans following them. Nina and Darrell turn and look at each
other wonderingly, inquisitively, for a long moment. Darrell remains standing and seems to be a little uneasy.*)

DARRELL—(*thinking with melancholy interest*)

And now? . . . what? . . . I can look into her eyes
. . . strange eyes that will never grow old . . . without desire or jealousy or bitterness . . . was she ever
my mistress? . . . can she be the mother of my child?
. . . is there such a person as my son? . . . I can't
think of these things as real any more . . . they must
have happened in another life. . . .

NINA—(*thinking sadly*)

My old lover . . . how well and young he looks . . .
now we no longer love each other at all . . . our account with God the Father is settled . . . afternoons
of happiness paid for with years of pain . . . love, passion, ecstasy . . . in what a far-off life were they alive!
. . . the only living life is in the past and future . . .
the present is an interlude . . . strange interlude in
which we call on past and future to bear witness we
are living! . . .

(*with a sad smile*) Sit down, Ned. When I heard you were
back I wrote you because I need a friend. It has been so long

since we loved each other we can now be friends again. Don't you feel that?

DARRELL—(*gratefully*) Yes. I do. (*He sits down in one of the chairs at left, drawing it up closer to her. Thinking cautiously*)

       I want to be her friend . . . but I will never . . .

NINA—(*thinking cautiously*)

       I must keep very cool and sensible or he won't help me. . . .

(*with a friendly smile*) I haven't seen you look so young and handsome since I first knew you. Tell me your secret. (*bitterly*) I need it! I'm old! Look at me! And I was actually looking forward to being old! I thought it would mean peace. I've been sadly disillusioned! (*then forcing a smile*) So tell me what fountain of youth you've found.

DARRELL—(*proudly*) That's easy. Work! I've become as interested in biology as I once was in medicine. And not selfishly interested, that's the difference. There's no chance of my becoming a famous biologist and I know it. I'm very much a worker in the ranks. But our Station is a "huge success," as Sam would say. We've made some damned important discoveries. I say "we." I really mean Preston. You may remember I used to write you about him with enthusiasm. He's justified it. He *is* making his name world-famous. He's what I might have been—I did have the brains, Nina!—if I'd had more guts and less vanity, if I'd hewn to the line! (*then forcing a smile*) But I'm not lamenting. I've found myself in helping him. In that way I feel I've paid my debt—that his work is partly my work. And he acknowledges it. He possesses the rare virtue of gratitude. (*with proud affection*) He's a fine boy, Nina! I suppose I should say man now he's in his thirties.

NINA—(*thinking with bitter sorrow*)

       So, Ned . . . you remember our love . . . with bitterness! . . . as a stupid mistake! . . . the proof of a gutless vanity that ruined your career! . . . oh! . . .

(*then controlling herself—thinking cynically*)

       Well, after all, how do I remember our love? . . . with no emotion at all, not even bitterness! . . .

(*then with sudden alarm*)

       He's forgotten Gordon for this Preston! . . .

(*thinking desperately*)

> I must make him remember Gordon is his child or I
> can never persuade him to help me! . . .

(*reproachfully*) So you have found a son while I was losing
mine—who is yours, too!

DARRELL—(*struck by this—impersonally interested*) That's
never occurred to me but now I think of it— (*smiling*) Yes,
perhaps unconsciously Preston is a compensating substitute.
Well, it's done both of us good and hasn't harmed anyone.

NINA—(*with bitter emphasis*) Except your real son—and
me—but we don't count, I suppose!

DARRELL—(*coolly*) Harmed Gordon? How? He's all right,
isn't he? (*with a sneer*) I should say from all I've been hearing
that he was your ideal of college hero—like his never-to-be-
forgotten namesake!

NINA—(*thinking resentfully*)

> He's sneering at his own son! . . .

(*then trying to be calculating*)

> But I mustn't get angry . . . I must make him help
> me. . . .

(*speaking with gentle reproach*) And am I the ideal of a happy
mother, Ned?

DARRELL—(*immediately moved by pity and ashamed of himself*) Forgive me, Nina. I haven't quite buried all my bitterness, I'm afraid. (*gently*) I'm sorry you're unhappy, Nina.

NINA—(*thinking with satisfaction*)

> He means that . . . he still does care a little . . . if
> only it's enough to . . . !

(*speaking sadly*) I've lost my son, Ned! Sam has made him all
his. And it was done so gradually that, although I realized
what was happening, there was never any way I could interfere. What Sam advised seemed always the best thing for
Gordon's future. And it was always what Gordon himself
wanted, to escape from me to boarding school and then to
college, to become Sam's athletic hero—

DARRELL—(*impatiently*) Oh, come now, Nina, you know
you've always longed for him to be like Gordon Shaw!

NINA—(*bursting out in spite of herself—violently*) He's not
like Gordon! He's forgotten me for that—! (*trying to be more
reasonable*) What do I care whether he's an athlete or not? It's

such nonsense, all this fuss! I'm not the slightest bit interested in this race today, for example! I wouldn't care if he came in last! (*stopping herself—thinking frightenedly*)

    Oh, if he should ever guess I said that! . . .

DARRELL—(*thinking keenly*)

    Hello! . . . she said that as if she'd like to see him come last! . . . why? . . .

(*then vindictively*)

    Well, so would I! . . . it's time these Gordons took a good licking from life! . . .

MADELINE—(*suddenly appears in the door from the cabin, her face flushed with excitement*) They're off! Mr. Evans is getting something—it's terribly faint but—Navy and Washington are leading—Gordon's third! (*She disappears back in the cabin.*)

NINA—(*looking after her with hatred*)

    Her Gordon! . . . she is so sure! . . . how I've come to detest her pretty face! . . .

DARRELL—(*thinking with a sneer*)

    "Gordon's third"! . . . you might think there was no one else pulling the shell! . . . what idiots women make of themselves about these Gordons! . . . she's pretty, that Madeline! . . . she's got a figure like Nina's when I first loved her . . . those afternoons . . . age is beginning to tell on Nina's face . . . but she's kept her wonderful body! . . .

(*with a trace of malice—dryly*) There's a young lady who seems to care a lot whether Gordon comes in last or not!

NINA—(*trying to be sorrowful and appealing*) Yes. Gordon is hers now, Ned. (*But she cannot bear this thought—vindictively*) That is, they're engaged. But, of course, that doesn't necessarily mean— Can you imagine him throwing himself away on a little fool like that? I simply can't believe he really loves her! Why, she's hardly even pretty and she's deadly stupid. I thought he was only flirting with her—or merely indulging in a passing physical affair. (*She winces.*) At his age, one has to expect—even a mother must face nature. But for Gordon to take her seriously, and propose marriage—it's too idiotic for words!

DARRELL—(*thinking cynically*)

    Oh, so you'll compromise on his sleeping with her

. . . if you have to . . . but she must have no real
claim to dispute your ownership, eh? . . . you'd like
to make her the same sort of convenient slave for him
that I was for you! . . .

(*resentfully*) I can't agree with you. I find her quite charming.
It seems to me if I were in Gordon's shoes I'd do exactly what
he has done. (*in confusion—thinking bitterly*)

In Gordon's shoes! . . . I always was in Gordon
Shaw's shoes! . . . and why am I taking this young
Gordon's part? . . . what is he to me, for God's
sake? . . .

NINA—(*unheedingly*) If he marries her, it means he'll forget me! He'll forget me as completely as Sam forgot his
mother! She'll keep him away from me! Oh, I know what
wives can do! She'll use her body until she persuades him to
forget me! My son, Ned! And your son, too! (*She suddenly
gets up and goes to him and takes one of his hands in both of hers.*)
The son of our old love, Ned!

DARRELL—(*thinking with a strange shudder of mingled attraction and fear as she touches him*)

Our love . . . old love . . . old touch of her flesh
. . . we're old . . . it's silly and indecent . . . does
she think she still can own me? . . .

NINA—(*in the tone a mother takes in speaking to her husband
about their boy*) You'll have to give Gordon a good talking to,
Ned.

DARRELL—(*still more disturbed—thinking*)

Old . . . but she's kept her wonderful body . . . how
many years since? . . . she has the same strange influence over me . . . touch of her flesh . . . it's dangerous . . . bosh, I'm only humoring her as a friend . . .
as her doctor . . . and why shouldn't I have a talk
with Gordon? . . . a father owes something to his son
. . . he ought to advise him. . . .

(*then alarmed*)

But I was never going to meddle again . . .

(*sternly*) I swore I'd never again meddle with human lives,
Nina!

NINA—(*unheedingly*) You must keep him from ruining his
life.

DARRELL—(*doggedly—struggling with himself*) I won't touch a life that has more than one cell! (*harshly*) And I wouldn't help you in this, anyway! You've got to give up owning people, meddling in their lives as if you were God and had created them!

NINA—(*strangely forlorn*) I don't know what you mean, Ned. Gordon is my son, isn't he?

DARRELL—(*with a sudden strange violence*) And mine! Mine, too! (*He stops himself. Thinking*)

> Shut up, you fool! . . . is that the way to humor her? . . .

NINA—(*with strange quiet*) I think I still love you a little, Ned.

DARRELL—(*in her tone*) And I still love you a little, Nina. (*then sternly*) But I will not meddle in your life again! (*with a harsh laugh*) And you've meddled enough with human love, old lady! Your time for that is over! I'll send you a couple of million cells you can torture without harming yourself! (*regaining control—shamefacedly*) Nina! Please forgive me!

NINA—(*starts as if out of a dream—anxiously*) What were you saying, Ned? (*She lets go of his hand and goes back to her chair.*)

DARRELL—(*dully*) Nothing.

NINA—(*strangely*) We were talking about Sam, weren't we? How do you think he looks?

DARRELL—(*confusedly casual*) Fine. A bit too fat, of course. He looks as though his blood pressure might be higher than it ought to be. But that's not unusual in persons of his build and age. It's nothing to hope—I meant, to worry over! (*then violently*) God damn it, why did you make me say hope?

NINA—(*calmly*) It may have been in your mind, too, mayn't it?

DARRELL—No! I've nothing against Sam. I've always been his best friend. He owes his happiness to me.

NINA—(*strangely*) There are so many curious reasons we dare not think about for thinking things!

DARRELL—(*rudely*) Thinking doesn't matter a damn! Life is something in one cell that doesn't need to think!

NINA—(*strangely*) I know! God the Mother!

DARRELL—(*excitedly*) And all the rest is gutless egotism!

But to hell with it! What I started to say was, what possible reason could I have for hoping for Sam's death?

NINA—(*strangely*) We're always desiring death for ourselves or others, aren't we—while we while away our lives with the old surface ritual of coveting our neighbor's ass?

DARRELL—(*frightenedly*) You're talking like the old Nina now—when I first loved you. Please don't! It isn't decent—at our age! (*thinking in terror*)

> The old Nina! . . . am I the old Ned? . . . then that means? . . . but we must not meddle in each other's lives again! . . .

NINA—(*strangely*) I am the old Nina! And this time I will not let my Gordon go from me forever!

EVANS—(*appears in the doorway of the cabin—excited and irritated*) Madeline's listening in now. It went dead on me. (*Raising the binoculars as he goes to the rail, he looks up the river.*) Last I got, Gordon third, Navy and Washington leading. They're the ones to fear, he said—Navy especially. (*putting down the glasses—with a groan*) Damned haze! My eyes are getting old. (*then suddenly with a grin*) You ought to see Charlie! He started throwing Scotch into him as if he were drinking against time. I had to take the bottle away from him. It's hit him an awful wallop. (*then looking from one to the other—resentfully*) What's the matter with you two? There's a race going on, don't you know it? And you sit like dead clams!

DARRELL—(*placatingly*) I thought someone'd better stay out here and let you know when they get in sight.

EVANS—(*relieved*) Oh, sure, that's right! Here, take the glasses. You always had good eyes. (*Darrell gets up and takes the glasses and goes to the rail and begins adjusting them.*)

DARRELL—Which crew was it you said Gordon feared the most?

EVANS—(*has gone back to the cabin doorway*) Navy. (*then proudly*) Oh, he'll beat them! But it'll be damn close. I'll see if Madeline's getting— (*He goes back in the cabin.*)

DARRELL—(*looking up the river—with vindictive bitterness—thinking*)

> Come on, Navy! . . .

NINA—(*thinking bitterly*)

Madeline's Gordon! . . . Sam's Gordon! . . . the thanks I get for saving Sam at the sacrifice of my own happiness! . . . I won't have it! . . . what do I care what happens to Sam now? . . . I hate him! . . . I'll tell him Gordon isn't his child! . . . and threaten to tell Gordon too, unless! . . . he'll be in deadly fear of that! . . . he'll soon find some excuse to break their engagement! . . . he can! . . . he has the strangest influence over Gordon! . . . but Ned must back me up or Sam won't believe me! . . . Ned must tell him too! . . . but will Ned? . . . he'll be afraid of the insanity! . . . I must make him believe Sam's in no danger . . .

(*intensely*) Listen, Ned, I'm absolutely sure, from things she wrote me before she died, that Sam's mother must have been deliberately lying to me about the insanity that time. She was jealous because Sam loved me and she simply wanted to be revenged, I'm sure.

DARRELL—(*without lowering glasses—dryly*) No. She told you the truth. I never mentioned it, but I went up there once and made a thorough investigation of his family.

NINA—(*with resentful disappointment*) Oh—I suppose you wanted to make sure so you could hope he'd go insane?

DARRELL—(*simply*) I needed to be able to hope that, then. I loved you horribly at that time, Nina—horribly!

NINA—(*putting her hands on his arm*) And you don't—any more, Ned? (*thinking intensely*)

Oh, I must make him love me again . . . enough to make him tell Sam! . . .

DARRELL—(*thinking strangely—struggling with himself*)
She'd like to own me again . . . I wish she wouldn't touch me . . . what is this tie of old happiness between our flesh? . . .

(*harshly—weakly struggling to shake off her hands, without lowering the glasses*) I won't meddle again with human lives, I told you!

NINA—(*unheeding, clinging to him*) And I loved you horribly! I still do love you, Ned! I used to hope he'd go insane myself because I loved you so! But look at Sam! He's sane as a pig! There's absolutely no danger now!

DARRELL—(*thinking—alarmed*)

> What is she after now—what does she want me
> for? . . .

(*stiffly*) I'm no longer a doctor but I should say he's a healthy
miss of Nature's. It's a thousand to one against it at this late
day.

NINA—(*with sudden fierce intensity*) Then it's time to tell
him the truth, isn't it? We've suffered all our lives for his sake!
We've made him rich and happy! It's time he gave us back
our son!

DARRELL—(*thinking*)

> Aha . . . so that's it! . . . tell Sam the truth? . . . at
> last! . . . by God, I'd like to tell him, at that! . . .

(*with a sneer*) Our son? You mean yours, my dear! Kindly
count me out of any further meddling with—

NINA—(*unruffledly—obsessed*) But Sam won't believe me if
I'm the only one to tell him! He'll think I'm lying for spite,
that it's only my crazy jealousy! He'll ask you! You've got to
tell him too, Ned!

DARRELL—(*thinking*)

> I'd like to see his face when I told him this famous
> oarsman isn't his son but mine! . . . that might pay
> me back a little for all he's taken from me! . . .

(*harshly*) I've stopped meddling in Sam's life, I tell you!

NINA—(*insistently*) Think of what Sam has made us go
through, of how he's made us suffer! You've got to tell him!
You still love me a little, don't you, Ned? You must when you
remember the happiness we've known in each other's arms!
You were the only happiness I've ever known in life!

DARRELL—(*struggling weakly—thinking*)

> She lies! . . . there was her old lover, Gordon! . . .
> he was always first! . . . then her son, Gordon! . . .

(*with desperate rancor—thinking*)

> Come on, Navy! . . . beat her Gordons for me! . . .

NINA—(*intensely*) Oh, if I'd only gone away with you that
time when you came back from Europe! How happy we
would have been, dear! How our boy would have loved
you—if it hadn't been for Sam!

DARRELL—(*thinking—weakly*)

> Yes, if it hadn't been for Sam I would have been

happy! . . . I would have been the world's greatest neurologist! . . . my boy would have loved me and I'd have loved him! . . .

NINA—(*with a crowning intensity to break down his last resistance*) You must tell him, Ned! For my sake! Because I love you! Because you remember our afternoons—our mad happiness! Because you love me!

DARRELL—(*beaten—dazedly*) Yes—what must I do?—meddle again? (*The noise of Madeline's excited voice cheering and clapping her hands, of Marsden's voice yelling drunkenly, of Evans', all shouting* "Gordon! Gordon! Come on, Gordon!" *comes from the cabin. Marsden appears swaying in the cabin doorway yelling* "Gordon!" *He is hectically tipsy. Darrell gives a violent shudder as if he were coming out of a nightmare and pushes Nina away from him.*)

DARRELL—(*thinking—dazedly still, but in a tone of relief*)
          Marsden again! . . . thank God! . . . he's saved me!
          . . . from her! . . . and her Gordons! . . .

(*turning on her triumphantly*) No, Nina—sorry—but I can't help you. I told you I'd never meddle again with human lives! (*more and more confidently*) Besides, I'm quite sure Gordon isn't my son, if the real deep core of the truth were known! I was only a body to you. Your first Gordon used to come back to life. I was never more to you than a substitute for your dead lover! Gordon is really Gordon's son! So you see I'd be telling Sam a lie if I boasted that I— And I'm a man of honor! I've proved that, at least! (*He raises his glasses and looks up the river. Thinking exultantly*)
          I'm free! . . . I've beaten her at last! . . . now come
          on, Navy! . . . you've got to beat her Gordons for
          me! . . .

NINA—(*after staring at him for a moment—walking away from him—thinking with a dull fatalism*)
          I've lost him . . . he'll never tell Sam now . . . is
          what he said right? . . . is Gordon Gordon's? . . . oh,
          I hope so! . . . oh, dear, dead Gordon, help me to get
          back your son! . . . I must find some way. . . .

(*She sits down again.*)

MARSDEN—(*who has been staring at them with a foolish grin*) Hello, you two! Why do you look so guilty? You don't love each other any more! It's all nonsense! I don't feel the slightest twinge of jealousy. That's proof enough, isn't it? (*then blandly apologetic*) Pardon me if I sound a bit pipped— a good bit! Sam said ten and then took the bottle away when I'd had only five! But it's enough! I've forgotten sorrow! There's nothing in life worth grieving about, I assure you, Nina! And I've gotten interested in this race now. (*He sings raucously*) "Oh we'll row, row, row, right down the river! And we'll row, row, row—" Remember that old tune— when you were a little girl, Nina? Oh, I'm forgetting Sam said to tell you Gordon was on even terms with the leaders! A gallant spurt did it! Nip and tuck now! I don't care who wins—as long as it isn't Gordon! I don't like him since he's grown up! He thinks I'm an old woman! (*sings*) "Row, row, row." The field against Gordon!

DARRELL—(*hectically*) Right! (*He looks through the glasses— excitedly*) I see a flashing in the water way up there! Must be their oars! They're coming! I'll tell Sam! (*He hurries into the cabin.*)

NINA—(*thinking dully*)
> He'll tell Sam . . . no, he doesn't mean that . . . I
> must find some other way . . .

MARSDEN—(*walks a bit uncertainly to Nina's chair*) Gordon really should get beaten today—for the good of his soul, Nina. That Madeline is pretty, isn't she? These Gordons are too infernally lucky—while we others—(*he almost starts to blubber—angrily*) we others have got to beat him today! (*He slumps clumsily down to a sitting position on the deck by her chair and takes her hand and pats it.*) There, there, Nina Cara Nina! Don't worry your pretty head! It will all come out all right! We'll only have a little while longer to wait and then you and I'll be quietly married! (*thinking frightenedly*)
> The devil! . . . what am I saying? . . . I'm drunk!
> . . . all right, all the better! . . . I've wanted all my
> life to tell her! . . .

Of course, I realize you've got a husband at present but, never mind, I can wait. I've waited a lifetime already; but for a long while now I've had a keen psychic intuition that I wasn't born to die before— (*Evans and Madeline and Darrell come rushing out of the cabin. They all have binoculars. They run to the rail and train their glasses up the river.*)

MADELINE—(*excitedly*) I see them! (*grabbing his arm and pointing*) Look, Mr. Evans—there—don't you see?

EVANS—(*excitedly*) No—not yet— Yes! Now I see them! (*pounding on the rail*) Come on, Gordon boy!

MADELINE—Come on, Gordon! (*The whistles and sirens from the yachts up the river begin to be heard. This grows momentarily louder as one after another other yachts join in the chorus as the crews approach nearer and nearer until toward the close of the scene there is a perfect pandemonium of sound.*)

NINA—(*with bitter hatred—thinking*)

How I hate her! . . .

(*then suddenly with a deadly calculation—thinking*)

Why not tell her? . . . as Sam's mother told me? . . . of the insanity? . . . she thinks Gordon is Sam's son. . . .

(*with a deadly smile of triumph*)

That will be poetic justice! . . . that will solve everything! . . . she won't marry him! . . . he will turn to me for comfort! . . . but I must plan it out carefully! . . .

MARSDEN—(*driven on—extravagantly*) Listen, Nina! After we're married I'm going to write a novel—my first real novel! All the twenty odd books I've written have been long-winded fairy tales for grown-ups—about dear old ladies and witty, cynical bachelors and quaint characters with dialects, and married folk who always admire and respect each other, and lovers who avoid love in hushed whispers! That's what I've been, Nina—a hush-hush whisperer of lies! Now I'm going to give an honest healthy yell—turn on the sun into the shadows of lies—shout "This is life and this is sex, and here are passion and hatred and regret and joy and pain and ecstasy, and these are men and women and sons and daughters whose hearts are weak and strong, whose blood is blood and not a soothing syrup!" Oh, I can do it, Nina! I can write the truth! I've seen it in you, your father, my mother, sister, Gordon, Sam, Darrell and myself. I'll write the book of us! But here I am talking while my last chapters are in the making—right here and now— (*hurriedly*) You'll excuse me, won't you,

Nina? I must watch—my duty as an artist! (*He scrambles to his feet and peers about him with a hectic eagerness. Nina pays no attention to him.*)

EVANS—(*exasperatedly, taking down his glasses*) You can't tell a damn thing—which is which or who's ahead—I'm going to listen in again. (*He hurries into the cabin.*)

NINA—(*with a smile of cruel triumph—thinking*)

> I can tell her . . . confidentially . . . I can pretend I'm forced to tell her . . . as Sam's mother did with me . . . because I feel it's due to her happiness and Gordon's . . . it will explain my objection to the engagement . . . oh, it can't help succeeding . . . my Gordon will come back! . . . I'll see he never gets away again! . . .

(*She calls*) Madeline!

MARSDEN—(*thinking*)

> Why is she calling Madeline? . . . I must watch all this carefully! . . .

EVANS—(*comes rushing out in wild alarm*) Bad news! Navy has drawn ahead—half a length—looks like Navy's race, he said— (*then violently*) But what does he know, that damn fool announcer—some poor boob—!

MADELINE—(*excitedly*) He doesn't know Gordon! He's always best when he's pushed to the limit!

NINA—(*She calls more sharply.*) Madeline!

DARRELL—(*turns around to stare at her—thinking*)

> Why is she calling Madeline? . . . she's bound she'll meddle in their lives . . . I've got to watch her . . . well, let's see. . . .

(*He touches Madeline on the shoulder.*) Mrs. Evans is calling you, Miss Arnold.

MADELINE—(*impatiently*) Yes, Mrs. Evans. But they're getting closer. Why don't you come and watch?

NINA—(*not heeding—impressively*) There's something I must tell you.

MADELINE—(*in hopeless irritation*) But— Oh, all right. (*She hurries over to her, glancing eagerly over her shoulder towards the river.*) Yes, Mrs. Evans?

DARRELL—(*moves from the rail toward them—thinking keenly*)

I must watch this . . . she's in a desperate meddling mood! . . .

NINA—(*impressively*) First, give me your word of honor that you'll never reveal a word of what I'm going to tell you to a living soul—above all not to Gordon!

MADELINE—(*looking at her in amazement—soothingly*) Couldn't you tell me later, Mrs. Evans—after the race?

NINA—(*sternly—grabbing her by the wrist*) No, now! Do you promise?

MADELINE—(*with helpless annoyance*) Yes, Mrs. Evans.

NINA—(*sternly*) For the sake of your future happiness and my son's I've got to speak! Your engagement forces me to! You've probably wondered why I objected. It's because the marriage is impossible. You can't marry Gordon! I speak as your friend! You must break your engagement with him at once!

MADELINE—(*cannot believe her ears—suddenly panic-stricken*) But why—why?

DARRELL—(*who has come closer—resentfully thinking*)
    She wants to ruin my son's life as she ruined
    mine! . . .

NINA—(*relentlessly*) Why? Because—

DARRELL—(*steps up suddenly beside them—sharply and sternly commanding*) No, Nina! (*He taps Madeline on the shoulder and draws her aside. Nina lets go of her wrist and stares after them in a sort of stunned stupor.*) Miss Arnold, as a doctor I feel it my duty to tell you that Mrs. Evans isn't herself. Pay no attention to anything she may say to you. She's just passed through a crucial period in a woman's life and she's morbidly jealous of you and subject to queer delusions! (*He smiles kindly at her.*) So get back to the race! And God bless you! (*He grips her hand, strangely moved.*)

MADELINE—(*gratefully*) Thank you. I understand, I think. Poor Mrs. Evans! (*She hurries back to the rail, raising her glasses.*)

NINA—(*springing to her feet and finding her voice—with despairing accusation*) Ned!

DARRELL—(*steps quickly to her side*) I'm sorry, Nina, but I warned you not to meddle. (*then affectionately*) And Gordon is—well—sort of my stepson, isn't he? I really want him to be happy. (*then smiling good-naturedly*) All the same, I can't help hoping he'll be beaten in this race. As an oarsman he recalls his father, Gordon Shaw, to me. (*He turns away and raises his glasses, going back to the rail. Nina slumps down in her chair again.*)

EVANS—Damn! They all look even from here! Can you tell which is which, Madeline?

MADELINE—No—not yet—oh, dear, this is awful! Gordon!

NINA—(*looking about her in the air—with a dazed question*) Gordon?

MARSDEN—(*thinking*)

> Damn that Darrell! . . . if he hadn't interfered Nina would have told . . . something of infinite importance, I know! . . .

(*He comes and again sits on the deck by her chair and takes her hand.*) Because what, Nina—my dear little Nina Cara Nina—because what? Let me help you!

NINA—(*staring before her as if she were in a trance—simply, like a young girl*) Yes, Charlie. Yes, Father. Because all of Sam's father's family have been insane. His mother told me that time so I wouldn't have his baby. I was going to tell Madeline that so she wouldn't marry Gordon. But it would have been a lie because Gordon isn't really Sam's child at all, he's Ned's. Ned gave him to me and I gave him to Sam so Sam could have a healthy child and be well and happy. And Sam is well and happy, don't you think? (*childishly*) So I haven't been such an awfully wicked girl, have I, Father?

MARSDEN—(*horrified and completely sobered by what he has heard—stares at her with stunned eyes*) Nina! Good God! Do you know what you're saying?

MADELINE—(*excitedly*) There! The one on this side! I saw the color on their blades just now!

EVANS—(*anxiously*) Are you sure? Then he's a little behind the other two!

DARRELL—(*excitedly*) The one in the middle seems to be ahead! Is that the Navy? (*But the others pay no attention to him. All three are leaning over the rail, their glasses glued to their eyes, looking up the river. The noise from the whistles is now very loud. The cheering from the observation trains can be heard.*)

MARSDEN—(*stares into her face with great pity now*) Merciful God, Nina! Then you've lived all these years—with this horror! And you and Darrell deliberately—?

NINA—(*without looking at him—to the air*) Sam's mother said I had a right to be happy too.

MARSDEN—And you didn't love Darrell then—?

NINA—(*as before*) I did afterwards. I don't now. Ned is dead, too. (*softly*) Only you are alive now, Father—and Gordon.

MARSDEN—(*gets up and bends over her paternally, stroking her hair with a strange, wild, joyous pity*) Oh, Nina—poor little Nina—my Nina—how you must have suffered! I forgive you! I forgive you everything! I forgive even your trying to tell Madeline—you wanted to keep Gordon—oh, I understand that—and I forgive you!

NINA—(*as before—affectionately and strangely*) And I forgive you, Father. It was all your fault in the beginning, wasn't it? You mustn't ever meddle with human lives again!

EVANS—(*wildly excited*) Gordon's sprinting, isn't he? He's drawing up on that middle one!

MADELINE—Yes! Oh, come on, Gordon!

DARRELL—(*exultantly*) Come on, Navy!

EVANS—(*who is standing next to Ned, whirls on him in a furious passion*) What's that? What the hell's the matter with you?

DARRELL—(*facing him—with a strange friendliness slaps him on the back*) We've got to beat these Gordons, Sam! We've got to beat—

EVANS—(*raging*) You—! (*He draws back his fist—then suddenly horrified at what he is doing but still angry, grabs Darrell by both shoulders and shakes him.*) Wake up! What the hell's got into you? Have you gone crazy?

DARRELL—(*mockingly*) Probably! It runs in my family! All of my father's people were happy lunatics—not healthy, country folk like yours, Sam! Ha!

EVANS—(*staring at him*) Ned, old man, what's the trouble? You said "Navy."

DARRELL—(*ironically—with a bitter hopeless laugh*) Slip of the tongue! I meant Gordon! Meant Gordon, of course! Gordon is always meant—meant to win! Come on, Gordon! It's fate!

MADELINE—Here they come! They're both spurting! I can see Gordon's back!

EVANS—(*forgetting everything else, turns back to the race*) Come on, boy! Come on, son! (*The chorus of noise is now a bedlam as the crews near the finish line. The people have to yell and scream to make themselves heard.*)

NINA—(*getting up—thinking with a strange, strident, wild passion*)

> I hear the Father laughing! . . . O Mother God, protect my son! . . . let Gordon fly to you in heaven! . . . quick, Gordon! . . . love is the Father's lightning! . . . Madeline will bring you down in flames! . . . I hear His screaming laughter! . . . fly back to me! . . .

(*She is looking desperately up into the sky as if some race of life and death were happening there for her.*)

EVANS—(*holding on to a stanchion and leaning far out at the imminent risk of falling in*) One spurt more will do it! Come on, boy, come on! It took death to beat Gordon Shaw! You can't be beaten either, Gordon! Lift her out of the water, son! Stroke! Stroke! He's gaining! Now! Over the line, boy! Over with her! Stroke! That's done it! He's won! He's won!

MADELINE—(*has been shrieking at the same time*) Gordon! Gordon! He's won! Oh, he's fainted! Poor dear darling! (*She remains standing on the rail, leaning out dangerously, holding on with one hand, looking down longingly toward his shell.*)

EVANS—(*bounding back to the deck, his face congested and purple with a frenzy of joy, dancing about*) He's won! By God, it was close! Greatest race in the history of rowing! He's the greatest oarsman God ever made! (*embracing Nina and kissing her frantically*) Aren't you happy, Nina? Our Gordon! The greatest ever!

NINA—(*torturedly—trying incoherently to force out a last despairing protest*) No!—not yours!—mine!—and Gordon's!—Gordon is Gordon's!—he was my Gordon!—his Gordon is mine!

EVANS—(*soothingly, humoring her—kissing her again*) Of course he's yours, dear—and a dead ringer for Gordon Shaw, too! Gordon's body! Gordon's spirit! Your body and spirit, too, Nina! He's not like me, lucky for him! I'm a poor boob!

I never could row worth a damn! (*He suddenly staggers as if he were very drunk, leaning on Marsden—then gives a gasp and collapses inertly to the deck, lying on his back.*)

MARSDEN—(*stares down at him stupidly—then thinking strangely*)

 I knew it! . . . I saw the end beginning! . . .

(*He touches Nina's arm—in a low voice*) Nina—your husband! (*touching Darrell who has stood staring straight before him with a bitter ironical smile on his lips*) Ned—your friend! Doctor Darrell—a patient!

NINA—(*stares down at Evans—slowly, as if trying to bring her mind back to him*) My husband? (*suddenly with a cry of pain, sinks on her knees beside the body*) Sam!

DARRELL—(*looking down at him—thinking yearningly*)

 Is her husband dead . . . at last? . . .

(*then with a shudder at his thoughts*)

 No! . . . I don't hope! . . . I don't! . . .

(*He cries.*) Sam! (*He kneels down, feels of his heart, pulse, looks into his face—with a change to a strictly professional manner*) He's not dead. Only a bad stroke.

NINA—(*with a cry of grief*) Oh, Ned, did all our old secret hopes do this at last?

DARRELL—(*professionally, staring at her coldly*) Bosh, Mrs. Evans! We're not in the Congo that we can believe in evil charms! (*sternly*) In his condition, Mr. Evans must have absolute quiet and peace of mind or— And perfect care! You must tend him night and day! And I will! We've got to keep him happy!

NINA—(*dully*) Again? (*then sternly in her turn, as if swearing a pledge to herself*) I will never leave his side! I will never tell him anything that might disturb his peace!

MARSDEN—(*standing above them—thinking exultantly*)

 I will not have long to wait now! . . .

(*then ashamed*)

 How can I think such things . . . poor Sam! . . . he was . . . I mean he is my friend . . .

(*with assertive loyalty*) A rare spirit! A pure and simple soul! A good man—yes, a good man! God bless him! (*He makes a motion over the body like a priest blessing.*)

DARRELL—(*his voice suddenly breaking with a sincere human*

grief) Sam, old boy! I'm so damned sorry! I will give my life to save you!

NINA—(*in dull anguish*) Save—again? (*then lovingly, kissing Evans' face*) Dear husband, you have tried to make me happy, I will give you my happiness again! I will give you Gordon to give to Madeline!

MADELINE—(*still standing on the rail, staring after Gordon's shell*)

> Gordon! . . . dear lover . . . how tired . . . but you'll rest in my arms . . . your head will lie on my breast . . . soon! . . .

(*Curtain*)

ACT NINE

SCENE—*Several months later. A terrace on the Evans' estate on Long Island. In the rear, the terrace overlooks a small harbor with the ocean beyond. On the right is a side entrance of the pretentious villa. On the left is a hedge with an arched gateway leading to a garden. The terrace is paved with rough stone. There is a stone bench at center, a recliner at right, a wicker table and armchair at left.*

It is late afternoon of a day in early fall. Gordon Evans is sitting on the stone bench, his chin propped on his hands, Madeline standing behind him, her arm about his shoulders. Gordon is over six feet tall with the figure of a trained athlete. His sun-bronzed face is extremely handsome after the fashion of the magazine cover American collegian. It is a strong face but of a strength wholly material in quality. He has been too thoroughly trained to progress along a certain groove to success ever to question it or be dissatisfied with its rewards. At the same time, although entirely an unimaginative code-bound gentleman of his groove, he is boyish and likable, of an even, modest, sporting disposition. His expression is boyishly forlorn, but he is making a manly effort to conceal his grief.

Madeline is much the same as in the previous Act except that there is now a distinct maternal older feeling in her attitude toward Gordon as she endeavors to console him.

MADELINE—(*tenderly, smoothing his hair*) There, dear! I know how horribly hard it is for you. I loved him, too. He was so wonderful and sweet to me.

GORDON—(*his voice trembling*) I didn't really realize he was gone—until out at the cemetery— (*His voice breaks.*)

MADELINE—(*kissing his hair*) Darling! Please don't!

GORDON—(*rebelliously*) Damn it, I don't see why he had to die! (*with a groan*) It was that constant grind at the office! I ought to have insisted on his taking better care of himself. But I wasn't home enough, that's the trouble. I couldn't watch him. (*then bitterly*) But I can't see why Mother didn't!

MADELINE—(*reprovingly but showing she shares his feeling*) Now! You mustn't start feeling bitter toward her.

GORDON—(*contritely*) I know I shouldn't. (*but returning to his bitter tone*) But I can't help remembering how unreasonably she's acted about our engagement.

MADELINE—Not since your father was taken sick, she hasn't, dear. She's been wonderfully nice.

GORDON—(*in the same tone*) Nice? Indifferent, you mean! She doesn't seem to care a damn one way or the other any more!

MADELINE—You could hardly expect her to think of anyone but your father. She's been with him every minute. I never saw such devotion. (*thinking*)

> Will Gordon ever get old and sick like that? . . . oh, I hope we'll both die before! . . . but I'd nurse him just as she did his father . . . I'll always love him! . . .

GORDON—(*consoled—proudly*) Yes, she sure was wonderful to him, all right! (*then coming back to his old tone*) But—this may sound rotten of me—I always had a queer feeling she was doing it as a duty. And when he died, I felt her grief was—not from love for him—at least, only the love of a friend, not a wife's love. (*as if under some urgent compulsion from within*) I've never told you, but I've always felt, ever since I was a little kid, that she didn't really love Dad. She liked him and respected him. She was a wonderful wife. But I'm sure she didn't love him. (*blurting it out as if he couldn't help it*) I'll tell you, Madeline! I've always felt she cared a lot for—Darrell. (*hastily*) Of course, I might be wrong. (*then bursting out*) No, I'm not wrong! I've felt it too strongly, ever since I was a kid. And then when I was eleven—something happened. I've been sure of it since then.

MADELINE—(*thinking in amazement, but not without a queer satisfaction*)

> Does he mean that she was unfaithful to his father? . . . no, he'd never believe that . . . but what else could he mean? . . .

(*wonderingly*) Gordon! Do you mean you've been sure that your mother was—

GORDON—(*outraged by something in her tone—jumping to his feet and flinging her hand off—roughly*) Was what? What do you mean, Madeline?

MADELINE—(*frightened—placatingly puts her arms around*

him) I didn't mean anything, dear. I simply thought you meant—

GORDON—(*still indignant*) All I meant was that she must have fallen in love with Darrell long after she was married— and then she sent him away for Dad's sake—and mine, too, I suppose. He kept coming back every couple of years. He didn't have guts enough to stay away for good! Oh, I suppose I'm unfair. I suppose it was damned hard on him. He fought it down, too, on account of his friendship for Dad. (*then with a bitter laugh*) I suppose they'll be getting married now! And I'll have to wish them good luck. Dad would want me to. He was game. (*with a bitter gloomy air*) Life is damn queer, that's all I've got to say!

MADELINE—(*thinking with a sort of tender, loving scorn for his boyish naïveté*)

> How little he knows her! . . . Mr. Evans was a fine man but . . . Darrell must have been fascinating once . . . if she loved anyone she isn't the kind who would hesitate . . . any more than I have with Gordon . . . oh, I'll never be unfaithful to Gordon . . . I'll love him always! . . .

(*She runs her fingers through his hair caressingly—comfortingly*) You must never blame them, dear. No one can help love. We couldn't, could we? (*She sits beside him. He takes her in his arms. They kiss each other with rising passion. Marsden comes in noiselessly from the garden, a bunch of roses and a pair of shears in his hands. He looks younger, calm and contented. He is dressed in his all black, meticulous, perfectly tailored mourning costume. He stands looking at the two lovers, a queer agitation coming into his face.*)

MARSDEN—(*scandalized as an old maid—thinking*)

> I must say! . . . his father hardly cold in his grave! . . . it's positively bestial! . . .

(*then struggling with himself—with a defensive self-mockery*)

> Only it wasn't his father . . . what is Sam to Darrell's son? . . . and even if he were Sam's son, what have the living to do with the dead? . . . his duty is to love that life may keep on living . . . and what has their loving to do with me? . . . my life is cool green shade wherein comes no scorching zenith sun of passion and

possession to wither the heart with bitter poisons . . .
my life gathers roses, coolly crimson, in sheltered gar-
dens, on late afternoons in love with evening . . .
roses heavy with after-blooming of the long day, desiring evening . . . my life is an evening . . . Nina is a
rose, my rose, exhausted by the long, hot day, leaning
wearily toward peace. . . .

(*He kisses one of the roses with a simple sentimental smile—then
still smiling, makes a gesture toward the two lovers.*)

That is on another planet, called the world . . . Nina
and I have moved on to the moon. . . .

MADELINE—(*passionately*) Dear one! Sweetheart!

GORDON—Madeline! I love you!

MARSDEN—(*looking at them—gaily mocking—thinking*)
Once I'd have felt jealous . . . cheated . . . swindled
by God out of joy! . . . I would have thought bitterly,
"The Gordons have all the luck!" . . . but now I
know that dear old Charlie . . . yes, poor dear old
Charlie!—passed beyond desire, has all the luck at
last! . . .

(*then matter-of-factly*)

But I'll have to interrupt their biological preparations
. . . there are many things still to be done this evening . . . Age's terms of peace, after the long interlude of war with life, have still to be concluded . . .
Youth must keep decently away . . . so many old
wounds may have to be unbound, and old scars
pointed to with pride, to prove to ourselves we have
been brave and noble! . . .

(*He lets the shears drop to the ground. They jump startledly and
turn around. He smiles quietly.*) Sorry to disturb you. I've been
picking some roses for your mother, Gordon. Flowers really
have the power to soothe grief. I suppose it was that discovery that led to their general use at funerals—and weddings!
(*He hands a rose to Madeline.*) Here, Madeline, here's a rose
for you. Hail, Love, we who have died, salute you! (*He smiles
strangely. She takes the rose automatically, staring at him uncom-
prehendingly.*)

MADELINE—(*thinking suspiciously*)
What a queer creature! . . . there's something un-

canny! . . . oh, don't be silly! . . . it's only poor old Charlie! . . .

(*She makes him a mocking curtsey.*) Thank you, Uncle Charlie!

GORDON—(*thinking with sneering pity*)

> Poor old guy! . . . he means well . . . Dad liked him. . . .

(*pretending an interest in the roses*) They're pretty. (*then suddenly*) Where's Mother—still in the house?

MARSDEN—She was trying to get rid of the last of the people. I'm going in. Shall I tell her you want to see her? It would give her an excuse to get away.

GORDON—Yes. Will you? (*Marsden goes into the house on right.*)

MADELINE—You'd better see your mother alone. I'll go down to the plane and wait for you. You want to fly back before dark, don't you?

GORDON—Yes, and we ought to get started soon. (*moodily*) Maybe it would be better if you weren't here. There are some things I feel I ought to say to her—and Darrell. I've got to do what I know Dad would have wanted. I've got to be fair. He always was to everyone all his life.

MADELINE—You dear, you! You couldn't be unfair to anyone if you tried! (*She kisses him.*) Don't be too long.

GORDON—(*moodily*) You bet I won't! It won't be so pleasant I'll want to drag it out!

MADELINE—Good-bye for a while then.

GORDON—So long. (*He looks after her lovingly as she goes out right, rear, around the corner of the house. Thinking*)

> Madeline's wonderful! . . . I don't deserve my luck . . . but, God, I sure do love her! . . .

(*He sits down on the bench again, his chin on his hands.*)

> It seems rotten and selfish to be happy . . . when Dad . . . oh, he understands, he'd want me to be . . . it's funny how I got to care more for Dad than for Mother . . . I suppose it was finding out she loved Darrell . . . I can remember that day seeing her kiss him . . . it did something to me I never got over . . . but she made Dad happy . . . she gave up her own happiness for his sake . . . that was certainly damn

fine . . . that was playing the game . . . I'm a hell of
a one to criticize . . . my own mother! . . .
(*changing the subject of his thoughts abruptly*)
Forget it! . . . think of Madeline . . . we'll be married . . . then two months' honeymoon in Europe
. . . God, that'll be great! . . . then back and dive
into the business . . . Dad relied on me to carry on
where he left off . . . I'll have to start at the bottom
but I'll get to the top in a hurry, I promise you that,
Dad! . . .
(*Nina and Darrell come out of the house on the right. He hears
the sound of the door and looks around. Thinking resentfully*)
Funny! . . . I can't stand it even now! . . . when
I see him with Mother! . . . I'd like to beat him
up! . . .
(*He gets to his feet, his face unconsciously becoming older and cold
and severe. He stares accusingly at them as they come slowly toward him in silence. Nina looks much older than in the preceding
Act. Resignation has come into her face, a resignation that uses
no make-up, that has given up the struggle to be sexually attractive and look younger. She is dressed in deep black. Darrell's deep
sunburn of the tropics has faded, leaving his skin a Mongolian
yellow. He, too, looks much older. His expression is sad and bitter.*)
NINA—(*glancing at Gordon searchingly—thinking sadly*)
He sent for me to say good-bye . . . really good-bye
forever this time . . . he's not my son now, nor Gordon's son, nor Sam's, nor Ned's . . . he has become
that stranger, another woman's lover. . . .
DARRELL—(*also after a quick keen glance at Gordon's face—
thinking*)
There's something up . . . some final accounting . . .
(*thinking resignedly*)
Well, let's get it over . . . then I can go back to
work. . . . I've stayed too long up here . . . Preston
must be wondering if I've deserted him. . . .
(*then with a wondering sadness*)
Is that my son? . . . my flesh and blood? . . . staring
at me with such cold enmity? . . . how sad and idiotic
this all is! . . .

NINA—(*putting on a tone of joking annoyance*) Your message was a godsend, Gordon. Those stupid people with their social condolences were killing me. Perhaps I'm morbid but I always have the feeling that they're secretly glad someone is dead—that it flatters their vanity and makes them feel superior because they're living. (*She sits wearily on the bench. Darrell sits on side of the recliner at right.*)

GORDON—(*repelled by this idea—stiffly*) They were all good friends of Dad's. Why shouldn't they be sincerely sorry? His death ought to be a loss to everyone who knew him. (*His voice trembles. He turns away and walks to the table. Thinking bitterly*)

> She doesn't care a damn! . . . she's free to marry Darrell now! . . .

NINA—(*thinking sadly, looking at his back*)

> He's accusing me because I'm not weeping . . . well,
> I did weep . . . all I could . . . there aren't many
> tears left . . . it was too bad Sam had to die . . .
> living suited him . . . he was so contented with him-
> self . . . but I can't feel guilty . . . I helped him to
> live . . . I made him believe I loved him . . . his
> mind was perfectly sane to the end . . . and just be-
> fore he died, he smiled at me . . . so gratefully and
> forgivingly, I thought . . . closing our life together
> with that smile . . . that life is dead . . . its regrets
> are dead . . . I am sad but there's comfort in the
> thought that now I am free at last to rot away in peace
> . . . I'll go and live in Father's old home . . . Sam
> bought that back . . . I suppose he left it to me . . .
> Charlie will come in every day to visit . . . he'll com-
> fort and amuse me . . . we can talk together of the
> old days . . . when I was a girl . . . when I was
> happy . . . before I fell in love with Gordon Shaw
> and all this tangled mess of love and hate and pain and
> birth began! . . .

DARRELL—(*staring at Gordon's back resentfully*)

> It gets under my skin to see him act so unfeelingly
> toward his mother! . . . if he only knew what she's
> suffered for his sake! . . . the Gordon Shaw ideal

    passed on through Sam has certainly made my son an insensitive clod! . . .

(with disgust)

    Bah, what has that young man to do with me? . . . compared to Preston he's only a well-muscled, handsome fool! . . .

(with a trace of anger)

    But I'd like to jolt his stupid self-complacency! . . . if he knew the facts about himself, he wouldn't be sobbing sentimentally about Sam . . . he'd better change his tune or I'll certainly be tempted to tell him . . . there's no reason for his not knowing now . . .

(His face is flushed. He has worked himself into a real anger.)

GORDON—*(suddenly, having got back his control, turns to them—coldly)* There are certain things connected with Dad's will I thought I ought to— *(with a tinge of satisfied superiority)* I don't believe Dad told you about his will, did he, Mother?

NINA—*(indifferently)* No.

GORDON—Well, the whole estate goes to you and me, of course. I didn't mean that. *(with a resentful look at Darrell)* But there is one provision that is peculiar, to say the least. It concerns you, Doctor Darrell—a half-million for your Station to be used in biological research work.

DARRELL—*(his face suddenly flushing with anger)* What's that? That's a joke, isn't it? *(thinking furiously)*

    It's worse! . . . it's a deliberate insult! . . . a last sneer of ownership! . . . of my life! . . .

GORDON—*(coldly sneering)* I thought it must be a joke myself—but Dad insisted.

DARRELL—*(angrily)* Well, I won't accept it—and that's final!

GORDON—*(coldly)* It's not left to you but to the Station. Your supervision is mentioned but I suppose if you won't carry on, whoever is in real charge down there will be only too glad to accept it.

DARRELL—*(stupefied)* That means Preston! But Sam didn't even know Preston—except from hearing me talk about him! What had Sam to do with Preston? Preston is none of his business! I'll advise Preston to refuse it! *(thinking torturedly)*

    But it's for science! . . . he has no right to refuse!

... I have no right to ask him to! ... God damn Sam! ... wasn't it enough for him to own my wife, my son, in his lifetime? ... now in death he reaches out to steal Preston! ... to steal my work! ...

NINA—(*thinking bitterly*)

Even in death Sam makes people suffer ...

(*sympathetically*) It isn't for you—nor for Preston. It's for science, Ned. You must look at it that way.

GORDON—(*thinking resentfully*)

What a tender tone she takes toward him! ... she's forgotten Dad already! ...

(*with a sneer*) You'd better accept. Half-millions aren't being thrown away for nothing every day.

NINA—(*in anguish—thinking*)

How can Gordon insult poor Ned like that! ... his own father! ... Ned has suffered too much! ...

(*sharply*) I think you've said about enough, Gordon!

GORDON—(*bitterly, but trying to control himself—meaningly*) I haven't said all I'm going to say, Mother!

NINA—(*thinking—at first frightenedly*)

What does he mean? ... does he know about Ned being ... ?

(*then with a sort of defiant relief*)

Well, what does it matter what he thinks of me? ... he's hers now, anyway. ...

DARRELL—(*thinking vindictively*)

I hope he knows the truth, for if he doesn't, by God, I'll tell him! ... if only to get something back from Sam of all he's stolen from me! ...

(*authoritatively—as Gordon hesitates*) Well, what have you got to say? Your mother and I are waiting.

GORDON—(*furiously, taking a threatening step toward him*) Shut up, you! Don't take that tone with me or I'll forget your age—(*contemptuously*) and give you a spanking!

NINA—(*thinking hysterically*)

Spanking! ... the son spanks the father! ...

(*laughing hysterically*) Oh, Gordon, don't make me laugh! It's all so funny!

DARRELL—(*jumps from his chair and goes to her—solicitously*) Nina! Don't mind him! He doesn't realize—

GORDON—(*maddened, comes closer*) I realize a lot! I realize you've acted like a cur! (*He steps forward and slaps Darrell across the face viciously. Darrell staggers back from the force of the blow, his hands to his face. Nina screams and flings herself on Gordon, holding his arms.*)

NINA—(*piteously—hysterically*) For God's sake, Gordon! What would your father say? You don't know what you're doing! You're hitting your father!

DARRELL—(*suddenly breaking down—chokingly*) No—it's all right, son—all right—you didn't know—

GORDON—(*crushed, overcome by remorse for his blow*) I'm sorry—sorry—you're right, Mother—Dad would feel as if I'd hit him—just as bad as if I'd hit him!

DARRELL—It's nothing, son—nothing!

GORDON—(*brokenly*) That's damn fine, Darrell—damn fine and sporting of you! It was a rotten, dirty trick! Accept my apology, Darrell, won't you?

DARRELL—(*staring at him stupidly—thinking*)

> Darrell? . . . he calls me Darrell! . . . but doesn't he know? . . . I thought she told him. . . .

NINA—(*laughing hysterically—thinking*)

> I told him he hit his father . . . but he can't understand me! . . . why, of course he can't! . . . how could he? . . .

GORDON—(*insistently holding out his hand*) I'm damned sorry! I didn't mean it! Shake hands, won't you?

DARRELL—(*doing so mechanically—stupidly*) Only too glad—pleased to meet you—know you by reputation—the famous oarsman—great race you stroked last June—but I was hoping the Navy would give you a beating.

NINA—(*thinking in desperate hysterical anguish*)

> Oh, I wish Ned would go away and stay away forever! . . . I can't bear to watch him suffer any more! . . . it's too frightful! . . . yes, God the Father, I hear you laughing . . . you see the joke . . . I'm laughing too . . . it's all so crazy, isn't it? . . .

(*laughing hysterically*) Oh, Ned! Poor Ned! You were born unlucky!

GORDON—(*making her sit down again—soothing her*) Mother! Stop laughing! Please! It's all right—all right between us! I've apologized! (*as she has grown calmer*) And now I want to say what I was going to say. It wasn't anything bad. It was just that I want you to know how fine I think you've both acted. I've known ever since I was a kid that you and Darrell were in love with each other. I hated the idea on Father's account—that's only natural, isn't it?—but I knew it was unfair, that people can't help loving each other any more than Madeline and I could have helped ourselves. And I saw how fair you both were to Dad—what a good wife you were, Mother—what a true friend you were, Darrell—and how damn much he loved you both! So all I wanted to say is, now he's dead, I hope you'll get married and I hope you'll be as happy as you both deserve— (*Here he breaks down, kissing her and then breaking away.*) I've got to say good-bye—got to fly back before dark—Madeline's waiting. (*He takes Darrell's hand and shakes it again. They have both been staring at him stupidly.*) Good-bye, Darrell! Good luck!

DARRELL—(*thinking sufferingly*)
      Why does he keep on calling me Darrell . . . he's my boy . . . I'm his father . . . I've got to make him realize I'm his father! . . .

(*holding Gordon's hand*) Listen, son. It's my turn. I've got to tell you something—

NINA—(*thinking torturedly*)
      Oh, he mustn't! . . . I feel he mustn't! . . .

(*sharply*) Ned! First, let me ask Gordon a question. (*then looking her son in the eyes, slowly and impressively*) Do you think I was ever unfaithful to your father, Gordon?

GORDON—(*startled, stares at her—shocked and horrified—then suddenly he blurts out indignantly*) Mother, what do you think I am—as rotten-minded as that! (*pleadingly*) Please, Mother, I'm not as bad as that! I know you're the best woman that ever lived—the best of all! I don't even except Madeline!

NINA—(*with a sobbing triumphant cry*) My dear Gordon! You do love me, don't you?

GORDON—(*kneeling beside her and kissing her*) Of course!

NINA—(*pushing him away—tenderly*) And now go! Hurry! Madeline is waiting! Give her my love! Come to see me once in a while in the years to come! Good-bye, dear!

(*turning to Darrell, who is standing with a sad resigned expression—imploringly*) Did you still want to tell Gordon something, Ned?

DARRELL—(*forcing a tortured smile*) Not for anything in the world! Good-bye, son.

GORDON—Good-bye, sir. (*He hurries off around the corner of the house at left, rear, thinking troubledly*)

> What does she think I am? . . . I've never thought that! . . . I couldn't! . . . my own mother! I'd kill myself if I ever even caught myself thinking . . . !

(*He is gone.*)

NINA—(*turns to Ned, gratefully taking his hand and pressing it*) Poor dear Ned, you've always had to give! How can I ever thank you?

DARRELL—(*with an ironical smile—forcing a joking tone*) By refusing me when I ask you to marry me! For I've got to ask you! Gordon expects it! And he'll be so pleased when he knows you turned me down. (*Marsden comes out of the house.*) Hello, here comes Charlie. I must hurry. Will you marry me, Nina?

NINA—(*with a sad smile*) No. Certainly not. Our ghosts would torture us to death! (*then forlornly*) But I wish I did love you, Ned! Those were wonderful afternoons long ago! The Nina of those afternoons will always live in me, will always love her lover, Ned, the father of her baby!

DARRELL—(*lifting her hand to his lips—tenderly*) Thank you for that! And that Ned will always adore his beautiful Nina! Remember him! Forget me! I'm going back to work. (*He laughs softly and sadly.*) I leave you to Charlie. You'd better marry him, Nina—if you want peace. And after all, I think you owe it to him for his life-long devotion.

MARSDEN—(*thinking uneasily*)

> They're talking about me . . . why doesn't he go? . . . she doesn't love him any more . . . even now he's all heat and energy and the tormenting drive of noon . . . can't he see she is in love with evening? . . .

(*clearing his throat uneasily*) Do I hear my name taken in vain?

NINA—(*looking at Marsden with a strange yearning*)

> Peace! . . . yes . . . that is all I desire . . . I can no

longer imagine happiness . . . Charlie has found
peace . . . he will be tender . . . as my father was
when I was a girl . . . when I could imagine happiness . . .

*(with a girlish coquettishness and embarrassment—making way
for him on the bench beside her—strangely)* Ned's just proposed
to me. I refused him, Charlie. I don't love him any more.

MARSDEN—*(sitting down beside her)* I suspected as much.
Then whom do you love, Nina Cara Nina?

NINA—*(sadly smiling)* You, Charlie, I suppose. I have always loved your love for me. *(She kisses him—wistfully)* Will
you let me rot away in peace?

MARSDEN—*(strongly)* All my life I've waited to bring you
peace.

NINA—*(sadly teasing)* If you've waited that long, Charlie,
we'd better get married tomorrow. But I forgot. You haven't
asked me yet, have you? Do you want me to marry you,
Charlie?

MARSDEN—*(humbly)* Yes, Nina. *(thinking with a strange
ecstasy)*

I knew the time would come at last when I would hear
her ask that! . . . I could never have said it, never!
. . . oh, russet-golden afternoon, you are a mellow
fruit of happiness ripely falling! . . .

DARRELL—*(amused—with a sad smile)* Bless you, my children! *(He turns to go.)*

NINA—I don't suppose we'll ever see you again, Ned.

DARRELL—I hope not, Nina. A scientist shouldn't believe
in ghosts. *(with a mocking smile)* But perhaps we'll become
part of cosmic positive and negative electric charges and meet
again.

NINA—In our afternoons—again?

DARRELL—*(smiling sadly)* Again. In our afternoons.

MARSDEN—*(coming out of his day dream)* We'll be married
in the afternoon, decidedly. I've already picked out the
church, Nina—a gray ivied chapel, full of restful shadow,
symbolical of the peace we have found. The crimsons and
purples in the windows will stain our faces with faded passion. It must be in the hour before sunset when the earth
dreams in afterthoughts and mystic premonitions of life's

beauty. And then we'll go up to your old home to live. Mine wouldn't be suitable for us. Mother and Jane live there in memory. And I'll work in your father's old study. He won't mind me. (*From the bay below comes the roaring hum of an airplane motor. Nina and Darrell jump startledly and go to the rear of the terrace to watch the plane ascend from the water, standing side by side. Marsden remains oblivious.*)

NINA—(*with anguish*) Gordon! Good-bye, dear! (*pointing as the plane climbs higher moving away off to the left—bitterly*) See, Ned! He's leaving me without a backward look!

DARRELL—(*joyfully*) No! He's circling. He's coming back! (*The roar of the engine grows steadily nearer now.*) He's going to pass directly over us! (*Their eyes follow the plane as it comes swiftly nearer and passes directly over them.*) See! He's waving to us!

NINA—Oh, Gordon! My dear son! (*She waves frantically.*)

DARRELL—(*with a last tortured protest*) Nina! Are you forgetting? He's my son, too! (*He shouts up at the sky*) You're my son, Gordon! You're my— (*He controls himself abruptly—with a smile of cynical self-pity*) He can't hear! Well, at least I've done my duty! (*then with a grim fatalism—with a final wave of his hand at the sky*) Good-bye, Gordon's son!

NINA—(*with tortured exultance*) Fly up to heaven, Gordon! Fly with your love to heaven! Fly always! Never crash to earth like my old Gordon! Be happy, dear! You've got to be happy!

DARRELL—(*sardonically*) I've heard that cry for happiness before, Nina! I remember hearing myself cry it—once—it must have been long ago! I'll get back to my cells—sensible unicellular life that floats in the sea and has never learned the cry for happiness! I'm going, Nina. (*as she remains oblivious, staring after the plane—thinking fatalistically*)

She doesn't hear, either. . . .

(*He laughs up at the sky.*)

Oh, God, so deaf and dumb and blind! . . . teach me to be resigned to be an atom! . . .

(*He walks off, right, and enters the house.*)

NINA—(*finally lowering her eyes—confusedly*) Gone. My eyes are growing dim. Where is Ned? Gone, too. And Sam is gone. They're all dead. Where are Father and Charlie? (*With a shiver of fear she hurries over and sits on the bench beside Marsden, huddling against him.*) Gordon is dead, Father. I've just had a cable. What I mean is, he flew away to another life—my son, Gordon, Charlie. So we're alone again—just as we used to be.

MARSDEN—(*putting his arm around her—affectionately*) Just as we used to be, dear Nina Cara Nina, before Gordon came.

NINA—(*looking up at the sky—strangely*) My having a son was a failure, wasn't it? He couldn't give me happiness. Sons are always their fathers. They pass through the mother to become their father again. The Sons of the Father have all been failures! Failing they died for us, they flew away to other lives, they could not stay with us, they could not give us happiness!

MARSDEN—(*paternally—in her father's tone*) You had best forget the whole affair of your association with the Gordons. After all, dear Nina, there was something unreal in all that has happened since you first met Gordon Shaw, something extravagant and fantastic, the sort of thing that isn't done, really, in our afternoons. So let's you and me forget the whole distressing episode, regard it as an interlude, of trial and preparation, say, in which our souls have been scraped clean of impure flesh and made worthy to bleach in peace.

NINA—(*with a strange smile*) Strange interlude! Yes, our lives are merely strange dark interludes in the electrical display of God the Father! (*resting her head on his shoulder*) You're so restful, Charlie. I feel as if I were a girl again and you were my father and the Charlie of those days made into one. I wonder is our old garden the same? We'll pick flowers together in the aging afternoons of spring and summer, won't we? It will be a comfort to get home—to be old and to be home again at last—to be in love with peace together—to love each other's peace—to sleep with peace together—! (*she kisses him—then shuts her eyes with a deep sigh of requited weariness*)—to die in peace! I'm so contentedly weary with life!

MARSDEN—(*with a serene peace*) Rest, dear Nina. (*then*

tenderly) It has been a long day. Why don't you sleep now—as you used to, remember?—for a little while?

NINA—(*murmurs with drowsy gratitude*) Thank you, Father—have I been wicked?—you're so good—dear old Charlie!

MARSDEN—(*reacting automatically and wincing with pain—thinking mechanically*)

God damn dear old . . . !

(*then with a glance down at Nina's face, with a happy smile*)

No, God bless dear old Charlie . . . who, passed beyond desire, has all the luck at last! . . .

(*Nina has fallen asleep. He watches with contented eyes the evening shadows closing in around them.*)

(*Curtain*)

DYNAMO

CHARACTERS

Reverend Hutchins Light
Amelia, *his wife*
Reuben, *their son*
Ramsay Fife, *superintendent of a hydro-electric plant*
May, *his wife*
Ada, *their daughter*
Jennings, *an operator at the plant*

GENERAL SCENE

ACT ONE

The exterior of the homes of the Lights and the Fifes in a small town in Connecticut. These houses stand side by side, facing front, on the street. They are separated by narrow strips of lawn, with a lilac hedge at center marking the boundary-line between the two properties, and a row of tall maples in the background behind the yards and the two houses. The Fife house, a small brownish-tinted modern stucco bungalow type, recently built, is at left; the Light home, a little old New England white frame cottage with green shutters, at right. Only the half sections of the two houses are visible which are nearest to each other, the one containing the Fife sitting room, with Ramsay's and May's bedroom directly above it, and the section of the Lights' home in which are their sitting room and Reuben's bedroom on the floor above.

As the separate scenes require, the front walls of these rooms are removed to show the different interiors. All these rooms are small, the ones in the Light home particularly so.

It is the month of May of the present day. The lilacs are in bloom, the grass is a fresh green.

SCENE 1: The Light sitting room and Reuben's bedroom above it.

SCENE 2: The Fife sitting room with Ramsay's and May's bedroom on the floor above.

SCENE 3: The Light and Fife sitting rooms.

SCENE 4: Reuben's bedroom.

ACT TWO

SCENE 1: Same as Act One, Scene One. The Light sitting room. Fifteen months later.

SCENE 2: Same as Scene One, except that Reuben's bedroom is revealed.

SCENE 3: Exterior of the Light and Power Company's hydro-electric plant. A half hour later.

Act Three

Dynamo

ACT ONE

SCENE ONE—*It is evening. In the background between the two houses the outlines of the maples are black against a sky pale with the light of a quarter-moon. Now and then there is a faint flash of lightning from far off and a low rumble of thunder.*

The Light sitting room and Reuben's bedroom are revealed. Both are sparsely furnished with the bare necessities. Reuben's bedroom contains an old four poster bed, front, facing left, a small table on which are stacked his textbooks, and a chair in left corner, front. In the left wall is a window. A washstand with bowl and pitcher is in the left corner, rear, and an old-fashioned bureau in the middle of the rear wall. To the right of this is the door of a clothes closet. The door to the hall and the stairs is at right, rear. There is a lighted kerosene lamp on the table.

In the sitting room below there is a table at center, front. The minister's armchair is beside this on the left. His wife's rocker is at the right of the table. Farther right is another chair. Three small hooked rugs are on the floor. Several framed prints of scenes from the Bible hang on the walls. The minister's small desk is placed against the left wall beside the window. On the table at center are a cheap oil reading lamp, a Bible, and some magazines. There is a door to the hall in the right wall, rear.

The ceilings of both rooms are low, the wall paper so faded that the ugliness of its color and design has been toned down into a neutral blur. But everything in this home is spotlessly clean and in order, the old furniture and floors are oiled and polished.

The Reverend Hutchins Light is seated in his armchair, his wife in her rocker. He is a man in his early sixties, slightly under medium height, ponderously built. His face is square, ribbed with wrinkles, the forehead low, the nose heavy, the eyes small and gray-blue, the reddish hair grizzled and bushy, the stubborn jaw weakened by a big indecisive mouth. His voice is the bullying one of a sermonizer who is the victim of an inner uncertainty that compensates itself by being boomingly overassertive.

His wife, Amelia, is fifteen years his junior and appears even younger. Her stout figure is still firm and active, with large breasts and broad, round hips. She must have been pretty as a

*girl. Even now her dark-complected face, with its big brown eyes
and wavy black hair, retains its attractiveness although it has
grown fleshy. Her expression is one of virtuous resignation. Only
her mouth is rebellious. It is a thin small mouth, determined and
stubborn.*

*In the bedroom above, their son, Reuben, is sitting in his shirt
sleeves on the side of his bed. He is seventeen, tall and thin. His
eyes are large, shy and sensitive, of the same gray-blue as his
father's. His mouth is like his father's. His jaw is stubborn, his
thick hair curly and reddish-blond. He speaks timidly and hesitatingly, as a much younger boy might. His natural voice has an
almost feminine gentleness. In intercourse with the world, however, he instinctively imitates his father's tone, booming self-
protectively.*

*Hutchins Light has a pad on which he has been trying to make
notes for his next sermon, but his mind is abstracted. He stares
before him with the resentful air of one brooding over a wrong
done him and unsuccessfully plotting revenge. His wife is pretending to read, but her thoughts are actively elsewhere, and she
glances calculatingly at her husband from under lowered lids.*

*In the bedroom above, Reuben's eyes are turned toward the
window, his face eager with dreams.*

LIGHT—(*arguing tormentedly within himself*)
    What did he mean about Reuben? . . . that foul-
    mouthed scoundrel! . . . "Better call in your son or
    some night I might mistake his odor of sanctity for a
    skunk's and fill his" . . . filthy word belching from his
    grinning mouth! . . . "full of buckshot" . . . I heard
    the corner loafers laugh . . . and I had to slink by and
    pretend not to hear! . . . If it weren't for my cloth I'd
    have beaten his face to a bloody pulp! . . . I'd . . .
(*suddenly horrified at himself*)
    A murderer's thoughts! . . . Lord God, forgive
    me! . . .
MRS. LIGHT—(*glances at him and speaks in a gentle tone
that carries a challenging quality*) Hutchins, do you realize
Reuben will graduate from school in less than a month?
LIGHT—(*oblivious*)
    But, Lord, Thou knowest what a thorn in the flesh

that atheist, Fife, has been since the devil brought him next door! . . .

(*protesting petulantly to his God*)

How long, O Lord? . . . does not his foul ranting begin to try Thy patience? . . . is not the time ripe to smite this blasphemer who defies Thee publicly to strike him dead? . . . Lord God of Hosts, why dost Thou not strike him? . . . If Thou didst, I would proclaim the awful warning of it over all America! . . . I would convert multitudes, as it was once my dream to do! . . .

MRS. LIGHT—Hutchins, please pay attention to what I'm saying. Don't you think we ought to decide definitely about Reuben's future?

LIGHT—(*turns to her with a frown*) I have decided. He shall follow in my footsteps—mine and those of my father before me and his father before him. It is God's manifest will! (*He presses his lips tightly together—an effort to appear implacable that gives his face the expression of a balky animal's.*)

MRS. LIGHT—(*thinks scornfully*)

He is always so sure of what God wills! . . . but Reuben'll never be a minister if I can prevent it! . . . I'd rather see him dead than go through the poverty and humiliation I've had to face! . . . Reuben's got to go to college . . . then into business . . . marry a nice girl with money . . . he doesn't care anything about girls yet, thank goodness!

(*She speaks in a meek, persuasive tone.*) Each of us must judge about Reuben according to the light vouchsafed by God. He doesn't feel any call to the ministry and I think it would be a great sin if—

LIGHT—(*his voice booming*) And I tell you, Amelia, it is God's will!

REUBEN—(*hearing his father's voice, jumps to his feet and stares down toward the room with an expression of boyish apprehension*)

What's he shouting about? . . . has he heard about Ada and me? . . . he'll raise the roof! . . . but Mother'll take my side against him . . . she's always sided with me . . .

(*then resentfully*)

What do I care about him anyway? . . . he hates Fife because he's scared of him . . . he's scared to take up Fife's challenge to debate about whether there's a God or not . . . when Fife took out his watch and said if there was a God let Him prove it by striking him dead in five minutes, why was it nothing happened? . . . I should think if . . .

(*He looks around uneasily, afraid of where his thoughts are leading him. A faint flash of lightning from the distant storm flickers through his window. He starts guiltily and hastily makes a reassuring declaration of faith.*)

Of course there's a God . . . He wouldn't pay any attention to a fool like Fife, that's all . . .

LIGHT—I believe that storm must be coming this way. (*He gets to his feet—a bit shamefacedly*) I think I'll close the shutters.

MRS. LIGHT—But it'll make it so dreadfully close in here! (*Then seeing his ashamed look, she smiles.*) Oh, all right, close them if you're getting scared.

LIGHT—(*his dignity ruffled, turns his back on her and goes to the window*) Lightning gets on lots of people's nerves without their being afraid of it.

REUBEN—

Aw, what's the matter with me? . . . that lightning had nothing to do with what I was thinking . . .

(*He goes to the window and looks over toward the Fife home.*)

Ada said she'd put a record on the Victrola as soon as she was free . . . then I was to meet her down by the lilacs . . .

(*He breathes in the spring.*)

Gee, those lilacs smell sweet . . . I wish she'd hurry up . . . I've got to get up my nerve and tell her I love her . . .

LIGHT—(*stands by the window and sniffs the air*) Can you smell the perfume of the lilacs, Amelia? Do you remember our first spring here?

MRS. LIGHT—Of course. (*then, after a pause, her voice turned bitter*) Twenty-three years! It's a long time to live in this awful little house! Hutchins, are you ever going to insist that they install electric lighting here? It's a shame the way they deny you the ordinary comforts of life!

LIGHT—(*turns away and leans out of the window staring into the night*)

Comforts of life . . . she has always desired the comfortable path . . . where the spirit decays in the sinful sloth of the flesh . . .

(*From the open, curtained windows of the Fife living room a burst of laughter is heard—Fife's voice, sardonic and malicious. Light draws back into the room, muttering viciously*) Scum of the earth! (*then turning on his wife*) Tell me, has Reuben been having anything to do with that cursed pack next door? That scoundrel called something at me on the street to-day—

MRS. LIGHT—(*impatiently*) Don't you know that man well enough by this time not to pay attention to his trying to rile you?

LIGHT—Then answer me this: why has Reuben taken such a sudden notion to going out in the evening lately?

MRS. LIGHT—Do you expect a boy of his age to stay in like a poor stick-in-the-mud just because he happens to be a minister's son—especially when it's spring?

LIGHT—I remembered that it's spring—and I've just remembered that Fife has a daughter!

MRS. LIGHT—That painted flapper with her skirts hitched up over her knees! Do you think for one moment that Reuben, who never looks at girls anyway—and knowing what her father is— Really, Hutchins, you're getting just too stupid! (*From the Fife house comes the sound of a Victrola starting a jazz record.*)

REUBEN—(*starts from his dream by the window upstairs*)

That's her signal! . . .

(*He hurriedly puts on his coat.*)

I better sneak out the back . . .

(*He blows out the light and makes his way carefully out the bedroom door in right, rear.*)

LIGHT—(*listening to the Victrola, fixes his eyes on his wife combatively*) You may call me as stupid as you like but I insist there was something back of what Fife said about Reuben. He sneered that we'd better keep him home at night and insinuated he was hanging around their place. The thought of that girl of his never entered my head until a moment ago— but what else could he mean? I'm going to face Reuben with it right now and we'll see what he has to say for himself.

MRS. LIGHT—(*sharply*) Now don't you go preaching at him again. You better let me talk to him first. He's never lied to me. (*She goes toward the door in rear, plainly worried now but trying to make little of it.*) You're always so ready to believe the worst of him. I know it's all nonsense. (*She goes out.*)

LIGHT—(*sits thinking gloomily*)
    Never lied to her . . . she means he does to me . . . why? . . . have I been too stern? . . . but even when he was little I sensed in him his mother's rebellious spirit . . . and now . . . if it is Fife's daughter . . . what a feather in that blasphemer's cap to corrupt my son! . . . how the gossips would sneer at me! . . .

(*This thought drives him frantic—he paces up and down trying vainly to calm himself.*)
    No, no! . . . Reuben could never be guilty of so base a treachery! . . .

(*He sits down by the table and, picking up his Bible, begins to read in a determined effort to get his mind off the subject.*)

MRS. LIGHT—(*can be dimly made out entering the bedroom above just as Reuben, coming from the back door of the house, slinks stealthily around the rear corner across the patch of moonlit lawn to the shadow of the lilacs. Keeping in this shadow he moves down until he comes to a small gap that is almost at the end of the hedge, front. He stands by this, waiting nervously, peering through the gap at the Fife house. Mrs. Light thinks worriedly*)
    Gone to bed? . . . so early? . . . was he sick and didn't tell me? . . .

(*She has come to the bed—with sudden fear*)
    He's not here! . . . he sneaked out! . . . the first time he ever did such a thing! . . . but how do I know it's the first? . . . all the evenings I thought he was here studying . . . it can only mean one thing! . . . a girl! . . . not a good girl! . . . it must be that Fife girl! . . .

(*She goes to the window, peering out but keeping her head carefully inside—with fierce jealousy*)

That dirty little . . . I'd like to see her try to catch my Reuben! . . .

(There is a strong flash of distant lightning that suddenly reveals Reuben in his hiding place by the hedge. She gives a gasp.)

Oh! . . . there he is! . . . watching their house! . . . I'll just watch him and make sure. . . . Oh, Reuben, I can't believe it, you've never noticed girls! . . .

There is darkness for a moment—(as if the moon had passed behind a cloud)—to mark the end of Scene One. No time elapses between Scenes One and Two.

SCENE TWO—*When it grows light again the outer walls of the two rooms in the Light home have been replaced, while the interiors of the Fife sitting room and the couple's bedroom above it are now revealed. There is one small window on the top floor front of the Light home, two on the ground floor. Mrs. Light's head can be seen peering out of the side bedroom window at Reuben, crouched in the shadow of the lilacs. The two rooms in the Fife home, bright with all their electric lights on, are of a glaring newness. There is a table at center, front, in the sitting room, a Victrola in the rear corner, left, near the door in the left wall which leads to the hall. In the right wall are three windows looking out on the lawn toward the lilac hedge and the Light home. These windows are repeated in the same series in the bedroom above. The bed is at left, front, its head against the left wall. In the same wall, to the rear of the bed, is the door. There is a dressing table with a big mirror against the rear wall, right, near the windows.*

Ramsay Fife is seated at the left of the table, glancing through the pages of a technical book on Hydro-Electric Engineering. His wife is lying back in a chaise longue that she has pushed close to the windows on the right so she can stare out up at the sky.

Fife is a small wiry man of fifty, of Scotch-Irish origin, with a sharp face and keen black eyes. His thin mouth is full of the malicious humor of the practical joker. He has a biting tongue, but at bottom is a good-natured man except where the religious bigotry of his atheism is concerned. His wife is tall and stout, weighing well over two hundred. Her face must have once been one of those rosy-cheeked pretty doll-like faces and in spite of its fat, it has kept its girlish naïveté and fresh complexion. Her figure is not formless nor flabby. It suggests, rather, an inert strength. A mass of heavy copper-colored hair is piled without apparent design around her face. Her mouth is small with full lips. Her eyes are round and dark blue. Their expression is blank and dreamy. Her voice is sentimental and wondering. She is about forty years old.

Their daughter, Ada, sixteen, who is upstairs in the bedroom putting on a heavy make-up of rouge and mascara, resembles her father more than her mother. She has his alert quality. Her pretty face, with her mother's big blue eyes, is alive and keen, her mouth has a touch of her father's malicious humor. Her brown hair is boyishly bobbed. Her speech is self-assertive and consciously slangy. Beneath her flip talk, however, one senses a strong trace of her mother's sentimentality.

MRS. FIFE—(*dreaming sentimentally*)

    I hear Ada upstairs . . . she's primping up before my mirror . . . she's falling in love . . . it's nice to be in love in May . . . I love May better than any other month . . . May is when I first met Ramsay . . . it's warm to-night . . . I mustn't forget to make Ramsay change to his summer underwear this week . . . he always wears his heavies too long and gets prickly heat and then he's terrible cross . . .

FIFE—(*reading—disgustedly*)

    "Hydro-Electric engineering" . . . it's studying this stuff gives those stuck-up engineers their diplomas . . . "Frequency and number of phases" . . . "Inherent Regulations" . . . "Parallel Working" . . . "Wave Form" . . . diagrams and equations! . . . "The kinetic energy of a rotor of diameter D and axial length L, running at a speed of rotation n, is theoretically proportional to $D4\ Ln2$" . . . arrh! . . . the devil take their theories! . . . when anything goes wrong at the plant it's me who fixes it without any theory! . . .

(*He tosses the book on the table and speaks to his wife.*) I wish Townsend wouldn't go forcing his books on me, telling me I owe it to myself to pass for engineer's papers. (*with a chuckle*)

Him arguing with me and at the same time admitting "Fife, you know a damn sight more about this game than I do."

MRS. FIFE—(*mooning at him with adoring eyes*) You know more than any one, Ramsay.

FIFE—(*pleased but amused—teasing her as he would a big child*) Oho, I do, do I? How the hell do you know? (*then complacently*) Well, I do know more than most. There isn't a damn job in the game I haven't had a hand at sometime or another. (*He looks at her and sees she is not listening any more.*)

    Look at her . . . in a dope dream again . . . I might as well be married to a cow . . .

(*then amusedly*)

    Well, she's a damn funny woman . . . I've never seen her equal anywhere . . .

(*He sees the newspaper on the table and reaches for it, glances at the headlines and settles down to reading with a grunt of awakened interest.*)

MRS. FIFE—(*has again fallen to dreaming sentimentally of the past*)

    When I first met Ramsay he was a linesman . . . I loved him at first sight . . . he was so romantic looking with those steel climbing things on his legs . . . and he wore a colored handkerchief round his neck just like a cowboy . . . Pa and Ma warned me linesmen were no good . . . they just ruined you and went their way . . . they were wrong about Ramsay . . . except he did ruin me . . . I said, why is it wrong when I love him? . . . Pa yelled to get out, I'd disgraced the family . . . I never expected Ramsay'd marry me . . . he was the roving kind . . . but as soon as he knew he'd got me into trouble he spoke right up . . . "Oh, hell, then I guess I've got to marry you" . . . and I said yes, and I was awful happy . . . and five months after Ada was born and he was crazy about her from the first . . . and we've all been happy ever since . . .

(*She sighs contentedly.*)

ADA—(*in the bedroom above, finishes making up and inspects herself critically in the mirror—approvingly*)

    I got to hand it to you, baby, you're there! . . . Gosh,

how long is it since I put on that record? . . . Rube'll
be waiting . . . he's as bashful as a kid . . . but that's
what I like about him . . . I'm sick of these fresh guys
that think all they have to do is wink and you fall! . . .
Rube has got honest-to-God feelings . . . but of
course, I'd never love him . . . he's too big a Mama's
boy for me . . .

(*She goes to the door and puts her hand on the switch.*)

Well, let's go . . . I'm dying to see if he'll have nerve
enough to kiss me . . .

(*She turns out the light.*)

REUBEN—(*crouched by the hedge, gives a start as a flash of
lightning flickers over the sky*)

Gosh, I wish Ada'd hurry up . . . this isn't much fun
. . . I'm losing all my nerve waiting . . .

MRS. LIGHT—(*bending out of the window in Reuben's bedroom—in suspense between suspicion and hope*)

She doesn't seem to be coming . . . maybe it's only
some game he's playing . . . waiting to scare some
friend of his . . .

FIFE—(*looking up from his paper with a snort of disgust just
as Ada enters the room*) The bloody swinepot!

ADA—(*comes and puts an arm around his shoulder—teasingly*) What's the bad news, Pop? Has another Fundamen-
talist been denying Darwin?

FIFE—(*boiling over with indignation, thrusting the paper on
her, his finger pointing out the article*) Read this and you won't
joke about it! (*As Ada begins to read, he speaks to his wife.*) Of
all the yellow tricks!

MRS. FIFE—(*coming out of her dream with a start*) What,
Ramsay?

FIFE—This story in the paper! There was a man in Ohio
many years back killed another fellow in a fight about a girl.
He got twenty years for it, but the girl helped him to escape
and they both got clean away to the Coast, where he settled
down under another name and they were married and had a
daughter. He became one of the town's best citizens, and
damned if his daughter didn't get engaged to the minister's
son! Then, just before the wedding, the old man feels he's
honor bound to tell his future son-in-law the secret of his

past; so the damned idiot blathers the whole story of his killing the man and breaking jail! And what do you suppose that young skunk does? Breaks off with the girl and goes to the police with the story, saying he's bound by his conscience to squeal on him!

ADA—(*who has finished reading the story*) Phew! Some louse, that boy!

FIFE—Arrh! They're all the same, the Bible-punching breed! (*then with a touch of severity*) And mind you bear that in mind, young lady, when you're fooling with that young ass next door!

ADA—Hey, listen, Pop! Honestly, I think you've got a nerve to— Why, it was you said to start up an acquaintance with him, when I told you I'd caught him staring at me, because you knew how it'd get his old man's goat!

FIFE—(*his sense of humor returning—with a malicious grin*) Aye, it will that! I gave him a strong hint on the street to-day that upset him. Oh, if you'd only make a prize jackass of that yellow Nancy son of his!

ADA—Say, why have you got it in for Rube so? He's not to blame for his father. (*then hastily*) Not that it's anything in my young life. I'm simply having fun kidding him along. (*then defensively again*) But Rube's a good scout—in his way. He isn't yellow.

MRS. FIFE—(*suddenly—with a placid certainty*) You're falling in love, Ada.

ADA—(*confused*) Aw, Mom, where d'you get that stuff?

FIFE—(*has glanced at her with suspicion*) So you don't believe that lad's yellow, don't you? What'll you bet he isn't? (*then as she doesn't answer*) I dare you to bring him in tonight, and let me talk to him and you listen, and if I don't show him up yellow then I'll buy you the best dress you can find in the town! (*as she hesitates—tauntingly*) Are you afraid to take me up?

ADA—(*with defensive flippancy, turns to go*) I'll think about it. There's a dress in Steele's I've had my eye on. (*She goes out the door at left.*)

FIFE—(*looks after her—frowning*)

She acts queer about him . . . it's time I took a hand in this . . . I've got to fix up a scheme on him quick . . . she'll bring him back if she has to drag him . . .

ADA—(*has come out of the house by the front door, off left, and enters from the left, then hesitates for a moment, debating with herself*)

Shall I make him come in? . . . he'll be scared stiff! . . . but Pop was only bluffing . . . well, I'll just call his bluff! . . . he can't get away with that stuff with me! . . .

(*She walks toward the gap in the hedge.*)

MRS. LIGHT—(*can see her now from the window*)

There she comes . . . the little harlot! . . .

ADA—(*calling*) Rube.

REUBEN—(*comes through the hedge to her—sheepishly*) Hello, Ada. (*Then, as he stands beside her, looking down into her face, a sudden thrill of desire almost overcomes his timidity.*) Gosh, Ada,—you're pretty in the moonlight. I—I wish— (*His courage fails him—lamely*) It's certainly grand to-night, isn't it?

ADA—Yeah. It's great. (*She takes one of his hands.*) Come on in my house and meet Pop. I want you to see he isn't the devil out of hell your old man makes him out to be.

REUBEN—(*immediately terrified*) I can't, Ada! You know I can't. Why don't we walk the same as—

ADA—I'm sick of walking. (*as he still holds back—tauntingly*) Are you scared Pop will eat you? You make me sick, Rube!

REUBEN—It's not because I'm scared of your father; it's because—

ADA—Afraid your Mama would spank you if she found out? (*then as he still hesitates*) Oh, very well, you know what you can do, don't you? (*She turns her back on him and walks away.*)

REUBEN—Ada! Wait a minute! Please don't get sore! I'll come!

ADA—Good boy! (*She suddenly raises herself on tiptoe and kisses him—with a little laugh*) There! That's to help keep your nerve up!

REUBEN—(*a wave of passion coming over him, grabs her by the shoulders and bends his face close to hers*) Ada!

ADA—Ouch! That hurts, Rube!

REUBEN—I don't care if it does! I love you, Ada! (*He tries to kiss her.*)

ADA—(*struggling away from him*) Hey, cut it out! What do you think I am? (*Then, as, brought back to himself, he releases her in shamefaced confusion, she adds tartly, her confidence restored and her temper a bit ruffled*) Listen here, Rube, just because I kissed you in fun, don't get too fresh!

REUBEN—I—I didn't mean nothing bad—honest I didn't!

ADA—All right, only don't get rough again. (*taking his hand—in a bullying tone*) Come on. Let's go in. (*Reuben follows her off left mechanically, a look of growing dread on his face.*)

MRS. LIGHT—

    She kissed him! . . . the brazen little harlot! . . .
    where is she taking him? . . . I've got to stop her! . . .

(*She draws back quickly from the window and can be made out going hurriedly from the bedroom.*)

FIFE—(*irritably*)

    May the devil kill me if I can think up a good
    scheme . . .

(*He turns his exasperation on his wife.*) How can I think in the same room with you? It's like trying to swim in glue! For God's sake, get out of here!

MRS. FIFE—(*raises herself to her feet placidly, without a trace of resentment*) I'll go upstairs and read the paper.

FIFE—(*starts to thrust the paper on her*) Here you are then! (*But as he does so his eye lights on the same headline that had attracted his attention before and suddenly he has an inspiration and grins elatedly.*) By God, I've got it, May! I'll try that on him! All the pious folks in this town think I've a bad record behind me— (*He pushes the paper into her hands.*) Get out of here quick! I don't want you around to give me away! (*She goes out. He waits, looking at the door, a grin of malicious expectancy on his face. At this moment Mrs. Light, who has come out by her kitchen door, appears around the corner of her house and slinks hurriedly across the patch of lawn to the shadow of the lilacs at the extreme edge of the hedge, front.*)

MRS. LIGHT—(*peers stealthily around the corner of the hedge*

down the street—in an extreme state of agitation)
> I can't see them . . . they're hiding somewheres . . .
> she'll be kissing him . . . oh, just wait till I tell her
> what I think of her! . . .

(*She starts out of the shadow of the lilacs as if to go down the street
but the brightness of the moonlight frightens her and she moves
quickly back into the shadow.*)
> Supposing any one should see me . . . oh, I don't
> know what to do! . . . that nasty wicked boy! . . .
> he'll be punished good for this! . . .

*There is darkness again for a moment, to mark the end of Scene
Two. No time elapses between Scenes Two and Three.*

SCENE THREE—*When the light comes on again, the wall of the
Fife bedroom has been replaced. Their sitting room is revealed as
before with Fife still sitting looking expectantly at the door. And
now the interior of the Light sitting room is again shown with
Light sitting as at the end of Scene One. He holds the open Bible
but he is staring moodily over it. Mrs. Light, as before, is hiding
in the shadow of the lilac hedge, peering down the road, ashamed
of her position and afraid she will be discovered.*

LIGHT—(*thinking gloomily*)
> I must be honest with myself . . . who am I to cast
> the first stone at Reuben if he desires a woman? . . .
> hasn't my love for Amelia been one long desire of the
> senses? . . . I should understand Reuben's weakness
> and forgive him . . .

(*then his resentment smoldering up*)
> But to betray me to Fife! . . . that would go deeper!
> . . . it would be treachery to God! . . .

MRS. FIFE—(*leans out of the front window of the bedroom
upstairs*)
> I don't want to read the paper . . . I'd rather look at
> the moon . . .

(*mooning up at the moon*)
> Ada loves that Light boy . . . he must be nice . . .
> he isn't to blame because his father believes in religion

. . . maybe his father is nice too if you got to know him off the job . . . Ramsay is always so cranky when he's at the plant . . . I love the plant . . . I love the dynamos . . . I could sit forever and listen to them sing . . . they're always singing about everything in the world . . .

(*She hums to herself for a moment—an imitation of the whirring purr of a dynamo.*)

MRS. LIGHT—(*hearing this noise, looks up around the corner of the hedge and sees her and immediately dissolves into abject shame and fright*) Oh, my God! . . . did she see me? . . . she'll tell the whole town I was spying! . . . oh, this is terrible! . . . I ought to get Hutchins . . . but I can't move while she's watching . . .

FIFE—(*standing up and looking at the door*) Ada's a long time bringing him . . . there's a lot of whispering in the hall . . . he's afraid, I'm thinking . . . about to enter the presence of Satan . . . I'll have to start in making him think I'm the devil himself! . . .

(*Ada comes in the doorway of the sitting room, left, followed by Reuben.*)

FIFE—(*without waiting for an introduction, goes up and shakes Reuben's hand with an exaggerated cordiality*) So you're young Mr. Light, are you? I'm damned glad to make your acquaintance. Sit down and make yourself at home. (*All the time he is talking, he stares at Reuben's flustered face, keenly sizing him up. He forces him to sit in the chair across the table from him. Ada sits down at right, watching her father with a challenging smile.*)

REUBEN—(*stammers*) Pleased to meet you. Thank you. Thanks.

FIFE—(*with a sudden change to severity*) I want a damned serious talk with you, young man! That's why I had Ada invite you in! (*as Reuben stares at him bewilderedly*) But before we start that, let me ask you, is your reverend father ever going to take up my challenge to debate with me?

REUBEN—(*shamefacedly*) I—I don't think so.

FIFE—(*jeeringly*) He's afraid I'd beat him!

REUBEN—(*defensively*) No, he isn't! He can answer all your arguments easy—with things right out of the Bible! He's only scared that folks'd think he was wrong to argue with you! (*then raising his voice defiantly*) But I'd argue if I was in his place!

MRS. LIGHT—(*from her hiding place by the hedge has caught Reuben's raised voice—with horrified stupefaction*)

  That was Reuben's voice! . . . he's actually in there talking to that atheist! . . . oh, I wish I could get closer to the window! . . . but she'd see me! . . .

(*But she comes around the end of the hedge as far as she can get and strains her ears.*)

FIFE—(*smiling mockingly at Reuben*) Well, maybe after you're a minister you and me'll argue it out sometime.

REUBEN—(*glad to make a show of his independence before Fife*) I'm not going to be a minister! Father wants me to but Mother doesn't—and I don't want to be. Besides, I've never felt the call. You have to feel God calling you to His service.

FIFE—(*with a leer*) And how does God call you, tell me? I'm thinkin' He wouldn't use the telegraph or telephone or radio for they're contraptions that belong to His archenemy Lucifer, the God of Electricity. (*Reuben's face has flushed with mingled indignation and fear. He looks up at the ceiling apprehensively, then opens his mouth to make some retort to Fife when there is a vivid flash of lightning. He gives a start and half rises from his chair, controlling an impulse to run from the room. Fife's keen eyes are watching him and he grins with satisfaction.*)

REUBEN—(*stammers*) You better not—talk like that, or— you better look out!

FIFE—What's the trouble, young fellow? Are you afraid of a bit of lightning? Don't worry about me. The devil looks after his own! But a minister's son has reason to worry, maybe, when he's in a den of atheism, holding intimate converse with a damned man! I'm thinking your Jehovah might aim a thunderbolt at me but Lucifer would deflect it on to you—and he's the better electrical expert of the two, being more modern in his methods than your God!

REUBEN—(*in a turmoil of guilt and fright*)

  I wish I'd never come here! . . . God may strike him!

. . . He certainly ought to! . . . if I was God, I'd kill him for blaspheming like that! . . .

ADA—(*observing Reuben—worriedly*)

Why did the poor boob let Pop get wise he was scared of lightning? . . .

(*then indignantly*)

Pop has no right to pick on religion! . . . that's hitting below the belt! . . .

(*protestingly*) Aw, Pop, lay off religion, can't you!

FIFE—(*glances at her irritably—then with a calculating tone to Reuben*) Ada's right, Mr. Light. I didn't have you in to convert you to atheism. This is a free country and you're free to believe any God-forsaken lie you like—even the book of Genesis! (*then solemnly*) But here's what I did have you in for, and I'll come right to the point. As a father I want to know what your intentions are regarding my daughter! (*Reuben stares at him in open-mouthed amazement.*)

ADA—(*embarrassed but cannot help a giggle of amusement when she looks at Reuben*) Aw, Pop, what—

FIFE—Keep your tongue out of this! (*sternly to Reuben*) I trust you mean honorably by her, young fellow, or it'll be the worse for you! I'll have no young spark seducing my daughter—getting her with child, maybe, and then deserting her with no marriage lines to save her from disgrace! (*Ada begins to see this as a huge joke and she has to bury her face in her hands to choke back her laughter as she looks at Reuben's face on which is at first a shocked look of stupefaction. But this gives way to a fit of indignation that any one could think him so low.*)

REUBEN—What do you think I am? You have no right to say that about me! I'm not that kind of— (*then his voice booming like his father's with moral self-righteousness*) I respect Ada just as much as I do my mother! I'm going to marry her!

ADA—(*genuinely flustered—trying to laugh it off*) Gee, Rube, did I say you had no nerve? I take it all back! (*Reuben's nerve immediately deserts him. He hangs his head in acute embarrassment, his eyes on the floor.*)

MRS. LIGHT—(*by the end of the hedge*)

Marry her! . . . I heard it clear as day! . . . respect her like he does me! . . . damn her! . . . Oh, I

didn't mean to swear! . . . I don't know what I'm
doing! . . .

(*then weeping hysterically and trying to stifle it*)

Oh, I'll get Hutchins to beat him within an inch of his
life! . . .

(*She sinks down on the ground, her hands over her face.*)

I've got to stop! . . . she'll hear me up there! . . .
she'll tell how I was crying! . . .

MRS. FIFE—(*has noticed the noise of Mrs. Light's movements
and looks down vaguely*)

Some animal's in the garden . . . maybe it's a skunk
. . . I'd love to have a skunk skin coat next winter
. . . maybe Ramsay'll give me one for Christmas . . .
Ramsay calls the minister a skunk . . . poor Mr.
Light! . . . Ramsay says awful mean things sometimes
. . . but it's only because he loves to make jokes . . .
he's the kindest man in the world . . .

FIFE—(*pretending to be sunk in thought has been staring calculatingly at Reuben—solemnly*) Young man, I'll be honest
with you. In view of your honorable intentions I feel bound
by my conscience to let you know the secret of the family
you're wanting to marry into. But you must give me your
word of honor, as man to man—I don't ask you to swear on
the Bible—that you'll never repeat what I'm saying to any
one, no matter how dreadful it seems to you! Will you give
me your word?

REUBEN—(*made visibly uneasy but forcing a manly tone*)
Sure. I wouldn't ever say anything.

ADA—(*leaning forward in her chair and watching her father
worriedly*)

What's Pop going to spring? . . . Rube's looking pale
behind the gills, poor guy! . . . aw, poor nothing!
. . . he ought to have more guts! . . .

FIFE—(*with a tragic sigh*) There's not a living soul knows
it, barring my wife and Ada. It's like putting my life in your
hands. You know, don't you, that no one knows what I done
before I came to this town, nor where I came from. I've good
reason for keeping it dark. Listen now. Twenty years ago
there was a man by the name of Andrew Clark lived in the
town of Arming, Ohio. (*He pauses significantly, giving a quick*

side glance at Ada to see if she's caught the joke—*then goes on with a guilty furtiveness*—*lowering his voice*) Now Clark was in love with a girl whose family had got her engaged to another fellow, but she loved Clark and used to meet him in the woods. But this fellow who was engaged to her got suspicious and one night he sneaked up on them lying in each other's arms—in sin, as you'd call it—and he rushed out with a knife at them both, but Clark picked up an ax and split his skull! (*He finishes up with well-feigned savagery.*) And serve him right, the bloody sneak!

REUBEN—(*stares at Fife with horror*) You mean—Clark murdered him?

FIFE—(*with a great pretense of guilt-stricken protest*) Oh, don't say that! Not murder! He killed him in self-defense! Wouldn't you do the same if Ada was the girl and you was Clark?

REUBEN—

What is he asking? . . . Ada? . . . would I? . . .

(*then his horror turning to a confused rage*)

I'd kill Ada if I caught her! . . . but it was the other man who caught! . . . and they were engaged, too! . . . she belonged to him! . . .

(*harshly and condemningly*—*in his father's tone*) That other fellow should have killed them, that's what I think! That girl was engaged to the other fellow! She had no right to love Clark! That wasn't love, it was lust! She was an adulteress! It would have been only her just punishment if that fellow had killed her! I would have!

FIFE—For the love of God, don't be so hard on me—for what I was coming to tell you was that I was Clark! (*As if to punctuate this dramatic confession, there is a flash of lightning, brighter than any that has gone before.*)

REUBEN—(*clutches the arms of his chair in superstitious terror, all the passion drained out of him instantly, leaving him weak and penitent*)

Oh, God, please forgive me! . . . I didn't mean it! . . . I wouldn't ever kill her! . . .

(*then glancing at Fife with fear*)

He's a murderer! . . . he said himself he was damned! . . .

FIFE—(*eyeing Reuben keenly*) After I'd killed him I gave myself up. The jury said it was murder in the second degree and gave me twenty years—but I fooled 'em with the help of the girl and escaped and we both ran off to the far west and settled down in Niclum, California, and I married her under the name of Fife and we had a daughter. That's Ada.

REUBEN—(*keeping his eyes averted from Ada*)
        Then that's her mother! . . . she's the daughter of an adulteress! . . . and a murderer! . . . how can I ever trust her? . . . she's gone around with lots of fellows . . . how do I know she never—? . . .
(*then torturedly*)
        Oh, God, why did I ever come here to-night? . . .

FIFE—(*with a great pretense of uneasiness*) You don't say a word. Well, maybe I shouldn't have told you, because now I've made you an accessory in the murder for you'll be shielding me unlawfully by keeping silence. And the devil knows what sin you'll think it in the sight of God! (*The clap of thunder from the preceding flash comes with a great rumble.*)

REUBEN—
        Accessory! . . . the police can arrest me! . . .
(*then summoning his manhood*)
        but I won't tell them! . . . ever! . . . I gave my word! . . .
(*then conscience-strickenly*)
        but God! . . . I'll be guilty before God! . . . but He knows I gave my word! . . . but does that count with Him? . . . when I didn't swear on the Bible? . . .
(*then frantically*)
        But He knows I love Ada . . . He wouldn't want me to tell on her father . . .
(*He suddenly jumps up and mumbles to Fife*) I won't tell the police, you needn't worry.

ADA—(*with a triumphant glance at her father*) Good for you, Rube!

REUBEN—(*avoiding her eyes*) I've got to go home now.

FIFE—(*searching Reuben's face—insistently*) I'm sorry to put such a load on your conscience, Mr. Light, but I felt it was only right of me.

REUBEN—

Why does he rub it in? . . . God, I hate him! . . . I wish they'd hung him! . . .

(*angrily—his voice booming denouncingly like his father's*) You needn't be afraid I'll tell—but you ought to go and tell yourself! You know you're guilty in the sight of God! Do you want to burn forever in hell?

FIFE—(*jeeringly*) Your hell and God mean no more to me than old women's nonsense when they're scared of the dark!

REUBEN—Don't you dare talk like that! I won't stand for it—not now! If you don't stop your blaspheming, I'll—I mean, it'd serve you right if I— (*hurrying toward the door as if in flight*) I got to get home. (*He stops at the door and turns to Ada, but keeps his eyes averted.*) Good night, Ada. (*He goes out.*)

ADA—

He was threatening Pop already he'd tell on him! . . . gee, he is yellow all right! . . .

(*Tears of mortification and genuine hurt come to her eyes—she brushes them back.*)

Aw, what do I care about him? . . .

FIFE—(*with a chuckle*) He'll be blabbin' my dreadful secret to his old man yet, wait and see!

ADA—(*to his surprise, turns on him angrily*) It wasn't fair! He never had a chance! (*She flings herself on the chaise longue and begins to cry.*)

FIFE—(*stares at her in astonishment*) Are you turning against me—for that lump! (*Then he comes and pats her on the shoulder.*) I was only doing it for your sake, Ada. You ought to see him in his true colors so you'd not be thinking too much about him.

ADA—(*forces back her tears and jumps up*) I didn't think anything! Leave me alone about him, can't you? (*With a great pretense of indifference she gets a book from the table and sits down again.*) I should worry about that poor fish! I've got to study my algebra. (*Her father stares at her puzzledly. There is a bright flash of lightning and Light, sitting as before in the sitting room of the other house reading the Bible, jumps nervously to his feet.*)

LIGHT—

I ought to conquer that silly fear in myself . . . the

lightning is God's will . . . what on earth can Amelia
be doing with Reuben all this time? . . .

(*He listens for a moment—uneasily*)

I'll go upstairs to them . . . she should be more considerate than to leave me alone when . . .

(*He walks toward the door on right.*)

*There is a pause of darkness here to mark the end of Scene Three.
In this darkness the clap of thunder from the preceding flash comes.
No time elapses between Scenes Three and Four.*

SCENE FOUR—*When the light comes on again—but this time
very dimly, as if the moon were behind clouds—the walls of the
Fife and Light sitting rooms have been replaced while the interior
of Reuben's bedroom is now revealed. Mrs. Fife still leans out of
her bedroom window and Mrs. Light sits crouching by the hedge.*

MRS. LIGHT—(*suddenly jumping to her feet and peering up
through the leaves at Mrs. Fife*)

Oh, God, isn't she ever going in? . . . I'll scream in a
minute! . . .

MRS. FIFE—

I love to watch lightning . . . the thunder clouds are
getting nearer the moon . . . I'd like to be a cloud
. . . it must be nice to float in the wind . . . but it
must be getting bedtime . . .

(*She slowly backs herself into her room.*)

MRS. LIGHT—(*as Mrs. Fife disappears*)

Now I can get Hutchins . . .

(*She slinks back along the hedge and then quickly across the lawn
around the corner of her house just as Reuben enters from the left
by the Fife house.*)

REUBEN—(*stands hesitating—uneasily*)

I thought I'd walk around and think up some lie . . .
Mother'll guess something is wrong as soon as she
looks at me . . . but I'm not going to stay out in the
storm . . .

(*He walks slowly over to where he had stood with Ada—dully*)

Here's where she kissed me . . . why couldn't we have

gone for a walk? . . . she'd have let me kiss her . . . I'd have had her in my arms . . . like her mother was with Clark? . . . no, I didn't mean that! . . . I didn't mean sin! . . .

(*then with desperate bravado*)

Aw, what is sin, anyway? . . . maybe that's just old women's nonsense, like Fife says! . . . why should I have a guilty conscience? . . . it's God's fault! . . . why hasn't He done something to Fife? . . . I should think He'd have to punish adultery and murder . . . if there is any God . . .

(*There is a great flash of lightning and he stands paralyzed with superstitious terror.*)

It comes every time! . . . when I deny! . . .

(*more and more obsessed by a feeling of guilt, of being a condemned sinner alone in the threatening night*)

Fife's damned me with him! . . . there's no use praying! . . . it's getting black! . . . I'm afraid of God! . . .

(*There is a crash of thunder. He cowers, trembling—then cries like a frightened little boy*) Mother! Mother! (*He runs off right, forgetting that he has sneaked out by the back, making for the front door. At the same moment Light can be dimly made out as he enters Reuben's bedroom, and Fife sticks his head out of his sitting-room window and looks toward the Light home.*)

FIFE—

That was him I heard passing . . . I'll wait here and watch the fun . . .

(*He chuckles to himself.*)

LIGHT—(*pauses just inside Reuben's bedroom door in alarm at finding the room dark and empty—calls uneasily*) Amelia! Reuben! (*He lights a match with trembling fingers and hurries over to the lamp and lights it. His wife's voice comes excitedly from below and then from the stairs in the hallway.*)

MRS. LIGHT—Hutchins! Hutchins! Where are you?

LIGHT—(*hurries to the door calling*) Here—upstairs.

MRS. LIGHT—(*a moment later hurries in excitedly, her words pouring out*) Oh, Hutchins, something awful has happened—that Fife girl—I heard Reuben asking Fife if he could marry her! (*Light, completely stunned, stares at her blankly. There is the noise of the front door being slammed and Reuben's voice calling desperately*)

REUBEN—Mother! Where are you?

MRS. LIGHT—Sshh! Let him come up here. (*pushing him toward the closet in rear*) You hide in that closet and listen! I'll make him acknowledge everything! He'd only lie to you! (*vindictively*) I promise I won't stand between him and punishment this time! (*She gives him a final shove inside the door and closes it.*)

REUBEN—(*His voice comes from the hall as he rushes upstairs.*) Mother! (*A second later he runs in and, too distracted to notice her expression, throws his arms around her.*) Mother! (*He breaks down and sobs.*)

MRS. LIGHT—(*alarmed by the state he is in, puts her arms around him, her immediate reaction one of maternal tenderness. She leads him front and sits on the side of the bed.*) There, there! It's all right, Reuben! Mother's here! (*then indignantly*) What have those awful people been doing to my boy to get him in such a state? (*as he gives a start—sharply*) Now don't deny you were there! Don't make matters worse by lying! What happened between you and that man? Tell Mother!

REUBEN—(*brokenly*) I can't! I promised him I wouldn't. I can't tell any one!

MRS. LIGHT—(*changing to a tone of wheedling affection*) Yes you can, Reuben. You can always tell Mother everything. You always have.

REUBEN—(*clinging to her*)

I love Mother better'n anything in the world . . . she always forgives me . . . I wish I could tell her . . . she'd know what was right . . .

(*There is a bright flash of lightning. He shrinks closer to her and blurts out*) I'm scared, Mother! I'm guilty! I'm damned!

MRS. LIGHT—(*startled*)

Guilty? . . . does he mean he? . . .

(*with sudden strong revulsion*)

And to think he's had those same arms hugging that little filthpot this very evening! . . .

(*She pushes him away, but, holding his shoulders, stares down into his face.*) Do you mean to say you refuse to tell your own mother, just because you were forced into promising not to by that atheist? Then all I can say is that my boy I thought I could trust has turned into a liar and a sneak, and I don't wonder you feel guilty in God's sight! (*As she finishes speaking, the roll of the thunder from the preceding flash comes crashing and rumbling. Reuben sinks down on his knees beside her, hiding his face in her lap.*)

REUBEN—(*stammers*) I'll tell you, Mother—if you promise to keep it a secret—just between me and you—and never tell Father.

MRS. LIGHT—All right. I'll promise.

REUBEN—(*made uneasy by something in her tone—insistently*) You'll swear it on the Bible?

MRS. LIGHT—Yes, I'll swear on the Bible I won't tell him.

REUBEN—(*in a passion of eagerness to get the guilty tale off his conscience*) His name isn't even Fife, it's Clark! He changed it because he'd murdered a man out in Ohio where he used to live. He got twenty years but he escaped and ran away to California! Fife's a murderer, that's what he really is! (*While he has been telling this story, the closet door has opened and Light stands there, listening greedily. In his hand is a belt of Reuben's.*)

LIGHT—(*thinking with a fierce, revengeful joy*)
　　　　Lord God of Righteous Vengeance, I thank Thee!
　　　　. . . at last Thou strikest! . . .

MRS. LIGHT—(*dumbfounded, not knowing what to make of this strange tale—and disappointed that it is not a confession about Ada*) Wherever did you get hold of this story?

REUBEN—He told me himself.

MRS. LIGHT—Do you expect me to believe Fife's such an idiot as to confess such things to you?

REUBEN—He had a good reason to tell me! I asked him if I could marry Ada and he thought he was honor bound to tell me! He knew it'd be safe with me when I gave him my word— (*then thinking with guilty shame*)
　　　　But I've told! . . . I've just told! . . . why did I? . . .
　　　　Oh, how Ada would hate me if she knew! . . .
(*pleadingly*) Remember you swore on the Bible you'd never tell! Remember, Mother!

MRS. LIGHT—(*glaring into his face vindictively*) So you want to marry that little harlot, do you?

REUBEN—(*shakes her hands off his shoulders—shrinking back from her, still on his knees*) Don't you say that, Mother! I love Ada, Mother! I love her with all my heart!

MRS. LIGHT—(*calls over her shoulder*) Do you hear that, Hutchins?

LIGHT—(*grimly*) Yes, I hear. (*He takes a threatening step forward.*)

REUBEN—Father! (*Then his eyes turn to his mother's vindictive face and he thinks in a tortured agony of spirit*)

> He was hiding in the closet! . . . she knew it! . . . she cheated me! . . . when I trusted her! . . . when I loved her better than any one in the world! . . .

(*He cries out in a passion of reproach*) Oh, Mother! Mother!

MRS. LIGHT—(*misunderstanding this as a plea*) No, you needn't think I'm going to get you off this time! You punish him good, Hutchins! The very idea—kissing that dirty little—!

REUBEN—Don't you say that!

LIGHT—(*walks toward him*) Hold your tongue! How dare you address your mother—!

REUBEN—(*his thoughts whirling in his head*)

> Mother's face . . . she looks terrible . . . she wants him to beat me . . . she wants to hear me yell . . .

(*then with a defiant determination as if some hidden strength in him had suddenly been tapped*)

> But I won't give her the satisfaction! . . . no matter how it hurts! . . .

LIGHT—Let this put back the fear of God into your sinful heart, Reuben! (*He brings the belt down heavily across Reuben's back. Reuben quivers but not a sound comes from his lips. At the same moment there is a glaring flash of lightning and Light cringes back with a frightened exclamation.*)

MRS. LIGHT—(*has winced when Reuben was hit—conscience-strickenly*)

> That must have hurt dreadfully! . . . poor Reuben! . . .

(*then with an exasperated sense of frustration, gazing at Reuben's set face*)

> Why doesn't he cry? . . . if he'd cry I'd stop Hutchins . . . that girl has changed him! . . .

REUBEN—(*expecting the next blow, thinking with a grim elation*)

Come on! . . . hit again! . . . hit a million times! . . . you can't make me show her you hurt me! . . .

(*then stealing a glance up at his father's face*)

He looks scared! . . . it was that lightning! . . . I'll never be scared of lightning again! . . .

(*then resolutely*)

I'll be damned if I'm going to let him beat me! . . .

(*He jumps to his feet and faces his father defiantly.*)

LIGHT—(*guiltily*)

I can't bear him looking at me like that . . . I really ought to feel grateful to him . . . his folly has delivered Fife into my hands . . .

(*He throws the belt on the bed—to his wife*) Reuben's punishment can wait. I have my duty of denouncing that murderer to the proper authorities. (*triumphantly*) Haven't I always said, if the truth were known, that man was a criminal! (*turning toward the door*) Keep Reuben here. He might warn Fife. I'll lock this door after me. (*then hurriedly, as a crash of thunder comes*) I must hurry. I want to get to the police station before the rain. (*He shuts the door behind him and locks it.*)

REUBEN—(*staring after him with the same look of defiance—calls jeeringly*) Look out for the lightning! (*Then he turns to his mother with a sneer—contemptuously*) Picture my being scared of that boob all my life! What did you ever see in him, to marry him? He's yellow!

MRS. LIGHT—(*frightened by the change in him but attempting a bullying tone*) How dare you talk so disrespectfully—!

REUBEN—But you're yellow, too. And I'm yellow. How could I help being? It's in my blood. (*harshly*) But I'll get him out of my blood, by God! And I'll get you out, too!

MRS. LIGHT—(*pitiably now*) What have I done, Reuben?

REUBEN—(*bitterly*) You knew he was in that closet! You led me on to tell! I thought you loved me better'n any one, and you'd never squeal on me to him! (*He starts to break down miserably.*)

MRS. LIGHT—(*goes to him as if to take him in her arms*) I do love you better than any one, Reuben! I didn't mean—

REUBEN—(*steps back from her—accusingly*) And you called

Ada a harlot—after I told you I loved her with all my heart!
(*then a note of pleading*) Do you mean you didn't mean that
part of it—about her?

MRS. LIGHT—(*immediately furious again*) Yes, I did mean
it about her! I meant it and a lot more!

REUBEN—Then I'm through with you! And as for him—!
(*He suddenly is reminded of something—thinking wildly*)

He went! . . . police station! . . . that'll finish me
with Ada! . . .

(*There is the noise of the front door slamming.*)

He's leaving! . . .

(*He rushes to the door but finds it locked—pushes and pulls at it,
trying to force it open.*)

MRS. LIGHT—I suppose you want to run over and warn
your fine friends! Fife'll be in a cell before long, please God,
and if there was any real justice his girl'd be put in along with
him for she's no better than a street-walker!

REUBEN—(*turns and glares at her*) I'm glad you're talking
like that! It shows you up and I can hate you now!

MRS. LIGHT—(*breaking down*) Reuben! For God's sake,
don't say that—to your mother!

REUBEN—You're not my mother any more! I'll do without
a mother rather than have your kind! (*He turns from her to the
window and looks out. As he does so, his father appears from right,
coming from the front door. He is buttoned up to the neck in an
old raincoat and carries an umbrella.*)

FIFE—(*still leaning out of his sitting room window, catches
sight of Light—calls excitedly over his shoulder*) Here's the old
man now! Come quick, Ada! (*A moment later, just as Light
comes up, she appears at the window next to her father. Her face
is set in an ugly, sneering expression. Fife calls to Light in a mocking tone*) Good evening, Your Holiness.

LIGHT—(*stops short and stares at Fife with a rage that chokes
him so that for a moment his lips move, forming words, but he
can't utter them—finally finding his voice, he stammers*) You—
you murderer!

FIFE—(*nudging Ada—with a great pretense of guilt*) Murderer? In the name of God, has your son—? after he'd sworn
his word of honor—!

LIGHT—(*triumphantly*) You thought you had him caught

in your snares, did you?—but God was simply using Reuben to bring retribution on your head! (*in a booming triumph*) "Vengeance is mine, saith the Lord!"

REUBEN—(*watching from his window*)

He's talking to Fife! . . . he's telling! . . .

(*then cursing his father aloud*) God damn him! I'll show him! (*He drives back at the door with the weight of his whole body, and it crashes open and he stumbles over it and disappears in the hall.*)

MRS. LIGHT—(*starts after him, calling frightenedly*) Reuben! Don't! Reuben!

FIFE—(*enjoying himself hugely*) You wouldn't give me up to the police, would you—a kind-hearted Shepherd of the Lord like you?

ADA—(*suddenly flares up into a temper*) Aw, cut it out, Pop! This has gone far enough! (*to Light with sneering contempt*) No wonder your son is a sap! Can't you see this is only a joke on you? Why, you poor fish, that murder story is in to-day's *Star*—the name Clark and everything! Pop simply copied that story—and if you go to the police you'll only be making a boob of yourself—but go ahead if you like! (*As she speaks Reuben runs in from the right. He advances threateningly on his father who is staring at Ada stupidly, overwhelmed by the conviction that what she has told him is true.*)

REUBEN—Did you tell—?

ADA—Look who's here! I was just telling your old man it was only a murder story out of the paper Pop told you to prove you were yellow! And you are, all right! Don't you ever dare speak to me again! You're a yellow rat! (*She breaks down, weeping, and rushes back into the room.*)

FIFE—(*following her*) Ada! Don't waste crying over—

REUBEN—Ada! Listen! I didn't mean—I didn't know—! (*He takes a few steps toward the window, then stops, thinking bitterly*)

So it was all a lie! . . . a joke she played on me! . . . that's why she made me meet her old man! . . . so she could make a fool of me! . . .

(*He yells at the window*) It's you who're the rat, Ada! You can go to hell!

MRS. LIGHT—(*hurrying in from the right. She runs to him and tries to put her arms around him.*) Reuben!

REUBEN—(*pushing her away from him—furiously*) Leave me alone! You're to blame for this! You cheated me! I hate you!

MRS. LIGHT—For God's sake, Reuben!

LIGHT—(*comes out of the state of humiliated stupefaction into which the knowledge of the joke has thrown him—bursting into a fatuous rage—to his wife*) As if I have not had enough to bear of humiliation! (*He points a shaking finger at Reuben.*) This dunce—this stupid dolt—now I shall be the butt of all their sneers! And to think I stayed my hand—! But wait! I'll show him what a real whipping is!

REUBEN—(*fiercely*) You'll never dare touch me again, you old fool! I'm not scared of you or your God any more! (*There is a blinding flash of lightning. Light, his nerves already at the breaking point, gives a gasp of superstitious fright.*)

LIGHT—God have mercy!

REUBEN—(*with a sneer*) What God? Fife's God? Electricity? Are you praying to It for mercy? It can't hear you! It doesn't give a damn about you! (*There is a tremendous crash of thunder. Reuben looks up and gives a wild laugh as though the thunder elated him. His mother and father shrink back from him as he shouts up at the sky*) Shoot away, Old Bozo! I'm not scared of You!

MRS. LIGHT—Reuben! You don't know what you're saying!

REUBEN—(*with a hard, mocking laugh—to his mother*) What's the matter? Do you still believe in his fool God? I'll show you! (*He jumps to his father's side and grabs his raincoat by the lapel—addressing the sky with insulting insolence*) If there is his God let Him strike me dead this second! I dare Him! (*His father squeals with terror and tries to break away from his hold. His mother screams. He laughs triumphantly.*) There! Didn't I tell you! (*Light finally tears his coat from Reuben's grip and runs panic-stricken off right, dragging his moaning wife by the arm. Reuben turns his back on his home determinedly and starts walking off left—with bitter defiance*) There is no God! No God but Electricity! I'll never be scared again! I'm through with the lot of you! (*As he disappears off left, the sound of wind and rain sweeping down on the town from the hills is heard.*)

(*Curtain*)

ACT TWO

SCENE ONE—*The same as Act One, Scene One. The interior of the Light sitting room is revealed.*

It is an early morning of a hot day in August. Fifteen months have elapsed.

Mrs. Fife is leaning out of one of the windows of their sitting room, basking contentedly in the sun. She wears a faded blue wrapper.

MRS. FIFE—(*thinking with a sleepy content*)
    The sun is hot . . . I feel so dozy . . . I know why
    dogs love to lie in the sun . . . and cats and chickens
    . . . they forget to think they're living . . . they're
    just alive . . .

(*She looks toward the Light house—with drowsy melancholy*)
    Alive . . . poor Mrs. Light is dead . . . what is death
    like, I wonder? . . . I suppose I'll have to die some-
    time . . . I don't want to die before Ramsay . . . he
    wouldn't know how to take care of himself . . .

(*At a noise in the room behind her she half turns her head—then Ada leans out of the window next to her mother. Her face has a peaked look. Her manner is touchy and irritable and she has lost her former air of flippancy. There is no rouge on her face and she is dressed as if she had grown indifferent about her personal appearance.*)

ADA—For heaven's sake, what're you dope-dreaming about now, Mom?

MRS. FIFE—I was thinking of poor Mrs. Light—

ADA—Poor nothing! She hated us worse than poison! She'd have sung hymns of joy if any of us had died! And why feel sorry for her, anyway? She's lucky, if you ask me! Life is the bunk!

MRS. FIFE—(*looks at her worriedly—with a sigh*) I wish that Light boy would come back.

ADA—(*immediately flying into a temper*) For God's sake, shut up! I've told you a million times how dumb that talk is and yet you keep on harping—!

MRS. FIFE—All right, Ada. I won't say anything.

ADA—What do I care about that poor fish! He can be

dead for all I care! (*then, as Fife's voice is heard calling from somewhere in the house*) There's Pop howling his head off about something. You go in and smooth him down, Mom. I'm sick of his grouches.

MRS. FIFE—(*as she turns to go*) I wish you'd make it up with your Pop, Ada. He feels so bad about it. You've kept a grudge against him ever since the night that Light boy—

ADA—There you go again! For Pete's sake, leave me alone! (*Mrs. Fife disappears meekly without another word. Ada stares before her, thinking resentfully*)

> I've got a good right to have a grudge against him . . . what he did that night wasn't on the level . . . it isn't a question of Rube . . . I don't give a darn about him . . . then why are you all the time thinking about him? . . . I'm not! . . . I liked him but that was all . . . and he was yellow, wasn't he? . . . well, maybe you'd be worse if everything was framed against you the way Pop got him! . . . poor Rube! . . . what's he been doing all this time, I wonder? . . .

(*with a sad smile of scorn for herself*)

> You poor boob! . . . it must be love! . . .

(*In the sitting room of the Light home, Hutchins Light enters from the rear, right. The grief over his wife's death has made him an old man. His hair has turned almost white, his mouth droops forlornly, his eyes are dull, his whole face is a mask of stricken loneliness. He comes and sits in his old chair and mechanically picks up his Bible from the table but lets it drop again and stares before him.*)

LIGHT—(*thinking dully*)

> Another day . . . empty . . . all days are empty now . . . how long, O Lord? . . .

(*He sighs heavily.*)

> No sleep again last night except for a few minutes . . . and then nightmare . . . I dreamed Amelia was in my arms . . . and Reuben came and beckoned her and she went away with him . . .

(*He shudders, flinging off the memory—then wondering bitterly*)

> Does that dream mean Reuben is dead, too? . . . what does it matter? . . . ever since that night he has been dead for me . . . but he never gave Amelia a

chance to forget him . . . a postal card every month
or so . . . each with the same blasphemy . . . "We
have electrocuted your God. Don't be a fool!" . . .
her last words! . . . "Don't be a fool," she kept saying
to me . . . she couldn't have known what she was
saying . . .

(*He breaks down, sobbing, and buries his head in his arms on the
table.*)

MRS. FIFE—(*reappears in the window beside Ada. She is smiling with a doting good nature.*) Your Pop told me to get out
of the room and stop looking at him or he'd start breaking
plates. My, but he's in a breakfast temper, though! The men
at the plant'll catch it—but they don't mind him. They know,
like I do, that he's really the kindest man in the world.

ADA—(*resentfully*) Oh, is he? I suppose that's why he acted
the way he did to Rube!

MRS. FIFE—He couldn't help being mean then. He'd be
mean at first to any man he thought you cared for—especially
a minister's son. But he'd get over it, you'd see. He'd like to
see you happy, before everything. I'm sure he's been wishing
for a long time that Light boy'd come home so he could
make friends with him.

ADA—Aw, you're crazy, Mom. (*Suddenly she leans over and
kisses her mother affectionately.*) It's you who are the kindest in
the world. (*then embarrassed—irritably*) Gosh, this sun's hot!
I don't see how you stand it. (*She retreats into the house.*)

MRS. FIFE—(*blinking placidly in the sun*)

It was awful nice the way Ada kissed me . . . I wish
she'd get to kissing her Pop again that way . . . she
does it now as if she wished she was a mosquito with
a stinger . . . the screen up in her room has a hole
rusted in it . . . I must remember to get it fixed or
they'll be flying in keeping her awake . . .

(*A pause—then Reuben Light comes slowly in from the left and
stands there, his eyes fixed for a while on his home, taking in every
detail. He does not for a moment notice Mrs. Fife nor she him. A
great change has come over him; he is hardly recognizable as the
Reuben of Act One. Nearly nineteen now, his body has filled out,
his skin is tanned and weather-beaten. In contrast to his diffident,
timid attitude of before, his manner is now consciously hard-boiled.*)

The look on his face emphasizes the change in him. It is much older than his years, and it is apparent that he has not grown its defensive callousness without a desperate struggle to kill the shrinking boy in him. But it is in his eyes that the greatest change has come. Their soft gray-blue has become chilled and frozen, and yet they burn in their depths with a queer devouring intensity. He is dressed roughly in battered shoes, dungaree trousers faded by many washings, a blue flannel shirt open at the neck, with a dirty colored handkerchief knotted about his throat, and wears the coat of his old suit. Under his arm he carries six books, bound together with a strap.)

REUBEN—(*thinking jeeringly*)

> Home, Sweet Home! . . . the prodigal returns! . . . what for? . . . I felt a sudden hunch I had to come . . . to have a talk with Mother, anyway . . . well, I'll soon know what it's all about . . . and won't the old man be glad to see me! . . . yes! . . . he'll poison the fatted calf! . . .

(*He laughs aloud. Mrs. Fife turns and gives a startled exclamation as she recognizes him. He turns and looks at her for a moment—then with a swaggering impudence*) Fine day, isn't it?

MRS. FIFE—(*her eyes mooning at him, with a simple, pleased smile*) I'm glad you've come home. Ada'll be glad. (*She stirs as if to go into the house.*) I'll tell her you're here.

REUBEN—(*frowning*) No. I've got no time for her now. (*then with a peculiar air of indifferent curiosity*) Are you sure Ada'll be glad I'm back? I shouldn't think she would after what happened.

MRS. FIFE—That wasn't her doing. She's been sorry about it ever since.

REUBEN—(*with the same detached interest*) She called me a yellow rat—and she had the right dope. I sure was dumb when it came to guessing what she really wanted or I would have— (*with a cold smile*) Well, never mind what—but you can tell her I've changed. I've lived a lot and read a lot to find out for myself what's really what—and I've found out all right! You can tell her I've read up on love in biology, and I know what it is now, and I've proved it with more than one female.

MRS. FIFE—(*preoccupied with her own thoughts*) It was just one of Ramsay's jokes.

REUBEN—He's a great little joker! And I certainly fell for it. Well, there's no hard feelings. He did me a favor. He woke me up. (*with a laugh, a queer expression coming into his eyes*) You can tell him I've joined his church. The only God I believe in now is electricity.

MRS. FIFE—(*simply*) Ramsay'll be glad.

REUBEN—(*indicating the books he carries*) I'm studying a lot of science. Sometimes I've gone without eating to buy books—and often I've read all night—books on astronomy and biology and physics and chemistry and evolution. It all comes down to electricity in the end. What the fool preachers call God is in electricity somewhere. (*He breaks off—then strangely*) Did you ever watch dynamos? What I mean is in them—somehow.

MRS. FIFE—(*dreamily*) I love dynamos. I love to hear them sing. They're singing all the time about everything in the world! (*She hums her imitation of a dynamo's whirring purr.*)

REUBEN—(*startled—looks at her with growing interest*) "Singing all the time about everything in the world" . . . she gets them all right . . . listen to her . . . she's caught the sound . . .

(*Abruptly he puts down his books and walks up to Mrs. Fife.*) Say, you're all right! (*He takes one of her hands in his clumsily—then lets go of it, grinning awkwardly.*)

MRS. FIFE—(*sentimentally touched—beaming on him*) I always knew you must be a nice boy. (*with a coquettish, incongruously girlish air*) But you save your holding hands for Ada! (*Then she half turns around at some sound in the room behind her—in a hurried whisper to Reuben*) She's coming! You hide behind those bushes and we'll surprise her! (*Mechanically, reacting instinctively for a moment as the timid boy of formerly, he runs to the gap in the lilac bushes and hides in the old place. Ada appears in the window beside her mother. Her face wears an expression of eager expectation. Her eyes glance quickly on all sides as if searching for some one.*)

ADA—(*flusteredly*) I'm sure I heard some one . . . it sounded like . . .

REUBEN—(*almost as soon as he reaches his old hiding place is overcome by shame*)

> What'd I do that for? . . . hide! . . . the old stuff! . . .

(*savagely*)

> No, by God! . . . her mother put it in my head . . . but I'll soon show Ada! . . . she'll find out if I'm yellow now! . . .

(*With a swagger and a cold smile on his lips he walks through the gap just as Mrs. Fife speaks to Ada.*)

MRS. FIFE—(*with a teasing smile*) Ada, I've got a big surprise for you. Guess— (*But Ada has already seen him.*)

ADA—(*with a cry of joy*) Rube!

REUBEN—(*walks toward her, the smile frozen on his lips, his eyes fixed on hers*)

> Go right up and kiss her! . . . look at the way she's looking at you! . . . she's easy now! . . .

ADA—(*staring at him, stammers his name again in a tone in which there is now a note of panic*) Rube!

REUBEN—(*pulls her head down and kisses her, keeping his lips on hers while she struggles instinctively for a moment, until she gives up and returns his kiss—then he pushes her a little away from him and laughs quietly, his confidence in himself completely restored.*) Well, this prodigal gets the fatted kiss even if "there ain't no calf." Hello, Ada! How's every little thing?

MRS. FIFE—(*sentimentally*) That's right. You two kiss and make up. I'll leave you alone. (*She goes back into the room.*)

ADA—(*is staring at him with eyes that search his face apprehensively*) Rube! You—you've changed. I—I hardly know you! I shouldn't have kissed you—like that. I don't know why I—

REUBEN—Well, I know. (*He takes her face between his hands again and brings his close to it.*) Because you love me. Isn't that right? (*as she hesitates—insistently, giving her head a little shake*) Isn't it?

ADA—(*helplessly*) I guess it is, Rube.

REUBEN—Guess, nothing! You loved me before I went away—even when you were bawling me out for a yellow rat. That was what made you so mad, wasn't it? You were ashamed of loving me when I was so dumb and didn't get what you wanted and was so damned scared to touch you. (*He laughs—a self-assured, insinuating laugh that for her has something at once fascinating and frightening about it.*) But you needn't worry any more, Ada. I've learned a lot about love since I left—and I get you now, all right! (*then with a sudden burst of threatening assertiveness*) You're damned right I've changed! I'm not yellow about you or God or anything else! Don't forget that, Ada! (*then as suddenly changing to a passionate tone of desire*) Gosh, you're pretty! I'd forgotten how pretty you were! You make all the girls I've been playing around with look like mistakes! Your eyes are grand—and your hair—and your mouth—! (*He kisses them hungrily as he speaks—then controls himself and breaks away from her, forcing a laugh.*) Continued in our next! Let's take a walk to-night.

ADA—(*staring at him helplessly*) Yes—no—I don't think—

REUBEN—Sure you will. We'll walk out to the top of Long Hill. That's where I was all during the storm that night after I left here. I made myself stand there and watch the lightning. After that storm was over I'd changed, believe me! I knew nothing could ever scare me again—and a whole lot of me was dead and a new lot started living. And that's the right place for us to love—on top of that hill—close to the sky—driven to love by what makes the earth go round—by what drives the stars through space! Did you ever think that all life comes down to electricity in the end, Ada? Did you ever watch dynamos? (*She stares at him, frightened and fascinated, and shakes her head.*) I've watched them for hours. Sometimes I'd go in a plant and get talking to the guys just to hang around, and I tried everywhere to get a job in a plant but never had any luck. But every job I've had—I never stuck to one long, I wanted to keep moving and see everything—every job was connected with electricity some way. I've worked for electricians, I've gone out helping linesmen, I shoveled sand on a big water-power job out West. (*then with sudden eagerness*) Say, Ada, I've just had a hunch! I know now what drove me back here, all right! You've got to get your old man to give me a job in his plant—any job, I don't care what!

ADA—Sure—I'll try, Rube.

REUBEN—(*with a cold assurance*) You've got to, Ada. Because I can't stay on here without a job. I'm broke and I won't live home—even if the old gent would let me. And that reminds me, I better go and pay my little visit. I don't want to see him but I want to have a talk with Mother. I've got over my hard feelings about her. She was so crazy jealous of you she didn't care what she did. I can make allowances for her—now. So I'll be friends again if she wants to—and then you watch me convert her over from that old God stuff of his! (*He grins with resentful anticipation.*)

ADA—(*has listened with blank astonishment—pityingly*) Then you don't—? Why, I thought— Didn't they send for you?

REUBEN—(*unsuspectingly—with a grin*) Send for me to come home and be good? I never gave them my address, kid. I didn't want them bothering me. I never wrote, except some postcards to Mother I sent to get her goat—and his. (*then picking up his books and turning toward his home*) Guess I'll go round by the back. I don't want to run into him unless I have to. So long, Ada. Tell your old man I'd sure like that job! (*He walks to the hedge and then, stealthily, across the lawn and disappears behind the house.*)

ADA—(*looking after him*)
> He doesn't know she's dead . . . ought I to have told
> him? . . . oh, I couldn't! . . . poor Rube! . . .

(*then admiringly*)
> How strong he's gotten! . . . but it makes me afraid,
> too . . . his eyes seemed to take all the clothes off me
> . . . and I didn't feel ashamed . . . I felt glad! . . .

(*defiantly*)
> I love him! . . . I want him as much as he wants me!
> . . . what of it? . . .

(*then with a shudder she cannot repress*)
> But his eyes are so queer . . . like lumps of ice with
> fire inside them . . . and he never said he loved me
> . . . aw, of course he does! . . . he was nuts about
> me before he went away, wasn't he? . . .

(*determinedly*)
> I've got to make Pop give him that job or he might
> beat it again . . . he owes it to Rube to do something
> for him . . . I'll talk to him right now . . .

(*She disappears inside the house just as Reuben slowly opens the door of the Light sitting room. There is an expression of puzzled uneasiness on his face as he peers around the half-opened door, then slinks in as if he were a burglar. Light is still sitting, his face hidden in his arms on the table, in an attitude of exhausted grief. Reuben does not at first see him.*)

REUBEN—

Something's all wrong here . . . where the hell is every one? . . . where's Mother? . . .

(*He has stepped on tiptoe into the room and now suddenly he sees his father and a sneering smile immediately comes to his lips.*)

There he is, anyway . . . praying as usual . . . the poor boob . . . there isn't a damn prayer ever got him a thing . . . Mother used to make him pray for electric lights in the house . . .

(*suddenly with a pleased grin*)

That's a good hunch . . . I'll get them put in the first money I save . . . it'll be like bringing my gospel to the heathen . . . let there be electric light! . . .

(*He chuckles, then bends closer to look at his father.*)

He must be asleep . . . that's one on him to catch him . . .

(*He speaks with mocking geniality.*) Hello! (*His father gives a frightened start, as if dodging a blow, and stares at his son's face with stupefied bewilderment.*) Sorry to disturb your little snooze. (*His father continues to look at him, as if he can't believe his eyes.*) Oh, this is me, all right. (*Then the fact of his father's changed appearance strikes him for the first time, and he blurts out in a tone that is almost kindly*) Say, you look all in. What's the trouble? Been sick?

LIGHT—(*thinking gropingly*)

It's Reuben . . . Reuben . . . but he doesn't seem like Reuben . . .

REUBEN—(*misunderstanding his father's silence as intentional, immediately becomes resentful*) What's the matter? Don't you want to talk to me? Well, I'm not here to talk to you, either. I was just passing this way and thought I'd drop in to say hello to Mother. Where is she?

LIGHT—(*thinking more clearly now—an unstrung fury rising within him*)

Oh, yes, it's Reuben! . . . I recognize him now! . . .
the same as that night! . . . cruel and evil! . . .
and now he's asking for the mother he . . . my poor
Amelia! . . . he killed her! . . .

(*He lurches to his feet and leans against the back of his chair
weakly, glaring at his son.*) Murderer! You killed her!

REUBEN—(*stares at him with a stunned look*) What the hell
do you mean? (*then harshly, taking a threatening step forward*)
Where's Mother, I'm asking you!

LIGHT—(*his strength failing him—in a faltering tone hardly
above a whisper*) She's dead—Reuben.

REUBEN—(*terribly shaken*) You're a liar! You're just saying
that to get my goat!

LIGHT—(*going on as if he hadn't heard—in a tone of monotonous grief*) You can't see her—I can't—never—never see
her again! (*He breaks down abjectly, sinking on his chair and
sobbing, his face in his hands.*)

REUBEN—(*stands looking at him stupidly, convinced now of
the truth and trying to make himself realize it and accept it*)
Then it's straight goods . . . she is dead . . . gone
. . . no use making a fuss . . . let him cry . . . why
can't his religion buck him up now? . . . he ought to
feel sure he's going to see her again soon . . . in
heaven . . . I'd like to see her again . . . tell her I'm
sorry for acting so rough to her that night . . .

(*He gulps and his lips twitch.*)
I wish he'd stop crying . . .

(*He goes forward and pats his father on the back gingerly.*) Buck
up. (*His father doesn't seem to hear him. He turns and slumps
into the chair at the far side of the table.*)
Why couldn't I have seen her just once again . . . this
is a rotten break . . .

(*He asks mechanically*) How long ago did she die?

LIGHT—(*mechanically in his turn—without lifting his head*)
Two weeks ago yesterday.

REUBEN—
Two weeks . . . it was about then I first felt that
hunch to come home and see her . . . that's damn
queer . . .

(*He stares at his father—uneasily*)

    He said I killed her . . . what the hell did he mean? . . . (*forcing a casual tone*) What did she die of?

    LIGHT—(*dully*) Pneumonia.

    REUBEN—(*heaving a sigh of relief*)

        Sure . . . I knew he was only saying that to get my
        goat . . .

(*He speaks to his father in a defensive, accusing tone.*) Pneumonia, eh? Well, it's a damn wonder we didn't all die of it years ago, living in this dump! Ever since I can remember the cellar's leaked like a sieve. You never could afford to get it fixed right. Mother was always after you about it. And I can remember the ceiling in my room. Every storm the water'd begin to drip down and Mother'd put the wash basin on the floor to catch it. It was always damp in this house. Mother was always after you to make them put in a decent furnace instead of—

    LIGHT—(*has lifted his head and is glaring at his son*) Are you trying to say I killed her? It was you! She'd been pining away for almost a year. Her heart was broken because you'd gone. She hoped for a time you'd come back but finally she gave up hoping—and gave up wanting to live! And your horrible blasphemous postcards kept coming! She blamed herself for your ruin and she wrote long letters begging your forgiveness, and asking you to come home! But you'd never given her an address! She couldn't mail them, she knew you'd never read them, and that broke her heart most of all! You killed her as surely as if you'd given her poison, you unnatural accursed son!

    REUBEN—(*deeply disturbed but trying desperately to conceal it*) I never gave her my address because I thought she'd only write bawling me out. (*then harshly*) Where are those letters she wrote? They're mine!

    LIGHT—I destroyed them! I burnt them to the last scrap!

    REUBEN—(*starts for his father threateningly, his fists clenched*) You rotten son of a— (*He chokes it back—then helplessly, with a wounded look*) Say, that was a dirty trick! I'd like to have read— (*Light averts his eyes and suddenly hides his face in his hands.*)

LIGHT—(*remorsefully now*)

He's right . . . I had no right . . . no right even to read them . . . how I wish I'd never read them! . . . (*lifting his head*) I destroyed them in a fit of anger. When I read them I realized that Amelia had been thinking of you all the time. And I felt betrayed! I hated her and you! I was insane with hatred! God forgive me!

REUBEN—(*after a pause—dully*) Did she ever talk about me?

LIGHT—(*immediately jealous again*) She never mentioned your name! (*then forcing himself to say it*) I—I had forbidden her to.

REUBEN—(*His face lights up with anger again but he controls it.*) Sure, you had to, didn't you?—so what the hell? (*then insistently*) But—didn't she?—at the last?—when she was dying?—say anything?

LIGHT—(*fighting a furious battle with himself*)

Have I got to tell him? . . . that she'd even forgotten God? . . . that her last words were his words? . . . even her soul lost to me? . . . must I tell this? . . .

(*savagely*)

No! . . . I don't owe him the truth! . . . I must make him feel he is accursed! . . .

(*He springs from his chair and leaning across the table, points his finger at Reuben denouncingly.*) Yes, with her last breath she cursed you for all the ruin and suffering you had brought on her—and on me! (*Then as he sees Reuben shrinking back in his chair, a haunted look of horror on his face, the consciousness of the evil of the lie he is telling overwhelms him with guilty remorse. He stammers*) No!—that's a lie, Reuben!—a terrible lie!—don't listen!—don't believe me! (*He stumbles hastily around the table to the dazed Reuben and with a pitiful gesture puts a trembling hand on his head—pleadingly*) Forgive me, Reuben! You are my son as well as hers, remember. I haven't the strength to resist evil. I wanted to punish you. She didn't curse you. Her last words were the very words you had written her. "Don't be a fool!" she kept saying to me! (*He shudders.*)

REUBEN—(*springs from his chair in extreme agitation and grabbing his father by both shoulders, stares hungrily in his face*) What? What's that? Mother said that?

LIGHT—(*seeming to shrivel up in his son's grip—trying unconvincingly to reassure himself*) She was delirious. She must have been delirious.

REUBEN—(*lets go of his father. The old man turns and stumbles back to his chair. Reuben stares before him, thinking excitedly*)

> "We have electrocuted your God. Don't be a fool" . . . that's what I kept writing her . . . her last words! . . . then I'd converted her away from his God! . . . the dying see things beyond . . . she saw I'd found the right path to the truth! . . .

(*His eyes shine with a new elation.*)

> By God, I'll go on now all right! . . .

(*He laughs aloud to himself exultantly.*)

LIGHT—Don't, for the love of God!

REUBEN—(*immediately ashamed of himself*) I wasn't laughing at you, honest. (*then suddenly*) Say, I think I'll go and visit Mother's grave. There's some things I'd like to get off my chest—even if she can't hear me. (*turning to the door*) Well, so long.

LIGHT—(*dully*) Shall I have your room put in order for you?

REUBEN—(*frowning*) No. It isn't my room now. That me is dead. (*Then an idea comes to him—thinking*)

> But maybe Mother'd want me to? . . . maybe I'd get some message from her if I stayed here? . . .

(*then casually to his father*) All right. I'll stay for a couple of days. After that I'm going to get a room out near the plant. Say, I might as well break the bad news to you. I'm getting a job in Fife's power house. (*then quickly*) I suppose you think I'm doing it to spite you, but I'm not.

LIGHT—(*dully*) You have sold your soul to Satan, Reuben.

REUBEN—(*immediately resentful—with his cold smile*) Your Satan is dead. We electrocuted him along with your God. Electricity is God now. And we've got to learn to know God, haven't we? Well, that's what I'm after! (*in a lighter tone—mockingly*) Did you ever watch dynamos? Come down to the plant and I'll convert you! (*He cannot restrain a parting shot.*) I converted Mother, didn't I? Well, so long. (*He goes out and a moment later walks past the front of the house from the right.*

He is off guard and the callousness has gone from his face, which is now very like that of the boy of Act One.)

I wish she hadn't died . . . but she forgave me . . .

ADA—(*sticks her head out of their sitting-room window as he passes the lilac hedge. Her face is flushed with excitement, happy and pretty now. She calls*) It's all right, Rube. Pop's got a job for you. A floor man is leaving Saturday.

REUBEN—(*startled out of his thoughts, at first frowns, then forces the cold smile to his lips*) That's great.

ADA—(*coquettishly*) Well, don't I get anything?

REUBEN—(*with his cold smile*) Sure! (*He goes to her and reaches up as if to kiss her—then checks himself, thinking remorsefully*)

What the hell am I doing? . . . I'm going out to Mother's grave . . . she hated her . . .

(*He steps back, frowning.*) Wait till later, Ada. Well, so long. See you to-night. (*He turns his back on her abruptly and walks off left. She looks after him, bewildered and hurt.*)

(*Curtain*)

SCENE TWO—*The same except that Reuben's bedroom is now revealed while the wall of the sitting room has been replaced. It is about half past eleven on the same night—a sultry, hazy sky with few stars visible. There is no light in either house.*

Reuben and Ada come in from the left. She is hanging on his arm, pressing close to him as if she were afraid of his leaving her, glancing up into his face with a timid look of mingled happiness and apprehension.

Reuben's face shows that he also is struggling with conflicting emotions. There is a fixed smile of triumph and gratified vanity on his lips, but his eyes are restless and there is a nervous uneasiness apparent in his whole manner.

ADA—You're sure you don't hate me now—because I let you—maybe I shouldn't have—but oh, Rube, I do love you so much! Say you love me just as much—that you always will!

REUBEN—(*preoccupiedly*) Sure I will.

ADA—(*pleadingly*) Put your arms around me tight and kiss me again. Then I won't be scared—or sorry.

REUBEN—(*mechanically puts his arms around her and kisses her at first perfunctorily, then with reawakening passion*) Gee, you're pretty, Ada! You've certainly got me going!

ADA—(*happily now*) Oh, Rube, when you kiss me like that nothing in the world matters but you! Up on the hill when we—oh, I felt I was just you, a part of you and you were part of me! I forgot everything!

REUBEN—(*suddenly moves away from her and stares around him nervously—in a strange voice*) Sure. You forget everything for a minute. You're happy. Then something has to wake you up—and start you thinking again.

ADA—What is it you're thinking about? Tell me and maybe I can help you forget it.

REUBEN—(*shaking his head*) I can't forget. (*then determinedly*) And I don't want to. I want to face things. I won't ever be satisfied now until I've found the truth about everything.

ADA—(*trying to force a joking tone*) And where do I come in?

REUBEN—(*coldly*) You don't come in.

ADA—Rube! Don't say that—not after— You scare me!

REUBEN—(*irritatedly*) Cut out that talk of being scared! What are you scared about? Scared what we did was a sin? You're the hell of an atheist! (*then jeeringly*) And you're the one that used to be always kidding me about being a goody boy! There's nothing to be scared about or sorry for. What we did was just plain sex—an act of nature—and that's all there is to it!

ADA—(*pitifully—her voice trembling*) Is that all—it means to you?

REUBEN—That's all it means to any one! What people call love is just sex—and there's no sin about it!

ADA—I wasn't saying there was, was I? I've proved to you I don't—only— (*then frightenedly*) It's you, Rube. I can't get used to you talking like that. You've changed so.

REUBEN—(*with a coarse grin*) Well, you've got no kick coming. If I'd stayed the same poor boob I used to be you might have died an old maid.

ADA—But—you wanted to marry me then, Rube.

REUBEN—(*roughly*) And a lot that got me, didn't it?

ADA—(*faintly*) Don't you want to—any more?

REUBEN—Don't I what? Talk sense, Ada! We're married by Nature now. We don't need any old fool of a minister saying prayers over us! (*then after a moment's pause—with a forced laugh*) Say, here's one on me, Ada—speaking of praying. It was out at Mother's grave. Before I thought, I started to do a prayer act—and then suddenly it hit me that there was nothing to pray to. (*He forces another laugh.*) It just goes to show you what a hold that bunk gets on you when you've had it crammed down your throat from the time you were born! You can't pray to electricity unless you're foolish in the head, can you? (*then strangely*) But maybe you could, at that—if you knew how!

ADA—Is that where you went this afternoon—out to her grave?

REUBEN—(*with affected indifference*) Sure. What of it?

ADA—(*pityingly*) Poor Rube!

REUBEN—(*frowning*) Poor nothing! She's dead, and that's all there is about it. You've got to face death as well as life.

ADA—I'm sorry she hated me so. I hope now she forgives us—for loving each other.

REUBEN—(*with his cold smile*) You mean forgives us for what we did to-night? You don't know her! She never would! But what's the use of talking about it? Who gives a damn? Good night, Ada. I'm tired. I'm going to bed. See you to-morrow. (*He turns his back on her abruptly and walks off right toward the front door of his house.*)

ADA—(*stands looking after him with bewildered hurt for a moment, then turns back toward her own front door and begins to cry softly, at the same time trying to reassure herself*)

I mustn't . . . feel bad . . . he doesn't mean to hurt me . . . he's changed, that's all . . .

(*She disappears off left. A moment later, Reuben appears in his bedroom and lights the lamp. He sits down on the bed and stares before him.*)

REUBEN—(*looking about the room now, thinking bitterly*)

The last time I was here . . . there's the closet where

she hid him . . . here's where she sat lying to me . . .
watching him beat me . . .

(*He springs to his feet—viciously*)

I'm glad she's dead! . . .

(*then immediately remorseful*)

No . . . I don't mean that, Mother . . . I was thinking of how you acted that night . . . I wish I could
have seen you after you'd changed . . . after you'd
come back to my side . . .

(*He goes to the window on the left and looks out.*)

Here's where I was looking out, waiting for Ada to
signal on the Victrola . . . gosh, that seems a million
years ago! . . . how scared I was of even kissing her!
. . . and to-night she was dead easy . . . like rolling
off a log! . . .

(*He comes back to the bed and sits down.*)

Mother said she was no better than a street-walker
. . . she certainly didn't put up a fight . . . marry her!
. . . what does she think I am, a boob? . . . she put
one over on me and now I've put one over on her!
. . . we're square . . . and whatever's going to happen, will happen, but it won't be a wedding! . . .

(*then with coarse sensuality*)

But it's grand to have her around handy whenever I
want . . . the flesh, as the old man would call it! . . .
and she's all right other ways, too . . . I like her . . .
she got me the job . . . she'll be useful . . . and I'll
treat her decent . . . maybe it's love . . . whatever
the hell love is! . . . did Mother really love the old
man? . . . she must have or how could she stand him?
. . . and she made me with him . . . act of Nature
. . . like me and Ada . . .

(*He jumps to his feet distractedly.*)

God, that seems lousy somehow! . . . I don't want to
think of it! . . .

(*He paces up and down—then pauses and appears to be listening
for something.*)

There's something queer about this dump now . . . as
if no one was living here . . . I suppose that's because
Mother's gone . . . I'd like to reach her somehow

. . . no one knows what happens after death . . .
even science doesn't . . . there may be some kind of
hereafter . . . I used to kneel down here and say my
prayers . . . she taught them to me . . . then she'd
tuck me in, even after I'd grown up . . . and kiss me
good night . . .

(*As if automatically he slips to his knees by the bed.*)

I'm sorry, Mother . . . sorry you're dead . . . I wish
I could talk to you . . .

(*He scrambles to his feet—angry at himself.*)

You damn fool! . . . what's come over you, anyway? . . . what are you praying to? . . . when there's
nothing . . .

(*then strangely*)

Funny, that hunch I got when I was talking to Ada
. . . about praying to electricity, if you knew how
. . . it was like a message . . . Mother believed what
I believed when she died . . . maybe it came from
her . . .

(*then suspicious of himself again*)

Aw, that's just superstitious junk . . . but why is it?
. . . look at how mysterious all this electrical wave
stuff is in radio and everything . . . that's scientific
fact . . . and why couldn't something like that that no
one understands yet? . . . between the dead and the
living? . . .

(*He walks around nervously.*)

No use trying to go to sleep . . . and I want to keep
on thinking . . . but not in here . . . I'll go for a walk
. . . why not go down to the plant? . . . take a look
in at the dynamos . . . watching them always helps
me somehow . . . sure, that's the stuff! . . .

(*He turns down the light and blows it out and can be seen going
through the door in rear.*)

(*Curtain*)

SCENE THREE—*A half hour later. Exterior of the Light and
Power Company's hydro-electric plant about two miles from the*

town. The plant is comparatively a small one. The building is red brick. The section on the left, the dynamo room, is much wider than the right section but is a story less in height. An immense window and a big sliding door are in the lower part of the dynamo-room wall, and there is a similar window in the upper part of the section on right. Through the window and the open door of the dynamo room, which is brilliantly lighted by a row of powerful bulbs in white globes set in brackets along both walls, there is a clear view of a dynamo, huge and black, with something of a massive female idol about it, the exciter set on the main structure like a head with blank, oblong eyes above a gross, rounded torso.

Through the upper window of the right section of the building, in the switch galleries, by a dim light, one gets a glimpse of the mathematically ordered web of the disconnecting switches, double busses, and other equipment stretching up through the roof to the outgoing feeders leading to the transmission towers.

The air is full of sound, a soft overtone of rushing water from the dam and the river bed below, penetrated dominatingly by the harsh, throaty, metallic purr of the dynamo.

Reuben comes in from the right and approaches until he is opposite the open doorway. He stands there staring at the dynamo and listening to it.

REUBEN—*(after a pause—fascinatedly)*
    It's so mysterious . . . and grand . . . it makes you feel things . . . you don't need to think . . . you almost get the secret . . . what electricity is . . . what life is . . . what God is . . . it's all the same thing . . .
(A pause—then he goes on in the same fascinated tone.)
    It's like a great dark idol . . . like the old stone statues of gods people prayed to . . . only it's living and they were dead . . . that part on top is like a head . . . with eyes that see you without seeing you . . . and below it is like a body . . . not a man's . . . round like a woman's . . . as if it had breasts . . . but not like a girl . . . not like Ada . . . no, like a woman . . . like her mother . . . or mine . . . a great, dark mother! . . . that's what the dynamo is! . . . that's what life is! . . .

(*He stares at it raptly now.*)

> Listen to her singing . . . that beats all organs in
> church . . . it's the hymn of electricity . . . "always
> singing about everything in the world" . . . if you
> could only get back into that . . . know what it means
> . . . then you'd know the real God! . . .

(*then longingly*)

> There must be some way! . . . there must be some-
> thing in her song that'd tell you if you had ears to
> hear! . . . some way that she'd teach you to know
> her . . .

(*He begins to hum, swaying his body—then stops when he can't
catch the right tone.*)

> No, you can't get it! . . . it's as far off as the sky and
> yet it's all around you! . . . in you! . . .

(*excitedly*)

> I feel like praying now! . . . I feel there is something
> in her to pray to! . . . something that'll answer
> me! . . .

(*He looks around him and moves to the right out of the square of
light from the open doorway.*)

> Supposing any one saw me . . . they'd think I was
> nutty . . . the old prayer stuff! . . .

(*then arguing tormentedly with himself*)

> But I feel it's right . . . I feel Mother wants me
> to . . . it's the least I can do for her . . . to say a
> prayer . . .

(*He gets down on his knees and prays aloud to the dynamo.*) Oh,
Mother of Life, my mother is dead, she has passed back into
you, tell her to forgive me, and to help me find your truth!
(*He pauses on his knees for a moment, then gets slowly to his feet.
There is a look of calm and relief on his face now. He thinks rev-
erentially*)

> Yes, that did it . . . I feel I'm forgiven . . . Mother
> will help me . . . I can sleep . . . I'll go home . . .

(*He walks slowly off right.*)

(*Curtain*)

ACT THREE

SCENE ONE—*Same as Act Two, Scene Three—Exterior of the power house four months later. It is a little after sunset and the equipment on the roof is outlined blackly against a darkening crimson sky.*

The door of the dynamo room is shut but the interior is brilliantly lighted and the dynamo can be partly seen through the window. There is a dim light above in the switch galleries as in the previous scene. The overtone of rushing water from the dam sounds louder because of the closed door which muffles the noise of the dynamo to a minor strain.

Reuben enters from the left accompanied by Mrs. Fife. He has grown very thin, his dungarees sag about his angular frame. His face is gaunt and pale. His eyes are deeply sunken. He is talking with unnatural excitement as they come in. Mrs. Fife is unchanged. If anything, her moony dreaminess is more pronounced. She listens to Reuben with a fascinated, far-away look, as if the sound of his voice hypnotized her rather than the meaning of the words.

REUBEN—(*insistently*) You understood all I explained to you up on the dam, didn't you?—about how life first came out of the sea?

MRS. FIFE—(*nods dreamily*) Yes, Reuben. It sounds like poetry—"life out of the sea."

REUBEN—It is like poetry. Her song in there—Dynamo's—isn't that the greatest poem of all—the poem of eternal life? And listen to the water rushing over the dam! Like music! It's as if that sound was cool water washing over my body!—washing all dirt and sin away! Like some one singing me to sleep—my mother—when I was a kid—calling me back to somewhere far off where I'd been once long ago and known peace! (*He sighs with longing, his body suddenly gone limp and weary.*)

MRS. FIFE—(*dreamily*) That's awful pretty, Reuben. (*She puts her arm around him—sentimentally*) I'll be your mother—yours and Ada's. I've always wanted a boy.

REUBEN—(*leans against her gratefully, his head almost on her shoulder, his eyes half closed*) Yes. You're like her—

Dynamo—the Great Mother—big and warm— (*with a sudden renewal of his unnatural excitement, breaks away from her*) But I've got to finish telling you all I've come to know about her—how all things end up in her! Did I tell you that our blood plasm is the same right now as the sea was when life came out of it? We've got the sea in our blood still! It's what makes our hearts live! And it's the sea rising up in clouds, falling on the earth in rain, made that river that drives the turbines that drive Dynamo! The sea makes her heart beat, too!—but the sea is only hydrogen and oxygen and minerals, and they're only atoms, and atoms are only protons and electrons—even our blood and the sea are only electricity in the end! And think of the stars! Driving through space, round and round, just like the electrons in the atom! But there must be a center around which all this moves, mustn't there? There is in everything else! And that center must be the Great Mother of Eternal Life, Electricity, and Dynamo is her Divine Image on earth! Her power houses are the new churches! She wants us to realize the secret dwells in her! She wants some one man to love her purely and when she finds him worthy she will love him and give him the secret of truth and he will become the new saviour who will bring happiness and peace to men! And I'm going to be that saviour—that's why I asked you to come—I want you to be a witness! I know the miracle will happen to me to-night because I had a message from my mother last night. I woke up and saw her standing beside my bed—just as she used to when she came in to kiss me good night—and she smiled and held out her arms to me. I know she came from the spirit of the Great Mother into which she passed when she died to tell me she had at last found me worthy of her love.

MRS. FIFE—(*sentimentally*) Most people don't believe in ghosts. Ramsay don't. But I do. Has she come many times, Reuben?

REUBEN—(*strangely*) Not lately—not since I gave up seeing Ada. Before that she used to come almost every night to warn me.

MRS. FIFE—Warn you about what, Reuben?

REUBEN—That I was living in sin—that Dynamo would never find me worthy of her secret until I'd given up the flesh and purified myself! (*then proudly*) And I found the strength to do it. It was hard! I was beginning to really love Ada.

MRS. FIFE—(*simply*) Of course, you love Ada—and you shouldn't act so mean to her, Reuben. You haven't been around in a month or more. She's making herself sick worrying.

REUBEN—(*intensely*) I'd like to see her! I'd love to! But I can't. Don't you understand I can't—that my finding the secret is more important than—? (*then thinking with sudden fear and doubt*)

> But supposing the miracle doesn't happen to-night? . . . Ada keeps coming in dreams . . . her body . . . I've beaten myself with my belt . . . I can't keep on much longer . . .

(*He sways dizzily on his feet, passing his hand over his eyes—then straightens himself and turns to Mrs. Fife.*) I've got to go in. They'll be missing me. And I've got to pray to her. (*He goes to the door.*) You wait until your husband's gone home. Then you come in.

MRS. FIFE—All right, Reuben. (*Reuben slides back the dynamo-room door a few feet and enters, closing it behind him. Mrs. Fife stares after him mooningly. A moment later the door from the dynamo room is opened again and Fife comes out, closing it behind him. He hasn't changed since his last appearance. He starts to walk hesitatingly off right—then stops without looking around him and does not notice his wife.*)

FIFE—(*thinking exasperatedly*)

> That damned Rube! . . . there's a queer look in those cold eyes of his lately! . . . by God, I'd fire him to-night if Ada wouldn't make my life a hell for it! . . . but he does his work good . . . too damned good! . . . he's always pawing around a dynamo when he's no business . . .

MRS. FIFE—Hello, Ramsay. You better get home to supper. I had mine early. I had to go out.

FIFE—(*turns on her with an irritated start*) Oh, you did, did you? You're always having to go out these days, it seems! I won't have you gallivanting down here at all hours and staring at the dynamos and humming like a half-wit! What the hell's come over you, anyway?

MRS. FIFE—Nothing's come over me, Ramsay. I was talking to Reuben. He took me up on the dam and told me about how we all used to live in the ocean once. (*then in her tone of childish mooning*) D'you suppose I ever was a fish, Ramsay?

FIFE—Aye, a jellyfish, I'm thinking! You've the brains for that! (*then angrily*) You do too much gabbing with that Rube! He'll addle the little sense you've left! But if you've got to talk to him, make him talk turkey and say when is he planning to marry Ada! Aren't you her mother, and don't you see she's worrying her heart out? (*lowering his voice*) D'you think it's happened between them—you know what I mean?

MRS. FIFE—(*with naïve simplicity*) Yes, of course it has, Ramsay. She loves him the same as I did you when we—

FIFE—Don't be comparing him to me! I was more of a decent man than he ever will be! (*in a passion*) I'll have a talk with that lad and if he don't do the decent thing by her, I'll beat decency into him! (*He turns from her in a tantrum.*) To hell with you! I'm hungry! I'm going home! (*He goes off right. Mrs. Fife looks after him with a placid smile—then she gives the big door a push that slides it open to its full width and steps inside and, as she sees Reuben, stops as she is about to pull the door closed again. He is kneeling just inside the doorway before the dynamo in the foreground, his arms stretched out to it supplicatingly.*)

REUBEN—(*suddenly cries out with a note of despair*) Mother! Don't you hear me? Can't you give me some sign? O Dynamo, who gives life to things, hear my prayer! Grant me the miracle of your love! (*He waits, his body strained with suspense, listening as if he expected the dynamo to answer him. Ada comes from around the corner of the building at the left. Her manner is furtive as if she were doing something she is ashamed of. She looks worried and run down, although she has made a defiant effort with rouge and mascara to hide this.*)

ADA—

He must be around some place . . .

(*She moves cautiously to the window and peeks in, but cannot see him.*)

I don't want no one to see me . . . I'll knock on the window when I see him and get him to come out . . .

(*then with bitter self-contempt*)

> Here I am chasing after him! . . . but I couldn't stand
> it any more, waiting . . . oh, what a damn fool I was
> to give in so easy! . . . no wonder he's sick of me!
> . . . but he can't throw me over this way! . . .

(*She looks in the window again.*)

REUBEN—(*his tense, supplicating attitude suddenly relaxing dejectedly*)

> She won't answer me . . . there must still be some-
> thing I've got to do . . .

(*then guiltily*)

> Maybe she feels I haven't killed all desire for Ada yet?
> . . . that I ought to face her and conquer the flesh
> once for all . . .

(*He jumps to his feet and turns to Mrs. Fife pleadingly.*) Can't
you tell me? You know what she means sometimes. (*He lowers
his voice cautiously as if he didn't want the dynamo to overhear.*)
Do you think it's something I've got to do about Ada?

MRS. FIFE—(*simply*) Yes, you've got to do the right thing
by Ada, Reuben.

REUBEN—(*thinking with unnatural excitement*)

> Then that is it! . . . I'll have to go and face Ada right
> now! . . .

(*turning to Mrs. Fife*) You stay here! I'll be back. (*He comes
out, sliding the door closed after him.*)

ADA—(*turns at the noise of the door closing from where she is
looking in the window and calls to him*) Rube!

REUBEN—(*whirls around and stands staring at her with
strange fixity for a moment, his thoughts seizing on this coinci-
dence*)

> It's Ada! . . . Dynamo sent her here! . . . she wanted
> to prove I've conquered the flesh! . . .

ADA—(*frightenedly*) What's the matter? Don't look at me
like that, Rube!

REUBEN—(*moved in spite of himself, instinctively takes a
step toward her—in a queer, detached tone*) I didn't mean to
scare you, Ada. You gave me a start, seeing you all of a
sudden.

ADA—(*looking at him hopefully*) You're not sore at me for
coming, are you?

REUBEN—No. It's as if you'd been sent. Didn't you feel something driving you to come here right now?

ADA—(*quickly*) Yes, I just had to come!

REUBEN—(*strangely*) It was she who made you come.

ADA—She? Who's she?

REUBEN—(*A lightning change comes over his face. He takes a threatening step toward her—denouncingly, his voice booming like his father's*) You blasphemous fool, you! Do you dare to deny her! "The fool saith in his heart—" (*He suddenly checks himself and forces a strange, shamefaced laugh.*) Say, did you get me quoting from the Bible, Ada? That's one on me! That comes from arguing with the old man lately. He's got some fool notion that Dynamo is the devil. (*then his expression abruptly changing again—fiercely*) But I'll make the old fool get down on his knees to her yet before I'm through with him! And I'll make you, too, Ada! (*This puts a sudden idea into his head—thinking excitedly*)

> What made me say that? . . . you, Mother? . . . not only conquer her flesh, but convert her? . . . make her pray to you? . . .

Listen to me, Ada! To-night the miracle will happen!—and then there will be only the kingdom of happiness on earth— my kingdom!—for us, Ada! (*then suddenly grabbing her by the arm*) Only you've got to help me!

ADA—(*thinking frightenedly*)

> For God's sake, what's come over him? . . . the damned dynamo! . . . it's driving him crazy! . . .

(*She puts her arms around him pityingly and tries to hug him to her.*) I'll do anything, Rube! Don't you know how much I love you?

REUBEN—(*pushing her away from him—in a stammering panic*) Don't do that! (*then pleadingly*) Why can't you understand? You've got to believe in Dynamo, and bow down to her will!

ADA—(*soothingly*) All right, Rube.

REUBEN—(*taking her hand—insistently*) Come with me! I want to explain everything to you—to prove everything!— all this plant means about her—you've got to believe in her, Ada! (*She follows him off left, frightened but pitying and resolved to humor him. His voice is heard explaining excitedly as they climb to the dam. It recedes and then grows louder as they cross from the dam to the dynamo-room roof, and a moment later he is seen there. He comes forward until he stands by the coping, front. He still has Ada by the hand. She follows him, holding back as much as she dares, a nervous look on her face. His unnatural excitement has increased, he looks around him with the rapt expression of one in a trance.*) Oh, Ada, you simply can't help believing in her! You only have to listen to her! Her song is the hymn of eternal generation, the song of eternal life!

ADA—(*uneasily*) Rube! I'm scared up here!

REUBEN—(*turns and looks at her like a sleepwalker for a second—then with a sudden hungry passion*) You're so damned pretty! God, how I wish the miracle was over and we could—!

ADA—(*persuasively*) I'm scared on this roof, Rube. Let's go down!

REUBEN—(*excitedly*) Yes, down to her! I was forgetting her! She's waiting for me! (*Then as she starts to go back the way they have come, he takes her hand again and pulls her through the door from the roof to the galleries.*)

ADA—(*frightenedly*) Rube! I don't want to go— (*He slams the door behind them.*)

There is a pause of darkness here to indicate the end of Scene One. No time elapses between Scenes One and Two.

SCENE TWO—*When the light comes on again the interiors of the upper and lower switch galleries are revealed. The lower gallery of the oil switches is a deep but narrow compartment with red brick walls. The oil switches, with their spindly steel legs, their square, crisscrossed steel bodies (the containers inside looking like bellies), their six cupped arms stretching upward, seem like queer Hindu idols tortured into scientific supplications. These switches extend in a straight row backward down the middle of the gallery, but in the dim light of one bulb in a bracket in the left wall only the front one in the foreground can be made out. Against the wall on the right is a stairway that extends backward halfway up this wall, then turns and ascends diagonally toward the left to the upper gallery, and from thence up to the door from the roof of the dynamo room.*

The upper gallery contains the disconnecting switches and the double busses. It is of double width and extends over the switchboard room also. This second gallery, dimly lighted like the one below, is a fretwork of wires, steel work, insulators, busses, switches, etc., stretching upward to the roof. Below the disconnecting switches is a raised platform.

Reuben and Ada are discovered by the dim light of this upper gallery standing just inside the door to the dynamo-room roof at the top of the stairway.

ADA—(*looking around her frightenedly at the weird shadows of the equipment writhing upward in the dimly lighted gallery— shrinking close to Reuben, who is staring at all this with a rapt, questioning, listening look*) All this stuff scares me. I've only seen it in daylight before. It looks as if it was alive!

REUBEN—(*strangely*) You're beginning to see, Ada! It is alive! Alive with the mighty spirit of her eternal life! (*Then with a start, he pushes her away from him roughly.*) What the hell are you doing? Don't press against me, I tell you! I'm wise to your dirty game—and I won't stand for it! Don't you realize we're in her temple now!

ADA—(*pitifully*) Rube! Please don't talk like that—when you know how I love you!

REUBEN—(*clutching her arm fiercely*) You mustn't say you love me in here, you fool you! Don't you know all this is watching—listening—that she knows everything! Sssh! I want to hear if she's angry at me! (*He stands in a strained attitude of attention, listening to the dynamo's hum sounding from below—then evidently satisfied, turns to Ada with a relieved air.*) No, she isn't angry on account of you being here because she knows you're beginning to believe in her! It's all right for you to come close to me now, Ada. (*He puts an arm around her and pulls her to him.*)

ADA—(*persuasively*) Please let's go down, Rube.

REUBEN—(*gently*) All right, Ada. (*They go down the first flight of steps. He stops as they get to the bottom and glances up and around him.*) You know, Ada, there used to be times when I was scared here too—when all these switches and busses and wires seemed like the arms of a devil fish—stretching out to suck me in— (*He gives a shudder and presses her to him.*)

ADA—(*soothingly*) You mustn't be afraid. I'm here with you.

REUBEN—(*pleadingly—pointing to the platform beneath the disconnecting switches*) Listen, Ada! I want you to pray to her—up there where I pray sometimes—under her arms—with your arms like her arms, stretching out for me! (*He suddenly bends his face to her face, his eyes devouring it desirously.*) God, you're pretty! (*He controls himself with a violent effort and pushes her away from him, keeping his face averted from hers—in a voice that is almost supplicating*) You must pray that she may find me worthy. You must pray for me, if you love me!

ADA—(*soothingly—humoring him*) All right, Rube. (*She goes up the stairs to the platform and stands directly under the switches, stretching her arms up in the same position as the switch arms.*)

REUBEN—(*remains standing below—thinking confusedly*) Mother would warn me if I was doing wrong . . . Dynamo means all this to happen to me . . . it's the great temptation . . . perhaps she wants me even to kiss Ada . . .

(*He ascends to the platform and stands before her.*)

ADA—(*tenderly and soothingly*) Why did you say a minute ago, if I loved you? Don't you know I do? Why have you stayed away from me so long, Rube? I've almost died, longing for you!

REUBEN—(*without looking at her—dully*) You believe in her now, don't you? You wouldn't do anything to make me unworthy in her sight, would you?—when it means happiness for me—and for all mankind? You couldn't, could you?

ADA—(*humoring him—gently*) Of course not.

REUBEN—(*mechanically*) You swear to her?

ADA—(*in the same tone*) Yes, I swear.

REUBEN—(*mechanically*) Then I'm going to kiss you, Ada—just once—only kiss you—she wants me to—as a final test—to prove I'm purified— (*He looks up at her now and*

lurches forward with a moan of passion and takes her in his arms.)
Ada! *(He kisses her frantically, bending her backward and down toward the floor of the platform. She cries out frightenedly.)*

There is a pause of darkness to indicate the end of Scene Two. A short time is supposed to elapse between Scenes Two and Three.

SCENE THREE—*As the light slowly comes on again, Reuben is heard sobbing brokenly from the gallery. The interiors of the dynamo and switchboard rooms are now also revealed.*

The dynamo room is high and wide with red brick walls and a row of great windows in the left wall. The floor and an observation balcony which projects into the dynamo room from the switchboard room on the right (one story up) are of concrete. The nearest dynamo, which we have seen previously through the doorway, occupies most of the floor space in the foreground. A steel ladder runs up its side on the right to a platform around the exciter.

The switchboard room is a small compartment to the right of the dynamo room, one story up in the other section of the building. In it are the switchboard and a couple of chairs. It is lighted by a shaded drop light over the desk. Jennings, the operator on duty, a man of thirty or so, is seated at the desk.

Mrs. Fife is sitting in the dynamo room just under and to the left of the observation balcony. She is staring dreamily at the front dynamo, humming to herself, her big body relaxed as if she had given herself up completely to the spell of its hypnotic, metallic purr which flows insistently through the ears, numbing the brain, charging the nerves with electricity, making the heart strain with the desire to beat in its rhythm of unbroken, eternal continuity.

In the gallery, Ada and Reuben are still on the platform beneath the disconnecting switches. Reuben is on his knees, his back bowed, his face covered by his hands. Ada is standing before him, directly beneath the switches as before. She is bending over him in a tender attitude, one hand reaching down, touching his hair.

REUBEN—*(thinking torturedly)*
Mother! . . . I've betrayed you . . . you will never

bless me with the miracle now! . . . you have shut me
from your heart forever! . . .

(*He groans and beats his head against the floor.*)

ADA—(*pats him on the back consolingly*) Poor Rube! I love
you. You'll be all right, dear.

REUBEN—(*shrinking away*) Don't touch me! (*He springs to
his feet, and shielding his face with one hand from the sight of her,
runs down the stairs to the lower oil switch gallery. He stops there,
looking around him distractedly as if he didn't know where to hide,
his thoughts hounded by remorse.*)

Mother! . . . have mercy on me! . . . I hate her now!
. . . as much as you hate her! . . . give me one more
chance! . . . what can I do to get you to forgive me?
. . . tell me! . . . yes! . . . I hear you, Mother! . . .
and then you'll forgive me? . . . and I can come to
you? . . .

(*A terrible look of murder comes on his face. He starts for the
stairs, his hands outstretched as if he were already strangling
her—then stops.*)

No . . . not with my hands. . . . Never touch her
flesh again . . . how? . . . I see. . . . Switchboard
room . . . in the desk. . . .

(*He dashes over into the switchboard room through the door at left
of the gallery. He has the startled and terrified Jennings by the
throat before the latter knows it and flings him away from the
desk, tears out a drawer and gets the revolver and with it motions
him to the door of the office in the rear.*) Get in there! Quick!
(*Jennings obeys hastily. Reuben turns the key in the lock after him.
In contrast to his furious haste of a moment before, he now walks
deliberately back through the door to the oil switch gallery. His
face is as drained of all human feeling as a plaster mask.*)

I won't be a murderer . . . I'm your executioner,
Mother . . . that's why I'm so calm . . .

(*He glides stealthily across toward the foot of the stairs.*)

ADA—(*worried about him has come down from the platform
and is beginning to descend the stairs to the lower switch gallery—
she calls uneasily*) Rube! Where are you?

REUBEN—

Harlot! . . . that's what Mother called her! . . .

(*He springs up the stairs to her, shouting fiercely*) Harlot!

ADA—(*She sees the revolver aimed at her breast as he stops directly beneath her—in a terrified whisper*) Rube! (*Reuben fires twice and she jerks back and pitches sideways on the stairs.*)

REUBEN—(*stares down at her body for a moment and lets the gun fall from his hand and begins to tremble all over. He calls pitifully*) Ada! I didn't mean to hurt you! (*then thinking with an anguished appeal*)

Mother! . . . where are you? . . . I did it for your sake! . . . why don't you call to me? . . . don't leave me alone! . . .

(*He turns and runs headlong through the switchboard room, and down the stairs to the dynamo-room floor, where he lunges for the rungs on the dynamo's side and clambers up frenziedly. Up on the platform, he stops for a moment, gasping for breath, stretching out his arms to the exciter-head of his Dynamo-Mother with its whirling metal brain and its blank, oblong eyes.*)

MRS. FIFE—(*dimly aware of him—dreamily*) What was that noise up there, Reuben? It sounded like a shot.

REUBEN—(*pleading to the dynamo like a little boy*) I don't want any miracle, Mother! I don't want to know the truth! I only want you to hide me, Mother! Never let me go from you again! Please, Mother! (*He throws his arms out over the exciter, his hands grasp the carbon brushes. There is a flash of bluish light about him and all the lights in the plant dim down until they are almost out and the noise of the dynamo dies until it is the faintest purring hum. Simultaneously Reuben's voice rises in a moan that is a mingling of pain and loving consummation, and this cry dies into a sound that is like the crooning of a baby and merges and is lost in the dynamo's hum. Then his body crumples to the steel platform and from there falls heavily to the floor. There is a startled cry from Mrs. Fife as she runs to the body. The dynamo's throaty metallic purr rises slowly in volume and the lights begin to come up again in the plant.*)

MRS. FIFE—(*kneeling beside Reuben, one hand on the forehead of his upturned face*) Reuben! Are you hurt bad? (*She turns with childish bewildered resentment and hurt to the dynamo.*) What are you singing for? I should think you'd be ashamed! And I thought you was nice and loved us! (*The dynamo's purr has regained its accustomed pitch now. The lights in the plant are again at their full brightness. Everything is as before. Mrs. Fife pounds the steel body of the generator in a fit of childish anger.*) You hateful old thing, you! (*Then she leaves off, having hurt her hands, and begins to cry softly.*)

(*Curtain*)

MOURNING BECOMES ELECTRA

A Trilogy

To
Carlotta
my wife

Contents

General Scene of the Trilogy

The action of the trilogy, with the exception of an act of the second play, takes place in or immediately outside the Mannon residence, on the outskirts of one of the smaller New England seaport towns.

A special curtain shows the house as seen from the street. From this, in each play, one comes to the exterior of the house in the opening act and enters it in the following act.

This curtain reveals the extensive grounds—about thirty acres—which surround the house, a heavily wooded ridge in the background, orchards at the right and in the immediate rear, a large flower garden and a greenhouse to the left.

In the foreground, along the street, is a line of locust and elm trees. The property is enclosed by a white picket fence and a tall hedge. A driveway curves up to the house from two entrances with white gates. Between the house and the street is a lawn. By the right corner of the house is a grove of pine trees. Farther forward, along the driveway, maples and locusts. By the left corner of the house is a big clump of lilacs and syringas.

The house is placed back on a slight rise of ground about three hundred feet from the street. It is a large building of the Greek temple type that was the vogue in the first half of the nineteenth century. A white wooden portico with six tall columns contrasts with the wall of the house proper which is of gray cut stone. There are five windows on the upper floor and four on the ground floor, with the main entrance in the middle, a doorway with squared transom and sidelights flanked by intermediate columns. The window shutters are painted a dark green. Before the doorway a flight of four steps leads from the ground to the portico.

The three plays take place in either spring or summer of the years 1865–1866.

HOMECOMING

A Play in Four Acts

Part One of the Trilogy

MOURNING BECOMES ELECTRA

CHARACTERS

BRIGADIER-GENERAL EZRA MANNON
CHRISTINE, *his wife*
LAVINIA, *their daughter*
CAPTAIN ADAM BRANT, *of the clipper "Flying Trades"*
CAPTAIN PETER NILES, *U.S. Artillery*
HAZEL NILES, *his sister*
SETH BECKWITH
AMOS AMES
LOUISA, *his wife*
MINNIE, *her cousin*

SCENES

ACT ONE: Exterior of the Mannon house in New England
—April, 1865.
ACT TWO: Ezra Mannon's study in the house—no time has
elapsed.
ACT THREE: The same as Act One—exterior of the house—
a night a week later.
ACT FOUR: A bedroom in the house—later the same night.

Homecoming

ACT ONE

SCENE—*Exterior of the Mannon house on a late afternoon in April, 1865. At front is the driveway which leads up to the house from the two entrances on the street. Behind the driveway the white Grecian temple portico with its six tall columns extends across the stage. A big pine tree is on the lawn at the edge of the drive before the right corner of the house. Its trunk is a black column in striking contrast to the white columns of the portico. By the edge of the drive, left front, is a thick clump of lilacs and syringas. A bench is placed on the lawn at front of this shrubbery which partly screens anyone sitting on it from the front of the house.*

It is shortly before sunset and the soft light of the declining sun shines directly on the front of the house, shimmering in a luminous mist on the white portico and the gray stone wall behind, intensifying the whiteness of the columns, the somber grayness of the wall, the green of the open shutters, the green of the lawn and shrubbery, the black and green of the pine tree. The white columns cast black bars of shadow on the gray wall behind them. The windows of the lower floor reflect the sun's rays in a resentful glare. The temple portico is like an incongruous white mask fixed on the house to hide its somber gray ugliness.

In the distance, from the town, a band is heard playing "John Brown's Body." Borne on the light puffs of wind this music is at times quite loud, then sinks into faintness as the wind dies.

From the left rear, a man's voice is heard singing the chanty "Shenandoah"—a song that more than any other holds in it the brooding rhythm of the sea. The voice grows quickly nearer. It is thin and aged, the wraith of what must once have been a good baritone.

> "Oh, Shenandoah, I long to hear you
> A-way, my rolling river
> Oh, Shenandoah, I can't get near you
> Way-ay, I'm bound away
> Across the wide Missouri."

The singer, Seth Beckwith, finishes the last line as he enters from around the corner of the house. Closely following him are Amos Ames, his wife Louisa, and her cousin Minnie.

Seth Beckwith, the Mannons' gardener and man of all work, is an old man of seventy-five with white hair and beard, tall, raw-boned and stoop-shouldered, his joints stiffened by rheumatism, but still sound and hale. He has a gaunt face that in repose gives one the strange impression of a life-like mask. It is set in a grim expression, but his small, sharp eyes still peer at life with a shrewd prying avidity and his loose mouth has a strong suggestion of ribald humor. He wears his earth-stained working clothes.

Amos Ames, carpenter by trade but now taking a holiday and dressed in his Sunday best, as are his wife and her cousin, is a fat man in his fifties. In character he is the townsfolk type of garrulous gossip-monger who is at the same time devoid of evil intent, scandal being for him merely the subject most popular with his audience.

His wife, Louisa, is taller and stouter than he and about the same age. Of a similar scandal-bearing type, her tongue is sharpened by malice.

Her cousin, Minnie, is a plump little woman of forty, of the meek, eager-listener type, with a small round face, round stupid eyes, and a round mouth pursed out to drink in gossip.

These last three are types of townsfolk rather than individuals, a chorus representing the town come to look and listen and spy on the rich and exclusive Mannons.

Led by Seth, they come forward as far as the lilac clump and stand staring at the house. Seth, in a mood of aged playfulness, is trying to make an impression on Minnie. His singing has been for her benefit. He nudges her with his elbow, grinning.

SETH—How's that fur singin' fur an old feller? I used to be noted fur my chanties. (*Seeing she is paying no attention to him but is staring with open-mouthed awe at the house, he turns to Ames—jubilantly*) By jingo, Amos, if that news is true, there won't be a sober man in town tonight! It's our patriotic duty to celebrate!

AMES—(*with a grin*) We'd ought to, that's sartin!

LOUISA—You ain't goin' to git Amos drunk tonight, surrender or no surrender! An old reprobate, that's what you be!

SETH—(*pleased*) Old nothin'! On'y seventy-five! My old man lived to be ninety! Licker can't kill the Beckwiths! (*He and Ames laugh. Louisa smiles in spite of herself. Minnie is oblivious, still staring at the house.*)

MINNIE—My sakes! What a purty house!

SETH—Wal, I promised Amos I'd help show ye the sights when you came to visit him. 'Taint everyone can git to see the Mannon place close to. They're strict about trespassin'.

MINNIE—My! They must be rich! How'd they make their money?

SETH—Ezra's made a pile, and before him, his father, Abe Mannon, he inherited some and made a pile more in shippin'. Started one of the fust Western Ocean packet lines.

MINNIE—Ezra's the General, ain't he?

SETH—(*proudly*) Ayeh. The best fighter in the hull of Grant's army!

MINNIE—What kind is he?

SETH—(*boastfully expanding*) He's able, Ezra is! Folks think he's cold-blooded and uppish, 'cause he's never got much to say to 'em. But that's only the Mannons' way. They've been top dog around here for near on two hundred years and don't let folks fergit it.

MINNIE—How'd he come to jine the army if he's so rich?

SETH—Oh, he'd been a soldier afore this war. His paw made him go to West P'int. He went to the Mexican war and come out a major. Abe died that same year and Ezra give up the army and took holt of the shippin' business here. But he didn't stop there. He learned law on the side and got made a judge. Went in fur politics and got 'lected mayor. He was mayor when this war broke out but he resigned to once and jined the army again. And now he's riz to be General. Oh, he's able, Ezra is!

AMES—Ayeh. This town's real proud of Ezra.

LOUISA—Which is more'n you kin say fur his wife. Folks all hates her! She ain't the Mannon kind. French and Dutch descended, she is. Furrin lookin' and queer. Her father's a doctor in New York, but he can't be much of a one 'cause she didn't bring no money when Ezra married her.

SETH—(*his face growing grim—sharply*) Never mind her. We ain't talkin' 'bout her. (*then abruptly changing the subject*)

Wal, I've got to see Vinnie. I'm goin' round by the kitchen. You wait here. And if Ezra's wife starts to run you off fur trespassin', you tell her I got permission from Vinnie to show you round. (*He goes off around the corner of the house, left. The three stare about them gawkily, awed and uncomfortable. They talk in low voices.*)

LOUISA—Seth is so proud of his durned old Mannons! I couldn't help givin' him a dig about Ezra's wife.

AMES—Wal, don't matter much. He's allus hated her.

LOUISA—Ssshh! Someone's comin' out. Let's get back here! (*They crowd to the rear of the bench by the lilac clump and peer through the leaves as the front door is opened and Christine Mannon comes out to the edge of the portico at the top of the steps. Louisa prods her cousin and whispers excitedly*) That's her! (*Christine Mannon is a tall striking-looking woman of forty but she appears younger. She has a fine, voluptuous figure and she moves with a flowing animal grace. She wears a green satin dress, smartly cut and expensive, which brings out the peculiar color of her thick curly hair, partly a copper brown, partly a bronze gold, each shade distinct and yet blending with the other. Her face is unusual, handsome rather than beautiful. One is struck at once by the strange impression it gives in repose of being not living flesh but a wonderfully life-like pale mask, in which only the deep-set eyes, of a dark violet blue, are alive. Her black eyebrows meet in a pronounced straight line above her strong nose. Her chin is heavy, her mouth large and sensual, the lower lip full, the upper a thin bow, shadowed by a line of hair. She stands and listens defensively, as if the music held some meaning that threatened her. But at once she shrugs her shoulders with disdain and comes down the steps and walks off toward the flower garden, passing behind the lilac clump without having noticed Ames and the women.*)

MINNIE—(*in an awed whisper*) My! She's awful handsome, ain't she?

LOUISA—Too furrin lookin' fur my taste.

MINNIE—Ayeh. There's somethin' queer lookin' about her face.

AMES—Secret lookin'—'s if it was a mask she'd put on. That's the Mannon look. They all has it. They grow it on their wives. Seth's growed it on too, didn't you notice—from bein' with 'em all his life. They don't want folks to guess their secrets.

MINNIE—(*breathlessly eager*) Secrets?

LOUISA—The Mannons got skeletons in their closets same as others! Worse ones. (*lowering her voice almost to a whisper—to her husband*) Tell Minnie about old Abe Mannon's brother David marryin' that French Canuck nurse girl he'd got into trouble.

AMES—Ssshh! Shet up, can't you? Here's Seth comin'. (*But he whispers quickly to Minnie*) That happened way back when I was a youngster. I'll tell you later. (*Seth has appeared from around the left corner of the house and now joins them.*)

SETH—That durned nigger cook is allus askin' me to fetch wood fur her! You'd think I was her slave! That's what we get fur freein' 'em! (*then briskly*) Wal, come along, folks. I'll show you the peach orchard and then we'll go to my greenhouse. I couldn't find Vinnie. (*They are about to start when the front door of the house is opened and Lavinia comes out to the top of the steps where her mother had stood. She is twenty-three but looks considerably older. Tall like her mother, her body is thin, flatbreasted and angular, and its unattractiveness is accentuated by her plain black dress. Her movements are stiff and she carries herself with a wooden, square-shouldered, military bearing. She has a flat dry voice and a habit of snapping out her words like an officer giving orders. But in spite of these dissimilarities, one is immediately struck by her facial resemblance to her mother. She has the same peculiar shade of copper-gold hair, the same pallor and dark violet-blue eyes, the black eyebrows meeting in a straight line above her nose, the same sensual mouth, the same heavy jaw. Above all, one is struck by the same strange, life-like mask impression her face gives in repose. But it is evident Lavinia does all in her power to emphasize the dissimilarity rather than the resemblance to her parent. She wears her hair pulled tightly back, as if to conceal its natural curliness, and there is not a touch of feminine allurement to her severely plain get-up. Her head is the same size as her mother's, but on her thin body it looks too large and heavy.*)

SETH—(*seeing her*) There she be now. (*He starts for the steps—then sees she has not noticed their presence, and stops and stands waiting, struck by something in her manner. She is looking off right, watching her mother as she strolls through the garden to the greenhouse. Her eyes are bleak and hard with an intense, bitter enmity. Then her mother evidently disappears in the greenhouse, for Lavinia turns her head, still oblivious to Seth and his friends, and looks off left, her attention caught by the band, the music of which, borne on a freshening breeze, has suddenly become louder. It is still playing "John Brown's Body." Lavinia listens, as her mother had a moment before, but her reaction is the direct opposite to what her mother's had been. Her eyes light up with a grim satisfaction, and an expression of strange vindictive triumph comes into her face.*)

LOUISA—(*in a quick whisper to Minnie*) That's Lavinia!

MINNIE—She looks like her mother in face—queer lookin'—but she ain't purty like her.

SETH—You git along to the orchard, folks. I'll jine you there. (*They walk back around the left of the house and disappear. He goes to Lavinia eagerly.*) Say, I got fine news fur you, Vinnie. The telegraph feller says Lee is a goner sure this time! They're only waitin' now fur the news to be made official. You can count on your paw comin' home!

LAVINIA—(*grimly*) I hope so. It's time.

SETH—(*with a keen glance at her—slowly*) Ayeh.

LAVINIA—(*turning on him sharply*) What do you mean, Seth?

SETH—(*avoiding her eyes—evasively*) Nothin'—'cept what you mean. (*Lavinia stares at him. He avoids her eyes—then heavily casual*) Where was you gallivantin' night afore last and all yesterday?

LAVINIA—(*starts*) Over to Hazel and Peter's house.

SETH—Ayeh. There's where Hannah said you'd told her you was goin'. That's funny now—'cause I seen Peter upstreet yesterday and he asked me where you was keepin' yourself.

LAVINIA—(*again starts—then slowly as if admitting a secret understanding between them*) I went to New York, Seth.

SETH—Ayeh. That's where I thought you'd gone, mebbe. (*then with deep sympathy*) It's durned hard on you, Vinnie. It's a durned shame.

LAVINIA—(*stiffening—curtly*) I don't know what you're talking about.

SETH—(*nods comprehendingly*) All right, Vinnie. Just as you say. (*He pauses—then after hesitating frowningly for a moment, blurts out*) There's somethin' been on my mind lately I want to warn you about. It's got to do with what's worryin' you—that is, if there's anythin' in it.

LAVINIA—(*stiffly*) There's nothing worrying me. (*then sharply*) Warn me? About what?

SETH—Mebbe it's nothin'—and then again mebbe I'm right, and if I'm right, then you'd ought t'be warned. It's to do with that Captain Brant.

LAVINIA—(*starts again but keeps her tone cold and collected*) What about him?

SETH—Somethin' I calc'late no one'd notice 'specially 'ceptin' me, because— (*then hastily as he sees someone coming up the drive*) Here's Peter and Hazel comin'. I'll tell you later, Vinnie. I ain't got time now anyways. Those folks are waitin' for me.

LAVINIA—I'll be sitting here. You come back afterwards. (*then her cold disciplined mask breaking for a moment—tensely*) Oh, why do Peter and Hazel have to come now? I don't want to see anyone! (*She starts as if to go into the house.*)

SETH—You run in. I'll git rid of 'em fur you.

LAVINIA—(*recovering herself—curtly*) No. I'll see them. (*Seth goes back around the corner of the house, left. A moment later Hazel and Peter Niles enter along the drive from left, front. Hazel is a pretty, healthy girl of nineteen, with dark hair and eyes. Her features are small but clearly modelled. She has a strong chin and a capable, smiling mouth. One gets a sure impression of her character at a glance—frank, innocent, amiable and good—not in a negative but in a positive, self-possessed way. Her brother, Peter, is very like her in character—straightforward, guileless and good-natured. He is a heavily built young fellow of twenty-two, awkward in movement and hesitating in speech. His face is broad, plain, with a snubby nose, curly brown hair, fine gray eyes and a big mouth. He wears the uniform of an artillery captain in the Union Army.*)

LAVINIA—(*with forced cordiality*) Good afternoon. How are you? (*She and Hazel kiss and she shakes hands with Peter.*)

HAZEL—Oh, we're all right. But how are you, Vinnie,

that's the question? Seems as if we hadn't seen you in ages! You haven't been sick, I hope!

LAVINIA—Well—if you call a pesky cold sick.

PETER—Gosh, that's too bad! All over it now?

LAVINIA—Yes—almost. Do sit down, won't you? (*Hazel sits at left of bench, Lavinia beside her in the middle. Peter sits gingerly on the right edge so that there is an open space between him and Lavinia.*)

HAZEL—Peter can stay a while if you want him to, but I just dropped in for a second to find out if you'd had any more news from Orin.

LAVINIA—Not since the letter I showed you.

HAZEL—But that was ages ago! And I haven't had a letter in months. I guess he must have met another girl some place and given me the go by. (*She forces a smile but her tone is really hurt.*)

PETER—Orin not writing doesn't mean anything. He never was much of a hand for letters.

HAZEL—I know that, but—you don't think he's been wounded, do you, Vinnie?

LAVINIA—Of course not. Father would have let us know.

PETER—Sure he would. Don't be foolish, Hazel! (*then after a little pause*) Orin ought to be home before long now. You've heard the good news, of course, Vinnie?

HAZEL—Peter won't have to go back. Isn't that fine?

PETER—My wound is healed and I've got orders to leave tomorrow but they'll be cancelled, I guess. (*grinning*) I won't pretend I'm the sort of hero that wants to go back, either! I've had enough!

HAZEL—(*impulsively*) Oh, it will be so good to see Orin again. (*then embarrassed, forces a self-conscious laugh and gets up and kisses Lavinia*) Well, I must run. I've got to meet Emily. Good-bye, Vinnie. Do take care of yourself and come to see us soon. (*with a teasing glance at her brother*) And be kind to Peter. He's nice—when he's asleep. And he has something he's just dying to ask you!

PETER—(*horribly embarrassed*) Darn you! (*Hazel laughs and goes off down the drive, left front. Peter fidgets, his eyes on the ground. Lavinia watches him. Since Hazel's teasing statement, she has visibly withdrawn into herself and is on the defensive. Finally*

Peter looks up and blurts out awkwardly) Hazel feels bad about Orin not writing. Do you think he really—loves her?

LAVINIA—(*stiffening—brusquely*) I don't know anything about love! I don't want to know anything! (*intensely*) I hate love!

PETER—(*crushed by this but trying bravely to joke*) Gosh, then, if that's the mood you're in, I guess I better not ask— something I'd made up my mind to ask you today.

LAVINIA—It's what you asked me a year ago when you were home on leave, isn't it?

PETER—And you said wait till the war was over. Well, it's over now.

LAVINIA—(*slowly*) I can't marry anyone, Peter. I've got to stay home. Father needs me.

PETER—He's got your mother.

LAVINIA—(*sharply*) He needs me more! (*A pause. Then she turns pityingly and puts her hand on his shoulder.*) I'm sorry, Peter.

PETER—(*gruffly*) Oh, that's all right.

LAVINIA—I know it's what girls always say in books, but I do love you as a brother, Peter. I wouldn't lose you as a brother for anything. We've been like that ever since we were little and started playing together—you and Orin and Hazel and I. So please don't let this come between us.

PETER—'Course it won't. What do you think I am? (*doggedly*) Besides, I'm not giving up hope but what you'll change your mind in time. That is, unless it's because you love someone else—

LAVINIA—(*snatching her hand back*) Don't be stupid, Peter!

PETER—But how about this mysterious clipper captain that's been calling?

LAVINIA—(*angrily*) Do you think I care anything about that—that—!

PETER—Don't get mad. I only meant, folks say he's court-ing you.

LAVINIA—Folks say more than their prayers!

PETER—Then you don't—care for him?

LAVINIA—(*intensely*) I hate the sight of him!

PETER—Gosh! I'm glad to hear you say that, Vinnie. I was

afraid—I imagined girls all liked him. He's such a darned romantic-looking cuss. Looks more like a gambler or a poet than a ship captain. I got a look as he was coming out of your gate—I guess it was the last time he was here. Funny, too. He reminded me of someone. But I couldn't place who it was.

LAVINIA—(*startled, glances at him uneasily*) No one around here, that's sure. He comes from out West. Grandfather Hamel happened to meet him in New York and took a fancy to him, and Mother met him at Grandfather's house.

PETER—Who is he, anyway, Vinnie?

LAVINIA—I don't know much about him in spite of what you think. Oh, he did tell me the story of his life to make himself out romantic, but I didn't pay much attention. He went to sea when he was young and was in California for the Gold Rush. He's sailed all over the world—he lived on a South Sea island once, so he says.

PETER—(*grumpily*) He seems to have had plenty of romantic experience, if you can believe him!

LAVINIA—(*bitterly*) That's his trade—being romantic! (*then agitatedly*) But I don't want to talk any more about him. (*She gets up and walks toward right to conceal her agitation, keeping her back turned to Peter.*)

PETER—(*with a grin*) Well, I don't either. I can think of more interesting subjects. (*Christine Mannon appears from left, between the clump of lilacs and the house. She is carrying a big bunch of flowers. Lavinia senses her presence and whirls around. For a moment, mother and daughter stare into each other's eyes. In their whole tense attitudes is clearly revealed the bitter antagonism between them. But Christine quickly recovers herself and her air resumes its disdainful aloofness.*)

CHRISTINE—Ah, here you are at last! (*Then she sees Peter, who is visibly embarrassed by her presence.*) Why, good afternoon, Peter, I didn't see you at first.

PETER—Good afternoon, Mrs. Mannon. I was just passing and dropped in for a second. I guess I better run along now, Vinnie.

LAVINIA—(*with an obvious eagerness to get him off—quickly*) All right. Good-bye, Peter.

PETER—Good-bye. Good-bye, Mrs. Mannon.

CHRISTINE—Good-bye, Peter. (*He disappears from the drive, left. Christine comes forward.*) I must say you treat your one devoted swain pretty rudely. (*Lavinia doesn't reply. Christine goes on coolly.*) I was wondering when I was going to see you. When I returned from New York last night you seemed to have gone to bed.

LAVINIA—I had gone to bed.

CHRISTINE—You usually read long after that. I tried your door—but you had locked yourself in. When you kept yourself locked in all day I was sure you were intentionally avoiding me. But Annie said you had a headache. (*While she has been speaking she has come toward Lavinia until she is now within arm's reach of her. The facial resemblance, as they stand there, is extraordinary. Christine stares at her coolly, but one senses an uneasy wariness beneath her pose.*) Did you have a headache?

LAVINIA—No. I wanted to be alone—to think over things.

CHRISTINE—What things, if I may ask? (*Then, as if she were afraid of an answer to this question, she abruptly changes the subject.*) Who are those people I saw wandering about the grounds?

LAVINIA—Some friends of Seth's.

CHRISTINE—Because they know that lazy old sot, does it give them the privilege of trespassing?

LAVINIA—I gave Seth permission to show them around.

CHRISTINE—And since when have you the right without consulting me?

LAVINIA—I couldn't very well consult you when Seth asked me. You had gone to New York—(*she pauses a second—then adds slowly, staring fixedly at her mother*) to see Grandfather. Is he feeling any better? He seems to have been sick so much this past year.

CHRISTINE—(*casually, avoiding her eyes*) Yes. He's much better now. He'll soon be going the rounds to his patients again, he hopes. (*as if anxious to change the subject, looking at the flowers she carries*) I've been to the greenhouse to pick these. I felt our tomb needed a little brightening. (*She nods scornfully toward the house.*) Each time I come back after being away it appears more like a sepulchre! The "whited" one of the Bible—pagan temple front stuck like a mask on Puritan gray ugliness! It was just like old Abe Mannon to build such a monstrosity—as a temple for his hatred. (*then with a little mocking laugh*) Forgive me, Vinnie. I forgot you liked it. And you ought to. It suits your temperament. (*Lavinia stares at her but remains silent. Christine glances at her flowers again and turns toward the house.*) I must put these in water. (*She moves a few steps toward the house—then turns again—with a studied casualness*) By the way, before I forget, I happened to run into Captain Brant on the street in New York. He said he was coming up here today to take over his ship and asked me if he might drop in to see you. I told him he could—and stay to supper with us. (*without looking at Lavinia, who is staring at her with a face grown grim and hard*) Doesn't that please you, Vinnie? Or do you remain true to your one and only beau, Peter?

LAVINIA—Is that why you picked the flowers—because he is coming? (*Her mother does not answer. She goes on with a threatening undercurrent in her voice.*) You have heard the news, I suppose? It means Father will be home soon!

CHRISTINE—(*without looking at her—coolly*) We've had so many rumors lately. This report hasn't been confirmed yet, has it? I haven't heard the fort firing a salute.

LAVINIA—You will before long!

CHRISTINE—I'm sure I hope so as much as you.

LAVINIA—You can say that!

CHRISTINE—(*concealing her alarm—coldly*) What do you mean? You will kindly not take that tone with me, please! (*cuttingly*) If you are determined to quarrel, let us go into the house. We might be overheard out here. (*She turns and sees Seth who has just come to the corner of the house, left, and is standing there watching them.*) See. There is your old crony doing his best to listen now! (*moving to the steps*) I am going in and rest a while. (*She walks up the steps.*)

LAVINIA—(*harshly*) I've got to have a talk with you, Mother—before long!

CHRISTINE—(*turning defiantly*) Whenever you wish. To-night after the Captain leaves you, if you like. But what is it you want to talk about?

LAVINIA—You'll know soon enough!

CHRISTINE—(*staring at her with a questioning dread—*

forcing a scornful smile) You always make such a mystery of things, Vinnie. (*She goes into the house and closes the door behind her. Seth comes forward from where he had withdrawn around the corner of the house. Lavinia makes a motion for him to follow her, and goes and sits on the bench at left. A pause. She stares straight ahead, her face frozen, her eyes hard. He regards her understandingly.*)

LAVINIA—(*abruptly*) Well? What is it about Captain Brant you want to warn me against? (*then as if she felt she must defend her question from some suspicion that she knows is in his mind*) I want to know all I can about him because—he seems to be calling to court me.

SETH—(*managing to convey his entire disbelief of this statement in one word*) Ayeh.

LAVINIA—(*sharply*) You say that as if you didn't believe me.

SETH—I believe anything you tell me to believe. I ain't been with the Mannons for sixty years without learning that. (*A pause. Then he asks slowly*) Ain't you noticed this Brant reminds you of someone in looks?

LAVINIA—(*struck by this*) Yes. I have—ever since I first saw him—but I've never been able to place who— Who do you mean?

SETH—Your Paw, ain't it, Vinnie?

LAVINIA—(*startled—agitatedly*) Father? No! It can't be! (*then as if the conviction were forcing itself on her in spite of herself*) Yes! He does—something about his face—that must be why I've had the strange feeling I've known him before— why I've felt— (*then tensely as if she were about to break down*) Oh! I won't believe it! You must be mistaken, Seth! That would be too—!

SETH—He ain't only like your Paw. He's like Orin, too—and all the Mannons I've known.

LAVINIA—(*frightenedly*) But why—why should he—?

SETH—More speshully he calls to my mind your Grandpaw's brother, David. How much do you know about David Mannon, Vinnie? I know his name's never been allowed to be spoke among Mannons since the day he left—but you've likely heard gossip, ain't you—even if it all happened before you was born.

LAVINIA—I've heard that he loved the Canuck nurse girl who was taking care of Father's little sister who died, and had to marry her because she was going to have a baby; and that Grandfather put them both out of the house and then afterwards tore it down and built this one because he wouldn't live where his brother had disgraced the family. But what has that old scandal got to do with—

SETH—Wait. Right after they was throwed out they married and went away. There was talk they'd gone out West, but no one knew nothin' about 'em afterwards—'ceptin' your Grandpaw let out to me one time she'd had the baby—a boy. He was cussin' it. (*then impressively*) It's about her baby I've been thinkin', Vinnie.

LAVINIA—(*a look of appalled comprehension growing on her face*) Oh!

SETH—How old is that Brant, Vinnie?

LAVINIA—Thirty-six, I think.

SETH—Ayeh! That'd make it right. And here's another funny thing—his name. Brant's sort of queer fur a name. I ain't never heard tell of it before. Sounds made up to me—like short fur somethin' else. Remember what that Canuck girl's name was, do you, Vinnie? Marie Brantôme! See what I'm drivin' at?

LAVINIA—(*agitatedly, fighting against a growing conviction*) But—don't be stupid, Seth—his name would be Mannon and he'd be only too proud of it.

SETH—He'd have good reason not to use the name of Mannon when he came callin' here, wouldn't he? If your Paw ever guessed—!

LAVINIA—(*breaking out violently*) No! It can't be! God wouldn't let it! It would be too horrible—on top of—! I won't even think of it, do you hear? Why did you have to tell me?

SETH—(*calmingly*) There now! Don't take on, Vinnie. No need gettin' riled at me. (*He waits—then goes on insistently.*) All I'm drivin' at is that it's durned funny—his looks and the name—and you'd ought fur your Paw's sake to make sartin.

LAVINIA—How can I make certain?

SETH—Catch him off guard sometime and put it up to him strong—as if you knowed it—and see if mebbe he don't give himself away. (*He starts to go—looks down the drive at left.*) Looks like him comin' up the drive now, Vinnie. There's somethin' about his walk calls back David Mannon, too. If I didn't know it was him I'd think it was David's ghost comin' home. (*He turns away abruptly.*) Wal, calc'late I better git back to work. (*He walks around the left corner of the house. A pause. Then Captain Adam Brant enters from the drive, left, front. He starts on seeing Lavinia but immediately puts on his most polite, winning air. One is struck at a glance by the peculiar quality his face in repose has of being a life-like mask rather than living flesh. He has a broad, low forehead, framed by coal-black straight hair which he wears noticeably long, pushed back carelessly from his fore- head as a poet's might be. He has a big aquiline nose, bushy eye- brows, swarthy complexion, hazel eyes. His wide mouth is sensual and moody—a mouth that can be strong and weak by turns. He wears a mustache, but his heavy cleft chin is clean-shaven. In fig- ure he is tall, broad-shouldered and powerful. He gives the impres- sion of being always on the offensive or defensive, always fighting life. He is dressed with an almost foppish extravagance, with touches of studied carelessness, as if a romantic Byronic appearance were the ideal in mind. There is little of the obvious ship captain about him, except his big, strong hands and his deep voice.*)

BRANT—(*bowing with an exaggerated politeness*) Good after- noon. (*coming and taking her hand which she forces herself to hold out to him*) Hope you don't mind my walking in on you without ceremony. Your mother told me—

LAVINIA—I know. She had to go out for a while and she said I was to keep you company until she returned.

BRANT—(*gallantly*) Well, I'm in good luck, then. I hope she doesn't hurry back to stand watch over us. I haven't had a chance to be alone with you since—that night we went walking in the moonlight, do you remember? (*He has kept her hand and he drops his voice to a low, lover-like tone. Lavinia can- not repress a start, agitatedly snatching her hand from his and turning away from him.*)

LAVINIA—(*regaining command of herself—slowly*) What do you think of the news of Lee surrendering, Captain? We expect my father home very soon now. (*At something in her tone he stares at her suspiciously, but she is looking straight before her.*) Why don't you sit down?

BRANT—Thank you. (*He sits on the bench at her right. He has become wary now, feeling something strange in her attitude but not able to make her out—casually*) Yes, you must be very happy at the prospect of seeing your father again. Your mother has told me how close you've always been to him.

LAVINIA—Did she? (*then with intensity*) I love Father better than anyone in the world. There is nothing I wouldn't do—to protect him from hurt!

BRANT—(*watching her carefully—keeping his casual tone*) You care more for him than for your mother?

LAVINIA—Yes.

BRANT—Well, I suppose that's the usual way of it. A daughter feels closer to her father and a son to his mother. But I should think you ought to be a born exception to that rule.

LAVINIA—Why?

BRANT—You're so like your mother in some ways. Your face is the dead image of hers. And look at your hair. You won't meet hair like yours and hers again in a month of Sundays. I only know of one other woman who had it. You'll think it strange when I tell you. It was my mother.

LAVINIA—(*with a start*) Ah!

BRANT—(*dropping his voice to a reverent, hushed tone*) Yes, she had beautiful hair like your mother's, that hung down to her knees, and big, deep, sad eyes that were blue as the Caribbean sea!

LAVINIA—(*harshly*) What do looks amount to? I'm not a bit like her! Everybody knows I take after Father!

BRANT—(*brought back with a shock, astonished at her tone*) But—you're not angry at me for saying that, are you? (*then filled with uneasiness and resolving he must establish himself on an intimate footing with her again—with engaging bluntness*) You're puzzling today, Miss Lavinia. You'll excuse me if I come out with it bluntly. I've lived most of my life at sea and in camps and I'm used to straight speaking. What are you holding against me? If I've done anything to offend you, I swear it wasn't meant. (*She is silent, staring before her with hard eyes, rigidly upright. He appraises her with a calculating look, then goes on.*) I wouldn't have bad feeling come between us for the world. I may only be flattering myself, but I thought you liked me. Have you forgotten that night walking along the shore?

LAVINIA—(*in a cold, hard voice*) I haven't forgotten. Did Mother tell you you could kiss me?

BRANT—What—what do you mean? (*But he at once attributes the question to her naïveté—laughingly*) Oh! I see! But, come now, Lavinia, you can't mean, can you, I should have asked her permission?

LAVINIA—Shouldn't you?

BRANT—(*again uneasy—trying to joke it off*) Well, I wasn't brought up that strictly and, should or shouldn't, at any rate, I didn't—and it wasn't the less sweet for that! (*Then at something in her face he hurriedly goes off on another tack.*) I'm afraid I gabbed too much that night. Maybe I bored you with my talk of clipper ships and my love for them?

LAVINIA—(*dryly*) "Tall, white clippers," you called them. You said they were like beautiful, pale women to you. You said you loved them more than you'd ever loved a woman. Is that true, Captain?

BRANT—(*with forced gallantry*) Aye. But I meant, before I met you. (*then thinking he has at last hit on the cause of her changed attitude toward him—with a laugh*) So that's what you're holding against me, is it? Well, I might have guessed. Women are jealous of ships. They always suspect the sea. They know they're three of a kind when it comes to a man! (*He laughs again but less certainly this time, as he regards her grim, set expression.*) Yes, I might have seen you didn't appear much taken by my sea gamming that night. I suppose clippers are too old a story to the daughter of a ship builder. But unless I'm much mistaken, you were interested when I told you of the islands in the South Seas where I was shipwrecked my first voyage at sea.

LAVINIA—(*in a dry, brittle tone*) I remember your admiration for the naked native women. You said they had found the secret of happiness because they had never heard that love can be a sin.

BRANT—(*surprised—sizing her up puzzledly*) So you remember that, do you? (*then romantically*) Aye! And they live in as near the Garden of Paradise before sin was discovered as you'll find on this earth! Unless you've seen it, you can't picture the green beauty of their land set in the blue of the sea! The clouds like down on the mountain tops, the sun drowsing in your blood, and always the surf on the barrier reef singing a croon in your ears like a lullaby! The Blessed Isles, I'd call them! You can forget there all men's dirty dreams of greed and power!

LAVINIA—And their dirty dreams—of love?

BRANT—(*startled again—staring at her uneasily*) Why do you say that? What do you mean, Lavinia?

LAVINIA—Nothing. I was only thinking—of your Blessed Isles.

BRANT—(*uncertainly*) Oh! But you said— (*Then with a confused, stupid persistence he comes closer to her, dropping his voice again to his love-making tone.*) Whenever I remember those islands now, I will always think of you, as you walked beside me that night with your hair blowing in the sea wind and the moonlight in your eyes! (*He tries to take her hand, but at his touch she pulls away and springs to her feet.*)

LAVINIA—(*with cold fury*) Don't you touch me! Don't you dare—! You liar! You—! (*Then as he starts back in confusion, she seizes this opportunity to follow Seth's advice—staring at him with deliberately insulting scorn*) But I suppose it would be foolish to expect anything but cheap romantic lies from the son of a low Canuck nurse girl!

BRANT—(*stunned*) What's that? (*then rage at the insult to his mother overcoming all prudence—springs to his feet threateningly*) Belay, damn you!—or I'll forget you're a woman—no Mannon can insult her while I—

LAVINIA—(*appalled now she knows the truth*) So—it is true— You are her son! Oh!

BRANT—(*fighting to control himself—with harsh defiance*) And what if I am? I'm proud to be! My only shame is my dirty Mannon blood! So that's why you couldn't stand my touching you just now, is it? You're too good for the son of a servant, eh? By God, you were glad enough before—!

LAVINIA—(*fiercely*) It's not true! I was only leading you on to find out things!

BRANT—Oh, no! It's only since you suspected who I was! I suppose your father has stuffed you with his lies about my mother! But, by God, you'll hear the truth of it, now you know who I am— And you'll see if you or any Mannon has the right to look down on her!

LAVINIA—I don't want to hear— (*She starts to go toward the house.*)

BRANT—(*grabbing her by the arm—tauntingly*) You're a coward, are you, like all Mannons, when it comes to facing the truth about themselves? (*She turns on him defiantly. He drops her arm and goes on harshly.*) I'll bet he never told you your grandfather, Abe Mannon, as well as his brother, loved my mother!

LAVINIA—It's a lie!

BRANT—It's the truth. It was his jealous revenge made him disown my father and cheat him out of his share of the business they'd inherited!

LAVINIA—He didn't cheat him! He bought him out!

BRANT—Forced him to sell for one-tenth its worth, you mean! He knew my father and mother were starving! But the money didn't last my father long! He'd taken to drink. He was a coward—like all Mannons—once he felt the world looked down on him. He skulked and avoided people. He grew ashamed of my mother—and me. He sank down and down and my mother worked and supported him. I can remember when men from the corner saloon would drag him home and he'd fall in the door, a sodden carcass. One night when I was seven he came home crazy drunk and hit my mother in the face. It was the first time he'd ever struck her. It made me blind mad. I hit at him with the poker and cut his head. My mother pulled me back and gave me a hiding. Then she cried over him. She'd never stopped loving him.

LAVINIA—Why do you tell me this? I told you once I don't want to hear—

BRANT—(*grimly*) You'll see the point of it damned soon! (*unheeding—as if the scene were still before his eyes*) For days after, he sat and stared at nothing. One time when we were alone he asked me to forgive him hitting her. But I hated him and I wouldn't forgive him. Then one night he went out and he didn't come back. The next morning they found him hanging in a barn!

LAVINIA—(*with a shudder*) Oh!

BRANT—(*savagely*) The only decent thing he ever did!

LAVINIA—You're lying! No Mannon would ever—

BRANT—Oh, wouldn't they? They are all fine, honorable gentlemen, you think! Then listen a bit and you'll hear something about another of them! (*then going on bitterly with his story*) My mother sewed for a living and sent me to school. She was very strict with me. She blamed me for his killing himself. But she was bound she'd make a gentleman of me—like he was!—if it took her last cent and her last strap! (*with a grim smile*) She didn't succeed, as you notice! At seventeen I ran away to sea—and forgot I had a mother, except I took part of her name—Brant was short and easy on ships—and I wouldn't wear the name of Mannon. I forgot her until two years ago when I came back from the East. Oh, I'd written to her now and then and sent her money when I happened to have any. But I'd forgotten her just the same—and when I got to New York I found her dying—of sickness and starvation! And I found out that when she'd been laid up, not able to work, not knowing where to reach me, she'd sunk her last shred of pride and written to your father asking for a loan. He never answered her. And I came too late. She died in my arms. (*with vindictive passion*) He could have saved her—and he deliberately let her die! He's as guilty of murder as anyone he ever sent to the rope when he was a judge!

LAVINIA—(*springing to her feet—furiously*) You dare say that about Father! If he were here—

BRANT—I wish to God he was! I'd tell him what I tell you now—that I swore on my mother's body I'd revenge her death on him.

LAVINIA—(*with cold deadly intensity*) And I suppose you boast that now you've done so, don't you?—in the vilest, most cowardly way—like the son of a servant you are!

BRANT—(*again thrown off guard—furiously*) Belay, I told you, with that kind of talk!

LAVINIA—She is only your means of revenge on Father, is that it?

BRANT—(*stunned—stammers in guilty confusion*) What?— She?— Who?— I don't know what you're talking about!

LAVINIA—Then you soon will know! And so will she! I've

found out all I wanted to from you. I'm going in to talk to her now. You wait here until I call you!

BRANT—(*furious at her tone*) No! Be damned if you can order me about as if I was your servant!

LAVINIA—(*icily*) If you have any consideration for her, you'll do as I say and not force me to write my father. (*She turns her back on him and walks to the steps woodenly erect and square-shouldered.*)

BRANT—(*desperately now—with a grotesque catching at his lover's manner*) I don't know what you mean, Lavinia. I swear before God it is only you I— (*She turns at the top of the steps at this and stares at him with such a passion of hatred that he is silenced. Her lips move as if she were going to speak, but she fights back the words, turns stiffly and goes into the house and closes the door behind her.*)

(*Curtain*)

ACT TWO

SCENE—*In the house—Ezra Mannon's study. No time has elapsed.*

The study is a large room with a stiff, austere atmosphere. The furniture is old colonial. The walls are plain plastered surfaces tinted a dull gray with a flat white trim. At rear, right, is a door leading to the hall. On the right wall is a painting of George Washington in a gilt frame, flanked by smaller portraits of Alexander Hamilton and John Marshall. At rear, center, is an open fireplace. At left of fireplace, a bookcase filled with law books. Above the fireplace, in a plain frame, is a large portrait of Ezra Mannon himself, painted ten years previously. One is at once struck by the startling likeness between him and Adam Brant. He is a tall man in his early forties, with a spare, wiry frame, seated stiffly in an armchair, his hands on the arms, wearing his black judge's robe. His face is handsome in a stern, aloof fashion. It is cold and emotionless and has the same strange semblance of a life-like mask that we have already seen in the faces of his wife and daughter and Brant.

On the left are two windows. Between them a desk. A large table with an armchair on either side, right and left, stands at left center, front. At right center is another chair. There are hooked rugs on the floor.

Outside the sun is beginning to set and its glow fills the room with a golden mist. As the action progresses this becomes brighter, then turns to crimson, which darkens to somberness at the end.

Lavinia is discovered standing by the table. She is fighting to control herself, but her face is torn by a look of stricken anguish. She turns slowly to her father's portrait and for a moment stares at it fixedly. Then she goes to it and puts her hand over one of his hands with a loving, protecting gesture.

LAVINIA—Poor Father! (*She hears a noise in the hall and moves hastily away. The door from the hall is opened and Christine enters. She is uneasy underneath, but affects a scornful indignation.*)

CHRISTINE—Really, this unconfirmed report must have turned your head—otherwise I'd find it difficult to understand your sending Annie to disturb me when you knew I was resting.

LAVINIA—I told you I had to talk to you.

CHRISTINE—(*looking around the room with aversion*) But why in this musty room, of all places?

LAVINIA—(*indicating the portrait—quietly*) Because it's Father's room.

CHRISTINE—(*starts, looks at the portrait and quickly drops her eyes. Lavinia goes to the door and closes it. Christine says with forced scorn*) More mystery?

LAVINIA—You better sit down. (*Christine sits in the chair at rear center. Lavinia goes back to her father's chair at left of table.*)

CHRISTINE—Well—if you're quite ready, perhaps you will explain.

LAVINIA—I suppose Annie told you I'd been to visit Hazel and Peter while you were away.

CHRISTINE—Yes. I thought it peculiar. You never visit anyone overnight. Why did you suddenly take that notion?

LAVINIA—I didn't.

CHRISTINE—You didn't visit them?

LAVINIA—No.

CHRISTINE—Then where did you go?

LAVINIA—(*accusingly*) To New York! (*Christine starts. Lavinia hurries on a bit incoherently.*) I've suspected something— lately—the excuse you've made for all your trips there the past year, that Grandfather was sick— (*as Christine is about to protest indignantly*) Oh! I know he has been—and you've stayed at his house—but I've suspected lately that wasn't the real reason—and now I can prove it isn't! Because I waited outside Grandfather's house and followed you. I saw you meet Brant!

CHRISTINE—(*alarmed but concealing it—coolly*) Well, what if you did? I told you myself I ran into him by accident—

LAVINIA—You went to his room!

CHRISTINE—(*shaken*) He asked me to meet a friend of his—a lady. It was her house we went to.

LAVINIA—I asked the woman in the basement. He had hired the room under another name, but she recognized his description. And yours too. She said you had come there often in the past year.

CHRISTINE—(*desperately*) It was the first time I had ever been there. He insisted on my going. He said he had to talk to me about you. He wanted my help to approach your father—

LAVINIA—(*furiously*) How can you lie like that? How can you be so vile as to try to use me to hide your adultery?

CHRISTINE—(*springing up—with weak indignation*) Vinnie!

LAVINIA—Your adultery, I said!

CHRISTINE—No!

LAVINIA—Stop lying, I tell you! I went upstairs! I heard you telling him—"I love you, Adam"—and kissing him! (*with a cold bitter fury*) You vile—! You're shameless and evil! Even if you are my mother, I say it! (*Christine stares at her, overwhelmed by this onslaught, her poise shattered for the moment. She tries to keep her voice indifferent but it trembles a little.*)

CHRISTINE—I—I knew you hated me, Vinnie—but not as bitterly as that! (*then with a return of her defiant coolness*) Very well! I love Adam Brant. What are you going to do?

LAVINIA—How you say that—without any shame! You don't give one thought to Father—who is so good—who trusts you! Oh, how could you do this to Father? How could you?

CHRISTINE—(*with strident intensity*) You would understand if you were the wife of a man you hated!

LAVINIA—(*horrified—with a glance at the portrait*) Don't! Don't say that—before him! I won't listen!

CHRISTINE—(*grabbing her by the arm*) You will listen! I'm talking to you as a woman now, not as mother to daughter! That relationship has no meaning between us! You've called me vile and shameless! Well, I want you to know that's what I've felt about myself for over twenty years, giving my body to a man I—

LAVINIA—(*trying to break away from her, half putting her hands up to her ears*) Stop telling me such things! Let me go! (*She breaks away, shrinking from her mother with a look of sick repulsion. A pause. She stammers*) You—then you've always hated Father?

CHRISTINE—(*bitterly*) No. I loved him once—before I married him—incredible as that seems now! He was handsome in his lieutenant's uniform! He was silent and mysterious and romantic! But marriage soon turned his romance into—disgust!

LAVINIA—(*wincing again—stammers harshly*) So I was born of your disgust! I've always guessed that, Mother—ever since I was little—when I used to come to you—with love—but you would always push me away! I've felt it ever since I can remember—your disgust! (*then with a flare-up of bitter hatred*) Oh, I hate you! It's only right I should hate you!

CHRISTINE—(*shaken—defensively*) I tried to love you. I told myself it wasn't human not to love my own child, born of my body. But I never could make myself feel you were born of any body but his! You were always my wedding night to me—and my honeymoon!

LAVINIA—Stop saying that! How can you be so—! (*then suddenly—with a strange jealous bitterness*) You've loved Orin! Why didn't you hate him, too?

CHRISTINE—Because by then I had forced myself to become resigned in order to live! And most of the time I was carrying him, your father was with the army in Mexico. I had forgotten him. And when Orin was born he seemed my child, only mine, and I loved him for that! (*bitterly*) I loved him until he let you and your father nag him into the war, in spite of my begging him not to leave me alone. (*staring at Lavinia with hatred*) I know his leaving me was your doing principally, Vinnie!

LAVINIA—(*sternly*) It was his duty as a Mannon to go! He'd have been sorry the rest of his life if he hadn't! I love him better than you! I was thinking of him!

CHRISTINE—Well, I hope you realize I never would have fallen in love with Adam if I'd had Orin with me. When he had gone there was nothing left—but hate and a desire to be revenged—and a longing for love! And it was then I met Adam. I saw he loved me—

LAVINIA—(*with taunting scorn*) He doesn't love you! You're only his revenge on Father! Do you know who he really is? He's the son of that low nurse girl Grandfather put out of our house!

CHRISTINE—(*concealing a start—coolly*) So you've found that out? Were you hoping it would be a crushing surprise to me? I've known it all along. He told me when he said he loved me.

LAVINIA—Oh! And I suppose knowing who he was gave you all the more satisfaction—to add that disgrace!

CHRISTINE—(*cuttingly*) Will you kindly come to the point and tell me what you intend doing? I suppose you'll hardly let your father get in the door before you tell him!

LAVINIA—(*suddenly becoming rigid and cold again—slowly*) No. Not unless you force me to. (*then as she sees her mother's astonishment—grimly*) I don't wonder you're surprised! You know you deserve the worst punishment you could get. And Father would disown you publicly, no matter how much the scandal cost him!

CHRISTINE—I realize that. I know him even better than you do!

LAVINIA—And I'd like to see you punished for your wickedness! So please understand this isn't for your sake. It's for Father's. He hasn't been well lately. I'm not going to have him hurt! It's my first duty to protect him from you!

CHRISTINE—I know better than to expect any generosity on my account.

LAVINIA—I won't tell him, provided you give up Brant and never see him again—and promise to be a dutiful wife to Father and make up for the wrong you've done him!

CHRISTINE—(*stares at her daughter—a pause—then she laughs dryly*) What a fraud you are, with your talk of your father and your duty! Oh, I'm not denying you want to save his pride—and I know how anxious you are to keep the family from more scandal! But all the same, that's not your real reason for sparing me!

LAVINIA—(*confused—guiltily*) It is!

CHRISTINE—You wanted Adam Brant yourself!

LAVINIA—That's a lie!

CHRISTINE—And now you know you can't have him, you're determined that at least you'll take him from me!

LAVINIA—No!

CHRISTINE—But if you told your father, I'd have to go

away with Adam. He'd be mine still. You can't bear that thought, even at the price of my disgrace, can you?

LAVINIA—It's your evil mind!

CHRISTINE—I know you, Vinnie! I've watched you ever since you were little, trying to do exactly what you're doing now! You've tried to become the wife of your father and the mother of Orin! You've always schemed to steal my place!

LAVINIA—(*wildly*) No! It's you who have stolen all love from me since the time I was born! (*then her manner becoming threatening*) But I don't want to listen to any more of your lies and excuses! I want to know right now whether you're going to do what I told you or not!

CHRISTINE—Suppose I refuse! Suppose I go off openly with Adam! Where will you and your father and the family name be after that scandal? And what if I were disgraced myself? I'd have the man I love, at least!

LAVINIA—(*grimly*) Not for long! Father would use all his influence and get Brant blacklisted so he'd lose his command and never get another! You know how much the "Flying Trades" means to him. And Father would never divorce you. You could never marry. You'd be an anchor around his neck. Don't forget you're five years older than he is! He'll still be in his prime when you're an old woman with all your looks gone! He'd grow to hate the sight of you!

CHRISTINE—(*stung beyond bearing—makes a threatening move as if to strike her daughter's face*) You devil! You mean little—! (*But Lavinia stares back coldly into her eyes and she controls herself and drops her hand.*)

LAVINIA—I wouldn't call names if I were you! There is one you deserve!

CHRISTINE—(*turning away—her voice still trembling*) I'm a fool to let you make me lose my temper—over your jealous spite! (*A pause. Lavinia stares at her. Christine seems considering something. A sinister expression comes to her face. Then she turns back to Lavinia—coldly*) But you wanted my answer, didn't you? Well, I agree to do as you said. I promise you I'll never see Adam again after he calls this evening. Are you satisfied?

LAVINIA—(*stares at her with cold suspicion*) You seem to take giving him up pretty easily!

CHRISTINE—(*hastily*) Do you think I'll ever give you the

satisfaction of seeing me grieve? Oh, no, Vinnie! You'll never have a chance to gloat!

LAVINIA—(*still suspiciously—with a touch of scorn*) If I loved anyone—!

CHRISTINE—(*tauntingly*) If? I think you do love him—as much as you can love! (*with a sudden flurry of jealousy*) You little fool! Don't you know I made him flirt with you, so you wouldn't be suspicious?

LAVINIA—(*gives a little shudder—then fiercely*) He didn't fool me! I saw what a liar he was! I just led him on—to find out things! I always hated him! (*Christine smiles mockingly and turns away, as if to go out of the room. Lavinia's manner becomes threatening again.*) Wait! I don't trust you! I know you're thinking already how you can fool me and break the promise you've just made! But you better not try it! I'll be watching you every minute! And I won't be the only one! I wrote to Father and Orin as soon as I got back from New York!

CHRISTINE—(*startled*) About Adam?

LAVINIA—Only enough so they'd be suspicious and watch you too. I said a Captain Brant had been calling and folks had begun to gossip.

CHRISTINE—Ah! I see what it's going to mean—that you'll always have this to hold over me and I'll be under your thumb for the rest of my life! (*She cannot restrain her rage—threateningly*) Take care, Vinnie! You'll be responsible if—! (*She checks herself abruptly.*)

LAVINIA—(*suspiciously*) If what?

CHRISTINE—(*quickly*) Nothing. I only meant if I went off with Adam. But of course you know I won't do that. You know there's nothing I can do now—but obey your orders!

LAVINIA—(*continues to stare at her suspiciously—grimly*) You ought to see it's your duty to Father, not my orders—if you had any honor or decency! (*then brusquely*) Brant is waiting outside. You can tell him what you've got to do—and tell him if he ever dares come here again—! (*forcing back her anger*) And see that you get rid of him right now! I'm going upstreet to get the latest news. I won't be gone more than a half-hour and I want him out of the house by the time I get back, do you hear? If he isn't, I'll write Father again. I won't even wait for him to come home! (*She turns her back on her*

*mother and marches out the door, square-shouldered and stiff,
without a backward glance. Christine looks after her, waiting
until she hears the side door of the house close after her. Then she
turns and stands in tense calculating thought. Her face has become like a sinister evil mask. Finally, as if making up her mind
irrevocably, she comes to the table, tears off a slip of paper and
writes two words on it. She tucks this paper in the sleeve of her
dress and goes to the open window and calls)*

CHRISTINE—Adam! *(She moves toward the door to wait for
him. Her eyes are caught by the eyes of her husband in the portrait
over the fireplace. She stares at him with hatred and addresses him
vindictively, half under her breath.)* You can thank Vinnie, Ezra!
*(She goes to the door and reaches it just as Brant appears from
the hall. She takes his hand and draws him into the room, closing
the door behind him. One is immediately struck by the resemblance between his face and that of the portrait of Ezra Mannon.)*

BRANT—*(glancing uneasily at her, as they come to the center
of the room)* She knows—?

CHRISTINE—Yes. She followed me to New York. And
she's found out who you are too, Adam.

BRANT—*(with a grim smile)* I know. She got that out of
me—the proof of it, at any rate. Before I knew what was up
I'd given myself away.

CHRISTINE—She must have noticed your resemblance to
Orin. I was afraid that might start her thinking.

BRANT—*(sees the portrait for the first time. Instantly his body
shifts to a fighting tenseness. It is as if he were going to spring at
the figure in the painting. He says slowly)* That, I take it, is
General Mannon?

CHRISTINE—Judge Mannon then. Don't forget he used to
be a judge. He won't forget it.

BRANT—*(his eyes still fixed on the portrait—comes and sits in
Mannon's chair on the left of table. Unconsciously he takes the
same attitude as Mannon, sitting erect, his hands on the arms of
the chair—slowly)* Does Orin by any chance resemble his
father?

CHRISTINE—*(stares at him—agitatedly)* No! Of course
not! What put such a stupid idea in your head?

BRANT—It would be damned queer if you fell in love with
me because I recalled Ezra Mannon to you!

CHRISTINE—(*going to him and putting an arm around his shoulder*) No, no, I tell you! It was Orin you made me think of! It was Orin!

BRANT—I remember that night we were introduced and I heard the name Mrs. Ezra Mannon! By God, how I hated you then for being his! I thought, by God, I'll take her from him and that'll be part of my revenge! And out of that hatred my love came! It's damned queer, isn't it?

CHRISTINE—(*hugging him to her*) Are you going to let him take me from you now, Adam?

BRANT—(*passionately*) You ask that!

CHRISTINE—You swear you won't—no matter what you must do?

BRANT—By God, I swear it!

CHRISTINE—(*kisses him*) Remember that oath! (*She glances at the portrait—then turns back to Brant with a little shiver—nervously*) What made you sit there? It's his chair. I've so often seen him sitting there— (*forcing a little laugh*) Your silly talk about resemblances— Don't sit there. Come. Bring that chair over here. (*She moves to the chair at right center. He brings the chair at right of table close to hers.*)

BRANT—We've got to decide what we must do. The time for skulking and lying is over—and by God I'm glad of it! It's a coward's game I have no stomach for! (*He has placed the chair beside hers. She is staring at the portrait.*) Why don't you sit down, Christine?

CHRISTINE—(*slowly*) I was thinking—perhaps we had better go to the sitting-room. (*then defiantly*) No! I've been afraid of you long enough, Ezra! (*She sits down.*)

BRANT—I felt there was something wrong the moment I saw her. I tried my damnedest to put her off the course by giving her some softsoap—as you'd told me to do to blind her. (*frowning*) That was a mistake, Christine. It made her pay too much attention to me—and opened her eyes!

CHRISTINE—Oh, I know I've made one blunder after another. It's as if love drove me on to do everything I shouldn't. I never should have brought you to this house. Seeing you in New York should have been enough for me. But I loved you too much. I wanted you every possible moment we could steal! And I simply couldn't believe that he ever would come home. I prayed that he should be killed in the war so intensely that I finally believed it would surely happen! (*with savage intensity*) Oh, if he were only dead!

BRANT—That chance is finished now.

CHRISTINE—(*slowly—without looking at him*) Yes—in that way.

BRANT—(*stares at her*) What do you mean? (*She remains silent. He changes the subject uneasily.*) There's only one thing to do! When he comes home I'll wait for him and not give Vinnie the satisfaction of telling him. I'll tell him myself. (*vindictively*) By God! I'd give my soul to see his face when he knows you love Marie Brantôme's son! And then I'll take you away openly and laugh at him! And if he tries to stop me—! (*He stops and glances with savage hatred at the portrait.*)

CHRISTINE—What would you do then?

BRANT—If ever I laid hands on him, I'd kill him!

CHRISTINE—And then? You would be hanged for murder! And where would I be? There would be nothing left for me but to kill myself!

BRANT—If I could catch him alone, where no one would interfere, and let the best man come out alive—as I've often seen it done in the West!

CHRISTINE—This isn't the West.

BRANT—I could insult him on the street before everyone and make him fight me! I could let him shoot first and then kill him in self-defense.

CHRISTINE—(*scornfully*) Do you imagine you could force him to fight a duel with you? Don't you know duelling is illegal? Oh, no! He'd simply feel bound to do his duty as a former judge and have you arrested! (*She adds calculatingly, seeing he is boiling inside*) It would be a poor revenge for your mother's death to let him make you a laughing stock!

BRANT—But when I take you off, the laugh will be on him! You can come on the "Flying Trades."

CHRISTINE—(*calculatingly reproachful*) I don't think you'd propose that, Adam, if you stopped thinking of your revenge for a moment and thought of me! Don't you realize he would never divorce me, out of spite? What would I be in the world's eyes? My life would be ruined and I would ruin yours! You'd grow to hate me!

BRANT—(*passionately*) Don't talk like that! It's a lie and you know it!

CHRISTINE—(*with bitter yearning*) If I could only believe that, Adam! But I'll grow old so soon! And I'm afraid of time! (*then abruptly changing tone*) As for my sailing on your ship, you'll find you won't have a ship! He'll see to it you lose this command and get you blacklisted so you'll have no chance of getting another.

BRANT—(*angrily*) Aye! He can do that if he sets about it. There are twice as many skippers as ships these days.

CHRISTINE—(*calculatingly—without looking at him*) If he had only been killed, we could be married now and I would bring you my share of the Mannon estate. That would only be justice. It's yours by right. It's what his father stole from yours.

BRANT—That's true enough, damn him!

CHRISTINE—You wouldn't have to worry about commands or owners' favors then. You could buy your own ship and be your own master!

BRANT—(*yearningly*) That's always been my dream—some day to own my own clipper! And Clark and Dawson would be willing to sell the "Flying Trades." (*then forgetting everything in his enthusiasm*) You've seen her, Christine. She's as beautiful a ship as you're a woman. Aye, the two of you are like sisters. If she was mine, I'd take you on a honeymoon then! To China—and on the voyage back, we'd stop at the South Pacific Islands I've told you about. By God, there's the right place for love and a honeymoon!

CHRISTINE—(*slowly*) Yes—but Ezra is alive!

BRANT—(*brought back to earth—gloomily*) I know it's only a dream.

CHRISTINE—(*turning to stare at him—slowly*) You can have your dream—and I can have mine. There is a way. (*then turning away again*) You remember my telling you he had written complaining of pains about his heart?

BRANT—You're surely not hoping—

CHRISTINE—No. He said it was nothing serious. But I've let it be known that he has heart trouble. I went to see our old family doctor and told him about Ezra's letter. I pretended to be dreadfully worried, until I got him worried too.

He's the town's worst old gossip. I'm sure everyone knows about Ezra's weak heart by this time.

BRANT—What are you driving at, Christine?

CHRISTINE—Something I've been thinking of ever since I realized he might soon come home. And now that Vinnie— but even if we didn't have to consider her, it'd be the only way! I couldn't fool him long. He's a strange, hidden man. His silence always creeps into my thoughts. Even if he never spoke, I would feel what was in his mind and some night, lying beside him, it would drive me mad and I'd have to kill his silence by screaming out the truth! (*She has been staring before her—now she suddenly turns on Brant—slowly*) If he died suddenly now, no one would think it was anything but heart failure. I've been reading a book in Father's medical library. I saw it there one day a few weeks ago—it was as if some fate in me forced me to see it! (*She reaches in the sleeve of her dress and takes out the slip of paper she had written on.*) I've written something here. I want you to get it for me. (*His fingers close on it mechanically. He stares at it with a strange stupid dread. She hurries on so as not to give him time for reflection.*) The work on the "Flying Trades" is all finished, isn't it? You sail to Boston tomorrow, to wait for cargo?

BRANT—(*dully*) Aye.

CHRISTINE—Get this at some druggist's down by the waterfront the minute you reach there. You can make up some story about a sick dog on your ship. As soon as you get it, mail it to me here. I'll be on the lookout, so Vinnie will never know it came. Then you must wait on the "Flying Trades" until you hear from me or I come to you—afterward!

BRANT—(*dully*) But how can you do it—so no one will suspect?

CHRISTINE—He's taking medicine. I'll give him his medicine. Oh, I've planned it carefully.

BRANT—But—if he dies suddenly, won't Vinnie—

CHRISTINE—There'll be no reason for her to suspect. She's worried already about his heart. Besides, she may hate me, but she would never think—

BRANT—Orin will be coming home, too.

CHRISTINE—Orin will believe anything I want him to. As for the people here, they'd never dream of such a thing in the

Mannon house! And the sooner I do it, the less suspicion there'll be! They will think the excitement of coming home and the reaction were too much for his weak heart! Doctor Blake will think so. I'll see that's what he thinks.

BRANT—(*harshly*) Poison! It's a coward's trick!

CHRISTINE—(*with fierce scorn now, seeing the necessity of goading him*) Do you think you would be braver to give me up to him and let him take away your ship?

BRANT—No!

CHRISTINE—Didn't you say you wanted to kill him?

BRANT—Aye! But I'd give him his chance!

CHRISTINE—Did he give your mother her chance?

BRANT—(*aroused*) No, damn him!

CHRISTINE—Then what makes you suddenly so scrupulous about his death? (*with a sneer*) It must be the Mannon in you coming out! Are you going to prove, the first time your love is put to a real test, that you're a weak coward like your father?

BRANT—Christine! If it was any man said that to me—!

CHRISTINE—(*passionately*) Have you thought of this side of his homecoming—that he's coming back to my bed? If you love me as much as you claim, I should think that would rid you of any scruples! If it was a question of some woman taking you from me, I wouldn't have qualms about which was or wasn't the way to kill her! (*more tauntingly*) But perhaps your love has been only a lie you told me—to take the sneaking revenge on him of being a backstairs lover! Perhaps—

BRANT—(*stung, grabbing her by the shoulders—fiercely*) Stop it! I'll do anything you want! You know it! (*then with a change to somber grimness—putting the paper in his pocket*) And you're right. I'm a damn fool to have any feeling about how Ezra Mannon dies!

CHRISTINE—(*A look of exultant satisfaction comes to her face as she sees he is definitely won over now. She throws her arms around him and kisses him passionately.*) Ah! Now you're the man I love again, not a hypocritical Mannon! Promise me, no more cowardly romantic scruples! Promise me!

BRANT—I promise. (*The boom of a cannon sounds from the fort that guards the harbor. He and Christine start frightenedly and stand staring at each other. Another boom comes, reverberating, rattling the windows. Christine recovers herself.*)

CHRISTINE—You hear? That's the salute to his homecoming! (*She kisses him—with fierce insistence*) Remember your mother's death! Remember your dream of your own ship! Above all, remember you'll have me!—all your own—your wife! (*then urgently*) And now you must go! She'll be coming back—and you're not good at hiding your thoughts. (*urging him toward the door*) Hurry! I don't want you to meet her! (*The cannon at the fort keep booming at regular intervals until the end of the scene. Brant goes out in the hall and a moment later the front door is heard closing after him. Christine hurries from the door to the window and watches him from behind the curtains as he goes down the drive. She is in a state of tense, exultant excitement. Then, as if an idea had suddenly come to her, she speaks to his retreating figure with a strange sinister air of elation.*) You'll never dare leave me now, Adam—for your ships or your sea or your naked Island girls—when I grow old and ugly! (*She turns back from the window. Her eyes are caught by the eyes of her husband in the portrait and for a moment she stares back into them, as if fascinated. Then she jerks her glance away and, with a little shudder she cannot repress, turns and walks quickly from the room and closes the door behind her.*)

(*Curtain*)

ACT THREE

SCENE—*The same as Act One, Scene One—exterior of the Mannon house. It is around nine o'clock of a night a week later. The light of a half moon falls on the house, giving it an unreal, detached, eerie quality. The pure white temple front seems more than ever like an incongruous mask fixed on the somber, stone house. All the shutters are closed. The white columns of the portico cast black bars of shadow on the gray wall behind them. The trunk of the pine at right is an ebony pillar, its branches a mass of shade.*

Lavinia is sitting on the top of the steps to the portico. She is dressed, as before, severely in black. Her thin figure, seated stiffly upright, arms against her sides, the legs close together, the shoulders square, the head upright, is like that of an Egyptian statue. She is staring straight before her. The sound of Seth's thin, aged baritone mournfully singing the chanty "Shenandoah" is heard from down the drive, off right front. He is approaching the house and the song draws quickly nearer:

> "Oh, Shenandoah, I long to hear you
> A-way, my rolling river.
> Oh, Shenandoah, I can't get near you
> Way-ay, I'm bound away
> Across the wide Missouri.

> "Oh, Shenandoah, I love your daughter
> A-way, my rolling river."

He enters right front. He is a bit drunk but holding his liquor well. He walks up by the lilacs starting the next line "Oh, Shenandoah"—then suddenly sees Lavinia on the steps and stops abruptly, a bit sheepish.

LAVINIA—(*disapprovingly*) This is the second time this week I've caught you coming home like this.

SETH—(*unabashed, approaches the steps—with a grin*) I'm aimin' to do my patriotic duty, Vinnie. The first time was celebratin' Lee's surrender and this time is drownin' my sorrow for the President gittin' shot! And the third'll be when your Paw gits home!

LAVINIA—Father might arrive tonight.

928

SETH—Gosh, Vinnie, I never calc'lated he could git here so soon!

LAVINIA—Evidently you didn't. He'd give you fits if he caught you drunk. Oh, I don't believe he'll come, but it's possible he might.

SETH—(*is evidently trying to pull himself together. He suddenly leans over toward her and, lowering his voice, asks soberly*) Did you find out anything about that Brant?

LAVINIA—(*sharply*) Yes. There's no connection. It was just a silly idea of yours.

SETH—(*stares at her—then understandingly*) Wal, if you want it left that way, I'll leave it that way. (*A pause. He continues to stand looking at her, while she stares in front of her.*)

LAVINIA—(*in a low voice*) What was that Marie Brantôme like, Seth?

SETH—Marie? She was always laughin' and singin'—frisky and full of life—with something free and wild about her like an animile. Purty she was, too! (*then he adds*) Hair just the color of your Maw's and yourn she had.

LAVINIA—I know.

SETH—Oh, everyone took to Marie—couldn't help it. Even your Paw. He was only a boy then, but he was crazy about her, too, like a youngster would be. His mother was stern with him, while Marie, she made a fuss over him and petted him.

LAVINIA—Father, too!

SETH—Ayeh—but he hated her worse than anyone when it got found out she was his Uncle David's fancy woman.

LAVINIA—(*in a low voice, as if to herself, staring at the house*) It's all so strange! It frightens me! (*She checks herself abruptly—turns to Seth, curtly*) I don't believe that about Father. You've had too much whiskey. Go to bed and sleep it off. (*She walks up the steps again.*)

SETH—(*gazes at her with understanding*) Ayeh. (*then warningly, making a surreptitious signal as he sees the front door opening behind her*) Ssstt! (*Christine appears outlined in the light from the hall. She is dressed in a gown of green velvet that sets off her hair. The light behind her glows along the edges of the dress and in the color of her hair. She closes the door and comes into the moonlight at the edge of the steps, standing above and a little to the right of Lavinia. The moonlight, falling full on them, accentuates strangely the resemblance between their faces and at the same time the hostile dissimilarity in body and dress. Lavinia does not turn or give any sign of knowing her mother is behind her. There is a second's uncomfortable silence. Seth moves off left.)* Wal, I'll trot along! (*He disappears around the corner of the house. There is a pause. Then Christine speaks in a dry mocking tone.*)

CHRISTINE—What are you moongazing at? Puritan maidens shouldn't peer too inquisitively into Spring! Isn't beauty an abomination and love a vile thing? (*She laughs with bitter mockery—then tauntingly*) Why don't you marry Peter? You don't want to be left an old maid, do you?

LAVINIA—(*quietly*) You needn't hope to get rid of me that way. I'm not marrying anyone. I've got my duty to Father.

CHRISTINE—Duty! How often I've heard that word in this house! Well, you can't say I didn't do mine all these years. But there comes an end.

LAVINIA—(*grimly*) And there comes another end—and you must do your duty again!

CHRISTINE—(*starts as if to retort defiantly—then says calmly*) Yes, I realize that.

LAVINIA—(*after a pause—suspiciously*) What's going on at the bottom of your mind? I know you're plotting something!

CHRISTINE—(*controlling a start*) Don't be stupid, please!

LAVINIA—Are you planning how you can see Adam again? You better not!

CHRISTINE—(*calmly*) I'm not so foolish. I said good-bye once. Do you think I want to make it harder for myself?

LAVINIA—Has it been hard for you? I'd never guess it—and I've been watching you.

CHRISTINE—I warned you you would have no chance to gloat! (*after a pause*) When do you expect your father home? You want me to play my part well when he comes, don't you?—for his sake. I'd like to be forewarned.

LAVINIA—His letter said he wouldn't wait until his brigade was disbanded but would try to get leave at once. He might arrive tonight—or tomorrow—or the next day. I don't know.

CHRISTINE—You think he might come tonight? (*then with*

a mocking smile) So he's the beau you're waiting for in the spring moonlight! (*then after a pause*) But the night train got in long ago.

LAVINIA—(*glances down the drive, left front—then starts to her feet excitedly*) Here's someone! (*Christine slowly rises. There is the sound of footsteps. A moment later Ezra Mannon enters from left, front. He stops short in the shadow for a second and stands, erect and stiff, as if at attention, staring at his house, his wife and daughter. He is a tall, spare, big-boned man of fifty, dressed in the uniform of a Brigadier-General. One is immediately struck by the mask-like look of his face in repose, more pronounced in him than in the others. He is exactly like the portrait in his study, which we have seen in Act Two, except that his face is more lined and lean and the hair and beard are grizzled. His movements are exact and wooden and he has a mannerism of standing and sitting in stiff, posed attitudes that suggest the statues of military heroes. When he speaks, his deep voice has a hollow repressed quality, as if he were continually withholding emotion from it. His air is brusque and authoritative.*)

LAVINIA—(*seeing the man's figure stop in the shadow—calls excitedly*) Who's that?

MANNON—(*stepping forward into the moonlight*) It's I.

LAVINIA—(*with a cry of joy*) Father! (*She runs to him and throws her arms around him and kisses him.*) Oh, Father! (*She bursts into tears and hides her face against his shoulder.*)

MANNON—(*embarrassed—patting her head—gruffly*) Come! I thought I'd taught you never to cry.

LAVINIA—(*obediently forcing back her tears*) I'm sorry, Father—but I'm so happy!

MANNON—(*awkwardly moved*) Tears are queer tokens of happiness! But I appreciate your—your feeling.

CHRISTINE—(*has slowly descended the steps, her eyes fixed on him—tensely*) Is it really you, Ezra? We had just given up hope of your coming tonight.

MANNON—(*going stiffly to meet her*) Train was late. The railroad is jammed up. Everybody has got leave. (*He meets her at the foot of the steps and kisses her with a chill dignity—formally*) I am glad to see you, Christine. You are looking well. (*He steps back and stares at her—then in a voice that betrays a deep undercurrent of suppressed feeling*) You have changed, somehow. You are prettier than ever— But you always were pretty.

CHRISTINE—(*forcing a light tone*) Compliments from one's husband! How gallant you've become, Ezra! (*then solicitously*) You must be terribly tired. Wouldn't you like to sit here on the steps for a while? The moonlight is so beautiful.

LAVINIA—(*who has been hovering about jealously, now manages to worm herself between them—sharply*) No. It's too damp out here. And Father must be hungry. (*taking his arm*) Come inside with me and I'll get you something to eat. You poor dear! You must be starved.

MANNON—(*really revelling in his daughter's coddling but embarrassed before his wife—pulling his arm back—brusquely*) No, thanks! I would rather rest here for a spell. Sit down, Vinnie. (*Christine sits on the top step at center; he sits on the middle step at right; Lavinia on the lowest step at left. While they are doing this he keeps on talking in his abrupt sentences, as if he were trying to cover up some hidden uneasiness.*) I've got leave for a few days. Then I must go back and disband my brigade. Peace ought to be signed soon. The President's assassination is a frightful calamity. But it can't change the course of events.

LAVINIA—Poor man! It's dreadful he should die just at his moment of victory.

MANNON—Yes! (*then after a pause—somberly*) All victory ends in the defeat of death. That's sure. But does defeat end in the victory of death? That's what I wonder! (*They both stare at him, Lavinia in surprise, Christine in uneasy wonder. A pause.*)

CHRISTINE—Where is Orin? Couldn't you get leave for him too?

MANNON—(*hesitates—then brusquely*) I've been keeping it from you. Orin was wounded.

LAVINIA—Wounded! You don't mean—badly hurt?

CHRISTINE—(*half starting to her feet impulsively—with more of angry bitterness than grief*) I knew it! I knew when you forced him into your horrible war—! (*then sinking back— tensely*) You needn't trouble to break the news gradually, Ezra. Orin is dead, isn't he?

LAVINIA—Don't say that! It isn't true, is it, Father?

MANNON—(*curtly—a trace of jealousy in his tone*) Of course it isn't! If your mother would permit me to finish instead of jumping at conclusions about her baby—! (*with a grim, proud satisfaction*) He's no baby now. I've made a man of him. He did one of the bravest things I've seen in the war. He was wounded in the head—a close shave but it turned out only a scratch. But he got brain fever from the shock. He's all right now. He was in a rundown condition, they say at the hospital. I never guessed it. Nerves. I wouldn't notice nerves. He's always been restless. (*half turning to Christine*) He gets that from you.

CHRISTINE—When will he be well enough to come home?

MANNON—Soon. The doctor advised a few more days' rest. He's still weak. He was out of his head for a long time. Acted as if he were a little boy again. Seemed to think you were with him. That is, he kept talking to "Mother."

CHRISTINE—(*with a tense intake of breath*) Ah!

LAVINIA—(*pityingly—with a tinge of scorn in her voice*) Poor Orin!

MANNON—I don't want you to baby him when he comes home, Christine. It would be bad for him to get tied to your apron strings again.

CHRISTINE—You needn't worry. That passed—when he left me. (*Another pause. Then Lavinia speaks.*)

LAVINIA—How is the trouble with your heart, Father? I've been so afraid you might be making it out less serious than it really was to keep us from worrying.

MANNON—(*gruffly*) If it was serious, I'd tell you, so you'd be prepared. If you'd seen as much of death as I have in the past four years, you wouldn't be afraid of it. (*suddenly jumping to his feet—brusquely*) Let's change the subject! I've had my fill of death. What I want now is to forget it. (*He turns and paces up and down to the right of steps. Lavinia watches him worriedly.*) All I know is the pain is like a knife. It puts me out of commission while it lasts. The doctor gave me orders to avoid worry or any over-exertion or excitement.

CHRISTINE—(*staring at him*) You don't look well. But probably that's because you're so tired. You must go to bed soon, Ezra.

MANNON—(*comes to a stop in his pacing directly before her*

and looks into her eyes—a pause—then he says in a voice that he tries to make ordinary) Yes, I want to—soon.

LAVINIA—(*who has been watching him jealously—suddenly pulling him by the arm—with a childish volubility*) No! Not yet! Please, Father! You've only just come! We've hardly talked at all! (*defiantly to her mother*) How can you tell him he looks tired? He looks as well as I've ever seen him. (*then to her father, with a vindictive look at Christine*) We've so much to tell you. All about Captain Brant. (*If she had expected her mother to flinch at this, she is disappointed. Christine is prepared and remains unmoved beneath the searching, suspicious glance Mannon now directs at her.*)

MANNON—Vinnie wrote me you'd had company. I never heard of him. What business had he here?

CHRISTINE—(*with an easy smile*) You had better ask Vinnie! He's her latest beau! She even went walking in the moonlight with him!

LAVINIA—(*with a gasp at being defied so brazenly*) Oh!

MANNON—(*now jealous and suspicious of his daughter*) I notice you didn't mention that in your letter, young lady!

LAVINIA—I only went walking once with him—and that was before— (*She checks herself abruptly.*)

MANNON—Before what?

LAVINIA—Before I knew he's the kind who chases after every woman he sees.

MANNON—(*angrily to Christine*) A fine guest to receive in my absence!

LAVINIA—I believe he even thought Mother was flirting with him. That's why I felt it my duty to write you. You know how folks in town gossip, Father. I thought you ought to warn Mother she was foolish to allow him to come here.

MANNON—Foolish! It was downright—!

CHRISTINE—(*coldly*) I would prefer not to discuss this until we are alone, Ezra—if you don't mind! And I think Vinnie is extremely inconsiderate the moment you're home —to annoy you with such ridiculous nonsense! (*She turns to Lavinia.*) I think you've done enough mischief. Will you kindly leave us?

LAVINIA—No.

MANNON—(*sharply*) Stop your squabbling, both of you! I

hoped you had grown out of that nonsense! I won't have it in my house!

LAVINIA—(*obediently*) Yes, Father.

MANNON—It must be your bedtime, Vinnie.

LAVINIA—Yes, Father. (*She comes and kisses him—excitedly*) Oh, I'm so happy you're here! Don't let Mother make you believe I— You're the only man I'll ever love! I'm going to stay with you!

MANNON—(*patting her hair—with gruff tenderness*) I hope so. I want you to remain my little girl—for a while longer, at least. (*then suddenly catching Christine's scornful glance—pushes Lavinia away—brusquely*) March now!

LAVINIA—Yes, Father. (*She goes up the steps past her mother without a look. Behind her mother, in the portico, she stops and turns.*) Don't let anything worry you, Father. I'll always take care of you. (*She goes in. Mannon looks at his wife who stares before her. He clears his throat as if about to say something—then starts pacing self-consciously up and down at the right of steps.*)

CHRISTINE—(*forcing a gentle tone*) Sit down, Ezra. You will only make yourself more tired, keeping on your feet. (*He sits awkwardly two steps below her, on her left, turned sideways to face her. She asks with disarming simplicity*) Now please tell me just what it is you suspect me of?

MANNON—(*taken aback*) What makes you think I suspect you?

CHRISTINE—Everything! I've felt your distrust from the moment you came. Your eyes have been probing me, as if you were a judge again and I were the prisoner.

MANNON—(*guiltily*) I—?

CHRISTINE—And all on account of a stupid letter Vinnie had no business to write. It seems to me a late day, when I am an old woman with grown-up children, to accuse me of flirting with a stupid ship captain!

MANNON—(*impressed and relieved—placatingly*) There's no question of accusing you of that. I only think you've been foolish to give the gossips a chance to be malicious.

CHRISTINE—Are you sure that's all you have in your heart against me?

MANNON—Yes! Of course! What else? (*patting her hand*

embarrassedly) We'll say no more about it. (*Then he adds gruffly*) But I'd like you to explain how this Brant happened—

CHRISTINE—I'm only too glad to! I met him at Father's. Father has taken a fancy to him for some reason. So when he called here I couldn't be rude, could I? I hinted that his visits weren't welcome, but men of his type don't understand hints. But he's only been here four times in all, I think. And as for there having been gossip, that's nonsense! The only talk has been that he came to court Vinnie! You can ask anyone in town.

MANNON—Damn his impudence! It was your duty to tell him flatly he wasn't wanted!

CHRISTINE—(*forcing a contrite air*) Well, I must confess I didn't mind his coming as much as I might have—for one reason. He always brought me news of Father. Father's been sick for the past year, as I wrote you. (*then with a twitch of the lips, as if she were restraining a derisive smile*) You can't realize what a strain I've been under—worrying about Father and Orin and—you.

MANNON—(*deeply moved, turns to her and takes her hand in both of his—awkwardly*) Christine—I deeply regret—having been unjust. (*He kisses her hand impulsively—then embarrassed by this show of emotion, adds in a gruff, joking tone*) Afraid old Johnny Reb would pick me off, were you?

CHRISTINE—(*controlling a wild impulse to burst into derisive laughter*) Do you need to ask that? (*A pause. He stares at her, fascinated and stirred.*)

MANNON—(*finally blurts out*) I've dreamed of coming home to you, Christine! (*leans toward her, his voice trembling with desire and a feeling of strangeness and awe—touching her hair with an awkward caress*) You're beautiful! You look more beautiful than ever—and strange to me. I don't know you. You're younger. I feel like an old man beside you. Only your hair is the same—your strange beautiful hair I always—

CHRISTINE—(*with a start of repulsion, shrinking from his hand*) Don't! (*then as he turns away, hurt and resentful at this rebuff—hastily*) I'm sorry, Ezra. I didn't mean—I—I'm nervous tonight. (*Mannon paces to the right and stands looking at*

*the trees. Christine stares at his back with hatred. She sighs with
affected weariness and leans back and closes her eyes.*)

CHRISTINE—I'm tired, Ezra.

MANNON—(*blurts out*) I shouldn't have bothered you with
that foolishness about Brant tonight. (*He forces a strained
smile.*) But I was jealous a mite, to tell you the truth. (*He
forces himself to turn and, seeing her eyes are shut, suddenly comes
and leans over her awkwardly, as if to kiss her, then is stopped by
some strangeness he feels about her still face.*)

CHRISTINE—(*feeling his desire and instinctively shrinking—
without opening her eyes*) Why do you look at me like that?

MANNON—(*turns away guiltily*) Like what? (*uneasily*) How
do you know? Your eyes are shut. (*Then, as if some burden of
depression were on him that he had to throw off, he blurts out
heavily*) I can't get used to home yet. It's so lonely. I've got
used to the feel of camps with thousands of men around me
at night—a sense of protection, maybe! (*suddenly uneasy
again*) Don't keep your eyes shut like that! Don't be so still!
(*then, as she opens her eyes—with an explosive appeal*) God, I
want to talk to you, Christine! I've got to explain some
things—inside me—to my wife—try to, anyway! (*He sits
down beside her.*) Shut your eyes again! I can talk better. It has
always been hard for me to talk—about feelings. I never
could when you looked at me. Your eyes were always so—so
full of silence! That is, since we've been married. Not before,
when I was courting you. They used to speak then. They
made me talk—because they answered.

CHRISTINE—(*her eyes closed—tensely*) Don't talk, Ezra.

MANNON—(*as if he had determined, once started, to go on
doggedly without heeding any interruption*) It was seeing death
all the time in this war got me to thinking these things. Death
was so common, it didn't mean anything. That freed me to
think of life. Queer, isn't it? Death made me think of life.
Before that life had only made me think of death!

CHRISTINE—(*without opening her eyes*) Why are you talking of death?

MANNON—That's always been the Mannons' way of
thinking. They went to the white meeting-house on Sabbaths
and meditated on death. Life was a dying. Being born was

starting to die. Death was being born. (*shaking his head with a dogged bewilderment*) How in hell people ever got such notions! That white meeting-house. It stuck in my mind—clean-scrubbed and whitewashed—a temple of death! But in this war I've seen too many white walls splattered with blood that counted no more than dirty water. I've seen dead men scattered about, no more important than rubbish to be got rid of. That made the white meeting-house seem meaningless—making so much solemn fuss over death!

CHRISTINE—(*opens her eyes and stares at him with a strange terror*) What has this talk of death to do with me?

MANNON—(*avoiding her glance—insistently*) Shut your eyes again. Listen and you'll know. (*She shuts her eyes. He plods on with a note of desperation in his voice.*) I thought about my life—lying awake nights—and about your life. In the middle of battle I'd think maybe in a minute I'll be dead. But my life as just me ending, that didn't appear worth a thought one way or another. But listen, me as your husband being killed that seemed queer and wrong—like something dying that had never lived. Then all the years we've been man and wife would rise up in my mind and I would try to look at them. But nothing was clear except that there'd always been some barrier between us—a wall hiding us from each other! I would try to make up my mind exactly what that wall was but I never could discover. (*with a clumsy appealing gesture*) Do you know?

CHRISTINE—(*tensely*) I don't know what you're talking about.

MANNON—But you've known it was there! Don't lie, Christine! (*He looks at her still face and closed eyes, imploring her to reassure him—then blunders on doggedly*) Maybe you've always known you didn't love me. I call to mind the Mexican War. I could see you wanted me to go. I had a feeling you'd grown to hate me. Did you? (*She doesn't answer.*) That was why I went. I was hoping I might get killed. Maybe you were hoping that too. Were you?

CHRISTINE—(*stammers*) No, no, I— What makes you say such things?

MANNON—When I came back you had turned to your new baby, Orin. I was hardly alive for you any more. I saw that. I tried not to hate Orin. I turned to Vinnie, but a daughter's not a wife. Then I made up my mind I'd do my work in the world and leave you alone in your life and not care. That's why the shipping wasn't enough—why I became a judge and a mayor and such vain truck, and why folks in town look on me as so able! Ha! Able for what? Not for what I wanted most in life! Not for your love! No! Able only to keep my mind from thinking of what I'd lost! (*He stares at her—then asks pleadingly*) For you did love me before we were married. You won't deny that, will you?

CHRISTINE—(*desperately*) I don't deny anything!

MANNON—(*drawing himself up with a stern pride and dignity and surrendering himself like a commander against hopeless odds*) All right, then. I came home to surrender to you— what's inside me. I love you. I loved you then, and all the years between, and I love you now.

CHRISTINE—(*distractedly*) Ezra! Please!

MANNON—I want that said! Maybe you have forgotten it. I wouldn't blame you. I guess I haven't said it or showed it much—ever. Something queer in me keeps me mum about the things I'd like most to say—keeps me hiding the things I'd like to show. Something keeps me sitting numb in my own heart—like a statue of a dead man in a town square. (*Suddenly he reaches over and takes her hand.*) I want to find what that wall is marriage put between us! You've got to help me smash it down! We have twenty good years still before us! I've been thinking of what we could do to get back to each other. I've a notion if we'd leave the children and go off on a voyage together—to the other side of the world—find some island where we could be alone a while. You'll find I have changed, Christine. I'm sick of death! I want life! Maybe you could love me now! (*in a note of final desperate pleading*) I've got to make you love me!

CHRISTINE—(*pulls her hand away from him and springs to her feet wildly*) For God's sake, stop talking. I don't know what you're saying. Leave me alone! What must be, must be! You make me weak! (*then abruptly*) It's getting late.

MANNON—(*terribly wounded, withdrawn into his stiff soldier armor—takes out his watch mechanically*) Yes—six past eleven. Time to turn in. (*He ascends two steps, his face toward the door.*

He says bitterly) You tell me to stop talking! By God, that's funny!

CHRISTINE—(*collected now and calculating—takes hold of his arm, seductively*) I meant—what is the good of words? There is no wall between us. I love you.

MANNON—(*grabs her by the shoulders and stares into her face*) Christine! I'd give my soul to believe that—but—I'm afraid! (*She kisses him. He presses her fiercely in his arms—passionately*) Christine! (*The door behind him is opened and Lavinia appears at the edge of the portico behind and above him. She wears slippers over her bare feet and has a dark dressing-gown over her night dress. She shrinks back from their embrace with aversion. They separate, startled.*)

MANNON—(*embarrassed—irritably*) Thought you'd gone to bed, young lady!

LAVINIA—(*woodenly*) I didn't feel sleepy. I thought I'd walk a little. It's such a fine night.

CHRISTINE—We are just going to bed. Your father is tired. (*She moves up, past her daughter, taking Mannon's hand, leading him after her to the door.*)

MANNON—No time for a walk, if you ask me. See you turn in soon.

LAVINIA—Yes, Father.

MANNON—Good night. (*The door closes behind them. Lavinia stands staring before her—then walks stiffly down the steps and stands again. Light appears between the chinks of the shutters in the bedroom on the second floor to the left. She looks up.*)

LAVINIA—(*in an anguish of jealous hatred*) I hate you! You steal even Father's love from me again! You stole all love from me when I was born! (*then almost with a sob, hiding her face in her hands*) Oh, Mother! Why have you done this to me? What harm had I done you? (*then looking up at the window again—with passionate disgust*) Father, how can you love that shameless harlot? (*then frenziedly*) I can't bear it! I won't! It's my duty to tell him about her! I will! (*She calls desperately*) Father! Father! (*The shutter of the bedroom is pushed open and Mannon leans out.*)

MANNON—(*sharply*) What is it? Don't shout like that!

LAVINIA—(*stammers lamely*) I—I remembered I forgot to say good night, Father.

MANNON—(*exasperated*) Good heavens! What— (*then gently*) Oh—all right—good night, Vinnie. Get to bed soon, like a good girl.

LAVINIA—Yes, Father. Good night. (*He goes back in the bedroom and pulls the shutter closed. She stands staring fascinatedly up at the window, wringing her hands in a pitiful desperation.*)

(*Curtain*)

ACT FOUR

SCENE—*Ezra Mannon's bedroom. A big four-poster bed is at rear, center, the foot front, the head against the rear wall. A small stand, with a candle on it, is by the head of the bed on the left. To the left of the stand is a door leading into Christine's room. The door is open. In the left wall are two windows. At left, front, is a table with a lamp on it and a chair beside it. In the right wall, front, is a door leading to the hall. Further back, against the wall, is a bureau.*

None of these details can be discerned at first because the room is in darkness, except for what moonlight filters feebly through the shutters. It is around dawn of the following morning.

Christine's form can be made out, a pale ghost in the darkness, as she slips slowly and stealthily from the bed. She tiptoes to the table, left front, and picks up a light-colored dressing-gown that is flung over the chair and puts it on. She stands listening for some sound from the bed. A pause. Then Mannon's voice comes suddenly from the bed, dull and lifeless.

MANNON—Christine.

CHRISTINE—(*starts violently—in a strained voice*) Yes.

MANNON—Must be near daybreak, isn't it?

CHRISTINE—Yes. It is beginning to get gray.

MANNON—What made you jump when I spoke? Is my voice so strange to you?

CHRISTINE—I thought you were asleep.

MANNON—I haven't been able to sleep. I've been lying here thinking. What makes you so uneasy?

CHRISTINE—I haven't been able to sleep either.

MANNON—You slunk out of bed so quietly.

CHRISTINE—I didn't want to wake you.

MANNON—(*bitterly*) Couldn't you bear it—lying close to me?

CHRISTINE—I didn't want to disturb you by tossing around.

MANNON—We'd better light the light and talk a while.

CHRISTINE—(*with dread*) I don't want to talk! I prefer the dark.

MANNON—I want to see you. (*He takes matches from the*

stand by the bed and lights the candle on it. Christine hastily sits down in the chair by the table, pushing it so she sits facing left, front, with her face turned three-quarters away from him. He pushes his back up against the head of the bed in a half-sitting position. His face, with the flickering candle light on its side, has a grim, bitter expression.) You like the dark where you can't see your old man of a husband, is that it?

CHRISTINE—I wish you wouldn't talk like that, Ezra. If you are going to say stupid things, I'll go in my own room. (*She gets to her feet but keeps her face turned away from him.*)

MANNON—Wait! (*then a note of pleading in his voice*) Don't go. I don't want to be alone. (*She sits again in the same position as before. He goes on humbly.*) I didn't mean to say those things. I guess there's bitterness inside me—my own cussedness, maybe—and sometimes it gets out before I can stop it.

CHRISTINE—You have always been bitter.

MANNON—Before we married?

CHRISTINE—I don't remember.

MANNON—You don't want to remember you ever loved me!

CHRISTINE—(*tensely*) I don't want to talk of the past! (*abruptly changing the subject*) Did you hear Vinnie the first part of the night? She was pacing up and down before the house like a sentry guarding you. She didn't go to bed until two. I heard the clock strike.

MANNON—There is one who loves me, at least! (*then after a pause*) I feel strange, Christine.

CHRISTINE—You mean—your heart? You don't think you are going to be—taken ill, do you?

MANNON—(*harshly*) No! (*a pause—then accusingly*) Is that what you're waiting for? Is that why you were so willing to give yourself tonight? Were you hoping—?

CHRISTINE—(*springing up*) Ezra! Stop talking like that! I can't stand it! (*She moves as if to go into her own room.*)

MANNON—Wait! I'm sorry I said that. (*Then, as she sits down again, he goes on gloomily.*) It isn't my heart. It's something uneasy troubling my mind—as if something in me was listening, watching, waiting for something to happen.

CHRISTINE—Waiting for what to happen?

MANNON—I don't know. (*A pause—then he goes on som-*

berly.) This house is not my house. This is not my room nor my bed. They are empty—waiting for someone to move in! And you are not my wife! You are waiting for something!

CHRISTINE—(*beginning to snap under the strain—jumps to her feet again*) What would I be waiting for?

MANNON—For death—to set you free!

CHRISTINE—Leave me alone! Stop nagging at me with your crazy suspicions! (*then anger and hatred come into her voice*) Not your wife! You acted as if I were your wife—your property—not so long ago!

MANNON—(*with bitter scorn*) Your body? What are bodies to me? I've seen too many rotting in the sun to make grass greener! Ashes to ashes, dirt to dirt! Is that your notion of love? Do you think I married a body? (*then, as if all the bitterness and hurt in him had suddenly burst its dam*) You were lying to me tonight as you've always lied! You were only pretending love! You let me take you as if you were a nigger slave I'd bought at auction! You made me appear a lustful beast in my own eyes!—as you've always done since our first marriage night! I would feel cleaner now if I had gone to a brothel! I would feel more honor between myself and life!

CHRISTINE—(*in a stifled voice*) Look out, Ezra! I won't stand—

MANNON—(*with a harsh laugh*) And I had hoped my homecoming would mark a new beginning—new love between us! I told you my secret feelings. I tore my insides out for you—thinking you'd understand! By God, I'm an old fool!

CHRISTINE—(*her voice grown strident*) Did you think you could make me weak—make me forget all the years? Oh no, Ezra! It's too late! (*Then her voice changes, as if she had suddenly resolved on a course of action, and becomes deliberately taunting.*) You want the truth? You've guessed it! You've used me, you've given me children, but I've never once been yours! I never could be! And whose fault is it? I loved you when I married you! I wanted to give myself! But you made me so I couldn't give! You filled me with disgust!

MANNON—(*furiously*) You say that to me! (*then trying to calm himself—stammers*) No! Be quiet! We mustn't fight! I mustn't lose my temper! It will bring on—!

CHRISTINE—(*goading him with calculating cruelty*) Oh, no! You needn't adopt that pitiful tone! You wanted the truth and you're going to hear it now!

MANNON—(*frightened—almost pleading*) Be quiet, Christine!

CHRISTINE—I've lied about everything! I lied about Captain Brant! He is Marie Brantôme's son! And it was I he came to see, not Vinnie! I made him come!

MANNON—(*seized with fury*) You dared—! You—! The son of that—!

CHRISTINE—Yes, I dared! And all my trips to New York weren't to visit Father but to be with Adam! He's gentle and tender, he's everything you've never been. He's what I've longed for all these years with you—a lover! I love him! So now you know the truth!

MANNON—(*in a frenzy—struggling to get out of bed*) You—you whore—I'll kill you! (*Suddenly he falls back, groaning, doubled up on his left side, with intense pain.*)

CHRISTINE—(*with savage satisfaction*) Ah! (*She hurries through the doorway into her room and immediately returns with a small box in her hand. He is facing away from her door, and, even if the intense pain left him any perception, he could not notice her departure and return, she moves so silently.*)

MANNON—(*gaspingly*) Quick—medicine!

CHRISTINE—(*turned away from him, takes a pellet from the box, asking tensely as she does so*) Where is your medicine?

MANNON—On the stand! Hurry!

CHRISTINE—Wait. I have it now. (*She pretends to take something from the stand by the head of the bed—then holds out the pellet and a glass of water which is on the stand.*) Here. (*He turns to her, groaning and opens his mouth. She puts the pellet on his tongue and presses the glass of water to his lips.*) Now drink.

MANNON—(*takes a swallow of water—then suddenly a wild look of terror comes over his face. He gasps*) That's not—my medicine! (*She shrinks back to the table, the hand with the box held out behind her, as if seeking a hiding place. Her fingers release the box on the table top and she brings her hand in front of her as if instinctively impelled to prove to him she has nothing. His eyes are fixed on her in a terrible accusing glare. He tries to call for help but his voice fades to a wheezy whisper.*) Help! Vinnie!

(*He falls back in a coma, breathing stertorously. Christine stares at him fascinatedly—then starts with terror as she hears a noise from the hall and frantically snatches up the box from the table and holds it behind her back, turning to face the door as it opens and Lavinia appears in the doorway. She is dressed as at the end of Act Three, in nightgown, wrapper and slippers. She stands, dazed and frightened and hesitating, as if she had just awakened.*)

LAVINIA—I had a horrible dream—I thought I heard Father calling me—it woke me up—

CHRISTINE—(*trembling with guilty terror—stammers*) He just had—an attack.

LAVINIA—(*hurries to the bed*) Father! (*She puts her arms around him.*) He's fainted!

CHRISTINE—No. He's all right now. Let him sleep. (*At this moment Mannon, with a last dying effort, straightens up in a sitting position in Lavinia's arms, his eyes glaring at his wife and manages to raise his arm and point an accusing finger at her.*)

MANNON—(*gasps*) She's guilty—not medicine! (*He falls back limply.*)

LAVINIA—Father! (*Frightenedly she feels for his pulse, puts her ear against his chest to listen for a heartbeat.*)

CHRISTINE—Let him alone. He's asleep.

LAVINIA—He's dead!

CHRISTINE—(*repeats mechanically*) Dead? (*then in a strange flat tone*) I hope—he rests in peace.

LAVINIA—(*turning on her with hatred*) Don't you dare pretend—! You wanted him to die! You— (*She stops and stares at her mother with a horrified suspicion—then harshly accusing*) Why did he point at you like that? Why did he say you were guilty? Answer me!

CHRISTINE—(*stammers*) I told him—Adam was my lover.

LAVINIA—(*aghast*) You told him that—when you knew his heart—! Oh! You did it on purpose! You murdered him!

CHRISTINE—No—it was your fault—you made him suspicious—he kept talking of love and death—he forced me to tell him! (*Her voice becomes thick, as if she were drowsy and fighting off sleep. Her eyes half close.*)

LAVINIA—(*grabbing her by the shoulders—fiercely*) Listen! Look at me! He said "not medicine"! What did he mean?

CHRISTINE—(*keeping the hand with the poison pressed against her back*) I—I don't know.

LAVINIA—You do know! What was it? Tell me!

CHRISTINE—(*with a last effort of will manages to draw herself up and speak with a simulation of outraged feeling*) Are you accusing your mother of—

LAVINIA—Yes! I—! (*then distractedly*) No—you can't be that evil!

CHRISTINE—(*her strength gone—swaying weakly*) I don't know what—you're talking about. (*She edges away from Lavinia toward her bedroom door, the hand with the poison stretched out behind her—weakly*) I—feel faint. I must go—and lie down. I— (*She turns as if to run into the room, takes a tottering step—then her knees suddenly buckle under her and she falls in a dead faint at the foot of the bed. As her hand strikes the floor the fingers relax and the box slips out onto one of the hooked rugs.*)

LAVINIA—(*does not notice this. Startled by Christine's collapse, she automatically bends on one knee beside her and hastily feels for her pulse. Then satisfied she has only fainted, her anguished hatred immediately returns and she speaks with strident denunciation.*) You murdered him just the same—by telling him! I suppose you think you'll be free to marry Adam now! But you won't! Not while I'm alive! I'll make you pay for your crime! I'll find a way to punish you! (*She is starting to her feet when her eyes fall on the little box on the rug. Immediately she snatches it up and stares at it, the look of suspicion changing to a dreadful, horrified certainty. Then with a shuddering cry she shrinks back along the side of the bed, the box clutched in her hand, and sinks on her knees by the head of the bed, and flings her arms around the dead man. With anguished beseeching*) Father! Don't leave me alone! Come back to me! Tell me what to do!

(*Curtain*)

THE HUNTED

A Play in Five Acts

Part Two of the Trilogy
MOURNING BECOMES ELECTRA

CHARACTERS

CHRISTINE, *Ezra Mannon's widow*
LAVINIA (VINNIE), *her daughter*
ORIN, *her son, First Lieutenant of Infantry*
CAPTAIN ADAM BRANT
HAZEL NILES
PETER, *her brother, Captain of Artillery*
JOSIAH BORDEN, *manager of the shipping company*
EMMA, *his wife*
EVERETT HILLS, D.D., *of the First Congregational Church*
HIS WIFE
DOCTOR JOSEPH BLAKE
THE CHANTYMAN

SCENES

ACT ONE: Exterior of the Mannon house—a moonlight night two days after the murder of Ezra Mannon.

ACT TWO: Sitting-room in the house—immediately follows Act One.

ACT THREE: Ezra Mannon's study—immediately follows Act Two.

ACT FOUR: The stern of the clipper ship "Flying Trades," at a wharf in East Boston—a night two days later.

ACT FIVE: Same as Act One—Exterior of the Mannon house the night of the following day.

The Hunted

ACT ONE

Scene—*The same as Acts One and Three of "Homecoming"*—*Exterior of the Mannon House.*

It is a moonlight night two days after the murder of Ezra Mannon. The house has the same strange eerie appearance, its white portico like a mask in the moonlight, as it had on that night. All the shutters are closed. A funeral wreath is fixed to the column at the right of steps. Another wreath is on the door.

There is a sound of voices from inside the house, the front door is opened and Josiah Borden and his wife, Everett Hills, the Congregational minister, and his wife, and Doctor Joseph Blake, the Mannons' family physician, come out. Christine can be seen in the hall just inside the door. There is a chorus of "Good night, Mrs. Mannon," and they turn to the steps and the door is closed.

These people—the Bordens, Hills and his wife and Doctor Blake—are, as were the Ames of Act One of "Homecoming," types of townsfolk, a chorus representing as those others had, but in a different stratum of society, the town as a human background for the drama of the Mannons.

Josiah Borden, the manager of the Mannon shipping company, is shrewd and competent. He is around sixty, small and wizened, white hair and beard, rasping nasal voice, and little sharp eyes. His wife, about ten years his junior, is a typical New England woman of pure English ancestry, with a horse face, buck teeth and big feet, her manner defensively sharp and assertive. Hills is the type of well-fed minister of a prosperous small-town congregation—stout and unctuous, snobbish and ingratiating, conscious of godliness, but timid and always feeling his way. He is in the fifties, as is his wife, a sallow, flabby, self-effacing minister's wife. Doctor Blake is the old kindly best-family physician—a stout, self-important old man with a stubborn opinionated expression.

They come down the steps to the drive. Mrs. Borden and Mrs. Hills walk together toward left front until they are by the bench. There they stop to wait for the men who stand at the foot of the steps while Borden and Blake light cigars.

MRS. BORDEN—(*tartly*) I can't abide that woman!

MRS. HILLS—No. There's something queer about her.

MRS. BORDEN—(*grudgingly honest*) Still and all, I come nearer to liking her now than I ever did before when I see how broken down she is over her husband's death.

MRS. HILLS—Yes. She looks terrible, doesn't she? Doctor Blake says she will have herself in bed sick if she doesn't look out.

MRS. BORDEN—I'd never have suspected she had that much feeling in her. Not but what she hasn't always been a dutiful wife, as far as anyone knows.

MRS. HILLS—Yes. She's seemed to be.

MRS. BORDEN—Well, it only goes to show how you can misjudge a person without meaning to—especially when that person is a Mannon. They're not easy to make head or tail of. Queer, the difference in her and Lavinia—the way they take his death. Lavinia is cold and calm as an icicle.

MRS. HILLS—Yes. She doesn't seem to feel as much sorrow as she ought.

MRS. BORDEN—That's where you're wrong. She feels it as much as her mother. Only she's too Mannon to let anyone see what she feels. But did you notice the look in her eyes?

MRS. HILLS—I noticed she never said a word to anyone. Where did she disappear to all of a sudden?

MRS. BORDEN—Went to the train with Peter Niles to meet Orin. I overheard her mother talking to Lavinia in the hall. She was insisting Peter should escort her to meet the train. Lavinia must have been starting to go alone. Her mother seemed real angry about it. (*then glancing toward the men who have moved a little away from the steps and are standing talking in low tones*) Whatever are those men gossiping about? (*She calls*) Josiah! It's time we were getting home.

BORDEN—I'm coming, Emma. (*The three men join the women by the bench, Borden talking as they come.*) It isn't for me to question the arrangements she's made, Joe, but it does seem as if Ezra should have been laid out in the town hall where the whole town could have paid their respects to him, and had a big public funeral tomorrow.

HILLS—That's my opinion. He was mayor of the town and a national war hero—

BLAKE—She says it was Ezra's wish he'd often expressed

that everything should be private and quiet. That's just like Ezra. He never was one for show. He did the work and let others do the showing-off.

HILLS—(*unctuously*) He was a great man. His death is a real loss to everyone in this community. He was a power for good.

BORDEN—Yes. He got things done.

HILLS—What a tragedy to be taken his first night home after passing unharmed through the whole war!

BORDEN—I couldn't believe the news. Who'd ever suspect— It's queer. It's like fate.

MRS. HILLS—(*breaks in tactlessly*) Maybe it is fate. You remember, Everett, you've always said about the Mannons that pride goeth before a fall and that some day God would humble them in their sinful pride. (*Everyone stares at her, shocked and irritated.*)

HILLS—(*flusteredly*) I don't remember ever saying—

BLAKE—(*huffily*) If you'll excuse me, that's darn nonsense! I've known Ezra Mannon all my life, and to those he wanted to know he was as plain and simple—

HILLS—(*hastily*) Of course, Doctor. My wife entirely misunderstood me. I was, perhaps wrongly, referring to Mrs. Mannon.

BLAKE—She's all right too—when you get to know her.

HILLS—(*dryly*) I have no doubt.

BLAKE—And it's a poor time, when this household is afflicted by sudden death, to be—

HILLS—You are quite right, Doctor. My wife should have remembered—

MRS. HILLS—(*crushed*) I didn't mean anything wrong, Doctor.

BLAKE—(*mollifiedly*) Let's forget it then. (*turning to Borden—with a self-satisfied, knowing air*) As for your saying who'd ever expect it—well, you and Emma know I expected Ezra wouldn't last long.

BORDEN—Yes. I remember you said you were afraid his heart was bad.

MRS. BORDEN—I remember you did too.

BLAKE—From the symptoms Mrs. Mannon described from his letter to her, I was as certain as if I'd examined him he had angina. And I wasn't surprised neither. I'd often told Ezra he was attempting more than one man could handle and if he didn't rest he'd break down. The minute they sent for me I knew what'd happened. And what she told me about waking up to find him groaning and doubled with pain confirmed it. She'd given him his medicine—it was what I would have prescribed myself—but it was too late. And as for dying his first night home—well, the war was over, he was worn out, he'd had a long, hard trip home—and angina is no respecter of time and place. It strikes when it has a mind to.

BORDEN—(*shaking his head*) Too bad. Too durned bad. The town won't find another as able as Ezra in a hurry. (*They all shake their heads and look sad. A pause.*)

MRS. BORDEN—Well, we aren't doing anyone any good standing here. We ought to get home, Josiah.

MRS. HILLS—Yes. We must, too, Everett. (*They begin moving slowly off left, Hills going with the two women. Doctor Blake nudges Borden and motions him to stay behind. After the others disappear, he whispers with a meaning grin*)

BLAKE—I'll tell you a secret, Josiah—strictly between you and me.

BORDEN—(*sensing something from his manner—eagerly*) Of course. What is it, Joe?

BLAKE—I haven't asked Christine Mannon any embarrassing questions, but I have a strong suspicion it was love killed Ezra!

BORDEN—Love?

BLAKE—That's what! Leastways, love made angina kill him, if you take my meaning. She's a damned handsome woman and he'd been away a long time. Only natural between man and wife—but not the treatment I'd recommend for angina. He should have known better, but—well—he was human.

BORDEN—(*with a salacious smirk*) Can't say as I blame him! She's a looker! I don't like her and never did but I can imagine worse ways of dying! (*They both chuckle.*) Well, let's catch up with the folks. (*They go off, left. They have hardly disappeared before the door of the house is opened and Christine Mannon comes out and stands at the head of the steps a moment, then descends to the drive. She is obviously in a terrible state of strained nerves. Beneath the mask-like veneer of her face there are deep lines about her mouth, and her eyes burn with a feverish light. Feeling herself free from observation for a moment she lets go, her mouth twitches, her eyes look desperately on all sides, as if she longed to fly from something. Hazel Niles comes out of the house to the head of the steps. She is the same as in "Homecoming." Christine at once senses her presence behind her and regains her tense control of herself.)*

HAZEL—(*with a cheering, sympathetic air*) So here you are. I looked everywhere around the house and couldn't find you.

CHRISTINE—(*tensely*) I couldn't stay in. I'm so nervous. It's been a little harrowing—all these people coming to stand around and stare at the dead—and at me.

HAZEL—I know. But there won't be any more now. (*then a tone of eagerness breaking through in spite of herself*) Peter and Vinnie ought to be back soon, if the train isn't late. Oh, I hope Orin will surely come!

CHRISTINE—(*strangely*) The same train! It was late that night he came! Only two days ago! It seems a lifetime! I've grown old.

HAZEL—(*gently*) Try not to think of it.

CHRISTINE—(*tensely*) As if I hadn't tried! But my brain keeps on—over and over and over!

HAZEL—I'm so afraid you will make yourself sick.

CHRISTINE—(*rallying herself and forcing a smile*) There, I'm all right. I mustn't appear too old and haggard when Orin comes, must I? He always liked me to be pretty.

HAZEL—It will be so good to see him again! (*then quickly*) He ought to be such a comfort to you in your grief.

CHRISTINE—Yes. (*then strangely*) He used to be my baby, you know—before he left me. (*suddenly staring at Hazel, as if struck by an idea*) You love Orin, don't you?

HAZEL—(*embarrassed—stammers shyly*) I—I—

CHRISTINE—I am glad. I want you to. I want him to marry you. (*putting an arm around her—in a strained tone*) We'll be secret conspirators, shall we, and I'll help you and you'll help me?

HAZEL—I don't understand.

CHRISTINE—You know how possessive Vinnie is with Orin. She's always been jealous of you. I warn you she'll do everything she can to keep him from marrying you.

HAZEL—(*shocked*) Oh, Mrs. Mannon, I can't believe Vinnie—!

CHRISTINE—(*unheeding*) So you must help me. We mustn't let Orin come under her influence again. Especially now in the morbid, crazy state of grief she's in! Haven't you noticed how queer she's become? She hasn't spoken a single word since her father's death! When I talk to her she won't answer me. And yet she follows me around everywhere—she hardly leaves me alone a minute. (*forcing a nervous laugh*) It gets on my nerves until I could scream!

HAZEL—Poor Vinnie! She was so fond of her father. I don't wonder she—

CHRISTINE—(*staring at her—strangely*) You are genuinely good and pure of heart, aren't you?

HAZEL—(*embarrassed*) Oh no! I'm not at all—

CHRISTINE—I was like you once—long ago—before— (*then with bitter longing*) If I could only have stayed as I was then! Why can't all of us remain innocent and loving and trusting? But God won't leave us alone. He twists and wrings and tortures our lives with others' lives until—we poison each other to death! (*seeing Hazel's look, catches herself— quickly*) Don't mind what I said! Let's go in, shall we? I would rather wait for Orin inside. I couldn't bear to wait and watch him coming up the drive—just like—he looks so much like his father at times—and like—but what nonsense I'm talking! Let's go in. I hate moonlight. It makes everything so haunted. (*She turns abruptly and goes into the house. Hazel follows her and shuts the door. There is a pause. Then footsteps and voices are heard from off right front and a moment later Orin Mannon enters with Peter and Lavinia. One is at once struck by his startling family resemblance to Ezra Mannon and Adam Brant [whose likeness to each other we have seen in "Homecoming"]. There is the same lifelike mask quality of his face in repose, the same aquiline nose, heavy eyebrows, swarthy complexion, thick straight black hair, light hazel eyes. His mouth and chin have the same general characteristics as his father's had, but the expression of his mouth gives an impression of tense oversensitiveness quite foreign to the General's, and his chin is a refined, weakened version of the dead man's. He is about the same height as Mannon and Brant, but his body is thin and his swarthy complexion sallow. He wears a bandage around his head high up on his forehead. He carries himself by turns with a marked slouchiness or with a self-conscious square-shouldered stiffness that indicates a soldierly bearing is unnatural to him. When he speaks it is jerkily, with a strange, vague, preoccupied air. But when he smiles naturally his face has a gentle boyish charm which makes women immediately want to mother him. He wears a mustache similar to Brant's which serves to increase their resemblance to each other. Although he is only twenty, he looks thirty. He is dressed in a baggy, ill-fitting uniform—that of a first lieutenant of infantry in the Union Army.*)

ORIN—(*as they enter looks eagerly toward the house—then with bitter, hurt disappointment in his tone*) Where's Mother? I thought she'd surely be waiting for me. (*He stands staring at the house.*) God, how I've dreamed of coming home! I thought it would never end, that we'd go on murdering and being murdered until no one was left alive! Home at last! No, by God, I must be dreaming again! (*then in an awed tone*) But the house looks strange. Or is it something in me? I was out of my head so long, everything has seemed queer since I came back to earth. Did the house always look so ghostly and dead?

PETER—That's only the moonlight, you chump.

ORIN—Like a tomb. That's what mother used to say it reminded her of, I remember.

LAVINIA—(*reproachfully*) It is a tomb—just now, Orin.

ORIN—(*hurriedly—shamefacedly*) I—I'd forgotten. I simply can't realize he's dead yet. I suppose I'd come to expect he would live forever. (*A trace of resentment has crept into his tone.*) Or, at least outlive me. I never thought his heart was weak. He told me the trouble he had wasn't serious.

LAVINIA—(*quickly*) Father told you that, too? I was hoping he had. (*then turning to Peter*) You go ahead in, Peter. Say we're coming a little behind. I want to speak to Orin a moment.

PETER—Sure thing, Vinnie. (*He goes in the front door, closing it behind him.*)

ORIN—I'm glad you got rid of him. Peter is all right but—I want to talk to you alone. (*with a boyish brotherly air—putting an arm around her*) You certainly are a sight for sore eyes, Vinnie! How are you, anyway, you old bossy fuss-buzzer! Gosh, it seems natural to hear myself calling you that old nickname again. Aren't you glad to see me?

LAVINIA—(*affectionately*) Of course I am!

ORIN—I'd never guess it! You've hardly spoken a word since you met me. What's happened to you? (*Then, as she looks at him reproachfully, he takes away his arm—a bit impatiently*) I told you I can't get used to the idea of his being dead. Forgive me, Vinnie. I know what a shock it must be to you.

LAVINIA—Isn't it a shock to you, Orin?

ORIN—Certainly! What do you think I am? But—oh, I can't explain! You wouldn't understand, unless you'd been at the front. I hardened myself to expect my own death and everyone else's, and think nothing of it. I had to—to keep alive! It was part of my training as a soldier under him. He taught it to me, you might say! So when it's his turn he can hardly expect— (*He has talked with increasing bitterness. Lavinia interrupts him sharply.*)

LAVINIA—Orin! How can you be so unfeeling?

ORIN—(*again shamefaced*) I didn't mean that. My mind is still full of ghosts. I can't grasp anything but war, in which he was so alive. He was the war to me—the war that would never end until I died. I can't understand peace—his end! (*then with exasperation*) God damn it, Vinnie, give me a chance to get used to things!

LAVINIA—Orin!

ORIN—(*resentfully*) I'm sorry! Oh, I know what you're thinking! I used to be such a nice gentlemanly cuss, didn't I?—and now— Well, you wanted me to be a hero in blue, so you better be resigned! Murdering doesn't improve one's manners! (*abruptly changing the subject*) But what the devil are we talking about me for? Listen, Vinnie. There's something I want to ask you before I see Mother.

LAVINIA—Hurry then! She'll be coming right out! I've got to tell you something too!

ORIN—What was that stuff you wrote about some Captain Brant coming to see Mother? Do you mean to tell me there's actually been gossip started about her? (*then without waiting for a reply, bursting into jealous rage*) By God, if he dares come here again, I'll make him damned sorry he did!

LAVINIA—(*grimly*) I'm glad you feel that way about him. But there's no time to talk now. All I want to do is warn you to be on your guard. Don't let her baby you the way she used to and get you under her thumb again. Don't believe the lies she'll tell you! Wait until you've talked to me! Will you promise me?

ORIN—(*staring at her bewilderedly*) You mean—Mother? (*then angrily*) What the hell are you talking about, anyway? Are you loony? Honestly, Vinnie, I call that carrying your everlasting squabble with Mother a bit too far! You ought to be ashamed of yourself! (*then suspiciously*) What are you being so mysterious about? Is it Brant—?

LAVINIA—(*at a sound from inside the house*) Ssshh! (*The front door of the house is opened and Christine hurries out.*)

CHRISTINE—(*angrily to Peter who is in the hall*) Why didn't you call me, Peter? You shouldn't have left him alone! (*She calls uncertainly*) Orin.

ORIN—Mother! (*She runs down the steps and flings her arms around him.*)

CHRISTINE—My boy! My baby! (*She kisses him.*)

ORIN—(*melting, all his suspicion forgotten*) Mother! God, it's good to see you! (*then almost roughly, pushing her back and staring at her*) But you're different! What's happened to you?

CHRISTINE—(*forcing a smile*) I? Different? I don't think so, dear. Certainly I hope not—to you! (*touching the bandage on his head—tenderly*) Your head! Does it pain dreadfully? You poor darling, how you must have suffered! (*She kisses him.*) But it's all over now, thank God. I've got you back again! (*Keeping her arm around him, she leads him up the steps.*) Let's go in. There's someone else waiting who will be so glad to see you.

LAVINIA—(*who has come to the foot of the steps—harshly*) Remember, Orin! (*Christine turns around to look down at her. A look of hate flashes between mother and daughter. Orin glances at his mother suspiciously and draws away from her.*)

CHRISTINE—(*immediately recovers her poise—to Orin, as if Lavinia hadn't spoken*) Come on in, dear. It's chilly. Your poor head— (*She takes his hand and leads him through the door and closes it behind them. Lavinia remains by the foot of the steps, staring after them. Then the door is suddenly opened again and Christine comes out, closing it behind her, and walks to the head of the steps. For a moment mother and daughter stare into each other's eyes. Then Christine begins haltingly in a tone she vainly tries to make kindly and persuasive.*) Vinnie, I—I must speak with you a moment—now Orin is here. I appreciate your grief has made you—not quite normal—and I make allowances. But I cannot understand your attitude toward me. Why do you keep following me everywhere—and stare at me like that? I had been a good wife to him for twenty-three years—until I met Adam. I was guilty then, I admit. But I repented and put him out of my life. I would have been a good wife again as long as your father had lived. After all, Vinnie, I am your mother. I brought you into the world. You ought to have some feeling for me. (*She pauses, waiting for some response, but Lavinia simply stares at her, frozen and silent. Fear creeps into Christine's tone.*) Don't stare like that! What are you thinking? Surely you can't still have that insane suspicion—that I— (*then guiltily*) What did you do that night after I fainted? I—I've missed something—some medicine I take to put me to sleep— (*Something like a grim smile of satisfaction forms on Lavinia's lips. Christine exclaims frightenedly*) Oh, you did—you found—and I suppose you connect that—but don't you see how insane—to suspect—when Doctor Blake knows he died of—! (*then angrily*) I know what you've been waiting for—to tell Orin your lies and get him to go to the police! You don't dare do that on your own responsibility—but if you can make Orin— Isn't that it? Isn't that what you've been planning the last two days? Tell me! (*Then, as Lavinia remains silent, Christine gives way to fury and rushes down the steps and grabs her by the arm and shakes her.*) Answer me when I speak to you! What are you plotting? What are you going to do? Tell me! (*Lavinia keeps her body rigid, her eyes staring into her mother's. Christine lets go and steps away from her. Then Lavinia, turning her back, walks slowly and woodenly off left between the lilac clump and the house. Christine stares after her, her strength seems to leave her, she trembles with dread. From inside the house comes the sound of Orin's voice calling sharply* "Mother! Where are you?" *Christine starts and immediately by an effort of will regains control over herself. She hurries up the steps and opens the door. She speaks to Orin and her voice is tensely quiet and normal.*) Here I am, dear! (*She shuts the door behind her.*)

(*Curtain*)

ACT TWO

SCENE—*The sitting-room of the Mannon house. Like the study, but much larger, it is an interior composed of straight severe lines with heavy detail. The walls are plain plastered surfaces, light gray with a white trim. It is a bleak room without intimacy, with an atmosphere of uncomfortable, stilted stateliness. The furniture is stationed about with exact precision. On the left, front, is a doorway leading to the dining-room. Further back, on the left, are a wall table and chair and a writing desk and chair. In the rear wall, center, is the doorway giving on the main hall and the stairs. At right is a fireplace with a chimneypiece of black marble, flanked by two windows. Portraits of ancestors hang on the walls. At the rear of the fireplace, on the right, is one of a grim-visaged minister of the witch-burning era. Between fireplace and front is another of Ezra Mannon's grandfather, in the uniform of an officer in Washington's army. Directly over the fireplace is the portrait of Ezra's father, Abe Mannon, done when he was sixty. Except for the difference in ages, his face looks exactly like Ezra's in the painting in the study.*

Of the three portraits on the other walls, two are of women — Abe Mannon's wife and the wife of Washington's officer. The third has the appearance of a prosperous shipowner of Colonial days. All the faces in the portraits have the same mask quality of those of the living characters in the play.

At the left center of the room, front, is a table with two chairs. There is another chair at center, front, and a sofa at right, front, facing left.

The opening of this scene follows immediately the close of the preceding one. Hazel is discovered sitting on the chair at center, front. Peter is sitting on the sofa at right. From the hall Orin is heard calling "Mother! Where are you?" as at the close of the preceding act.

HAZEL—Where can she have gone? She's worked herself into such a state of grief I don't think she knows what she's doing.

PETER—Vinnie's completely knocked out, too.

HAZEL—And poor Orin! What a terrible homecoming this is for him! How sick and changed he looks, doesn't he, Peter?

PETER—Head wounds are no joke. He's darned lucky to have come out alive. (*They stop talking self-consciously as Orin and Christine enter from the rear. Orin is questioning her suspiciously.*)

ORIN—Why did you sneak away like that? What were you doing?

CHRISTINE—(*forcing a wan smile*) The happiness of seeing you again was a little too much for me, I'm afraid, dear. I suddenly felt as if I were going to faint, so I rushed out in the fresh air.

ORIN—(*immediately ashamed of himself—tenderly, putting his arm around her*) Poor Mother! I'm sorry— Look here, then. You sit down and rest. Or maybe you better go right to bed.

HAZEL—That's right, Orin, you make her. I've been trying to get her to but she won't listen to me.

CHRISTINE—Go to bed the minute he comes home! I should say not!

ORIN—(*worried and pleased at the same time*) But you mustn't do anything to—

CHRISTINE—(*patting his cheek*) Fiddlesticks! Having you again is just the medicine I need to give me strength—to bear things. (*She turns to Hazel.*) Listen to him, Hazel! You'd think I was the invalid and not he.

HAZEL—Yes. You've got to take care of yourself, too, Orin.

ORIN—Oh, forget me. I'm all right.

CHRISTINE—We'll play nurses, Hazel and I, and have you your old self again before you know it. Won't we, Hazel?

HAZEL—(*smiling happily*) Of course we will.

CHRISTINE—Don't stand, dear. You must be worn out. Wait. We'll make you comfortable. Hazel, will you bring me a cushion? (*Hazel gets a cushion and helps to place it behind his back in the chair at right of table. Orin's eyes light up and he grins boyishly, obviously revelling in being coddled.*)

ORIN—How's this for the comforts of home, Peter? The front was never like this, eh?

PETER—Not so you'd notice it!

ORIN—(*with a wink at Hazel*) Peter will be getting jealous! You better call Vinnie in to put a pillow behind him!

HAZEL—(*with a smile*) I can't picture Vinnie being that soft.

ORIN—(*a jealous resentment creeping into his voice*) She can be soft—on occasion. She's always coddling Father and he likes it, although he pretends—

CHRISTINE—(*turning away and restraining a shudder*) Orin! You're talking as if he were—alive! (*There is an uncomfortable silence. Hazel goes quietly back to her chair at center. Christine goes around the table to the chair opposite Orin and sits down.*)

ORIN—(*with a wry smile*) We'd all forgotten he's dead, hadn't we? Well, I can't believe it even yet. I feel him in this house—alive!

CHRISTINE—Orin!

ORIN—(*strangely*) Everything is changed—in some queer way—this house, Vinnie, you, I—everything but Father. He's the same and always will be—here—the same! Don't you feel that, Mother? (*She shivers, looking before her but doesn't answer.*)

HAZEL—(*gently*) You mustn't make your mother think of it, Orin.

ORIN—(*staring at her—in a queer tone of gratitude*) You're the same, Hazel—sweet and good. (*He turns to his mother accusingly.*) At least Hazel hasn't changed, thank God!

CHRISTINE—(*rousing herself—turns to force a smile at him*) Hazel will never change, I hope. I am glad you appreciate her. (*Hazel looks embarrassed. Christine goes on—with motherly solicitude*) Wasn't the long train trip terribly hard on you, dear?

ORIN—Well, it wasn't a pleasure trip exactly. My head got aching till I thought it would explode.

CHRISTINE—(*leans over and puts her hand on his forehead*) Poor boy! Does it pain now?

ORIN—Not much. Not at all when your hand is there. (*Impulsively he takes her hand and kisses it—boyishly*) Gosh, Mother, it feels so darned good to be home with you! (*then staring at her suspiciously again*) Let me have a good look at you. You're so different. I noticed it even outside. What is it?

CHRISTINE—(*avoiding his eyes—forcing a smile*) It's just that I'm getting old, I'm afraid, dear.

ORIN—No. You're more beautiful than ever! You're younger, too, somehow. But it isn't that. (*almost pushing her hand away—bitterly*) Maybe I can guess!

CHRISTINE—(*forces a laugh*) Younger and more beautiful! Do you hear him going on, Hazel? He has learned to be very gallant, I must say! (*Lavinia appears in the doorway at rear. She enters but remains standing just inside the doorway and keeps her eyes fixed on her mother and Orin.*)

ORIN—(*who is again looking at Hazel, breaks out harshly*) Do you remember how you waved your handkerchief, Hazel, the day I set off to become a hero? I thought you would sprain your wrist! And all the mothers and wives and sisters and girls did the same! Sometime in some war they ought to make the women take the men's place for a month or so. Give them a taste of murder!

CHRISTINE—Orin!

ORIN—Let them batter each other's brains out with rifle butts and rip each other's guts with bayonets! After that, maybe they'd stop waving handkerchiefs and gabbing about heroes! (*Hazel gives a shocked exclamation.*)

CHRISTINE—Please!

PETER—(*gruffly*) Give it a rest, Orin! It's over. Give yourself a chance to forget it. None of us liked it any more than you did.

ORIN—(*immediately shamefaced*) You're right, Peter. I'm a damned whining fool! I'm sorry, Hazel. That was rotten of me.

HAZEL—It was nothing, Orin. I understand how you feel. Really I do.

ORIN—I—I let off steam when I shouldn't. (*then suddenly*) Do you still sing, Hazel? I used to hear you singing—down there. It made me feel life might still be alive somewhere—that, and my dreams of Mother, and the memory of Vinnie bossing me around like a drill sergeant. I used to hear you singing at the queerest times—so sweet and clear and pure! It would rise above the screams of the dying—

CHRISTINE—(*tensely*) I wish you wouldn't talk of death!

LAVINIA—(*from the doorway—in a brusque commanding tone like her father's*) Orin! Come and see Father.

ORIN—(*starts up from his chair and makes an automatic motion as if to salute—mechanically*) Yes, sir. (*then confusedly*)

What the devil—? You sounded just like him. Don't do that again, for heaven's sake! (*He tries to force a laugh—then shamefacedly*) I meant to look at him the first thing—but I got talking—I'll go in right now.

CHRISTINE—(*her voice tense and strained*) No! Wait! (*angrily to Lavinia*) Can't you let your brother have a minute to rest? You can see how worn out he is! (*then to Orin*) I've hardly had a chance to say a word to you yet—and it has been so long! Stay with me a little while, won't you?

ORIN—(*touched, coming back to her*) Of course, Mother! You come before everything!

LAVINIA—(*starts to make a bitter retort, glances at Peter and Hazel, then remarks evenly*) Very well. Only remember what I said, Orin. (*She turns her back and starts to go into the hall.*)

CHRISTINE—(*frightenedly*) Vinnie! Where are you going?

LAVINIA—(*does not answer her but calls back to her brother over her shoulder*) You'll come in a little while, won't you? (*She disappears across the hall. Orin gives his mother a sidelong glance of uneasy suspicion. Christine is desperately trying to appear calm. Peter and Hazel stand up, feeling uncomfortable.*)

HAZEL—Peter, we really must be getting home.

PETER—Yes.

CHRISTINE—It was so kind of you to come.

HAZEL—(*giving her hand to Orin*) You must rest all you can now, Orin—and try not to think about things.

ORIN—You're darned kind, Hazel. It's fine to see you again—the same as ever!

HAZEL—(*delighted but pulling her hand away shyly*) I'm glad, too. Good night, Orin.

PETER—(*shakes his hand*) Good night. Rest up and take it easy.

ORIN—Good night, Peter. Thanks for meeting me.

CHRISTINE—(*goes with them to the hall*) I'm afraid this isn't a very cheerful house to visit just now—but please come soon again. You will do Orin more good than anyone, Hazel. (*The look of suspicion again comes to Orin's eyes. He sits down in the chair at left of table and stares before him bitterly. Christine returns from the hall, closing the sliding doors behind her silently. She stands for a moment looking at Orin, visibly bracing herself for the ordeal of the coming interview, her eyes full of tense calculating fear.*)

ORIN—(*without looking at her*) What's made you take such a fancy to Hazel all of a sudden? You never used to think much of her. You didn't want me going around with her.

CHRISTINE—(*coming forward and sitting across the table from him—in her gentle motherly tone*) I was selfish then. I was jealous, too, I'll confess. But all I want now is your happiness, dear. I know how much you used to like Hazel—

ORIN—(*blurts out*) That was only to make you jealous! (*then bitterly*) But now you're a widow, I'm not home an hour before you're trying to marry me off! You must be damned anxious to get rid of me again! Why?

CHRISTINE—You mustn't say that! If you knew how horribly lonely I've been without you—

ORIN—So lonely you've written me exactly two letters in the last six months!

CHRISTINE—But I wrote you much more! They must have been lost—

ORIN—I received all of Hazel's letters—and Vinnie's. It's darned funny yours should be the only ones to get lost! (*Unable to hold back any longer, he bursts forth*) Who is this Captain Brant who's been calling on you?

CHRISTINE—(*prepared for this—with well-feigned astonishment*) On me? You mean on Vinnie, don't you? (*then as Orin looks taken aback*) Wherever did you get that silly idea? Oh, of course, I know! Vinnie must have written you the same nonsense she did your father.

ORIN—She wrote him? What did he do?

CHRISTINE—Why, he laughed at it, naturally! Your father was very fond of Vinnie but he knew how jealous she's always been of me and he realized she'd tell any lie she could to—

ORIN—Oh, come on now, Mother! Just because you're always getting on each other's nerves it doesn't mean Vinnie would ever deliberately—

CHRISTINE—Oh, doesn't it though? I think you'll discover before you're much older that there isn't anything your sister will stop at—that she will even accuse me of the vilest, most horrible things!

ORIN—Mother! Honestly now! You oughtn't to say that!

CHRISTINE—(*reaching out and taking his hand*) I mean it, Orin. I wouldn't say it to anyone but you. You know that. But we've always been so close, you and I. I feel you are really—my flesh and blood! She isn't! She is your father's! You're a part of me!

ORIN—(*with strange eagerness*) Yes! I feel that, too, Mother!

CHRISTINE—I know I can trust you to understand now as you always used to. (*with a tender smile*) We had a secret little world of our own in the old days, didn't we?—which no one but us knew about.

ORIN—(*happily*) You bet we did! No Mannons allowed was our password, remember!

CHRISTINE—And that's what your father and Vinnie could never forgive us! But we'll make that little world of our own again, won't we?

ORIN—Yes!

CHRISTINE—I want to make up to you for all the injustice you suffered at your father's hands. It may seem a hard thing to say about the dead, but he was jealous of you. He hated you because he knew I loved you better than anything in the world!

ORIN—(*pressing her hand in both of his—intensely*) Do you, Mother? Do you honestly? (*Then he is struck by what she said about his father—woundedly*) I knew he had it in for me. But I never thought he went as far as to—hate me.

CHRISTINE—He did, just the same!

ORIN—(*with resentful bitterness*) All right then! I'll tell you the truth, Mother! I won't pretend to you I'm sorry he's dead!

CHRISTINE—(*lowering her voice to a whisper*) Yes. I am glad, too!—that he has left us alone! Oh, how happy we'll be together, you and I, if you only won't let Vinnie poison your mind against me with her disgusting lies!

ORIN—(*immediately uneasy again*) What lies? (*He releases her hand and stares at her, morbidly suspicious.*) You haven't told me about that Brant yet.

CHRISTINE—There's nothing to tell—except in Vinnie's morbid revengeful mind! I tell you, Orin, you can't realize how she's changed while you've been away! She's always been a moody and strange girl, you know that, but since you've gone she has worried and brooded until I really believe she went a little out of her head. She got so she'd say the most terrible things about everyone. You simply wouldn't believe it, if I told you some of the things. And now, with the shock of your father's death on top of everything, I'm convinced she's actually insane. Haven't you noticed how queerly she acts? You must have!

ORIN—I saw she'd changed a lot. She seemed strange. But—

CHRISTINE—And her craziness all works out in hatred for me! Take this Captain Brant affair, for example—

ORIN—Ah!

CHRISTINE—A stupid ship captain I happened to meet at your grandfather's who took it into his silly head to call here a few times without being asked. Vinnie thought he was coming to court her. I honestly believe she fell in love with him, Orin. But she soon discovered that he wasn't after her at all!

ORIN—Who was he after—you?

CHRISTINE—(sharply) Orin! I'd be very angry with you if it weren't so ridiculous! (She forces a laugh.) You don't seem to realize I'm an old married woman with two grown-up children! No, all he was after was to insinuate himself as a family friend and use your father when he came home to get him a better ship! I soon saw through his little scheme and he'll never call here again, I promise you that! (She laughs—then with a teasing air) And that's the whole of the great Captain Brant scandal! Are you satisfied now, you jealous goose, you?

ORIN—(penitent and happy) I'm a fool! The war has got me silly, I guess! If you knew all the hell I've been through!

CHRISTINE—It was Vinnie's fault you ever went to war! I'll never forgive her for that! It broke my heart, Orin! (then quickly) But I was going to give you an example of her insane suspicions from the Captain Brant incident. Would you believe it that she has worked it all out that because his name is Brant, he must be the son of that nurse girl Marie Brantôme? Isn't that crazy? And to imagine for a moment, if he were, he'd ever come here to visit!

ORIN—(*his face hardening*) By God, I'd like to see him! His mother brought disgrace enough on our family without—

CHRISTINE—(*frightened, shrinking from him*) Orin! Don't look like that! You're so like your father! (*then hurrying on*) But I haven't told you the worst yet. Vinnie actually accuses me—your mother—of being in love with that fool and of having met him in New York and gone to his room! I am no better than a prostitute in your sister's eyes!

ORIN—(*stunned*) I don't believe it! Vinnie couldn't!

CHRISTINE—I told you she'd gone crazy! She even followed me to New York, when I went to see your sick grandfather, to spy on me. She saw me meet a man—and immediately to her crazy brain the man was Brant. Oh, it's too revolting, Orin! You don't know what I've had to put up with from Vinnie, or you'd pity me!

ORIN—Good God! Did she tell Father that? No wonder he's dead! (*then harshly*) Who was this man you met in New York?

CHRISTINE—It was Mr. Lamar, your grandfather's old friend who has known me ever since I was a baby! I happened to meet him and he asked me to go with him to call on his daughter. (*then, seeing Orin wavering, pitifully*) Oh, Orin! You pretend to love me! And yet you question me as if you suspected me, too! And you haven't Vinnie's excuse! You aren't out of your mind! (*She weeps hysterically.*)

ORIN—(*overcome at once by remorse and love*) No! I swear to you! (*He throws himself on his knees beside her and puts his arm around her.*) Mother! Please! Don't cry! I do love you! I do!

CHRISTINE—I haven't told you the most horrible thing of all! Vinnie suspects me of having poisoned your father!

ORIN—(*horrified*) What! No, by God, that's too much! If that's true, she ought to be put in an asylum!

CHRISTINE—She found some medicine I take to make me sleep, but she is so crazy I know she thinks— (*then, with real terror, clinging to him*) Oh, Orin, I'm so afraid of her! God knows what she might do, in her state! She might even go to the police and— Don't let her turn you against me! Remember you're all I have to protect me! You are all I have in the world, dear!

ORIN—(*tenderly soothing her*) Turn me against you? She can't be so crazy as to try that! But listen. I honestly think you— You're a little hysterical, you know. That—about Father—is all such damned nonsense! And as for her going to the police—do you suppose I wouldn't prevent that—for a hundred reasons—the family's sake—my own sake and Vinnie's, too, as well as yours—even if I knew—

CHRISTINE—(*staring at him—in a whisper*) Knew? Orin, you don't believe—?

ORIN—No! For God's sake! I only meant that no matter what you ever did, I love you better than anything in the world and—

CHRISTINE—(*in an outburst of grateful joy—pressing him to her and kissing him*) Oh, Orin, you are my boy, my baby! I love you!

ORIN—Mother! (*then seizing her by the shoulders and staring into her eyes—with somber intensity*) I could forgive anything—anything!—in my mother—except that other—that about Brant!

CHRISTINE—I swear to you—!

ORIN—If I thought that damned—! (*with savage vengefulness*) By God, I'd show you then I hadn't been taught to kill for nothing!

CHRISTINE—(*full of new terror now—for Brant's life—distractedly*) For God's sake, don't talk like that! You're not like my Orin! You're cruel and horrible! You frighten me!

ORIN—(*immediately contrite and soothing, petting her*) There, there, Mother! We won't ever think about it again! We'll talk of something else. I want to tell you something. (*He sits on the floor at her feet and looks up into her face. A pause. Then he asks tenderly, taking her hand*) Did you really want me to come back, Mother?

CHRISTINE—(*has calmed herself, but her eyes are still terrified and her voice trembles*) What a foolish question, dear.

ORIN—But your letters got farther and farther between—and they seemed so cold! It drove me crazy! I wanted to desert and run home—or else get killed! If you only knew how

I longed to be here with you—like this! (*He leans his head against her knee. His voice becomes dreamy and low and caressing.*) I used to have the most wonderful dreams about you. Have you ever read a book called "Typee"—about the South Sea Islands?

CHRISTINE—(*with a start—strangely*) Islands! Where there is peace?

ORIN—Then you did read it?

CHRISTINE—No.

ORIN—Someone loaned me the book. I read it and reread it until finally those Islands came to mean everything that wasn't war, everything that was peace and warmth and security. I used to dream I was there. And later on all the time I was out of my head I seemed really to be there. There was no one there but you and me. And yet I never saw you, that's the funny part. I only felt you all around me. The breaking of the waves was your voice. The sky was the same color as your eyes. The warm sand was like your skin. The whole island was you. (*He smiles with a dreamy tenderness.*) A strange notion, wasn't it? But you needn't be provoked at being an island because this was the most beautiful island in the world—as beautiful as you, Mother!

CHRISTINE—(*has been staring over his head, listening fascinatedly, more and more deeply moved. As he stops, an agonizing tenderness for him wells up in her—with tortured longing*) Oh, if only you had never gone away! If you only hadn't let them take you from me!

ORIN—(*uneasily*) But I've come back. Everything is all right now, isn't it?

CHRISTINE—(*hastily*) Yes! I didn't mean that. It had to be.

ORIN—And I'll never leave you again now. I don't want Hazel or anyone. (*with a tender grin*) You're my only girl!

CHRISTINE—(*again with tenderness, stroking his hair—smiling*) You're a big man now, aren't you? I can't believe it. It seems only yesterday when I used to find you in your nightshirt hiding in the hall upstairs on the chance that I'd come up and you'd get one more good-night kiss! Do you remember?

ORIN—(*with a boyish grin*) You bet I remember! And what a row there was when Father caught me! And do you remember how you used to let me brush your hair and how I loved to? He hated me doing that, too. You've still got the same beautiful hair, Mother. That hasn't changed. (*He reaches up and touches her hair caressingly. She gives a little shudder of repulsion and draws away from him but he is too happy to notice.*) Oh, Mother, it's going to be wonderful from now on! We'll get Vinnie to marry Peter and there will be just you and I! (*The sliding doors in rear are opened a little and Lavinia slips silently in and stands looking at them.*)

CHRISTINE—(*immediately senses her presence—controlling a start, harshly*) What do you want? (*Orin turns to look at his sister resentfully.*)

LAVINIA—(*in a flat, emotionless voice*) Aren't you coming in to see Father, Orin?

ORIN—(*scrambling to his feet—irritably*) Oh, all right, I'll come now. (*He hurries out past Lavinia with the air of one with a disagreeable duty he wants to get over quickly and closes the door with a bang behind him. Lavinia stares at her mother a moment—then about-faces stiffly to follow him.*)

CHRISTINE—(*springs to her feet*) Vinnie! (*as Lavinia turns to face her—sharply*) Come here—please. I don't want to shout across the room. (*Lavinia comes slowly forward until she is at arm's length. Her eyes grow bleak and her mouth tightens to a thin line. The resemblance between mother and daughter as they stand confronting each other is strikingly brought out. Christine begins to speak in a low voice, coolly defiant, almost triumphant.*) Well, you can go ahead now and tell Orin anything you wish! I've already told him—so you might as well save yourself the trouble. He said you must be insane! I told him how you lied about my trips to New York—for revenge!—because you loved Adam yourself! (*Lavinia makes a movement like a faint shudder but is immediately stiff and frozen again. Christine smiles tauntingly.*) So hadn't you better leave Orin out of it? You can't get him to go to the police for you. Even if you convinced him I poisoned your father, you couldn't! He doesn't want—any more than you do, or your father, or any of the Mannon dead—such a public disgrace as a murder trial would be! For it would all come out! Everything! Who Adam is and my adultery and your knowledge of it—and your love for Adam! Oh, believe me, I'll see to it that comes out if anything ever gets to a trial! I'll show you to the world as a daughter who desired her mother's lover and then tried to get her mother hanged out of hatred and jealousy! (*She laughs tauntingly. Lavinia is trembling but her face remains hard and emotionless. Her lips open as if to speak but she closes them again. Christine seems drunk with her own defiant recklessness.*) Go on! Try and convince Orin of my wickedness! He loves me! He hated his father! He's glad he's dead! Even if he knew I had killed him, he'd protect me! (*Then all her defiant attitude collapses and she pleads, seized by an hysterical terror, by some fear she has kept hidden*) For God's sake, keep Orin out of this! He's still sick! He's changed! He's grown hard and cruel! All he thinks of is death! Don't tell him about Adam! He would kill him! I couldn't live then! I would kill myself! (*Lavinia starts and her eyes light up with a cruel hatred. Again her pale lips part as if she were about to say something but she controls the impulse and about-faces abruptly and walks with jerky steps from the room like some tragic mechanical doll. Christine stares after her—then as she disappears, collapses, catching at the table for support—terrifiedly*) I've got to see Adam! I've got to warn him! (*She sinks in the chair at right of table.*)

(*Curtain*)

ACT THREE

SCENE—*The same as Act Two of "Homecoming"—Ezra Mannon's study. His body, dressed in full uniform, is laid out on a bier draped in black which is placed lengthwise directly before the portrait of him over the fireplace. His head is at right. His mask-like face is a startling reproduction of the face in the portrait above him, but grimly remote and austere in death, like the carven face of a statue.*

The table and chairs which had been at center have been moved to the left. There is a lamp on this table. Two stands of three lighted candles are at each end of the black marble chimneypiece, throwing their light above on the portrait and below on the dead man. There is a chair by the dead man's head, at front of bier.

Orin is standing by the head of the bier, at the rear of it, stiffly-erect like a sentinel at attention. He is not looking down at his father but is staring straight before him, deep in suspicious brooding. His face in the candlelight bears a striking resemblance to that of the portrait above him and the dead man's.

The time of the opening of this act precedes by a few moments that of the end of the previous act.

ORIN—(*ashamed and guilty—bursts out angrily at himself*) Christ, I won't have such thoughts! I am a rotten swine to— Damn Vinnie! She must be crazy! (*Then, as if to distract his mind from these reflections, he turns to gaze down at his father. At the same moment Lavinia appears silently in the doorway from the hall and stands looking at him. He does not notice her entrance. He stares at his father's mask-like face and addresses it with a strange friendly mockery.*) Who are you? Another corpse! You and I have seen fields and hillsides sown with them— and they meant nothing!—nothing but a dirty joke life plays on life! (*then with a dry smile*) Death sits so naturally on you! Death becomes the Mannons! You were always like the statue of an eminent dead man—sitting on a chair in a park or straddling a horse in a town square—looking over the head of life without a sign of recognition—cutting it dead for the impropriety of living! (*He chuckles to himself with a queer affectionate amusement.*) You never cared to know me in life—but I really think we might be friends now you are dead!

LAVINIA—(*sternly*) Orin!

ORIN—(*turns to her startledly*) Damn it, don't sneak around like that! What are you trying to do, anyway? I'm jumpy enough without— (*then as she turns and locks the door behind her—suspiciously*) What are you locking the door for?

LAVINIA—I've got to talk to you—and I don't want to be interrupted. (*then sternly*) What made you say such things just then? I wouldn't believe you could have grown so callous to all feeling of respect—

ORIN—(*guilty and resentful*) You folks at home take death so solemnly! You would have soon learned at the front that it's only a joke! You don't understand, Vinnie. You have to learn to mock or go crazy, can't you see? I didn't mean it in an unkind way. It simply struck me he looks so strangely familiar—the same familiar stranger I've never known. (*then glancing at the dead man with a kindly amused smile*) Do you know his nickname in the army? Old Stick—short for Stick-in-the-Mud. Grant himself started it—said Father was no good on an offensive but he'd trust him to stick in the mud and hold a position until hell froze over!

LAVINIA—Orin! Don't you realize he was your father and he is dead?

ORIN—(*irritably*) What Grant said was a big compliment in a way.

LAVINIA—When I think of how proud of you he was when he came home! He boasted that you had done one of the bravest things he'd seen in the war!

ORIN—(*astonished—then grins with bitter mockery*) One of the bravest things he'd seen! Oh, that's too rich! I'll tell you the joke about that heroic deed. It really began the night before when I sneaked through their lines. I was always volunteering for extra danger. I was so scared anyone would guess I was afraid! There was a thick mist and it was so still you could hear the fog seeping into the ground. I met a Reb crawling toward our lines. His face drifted out of the mist toward mine. I shortened my sword and let him have the point under the ear. He stared at me with an idiotic look as if he'd sat on a tack—and his eyes dimmed and went out— (*His voice has sunk lower and lower, as if he were talking to him-*

self. He pauses and stares over his father's body fascinatedly at nothing.)

LAVINIA—(*with a shudder*) Don't think of that now!

ORIN—(*goes on with the same air*) Before I'd gotten back I had to kill another in the same way. It was like murdering the same man twice. I had a queer feeling that war meant murdering the same man over and over, and that in the end I would discover the man was myself! Their faces keep coming back in dreams—and they change to Father's face—or to mine— What does that mean, Vinnie?

LAVINIA—I don't know! I've got to talk to you! For heaven's sake, forget the war! It's over now!

ORIN—Not inside us who killed! (*then quickly—with a bitter, joking tone*) The rest is all a joke! The next morning I was in the trenches. This was at Petersburg. I hadn't slept. My head was queer. I thought what a joke it would be on the stupid Generals like Father if everyone on both sides suddenly saw the joke war was on them and laughed and shook hands! So I began to laugh and walked toward their lines with my hand out. Of course, the joke was on me and I got this wound in the head for my pains. I went mad, wanted to kill, and ran on, yelling. Then a lot of our fools went crazy, too, and followed me and we captured a part of their line we hadn't dared tackle before. I had acted without orders, of course—but Father decided it was better policy to overlook that and let me be a hero! So do you wonder I laugh!

LAVINIA—(*soothingly, coming to him and taking his arm*) You were brave and you know it. I'm proud of you, too.

ORIN—(*helplessly*) Oh, all right! Be proud, then! (*He leaves her and sprawls in the chair at left of table. She stands by the head of the bier and faces him. He says resentfully*) Well? Fire away and let's get this over! But you're wasting your breath. I know what you're going to say. Mother warned me. (*The whole memory of what his mother had said rushes over him.*) My God, how can you think such things of Mother? What the hell's got into you? (*then humoringly*) But I realize you're not yourself. I know how hard his death has hit you. Don't you think it would be better to postpone our talk until—

LAVINIA—No! (*bitterly*) Has she succeeded in convincing

you I'm out of my mind? Oh, Orin, how can you be so stupid? (*She goes to him and, grasping him by his shoulders, brings her face close to him—compellingly*) Look at me! You know in your heart I'm the same as I always was—your sister—who loves you, Orin!

ORIN—(*moved*) I didn't mean— I only think the shock of his death—

LAVINIA—I've never lied to you, have I? Even when we were little you always knew I told you the truth, didn't you?

ORIN—Yes—but—

LAVINIA—Then you must believe I wouldn't lie to you now!

ORIN—No one is saying you'd deliberately lie. It's a question of—

LAVINIA—And even if she's got you so under her thumb again that you doubt my word, you can't doubt the absolute proof!

ORIN—(*roughly*) Never mind what you call proofs! I know all about them already! (*then excitedly*) Now, listen here, if you think you're going to tell me a lot of crazy stuff about Mother, I warn you I won't listen! So shut up before you start!

LAVINIA—(*threateningly now*) If you don't, I'll go to the police!

ORIN—Don't be a damn fool!

LAVINIA—As a last resort I will—if you force me to!

ORIN—By God, you must be crazy even to talk of—!

LAVINIA—They won't think so!

ORIN—Vinnie! Do you realize what it would mean—?

LAVINIA—I realize only too well! You and I, who are innocent, would suffer a worse punishment than the guilty— for we'd have to live on! It would mean that Father's memory and that of all the honorable Mannon dead would be dragged through the horror of a murder trial! But I'd rather suffer that than let the murder of our father go unpunished!

ORIN—Good God, do you actually believe—?

LAVINIA—Yes! I accuse her of murder! (*She takes the little box she has found in Christine's room right after the murder [Act Four "Homecoming"] from the bosom of her dress and holds it out to him.*) You see this? I found it right after Father died!

ORIN—Don't be a damned lunatic! She told me all about that! It's only some stuff she takes to make her sleep!

LAVINIA—(*goes on implacably, ignoring his interruptions*) And Father knew she'd poisoned him! He said to me, "She's guilty!"

ORIN—That's all your crazy imagination! God, how can you think—? Do you realize you're deliberately accusing your own mother— It's too horrible and mad! I'll have you declared insane by Doctor Blake and put away in an asylum!

LAVINIA—I swear by our dead father I am telling you the truth! (*She puts her hand on the dead man and addresses him.*) Make Orin believe me, Father!

ORIN—(*harshly*) Don't drag him in! He always sided with you against Mother and me! (*He grabs her arm and forces the box from her hand.*) Here! Give me that! (*He slips it into his coat pocket.*)

LAVINIA—Ah! So you are afraid it's true!

ORIN—No! But I'm going to stop your damned— But I'm a fool to pay any attention to you! The whole thing is too insane! I won't talk to a crazy woman! But, by God, you look out, Vinnie! You leave Mother alone or—!

LAVINIA—(*regarding him bitterly*) Poor Father! He thought the war had made a man of you! But you're not! You're still the spoiled crybaby that she can make a fool of whenever she pleases!

ORIN—(*stung*) That's enough from you!

LAVINIA—Oh, she warned me just now what to expect! She boasted that you wouldn't believe me, and that even if you knew she'd murdered Father you would be glad because you hated him! (*then a note of entreaty in her voice*) Orin! For God's sake—here, before him!—tell me that isn't true, at least!

ORIN—(*overcome by a sense of guilt—violently defensive*) Of course, I never said that—and I don't believe she did. But Mother means a thousand times more to me than he ever did! I say that before him now as I would if he could hear me!

LAVINIA—(*with a calculated scornful contempt now*) Then if I can't make you see your duty one way, I will another! If you won't help me punish her, I hope you're not such a coward that you're willing to let her lover escape!

ORIN—(*in a tone of awakening suspicion*) Lover? Who do you mean?

LAVINIA—I mean the man who plotted Father's murder with her, who must have got the poison for her! I mean the Captain Brant I wrote you about!

ORIN—(*thickly, trying to fight back his jealous suspicion*) You lie! She told me your rotten lies—about him—about following her to New York. That was Mr. Lamar she met.

LAVINIA—So that's what she told you! As if I could mistake Lamar for Adam Brant! What a fool you are, Orin! She kisses you and pretends she loves you—when she'd forgotten you were ever alive, when all she's thought of is this low lover of hers—!

ORIN—(*wildly*) Stop! I won't stand—!

LAVINIA—When all she is thinking of right now is how she can use you to keep me from doing anything, so she'll get a chance to run off and marry him!

ORIN—You lie!

LAVINIA—She pets you and plays the loving mother and you're so blind you can't see through her! I tell you she went to his room! I followed them upstairs. I heard her telling him, "I love you, Adam." She was kissing him!

ORIN—(*grabs her by the shoulder and shakes her, forcing her to her knees—frenziedly*) Damn you! Tell me you're lying or—!

LAVINIA—(*unafraid—looking up into his eyes—coldly*) You know I'm not lying! She's been going to New York on the excuse of visiting Grandfather Hamel, but really to give herself to—!

ORIN—(*in anguish*) You lie, damn you! (*threateningly*) You dare say that about Mother! Now you've got to prove it or else—! You're not insane! You know what you're saying! So you prove it—or by God, I'll—!

LAVINIA—(*taking his hands off her shoulders and rising*) All I ask is a chance to prove it! (*then intensely*) But when I do, will you help me punish Father's murderers?

ORIN—(*in a burst of murderous rage*) I'll kill that bastard! (*in anguished uncertainty again*) But you haven't proved anything yet! It's only your word against hers! I don't believe you! You say Brant is her lover! If that's true, I'll hate her!

I'll know she murdered Father then! I'll help you punish her! But you've got to prove it!

LAVINIA—(*coldly*) I can do that very soon. She's frightened out of her wits! She'll go to see Brant the first chance she gets. We must give her that chance. Will you believe me when you find them together?

ORIN—(*torturedly*) Yes. (*then in a burst of rage*) God damn him, I'll—!

LAVINIA—(*sharply*) Ssshh! Be quiet. There's someone in the hall! (*They wait, staring at the door. Then someone knocks loudly.*)

CHRISTINE—(*Her voice comes through the door, frightened and strained.*) Orin!

ORIN—(*stammers*) God! I can't face her now!

LAVINIA—(*in a quick whisper*) Don't let her know you suspect her. Pretend you think I'm out of my mind, as she wanted you to.

CHRISTINE—Orin! Why don't you answer me? (*She tries the doorknob, and finding the door locked, her voice becomes terrified.*) Why have you locked me out? Let me in! (*She pounds on the door violently.*)

LAVINIA—(*in a whisper*) Answer her. Let her in.

ORIN—(*obeying mechanically—calls in a choked voice*) All right. I'm coming. (*He moves reluctantly toward the door.*)

LAVINIA—(*struck by a sudden idea—grasps his arm*) Wait! (*Before he can prevent it, she reaches in his pocket and gets possession of the box and puts it conspicuously on the body over the dead man's heart.*) Watch her when she sees that—if you want proof!

CHRISTINE—Open the door! (*He forces himself to open the door and steps aside. Christine almost falls in. She is in a state bordering on collapse. She throws her arms around Orin as if seeking protection from him.*) Orin! I got so afraid—when I found the door locked!

ORIN—(*controls a furious jealous impulse to push her violently away from him—harshly*) What made you afraid, Mother?

CHRISTINE—(*stammers*) Why do you look at me—like that? You look—so like—your father!

ORIN—I am his son, too, remember that!

LAVINIA—(*warningly*) Orin!

CHRISTINE—(*turning on Lavinia who stands by the head of the bier*) I suppose you've been telling him your vile lies, you—

ORIN—(*remembering his instructions, forces himself to blurt out*) She—she's out of her head, Mother.

CHRISTINE—Didn't I tell you! I knew you'd see that! (*then anxiously, keeping her eyes on Lavinia*) Did she tell you what she's going to do, Orin? I know she's plotting something—crazy! Did she threaten to go to the police? They might not believe she's crazy— (*pleading desperately, her eyes still on Lavinia*) You won't let her do anything dreadful like that, will you?

ORIN—(*feeling her guilt, stammers*) No, Mother.

CHRISTINE—(*Her eyes, which have been avoiding the corpse, now fasten on the dead man's face with fascinated horror.*) No—remember your father wouldn't want—any scandal—he mustn't be worried, he said—he needs rest and peace— (*She addresses the dead man directly in a strange tone of defiant scorn.*) You seem the same to me in death, Ezra! You were always dead to me! I hate the sight of death! I hate the thought of it! (*Her eyes shift from his face and she sees the box of poison. She starts back with a stifled scream and stares at it with guilty fear.*)

ORIN—Mother! For God's sake, be quiet! (*The strain snaps for him and he laughs with savage irony.*) God! To think I hoped home would be an escape from death! I should never have come back to life—from my island of peace! (*then staring at his mother strangely*) But that's lost now! You're my lost island, aren't you, Mother? (*He turns and stumbles blindly from the room. Lavinia reaches out stealthily and snatches up the box. This breaks the spell for Christine whose eyes have been fixed on it hypnotically. She looks wildly at Lavinia's frozen accusing face.*)

LAVINIA—(*in a cold, grim voice*) It was Brant who got you this—medicine to make you sleep—wasn't it?

CHRISTINE—(*distractedly*) No! No! No!

LAVINIA—You're telling me it was. I knew it—but I wanted to make sure. (*She puts the box back in the bosom of her dress—turns, rigid and square-shouldered, and walks woodenly from the room.*)

CHRISTINE—(*stares after her wildly, then her eyes fasten again on the dead man's face. Suddenly she appeals to him dis-*

tractedly.) Ezra! Don't let her harm Adam! I am the only guilty one! Don't let Orin—! (*Then, as if she read some answer in the dead man's face, she stops in terror and, her eyes still fixed on his face, backs to the door and rushes out.*)

(*Curtain*)

ACT FOUR

The stern section of a clipper ship moored alongside a wharf in East Boston, with the floor of the wharf in the foreground. The vessel lies with her bow and amidships off left and only the part aft of the mizzenmast is visible with the curve of the stern at right. The ship is unloaded and her black side rises nine or ten feet above the level of the wharf. On the poop deck above, at right, is the wheel. At left is the chart room and the entrance to the companionway stairs leading below to the cabin. At extreme left is the mizzenmast, the lowest yard just visible above, the boom of the spanker extending out above the deck to the right. Below the deck the portholes show a faint light from the interior of the cabin. On the wharf the end of a warehouse is at left front.

It is a night two days after Act Two—the day following Ezra Mannon's funeral. The moon is rising above the horizon off left rear, its light accentuating the black outlines of the ship.

Borne on the wind the melancholy refrain of the capstan chanty "Shenandoah," sung by a chantyman with the crew coming in on the chorus, drifts over the water from a ship that is weighing anchor in the harbor. Half in and half out of the shadow of the warehouse, the chantyman lies sprawled on his back, snoring in a drunken slumber. The sound of the singing seems to strike a responsive chord in his brain, for he stirs, grunts, and with difficulty raises himself to a sitting position in the moonlight beyond the shadow.

He is a thin, wiry man of sixty-five or so, with a tousled mop of black hair, unkempt black beard and mustache. His weather-beaten face is dissipated, he has a weak mouth, his big round blue eyes are bloodshot, dreamy and drunken. But there is something romantic, a queer troubadour-of-the-sea quality about him.

CHANTYMAN—(*listens to the singing with critical disapproval*) A hell of a chantyman that feller be! Screech owls is op'ry singers compared to him! I'll give him a taste of how "Shenandoah" ought t' be sung! (*He begins to sing in a surprisingly good tenor voice, a bit blurry with booze now and sentimentally mournful to a degree, but still managing to get full value out of the chanty.*)

"Oh, Shenandoah, I long to hear you—
A-way, my rolling river!
Oh, Shenandoah, I can't get near you—
Way—ay, I'm bound away
Across the wide Missouri!

"Oh, Shenandoah, I love your daughter
A-way, my rolling river!"

(*He stops abruptly, shaking his head—mournfully*) No good! Too drunk to do myself jestice! Pipe down, my John! Sleep it off! (*He sprawls back on his elbows—confusedly*) Where am I? What the hell difference is it? There's plenty o' fresh air and the moon fur a glim. Don't be so damn pertic'lar! What ye want anyways? Featherbed an' a grand piany? (*He sings with a maudlin zest*)

"A bottle o' wine and a bottle o' beer
And a bottle of Irish whiskey oh!
So early in the morning
The sailor likes his bottle oh!"

(*He stops and mutters*) Who'll buy a drink fur the slickest chantyman on the Western or any other damn ocean? Go to hell then! I kin buy it myself! (*He fumbles in his pants pocket.*) I had it in this pocket—I remember I put it there pertic'lar—ten dollars in this pocket— (*He pulls the pocket inside out—with bewildered drunken anger*) By Christ, it's gone! I'm plucked clean! (*He struggles to a sitting position.*) Where was I last? Aye, I remember! That yaller-haired pig with the pink dress on! Put her arm around me so lovin'! Told me how fine I could sing! (*He scrambles unsteadily to his feet.*) By Christ, I'll go back an' give her a seaboot in her fat tail that'll learn her—! (*He takes a step but lurches into the shadow and leans against the warehouse.*) Hard down! Heavy gales around Cape Stiff! All is sunk but honor, as the feller says, an' there's damn little o' that afloat! (*He stands against the warehouse, waiting for the swaying world to subside. The companionway door on the poop deck of the vessel is opened and Adam Brant comes cautiously out. He looks around him quickly with an uneasy suspicious air. He is dressed in a merchant captain's blue uniform. Satisfied that there is no one on the deck, he comes to the rail and stares expec-*

tantly up the wharf, off left. His attitude is tense and nervous and he keeps one hand in his coat pocket. The chantyman loses his balance, lurches forward, then back against the warehouse with a thump. Brant leaps back from the rail startledly, jerking a revolver from his coat pocket—then leans over the rail again and calls threateningly)

BRANT—Who's there? Come out and let me have a look at you or by God I'll shoot!

CHANTYMAN—(*stares up, startled in his turn and momentarily sobered—hastily*) Easy goes, shipmate! Stow that pistol! I'm doin' you no harm. (*He lurches out into the moonlight—suddenly pugnacious*) Not that I'm skeered o' you or your shooter! Who the hell are you to be threatenin' the life of an honest chantyman? Tryin' to hold me up, air ye? I been robbed once tonight! I'll go to the police station and tell 'em there's a robber here—

BRANT—(*hastily, with a placating air*) No harm meant. I'm skipper of this vessel and there have been a lot of waterfront thieves around here lately. I'm lacking a watchman and I've got to keep my weather eye open.

CHANTYMAN—(*again momentarily sobered—touching his forehead*) Aye—aye, sir. Mind your eye. I heer'd tell robbers broke in the "Annie Lodge's" cabin two nights back. Smashed everything and stole two hundred dollars off her skipper. Murderous, too, they be! Near beat the watchman's brains out! (*Then drunken pugnaciousness comes over him again.*) Think I'm one o' that gang, do ye? Come down out o' that and I'll show ye who's a thief! I don't give a damn if ye air a skipper! Ye could be Bully Watermann himself an' I'd not let you insult me! I ain't signed on your old hooker! You've got no rights over me! I'm on dry land, by Christ, and this is a free country and— (*His voice has risen to a shout. Brant is alarmed that this uproar will attract someone. He puts the pistol back in his pocket hastily and peers anxiously down the wharf. Then he interrupts the chantyman's tirade by a sharp command.*)

BRANT—Stow your damned jaw! Or, by the Eternal, I'll come down and pound some sense in your head!

CHANTYMAN—(*automatically reacts to the voice of authority—quietly*) Aye—aye, sir. (*then inconsequentially*) You ain't needin' a chantyman fur your next vi'ge, are ye, sir?

BRANT—I'm not sailing for a month yet. If you're still out of a job then—

CHANTYMAN—(*proudly*) You don't know me, that's plain! I'm the finest damn chantyman that ever put a tune to his lip! I ain't lookin' fur berths—they're lookin' fur me! Aye! Skippers are on'y too glad to git me! Many's a time I've seed a skipper an' mates sweatin' blood to beat work out of a crew but nary a lick could they git into 'em till I raised a tune— and then there'd be full sail on her afore ye knowed it!

BRANT—(*impatiently*) I'm not doubting your ability. But I'd advise you to turn in and sleep it off.

CHANTYMAN—(*not heeding this—sadly*) Aye, but it ain't fur long, steam is comin' in, the sea is full o' smoky teakettles, the old days is dyin', an' where'll you an' me be then? (*lugubriously drunken again*) Everything is dyin'! Abe Lincoln is dead. I used to ship on the Mannon packets an' I seed in the paper where Ezra Mannon was dead! (*Brant starts guiltily. The chantyman goes on maudlinly.*) Heart failure killed him, it said, but I know better! I've sailed on Mannon hookers an' been worked t' death and gotten swill fur grub, an' I know he didn't have no heart in him! Open him up an' you'd find a dried turnip! The old skinflint must have left a pile o' money. Who gits it, I wonder? Leave a widder, did he?

BRANT—(*harshly*) How would I know? (*changing the subject calculatingly*) What are you doing here, Chantyman? I'd expect a man with your voice would be in a saloon, singing and making merry!

CHANTYMAN—So I would! So I would! But I was robbed, sir—aye—an' I know who done it—a yaller-haired wench had her arm around me. Steer clear o' gals or they'll skin your hide off an' use it fur a carpet! I warn ye, skipper! They're not fur sailormen like you an' me, 'less we're lookin' fur sorrow! (*then insinuatingly*) I ain't got the price of a drink, that's why I'm here, sir.

BRANT—(*reaches in his pocket and tosses him down a silver dollar*) Here!

CHANTYMAN—(*fumbles around and finds the dollar*) Thank ye, sir. (*then flatteringly*) It's a fine ship you've got there, sir. Crack sail on her and she'll beat most of 'em—an' you're the kind to crack sail on, I kin tell by your cut.

BRANT—(*pleased, glancing up at his ship's lofty rig*) Aye! I'll make her go right enough!

CHANTYMAN—All you need is a good chantyman to help ye. Here's "Hanging Johnny" fur ye! (*Brant starts at this. The chantyman suddenly begins to sing the chanty "Hanging Johnny" with sentimental mournfulness.*)

> "Oh, they call me Hanging Johnny
> Away—ay—i—oh!
> They says I hangs for money
> Oh, hang, boys, hang!"

BRANT—(*harshly*) Stop that damned dirge! And get out of here! Look lively now!

CHANTYMAN—(*starting to go*) Aye—aye, sir. (*then resentfully*) I see ye ain't got much ear fur music. Good night.

BRANT—(*with exasperated relief*) Good night. (*The chantyman goes unsteadily off left, between the warehouse and the ship. He bursts again into his mournful dirge, his voice receding.*)

> "They say I hanged my mother
> Away—ay—i—oh!
> They say I hanged my mother
> Oh, hang, boys, hang!"

(*Brant, standing by the rail looking after him, mutters a curse and starts pacing up and down the deck.*) Damn that chanty! It's sad as death! I've a foreboding I'll never take this ship to sea. She doesn't want me now—a coward hiding behind a woman's skirts! The sea hates a coward! (*A woman's figure dressed in black, heavily veiled, moves stealthily out from the darkness between the ship and the warehouse, left. She sees the figure on the deck above her and shrinks back with a stifled gasp of fear. Brant hears the noise. Immediately his revolver is in his hand and he peers down into the shadows of the warehouse.*) Who's there?

CHRISTINE—(*with a cry of relief*) Adam!

BRANT—Christine! (*then quickly*) Go back to the gangplank. I'll meet you there. (*She goes back. He hurries along the deck and disappears off left to meet her. Their voices are heard and a moment later they enter on the poop deck, from left. She leans against him weakly and he supports her with his arm around her.*)

I have to bring you this way. I bolted the door to the main deck.

CHRISTINE—I was so frightened! I wasn't sure which ship! Some drunken man came along singing—

BRANT—Aye. I just got rid of him. I fired the watchman this morning so I'd be alone at night. I was hoping you'd come soon. Did that drunk see you?

CHRISTINE—No. I hid behind some boxes. (*then frightenedly*) Why have you got that pistol?

BRANT—(*grimly*) I was going to give them a fight for it— if things went wrong.

CHRISTINE—Adam!

BRANT—By God, you don't think I'll ever let them take me alive, do you?

CHRISTINE—Please, please! Don't talk of that for a moment! Only hold me close to you! Tell me you love me!

BRANT—(*harshly*) It's no time! I want to know what's happened! (*Then immediately repentant he kisses her—with rough tenderness*) Don't mind me! My nerves are gone from waiting alone here not knowing anything but what I read in the papers—that he was dead. These last days have been hell!

CHRISTINE—If you knew what they have been for me!

BRANT—There's something gone wrong! I can read that in your face! What is it, Christine?

CHRISTINE—(*falteringly*) Vinnie knows—! She came into the room when he was dying! He told her—

BRANT—(*harshly*) God! What is she going to do? (*Then, without giving her time to answer his question, he suddenly looks around uneasily.*) Christine! How did you get away? She'd suspect you weren't going to your father's now. She followed you once before—

CHRISTINE—No. It's all right. This morning Orin said his cousins, the Bradfords, had invited him and Vinnie to visit them overnight at Blackridge and he was taking Vinnie with him because he thought a change would bring her back to her senses. I've made him think she's out of her head with grief—so he wouldn't listen to her—

BRANT—(*eagerly*) And he believes that?

CHRISTINE—(*weakly*) Yes—he does—now—but I don't know how long—

BRANT—Ah!

CHRISTINE—So I told him by all means to go. It gave me the chance I wanted to come to you. They went this morning. They don't know I've gone and even after they've found out they can't prove where I went. I can only stay a little while, Adam—we've got to plan—so many things have happened I couldn't foresee—I came to warn you—

BRANT—Ssshh! Come below in the cabin! We're fools to be talking out here. (*He guides her with his arm around her through the door to the companionway stairs and closes it quietly behind them. A pause in which the singing of the crew on the ship in the harbor comes mournfully over the water. Then Orin and Lavinia come in stealthily along the deck from the left. She is dressed in black as before. He wears a long cloak over his uniform and has a slouch hat pulled down over his eyes. Her manner is cold and grim. Orin is holding in a savage, revengeful rage. They approach the cabin skylight silently. Orin bends down by it to listen. His face, in the light from the skylight, becomes distorted with jealous fury. Lavinia puts a restraining hand on his arm.*

(*The scene fades out into darkness. Several minutes are supposed to elapse. When the light comes on again, a section of the ship has been removed to reveal the interior of the cabin, a small compartment, the walls newly painted a light brown. The skylight giving on the deck above is in the middle of the ceiling. Suspended in the skylight is a ship's compass. Beneath it is a pine table with three chairs, one at rear, the other two at the table ends, left and right. On the table is a bottle of whiskey, half full, with a glass and a pitcher of water.*

(*Built against the right wall of the cabin is a long narrow couch, like a bunk, with leather cushions. In the rear wall, at right, is a door leading into the captain's stateroom. A big sideboard stands against the left wall, center. Above it, a ship's clock. Farther back is a door opening on the alleyway leading to the main deck. The companionway stairs lead down to this alleyway.*

(*There is a lighted lamp on the sideboard and a ship's lantern, also lighted, at the right end of the table.*

(*In the cabin, Brant is seated at the right of table, Christine to the rear of it. Her face looks haggard and ageing, the mouth pinched and drawn down at the corners, and her general appearance, the arrangement of her hair and clothes, has the dishevelled touch of the fugitive. She is just finishing her story of the murder and the events following it. He is listening tensely.*

(*On the deck above, Orin and Lavinia are discovered as before, with Orin bending down by the transom, listening.*)

CHRISTINE—When he was dying he pointed at me and told her I was guilty! And afterwards she found the poison—

BRANT—(*springing to his feet*) For God's sake, why didn't you—

CHRISTINE—(*pitifully*) I fainted before I could hide it! And I had planned it all so carefully. But how could I foresee that she would come in just at that moment? And how could I know he would talk to me the way he did? He drove me crazy! He kept talking of death! He was torturing me! I only wanted him to die and leave me alone!

BRANT—(*his eyes lighting up with savage satisfaction*) He knew before he died whose son I was, you said? By God, I'll bet that maddened him!

CHRISTINE—(*repeats pitifully*) I'd planned it so carefully— but something made things happen!

BRANT—(*overcome by gloomy dejection, sinks down on his chair again*) I knew it! I've had a feeling in my bones! It serves me right, what has happened and is to happen! It wasn't that kind of revenge I had sworn on my mother's body! I should have done as I wanted—fought with Ezra Mannon as two men fight for love of a woman! (*with bitter self-contempt*) I have my father's rotten coward blood in me, I think! Aye!

CHRISTINE—Adam! You make me feel so guilty!

BRANT—(*rousing himself—shamefacedly*) I didn't mean to blame you, Christine. (*then harshly*) It's too late for regrets now, anyway. We've got to think what to do.

CHRISTINE—Yes! I'm so terrified of Vinnie! Oh, Adam, you must promise me to be on your guard every minute! If she convinces Orin you are my lover— Oh, why can't we go away, Adam? Once we're out of her reach, she can't do anything.

BRANT—The "Flying Trades" won't be sailing for a month or more. We can't get cargo as soon as the owners thought.

CHRISTINE—Can't we go on another ship—as passengers—to the East—we could be married out there—

BRANT—(*gloomily*) But everyone in the town would know you were gone. It would start suspicion—

CHRISTINE—No. Orin and Vinnie would lie to people. They'd have to for their own sakes. They'd say I was in New York with my father. Oh, Adam, it's the only thing we can do! If we don't get out of Vinnie's reach right away I know something horrible will happen!

BRANT—(*dejectedly*) Aye. I suppose it's the only way out for us now. The "Atlantis" is sailing on Friday for China. I'll arrange with her skipper to give us passage—and keep his mouth shut. She sails at daybreak Friday. You'd better meet me here Thursday night. (*then with an effort*) I'll write Clark and Dawson tonight they'll have to find another skipper for the "Flying Trades."

CHRISTINE—(*noticing the hurt in his tone—miserably*) Poor Adam! I know how it hurts you to give up your ship.

BRANT—(*rousing himself guiltily—pats her hand—with gruff tenderness*) There are plenty of ships—but there is only one you, Christine!

CHRISTINE—I feel so guilty! I've brought you nothing but misfortune!

BRANT—You've brought love—and the rest is only the price. It's worth it a million times! You're all mine now, anyway! (*He hugs her to him, staring over her head with sad blank eyes.*)

CHRISTINE—(*her voice trembling*) But I'm afraid I'm not much to boast about having—now. I've grown old in the past few days. I'm ugly. But I'll make myself beautiful again—for you—! I'll make up to you for everything! Try not to regret your ship too much, Adam!

BRANT—(*gruffly*) Let's not talk of her any more. (*then forcing a wry smile*) I'll give up the sea. I think it's through with me now, anyway! The sea hates a coward.

CHRISTINE—(*trying pitifully to cheer him*) Don't talk like that! You have me, Adam! You have me! And we will be happy—once we're safe on your Blessed Islands! (*then suddenly, with a little shudder*) It's strange. Orin was telling me of an island— (*On the deck above, Orin, who has bent closer to the transom, straightens up with a threatening movement. Lavinia grips his arm, restraining him.*)

BRANT—(*with a bitter, hopeless yearning*) Aye—the Blessed Isles— Maybe we can still find happiness and forget! (*then strangely, as if to himself*) I can see them now—so close—and a million miles away! The warm earth in the moonlight, the trade winds rustling the coco palms, the surf on the barrier reef singing a croon in your ears like a lullaby! Aye! There's peace, and forgetfulness for us there—if we can ever find those islands now!

CHRISTINE—(*desperately*) We will find them! We will! (*She kisses him. A pause. Suddenly she glances frightenedly at the clock.*) Look at the time! I've got to go, Adam!

BRANT—For the love of God, watch out for Vinnie. If anything happened to you now—!

CHRISTINE—Nothing will happen to me. But you must be on your guard in case Orin— Good-bye, my lover! I must go! I must! (*She tears herself from his arms but immediately throws herself in them again—terrifiedly*) Oh! I feel so strange—so sad—as if I'd never see you again! (*She begins to sob hysterically.*) Oh, Adam, tell me you don't regret! Tell me we're going to be happy! I can't bear this horrible feeling of despair!

BRANT—Of course we'll be happy! Come now! It's only a couple of days. (*They start for the door.*) We'll go by the main deck. It's shorter. I'll walk to the end of the wharf with you. I won't go further. We might be seen.

CHRISTINE—Then we don't have to say good-bye for a few minutes yet! Oh, thank God! (*They go out to the alleyway, Brant closing the door behind him. A pause. On the deck above Orin pulls a revolver from under his cloak and makes a move, as if to rush off left down to the main deck after them. Lavinia has been dreading this and throws herself in his way, grasping his arm.*)

ORIN—(*in a furious whisper*) Let me go!

LAVINIA—(*struggling with him*) No! Be quiet! Ssshh! I hear them on the main deck! Quick! Come to his cabin! (*She urges him to the companionway door, gets him inside and shuts the door behind them. A moment later the door on the left of the cabin below is opened and they enter.*)

LAVINIA—He's going to the end of the wharf. That gives us a few minutes. (*grimly*) You wanted proof! Well, are you satisfied now?

ORIN—Yes! God damn him! Death is too good for him! He ought to be—

LAVINIA—(*sharply commanding*) Orin! Remember you promised not to lose your head. You've got to do everything exactly as we planned it, so there'll be no suspicion about us. There would be no justice if we let ourselves—

ORIN—(*impatiently*) You've said all that before! Do you think I'm a fool? I'm not anxious to be hanged—for that skunk! (*then with bitter anguish*) I heard her asking him to kiss her! I heard her warn him against me! (*He gives a horrible chuckle.*) And my island I told her about—which was she and I—she wants to go there—with him! (*then furiously*) Damn you! Why did you stop me? I'd have shot his guts out in front of her!

LAVINIA—(*scornfully*) Outside on deck where the shot would be sure to be heard? We'd have been arrested—and then I'd have to tell the truth to save us. She'd be hanged, and even if we managed to get off, our lives would be ruined! The only person to come off lucky would be Brant! He could die happy, knowing he'd revenged himself on us more than he ever dared hope! Is that what you want?

ORIN—(*sullenly*) No.

LAVINIA—Then don't act like a fool again. (*looks around the cabin calculatingly—then in a tone of command*) Go and hide outside. He won't see you when he passes along the alleyway in the dark. He'll come straight in here. That's the time for you—

ORIN—(*grimly*) You needn't tell me what to do. I've had a thorough training at this game—thanks to you and Father.

LAVINIA—Quick! Go out now! He won't be long!

ORIN—(*goes to the door—then quickly*) I hear him coming. (*He slips out silently. She hurriedly hides herself by the sideboard at left, front. A moment later Brant appears in the doorway and stands just inside it blinking in the light. He looks around the cabin sadly.*)

BRANT—(*huskily*) So it's good-bye to you, "Flying Trades"! And you're right! I wasn't man enough for you!

(*Orin steps through the door and with the pistol almost against Brant's body fires twice. Brant pitches forward to the floor by the table, rolls over, twitches a moment on his back and lies still. Orin*) *springs forward and stands over the body, his pistol aimed down at it, ready to fire again.*)

LAVINIA—(*stares fascinatedly at Brant's still face*) Is he— dead?

ORIN—Yes.

LAVINIA—(*sharply*) Don't stand there! Where's the chisel you brought? Smash open everything in his stateroom. We must make it look as if thieves killed him, remember! Take anything valuable! We can sink it overboard afterwards! Hurry! (*Orin puts his revolver on the table and takes a chisel that is stuck in his belt under his cloak and goes into the stateroom. A moment later there is the sound of splintering wood as he pries open a drawer.*)

LAVINIA—(*goes slowly to the body and stands looking down into Brant's face. Her own is frozen and expressionless. A pause. Orin can be heard in the stateroom prying open Brant's desk and scattering the contents of drawers around. Finally Lavinia speaks to the corpse in a grim bitter tone.*) How could you love that vile old woman so? (*She throws off this thought—harshly*) But you're dead! It's ended! (*She turns away from him resolutely— then suddenly turns back and stands stiffly upright and grim beside the body and prays coldly, as if carrying out a duty*) May God find forgiveness for your sins! May the soul of our cousin, Adam Mannon, rest in peace! (*Orin comes in from the stateroom and overhears the last of her prayer.*)

ORIN—(*harshly*) Rest in hell, you mean! (*He comes to her.*) I've pried open everything I could find.

LAVINIA—Then come along. Quick. There's your pistol. Don't forget that. (*She goes to the door.*)

ORIN—(*putting it in his pocket*) We've got to go through his pockets to make everything look like a burglary. (*He quickly turns Brant's pockets inside out and puts the revolver he finds, along with bills and coins, watch and chain, knife, etc., into his own.*) I'll sink these overboard from the dock, along with what was in his stateroom. (*Having finished this, he still remains stooping over the body and stares into Brant's face, a queer fascinated expression in his eyes.*)

LAVINIA—(*uneasily*) Orin!

ORIN—By God, he does look like Father!

LAVINIA—No! Come along!

ORIN—(*as if talking to himself*) This is like my dream. I've killed him before—over and over.

LAVINIA—Orin!

ORIN—Do you remember me telling you how the faces of the men I killed came back and changed to Father's face and finally became my own? (*He smiles grimly.*) He looks like me, too! Maybe I've committed suicide!

LAVINIA—(*frightenedly—grabbing his arm*) Hurry! Someone may come!

ORIN—(*not heeding her, still staring at Brant—strangely*) If I had been he I would have done what he did! I would have loved her as he loved her—and killed Father too—for her sake!

LAVINIA—(*tensely—shaking him by the arm*) Orin, for God's sake, will you stop talking crazy and come along? Do you want us to be found here? (*She pulls him away forcibly.*)

ORIN—(*with a last look at the dead man*) It's queer! It's a rotten dirty joke on someone! (*He lets her hustle him out to the alleyway.*)

(*Curtain*)

ACT FIVE

SCENE—*The same as Act Three of "Homecoming"—exterior of the Mannon house. It is the following night. The moon has just risen. The right half of the house is in the black shadow cast by the pine trees but the moonlight falls full on the part to the left of the doorway. The door at center is open and there is a light in the hall behind. All the shutters of the windows are closed.*

Christine is discovered walking back and forth on the drive before the portico, passing from moonlight into the shadow of the pines and back again. She is in a frightful state of tension, unable to keep still.

She sees someone she is evidently expecting approaching the house from up the drive, off left, and she hurries down as far as the bench to meet her.

HAZEL—(*enters from left—with a kindly smile*) Here I am! Seth brought your note and I hurried right over.

CHRISTINE—(*kissing her—with unnatural effusiveness*) I'm so glad you've come! I know I shouldn't have bothered you.

HAZEL—It's no bother at all, Mrs. Mannon. I'm only too happy to keep you company.

CHRISTINE—I was feeling so terribly sad—and nervous here. I had let Hannah and Annie have the night off. I'm all alone. (*She sits on the bench.*) Let's sit out here. I can't bear it in the house. (*Hazel sits beside her.*)

HAZEL—(*pityingly*) I know. It must be terribly lonely for you. You must miss him so much.

CHRISTINE—(*with a shudder*) Please don't talk about— He is buried! He is gone!

HAZEL—(*gently*) He is at peace, Mrs. Mannon.

CHRISTINE—(*with bitter mockery*) I was like you once! I believed in heaven! Now I know there is only hell!

HAZEL—Ssshh! You mustn't say that.

CHRISTINE—(*rousing herself—forcing a smile*) I'm not fit company for a young girl, I'm afraid. You should have youth and beauty and freedom around you. I'm old and ugly and haunted by death! (*then, as if to herself—in a low desperate tone*) I can't let myself get ugly! I can't!

997

HAZEL—You're only terribly worn out. You ought to try and sleep.

CHRISTINE—I don't believe there's such a thing on this earth as sleep! It's only in the earth one sleeps! One must feel so at peace—at last—with all one's fears ended! (*then forcing a laugh*) Good heavens, what a bore it must be for you, listening to my gloomy thoughts! I honestly didn't send for you to— I wanted to ask if you or Peter had heard anything from Orin and Vinnie.

HAZEL—(*surprised*) Why, no. We haven't seen them since the funeral.

CHRISTINE—(*forcing a smile*) They seem to have deserted me. (*then quickly*) I mean they should have been home before this. I can't imagine what's keeping them. They went to Blackridge to stay overnight at the Bradfords'.

HAZEL—Then there's nothing to worry about. But I don't see how they could leave you alone—just now.

CHRISTINE—Oh, that part is all right. I urged them to go. They left soon after the funeral, and afterwards I thought it would be a good opportunity for me to go to New York and see my father. He's sick, you know, but I found him so much better I decided to come home again last night. I expected Vinnie and Orin back this noon, but here it's night and no sign of them. I—I must confess I'm worried—and frightened. You can't know the horror of being all night—alone in that house! (*She glances at the house behind her with a shudder.*)

HAZEL—Would it help you if I stayed with you tonight— I mean if they don't come?

CHRISTINE—(*eagerly*) Oh, would you? (*Hysterical tears come to her eyes. She kisses Hazel with impulsive gratitude.*) I can't tell you how grateful I'd be! You're so good! (*then forcing a laugh*) But it's an imposition to ask you to face such an ordeal. I can't stay still. I'm terrified at every sound. You would have to sit up.

HAZEL—Losing a little sleep won't hurt me any.

CHRISTINE—I mustn't sleep! If you see me falling asleep you must promise to wake me!

HAZEL—But it's just what you need.

CHRISTINE—Yes—afterwards—but not now. I must keep

awake. (*in tense desperation*) I wish Orin and Vinnie would come!

HAZEL—(*worriedly*) Perhaps Orin got so sick he wasn't able to. Oh, I hope that isn't it! (*then getting up*) If I'm going to stay all night I'll have to run home and tell Mother, so she won't worry.

CHRISTINE—Yes—do. (*then frightenedly*) You won't be long, will you? I'm afraid—to be alone.

HAZEL—(*kisses her—pityingly*) I'll be as quick as I possibly can. (*She walks down the drive, off left, waving her hand as she disappears. Christine stands by the bench—then begins to pace back and forth again.*)

CHRISTINE—(*her eyes caught by something down the drive— in a tense whisper*) She's met someone by the gate! Oh, why am I so afraid! (*She turns, seized by panic, and runs to the house—then stops at the top of the steps and faces around, leaning against a column for support.*) Oh, God, I'm afraid to know! (*A moment later Orin and Lavinia come up the drive from the left. Lavinia is stiffly square-shouldered, her eyes hard, her mouth grim and set. Orin is in a state of morbid excitement. He carries a newspaper in his hand.*)

ORIN—(*speaking to Vinnie as they enter—harshly*) You let me do the talking! I want to be the one— (*He sees his mother—startledly*) Mother! (*then with vindictive mockery*) Ah! So this time at least you are waiting to meet me when I come home!

CHRISTINE—(*stammers*) Orin! What kept you—?

ORIN—We just met Hazel. She said you were terribly frightened at being alone here. That is strange—when you have the memory of Father for company!

CHRISTINE—You—you stayed all this time—at the Bradfords'?

ORIN—We didn't go to the Bradfords'!

CHRISTINE—(*stupidly*) You didn't go—to Blackridge?

ORIN—We took the train there but we decided to stay right on and go to Boston instead.

CHRISTINE—(*terrifiedly*) To—Boston—?

ORIN—And in Boston we waited until the evening train got in. We met that train.

CHRISTINE—Ah!

ORIN—We had an idea you would take advantage of our being in Blackridge to be on it—and you were! And we followed you when you called on your lover in his cabin!

CHRISTINE—(*with a pitiful effort at indignation*) Orin! How dare you talk—! (*then brokenly*) Orin! Don't look at me like that! Tell me—

ORIN—Your lover! Don't lie! You've lied enough, Mother! I was on deck, listening! What would you have done if you had discovered me? Would you have gotten your lover to murder me, Mother? I heard you warning him against me! But your warning was no use!

CHRISTINE—(*chokingly*) What—? Tell me—!

ORIN—I killed him!

CHRISTINE—(*with a cry of terror*) Oh—oh! I knew! (*then clutching at Orin*) No—Orin! You—you're just telling me that—to punish me, aren't you? You said you loved me— you'd protect me—protect your mother—you couldn't murder—!

ORIN—(*harshly, pushing her away*) You could murder Father, couldn't you? (*He thrusts the newspaper into her hands, pointing to the story.*) Here! Read that, if you don't believe me! We got it in Boston to see whom the police would suspect. It's only a few lines. Brant wasn't important—except to you! (*She looks at the paper with fascinated horror. Then she lets it slip through her fingers, sinks down on the lowest step and begins to moan to herself, wringing her hands together in stricken anguish. Orin turns from her and starts to pace up and down by the steps. Lavinia stands at the left of the steps, rigid and erect, her face mask-like.*)

ORIN—(*harshly*) They think exactly what we planned they should think—that he was killed by waterfront thieves. There's nothing to connect us with his death! (*He stops by her. She stares before her, wringing her hands and moaning. He blurts out*) Mother! Don't moan like that! (*She gives no sign of having heard him. He starts to pace up and down again—with savage resentment*) Why do you grieve for that servant's bastard? I know he was the one who planned Father's murder! You couldn't have done that! He got you under his influence to revenge himself! He hypnotized you! I saw you weren't yourself the minute I got home, remember? How else could you ever have imagined you loved that low swine! How else could you ever have said the things— (*He stops before her.*) I heard you planning to go with him to the island I had told you about—our island—that was you and I! (*He starts to pace up and down again distractedly. She remains as before except that her moaning has begun to exhaust itself. Orin stops before her again and grasps her by the shoulders, kneeling on the steps beside her—desperately pleading now*) Mother! Don't moan like that! You're still under his influence! But you'll forget him! I'll make you forget him! I'll make you happy! We'll leave Vinnie here and go away on a long voyage—to the South Seas—

LAVINIA—(*sharply*) Orin!

ORIN—(*not heeding her, stares into his mother's face. She has stopped moaning, the horror in her eyes is dying into blankness, the expression of her mouth congealing to one of numbed grief. She gives no sign of having heard him. Orin shakes her—desperately*) Mother! Don't you hear me? Why won't you speak to me? Will you always love him? Do you hate me now? (*He sinks on his knees before her.*) Mother! Answer me! Say you forgive me!

LAVINIA—(*with bitter scorn*) Orin! After all that's happened, are you becoming her crybaby again? (*Orin starts and gets to his feet, staring at her confusedly, as if he had forgotten her existence. Lavinia speaks again in curt commanding tone that recalls her father.*) Leave her alone! Go in the house! (*as he hesitates—more sharply*) Do you hear me? March!

ORIN—(*automatically makes a confused motion of military salute—vaguely*) Yes, sir. (*He walks mechanically up the steps—gazing up at the house—strangely*) Why are the shutters still closed? Father has gone. We ought to let in the moonlight. (*He goes into the house. Lavinia comes and stands beside her mother. Christine continues to stare blankly in front of her. Her face has become a tragic death mask. She gives no sign of being aware of her daughter's presence. Lavinia regards her with bleak, condemning eyes.*)

LAVINIA—(*finally speaks sternly*) He paid the just penalty for his crime. You know it was justice. It was the only way true justice could be done. (*Her mother starts. The words shatter her merciful numbness and awaken her to agony again. She springs to her feet and stands glaring at her daughter with a terrible look in which a savage hatred fights with horror and fear. In spite of her frozen self-control, Lavinia recoils before this. Keeping her eyes on her, Christine shrinks backward up the steps until she stands at the top between the two columns of the portico before the front door. Lavinia suddenly makes a motion, as if to hold her back. She calls shakenly as if the words were wrung out of her against her will)* Mother! What are you going to do? You can live!

CHRISTINE—*(glares at her as if this were the last insult—with strident mockery)* Live! *(She bursts into shrill laughter, stops it abruptly, raises her hands between her face and her daughter and pushes them out in a gesture of blotting Lavinia forever from her sight. Then she turns and rushes into the house. Lavinia again makes a movement to follow her. But she immediately fights down this impulse and turns her back on the house determinedly, standing square-shouldered and stiff like a grim sentinel in black.)*

LAVINIA—*(implacably to herself)* It is justice! *(From the street, away off right front, Seth's thin wraith of a baritone is raised in his favorite mournful "Shenandoah," as he nears the gateway to the drive, returning from his nightly visit to the saloon.)*

> "Oh, Shenandoah, I long to hear you
> A-way, my rolling river!
> Oh, Shenandoah, I can't get near you
> Way—ay, I'm bound away
> Across the wide—"

(There is the sharp report of a pistol from the left ground floor of the house where Ezra Mannon's study is. Lavinia gives a shuddering gasp, turns back to the steps, starts to go up them, stops again and stammers shakenly) It is justice! It is your justice, Father! *(Orin's voice is heard calling from the sitting-room at right* "What's that"! *A door slams. Then Orin's horrified cry comes from the study as he finds his mother's body, and a moment later he rushes out frantically to Lavinia.)*

ORIN—Vinnie! *(He grabs her arm and stammers distractedly)* Mother—shot herself—Father's pistol—get a doctor— *(then with hopeless anguish)* No—it's too late—she's dead! *(then wildly)* Why—why did she, Vinnie? *(with tortured self-accusation)* I drove her to it! I wanted to torture her! She couldn't forgive me! Why did I have to boast about killing him? Why—?

LAVINIA—(*frightenedly, puts her hand over his mouth*) Be quiet!

ORIN—(*tears her hand away—violently*) Why didn't I let her believe burglars killed him? She wouldn't have hated me then! She would have forgotten him! She would have turned to me! (*in a final frenzy of self-denunciation*) I murdered her!

LAVINIA—(*grabbing him by the shoulders*) For God's sake, will you be quiet?

ORIN—(*frantically—trying to break away from her*) Let me go! I've got to find her! I've got to make her forgive me! I—! (*He suddenly breaks down and weeps in hysterical anguish. Lavinia puts her arm around him soothingly. He sobs despairingly.*) But she's dead— She's gone—how can I ever get her to forgive me now?

LAVINIA—(*soothingly*) Ssshh! Ssshh! You have me, haven't you? I love you. I'll help you to forget. (*He turns to go back into the house, still sobbing helplessly. Seth's voice comes from the drive, right, close at hand:*

> "She's far across the stormy water
> Way-ay, I'm bound away—"

He enters right, front. Lavinia turns to face him.)

SETH—(*approaching*) Say, Vinnie, did you hear a shot—?

LAVINIA—(*sharply*) I want you to go for Doctor Blake. Tell him Mother has killed herself in a fit of insane grief over Father's death. (*then as he stares, dumbfounded and wondering, but keeping his face expressionless—more sharply*) Will you remember to tell him that?

SETH—(*slowly*) Ayeh. I'll tell him, Vinnie—anything you say. (*His face set grimly, he goes off, right front. Lavinia turns and, stiffly erect, her face stern and mask-like, follows Orin into the house.*)

(*Curtain*)

THE HAUNTED

A Play in Four Acts

Part Three of the Trilogy

MOURNING BECOMES ELECTRA

CHARACTERS

LAVINIA MANNON
ORIN, *her brother*
PETER NILES
HAZEL, *his sister*
SETH
AMOS AMES
IRA MACKEL
JOE SILVA
ABNER SMALL

SCENES

ACT ONE: SCENE ONE—Exterior of the Mannon house—
an evening in the summer of 1866.

ACT ONE: SCENE TWO—Sitting-room in the house
(immediately follows Scene One).

ACT TWO: The study—an evening a month later.

ACT THREE: The sitting-room (immediately follows Act
Two).

ACT FOUR: Same as Act One, Scene One—Exterior of the
Mannon house—a late afternoon three days later.

The Haunted

ACT ONE

SCENE ONE

Exterior of the Mannon house (as in the two preceding plays) on an evening of a clear day in summer a year later. It is shortly after sunset but the afterglow in the sky still bathes the white temple portico in a crimson light. The columns cast black bars of shadow on the wall behind them. All the shutters are closed and the front door is boarded up, showing that the house is unoccupied.

A group of five men is standing on the drive by the bench at left, front. Seth Beckwith is there and Amos Ames, who appeared in the first Act of "Homecoming." The others are Abner Small, Joe Silva and Ira Mackel.

These four—Ames, Small, Silva and Mackel—are, as were the townsfolk of the first acts of "Homecoming" and "The Hunted," a chorus of types representing the town as a human background for the drama of the Mannons.

Small is a wiry little old man of sixty-five, a clerk in a hardware store. He has white hair and a wispy goat's beard, bright inquisitive eyes, ruddy complexion, and a shrill rasping voice. Silva is a Portuguese fishing captain—a fat, boisterous man, with a hoarse bass voice. He has matted gray hair and a big grizzled mustache. He is sixty. Mackel, who is a farmer, hobbles along with the aid of a cane. His shiny wrinkled face is oblong with a square white chin whisker. He is bald. His yellowish brown eyes are sly. He talks in a drawling wheezy cackle.

All five are drunk. Seth has a stone jug in his hand. There is a grotesque atmosphere of boys out on a forbidden lark about these old men.

SMALL—God A'mighty, Seth, be you glued to that jug?
MACKEL—Gol durn him, he's gittin' stingy in his old age!
SILVA—(*bursts into song*)

> "A bottle of beer and a bottle of gin
> And a bottle of Irish whiskey oh!
> So early in the morning
> A sailor likes his bottle oh!"

AMES—(*derisively*) You like your bottle 'ceptin' when your old woman's got her eye on ye!

SILVA—She's visitin' her folks to New Bedford. What the hell I care! (*bursts into song again*)

> "Hurrah! Hurrah! I sing the jubilee
> Hurrah! Hurrah! Her folks has set me free!"

AMES—(*slapping him on the back*) God damn you, Joe, you're gittin' to be a poet! (*They all laugh.*)

SMALL—God A'mighty, Seth, ain't ye got no heart in ye? Watch me perishin' fur lack o' whiskey and ye keep froze to that jug! (*He reaches out for it.*)

SETH—No, ye don't! I'm onto your game! (*with a wink at the others*) He's aimin' to git so full of Injun courage he wouldn't mind if a ghost sot on his lap! Purty slick you be, Abner! Swill my licker so's you kin skin me out o' my bet!

MACKEL—That's it, Seth! Don't let him play no skin games!

JOE—By God, if ghosts look like the livin', I'd let Ezra's woman's ghost set on my lap! M'm! (*He smacks his lips lasciviously.*)

AMES—Me, too! She was a looker!

SMALL—(*with an uneasy glance at the house*) It's her ghost folks is sayin' haunts the place, ain't it?

SETH—(*with a wink at the others*) Oh, hers and a hull passel of others. The graveyard's full of Mannons and they all spend their nights to hum here. You needn't worry but you'll have plenty o' company, Abner! (*The others laugh, their mirth a bit forced, but Small looks rather sick.*)

SMALL—It ain't in our bet for you to put sech notions in my head afore I go in, be it? (*then forcing a perky bravado*) Think you kin scare me? There ain't no sech thing as ghosts!

SETH—An' I'm sayin' you're scared to prove there ain't! Let's git our bet set out plain afore witnesses. I'm lettin' you in the Mannon house and I'm bettin' you ten dollars and a gallon of licker you dasn't stay there till moonrise at ten o'clock. If you come out afore then, you lose. An' you're to stay in the dark and not even strike a match! Is that agreed?

SMALL—(*trying to put a brave face on it*) That's agreed— an' it's like stealin' ten dollars off you!

SETH—We'll see! (*then with a grin*) An' you're supposed to go in sober! But I won't make it too dead sober! I ain't that hard-hearted. I wouldn't face what you'll face with a gallon under my belt! (*handing him the jug*) Here! Take a good swig! You're lookin' a mite pale about the gills a'ready!

SMALL—No sech thing! (*But he puts the jug to his lips and takes an enormous swallow.*)

MACKEL—Whoa thar! Ye ain't drinkin' fur all on us! (*Small hands the jug to him and he drinks and passes it around until it finally reaches Seth again. In the meantime Small talks to Seth.*)

SMALL—Be it all right fur me to go in afore dark? I'd like to know where I'm at while I kin see.

SETH—Wal, I calc'late you kin. Don't want you runnin' into furniture an' breakin' things when them ghosts git chasin' you! Vinnie an' Orin's liable to be back from Chiny afore long an' she'd give me hell if anythin' was broke. (*The jug reaches him. He takes a drink—then sets it down on the drive.*) Come along! I've took the screws out o' that door. I kin let you right in. (*He goes toward the portico, Small following him, whistling with elaborate nonchalance.*)

SMALL—(*to the others who remain where they are*) So long, fellers. We'll have a good spree on that ten dollars.

MACKEL—(*with a malicious cackle*) Mebbe! Would you like me fur one o' your pallbearers, Abner?

AMES—I'll comfort your old woman—providin' she'll want comfortin', which ain't likely!

SILVA—And I'll water your grave every Sunday after church! That's the kind of man I be, by God. I don't forget my friends when they're gone!

SETH—(*from the portico*) We'll all jine in, Joe! If he ain't dead, by God, we'll drown him! (*They all roar with laughter. Small looks bitter. The jest strikes him as being unfeeling— All glow has faded from the sky and it is getting dark.*)

SMALL—To hell with ye! (*Seth pries off the board door and unlocks the inner door.*)

SETH—Come on. I'll show you the handiest place to say your prayers. (*They go in. The group outside becomes serious.*)

AMES—(*voicing the opinion of all of them*) Wal, all the same,

I wouldn't be in Abner's boots. It don't do to monkey with them thin's.

MACKEL—You believe in ghosts, Amos?

AMES—Mebbe. Who knows there ain't?

MACKEL—Wal, I believe in 'em. Take the Nims' place out my way. Asa Nims killed his wife with a hatchet—she'd nagged him—then hung himself in the attic. I knew Ben Willett that bought the place. He couldn't live thar—had to move away. It's fallen to ruins now. Ben used to hear things clawin' at the walls an' winders and see the chairs move about. He wasn't a liar nor chicken-hearted neither.

SILVA—There is ghosts, by God! My cousin, Manuel, he seen one! Off on a whaler in the Injun Ocean, that was. A man got knifed and pushed overboard. After that, on moonlight nights, they'd see him a-settin' on the yards and hear him moanin' to himself. Yes, sir, my cousin Manuel, he ain't no liar neither—'ceptin' when he's drunk—and he seen him with his own eyes!

AMES—(*with an uneasy glance around, reaching for the jug*) Wal, let's have a drink. (*He takes a swig just as Seth comes out of the house, shutting the door behind him.*)

MACKEL—That's Seth. He ain't anxious to stay in thar long, I notice! (*Seth hurries down to them, trying to appear to saunter.*)

SETH—(*with a forced note to his joking*) God A'mighty, ye'd ought to see Abner! He's shyin' at the furniture covers an' his teeth are clickin' a'ready. He'll come runnin' out hell fur leather afore long. All I'm wonderin' is, has he got ten dollars.

MACKEL—(*slyly*) You seem a mite shaky.

SETH—(*with a scowl*) You're a liar. What're ye all lookin' glum as owls about?

MACKEL—Been talkin' of ghosts. Do you really believe that there house is haunted, Seth, or are ye only jokin' Abner?

SETH—(*sharply*) Don't be a durned fool! I'm on'y jokin' him, of course!

MACKEL—(*insistently*) Still, it'd be only natural if it was haunted. She shot herself there. Do you think she done it fur grief over Ezra's death, like the daughter let on to folks?

SETH—'Course she did!

MACKEL—Ezra dyin' sudden his first night to hum—that was durned queer!

SETH—(*angrily*) It's durned queer old fools like you with one foot in the grave can't mind their own business in the little time left to 'em. That's what's queer!

MACKEL—(*angry in his turn*) Wal, all I say is if they hadn't been Mannons with the town lickin' their boots, there'd have been queer doin's come out! And as fur me bein' an old fool, you're older an' a worse fool! An' your foot's deeper in the grave than mine be!

SETH—(*shaking his fist in Mackel's face*) It ain't so deep but what I kin whale the stuffin' out o' you any day in the week!

SILVA—(*comes between them*) Here, you old roosters! No fightin' allowed!

MACKEL—(*subsiding grumpily*) This is a free country, ain't it? I got a right to my opinions!

AMES—(*suddenly looking off down left*) Ssshh! Look, Seth! There's someone comin' up the drive.

SETH—(*peering*) Ayeh! Who the hell—? It's Peter'n Hazel. Hide that jug, durn ye! (*The jug is hidden under the lilacs. A moment later Hazel and Peter enter. They stop in surprise on seeing Seth and his friends. Seth greets them self-consciously.*) Good evenin'. I was just showin' some friends around—

PETER—Hello, Seth. Just the man we're looking for. We've just had a telegram. Vinnie and Orin have landed in New York and— (*He is interrupted by a muffled yell of terror from the house. As they all turn to look, the front door is flung open and Small comes tearing out and down the portico steps, his face chalky white and his eyes popping.*)

SMALL—(*as he reaches them—terrifiedly*) God A'mighty! I heard 'em comin' after me, and I run in the room opposite, an' I seed Ezra's ghost dressed like a judge comin' through the wall—and, by God, I run! (*He jerks a bill out of his pocket and thrusts it on Seth.*) Here's your money, durn ye! I wouldn't stay in there fur a million! (*This breaks the tension, and the old men give way to an hysterical, boisterous, drunken mirth, roaring with laughter, pounding each other on the back.*)

PETER—(*sharply*) What's this all about? What was he doing in there?

SETH—(*controlling his laughter—embarrassedly*) Only a joke, Peter. (*then turning on Small—scornfully*) That was Ezra's picture hangin' on the wall, not a ghost, ye durned idjut!

SMALL—(*indignantly*) I know pictures when I see 'em an' I knowed him. This was him! Let's get out o' here. I've had enough of this durned place!

SETH—You fellers trot along. I'll jine you later. (*They all mutter good evenings to Peter and Hazel and go off, left front. Small's excited voice can be heard receding as he begins to embroider on the horrors of his adventure. Seth turns to Peter apologetically.*) Abner Small's always braggin' how brave he is—so I bet him he dasn't stay in there—

HAZEL—(*indignantly*) Seth! What would Vinnie say if she knew you did such things?

SETH—There ain't no harm done. I calc'late Abner didn't break nothin'. And Vinnie wouldn't mind when she knew why I done it. I was aimin' to stop the durned gabbin' that's been goin' round town about this house bein' haunted. You've heard it, ain't ye?

PETER—I heard some silly talk but didn't pay any attention—

SETH—That durned idjut female I got in to clean a month after Vinnie and Orin sailed started it. Said she'd felt ghosts around. You know how them things grow. Seemed to me Abner's braggin' gave me a good chance to stop it by turnin' it all into a joke on him folks'd laugh at. An' when I git through tellin' my story of it round town tomorrow you'll find folks'll shet up and not take it serious no more.

PETER—(*appreciatively*) You're right, Seth. That was a darned slick notion! Nothing like a joke to lay a ghost!

SETH—Ayeh. But— (*He hesitates—then decides to say it.*) Between you 'n' me 'n' the lamp-post, it ain't all sech a joke as it sounds—that about the hauntin', I mean.

PETER—(*incredulously*) You aren't going to tell me you think the house is haunted too!

SETH—(*grimly*) Mebbe, and mebbe not. All I know is I wouldn't stay in there all night if you was to give me the town!

HAZEL—(*impressed but forcing a teasing tone*) Seth! I'm ashamed of you!

PETER—First time I ever heard you say you were afraid of anything!

SETH—There's times when a man's a darn fool not to be scared! Oh, don't git it in your heads I take stock in spirits trespassin' round in windin' sheets or no sech lunatic doin's. But there is such a thing as evil spirit. An' I've felt it, goin' in there daytimes to see to things—like somethin' rottin' in the walls!

PETER—Bosh!

SETH—(*quietly*) 'Taint bosh, Peter. There's been evil in that house since it was first built in hate—and it's kept growin' there ever since, as what's happened there has proved. You understand I ain't sayin' this to no one but you two. An' I'm only tellin' you fur one reason—because you're closer to Vinnie and Orin than anyone and you'd ought to persuade them, now they're back, not to live in it. (*He adds impressively*) Fur their own good! (*then with a change of tone*) An' now I've got that off my chest, tell me about 'em. When are they comin'?

PETER—Tomorrow. Vinnie asked us to open the house. So let's start right in.

SETH—(*with evident reluctance*) You want to do it tonight?

HAZEL—We must, Seth. We've got so little time. We can at least tidy up the rooms a little and get the furniture covers off.

SETH—Wal, I'll go to the barn and git lanterns. There's candles in the house. (*He turns abruptly and goes off left between the lilacs and the house.*)

HAZEL—(*looking after him—uneasily*) I can't get over Seth acting so strangely.

PETER—Don't mind him. It's rum and old age.

HAZEL—(*shaking her head—slowly*) No. There is something queer about this house. I've always felt it, even before the General's death and her suicide. (*She shudders.*) I can still see her sitting on that bench as she was that last night. She was so frightened of being alone. But I thought when Vinnie and Orin came back she would be all right. (*then sadly*) Poor Orin! I'll never forget to my dying day the way he looked when we saw him at the funeral. I hardly recognized him, did you?

PETER—No. He certainly was broken up.

HAZEL—And the way he acted—like someone in a trance! I don't believe when Vinnie rushed him off on this trip to the East he knew what he was doing or where he was going or anything.

PETER—A long voyage like that was the best thing to help them both forget.

HAZEL—(*without conviction*) Yes. I suppose it was—but— (*She stops and sighs—then worriedly*) I wonder how Orin is. Vinnie's letters haven't said much about him, or herself, for that matter—only about the trip. (*She sees Seth approaching, whistling loudly, from left, rear, with two lighted lanterns.*) Here's Seth. (*She walks up the steps to the portico. Peter follows her. She hesitates and stands looking at the house—in a low tone, almost of dread*) Seth was right. You feel something cold grip you the moment you set foot—

PETER—Oh, nonsense! He's got you going, too! (*then with a chuckle*) Listen to him whistling to keep his courage up! (*Seth comes in from the left. He hands one of the lanterns to Peter.*)

SETH—Here you be, Peter.

HAZEL—Well, let's go in. You better come out to the kitchen and help me first, Peter. We ought to start a fire. (*They go in. There is a pause in which Peter can be heard opening windows behind the shutters in the downstairs rooms. Then silence. Then Lavinia enters, coming up the drive from left, front, and stands regarding the house. One is at once aware of an extraordinary change in her. Her body, formerly so thin and undeveloped, has filled out. Her movements have lost their square-shouldered stiffness. She now bears a striking resemblance to her mother in every respect, even to being dressed in the green her mother had affected. She walks to the clump of lilacs and stands there staring at the house.*)

LAVINIA—(*turns back and calls coaxingly in the tone one would use to a child*) Don't stop there, Orin! What are you afraid of? Come on! (*He comes slowly and hesitatingly in from left, front. He carries himself woodenly erect now like a soldier. His movements and attitudes have the statue-like quality that was so marked in his father. He now wears a close-cropped beard in addition to his mustache, and this accentuates his resemblance to his father. The Mannon semblance of his face in repose to a mask*) *is more pronounced than ever. He has grown dreadfully thin and his black suit hangs loosely on his body. His haggard swarthy face is set in a blank lifeless expression.*)

LAVINIA—(*glances at him uneasily—concealing her apprehension under a coaxing motherly tone*) You must be brave! This is the test! You have got to face it! (*then anxiously as he makes no reply*) Do you feel you can—now we're here?

ORIN—(*dully*) I'll be all right—with you.

LAVINIA—(*takes his hand and pats it encouragingly*) That's all I wanted—to hear you say that. (*turning to the house*) Look, I see a light through the shutters of the sitting-room. That must be Peter and Hazel. (*then as she sees he still keeps his eyes averted from the house*) Why don't you look at the house? Are you afraid? (*then sharply commanding*) Orin! I want you to look now! Do you hear me?

ORIN—(*dully obedient*) Yes, Vinnie. (*He jerks his head around and stares at the house and draws a deep shuddering breath.*)

LAVINIA—(*her eyes on his face—as if she were willing her strength into him*) Well? You don't see any ghosts, do you? Tell me!

ORIN—(*obediently*) No.

LAVINIA—Because there are none! Tell me you know there are none, Orin!

ORIN—(*as before*) Yes.

LAVINIA—(*searches his face uneasily—then is apparently satisfied*) Come. Let's go in. We'll find Hazel and Peter and surprise them— (*She takes his arm and leads him to the steps. He walks like an automaton. When they reach the spot where his mother had sat moaning, the last time he had seen her alive [Act Five of "The Hunted"] he stops with a shudder.*)

ORIN—(*stammers—pointing*) It was here—she—the last time I saw her alive—

LAVINIA—(*quickly, urging him on commandingly*) That is all past and finished! The dead have forgotten us! We've forgotten them! Come! (*He obeys woodenly. She gets him up the steps and they pass into the house.*)

(*Curtain*)

SCENE TWO

*Same as Act Two of "The Hunted"—The sitting-room in the
Mannon house. Peter has lighted two candles on the mantel and
put the lantern on the table at front. In this dim, spotty light the
room is full of shadows. It has the dead appearance of a room long
shut up, and the covered furniture has a ghostly look. In the flickering candlelight the eyes of the Mannon portraits stare with a
grim forbiddingness.*

*Lavinia appears in the doorway at rear. In the lighted room,
the change in her is strikingly apparent. At a first glance, one
would mistake her for her mother as she appeared in the First Act
of "Homecoming." She seems a mature woman, sure of her feminine attractiveness. Her brown-gold hair is arranged as her mother's had been. Her green dress is like a copy of her mother's in Act
One of "Homecoming." She comes forward slowly. The movements
of her body now have the feminine grace her mother's had possessed.
Her eyes are caught by the eyes of the Mannons in the portraits
and she approaches as if compelled in spite of herself until she
stands directly under them in front of the fireplace. She suddenly
addresses them in a harsh resentful voice.)*

LAVINIA—Why do you look at me like that? I've done my
duty by you! That's finished and forgotten! *(She tears her eyes
from theirs and, turning away, becomes aware that Orin has not
followed her into the room, and is immediately frightened and uneasy and hurries toward the door, calling)* Orin!

ORIN—*(His voice comes from the dark hall.)* I'm here.

LAVINIA—What are you doing out there? Come here!
*(Orin appears in the doorway. His face wears a dazed expression
and his eyes have a wild, stricken look. He hurries to her as if
seeking protection. She exclaims frightenedly)* Orin! What is it?

ORIN—*(strangely)* I've just been in the study. I was sure
she'd be waiting for me in there, where— *(torturedly)* But she
wasn't! She isn't anywhere. It's only they— *(He points to the
portraits.)* They're everywhere! But she's gone forever. She'll
never forgive me now!

LAVINIA—*(harshly)* Orin! Will you be quiet!

ORIN—*(unheeding—with a sudden turn to bitter resentful
defiance)* Well, let her go! What is she to me? I'm not her son

any more! I'm Father's! I'm a Mannon! And they'll welcome me home!

LAVINIA—(*angrily commanding*) Stop it, do you hear me!

ORIN—(*shocked back to awareness by her tone—pitifully confused*) I—I didn't—don't be angry, Vinnie!

LAVINIA—(*soothing him now*) I'm not angry, dear—only do get hold of yourself and be brave. (*leading him to the sofa*) Here. Come. Let's sit down for a moment, shall we, and get used to being home? (*They sit down. She puts an arm around him—reproachfully*) Don't you know how terribly you frighten me when you act so strangely? You don't mean to hurt me, do you?

ORIN—(*deeply moved*) God knows I don't, Vinnie! You're all I have in the world! (*He takes her hand and kisses it humbly.*)

LAVINIA—(*soothingly*) That's a good boy. (*then with a cheerful matter-of-fact note*) Hazel and Peter must be back in the kitchen. Won't you be glad to see Hazel again?

ORIN—(*dully now*) You've kept talking about them all the voyage home. Why? What can they have to do with us—now?

LAVINIA—A lot. What we need most is to get back to simple normal things and begin a new life. And their friendship and love will help us more than anything to forget.

ORIN—(*with sudden harshness*) Forget? I thought you'd forgotten long ago—if you ever remembered, which you never seemed to! (*then with somber bitterness*) Love! What right have I—or you—to love?

LAVINIA—(*defiantly*) Every right!

ORIN—(*grimly*) Mother felt the same about— (*then with a strange, searching glance at her*) You don't know how like Mother you've become, Vinnie. I don't mean only how pretty you've gotten—

LAVINIA—(*with a strange shy eagerness*) Do you really think I'm as pretty now as she was, Orin?

ORIN—(*as if she hadn't interrupted*) I mean the change in your soul, too. I've watched it ever since we sailed for the East. Little by little it grew like Mother's soul—as if you were stealing hers—as if her death had set you free—to become her!

LAVINIA—(*uneasily*) Now don't begin talking nonsense again, please!

ORIN—(*grimly*) Don't you believe in souls any more? I think you will after we've lived in this house awhile! The Mannon dead will convert you. (*He turns to the portraits— mockingly*) Ask them if I'm not right!

LAVINIA—(*sharply*) Orin! What's come over you? You haven't had one of these morbid spells since we left the Islands. You swore to me you were all over them, or I'd never have agreed to come home.

ORIN—(*with a strange malicious air*) I had to get you away from the Islands. My brotherly duty! If you'd stayed there much longer— (*He chuckles disagreeably.*)

LAVINIA—(*with a trace of confusion*) I don't know what you're talking about. I only went there for your sake.

ORIN—(*with another chuckle*) Yes—but afterwards—

LAVINIA—(*sharply*) You promised you weren't going to talk any more morbid nonsense. (*He subsides meekly. She goes on reproachfully.*) Remember all I've gone through on your account. For months after we sailed you didn't know what you were doing. I had to live in constant fear of what you might say. I wouldn't live through those horrible days again for anything on earth. And remember this homecoming is what you wanted. You told me that if you could come home and face your ghosts, you knew you could rid yourself forever of your silly guilt about the past.

ORIN—(*dully*) I know, Vinnie.

LAVINIA—And I believed you, you seemed so certain of yourself. But now you've suddenly become strange again. You frighten me. So much depends on how you start in, now we're home. (*then sharply commanding*) Listen, Orin! I want you to start again—by facing all your ghosts right now! (*He turns and his eyes remain fixed on hers from now on. She asks sternly*) Who murdered Father?

ORIN—(*falteringly*) Brant did—for revenge because—

LAVINIA—(*more sternly*) Who murdered Father? Answer me!

ORIN—(*with a shudder*) Mother was under his influence—

LAVINIA—That's a lie! It was he who was under hers. You know the truth!

ORIN—Yes.

LAVINIA—She was an adulteress and a murderess, wasn't she?

ORIN—Yes.

LAVINIA—If we'd done our duty under the law, she would have been hanged, wouldn't she?

ORIN—Yes.

LAVINIA—But we protected her. She could have lived, couldn't she? But she chose to kill herself as a punishment for her crime—of her own free will! It was an act of justice! You had nothing to do with it! You see that now, don't you? (*As he hesitates, trembling violently, she grabs his arm fiercely.*) Tell me!

ORIN—(*hardly above a whisper*) Yes.

LAVINIA—And your feeling of being responsible for her death was only your morbid imagination! You don't feel it now! You'll never feel it again!

ORIN—No.

LAVINIA—(*gratefully—and weakly because the strength she has willed into him has left her exhausted*) There! You see! You can do it when you will to! (*She kisses him. He breaks down, sobbing weakly against her breast. She soothes him.*) There! Don't cry! You ought to feel proud. You've proven you can laugh at your ghosts from now on. (*then briskly, to distract his mind*) Come now. Help me to take off these furniture covers. We might as well start making ourselves useful. (*She starts to work. For a moment he helps. Then he goes to one of the windows and pushes back a shutter and stands staring out. Peter comes in the door from rear. At the sight of Lavinia he stops startledly, thinks for a second it is her mother's ghost and gives an exclamation of dread. At the same moment she sees him. She stares at him with a strange eager possessiveness. She calls softly*)

LAVINIA—Peter! (*She goes toward him, smiling as her mother might have smiled.*) Don't you know me any more, Peter?

PETER—(*stammers*) Vinnie! I—I thought you were—! I can't realize it's you! You've grown so like your— (*checking himself awkwardly*) I mean you've changed so—and we weren't looking for you until— (*He takes her hand automatically, staring at her stupidly.*)

LAVINIA—I know. We had intended to stay in New York tonight but we decided later we'd better come right home. (*then taking him in with a smiling appreciative possessiveness*) Let me look at you, Peter. You haven't gone and changed, have you? No, you're the same, thank goodness! I've been thinking of you all the way home and wondering—I was so afraid you might have.

PETER—(*plucking up his courage—blurts out*) You—you ought to know I'd never change—with you! (*Then, alarmed by his own boldness, he hastily looks away from her.*)

LAVINIA—(*teasingly*) But you haven't said yet you're glad to see me!

PETER—(*has turned back and is staring fascinatedly at her. A surge of love and desire overcomes his timidity and he bursts out*) I—you know how much I—! (*Then he turns away again in confusion and takes refuge in a burst of talk.*) Gosh, Vinnie, you ought to have given us more warning. We've only just started to open the place up. I was with Hazel, in the kitchen, starting a fire—

LAVINIA—(*laughing softly*) Yes. You're the same old Peter! You're still afraid of me. But you mustn't be now. I know I used to be an awful old stick, but—

PETER—Who said so? You were not! (*then with enthusiasm*) Gosh, you look so darned pretty—and healthy. Your trip certainly did you good! (*staring at her again, drinking her in*) I can't get over seeing you dressed in color. You always used to wear black.

LAVINIA—(*with a strange smile*) I was dead then.

PETER—You ought always to wear color.

LAVINIA—(*immensely pleased*) Do you think so?

PETER—Yes. It certainly is becoming. I— (*then embarrassedly changing the subject*) But where's Orin?

LAVINIA—(*turning to look around*) Why, he was right here. (*She sees him at the window.*) Orin, what are you doing there? Here's Peter. (*Orin closes the shutter he has pushed open and turns back from the window. He comes forward, his eyes fixed in a strange preoccupation, as if he were unaware of their presence. Lavinia watches him uneasily and speaks sharply.*) Don't you see Peter? Why don't you speak to him? You mustn't be so rude.

PETER—(*good-naturedly*) Give him a chance. Hello, Orin. Darned glad to see you back. (*They shake hands. Peter has difficulty in hiding his pained surprise at Orin's sickly appearance.*)

ORIN—(*rousing himself, forces a smile and makes an effort at his old friendly manner with Peter*) Hello, Peter. You know I'm glad to see you without any polite palaver. Vinnie is the same old bossy fuss-buzzer—you remember—always trying to teach me manners!

PETER—You bet I remember! But say, hasn't she changed, though? I didn't know her, she's grown so fat! And I was just telling her how well she looked in color. Don't you agree?

ORIN—(*in a sudden strange tone of jeering malice*) Did you ask her why she stole Mother's colors? I can't see why—yet—and I don't think she knows herself. But it will prove a strange reason, I'm certain of that, when I do discover it!

LAVINIA—(*making a warning sign to Peter not to take this seriously—forcing a smile*) Don't mind him, Peter.

ORIN—(*his tone becoming sly, insinuating and mocking*) And she's become romantic! Imagine that! Influence of the "dark and deep blue ocean"—and of the Islands, eh, Vinnie?

PETER—(*surprised*) You stopped at the Islands?

ORIN—Yes. We took advantage of our being on a Mannon ship to make the captain touch there on the way back. We stopped a month. (*with resentful bitterness*) But they turned out to be Vinnie's islands, not mine. They only made me sick—and the naked women disgusted me. I guess I'm too much of a Mannon, after all, to turn into a pagan. But you should have seen Vinnie with the men—!

LAVINIA—(*indignantly but with a certain guiltiness*) How can you—!

ORIN—(*jeeringly*) Handsome and romantic-looking, weren't they, Vinnie?—with colored rags around their middles and flowers stuck over their ears! Oh, she was a bit shocked at first by their dances, but afterwards she fell in love with the Islanders. If we'd stayed another month, I know I'd have found her some moonlight night dancing under the palm trees—as naked as the rest!

LAVINIA—Orin! Don't be disgusting!

ORIN—(*points to the portraits mockingly*) Picture, if you can, the feelings of the God-fearing Mannon dead at that spectacle!

LAVINIA—(*with an anxious glance at Peter*) How can you make up such disgusting fibs?

ORIN—(*with a malicious chuckle*) Oh, I wasn't as blind as I pretended to be! Do you remember Avahanni?

LAVINIA—(*angrily*) Stop talking like a fool! (*He subsides meekly again. She forces a smile and a motherly tone.*) You're a naughty boy, do you know it? What will Peter think? Of course, he knows you're only teasing me—but you shouldn't go on like that. It isn't nice. (*then changing the subject abruptly*) Why don't you go and find Hazel? Here. Let me look at you. I want you to look your best when she sees you. (*She arranges him as a mother would a boy, pulling down his coat, giving a touch to his shirt and tie. Orin straightens woodenly to a soldierly attention. She is vexed by this.*) Don't stand like a ramrod! You'd be so handsome if you'd only shave off that silly beard and not carry yourself like a tin soldier!

ORIN—(*with a sly cunning air*) Not look so much like Father, eh? More like a romantic clipper captain, is that it? (*As she starts and stares at him frightenedly, he smiles an ugly taunting smile.*) Don't look so frightened, Vinnie!

LAVINIA—(*with an apprehensive glance at Peter—pleading and at the same time warning*) Ssshh! You weren't to talk nonsense, remember! (*giving him a final pat*) There! Now run along to Hazel.

ORIN—(*looks from her to Peter suspiciously*) You seem damned anxious to get rid of me. (*He turns and stalks stiffly with hurt dignity from the room. Lavinia turns to Peter. The strain of Orin's conduct has told on her. She seems suddenly weak and frightened.*)

PETER—(*in shocked amazement*) What's come over him?

LAVINIA—(*in a strained voice*) It's the same thing—what the war did to him—and on top of that Father's death—and the shock of Mother's suicide.

PETER—(*puts his arm around her impulsively—comfortingly*) It'll be all right! Don't worry, Vinnie!

LAVINIA—(*nestling against him gratefully*) Thank you,

Peter. You're so good. (*then looking into his eyes*) Do you still love me, Peter?

PETER—Don't have to ask that, do you? (*He squeezes her awkwardly—then stammers*) But do you—think now—you maybe—can love me?

LAVINIA—Yes!

PETER—You really mean that!

LAVINIA—Yes! I do! I've thought of you so much! Things were always reminding me of you—the ship and the sea—everything that was honest and clean! And the natives on the Islands reminded me of you too. They were so simple and fine— (*then hastily*) You mustn't mind what Orin was saying about the Islands. He's become a regular bigoted Mannon.

PETER—(*amazed*) But, Vinnie—!

LAVINIA—Oh, I know it must sound funny hearing me talk like that. But remember I'm only half Mannon. (*She looks at the portraits defiantly.*) And I've done my duty by them! They can't say I haven't!

PETER—(*mystified but happy*) Gosh, you certainly have changed! But I'm darned glad!

LAVINIA—Orin keeps teasing that I was flirting with that native he spoke about, simply because he used to smile at me and I smiled back.

PETER—(*teasingly*) Now, I'm beginning to get jealous, too.

LAVINIA—You mustn't. He made me think of you. He made me dream of marrying you—and everything.

PETER—Oh, well then, I take it all back! I owe him a vote of thanks! (*He hugs her.*)

LAVINIA—(*dreamily*) I loved those Islands. They finished setting me free. There was something there mysterious and beautiful—a good spirit—of love—coming out of the land and sea. It made me forget death. There was no hereafter. There was only this world—the warm earth in the moonlight—the trade wind in the coco palms—the surf on the reef—the fires at night and the drum throbbing in my heart—the natives dancing naked and innocent—without knowledge of sin! (*She checks herself abruptly and frightenedly.*) But what in the world! I'm gabbing on like a regular chatterbox. You must think I've become awfully scatter-brained!

PETER—(*with a chuckle*) Gosh no! I'm glad you've grown that way! You never used to say a word unless you had to!

LAVINIA—(*suddenly filled with grateful love for him, lets herself go and throws her arms around him*) Oh, Peter, hold me close to you! I want to feel love! Love is all beautiful! I never used to know that! I was a fool! (*She kisses him passionately. He returns it, aroused and at the same time a little shocked by her boldness. She goes on longingly.*) We'll be married soon, won't we, and settle out in the country away from folks and their evil talk. We'll make an island for ourselves on land, and we'll have children and love them and teach them to love life so that they can never be possessed by hate and death! (*She gives a start—in a whisper as if to herself*) But I'm forgetting Orin!

PETER—What's Orin got to do with us marrying?

LAVINIA—I can't leave him—until he's all well again. I'd be afraid—

PETER—Let him live with us.

LAVINIA—(*with sudden intensity*) No! I want to be rid of the past! (*then after a quick look at him—in a confiding tone*) I want to tell you what's wrong with Orin—so you and Hazel can help me. He feels guilty about Mother killing herself. You see, he'd had a quarrel with her that last night. He was jealous and mad and said things he was sorry for after and it preyed on his mind until he blames himself for her death.

PETER—But that's crazy!

LAVINIA—I know it is, Peter, but you can't do anything with him when he gets his morbid spells. Oh, I don't mean he's the way he is tonight most of the time. Usually he's like himself, only quiet and sad—so sad it breaks my heart to see him—like a little boy who's been punished for something he didn't do. Please tell Hazel what I've told you, so she'll make allowances for any crazy thing he might say.

PETER—I'll warn her. And now don't you worry any more about him. We'll get him all right again one way or another.

LAVINIA—(*again grateful for his simple goodness—lovingly*) Bless you, Peter! (*She kisses him. As she does so, Hazel and Orin appear in the doorway at rear. Hazel is a bit shocked, then smiles happily. Orin starts as if he'd been struck. He glares at them with jealous rage and clenches his fists as if he were going to attack them.*)

HAZEL—(*with a teasing laugh*) I'm afraid we're interrupting, Orin. (*Peter and Vinnie jump apart in confusion.*)

ORIN—(*threateningly*) So that's it! By God—!

LAVINIA—(*frightened but managing to be stern*) Orin!

ORIN—(*pulls himself up sharply—confusedly, forcing a sickly smile*) Don't be so solemn—Fuss Buzzer! I was only trying to scare you—for a joke! (*turning to Peter and holding out his hand, his smile becoming ghastly*) I suppose congratulations are in order. I—I'm glad. (*Peter takes his hand awkwardly. Hazel moves toward Lavinia to greet her, her face full of an uneasy bewilderment. Lavinia stares at Orin with eyes full of dread.*)

(*Curtain*)

ACT TWO

SCENE—*Same as Act Three of "The Hunted"—Ezra Mannon's study—on an evening a month later. The shutters of the windows are closed. Candles on the mantel above the fireplace light up the portrait of Ezra Mannon in his judge's robes. Orin is sitting in his father's chair at left of table, writing by the light of a lamp. A small pile of manuscript is stacked by his right hand. He is intent on his work. He has aged in the intervening month. He looks almost as old now as his father in the portrait. He is dressed in black and the resemblance between the two is uncanny. A grim smile of satisfaction twitches his lips as he stops writing and reads over the paragraph he has just finished. Then he puts the sheet down and stares up at the portrait, sitting back in his chair.*

ORIN—(*sardonically, addressing the portrait*) The truth, the whole truth and nothing but the truth! Is that what you're demanding, Father? Are you sure you want the whole truth? What will the neighbors say if this whole truth is ever known? (*He chuckles grimly.*) A ticklish decision for you, Your Honor! (*There is a knock on the door. He hastily grabs the script and puts it in the drawer of the desk.*) Who's there?

LAVINIA—It's I.

ORIN—(*hastily locking the drawer and putting the key in his pocket*) What do you want?

LAVINIA—(*sharply*) Please open the door!

ORIN—All right. In a minute. (*He hurriedly straightens up the table and grabs a book at random from the bookcase and lays it open on the table as if he had been reading. Then he unlocks the door and comes back to his chair as Lavinia enters. She wears a green velvet gown similar to that worn by Christine in Act Three of "Homecoming." It sets off her hair and eyes. She is obviously concealing beneath a surface calm a sense of dread and desperation.*)

LAVINIA—(*glances at him suspiciously, but forces a casual air*) Why did you lock yourself in? (*She comes over to the table.*) What are you doing?

ORIN—Reading.

LAVINIA—(*picks up the book*) Father's law books?

ORIN—(*mockingly*) Why not? I'm considering studying law. He wanted me to, if you remember.

LAVINIA—Do you expect me to believe that, Orin? What is it you're really doing?

ORIN—Curious, aren't you?

LAVINIA—(*forcing a smile*) Good gracious, why wouldn't I be? You've acted so funny lately, locking yourself in here with the blinds closed and the lamp burning even in the daytime. It isn't good for you staying in this stuffy room in this weather. You ought to get out in the fresh air.

ORIN—(*harshly*) I hate the daylight. It's like an accusing eye! No, we've renounced the day, in which normal people live—or rather it has renounced us. Perpetual night—darkness of death in life—that's the fitting habitat for guilt! You believe you can escape that, but I'm not so foolish!

LAVINIA—Now you're being stupid again!

ORIN—And I find artificial light more appropriate for my work—man's light, not God's—man's feeble striving to understand himself, to exist for himself in the darkness! It's a symbol of his life—a lamp burning out in a room of waiting shadows!

LAVINIA—(*sharply*) Your work? What work?

ORIN—(*mockingly*) Studying the law of crime and punishment, as you saw.

LAVINIA—(*forcing a smile again and turning away from him*) All right, if you won't tell me. Go on being mysterious, if you like. (*in a tense voice*) It's so close in here! It's suffocating! It's bad for you! (*She goes to the window and throws the shutters open and looks out.*) It's black as pitch tonight. There isn't a star.

ORIN—(*somberly*) Darkness without a star to guide us! Where are we going, Vinnie? (*then with a mocking chuckle*) Oh, I know you think you know where you're going, but there's many a slip, remember!

LAVINIA—(*her voice strident, as if her will were snapping*) Be quiet! Can't you think of anything but— (*then controlling herself, comes to him—gently*) I'm sorry. I'm terribly nervous tonight. It's the heat, I guess. And you get me so worried with your incessant brooding over the past. It's the worst thing for your health. (*She pats him on the arm—soothingly*) That's all I'm thinking about, dear.

ORIN—Thank you for your anxiety about my health! But I'm afraid there isn't much hope for you there! I happen to feel quite well!

LAVINIA—(*whirling on him—distractedly*) How can you insinuate such horrible—! (*again controlling herself with a great effort, forcing a smile*) But you're only trying to rile me—and I'm not going to let you. I'm so glad you're feeling better. You ate a good supper tonight—for you. The long walk we took with Hazel did you good.

ORIN—(*dully*) Yes. (*He slumps down in his chair at left of table.*) Why is it you never leave me alone with her more than a minute? You approved of my asking her to marry me—and now we're engaged you never leave us alone! (*then with a bitter smile*) But I know the reason well enough. You're afraid I'll let something slip.

LAVINIA—(*sits in the chair opposite him—wearily*) Can you blame me, the way you've been acting?

ORIN—(*somberly*) No. I'm afraid myself of being too long alone with her—afraid of myself. I have no right in the same world with her. And yet I feel so drawn to her purity! Her love for me makes me appear less vile to myself! (*then with a harsh laugh*) And, at the same time, a million times more vile, that's the hell of it! So I'm afraid you can't hope to get rid of me through Hazel. She's another lost island! It's wiser for you to keep Hazel away from me, I warn you. Because when I see love for a murderer in her eyes my guilt crowds up in my throat like poisonous vomit and I long to spit it out— and confess!

LAVINIA—(*in a low voice*) Yes, that is what I live in terror of—that in one of your fits you'll say something before some-one—now after it's all past and forgotten—when there isn't the slightest suspicion—

ORIN—(*harshly*) Were you hoping you could escape retribution? You can't! Confess and atone to the full extent of the law! That's the only way to wash the guilt of our mother's blood from our souls!

LAVINIA—(*distractedly*) Ssshh! Will you stop!

ORIN—Ask our father, the Judge, if it isn't! He knows! He keeps telling me!

LAVINIA—Oh, God! Over and over and over! Will you never lose your stupid guilty conscience! Don't you see how you torture me? You're becoming my guilty conscience, too! (*with an instinctive flare-up of her old jealousy*) How can you still love that vile woman so—when you know all she wanted was to leave you without a thought and marry that—

ORIN—(*with fierce accusation*) Yes! Exactly as you're scheming now to leave me and marry Peter! But, by God, you won't! You'll damn soon stop your tricks when you know what I've been writing!

LAVINIA—(*tensely*) What have you written?

ORIN—(*his anger turned to gloating satisfaction*) Ah! That frightens you, does it? Well, you better be frightened!

LAVINIA—Tell me what you've written!

ORIN—None of your damned business.

LAVINIA—I've got to know!

ORIN—Well, as I've practically finished it—I suppose I might as well tell you. At his earnest solicitation—(*he waves a hand to the portrait mockingly*) as the last male Mannon— thank God for that, eh!—I've been writing the history of our family! (*He adds with a glance at the portrait and a malicious chuckle*) But I don't wish to convey that he approves of all I've set down—not by a damned sight!

LAVINIA—(*trying to keep calm—tensely*) What kind of history do you mean?

ORIN—A true history of all the family crimes, beginning with Grandfather Abe's—all of the crimes, including ours, do you understand?

LAVINIA—(*aghast*) Do you mean to tell me you've actually written—

ORIN—Yes! I've tried to trace to its secret hiding place in the Mannon past the evil destiny behind our lives! I thought if I could see it clearly in the past I might be able to foretell what fate is in store for us, Vinnie—but I haven't dared predict that—not yet—although I can guess— (*He gives a sinister chuckle.*)

LAVINIA—Orin!

ORIN—Most of what I've written is about you! I found
you the most interesting criminal of us all!

LAVINIA—(*breaking*) How can you say such dreadful
things to me, after all I—

ORIN—(*as if he hadn't heard—inexorably*) So many strange
hidden things out of the Mannon past combine in you! For
one example, do you remember the first mate, Wilkins, on the
voyage to Frisco? Oh, I know you thought I was in a stupor
of grief—but I wasn't blind! I saw how you wanted him!

LAVINIA—(*angrily, but with a trace of guilty confusion*) I
never gave him a thought! He was an officer of the ship to
me, and nothing more!

ORIN—(*mockingly*) Adam Brant was a ship's officer, too,
wasn't he? Wilkins reminded you of Brant—

LAVINIA—No!

ORIN—And that's why you suddenly discarded mourning
in Frisco and bought new clothes—in Mother's colors!

LAVINIA—(*furiously*) Stop talking about her! You'd think,
to hear you, I had no life of my own!

ORIN—You wanted Wilkins just as you'd wanted Brant!

LAVINIA—That's a lie!

ORIN—You're doing the lying! You know damned well
that behind all your pretense about Mother's murder being
an act of justice was your jealous hatred! She warned me of
that and I see it clearly now! You wanted Brant for yourself!

LAVINIA—(*fiercely*) It's a lie! I hated him!

ORIN—Yes, after you knew he was her lover! (*He chuckles
with a sinister mockery.*) But we'll let that pass for the present—I know it's the last thing you could ever admit to yourself!—and come to what I've written about your adventures
on my lost islands. Or should I say, Adam Brant's islands! He
had been there too, if you'll remember! Probably he'd lived
with one of the native women! He was that kind! Were you
thinking of that when we were there?

LAVINIA—(*chokingly*) Stop it! I—I warn you—I won't
bear it much longer!

ORIN—(*as if he hadn't heard—in the same sinister mocking
tone*) What a paradise the Islands were for you, eh? All those
handsome men staring at you and your strange beautiful hair!
It was then you finally became pretty—like Mother! You

knew they all desired you, didn't you? It filled you with pride! Especially Avahanni! You watched him stare at your body through your clothes, stripping you naked! And you wanted him!

LAVINIA—No!

ORIN—Don't lie! (*He accuses her with fierce jealousy.*) What did you do with him the night I was sick and you went to watch their shameless dance? Something happened between you! I saw your face when you came back and stood with him in front of our hut!

LAVINIA—(*quietly—with simple dignity now*) I had kissed him good night, that was all—in gratitude! He was innocent and good. He had made me feel for the first time in my life that everything about love could be sweet and natural.

ORIN—So you kissed him, did you? And that was all?

LAVINIA—(*with a sudden flare of deliberately evil taunting that recalls her mother in the last act of "Homecoming," when she was goading Ezra Mannon to fury just before his murder*) And what if it wasn't? I'm not your property! I have a right to love!

ORIN—(*reacting as his father had—his face grown livid—with a hoarse cry of fury grabs her by the throat*) You—you whore! I'll kill you! (*Then suddenly he breaks down and becomes weak and pitiful.*) No! You're lying about him, aren't you? For God's sake, tell me you're lying, Vinnie!

LAVINIA—(*strangely shaken and trembling—stammers*) Yes —it was a lie—how could you believe I— Oh, Orin, something made me say that to you—against my will—something rose up in me—like an evil spirit!

ORIN—(*laughs wildly*) Ghosts! You never seemed so much like Mother as you did just then!

LAVINIA—(*pleading distractedly*) Don't talk about it! Let's forget it ever happened! Forgive me! Please forget it!

ORIN—All right—if the ghosts will let us forget! (*He stares at her fixedly for a moment—then satisfied*) I believe you about Avahanni. I never really suspected, or I'd have killed him—and you, too! I hope you know that! (*then with his old obsessed insistence*) But you were guilty in your mind just the same!

LAVINIA—(*in a flash of distracted anger*) Stop harping on that! Stop torturing me or I—! I've warned you! I warn you again! I can't bear any more! I won't!

ORIN—(*with a mocking diabolical sneer—quietly*) Then why don't you murder me? I'll help you plan it, as we planned Brant's, so there will be no suspicion on you! And I'll be grateful! I loathe my life!

LAVINIA—(*speechless with horror—can only gasp*) Oh!

ORIN—(*with a quiet mad insistence*) Can't you see I'm now in Father's place and you're Mother? That's the evil destiny out of the past I haven't dared predict! I'm the Mannon you're chained to! So isn't it plain—

LAVINIA—(*putting her hands over her ears*) For God's sake, won't you be quiet! (*then suddenly her horror turning into a violent rage—unconsciously repeating the exact threat she had goaded her mother to make to her in Act Two of "Homecoming"*) Take care, Orin! You'll be responsible if—! (*She stops abruptly, terrified by her own words.*)

ORIN—(*with a diabolical mockery*) If what? If I should die mysteriously of heart failure?

LAVINIA—Leave me alone! Leave me alone! Don't keep saying that! How can you be so horrible? Don't you know I'm your sister, who loves you, who would give her life to bring you peace?

ORIN—(*with a change to a harsh threatening tone*) I don't believe you! I know you're plotting something! But you look out! I'll be watching you! And I warn you I won't stand your leaving me for Peter! I'm going to put this confession I've written in safe hands—to be read in case you try to marry him—or if I should die—

LAVINIA—(*frantically grabbing his arm and shaking him fiercely*) Stop having such thoughts! Stop making me have them! You're like a devil torturing me! I won't listen! (*She breaks down and sobs brokenly. Orin stares at her dazedly—seems half to come back to his natural self and the wild look fades from his eyes leaving them glazed and lifeless.*)

ORIN—(*strangely*) Don't cry. The damned don't cry. (*He slumps down heavily in his father's chair and stares at the floor. Suddenly he says harshly again*) Go away, will you? I want to be alone—to finish my work. (*Still sobbing, her hand over her eyes, Lavinia feels blindly for the door and goes out closing it after her. Orin unlocks the table drawer, pulls out his manuscript, and takes up his pen.)*

(*Curtain*)

ACT THREE

SCENE—*Same as Act One, Scene Two—the sitting-room. The lamp on the table is lighted but turned low. Two candles are burning on the mantel over the fireplace at right, shedding their flickering light on the portrait of Abe Mannon above, and of the other Mannons on the walls on each side of him. The eyes of the portraits seem to possess an intense bitter life, with their frozen stare "looking over the head of life, cutting it dead for the impropriety of living," as Orin had said of his father in Act Two of "The Hunted."*

No time has elapsed since the preceding act. Lavinia enters from the hall in the rear, having just come from the study. She comes to the table and turns up the lamp. She is in a terrific state of tension. The corners of her mouth twitch, she twines and untwines the fingers of her clasped hands with a slow wringing movement which recalls her mother in the last Act of "The Hunted."

LAVINIA—(*torturedly—begins to pace up and down, muttering her thoughts aloud*) I can't bear it! Why does he keep putting his death in my head? He would be better off if— Why hasn't he the courage—? (*then in a frenzy of remorseful anguish, her eyes unconsciously seeking the Mannon portraits on the right wall, as if they were the visible symbol of her God*) Oh God, don't let me have such thoughts! You know I love Orin! Show me the way to save him! Don't let me think of death! I couldn't bear another death! Please! Please! (*At a noise from the hall she controls herself and pretends to be glancing through a book on the table. Seth appears in the doorway.*)

SETH—Vinnie!

LAVINIA—What is it, Seth?

SETH—That durned idjut, Hannah, is throwin' fits agin. Went down cellar and says she felt ha'nts crawlin' behind her. You'd better come and git her calmed down—or she'll be leavin'. (*Then he adds disgustedly*) That's what we git fur freein' 'em!

LAVINIA—(*wearily*) All right. I'll talk to her. (*She goes out with Seth. A pause. Then a ring from the front door bell. A moment later Seth can be seen coming back along the hall. He opens*

*the front door and is heard greeting Hazel and Peter and follows
them in as they enter the room.)*

SETH—Vinnie's back seein' to somethin'. You set down
and she'll be here soon as she kin.

PETER—All right, Seth. (*Seth goes out again. They come forward and sit down. Peter looks hearty and good-natured, the same
as ever, but Hazel's face wears a nervous, uneasy look although her
air is determined.)*

PETER—I'll have to run along soon and drop in at the
Council meeting. I can't get out of it. I'll be back in half an
hour—maybe sooner.

HAZEL—(*suddenly with a little shiver*) I hate this house
now. I hate coming here. If it wasn't for Orin— He's getting
worse. Keeping him shut up here is the worst thing Vinnie
could do.

PETER—He won't go out. You know very well she has to
force him to walk with you.

HAZEL—And comes along herself! Never leaves him alone
hardly a second!

PETER—(*with a grin*) Oh, that's what you've got against
her, eh?

HAZEL—(*sharply*) Don't be silly, Peter! I simply think, and
I'd say it to her face, that she's a bad influence for Orin! I feel
there's something awfully wrong—somehow. He scares me
at times—and Vinnie—I've watched her looking at you.
She's changed so. There's something bold about her.

PETER—(*getting up*) If you're going to talk like that—!
You ought to be ashamed, Hazel!

HAZEL—Well, I'm not! I've got some right to say something about how he's cared for! And I'm going to from now
on! I'm going to make her let him visit us for a spell. I've
asked Mother and she'll be glad to have him.

PETER—Say, I think that's a darned good notion for both
of them. She needs a rest from him, too.

HAZEL—Vinnie doesn't think it's a good notion! I mentioned it yesterday and she gave me such a look! (*determinedly*) But I'm going to make him promise to come over
tomorrow, no matter what she says!

PETER—(*soothingly, patting her shoulder*) Don't get angry
now—about nothing. I'll help you persuade her to let him

come. (*then with a grin*) I'll help you do anything to help Orin get well—if only for selfish reasons. As long as Vinnie's tied down to him we can't get married.

HAZEL—(*stares at him—slowly*) Do you really want to marry her—now?

PETER—Why do you ask such a fool question? What do you mean, do I want to now?

HAZEL—(*Her voice trembles and she seems about to burst into tears.*) Oh, I don't know, Peter! I don't know!

PETER—(*sympathetic and at the same time exasperated*) What in the dickens is the matter with you?

HAZEL—(*hears a noise from the hall and collects herself—warningly*) Ssshh! (*Orin appears in the doorway at rear. He glances at them, then quickly around the room to see if Lavinia is there. They both greet him with "Hello, Orin".*)

ORIN—Hello! (*then in an excited whisper, coming to them*) Where's Vinnie?

HAZEL—She's gone to see to something, Seth said.

PETER—(*glancing at his watch*) Gosh, I've got to hurry to that darned Council meeting.

ORIN—(*eagerly*) You're going?

PETER—(*jokingly*) You needn't look so darned tickled about it! It isn't polite!

ORIN—I've got to see Hazel alone!

PETER—All right! You don't have to put me out! (*He grins, slapping Orin on the back and goes out. Orin follows him with his eyes until he hears the front door close behind him.*)

ORIN—(*turning to Hazel—with queer furtive excitement*) Listen, Hazel! I want you to do something! But wait! I've got to get— (*He rushes out and can be heard going across the hall to the study. Hazel looks after him worriedly. A moment later he hurries back with a big sealed envelope in his hand which he gives to Hazel, talking breathlessly, with nervous jerks of his head, as he glances apprehensively at the door.*) Here! Take this! Quick! Don't let her see it! I want you to keep it in a safe place and never let anyone know you have it! It will be stolen if I keep it here! I know her! Will you promise?

HAZEL—But—what is it, Orin?

ORIN—I can't tell you. You mustn't ask me. And you must promise never to open it—unless something happens to me.

HAZEL—(*frightened by his tone*) What do you mean?

ORIN—I mean if I should die—or—but this is the most important, if she tries to marry Peter—the day before the wedding—I want you to make Peter read what's inside.

HAZEL—You don't want her to marry Peter?

ORIN—No! She can't have happiness! She's got to be punished! (*suddenly taking her hand—excitedly*) And listen, Hazel! You mustn't love me any more. The only love I can know now is the love of guilt for guilt which breeds more guilt—until you get so deep at the bottom of hell there is no lower you can sink and you rest there in peace! (*He laughs harshly and turns away from her.*)

HAZEL—Orin! Don't talk like that! (*then conquering her horror—resolutely tender and soothing*) Ssshh! Poor boy! Come here to me. (*He comes to her. She puts an arm around him.*) Listen. I know something is worrying you—and I don't want to seem prying—but I've had such a strong feeling at times that it would relieve your mind if you could tell me what it is. Haven't you thought that, Orin?

ORIN—(*longingly*) Yes! Yes! I want to confess to your purity! I want to be forgiven! (*then checking himself abruptly as he is about to speak—dully*) No. I can't. Don't ask me. I love her.

HAZEL—But, you silly boy, Vinnie told Peter herself what it is and told him to tell me.

ORIN—(*staring at her wildly*) What did she tell?

HAZEL—About your having a quarrel with your poor mother that night before she—and how you've brooded over it until you blame yourself for her death.

ORIN—(*harshly*) I see! So in case I did tell you—oh, she's cunning! But not cunning enough this time! (*vindictively*) You remember what I've given you, Hazel, and you do exactly what I said with it. (*then with desperate pleading*) For God's sake, Hazel, if you love me help me to get away from here— or something terrible will happen!

HAZEL—That's just what I want to do! You come over tomorrow and stay with us.

ORIN—(*bitterly*) Do you suppose for a moment she'll ever let me go?

HAZEL—But haven't you a right to do as you want to?

ORIN—(*furtively*) I could sneak out when she wasn't look-ing—and then you could hide me and when she came for me tell her I wasn't there.

HAZEL—(*indignantly*) I won't do any such thing! I don't tell lies, Orin! (*then scornfully*) How can you be so scared of Vinnie?

ORIN—(*hearing a noise from the hall—hastily*) Ssshh! She's coming! Don't let her see what I gave you. And go home right away and lock it up! (*He tiptoes away as if he were afraid of being found close to her and sits on the sofa at right, adopting a suspiciously careless attitude. Hazel looks self-conscious and stiff. Lavinia appears in the doorway and gives a start as she sees Hazel and Orin are alone. She quickly senses something in the atmo-sphere and glances sharply from one to the other as she comes into the room.*)

LAVINIA—(*to Hazel, forcing a casual air*) I'm sorry being so long.

HAZEL—I didn't mind waiting.

LAVINIA—(*sitting down on the chair at center*) Where's Peter?

HAZEL—He had to go to a Council meeting. He's coming back.

LAVINIA—(*uneasiness creeping into her tone*) Has he been gone long?

HAZEL—Not very long.

LAVINIA—(*turning to Orin—sharply*) I thought you were in the study.

ORIN—(*sensing her uneasiness—mockingly*) I finished what I was working on.

LAVINIA—You finished—? (*She glances sharply at Hazel—forcing a joking tone*) My, but you two look mysterious! What have you been up to?

HAZEL—(*trying to force a laugh*) Why, Vinnie? What makes you think—?

LAVINIA—You're hiding something. (*Hazel gives a start and instinctively moves the hand with the envelope farther behind her back. Lavinia notices this. So does Orin who uneasily comes to Hazel's rescue.*)

ORIN—We're not hiding anything. Hazel has invited me over to their house to stay for a while—and I'm going.

HAZEL—(*backing him up resolutely*) Yes. Orin is coming tomorrow.

LAVINIA—(*alarmed and resentful—coldly*) It's kind of you. I know you mean it for the best. But he can't go.

HAZEL—(*sharply*) Why not?

LAVINIA—I don't care to discuss it, Hazel. You ought to know—

HAZEL—(*angrily*) I don't know! Orin is of age and can go where he pleases!

ORIN—Let her talk all she likes, Hazel. I'll have the upper hand for a change, from now on! (*Lavinia looks at him, frightened by the triumphant satisfaction in his voice.*)

HAZEL—(*anxious to score her point and keep Orin's mind on it*) I should think you'd be glad. It will be the best thing in the world for him.

LAVINIA—(*turns on her—angrily*) I'll ask you to please mind your own business, Hazel!

HAZEL—(*springs to her feet, in her anger forgetting to hide the envelope which she now holds openly in her hand*) It is my business! I love Orin better than you! I don't think you love him at all, the way you've been acting!

ORIN—(*sees the envelope in plain sight and calls to her warningly*) Hazel! (*She catches his eye and hastily puts her hand behind her. Lavinia sees the movement but doesn't for a moment realize the meaning of it. Orin goes on warningly.*) You said you had to go home early. I don't want to remind you but—

HAZEL—(*hastily*) Yes, I really must. (*starting to go, trying to keep the envelope hidden, aware that Lavinia is watching her suspiciously—defiantly to Orin*) We'll expect you tomorrow, and have your room ready. (*then to Lavinia—coldly*) After the way you've insulted me, Vinnie, I hope you realize there's no more question of any friendship between us. (*She tries awkwardly to sidle toward the door.*)

LAVINIA—(*suddenly gets between her and the door—with angry accusation*) What are you hiding behind your back? (*Hazel flushes guiltily, but refusing to lie, says nothing. Lavinia turns on Orin.*) Have you given her what you've written? (*as he hesitates—violently*) Answer me!

ORIN—That's my business! What if I have?

LAVINIA—You—you traitor! You coward! (*fiercely to Hazel*) Give it to me! Do you hear?

HAZEL—Vinnie! How dare you talk that way to me! (*She tries to go but Lavinia keeps directly between her and the door.*)

LAVINIA—You shan't leave here until—! (*then breaking down and pleading*) Orin! Think what you're doing! Tell her to give it to me!

ORIN—No!

LAVINIA—(*goes and puts her arms around him—beseechingly as he avoids her eyes*) Think sanely for a moment! You can't do this! You're a Mannon!

ORIN—(*harshly*) It's because I'm one!

LAVINIA—For Mother's sake, you can't! You loved her!

ORIN—A lot she cared! Don't call on her!

LAVINIA—(*desperately*) For my sake, then! You know I love you! Make Hazel give that up and I'll do anything—anything you want me to!

ORIN—(*stares into her eyes, bending his head until his face is close to hers—with morbid intensity*) You mean that?

LAVINIA—(*shrinking back from him—falteringly*) Yes.

ORIN—(*laughs with a crazy triumph—checks this abruptly—and goes to Hazel who has been standing bewilderedly, not understanding what is behind their talk but sensing something sinister, and terribly frightened. Orin speaks curtly, his eyes fixed on Lavinia.*) Let me have it, Hazel.

HAZEL—(*hands him the envelope—in a trembling voice*) I'll go home. I suppose—we can't expect you tomorrow—now.

ORIN—No. Forget me. The Orin you loved was killed in the war. (*with a twisted smile*) Remember only that dead hero and not his rotting ghost! Good-bye! (*then harshly*) Please go! (*Hazel begins to sob and hurries blindly from the room. Orin comes back to Lavinia who remains kneeling by the chair. He puts the envelope in her hand—harshly*) Here! You realize the promise you made means giving up Peter? And never seeing him again?

LAVINIA—(*tensely*) Yes.

ORIN—And I suppose you think that's all it means, that I'll be content with a promise I've forced out of you, which you'll always be plotting to break? Oh, no! I'm not such a fool! I've got to be sure— (*She doesn't reply or look at him. He stares at her and slowly a distorted look of desire comes over his face.*) You said you would do anything for me. That's a large promise, Vinnie—anything!

LAVINIA—(*shrinking from him*) What do you mean? What terrible thing have you been thinking lately—behind all your crazy talk? No, I don't want to know! Orin! Why do you look at me like that?

ORIN—You don't seem to feel all you mean to me now—all you have made yourself mean—since we murdered Mother!

LAVINIA—Orin!

ORIN—I love you now with all the guilt in me—the guilt we share! Perhaps I love you too much, Vinnie!

LAVINIA—You don't know what you're saying!

ORIN—There are times now when you don't seem to be my sister, nor Mother, but some stranger with the same beautiful hair— (*He touches her hair caressingly. She pulls violently away. He laughs wildly.*) Perhaps you're Marie Brantôme, eh? And you say there are no ghosts in this house?

LAVINIA—(*staring at him with fascinated horror*) For God's sake—! No! You're insane! You can't mean—!

ORIN—How else can I be sure you won't leave me? You would never dare leave me—then! You would feel as guilty then as I do! You would be as damned as I am! (*then with sudden anger as he sees the growing horrified repulsion on her face*) Damn you, don't you see I must find some certainty some way or go mad? You don't want me to go mad, do you? I would talk too much! I would confess! (*Then as if the word stirred something within him his tone instantly changes to one of passionate pleading.*) Vinnie! For the love of God, let's go now and confess and pay the penalty for Mother's murder, and find peace together!

LAVINIA—(*tempted and tortured, in a longing whisper*) Peace! (*then summoning her will, springs to her feet wildly*) No! You coward! There is nothing to confess! There was only justice!

ORIN—(*turns and addresses the portraits on the wall with a crazy mockery*) You hear her? You'll find Lavinia Mannon harder to break than me! You'll have to haunt and hound her for a lifetime!

LAVINIA—(*her control snapping—turning on him now in a burst of frantic hatred and rage*) I hate you! I wish you were dead! You're too vile to live! You'd kill yourself if you weren't a coward!

ORIN—(*starts back as if he'd been struck, the tortured mad look on his face changing to a stricken terrified expression*) Vinnie!

LAVINIA—I mean it! I mean it! (*She breaks down and sobs hysterically.*)

ORIN—(*in a pitiful pleading whisper*) Vinnie! (*He stares at her with the lost stricken expression for a moment more—then the obsessed wild look returns to his eyes—with harsh mockery*) Another act of justice, eh? You want to drive me to suicide as I drove Mother! An eye for an eye, is that it? But— (*He stops abruptly and stares before him, as if this idea were suddenly taking hold of his tortured imagination and speaks fascinatedly to himself.*) Yes! That would be justice—now you are Mother! She is speaking now through you! (*more and more hypnotized by this train of thought*) Yes! It's the way to peace—to find her again—my lost island—Death is an Island of Peace, too— Mother will be waiting for me there— (*with excited eagerness now, speaking to the dead*) Mother! Do you know what I'll do then? I'll get on my knees and ask your forgiveness—and say— (*His mouth grows convulsed, as if he were retching up poison.*) I'll say, I'm glad you found love, Mother! I'll wish you happiness—you and Adam! (*He laughs exultantly.*) You've heard me! You're here in the house now! You're calling me! You're waiting to take me home! (*He turns and strides toward the door.*)

LAVINIA—(*who has raised her head and has been staring at him with dread during the latter part of his talk—torn by remorse, runs after him and throws her arms around him*) No, Orin! No!

ORIN—(*pushes her away—with a rough brotherly irritation*) Get out of my way, can't you? Mother's waiting! (*He gets to the door. Then he turns back and says sharply*) Ssshh! Here's Peter! Shut up, now! (*He steps back in the room as Peter appears in the doorway.*)

PETER—Excuse my coming right in. The door was open. Where's Hazel?

ORIN—(*with unnatural casualness*) Gone home. (*then with a quick, meaning, mocking glance at Lavinia*) I'm just going in the study to clean my pistol. Darn thing's gotten so rusty. Glad you came now, Peter. You can keep Vinnie company. (*He turns and goes out the door. Peter stares after him puzzledly.*)

LAVINIA—(*with a stifled cry*) Orin! (*There is no answer but the sound of the study door being shut. She starts to run after him, stops herself, then throws herself into Peter's arms, as if for protection against herself and begins to talk volubly to drown out thought.*) Hold me close, Peter! Nothing matters but love, does it? That must come first! No price is too great, is it? Or for peace! One must have peace—one is too weak to forget—no one has the right to keep anyone from peace! (*She makes a motion to cover her ears with her hands.*)

PETER—(*alarmed by her hectic excitement*) He's a darned fool to monkey with a pistol—in his state. Shall I get it away from him?

LAVINIA—(*holding him tighter—volubly*) Oh, won't it be wonderful, Peter—once we're married and have a home with a garden and trees! We'll be so happy! I love everything that grows simply—up toward the sun—everything that's straight and strong! I hate what's warped and twists and eats into itself and dies for a lifetime in shadow. (*then her voice rising as if it were about to break hysterically—again with the instinctive movement to cover her ears*) I can't bear waiting— waiting and waiting and waiting—! (*There is a muffled shot from the study across the hall.*)

PETER—(*breaking from her and running for the door*) Good God! What's that? (*He rushes into the hall.*)

LAVINIA—(*sags weakly and supports herself against the table—in a faint, trembling voice*) Orin! Forgive me! (*She controls herself with a terrible effort of will. Her mouth congeals into a frozen line. Mechanically she hides the sealed envelope in a drawer of the table and locks the drawer.*) I've got to go in— (*She turns to go and her eyes catch the eyes of the Mannons in the portraits fixed accusingly on her—defiantly*) Why do you look at me like that? Wasn't it the only way to keep your secret, too? But I'm through with you forever now, do you hear? I'm Mother's daughter—not one of you! I'll live in spite of you! (*She squares her shoulders, with a return of the abrupt military movement copied from her father which she had of old— as if by the very act of disowning the Mannons she had returned to the fold—and marches stiffly from the room.*)

(*Curtain*)

ACT FOUR

SCENE—*Same as Act One, Scene One—exterior of the house. It is in the late afternoon of a day three days later. The Mannon house has much the same appearance as it had in the first act of "Homecoming." Soft golden sunlight shimmers in a luminous mist on the Greek temple portico, intensifying the whiteness of the columns, the deep green of the shutters, the green of the shrubbery, the black and green of the pines. The columns cast black bars of shadow on the gray stone wall behind them. The shutters are all fastened back, the windows open. On the ground floor, the upper part of the windows, raised from the bottom, reflect the sun in a smouldering stare, as of brooding revengeful eyes.*

Seth appears walking slowly up the drive from right, front. He has a pair of grass clippers and potters along pretending to trim the edge of the lawn along the drive. But in reality he is merely killing time, chewing tobacco, and singing mournfully to himself, in his aged, plaintive wraith of a once good baritone, the chanty "Shenandoah":

SETH—"Oh, Shenandoah, I long to hear you
      A-way, my rolling river,
      Oh, Shenandoah, I can't get near you
      Way-ay, I'm bound away
      Across the wide Missouri.

      "Oh, Shenandoah, I love your daughter
      A-way, you rolling river."

(stops singing and stands peering off left toward the flower garden—shakes his head and mutters to himself) There she be pickin' my flowers agin. Like her Maw used to—on'y wuss. She's got every room in the house full of 'em a'ready. Durn it, I hoped she'd stop that once the funeral was over. There won't be a one left in my garden! *(He looks away and begins pottering about again, and mutters grimly)* A durn queer thin' fur a sodger to kill himself cleanin' his gun, folks is sayin'. They'll fight purty shy of her now. A Mannon has come to mean sudden death to 'em. *(then with a grim pride)* But Vinnie's able fur 'em. They'll never git her to show nothin'. Clean Mannon strain!

(*Lavinia enters from the left. The three days that have inter-
vened have effected a remarkable change in her. Her body, dressed
in deep mourning, again appears flat-chested and thin. The Mannon mask-semblance of her face appears intensified now. It is deeply
lined, haggard with sleeplessness and strain, congealed into a stony
emotionless expression. Her lips are bloodless, drawn taut in a grim
line. She is carrying a large bunch of flowers. She holds them out
to Seth and speaks in a strange, empty voice.*)

LAVINIA—Take these, Seth, and give them to Hannah. Tell
her to set them around inside. I want the house to be full of
flowers. Peter is coming, and I want everything to be pretty
and cheerful. (*She goes and sits at the top of the steps, bolt
upright, her arms held stiffly to her sides, her legs and feet pressed
together, and stares back into the sun-glare with unblinking,
frozen, defiant eyes.*)

SETH—(*stands holding the flowers and regarding her worriedly*) I seed you settin' out here on the steps when I got up
at five this mornin'—and every mornin' since Orin— Ain't
you been gittin' no sleep? (*She stares before her as if she had not
heard him. He goes on coaxingly.*) How'd you like if I hauled
one of them sofas out fur you to lie on, Vinnie? Mebbe you
could take a couple o' winks an' it'd do you good.

LAVINIA—No, thank you, Seth. I'm waiting for Peter.
(*then after a pause, curiously*) Why didn't you tell me to go in
the house and lie down? (*Seth pretends not to hear the question,
avoiding her eyes.*) You understand, don't you? You've been
with us Mannons so long! You know there's no rest in this
house which Grandfather built as a temple of Hate and
Death!

SETH—(*blurts out*) Don't you try to live here, Vinnie! You
marry Peter and git clear!

LAVINIA—I'm going to marry him! And I'm going away
with him and forget this house and all that ever happened in
it!

SETH—That's talkin', Vinnie!

LAVINIA—I'll close it up and leave it in the sun and rain
to die. The portraits of the Mannons will rot on the walls and
the ghosts will fade back into death. And the Mannons will
be forgotten. I'm the last and I won't be one long. I'll be Mrs.
Peter Niles. Then they're finished! Thank God! (*She leans back*

in the sunlight and closes her eyes. Seth stares at her worriedly, shakes his head and spits. Then he hears something and peers down the drive, off left.)

SETH—Vinnie. Here's Hazel comin'.

LAVINIA—(*jerks up stiffly with a look of alarm*) Hazel? What does she want? (*She springs up as if she were going to run in the house, then stands her ground on the top of the steps—her voice hardening*) Seth, you go work in back, please!

SETH—Ayeh. (*He moves slowly off behind the lilacs as Hazel enters from left, front—calling back*) Evenin', Hazel.

HAZEL—Good evening, Seth. (*She stops short and stares at Lavinia. Lavinia's eyes are hard and defiant as she stares back. Hazel is dressed in mourning. Her face is sad and pale, her eyes show evidence of much weeping, but there is an air of stubborn resolution about her as she makes up her mind and walks to the foot of the steps.*)

LAVINIA—What do you want? I've got a lot to attend to.

HAZEL—(*quietly*) It won't take me long to say what I've come to say, Vinnie. (*Suddenly she bursts out*) It's a lie about Orin killing himself by accident! I know it is! He meant to!

LAVINIA—You better be careful what you say. I can prove what happened. Peter was here—

HAZEL—I don't care what anyone says!

LAVINIA—I should think you'd be the last one to accuse Orin—

HAZEL—I'm not accusing him! Don't you dare say that! I'm accusing you! You drove him to it! Oh, I know I can't prove it—any more than I can prove a lot of things Orin hinted at! But I know terrible things must have happened— and that you're to blame for them, somehow!

LAVINIA—(*concealing a start of fear—changing to a forced reproachful tone*) What would Orin think of you coming here the day of his funeral to accuse me of the sorrow that's afflicted our family?

HAZEL—(*feeling guilty and at the same time defiant and sure she is right*) All right, Vinnie. I won't say anything more. But I know there's something—and so do you—something that was driving Orin crazy— (*She breaks down and sobs.*) Poor Orin!

LAVINIA—(*stares straight before her. Her lips twitch. In a stifled voice between her clenched teeth*) Don't—do that!

HAZEL—(*controlling herself—after a pause*) I'm sorry. I didn't come to talk about Orin.

LAVINIA—(*uneasily*) What did you come for?

HAZEL—About Peter.

LAVINIA—(*as if this were something she had been dreading—harshly*) You leave Peter and me alone!

HAZEL—I won't! You're not going to marry Peter and ruin his life! (*pleading now*) You can't! Don't you see he could never be happy with you, that you'll only drag him into this terrible thing—whatever it is—and make him share it?

LAVINIA—There is no terrible thing!

HAZEL—I know Peter can't believe evil of anyone, but living alone with you, married, you couldn't hide it, he'd get to feel what I feel. You could never be happy because it would come between you! (*pleading again*) Oh, Vinnie, you've got to be fair to Peter! You've got to consider his happiness—if you really love him!

LAVINIA—(*hoarsely*) I do love him!

HAZEL—It has started already—his being made unhappy through you!

LAVINIA—You're lying!

HAZEL—He fought with Mother last night when she tried to talk to him—the first time he ever did such a thing! It isn't like Peter. You've changed him. He left home and went to the hotel to stay. He said he'd never speak to Mother or me again. He's always been such a wonderful son before—and brother. We three have been so happy. It's broken Mother's heart. All she does is sit and cry. (*desperately*) Oh, Vinnie, you can't do it! You will be punished if you do! Peter would get to hate you in the end!

LAVINIA—No!

HAZEL—Do you want to take the risk of driving Peter to do what Orin did? He might—if he ever discovered the truth!

LAVINIA—(*violently*) What truth, you little fool! Discover what?

HAZEL—(*accusingly*) I don't know—but you know! Look

in your heart and ask your conscience before God if you ought to marry Peter!

LAVINIA—(*desperately—at the end of her tether*) Yes! Before God! Before anything! (*then glaring at her—with a burst of rage*) You leave me alone—go away—or I'll get Orin's pistol and kill you! (*Her rage passes, leaving her weak and shaken. She goes to her chair and sinks on it.*)

HAZEL—(*recoiling*) Oh! You are wicked! I believe you would—! Vinnie! What's made you like this?

LAVINIA—Go away!

HAZEL—Vinnie! (*Lavinia closes her eyes. Hazel stands staring at her. After a pause—in a trembling voice*) All right. I'll go. All I can do is trust you. I know in your heart you can't be dead to all honor and justice—you, a Mannon! (*Lavinia gives a little bitter laugh without opening her eyes.*) At least you owe it to Peter to let him read what Orin had in that envelope. Orin asked me to make him read it before he married you. I've told Peter about that, Vinnie.

LAVINIA—(*without opening her eyes—strangely, as if to herself*) The dead! Why can't the dead die!

HAZEL—(*stares at her frightenedly, not knowing what to do—looks around her uncertainly and sees someone coming from off left, front—quickly*) Here he comes now. I'll go by the back. I don't want him to meet me. (*She starts to go but stops by the clump of lilacs—pityingly*) I know you're suffering, Vinnie—and I know your conscience will make you do what's right—and God will forgive you. (*She goes quickly behind the lilacs and around the house to the rear.*)

LAVINIA—(*looks after her and calls defiantly*) I'm not asking God or anybody for forgiveness. I forgive myself! (*She leans back and closes her eyes again—bitterly*) I hope there is a hell for the good somewhere! (*Peter enters from the left, front. He looks haggard and tormented. He walks slowly, his eyes on the ground—then sees Lavinia and immediately makes an effort to pull himself together and appear cheerful.*)

PETER—Hello, Vinnie. (*He sits on the edge of the portico beside her. She still keeps her eyes closed, as if afraid to open them. He looks at her worriedly.*) You look terribly worn out. Haven't you slept? (*He pats her hand with awkward tenderness. Her*

*mouth twitches and draws down at the corners as she stifles a sob.
He goes on comfortingly.*) You've had an awfully hard time of
it, but never mind, we'll be married soon.

LAVINIA—(*without opening her eyes—longingly*) You'll love
me and keep me from remembering?

PETER—You bet I will! And the first thing is to get you
away from this darned house! I may be a fool but I'm beginning to feel superstitious about it myself.

LAVINIA—(*without opening her eyes—strangely*) Yes. Love
can't live in it. We'll go away and leave it alone to die—and
we'll forget the dead.

PETER—(*a bitter resentful note coming into his voice*) We
can't move too far away to suit me! I hate this damned town
now and everyone in it!

LAVINIA—(*opens her eyes and looks at him startledly*) I never
heard you talk that way before, Peter—bitter!

PETER—(*avoiding her eyes*) Some things would make anyone bitter!

LAVINIA—You've quarrelled with your mother and Hazel
—on account of me—is that it?

PETER—How did you know?

LAVINIA—Hazel was just here.

PETER—She told you? The darned fool! What did she do
that for?

LAVINIA—She doesn't want me to marry you.

PETER—(*angrily*) The little sneak! What right has she—?
(*then a bit uneasily—forcing a smile*) Well, you won't pay any
attention to her, I hope.

LAVINIA—(*more as if she were answering some voice in herself
than him—stiffening in her chair—defiantly*) No!

PETER—She and Mother suddenly got a lot of crazy notions in their heads. But they'll get over them.

LAVINIA—(*staring at him searchingly—uneasily*) Supposing
they don't?

PETER—They will after we are married—or I'm through
with them!

LAVINIA—(*A pause. Then she takes his face in her hands and
turns it to hers.*) Peter! Let me look at you! You're suffering!
Your eyes have a hurt look! They've always been so trustful!
They look suspicious and afraid of life now! Have I done this

to you already, Peter? Are you beginning to suspect me? Are you wondering what it was Orin wrote?

PETER—(*protesting violently*) No! Of course I'm not! Don't I know Orin was out of his mind? Why would I pay any attention—?

LAVINIA—You swear you'll never suspect me—of anything?

PETER—What do you think I am?

LAVINIA—And you'll never let anyone come between us? Nothing can keep us from being happy, can it? You won't let anything, will you?

PETER—Of course I won't!

LAVINIA—(*more and more desperately*) I want to get married right away, Peter! I'm afraid! Would you marry me now—this evening? We can find a minister to do it. I can change my clothes in a second and put on the color you like! Marry me today, Peter! I'm afraid to wait!

PETER—(*bewildered and a bit shocked*) But—you don't mean that, do you? We couldn't. It wouldn't look right the day Orin—out of respect for him. (*then suspicious in spite of himself*) I can't see why you're so afraid of waiting. Nothing can happen, can it? Was there anything in what Orin wrote that would stop us from—?

LAVINIA—(*with a wild beaten laugh*) The dead coming between! They always would, Peter! You trust me with your happiness! But that means trusting the Mannon dead—and they're not to be trusted with love! I know them too well! And I couldn't bear to watch your eyes grow bitter and hidden from me and wounded in their trust of life! I love you too much!

PETER—(*made more uneasy and suspicious by this*) What are you talking about, Vinnie? You make me think there was something—

LAVINIA—(*desperately*) No—nothing! (*then suddenly throwing her arms around him*) No! Don't think of that—not yet! I want a little while of happiness—in spite of all the dead! I've earned it! I've done enough—! (*growing more desperate—pleading wildly*) Listen, Peter! Why must we wait for marriage? I want a moment of joy—of love—to make up for what's coming! I want it now! Can't you be strong, Peter?

Can't you be simple and pure? Can't you forget sin and see that all love is beautiful? (*She kisses him with desperate passion.*) Kiss me! Hold me close! Want me! Want me so much you'd murder anyone to have me! I did that—for you! Take me in this house of the dead and love me! Our love will drive the dead away! It will shame them back into death! (*at the topmost pitch of desperate, frantic abandonment*) Want me! Take me, Adam! (*She is brought back to herself with a start by this name escaping her—bewilderedly, laughing idiotically*) Adam? Why did I call you Adam? I never even heard that name before— outside of the Bible! (*then suddenly with a hopeless, dead finality*) Always the dead between! It's no good trying any more!

PETER—(*convinced she is hysterical and yet shocked and repelled by her display of passion*) Vinnie! You're talking crazy! You don't know what you're saying! You're not—like that!

LAVINIA—(*in a dead voice*) I can't marry you, Peter. You mustn't ever see me again. (*He stares at her, stunned and stupid.*) Go home. Make it up with your mother and Hazel. Marry someone else. Love isn't permitted to me. The dead are too strong!

PETER—(*his mind in a turmoil*) Vinnie! You can't—! You've gone crazy—! What's changed you like this? (*then suspiciously*) Is it—what Orin wrote? What was it? I've got a right to know, haven't I? (*then as she doesn't answer—more suspiciously*) He acted so queer about—what happened to you on the Islands. Was it something there—something to do with that native—?

LAVINIA—(*her first instinctive reaction one of hurt insult*) Peter! Don't you dare—! (*then suddenly seizing on this as a way out—with calculated coarseness*) All right! Yes, if you must know! I won't lie any more! Orin suspected I'd lusted with him! And I had!

PETER—(*shrinking from her aghast—brokenly*) Vinnie! You've gone crazy! I don't believe— You—you couldn't!

LAVINIA—(*stridently*) Why shouldn't I? I wanted him! I wanted to learn love from him—love that wasn't a sin! And I did, I tell you! He had me! I was his fancy woman!

PETER—(*wincing as if she had struck him in the face, stares at her with a stricken look of horrified repulsion—with bitter, broken anger*) Then—Mother and Hazel were right about you—

you are bad at heart—no wonder Orin killed himself—God, I—I hope you'll be punished—I—! (*He hurries blindly off down the drive to the left.*)

LAVINIA—(*watches him go—then with a little desperate cry starts after him*) Peter! It's a lie! I didn't—! (*She stops abruptly and stiffens into her old, square-shouldered attitude. She looks down the drive after him—then turns away, saying in a lost, empty tone*) Good-bye, Peter. (*Seth enters from the left rear, coming around the corner of the house. He stands for a moment watching her, grimly wondering. Then to call her attention to his presence, he begins singing half under his breath his melancholy "Shenandoah" chanty, at the same time looking at the ground around him as if searching for something.*)

SETH—"Oh, Shenandoah, I can't get near you
        Way-ay, I'm bound away—"

LAVINIA—(*without looking at him, picking up the words of the chanty—with a grim writhen smile*) I'm not bound away— not now, Seth. I'm bound here—to the Mannon dead! (*She gives a dry little cackle of laughter and turns as if to enter the house.*)

SETH—(*frightened by the look on her face, grabs her by the arm*) Don't go in there, Vinnie!

LAVINIA—(*grimly*) Don't be afraid. I'm not going the way Mother and Orin went. That's escaping punishment. And there's no one left to punish me. I'm the last Mannon. I've got to punish myself! Living alone here with the dead is a worse act of justice than death or prison! I'll never go out or see anyone! I'll have the shutters nailed closed so no sunlight can ever get in. I'll live alone with the dead, and keep their secrets, and let them hound me, until the curse is paid out and the last Mannon is let die! (*with a strange cruel smile of gloating over the years of self-torture*) I know they will see to it I live for a long time! It takes the Mannons to punish themselves for being born!

SETH—(*with grim understanding*) Ayeh. And I ain't heard a word you've been sayin', Vinnie. (*pretending to search the ground again*) Left my clippers around somewheres.

LAVINIA—(*turns to him sharply*) You go now and close the shutters and nail them tight.

SETH—Ayeh.

LAVINIA—And tell Hannah to throw out all the flowers.

SETH—Ayeh. (*He goes past her up the steps and into the house. She ascends to the portico—and then turns and stands for a while, stiff and square-shouldered, staring into the sunlight with frozen eyes. Seth leans out of the window at the right of the door and pulls the shutters closed with a decisive bang. As if this were a word of command, Lavinia pivots sharply on her heel and marches woodenly into the house, closing the door behind her.*)

(*Curtain*)

Chronology

1900   Makes First Communion on May 25. Autumn, enters De La Salle Institute in New York City, taught by Christian Brothers; lives in family's hotel apartment on West 68th Street near Central Park West.

1901   Becomes boarding student at De La Salle Institute in fall, living at school on West 58th Street near Sixth Avenue. Does well in history, English, and religion and poorly in mathematics.

1902   Fall, enters Betts Academy, non-sectarian boarding school in Stamford, Connecticut. Takes long walks in surrounding countryside, enjoys rowing, but does not participate in team sports.

1903–05   Summer 1903, learns that mother is morphine addict when she attempts to throw herself into Thames River outside cottage while undergoing withdrawal. Renounces religious faith and refuses to attend Mass with father. Returns to Betts and explores theaters, restaurants, saloons, and brothels of New York City with brother Jamie (now acting with father's company). Begins drinking. Patronizes Unique Book Shop in New York, owned by anarchist journalist Benjamin Tucker, and reads radical political tracts, including those of Emma Goldman, as well as works by Shaw, Ibsen, Nietzsche, Baudelaire, Wilde, Swinburne, Ernest Dowson, and Edward FitzGerald. Corresponds with New London friend Marion Welch about school life and his enjoyment of musicals (*The Rogers Brothers in Ireland*, *Pearl and Pumpkin*) and popular novels (including works by Thomas Dixon, Henry Harland, George Barr McCutcheon, and Harold McGrath).

1906   Passes entrance examinations for Princeton University in spring and enters college in fall. Frequents bars and brothels of Trenton and explores Hell's Kitchen and Greenwich Village sections of New York City. Reads *Thus Spake Zarathustra* by Nietzsche, *The Ego and His Own* by Max Stirner, Tolstoy, Dostoyevsky, and Maxim Gorky.

1907   Sees Alla Nazimova in Ibsen's *Hedda Gabler* ten times. Suspended at end of second semester for "poor scholastic standing" after failing to take any final examinations.

Takes secretarial job father finds him with mail-order firm, the New York–Chicago Supply Company, for $25 a week. Lives in parents' apartment in Hotel Lucerne on Amsterdam Avenue and 79th Street. Explores saloons and brothels of Tenderloin district. Becomes friends with Greenwich Village restaurant owner Polly Holladay and her brother Louis, painters Edward Keefe and George Bellows, and theater publicist James Findlater Byth. Reads Schopenhauer.

1908   Leaves job and begins receiving $7 a week allowance from parents. Stays with friends as relationship with father becomes increasingly strained.

1909   Spends January with Keefe and Bellows on farm owned by father in Zion, New Jersey, writing sonnets while they paint (later describes poems as "bad imitations of Dante Gabriel Rossetti"). Returns to New York and becomes romantically involved with twenty-year-old Kathleen Jenkins, daughter of prosperous middle-class family. Agrees when father, who disapproves of her Episcopalian background, proposes that he accompany mining engineer Fred C. Stevens on gold prospecting trip to Honduras. Marries Kathleen Jenkins in Hoboken, New Jersey, October 2; ceremony is kept secret from both families. Reads Jack London and Joseph Conrad before leaving for San Francisco in early October. Sails with Stevens and his wife, Ann, to Amapala, Honduras, travels on muleback to Tegucigalpa, and begins prospecting along Rio Seale without success in mid-November. Dislikes Honduran food and is plagued by insect bites.

1910   Contracts malaria and spends three weeks ill with fever in Tegucigalpa before returning to New York in March. Takes job as assistant stage manager with father's company, now touring with play *The White Sister*. Son Eugene Gladstone O'Neill, Jr., born May 4; O'Neill does not see him or Kathleen. Sails from Boston on Norwegian steel barque *Charles Racine* June 4, and arrives in Buenos Aires August 4. Works at Singer sewing machine factory, Swift meat packing plant, and on docks loading ships. Lives in cheap hotels and onboard moored *Charles Racine*, and frequents brothels and rough waterfront bars.

1911   Leaves Buenos Aires March 21 as ordinary seaman on British freighter *Ikala*, arriving in New York April 15. Calls once on Kathleen and sees his son, but does not return and never sees her again. Moves to waterfront saloon and flophouse run by James "Jimmy the Priest" Condon at 252 Fulton Street, where he stays for $3 a month. Sails for Southampton, England, July 22 as ordinary seaman on liner *New York* and returns August 26 as able-bodied seaman on liner *Philadelphia*. Visits New London, but returns by mid-September to Jimmy the Priest's saloon. December, Kathleen requests divorce without asking for alimony or child support. O'Neill arranges to substantiate adultery charges by being discovered in hotel room with prostitute. Sees all of the plays performed by Abbey Players from Dublin during six-week New York engagement, including T. C. Murray's *Birthright* and J. M. Synge's *Riders to the Sea* and *The Playboy of the Western World*.

1912   Attempts suicide with overdose of sleeping drug Veronal at Jimmy the Priest's in early January, but is saved by roommate James Byth (Byth will commit suicide at flophouse in 1913). Joins family on western vaudeville circuit, where father is touring in abridged version of *Monte Cristo*, and plays roles of courier and jailer of the Château d'If. Returns to New York in March and goes to New London in April. Divorce from Kathleen becomes final in July. Joins staff of *New London Telegraph* in August, covers local events and writes poetry for the paper, and becomes friends with editor Frederick Latimer. Falls in love with Maibelle Scott, eighteen-year-old neighbor; both families disapprove of romance. Develops persistent cough in October, and is diagnosed as having tuberculosis in November. Resigns newspaper job and enters Fairfield County State Sanatorium in Shelton, Connecticut, December 9, but leaves after two days. December 24, enters Gaylord Farm, private sanatorium in Wallingford, Connecticut.

1913   Has brief romance with fellow patient Catherine MacKay. Reads plays of Synge, Eugène Brieux, Gerhart Hauptmann, and August Strindberg. June 3, leaves Gaylord Farm with tuberculosis arrested and returns to New London. Writes vaudeville sketch, *A Wife for a Life*, and four one-act plays, *The Web*, *Thirst*, *Recklessness*, and *Warnings*.

Moves in autumn into boarding house run by Rippin family near Monte Cristo cottage. Resumes romance with Maibelle Scott. Writes film scenarios to make money, but none are accepted.

1914 Mother overcomes morphine addiction during stay at convent. Romance with Maibelle Scott ends and O'Neill begins to see Beatrice Ashe, eighteen-year-old daughter of New London trolley-car superintendent. Completes two full-length plays, *Bread and Butter* and *Servitude*, and four one-act plays, *Fog*, *Bound East for Cardiff* (then titled *Children of the Sea*), *Abortion*, and *The Movie Man*. First book, *Thirst and Other One Act Plays*, containing *Thirst*, *The Web*, *Warnings*, *Fog*, and *Recklessness*, published by Gorham Press of Boston in August (father pays printing costs). Fall, enrolls as special student in English 47 play-writing workshop at Harvard University, taught by Pro-fessor George Pierce Baker. Lives in boarding house at 1105 Massachusetts Avenue. Learns from Baker practice of writing detailed scenario of play before working on the dialogue (will follow this procedure for remainder of career). Writes one-act play "The Dear Doctor" (later destroyed) and full-length play "Belshazzar" (later de-stroyed), a collaboration with classmate Colin Ford. Stud-ies French and German on his own.

1915 Completes one-act play *The Sniper* and full-length play *The Personal Equation* for course. Spends summer in New London. Father becomes increasingly concerned about fi-nancial situation after his producers declare bankruptcy, and O'Neill is unable to study further with Baker. Goes to New York in fall and lives at the Garden Hotel, Madi-son Avenue and 27th Street. Drinks heavily in hotel saloon and at The Golden Swan (known to patrons as the "Hell Hole") at Sixth Avenue and 4th Street. Becomes friendly at the Hell Hole with the "Hudson Dusters," Irish-Amer-ican street gang, and Terry Carlin, an anarchistic, alcoholic drifter deeply influenced by Nietzsche. Writes poetry in-termittently.

1916 Sees production of Hauptmann's *The Weavers* six times. Watches six-day bicycle races at Madison Square Garden (event becomes a favorite New York pastime of O'Neill's). Goes with Carlin to Provincetown, Massachusetts, in

June. Meets summer colony of writers, including George Cram Cook, his wife, Susan Glaspell, radical journalist John Reed, Louise Bryant, Hutchins and Neith Boyce Hapgood, and Wilbur Daniel Steele, who had started amateur theater in Provincetown wharf shed the previous year. Led by Cook, group stages series of original one-act plays, including *Bound East for Cardiff* on July 28 and *Thirst* in August; O'Neill appears in both plays. Completes one-act plays *Before Breakfast* and "The G.A.N." (later destroyed), three-act *Now I Ask You*, and short story "Tomorrow." Forms friendship with medical student Saxe Commins. Begins affair with Louise Bryant. September, joins others in organizing The Provincetown Players: The Playwrights' Theatre, dedicated to the production of new American plays. Group moves to New York in fall and opens 140-seat theater, The Provincetown Playhouse, at 139 Macdougal Street in Greenwich Village. Provincetown Players stage *Bound East for Cardiff*, November 3, and *Before Breakfast*, December 1. Affair with Louise Bryant continues after she marries John Reed in November.

1917 Provincetown Players stage *Fog*, January 5, and *The Sniper*, February 16. Goes to Provincetown in March. Writes four one-act plays, *In the Zone*, *Ile*, *The Long Voyage Home*, and *The Moon of the Caribbees*, and short story "The Hairy Ape" (later destroyed). "Tomorrow" published in *Seven Arts* magazine, June, earning O'Neill $50. Louise Bryant and John Reed leave for Russia. O'Neill returns to New York in fall and becomes friends with journalist Dorothy Day. October, *The Long Voyage Home* appears in *The Smart Set*. The Washington Square Players stage *In the Zone*, October 31, and Provincetown Players stage *The Long Voyage Home*, November 2, and *Ile*, November 30. Introduced to Agnes Boulton, twenty-four-year-old writer of magazine stories and novelettes, at the Hell Hole in late autumn.

1918 Shaken by death of Louis Holladay from heroin overdose, January. Goes to Provincetown with Agnes Boulton in late winter. Ends affair with Louise Bryant after her return from Russia. Marries Agnes, April 12. Earns money from vaudeville production of *In the Zone*. Completes *Beyond the Horizon* and "Till We Meet" (later destroyed) and four one-act plays, *The Rope* (staged by Provincetown Players

April 26), *Shell Shock*, *Where the Cross Is Made*, and *The Dreamy Kid*. Broadway producer J. D. Williams options *Beyond the Horizon* for $500. Reads *Dubliners* and *A Portrait of the Artist as a Young Man* by James Joyce. Moves in autumn to house owned by Agnes in West Point Pleasant, New Jersey. Provincetown Players stage *Where the Cross Is Made*, November 22, and *The Moon of the Caribbees*, December 20, at their new location, 133 Macdougal Street.

1919   Engages Richard Madden of the American Play Company as literary agent and Harry Weinberger as his attorney; both become trusted friends. *The Moon of the Caribbees and Six Other Plays of the Sea*, published by Boni & Liveright, Inc., receives good reviews (Boni & Liveright will continue to publish his plays, generally coinciding with their first production). Begins long friendship with drama critic George Jean Nathan. Grows closer to father and spends time playing cards with him. Returns to Provincetown in late May and moves to Peaked Hill Bar on eastern side of Cape Cod, living in former Coast Guard station bought for him by father as wedding present (purchase includes furnishings of previous occupant, Mabel Dodge). Becomes enthusiastic kayaker. Completes *The Straw*, *Chris Christophersen*, and three one-act plays, "Exorcism," "Honor Among the Bradleys," and "The Trumpet" (all later destroyed). Broadway producer George C. Tyler options *Chris Christophersen*. Rents cottage in Provincetown at end of summer. Second son, Shane Rudraighe O'Neill, born October 30. Provincetown Players stage *The Dreamy Kid*, October 31, with all-black cast (one of the first productions by a white theater company to cast black actors in black roles).

1920   Goes to New York in early January for rehearsals of *Beyond the Horizon*, which begins series of matinees on February 3. Play is critically praised and runs for 144 evening performances, earning O'Neill $5,264. Father is deeply gratified by play's success, but soon has stroke and is discovered to have intestinal cancer. Production of *Chris Christophersen* is not brought to New York after performances in Atlantic City and Philadelphia. Provincetown Players stage "Exorcism" (O'Neill later recalls and destroys all copies of play, which depicts young man's suicide attempt). Returns to Provincetown in early March and completes *Gold*, longer version of *Where the Cross Is Made*. *Beyond the Horizon* receives Pulitzer Prize for drama in June. Goes to New London in late July and is at father's bedside when he slips into coma. Father dies of cancer, August 10. Jamie stops drinking and stays with mother, who proves capable of managing father's complex estate. Returns to Peaked Hill Bar, completes *"Anna Christie"* (revised version of *Chris Christophersen*), and writes *The Emperor Jones* and *Diff'rent*. *The Emperor Jones*, staged by Provincetown Players, November 1, is widely acclaimed and later moves to Broadway under commercial management, running for 204 performances. *Diff'rent*, produced by Provincetown Players, opens December 27 and runs for 100 performances in Village and on Broadway.

1921   Becomes friends with theatrical critic Kenneth Macgowan and stage designer Robert Edmond Jones. Writes draft of *The First Man* in March. Joins successful protest against New York Drama League's decision not to invite black actor Charles Gilpin, lead player in *The Emperor Jones*, to its annual awards dinner. Has teeth worked on by Saxe Commins, now practicing dentistry in Rochester, New York (O'Neill will continue to have serious dental problems for remainder of his life). *Gold* opens on Broadway June 1 and closes after 13 performances. Finishes draft of *The Fountain* in late August. Agrees to pay child support when Kathleen Jenkins, now married to George Pitt-Smith, contacts him through her lawyer. Goes to New York for rehearsals in October. Meets Eugene, Jr., who had been given name of Richard Pitt-Smith, now attending military school; O'Neill and son both enjoy visit. *"Anna Christie"* opens on Broadway November 2 and runs for 177 performances. *The Straw* opens November 10 at Greenwich Village Theatre and closes after 20 performances. Impressed by German film *The Cabinet of Dr. Caligari*. Returns to Provincetown. Writes *The Hairy Ape* in December.

1922   January, attends rehearsals in New York. Mother dies in Los Angeles after series of strokes, February 28. *The First Man* opens March 4 and closes after 27 performances. March 9, Provincetown Players staging of *The Hairy Ape* opens on same evening that mother's body arrives in New

York, accompanied by Jamie, who has suffered severe alcoholic relapse. O'Neill does not attend opening and remains at his hotel, sending family friend to meet train. *The Hairy Ape* moves to Broadway in April and runs for 120 performances. Returns to Provincetown and completes *The Fountain.* *"Anna Christie"* wins Pulitzer Prize. Visited by Eugene, Jr., and by Jamie, who is drinking heavily. Begins *Welded* in September. Buys Brook Farm, thirty-acre estate with fifteen-room house in Ridgefield, Connecticut, for $32,500, and moves there in autumn. Earns $44,000 during year.

1923　　Awarded gold medal by National Institute of Arts and Letters. Successful production of *"Anna Christie"* in London helps establish European reputation. Finishes *Welded* in spring. Lives at Peaked Hill Bar for summer and begins *Marco Millions.* Jamie is committed to sanatorium in June after suffering acute alcoholic breakdown. O'Neill joins Kenneth Macgowan and Robert Edmond Jones in assuming control of Provincetown Players, who have become inactive due to financial difficulties and artistic differences (later adopt name of The Experimental Theatre, Inc., for their productions). Begins *All God's Chillun Got Wings* in September and finishes it after returning to Brook Farm in fall. Visited by Hart Crane and Malcolm Cowley in early November. Jamie dies in Paterson, New Jersey, sanatorium, November 8. O'Neill, recovering from severe drinking episode, does not attend service or burial.

1924　　Begins *Desire Under the Elms* in January. Saddened by death in Greece of George Cram Cook. Rehearsals for *All God's Chillun Got Wings* begin in February amid newspaper controversy over play's depiction of interracial marriage, centering on scene in which white actress Mary Blair kisses black actor Paul Robeson's hand. O'Neill, Blair, and Robeson receive hate mail and death threats from Ku Klux Klan and others. *Welded,* produced by O'Neill, Macgowan, Jones, and Edgar Selwyn, opens March 17 and runs for 24 performances. *The Ancient Mariner,* O'Neill's dramatic arrangement of Coleridge's poem, opens April 6 at Provincetown Playhouse and closes after 33 performances. *All God's Chillun Got Wings* opens at Provincetown Playhouse May 15 and runs for 100 performances; first scene is read aloud by director James Light after city refuses to issue permits needed by child actors appearing in production. Finishes *Desire Under the Elms* in June. Resumes work on *Marco Millions* at Peaked Hill Bar in July. Revises and corrects previously published plays for *The Complete Works of Eugene O'Neill*, two-volume limited edition published by Boni & Liveright. Goes to New York in October for rehearsals. *Desire Under the Elms* opens November 11 at Greenwich Village Theatre. O'Neill is dissatisfied with stage set (which is based on his own sketches) but pleased by Walter Huston's performance (tells interviewer for 1948 profile that Huston, Charles Gilpin in *The Emperor Jones*, and Louis Wolheim in *The Hairy Ape* were the only actors in his plays who "lived up to the conceptions I had as I wrote"). Sails to Bermuda November 29 and rents cottage in Paget Parish on south shore.

1925   January, condenses *Marco Millions* from original eight-act length and begins *The Great God Brown*. *Desire Under the Elms* moves to Broadway and is threatened with prosecution for indecency by Manhattan district attorney Joab Banton until panel of citizens serving as "play-jury" clears it; production runs for 208 performances. (Play is later banned in Boston and England.) Finishes *The Great God Brown* in late March. Reads Nietzsche (*The Birth of Tragedy*, *Joyful Wisdom*) and Freud (*Beyond the Pleasure Principle*, *Group Psychology and the Analysis of the Ego*). Begins extended period of heavy drinking in April. Daughter Oona born, May 14. Goes to Nantucket in late July and writes scenarios for *Lazarus Laughed* and *Strange Interlude*. Returns to Ridgefield in October and works on *Lazarus Laughed* for remainder of year. *The Fountain*, produced by Macgowan, Jones, and O'Neill, opens at the Greenwich Village Theatre on December 10 and runs for 24 performances. Continues to drink heavily; Macgowan arranges for him to see psychoanalyst Dr. G. V. Hamilton.

1926   Participates in Hamilton's survey of marital sexual behavior and psychological attitudes (published in 1929 as *A Research in Marriage*) and undergoes six weeks of psychoanalytic treatment with him. Stops drinking (except for intense, short episodes, will abstain for remainder of life). *The Great God Brown*, produced by Macgowan, Jones, and O'Neill, opens on January 23 and runs for 278 perfor-

mances. Returns to Bermuda in late February and moves
to Bellevue, rented estate in Paget Parish. Works on *Lazarus Laughed* and finishes first draft in May. Reads Joyce's
Ulysses. Buys Spithead, 200-year-old house on Little Turtle
Bay, for $17,500. Begins writing *Strange Interlude* in late
May. Receives D. Litt. degree from Yale University, June
23, and sees George Pierce Baker, now teaching at Yale.
Visits New London before spending summer in Belgrade
Lakes, Maine, where he works steadily on *Strange Interlude*. Visited by Eugene, Jr., and Barbara Boulton, Agnes's
eleven-year-old daughter by earlier marriage (Barbara lives
with her grandparents). Meets again actress Carlotta
Monterey (born Hazel Neilson Tharsing, 1888), who had
played Mildred in *The Hairy Ape* on Broadway. Inter-
viewed by journalist Elizabeth Shepley Sergeant for profile
in *The New Republic*, beginning friendship. Goes to New
York in October, sees Carlotta Monterey frequently, and
writes film scenarios for *The Hairy Ape* and *Desire Under
the Elms* (neither of his scenarios are ever produced). Returns to Bermuda in November and moves into guest cottage at Spithead while main house is renovated. Revises
Marco Millions for publication by Boni & Liveright in
hopes of encouraging its production (appears April 1927).

1927   Finishes first draft of *Strange Interlude* in February. Visited in March by Lawrence Langner, a director of the
Theatre Guild, New York producers' organization, who
reads first six acts of *Strange Interlude*. April, Theatre
Guild board accepts *Marco Millions* for production and options *Strange Interlude*. Revises *Lazarus Laughed* (published in November by Boni & Liveright) and *Strange
Interlude* during summer before going to New York at end
of August. Suffers from depression and extreme nervousness; consults doctors and is diagnosed as having prostate
condition and thyroid deficiency (weighs 137 pounds at
height of five feet eleven inches). Eugene, Jr., enters Yale.
O'Neill goes to Bermuda in late October before returning
to New York in November for rehearsals. Writes increasingly angry letters to Agnes as affair with Carlotta Monterey intensifies.

1928   *Marco Millions* opens January 9 and runs for 92 performances. *Strange Interlude* opens January 30 and runs for
426 performances (published version sells over 100,000

copies by 1931, and O'Neill eventually earns $275,000 from play). Leaves with Carlotta Monterey for Europe on February 10. Goes to London and Paris before renting villa at Guéthary in southern France, March. Keeps whereabouts secret from Agnes and most friends. Begins writing *Dynamo*, first in planned trilogy "Myths for the God-forsaken," to be completed by *Days Without End* (originally titled *Without Endings of Days*) and "It Cannot Be Mad." *Lazarus Laughed* staged by Pasadena Community Playhouse, April 9, and runs for 28 performances. Receives Pulitzer Prize for *Strange Interlude*. Becomes enraged by Agnes's demands in divorce settlement negotiations and by newspaper interview she gives, discussing separation. Finishes draft of *Dynamo* in August and sends it to Saxe Commins, who is living in Paris, to be typed. Leaves with Carlotta Monterey for China, October 5. Becomes ill with influenza during brief stay in Saigon. Arrives in Shanghai, November 9. Drinks heavily and is briefly separated from Carlotta before being hospitalized. Leaves for Manila under assumed name to avoid newspaper reporters, December 12. Resumes drinking onboard ship bound for Singapore.

1929   Carlotta leaves him in Colombo, Ceylon, January 1, but they are reunited in Port Said, Egypt, January 15. Rents villa in late January at Cap d'Ail, on French Riviera near Monte Carlo. Works on scenario for "It Cannot Be Mad." Theatre Guild production of *Dynamo* opens February 11 and receives harsh reviews; runs for 50 performances, mostly to Guild subscribers. O'Neill regrets having had play produced in his absence and makes extensive changes in text while reviewing proofs of published version. Sets trilogy aside in May and begins writing scenarios for *Mourning Becomes Electra*. Sued for $1,250,000 by Gladys Lewis, who claims that *Strange Interlude* was plagiarized from her privately published novel *The Temple of Pallas-Athenæ*, written under name of Georges Lewys. Moves in early June to Château Le Plessis in St. Antoine-du-Rocher, near Tours. Agnes is granted divorce on grounds of desertion in Reno, Nevada, July 2; settlement gives her life interest in Spithead and $6,000–$10,000 per year alimony, depending on O'Neill's income. Marries Carlotta in Paris, July 22. Finishes scenarios for *Mourning Becomes Electra* in early August. Visited by Eugene, Jr. Fall, buys

Bugatti sports car, which he enjoys driving at high speed, and Silverdene Emblem ("Blemie"), prize Dalmatian (dog becomes O'Neill's favorite of several he has owned).

1930　　Completes first draft of *Mourning Becomes Electra* in late February. Visits Paris and tours France before beginning second draft at end of March. Film version of *"Anna Christie,"* directed by Clarence Brown and starring Greta Garbo in her first talking role, is popular success (earlier silent version, released in 1923, had starred Blanche Sweet). May, sees *All God's Chillun Got Wings* and *Desire Under the Elms* performed in Russian by Kamerny, experimental Soviet theater company that uses music, dance, and stylized decor in its stagings. Meets its founder, Aleksandr Tairov, and writes letter praising productions. Finishes third draft of *Mourning Becomes Electra* in September and fourth draft in October. Travels in Spain and Morocco. Returns in November and begins fifth draft.

1931　　Completes fifth draft in February. Writes sixth draft at Las Palmas in the Canary Islands in March before mailing typescript to Theatre Guild from Paris, April 7. Federal district judge John W. Woolsey rules for defendants in plagiarism case and awards O'Neill $7,500 costs (is unable to collect from bankrupt plaintiff). Resolution of suit allows sale of film rights to *Strange Interlude*, from which O'Neill receives $37,500 (released in 1932, film stars Norma Shearer, Clark Gable, Frank Morgan, and Robert Young, and is directed by Robert Z. Leonard). Returns to United States with Carlotta to prepare for production of *Mourning Becomes Electra*, May 17. Artist Ralph Barton, Carlotta's third husband, commits suicide May 19, leaving note declaring love for her; O'Neills are upset by resulting publicity. Rents house in Northport, Long Island, in June. Takes pride in Eugene, Jr., who recently has won Yale prize for his scholarship in classics. Visited for two weeks in August by Shane, who is entering Lawrenceville School in New Jersey. Works on proofs for published version of *Mourning Becomes Electra* with Saxe Commins, now editor at Horace Liveright, Inc. (formerly Boni & Liveright). Takes duplex apartment at 1095 Park Avenue when rehearsals begin in early September. *Mourning Becomes Electra* opens October 26 to wide critical acclaim and runs for 150 performances. O'Neill is "overjoyed" the following day, but soon writes in work diary: "Reaction—sunk—worn out—depressed—sad that the Mannons exist no more—for me!" November, goes with Carlotta to Sea Island, Georgia, where they decide to build house. Returns to New York in December and meets Mexican artist and writer Miguel Covarrubias.

1932   January, meets Nellie Tharsing, Carlotta's mother, and Cynthia Chapman, Carlotta's fourteen-year-old daughter by her second husband. Sees Oona and Shane. Begins work in February on scenario for *Days Without End*. Sees George Jean Nathan, actress Lillian Gish, Saxe and Dorothy Commins, and James Speyer, wealthy banker and former lover of Carlotta's, who had established trust fund that pays her $14,000 a year. (O'Neill is unaware of Speyer's affair with Carlotta and believes aunt in California is source of her annuity.) Meets German playwright Gerhart Hauptmann. Goes with Carlotta to Sea Island in May, staying in cottage while house is finished. Begins writing *Days Without End*, but work is difficult and he makes little progress. Twenty-room house, costing $100,000 (including land), is finished in late June; O'Neills name it Casa Genotta (name derived from "Eugene" and "Carlotta"). Enjoys swimming and surf fishing. Becomes associate editor of new literary journal *The American Spectator*, edited by George Jean Nathan, and contributes "Memoranda on Masks," "Second Thoughts," and "A Dramatist's Notebook," essays on use of masks in contemporary theater (series appears November 1932–January 1933). Writes in "Memoranda on Masks": "One's outer life passes in a solitude haunted by the masks of others; one's inner life passes in a solitude hounded by the masks of oneself." Resumes work on *Days Without End*, but sets it aside on morning of September 1 to begin *Ah, Wilderness!* (writes in work diary: "Awoke with idea for this 'Nostalgic Comedy' & worked out tentative outline—seems fully formed & ready to write"). Completes first draft by end of September. Returns to *Days Without End* and with difficulty finishes third draft by end of year.

1933   Works on "The Life of Bessie Bowen" (formerly "It Cannot Be Mad") in January, then returns to *Days Without End* in early February and finishes fifth draft by end of March. Sale of film rights to *The Emperor Jones* for $30,000 lessens worries over continuing expenses, which include financial support for Terry Carlin and other friends. (Film, released later in year, is directed by Dudley Murphy and stars Paul Robeson and Dudley Digges.) Saxe Commins secures royalties owed O'Neill by Liveright, Inc., before firm declares bankruptcy in May. O'Neill signs with Bennett Cerf, co-founder of Random House, on condition that Cerf hire Commins as editor (Commins later becomes editor-in-chief of Random House). Contract provides for 20 percent royalty rate and $10,000 advance. Revises *Ah, Wilderness!* in June before beginning sixth draft of *Days Without End*. August, vacations at Big Wolf Lake in Adirondack Mountains. Attends rehearsals of *Ah, Wilderness!* and becomes friends with Russel Crouse, publicist for the Theatre Guild. Play opens in New York, October 2, and runs for 289 performances. Returns to Sea Island in mid-October and revises *Days Without End*. Enjoys player piano "Rosie" given him by Carlotta. Receives $37,500 for screen rights to *Ah, Wilderness!* (film, directed by Clarence Brown and starring Lionel Barrymore, Wallace Beery, and Mickey Rooney, is released in 1935; a musical version, *Summer Holiday*, is released in 1948). Goes to New York in late November for rehearsals.

1934   Theatre Guild production of *Days Without End* opens in New York January 8 and runs for 57 performances; O'Neill is angered by "very prejudiced" reviews. (Play is well received in Ireland when Abbey Theatre stages it later in the year.) Returns to Sea Island at end of January and suffers from severe nervousness and digestive troubles. Told by doctor during visit to New York in March that he must rest for six months to avoid nervous breakdown. Begins taking insulin to gain weight and buys kayak. Has several ship models made for his use in planning "The Calms of Capricorn," play set aboard clipper ship rounding Cape Horn. Goes to Big Wolf Lake in early August and stays until end of September. October, meets Irish playwright Sean O'Casey in New York. Works on notes and outlines for several plays at Sea Island during fall. Visited in December by Shane, now student at Florida Military Academy after doing poorly at Lawrenceville.

1935   January, begins planning cycle of seven plays, incorporating "The Life of Bessie Bowen" and "The Calms of

Capricorn," examining American life since the early nineteenth century through several generations of the Harford family (will eventually adopt title "A Tale of Possessors Self-Dispossessed" for cycle). Writes scenarios for first two plays, *A Touch of the Poet* (originally titled *The Hair of the Dog*) and *More Stately Mansions*, February–April. Visited by Sherwood Anderson and by Eugene, Jr., now graduate student in classics. Works on notes and outlines for scenario through summer and fall despite episodes of nervousness and depression and series of minor ailments. Begins writing draft of *A Touch of the Poet* in November. Visited by Somerset Maugham in December.

1936   Hospitalized with gastritis during visit to New York in February. Suffers from depression, extreme nervousness, and continuing stomach pains after returning to Sea Island. Leaves draft of *A Touch of the Poet* unfinished to work on other plays in cycle. Expands plan to include nine plays, beginning in late eighteenth century. Blames poor health on hot Sea Island climate. Goes to New York in October for medical treatment and is told to rest. November, moves with Carlotta to Seattle at invitation of friend Sophus Keith Winther, professor at University of Washington and author of study of O'Neill's work, who finds house they rent at 4701 West Ruffner Street, overlooking Puget Sound. Awarded Nobel Prize for Literature, November 12. Writes acceptance letter acknowledging influence of Strindberg. Moves with Carlotta to San Francisco in December. Enters Merritt Hospital in Oakland, suffering from abdominal pain and prostate trouble, on December 26, and has appendix removed December 29.

1937   Nearly dies from infection in mid-January, then begins slow recovery. Sells Casa Genotta for $75,000. Leaves hospital in early March but continues to suffer from prostate and stomach ailments. April, moves from San Francisco hotel to house at 2909 Avalon Avenue in Berkeley. Buys 160 acres of land for new home in Las Trampas Hills near Danville, California. Rents house in nearby Lafayette while Danville house is being built, June. Resumes work despite poor health. Writes draft of new first play in cycle that is longer than nine-act *Strange Interlude*, but is uncertain about cutting it. Develops painful neuritis in arm,

November. Moves to Tao House, new Danville home, at end of year.

1938 Neuritis prevents work until late March. Begins draft of *More Stately Mansions*, April. Visited by Shane, now attending ranch school in Colorado. Finishes draft in September and begins rewriting. Disturbed when he learns that Shane is returning to Lawrenceville School, but feels powerless to intervene in his education.

1939 Completes and revises second draft of *More Stately Mansions* in January. Begins rewriting *A Touch of the Poet*, now third play in cycle. Suffers from neuritis, melancholia, low blood pressure, and anxiety over eye operation Carlotta must undergo (surgery is successful). Finishes third draft of *A Touch of the Poet* in mid-May. Decides June 5 to set cycle aside and work on plays outside it. Reviews notes on June 6 and chooses two autobiographical ideas to develop. Finishes outline of first, *The Iceman Cometh*, in late June and of the second, *The Long Day's Journey* (later retitled *Long Day's Journey into Night*), in early July. Visited by Eugene, Jr., now teaching classics at Yale, in July and by Oona in August ("really a charming girl, both in looks and manner—And she has intelligence, too"). Follows outbreak of World War II; writes in diary, "Spengler was right." Finishes first draft of *The Iceman Cometh* in mid-October. Tremor in hands, present intermittently since childhood, becomes more pronounced. Completes third draft of *The Iceman Cometh* in mid-December and considers play to be essentially finished.

1940 Exhaustion prevents steady work on cycle. February, meets director John Ford and screenwriter Dudley Nichols to discuss their plans for filming S. S. *Glencairn* plays (*Bound East for Cardiff*, *The Moon of the Caribbees*, *In the Zone*, and *The Long Voyage Home*) under title *The Long Voyage Home* (O'Neill will see film, which stars John Wayne, Thomas Mitchell, and Barry Fitzgerald, in July and praise it as the best screen adaptation of his work). Begins draft of *Long Day's Journey into Night* in late March, but writes slowly due to continued poor health. Injures back at end of April. Develops "war obsession" after German invasion of France and the Low Countries, May 10, closely following news and doing no writing. Resumes work on *Long Day's Journey into Night* June 26 and finishes first draft in late September. Writes second draft before returning to cycle in late October. Decides to divide first two plays into four, creating eleven-play cycle. November, plans "By Way of Obit.", series of one-act monologue plays. Dalmatian "Blemie" dies December 17. O'Neill and Carlotta are deeply grieved; O'Neill writes "The Last Will and Testament of Silverdene Emblem O'Neill" as tribute.

1941 Ill with prostate and digestive disorders and bronchitis. Begins notes in February for non-cycle play "The Thirteenth Apostle." Works on *Long Day's Journey into Night* in March (writes that play "does most with the least—a quiet play!—and a great one, I believe"). Writes draft of *Hughie*, one-act play in "By Way of Obit." series, April. Has increasing difficulty controlling pencil as hand tremor worsens. Tremor diagnosed as Parkinson's disease; receives vitamin shots that prove ineffective and doubts that he will be able to complete cycle. Visited by Oona in July. Eugene, Jr., is deeply moved by reading *Long Day's Journey into Night* and *The Iceman Cometh* during visit in September, which pleases O'Neill. Makes notes at end of October for *A Moon for the Misbegotten*. Works on draft for remainder of year. Preoccupation with war grows after Japanese attack on Pearl Harbor, December 7. Shane joins merchant marine.

1942 Finishes first draft of *A Moon for the Misbegotten* in January. Able to work only sporadically on *A Touch of the Poet*, "The Thirteenth Apostle," and *Hughie* as tremor, prostate, and other health problems worsen. Carlotta develops serious back problem. O'Neill is intensely angered by news in April that Oona has been chosen "Debutante No. 1" at the Stork Club in New York, considering distinction frivolous and inappropriate during wartime. Eugene, Jr., leaves Yale faculty to do war work (rejected for intelligence and military service, will work in cable factory and begin drinking heavily). Sends manuscripts, typescripts, and other materials to Princeton and Yale libraries for safekeeping. Finishes revising *Hughie* in June. Suffers from effects of drugs taken to control Parkinson's (writes in diary in late July: "Tough game—take sedatives and feel a dull dope—don't take, and feel as if maggots were crawling all over inside your skin"). Finishes revision of *A Touch of the Poet* in mid-November. Refuses to see Oona when she comes to California to pursue a screen career and writes letter threatening permanent break in relations. Works on "The Last Conquest" (formerly "The Thirteenth Apostle"). Departure of servants for war work, gasoline rationing, and O'Neills' inability to drive leaves them increasingly isolated at Tao House.

1943   Begins second draft of *A Moon for the Misbegotten* in January and finishes in May, working three hours a day despite worsening tremor. Destroys notes for seven plays he no longer expects to write. Tries to begin play "Blind Alley Guy" in June but is forced to stop, no longer capable of controlling pencil and unable to compose on typewriter or dictate. Oona attempts reconciliation with O'Neill after her marriage to Charlie Chaplin on June 16, but he does not respond (will not reply to several other letters from her and never sees any of the five children she will have in his lifetime). Financial worries reduced by sale of film rights to *The Hairy Ape* for $30,000 (film, directed by Alfred Santell and starring William Bendix and Susan Heyward, is released in 1944). Shane suffers nervous collapse after extensive service in North Atlantic and is hospitalized.

1944   Sells Tao House in February and moves to Huntington Hotel in San Francisco. Burns manuscripts of two unfinished cycle plays. Carlotta dangerously ill from kidney infection. Saddened by death of friend and attorney Harry Weinberger. Hires Jane Caldwell, daughter of Carlotta's school friend Myrtle Caldwell, as typist. Revises *A Moon for the Misbegotten* and *A Touch of the Poet*. Meets with Lawrence Langner during summer to discuss production of completed plays, recommending that *The Iceman Cometh* be staged after anticipated mood of post-war optimism recedes. Tremor causes occasional shaking of entire body.

1945   O'Neill's minor flirtation with Jane Caldwell leads to exchange of bitter accusations between him and Carlotta. Moves with Carlotta to New York in October, taking suite at Hotel Barclay. Goes to jazz clubs and sporting events with George Jean Nathan and new attorney, Winfield Aronberg. Sees Eugene, Jr., now pursuing erratic teaching and radio broadcasting career in New York, and Shane, who is drinking heavily, drifting between jobs, and has twice attempted suicide. Grandson Eugene O'Neill III born to Shane and his wife, Catherine Givens, November 19 (O'Neill never sees child, who dies in crib February 10, 1946). Deposits sealed copy of *Long Day's Journey into Night* in Random House safe, November 29, with instructions that it not be published until twenty-five years after his death and never be staged (Carlotta, his literary executor, has play published and produced in 1956; it wins Pulitzer Prize).

1946   Sees Shane and Catherine before they go to Spithead to recover from death of their son. Continuing tension with Carlotta eased when they move in spring into six-room penthouse apartment at 35 East 84th Street. Sees Dudley Nichols about his screen adaptation of *Mourning Becomes Electra* (film, directed by Nichols and starring Rosalind Russell, Michael Redgrave, and Katina Paxinou, is released following year). Works on design and casting of Theatre Guild production of *The Iceman Cometh* and with Saxe Commins on published version. Attends afternoon rehearsals, beginning in early September. Play opens to mixed reviews October 9 and runs for 136 performances.

1947   Attends rehearsals for Theatre Guild staging of *A Moon for the Misbegotten*. Becomes dissatisfied with production, which the Guild decides to try out on tour. Play opens in Columbus, Ohio, February 20 and is performed in Pittsburgh, Detroit, and St. Louis, where it closes March 29. O'Neill does not press for another production and asks Guild to postpone planned staging of *A Touch of the Poet*. Settles remaining alimony claims with Agnes for $17,000. Relationship with Carlotta becomes increasingly strained during fall.

1948   Carlotta leaves after quarrel, January 18. O'Neill drinks, stumbles, and breaks left arm, January 27. Considers leaving Carlotta while in hospital (tells friends that he has learned of her true relationship with James Speyer), but they are reconciled in March. Moves with Carlotta to Boston in April, where they buy shorefront cottage on Point O'Rocks Lane in nearby Marblehead Neck. Purchase and renovation ultimately cost about $85,000 (half coming from Carlotta's savings). Shane is arrested for possession of three vials of heroin, August 10. O'Neill refuses to send $500 bail and breaks off relations (Shane spends four months in federal hospital in Lexington, Kentucky, but is not cured of his addiction). Tremor worsens in legs, making walking difficult, but lessens in hands; O'Neill expresses hope that he may begin writing again. Moves into cottage in fall.

1949   Worsening tremor in hands makes resumption of writing impossible, though O'Neill's desk remains arranged for work. Listens to large collection of jazz and blues records and occasionally visits Boston.

1950   Eugene, Jr., after years of heavy drinking and failed attempt at television career, commits suicide in Woodstock, New York, September 25.

1951   Leaves house, thinly dressed and without cane, after quarrel with Carlotta on night of February 5. Trips over rock beneath snow in garden and breaks right leg at knee. Lies outside for nearly an hour before family doctor arrives and takes him to Salem Hospital (O'Neill later tells friends that Carlotta had tauntingly refused to assist him). Carlotta, severely disoriented, is hospitalized as psychiatric patient February 6, suffering effects of bromide poisoning caused by over-medication (remains in hospital until March 29). O'Neill is visited by New York friends, including Commins, Aronberg, and Langner, who try to arrange permanent separation from Carlotta. Signs petition alleging that Carlotta is insane and incapable, March 23, and enters Doctors' Hospital in New York, March 31. Weighs less than 100 pounds and occasionally hallucinates (is diagnosed as having bromide poisoning less severe than Carlotta's). Develops pneumonia in early April, but responds to penicillin treatment. Declines offer from Saxe and Dorothy Commins to live with them in Princeton. Withdraws petition, April 23. Rejoins Carlotta in Boston on May 17, moving into Suite 401 of Shelton Hotel at 91 Bay State Road (will not leave suite, except for medical reasons, for remainder of his life). Marblehead Neck cottage is sold; O'Neill donates large archive of literary material to Yale, including typescript of *More Stately Mansions*. Visited by Russel Crouse, his only friend still on good terms with Carlotta. Reads mysteries, listens to baseball games on the radio, and takes increasing amounts of sedatives.

1952   Makes Carlotta sole literary executor of his published and unpublished writings. Destroys drafts and scenarios of unfinished cycle plays. *A Moon for the Misbegotten*, published by Random House, receives mixed reviews and sells poorly.

1953   Health deteriorates until he is confined to bed in September. Dies of pneumonia at the Shelton at 4:37 P.M., November 27. Post-mortem examination reveals rare degenerative disease of the cerebellum, possibly inherited and superficially resembling Parkinson's, as primary cause of tremor. Buried at Forest Hills Cemetery in Boston, December 2.

Note on the Texts

For Eugene O'Neill, the publication of a play was at least as important as its stage production. He had more control over the printed form than was possible on the stage, where individual characterizations by actors and cuts to shorten the running time often made the play different from what he had wanted it to be. He attended rehearsals of his plays whenever possible; if revisions were considered necessary, he wanted to make them himself. Some of his revisions, made to fit particular productions, were retained in the published plays because he thought they were improvements. A few plays were published before he could incorporate his revisions in them, and in these instances he inserted the revisions in the next publication. All thirteen plays in this volume were staged during O'Neill's lifetime; he was able to attend rehearsals for all but two of them, *Lazarus Laughed* and *Dynamo*. The plays went through several editions and printings, but O'Neill did not proofread all of the new editions and he seldom made further revisions in a play once he had revised it for publication. The plays in this volume are arranged in the order O'Neill wrote them rather than in the order of their first publication.

Diff'rent was written in October 1920 and had its first production December 27, 1920. It was first published in *The Emperor Jones, Diff'rent, The Straw* by Boni & Liveright, April 7, 1921. A second edition was published by Boni & Liveright in *The Complete Works of Eugene O'Neill* (two volumes, limited to 1250 autographed sets; dated 1924, but not distributed until early 1925). O'Neill took particular care correcting the proofs for this edition in October 1924, revising most of the plays, some extensively. *Diff'rent* was one of the plays only slightly revised; a few words were deleted and some punctuation was changed. No further revisions were made in later editions of the play. This volume prints the text of *Diff'rent* from *The Complete Works* edition (1924).

O'Neill finished writing *The First Man* (copyrighted originally as *The Oldest Man*) in October 1921; it was produced March 4, 1922, and published in *The Hairy Ape, Anna Christie, The First Man* by Boni & Liveright, July 24, 1922. In preparing the proofs for *The Complete Works* edition in October 1924, O'Neill cut and tightened some of the speeches. No other authorial changes were made in later editions; the text of the play in *The Complete Works of Eugene O'Neill* (1924) is printed here.

O'Neill wrote *The Hairy Ape* in less than three weeks in December 1921. The play was produced March 9, 1922, and published July 24, 1922, by Boni & Liveright in *The Hairy Ape, Anna Christie, The First Man*. Although O'Neill did not make many revisions in this play for *The Complete Works* edition, there is evidence that he corrected some punctuation and spelling. Therefore the text of *The Hairy Ape* from *The Complete Works of Eugene O'Neill* (1924) is printed here.

O'Neill began work on *The Fountain* in the spring of 1921 and completed it in the fall of 1922. The play was not included in *The Complete Works* edition, perhaps because O'Neill wanted to see it in rehearsal before he published it. The play was produced December 10, 1925, and was published in *The Great God Brown, The Fountain, The Moon of the Caribbees, and Other Plays* by Boni & Liveright, March 15, 1926. In correcting proofs, O'Neill overlooked the omission of the name "Christopher Columbus" from the character list; it was added when Charles Scribner's Sons brought out a second edition (1934–35), but the name was left out again in the Random House third edition (1941). O'Neill made no changes in these later editions and there is no evidence that he ever went over proofs of the play again. The text printed here is that of the first edition published by Boni & Liveright (1926), with the addition of "Christopher Columbus" in the list of characters.

Welded was written between the fall of 1922 and the spring of 1923, but was not produced in New York until March 17, 1924. The play had been tried out first in Baltimore, where on March 5 O'Neill saw a performance he disliked. He attended rehearsals in New York but was still dissatisfied with the presentation. The first edition, *All God's Chillun Got Wings and Welded*, was published by Boni & Liveright, April 17, 1924, too soon after the production to allow the insertion of revisions. On July 14, 1924, he reported in his work diary that he had "worked cutting '*Welded*' for Collected Works edition Liveright is to get out." This cutting was done on tear sheets from the first edition. In October, he made further revisions in the play when he was going over proofs for *The Complete Works of Eugene O'Neill*. As he made no other changes in later editions, the text of *Welded* in *The Complete Works* (1924) is printed here.

O'Neill finished writing *All God's Chillun Got Wings* in the late fall of 1923. It was published in the February 1924 issue of *The American Mercury* (O'Neill received his copy January 22). Boni & Liveright brought out the first book edition, *All God's Chillun Got Wings and Welded*, on April 17, 1924. The play was produced May 15, 1924. Though O'Neill had not seen the play in production before its first two editions, he made only a few revisions in it for *The Complete Works of Eugene O'Neill*: two lines were added to the chorus of a song, two spoken words and a stage direction were changed. These were the last changes he made in the play; therefore the text from *The Complete Works* (1924) is printed here.

O'Neill began writing *Desire Under the Elms* in January 1924 and completed it on July 2, 1924, in time for inclusion in his *Complete Works* edition. The play was produced November 11, 1924. A separate edition of *Desire Under the Elms* was published by Boni & Liveright April 11, 1925. O'Neill read the proofs and made some revisions both in stage directions and speeches in the second edition; the text of this edition is printed here.

O'Neill began work on *Marco Millions* in the summer of 1923, then put it aside to work on *Desire Under the Elms*. After finishing that play, he again worked on *Marco Millions* until it was completed in October 1924, but by that time it was the length of two four-act plays and had a cast of thirty-four characters. Because he was anxious to have it produced, he spent January 1925 making it into one long play. As no production was in sight by December 1926, O'Neill decided to prepare the play for publication. (The play was finally produced January 9, 1928.) Boni & Liveright brought it out on April 23, 1927, with a limited autographed printing following in May. No other edition was ever prepared by O'Neill, and this first edition text is printed here.

The Great God Brown was written by O'Neill between January and March 1925. Rehearsals of the play began January 4,

1926, a performance was given for an invited audience on January 22, and it opened on January 23, 1926. O'Neill corrected proofs of the play early in February but apparently did not notice that the list of characters still reflected an earlier version of the play: "a stenographer" was listed and "a client," "three committeemen," and "a police captain" were omitted. (Only the third edition brought out by Charles Scribner's Sons, 1934–35, corrects the list of characters.) The play was published in *The Great God Brown, The Fountain, The Moon of the Caribbees, and Other Plays* by Boni & Liveright, March 15, 1926. O'Neill took no part in the preparation of later editions; the text of the first edition, with the list of characters corrected, is printed here.

O'Neill began the scenario of *Lazarus Laughed* in September 1925 and continued to work on the play until late November. He picked it up again in March of the following year and finished it in June 1926. In June 1927, he revised Act One for publication in *The American Caravan: A Yearbook of American Literature*, edited by Van Wyck Brooks, Lewis Mumford, Alfred Kreymborg, and Paul Rosenfeld (New York: The Macaulay Company, 1927). In July 1927, he again revised the play, this time in preparation for book publication by Boni & Liveright, November 12, 1927; a limited autographed printing of this edition came out two weeks later. O'Neill was unable to get the play produced in New York; the first production was given by The Community Playhouse in Pasadena, California, April 9, 1928, while he was living in France. No further editions were supervised by O'Neill. The text of the Boni & Liveright edition of *Lazarus Laughed* (1927) is printed here.

O'Neill worked on *Strange Interlude* from May 1926 until July 25, 1927, when he wrote in his diary that he would "call this play finally finished now!" He corrected first proofs from October 31 to November 6, 1927, and went over the last proofs in January 1928 while attending rehearsals for the Theatre Guild's production, which opened on January 30, 1928. Boni & Liveright published the trade edition on March 3, 1928, and later that month produced a special autographed two-color edition, which for some reason failed to incorporate O'Neill's last proof corrections in the early pages. Therefore, it is the text of the trade edition of *Strange Interlude* that is printed in this volume.

O'Neill had done some work on *Dynamo* in 1927 and then put it aside for other projects. In March 1928, soon after he and Carlotta had settled in France, he began working on the play in earnest. By September 10, 1928, he considered the play finished and sent it off both for publication by Horace Liveright, Inc. (the firm had been reorganized and changed its name) and for production by the Theatre Guild. After learning when the play was to be produced, he reviewed the script and was very dissatisfied, writing in his work diary on February 4, 1929, that he "would like to rewrite entirely but too late now—opens 11th." When he received proofs from Horace Liveright in March, he decided to rewrite and revise some portions of it, to add new scenes to the second act, and to change the opening of Act Three. The revised play was therefore very different from the play that had been performed; the program bill, for example, included some characters who no longer appear in the printed version. He made further corrections on page proofs June 10–14 (these late corrections, unlike corrections he made for other plays, were not incorporated into the text published in England). The book was published in two editions again, the trade edition on October 5, 1929, and the autographed limited edition soon after. Though O'Neill often said that he would like to revise the play further, he made no more changes. The text printed here is that of the Horace Liveright first edition (1929).

Between May 1929 and April 7, 1931, when he sent the script to the Theatre Guild, O'Neill wrote six drafts of *Mourning Becomes Electra*. He continued making extensive revisions in proofs from July 26 to October 13, 1931. The Theatre Guild began rehearsals of the play on September 7, so O'Neill was able to continue making revisions in the proofs while attending rehearsals. The play opened October 26, and the first trade printing was published by Horace Liveright on November 3. A limited autographed printing from the same plates, in which a first-printing error was corrected and a separate section ("Working Notes and Extracts from a Fragmentary Work Diary") added, was published late in November. This corrected second printing, without the added section, is the text printed in this volume.

This volume presents the texts of the original editions chosen for inclusion here. It does not attempt to reproduce features of the physical layout or design of these documents, such as the typography of speech headings and stage directions. The texts are reproduced without change, except for the correction of lists of characters and typographical errors. O'Neill's own usage in spelling (for example "ballin'" for "bawlin'") and his handling of apostrophes ("on'y" or "o'ny," "its" for "it's," "your's" for "yours," etc.) are retained. Spelling, punctuation, and capitalization are often expressive features, and they are not altered, even when inconsistent or irregular. The following is a list of typographical errors corrected, cited by page and line number: 22.9, joshin,'; 28.5, *records*; 56.12, RICHARD; 62.9, Bill; 66.36, *coach*; 99.29–30, *him. Shuddering*); 106.39, know!; 129.30, mix; 137.11, *branishes*; 139.28, *hecticly*; 142.31, se; 143.6, nothin,'; 145.4, trough; 156.22, SERETARY; 223.4, death; 225.35, *envelopes*; 266.10, *hyterical*; 344.37, saying; 349.9, sayin; 349.27, awaw; 352.14, thar;; 372.12, Morning'; 388.21, sir; 426.34, yens'; 448.4, *runinng*; 453.29, wooes; 488.9–10, children hurry; 507.17, Shöal!; 570.12, *wreathes*; 586.7, sake!' "; 611.39, like; 619.24, *smoothes*; 677.9, must; 945.31, *put*; 980.37, *muderous*; 1011.8, an'.

Notes

In the notes below, the reference numbers denote page and line of the present volume (the line count includes act and scene headings). No note is made for material included in a standard desk-reference book. For more detailed notes, references to other studies, and further biographical background, see: *The Unknown O'Neill*, edited by Travis Bogard (New Haven: Yale University Press, 1988); *Selected Letters of Eugene O'Neill*, edited by Travis Bogard and Jackson R. Bryer (New Haven: Yale University Press, 1988); *"Love and Admiration and Respect": The O'Neill-Commins Correspondence*, edited by Dorothy Commins (Durham: Duke University Press, 1986); *"As Ever, Gene": The Letters of Eugene O'Neill to George Jean Nathan*, edited by Nancy L. Roberts and Arthur W. Roberts (Rutherford, New Jersey: Farleigh Dickinson University Press, 1987); *"The Theatre We Worked For": The Letters of Eugene O'Neill to Kenneth Macgowan*, edited by Jackson R. Bryer, introductions by Travis Bogard (New Haven: Yale University Press, 1982); *Eugene O'Neill Work Diary 1924–1943*, preliminary edition, edited by Donald Gallup (2 vols.; New Haven: Yale University Library, 1981); Jennifer McCabe Atkinson, *Eugene O'Neill: A Descriptive Bibliography* (Pittsburgh: University of Pittsburgh Press, 1974); Travis Bogard, *Contour in Time: The Plays of Eugene O'Neill*, revised edition (New York: Oxford University Press, 1987); Arthur and Barbara Gelb, *O'Neill*, enlarged edition (New York: Harper & Row, 1973); Jordan Y. Miller, *Playwright's Progress: O'Neill and the Critics* (Chicago: Scott, Foresman and Company, 1965); Margaret Loftus Ranald, *The Eugene O'Neill Companion* (Westport, Connecticut: Greenwood Press, 1984); Louis Sheaffer, *O'Neill: Son and Playwright* (Boston: Little, Brown and Company, 1968) and *O'Neill: Son and Artist* (Boston: Little, Brown and Company, 1973).

The cast lists of the first productions below are supplied from the opening-night playbills and do not always correspond exactly with the character lists in the texts of the plays.

Contrary to current practice, O'Neill described stage settings from the point of view of the audience rather than the actors.

DIFF'RENT

First produced by The Provincetown Players, December 27, 1920, at The Playwrights' Theatre, New York City.

    Direction: Charles O'Brien   *Design:* Cleon Throckmorton
        Kennedy

Captain Caleb Williams: James Light
Emma Crosby: Mary Blair
Captain John Crosby: H. B. Tisdale
Mrs. Crosby: Alice Rostetter

Jack Crosby: Eugene Lincoln
Harriet Williams: Elizabeth Brown
Alfred Rogers: Iden Thompson
Benny Rogers: Charles Ellis

THE FIRST MAN

First produced by Augustin Duncan, March 4, 1922, at The Neighborhood Playhouse of the Henry Street Settlement, New York City.

Direction: Augustin Duncan

Curtis Jayson: Augustin Duncan
Martha: Margaret Mower
John Jayson: Harry Andrews
John, Jr.: Gordon Burby
Richard: Alan Bunce
Esther: Margherita Sargent

Lily: Marjorie Vonnegut
Mrs. Davidson: Marie L. Day
Mark Sheffield: Eugene Powers
Emily: Eva Condon
Edward Bigelow: Frederic Burt
A Maid: I. Hill
A Trained Nurse: Isabel Stuart

THE HAIRY APE

First produced by The Provincetown Players, March 9, 1922, at The Provincetown Playhouse, New York City.

Direction: James Light with the assistance of Arthur Hopkins
Design: Cleon Throckmorton with the assistance of Robert Edmond Jones
Costumes: Blanche Hays

Robert Smith, "Yank": Louis Wolheim
Paddy: Henry O'Neill
Long: Harold West
Mildred Douglas: Mary Blair
Her Aunt: Eleanor Hutchison
Second Engineer: Jack Gude

A Guard: Harry Gottlieb
A Secretary of an Organization: Harold McGee
Stokers, Ladies, Gentlemen, etc.: Josephine Hutchinson, Greta Hoving, Esther Pinch, Lucy Shreve, Jack Gude, Clement O'Loughlen, Anterio Argondona, Em Jo Basshe, Allen Delano, Patrick Barnum, Harold McGee, Harry Gottlieb, Alexander Boije, and George Tobias

131.27   Whitechapel]   Poor neighborhood in London's East End.

145.4   Garden]   Madison Square Garden, New York City.

147.39   Tell it to Sweeney!]   An expression of disbelief. "Sweeney" was a legendary figure who would believe anything.

149.35–36   *Blackwells Island*]   Former name of Welfare Island, now Roosevelt Island, in the East River, New York City.

159.1–2   Burns or Pinkerton]   Private detective agencies.

159.35   Ingersoll]   A pocket watch.

163.13   Zybszko]   Stanislaus Zbyszko (1879–1967), a professional wrestler.

THE FOUNTAIN

First produced by Kenneth Macgowan, Robert Edmond Jones, and Eugene G. O'Neill, in association with A. L. Jones and Morris Green, December 10, 1925, at The Greenwich Village Theatre, New York City.

Direction/Design: Robert Edmond Jones
Costumes: Millia Davenport
Music: Macklin Marrow

Ibnu Aswad: Stanley Berry
Juan Ponce de Leon: Walter Huston
Pedro: William Stahl
Maria de Cordova: Pauline Moore
Luis de Alvaredo: Egon Brecher
Yusef: John Taylor
Diego Menendez: Crane Wilbur
Vincente de Cordova: Edgar Stehli
Alonzo de Oviedo: Perry Ivins
Manuel de Castillo: Morris Ankrum
Cristoval de Mendoza: Ralph Benzies

Christopher Columbus: Henry O'Neill
A Soldier: William Stahl
Helmsman: Philip Jones
Friar Quesada: Edgar Stehli
Beatrize de Cordova: Rosalinde Fuller
Her Duenna: Liza Dallet
Nano: Curtis Cooksey
A Chief of the Indians: Ray Corning
A Medicine Man: John Taylor
Father Superior: Henry O'Neill
Juan: John Taylor
His Servant: Philip Jones

176.15   Cipango and Cathay]   Japan and China.

176.37   Cambuluc]   Beijing.

189.5   Espaniola]   Hispaniola, which includes Haiti and the Dominican Republic.

WELDED

First produced by Kenneth Macgowan, Robert Edmond Jones, and Eugene G. O'Neill in association with Edgar and Arch Selwyn; after tryout March 3, in Baltimore, it opened March 17, 1924, at the Thirty-ninth Street Theatre, New York City.

Direction: Stark Young	*Eleanor:* Doris Keane
Design: Robert Edmond Jones	*John:* Curtis Cooksey
	A Woman: Catherine Collins
Michael Cape: Jacob Ben-Ami	

ALL GOD'S CHILLUN GOT WINGS

First produced by Kenneth Macgowan, Robert Edmond Jones, and Eugene G. O'Neill, May 15, 1924, at The Provincetown Playhouse, New York City. Because the mayor's office refused a permit allowing children to appear on stage, the first scene was not performed, but was read by James Light.

Direction: James Light   *Design:* Cleon Throckmorton

IN SCENE ONE:

Jim Harris: William Davis	*Mickey:* Jimmy Ward
Ella Downey: Virginia Wilson	*Little Girls:* Grace Burns, Alice
Shorty: George Finley	Nelson, and Evelyn Wynn
Joe: Malvin Myrck	

IN REMAINING SCENES:

Jim Harris: Paul Robeson	*Men and Women:* Kirk Ames,
Mrs. Harris: Lillian Greene	Eloise Anderson, Harold
Hattie: Dora Cole	Bryant, Polly Craig, Hume
Ella Downey: Mary Blair	Derr, Oscar Flannner, Lila
Shorty: John Taylor	Hawkins, Paul Jones, Spurgon
Joe: Frank Wilson	Lampert, Sadie Reynolds, and
Mickey: James Martin	Kathleen Roarke
Organ Grinder: James Meighan	
Salvationists: Barbara Benedict,	
Clement O'Laughlen, and	
William Stahl	

305.30   *Blackstone*]   *Commentaries on the Laws of England* (1765–69) by Sir William Blackstone.

DESIRE UNDER THE ELMS

First produced by Kenneth Macgowan, Robert Edmond Jones, and Eugene G. O'Neill, November 11, 1924, at The Greenwich Village Theatre, New York City.

Direction/Design: Robert Edmond Jones
Music: Macklin Marrow

Ephraim Cabot: Walter Huston
Simeon: Allen Nagle
Peter: Perry Ivins
Eben: Charles Ellis
Abbie Putnam: Mary Morris
Young Girl: Eloise Pendleton
Farmers: Romeyn Benjamin, Arthur Mack, William Stahl, and Jim Taylor

The Fiddler: Macklin Marrow
A Sheriff: Walter Abel
Old Woman: Norma Millay
Deputies: Arthur Mack and William Stahl
Other folk from the neighboring farms: Albert Brush, Hume Derr, Donald Oenslager, Alma O'Neill, Lucy Shreve, Mary Ture, and Ruza Wenclawska

320.15   Solomon's mines]   Fabled gold mines.

330.29−31   lilies . . . spin]   Cf. Matthew 6:28.

345.1−4   Rose . . . wheat]   Cf. Song of Solomon, chapters 2, 4, and 7.

347.20   God . . . Rachel]   Genesis 30:22.

349.13−15   Build . . . Peter!]   Cf. Matthew 16:18.

359.27−28   'Cause . . . born!]   Cf. Isaiah, 9:6.

MARCO MILLIONS

First produced by The Theatre Guild, January 9, 1928, at The Guild Theatre, New York City.

Direction: Rouben Mamoulian
Design: Lee Simonson

Music: Emerson Whithorne

CHRISTIANS

A Traveler: Philip Leigh
Marco Polo: Alfred Lunt
Donata: Natalie Browning
Nicolo Polo: Henry Travers
Maffeo Polo: Ernest Cossart
Tedaldo: Morris Carnovsky

A Dominican Monk: Albert Van Dekker
A Knight-Crusader: George Cotton
A Papal Courier: Sanford Meisner
Paulo Loredano: Philip Leigh

HEATHEN

A Magian Traveler: Mark
  Schweid
A Buddhist Traveler: Charles
  Romano
A Mahometan Captain: Robert
  Barrat
Corporal: Albert Van Dekker
First Ali Brother: H. H.
  McCollum
Older Ali Brother: Mark
  Schweid
A Prostitute: Mary Blair
Dervish: John Henry
Tartar Minstrel: William
  Edmonson
Emissary from Kublai: Albert
  Van Dekker

Kublai: Baliol Holloway
Princess Kukachin: Margalo
  Gillmore
Chu-Yin: Dudley Digges
General Bayan: Robert Barrat
A Messenger from Persia: Charles
  Romano
Ghazan: Morris Carnovsky
A Buddhist Priest: Philip Leigh
A Taoist Priest: Louis Veda
A Confucian Priest: Mark Schweid
A Moslem Priest: H. H. McCollum
Indian Snake Charmer: John
  Henry
A Tartar Chronicler: Philip Leigh

383.13   Cambaluc] See note to 176.37.

383.17   Zayton] Believed to be Chin-chiang (or Tsin-kiang), now Quan-zhou, commercial maritime center during the Yüan Dynasty (A.D. 1280–1368), in province of Fukien on inlet of Formosa Strait.

397.2   thistle . . . figs.] Cf. Matthew 7:16.

THE GREAT GOD BROWN

First produced by Kenneth Macgowan, Robert Edmond Jones, and Eugene G. O'Neill, January 23, 1926, at The Greenwich Village Theatre, New York City.

Direction/Design: Robert
  Edmond Jones

William A. Brown: William
  Harrigan
His Father: Milano Tilden
His Mother: Clifford Sellers
Dion Anthony: Robert Keith
His Father: Hugh Kidder
His Mother: Eleanor
  Wesselhoeft
Margaret: Leona Hogarth
Her Three Sons: Starr Jones,
  Paul Jones, and Teddy Jones

Cybel: Anne Shoemaker
Two Draftsmen: Frederick C.
  Packard, Jr., and John Mahin
Client ("Man"): Seth Kendall
Three Committeemen: Stanley
  Barry, Adrian Marsh, and
  William Stahl
Police Captain: Ellsworth Jones
Margaret's Sons (four years later):
  Tupper Jones, Starr Jones, and
  Paul Jones

470.12−14   CLIENT . . . CAPTAIN]   In revising this play for publication, O'Neill did not make final corrections in the character list. The "Client," "Three Committeemen," and "Police Captain" were not included and a "Stenographer," no longer in the play, appeared in the published version.

484.9   *Act One*]   Should be "the Prologue." Apparently overlooked when O'Neill was revising the play.

484.24−25   "Come . . . rest."]   Matthew 11:28.

485.23−24   "Suffer . . . ones!"]   Cf. Matthew 19:14.

487.34−35   Blessed . . . spirit]   Cf. Matthew 5:5 and 5:3; throughout the play, characters quote or adapt verses from this chapter of Matthew (the Sermon on the Mount).

492.27−28   "And He . . . them."]   Mark 6:5.

496.30−31   Lead . . . Light!]   Cf. John Henry Newman, "Lead Kindly Light" (1833).

497.27   Word . . . Beginning]   Cf. John 1:1.

499.17−18   "Into . . . Lord,"]   Luke 23:46.

499.22−23   "Swift . . . soon!"]   Percy Bysshe Shelley, "To Night" (1821).

500.26   homeward Christian Soldier]   Cf. Sabine Baring-Gould, "Onward Christian Soldiers."

503.16−17   'Because . . . come!']   Matthew 25:13.

503.21−22   Tomorrow . . . Paradise!]   Cf. Luke 23:43.

505.12   *Act . . . One*]   Should be "the Prologue"; see note to 484.9.

506.23−24   William . . . on!]   Cf. Thomas Brigham Bishop, "John Brown's Body."

509.8   best . . . born]   Cf. Sophocles, *Oedipus at Colonus*.

532.12   To . . . dead!]   From the Apostle's Creed.

LAZARUS LAUGHED

First produced by The Pasadena Community Players, April 9, 1928, at The
Pasadena Community Playhouse, Pasadena, California.

Direction: Gilmor Brown
Design: James Hyde
Music: Arthur Alexander
Direction of Movement:
  Katharane Edson

Lazarus: Irving Pichel
His Father: Maurice Wells
His Mother: Esther M.
  Cogswell
Martha: Margaret Morrow
Mary: Dorothy Warren
Miriam: Lenore Shanewise
An Orthodox Priest: William
  Earle
Messengers: Ralph Urmy and
  Charles Bruins
Aged Orthodox Jew: Jerome
  Coray

A Centurian: Richard Menefee
Gaius Caligula: Victor Jory
Crassus: Max Turner
Flavius: Richard Menefee
Marcellus: Maurice Wells
Tiberius Cæsar: Gilmor Brown
Pompeia: Dore Wilson
Soldier: Jerome Coray
Chorus of 159 persons, doubling
  in approximately 420 roles as
  Lazarus's guests, chorus of old
  men, Roman soldiers, orthodox
  Jews, Nazarenes, followers of
  Lazarus, Greeks, Roman
  legionaries, Roman senators,
  chorus of youths and girls,
  chorus of senile old men,
  Roman crowd.

543.3−4   Jesus . . . forth!] John, Chapter 11.

588.6   Blessed Isles] Cf. Friedrich Nietzsche, *Thus Spake Zarathustra*,
Part II, Chapter 2. O'Neill uses the phrase throughout *Mourning Becomes
Electra*.

STRANGE INTERLUDE

First produced by The Theatre Guild, January 30, 1928, at the John Golden
Theatre, New York City.

Direction: Philip Moeller
Design: Jo Mielziner

Charles Marsden: Tom Powers
Professor Henry Leeds: Philip
  Leigh
Nina Leeds: Lynn Fontanne
Edmund Darrell: Glenn Anders

Sam Evans: Earle Larimore
Mrs. Amos Evans: Helen Westley
Gordon Evans as a boy: Charles
  Walters
Madeline Arnold: Ethel Westley
Gordon Evans as a man: John J.
  Burns

636.19   "Nothing . . . dream,"] Cf. Thomas Moore, "Love's Young
Dream," in *Irish Melodies*.

652.11−14   "Stetit . . . Iovem;"] "He stood alone in the citadel; head
held high, and triumphant, he sent his bright glance to the stars and looked

more closely at Olympus and inquired for Jove." Marcus Manilius, early first century A.D., *Astronomica*, Book IV, lines 905–08.

678.27   "God's . . . world!"]   Robert Browning, "Song" from *Pippa Passes*, Scene 1.

700.7–8   "life . . . things!"]   Robert Louis Stevenson, "Happy Thoughts," *A Child's Garden of Verses*.

806.36   Hail, . . . you!]   Cf. Suetonius (Gaius Suetonius Tranquillus), *Lives of the Caesars*, "Life of Claudius," 21.

DYNAMO

First produced by The Theatre Guild, February 11, 1929, at the Martin Beck Theatre, New York City.

Direction: Philip Moeller	*Reuben:* Glenn Anders
Design: Lee Simonson	*Ramsay Fife:* Dudley Digges
	May: Catherine Calhoun Doucet
Reverend Hutchins Light:	*Ada:* Claudette Colbert
George Gaul	*Jennings:* Ross Forrester
Amelia: Helen Westley	*Rocco:* Edgar Kent

O'Neill eliminated the character Rocco when he revised *Dynamo* in proofs a month after it opened.

825.4   How . . . Lord?]   Cf. Isaiah 6:11.

851.3   "Vengeance . . . Lord!"]   Romans 12:19.

878.9   "The fool . . . heart—"]   Cf. Psalms 14:1.

MOURNING BECOMES ELECTRA

First produced by The Theatre Guild, October 26, 1931, at The Guild Theatre, New York City. (The cast for all three parts of the trilogy is given below.)

Direction: Philip Moeller	*Louisa:* Bernice Elliott
Design: Robert Edmond Jones	*Minnie:* Emily Lorraine
	Orin: Earle Larimore
Brigadier-General Ezra Mannon:	*Josiah Borden:* James Bosnell
Lee Baker	*Emma:* Augusta Durgeon
Christine: Alla Nazimova	*Everett Hills, D.D.:* Oliver Putnam
Lavinia: Alice Brady	*His Wife:* Janet Young
Captain Adam Brant: Thomas	*Doctor Joseph Blake:* Erskine
Chalmers	Sanford
Captain Peter Niles: Philip	*The Chantyman:* John Hendricks
Foster	*Ira Mackel:* Oliver Putnam
Hazel Niles: Mary Arbenz	*Joe Silva:* Grant Gordon
Seth Beckwith: Arthur Hughes	*Abner Small:* Erskine Sanford
Amos Ames: Jack Byrne	

903.39–40   sepulchre! . . . Bible]   Cf. Matthew 23:27.

972.4   "Typee"]   *Typee: A Peep at Polynesian Life* (1846), by Herman Melville.

986.29   Bully Watermann]   Robert H. Waterman (1808–84), sea captain noted for record runs in sailing vessels.

1021.22–23   "dark . . . ocean"]   Lord Byron, *Childe Harold's Pilgrimage*, Canto IV, Stanza 179.

CATALOGING INFORMATION

O'Neill, Eugene Gladstone, 1888–1953.
  Complete Plays 1920–1931.

  (The Library of America ; 41)
  Edited by Travis Bogard.
    Contents (v. 2): Diff'rent — First man — Hairy ape — Fountain —
Welded — All God's chillun — Desire under elms — Marco Millions —
Great God Brown — Lazarus laughed — Strange interlude — Dynamo —
Mourning becomes electra
  I. Theater—American—20th century. I. Title. II. Series.
PS3529.N5 1988   812'52   88-50686
ISBN 0–940450–49–6(v. 2)

This book is set in 10 point Linotron Galliard,
a face designed for photocomposition by Matthew Carter
and based on the sixteenth-century face Granjon. The paper
is acid-free Ecusta Nyalite and meets the requirements for perma-
nence of the American National Standards Institute. The binding
material is Brillianta, a 100% woven rayon cloth made by
Van Heek-Scholco Textielfabrieken, Holland. The com-
position is by Haddon Craftsmen, Inc., and The
Clarinda Company. Printing and binding
by R. R. Donnelley & Sons Company.
Designed by Bruce Campbell.